CONCORDIA UNIVERSITY

HN18.D43   C001 V
MAN AND MODERN SOCIETY NEW YORK

W9-DCU-592

3 4211 000041521

MAN AND

MODERN SOCIETY

MAN AND

Conflict and

KARL DE SCHWEINITZ, Jr.

NORTHWESTERN UNIVERSITY

HENRY HOLT

MODERN SOCIETY

Choice in the Industrial Era

KENNETH W. THOMPSON

UNIVERSITY OF CHICAGO

With the collaboration of PAUL K. HATT

NORTHWESTERN UNIVERSITY

AND COMPANY NEW YORK

COPYRIGHT, 1953, BY
HENRY HOLT AND COMPANY, INC.
LIBRARY OF CONGRESS CATALOG CARD NUMBER: 52-13893
PRINTED IN THE UNITED STATES OF AMERICA

39695

TO THE MEMORY OF
PAUL K. HATT

394 95

PREFACE

THIS BOOK is the outgrowth of our experiences in an integrated social science course at Northwestern University. Designed for freshmen and sophomores, the course had for its chief objective the examination of the underlying forces in " modern society." Our inquiries into the major institutions and problems of contemporary society were based on the collaboration of economists, geographers, political scientists and sociologists.

From the outset those engaged in this experiment were hampered by three fundamental defects in the materials and organization of such a course. First, there is today no conceptual framework for general social science as such. Economics, political science and sociology as independent and separate social sciences have extracted from society institutions and problems of a limited character for research and evaluation. Moreover, each has derived a methodology appropriate to its particular subject matter. Our overriding concern in organizing these materials has been to illustrate a possible conceptual framework for studying the whole of modern society that has proved fruitful in our experience. The methods employed by the separate contributors to this general scheme are those of the existing social sciences. But by asking distinguished scholars and writers in different fields to speak to a common problem, we have hoped to indicate the areas in which their assumptions and methods overlapped.

Second, many courses in the social sciences, in the zeal of their organizers to make them contemporary and relevant, have degenerated into mere current affairs or great issues courses. Conscious of this problem, we have deliberately postponed the discussion of problems and tensions until the main currents and underlying foundations of modern society have been explored. The working assumption underlying the whole of this study has been that present tensions, whether national or international, are the outcome of the interrelationship of the permanent foundations and institutions of society with the novel and unique forces at work in the world. Therefore we confront the reader for the first time in Part III with the supreme issues and problems which he must face as a citizen. Even here we have foresworn the impulse to present policy recommendations for concrete problems.

Third, the gravest problem for those engaged in general education courses is the absence of available readings. Our major endeavor in preparing this volume has been to assist others to cope with the three problems which were the main stumbling blocks in our experience.

There are certain individuals among many kind and helpful friends who deserve special thanks at this point. Professor Clarence Overbeck, Chairman of the Bachelor of Arts Committee at Northwestern University, gave wise counsel and encouragement at many stages along the way. Dean Simeon Leland and Vice President Payson S. Wild were staunch supporters of our phase of a broader general education program which they helped conceive and maintain at Northwestern. Professors Charles S. Hyneman, Rollin Posey, and Roy C. Macridis of Northwestern's Department of Political Science gave generously of their time and energy. Many features of the book bear the imprint of Charles S. Hyneman's influence as former chairman of the course. One of us is especially indebted to Professors Hans J. Morgenthau and Leo Strauss of the University of Chicago and Reinhold Niebuhr of Union Theological Seminary, wise teachers and inspiring friends. Professor Leonard D. White of the University of Chicago cooperated in several important ways. But above all we are indebted to Miss Myrtle Meyer, Secretary of the Bachelor of Arts Program at Northwestern and Lucille B. Thompson whose patience, understanding and intelligent editing and accurate typing brought the manuscript to a satisfactory completion. We also thank Mr. Richard Cox, an extraordinarily brilliant associate.

University of Chicago   K. W. T.
Northwestern University   K. de S.

CONTENTS

1. Introduction

The roots of most societies are embedded in their history and physical position. Among cultures, some have had greater interest and self-consciousness than others in their traditions and historic roles. Sometimes this awareness has been stimulated by a sudden recognition that an era of greatness was passing. Often it has been in the twilight of history that a civilization's poets and philosophers have written with surest strokes the truth about their societies. For example, the insights into history and politics that were concentrated in two brief periods totaling less than a century probably remain unsurpassed. One was the Athens of Plato and Aristotle in the two middle quarters of the fourth century before Christ. The other was England between 1640 and 1690 when Hobbes, Locke, and their contemporaries sought to interpret the dawning of the new era of the constitutional nation-state. Both were periods of momentous change caused by the breakdown of an older order. Indeed these societies were no longer enjoying a period of vibrant growth but *rigor mortis* had set in when the philosophers began to write. The collapse of the Greek city-state and the crumbling of the medieval order were historic facts to which sensitive and penetrating minds responded but which no force on earth could then have reversed or changed.

It is not surprising, therefore, that anxiety and fear have been the prevailing emotions with which we have faced our own era of political and moral upheaval. For most philosophers of history, whether friendly or antagonistic to the schools of thought that unexpectedly have grown up around the writings of Spengler and Toynbee, there are today signs that our own " Time of Troubles " may be approaching. It has become increasingly clear that we are experiencing twin revolutions in the political and moral spheres which may herald the decline of our civilization. There are signs, for instance, that the traditional modern state system has been shattered and destroyed by the overwhelming power of the two giants from East and West, the Soviet Union and the United States. The unity of the Western world based on a common moral code was severed originally by the displacement of the feudal-medieval order by that of sovereign nation-states. This change was only a prelude to the revolutions we have witnessed in our own time.

No one can deny that political and moral changes as far-reaching as the collapse of the nation-state system and the deterioration of the influence of the common ethical standards of Christendom require new insights and novel interpretations. The nature of the political order and the

I

forms of accommodating techniques appropriate to the functioning of that order have been transformed in the mid-twentieth century. The magnitude of Russian and American power have made impossible the simple restraining influence of the balance of power system as it operated over three centuries. There are no longer any powers or combinations of powers that can throw their strength to the weaker combination of nations to prevent the outbreak of conflict. In the same way, through the moral revolution the restraining influence of a common moral order or a community of interests such as existed among the eighteenth century aristocratic elite has been supplanted by the emergence of two separate and autonomous orders, those of the communist and democratic political religions. For communism in theory and practice and less obviously for democracy in practice the effective moral code is an immanent one in which ethics are determined by the objectives of the particular system of state. Virtue and justice are measured by the influence of the actor or action upon progress toward communist or democratic goals.

These revolutions, no less profound than the disintegration of the city-state system in the fourth century B.C., or the breakdown of the medieval order in the seventeenth century, call for new principles and theories if they are to be understood. The failure of the social sciences to provide such principles implies a fundamental defect in methodology or an indifference to the formulation

of theories. In the past century not organized social science but students on the periphery have presented the bold insights, such as the Marxian and Freudian theories, which social scientists have appropriated with varying shades of enthusiasm. While principles in the social sciences can be no more than tentative, they furnish a basis for understanding the present and a means for coping with the future. Moreover, in certain areas the relation of recurrent aspects of human behavior to permanent conditions in the environment make the formulation of principles more practical and feasible.

It can be shown that certain features in any society are relatively permanent and fundamental. They include the history and traditions, circumstances of geography, amplitude of resources, population patterns and goods supply. These elements blended together constitute the permanent environment, which sets the limits and boundaries within which the individual can work out his destiny. His importance and that of his society are largely determined by the interrelationship of these and similar factors.

The historic, demographic and geographic areas together make up the "natural environment." For a given culture or society, this environment tends to be relatively stable. Geography, for instance, limits historic and social growth. War and peace are frequently influenced, if not determined, by geography. Lord Curzon once wrote: "Frontiers are indeed the razor's edge on which hang suspended the modern issues of war and peace, of life and death to nations." The uniqueness of America's geographical position and the extent of its resources have made possible its unparalleled development to its present world role. France, by contrast, has never been able to erase the specter of a ubiquitous conqueror inspired and encouraged by the nature of her northeast frontier.

For any large and well-organized group, population trends can be discovered which furnish an estimate of the manpower component of a society's strength and determine in part the character of their prospective relations — whether of dominance or dependence — with others. France was the dominant power in Europe when every seventh European was a Frenchman. Germany endangered the security of France only in the nineteenth century, when its population had overtaken that of the third Napoleonic Empire. One persisting reason that the Soviet Union throws a menacing shadow over the world is because in 1970 its population is expected to reach 250,000,000. The promise or peril of cultures or nations are therefore frequently judged by the demographic aspect of their permanent environment.

Unless one believes in "natural" determinism, however, the historic, demographic, and geographic dimensions of society do not predetermine its development. The "natural" environment merely delimits the boundaries of development and within these boundaries the decisions made consciously and unconsciously by society control the direction and extent of its change. Decision-making, therefore, can be viewed as the adaptation of social institutions to the "natural" environment in which they take roots.

Of the many decisions that any society must make, political decision-making is most crucial in terms of its influence on the character of social institutions. The type of state a society develops precludes the existence of some institutions, places strictures on the growth of others, and stimulates the growth of still others. Independent unionism was an anathema to Nazi Germany but a boon to the New Deal of the United States. Organized religion flourishes in the United States but is severely circumscribed in the Soviet Union.

Perhaps more significantly, the means of political choice establishes a pattern of power relationships in society between the many and the few — the many who are controlled by the state and the few who administer the affairs of the state. In democratic society sovereignty rests with the people who thus have the power through political choice of discharging irresponsible leaders. On the other hand, the citizens of totalitarian society must passively accept the decisions of a ruling elite, whether responsible or not.

Since the flowering of the Greek tradition in the fourth century before Christ, mankind has continuously addressed itself to the problem of political choice. Although institutions have changed and society in consequence has evolved from small personal organization to large impersonal organization the questions asked have remained the same — how *should* political decisions be made, on the one hand, and how *are* political decisions made, on the other? The answers to these questions have varied from historical era to historical era and from society to society. That these questions have not been answered once and for all does not prove the stupidity of man. Rather it proves the profound importance of the questions raised and the necessity for each new generation to struggle with the questions and attempt to answer them in the light of the values it holds important.

The search for a solution, however, is not pursued in the abstract. The recognition of the problem of political choice in any given society compels man to examine the historical tradition and the ideological heritage which have molded the existing political institutions. Moreover, men are schooled to look at problems in similar ways through the possession of common traditions. Present solutions will be guided by past answers. Consequently society will exhibit a continuity in its political growth that can only be disrupted by its demise. Nations and societies are more than artificial growths or synthetic creations. The Bolshevik revolution of 1917, which shattered the structure of Tsarist society, did not and could not destroy the unique historical conditions that comprise the Russian tradition. Similarly the French revolution did not deprive the French of the influence of their past. Thus political choices determine the direction

in which a society will grow but are in turn reflections of the traditions and history of its past and present generations.

If political choice is of fundamental importance in shaping the institutions within which man lives, economic choice is hardly of less importance. The resources available for transformation into goods and services are not plentiful enough to satisfy the multitudinous wants of man. Society must develop organizations through which decisions can be made about the utilization of limited resources among unlimited alternative employments. Through the sweep of historical time, many different types of economic organization have facilitated the production and distribution of goods and services. Each particular society evolves its own unique system of economic choice. The feudal system submerged economic choice in the contractual relationships existing between lords and villeins, lords and serfs. The choice of how to utilize resources and how to distribute the product of resources was not made consciously but rather was bound up with the status hierarchy of the feudal community. In an enterprise system, theoretically at least, the significant economic decisions are made consciously by all the members of society who meet in the markets as buyers and sellers. At the opposite extreme, a centrally planned economy delegates the important decision-making functions to a central authority. Although the specific methods utilized in these economic organizations are different, the nature of the decisions that must be made is the same in each.

Obviously, success in the performance of these functions is vital to society. The failure to meet the challenge of economic choice accentuates the other social problems that society faces. Material wealth opens up to a society a whole range of policy measures denied to societies of lesser wealth. The " welfare state " — the product of western liberalism — is dependent on the productivity increases that generate a large surplus over subsistence. The " welfare state " cannot function in a society that consumes all it produces and still does not maintain a subsistence standard of living.

Choice, whether political or economic, democratic or totalitarian, depends upon the transmission of the natural and social environment to the minds of those who make decisions. In other words, society must have some system for exchanging ideas and registering its mind on concrete issues. This function is performed by the media of communication.

The media of communication are essential for choice. Yet they always pose the threat of a perversion of choice, for the real world of daily occurrence is seen and evaluated not as objective reality but as a picture of reality implanted in men's minds by the controllers of communication. For any people, therefore, the real world is twice removed and twice mediated. The images in our minds are the grains and kernels of history that filter through the sieve of men's beliefs,

opinions, and prejudices. They are the stereotypes with which uncertain men confront reality. Moreover, in mass societies the reality presented to the mind is one that has been sorted and interpreted by other minds. No individual can be on the scene for more than a fraction of history's significant events. His picture of truth is thus slanted not alone by his well-guarded bias and beliefs but by the men and institutions that deal in the commerce of ideas.

The social-psychological environment of mass communication is therefore the world we feel and breathe rather than the world-in-itself. The mass media provide instantaneous translations, through which men learn about current events. In contemporary society mass communications are big business. By contrast, in a face-to-face society where contacts are limited and firsthand, communication is diffused through the institutions of varying and competing influence such as kinship, religious, and family groups. These institutions rather than the mechanized and organized activities of vast instruments of mass communication carry the news. Their limitation is in the range and scope of their technique of newscoverage. But the shortcomings of the mass media of communication are sociological not technical, qualitative not quantitative. The risk of great efficiency is that a limited few will give the answer to the timeless question " what is truth? " If members of a common social group administer the business of reporting the news, it is always possible that

they will tend to look through uni-
focal lenses at a multi-colored panorama of the deeds and aspirations
constituting the experiences of
groups and nations.

To summarize, any society is embedded in a " natural " environment,
which is a compound of the geographical location, the resources base,
the demographic pattern, and the historical tradition of that society.
Within the limits established by the
" natural " environment, the choices
society makes with respect to political organization and the utilization
of scarce resources determine the specific character of many of the institutions by which and within which
man lives. Thus, communication,
which must be central to any system
of choice, can exert a profound influence on the organization of society.

If it were necessary to isolate the
single most important phenomenon
distinguishing modern society from
its progenitors, one could make a
good case for the Industrial Revolution, which flourished in England at
the end of the eighteenth century.
The changes wrought by this rapid
transformation in the technological
and economic basis of society still
make their impression. Because of
the Industrial Revolution man lives
in a world of specialization and is excluded from a range of knowledge
much wider than that afforded by his
particular occupation. More often
than not his contribution to society is
lost in the complexities of industrial
organization and can only be estimated by a normative interpretation of
wages and income. And as indus-

trialization has proceeded apace, man
has become further removed from the
vital center of the institutions within
which he lives. The boss he once
knew by sight and name he now
knows only by reputation. His political representative is immersed in
a large bureaucracy, which threatens
to become even larger in response to
the inexorable problems of industrial
society. His home, which was once
the fulcrum of his total existence,
now becomes the way station between the world of work and the
world of entertainment.

Yet industrialization has brought
the amenities of material wealth to
many more people than was ever before considered possible. It has shattered the belief that poverty is ordained by a super being and that the
poor exist to serve the rich. Man
is now held responsible for the plight
of mankind and it has sometimes
seemed to many that the energies
erupting in industrialization portend
the millennium when poverty, ignorance, and squalor will be banished
from the earth.

Industrialization has not yet exorcised the specter of hunger and poverty. We do not live in utopia. The
problems of political and economic
choice, therefore, become even more
important in the milieu of an industrial order. For, having cast aside
the shackles of a traditionalistic belief in the inevitability of man's fate,
the members of industrial society
consciously strive to achieve the better life. Choice then becomes an
explicit and intended part of the design of living.

In the industrial civilization of today there are numerous systems of economic and political choice, all of which presumably are attempting to achieve similar objectives. The social organizations of the United States are characterized by a predominant emphasis on individual choice, the social organizations of the Soviet Union by collective choice. In the former individuals make the significant decisions, which in the aggregate represent the ultimate arbiter of policy. In the latter a collectivity, which presumably represents the members of society, makes the significant decisions. Between these extremes the societies of the world form a continuum, which links the systems of individual and collective choice; some nations eschew political collectivism but depend on economic collectivism while other nations eschew economic collectivism but accept political collectivism.

Vast areas of the world, struggling to break out of the vicious circle of subsistence-living, are now compelled consciously to place themselves in this continuum of systems of choice. For any given society the appropriate system of choice is conditioned by its "natural" environment and by the rate at which the society wishes to make the transformations implied in industrialization. The solution is not simple and at the present juncture of world affairs the problem provides one of the focal points of antagonism between East and West.

As we have suggested, industrialization has been a mixed blessing. Although material levels of living have been raised, new social problems have appeared that should temper the optimism of the hopeful. The industrial order brought into urban centers a surge of population, which inundated urban facilities and thus created the blight of the slum. The slum deprived the individual of the stability of family existence and compensated him with the harsh and metallic order of street lights, pavements, and honky tonks.

The slum, which is a living memorial to the destruction of the individual in modern industrial society, also dramatizes the extreme contrast between rich and poor. The South Side and the North Shore in Chicago, Harlem and Westchester County in New York are paradoxically enough by-products of the very process that has made the United States the wealthiest nation in the world. It is part of our history that those who rode the crest of the industrial expansion prospered, but many fell and floundered in hopeless poverty.

Yet income inequality apparently is a malignant growth in industrial society, which cannot be removed by the surgery of social policy. The Soviet Union, whose early leaders had equalitarian predilections, has apparently found under the duress of economic reality that it had progressively to widen income inequality in order to achieve satisfactory rates of industrialization. The material wealth of industrial society breeds a dependence on the material forms of motivation.

Modern man has chosen to solve these and other social problems associated with industrial society. The attempt to do so, however, has posed still other problems. Since the existence of social ills is symptomatic of the loss of the individual capacity for self-adjustment, society has chosen to expand the role of the state in order to compensate the individual for his weaknesses in mass industrial organization. In the past twenty years the agencies of the United States government have proliferated at an uncommon rate. Some of the less favorable consequences of this development have been ameliorated but the cost has been high — the erection of a large bureaucracy.

Bureaucracy, wherever it exists, can become a threat to individual political choice. The bureaucrat may be an expert required to deal with technical problems about which the average individual cannot be expected to hold an opinion. That the expert plays a role in the bureaucracy is not the result of malevolent design, however, but rather the result of the immense range and complexity of the underlying social problems that society is attempting to resolve. A large bureaucracy removes high governmental officials from the immediate pressures of political choice by surrounding him with offices, secretaries, and lesser bureaucrats who function in part to maintain the sanctity and privacy of the inner office. The top official thus looks at the world through an institution which protects him from the world. In short, bureaucracy may create conditions favorable to irresponsible behavior on the part of governmental officials.

However, bureaucracy is not peculiar to democratic society; it is peculiar to large industrial society. Whenever and wherever man has directed his energies to the transformation of agricultural society into industrial society, governmental bureaucracy has been an inevitable concomitant. The issues raised by bureaucracy, however, vary with the conditions of social and economic organization. In any democratic society bureaucracy may vitiate the vitality of democratic choice. Therefore it compels the society constantly to improvise methods of enforcing responsible behavior on the part of governmental officials. In totalitarian society this aspect of bureaucracy is not a problem. But the totalitarian leader's unconcern about the preferences of the people cannot blind him to the impediments a bureaucracy can build up around his chosen policy. Responsible to the leader in theory, it may engulf him in practice. The leader, therefore, must improvise methods of keeping his bureaucracy " pure," loyal, and devoted to the values he symbolizes.

Industrialization, urbanism, and big government — this is the background against which social policy is formulated in an ever-larger and growing part of the world. Out of this background, however, tensions are fermented within nations and among nations, which complicate the formulation of policy. These tensions can be viewed as conflicts in the patterns of choice and as rivalries among groups and individuals striving for the right to make such choices.

Within any given society there may be complete agreement about the ultimate ends of life, but there can scarcely be complete agreement about the means for achieving these ends. We may all agree that the slum is a blight on modern society, but we may differ when we seek a solution to the problem.

Disagreement with respect to means is inherent in the social structure of society. The attitudes of individuals, and hence the decisions they make, will be conditioned by the roles they perform in the social life. Industrial society through specialization of function multiplies the number of these roles. The unskilled worker, the skilled worker, the secretary, the lawyer, the chemist, the industrialist, and the professor have different positions in the social hierarchy and view social processes from different vantage points. Minimum wage legislation may appear to be the height of lunacy to the industrialist but the ultimate virtue to the unskilled worker.

The decisions or the choices individuals make with respect to social policy, however, are not rigidly determined by *a* role. For any individual assumes a number of roles. He may be a skilled worker, but he is also a head of a family, a member of a community, a ward heeler for a political party, or a paid-up member of a fraternal organization. The individual sees life through these roles and the decisions he makes represent the distillation of the forces that impinge on him through these roles. The multiplicity of roles that any individual plays dulls the sharp edges of tensions among occupational statuses. The worker and his employer

may be in inalterable opposition about the merits of a wage increase, but as heads of families they may be in hearty accord about the necessity of building a new school. Since policies normally affect the way one can perform more than one role, the vested interest of one particular role does not always dominate one's policy decisions.

In democratic organization the tensions arising from the structure of society are institutionalized in a political process which defines rules of political conduct. The members of society agree to disagree. Tensions which exist between groups are brought to the surface and given public hearing. In making tensions explicit it becomes possible, therefore, to apply remedial measures that have been discussed by all and agreed to by at least a majority.

In totalitarian society the tensions that exist among groups and individuals are hidden behind the symbolism of unanimity, as, for example, the symbol of the classless society. In other words, tensions are repressed by elevating one role in society to a dominant and pre-eminent position — the role of the individual as an organic member of total society. The role of the individual as a father or a worker becomes subservient to this all-pervasive role. Tensions, then, rather than being made explicit, are repressed in order to maintain the illusion of unanimity.

Industrialization, in addition to proliferating the number of roles men can perform in society, has also increased the importance of some roles. The industrial workers who man the expanding factories become more numerous relative to other occupational groups. The managerial groups, who are responsible for the organization of production, become increasingly important as society becomes more dependent on the maintenance of industrial employment. The concentration of these groups in an industrial order, however, gives rise to a formalization of the tensions between them.

The individual worker, unable to cope with the problems he meets, turns to a group — the union — which can compensate him for his weaknesses as an individual. The union in acting for the worker is primarily concerned with the individual's role as a worker and only secondarily with the other roles that he plays. The decisions of the union group, therefore, stem from a more unequivocal source than do the decisions of an individual. The demands for the amelioration of the conditions of work become strong and persistent.

The persistent demands of unions appear to management to be encroachments on their prerogatives, on their decision-making authority. Management therefore strives to protect its position. This protection was achieved at one time in the United States by forcibly denying the union entrance into industry. Now it is sought by collective bargaining around the conference table.

Collective bargaining can be construed as the formalization of the tensions between labor and management. If industrialization hardens class lines, collective bargaining brings to the surface the tensions between industrial classes and thus makes possible their relaxation through compromise.

The tensions within nations will not disappear so long as individuals and groups possess the powers of choice and attempt to achieve their ends in the light of the various roles they perform. Tensions, however, can be minimized and prevented from deteriorating into overt conflict. The success of social policy may in part be measured by its influence in adjusting tensions and preventing the outbreak of debilitating conflict.

If the tensions within nations can be minimized, it is because individuals accept some dominant set of values that restrain and limit their behavior. If tensions among nations frequently manifest themselves in war, it is because the nations of the world do not accept a common and dominant set of values and therefore the behavior of each nation is only restrained by the behavior of other nations. In short, each nation considers itself the sovereign judge of its own conduct.

The choices each sovereign nation makes in the development of its foreign policy generates a nexus of power relationships among the nations of the world. These power relationships are at once the symptom of tensions among nations and the means of reducing them. Nations combine in formal or informal alliance to protect themselves from the adverse decisions of what they conceive to be unfriendly nations.

These adverse decisions are the source of tensions in international politics and therefore the source of alliance. The power relationships among nations, however, can prevent tensions from breaking out into open war. For it is only through power that nations can constrain the behavior of other nations, and the maintenance of peace requires an international order of the kind that would discourage any nation from the temptation to wage overt military campaigns to achieve its objectives. War, the resort to naked power, paradoxically enough is a manifestation of the breakdown of a power system capable of exerting international restraint.

The interwar period of international diplomacy was both noble and tragic, noble because the moral revulsion against war — the pre-eminence of pacificism — guided the policies of the Western nations and tragic because these noble aspirations were not supported by an effective system of power which could have made them come true. Time and time again the allied nations were to shrink from making decisions that might have prevented the ruthless and unbridled behavior of Nazi Germany. They were reluctant to act because these decisions seemed morally indefensible. The rearmament of Germany, the militarization of the Rhineland, the Austrian coup d'état, the Nazi-Fascist alliance, the Sudeten crisis, and the Nazi-Soviet pact were in effect accomplished with the acquiescence of the Western nations. The fear of using the techniques of power stimulated the growth of a malignant cancer in Central Europe that eventually engulfed the world in total war. The United States in particular set itself firmly against an involvment in what it considered the evil power politics of Western Europe.

Industrialization has influenced international politics in three important respects. First, a revolution in the technique of production, transportation, and communication has reduced the effective size of the world. The stage in which international politics is played has become smaller and therefore the decisions made by the players have universal repercussions. No longer can the United States look upon Europe or Asia as remote continents far removed from its national interests. Second, the strength of industrial nations has increased to such an extent that for the first time in history mankind possesses the means of destroying itself. It is no longer farfetched to assert that survival depends on the types of decisions made in international politics. Third, industrialization has widened the philosophical gulf that separates the participants in international politics. Marxism, the critical offshoot of industrial capitalism, fosters a belief in determinism that is in sharp conflict with the indeterminism of liberal democracy. The Marxist also views life through the prism of dialectical materialism, which does not square with the spirit of compromise that normally prevails in liberal democracy.

Because of these influences the structure of power in international politics has polarized. The United

States dominates one pole, the USSR the other, and the nations of the world gravitate to one pole or the other in accordance with the dictates of their national interests. Clearly the responsibilities for the decisions or choices that will maintain or break the peace devolve more and more on these two great powers. The areas of the world, therefore, where the national interests of the United States and the USSR meet head on assume added significance. The conduct of international affairs in Germany, the Middle East, and the Far East provide the clues to the eventual development of world politics, and Lord Curzon's axiom that foreign affairs are in practice the most domestic of all affairs since they affect the individual most vitally and intimately has come true.

The readings which follow do not pretend to solve the manifold problems of modern society. They have been chosen because they elucidate and expand the topics outlined in this introduction. Part I is devoted to the development of the thesis that choice is essential to any society regardless of its institutional organization. Part II explores the modern context in which choices are made — industrialization, urbanism, and big government. In conclusion, Part III considers the tensions which arise within nations and among nations in consequence of the decisions made in industrial society. It is hoped that an understanding and appreciation of choice will prepare the student to think more intelligently about the problems his own society and the world face.

PART I

THE FOUNDATIONS
OF MODERN SOCIETY

1 THE PERMANENT FOUNDA-
TIONS OF SOCIETY

A. Historic Roots

2. The Historic Basis of Modern Society

Any study of society first must chart the subject's location in time and in space. The former is a task for the historian; the latter for the geographer. In a profoundly incisive little lecture on " The Study of History " delivered at Cambridge on June 11, 1895, Lord Acton observed: " I describe as modern history that which begins four hundred years ago, which is marked off by an evident and intelligible line from the time immediately preceding, and displays in its course specific and distinctive characteristics of its own."

Modern society, as we conceive it, had its genesis in the fifteenth and sixteenth centuries. It fell heir at this time to certain medieval traditions but was an apostate from others. The old order had been weakened by forces that would not be arrested. We may say that its disappearance was hastened by five figures who became spokesmen of the new epoch. They were the architects of the Renaissance and Reformation. Columbus shattered the most stubborn of illusions about the shape of the world and its boundaries. Ma-

chiavelli probed to the bedrock of emerging government and statecraft as it has been practiced down to the present day. Erasmus redirected the study of classical sources into new channels. Luther challenged and helped overthrow the once powerful and unified Corpus Christianum. Copernicus sapped at the vitals of the earth-centered concept of the universe, which had offered an impressive but misguided basis for estimating the importance of man and his earth. The transformation of commerce, government, learning, religion, and science over several centuries was responsible for the fact that the new civilization was ushered in almost imperceptibly by the operation of forces too powerful to allow the survival of the old.

In space, the modern society we shall consider had its origins in Western Europe. It is true that in practice, the geographic locations of medieval and modern society are substantially the same. In contrast to the Hellenic world, whose interests faced chiefly toward the Mediterranean, medieval and modern societies looked both north and south to the Mediterranean and the North Sea. In its expansion Europe thrust out many spokes from the area that to-day is Germany. Its first thrust was toward the east. Soon it collided with a Russian power, which then as now was partly European and partly non-European. Of this power, Henry Adams wrote to his brother Brooks on July 6, 1898: "France must follow Spain to the seclusion of local interests; and Germany must merge in Russia. So we can foresee a new centralization, of which Russia is one pole, and we the other, with England between." Moreover, there has been a third crucial area. Between the millstone of the West and netherstone of Russia, the area of Eastern Europe has been ground and crushed until it has become the traditional "shatter-zone" in world politics, the victim of pressures from east and west.

Modern society has likewise expanded westward and in this process England became the major peripheral or rim-land area. Then the emergence, at the turn of this century, of the United States as potentially the strongest world power took place. To the east Japan, China, and India, unlike one another in many respects, shared a common experience of subjection to the impact of westernization. We can say in general terms that modern society has tended to subvert older cultures and alien customs to its own ways through the intervention of Western technology. But "Westernization" is usually incomplete. The position of those areas for whom industrialization has

been most recent — notably Japan and certain countries in Latin America — or has not yet been consummated — as India, Africa, and Southeast Asia — is in a crude way no different from pre-Bolshevik-Russia. From Peter the Great to the present, Russia by technology has been a member of the West, but by choice has remained the "Twentieth Century Byzantium." Cultures and civilizations have tried to retain their prerogatives of importing certain aspects but not others of alien societies.

The resulting disparity between industrial development and political practices in these areas as contrasted to the core of modern society in the West has created tragic and nearly intractable problems. We shall return to them in Part III. Here we have tried merely to suggest that the scope and sweep of modern society extends over the whole world to the extent that Western technology has become universal. It is something less than world-wide in so far as some areas have rejected the more far-reaching cultural and political changes which in the past accompanied industrialization. Even those areas that in part might be considered outside of modern society, must in practice be included since their institutions are unceasingly in jeopardy from the transforming encroachment of Western techniques and attitudes.

Historically modern society had its genesis in the fifteenth and sixteenth centuries; geographically it extends over most of the world about which we know. The first selection is a paper presented to a conference at the Royal Institute of International

Affairs in 1931. It is remarkable from at least two points of view. Mr. Arnold Toynbee, Director of Studies at the Royal Institute of International Affairs and Research Professor of International History at the University of London, has selected from the past episodes that parallel contemporary crises. By dealing with epochs whose final chapters have been completed, he dramatizes the consequences of steps taken or avoided then and compares them with the alternatives facing us today. The prophetic character of this paper written in 1931 rests chiefly in the author's prediction that communism then was destined to become a crusading political religion and that world politics operating without regulation under a world government can be limited solely by the machinery of the balance of power. It is a tendency of the balance to shift to the periphery, as indeed the European center of gravity has moved to Washington and Moscow, but in a crude and imperfect way it must continue to operate if we are to keep the peace.

More important than the accuracy of his prophecies are Mr. Toynbee's principles of history. While sometimes controversial and unproven, they are never irrelevant or pointless. The great merit of this selection lies in its clear ringing emphasis on the enduring character of certain forces in history. When order was maintained in the Greek world it was by means of the balance of power. The crusading character now associated with the communist political religion was felt before among those of the Moslem faith. These parallels are important in throwing light on the basic character and risks or pitfalls of our present position.

Our second selection reiterates a series of important questions. Historians and philosophers have long puzzled over the relationships between separate but affiliated civilizations succeeding one another in time. How does history cross the boundaries of successive cultures? What is the nature of the process by which a society appropriates or rejects wholly or partly the customs and institutions of its predecessors? To what extent does the one re-establish the practices of the other? Professor George M. Trevelyan, since 1940 Master of Trinity College, Cambridge, tries to answer these questions by tracing the emergence of contemporary society as a child of medieval culture and by indicating specifically the points at which it has diverged from its parent. By implication, he deals with the basic problems of historical continuity, cultural penetration, and the recurrence of historical patterns in the forms of cycles or spirals.

3. Historical Parallels to Current International Problems*

I daresay many people in this room will want to ask the preliminary question whether there really are any historical parallels to current problems. The very title of my talk may possibly be challenged, because we people of the West, in our generation, are inclined to believe that our present situation is unprecedented: that we are "not as other men are." Of course every generation, everywhere, in its day, is inclined to feel the same about its own life. The present is practically more important than the past or the future for those living in the present, and so it is natural to feel that it is more important for all time. Yet history shows that all our predecessors have been mistaken about their own uniqueness. Have we any better justification for our megalomania?

I am convinced that our belief in our own uniqueness is an illusion. On what is this belief based? Almost entirely on the recent increase in our command over Physical Nature — on our knack for clockwork, to put it in less exalted terms.

I suggest that Man is still the measure of all things, and that the importance of human inventions must be measured by their effect on human life. None of our recent inventions has had such a profound ef-

fect on human life as the great prehistoric inventions. Take wireless and gramophones: well, somebody once invented language. Or take our marvelous astronomical discoveries: well, somebody once discovered the calendar — the movements of the sun and moon. Take our domestication of steam and electricity: somebody once domesticated fire, plants and animals; and the calendar and the domestication of plants together produced agriculture and so revolutionized human life to an infinitely greater degree than any of the inventions of modern times. Motorcars are not so great an invention as the first wheel. Or compare a machine gun with the first bow and arrow — the idea of hitting something at a distance with a missile: the great creativeness was there. Compare a modern steel works with the first copper smith, or the first dugout with the latest liner. In every case the prehistoric invention puts the modern invention into the shade. If we base our claim to uniqueness on modern inventions, our case is weak.

But do not let us discuss the question on the basis of material inventions, ancient or modern. They merely give command over Physical Nature; and our relations with Physical Nature are child's play compared to our relations with Human Nature; our relations with ourselves and with our neighbours.

* From Arnold J. Toynbee, *International Affairs*, X (1931), pp. 477–88. Reprinted by permission of Arnold J. Toynbee and *International Affairs*.

By the Upper Palaeolithic Age, the Human Race had already attained such mastery over Physical Nature — not only inanimate Nature, but all the fauna and flora of the planet except Man himself — that Mankind was assured by then, not only of survival, but also of mastery over everything on the face of the planet except Mankind.

Since then, our relations with Human Nature have been the supremely important thing in human affairs. The advances which we have made since rather remote prehistoric times in our command over Physical Nature have been superfluities — luxuries — of no significance except for their effect upon our command over Human Nature.

Now, increases in our command over Physical Nature have as often as not upset and set back our command over Human Nature, our command over ourselves and over our relations with each other. If one considers our modern material inventions in order to ask whether they have made human relations easier or more difficult, happier or unhappier, better or worse, the answer is doubtful. Are our human relations in our day and in our society really different in kind from those of our predecessors?

I should like to suggest that our present situation, when looked at in the right perspective and measured with the right measure, is not unprecedented at all. Let us take one concrete set of human relations with which we particularly concern ourselves in this Institute: the relations between a multitude of local States, living side by side in the same world and in the same society, yet each possessing sovereign independence and all asserting their sovereignty by periodically going to war with one another.

Is that unprecedented? Why, history teems with parallels. Let us pick out two or three at random and look at them in comparison with our own present position in international politics: first, the warring States of mediaeval Italy during the four centuries ending with the fifteenth century of our era; then the warring States of the ancient Graeco-Roman world from the Peloponnesian War to the time of Augustus; then, going further away to a field which is rather vague to most of us, the warring States of the ancient Chinese world from the seventh century B.C. to the third century.

Let us consider, first of all, what bearing these three parallels to our modern Balance of Power have upon our greatest modern problem: the problem of peace. When we consider this problem, which rightly obsesses us all in our world — the problem: Will war be abolished? — what light do the historical parallels throw upon this question, on which our own future hangs?

Some people say that war is inseparable from Human Nature; that wherever two or three human beings are gathered together there will be war in the midst of them. I think the historical parallels show that this view is mistaken. I think they show that in every society that is war-ridden, war *is* abolished sooner or later and in one way or another. At first sight this seems encouraging, but it all depends on how soon and in which way. The usual way has been for war to be abolished, later rather than sooner, by a knockout blow.

In the Graeco-Roman world they fought war after war with each other, bringing upon themselves social disintegration and dissolution, until in the end all the other sovereign States, and there were a great many of them, were knocked out by Rome.

In the ancient Chinese world, as far as I know, the picture is much the same: centuries of war between contending States, ending again in a knockout blow delivered by the State corresponding to Rome — Ts'in.

This method is like bolting the stable door after the steed has fled; abolishing war after society has exhausted its vitality. It is not so difficult to do, but it is a kind of deathbed repentance, not a convalescence. If you look into the history of these parallels, I think you can see that the ancient Chinese and the ancient classical civilizations had ceased to be creative before the advent of peace. The great things in classical history certainly were done before the establishment of the Roman Peace, not after. So I believe it is in Chinese history: the whole of Chinese philosophy was thought out, as far as it ever went, before the establishment of the Chinese Universal Empire. I suggest that by the historic way of waiting until one State gives a knockout blow and establishes a Universal Empire, you do get peace for a short time; but almost everything which

makes life worth living has vanished before then.

The other way, the way we are trying to adopt in our society, in our generation, is to abolish war sooner rather than later, by agreement and not by force, by organization and not by conquest, at a time when our vitality is still strong, not waiting until war has exhausted it. What chances of success have we in trying to abolish war in this way — the only way that is worth while? You do find such attempts in the Graeco-Roman and Chinese worlds from time to time — attempts to stop war and organize peace — before the knockout blow — but the outcome of those attempts is not very encouraging for us.

Then, let me pass to another thing connected rather closely with the problem of war, which exercises us to-day: the dwarfing of Europe in the post-War world. It is most paradoxical and, to us Europeans, painful to watch. It is not a paradox that the region which is the cradle of our modern civilization is being dwarfed by the regions into which that civilization has spread — that the mother countries of Western Civilization are being dwarfed by their children? When I say children, I do not merely mean children after the flesh — the new countries built up by European settlers overseas, as on the American continent. I mean also children after the spirit: the Eastern civilizations which, without any infusion of blood, are becoming converts to Western Civilization. Countries like India and China, when they come into their own, will tower above Europe just as the United States and Canada tower above us already.

For this paradox we have striking parallels in the cases I have mentioned. Look at Greece in the ancient world after the conquests of Alexander, or Central China from the fifth century B.C. onwards, or Italy, the cradle of our modern Western Civilization, from the sixteenth century of our era onwards.

I was working once in the Foreign Office and had to deal with a pile of documents bearing upon the Peace Settlement. In the pile I came across a certain Minute of the Supreme War Council of the Allies. The record mentioned that on this occasion, before the Supreme Council got to business, Baron Sonnino bored his colleagues, as he had so often done before, by expounding his view that the European States were like the States of ancient Greece and that America was like Rome; the European States would go on fighting each other, and America would come in at the end, as Rome came in, and take the whole thing. His colleagues obviously sat through this prologue, feeling very much bored, and then the business of the day came on. But I wonder whether Baron Sonnino's prologue was not really more to the point than what followed.

Baron Sonnino was thinking about a certain speech recorded by the Greek historian Polybius as having been delivered by a certain Greek statesman at a moment when the future of the world was being decided by a great war between Rome and Carthage, the War of Hannibal.

The tiny Greek States, still the centers of civilization, were also still fighting innumerable wars, and now they happened to be holding a peace conference. One of the leading statesmen got up and said: "We must agree among ourselves. If we do not, we are lost. Look at that cloud in the west rising above our horizon." He made that speech, and for a moment they thought how nice it would be to make peace, and then they went on making war, and the cloud in the west rose until it overshadowed them. Yes, I am inclined to think that Baron Sonnino's boring prologue was one of the most important pieces of business in that Supreme Council meeting.

Then look at Machiavelli's "Prince": Was not the Florentine somehow trying to do the same thing as Polybius's Greek statesman, in order that the Italian States, the heart of the civilization of the day, might hold their own against the great surrounding barbarian States, France and England, the Hapsburg Power, and so on? He did not succeed.

In ancient China one has glimpses of the same thing; the small States in the heart of the Chinese world and the big new States on the edges which eventually engulfed them. And in our own time there is Count Coudenhove-Kalergi, or Monsieur Briand with his more official schemes, talking about Europe on the same lines. Cannot the tiny European States, instead of thwarting each other, get together? After all, they are still the heart of civilization; and if they are overshadowed and dominated by the big States round the edges, the world will be spiritually the poorer for it.

I think these ancient parallels do throw light on our own problems. Why did the Italian States in Machiavelli's time, or the States of ancient Greece in the time of the Punic Wars, fail to get together and hold their own? Why were the most intelligent people of the age, at the center of civilization, so inept in politics compared with the rising peoples on the edges? Obviously because of the continuance of chronic warfare. When you get chronic warfare the small States at the center will inevitably go under and the big States at the edges will inevitably come up.

That follows from the way in which the Balance of Power system works. It is a system of pressures between a number of States covering a given area of the earth's surface, and in any system of that sort the pressure is always greater at the center than at the edges. Take our world; think of the European wars of the last century. How very small the territories are which have changed hands, and how very hard the European States have fought for tiny areas like Alsace and Lorraine, while, almost unnoticed, the United States has expanded from the Atlantic to the Pacific and Russia from the Baltic to the Pacific. But, all the time, from the center of the civilized world, there is streaming out a current of civilization, flowing into the larger States on the edges which have been able to become large because they are not under the pressure which is greatest at the center. That

stream of civilization flowing — in our case, out of Europe — in the form of emigrants, capital, ideas, institutions, transforms the great States that arise in the outer darkness and gradually raises their standard of civilization and power, until the little States in the center, the mothers of civilization, are dwarfed by their children.

There is then a fatal divorce between the holders of material power and the holders of creative power. In the modern world the creative power is still in Europe as much as ever, but material power is passing to the States on the edges. The creative power at the center equips the outsiders with the means to dominate the creative center, and, even against their will, to sterilize it and, with it, the whole of society.

If we can get rid of war sooner rather than later and by agreement rather than by force, then material power may count for less than spiritual power and Europe may retain — or, rather, recover — her leadership in the modern world for the good of modern society as a whole. If we do not solve this problem of war, Europe will be the battlefield and the chief sufferer, and the State which finally plays the part of ancient Rome, whether it be American or Asiatic, will not be European.

Let us pass to another point — the contact of civilizations. That makes one look far ahead into the future. When we see the extraordinary psychological cultural effects of the contact between Western civilization and the other surviving civilizations — Byzantine, Islamic, Hindu, Far Eastern — going on under our eyes in our own day, we are bound to ask ourselves what, in the long run, is going to come about. One sees the ferment and wants to know the final chemical product. In our case we can only conjecture. We happen to be just at the beginning of the process, and for us the final outcome is far ahead. It is a process that takes place in the course of centuries and not in a lifetime.

Here there is the parallel of the contact between ancient Greek civilization and the ancient civilizations of Egypt, Syria, Mesopotamia, Persia and India. When Alexander the Great overran the Oriental world, the Greeks came in as the creative masters, the pushing force, into those relatively stagnant Oriental cultures, just as we Westerners have come into the East in the modern world.

The first phase we know: the passive civilizations, with which the active civilization collides, are turned upside down and thrown into a furore of revolution. We are familiar with that at present in contemporary China and Turkey. The Westernization of the modern East is paralleled with curious closeness by the Hellenization of the ancient East. In ancient Egypt under the Ptolemies there was the same attitude of the Egyptians to the Greeks as there is in modern Egypt towards the British and the other Westerners. The introduction of modern democratic institutions into Oriental countries — republics, parliaments, and so on — is paralleled in ancient times by the introduction of the Greek City State and all that it implied — a re-

grouping of Western Asia into city communities — and we know the ferment that it made. Again, we find Greek architecture at Baalbek in Syria, and Greek sculpture as far east as Afghanistan. The earliest statues of the Buddha are derived from a Greek type of Apollo, and the earliest representations of the Christ in the Catacombs at Rome are modelled on a traditional Greek representation of Orpheus.

Look at the violent collisions described in the Second Book of the Maccabees, between the forceful Hellenizer, Antiochus Epiphanes, and the zealous Jews who resisted him. The Hellenizing High Priest, Joshua, changed his name to the Greek Jason and made the young priests in the Temple go in for sports and gymnastics; and the final outrage was when they were made to wear felt hats with brims. We have had the very same thing in Afghanistan recently and in Turkey. On this issue of hats, Mustafa Kemal won in Turkey because he put some people to death; Amanullah was beaten and had to go into exile.

In the first phase, then, the intrusive civilization imposes its politics, economics, and even its art, upon the civilizations on which it intrudes; but there is a second phase. In our own case it is covered in darkness, but we know what it was in the ancient instance, because we know the whole story. The invaded civilizations make a counteroffensive by doing what would have struck the original Hellenizers as incredible — by imposing their religion, of all things, on the invaders. There was an invasion of the Graeco-Roman world by a number of Oriental religions. The cult of Isis from Egypt, Christianity from Syria, the worship of the stars from Mesopotamia, Mithra from Persia, and in the outskirts of the Greek world the new Mahayana form of Buddhism, all took part in this counterattack against the former masters of the world.

You know the sequel. In the ancient story it is the Greek who is now passive and the Oriental who is now active. The last chapter in the history of ancient Greek Civilization is the struggle between a number of competing Oriental religions for the conquest of the Graeco-Roman world. Christianity and Mithraism are the only two left in the last round, and finally Christianity conquers Hellenic Civilization. It would have seemed incredible, not only to Alexander and Caesar, but also to people as near the event as Marcus Aurelius.

On this analogy, we may forecast that, some centuries hence, the supreme social question in Europe and America will be: Shall we become converts to a new religion from Russia or to a new religion from India? Because we *must* have some religion to fill the void in our decaying civilization. I take it that Hinduism and the Russian version of Communism are the only serious competitors that we can see for the mission of filling our great void in the West. I do not think the Islamic world or the Far East will be in the running. As far as I can see, Islam and Buddhism and Confucianism are going the same way as Christianity. I have a

feeling that the future religion of the world will come out of Russia or India, where the religious spirit is strong; and, if it is a choice between Hinduism and Russian Communism, I should be inclined on present showing to back Russia rather than India. On the whole, I do not believe that Western Society, even in its dotage, will worship divinities with six arms and legs. I think we are more likely to deify Marx and Lenin and to accept *Das Kapital* and a selection from Lenin's works as our sacred books.

That, of course, raises the last question that I am going to put before you, and perhaps the most provocative: Is Communism, in the hands of the Russians, capable of being turned into a religion?

The suggestion that Communism is an incipient religion will seem to many people either ridiculous or shocking, and anyway paradoxical. Communism, they will say, denies the existence of God and the potency of spiritual forces in human affairs; one of its cardinal tenets is the materialist, determinist interpretation of history; and it is interested exclusively in material things: in redistributing the goods of this world, not in striving to attain the goods of another world. How can you call that a religion or expect it to turn into a religion?

Of course, all that is quite true; and if you were to ask me: " Was the Communism of Marx and Engels a religion? ", I should answer unhesitatingly: " No: it was a criticism — half philosophical and half political — of a particular phase in our Western social history, by certain Westerners of the day who were in revolt against the social system of their times." That is a simple answer to a simple question. But that simple question is not very important or interesting. The interesting and important question is: "What is this primitive Marxian Communism going to turn into now that the Russians have run away with it?" The Russians are a very religious people, and I fancy they can turn almost anything into a religion. Is there anything which will necessarily prevent Communism from being turned into a religion by them?

Let us see what light we can get from the historical parallels here. Let us glance, with this in view, at the history of religions which already have a long history behind them; for instance, Christianity and Buddhism. Communism is atheistic; does that exclude it from becoming a religion? Well, the Christians were regarded as atheists and blasphemers by the adherents of all the other religions in the Roman Empire, because they would tolerate no other religion but their own in a world which was accustomed to hosts of different cults, each tolerating the other. The fact that Christianity was a cult which would have no dealing with any of the others made Christianity seem atheistic by contrast with the pagan polytheistic toleration. The Christians differed from the others because they refused to live and let live, because they insisted on eradicating all the other cults and making Christianity the exclusive religion of society. Now that view of Christianity

as atheism, held by cultivated people of the time, was undoubtedly sincere; it was really how Christianity struck them. But of course we know that the view was quite mistaken; the Christians obviously did worship a God. Although Christianity seemed like atheism to the Greek and Roman pagans whose cults were threatened, it was very much of a religion, albeit an exclusive one. So now let us turn to Buddhism, which really did start in atheism. The atheism of Gautama was not an illusion but a fact. In the tenets of Buddhism, as expounded by Gautama himself, the central point was the denial of the existence of such a thing as personality either in Gods or in Men. Gautama taught that psychic existence consisted simply in a succession of psychic states which were only linked with one another — and this unnaturally and unhealthily — by the evil force of desire. His message was: "Get rid of desire, disintegrate the psychic states, and so attain the normal and healthy state of oblivion." What he taught was practical psychoanalysis. So far from dealing in theology, he discouraged his followers from attending even to metaphysics and advised them to concentrate on the practical psychic exercises which were calculated to enable them to attain oblivion.

That is what Primitive Buddhism was. And now if you go to Japan and attend a service in a Mahayan Buddhist temple you will have no doubt about Mahayana Buddhism being a religion. You would think you had walked into a Roman Catholic church. With the passage of time strange things happen; and no one would have been more surprised than the Buddha himself to see the transformation which, in the course of centuries, has overtaken his system. May we not also guess that nobody would be more surprised than Marx, if he could come to earth some centuries hence and see what had happened in the meantime to Marxian Communism?

Therefore I do not think that atheism will debar Communism from becoming a universal Religion. I suggest that the present " anti-God " campaign in the USSR is not a war of atheism against religion: if it were, one might have struck, here, a phenomenon in our present situation which really was without a parallel. It is very hard to think of any case of a systematic war waged by an atheistical system against religion. But I think what we actually see is simply one more example of a phenomenon that is quite familiar: an attempt by a new religion, Communism, to wipe out and supplant a number of old religions — Orthodox Christianity, Islam, Judaism, and certain forms of Buddhism — in the Soviet Union.

This campaign of the present Communist Government in the Soviet Union against all the non-Communistic religions under its jurisdiction is amazingly parallel to the campaign of the Christian Government in the Roman Empire during the fourth and fifth centuries against the non-Christian cults.

Let me touch upon the points of likeness: first, an active confident minority imposing its religion upon an apathetic majority; second, the towns imposing their religion upon the countryside. Communism in Russia comes out of the towns and is impressed or imposed upon a rather unwilling peasantry. Christianity in the Roman Empire came out of the towns. The pre-Christians or non-Christians in the Latin-speaking provinces were called pagans — people of the countryside; in the eastern provinces they were called Hellenes — adherents of the old Hellenic cults and culture which Christianity supplanted. Now the Russian name for peasant is " Chrestian," which corresponds to " Hellenes " (the adherents of the old religion) in the Roman Empire, while " peasant " itself corresponds to " pagan," which simply means peasant. These are striking parallels between what happened in the Roman Empire then and what we see taking place in the Soviet Union now.

Another obvious parallel is that the victorious religion does not win because it has the Government behind it; it captures the Government because it has spiritual fervor. It was not because that cold-blooded, calculating fellow, Constantine, sided with Christianity that Christianity conquered the Roman Empire; Constantine only sided with it because it was the winning force, and he had the wit to see it. Christianity captured the Roman Government because the spiritual force was on the side of the Christian Church. The ultimate test of whether a movement is a religion is not its theology but its zeal, zeal which eats up its adherents and draws every side of life into its ambit. On this test, Russian Communism is certainly a religion already.

Then there is the further question: when this new religion of Communism has made itself the exclusive religion of the U. S. S. R., perhaps it will find itself unable to spread beyond the Soviet frontiers into regions where the arm of the State will be not for it but against it? Though it may have conquered the Soviet Government by its own spiritual power, it is obviously now using the Government as a secular instrument to stamp out its opponents, just as, in the ancient parallel, though Christianity conquered the Empire by spiritual power, it used the secular power of Rome to stamp out the remnants of the rival religions. Suppose Communism conquers the whole of Russia, what will happen beyond the frontiers? Is Communism as a religion destined perhaps to reach the limits of the Soviet frontiers, but not to pass beyond them?

And if the Soviet Government were to fall in Russia itself, would that mean that Communism would fall with it and perish from the earth?

One can ask the same question in the parallel ancient case which I have suggested for comparison. When Christianity had stamped out all the other religions in the Roman Empire, did it stop at the Imperial frontiers, at the limits up to which the Roman power could support it? Of course not: it straightway conquered the outer barbarians. And when the Roman Empire fell, did the Christian Church fall too? Of course not: the Church rose from the ashes of the Roman Empire like a phoenix.

If this analogy has any force or value, I am inclined to think that something from Russia rather than something from India is the most likely candidate for becoming the new religion of the modern world some centuries hence. I must confess that the thought is very unpleasant.

4. Some Points of Contrast between Medieval and Modern Civilization*

We should all, I think, agree that it was impossible to describe everything that took place between — let us say — 1000 and 1500 A.D. as medieval, and everything subsequent as modern. The principal characteristics of

* From G. M. Trevelyan, *History*, XI, New Series (1926), pp. 1–14. Reprinted by permission of the Historical Association and Professor G. M. Trevelyan.

medieval society began long before 1000 in some places, and lingered long after 1500 in others. Just as the Bronze age succeeded the Neolithic age sooner in the Levant than in Britain, so the Middle Ages succeeded the Dark Ages somewhat sooner in Italy and in France than in England and Scandinavia; and when the end of the distinctively medieval period drew near, the Renaissance began to displace medieval learning and art sooner in Italy than in the North; while, on the other hand, in the sphere of politics and society, the England of the Hundred Years' War had developed national unity of a post-medieval type sooner than any other country in Christendom. The Neopolitan kingdom retained many institutions of a medieval type in full vigor till the Napoleonic era. In its social laws the France of 1788 was in part medieval, when politically, intellectually and economically she had long been modern. Our own constitution in Church and State to-day is very largely medieval in its forms, though no longer at all in its spirit.

So, when I speak of medieval civilization, I am not speaking with chronological precision, though my thoughts center round the twelfth century. I mean by, "medieval" the type of civilization which grew out of and displaced the confusions of the Dark Ages, and which was itself gradually replaced by the rise of national monarchies, the emancipation of the serfs, the geographic discoveries, the Renaissance and the Reformation.

To define "modern civilization" is even more difficult. There have been so many "modern civilizations." We, ourselves, are a part of modern times, yet our present civilization differs more from that of the seventeenth century than that period differed from the medieval. The Industrial Revolution introduced a new epoch, or rather a series of new epochs, which are succeeding one another with a rapidity unexampled in the slow movements of previous social evolution. The Industrial Revolution is still in process, transmuting the form and character of society afresh in each successive generation.

When, therefore, we seek a definition of "modern times," we cannot include the Stuart era and our own day as one civilization, for they are fundamentally different. Their chief similarity consists in their common divergence from the medieval, and that is the only reason why we ever think of them as one, under the all-embracing title of "modern times." In this lecture I am going to confine my remarks about modern civilization mainly to the period of the sixteenth to eighteenth centuries, when, roughly speaking, the Middle Ages had passed away and the Industrial Revolution had not yet come. Those centuries between Martin Luther and George Stephenson constitute a distinct epoch of civilization — at least as distinct as the Graeco-Roman epoch, the Dark Ages, or the medieval civilization. They will probably be accorded the honors of a separate epoch with a name of its own, when in a few years' time a slightly more distant perspective demands a further analysis of that makeshift expression "modern times." I do not propose to talk about our own world that is being created by the Industrial Revolution. It is still in flux, and as we live in it we cannot see it from outside. My contrast, therefore, is to be made between the medieval civilization and that which immediately succeeded it.

One of the first points to consider about any civilization is its geography. What, then, was the geographical area of medieval Christendom, say in the twelfth century, and with what other parts of the world had it dealings or acquaintance? The area was very much the same as that of modern Europe; but the extent of its knowledge and dealings with other lands, beyond its own boundaries, was very much smaller.

Both these facts are important. Let us consider the first, the geographic identity of medieval and modern Europe. If we take modern Europe, leaving out most of modern Spain and modern Russia, we get something very like the area of twelfth-century Christendom. This identity is worthy of remark, because the Graeco-Roman world had been very different in area: it had been a Mediterranean civilization. But the medieval world belonged only half to the Mediterranean, and half to the North Sea. It was half Latin, half Nordic. The medieval civilization was the first to be European of the Continent; it first laid out the ground-plan of the geographic Europe that we still recognize to-day. This came about because, during the Dark Ages, the Levant and North Africa had been lost to Christendom, and Germany had been gained instead. Germany was thenceforth, geographically, the trunk of the European body. Its northern limbs were Scandinavia and Britain.

Until the middle of the eleventh century, Scandinavia and Britain were somewhat loosely attached to the medieval civilization of Europe. Their own Nordic traditions and literature were connected with much that was manliest and noblest in the Dark Ages; the spirit of the Eddas and Sagas was not yet extinguished in the North. But the Norman Conquest severed Britain from Scandinavia and bound her to France for four hundred years.

This medieval civilization, to which England was so closely attached from 1066 onwards, found its unity in social, religious and cultural institutions. Unlike the ancient Roman world medieval Europe was not held together as a single political State. In that, at least, it resembles modern Europe. Its political structure was the legalized and regulated anarchy of the feudal system. The unity was not political but social, religious and cultural. The name by which Europe knew itself was Christendom, and its only capital was Papal Rome. Politically, there was no capital; the so-called Empire existed in theory, but had slender administrative force. In saying this, we must, of course, except the semi-detached portion of Christendom, the Byzantine or Eastern Roman Empire of Constantinople, where the State ruled the Church, and where an erastian despotism prevailed, in contrast to the feudalism and clericalism of Western Europe.

Outside the Balkan peninsula, medieval Europe had a remarkable unity, derived from the customs of feudalism, chivalry and Roman Christianity which were then common to all lands from the Forth to the Tagus, from the Carpathians to the Bay of Biscay. But it was a unity that could not persist when material and intellectual progress made society and thought more complex and more varied. The agrarian feudal economy, with its lords and serfs, the orders of the clergy, with their judicial powers and social privileges, the feudal law and the canon law, were universally accepted — as no equally important institutions could again be, after the rise of the middle classes and the rise of nationality had given greater variety to European life. The English knight, speaking French, and the English Churchman, speaking Latin, could travel through medieval Europe from castle to castle and from abbey to abbey, and find more that was familiar to them than English "milords" touring in the same parts in the eighteenth century.

The cultural leadership lay with Italy and France conjointly, but political and military power lay decisively to the north of the Alps, among the feudal knighthood of the French and German States. Indeed, Normandy, Flanders and Paris, closely connected with South England in commerce, literature and politics, were as much the hearth of medieval civilization as Italy herself. Because civilization was no longer Mediterranean, but European, the Norman Conquest left more permanent traces than the Roman had done upon the life of our island, by as much as Normandy is nearer to us than Rome.

But although Britain, under the Norman and Angevin kings, was for a while made part of the continent, she still lay at the extreme northwest angle of the world. Medieval Europe was almost as large as modern Europe, but its contacts with the outside world were very much smaller. No one dreamt that there were lands yet to be discovered beyond the Altantic rollers — unless, indeed, in remote fiords of Iceland and Norway tales about "Vineland" still lingered among the descendants of those bold Viking crews who had, a thousand years after Christ, beached their longships on some point in the North American shore. But that joyous venture had been the outcome, not of medieval organization, but of the barbaric vigor of the Dark Ages. The medieval mariner, as distinct from the Elizabethan, was thalassic, not oceanic. He coasted cautiously round Europe from the Baltic to the Euxine, but he crossed no ocean.

It is true that the treasures of the Far East came to Europe from the ports of China and India in ships that sailed up the Persian Gulf and the Red Sea. But those voyages were effected by Chinese junks and small Indian craft, while the overland journey was accomplished by the Asiatic "ship of the desert." The galleys of Venice only met the Eastern goods at the European terminus, at Alexandria or the Black Sea. Thence it was the profitable task of the Italian merchants to distribute them over Europe. In return for these precious goods, Europe was fain to send gold and silver to the East, denuding herself very seriously of the precious metals. For the bulky products of Europe could not be carried by the caravan routes which were able to cope with the lighter silks and spices of Asia.

It was, therefore, a very different sort of trade from that of modern times, when the large ocean-going sailing ships of Portugal, Holland and England,

Close sailing from Bengala, or the isles
Of ternate and Tidore, whence mer-
    chants bring
Their spicy drugs,

could carry English textiles or other bulky manufactures round the Cape to the East, or to the new European colonies in America.

This difference between the external trade of Europe in the Middle Ages and in modern times underlies many other differences between the two civilizations. Medieval trade was mainly a trade in luxuries for the rich. The poor, for the most part, fed, clothed and housed themselves locally in the village, and had no luxuries. Only in modern times were the daily requirements of the common man increasingly catered for by distant manufacturers and traders, with the result that the number of those engaged in trade and manufacture as distinct from agriculture was immensely increased. In the Middle Ages the village carpenter knocked up the peasants' huts; and the skins or coarse cloth that they wore were of village manufacture.

The Venetian trade in luxuries, and all other contacts with the East, both personal and intellectual, were greatly stimulated by the Crusades. The Crusades were the military and religious aspect of a general urge towards the East on the part of the reviving energies of Europe. The *Drang nach Osten* was the one outward effort possible for medieval Europe, because the Atlantic barred exploration and development to the West, and the Sahara barred it to the South. *Eastward Ho!* was necessarily the word of the medieval explorer, trader and adventurer.

Very great historical importance attaches to the Crusades and the *Drang nach Osten* of the eleventh to the thirteenth centuries, because until then, during the Dark Ages, Christendom had been the attacked and not the attacker; the explored and not the explorer. In the ninth and tenth centuries, Christendom had still been ringed round by foes encroaching from east, from south and from north. If her enemies no longer after the days of Charlemagne threatened her very life, they still, for another two hundred years, bade fair to deny her the use of the sea, the possession of her own coasts, and therewith the prospect of the commerce and the world expansion which we associate with the destiny of the European peoples. In the north, the heathen Vikings held both sea and shore. Most of Spain and Sicily were under Saracen rule. The Mediterranean was swept by Moslem and Viking craft. From the lower Danube the heathen Magyars pushed into the heart of Germany and invaded the Lombard plain. By sea and by land Western Europe was being cut off from everything outside herself, even Constantinople, the heart of Eastern Christianity and learning.

Feudalism arose to combat this condition of affairs. Feudalism was originally a method for the local organization of war, because central government had broken down. As such it served its purpose well. It did what the Roman system had left undone: it organized local resistance to the invader. If, for instance, there had been feudal knights and barons in the villas of Roman Britain, the island would not have fallen so easy a prey to savage Pict and half-armed Saxon as it did after the departure of the legions from the midst of helpless and unorganized civilians. Feudalism was developed to repel Viking, Magyar and Saracen invader, and with such success that in the course of the eleventh and twelfth centuries the situation was reversed, and Christendom resumed the offensive. The slow reconquest of Spain from north to south began. Norman instead of Saracen reigned in Sicily. The Vikings were repelled or converted, and their splendid energies, renewed in Norman warriors and statesmen, became the spearhead of Christian chivalry. The Magyars, too, were baptized, and their kingdom of Hungary gave the crusading armies free access by land to the Balkan territories, the Byzantine Empire and thence into Asia Minor, and on to the Holy Land. Sea power passed into the hands of the Italian maritime republics of Genoa and Venice, who were, therefore, able to convoy the soldiers of the Cross to the Levant and to establish their own trade there on a permanent footing.

The prize that Europe brought back from the crusades was not the permanent liberation of the Holy Sepulchre, or the fraternal unity of Christendom, of which the story of the crusades is one long negation. She brought back, instead, the finer arts and crafts, luxury, science and intellectual curiosity — everything that Peter the Hermit would most have despised. The rich, many-coloured fabric of later medieval life, the world of Dante and Chaucer, would never have come into existence if barbarous Europe had remained as much shut in upon herself as she had been when the crusades began.

It is with this emancipation and outward thrust of Europe reorganized by the feudal system that the medieval period begins as distinct from the Dark Ages. For good and for evil, feudalism is the characteristic institution of the Middle Ages; it implies a fixed and legalized subordination of certain classes of society to certain others, to obtain civilized order at the expense of barbaric liberty and equality — in so far, that is to say, as barbarism had been "free and equal." Feudal society divided up the surplus product of the labor of the rural serf among barons and knights, bishops and abbots. By stereotyping and regularizing the inequality of incomes derived from the land, it enabled wealth to accumulate in the hands of Lords and Prelates, and so stimulated the rich man's demand for luxuries, which stimulated the trade and the higher arts and crafts of the merchant cities. In this way the Dark Ages progressed into the Middle Ages, and barbarism grew into civilization — but decidedly not along the path of liberty and equality.

Another aspect of feudalism was that it organized military, political and judicial power on a local basis. Not the Empire as in Roman times, or the nation as in modern times, but the barony, or the manor, was the unit of organized power. Feudalism was a confession of the disintegration of the Empire and the non-existence of the secular State. Over against this disintegrated secular society of feudal barons and knights, each with an outlook limited to his province or his manor, stood the pan-European Church, organized from Rome, as centralized as secular society was decentralized, and, therefore, if for no other reason, its master. Furthermore, since the clergy enjoyed an almost complete monopoly of learning and clerkship, the mastery of Church over State was very nearly complete.

Europe owed an immense debt to the clergy during its emergence from barbarism, and just because of that debt Europe was in grave danger of becoming a theocratic society like ancient Egypt or Brahminical India. Those lands also, in emerging from barbarism, had owed immense debts to their priesthoods, and had thereupon settled down as priest-governed societies. But in Europe the subjection of the laity was not permanent, because the spirit of medieval Europe was not static but dynamic; not submissive but progressive. The crusades, the oriental trade, the constant wars and ambitions of barons, princes and cities, prevented a set-tling down under papal theocracy, or indeed any settling down at all. Forward, through strife and confusion to something new, was ever the watchword of Europe, that distinguishes it from India, China, Egypt and Islam.

Medieval society was always on the move. It never had the settled feeling of the Roman Empire. It was young and agile. Its institutionalism, for which it is justly famous, was not a sign of decrepitude, but was a vigorous onslaught against the realm of anarchy and old darkness. It loved to create abbeys, universities, colleges, schools, parliaments, town corporations, craft guilds, laws, law courts and inns of court. These, and many other noble manifestations of the corporate spirit which we owe to the Middle Ages, enriched English and European civilization between the eleventh and fifteenth centuries.

Medieval society began as a rude arrangement between knights, churchman and peasant serf, for the protection of a poverty-stricken rustic village against marauders and devils, and, in return, for its due exploitation for the benefit of knight and churchman. It was an arrangement in the making of which there were elements of force and fraud, as also of religious idealism and soldierly heroism in defence of the community. But out of these primitive arrangements of feudalism, the Middle Ages gradually built up the Europe of Dante and Chaucer; of the cathedrals and universities; of the English monarchy and Parliament; of the canon, civil and English law; of the merchant communities in Italy and Flanders, and of London, "the flower of cities all." Which of these two pictures is the true Middle Ages? The feudal village, with the ragged, frightened, superstitious, half-starved serf, leaving his chimneyless cabin to drive afield his meager team of oxen, and fleeing to the woods at the approach of armed horsemen — or the Florence of Dante, the Oxford of Grossetête and Wyclif, the Venice of Carpaccio? Which is the true Middle Ages, the barbarism or the civilization? The answer, surely, is "both." The one was developed out of the other and the two continued side by side. The Dark Ages were in four hundred eventful years transformed into the full splendour of the Renaissance, although the darkness of poverty and ignorance still lay thick in many districts of the new Europe.

The aim of the greatest minds of the Middle Ages was to provide man upon earth with a permanent resting place in unchangeable institutions and unchallengeable beliefs; but their real achievement was very different: the true merit of medieval Christendom was that as compared to Islam and Brahminism it was progressive and that society moved constantly forward from 1100 to 1500 towards new things — out of uniformity into variety; out of feudal cosmopolitanism into national monarchy; out of a well-earned hegemony of the priesthood into lay emancipation; out of the rule of the knight into the world of the craftsman, the capitalist and the yeoman. The best and the worst of the Mid-

dle Ages was that they were full of wolfish life and energy. Their sins were the vices not of decrepitude but of violence. It is useless to seek in the Middle Ages for a golden age of piety, peace and brotherly love, as some would fain do to-day. It would be an equal mistake to fall back into the error of the eighteenth century, of despising the great epoch that led man back out of barbarism into the renewed light of civilization. Do not think of the medieval era as a fixed state but as a living process; do not conceive it as a motionless picture in a Morris tapestry, but as a series of shifting scenes, some brilliant, some terrible, all full of life and passion.

It is sometimes asserted that the medieval unity of Christendom prevented such wars as those which have devastated Europe at intervals from the sixteenth to the twentieth centuries. But many small wars can be as bad as a few big ones. There was no unwillingness on the part of Christians to wage war on one another, and the cruelty with which war was waged was even greater than in our own day. The desire to kill, plunder and destroy was under less restraint of conscience or of custom, but the means of killing were more restricted. Piracy at sea and private war on land were practised as matters of course by respectable merchants and gentlemen. It was not the unity of Christendom but the limit of man's control over nature, the inferior methods of locomotion, and the want of administrative and financial machinery to keep and feed large bodies of men in distant campaigns that prevented wars on the colossal scale. Europe, still very poor and with no elaborate system of credit, could not pay for the withdrawal from agriculture of a large proportion of her youth to engage in destruction as a skilled trade. The small warrior class of feudal knights was all-powerful, because they and their paid followers held monopoly in the profession of arms as a whole-time occupation. Wars were numerous and local, instead of being few and large as in modern times. The arm of Mars was short, but it was kept in continual practice, and the peasant suffered as much from the soldier in the Middle Ages as during the century that witnessed the Thirty Years' War.

In the medieval State, anarchy was a greater danger than despotism, though the opposite was the case in the medieval Church. The medieval State was a " mixed polity " of King, Barons and Prelates. The relation between lord and man, which was the essence of feudal politics, was based on mutual obligation. A breach of contract on either side involved penalties, and as law was ill-defined and ill-administered, resort was continually had to war to decide points of feudal right, as in our own country in the reigns of Henry II, John and Henry III. Non-resistance to the Lord's anointed was opposed to the central current of theory and practice in the Middle Ages. In the mutual obligations of feudalism lay the historical reality of that " original contract between King and people," long afterwards proclaimed by the Whig philosophers in reaction against the renaissance despots. The political merit of the medieval period lay in its dislike of absolutism in the temporal sphere, its elaborate distribution of power, its sense of corporate life and its consultation of the various corporate interests through their representatives.

The gradual development of feudal constitutionalism into parliamentary constitutionalism is the history of English political growth out of medieval into modern conditions. It is in the Middle Ages that we must seek the origin of parliament, and of the English common law — that law which the ultimate victory of parliament over the royal power has made supreme in all English-speaking lands. Professor Holdsworth's *History of English Law,* which may be said to carry the spirit and idea of Maitland's work forward into the Tudor and Stuart period, is adding greatly to our knowledge of the transition from medieval to modern times. Volumes IV to VI are especially interesting on that subject.

On the passing away of feudalism, the Latin peoples read the message of the modern world to be Macchiavelli's despotic interpretation of the new nationalism — and at this very moment the dominant party in Italy is reverting to that opinion, in reaction against Cavour's Anglophil constitutionalism. England of the Tudors and Stuarts, alone of the great States, adapted to modern requirements the medieval parliament, and the medieval idea of representation, and the medieval limitation of princely power by law. But in the same epoch modern England made a greater change in the ecclesiastical system inherited from the Middle Ages than the Latin peoples were then willing to do. England put the State above the Church, and the layman on a level with the priest. The Tudors took the medieval parliament for the ally of the modern monarchy, and subjected the medieval Church to the laity. The Valois and Hapsburgs, on the other hand, took the medieval Church for their ally and subjugated the medieval parliaments. Therefore, the difference between England and the Continent, already considerable towards the close of the Middle Ages, became profound in modern times. England became semi-detached from the continental civilization of which in the twelfth century she had been a part. Her external interests and connections across the Atlantic also drew her away from interest in continental affairs, except when self-preservation demanded her attention to the power and designs of such people as Louis XIV or Napoleon. Close connection with the Continent had done much to develop England out of the barbarism of the eleventh century, but her national emancipation from foreign influence was equally necessary for the splendid efflorescence of English life from the time of Shakespeare onwards.

Modern Europe was divided perpendicularly into a number of separate States, each absolute sovereign in its own territories, and the more important States purporting to represent a racial or national idea. But in the Middle Ages Europe had been divided horizontally into Estates and corporations — clergy, nobles, villeins, burghers — governed locally by their own domestic laws, in convents, castles, manors and walled cities. In the shelter of that framework the arts of civilization, torn up by the barbarian inroads, took root again and flourished in new forms. But the individual had, by modern standards, little freedom in the feudal village and less in the monastery; while, even in the chartered town and guild, personal initiative was checked and the unprivileged stranger excluded. Expansion, progress and individuality were hampered, until these rigid corporations and institutions had lost much of their power, and until the close control of the medieval Church over the lives and thoughts of all men had been loosened.

The only power strong enough to effect a social revolution of such extent and gravity was the power of the national State, embodying the modern passion of patriotism. The despotism of the State laid indeed restraints of its own upon liberty, but it cleared more elbow-room for the individual than he had enjoyed in the medieval world, at any rate in England. The era of private enterprise and expanding genius which we associate with Drake and Raleigh, Shakespeare and Bacon was the outcome of two hundred years of social disruption and rebirth.

But in modern times, Tudor and Stuart England, while effecting a great revolution in the social system, characteristically preserved the form and even the spirit of much that was medieval. Most of the orders, corporations and institutions which had been the principal channels of medieval life remained intact in modern England, on condition of giving up their medieval " liberties " or exemptions, and submitting to the sovereign authority of the State. Universities, nobles, lawyers, parliaments, bishops, secular clergy and town corporations survived, ostensibly in the old forms. But some institutions, like the strictly cosmopolitan orders of monks and friars, could not be fitted into the new national scheme of things, and were ruthlessly destroyed by the State. Rights like those of Sanctuary and Benefit of Clergy, and much of the jurisdiction of the Church Courts were reduced or abolished because they set limits to the execution of the national law. Cosmopolitan feudalism and the cosmopolitan Church went down before the new idea of a national State with a national Church attached — further modified in the eighteenth century by the peculiarly modern idea of toleration for the individual conscience, to which the Middle Ages had been stone blind. The judicial and political " liberties " of the medieval clergy and aristocracy, slices of sovereignty held in private or corporate hands, were abolished in favor of the liberty of the ordinary English subject, sheltered behind the power of the State.

So, too, the regulation of trade, instead of being as in the Middle Ages an affair of each chartered town or guild, became the business of the national authorities. The law of apprenticeship was regulated no longer by local corporations, but by the Statute of Artificers passed by Queen Elizabeth's parliament. The provision for the poor, formerly left to monasteries, guilds and private charity, was provided for as a duty incumbent on society and enforced by the State. The chief agents in this statutory control of the nation's economic life — as indeed of its political life also — were the unpaid Justices of the Peace appointed by the Crown, who formed the link between the views of central authority and the facts of local administration. They performed, as servants of the State, many functions which in the Middle Ages the feudal baron had performed in his own personal right.

Under this modern system the heart had gone out of the great medieval corporations. The unit of the manor was of decreasing importance (its death the other day scarcely attracted the notice of our own busy age); and the progress of the enclosure movement in favor of compact farms gradually destroyed the corporate life of the village. The corporate towns were less important in the modern economy than they had been in the Middle Ages. The growth of the cloth trade favoured village industry, and avoided the area of the old town corporations, whose old-fashioned restrictions were often found very hampering to new business.

From the emancipation of the serfs to the coming of the Industrial Revolution, the English village was at its zenith of prosperity and vitality. Its medieval poverty and isolation had passed away. Well-to-do yeomen, tenant farmers and small squires were numerous and independent, in spite of the coexistence of the great estates. The crafts and manufactures were increasingly carried on, not in the corporate towns but in the country. Many villages and hamlets manufactured for the national and international market. The modern peasant came in contact in his own village with men of various occupations dealing much with distant shires and lands. Community of trade drew the whole nation together, sharpening the wits and broadening the outlook of the English villager. He was ready to play an independent part in any new development, religious or political, industrial or colonial.

The Pilgrim Fathers were most of them English villagers in origin. The medieval serf would never have planted the free, self-sufficient townships of New England. The English colonial movement was the migration of a modern society, mainly rural but already half industrial, awake to economic and intellectual change and with a strong instinct towards self-government. The Breton settlements in Canada of the same seventeenth century were made under royal, seigneurial and ecclesiastical supervision by a peasantry very much more medieval in its ideas and leadership than the settlers of New England. That is one of the reasons why, as I said at the beginning of the lecture, it is so dangerous to give a date to the passing of the Middle Ages. In 1620 they had passed in England, but not in Brittany — a fact that has had, and is still having, immense consequences to North America and to the world.

B. The Role of the Physical Environment

5. The Geographic Basis of Modern Society

The permanent land-resource features of various areas in the world are frequently taken for granted. It is often assumed that the objective conditions of an environment, such as area, access to bodies of water, or location in relation to other great land masses, are less important for a society's growth and development than basic inventions or dramatic leadership. This is an unwarranted view. Our problem in thinking about these issues arises from the fact that the persistent interrelations between the geographic foundations of a society and its public policy have not been systematically studied.

Historically, certain geographic factors have been of particular importance in affecting the growth and emergence of cultures. It is possible to consider them as elements in three sets of related factors. One element of immense importance is the location of a society — both world and regional. World location has determined whether or not an area would be athwart main lines of commerce and trade. A single map of the history of civilizations would indicate that the centers of culture have crept steadily along the fringes of the Mediterranean and Atlantic coasts. Those areas which have been exposed by their location to the conqueror, missionary, or trader have usually shown the most vitality in carving out a place for themselves in history. Or, as Arnold Toynbee has put it, the challenge of their position has evoked an audacious response. Then, in another connection, the regional location of an area affects its security and survival. It has made an enormous difference for the institutions, public policy, and economic growth of a country whether or not its development was protected by the regional geographic environment. For example, this is obviously true of England's insular position as contrasted with the location of Poland in the North European Plain. The foreign policies of most nations will reflect their peculiar geographic conditions.

An additional set of factors are size and topography, or land forms. Nations and societies have in general attained greatness when they were large enough to influence others. Size in itself is not sufficient to establish a people's future, but in its absence other factors such as diplomacy or force must be developed and exploited more fully. Even then, the smaller nation must live in deadly

fear of its potentially more powerful neighbors.

Just as size is vital to a nation's potential strength, its shape and topography are decisive for its security and defense. The creation of an effective communication network can be facilitated or complicated by the distances and the nature of the terrain between centers of trade and government. The ideal shape of a state for purposes of communication is a circular or oval territory where points on the periphery are equally accessible from points of control at the center. Mountains and rivers have traditionally both determined the main lines of contact among peoples and provided obstacles to commerce or aggression. Specialization within a region is frequently the outgrowth of this isolation of one community from another. Some areas have in the past been rendered inaccessible to habitation and settlement by natural environments too formidable for all but adventurers or explorers. It should be obvious to the reader of Professor Spykman's essay that history has been influenced in crucial and decisive terms by the direction of the slope of a mountain or the flow of a river.

The last pair of geographic features are natural resources and climate. It has long been common in diplomatic practice to assess the power of individual nations in terms of critical and strategic raw materials. Steel production is in our times the perennial index of strength on the world stage; iron and coal as its ingredients are therefore essential to world power. Recently, however, other resources have loomed up, most notably uranium, tin, and the so-called ferro-alloys, such as manganese and tungsten. Furthermore, any realistic estimate of military strength today must take into account the oil a nation has on hand to power its mechanized armies and the rubber for tires on which men and equipment must be moved. It is not by accident that the two most powerful nations in modern society are also the richest in natural resources. Nor should we be surprised that Germany in World War II should have set its sights on increasing its supply of strategic resources.

Less tangible than the influence of the resources of an area on its world position is its climate. Whole theories of civilization have been founded on patterns of climate. The most notable and controversial of these was Professor Ellsworth Huntington's (Yale) theory of world history. The historian Arnold Toynbee has also considered climate as one of the elements useful in explaining the rise of new civilizations. Whether or not one finds these theories to be fully convincing, he would be hard pressed to prove, in the light of the concentration in temperate zones of the majority of civilizations, that climate had not been a crucial element in past history.

Therefore the facts of geography must be recognized. While it is misleading to pretend that history is predetermined by the context of geography within which societies operate, no nation can escape its geography. In brief there are enduring possibilities and stubborn limits to which so-cieties must adjust or perish. In this sense, to ignore geography is to court final disaster.

Few students of history or politics have written with deep insight on geography. A conspicuous exception was Nicholas Spykman (1893–1943), Professor of International Relations at Yale University. His papers on methodology ushered in a new era for international studies. The main lines of his approach are the ones which have been followed in international politics since World War II. This selection represents one of the few pioneering attempts with which the editors are familiar to develop a systematic theory of geography for relations among states. It is a daring dissent from the prevailing view then and now that geography is primarily a descriptive science. It holds unswervingly to the attitude, more modest than the theories of Huntington and Toynbee, that geography merely establishes possibilities and limits rather than determines what a people are destined to be and to do.

Spykman indeed rejects three popular views about geography's function and purpose. Some say that geography should be purely descriptive in locating world areas and resources. Others in the pseudo-science of geopolitics have asserted that the successive policies of nations in a given situation in international politics may be explained and forecast in terms of the conquest of space. Finally, some philosophies go even farther and contend that the rise and fall of all civilizations can be accounted for exclusively in geographic terms, such as shifts in climate and rainfall. This essay takes its stand somewhere between the first and the latter two viewpoints. It is fair to say that its principal aim is to place geography in proper perspective.

By considering separate aspects — location, climate, and size — and observing their influence in concrete historic and current relations, we may provide the social sciences with the foundations, if not the substance, of an enduring theory of geography.

6. Geography and Foreign Policy *

I

"La politique de toutes les puissances est dans leur geographie," conceded the man whose famous retort, "Circonstances? Moi, je fais les circonstances," indicates his contempt for any agency but the human will as the arbiter of human destiny. But since the Red Sea parted for Moses and the sun obligingly paused for Joshua, the human will has been unable to recapture the control over topography and climate exhibited by those forceful gentlemen, and it is probably safe to say that it was by Russian geography rather than by men that the diminutive Corsican was finally defeated. If he is still living, there is at Waterloo even today a loyal guide who asserts with unshakable conviction that neither genius nor skill but a swampy ditch gave that victory to Wellington.

Unfortunately for the political scientist with a fondness for simplification, but fortunately for the statesman striving to overcome the geographic handicaps of his country, neither does

* From Nicholas J. Spykman, *The American Political Science Review*, XXXII (1938), pp. 28–50. Reprinted by permission of *The American Political Science Review*.

the entire foreign policy of a country lie in geography, nor does any part of that policy lie entirely in geography. The factors that condition the policy of states are many; they are permanent and temporary, obvious and hidden; they include, apart from the geographic factor, population density, the economic structure of the country, the ethnic composition of the people, the form of government, and the complexes and pet prejudices of foreign ministers; and it is their simultaneous action and interaction that create the complex phenomenon known as "foreign policy."

It is the task of the social scientist to try to find in the enormous mass of historical material correlations between conditioning factors and types of foreign policy. This means that the study of diplomatic history must be supplemented by a search for the behavior patterns of states under different stimuli and in various international environments. Scientific method requires that the search operate by means of abstraction, and common sense warns that correlations found by means of such abstraction can by themselves be only partial, not complete, explanations of concrete historical situations.

Of the various factors that condition the foreign policy of states, there is no question that Napoleon indicated the most significant. War was an instrument of national policy in his time and still is today, and, in a world where groups struggle for power by means of war, policy becomes high strategy.

In such a world, the geographic area of the state is the territorial base from which it operates in time of war and the strategic position which it occupies during the temporary armistice called peace. It is the most fundamentally conditioning factor in the formulation of national policy because it is the most permanent. Ministers come and ministers go, even dictators die, but mountain ranges stand unperturbed. George Washington defending thirteen states with a ragged army has been succeeded by Franklin Roosevelt with the resources of a continent at his command, but the Atlantic continues reassuringly to separate Europe from the United States and the ports of the Saint Lawrence are still blocked by winter ice. Alexander I, Czar of all the Russians, bequeathed to Joseph Stalin, simple member of the Communist party, not only his power but his endless struggle for access to the sea, and Clemenceau shared with Caesar and Louis XIV their anxiety over the open German frontier.

Because the geographic characteristics of states are relatively unchanging and unchangeable, the geographic demands of those states will re-main the same for centuries, and because the world has not yet reached that happy state where the wants of no man conflict with those of another, those demands will cause friction. Thus at the door of geography may be laid the blame for many of the age-long struggles which run persistently through history while governments and dynasties rise and fall.

Greece was divided by nature into small economic units, and she therefore developed small political units. The valleys were self-centered and the most fertile sections of the country were open to the sea but shut off from contact by land with the rest of the peninsula. She therefore exchanged ideas and commodities by sea rather than by land, and the Greek settlements became a string of cities many of which were enemies each of the other. A similar situation prevails in the Balkans peninsula today, where each valley or plain is isolated by a mountain wall, and the various groups preserve their own social, political, and religious characteristics. There is no natural center within the peninsula around which a great state might form, and rivalries between the small states are inevitable. The same influence of lowland and highland distribution can be traced in the disintegration of the Roman Empire in western Europe into comparatively small units, which are small because the low ground and high ground are distributed in small areas.

The factors of topography which create barriers to expansion will, should these barriers be overcome, continue to operate as obstacles to effective defense and successful integration of the new territory with the old domain. The effect of the nature of the border territory on the problems of defense and foreign policy in general will be discussed later. But at this point must be mentioned the problem of effective control quite apart from the danger of aggression, because only with effective centralized control does large size become an element of strength rather than of weakness. Such control depends primarily on two factors: on the existence of an effective system of communication from the center to the periphery, and on the absence or the successful counterbalancing of centrifugal forces of separatism. On the establishment of a communication system, which is in turn one of the most effective means of counteracting separatist tendencies, the shape and topography of a state has a direct influence.

Obviously, the ideal territorial shape for a state is that of a perfect circle. Given such a configuration, the greatest possible area is enclosed within the shortest possible boundary, facilitating defense, and all parts of the area are equi-distant from, and as near as possible to, a government located at the center of the circle. States that are long and narrow in shape — and this is particularly true for land powers — tend inevitably to disintegrate either by losing territory at the periphery where the centralizing influence of the government is least felt, or by splitting to reappear as separate states. Examples of the former tendency are to be found in the Ottoman Empire, which had lost

effective control of all northern Africa and most of the Balkans before those areas were taken by other powers, and in the Arabian, Mongol, and Macedonian Empires which preceded it.

A factor even more significant than shape in the establishment of centralized control over a given area is topography. On the height and configuration of mountain ranges, the depth and width of valleys, the direction of rivers, and the modifying effect of climate on all of these features, will depend the ease of communication within a country. Where mountains like the Andes or the Scandinavian or Swiss ranges bar the way or cut the country into disconnected sections as in the Balkan peninsula, communication will be slow to be established and will remain expensive and infrequent; where marshes or deserts divide two parts of a country, road building will be difficult; and where river systems run parallel instead of converging, they offer no convenient means of communication to a centrally located government and tend to separate rather than to unite.

Over those sections of the country with which it has but infrequent communication a government will have but slight control. Mountain distribution, the chief cause of the present ethnic distribution, has exercised on Switzerland a definitely decentralizing effect which is intensified by the river system. What is significant about this river system as a disunifying influence is not its direction, however, but the fact that all the rivers flow from the periphery outward, creating no network of communication within the country and tending to connect the peripheral sections more closely with foreign countries than with the central part of the homeland. For various political reasons this has not, in the case of Switzerland, resulted in actual political disunity. It has, however, been the cause of the cultural, linguistic, and economic decentralization that is such an outstanding characteristic of the Republic. The same phenomenon of parallel rivers, with the same disunifying effect, can be noted in Germany, where the Rhine, the Weser, the Elbe, the Oder, and the Weichsel all flow northwest along parallel lines, dividing the country into five valleys and converging near no point from which a central government might extend its unifying influence along the river valleys to the edge of the state. The smallest Chinese river basins have formed the tiny political units which are characteristic of all Chinese history, and the three large river valleys persistently maintained a regional separatism which has been an obstacle to political unification. In Siberia, climate adds its decentralizing influence to that of topography, and the rivers not only flow along parallel courses but flow to the Arctic and are closed by ice. It was no accident that Siberia did not become effectively a part of the Russian Empire until the development of the railroad.

Rivers can be, and often have been, however, the chief unifying influence, especially in early political organizations. The first states were without exception river states, centered around the Tigris and Euphrates and the Nile, and the French colonial empire in North America was established along the St. Lawrence and Mississippi valleys. From just northwest of Moscow, the Dnieper flows south to the Black Sea, the Volga flows east and south to the Caspian, and the Volkhof flows north through Lake Ladoga to reach the Gulf of Finland as the Neva. Because the cataracts on the Dnieper below Kiev formed a barrier to communication, Kiev gave way to Moscow as the seat of the government, which from its position on the Moscova, a tributary of the Oka, which in turn flows into the Volga, can extend its centralizing influence to all the corners of European Russia. A similar network of rivers converging on Paris makes that city the inevitable center of France and centers France inevitably about Paris.

From the beginning, governments have strengthened their control over territory by supplementing the natural means of communication and attempting to overcome the barriers posed by topography. The Incas unified their empire by roads, the Persians constructed a central highway from Sardes to Susa which interestingly followed practically the same route as the projected Berlin-to-Bagdad railroad about two thousand years later; the Chinese, the French, and the Russians supplemented their great rivers by a honeycomb of canals; and Rome retained contact with her distant empire by roads so well constructed that some of them exist today. Charlemagne built roads, and every forward step of the French kingdom toward centralization coincides with a step toward the perfection of communication within the country. In the period of reorganization after the Hundred Years' War, Louis XI established the first postal service; and at the beginning of the rapid national development that followed the religious wars Sully planned his first great highway system.

It was the railroad, however, that made possible effective integration over wider areas. Before its development, few states located in conflict areas were able to maintain control over territories lying more than three hundred miles from the center of government. For this reason, large states have availed themselves of this instrument and have built lines for strategic and political reasons long before the economic significance of the outlying areas justified such construction. The railroads of France, Germany, and Russia radiate from Paris, Berlin, and Moscow. In the same way, the large continental powers have confirmed their unity by the development of their railroad systems. Transcontinental lines stretch across the United States, Canada, and Australia, and the Trans-Siberian and the Turk-Sib lines have brought Asiatic Russia within reach of the central government. Madrid, which made a feeble attempt in the same direction, is realizing today to her sorrow the dangers of an inadequate railway net.

Indeed, so important have railroads become as the most effective means of establishing control over the territory through which they run that their ownership has become almost a symbol of sovereignty.

Closely following the development of the railroads and interior waterways have come the airways which now cover every continent and which, although still imperfect for the transportation of commodities, are the most perfect means of retaining constant contact between a central government and distant parts of the country. In this connection, the efficacy of radio as a means of cultural and ideological centralization should not be forgotten.

Conversely, the decline of large empires has often been accompanied by a neglect of the communication system. The European and Asiatic states of the Middle Ages used the existing means without troubling to improve or develop them, and therefore remained small in size. Where large states did exist, such as the Caliphate and the Mongol Empire, they were political units in name only, with no actual control over the peripheral sections of their territory. The new Turkish republic, with its ambitious plans for the development of an elaborate system of communications, has evidently profited by the example of its predecessor.

Although the strategic and political problem of integrating and retaining overseas territories is entirely different from that presented by distant sections of contiguous territory, it is undoubtedly true that here also distance in relation to existing forms of communication played a role in the loss of American colonies to the

British and Spanish mother countries.

In revolting against England the American colonies followed a recognized law of political geography. They constituted the remote western frontier of Europe; and a tendency toward defection manifests itself in all peripheral holdings . . . mere distance increases greatly the difficulty of governmental control. . . .

Topography, climate, and distance thus determine the ease of communication within a country and thereby greatly lessen or enhance the probability of the development of separatism. Sections cut off by mountains or deserts, or whose location in a river valley predisposes them toward economic identification with a foreign country rather than with other sections of the homeland, tend to develop local interests and a local policy and gradually to shake off the control of the central government. Regionalism will not lead necessarily to the actual severance of political connections unless it occurs on the periphery and in combination with ethnic differences. The regionalism which during the nineteenth and early twentieth centuries caused the disintegration of the Turkish and Austrian Empires and resulted in the establishment of independent states through rather than of topographically isolated areas, although topography played its part in the prevention of ethnic diffusions. When regionalism takes the virulent form of nationalism, as it did in these instances, it may break even a state like Austria-Hungary, which had an ele-

ment of natural geographic unity as the basin state of the Danube.

Regionalism which falls short of separatism nevertheless creates difficulties in the formulation of a unified national policy, for the interests of different regions will inevitably conflict, and national policy will then represent a compromise between these conflicts. A paradoxical characteristic of regionalism is that economic regionalism may be one of the strongest elements in the unity of a country because of the interchange of goods which it fosters and still be an element of disunity in foreign policy because of the difficulty of incorporating into the foreign commercial policy the conflicting demands of various regions for protection, markets, raw materials, and capital.

Thus it appears that regionalism is a complex phenomenon, the result of many contributing factors, of which topography and climate are not the least important. The regionalism to be found today in the United States, Brazil, and Australia is primarily that of economic specialization determined by topography and climate; in Germany, it is both topographically and ideologically conditioned; in France, it is geographic, economic, traditional, and ideological. At the present time, technological progress, as manifested in railroad, steamship, and aeroplane development, has made it possible to overcome almost all the topographical elements in regionalism, and therefore to integrate effectively an area of almost any size. It is probably safe to say, then, that it is economic regionalism that exerts the most apparent influence on foreign policy.

It appears, therefore, that great size, especially if combined with favorable climate and productive soil, is a decided element of strength, but that such strength can become effective only after centralized control has been established over the entire area by the creation of an efficient communication system. If topography and climate lend their aid in the development of communications the evolution from large state to strong state will be rapid. If topography and climate create barriers, the state must wait until the necessary elements of capital and technological skill are at hand to overcome the natural barriers by artificial means. It thus becomes clear why Turkey before 1914 and Brazil and China today, although among the largest states in the world, are still second-class powers. A large part of the Turkish territory was desert and, as we have already noted, the country had no adequate system of communication and no effective administration. The same lack of systems of communications, coupled in the case of China with a complete absence of industrial technique, has so far kept both Brazil and China from effectively integrating their vast territories. There is little escape from the conclusion that size means potential strength, and that with the diffusion of Western technology great size plus time and a will to power will almost inevitably mean actual strength. Unless the dreams of European Confederation should materialize, it may well be that fifty years from now the quadrumvirate of world powers will be China, India, the United States, and the U.S.S.R.

II. THE FACTOR OF LOCATION

Important as size may be, however, it does not exclusively determine the rank of a state in the hierarchy of world powers and may be less significant than location in determining its importance in international affairs and in defining its problem of foreign policy. The location of a state may be described from the point of view of world-location, that is, with reference to the land masses and oceans of the world as a whole, or from the point of view of regional location, that is, with reference to the territory of other states and immediate surroundings. The former description will be in terms of latitude, longitude, altitude, and distance from the sea; the latter will be in terms of relations to surrounding areas, distances, lines of communication, and the nature of border territory.

A complete description of the geographic location of a state will include not only both these points of view as facts of location, but an analysis of the meaning of those facts. The facts of location do not change. The significance of such facts changes with every shift in the means of communication, in routes of communication, in the technique of war, and in the centers of world power, and the full meaning of a given location can be obtained only by considering the specific area in relation to two systems of reference: a geographic system of reference from which we derive the facts of location, and a historical system of reference by which we evaluate those facts.

The geographic location of a state expressed, then, in terms of the facts and significance of its world and regional location is the most fundamental factor in its foreign policy. It can modify the significance of size and explain the historical importance of many small states. It conditions and influences all other factors for the reason that world location defines climatic zones and thereby economic structure, and regional location defines potential enemies and thereby the problem of territorial security and potential allies, and perhaps even the limits of a state's role as a participant in a system of collective security. If the British were willing to give up Empire, a shift of the Isles a thousand miles to the west might enable them to enjoy the luxury of "isolationism." With the present location, Empire or no Empire, they are inevitably enmeshed in the politics of continental Europe.

Since the French dug a ditch near Suez, and the French and the Americans blasted a trench near Panama, the great land masses of the world consist of two islands, Eurasia and North America, which because of navigation problems on the North Polar Sea, function as peninsulas, and three true islands, South America, Africa, and Australia. The world location of a state becomes therefore a question of its location with reference to these land masses. The fact that the greater land masses lie in the northern hemisphere, and

that the largest land masses that do exist in the southern hemisphere lie in the tropics, has certain obvious implications. Politically and industrially, the northern hemisphere will always be more important than the southern, and relations between various parts of the northern hemisphere will have more influence on the history of the world than relations between parts of the southern hemisphere or between the two hemispheres. The location of a state north or south of the equator will therefore play a large part in determining the political significance of that state, the nature of its international relations, and the problems of its foreign policy.

Location with reference to the equator will largely determine climate, and the political activity of the world is for the most part centered in the temperate zones, although where ocean currents or other modifying influences alter the normal climatic conditions, the significance of location will be modified to that extent. On the European coast, which is warmed by the Gulf Stream, states can exist as far north as the polar circle, but the mouth of the Amur and the ports of Kamtchatka and Labrador are closed by ice six months of the year. In general, however, history is made between the latitudes of 25° and 60°, and, because very little of the land mass of the southern hemisphere lies between these limits, history is made between 25° and 60° north latitude.

But the significance of world location does not become clear until it is expressed not only with reference to land masses but also in relation to oceans. The five major bodies of water are the South Polar Sea, the North Polar Sea, the Indian Ocean, the Pacific, and the Atlantic. The South Polar Sea has no land to drain, and location on the North Polar Sea will remain for a long time to come a tremendous obstacle notwithstanding the heroic efforts of the Soviet government to open up the North Siberian coast.

Of the remaining three oceans, the Atlantic is the most important because, due to the distribution of mountain ranges and the resulting river flow, it has the most favorable ratio of ocean surface to land surface. Thirty-five million square miles in area, it drains nineteen million square miles of land, and, except in Africa, the navigability of most of its rivers permits easy access to inland regions. On the shores of the Atlantic and its inland seas live nine hundred million people, or forty-four per cent of the total population of the globe, and it touches most of the areas with a high standard of living.

To the Atlantic world come at least two-thirds of the world exports, probably more. The traffic across the Atlantic is 75 per cent of the whole sea-going traffic. The production of the most important raw materials and finished goods is equally concentrated on the shores of the Atlantic within the Atlantic world.

The Atlantic area contains the seats of all the large powers and the principal naval bases of all the great sea-powers except Japan.

For the Pacific, the ratio of surface to drainage basin is less favorable. The ocean is sixty-eight million square miles in area and the surface drained only eight million square miles. " About 723,000,000 people, or about 35.4 per cent of the total population of the world, live on the shores of the Pacific." Most of these live in Asia on relatively low standards of living. It will be a very long time before the Pacific can compare with the Atlantic in trade significance, but not only the gold value but also the volume of the foreign trade of the Pacific countries is now definitely increasing, and the relative position of the Atlantic and the Pacific is shifting in favor of the latter.

Geographically, the world of the Indian Ocean lies between the other two, with the Straits of Malacca and the Suez Canal the connecting links. About 400 million people, i.e., 19.8 per cent of the total population, live here, the majority on a very low standard of living. Except for Australia, it is a colonial world which does not originate policy and is still today practically a British sea.

The northern Atlantic is today, therefore, the most desirable body of water on which a state can be located. The southern Atlantic ranks next in importance, followed by the northern and southern Pacific and the Indian Ocean. And our consideration of climate and the distribution of land masses has led to the conclusion that the political activity of the world is, and will continue to be, centered between 25° and 60° north latitude. In so far as world location is an element of strength and importance, those states will be most active politically and industrially, and will therefore rank as world powers, which are located in the temperate zone of the northern hemisphere with direct or indirect access to the northern Atlantic. Since men first crossed the Atlantic, Japan is the only great power to develop away from its shores.

The most favored state in the world from the point of view of location is the United States. It faces two oceans and has therefore direct access to the two most important trade areas of the world. Before the making of the Panama Canal, this fact had only limited significance, because the height and direction of the Rockies and the Sierras make the United States primarily an Atlantic drainage area. With the piercing of the Isthmus, however, the territory east of the Rockies, which will forever remain the heart and core of the continent, was given an easy route to the Pacific and the whole of the economic structure of the United States obtained access to two oceans.

Location is therefore defined first in terms of the great land and ocean masses. But it should be remembered that this global frame of reference is different for each state because for each state it has a different focus, namely, the capital of that state. Every Foreign Office, whatever may be the atlas it uses, operates mentally with a different map of the world. This means that a given area in the world will have for two states which lie far apart an entirely different strategic and political significance, a fact which is responsible for

the failure of our system of worldwide collective security. It is also responsible for the almost insurmountable difficulties which arise in attempts to achieve effective political cooperation between states with very different frames of reference, a fact usually forgotten in the heavy aroma of cigars and goodwill that fills the air after Pilgrim dinners.

The facts of location do not change. Tarquinius Superbus from his peninsular kingdom surveyed the same sea as does Mussolini from his peninsular kingdom; McKinley signed the Platt amendment and Roosevelt abrogated it, but the geographic location of Cuba with reference to the United States remains unaltered. The significance of such facts, however, does change. The frame of reference previously described to serve for evaluating world location has both a geographic and therefore fixed, and a historical and therefore changing, aspect. It should also be remembered that the significance of a given location is both a factor in the foreign policy of a specific state and the result of the past history of that same state. Position on the North Atlantic is a factor in the foreign policy of the United States, and it is the development of the United States that accounts for the present significance of the Atlantic. The latter is a problem for the historians; the former a factual *datum* for the statesman.

Slow but irrevocable in effect are the changes in the significance of location which derive from shifts in the centers of culture diffusion and military power. From the beginning of history, Western civilization has developed around large bodies of water. Hellenic civilization was circumferential to the Aegean Sea, Roman civilization encircled the Mediterranean, and the Western civilization of the present surrounds the Atlantic. Location is important, therefore, in relation to the body of water which at a given historical period contains the source area of cultural diffusion.

The general direction in which civilization has moved through the centuries has been from a sub-tropical latitude northward to a cool temperate zone, and from east to west. . . .

It is clear that such shifts in the center of world power may well seal the fate of a country with a considerable measure of finality. In the first century B.C., the center of power was in the Mediterranean, and that section of Europe now known as the Netherlands lay on the North Sea, unimportant and far removed from the spheres of activity. After 1500, the center of power moved to western Europe, and the Netherlands, in possession of the mouth of one of Europe's most important rivers and situated among those states destined to become world powers, has acquired a position of outstanding political and commercial importance for which it merits no more credit than it merited censure for its earlier isolation. Conversely, in 2000 B.C., Syria and Palestine lay at the heart of world civilization and activity between the great empires of Babylonia and Egypt, while two thousand years later they lay far to the east of the center of power. As time went on, they acquired, and will probably always retain in varying degrees, great significance as passage lands; for the shortest routes between Europe and Asia, whether caravan, motor, or air, must pass through Asia Minor. But until the cycle of the movement of civilization completes itself and political life is once more concentrated on the eastern shores of the Mediterranean, Syria and Palestine must reconcile themselves to the role of junction rather than of final destination.

During the Middle Ages, after the power of Rome declined, Europe still looked to the east and southeast, with its most prosperous ports and most cosmopolitan cities on the Mediterranean. With the discovery of America, however, the center of gravity moved northwestward, and from the beginning of the sixteenth century to the beginning of the twentieth, the centers of wealth, culture, and political life were in western Europe. Great Britain, taking advantage of her island location and employing consistently her continental balance of power policy, was able to dominate the world by her sea power. With the rise of the United States to the status of a world power after the Spanish-American war, the power of Great Britain in the western Atlantic and South America declined. Similarly, with the Japanese rise to power after the World War, and especially after the Washington conference established the rank of Japan on the seas, Great Britain and the United States lost their predominant position in the western Pacific.

The center of world power has left western Europe; or rather there is no longer a center of world power. An epoch in the world's history has come to an end. Characteristic of the new period is the decentralization of power and the creation of great spheres dominated from different centers — the Americas from the United States, the Far East from Japan, the heartland of Eurasia from Moscow, and the Eastern Atlantic and Indian Ocean from Europe. By such great shifts, the significance of the location of every area is affected and thereby the problems of foreign policy. Rome's problem is no longer Carthage but London, the Central American Republics exchange their worries about the intentions of London for worries about the plans of Washington, and the Chinese are faced, not with the demands of far distant European powers, but with an aggressive neighbor.

While shifts in centers of civilization and power occur only slowly, shifts in routes of communication may change the significance of location in a relatively short period of time. With the discovery of the sea-route to India, the old route through the Near East, the Mediterranean, and Central Europe was superseded. This, together with the discovery of America, made the Atlantic the scene of the world's most important activity, and the Mediterranean a minor inland sea. Venice yielded her place as queen of world commerce to Spain and Portugal. At the same time, the Baltic, formerly the center of northern European commerce, became cut off from the main trade routes. Nürnberg and Augsburg, which had prospered, sank into insignificance with Lübeck and the other Hanseatic cities, and Hamburg and Bremen, and even more the Netherlands and England, moved from the periphery of world trade to its center. As ships began to sail around the southern tip of Africa, Capetown came into prominence, only to lose its commercial significance in 1869 when the opening of the Suez Canal diverted trade once more into the Mediterranean, and the Near East regained its early importance, enhanced today because it is now the funnel for the air route from Europe to Asia. A large portion of the traffic which once flowed past the ports of Brazil and Argentina now flows through the Panama Canal, with benefit to Central America and the western coast of the United States, and to the corresponding detriment of the trade of the eastern coast of South America.

The construction of railroads as well as of canals may bring about a change in the significance of location. The opening of the trans-Siberian railroad in 1901 dealt a death-blow to Kjachta, the former center of the Chinese tea trade, for the road was unkind enough not to include Kjachta in its itinerary, while Chita, Irkutsk, and other slumbering Siberian towns found themselves by the side of the road from Petrograd to Vladivostok. And the construction of the Turk-Sib railroad from Novo Sibirsk to the Moscow-Tashkent line placed in direct communication with the Pacific coast on one side, and with Moscow and Petrograd on the other, a district that had been practically isolated for centuries. Yarkand, the point from which the trade of Sinkiang had formerly flowed to British India, yielded its place as a commercial center to Kashgar and Kuldja because the latter towns had access to the railroad. Nikolaievsk, at the mouth of the Amur, has become one terminus of the railroad from Taishet to the coast, and Komsomolsk, which until recently did not exist, is now the main terminus of the railroad and the junction of its three branches to Nikolaievsk, Khabarovsk, and a new and as yet nameless port to be created east of Komsomolsk, giving the maritime provinces a commercial and strategic importance undreamed of fifty years ago.

It seems almost axiomatic that a country or section should benefit from a shift in communication or trade routes which places it on or near the line of traffic. Although this is true from an economic point of view, it is not necessarily true politically. If the country through which the route runs be weak, and the route of great significance, the section in question may well become a bone of contention among the great powers of the world and may pay for its advantageous location with its independence. Egypt was not strong enough or stable enough to be trusted with the defense of the Suez Canal and was forced to submit to British occupation. The isthmian canal in the New World was too vital a route of communication between the eastern and western coasts of the United States to be left in the hands of Colombia, and the state of Panama accordingly declared its independence. The isthmus of Kra is the logical place for a canal from the Pacific to the Indian Ocean. The Japanese, with their gift for imitation, may some day like to copy their Anglo-Saxon sisters and run a canal of their own, thereby upsetting the existing power relation in the Indian Ocean and destroying the value of Singapore. For that reason, Siam may continue to expect a lively interest in her development both in London and in Tokyo.

Some of the changes in routes already indicated and their effect on the significance of geographic location are the result of technological development in the means of communication. It was not until the development of the steamship that men could follow the great circle routes on the sea. With the development of the aëroplane has come the possibility of following the great circle routes overland to a greater extent than ever before, although over the broader stretches of the sea the aëroplane, until its effective cruising radius has been increased, must follow routes where it can find island bases.

As such new routes of communication come into existence, new parts of the earth's surface will obviously gain, and other sections will decline, in importance. The future development of air transportation will mean that many now worthless and unclaimed bits of territory will become highly desirable. The United States, Great Britain, and Russia have long been disputing the possession of Wrangel Island, which was discovered in 1881, and which lies in the *Arctic* Ocean on the direct air route from New York to Tokyo. Great Britain claimed the island in 1916, the United States raised its flag in 1924, and three days later the Russian flag was raised. Russia proclaimed her annexation of the island in 1916, 1924, and 1926, and in 1927 established a colony there, but the United States has refused to recognize the annexation. The camping trips of the Hawaiian boy scouts to Baker, Jarvis, and Howland which strengthened legal titles to these coral specks by adding occupation to discovery is entered in the record of good deeds. The Bermudas, the Azores, the Cape Verde islands, St. Helena, Ascension, Tristan d'Acunha, Fernando Noronha, and St. Paul all lie on possible air routes of the future, and Midway, Wake, and Guam mark the route from the United States to the Philippines. Sections of the mainland hitherto excluded from world trade, such as northern Siberia, Ireland, and Greenland, which lie on the direct air route from New York to Europe, will find themselves in the center of the stream of world trade instead of far beyond its edges.

But the same geographic location will acquire a new strategic and political meaning with new means of communication even if it involves no change in route, for distance is defined not in miles but in hours, and therefore in concrete terms of movement possibilities. As we have progressed from the horse and cart through the railroad, the motor car, and tractor to the aëroplane and airship, and on sea from the sailing vessel through the steam and motor vessel to the hydroplane and airship, distances have grown consistently less. In the second half of the eighteenth century, the Atlantic Ocean was six weeks wide and the United States was practically isolated from Europe. The same ocean is now three days wide, with week-ends in Paris becoming not too remote a possibility for the restless New Yorker.

When the Greeks, after their victory over the Persians, stipulated that no Persian army should come nearer to the coast than the distance a horse could run in twenty-four hours, they provided a large degree of security for themselves. The same stipulation would today afford little security against a Turkish air attack from well behind the line that marked the cruising radius of the fleetest Persian steed. The English Channel, reinforced by the British navy, remained a barrier behind which the British felt secure even after the development of the swiftest ships. In terms of air transportation, London is now no more secure from attack than if it were on the Continent.

It is the application of such technological development to the weapons of war that causes the quickest variations in the strategic, and therefore political, significance of a specific area. In the days before aerial warfare, naval bases and naval stations performed their function if fleets could lie protected behind their land fortifications. Offshore islands or narrow peninsular points near weak powers were ideally suited for such purposes and much sought after by the British and other naval powers. During the post-war period, the bomb attack obtained a tactical advantage over air defense, and the latter was primarily dependent on counter-attack by fighting planes. This presupposed depth of territory before the objective to insure adequate warning. But many of the outlying naval stations had been obtained under different tactical conditions, when ease of defense suggested smallness of size. Under modern circumstances they are hardly a safe place in which to keep a fleet at anchor, if in the vicinity there be a potential enemy air fleet superior to the local air force. The changed position of Malta under these circumstances has not been without influence on recent Italian-British diplomacy. But it is not only Malta but also Aden, since the conquest of Ethiopia, that has undergone this change, and the future may create the same problem for Gibraltar and Hongkong. Should, however, the more recent development in anti-aircraft guns make possible adequate defense of a narrow territorial base, these points might regain their former significance.

The preceding pages have provided an analysis of the ways in which geography conditions foreign policy. The influence of size has been indicated, as modified by climate, topography, and technological development, and the significance of location has been demonstrated as modified by shifts in centers of power, changes in routes of communication, and new inventions in transportation and warfare. The emphasis has been on world location, and therefore the most immediate factor in foreign policy, regional location, remains to be treated. It is already clear, however, that, whatever aloofness the student of international law may permit himself, the student of international politics must deal with geography as basic reality.

C. Patterns of World Resources

7. Raw Materials are the Core of the Earth's Substance

It was commonplace in the years between World Wars I and II for students of world politics to designate certain areas as "The World that Matters." This phrase served to point out that control over natural resources is a prerequisite for exercising influence among nations. If an area possessed an abundance of coal and iron in close proximity, it was considered to have the basis for industrial development. This has been true for over a century. From the period of Great Britain's world supremacy, the center of power has shifted to lands enriched by or having close access to resources like coal and iron ore. In this century Central Europe and the United States succeeded Britain as the industrial heartlands of the world, only to be challenged by the Soviet Union. Today the industrial structures of the Soviet Union and the United States are both founded squarely on the hard core of their strategic natural resources.

It should be obvious that the relative value of individual resources is not constant. One merit of the essay by Professor Jan O. M. Broek, Chairman of the Department of Geography at the University of Minnesota, is his clear demonstration of this truth. Resources that were unimportant yesterday are crucial today, and tomorrow technological changes will place new demands calling for new resources from the earth's surface. It is an uncertain business, therefore, to identify world power too closely with one or the other particular resource.

A safer approach is to recognize there are two broad classes of raw materials. One is organic and includes foodstuffs, chemicals, fats and oils, forest products, and textile fibers. We have excluded it solely because of limits on space and content. The organic products of the *soil* make it in many respects the most vital of all resources. A full study of natural resources would above all seem to require the examination of types of soils and their characteristics. The other class of raw materials, however, is the vital area through which we have chosen to illustrate this topic. It is the inorganic class of raw materials which includes the minerals of the world. Some of these, such as coal, iron ore, petroleum, and conceivably uranium, are primary ingredients for industrial development. Others are secondary, such as nitrates for fertilizers, bauxite for aluminum, sulphur for chemicals, zinc for brass, and copper for electrical equipment. A third group — the ferro-alloy metals — serve to strengthen iron and steel products and add to their efficiency. This last group includes manganese, nickel, and tungsten, which have recently assumed roles of increasing importance among the earth's resources. The earth's substance, so unevenly scattered and dispersed, has been and will continue to be a vital element in modern society.

8. The Natural Endowment of the Nations: The Distribution of Population and Resources*

By physical resources I mean those elements of the natural environment that have utility for man. It is ob-

* From Jan O. M. Broek, *World Resources and Peace*, pp. 3–20. Copyright 1941 by The University of California Press. Reprinted by permission of Jan O. M. Broek and The University of California Press.

vious that this appraisal varies, depending upon the stage of civilization: a plant, an animal, a mineral which may not have had the slightest value for a primitive society may for our modern Western civilization be of the greatest significance.

It is this dynamic nature of the interplay between man and the land that explains why regions shift in economic value and often also in political strength. Each period of history has had its areas which were particularly favored by the dominant resource pattern. For example, the oases of Egypt and Mesopotamia, the Mediterranean, or the Atlantic margins of Europe and North America, each in turn became zones of economic energy, accumulating wealth and political power.

With the evolution of material civilization, man not only came to use more and more elements of his direct natural environment; he also became increasingly dependent upon commodities from other regions. Though the facts are obvious and hardly need supporting evidence, I should like to quote some examples from the field of mineral resources; it is in this field particularly that changes in evaluation of areas have been precipitous, in response to new technical uses of metals. Formerly, if a nation had coal and iron in large quantities it had the prerequisites for industrial development, provided its peoples had the science, technical skill, and capital. Today, a great many other minerals are just as vital to a modern nation. Ideally speaking, the lack of such minerals should not be a hindrance, because the exchange of goods and services can take care of this. We cannot ignore the reality, however, which shows that (for whatever reasons) ownership or effective political control is considered a great advantage.

Even so short a period as that lying between the beginning of the First World War and the present conflict shows some striking changes in production centers. For instance, we may consider petroleum, bauxite (which is the aluminum-bearing ore), copper, and chromium (one of the metals used for making steel alloys, especially stainless steel).

In 1913 the greatest producer of crude oil was the United States, followed by Russia with about one-fourth the United States production, then by Mexico, Rumania, and Netherlands East India. In response to the ever-increasing use of petroleum products for automobiles, airplanes, and ships, and for the lubrication of machinery, the world production is today over five times as large. The United States still has its dominant position, but Venezuela now contends with Russia for second place, and Iran (Persia) is fourth, followed by Netherlands East India, Rumania, and finally Mexico. The new fields in Arabia and Baluchistan may upset this list. [Editors' Note: Iran had by 1952 eclipsed Russia, which was fourth.]

Aluminum has become increasingly important, especially as a weight-saving material in transportation, and also for transmission cables and other purposes. For bauxite in 1913 the world was practically dependent upon France and the United States. Today France still is the largest producer, but now Hungary takes second place, and the other important countries exporting bauxite are Yugoslavia and Italy in Europe, British and Dutch Guiana in South America, and Netherlands East India.

As to copper, in 1913 the United States was the outstanding producer, with more than seven times the amount from the next on the list, Japan. At present the United States still is first, but it mines less than one-third of the world total. Chile and Canada in the Western Hemisphere, Northern Rhodesia and the adjacent Belgian Congo in Africa, in the order named now produce together almost half of the world's copper.

Chromium was of little consequence twenty-five years ago. In 1913 the prominent chrome-ore producers were British Southern Rhodesia and French New Caledonia in the Southwest Pacific. Today Russia heads the list, followed by Southern Rhodesia, the Union of South Africa, and Turkey, which together supply more than three-fourths of the world's total. [Editors' Note: Turkey had by 1952 taken first place.]

These examples show clearly the nature of the shifts in areas of strategic importance and demonstrate strikingly how the older European industrial countries have become more and more dependent upon other regions for the modern minerals.

Now let us turn from physical resources to the people. Here, too, we find significant changes in terms of time and space. We must, however, stretch our period of comparison to gain a true perspective. The outstanding fact of modern history is the expansion of the peoples of European stock, associated with the emergence of technological civilization. Though population data are notoriously unreliable for former centuries, and even today are far from complete, enough research has been done to justify some rough estimates.

We may take as a point of comparison the middle of the eighteenth century, when the European expansion was on its way but was as yet unaided by modern technology. The world population in 1750 was roughly 660 millions; at present it is some 2000 millions — three times as much. It was especially the peoples of European stock that caused this increase. In 1750 they formed slightly more than one-fifth of the world's population; today, of a far larger world total, one-third. In Europe the population grew from 140 to 500 millions, which is three and one-half times as much as it was two centuries ago. Besides this, there are now outside of Europe some 160 million people of pure European stock. The other peoples have, in general, also increased, but none so fast as the Europeans. Asia, which makes the best showing, seems to have had some 400 million inhabitants in 1750 and now has about 1000 millions, or two and one-half times as much.

It is well known that this rapid increase of European peoples is now coming to an end. As a matter of fact, some nations are already on the verge of a decline of population. The great push of the white man into various parts of the world draws to a close. One may even go further and say that in some parts of the world the white man is already on the defensive. This is, of course, not purely a matter of numbers, but just as much, or more, the result of other races' borrowing from the West the tools and techniques which once were its monopoly. This counter-move is most noticeable in eastern Asia, and one can have little doubt that it will spread to other areas. Naturally it will be the colonial powers, those which were most active in the European expansion, that will have to bear the brunt of this coming conflict.

From resources and peoples we turn to their product, the nation. A nation is a union between a people and its habitat. The land influences the people, the people change the land. A nation is a spiritual community of people, but such a community can maintain itself only if built upon a strong material foundation. It is difficult to say what is the most essential element in forming a nation. On the spiritual side, language, as the main vehicle of thought, is doubtless a strong factor, but it is not always decisive, as many exceptions show. (United States — England; South America — Spain, or Portugal; Belgium or Switzerland — France.) Race or religion may have their influence, but they are usually of minor importance.

The French historian Renan once defined a nation as " a large community based on a consciousness of sacrifices made for the common weal in the past and on a tacit agreement to stand together in the future in this same spirit of loyal collaboration." " In this sense," he remarks, " the existence of a nation is a plebiscite continued from day to day." The value of the definition lies in its stress on the spiritual ties as born from a common history, without emphasis upon any single factor. Of course, these spiritual ties must be taken to include the economic common interest, which, in my opinion, has played an important role in the formation of nations. (For example, the divorce of the Low Countries from the German Empire, mainly because of differing economic interests; the formation of national cores in Flanders and Holland, and the development of their own language and culture.)

Each nation has its nucleus from where its power emanates; usually this is the cradle of national consciousness where its traditions and customs were formed. If there are no physical barriers, like the ocean, the limits of a nation are often ill-defined, and political boundaries may cut through a no-man's-land of fluctuating loyalties. It is particularly in the transition zones between different culture areas that this continual plebiscite takes place. Here groups are apt to shift allegiance from one side to the other, depending on where the attraction — or pressure — is strongest, and the national sphere expands or contracts accordingly. If I may use the terminology of the geologist, such areas may be compared to fault zones between the more stable blocks on either side. Sometimes in this borderland separate national entities may crystallize, and thus the shatter belt may become stabilized. We have a good example of this in the region between Romance (Latin) and Germanic cultures where we find the strip of independent states: The Netherlands, Belgium, Luxemburg, and Switzerland.

But in Eastern Europe, on the margins of the former Russian, Turkish, German, and Austrian empires, from Baltic to Mediterranean, lies another fault zone — a fault zone still quite active. Here the crosscurrents of migrations have deposited a conglomerate of races, languages, and religion groups, and economic and social castes. There is constant strife between the various factions, and oppression of minorities by the national groups in power. So far, strong harmonious nations have not developed here; at present the region can only be characterized as being socially and politically immature. In my judgment, the continuation of this diversity is mainly due to economic conditions, a point to which I shall return later.

Now let us look at Europe as a whole, to see how these ideas of nations and of resources can be applied. I may start with a simple observation: if we look at a political world map, we see how the lion's share of the overseas colonies, protectorates, or other dependencies is in the hands of oceanic Europe, from Great Britain to Spain. This reveals a basic contrast in development between the Atlantic seaboard and the continental part of Europe.

Before the so-called "Industrial Revolution," water transportation was the only efficient means of moving goods in bulk beyond short distances. A people on the coast had its front door on the world's highway. The merchant cities of Venice and Genoa at one time dominated the Mediterranean; the Hanse merchants of the Baltic had their golden age; but no peoples gained such a wide sweep of trade and possibilities of conquest as those living on the shores of the Atlantic. Beginning with the great discoveries, this zone became a region of bustling economic activity; it had stimulating relations with all parts of the world; it accumulated wealth and power. In comparison, the rest of Europe was like a scattering of rustic peasant communities, mere provinces to the metropolis. Agriculture remained the mainstay of continental Europe, and local squabbles its main worry.

There is a close relationship between the rise of economic power in this oceanic zone and the development of strongly welded national states. Though other factors have played their part, there is no denying the correlation between the two phenomena: national units developed because some vital common interest transcended the conflicts of local groups, and in turn the powerful states tied the people closely together.

The idea of the nation and national state spread to other parts of Europe; as a matter of fact, here (as for instance, in Germany) the concept often was more ably expressed just because the lack of national unity was more keenly felt than in the seaboard nations to whom it had come almost as a matter of course. But without a broad material base the national states of Central Europe would have remained an idle dream.

It was toward 1800 that the so-called "Industrial Revolution" began to change our civilization. The term is incorrect in many respects, especially because new resources, functions, and forms are still being added, and the machine civilization is still spreading over the earth.

With this new technology an entirely different set of factors began to operate. New means of communication and transportation diminished the former handicaps of the continental areas, as compared to the maritime countries. New resources, especially minerals, such as coal, iron, and later copper, aluminum, nickel, manganese and oil, became a vital consequence. In short, the new technology revolutionized the appraisal of regions with respect to their material value and their strategic location.

We may turn a moment to the United States in order to realize fully the significance of this new complex of forces. This country was particularly fortunate in that its expansion took place during the period of rising technology. Perhaps it is more correct to say that the machine civilization made possible this expansion and consolidation of a nation of continental proportions. Anyway, the point is that this country was shaped in harmony with the new technical-economic forces. If America stands powerful in the world of today, and if it may hope for a still greater tomorrow, it is because it fits perfectly into this modern resource pattern.

Now let us consider Europe. Whatever the historical processes were that determined the political boundaries of Europe, they had, un-

til recently, nothing to do with the subsoil or with the modern means of communication. Even as late as 1870 Germany took Alsace-Lorraine from France principally for strategic reasons; today, though this function is still useful, the greatest value of the region lies in its iron deposits, a rich resource only after a technique had been developed (in the 1880's) to extract the phosphorus from these ores. Briefly, it is almost pure luck if a state has many or none of the minerals that today spell power or weakness.

New means of transportation have, of course, benefited all nations. But there is no denying that they have emancipated the landlocked regions. The railroad made possible the long-distance moving of bulky goods overland; the automobile and truck have served to complete the network; the airplane has added the atmosphere as a medium of transportation — a medium that lies over both land and water. Even now, while this new means of transport is only beginning to be developed, its tremendous significance has already become obvious. In a strategic sense, it has seriously diminished England's advantage in its island position: it has strengthened a semicontinental nation, like Germany, which can strike alike to east and west, over land and water.

Pointing out these changes in resources and in transportation is not prophesying any definite political changes, nor recommending a fatalistic attitude. It is recognizing that there are economic forces at work that diminish the superiority once enjoyed by the oceanic wing of Europe. It means the emergence of new areas of economic importance. Whether the potential political power will be transformed into kinetic energy will depend on many other factors.

The strategic nations in this emergence of continental Europe are Germany, Russia, and the shatter belt of peoples between them. I will attempt to sketch here in a few words some vital features of their resource structure. Russia as a continental power is the absolute European antithesis of maritime England. Its expansion from the Baltic and the Black Sea to the Pacific has been a territorial conquest. For all practical purposes it has always been a landlocked (or icelocked) state, reaching the open ocean of the Pacific only at its extreme eastern end, far away from the nation's core. It remained a feudal country of peasants and landed gentry until within the present century. Although certain beginnings were made before 1900, it is only in the most recent decades that the country has come to grips with the Industrial Revolution. . . .

The U.S.S.R. is more than self-sufficient in the production of such staple commodities as lumber, wood pulp, grains, coal, petroleum, iron, manganese, and chromium, and perhaps will be so for copper and nickel. In view of the large output, it is surprising to find in the trade statistics relatively small exports of these goods. Only lumber is a large item; several of the other commodities, such as oil and chromium, have even declined in their export in the most recent years. It is tempting to guess

at the reasons for this phenomenon and to speculate how far Russia is actually able or willing to supply Germany with raw materials, but such speculation would lead to a detailed discussion of current events which is outside the purpose of this lecture.

Germany is intermediate in structure between Britain and Russia. It is the outstanding example of a major industrial country that has very few of the raw materials it manufactures. Only coal and potash are abundantly available in Germany. Having lost the iron mines of Lorraine and of part of Silesia after the First World War, she . . . imported more than half of her iron-ore supplies. For all other metals and oil Germany must import from 60 to 100 per cent of its consumption. Besides the minerals, there are huge deficits in lumber, pulpwood, wool, and oils and fats, not to speak of the obvious lack of commodities which specifically come from the sub-tropics and tropics, as for example cotton, rubber, and such pleasant luxuries as coffee. In a normal economy all these goods were paid for by the impressive exports of processed metals, machinery, chemical products, and other merchandise.

The annexations of recent years have added a few mineral deposits, it is true, but this is largely offset by the greater imports necessary to continue the industries of the Czech country and Austria. The highly developed German chemical industry has been able to find numerous substitutes, but most of them are as yet more expensive and less satisfactory than the goods they must replace. Besides, the substitutes finally depend again on other raw materials and on the building of machinery to make them, which in turn means a new demand for metal and labor.

The wish to control sources of needed raw materials is not new. The German foreign policy before the First World War had Janus faces: one looked toward the ocean and an overseas colonial empire, while the other looked toward the East for continental expansion. The German navy and the projected Berlin-Bagdad railway were symbols as well as instruments of this dual policy. Nazi Germany has concentrated on a drive to the east. We will not speculate here whether this means that it has given up its demand for colonies or whether it will ask for them as soon as, or if, its plans for the east succeed. For the time being, at least, the continental expansion stands in the center of Germany's interest.

Before the World War, technical and industrial Europe reached east as far as the line Danzig, Silesia, over Vienna, to Trieste at the northern end of the Adriatic. In the most recent decades, Russia has been building up its machine civilization. In between lies the zone that is now becoming an anomaly in Europe, a zone overwhelmingly agricultural in economy and almost feudal in its social structure, a crazyquilt of culture, language, race, and religion groups. Since this region lacks the financial and technical equipment for autonomous internal development, some outside power is bound to take control and manage the peoples as well as the resources.

In my personal opinion, the happiest solution for the peoples concerned would have been a development with the help of Western European capital and technology, since it would have left them considerable latitude in matters of a national-political nature. Unfortunately, however, the Atlantic seaboard nations have never shown great economic interest in this belt, and quite naturally so, for their colonies, and such young sovereign states as the United States and Argentina, promised much safer investments and quicker profits than Eastern Europe. Postwar support was born of the political desire to set up a cordon of buffer states, directed against Germany as well as Russia; and most of the loans made to the new vassal states were intended to strengthen their military value. Such exploitation as that of the oil fields of Rumania and of various mineral deposits in the Balkans has been of an extractive nature and the social-economic benefits to the native population are quite limited. Besides, the nations of oceanic Europe have little need for the agricultural products of Southeastern Europe. France, with her North African resources, is almost self-sufficient in grains; England gets her food supply from the Dominions, Denmark, Holland, and the small Baltic states.

On the other hand, the markets of Central Europe are not only closer to the Balkan countries and to Poland, but also more complementary in character. Germany and the former Austria and Czechoslovakia need the agricultural and mineral raw materials, while Eastern Europe needs manufactured articles. The trade statistics prove the existence of this mutual relationship. Were it not for the constant and all too well justified fear of political domination following economic penetration, all parties concerned could only welcome this form of coöperation.

It is extremely difficult to look away from the present misery — and from that which is sure to come — and evaluate coolly the historical process. But it seems quite possible that eventually the political domination will further the economic development of the subjected peoples. As means of transportation and communication are extended, industrial equipment installed, and agricultural methods improved, they may for a time mainly serve the dominant power, but in the long run they will strengthen the economic structure and tend to reduce petty differences. And this process may be relatively rapid: the invader is not dealing here with primitive groups, such as the British found in most of their colonies, but with old European peoples who by geographic and historic circumstances have been left behind in the rush for economic and political power and who lack the national unity and relative prosperity that is part of the complex.

I will leave open the question of which power, Germany or Russia, is the more acceptable, or less objectionable, to the peoples concerned. It cannot be economic necessity that drives Russia to territorial expansion.

But it is vital to Germany — in her own view — to gain control over the larger part of Southeastern Europe, now that she has apparently lost all hope of expanding farther toward the east. The Balkans have a surplus of grains, animal products, olive oil, tobacco, and fruits; they have many metals, such as iron, copper, lead, zinc, and chromium, and especially attractive are the large deposits of aluminum ore. The oil of Rumania is another objective; however, one should note that the reserves here are apparently small. . . .

Let us summarize these observations. Before the Industrial Revolution the expansion of European peoples and the building up of colonial empires radiated from the Atlantic seaboard, where wealth accumulated and powerful national states developed. The Industrial Revolution brought a new set of forces into play which tended to offset the former handicaps of the continental areas. The new civilization spread to Central Europe, then to Russia, jumping the shatter belt in between. Now this " third Europe " is in a stage of transition to the new phase. Various circumstances have prevented Western Europe from taking an active part in this development, and it seems probable — whether one likes it or not — that Germany or Russia will take over the leadership in this zone. Germany needs this zone, certainly its southern half, more than Russia does, but it faces immense difficulties for any sustained dominance. The U.S.S.R., comparable to the United States in its broad territorial base and its wealth in minerals, may well, in time, become the real power of continental Eurasia.

We have seen how the boundaries of the European states are in the main based on the national criterion. These boundaries, as was pointed out, have little or no relation to present economic conditions — a discrepancy that will be further accentuated as time goes on. This is the dilemma of Europe: on the one hand, the wish for sovereign national states; on the other, the need of physical resources as a basis for material existence.

The cultural significance of a national life is not to be disputed, but it appears that the national idea has overreached itself. Is it not possible to save the spiritual values and at the same time provide a wider and more secure material foundation?

To answer this question we must remember that the idea of the national state is a relatively recent one. Being a historical concept, it may in time loose its grip again. This does not mean that Europe is likely to become a standardized, uniform civilization. Rather do I expect, or at least hope, that it will be possible to restrict the national spirit to its true function of cultural expression, in other words, to divest it of its power to make national boundaries into economic barriers. In short, the only solution is cultural autonomy for the different groups, with economic unity for the whole.

If we look at present-day Europe, it seems almost preposterous to express this hope. And yet, exhaustion following a long war, or fear for the rising eastern giant Russia, might well bring about what peace could never realize.

But whatever the solution, if Europe is to be saved from complete destruction, there must be established a new order: one different from that imposed at Versailles twenty years ago, and different from that dictated from Berchtesgaden today.

D. Demographic Factors

9. The Demographic Basis of Society

The philosopher's riddle has long been to discover why nations and societies thrive and grow, and, conversely, why they decline. The historian Gibbon attributed the fall of Rome to the influence of "barbarism and religion." Invaders threatened the Roman Empire from the outside and Christians undermined its social consciousness from within. Another theory maintains that decline was the price of failure in achieving political unity. In recent times, some population theorists, notably Gini, have put forth the thesis that the truest measure of growth and decline is the pattern of population growth or loss. If two societies are relatively equal in unity, industrialization, and technical advance, the factor that will tip the balance for one or the other will be superiority in numbers of persons in the productive years of life, or manpower.

Historically, evidence can be found to support this proposition. The society on the move frequently displays a steeply ascending curve of population growth. The miniature powers of the north Italian city-states in the fifteenth century were supreme on the peninsula until the rise of more populous nation-states within Europe. French power on the Continent was paramount until overtaken by Germany's rising population. Just as Germany eclipsed France in 1870, in our own day the Soviet Union has exceeded Germany in population and in power. Some demographers have concluded that a nation's power is greater or less than its neighbor's in proportion to the age structure and the size of their respective populations ". . . other things being equal."

The immortal phrase "other things being equal," however, sends up a warning signal against unqualified acceptance of the equation "population equals power." The fact is that the economic and political development of two countries never is identical and often is radically different. China and India possess vast reservoirs of available manpower but until recently lacked the most rudimentary basis of industrial development. Numbers are important to the extent that they can be vitalized through industrial techniques and skills. A realistic demography, therefore, accords recognition to the per capita production of a people and assesses strength on the basis of production as well as population data.

What are the reasons for differences among societies in numbers of population and rate of population growth? Why should Africa and India display a pattern of high birth and death rates whereas most countries in the West are experiencing declines? One answer can be found in the population policies of the countries concerned. From among three alternatives a nation may deliberately adopt or unconsciously pursue a certain population program. These alternatives are an expansive, a restrictive, or a eugenic policy. By following an expansive policy, nations deliberately introduce measures designed to increase population. Taxes are adjusted to reward prolific parents, birth premiums and family allowances are provided, and loans are granted on liberal terms. By contrast, restrictive population policies operate to achieve and encourage a declining birth rate and/or an increase in mortality. The policy of the United States, which on the face of it appears to be expansive, is in practice restrictive. The tax differential provided in exemptions for children reflects so inadequately the differences in cost that it punishes the prolific parent. Sweden through subventions has sought to restore balance to this ratio. The third alternative is the eugenic or qualitative policy which attempts to breed a superior race. It was avowedly the aim of the Nazis to follow this program.

This policy exploits or manufactures racial and linguistic differences and frequently becomes a rationalization for the special promotion of group interests and privileges. Some nations achieve the objectives of a particular policy through positive government directives. Others, by standing idly by while the cost of supporting large families becomes prohibitive, impose upon themselves unintended programs. Some say that this latter state of things is a crude but accurate description of the situation in this country today.

Population trends are also influenced by profound underlying forces. Industrialization exerts pressures that most societies appear unable to withstand. Mature industrial countries traditionally have witnessed declining birth rates, which rapidly overtake drops in mortality induced by advances in scientific medicine, sanitation, and communication. The Western powers are in this class. Groups for whom industrialization has been a recent experience frequently pass through a transitional stage wherein the drop in fertility fails to catch up immediately with a drop in the mortality rate. Japan and the Soviet Union exemplify this stage. Regions which have not yet undertaken programs of industrialization are known as high potential areas. Here high birth and death rates continue until technological change brings with it medical progress. India as it steadily pursues an industrialization policy is already moving from the high potential to the transitional stage in its population development.

Finally, population patterns reflect the influence of religion, literacy, and urbanization. The birth rate in a Catholic country tends to be higher than in a Protestant country although both Ireland and France are exceptions to this. Moreover, studies show that literacy can be positively correlated with low fertility. Illiterate populations manifest consistently higher birth rates throughout the world. In estimating and projecting population trends, the student of demography must employ such data in determining a country's position in the demographic cycle.

The age distribution in a society is still more intimately bound up with its demographic prospects. One needs only recall the significance attached to differences between the the youthful Soviet population contrasted with Western population configurations, where greater concentration is found in upper age groups. A young population is the essential basis of significant population growth. Partly because of the age distribution of the Russian people, demographers predict increases there which will greatly exceed those in the United States. In this way, the age distribution of a people, its religion and literacy, and the degree of industrialization and urbanization all contribute to its demographic pattern.

It is evident therefore that the demographic factor has played a significant role in the history of nations. The following essay seeks concretely to apply the principles of this science to current affairs. Mr. Dudley Kirk (1913–   ), a demographer in the Department of State, identifies the chief trend of our day as the eastward drift of population potential. Europe's population decline is matched by the increase of Asia's peoples. That this portends an irreversible end to the colonial era is evident today.

It should be pointed out that while the Kirk article presents what are essentially still valid and significant observations, some modifications may be necessary. This is particularly true with respect to his "continuum of demographic development." It is clear that we cannot expect the exact repetition by the growing Eastern powers of the nineteenth-century history of demographic growth as experienced by the Western world. Japan did not and probably will not duplicate exactly the industrial, commercial, and demographic development of England; nor can we expect China or India to recapitulate the precise history of the United States and Canada. Consequently, while in the large it is true that demographic patterns are largely predictable in terms of the process of industrialization, there is probably no rigid continuum of demographic evolution, but a series of types of balances, which various nations will tend to reach under changing internal and external pressures.

10. Population Changes and the Postwar World*

Great changes have occurred and are occurring in the size and distribution of the world's population. These changes are among the more fundamental and predictable determinants of the future. In their larger aspects population trends have shown a great deal of stability in the past and it seems reasonable to suppose that they will continue to do so in the future. They are one of the more certain elements in a most uncertain world. It is the purpose of this paper, first, to make some generalizations about population changes, occurring in modern times and, second, to indicate some directions in which they, in association with other social trends, may affect the postwar world.

A generation ago, behind every discussion of population problems there loomed the figure of Malthus. The writings of demography were filled with the dangers of overpopulation. These dangers have not disappeared; in most of the world there is still a heavy pressure of population on developed resources, and the Malthusian controls of famine, disease, and war are still the major checks to population growth. But a different interpretation of population phenomena has become more popular, partly owing to obvious changes in population trends, partly because of a re-evaluation of the relationship between population growth and eco-

* From Dudley Kirk, *American Sociological Review*, IX (1944), pp. 28–35. Reprinted by permission of Dudley Kirk and *American Sociological Review*.

nomic development in the modern world.

POPULATION TRENDS AS A FUNCTION OF " PROGRESS "

The dismal outlook of never-ending pressure of population on the food supply was dispelled in Western civilization by the achievements of the agricultural and industrial revolutions, and to a lesser extent by the exploitation of new lands and of old peoples. These have combined to provide the economic basis for both rising levels of living and extraordinarily rapid population growth. In the past three centuries the population of European races has increased sevenfold: from 100 millions in 1650 to 700 millions at the present time. In the same period it has increased from less than a fifth of the world's total to more than a third. But accompanying the achievement of higher levels of living, both as cause and consequence, has been the spread of the empirical outlook on life conducive to the restriction of family size and the termination of population growth. As is well known, the indefinite continuation of interwar trends would ultimately lead to the depopulation of Western Europe and of Europe overseas.

Rapid population growth and the subsequent slowing of growth arising from control of family size are intrinsic elements in the nexus of cultural traits that are valued as " progress." Their development has not been haphazard. Within Europe, for instance, there has been a clear pattern of cultural diffusion

from the initial locus of development in Northwestern and Central Europe. Modern education, improved health conditions, and economic advance are parts of the same cultural complex, indigenous to the West and for many decades past in the process of spreading across the continent. Progress flows along the lines of communication, is assisted by the presence of natural resources appropriate to industrialization, and is checked by natural and cultural barriers, but in general the level of material achievement of any given area in Europe is a function of its distance from the centers of diffusion in the West. Generally speaking, to go eastward in Europe is to go backward in time. The mode of life in some of the remote corners of Europe, as in the mountain districts of Yugoslavia, in Bessarabia, or in the Caucasus, has many points of resemblance to that existing in Western Europe several generations ago. Intermediate areas tend to blend toward one extreme or the other depending upon their geographical location and cultural associations. In these terms Europe is a cultural unit, all in the same stream of development, but with differences in the level of attainment growing from differences in the time at which the transition began from a peasant, self-sufficient society to an urban, industrial society.

Outside of Europe technological civilization has made progress likewise in relation to the accessibility, both cultural and geographical, to the centers of its development. It has now gained a solid foothold even among non-European peoples, and the time has long since passed when our arrogance will permit us to assert that Orientals, for instance, are racially or culturally incapable of establishing a modern industrial civilization. The spread of industry and the growth of cities have been well-nigh universal phenomena of recent times. Though in many countries these exist now only in embryonic form, it is questionable if there is a single country in the world that has not experienced some increase in industrial output and in modern urban influences during the twentieth century.

Demographic trends have shown an almost equal, and closely related, consistency in the direction of their development. Every country in the world with sufficiently good vital statistics to permit a judgment of trends displayed declining mortality rates in the interwar period. With few exceptions in the world, and none in the sphere of Western civilization, the birth rates likewise were lower at the end than at the beginning of the period.

The Continuum of Demographic Development

In regard to demographic matters the different countries of the world may be considered as on a single continuum of development, a continuum having both spatial and temporal significance. It is spatial in that the degree of development is related to the cultural and geographical accessibility to the most advanced countries. It is temporal in that each country in its development is following a general historical pattern common to all. In areas relatively untouched by Western influences, the typical demographic situation today is one of high birth rates and high death rates, with a low value placed on human life both in its inception and in its destruction. Of course this was also the demographic position of Europe at an earlier period. In normal years such areas have a substantial margin of natural increase, which is periodically checked by disasters of one sort or another. As modern influences increase, the beginnings of police control, better transportation, and the application of elementary public health measures all ameliorate the effects of these disasters. Before the war, the British in India, the Dutch in Java, the Japanese in Korea, we ourselves in the Philippines and Puerto Rico, had softened the impact of calamity, and had made effective the normally high rate of natural increase. This is the typical " colonial" situation today, characteristic of most of the Far East, the Mohammedan world, and much of Africa and Latin America. It was the condition of roughly half the population of the globe before the war.

In more developed countries further application of relatively elementary principles in the saving of lives had brought about further declines in the death rates. Later, the advance of modern influences, in the form of urban ways of life and the values which have accompanied this way of life in Western civilization, has resulted in the spread of the small family pattern, first among the upper classes and then among all the urban elements of the population. Such developments have yielded the beginnings of the decline of the birth rate, with clear indication that it would continue if unimpeded by a return to earlier values or by the inauguration of repressive population policies. In Southern and Eastern Europe, in the more progressive countries of Latin America, and in Japan, the decline of the death rate in the interwar period was accompanied by a declining birth rate. In these countries the pattern of fertility decline was established. However, the momentum of past growth, as reflected in the youth of their populations, and the inevitable lag in the decline of fertility from its present levels, posit substantial future growth of population in these areas for some years to come.

The countries nearer the centers of Western civilization have progressed further in the transition than those less fully caught up in the rising tide of material values. In the core of Western civilization in Northwestern Europe demographic evolution before the war had proceeded to the point where the birth rate was overtaking the death rate in its decline. The list of countries facing the likelihood of future population decline is a roster of the nations that have led the world in material progress.

The continuum of population development may be divided into three significant segments, each with its peculiar problems in the postwar world. About half the population of the world is in the first stage, the stage of great potential growth. Western influences have made possible a reduction in the death rate without compensating declines in the birth rate. In a relatively stable postwar world these areas will experience tremendous population growth, comparable in amount, though probably not in rate, to that experienced by the Western world at an earlier period of its history. A second, and transitional, stage has been achieved by those nations now caught up in the tide of industrialization and urbanization, but formerly, at least, on the peripheries of Western civilization. In these countries birth and death rates have both been declining, but the birth rates are still sufficiently high to support population growth for some time to come. Finally, there are those countries that face the prospect of depopulation if the net fertility declines of the interwar period are continued.

It would be tempting to consider a multitude of problems that may be encountered at each stage of economic and demographic evolution, but it would be impossible even to list them in the space allotted, and much less to analyze all the permutations and combinations represented in the various parts of the world. Perhaps what is most significant to us now, with the problems of planning a peace a public issue, is the political implications of the differing demographic trends, first, within Europe and, second, in the relationships between the Western peoples and the rest of the world.

Power Implications of Population Trends: Within Europe

It has been suggested that European peoples, and in fact almost all the nations of the earth, are moving on a continuum of economic and demographic development, representing greater or lesser change in the direction of an urban society. Within Europe, economic development and population change have gone hand in hand. Both have undoubtedly been elements in the changing distribution of political power.

The predominant position of France on the continent of Europe two or three centuries ago was partly a function of the fact that she was the wealthiest and in many respects the most advanced country in Europe. It is also undoubtedly associated with the fact that she was probably at the same time the most populous nation of the continent, not even excluding Russia, which now has four times her population. The economic and political position of France in relation to the remainder of Europe has changed enormously since 1800, and this change is probably not entirely unrelated to the fact that she now stands fifth rather than first among European nations in regard to population size.

The rise of Germany likewise has demographic foundations. In the Napoleonic period, Germans lived in a Europe dominated not only politically, but also numerically by the French. As the result of the economic development of Germany and the population increase made possible by this development, since the middle of the last century Germans have become much the most numerous of the European peoples aside from the Russians. As the largest single group, occupying a central position in Europe, it is natural that the Germans should have sought to bring the balance of political power into line with their growing numerical and industrial importance. That this could have been achieved more effectively through peaceful rather than through warlike means is now unfortunately beside the point.

By virtue of its more rapid natural increase and the Nazi annexation of German-speaking areas, Germany in 1939 had twice the population of France and a considerably larger population than that of Britain. However, from the demographic point of view, Germany had already passed the crest of the wave. The last war had serious consequences. But these were overshadowed by the effects of fertility declines. The population of the old Reich in 1939 was perhaps 6 million less because of World War I. It was 13 million less as the result of the decline of the birth rate since 1910. Prior to Hitler's accession to power the net reproduction rate had fallen to a lower level than that of France, the classic country of depopulation. The Nazi population policies, though moderately successful in their objective of increasing the number of births, nevertheless fell very far short of reestablishing 1910 fertility. The eastward wave of population increase has come and gone in Germany, and she is on the receding side of the tide in company with her Western neighbors. Demographically, Germany is in substantially the same position as England, France, and Scandinavia, all of which face the prospect of stationary or declining populations. War may speed the approach of population decline; population policies may retard it. But the underlying demographic situation will probably not be altered. Aside from an unforeseen volume of immigration the era of rapid population growth in these countries is past.

The populations of Eastern Europe grew much faster than those of Western European countries in the interwar period despite political disorder and the more severe effects of World War I in the East. At an earlier period the large population growth of this region was made possible by the fact that large areas were then in the process of initial agricultural settlement, or, put in other terms, in transition from a pastoral to a settled farm economy. In Russia there was new settlement not unlike that of our own frontier. This agricultural settlement represented a superior form of land utilization, and made possible the support of a far denser population than had formerly existed. More recently the wave of material progress represented by industrialization and an urban way of life has reached Eastern Europe from its centers of origin in the West. In Russia the contrast of the old and the new resulted in such severe stress on the old social order that it was swept away and the new technical civilization was ushered in with an impetus

previously unexampled in history. These developments have made possible rapid population increase such as existed in Western Europe at an earlier period. Despite war and revolution, which apparently cost Russia a total population deficit of 26 millions, including both deaths and loss of births, since 1900 the population of the territory of the Soviet Union has grown more rapidly than that of Western Europe. Its present age structure and fertility levels suggest that the present war will not have a serious retarding influence on her future rapid growth. The youth of the Russian population is suggested by the fact that the median age is under twenty-three years, as contrasted with thirty-two in Northwestern and Central Europe now and with a median age of 40 in that region by 1970 on a projection of interwar vital trends. The reported birth rate in the U.S.S.R. for 1938 was 38.3 per thousand population or over twice that of the United States in the same year.

Ignoring the war and assuming fertility declines comparable to those experienced in Western Europe at the same level of fertility, the population of the Soviet Union in 1970 would exceed 250 millions. The war will reduce the growth potential, but barring a demographic catastrophe greatly exceeding that of World War I and the Russian revolution, the U.S.S.R. gives every promise of growing more rapidly than the remainder of Europe. In 1939 the U.S.S.R. had twice the 80 millions living in the area of Greater Germany. In 1970 it will probably have three times as large a population, and there will probably be no Greater Germany. What these differences can mean in terms of military potential may be indicated from the trends of manpower. On the assumptions of growth suggested the U.S.S.R. by 1970 would have more men of prime military age, twenty to thirty-four, than its six closest rivals in Europe combined. The increase in the number of men of this military age by 1970 would alone be as large as the total German military manpower of that age today, or that to be expected from any reasonable demographic trends to 1970.

As long as the Russians were poor, illiterate, and thinly scattered over an enormous area, their numbers were not very effective against the industrialized nations of the West except in terms of resistance through sheer inertia of size. Even in the present war, distance and weight of numbers have been an important element in the Russian successes. But the Soviet Union is moving into a position in which it will be able to make its people as effective economically, person for person, as those of Western Europe in general and Germany in particular. Since the Russian manpower of a generation hence will almost certainly be greater proportionately than it is today, a future German challenge to Russia and the world along the lines of 1914 and 1939 seems improbable. Demographic trends alone suggest that this conflict is Germany's last chance for European and world domination.

To say that Russia will be powerful is, of course, not equivalent to saying that she will be a threat. Large population growth in Russia does not involve the serious difficulties that it would, for instance, in Germany. In the Soviet Union rapid growth for some time to come is probably necessary for the maximum development of large available resources in relation to existing population. It should present no greater problem than it did in the United States after the Civil War. Russia has ample resources, ample territory, and a great need for labor to develop unexploited areas in Asia and in the Arctic. The problem is not one of resources or of territory. It is rather that of converting a population only two or three generations from serfdom into a literate, physically healthy, technically competent, urban people. At least that is the job as seen by the Russians themselves according to many reports, and it is a job certainly appropriate to the predominant values of our own world.

Power Implications of Population Trends: Europe and Asia

A less certain, but ultimately equally significant development is the eastward movement of power, not only in Europe, but in the world. As long as Western European civilization was able to maintain an effective monopoly on the industrial techniques that give power in the modern world, numbers were relatively unimportant in the relations between Western countries and the densely populated Orient. Numbers are an element of power in any social group.

But to be effective they must be implemented with resources and skills, and cemented by social cohesion and unity of purpose. Clearly numbers are of little importance when two civilizations of very different values meet. The domination of India by a handful of Englishmen is an obvious case in point. The British had at their command a great technical superiority of weapons and a social organization directed at the achievement of material ends. The British and the Indians simply were not interested in the same things: the goals and values of their respective societies were almost diametrically opposed. To most Indians the assumption of political control by the British was a matter of complete indifference.

This is no longer the case. Whether through the success of our own efforts at indoctrination, or through frank admiration for our achievements, Oriental and other colored peoples are absorbing important elements of our civilization. Thus the Japanese have clearly demonstrated, first, that a non-European people can establish an astonishingly strong industrial civilization almost entirely on its own initiative, and, further, that a poor but industrious folk can accomplish this with a poverty of natural resources that would seem hopeless by Western standards. But in terms of a reasonable evaluation of its economic and political potential Japan seems no more formidable in relation to Asia as a whole than would England, shorn of its empire, in relation to a united Europe. And China, at least, seems on the way to achieving a unity that Europe was never able to accomplish.

It is commonly assumed that overpopulation in China, as indicated by the prevailing poverty of the people, will prove a great barrier to the economic progress of the country and hence to its rise as a world power. However, it needs to be pointed out that China is not so hopelessly overpopulated as is commonly supposed and that this condition does not represent an insuperable obstacle to industrialization. It is perhaps suprising to note that the over-all density of population in China is only half that of Europe west of Russia though her total population is roughly comparable in size. Even in China proper, population density is much less than in Western Europe. Overpopulation in China, as elsewhere, is indicated by a high ratio of population to developed resources. It has reality only in relation to a given stage of technological development. In other areas technical changes have obviously brought about enormous changes in the carrying capacity of the land. Four hundred years ago the present area of continental United States supported only 200 or 300 thousand Indians living on the margin of subsistence. With our present technological development, the same area readily supports 130 million or several hundred times as many people, and at a much higher standard of living. In existing circumstances the level of living in a country is much more closely related to its degree of technological development than it is to the absolute numbers of its population. Overpopulation is not a matter of too many people any more than it is a matter of too little economic production.

Considered in this light the problems of the densely populated countries of the Far East take on a much more hopeful aspect than has commonly been attributed to them. Given its present economic structure, it is undeniable that China is overcrowded. But it does not appear fanciful to suppose that at the level of technical efficiency now prevailing in Europe the present population of China could be maintained at something approximating Europe's levels of living. This would assume a potential resource base somewhat comparable to that of Europe west of Russia in an area more than twice as large.

It is obvious that the Chinese population does not now have either the capital or the trained personnel to achieve the present per capita production of Europe in the near future. However, there are compelling precedents in recent history demonstrating that neither of these are insuperable obstacles. In Russia a backward and illiterate peasantry is being converted almost in a single generation into a literate, forward-looking proletariat, rapidly acquiring the skills necessary for efficient industrial production. And on the other side of China is the convincing example of Japan, which has constructed an industrial economy with a paucity of natural resources that would be appalling to any Western people.

In China herself something of the possibilities both for industrialization and for higher per capita output in agriculture have been demonstrated in these war years. In this period China has built up an army of some 10 million men, chiefly taken from the peasantry and consequently withdrawn from agricultural production. At the same time agricultural production in Western China has apparently remained at least as high as before the war, partly because the men withdrawn from agriculture were inefficiently used in agriculture anyway, and partly because even in the space of five years some progress has been made, especially in the use of better seed. These factors combined are sufficient to free 10 million men as industrial workers in this area after the war. Furthermore, the army was provided with small arms, i.e., rifles and light machine guns, and the appropriate ammunition, almost entirely from domestic production. When it is considered that most of China's prewar industries were located in the coastal cities now occupied by the Japanese, such an accomplishment must be considered a remarkable one. The capital for this achievement was naturally obtained at great sacrifice. But the means of industrialization can be wrung from a people living as close to the margin of subsistence as the Chinese if there is a central government with the necessary will and unity.

In these war years China herself has given ample evidence that with a stable government she is capable of great economic progress, even without effective assistance from outside. However, it is certainly true that unless some check is placed on population growth, her growing masses will ultimately consume the margin of production created by technical progress. Past experience has demonstrated, as in Japan, that even in very poor countries technical progress can outstrip population growth for a time and bring about a rising level of living in the face of large increments of population. Yet this can be no ultimate solution. Population growth, if unchecked, must ultimately destroy the gains of more efficient production, and through that destruction hinder and perhaps eliminate further gains. China's problem, then, is a combination of the economic and the demographic. Her material progress will depend on how quickly she is able to make technical advances in production. It also depends upon how quickly she absorbs the pattern of birth control.

Whether Asia will follow the course set by Western Europe in the decline of the birth rate is obviously a crucial question. Where birth control runs counter to the prevailing values, as in India, its diffusion may be slow. However, the influences operating against the acceptance of birth control probably also operate against economic development and against further declines in the death rates. The only Asiatic country to have undergone sufficient industrialization and urbanization to offer a test case is Japan. In that country birth control had apparently established itself before the war. In Japanese cities, where birth control would most likely first achieve general use, the prewar fertility seems to have been only about five-eighths that in the rural areas. In the country as a whole the age distribution and vital trends in the interwar period were similar to those of England between 1880 and 1900, and indicate a stage of demographic evolution comparable to that of England in that period. . . . The Japanese case is not conclusive, but it is illuminating; it suggests that the barriers between the Western and Eastern worlds are not too great to prevent the diffusion of the birth control pattern.

The decline of the birth rate in Asia is eminently desirable as long as the continent faces elementary difficulties in feeding its huge population. Emigration is no real solution for the future. There are no longer empty countries either willing or able to welcome the surplus population on a scale sufficient to afford relief. The economic problems are serious. And yet it seems probable that given a modicum of political stability, the Oriental countries will be enabled to experience both a rising level of living and rapid population increase for a time. It is true that they have less of a margin above subsistence than the Western countries had at a comparable stage of economic development. But it is also true that they have the experience of the West to draw upon in the solution of their difficulties.

Asia as a whole appears to be on the verge of a great awakening. This awakening may take many generations and undoubtedly will not occur evenly throughout the continent. But the tempo of change has been so increased that it seems possible that this awakening will occur with tremendous explosive force, and much sooner than is commonly supposed. If the modernization of Asia follows the course that it took in Europe it will be accompanied by large population increase. Increase of population, and the very mass of the Asiatic population itself, could be ignored in the past as unimportant in the balance of world power. But with the prospect that the Asiatic masses will ultimately learn to forge the tools that will give them power, the differential population trends may become of very great importance. Population increase has been part and parcel of the spread of European populations over much of the globe. In the past European populations have been growing very rapidly in a relatively slowly growing world. The present outlook is for relatively stationary or declining populations among Western European peoples in a rapidly growing world. Western European peoples will almost certainly become a smaller part of the total population of the world. To the extent that numbers are a factor in the distribution of economic and political power, there will be some redistribution of power from old to new centers.

Conclusion

What all this means for the future is that we are not going to see again a world in which huge areas inhabited by non-European peoples may be casually regarded as the political playthings of Western European and American powers. The day is rapidly passing when a handful of Europeans, equipped with superior weapons and a complacent and somehow contagious faith in white supremacy, can expect indefinitely to dominate the half of the world that is occupied by the colored peoples. Either we must be prepared to meet the emerging nations halfway, helping them willingly along the road we have travelled to higher standards of living, and the more efficient creation of a better human product, or we must be prepared to maintain white supremacy by force of arms, and in defiance of our own conception of human rights. In the latter case, we would probably be faced with the prospect of an intercontinental conflict that might well dwarf the present war in ferocity and in its threat to the values that are considered the foundation of our society. If we choose to take the path of friendly assistance we will enjoy economic benefits through the rapid expansion of markets and trade. We will probably be serving our own ultimate political interests by speeding the social evolution that will bring about slower population growth. Most important of all, we shall have led all of humanity to new possibilities of life for the common man, freed from the degrading influences of hunger and grinding poverty.

E. Prospects for Survival: Population *v.* Food Supply

11. Food, People, and Survival

No society can survive without adequate supplies of food resources. In recent years many people have become increasingly alarmed by the possibility that the world's population might be outrunning its food supply. This same concern in 1798 inspired Thomas Malthus to write his *Essay on Principles of Population*. Today there has been a revival of the Malthusian theory that population increases in a geometric ratio, while the food supply only increases in an arithmetic ratio. The neo-Malthusian view is that this takes place not inevitably, as Malthus thought, but in consequence of the control over mortality. Some feel that this neo-Malthusian doctrine describes the problem facing the West in most of the so-called underdeveloped areas. It is argued that no outlay of technical and economic assistance or even the wisest form of counsel can arrest the consequences of unlimited population growth. On a world scale the increase required in food supply, it is alleged, is beyond the capacity of available land and other food-producing resources.

Professor M. K. Bennett, of Stanford University, in this selection takes a stand somewhere between the optimism of some of the disciples of progress and the pessimism of the neo-Malthusian school. There is a wide range of change which modern technology has made possible. Yet there remain limits beyond which man cannot now go. This selection holds its chief interest in indicating the points of difference between the neo-Malthusians and their opponents.

12. Population and Food Supply: The Current Scare*

The so-called "race between population and food supply" has again come forward as an absorbing topic of discussion, in popular and professional circles alike. Discussants mostly present a deeply pessimistic view of the future. At a press conference on May 18, 1948, Sir John Boyd Orr, retiring director of the Food and Agriculture Organization of the United Nations, is reported to have "pleaded with the correspond-

* From M. K. Bennett, *The Scientific Monthly*, LXVII (1949), pp. 17–26. Reprinted by permission of M. K. Bennett and *The Scientific Monthly*.

ents to help awaken the people to the fact that in the race between population and food, population was winning — 'and we do not know how to stop it.'" A few months earlier Sir John had said, "Taking account of the expected increase in world population, food production must be increased by 110 percent (more than doubled) in the next twenty-five years if sufficient food is to be provided for all mankind. Only co-operative international action can prevent the direst calamities."

Reiterating in July 1948 Sir John's estimate of what a tremendous twenty-five year increase in production would be required to provide the world with " sufficient food," and defining sufficiency as a meager 2,600 calories per person per day (meager for the U.S., that is, but not for Oriental populations), President Milton S. Eisenhower, of Kansas State College, added, " And I say in all earnestness that it is an open question whether food production, for all our science, can be increased that much." Reports in September 1948 from the Inter-American Conference on Renewable Natural Resources in Denver, and from meetings of both the American and the British Associations for the Advancement of Science were replete with similar pessimism. A Canadian publication stated in August,

it would seem, then, that perhaps never again — unless an unforeseen miracle occurs — will the white people of the world be able to enjoy the extremely high level of food that was available to them in 1938 and 1939. The white races . . . will have to adapt themselves . . . to a gradual change in their diet, consuming less livestock products and more cereals.

There is also William Vogt's recent book, *Road to Survival* described by its publishers as a " revelation of the fact that the earth, as abused by man, is unable to support the human race in terms of its most basic need — food." Fairfield Osborn's book *Our Plundered Planet* chants much the same lament.

The problem (he says) is now to conserve the remaining good natural soils that exist on the earth, together with the complementary resources of forest, water sources, and the myriads of beneficial forms of animal life. There is no other problem. If that is not solved the threat to human life will grow in intensity and the present conditions of starvation that are already apparent in various parts of the earth will seem as nothing in the years that lie ahead.

Examples need not be multiplied to indicate that we are in the midst of a resurgence of widespread discussion of the old problem of pressure of population upon the food supply. In the English-speaking world three waves of such discussion, heavily weighted with pessimism, have been recognizable, since the first one was touched off by Malthus' famous *An Essay on the Principle of Population* . . . , published anonymously in 1798. The second wave came in the late 1890's in connection with the German controversy about the relative merits of agrarian and industrial national economies. Perhaps an ephemeral shortage and high price of wheat was a contributing factor. It was in 1898 that Sir William Crookes delivered his famous address, " The Wheat Problem," to the British Association for the Advancement of Science; some people took it as a " cosmic scare." But again interest in the global food-supply problem waned, only to be stimulated for the third time, for a few years after World War I. We are now in the midst of the fourth wave.

I

What are the sources of this resurgence of interest, and what is new in current discussion?

It appears that many have recently become aware of an increase in births following the cessation of hostilities — at least here in the United States, in some countries of Western Europe, and in Japan. At the same time it has become clear that war casualties — deaths — were in many countries not so large as to slow down rates of population growth. Also, there has been in the past few years tremendous inventiveness in the field of lifesaving techniques, to mention only the use of the sulfa drugs, penicillin, Atabrine, and insecticides of the DDT type — all tending to reduce mortality rates and all tending to become cheaper and more widely available. Coupling these new developments with widening knowledge of the facts about world population growth during the past half century and more, many come to the conclusion that the population outlook for the next half century is for growth, very rapid and perhaps alarming because the earth's surface is limited in extent.

Certainly the available evidence on world population growth during the past two centuries is impressive. There were perhaps about 875 million people in the world in 1750. Now, as we near 1950, there are perhaps 2,350 million. The words " perhaps " and " about " are used advisedly, for the world's population has never actually been counted. But the estimates, imperfect as they are, seem sound enough to warrant the statements that the world now contains nearly three people to every one person existing two centuries ago, and that the increase, at least if one takes it by centuries since 1650, has been at an accelerating rate in the world as a whole though not in each of its parts.

If we take the present or 1950 world population as about 2,350 million, the probability is that the increase in the past fifty years has amounted to roughly 750 million people, and this in spite of two world wars in the interval. It is an increase of over 45 percent within the adult memories of a good many living men. Much of the world's population growth since 1900 has occurred in areas rather far out on the horizon of our vision, such as India, Burma, Japan, and the Netherlands Indies. Nevertheless, our own national population, helped by immigration, has approximately doubled since 1900, and there seems to be no large geographical area of the world where population increase has not been substantial in the past half century. The rates of natural increase, it is true, were lower in Western Europe, North America, and Australasia than in most other parts of the world. Indeed, not more than a decade ago these low rates of natural increase gave rise to concern about decline of certain national populations in the future. But recently that concern has diminished; the dates of probable maxima of populations have been postponed by the demographers.

One authoritative projection of population growth places the more or less probable world total in the year 2000 as about 3,300 million people. An increase of some 900 million is implied for the half century which we are about to enter — in absolute numbers, a larger increase than occurred in the half century just past. Of course this is not a firm prediction, but it represents the type of projection in the minds of many who currently discuss the problem of population and food supply. They regard population trends as rather intractable and stubborn; and from all we know this seems a proper attitude to assume. Current discussion of the question seems generally to take for granted a great and perhaps unprecedented increase of world population in the next half century, barring only the advent of events highly unpalatable to mankind. Birth rates, it is supposed, cannot reasonably be expected to fall as rapidly as death rates, which are more and more reduced by modern life-preserving techniques — unless indeed the death rate should be elevated by war, famine, or pestilence, all of which men of good will seek to avoid.

Some discussants recognize that rates of natural increase vary from nation to nation, and that the lower rates, presaging little or no augmentation of certain national populations if we neglect immigration, tend to appear in prosperous or advanced countries. Those are countries at once highly urbanized, highly industrialized, highly literate, highly productive economically. Among them are the United States and Canada, Australia and New Zealand, the United Kingdom, Belgium, the Netherlands, Switzerland, the Scandinavian countries, and France. Germany was of this group before the war, but may not in all respects be of it now. However, the population of the high-income countries of lowest rates of natural increase of population make up much less than half the world's population; so that an expectation of heavy increase in the world total population, in the absence of unwelcome types of checks, seems well justified.

The war, as everyone knows, tended in many though not all parts of the world to cut down agricultural production, and to curtail the international movement of food from surplus to deficit areas. Post-hostility shortages of many sorts, currency inflations, balance-of-payment difficulties, shifts of national boundaries and population groups, occupation policies, political revolutions, civil wars, and other influences have so far combined to hamper recovery. Additionally, in the world's great food-importing area of Western Europe, the weather was very bad for crops produced in 1945 and 1947. Only as the harvest of Northern Hemisphere crops of 1948 came to an end did the Western world begin to emerge from a food shortage of great severity. Here in the United States the shortage touched us in imagination and pocket, not in the stomach. But it has certainly struck the imagination hard. From all over the world for nearly a decade stories of the most urgent food needs, or of starvation itself, have poured into our consciousness. We have been made aware, to a degree hitherto unfamiliar, of the generally restricted diets of a billion and a half or more of the world's population even in prewar years. And population growth during the past decade of war and incomplete recovery has tended to accentuate the meagerness of food supplies in all but a few exceptionally situated food-exporting nations like our own. No wonder, on this count alone, that pessimism rules.

With growing population coupled with lagging recovery of food output and distribution, it appears difficult for the less fortunately situated nations to recoup the level of food intake prevailing before the war, in the late 1930's. But, in the minds of many, perhaps especially the nutrition-minded, such recovery is not enough, not what the world wants or needs. Rather, the desideratum is substantial improvement in the per capita food intake of most nations, perhaps of all — one aspect of " Freedom from Want." This is an idea for several years strongly espoused by the Food and Agriculture Organization of the United Nations. It has spent no little time and effort in publicizing the facts that even before the war, as measured against standards of adequacy set up by the nutritionists, the average per capita food intake of many nations, comprising in total far more than half the world's population, was sadly deficient in quality and not infrequently in quantity; and that even in the best-fed countries at least a modest fraction of the population was either undernourished or malnourished. Although evidence for these conclusions began to appear nearly two decades ago, it has lately been the FAO more than any other organized group that has broadcast information on the quantity and composition of national food supplies. And it has espoused as its foremost objective, its major *raison d'être,* the improvement of human nutrition throughout the world — not merely the recovery of prewar nutritional status.

If those who limit their hopes to a fairly prompt return of the world to its prewar nutritional status are nowadays pessimistic in outlook, we need not be surprised that those whose hearts are set on general improvement of nutritional status are even more so.

The jeremiads of the nutritional idealists, however, are hardly as frightening as those of the conservationists, notably the soil conservationists. Extremists of this group seem to take for granted the population projections of the demographers and the nutritional goals of FAO; and then they proceed to uncover, it would seem practically everywhere, evidence of permanent soil erosion by water and wind, and of depletion of soil fertility. Both are ascribed in dominant part to blind pursuit of profits by the farmers and graziers of the world, which is alleged to lead to mistreatment of the soil.

There seems to be a degree of historical coincidence in the rise of the soil-conservation school to its present degree of public prominence. Great dust storms afflicted our Great Plains in the middle 1930's. A bit earlier, in 1933, this nation had embarked upon the adventure of curing economic depression in part by supporting farm prices and incomes, and the method first chosen was to make Federal payments directly to farmers in exchange for acreage reduction. When the Supreme Court in January 1936 put a stop to this " gentle rain of checks," as a shrewd observer called it, a lawful way to continue became the object of political expediency. And so the payments earlier made to purchase acreage reduction became " agricultural conservation payments"; politics opened the door of the public treasury to conservationists; the great droughts carried conviction to the public of a crying need for conservation; and increasingly since then political leaders, soil conservationists, and the public seem to have been at one in viewing soil erosion as a dreadful threat domestically. As conservationists proliferated, the perception of threat to food supply through soil erosion spread so as to compass whole continents. The books by Vogt and Osborn provide outstanding, perhaps extreme, examples of literature originating with the ardent-conservation school. That group, of course, cries for " action

now," and for funds as well. Allusion is made to civilizations which, it is claimed, disappeared because their soil was swept away. It is sought to check or control erosion, thus saving civilization.

The soil-conservation school adds to the old concept that the food-producing land of the world is strictly limited in extent, the new concept that the land is actually being destroyed, and at a rapid rate. The argument is picked up in strange places. An advertisement of a British firm selling agricultural machinery reads in part: " To avert mass starvation and world strife, more food must be produced. Man in his ignorance, however, has raped vast areas of the good earth. Soil erosion, like a cancerous growth, has doomed miles of the land to sterility."

The broad and general tenor of current discussion is summed up in a sentence of Sir William Crookes, spoken in 1898: " As mouths multiply, food resources dwindle." A few points made in this fourth wave of pessimism, however, seem new. Concern has largely shifted, for example from " bread-eaters" of the Western world to the teeming populations of Asiatic countries. Again, interest has largely shifted from mere maintenance of accustomed diets to the improvement of diets. " Improved" diets usually involve enlargement of the proportion of calories derived from animal products; and this would involve extra drafts on productive resources because the animals burn up humanly edible grain when they convert it to meat, milk, or eggs. Sir John Orr may be thinking of such dietary improvement rather than maintenance, or even return to pre-World War II status, when he estimates that world food production must be increased by 110 percent in the next twenty-five years if sufficient food is to be provided for all mankind. New also in current discussion is the heavy emphasis on destruction of soil through erosion. And, finally, one sees little in earlier discussions the idea, often mentioned now, that there would be little purpose in fostering the international spread of new lifesaving techniques and sanitary measures, because resulting increased pressure of population on food supply would merely plunge into misery those whose lives were saved. The emergence of some of these new notes tends to intensify current pessimism. A vicious circle as perceived nowadays seems, if not altogether different from what it seemed before, to be more vicious than we used to think.

The consequences envisaged in current writings are various, some perhaps rather vague. Sir John Orr speaks of " direst calamities " in the absence of concerted international action, but is not specific about the nature of those calamities or about the international action. Eisenhower speaks of " the spector of permanent, world-wide hunger " as now seeming very real. Our British advertiser speaks of the necessity of greater food production if " mass starvation " and " world strife " are to be averted. Vogt, Osborn, and Eisenhower alike make much of the disappearance of earlier civilizations, as in Mesopo-

tamia, Syria, Rome, northwestern China, and Guatemala, and they suggest that modern civilization may be headed in the same direction. Deserts are said to be on the march, because men disturb and destroy natural vegetation. Less frightening though perhaps still unpalatable is the Searle Grain Company's opinion that the people of the world may never again enjoy as good a food supply as existed just before World War II, and that the white races in particular may have to cut down on ingestion of livestock products and resort more to grain.

II

It seems pertinent next to review sketchily what has happened to food supplies or intake over the world in the past fifty years or so when population increased by perhaps 750 million people. The recent past has some bearing on what may conceivably happen in the next fifty years when, the demographers suggest, a further increase of some 900 million may reasonably be expected in the absence of intolerable " positive " checks to population growth.

The question posed with respect to the past half century has to be stated with more precision. Not much is to be learned by asking what has happened to the average per capita calorie intake of the whole world, or what has happened to the composition of the diet of the world as a whole. We simply do not know, and cannot expect to find out. But there is no point in raising such a question. The world is nothing like a unit with reference to food intake, any more than it is with reference to per capita real income, and a per capita world average is next door to meaningless. Much more useful to raise are the questions: Where throughout the world has food intake become more plentiful and more varied in composition in the past half century? Where less so? Where unchanged? And why?

Simply because the only available information pertains to nations or colonies, the changes must be located mainly in terms of national boundaries — and even this only approximately because national boundaries themselves have changed.

A degree of precision will be added if we mainly consider two aspects of average national diets: (a) the average per capita intake of total food calories from whatever crude foodstuffs they may be derived; and (b) the proportion of national food intake derived from the grains and potatoes (including here such items as cassava and taro). It may be assumed that a long-persisting decline in the "cereal-potato" fraction of a national diet represents an improvement of diet unless that is evidence of accompanying exceptional decline in total calorie intake per capita. For the cereals and potatoes are almost universally the cheapest of all foods per thousand calories; and all population groups except the very wealthy clearly tend to reduce the proportion of total calories derived from cereals and potatoes whenever they can do so, expanding variously the proportions of their food-calorie intake derived from other principal and more expensive groups of foods: namely, sugars, vegetable oils, legumes or pulses, low-calorie fruits and vegetables, and animal products, including meat, dairy products, eggs and poultry, fish, and their accompanying fats. A decline in the proportion of calories derived from cereals and potatoes in a national diet does not constitute altogether conclusive evidence of nutritional improvement of diet; it may not, especially if only sugar or vegetable oil replaces the cereals and potatoes. But in general a decline of the cereal-potato fraction of a diet means increase of palatability and diversity and represents economic improvement of diet. On all the evidence we have, the mass behavior of people is to reduce the cereal-potato component of diets when that component is high, if they can afford it. Such evidence comes forward in all surveys of food consumption by differing income groups, in whatever places and at whatever dates the surveys are made. But the tendency does not run to complete displacement; perhaps 10–20 percent of cereal-potato foods would be retained by a mass of millionaires.

At the present time it happens to be impossible to ascertain, systematically, nation by nation for the whole world, exactly what changes have occurred in per capita calorie intake or in the proportion of calories derived respectively from cereals and potatoes and from other foods. If estimates of population growth over the past half century are commonly lacking or uncertain, the position is far worse with respect to food supply. We know most about the nations where the record keeping is best; where domestic crops have long been painstakingly estimated, and imports and exports systematically recorded. The measurement of a national food supply is fearfully complex to accomplish, not only because there are so many components in a food supply, but also because so many important foodstuffs are usable and are used both for food and for feed.

More is perhaps known about the United States than any other country. Elaborate official statistics and estimates cover, year by year, the period since 1909. They show, in the 30 years between 1909 and 1939, a small decline in total calories per capita "available . . . at the retail level: from about 3,500 to about 3,300. They show also a much more striking decline in the proportion of total calories derived from the grains and potatoes — from 44 to 29 percent. On the other hand, there were measurable increases in the proportions derived from sugar (from 12 to 16 percent), from fruits and the vegetables other than potatoes (from 7 to 10 percent), and from meat, fish, poultry, eggs, dairy products, and fats and oils (from 37 to 45 percent). Thus the proportion of national calories derived from grains and potatoes fell, and the proportion derived from other foodstuffs, more expensive per thousand calories as a group and with respect to nearly all individual items, reciprocally rose — at least from 1909 to 1939.

If one seeks now to push backward in time through the twenty years preceding 1909, the official statisti-

cians give less help. But Holbrook Working was able to establish convincing evidence of decline in the per capita consumption of the chief grain products, wheat flour and corn meal, and also an increase in per capita consumption of sugar, during those two decades. Flour and meal consumption fell from about 560,000 calories per person per year in 1889 to about 450,000 in 1909, a decline of nearly 20 percent. The rise in sugar consumption did not offset this. Working's incomplete findings are consistent with the interpretation that general trends known to exist from 1909 to 1939 existed also from 1889 to 1909 — a decline in total food calories per capita, a decline in the proportion derived from grains and potatoes, and an increase in the proportion derived from other foodstuffs than grains and potatoes, demonstrably from sugar.

These, then, were the tendencies in the United States for half a century preceding World War II. They represented a general sufficiency of total calories even with decline; that decline is reasonably attributable mainly to lowered requirement due to reduction of physical activity — machines increasingly working for men. They also represented wider freedom of choice in foods, greater variety and palatability — in short, an improvement of diet in the economic sense, whether or not in the nutritional sense. This could not have happened without increase in per capita real income, of which there is plenty of evidence that need not be brought forward.

But the United States is only a

part of the world. What happened elsewhere? Of this we know less. It is a proper subject for prolonged and intricate research. Yet a good many pieces of evidence can be tied together to indicate that decline in the cereal-potato fraction of national diets was rather widespread in the half century before World War II. Quite commonly we perceive in statistics declines in per capita human consumption of what are generally regarded as inferior cereals — rye, corn, barley, oats, and the millets and sorghums. In itself this indicates the existence of economic circumstances permitting wider choice of more expensive and desirable foodstuffs, among which the preferred cereals, wheat and rice commonly appear. Quite commonly we perceive increases in per capita consumption of sugar. Not uncommonly we perceive declines in per capita consumption of a preferred cereal, wheat; but this reflects a reciprocal rise in consumption of more expensive foods. Trends toward economic improvement of national diets can be demonstrated satisfactorily at least for Canada, Australasia, the British Isles, Scandinavia, Germany, the Low Countries, Switzerland, France, and Japan — in kind resembling the trends in the United States, in degree and details quite likely different. One need not much hesitate to add to this list such nations as Argentina, Brazil, Mexico, Cuba, the former Baltic States, Poland, Czechoslovakia, Austria, Hungary, Yugoslavia, Greece, Italy, Spain, and Turkey. In each of these, there appears to be no suggestion of a long-term

trend toward insufficiency of total calories per capita, even if there was slight decline as in the United States and for similar reasons; and there is some evidence of increasing diversity of diet.

Again looking at the half century preceding World War II, we see, though most dimly, developments which have the appearance of being somewhat different in several Oriental countries — India, Burma, Korea, Formosa, Java, the Philippines. The meager statistics for recent decades — one cannot press far back — suggest a gradual small reduction of per capita calorie supply, coupled with tendencies for inferior cereals and for sweet potatoes to increase while the favored grain, rice, declines in consumption. In spite of some small increase of wheat consumption, occasionally of sugar, and in spite of lessened incidence of local famines, one finds little direct statistical evidence of increasing per capita consumption of fats, meat, dairy products, and fish. The dependence on cereal-potato foodstuffs remains very high; if it declined, the decline was small. There is a suggestion here, though only a suggestion, of general tightening of the food situation — fewer calories where more were needed — rather than enlarged scope to diversity diet.

The largest population groups not yet mentioned are China, the African continent, and the USSR. On food developments in China and Africa, little useful statistical evidence is to be found. That northern China suffered sporadic localized famines in the course of the half century is certain. Whether there was important deterioration generally in calorie supply or in composition of the national average diet is unknown. There is perhaps evidence of improvement in African food supplies, but no conclusions need be drawn here.

In the USSR, from 1898 to World War I, there seems to have been general sufficiency of calories aside from local shortages, also a shift from rye to wheat, and possibly a degree of increased diversification of dietary composition. The First World War and the Revolution led to famine in 1921–23. Subsequent recovery was interrupted by the drive for collectivization and ensuing slaughter of livestock, and another famine occurred in 1932–33. Again came recovery, but Soviet statistics are not such as to tell us truly about calorie supplies and composition of diet just before World War II. There is ample reason, however, to believe that the rural fraction of the population was then less well fed than it had been before World War I; and the rural fraction remained, in spite of growing industrialization, much the larger fraction of total. Also, the urban population itself seems unlikely to have been as well fed before World War II as it was before World War I.

So much for the history of the relationship between population and food supply during the half century preceding World War II. The world population growth was enormous. But meanwhile food intake improved in a good many national populations. This, it should be em-phasized, is the fact so far as concerns the regions about which we know most and can have most confidence in the statistical evidence. As for the populations where deterioration of the food position is suggested, either the credible direct evidence on food supplies is decidedly meager, or we can be fairly certain that the deterioration sprang in large part from governmental interventions, as in Korea, Formosa, and the USSR.

Even with respect to India, one cannot feel confident that the food position really deteriorated progressively, although the statistics — such as they are — point in this direction. For we know that at the same time India unquestionably became increasingly urbanized and industrialized. Except as this comes about through a socialized control — investment squeezed from consumption — such as prevailed after 1917 in the USSR but never in India, urbanization and industrialization spell enlargement of national real income per capita; and that tends strongly to carry with it improvement of diet in the economic sense. It is difficult to believe, of India or any other non-socialized country, that city populations grew as they did in relation to rural populations for any other important reason than that the farm people saw a chance to improve their income status in the cities, and that the process of industrialization opened avenues for them. The people who migrated from farm to city were not jumping from frying pan to fire. On this line of reasoning, one cannot feel fully confident that India, and perhaps, though less probably, even China, were not enjoying a somewhat more diversified average national diet, albeit a poor one by our standards, in 1939 than fifty years before. The facts are not clear, whereas the facts are clear concerning the great majority of nations belonging to the commercial Western World.

The half century preceding World War II may then reasonably be regarded as one more accurately characterized as giving evidence of improvement in per capita food supplies than the opposite. Widespread indeed were demonstrable improvements, whereas positive deterioration suggested in some places is subject to doubts not readily dispelled, or can be explained in terms of political interference with economic development. That this is the picture that emerges is the more remarkable because a destructive world war occurred in the interval, to say nothing of minor yet devastating localized wars; and because a rather general economic paralysis beset the world toward the end of the fifty-year period. The forces that make for higher levels of living, with accompanying dietary improvement, must have been tremendously powerful.

III

It would be possible to review in a general way what happened in the fifty years preceding 1939 to improve national food situations in so many parts of the world. One would mention, as did Joseph S. Davis in his explanation of history's answer to Sir William Crookes, not only expansion of acreage but increase of yield per acre, through improved breeds and varieties, better rotations, the spread and cheapening of transportation, the invention of laborsaving machinery, and so on. It may be added as factual material that between 1888 and 1938, even in long-settled areas of the world excluding China and Russia, it proved possible for the yield per acre of wheat to increase fully 25 percent while acreage increased some 10 percent; and in the new areas of the world, although expansion of acreage supposedly to poorer and drier land was no less than sixfold — more than 100 million acres — the yield per acre nevertheless did not decline if one makes allowance for the unusual character of the droughts of the middle 1930's in the Great Plains.

But this approach is perhaps no more illuminating than to ask the question, What is it that was impeding before 1939, is now impeding, and may well continue to impede the growth of economic productivity in general and of agricultural production specifically? What, in particular, tends to prevent more food and more varied food from being produced and put into the hands of the multitudes who need or desire it?

Those impediments are overwhelmingly numerous if looked at one by one. Economists long since invented, however, a set of rubrics convenient for the discussion but including only four terms. They would say that agricultural productivity, with reference to an unchanging supply of land, must depend upon the application of the three other factors of production — labor, capital, and management. The rubrics — land, labor, capital, and management — are convenient, if only because bearing them all in mind precludes our focusing attention upon only one or the other of them as I suspect some soil conservationists do.

About any acre of agricultural land now in use in the world, theory and history tell us (1) that it has a *maximum* theoretical (economic) productivity, given the state of technology of the moment; (2) that its maximum theoretical productivity may or may not actually be achieved at the moment, depending upon whether the optimum combination of labor, capital, and management is being applied; and (3) that in all probability, as judged by history, the point of maximum productivity will be shifted upward as time passes because technological advances will be made, even if we cannot predict either the degree or the pace of advance. But nothing in history or theory tells us what the output may be, in volume or value, at the point of maximum productivity.

The most impressive probability about the acres of the world now devoted to agricultural use is that a truly enormous gap exists between actual productivity and maximum productivity under optimum application of labor, capital, and management. This refers to maximum economic productivity, not maximum physical productivity, which no doubt is the greater. In all probability a very large fraction of the managers of the world's agricultural land are inhibited from applying optimum doses of labor, capital, and management. Either they are not aware of the best in current technology, or they are helpless to make use of it, or they are unwilling even if able. The mere existence of cover crops and green manures, commercial fertilizers, effective sprays against weeds whether new or old, hybrid corn, rust-resistant wheats, inoculation against hog cholera, tests for animal tuberculosis, is literally unknown to thousands of land managers in the very areas of the world where population is alleged to be most obviously outrunning food supply. In those same areas and others are land managers who know of an improvement, but have no incentive to put it to use. Somewhere a large landholder, wealthy enough and socially important enough to satisfy all his ambitions, may remain content with farming methods reminiscent of the Middle Ages. Perhaps one could find instances in Spain or Chile. Elsewhere a lack of security of life and property — in essence, a lack of orderly government — may inhibit the application of improvements widely known. Bad though orderly government, exercising unwisely its power of taxation may inhibit improvements in farming, simply because the fruit of effort is not permitted to accrue to the men who make it. The Soviet Union is a case in point. Above all, perhaps, a great many land managers of the world cannot apply what they both know and are willing to try for the reason that they lack capital to cover the initial cost. The purchase of a pound of improved seed, to say nothing of a good spade or plow, may unfortunately be quite beyond the capacity of a great many who cultivate the world's soil.

For these and other reasons, the gap between agricultural potential and agricultural practice is unquestionably very wide, and has been very wide at any given point of time for far more than half a century. One of the other reasons, a most compelling one, is lack of demand or of the development of demand. There has to be an exchange of products between those who manage the land and those with whom they exchange produce; and the last must have something to exchange. Agricultural productivity not only responds to advances in economic productivity on other fronts, but stimulates it as well. The process is complex in the extreme, involving of necessity appropriate fluctuations in the relative prices of the factors of production; but its existence ought not to be overlooked merely because it is difficult to describe and trace. The invention and use of a pound of higher-yielding seed, of a longer-lived and sharper hoe, or of a way to twist rope at lesser cost, worked reciprocally to enhance both agricultural and industrial productivity. Multiplied in thousands of instances, such innovations exemplify economic development. More elaborate division of labor, a most excellent way of increasing economic productivity, is an accompanying phenomenon. The race is less accurately between population and food supply, than between population and economic development in every sphere. And even

here the analogy is imperfect, for the racers are hobbled together; economic development at some stage becomes associated with a slowing down of the rate of population growth.

Much that can be said about the gap between agricultural practice and agricultural potential may equally be said about a gap between food harvested and food eaten. Losses in storage and transportation are truly impressive, and are unquestionably subject to reduction as the effectiveness of inhibiting influences is removed or lessened.

So far the emphasis has been given to factors that impede the increase of food yield per acre on land under cultivation now. It remains briefly to speak about land itself, the lack and destruction of which are currently so heavily emphasized as impediments to improvement of per capita food supplies. Almost axiomatic is the fact that there is now less naturally good land for men to bring into use than ever (sic) there was before in historical time. Far from true would be a statement that there remains no unused land whatever subject to development for food crops. There are still areas of the world where lack of transportation hampers settlement, and where the presence of the tsetse fly or the malarial mosquito acts similarly. No one could reasonably suppose that the tropics are now fully developed, with reference especially to oil-bearing palms. Also the limit of land cultivation — at best a vague concept — is elastic, not fixed. It changes, for example, whenever a shorter-maturing variety of grain is invented, moving the limit both in latitude and in altitude — and even, perhaps, permitting double cropping of land once single-cropped. If the behavior of demand is such as to call all these reservoirs of food production into activity, their product will be huge indeed. Economic planners in Brazil estimate that Brazil has 150 million acres fit for growing wheat. Those acres may never or may not soon be settled, but the estimate itself is indicative of ideas held by some people that by no means all the productive land of the world is as yet under the plow. And land is not all. One cannot dismiss as inconceivable the profitable use of the plankton of the oceans as food or feed; and ways and means of utilizing solar radiation to provide the energy for artificial synthesis of the food elements remain to be speculated about.

Some writers such as Osborn and Vogt, who have espoused the cause of soil conservation, paint a picture of rapid contemporary destruction of soil resources through erosion by water and wind. The question here is not whether there is any erosion at all, for there is, but how important it may be; and this is a difficult question. If a man alleges, as Vogt does, that in this country we have lost a third of our topsoil in 150 years and that the future of our country is still within our control but will not be after only a few more decades of such abuse as we have subjected it to, no easy counterassertion comes to mind. It is comforting then to read the words of an experienced soil scientist, Charles E. Kellogg, chief of the Division of Soil survey in this country: ". . . a large part of the arable soils of the world are made better by good farming than they were naturally." And to have him say, "For a time, it almost seemed that each popular writer was trying to outdo the others in dramatic statement. Some even went so far as to assert that erosion had swallowed whole civilizations . . . It is sincerely to be hoped that the period of extreme statement on soil erosion is nearly over . . ."

One can hardly fail to be impressed not only by the tendency of the extremists to engage in what may be called spurious quantitative thinking, but also by their failure to make clear precisely where all the damage they see has been done, or to differentiate between geological and man-made erosion, or to stress what has happened on the great agricultural flatlands of the earth equally with what they say has occurred on the much less important sloping uplands, which are singled out as manifesting the soil-destroying evils of so-called " fire framing " or " shifting cultivation." On reading the extremists, one would never guess that the Missouri River was carrying silt — was called the " Big Muddy " — when men who knew the plow or herded domestic animals first saw it; or that beavers had ever made dams which silted up and formed mountain meadows long before the mountains above were grazed; or that dust storms had occurred in the Great Plains in the 1890's, before they felt the plow.

One who has no claim to expertness in this field may nevertheless find it impossible either to deny the existence of man-made soil erosion and the desirability of a degree of social action against it, or to become greatly exercised about it when he thinks of the impressive array of quite different factors which inhibit agricultural productivity.

IV

What need be said in conclusion? Certainly it seems futile to engage in unqualified prediction in so inexact a field of inquiry, and it would be irksome to state all the qualifications necessary in prediction. We must concede, perhaps, that the " direst calamities " lie in the realm of possibilities, though in appraising even possibilities it would be helpful to know more precisely what those calamities are thought to be. If one of the " direst calamities " is eventual reduction of the per capita ingestion of animal products among the white races, we must concede its possibility; and so with " mass starvation " if by that is meant what has long occurred locally and among relatively few people at any point in time. To concede possibility in these matters, however, is not to argue probability.

We need not concede the possibility within the foreseeable future of the emergence of " permanent worldwide hunger," if that phrase means everybody hungers at once. That cannot happen unless a world society develops and finds a way to achieve absolute equality of personal income, a possibility surely so remote as hardly to be called a possibility at all. In such a society the tremendous contents of the feedbin of the world could be utilized to assuage human hunger; humanly edible grain now lost to man in the conversion processes of animals could then be captured for human consumption.

We need not concede that possible localized national deterioration of diets of historical type leads at all certainly to world strife. Hungry nations are commonly economically weak and weak in military potential as nowadays measured in other terms than clubs or knives, and hence may be chary of assuming the risk of aggression; and in any event wars have other causes than scarcity of food.

We might not be wise to concede, on the other hand, the possibility of an increase of 110 percent in world food supplies within twenty-five years. That is a decidedly short time for so tremendous an increase.

And, yet, at the same time that we concede the possibilities both of deterioration of food supply and of the unlikelihood of hoped for extreme improvement, we need not exclude the possibility of a geographically spreading gradual improvement of national diets, doubtless unequal in pace among the several nations, resulting in generally firmer assurance of food supplies increasingly consistent with human aspirations. It is well to remember that the recent years of food shortage may, if a long stretch of peace lies before us, seem in retrospect merely transitory.

Pessimism about maintenance or improvement of per capita food supply, even where population is densest, is not intellectually necessary, not compelled on the basis of historical fact or logic. We know approximately what the trends have been. More important, enough is understood about the powerful forces lying behind economic productivity and dietary improvement to warrant the statement that the ultimate productivity of the earth's surface had best be regarded as incommensurabie and elastic, not fixed. It can be measured, and thereafter set in relation to a future growth of population itself not firmly predictable, only in terms of surface — square miles or square feet. The customary but spurious quantitative exercise — only 4 billion cultivable acres now, less than two acres per person, with two and a half acres estimated to be required per person to provide a minimum adequate diet, and with population growing while soil is washed away — ought not to mislead. The possible product of the earth defies measurement even on the assumption of stagnant technology, and the assumption itself gains no support from history.

Time may prove today's pessimists

to have been right in their attitude; the actual outcome remains to be seen. But if they prove right, the historical reasons are quite unlikely to be limited to an overrapid increase of population set against an overrapid destruction of soil resources. The future historian will need to inquire whether some other contributory causes were important — whether men and governments acted wisely in such directions as engaging in wars, keeping civil order, spending appropriately on education and research, taxing with propriety, intervening intelligently in economic life, nursing economic isolation, or freeing the channels of trade. To follow the wrong paths is to hamper invention, stifle capital accumulation, hinder investment domestically and internationally, and hence to retard the general economic development, one aspect of which is improvement of national diets. If the right paths are followed in these directions, and not only in human reproduction and in land use, time may prove today's pessimists to have been wrong, as with the pessimists of yesterday.

F. The Cultural Setting

13. Introduction

In the preceding five sections of this chapter it has been shown that a society and its behavior cannot be fully understood without seeing it in reference to its previous history, its

physical environment, its relation to material resources, and its pattern of population growth. One more point of view remains to be discussed. A society is not merely the creature of its historical past, its demographic structure, and its resource base; it is a *functioning* organization of people pursuing certain common ends, building on its past, employing available resources toward securing certain widely accepted values.

In other words it is essential to understand the meaning of any given form of collective behavior in terms of the society within which it occurs. Man essentially differs from other animals in his ability to use symbolic communication and by means of this, to store up knowledge and develop complex, diverse, but interrelated ways of behaving, which, when put together, constitute the particular quality of any society.

Taken in their broadest aspect the sum of these learned behaviors represents what is called "culture." Culture, however, is not merely a sum of isolated, separate series of simple behavior patterns or traits; it is integrated and organized into broad themes and patterns. Culture thus sets the goals to be pursued within a society, provides the means for their achievement, and determines the conditions within which such a pursuit will occur. In so doing, cultural factors operate to integrate a society in two quite opposite fashions.

First, there is the aspect of culture that provides for consistency and homogeneity within the society. Second, there are those cultural factors that lead to differentiation. It is quite clear that all societies are characterized by both types of norms. To take the simplest possible example, it is difficult to imagine a society

in which men and women, of all ages, are expected to perform in precisely the same ways. What actually happens, of course, is that each society develops what it considers "proper" behavior for young men, young women, older men, older women, etc.

On the other hand, it is equally difficult to imagine a society in which the way every individual behaves is unrelated to the way in which any other person reacts. Under such circumstances there could be no communication, no continuity, no predictability, and in short no human life.

Durkheim has referred to these two processes as *mechanical* versus *organic* solidarity. That is, those factors of similarity that hold a society together he considers as constituting a *mechanical* bond. Those factors of interdependent differentiation, however, such as the mutually interdependent roles of the various occupations, of buyer and seller, of teacher and student, of husband and wife, are considered to be *organic* bonds.

It is easy to see how social theorists such as Tönnies, Von Wiese, Becker and Redfield would use these two principles in classifying societies so that a simple, non-literate, homogeneous, stable society or community would be classed at one end of a continuum (*Gemeinschaft,* Sacred, Folk) and a complex, urban, industrial, rapidly changing society at the other (*Gesellschaft,* Secular, Urban). The first emphasizes mechanical solidarity, the second organic.

The usefulness of such a continuum in understanding modern society, which lies toward the secular, urban end is dependent on the degree to which it can help to understand the differences that exist among modern nations. Before discussing this point it is necessary to take up another question.

We need to know something about the question of the balance between consensus and homogeneity on the one hand and conflict and heterogeneity on the other in modern complex society. As the differences in function and mode of life increase, one would expect that agreement on both values and means to values would decrease. Thus we find modern society dominated by many types of *interest groups,* homogeneous with respect to many aspects of life, vying with one another to secure public policy decisions, each in accordance with its own particular values. Labor and management, the farmer and the urbanite, the wealthy and the poor, the seller and the buyer, the Catholic and the Protestant, the Westerner and the Southerner, and so on in a multitude of patterns, all are struggling to have their values taken as a basis for national policy.

This situation is true of all countries in modern society. The *way* in which these decisions are made is crucial in differences among countries and this depends on the *values* that dominate in a particular culture or nation. Thus when the value against which alternative decisions are measured is homogeneity, the decisions and their consequences will be quite different from those flowing from values favorable to heterogeneity.

It is easy to take examples from recent world history. Hitler's Germany openly stated that its policies were based on the value of homogeneity, and the slogan, " one empire, one pure race, one leader " (*ein Volk, ein Reich, ein Führer*) was their watchword. The consequences of such a value system are now only too apparent. The Soviet Union, too, in its early period emphasized homogeneity, this time in terms of social class. The value of the " classless society," however, seems to have given way to the kind of homogeneity inherent in Pan-Slavism.

What of the United States? Clearly our values as stated in the Declaration of Independence and the first ten Amendments to the Constitution are opposed to the idea of homogeneity and are in fact primarily concerned with protecting individuals and minorities from an insistence on homogeneity by majorities. Nevertheless, in our history, the *power* of particular groups, rather than the values of individuals and minority rights have, in some cases, prevailed. With changes in power, and the continuance of a rule of law, however, it is possible to say that the positive values of heterogeneity receive their greatest recognition in democratic nations.

Conflicts of value and the formation of antagonistic interest groups, together with the superior values which determine the mediation of those conflicts, are not the only problems with which a cultural analysis must deal. The social structure is, after all, composed of niches, but these are in fact filled by people. No two people can ever be exactly alike even in the most rigid and simple society. In the interaction between the growing, developing person and his culture, as well as in the conflict of interest groups, lie the seeds of culture change and the roots of human behavior.

Toward understanding this aspect of culture, the selection by Dr. Benedict (1887–1948) directs anthropological evidence toward an understanding of the unity of culture and personality. In doing so, this selection is concerned with the fact that culture determines " norms " thus making what is " right " a relative matter among cultures; and also with the problem that culture, while restric-

tive and regimenting in its effect on behavior, also provides variants and alternatives, and, in its own changes, flexibility. The data by which Dr. Benedict illustrates her points are taken from three widely divergent cultures; that of the Kwakiutl Indians of the coast of British Columbia; the Zuñi of the American Southwest; and the Dobuans on the island of New Guinea. Each of these cultures has developed a special cultural theme, so that the extreme competitive values of the Kwakiutl are compared to an idealization of the " golden mean " on the part of the Zuñi and the widespread use of magic, trickery, and treachery in Dobu.

14. The Individual and Patterns of Culture*

There is no proper antagonism between the role of society and that of the individual. One of the most misleading misconceptions due to this nineteenth-century dualism was the idea that what was subtracted from society was added to the individual and what was subtracted from the individual was added to society. Philosophies of freedom, political creeds of *laissez faire,* revolutions that have unseated dynasties, have been built on this dualism. The quarrel in anthropological theory between the importance of the culture pattern and of the individual is only a small

* From Ruth Benedict, *Patterns of Culture,* Boston: Houghton Mifflin Company, 1934, pp. 251–78. Reprinted by permission of Houghton Mifflin Company.

ripple from this fundamental conception of the nature of society.

The man in the street still thinks in terms of a necessary antagonism between society and the individual. In large measure this is because in our civilization the regulative activities of society are singled out, and we tend to identify society with the restrictions the law imposes upon us. The law lays down the number of miles per hour that I may drive an automobile. If it takes this restriction away, I am by that much the freer. This basis for a fundamental antagonism between society and the individual is naive indeed when it is extended as a basic philosophical and political notion. Society is only incidentally and in certain situations regulative, and law is not equivalent to the social order. In the simpler homogeneous cultures collective habit or custom may quite supersede the necessity for any development of formal legal authority. American Indians sometimes say: "In the old days, there were no fights about hunting grounds or fishing territories. There was no law then, so everybody did what was right." The phrasing makes it clear that in their old life they did not think of themselves as submitting to a social control imposed upon them from without. Even in our civilization the law is never more than a crude implement of society, and one it is often enough necessary to check in its arrogant career. It is never to be read off as if it were the equivalent of the social order.

Society in its full sense as we have discussed it in this volume is never an entity separable from the individuals who compose it. No individual can arrive even at the threshold of his potentialities without a culture in which he participates. Conversely, no civilization has in it any element which in the last analysis is not the contribution of an individual. Where else could any trait come from except from the behavior of a man or a woman or a child?

The vast proportion of all individuals who are born into any society always and whatever the idiosyncrasies of its institutions, assume, as we have seen, the behavior dictated by that society. This fact is always interpreted by the carriers of that culture as being due to the fact that their particular institutions reflect an ultimate and universal sanity. The actual reason is quite different. Most people are shaped to the form of their culture because of the enormous malleability of their original endowment. They are plastic to the molding force of the society into which they are born. It does not matter whether, with the Northwest Coast, it requires delusions of self-reference, or with our own civilization the amassing of possessions. In any case the great mass of individuals take quite readily the form that is presented to them.

They do not all, however, find it equally congenial, and those are favored and fortunate whose potentialities most nearly coincide with the type of behavior selected by their society. Those who, in a situation in which they are frustrated, naturally seek ways of putting the occasion out of sight as expeditiously as possible are well served in Pueblo culture. Southwest institutions, as we have seen, minimize the situations in which serious frustration can arise, and when it cannot be avoided, as in death, they provide means to put it behind them with all speed.

On the other hand, those who react to frustration as to an insult and whose first thought is to get even are amply provided for on the Northwest Coast. They may extend their native reaction to situations in which their paddle breaks or their canoe overturns or to the loss of relatives by death. They rise from their first reaction of sulking to thrust back in return, to "fight" with property or with weapons. Those who can assuage despair by the act of bringing shame to others can register freely and without conflict in this society, because their proclivities are deeply channeled in their culture. In Dobu those whose first impulse is to select a victim and project their misery upon him in procedures of punishment are equally fortunate.

It happens that none of the three cultures we have described meets frustration in a realistic manner by stressing the resumption of the original and interrupted experience. It might even seem that in the case of death this is impossible. But the institutions of many cultures nevertheless attempt nothing less. Some of the forms the restitution takes are repugnant to us, but that only makes it clearer that in cultures where frustration is handled by giving rein to this potential behavior, the institutions of that society carry this course to extraordinary lengths. Among the Eskimo, when one man has killed another, the family of the man who has been murdered may take the murderer to replace the loss within its own group. The murderer then becomes the husband of the woman who has been widowed by his act. This is an emphasis upon restitution that ignores all other aspects of the situation — those which seem to us the only important ones; but when tradition selects some such objective it is quite in character that it should disregard all else.

There is another possible attitude toward frustration. It is the precise opposite of the Pueblo attitude, and we have described it among the other Dionysian reactions of the Plains Indians. Instead of trying to get past

the experience with the least possible discomfiture, it finds relief in the most extravagant expression of grief. The Indians of the Plains capitalized the utmost indulgences and exacted violent demonstrations of emotion as a matter of course.

In any group of individuals we can recognize those to whom these different reactions to frustration and grief are congenial: ignoring it, indulging it by uninhibited expression, getting even, punishing a victim, and seeking restitution of the original situation. In the psychiatric records of our own society, some of these impulses are recognized as bad ways of dealing with the situation, some as good. These bad ones are said to lead to maladjustments and insanities, the good ones to adequate social functioning. It is clear, however, that the correlation does not lie between any one " bad " tendency and abnormality in any absolute sense. The desire to run away from grief, to leave it behind at all costs, does not foster psychotic behavior where, as among the Pueblos, it is mapped out by institutions and supported by every attitude of the group. The Pueblos are not a neurotic people. Their culture gives the impression of fostering mental health. Similarly, the paranoid attitudes so violently expressed among the Kwakiutl are known in psychiatric theory derived from our own civilization as thoroughly " bad "; that is, they lead in various ways to the breakdown of personality. But it is just those individuals among the Kwakiutl who find it congenial to give the freest expression to these attitudes who nevertheless are the leaders of Kwakiutl society and find greatest personal fulfilment in its culture.

The tribes we have described have all, of them their non-participating "abnormal" individuals. The individual in Dobu who was thoroughly disoriented was the man who was naturally friendly and found activity an end in itself. He was a pleasant fellow who did not seek to overthrow his fellows or to punish them. He worked for anyone who asked him, and he was tireless in carrying out their commands. He was not filled by a terror of the dark like his fellows, and he did not, as they did, utterly inhibit simple public responses of friendliness toward women closely related, like a wife or sister. He often patted them playfully in public. In any other Dobuan this was scandalous behavior, but in him it was regarded as merely silly. The village treated him in a kindly enough fashion, not taking advantage of him or making a sport of ridiculing him, but he was definitely regarded as one who was outside the game.

The behavior congenial to the Dobuan simpleton has been made the ideal in certain periods of our own civilization, and there are still vocations in which his responses are accepted in most Western communities. Especially if a woman is in question, she is well provided for even today in our *mores,* and functions honorably in her family and community. The fact that the Dobuan could not function in his culture was not a consequence of the particular responses that were con-

genial to him, but of the chasm between them and the cultural pattern.

The dilemma of such an individual is often most successfully solved by doing violence to his strongest natural impulses and accepting the rôle the culture honors. In case he is a person to whom social recognition is necessary, it is ordinarily his only possible course. One of the most striking individuals in Zuñi had accepted this necessity. In a society that thoroughly distrusts authority of any sort, he had a native personal magnetism that singled him out in any group. In a society that exalts moderation and the easiest way, he was turbulent and could act violently upon occasion. In a society that praises a pliant personality that "talks lots" — that is, that chatters in a friendly fashion — he was scornful and aloof. Zuñi's only reaction to such personalities is to brand them as witches. He was said to have been seen peering through a window from outside, and this is a sure mark of a witch. At any rate, he got drunk one day and boasted that they could not kill him. He was taken before the war priests who hung him by his thumbs from the rafters till he should confess to his witchcraft. This is the usual procedure in a charge of witchcraft. However, he dispatched a messenger to the government troops. When they came, his shoulders were already crippled for life, and the officer of the law was left with no recourse but to imprison the war priests who had been responsible for the enormity. One of these war priests was probably the most respected and important person in recent Zuñi history, and when he returned after imprisonment in the state penitentiary he never resumed his priestly offices. He regarded his power as broken. It was a revenge that is probably unique in Zuñi history. It involved, of course, a challenge to the priesthoods, against whom the witch by his act openly aligned himself.

The course of his life in the forty years that followed this defiance was not, however, what we might easily predict. A witch is not barred from his membership in cult groups because he has been condemned, and the way to recognition lay through such activity. He possessed a remarkable verbal memory and a sweet singing voice. He learned unbelievable stores of mythology, of esoteric ritual, of cult songs. Many hundreds of pages of stories and ritual poetry were taken down from his dictation before he died, and he regarded his songs as much more extensive. He became indispensable in ceremonial life and before he died was the governor of Zuñi. The congenial bent of his personality threw him into irreconcilable conflict with his society, and he solved his dilemma by turning an incidental talent to account. As we might well expect, he was not a happy man. As governor of Zuñi, and high in his cult groups, a marked man in his community, he was obsessed by death. He was a cheated man in the midst of a mildly happy populace.

It is easy to imagine the life he might have lived among the Plains Indians, where every institution fa-voured the traits that were native to him. The personal authority, the turbulence, the scorn, would all have been honored in the career he could have made his own. The unhappiness that was inseparable from his temperament as a successful priest and governor of Zuñi would have had no place as a war chief of the Cheyenne; it was not a function of the traits of his native endowment but of the standards of the culture in which he found no outlet for his native responses.

The individuals we have so far discussed are not in any sense psychopathic. They illustrate the dilemma of the individual whose congenial drives are not provided for in the institutions of his culture. This dilemma becomes of psychiatric importance when the behavior in question is regarded as categorically abnormal in a society. Western civilization tends to regard even a mild homosexual as an abnormal. The clinical picture of homosexuality stresses the neuroses and psychoses to which it gives rise, and emphasizes almost equally the inadequate functioning of the invert and his behavior. We have only to turn to other cultures, however, to realize that homosexuals have by no means been uniformly inadequate to the social situation. They have not always failed to function. In some societies they have even been especially acclaimed. Plato's *Republic* is, of course, the most convincing statement of the honorable estate of homosexuality. It is presented as a major means to the good life, and Plato's high ethical evaluation of this response was upheld in the customary behavior of Greece at that period.

The American Indians do not make Plato's high moral claims for homosexuality, but homosexuals are often regarded as exceptionally able. In most of North America there exists the institution of the *berdache,* as the French called them. These men-women were men who at puberty or thereafter took the dress and the occupations of women. Sometimes they married other men and lived with them. Sometimes they were men with no inversion, persons of weak sexual endowment who chose this rôle to avoid the jeers of the women. The berdaches were never regarded as of first-rate supernatural power, as similar men-women were in Siberia, but rather as leaders in women's occupations, good healers in certain diseases, or, among certain tribes, as the genial organizers of social affairs. They were usually, in spite of the manner in which they were accepted, regarded with a certain embarrassment. It was thought slightly ridiculous to address as "she" a person who was known to be a man and who, as in Zuñi, would be buried on the men's side of the cemetery. But they were socially placed. The emphasis in most tribes was upon the fact that men who took over women's occupations excelled by reason of their strength and initiative and were therefore leaders in women's techniques and in the accumulation of those forms of property made by women. One of the best known of all the Zuñis of a generation ago was the man-woman We-wha, who

was, in the words of his friend, Mrs. Stevenson, "certainly the strongest person in Zuñi, both mentally and physically." His remarkable memory for ritual made him a chief personage on ceremonial occasions, and his strength and intelligence made him a leader in all kinds of crafts.

The men-women of Zuñi are not all strong, self-reliant personages. Some of them take this refuge to protect themselves against their inability to take part in men's activities. One is almost a simpleton, and one, hardly more than a little boy, has delicate features like a girl's. There are obviously several reasons why a person becomes a berdache in Zuñi, but whatever the reason, men who have chosen openly to assume women's dress have the same chance as any other persons to establish themselves as functioning members of the society. Their response is socially recognized. If they have native ability, they can give it scope; if they are weak creatures, they fail in terms of their weakness of character, not in terms of their inversion.

Trance is a similar abnormality in our society. Even a very mild mystic is aberrant in Western civilization. In order to study trance or catalepsy within our own social groups, we have to go to the case histories of the abnormal. Therefore the correlation between trance experience and the neurotic and psychotic seems perfect. As in the case of the homosexual, however, it is a local correlation characteristic of our century. Even in our own cultural background other eras give different results. In the Middle Ages when

Catholicism made the ecstatic experience the mark of sainthood, the trance experience was greatly valued, and those to whom the response was congenial, instead of being overwhelmed by a catastrophe as in our century, were given confidence in the pursuit of their careers. It was a validation of ambitions, not a stigma of insanity. Individuals who were susceptible to trance, therefore, succeeded or failed in terms of their native capacities, but since trance experience was highly valued, a great leader was very likely to be capable of it.

Among primitive peoples, trance and catalepsy have been honored in the extreme. Some of the Indian tribes of California accorded prestige principally to those who passed through certain trance experiences. Not all of these tribes believed that it was exclusively women who were so blessed, but among the Shasta this was the convention. Their shamans were women, and they were accorded the greatest prestige in the community. They were chosen because of their constitutional liability to trance and allied manifestations. One day the woman who was so destined, while she was about her usual work, fell suddenly to the ground. She had heard a voice speaking to her in tones of the greatest intensity. Turning, she had seen a man with drawn bow and arrow. He commanded her to sing on pain of being shot through the heart by his arrow, but under the stress of the experience she fell senseless. Her family gathered. She was lying rigid, hardly breathing. They knew

that for some time she had had dreams of a special character which indicated a shamanistic calling, dreams of escaping grizzly bears, falling off cliffs or trees, or of being surrounded by swarms of yellow-jackets. The community knew therefore what to expect. After a few hours the woman began to moan gently and to roll about upon the ground, trembling violently. She was supposed to be repeating the song which she had been told to sing and which during the trance had been taught her by the spirit. As she revived, her moaning became more and more clearly the spirit's song until at last she called out the name of the spirit itself, and immediately blood oozed from her mouth.

When the woman had come to herself after the first encounter with her spirit, she danced that night her first initiatory shaman's dance. For three nights she danced, holding herself by a rope that was swung from the ceiling. On the third night she had to receive in her body her power from her spirit. She was dancing, and as she felt the approach of the moment she called out, " He will shoot me, he will shoot me." Her friends stood close, for when she reeled in a kind of cataleptic seizure, they had to seize her before she fell or she would die. From this time on she had in her body a visible materialization of her spirit's power, an icicle-like object which in her dances thereafter she would exhibit, producing it from one part of her body and returning it to another part. From this time on she continued to validate her supernatural power by further cataleptic demonstrations, and she was called upon in great emergencies of life and death, for curing and for divination and for counsel. She became, in other words, by this procedure a woman of great power and importance.

It is clear that, far from regarding cataleptic seizures as blots upon the family escutcheon and as evidences of dreaded disease, cultural approval had seized upon them and made of them the pathway to authority over one's fellows. They were the outstanding characteristic of the most respected social type, the type which functioned with most honour and reward in the community. It was precisely the cataleptic individuals who in this culture were singled out for authority and leadership.

The possible usefulness of "abnormal" types in a social structure, provided they are types that are culturally selected by that group, is illustrated from every part of the world. The shamans of Siberia dominate their communities. According to the ideas of these peoples, they are individuals who by submission to the will of the spirits have been cured of a grievous illness — the onset of the seizures — and have acquired by this means great supernatural power and incomparable vigor and health. Some, during the period of the call, are violently insane for several years; others irresponsible to the point where they have to be constantly watched lest they wander off in the snow and freeze to death; others ill and emaciated to the point of death, sometimes with bloody sweat. It is the shamanistic practice which constitutes their cure, and the extreme exertion of a Siberian séance leaves them, they claim, rested and able to enter immediately upon a similar performance. Cataleptic seizures are regarded as an essential part of any shamanistic performance.

It is clear that culture may value and make socially available even highly unstable human types. If it chooses to treat their peculiarities as the most valued variants of human behavior, the individuals in question will rise to the occasion and perform their social roles without reference to our usual ideas of the types who can make social adjustments and those who cannot. Those who function inadequately in any society are not those with certain fixed "abnormal" traits, but may well be those whose responses have received no support in the institutions of their culture. The weakness of these aberrants is in great measure illusory. It springs, not from the fact that they are lacking in necessary vigor, but that they are individuals whose native responses are not reaffirmed by society. They are, as Sapir phrases it, "alienated from an impossible world."

The person unsupported by the standards of his time and place and left naked to the winds of ridicule has been unforgettably drawn in European literature in the figure of Don Quixote. Cervantes turned upon a tradition still honored in the abstract the limelight of a changed set of practical standards, and his poor old man, the orthodox upholder of the romantic chivalry of another generation, became a simpleton. The windmills with which he tilted were the serious antagonists of a hardly vanished world, but to tilt with them when the world no longer called them serious was to rave. He loved his Dulcinea in the best traditional manner of chivalry, but another version of love was fashionable for the moment, and his fervor was counted to him for madness.

These contrasting worlds which, in the primitive cultures we have considered, are separated from one another in space, in modern Occidental history more often succeed one another in time. The major issue is the same in either case, but the importance of understanding the phenomenon is far greater in the modern world where we cannot escape if we would from the succession of configurations in time. When each culture is a world in itself, relatively stable like the Eskimo culture, for example, and geographically isolated from all others, the issue is academic. But our civilization must deal with cultural standards that go down under our eyes and new ones that arise from a shadow upon the horizon. We must be willing to take account of changing normalities even when the question is of the morality in which we were bred. Just as we are handicapped in dealing with ethical problems so long as we hold to an absolute definition of morality, so we are handicapped in dealing with human society so long as we identify our local normalities with the inevitable necessities of existence.

No society has yet attempted a self-conscious direction of the process by which its new normalities are created in the next generation. Dewey has pointed out how possible and yet how drastic such social engineering would be. For some traditional arrangements it is obvious that very high prices are paid, reckoned in terms of human suffering and frustration. If these arrangements presented themselves to us merely as arrangements and not as categorical imperatives, our reasonable course would be to adapt them by whatever means to rationally selected goals. What we do instead is to ridicule our Don Quixotes, the ludicrous embodiments of an outmoded tradition and continue to regard our own as final and prescribed in the nature of things.

In the meantime the therapeutic problem of dealing with our psycopaths of this type is often misunderstood. Their alienation from the actual world can often be more intelligently handled than by insisting that they adopt the modes that are alien to them. Two other courses are always possible. In the first place, the misfit individual may cultivate a greater objective interest in his own preferences and learn how to manage with greater equanimity his deviation from the type. If he learns to recognize the extent to which his suffering has been due to his lack of support in a traditional ethos, he may gradually educate himself to accept his degree of difference with less suffering. Both the exaggerated emotional disturbances of the manic depressive and the seclusion of the schizophrenic add certain values to existence which are not open to those differently constituted. The unsupported individual who valiantly accepts his favorite and native virtues may attain a feasible course of behavior that makes it unnecessary for him to take refuge in a private world he has fashioned for himself. He may gradually achieve a more independent and less tortured attitude toward his deviations and upon this attitude he may be able to build an adequately functioning existence.

In the second place, an increased tolerance in society toward its less usual types must keep pace with the self-education of the patient. The possibilities in this direction are endless. Tradition is as neurotic as any patient; its overgrown fear of deviation from its fortuitous standards conforms to all the usual definitions of the psychopathic. This fear does not depend upon observation of the limits within which conformity is necessary to the social good. Much more deviation is allowed to the individual in some cultures than in others, and those in which much is allowed cannot be shown to suffer from their peculiarity. It is probable that social orders of the future will carry this tolerance and encouragement of individual difference much further than any cultures of which we have experience.

The American tendency at the present time leans so far to the opposite extreme that it is not easy for us to picture the changes that such an attitude would bring about. Middletown is a typical example of our usual urban fear of seeming in however slight an act different from our neighbours. Eccentricity is more feared than parasitism. Every sacrifice of time and tranquillity is made in order that no one in the family may have any taint of nonconformity attached to him. Children in school make their great tragedies out of not wearing a certain kind of stockings, not joining a certain dancing-class, not driving a certain car. The fear of being different is the dominating motivation recorded in Middletown.

The Puritan divines of New England in the eighteenth century were the last persons whom contemporary opinion in the colonies regarded as psychopathic. Few prestige groups in any culture have been allowed such complete intellectual and emotional dictatorship as they were. They were the voice of God. Yet to a modern observer it is they, not the confused and tormented women they put to death as witches, who were the psychoneurotics of Puritan New England. A sense of guilt as extreme as they portrayed and demanded both in their own conversion experiences and in those of their converts is found in a slightly saner civilization only in institutions for mental diseases. They admitted no salvation without a conviction of sin that prostrated the victim, sometimes for years, with remorse and terrible anguish. It was the duty of the minister to put the fear of hell into the heart of even the youngest child, and to exact of every convert emotional acceptance of his damnation if God saw fit to damn him. It does not matter where we turn among the records of New England Puritan churches of this period, whether to those dealing with witches or with unsaved children not yet in their teens or with such themes as damnation and predestination, we are faced with the fact that the group of people who carried out to the greatest extreme and in the fullest honor the cultural doctrine of the moment are by the slightly altered standards of our generation the victims of intolerable aberrations. From the point of view of a comparative psychiatry they fall in the category of the abnormal.

In our own generation extreme forms of ego-gratification are culturally supported in a similar fashion. Arrogant and unbridled egoists as family men, as officers of the law and in business, have been again and again portrayed by novelists and dramatists, and they are familiar in every community. Like the behavior of Puritan divines, their courses of action are often more asocial than those of the inmates of penitentiaries. In terms of the suffering and frustration that they spread about them there is probably no comparison. There is very possibly at least as great a degree of mental warping. Yet they are entrusted with positions of great influence and importance and are as a rule fathers of families. Their impress both upon their own children and upon the structure of our society is indelible. They are not described in our manuals of psychiatry because they are supported by every tenet of our civilization. They are sure of themselves in real life in a way that is possible only to those who are oriented to the points of the compass laid down in their own cul-

ture. Nevertheless a future psychiatry may well ransack our novels and letters and public records for illumination upon a type of abnormality to which it would not otherwise give credence. In every society it is among this very group of the culturally encouraged and fortified that some of the most extreme types of human behavior are fostered.

Social thinking at the present time has no more important task before it than that of taking adequate account of cultural relativity. In the fields of both sociology and psychology the implications are fundamental, and modern thought about contacts of peoples and about our changing standards is greatly in need of sane and scientific direction. The sophisticated modern temper has made of social relativity, even in the small area which it has recognized, a doctrine of despair. It has pointed out its incongruity with the orthodox dreams of permanence and ideality and with the individual's illusions of autonomy. It has argued that if human experience must give up these, the nutshell of existence is empty. But to interpret our dilemma in these terms is to be guilty of an anachronism. It is only the inevitable cultural lag that makes us insist that the old must be discovered again in the new, that there is no solution but to find the old certainty and stability in the new plasticity. The recognition of cultural relativity carries with it its own values, which need not be those of the absolutist philosophies. It challenges customary opinions and causes those who have been bred to them acute discomfort. It rouses pessimism because it throws old formulas into confusion, not because it contains anything intrinsically difficult. As soon as the new opinion is embraced as customary belief, it will be another trusted bulwark of the good life. We shall arrive then at a more realistic social faith, accepting as grounds of hope and as new bases for tolerance the coexisting and equally valid patterns of life which mankind has created for itself from the raw materials of existence.

2 POLITICAL CHOICE IN MODERN SOCIETY

A. The Origin of Political Theory in the West

15. Introduction

The roots of political reflection in the West go back at least to the sixth century before Christ. Interest and speculation about politics, which is sometimes ascribed to the influence of the Renaissance and the Reformation, was actually in full flowering two thousand years before. In fact not only is the concept " political " derived from the Greek *polis* or city state, but the major unsolved problems of justice, law, and power with which every society ultimately must wrestle were explicitly formulated by the Greeks. Therefore to discover the beginnings of Western thinking and concern for political decisions we must consider some of the more salient characteristics of Greek political philosophy, especially as represented in the writings of Plato (427 to 347 B.C.) and Aristotle (384 to 322 B.C.).

Before we enumerate the particular principles of Greek political philosophy that have been a part of the Western legacy, it is essential that we refer to a problem basic to all social science. One of the greatest of contemporary philosophers, Sir Alfred North Whitehead, has declared that all philosophy since Plato has been essentially in the nature of a footnote. Yet Plato, as we know, wrote and reflected under circumstances which politically, socially, and morally were radically different from our own. We would hardly expect someone embarking upon the study of the physical or natural sciences to go back to the chemists, physicians, or physicists of Plato's time, and yet it is said that nothing new in the way of basic and fundamental problems has been thought of by social scientists since the fourth century B.C. Whitehead's viewpoint has indeed been sharply challenged by a new and ambitious trend in social thinking. It is said by the social scientists who are the spokesmen of this reaction that any reference to the Greeks or the ancients is a sign of backwardness and that unless the social sciences rid themselves of their antiquarianism they can never hope to match the accomplishments of natural science.

Yet this recent trend in social thinking has not proved fully satisfying or convincing. There has been, as has so often been true in the past, a counter-reaction against the school that would model the study of man on the methods employed in the study of nature. Within the past decade, a small group of writers have argued that progress in social science is qualitatively different from that in the physical sciences. They have claimed it is logical still today to study Greek philosophy since Plato and Aristotle dealt with human nature with its recurrent drives and with the problems growing out of man's relations with other men. Such issues as justice, political power, and revolution are as basic in our own day as they were for our precursors. It should be the task of social science to separate what is enduring in Greek writing and experience from those speculations relevant only to the unique conditions that prevailed at the time. And this is impossible if the Greek interval in world history is appraised and evaluated in terms of the standards of other discrete periods in history, as for example, the standards of nineteenth century liberalism. The confidence of some moderns that they can look at the past in their own terms and thereby understand it better than it understood itself has not contributed substantially to man's fund of knowledge about either the recurrent or the unique elements in history. It is maintained that to understand philosophy we must read it in the terms it was written.

Four general principles or beliefs constitute the pillars on which Greek political philosophy was founded. The first is a belief in the existence of objective truth. The second is the law that the individual can realize his true nature only through association with his fellows in the state. The third is an unwillingness to distinguish, as have most modern philosophers, between " facts " and " values," holding to the view instead that politics is a part of applied ethics. The fourth is the acceptance of an essential dualism in human nature.

The first of these principles emerged as a reaction to the precepts of the philosophical school of Sophism. Sophism at the time was the dominant trend of philosophy and the Sophists as a community of scholars had almost none of the negative coloration they subsequently acquired. Plato and Aristotle, however, found themselves in opposition to this group, who maintained that law and justice were mere conventions. The Sophists had claimed that the state and other aspects of human society were artifices of man and were entirely relative to his whims and preferences. Thrasymachus when asked in the dialogue of Plato's *Republic,* " What is justice? " replied that it was the right of the stronger. Justice, according to Sophists like Thrasymachus, depended solely on ever-changing relations of power. Political beliefs were interpreted as subjective creations of man bearing no resemblance to any underlying principles of truth.

Plato and Aristotle in answering these claims sought to uncover an objective basis for the main concepts and institutions of political life. The Sophists had argued that the state was essentially the same kind of product as a pair of shoes created deliberately and arbitrarily by man for his own use. Plato and Aristotle, in disputing this viewpoint, contended that the state as a natural phenomenon was both objective and necessary. In other words, the state as *physis* was an objective reality with criteria and standards which transcended at any particular time the will of the majority of the people. The task of the political philosopher was to undertake to discover the essence of the *real state,* which was reflected in current, visible states. The aim of classical thought was to establish a system of thought explaining the political reality which existed beyond the illusion of seeming reality.

In explaining this search for reality, Plato used the figure of a cave. Most men who observed the functions of their states were like slaves chained to the wall of a cave. The shadows they saw on the wall of the cave were merely reflections of the events taking place in the sunlight outside — images and reflections of reality. A few in the cave could discover reality through reason by turning from the wall of the cave to the sunlight outside. These few were the political philosophers. Most, by reason of their physical nature, would remain chained to the wall inside.

Objective reality, in so far as the state was concerned, was not a uto-pia. For a great gulf existed between the ideal state and the historic state of experience. The perfect state was a concept of higher reality and only by accident or through grace could it be achieved. For Plato there was an even more unbridgeable chasm between the "real" and the visible states than for later Christian philosophers between the City of God and the City of Man. For in Saint Augustine's system the final transformation depended not upon accident but upon salvation through God's grace. Yet there is another way in which the ideal is related to the visible. Thus for Plato a recognition of injustice points to the standard of justice against which every instance of imperfect justice may be measured. It should be the task of the political philosopher to determine the objective relationship between visible reality and the essential reality of politics. The historic state should be conceived in the light of the objective and ideal state as well as in terms of its particular historic circumstances.

When we consider the questions which are uppermost in the minds of modern political philosophers this interest appears to have almost disappeared. For contemporary philosophers are concerned with relations between the state and individual and not the state and its essence or ideal. Questions about the best political order or the best possible order are no longer accepted as the most appropriate concern of political philosophy.

The second general principle of classical philosophy relates to the individual. For the Greeks there could be no existence as such for the individual outside of the state. Only with the appearance of Stoicism and Christianity is there an emphasis on individual rights independent of and outside of the state. Yet if the individual could realize his true nature only in association with others in the state, the individual nevertheless did not, as he has in the totalitarian state, exist only for the state. For the state was a partnership in every mode of life. This life had an intimacy which was made possible by the size and the structure of the city-state. Art, religion, politics, and ethics were centered in the state, and the sharp divisions of compartments into which modern society has been fragmented were not present. Thus life in the state was all life in common, and individuals who were unwilling to participate were considered not harmless but useless. Political science was concerned with the wise handling of concrete, immediate situations in this common order. And in the pursuit of the communal life the individual gives expression to values which transcend his mere biological needs. The state is therefore not a necessary evil, as liberalism and Marxism assume, but an ethical and moral relationship in which individuals are able to realize their virtues.

A third principle that is central to the classical outlook is the belief that those questions that relate to values should not be excluded from political philosophy. For political philosophy was assumed to have its point of origin at the heart of political life where intelligent men asked questions regarding the good life and the best political order. Thus, the philosopher might ask the ultimate questions beyond those asked in the sphere of practical politics, but he could not abandon faith with the orientation of politics as such. When the value distinctions being made by statesmen and politicians were judged to be mere ideologies and not intrinsically a part of the essence of politics, the philosopher's orientation in politics was breached and destroyed. Political life and its observance leads to philosophy, and while philosophy is primarily concerned with those virtues that are good for all communities, political science involves the practical virtues which are best for the governing of a particular community. Method in these terms is subordinate to virtue and wisdom.

The fourth principle is the belief that man is to be understood primarily from the standpoint of his rational faculties. What is unique in man is essentially his capacity for thought and reason. The dualism of classical political thought results from an identification of the body with evil and of the mind with an idea of goodness and universality. Since the body alone is corrupted and corruptible, classical philosophy assumes an optimistic frame of mind in regard to what man can accomplish through reason. Here the Greeks part company with many of the great religious and political systems, which consider man as fallen and incapable of doing more than mitigating his political and social problems. The rationalism and dualism of classical thought would seem to deprive it of the tragic insights some other philosophies have attained. The two selections which follow should illustrate these general principles, and in particular the first three. Professor

Leo Strauss is Professor of Political Philosophy at the University of Chicago. The selection from Aristotle (384–322 B.C.) provides a brief concrete illustration of the spirit of classical political philosophy.

16. On Classical Political Philosophy*

The ancients "would therefore advise the moderns rather to raise their own side of the hill than dream of pulling down that of the ancients; to the former of which they would not only give license, but also largely contribute." *The Battle of the Books.*

Today the status of political philosophy is more precarious, and its meaning is more blurred, than at any time since political philosophy emerged many centuries ago, somewhere in Greece. Its present condition is sufficiently illustrated by the fact that it has become possible, and indeed customary, to speak of the "political philosophies" of vulgar imposters.

In the past political philosophy had a very precise meaning. The galaxy of political philosophers from Socrates to Rousseau, and even certain more recent thinkers, conceived of it as an attempt to replace opinions about political fundamentals. These fundamentals include two groups of subjects: "the nature of political things" (that is, of laws, institutions, power, authority, duties and

rights, conditions, actions, decisions, programs, aspirations and wishes, human beings as political agents or as objects of political action); and "the best, or the just, political order." Political philosophy, as formerly understood, was identical with political science, or, if not identical, then the relations between the two were regarded not as those between one field of inquiry and another, but as those between the way and the goal. Moreover, political philosophy was thought to be fundamentally distinguished from history: it was not considered a historical discipline.

The present crisis in political philosophy is due to the twofold fact that in one way or another a distinction is generally made between political philosophy and political science as two different fields of inquiry, and that the idea of an ahistorical political philosophy has become doubtful. It is due, in other words, to the unsolved problems raised by positivism and historicism.

In contrast to earlier political philosophy, positivism and, more obviously, historicism must regard the study of the history of political philosophy as an integral part of their

* From Leo Strauss, *Social Research,* XII (1945), pp. 98–117. Reprinted by permission of Leo Strauss and *Social Research.*

own philosophic effort. They naturally tend to interpret earlier political philosophy from a positivist or historicist point of view. The dangers of misinterpretation are perhaps greatest as regards classical political philosophy. It is safe to say that the typical present-day interpretation of classical political philosophy is not historical, but historicist. An historical interpretation is one that tries to understand the philosophy of the past exactly as that philosophy understood itself. The historicist interpretation is one form of the attempt to understand the philosophy of the past better than it understood itself; for it is based on the assumption, wholly alien to the thought of the classics, that each philosophy is essentially related to its time — to the "spirit" of its time or to the "material conditions" of its time, or to both. In trying to understand classical political philosophy in the light of this assumption one does not understand it as it understood itself: one does not understand it historically.

The purpose of the following remarks is to discuss especially those elements of classical political philosophy which are particularly likely to be overlooked or insufficiently stressed by the schools that are most influential in our time. These remarks are not intended to sketch the outlines of a truly historical interpretation of classical political philosophy. They will have fulfilled their purpose if they point to the way which, I believe, is the only one whereby such an interpretation can eventually be reached.

I

Classical political philosophy is characterized by the fact that it was related to political life directly. It was only after the classical philosophers had done their work that political philosophy became definitely "established" and thus acquired a certain independence of political life. Since that time the relationship of political philosophers to political life, and their grasp of it, has been determined by the existence of an inherited political philosophy: since then political philosophy has been related to political life through the medium of a tradition of political philosophy. The tradition that originated in classical Greece was rejected in the sixteenth and seventeenth centuries in favor of a new political philosophy. But this "revolution" did not restore the direct relation to political life that had existed in the beginning: the new political philosophy was related to political life through the medium of the inherited general notion of political philosophy or political science, and through the medium of a new concept of science. Today, political science may believe that by rejecting or by emancipating itself from political philosophy, it stands in the most direct relation to political life; actually it is related to political life through the medium of the inherited general notion of political philosophy or political science, and through the medium of a new concept of science. Today, political science may believe that by rejecting or by emancipating itself from political philosophy, it stands in the most direct relation to political life; actually it is related to political life through the medium of modern natural science, or of the reaction to modern natural science, and through a number of basic concepts inherited from the philosophic tradition, however despised or ignored.

It was its direct relation to political life which determined the orientation and scope of classical political philosophy. Accordingly, the tradition which was based on that philosophy, and which preserved its orientation and scope, preserved that direct relation to a certain extent. The fundamental change in this respect was prepared by the new political philosophy of the early modern period and reaches its climax in present-day political science. The most striking difference between classical political philosophy and present-day political science is that the latter is no longer concerned with what was the guiding question for the former: the question of the best form of government, or of the best political order. On the other hand, modern political science is greatly preoccupied with a type of question that was of much less importance to classical political philosophy: questions concerning method. Both differences must be traced to the same reason: to the different degree of directness in which classical political philosophy, on the one hand, and present-day political science, on the other, are related to political life.

Classical political philosophy attempted to reach its goal by accepting the basic distinctions made in political life exactly in the sense and with the orientation in which they are made in political life, and by thinking them through, by understanding them as perfectly as possible. It did not start from such basic distinctions as those between "the state of nature" and "the civil state," between "facts" and "values," or between "reality" and "ideologies," distinctions which are alien, and even unknown, to political life as such and which originate only in philosophic or scientific reflection. Nor did it try to bring order into that chaos of political "facts" which exists only for those who approach political life from a point of view outside of political life, that is to say, from the point of view of a science that is not itself essentially an element of political life. Instead, it followed carefully and even scrupulously the articulation which is inherent in, and natural to, political life and its objects.

The primary questions of classical political philosophy, and the terms in which it stated them, were not specifically philosophic or scientific; they were questions that are raised in assemblies, councils, clubs and cabinets, and they were stated in terms intelligible and familiar, at least to all sane adults, from everyday experience and everyday usage. These questions have a natural hierarchy which supplies political life, and hence political philosophy, with its fundamental orientation. No one can help distinguishing among questions of smaller, of greater, and of paramount importance, and between questions of the moment and questions that are always present in political communities; and intelligent men apply these distinctions intelligently.

Similarly it can be said that the method, too, of classical political philosophy was presented by political life itself. Political life is characterized by conflicts between men asserting opposed claims. Those who raise a claim usually believe that what they claim is good for them. In many cases they believe, and in most cases they say, that what they claim is good for the community at large. In practically all cases claims are raised, sometimes sincerely and sometimes insincerely, in the name of justice. The opposed claims are based, then, on opinions of what is good or just. To justify their claims, the opposed parties advance arguments. The conflict calls for arbitration, for an intelligent decision that will give each party what it truly deserves. Some of the material required for making such a decision is offered by the opposed parties themselves, and the very insufficiency of this partial material — an insufficiency obviously due to its partisan origin — points the way to its completion by the umpire. And the umpire par excellence is the political philosopher. He tries to settle those political controversies that are both of paramount and of permanent importance.

This view of the function of the political philosopher — that he must not be a " radical " partisan who prefers victory in civil war to arbitration — is also of political origin: it is the duty of the good citizen to make civil strife cease and to create, by persuasion, agreement among the citizens. The political philosopher first comes into sight as a good citizen who can perform this function of the good citizen in the best way and on the highest level. In order to perform his function he has to raise ulterior questions, questions that are never raised in the political arena; but in doing so he does not abandon his fundamental orientation, which is the orientation inherent in political life. Only if that orientation were abandoned, if the basic distinctions made by political life were considered merely " subjective " or " unscientific " and therefore disregarded, would the question of how to approach political things in order to understand them, that is to say, the question of method, become a fundamental question, and, indeed, *the* fundamental question.

It is true that political life is concerned primarily with the individual community to which the people happen to belong, and mostly even with individual situations, whereas political philosophy is concerned primarily with what is essential to all political communities. Yet there is a straight and almost continuous way leading from the pre-philosophic to the philosophic approach. Political life requires various kinds of skills, and in particular that apparently highest skill which enables a man to manage well the affairs of his political community as a whole. That skill — the art, the prudence, the practical wisdom, the specific understanding possessed by the excellent statesman or politician — and not " a body of true propositions " concerning political matters which is transmitted by teachers to pupils, is what was originally meant by "political science." A man who possesses "political science" is not merely able to deal properly with a large variety of situations in his own community; he can, in principle, manage well even the affairs of any other political community, be it "Greek" or "barbarian." While all political life is essentially the life of this or that political community, "political science," which essentially belongs to political life, is essentially "transferable" from one community to any other. A man like Themistocles was admired and listened to not only in Athens, but, after he had to flee from Athens, among the barbarians as well; such a man is admired because he is capable of giving sound political advice wherever he goes.

"Political science" designated originally the skill by virtue of which a man could manage well the affairs of political communities by deed and by speech. The skill of speaking differs from the skill of doing in that it is more capable of being taught. Accordingly, that part of political skill which first became the object of instruction was the skill of public speaking. "Political science" in a more precise sense, that is, as a skill that is essentially teachable, appeared first as rhetoric, or as a part of it. The teacher of rhetoric was not necessarily a politician or statesman; he was, however, a teacher of politicians or statesmen. Since his pupils belonged to the most different political communities, the content of his teaching could not possibly be bound up with the particular features of any individual political community.

"Political science," on the level which it reached as a result of the exertions of the rhetoricians, is more "universal," is to an even higher degree "transferable," than is "political science" as the skill of the excellent statesman or politician: whereas strangers as statesmen or political advisers were an exception, strangers as teachers of rhetoric were the rule.

Classical political philosophy rejected the identification of political science with rhetoric; it held that rhetoric, at its best, was only an instrument of political science. It did not, however, descend from the level of universality that had been reached by the rhetoricians. On the contrary, after that part of political skill which is the skill of speaking had been raised to the level of a distinct discipline, the classical philosophers could meet that challenge only by raising the whole of "political science," as far as possible or necessary, to the rank of a distinct discipline. By doing this they became the founders of political science in the precise and final sense of the term. And the way in which they did it was determined by the articulation natural to the political sphere.

"Political science" as the skill of the excellent politician or statesman consists in the right handling of individual situations; its immediate "products" are commands or decrees or advices effectively expressed, which are intended to cope with an individual case. Political life knows, however, a still higher kind of political understanding, which is concerned not with individual cases but, as regards each relevant subject, with all cases, and whose immediate "products" — laws and institutions — are meant to be permanent. The true legislators — "the fathers of the Constitution," as modern men would say — establish, as it were, the permanent framework within which the right handling of changing situations by excellent politicians or statesmen can take place. While it is true that the excellent statesman can act successfully within the most different frameworks of laws and institutions, the value of his achievement depends ultimately on the value of the cause in whose service he acts; and that cause is not his work but the work of him or those who made the laws and institutions of his community. The legislative skill is, therefore, the most "architectonic" political skill that is known to political life.

Every legislator is primarily concerned with the individual community for which he legislates, but he has to raise certain questions which regard all legislation. These most fundamental and most universal political questions are naturally fit to be made the subject of the most "architectonic," the truly "architectonic" political knowledge: of that political science which is the goal of the political philosopher. This political science is the knowledge which would enable a man to teach legislators. The political philosopher who has reached his goal is the teacher of legislators. The knowledge of the political philosopher is "transferable" in the highest degree. Plato demonstrated this *ad oculos* in his dialogue on legislation, by presenting in the guise of a stranger the philosopher who is a teacher of legislators. He illustrated it less ambiguously by the comparison which frequently occurs in his writings, of political science with medicine.

It is by being the teacher of legislators that the political philosopher is the umpire par excellence. All political conflicts that arise within the community are at least related to, if they do not proceed from, the most fundamental political controversy: the controversy as to what type of men should rule the community. And the right settlement of that controversy appears to be the basis of excellent legislation.

Classical political philosophy was related to political life directly, because its guiding subject was a subject of actual political controversy carried on in pre-philosophic political life. Since all political controversies presuppose the existence of the political community they are not primarily concerned with the question of whether and why there is, or should be, a political community; hence the question of the nature and purpose of the political community is not the guiding question for classical political philosophy. Similarly, to question the desirability or necessity of the survival and independence of one's political community normally means to commit the crime of treason; in other words, the ultimate aim of foreign policy is not essentially controversial. Hence classical political philosophy is not guided by questions concerning the external relations of the political community. It is concerned primarily with the inner structure of the political community, because that inner structure is essentially the subject of such political controversy as essentially involves the danger of civil war.

The actual conflict of groups struggling for political power within the community naturally gives rise to the question what group should rule, or what compromise would be the best solution — that is to say, what political order would be the best order. Either the opposed groups are merely factions made up of the same type of men (such as parties of noblemen or adherents of opposed dynasties), or each of the opposed groups represents a specific type. Only in the latter case does the political struggle go to the roots of political life; then it becomes apparent to everyone, from everyday political life, that the question as to what type of men should have the decisive say is the subject of the most fundamental political controversy.

The immediate concern of that controversy is the best political order for the given political community, but every answer to that immediate question implies an answer to the universal question of the best political order as such. It does not require the exertions of philosophers to lay bare this implication, for the political controversy has a natural tendency to express itself in universal terms. A man who rejects kingship for Israel cannot help using arguments against kingship as such; a man who defends democracy in Athens cannot help using arguments in favor of democracy as such. When they are confronted with the fact that monarchy is the best political order, say,

for Babylon, the natural reaction of such men will be that this fact shows the inferiority of Babylon and not that the question of the best political order does not make sense.

The groups, or types, whose claims to rule were considered by the classical philosophers were " the good " (men of merit), the rich, the noble, and the multitude, or the poor citizens; in the foreground of the political scene in the Greek cities, as well as in other places, was the struggle between the rich and the poor. The claim to rule which is based on merit, on human excellence, on " virtue," appeared to be least controversial: courageous and skilful generals, incorruptible and equitable judges, wise and unselfish magistrates, are generally preferred. Thus " aristocracy " (rule of the best) presented itself as the natural answer of all good men to the natural question of the best political order. As Thomas Jefferson put it, " That form of government is the best, which provides the most effectually for a pure selection of (the) natural aristoi into offices of the government."

What is to be understood by " good men " was known also from political life: good men are those who are willing, and able, to prefer the common interest to their private interest and to the objects of their passions, or those who, being able to discern in each situation what is the noble or right thing to do, do it because it is noble and right and for no ulterior reason. It was also generally recognized that this answer gives rise to further questions of almost overwhelming political significance: that results which are generally considered desirable can be achieved by men of dubious character or by the use of unfair means; that "just" and "useful" are not simply identical; that virtue may lead to ruin.

Thus the question guiding classical political philosophy, the typical answer that it gave, and the insight into the bearing of the formidable objections to it, belong to pre-philosophic political life, or precede political philosophy. Political philosophy goes beyond pre-philosophic political knowledge by trying to understand fully the implications of these pre-philosophic insights, and especially by defending the second of them against the more or less "sophisticated" attacks made by bad or perplexed men.

When the pre-philosophic answer is accepted, the most urgent question concerns the "materials" and institutions which would be most favorable to "the rule of the best." It is primarily by answering this question, by thus elaborating a "blueprint" of the best polity, that the political philosopher becomes the teacher of legislators. The legislator is strictly limited in his choice of institutions and laws by the character of the people for whom he legislates, by their traditions, by the nature of their territory, by their economic conditions, and so on. His choosing this or that law is normally a compromise between what he would wish and what circumstances permit. To effect that compromise intelligently, he must first know what he wishes, or, rather, what would be most desirable in itself. The political philosopher

can answer that question because he is not limited in his reflections by any particular set of circumstances, but is free to choose the most favorable conditions that are possible — ethnic, climatic, economic and other — and thus to determine what laws and institutions would be preferable under those conditions. After that, he tries to bridge the gulf between what is most desirable in itself and what is possible in given circumstances, by discussing what polity, and what laws, would be best under various types of more or less unfavorable conditions, and even what kinds of laws and measures are appropriate for preserving any kind of polity, however defective. By thus erecting on the "normative" foundation of political science a "realistic" structure, or, to speak somewhat more adequately, by thus supplementing political physiology with political pathology and therapeutics, he does not retract or even qualify, he rather confirms, his view that the question of the best polity is necessarily the guiding question.

By the best political order the classical philosopher understood that political order which is best always and everywhere. This does not mean that he conceived of that order as necessarily good for every community, as "a perfect solution for all times and for every place": a given community may be so rude or so depraved that only a very inferior type of order can "keep it going." But it does mean that the goodness of the political order realized anywhere and at any time can be judged only in terms of that political order which is best absolutely. "The best political order" is, then, not intrinsically Greek: it is no more intrinsically Greek than health, as is shown by the parallelism of political science and medicine. But just as it may happen that the members of one nation are more likely to be healthy and strong than those of others, it may also happen that one nation has a greater natural fitness for political excellence than others.

When Aristotle asserted that the Greeks had a greater natural fitness for political excellence than the nations of the north and those of Asia, he did not assert, of course, that political excellence was identical with the quality of being Greek: otherwise he could not have praised the institutions of Carthage as highly as the institutions of the most renowned Greek cities. When Socrates asked Glauco in the *Republic* whether the city that Glauco was founding would be a Greek city, and Glauco answered emphatically in the affirmative, neither of them said any more than that a city founded by Greeks would necessarily be a Greek city. The purpose of this truism, or rather of Socrates' question, was to induce the warlike Glauco to submit to a certain moderation of warfare: since a general prohibition of wars was not feasible, at least warfare among Greeks should keep within certain limits. The fact that a perfect city founded by Glauco would be a Greek city does not imply that any perfect city was necessarily Greek: Socrates considered it possible that the perfect city, which certainly did not exist at that time anywhere in

Greece, existed at that time "in some barbarian place." Xenophon went so far as to describe the Persian Cyrus as *the* perfect ruler, and to imply that the education Cyrus received in Persia was superior even to Spartan education; and he did not consider it impossible that a man of the rank of Socrates would emerge among the Armenians.

Because of its direct relation to political life classical political philosophy was essentially "practical"; on the other hand, it is no accident that modern political philosophy frequently calls itself political "theory." The primary concern of the former was not the description, or understanding, of political life, but its right guidance. Hegel's demand that political philosophy refrain from construing a state as it ought to be, or from teaching the state how it should be, and that it try to understand the present and actual state as something essentially rational, amounts to a rejection of the *raison d'être* of classical political philosophy. In contrast with present-day political science, or with well-known interpretations of present-day political science, classical political philosophy pursued practical aims and was guided by, and culminated in, "value judgments." The attempt to replace the quest for the best political order by a purely descriptive or analytical political science which refrains from "value judgments" is, from the point of view of the classics, as absurd as the attempt to replace the art of making shoes, that is, good and well-fitting shoes, by a museum of shoes made by apprentices, or as the idea of a medicine which refuses to distinguish between health and sickness.

Since political controversies are concerned with " good things " and " just things," classical political philosophy was naturally guided by considerations of " goodness " and " justice." It started from the moral distinctions as they are made in everyday life, although it knew better than the dogmatic skeptic of our time the formidable theoretical objections to which they are exposed. Such distinctions as those between courage and cowardice, justice and injustice, human kindness and selfishness, gentleness and cruelty, urbanity and rudeness, are intelligible and clear for all practical purposes, that is, in most cases, and they are of decisive importance in guiding our lives: this is a sufficient reason for considering the fundamental political questions in their light.

In the sense in which these distinctions are politically relevant, they cannot be " demonstrated," they are far from being perfectly lucid, and they are exposed to grave theoretical doubts. Accordingly, classical political philosophy limited itself to addressing men who, because of their natural inclinations as well as their upbringing, took those distinctions for granted. It knew that one can perhaps silence but not truly convince such people as have no " taste " for the moral distinctions and their significance: not even Socrates could convert, though he could silence, such men as Thrasymachus and Callicles, and he admitted the limits set to demonstrations in this sphere by taking recourse to " myths."

The political teaching of the classical philosophers, as distinguished from their theoretical teaching, was primarily addressed not to all intelligent men, but to all decent men. A political teaching which addressed itself equally to decent and indecent men would have appeared to them from the outset as unpolitical, that is, as politically, or socially, irresponsible; for if it is true that the well-being of the political community requires that its members be guided by considerations of decency or morality, the political community cannot tolerate a political science which is morally " neutral " and which therefore tends to loosen the hold of moral principles on the minds of those who are exposed to it. To express the same view somewhat differently, even if it were true that when men are talking of right they are thinking only of their interests, it would be equally true that that reserve is of the essence of political man, and that by emancipating oneself from it one would cease to be a political man or to speak his language.

Thus the attitude of classical political philosophy toward political things was always akin to that of the enlightened statesman; it was not the attitude of the detached observer who looks at political things in the way in which a zoologist looks at the big fishes swallowing the small ones, or that of the social " engineer " who thinks in terms of manipulating or conditioning rather than in terms of education or liberation, or that of the prophet who believes that he knows the future.

In brief, the root of classical political philosophy was the fact that political life is characterized by controversies between groups struggling for power within the political community. Its purpose was to settle those political controversies which are of a fundamental and typical character in the spirit not of the partisan but of the good citizen, and with a view to such an order as would be most in accordance with the requirements of human excellence. Its guiding subject was the most fundamental politically controversial subject, understood in the way, and in the terms, in which it was understood in pre-philosophic political life.

In order to perform his function the philosopher had to raise an ulterior question which is never raised in the political arena. That question is so simple, elementary and unobtrusive that it is, at first, not even intelligible, as is shown by a number of occurrences described in the Platonic dialogues. This distinctly philosophic question is "What is virtue?" What is that virtue whose possession — as everyone admits spontaneously or is reduced to silence by unanswerable arguments — gives a man the highest right to rule? In the light of this question the common opinions about virtue appear at the outset as unconscious attempts to answer an unconscious question. On closer examination their radical insufficiency is more specifically revealed by the fact that some of them are contradicted by other opinions which are equally common. To reach consistency the philosopher is compelled to maintain one part of common opinion and to give up the other part which contradicts it; he is thus driven to adopt a view that is no longer generally held, a truly paradoxical view, one that is generally considered " absurd " or " ridiculous."

Nor is that all. He is ultimately compelled to transcend not merely the dimension of common opinion, of political opinion, but the dimension of political life as such; for he is led to realize that the ultimate aim of political life cannot be reached by political life, but only by a life devoted to contemplation, to philosophy. This finding is of crucial importance for political philosophy, since it determines the limits set to political life, to all political action and all political planning. Moreover, it implies that the highest subject of political philosophy is the philosophic life: philosophy — not as a teaching or as a body of knowledge, but as a way of life — offers, as it were, the solution to the problem that keeps political life in motion. Ultimately, political philosophy transforms itself into a discipline that is no longer concerned with political things in the ordinary sense of the term: Socrates called his inquiries a quest for " the *true* political skill," and Aristotle called his discussion of virtue and related subjects "a *kind* of political science."

No difference between classical political philosophy and modern political philosophy is more telling than this: the philosophic life, or the life of " the wise," which was the highest subject of classical political philosophy, has in modern times almost completely ceased to be a subject of political philosophy. Yet even this ultimate step of classical political philosophy, however absurd it seemed to the common opinion, was nevertheless " divined " by pre-philosophic political life: men wholly devoted to the political life were sometimes popularly considered " busybodies," and their unresting habits were contrasted with the greater freedom and the higher dignity of the more retired life of men who were " minding their own business."

II

The direct relation of classical political philosophy to pre-philosophic political life was due not to the undeveloped character of classical philosophy or science, but to mature reflection. This reflection is summed up in Aristotle's description of political philosophy as " the philosophy concerning the human things." This description reminds us of the almost overwhelming difficulty which had to be overcome before philosophers could devote any serious attention to political things, to human things. The " human things " were distinguished from the " divine things " or the " natural things," and the latter were considered absolutely superior in dignity to the former. Philosophy, therefore, was at first exclusively concerned with the natural things: originally it was an attempt to replace opinions about the nature of the whole by genuine knowledge of the nature of the whole. Thus, in the beginning, philosophic effort was concerned only negatively, only accidentally, with political things. Soc-

rates himself, the founder of political philosophy, was famous as a philosopher before he ever turned to political philosophy. Left to themselves, the philosophers would not descend again to the " cave " of political life, but would remain outside in what they considered " the island of the blessed " — contemplation of the truth.

But philosophy, being an attempt to rise from opinion to science, is necessarily related to the sphere of opinion as its essential starting point, and hence to the political sphere. Therefore the political sphere is bound to advance into the focus of philosophic interest as soon as philosophy starts to reflect on its own doings. To understand fully its own purpose and nature, philosophy has to understand its essential starting point, and hence the nature of political things.

The philosophers, as well as other men who have become aware of the possibility of philosophy, are sooner or later driven to wonder " Why philosophy? " Why does human life need philosophy, why is it good, why is it right, that opinions about the nature of the whole should be replaced by genuine knowledge of the nature of the whole? Since human life is living together or, more exactly, is political life, the question " Why philosophy? " means " Why does political life need philosophy? " This question calls philosophy before the tribunal of the political community: it makes philosophy politically responsible. Like Plato's perfect city itself, which, once established, does not permit the philosophers to devote themselves any longer exclusively to contemplation, this question, once raised, forbids the philosophers any longer to disregard political life altogether. Plato's *Republic* as a whole as well as other political works of the classical philosophers, can best be described as an attempt to supply a political justification for philosophy by showing that the well-being of the political community depends decisively on the study of philosophy. Such a justification was all the more urgent since the meaning of philosophy was by no means generally understood, and hence philosophy was distrusted and hated by many well-meaning citizens. Socrates himself fell victim to the popular prejudice against philosophy. To justify philosophy before the tribunal of the political community means to justify philosophy in terms of the political community, that is to say, by means of a kind of argument which appeals not to philosophers as such, but to citizens as such. To prove to citizens that philosophy is permissible, desirable or even necessary, the philosopher has to follow the example of Odysseus and start from premises that are generally agreed upon, or from generally accepted opinions: he has to argue *ad hominem* or, more exactly, "dialectically." From this point of view the adjective "political" in the expression "political philosophy" designates not so much a subject matter as a manner of treatment; from this point of view, I say, "political philosophy" means primarily not the philosophic treatment of politics, but the political, or popular, treatment of philosophy, or the

political introduction to philosophy — the attempt to lead the qualified citizens, or rather their qualified sons, from the political life to the philosophic life. This deeper meaning of " political philosophy " tallies well with its ordinary meaning, for in both cases " political philosophy " culminates in praise of the philosophic life. At any rate, it is ultimately because he means to justify philosophy before the tribunal of the political community, and hence on the level of political discussion, that the philosopher has to understand the political things exactly as they are understood in political life.

In his political philosophy the philosopher starts, then, from that understanding of political things which is natural to pre-philosophic political life. At the beginning the fact that a certain habitual attitude or a certain way of acting is generally praised, is a sufficient reason for considering that attitude, or that way of acting, a virtue. But the philosopher is soon compelled, or able, to transcend the dimension of pre-philosophic understanding by raising the crucial question " What is virtue? " The attempt to answer this question leads to a critical distinction between the generally praised attitudes which are rightly praised, and those which are not; and it leads to the recognition of a certain hierarchy, unknown in pre-philosophic life, of the different virtues. Such a philosophic critique of the generally accepted views is at the bottom of the fact that Aristotle, for example, omitted piety and sense of shame from his list of virtues, and that his list starts with courage and moderation (the least intellectual virtues) and, proceeding via liberality, magnanimity and the virtues of private relations, to justice, culminates in the dianoetic virtues. Moreover, insight into the limits of the moral-political sphere as a whole can be expounded fully only by answering the question of the nature of political things. This question marks the limit of political philosophy while essentially practical in itself, the question functions as an entering wedge for others whose purpose is no longer to guide action but simply to understand things as they are.

17. The Subject of Ethics is the Good for Man *

Every art and every inquiry, and similarly every action and pursuit, is thought to aim at some good; and for this reason the good has rightly been declared to be that at which all things aim. But a certain difference is found among ends; some are activities, others are products apart from the activities that produce them. Where there are ends apart from the actions, it is the nature of the products to be better than the activities. Now, as there are many actions, arts, and sciences, their ends also are many; the end of the medical art is health, that of shipbuilding a vessel, that of strategy victory, that of economics wealth. But where such arts fall under a single capacity — as bridle-making and the other arts concerned with the equipment of horses fall under the art of riding, and this and every military action under strategy, in the same way other arts fall under yet others — in all of these the ends of the master arts are to be preferred to all the subordinate ends; for it is for the sake of the former that the latter are pursued. It makes no difference whether the activities themselves are the ends of the actions, or something else apart from the activities, as in the case of the sciences just mentioned.

If, then, there is some end of the things we do, which we desire for its own sake (everything else being desired for the sake of this), and if we do not choose everything for the sake of something else (for at that rate the process would go on to infinity, so that our desire would be empty and vain), clearly this must be the good and the chief good. Will not the knowledge of it, then, have a great influence on life? Shall we not, like archers who have a mark to aim at, be more likely to hit upon what is right? If so, we must try, in outline at least, to determine what it is, and of which of the sciences or capacities it is the object. It would seem to belong to the most authoritative art and that which is most truly the master art. And politics appears to be of this nature; for it is

* From Aristotle, *Selections*, pp. 218–20. Copyright 1938 by Charles Scribner's Sons, New York. Reprinted by permission of Charles Scribner's Sons.

this that ordains which of the sciences should be studied in a state, and which each class of citizens should learn and up to what point they should learn them; and we see even the most highly esteemed of capacities to fall under this, e.g. strategy, economics, rhetorics; now, since politics uses the rest of the sciences, and since, again, it legislates as to what we are to do and what we are to abstain from, the end of this science must include those of the others, so that this end must be the good for man. For even if the end is the same for a single man and for a state, that of the state seems at all events something greater and more complete whether to attain or to preserve; though it is worth while to attain the end merely for one man, it is finer and more godlike to attain it for a nation or for city-states. These, then, are the ends at which our inquiry aims, since it is political science, in one sense of that term.

B. The Turning Point in Western Thought

18. Introduction

The major link between classical thought and modern political theory is Christian philosophy of the medieval era. Broadly speaking, the church fathers rejected two of the general propositions of classical thought and added two. The dualism, which had characterized classical philosophy, was put aside, and in its place a concept of man's essential and total depravity was substituted. Not the body alone, but reason and all man's faculties had been corrupted. Neither through reason nor by physical effort could he transcend his human frailties. Moreover, the idea of the state as a positive good was replaced by a variety of attitudes all conceiving the state as a necessary evil. Man's perfection was not attainable in this world, and therefore the state was at best an earth-bound version of the City of God.

The novel features of Christian political thinking were its emphasis on the individual as the possessor of certain God-given rights and its doctrine of the "Two Swords." The essential idea of fundamental human rights which, at a time considerably in the future, were to be translated into political rights have their roots in Stoic and Christian philosophy. And the concept of two spheres, that of church and of state, possessing authority respectively in the spiritual and temporal realms, became the basis for a theory of limited powers, upset by the Renaissance but revived in political terms in the concept of the separation of powers within the system.

Modern political theory is commonly considered to have begun with the Renaissance and the Reformation in Western society. This impression is born out by a list of the personalities and concepts of political philosophy that appeared sometime during the fifteenth and sixteenth centuries. To begin with, there were far-reaching changes which took place in at least three basic concepts of political philosophy: the acceptance of a new concept of progress, the transformation of the role and position of the individual, and the abandonment of a belief in objective truth. The idea of progress has its origins in the Renaissance doctrine of human perfectibility. Man was considered by both classical and Christian philosophies to possess limited and particular aspects of ideal or divine perfection. But both groups were profoundly pessimistic concerning his chances of creating an ideal state, which, for Plato could come about only by accident or through the grace of the gods, or, for Christians, by approaching the City of God on this earth. Beginning with the Renaissance and developing more fully by the seventeenth century, a belief in uninterrupted social progress came to the fore. It was widely accepted that mankind's condition was growing better and better and that some novel political device would in all likelihood usher in a society freed of conflicts.

The second far-reaching change for modern political theory was the movement of the individual, in one sense at least, from the center to the periphery of philosophy — and this despite modern individualism. This change is perhaps the most basic and serious of the three, but its presence and impact have often been concealed or unsuspected. For it is paradoxical that the era of democracy and equality should be conceived as one in which, philosophically, individualism has been dropped. Yet it has been clear from recent political experience that the practice of politics can be grounded in appeals to the rights and privileges of *all* individuals at the same time that the philosophy which defines and explains the system and its meaning can depreciate the role and development of the individual. Indeed, in a profound sense this has been the trend since the Renaissance period. The paramount question for the classical writers was: what is the " best state " for the development and welfare of the individual — given certain assumptions regarding human nature? The state was assumed to exist for the welfare of the individual and therefore his natural rights against the state were considered unimportant. The chief interest in both classical and medieval thought was the relation of the state, not to the individual as such, but to objective truth or to the moral laws under which the individual could fulfill himself. Individuals could revolt only if the state violated or transgressed the moral laws.

The Renaissance led to a shattering of these particular concepts of individualism and objective truth. As a general intellectual and cultural movement it stressed the autonomy, beauty, and power of individuals as such. The rights of individuals as against the state was the political expression of this adoration of man. The first of the philosophers who articulated this view was Niccolo Machiavelli (1469-1527). Born in Florence, he served until 1512 as a diplomat, organizer of the militia, and political secretary in the Florentine republic. When the republic was overthrown by the party of the Medici, Machiavelli was forced to go into exile. He returned to participate in an ill-fated conspiracy, being thrown into prison in return for his troubles. Through the intervention of Cardinal Julian de Medici he was released. Thereafter he retired to a life of farming and writing and produced his best known work *The Prince*. In addition he wrote *Discourses on the First Ten Books of Titus Livius* as well as a study of the *Art of War* and a *History of Florence*.

In the medieval order there had been a hierarchy of communities of which the individual was an integral part receiving his rights and duties from the whole. These rights in turn found their " reason " in the furtherance of his true nature. This order and " reason " disintegrated in the fifteenth century and Machiavelli's main purpose was to build a new system based on the power of superior individuals. The territorial state, as foreshadowed in Machiavelli, reflected essentially the same principle. For the state was to arise as the powerful king or ruler freed himself from the dominance of church and emperor and subjugated the feudal barons. By destroying the old forces the king created a new order coextensive with his power. Machiavelli wrote primarily about such developments, but his efforts were directed at prescribing the methods for gaining and keeping power. His treatise on *The Prince* was a recipe on how to win elections, and his recipe was formulated from his comprehension of the full range of man's virtues. He was more frank than his successors in laying bare the conflict between moral principles and practical politics. Without adoring power as such, he warned that men must make up their minds whether success or morality are the goals that they prize most highly. If they choose power and office, Machiavelli said morality must become a matter of indifference — although he said it with regrets.

Thomas Hobbes (1588-1679) is a second philosopher of the period, who sought to confront and to resolve these new problems. He had been a tutor to the Prince of Wales who was subsequently to become Charles II. As a result, Hobbes' sympathy in the English Civil War was with the royalists who took some displeasure, however, in the implications of his writings. Indeed not until John Austin who propounded his theory of law and jurisprudence in the nineteenth century were Hobbes' views revived and given wide currency. His greatest work was the *Leviathan* (1651). Hobbes faced the dilemma that individualism as conceived by a Renaissance mind led to anarchy and the threatening of society as such. Individuals, if left to their own natural desires, make society impossible but a Leviathan or compulsory political order would be calculated to save them. The paradox of the political philosophy of Hobbes is that in his search for happiness and success, the individual is driven to postulate a totalitarian state which by its nature must be a negation of radical individualism. In truth, the one logical political structure for early Renaissance individualism is anarchy.

A third approach to the problem was that of the English philosopher John Locke (1632–1704). As the secretary to the founder of the Whig Party, the Earl of Shaftesbury, Locke wrote in the stormy last quarter of the seventeenth century. He was forced in 1683 to go into exile and returned only after the death of James II in 1689. His writings were begun during the years in exile, and the most important of his political works were *Two Treatises of Civil Government* (1690) and the *Letters on Toleration* (1689). The philosophy of Locke, in contrast to Hobbes, provided for limitations on the power of the state by preserving the rights of individuals in the social contract establishing the state. The ancient doctrines had held that the state was responsible to God alone, but Locke introduced the concept that the individual held certain rights given by nature as part of his natural endowment. These immanent rights, which were owed to no divine agency or power, could never be transgressed by the state. For if the state were to violate the individual's rights it would have violated its contract with him and he would then be freed of his contractual ob-

ligations. The right of revolution was thereby made legitimate and the principle was shortly thereafter invoked by the American Revolutionaries.

The final expression of modern political philosophy that we shall mention is perhaps the most important and significant one. Jean Jacques Rousseau (1712–1778) was a restless, impulsive, and erratic figure, whose life of debauchery in Parisian society contrasts sharply with the moral intent of most of his writings. His solution to the baffling issue of the reconciliation of individualism and political organization is the one which has persisted throughout much of contemporary Western society. In constructing an answer to the Hobbesian paradox that the freedom of the individual can only be safeguarded by devices that are the very antithesis of freedom, he set forth the concept of *volonté général*. Man could be free only when he was made subject to the impersonal will of society. Government by individuals or private groups would lead to selfishness and destruction. Government by the general will of all individuals in aggregate leads to the welfare of all. This common will is not actually the source of all moral law, but inasmuch as it can never in practice be wrong it does act in harmony with every general law. Indeed, in practice the majority decision reflects the *volonté général* and minorities who may not agree are merely deceived as to their real interests.

The implication of this fusion of moral principles and majority right for modern governments, which by control of the means of mass communication can manipulate and create their own majorities, is only too obvious. And totalitarian systems have actually invoked the doctrine of the infallibility of the majority of the people. It is not without import that the United States with its doctrine of the " Higher Law " and the Constitution has required that majorities, in order not to forfeit their right to govern, comply with the terms of their compact.

There is one final shift in the movement from classical to modern thought which deserves special mention. For the classical and medieval writers, men were not conceived of as equal in intellectual and rational attributes. Since these attributes were considered decisive to politics, men were by definition politically unequal in this system. In Renaissance thinking, by contrast, whatever inequalities were known to exist were considered politically irrelevant.

It was Rousseau who attempted to bridge the disagreement between the Renaissance and the ancients on this issue. Men were indeed unequal in their intellectual capacities, but in sentiments and passions their status was equal. All men have the same quality of moral sense and sentiment. And on this basis the general will can be expected to function, reflecting the good sentiments of society as a whole. But the law-giver with his qualities of superior intellect and wisdom must gain people's support by appealing to their sentiments through the device of a civil religion, and not by means of the reasoning process whereby he himself has reached his conclusions. Thus, in the philosophy of political rule by majorities that are always morally right in their choices, it is said, we can find the roots of some of the more decisive elements of modern totalitarianism. Yet this same philosophy is likewise the basis of liberal democratic government.

19. In What Way Princes Must Keep Faith*

How laudable it is for a prince to keep good faith and live with integrity, and not with astuteness, every one knows. Still the experience of our times shows those princes to have done great things who have had little regard for good faith, and have been able by astuteness to confuse

* From Niccoló Machiavelli, The Prince and The Discourses, XVIII, pp. 63–66. Copyright, 1940, by The Modern Library, Inc., New York.

men's brains, and who have ultimately overcome those who have made loyalty their foundation.

You must know, then, that there are two methods of fighting, the one by law, the other by force: the first method is that of men, the second of beasts; but as the first method is often insufficient, one must have recourse to the second. It is therefore necessary for a prince to know well how to use both the beast and the man. This was covertly taught to rulers by ancient writers, who relate how Achilles and many others of those ancient princes were given to Chiron the centaur to be brought up and educated under his discipline. The parable of this semi-animal, semi-human teacher is meant to indicate that a prince must know how to use both natures, and that the one without the other is not durable.

A prince being thus obliged to know well how to act as a beast must imitate the fox and the lion, for the lion cannot protect himself from traps, and the fox cannot defend himself from wolves. One must therefore be a fox to recognise traps, and a lion to frighten wolves. Those that wish to be only lions do not understand this. Therefore, a prudent ruler ought not to keep faith when by so doing it would be against his interest, and when the reasons which made him blind himself no longer exist. If men were all good, this precept would not be a good one; but as they are bad, and would not observe their faith with you, so you are not bound to keep faith with them. Nor have legitimate grounds ever failed a prince who wished to show colourable excuse for the non-fulfilment of his promise. Of this one could furnish an infinite number of modern examples, and show how many times peace has been broken, and how many promises rendered worthless, by the faithlessness of princes, and those that have been best able to imitate the fox have succeeded best. But it is necessary to be able to disguise this character well, and to be a great feigner and

dissembler; and men are so simple and so ready to obey present necessities, that one who deceives will always find those who allow themselves to be deceived.

I will only mention one modern instance. Alexander VI did nothing else but deceive men, he thought of nothing else, and found the occasion for it; no man was ever more able to give assurances, or affirmed things with stronger oaths, and no man observed them less; however, he always succeeded in his deceptions, as he well knew this aspect of things.

It is not, therefore, necessary for a prince to have all the above-named qualities, but it is very necessary to seem to have them. I would even be bold to say that to possess them and always to observe them is dangerous, but to appear to possess them is useful. Thus it is well to seem merciful, faithful, humane, sincere, religious, and also to be so; but you must have the mind so disposed that when it is needful to be otherwise you may be able to change to the opposite qualities. And it must be understood that a prince, and especially a new prince, cannot observe all those things which are considered good in men, being often obliged, in order to maintain the state, to act against faith, against charity, against humanity, and against religion. And, therefore, he must have a mind disposed to adapt itself according to the wind, and as the variations of fortune dictate, and, as I said before, not deviate from what is good, if possible, but be able to do evil if constrained.

A prince must take great care that

nothing goes out of his mouth which is not full of the above-named five qualities, and, to see and hear him, he should seem to be all mercy, faith, integrity, humanity, and religion. And nothing is more necessary than to seem to have this last quality, for men in general judge more by the eyes than by the hands, for everyone can see, but very few have to feel. Everybody sees what you appear to be, few feel what you are, and those few will not dare to oppose themselves to the many, who have the majesty of the state to defend them; and in the actions of men, and especially of princes, from which there is no appeal, the end justifies the means. Let a prince therefore aim at conquering and maintaining the state, and the means will always be judged honourable and praised by every one, for the vulgar is always taken by appearances and the issue of the event; and the world consists only of the vulgar, and the few who are not vulgar are isolated when the many have a rallying point in the prince. A certain prince of the present time, whom it is well not to name, never does anything but preach peace and good faith, but he is really a great enemy to both, and either of them, had he observed them, would have lost him state or reputation on many occasions.

C. The Liberal Tradition

20. Introduction

The liberal tradition was the political creed of the rising middle class and as such it reflects both their convictions and their interests. In the seventeenth century the enemy of the middle class was the state, which adhered to the practices of the feudal and mercantilist orders. The middle class attempted to erect a concept of limited state action, which would undermine resistance to its rise to power and influence. Ideally, it was held, the state ought to function as an umpire or night watchman, interfering as little as possible with the self-regulating processes of the market. Government was an evil and its activities should be restricted to a bare minimum. The sphere of state action should be distinct from the sphere of society as such and the rule of law would serve to effectuate this division.

If liberalism was an expression and rationalization of middle-class interests, there is at least one eternal truth to be found in its emphasis on individual freedom. In all human beings there is a creative urge for freedom, and the great historic function of liberalism was to identify the effective enemy of freedom in the seventeenth and eighteenth centuries. Today there are new enemies of individual freedom in new concentrations of power of industry and labor.

But the enduring principle of freedom as the basis of progress has never been more forcefully stated than in the liberal tradition. In Selection 21, we have quoted the famous defense of freedom of publication and the press by John Milton (1608–1674). *Areopagitica* (1644) has become, along with John Stuart Mill's essay *On Liberty,* the classic argument for free speech.

21. The Liberal Tradition*

If every action, which is good or evil in man at ripe years, were to be under pittance and prescription and compulsion, what were virtue but a name, what praise could be then due to well-doing, what gramercy to be sober, just, or continent? Many there be that complain of Divine Providence for suffering Adam to transgress; foolish tongues! When God gave him reason, He gave him freedom to choose, for reason is but choosing; he had been else a mere artificial Adam, such an Adam as he is in the motions. We ourselves esteem not of that obedience, or love, or gift, which is of force: God therefore left him free, set before him a provoking object, ever almost in his eyes; herein consisted his merit, herein the right of his reward, the praise of his abstinence. Wherefore did He create passions within us, pleasures round about us, but that these rightly tempered are the very ingredients of virtue?

They are not skilful considerers of human things, who imagine to remove sin by removing the matter of sin; for, besides that it is a huge heap increasing under the very act of diminishing, though some part of it may for a time be withdrawn from some persons, it cannot from all, in such a universal thing as books are; and when this is done, yet the sin remains entire. Though ye take from a covetous man all his treasure, he has yet one jewel left, ye cannot bereave him of his covetousness. Banish all objects of lust, shut up all youth into the severest discipline that can be exercised in any hermitage, ye cannot make them chaste, that came not thither so: such great care and wisdom is required to the right managing of this point. Suppose we could expel sin by this means; look how much we thus expel of sin, so much we expel of virtue: for the matter of them both is the same; remove that, and ye remove them both alike.

This justifies the high providence of God, who though He commands us temperance, justice, continence, yet pours out before us, even to a profuseness, all desirable things, and gives us minds that can wander beyond all limit and satiety. Why should we then affect a rigor contrary to the manner of God and of nature, by abridging or scanting

* From John Milton *Areopagitica,* edited by Ernest Rhys, (London: J. M. Dent & Sons Ltd., 1927), pp. 18–19, 22, 24, 31, 32, 36–37.

those means, which books freely permitted are, both to the trial of virtue and the exercise of truth? It would be better done, to learn that the law must needs be frivolous, which goes to restrain things, uncertainly and yet equally working to good and to evil. And were I the chooser, a dram of well-doing should be preferred before many times as much the forcible hindrance of evil-doing. For God sure esteems the growth and completing of one virtuous person more than the restraint of ten vicious. . . .

When a man writes to the world, he summons up all his reason and deliberation to assist him; he searches, meditates, is industrious, and likely consults and confers with his judicious friends; after all which done he takes himself to be informed in what he writes, as well as any that writ before him. If, in this the most consummate act of his fidelity and ripeness, no years, no industry, no former proof of his abilities can bring him to that state of maturity, as not to be still mistrusted and suspected, unless he carry all his considerate diligence, all his midnight watchings and expense of Palladian oil, to the hasty view of an unleisured licenser, perhaps much his younger, perhaps for his inferior in judgment, perhaps one who never knew the labour of bookwriting, and if he be not repulsed or slighted, must appear in print like a puny with his guardian, and his censor's hand on the back of his title to be his bail and surety that he is no idiot or seducer, it cannot be but a dishonour and derogation to the author, to the book, to the privilege and dignity of Learning. . . .

Truth and understanding are not such wares as to be monopolised and traded in by tickets and statutes and standards. We must not think to make a staple commodity of all the knowledge in the land, to mark and licence it like our broadcloth and our woolpacks. What is it but a servitude like that imposed by the Philistines, not to be allowed the sharpening of our own axes and coulters, but we must repair from all quarters to twenty licensing forges? . . .

They are the troublers, they are the dividers of unity, who neglect and permit not others to unite those dissevered pieces which are yet wanting to the body of Truth. To be still searching what we know not by what we know, still closing up truth to truth as we find it (for all her body is homogeneal and proportional), this is the golden rule in theology as well as in arithmetic, and makes up the best harmony in a Church; not the forced and outward union of cold and neutral, and inwardly divided minds. . . .

Where there is much desire to learn, there of necessity will be much arguing, much writing, many opinions; for opinion in good men is but knowledge in the making. Under these fantastic terrors of sect and schism, we wrong the earnest and zealous thirst after knowledge and understanding which God hath stirred up in this city. . . . And though all the winds of doctrine were let loose to play upon the earth, so Truth be in the field, we do injuriously, by licensing and prohibiting, to misdoubt her strength.

Let her and Falsehood grapple; who ever knew Truth put to the worse, in a free and open encounter? Her confuting is the best and surest suppressing. He who hears what praying there is for light and clearer knowledge to be sent down among us, would think of other matters to be constituted beyond the discipline of Geneva, framed and fabricked already to our hands. Yet when the new light which we beg for shines in upon us, there be who envy and oppose, if it come not first in at their casements. What a collusion is this, whenas we are exhorted by the wise man to use diligence, to seek for wisdom as for hidden treasures early and late, that another order shall enjoin us to know nothing but by statute? When a man hath been labouring the hardest labour in the deep mines of knowledge; hath furnished out his findings in all their equipage; drawn forth his reasons as it were a battle ranged; scattered and defeated all objections in his way; calls out his adversary into the plain, offers him the advantage of wind and sun, if he please, only that he may try the matter by dint of argument: for his opponents then to skulk, to lay ambushments, to keep a narrow bridge of licensing where the challenger should pass, though it be valour enough in soldiership, is but weakness and cowardice in the wars of Truth.

D. The Reaction to the Liberal Tradition

22. Introduction

The problems with which contemporary societies are confronted are partly an outgrowth of the discrepancy between a political philosophy developed in the seventeenth and eighteenth centuries and the social and economic conditions under which it has had to operate in the twentieth century. The practical application of the principles of laissez-faire has led to an immense accumulation of power in the hands of certain private groups, which have risen to authority within society. The safeguards erected at the behest of the middle class against state encroachments have had little effect in protecting the rest of society from great private corporations or from massive labor unions.

In the mid-nineteenth century, the first full-scale reaction against some of the consequences of liberalism as a political philosophy was launched. The findings of a number of Royal Commissions in England disclosed that the achievements of liberal capitalism had been paid for at the price of unbelievable oppression for those who were found at the base of the social pyramid. It was demonstrated that in the administration of the poor laws and the operations of the coal mines, liberal society had contributed to the degeneration of individuals in a manner that passed all description. Members of the lower classes had been alienated from the land, from the work of their hands, from their religion, and from themselves. By the Industrial Revolution all social relations had been reduced to one brutal and absolute relationship, namely that of the market. Human labor and skills were commodities to be sold to the highest bidder, and the safeguards and limitations that were exerted by religious attitudes and moral forces in the medieval period had disappeared with the Renaissance.

The full force of the Marxist reaction initially is to be found in the moral indignation and compassion it expressed against these conditions. By confronting modern liberalism with the pretenses of its theory and the brutality and misery of actual conditions for a great mass of the people, Marxism was able to capitalize on the humanitarianism of the eighteenth and nineteenth centuries.

In the same way, the leaders of Italian Fascism and National Socialism in Germany responded to the conditions of defeat and failure by liberal democratic regimes in twentieth century Europe. The Weimar Republic and its executive Chancellor Brüning acted out to the full the sacred doctrines of liberalism. In the grave socio-economic crisis of 1929, Brüning was more preoccupied with balancing the budget than with intervening effectively to alleviate the crisis. At a time when most industries hovered near the point of bankruptcy, a policy was invoked for increasing the taxes of industries and consumers. As unemployment approached a critical point, the demands of a balanced budget required that unemployment benefits should be curtailed. With the breakdown of democratic government, the reaction of fascism to this situation was to replace inaction with action and the regularities of the market with coercion and public works. Thus both communism and fascism were assisted in their rise to power and authority by the mistakes of liberal statesmen who had not learned that the postulates of the seventeenth century were not in themselves adequate for the twentieth.

These attacks upon the liberal tradition provide us with some clues as to the nature and dynamism of the communist and fascist movements. Their essential characteristics are at least partially reflected in the charges being made against liberal democracy. Fascism claimed (see selection 24) that democracy is specious and unreal, for the idea of rule by the people is habitually used as a pretense by selfish forces who in fact rule and govern behind this façade. Not only is it true in these situations that the people *do not* rule but in practice they *cannot* rule. For men in society are basically and fundamentally unequal and their inequality extends to matters that are of decisive importance for popular government. The best government at all times and not merely under certain circumstances — as classical philosophy had conceded — is a government based on the inequality of man. Here fascism went far beyond the ideas of classical philosophy. Political choices should forever be limited to those who by race and resolve would be the decisive conveyors and leaders in their societies' mission. In every society some are the rulers and the others their followers. The mission of fascism could be realized by rationalizing and channeling this natural tendency to serve its own aims and purposes.

Communism and fascism are not only reactions to the practice of liberalism in Western society. In a deeper sense they are expressions or caricatures of some of the underlying tendencies which emerged with the turn in modern political philosophy. Following Rousseau, the groundwork was laid for the emergence of Marxism and fascism with the philosophies of Immanuel Kant (1724–1804) and Georg Wilhelm Friedrich Hegel (1770–1831). Kant was a professor of logic and metaphysics at the University of Königsberg in East Prussia, and so precise were his habits that it was said neighbors set their clocks by his going and coming. In his works, especially the monumental *Critique of Pure Reason* and the *Critique of Practical Reason,* Kant attempted to show the essential dualism of life. The world of things as we perceive them by means of our senses is the world of *phenomena.* But our senses and intellect can never give us a knowledge of the *noumena* or things-in-themselves. Science can never tell us what we desire

to know about this world. Only by means of the moral will can the individual approach the world " as it really is." The supreme duty for every individual is to act in terms of the moral law which, however, is a law without specific content. The one guide to moral conduct is Kant's categorical imperative wherein individuals are exhorted to act in such a way that they can " will " their conduct to become a universal law for all mankind.

Yet in practice this category is as empty of objective content as is the general will. It would be impossible to deduce from it any guidance for individuals in concrete situations. In practice it becomes a ready-made instrument for authoritarian governments, which assert, to take but one example, that unquestioning obedience to the rulers should become universalized. Since the categorical imperative offers no objective standards they must be extracted from each situation. In politics the objective rules are to be found nowhere but in the authority of the state. As with Rousseau, the individual becomes for better or for worse a slave to the state.

The second link between Rousseau and the reactions to the liberal tradition is Hegel. He was prevented by the Napoleonic Wars and the pressures of his financial position from living out his years in the academic profession. In 1818 he was called to the University of Berlin as the one man who was capable of assuming the chair in philosophy that Fichte had held. He remained at the University until his death in 1831. His major contributions were probably the universal form he gave to the dialectical method and his attempt to fuse the two worlds of experience and reality, which Kant had divided. He maintained that the way in which men achieve understanding is by means of the technique of the dialectic. They formulate a thesis about a problem, which is always partly true but also partly false. It remains, therefore, for them or for other individuals to offer another proposition which is also made up both of truth and half-truth. This antithesis must be combined with the original proposition or thesis to establish a new synthesis which can reconcile the two. But the synthesis, in turn, becomes a new thesis to be verified or falsified by comparing it with a new antithesis from which another synthesis can be derived.

The process goes on, presumably, indefinitely, but it was Hegel's assumption that each succeeding synthesis is closer to the point of final and absolute truth. History is the manifestation of Reason being realized and fulfilling itself by the dialectical unfolding of the absolute, or God's will. Reason is immanent in history and is engaged in realizing itself as the absolute principle. Man can participate in the onward march of this principle in history either unconscious of its purposes, or in true freedom when his reason has become identified with absolute Reason. God is Reason immanent in the world and coextensive with history, for history is not a revelation of God's will for mankind but *is* in fact God's will, which is a universal idea. The state is the incarnation of this

" world spirit " or the Absolute idea in process of unfolding. It is the embodiment of reason and social morality and only by submitting to it can the individual achieve his true freedom. At this point it is clear that Kant's emphasis on individual conscience would find no place in Hegel's philosophy. For the moral order is discovered not in man's moral will but in the dialectic of history and in its highest expression the state. Since the design and details of all history is predetermined by the dialectic, individuals have no personal responsibility for their actions. Hegelianism is a kind of pantheistic religion wherein the world spirit replaces God.

The concept of dialectic was taken over by Karl Marx (1818–1883). Marx was the son of a moderately prominent Jewish lawyer, who had become a convert to Protestant Christianity in 1826. As a student of philosophy at the Universities of Berlin and Jena he wrote a dissertation on " The Difference between the Natural Philosophy of Democritus and of Epicurus." At the University he was a member of the " young Hegelians " and acquired a full knowledge of Hegelian dialectics. Failing to obtain a teaching appointment, Marx embarked upon the career of a free-lance journalist, but the views he expressed in the democratic *Rheinische Zeitung* were too liberal for the Prussian authorities. He married the daughter of a Prussian aristocrat, moved to Paris, and there met a fellow-contributor to the *Deutsch-Franzosiche Jahrbücher*, a publication of German exiles, named Friedrich

Engels. Engels, the son and partner of a wealthy textile manufacturer with mills in both Germany and England, became Marx's collaborator and frequently provided the means for his financial support. In 1847 the two formed a Communist League in London and in 1848 prepared the statement of principles which became known as the *Communist Manifesto*. In 1867 Marx completed the first volume of *Capital*, the "bible" of Marxian thought. In addition to this major work and other important writings, Marx was a contributor to the *New York* (Herald) *Tribune* wherein he extended his views to international problems, most notably the problem of Germany.

In all structural aspects the Marxian dialectic is an honest replica of Hegel's system. Yet there are three radical differences in the meaning of this system. According to Marxism the essence of the world is not spiritual but material. Hegel, Marx said, had turned philosophy on its head. Marx was going to restore it to its true material foundations. But materialism for Marx was more than the claim that men are motivated by economic considerations. By "material" Marx meant certain objective material conditions, which shape a man's conduct regardless of his individual motivations. The capitalist, irrespective of motives, is forced to act in a particular way by the objective conditions of capitalist society. The modes of production of a particular society create by an inner logic a class that reflects them and that in turn is opposed by its opposite class. Thus a feudalist class finds in the bourgeois its antithesis, until through a new synthesis the bourgeois society emerges. The antagonism between the capitalist mode of production and a new proletariat class will evoke a new synthesis. But the socialist revolution will be decisive, for whereas in the past the revolutionary groups had never been more than minorities, the submerged and rising lower class in this case will constitute an actual majority. The purpose of this socialist revolt will be not to conquer but to smash the state. For once the majority have risen in revolt and the state is unable to serve as an instrument in the class struggle, it will "wither away." For the domination of men by men there will be substituted the "administration of things."

A second difference between Hegelian and Marxian dialectic lies in the immediacy of their respective goals. For Hegel, the fulfillment of the world spirit was conceived in remote and ultimate terms; for Marx the classless society and "withering away" of the state, and especially the multiplication of revolts against capitalism, were seen to be just around the corner. It is perhaps one of the most serious weaknesses of their position that Marxists were incautious enough to make prophesies that salvation was to be had in the immediate future. This prediction, which has furnished the basis for a "fighting faith," becomes the subject for important revisions. The "classless society" has been postponed until some indeterminate future. If contemporary Marxism has not been weakened by the need to revise its time schedule and even its concepts, it has at least shown that, as with all past political doctrines that promised to liberate men from political power here and now, it has been corrupted in practice into a doctrine of oppression which justifies itself in terms of a distant utopia.

The third difference between Hegel and Marx rests in Marxism's claim to be utterly scientific. Marx tried to show that past principles of economics were merely reflections of the class interests of the time. He attempted to prove, for example, that the truths that liberalism had proclaimed as eternal principles actually reflected the political and social situation of the middle class. Much that is worthwhile in contemporary social science has resulted from Marx's emphasis on the influence of the social and historic situation on the formulation of " laws " of social behavior. Marxian materialism has been responsible for an emphasis on a point about which Hegel had little to say. But more than that, Marxism could claim that there is

only one remedy which, by the inevitable dialectic of historical materialism, is bound to come about. Given its assumptions and its rationalization of periods in history and the relationship of ideas to the modes of production, Marxism provided a complete system for prediction and control. Yet in its pretenses to be entirely scientific, Marxist determinism falls victim to the accidents and contingencies of history. If Stalin had been killed in the Bolshevik Revolution, or if the German generals had destroyed Hitler in 1944, Western history might well have taken another turn. Yet Marxism as science is unable to grapple with the role of accidents or contingencies in history.

We have included the *Communist Manifesto* in order that readers may appraise it as a call to political action and test its accuracy and scientific quality as a reliable prediction of political events. The polemic of Mussolini (1883–1944) is an example of the claims and the charges of Fascism.

23. Manifesto of the Communist Party, Part I*

MANIFESTO OF THE COMMUNIST PARTY

A specter is haunting Europe — the specter of Communism. All the Powers of old Europe have entered into a holy alliance to exorcise this

* From Karl Marx, *Capital, The Communist Manifesto and other Writings,* ed. by Max Eastman (New York: The Modern Library, Inc., 1932), pp. 320–34.

specter; Pope and Czar, Metternich and Guizot, French Radicals and German police-spies.

Where is the party in opposition that has not been decried as communistic by its opponents in power? Where the Opposition that has not hurled back the branding reproach of Communism against the more advanced opposition parties, as well as against its reactionary adversaries?

Two things result from this fact.

I. Communism is already acknowledged by all European Powers to be itself a Power.

II. It is high time that Communists should openly, in the face of the whole world, publish their views, their aims, their tendencies, and meet this nursery tale of the specter of Communism with a Manifesto of the party itself.

To this end, Communists of various nationalities have assembled in London and sketched the following Manifesto, to be published in the English, French, German, Italian, Flemish and Danish languages.

I. BOURGEOIS AND PROLETARIANS [1]

The history of all hitherto existing society is the history of class struggles.

Freeman and slave, patrician and plebeian, lord and serf, guild-master and journeyman, in a word, oppressor and oppressed, stood in constant opposition to one another, carried on uninterrupted, now hidden, now open fight, a fight that each time ended, either in a revolutionary reconstitution of society at large, or in the common ruin of the contending classes.

In the earlier epochs of history we find almost everywhere a complicated arrangement of society into various orders, a manifold gradation of social rank. In ancient Rome we have patricians, knights, plebeians, slaves; in the middle ages feudal lords, vassals, guild-masters, journeymen, apprentices, serfs; in almost all of these classes, again, subordinate gradations.

The modern bourgeois society that has sprouted from the ruins of feudal society, has not done away with class antagonism. It has but established new classes, new conditions of oppression, new forms of struggle in place of the old ones.

Our epoch, the epoch of the bourgeoisie, possesses, however, this distinctive feature; it has simplified the class antagonisms. Society as a whole is more and more splitting up into two great hostile camps, into two great classes directly facing each other: Bourgeoisie and Proletariat.

From the serfs of the middle ages sprang the chartered burghers of the earliest towns. From these burgesses the first elements of the bourgeoisie were developed.

The discovery of America, the rounding of the Cape, opened up fresh ground for the rising bourgeoisie. The East Indian and Chinese markets, the colonization of America, trade with the colonies, the increase in the means of exchange and in commodities generally, gave to commerce, to navigation, to industry, an impulse never before known, and thereby, to the revolutionary element in the tottering feudal society, a rapid development.

The feudal system of industry, un-

[1] By bourgeoisie is meant the class of modern Capitalists, owners of the means of social production and employers of wage-labor. By proletariat, the class of modern wage laborers who, having no means of production of their own, are reduced to selling their labor-power in order to live. [Author's note.]

der which industrial production was monopolized by closed guilds, now no longer sufficed for the growing wants of the new market. The manufacturing system took its place. The guild-masters were pushed on one side by the manufacturing middle-class: division of labor between the different corporate guilds vanished in the face of division of labor in each single workshop.

Meantime the markets kept ever growing, the demand ever rising. Even manufacture no longer sufficed. Thereupon, steam and machinery revolutionized industrial production. The place of manufacture was taken by the giant, Modern Industry, the place of the industrial middle-class, by industrial millionaires, the leaders of whole industrial armies, the modern bourgeois.

Modern industry has established the world market, for which the discovery of America paved the way. This market has given an immense development to commerce, to navigation, to communication by land. This development has, in its turn, reacted on the extension of industry; and in proportion as industry, commerce, navigation, railways extended, in the same proportion the bourgeoisie developed, increased its capital, and pushed into the background every class handed down from the Middle Ages.

We see, therefore, how the modern bourgeoisie is itself the product of a long course of development, of a series of revolutions in the modes of production and of exchange.

Each step in the development of the bourgeoisie was accompanied by a corresponding political advance of that class. An oppressed class under the sway of the feudal nobility, an armed and self-governing association in the medieval commune, here independent urban republic (as in Italy and Germany), there taxable " third estate " of the monarchy (as in France), afterwards, in the period of manufacture proper, serving either the semi-feudal or the absolute monarchy as a counterpoise against nobility, and, in fact, cornerstone of the great monarchies in general, the bourgeoisie has at last, since the establishment of Modern Industry and of the world-market, conquered for itself, in the modern representative State, exclusive political sway. The executive of the modern State is but a committee for managing the common affairs of the whole bourgeoisie.

The bourgeoisie, historically, has played a most revolutionary part.

The bourgeoisie, wherever it has got the upper hand, has put an end to all feudal, patriarchal, idyllic relations. It has pitilessly torn asunder the motley feudal ties that bound man to his " natural superiors," and has left no other nexus between man and man than naked self-interest, than callous " cash payment." It has drowned the most heavenly ecstasies of religious fervor, of chivalrous enthusiasm, of Philistine sentimentalism, in the icy water of egotistical calculation. It has resolved personal worth into exchange value, and in place of the numberless indefeasible chartered freedom, has set up that single, unconscionable freedom — Free Trade. In one word, for exploitation, veiled by religious and political illusions, it has substituted naked, shameless, direct, brutal exploitation.

The bourgeoisie has stripped of its halo every occupation hitherto honored and looked up to with reverent awe. It has converted the physician, the lawyer, the priest, the poet, the man of science, into its paid wage laborers.

The bourgeoisie has torn away from the family its sentimental veil, and has reduced the family relation to a mere money relation.

The bourgeoisie has disclosed how it came to pass that the brutal display of vigor in the Middle Ages, which reactionists so much admire, found its fitting complement in the most slothful indolence. It has been the first to show what man's activity can bring about. It has accomplished wonders far surpassing Egyptian pyramids, Roman aqueducts and Gothic cathedrals; it has conducted expeditions that put in the shade all former Exoduses of nations and crusades.

The bourgeoisie cannot exist without constantly revolutionizing the instruments of production, and thereby the relations of production, and with them the whole relations of society. Conservation of the old modes of production in unaltered form was, on the contrary, the first condition of existence for all earlier industrial classes. Constant revolutionizing of production, uninterrupted disturbance of all social conditions, everlasting uncertainty and agitation distinguish the bourgeois epoch from all earlier ones. All fixed, fast frozen relations, with their train of ancient and venerable prejudices and opinions, are swept away, all new formed ones become antiquated before they can ossify. All that is solid melts into the air, all that is holy is profaned, and man is at last compelled to face with sober senses, his real conditions of life, and his relations with his kind.

The need of a constantly expanding market for its products chases the bourgeoisie over the whole surface of the globe. It must nestle everywhere, settle everywhere, establish connections everywhere.

The bourgeoisie has through its exploitation of the world-market given a cosmopolitan character to production and consumption in every country. To the great chagrin of reactionists, it has drawn from under the feet of industry the national ground on which it stood. All old-established national industries have been destroyed or are daily being destroyed. They are dislodged by new industries, whose introduction becomes a life and death question for all civilized nations, by industries that no longer work up indigenous raw material, but raw material drawn from the remotest zones; industries whose products are consumed, not only at home, but in every quarter of the globe. In place of the old wants, satisfied by the productions of the country, we find new wants, requiring for their satisfaction the products of distant lands and climes. In place of the old local and national seclusion and self-sufficiency, we have intercourse in every direction, universal interdependence of nations. And as in material, so also in intellectual production. The intellectual creations of individual nations become common property. National onesidedness and narrowmindedness become more and more impossible, and from the numerous national and local literatures there arises a world-literature.

The bourgeoisie, by the rapid improvement of all instruments of production, by the immensely facilitated means of communication, draws all, even the most barbarian nations into civilization. The cheap prices of its commodities are the heavy artillery with which it batters down all Chinese walls, with which it forces the barbarians' intensely obstinate hatred of foreigners to capitulate. It compels all nations, on pain of extinction, to adopt the bourgeois mode of production; it compels them to introduce what it calls civilization into their midst, i.e., to become bourgeois themselves. In a word, it creates a world after its own image.

The bourgeoisie has subjected the country to the rule of the towns. It has created enormous cities, has greatly increased the urban population as compared with the rural, and has thus rescued a considerable part of the population from the idiocy of rural life. Just as it has made the country dependent on the towns, so it has made barbarian and semibarbarian countries dependent on civilized ones, nations of peasants on nations of bourgeois, the East on the West.

The bourgeoisie keeps more and more doing away with the scattered state of the population, of the means of production, and of property. It has agglomerated population, centralized means of production, and has concentrated property in a few hands. The necessary consequence of this was political centralization. Independent, or but loosely connected provinces, with separate interests, laws, governments, and systems of taxation, became lumped together in one nation, with one government, one code of laws, one national class interest, one frontier and one customs tariff.

The bourgeoisie, during its rule of scarce one hundred years, has created more massive and more colossal productive forces than have all preceding generations together. Subjection of Nature's forces to man, machinery, application of chemistry to industry and agriculture, steam-navigation, railways, electric telegraphs, clearing of whole continents for cultivation, canalization of rivers, whole populations conjured out of the ground — what earlier century had even a presentiment that such productive forces slumbered in the lap of social labor?

We see then: the means of production and of exchange on whose foundation the bourgeoisie built itself up, were generated in feudal society. At a certain stage in the development of these means of production and of exchange, the conditions under which feudal society produced and exchanged, the feudal organization of agriculture and manufacturing industry, in one word, the feudal relations of property became no longer compatible with the already developed productive forces; they became so many fetters. They had to burst asunder; they were burst asunder.

Into their places stepped free competition, accompanied by social and political constitution adapted to it, and by economical and political sway of the bourgeois class.

A similar movement is going on before our own eyes. Modern bourgeois society with its relations of production, of exchange and of property, a society that has conjured up such gigantic means of production and of exchange, is like the sorcerer, who is no longer able to control the powers of the nether world whom he has called up by his spells. For many a decade past, the history of industry and commerce is but the history of the revolt of modern productive forces against modern conditions of production, against the property relations that are the conditions for the existence of the bourgeoisie and of its rule. It is enough to mention the commercial crises that by their periodical return put on its trial, each time more threateningly, the existence of the entire bourgeois society. In these crises a great part not only of the existing products, but also of the previously created productive forces, are periodically destroyed. In these crises there breaks out an epidemic that, in all earlier epochs, would have seemed an absurdity — the epidemic of overproduction. Society suddenly finds itself put back into a state of momentary barbarism; it appears as if a famine, a universal war of devastation, had cut off the supply of every means of subsistence; industry and commerce seem to be destroyed; and why? Because there is too much civilization, too much means of subsistence, too much industry, too much commerce. The productive forces at the disposal of society no longer tend to further the development of the conditions of the bourgeois property; on the contrary, they have become too powerful for these conditions by which they are fettered, and as soon as they overcome these fetters they bring disorder into the whole of bourgeois society, endanger the existence of bourgeois property. The conditions of bourgeois society are too narrow to comprise the wealth created by them. And how does the bourgeoisie get over these crises? On the one hand by enforced destruction of a mass of productive forces; on the other, by the conquest of new markets, and by the more thorough exploitation of the old ones. That is to say, by paving the way for more extensive and more destructive crises, and by diminishing the means whereby crises are prevented.

The weapons with which the bourgeoisie felled feudalism to the ground are now turned against the bourgeoisie itself.

But not only has the bourgeoisie forged the weapons that bring death to itself; it has also called into existence the men who are to wield those weapons — the modern working-class — the proletarians.

In proportion as the bourgeoisie, *i.e.,* capital, is developed, in the same proportion is the proletariat, the modern working-class, developed, a class of laborers who live only so long as they find work, and who find work only so long as their labor increases capital. These laborers, who must sell themselves piecemeal, are a commodity, like every other article of commerce, and are consequently exposed to all the vicissitudes of competition, to all the fluctuations of the market.

Owing to the extensive use of machinery and to division of labor, the work of the proletarians has lost all individual character, and, consequently, all charm for the workman. He becomes an appendage of the machine, and it is only the most simple, most monotonous and most easily acquired knack that is required of him. Hence, the cost of production of a workman is restricted almost entirely to the means of subsistence that he requires for his maintenance, and for the propagation of his race. But the price of a commodity, and also of labor, is equal to its cost of production. In proportion, therefore, as the repulsiveness of the work increases the wage decreases. Nay more, in proportion as the use of machinery and division of labor increases, in the same proportion the burden of toil increases, whether by prolongation of the working hours, by increase of the work enacted in a given time, or by increased speed of the machinery, etc.

Modern industry has converted the little workshop of the patriarchal master into the great factory of the industrial capitalist. Masses of laborers, crowded into factories, are organized like soldiers. As privates of the industrial army they are placed under the command of a perfect hierarchy of officers and sergeants.

Not only are they the slaves of the bourgeois class and of the bourgeois state, they are daily and hourly enslaved by the machine, by the overlooker, and, above all, by the individual bourgeois manufacturer himself. The more openly this despotism proclaims gain to be its end and aim, the more petty, the more hateful and the more embittering it is.

The less the skill and exertion or strength implied in manual labor, in other words, the more modern industry becomes developed, the more is the labor of men superseded by that of women. Differences of age and sex have no longer any distinctive social validity for the working class. All are instruments of labor, more or less expensive to use, according to their age and sex.

No sooner is the exploitation of the laborer by the manufacturer, so far at an end, that he receives his wages in cash, than he is set upon by the other portions of the bourgeoisie, the landlord, the shopkeeper, the pawnbroker, etc.

The lower strata of the middle class — the small tradespeople, shopkeepers and retired tradesmen generally, the handicraftsmen and peasants — all these sink gradually into the proletariat, partly because their diminutive capital does not suffice for the scale on which Modern Industry is carried on, and is swamped in the competition with the large capitalists, partly because their specialized skill is rendered worthless by new methods of production. Thus the proletariat is recruited from all classes of the population.

The proletariat goes through various stages of development. With its birth begins its struggle with the bourgeoisie. At first the contest is carried on by individual laborers, then by the workpeople of a factory, then by the operatives of one trade, in one locality, against the individual bourgeois who directly exploits them. They direct their attacks not against the bourgeois conditions of production, but against the instruments of production themselves; they destroy imported wares that compete with their labor, they smash to pieces machinery, they set factories ablaze, they seek to restore by force the vanished status of the workman of the Middle Ages.

At this stage the laborers still form an incoherent mass scattered over the whole country, and broken up by their mutual competition. If anywhere they unite to form more compact bodies, this is not yet the consequence of their own active union, but of the union of the bourgeoisie, which class, in order to attain its own political ends, is compelled to set the whole proletariat in motion, and is moreover yet, for a time, able to do so. At this stage, therefore the proletarians do not fight their enemies, but the enemies of their enemies, the remnants of absolute monarchy, the landowners, the non-industrial bourgeois, the petty bourgeoisie. Thus the whole historical movement is concentrated in the hands of the bourgeoisie, every victory so obtained is a victory for the bourgeoisie.

But with the development of industry the proletariat not only increases in number; it becomes concentrated in greater masses, its strength grows and it feels that strength more. The various interests and conditions of life within the ranks of the proletariat are more and more equalized, in proportion as machinery obliterates all distinctions of labor, and nearly everywhere reduces wages to the same low level. The growing competition among the bourgeois, and the resulting commercial crisis, make the wages of the workers even more fluctuating. The unceasing improvement of machinery, ever more rapidly developing, makes their livelihood more and more precarious; the collisions between individual workmen and individual bourgeois take more and more the character of collisions between two classes. Thereupon the workers begin to form combinations (Trades' Unions) against the bourgeois; they club together in order to keep up the rate of wages; they found permanent associations in order to make provision beforehand for these occasional revolts. Here and there the contest breaks out into riots.

Now and then the workers are victorious, but only for a time. The real fruit of their battle lies not in the immediate result but in the ever-expanding union of workers. This union is helped on by the improved means of communication that are created by modern industry, and that places the workers of different localities in contact with one another. It was just this contact that was needed to centralize the numerous local struggles, all of the same character, into one national struggle between classes. But every class struggle is a political struggle. And that union, to attain which the burghers of the Middle Ages with their miserable highways, required centuries, the modern proletarians, thanks to railways, achieve in a few years.

This organization of the proletarians into a class, and consequently into a political party, is continually being upset again by the competition between the workers themselves. But it ever rises up again, stronger, firmer, mightier. It compels legislative recognition of particular interests of the workers by taking advantage of the divisions among the bourgeoisie itself. Thus the ten hours' bill in England was carried.

Altogether collisions between the classes of the old society further, in many ways, the course of development of the proletariat. The bourgeoisie finds itself involved in a constant battle. At first with the aristocracy; later on, with those portions of the bourgeoisie itself whose interests have become antagonistic to the progress of industry; at all times, with the bourgeoisie of foreign countries. In all these battles it sees itself compelled to appeal to the proletariat, to ask for its help, and thus, to drag it into the political arena. The bourgeoisie itself, therefore, supplies the proletariat with its own elements of political and general education; in other words, it furnishes the proletariat with weapons for fighting the bourgeoisie.

Further, as we have already seen, entire sections of the ruling classes are, by the advance of industry, precipitated into the proletariat, or are at least threatened in their condi- tions of existence. These also supply the proletariat with fresh elements of enlightenment and progress.

Finally, in times when the class-struggle nears the decisive hour, the process of dissolution going on within the ruling class — in fact, within the whole range of an old society — assumes such a violent, glaring character that a small section of the ruling class cuts itself adrift and joins the revolutionary class, the class that holds the future in its hands. Just as, therefore, at an earlier period, a section of the nobility went over to the bourgeoisie, so now a portion of the bourgeoisie goes over to the proletariat, and in particular, a portion of the bourgeois ideologists, who have raised themselves to the level of comprehending theoretically the historical movements as a whole.

Of all the classes that stand face to face with the bourgeoisie today the proletariat alone is a really revolutionary class. The other classes decay and finally disappear in the face of modern industry; the proletariat is its special and essential product.

The lower middle class, the small manufacturer, the shopkeeper, the artisan, the peasant, all these fight against the bourgeoisie, to save from extinction their existence as fractions of the middle class. They are therefore not revolutionary, but conservative. Nay, more; they are reactionary, for they try to roll back the wheel of history. If by chance they are revolutionary, they are so only in view of their impending transfer into the proletariat; they thus defend not their present, but their future interests; they desert their own standpoint to place themselves at that of of the proletariat.

The "dangerous class," the social scum, that passively rotting mass thrown off by the lowest layers of old society, may, here and there, be swept into the movement by a proletarian revolution; its conditions of life, however, prepare it far more for the part of a bribed tool of reactionary intrigue.

In the conditions of the proletariat, those of the old society at large are already virtually swamped. The proletarian is without property; his relation to his wife and children has no longer anything in common with the bourgeois family relations; modern industrial labor, modern subjection to capital, the same in England as in France, in America as in Germany, has stripped him of every trace of national character. Law, morality, religion, are to him so many bourgeois prejudices, behind which lurk in ambush just as many bourgeois interests.

All the preceding classes that got the upper hand sought to fortify their already acquired status by subjecting society at large to their conditions of appropriation. The proletarians cannot become masters of the productive forces of society, except by abolishing their own previous mode of appropriation, and thereby also every other previous mode of appropriation. They have nothing of their own to secure and to fortify; their mission is to destroy all previous securities for and insurances of individual property.

All previous historical movements were movements of minorities, or in the interest of minorities. The proletarian movement is the self-conscious, independent movement of the immense majority. The proletariat, the lowest stratum of our present society, cannot stir, cannot raise itself up without the whole superincumbent strata of official society being sprung into the air.

Though not in substance, yet in form, the struggle of the proletariat with the bourgeoisie is at first a national struggle. The proletariat of each country must, of course, first of all settle matters with its own bourgeoisie.

In depicting the most general phases of the development of the proletariat, we traced the more or less veiled civil war, raging within existing society, up to the point where that war breaks out into open revolution, and where the violent overthrow of the bourgeoisie, lays the foundations for the sway of the proletariat.

Hitherto every form of society has been based, as we have already seen, on the antagonism of oppressing and oppressed classes. But in order to oppress a class, certain conditions must be assured to it under which it can, at least continue its slavish existence. The serf, in the period of serfdom, raised himself to membership in the commune, just as the petty bourgeois, under the yoke of feudal absolutism, managed to develop into a bourgeois. The modern laborer, on the contrary, instead of rising with the progress of industry, sinks deeper and deeper below the conditions of existence of his own class. He becomes a pauper, and pauperism develops more rapidly than population and wealth. And here it becomes evident that the bourgeoisie is unfit any longer to be the ruling class in society, and to impose its conditions of existence upon society as an over-riding law. It is unfit to rule, because it is incompetent to assure an existence to its slave within his slavery, because it cannot help letting him sink into such a state that it has to feed him, instead of being fed by him. Society can no longer live under this bourgeoisie; in other words, its existence is no longer compatible with society.

The essential condition for the existence, and for the sway of the bourgeois class, is the formation and augmentation of capital; the condition for capital is wage labor. Wage labor rests exclusively on competition between the laborers. The advance of industry, whose involuntary promoter is the bourgeoisie, replaces the isolation of the laborers, due to competition, by their involuntary combination, due to association. The development of Modern Industry, therefore, cuts from under its feet the very foundation on which the bourgeoisie produces and appropriates products. What the bourgeoisie therefore produces, above all, are its own grave diggers. Its fall and the victory of the proletariat are equally inevitable.

24. The Doctrine of Fascism *

Fascism combats the whole complex system of democratic ideology, and repudiates it, whether in its theoretical premises or in its practical application. Fascism denies that the majority, by the simple fact that it is a majority, can direct human society; it denies that numbers alone can govern by means of a periodical consultation, and it affirms the immutable, beneficial, and fruitful inequality of mankind, which can never be permanently leveled through the mere operation of a mechanical proc-

ess such as universal suffrage. The democratic régime may be defined as from time to time giving the people the illusion of sovereignty, while the real effective sovereignty lies in the hands of other concealed and irresponsible forces. Democracy is a régime nominally without a king, but it is ruled by many kings — more absolute, tyrannical, and ruinous than one sole king, even though a tyrant. This explains why Fascism, having first in 1922 (for reasons of expediency) assumed an attitude tending towards republicanism, renounced this point of view before the march to Rome, being convinced that the question of political form is not today of prime importance, and

* From Benito Mussolini, *The Political and Social Doctrine of Fascism* (translation by Jane Soames), pp. 14–19, 21–24, 11–13, and 25–26. Reprinted by permission of The Hogarth Press.

after having studied the examples of monarchies and republics past and present reached the conclusion that monarchy or republicanism are not to be judged, as it were, by an absolute standard; but that they represent forms in which the evolution — political, historical, traditional, or psychological — of a particular country has expressed itself. Fascism supersedes the antithesis monarchy or republicanism, while democracy still tarries beneath the domination of this idea, forever pointing out the insufficiency of the first and forever the praising of the second as the perfect régime. Today, it can be seen that there are republics innately reactionary and absolutist, and also monarchies which incorporate the most ardent social and political hopes of the future.

"Reason and science," says Renan (one of the inspired pre-Fascists) in his philosophical meditations, "are products of humanity, but to expect reason as a direct product of the people and a direct result of their action is to deceive oneself by a chimera. It is not necessary for the existence of reason that everybody should understand it. And in any case, if such a decimation of truth were necessary, it could not be achieved in a low-class democracy, which seems as though it must of its very nature extinguish any kind of noble training. The principle that society exists solely through the well-being and the personal liberty of all the individuals of which it is composed does not appear to be conformable to the plans of nature, in whose workings the race alone seems to be taken into consideration, and the individual sacrificed to it. It is greatly to be feared that the last stage of such a conception of democracy (though I must hasten to point out that the term 'democracy' may be interpreted in various ways) would end in a condition of society in which a degenerate herd would have no other preoccupation but the satisfaction of the lowest desires of common men." Thus Renan. Fascism denies, in democracy, the absurd conventional untruth of political equality dressed out in the garb of collective irresponsibility, and the myth of "happiness" and indefinite progress. But, if democracy may be conceived in diverse forms — that is to say, taking democracy to mean a state of society in which the populace are not reduced to impotence in the State — Fascism may write itself down as "an organized, centralized, and authoritative democracy."

Fascism has taken up an attitude of complete opposition to the doctrines of Liberalism, both in the political field and the field of economics. There should be no undue exaggeration (simply with the object of immediate success in controversy) of the importance of Liberalism in the last century, nor should what was but one among many theories which appeared in that period be put forward as a religion for humanity for all time, present and to come. Liberalism only flourished for half a century. It was born in 1830 in reaction against the Holy Alliance, which had been formed with the object of diverting the destinies of Europe back to the period before 1789, and the highest point of its success was the year 1848, when even Pius IX was a Liberal. Immediately after that date it began to decay, for if the year 1848 was a year of light and hope, the following year, 1849, was a year of darkness and tragedy. The Republic of Rome was dealt a mortal blow by a sister republic — that of France — and in the same year Marx launched the gospel of Socialist religion, the famous Communist Manifesto. In 1851 Napoleon III carried out his far from Liberal *coup d'état* and reigned in France until 1870, when he was deposed by a popular movement as the consequence of a military defeat which must be counted as one of the most decisive in history. The victor was Bismarck, who knew nothing of the religion of liberty, or the prophets by which that faith was revealed. And it is symptomatic that such a highly civilized people as the Germans were completely ignorant of the religion of liberty during the whole of the nineteenth century. It was nothing but a parenthesis, represented by that body which has been called " The ridiculous Parliament of Frankfort," which lasted only for a short period. Germany attained her national unity quite outside the doctrines of Liberalism — a doctrine which seems entirely foreign to the German mind, a mind essentially monarchic — while Liberalism is the logical and, indeed, historical forerunner of anarchy. The stages in the achievement of German unity are the three wars of '64, '66, and '70, which were guided by such " Liberals " as Von Moltke and Bismarck. As for Italian unity,

its debt to Liberalism is completely inferior in contrast to that which it owes to the work of Mazzini and Garibaldi, who were not Liberals. Had it not been for the intervention of the anti-Liberal Napoleon, we should not have gained Lombardy; and without the help of the again anti-Liberal Bismarck at Sadowa and Sedan it is very probable that we should never have gained the province of Venice in '66, or been able to enter Rome in '70. From 1870 to 1914 a period began during which even the very high priests of the religion themselves had to recognize the gathering twilight of their faith — defeated as it was by the decadence of literature and atavism in practice — that is to say, Nationalism, Futurism, Fascism. The era of Liberalism, after having accumulated an infinity of Gordian knots, tried to untie them in the slaughter of the World War — and never has any religion demanded of votaries such a monstrous sacrifice. Perhaps the Liberal Gods were athirst for blood? But now, today, the Liberal faith must shut the doors of its deserted temples, deserted because the peoples of the world realize that its worship — agnostic in the field of economics and indifferent in the field of politics and morals — will lead, as it has already led, to certain ruin. In addition to this, let it be pointed out that all the political hopes of the present day are anti-Liberal, and it is therefore supremely ridiculous to try to classify this sole creed as outside the judgment of history, as though history were a hunting ground reserved for the professors of Liberalism — as though Liberalism were the final unalterable verdict of civilization. . . .

The foundation of Fascism is the conception of the State, its character, its duty, and its aim. Fascism conceives of the State as an absolute, in comparison with which all individuals or groups are relative, only to be conceived of in their relation to the State. The conception of the Liberal State is not that of a directing force, guiding the play and development, both material and spiritual, of a collective body, but merely a force limited to the function of recording results; on the other hand, the Fascist State is itself conscious, and has itself a will and a personality — thus it may be called the " ethic " State. In 1929, at the first five-yearly assembly of the Fascist régime, I said: " For us Fascists, the State is not merely a guardian, preoccupied solely with the duty of assuring the personal safety of the citizens; nor is it an organization with purely material aims, such as to guarantee a certain level of well-being and peaceful conditions of life; for a mere council of administration would be sufficient to realize such objects. Nor is it a purely political creation, divorced from all contact with the complex material reality which makes up the life of the individual and the life of the people as a whole. The State, as conceived of and as created by Fascism, is a spiritual and moral fact in itself, since its political, juridical, and economic organization of the nation is a concrete thing: and such an organization must be in its origins and development a manifestation of the spirit. The State is the guarantor of security both internal and external, but it is also the custodian and transmitter of the spirit of the people, as it has grown up through the centuries in language, in custom, and in faith. And the State is not only a living reality of the present, it is also linked with the past and above all with the future, and thus transcending the brief limits of individual life, it represents the immanent spirit of the nation. The forms in which States express themselves may change, but the necessity for such forms is eternal. It is the State which educates its citizens in civic virtue, gives them a consciousness of their mission and welds them into unity; harmonizing their various interests through justice, and transmitting to future generations the mental conquests of science, or art, of law and the solidarity of humanity. It leads men from primitive tribal life to that highest expression of human power which is Empire: it links up through the centuries the names of those of its members who have died for its existence and to obedience to its laws, it holds up the memory of the leaders who have increased its territory and the geniuses who have illumined it with glory as an example to be followed by future generations. When the conception of the State declines, and disunifying and centrifugal tendencies prevail, whether of individuals or of particular groups, the nations where such phenomena appear are in their decline."

From 1929 until today, evolution,

both political and economic, has everywhere gone to prove the validity of these doctrinal promises. Of such gigantic importance is the State. It is the force which alone can provide a solution to the dramatic contradictions of capitalism, and that state of affairs which we call the shade of Jules Simon, who in the dawn of Liberalism proclaimed that, "The State must labor to make itself unnecessary, and prepare the way for its own dismissal." Or of McCulloch, who, in the second half of the last century, affirmed that the State must guard against the danger of governing too much? What would the Englishman, Bentham, say today to the continual and inevitably invoked intervention of the State in the sphere of economics, while according to his theories industry should ask no more of the State than to be left in peace? Or the German, Humboldt, according to whom the "lazy" State should be considered the best? It is true that the second wave of Liberal economists were less extreme than the first, and Adam Smith himself opened the door — if only very cautiously — which leads to State intervention in the economic field: but whoever says Liberalism implies individualism, and whoever says Fascism implies the State. Yet the Fascist State is unique, and an original creation. It is not reactionary, but revolutionary, in that it anticipates the solution of the universal political problems which elsewhere have to be settled in the political field by the rivalry of parties, the excessive power of the parliamentary régime and the irresponsibility of political assemblies; while it meets the problems of the economic field by a system of syndicalism which is continually increasing in importance, as much in the sphere of labor as of industry: and in the moral field enforces order, discipline, and obedience to that which is the determined moral code of the country. Fascism desires the State to be a strong and organic body, at the same time reposing upon broad and popular support. The Fascist State has drawn into itself even the economic activities of the nation, and, through the corporative social and educational institutions created by it, its influence reaches every aspect of the national life and includes, framed in their respective organizations, all the political, economic and spiritual forces of the nation. A State which reposes upon the support of millions of individuals who recognize its authority, are continually conscious of its power and are ready at once to serve it, is not the old tyrannical State of the medieval lord nor has it anything in common with the absolute governments either before or after 1789. The individual in the Fascist State is not annulled but rather multiplied, just in the same way that a soldier in a regiment is not diminished but rather increased by the number of his comrades. The Fascist State organizes the nation, but leaves a sufficient margin of liberty to the individual; the latter is deprived of all useless and possibly harmful freedom, but retains what is essential; the deciding power in this question cannot be the individual, but the State alone.

And above all, Fascism, the more it considers and observes the future and the development of humanity quite apart from political considerations of the moment, believes neither in the possibility nor the utility of perpetual peace. It thus repudiates the doctrine of Pacifism — born of a renunciation of the struggle and an act of cowardice in the face of sacrifice. War alone brings up to its highest tension all human energy and puts the stamp of nobility upon the peoples who have the courage to meet it. All other trials are substitutes, which never really put men into the position where they have to make the great decision — the alternative of life or death. Thus a doctrine which is founded upon this harmful postulate of peace is hostile to Fascism. And thus hostile to the spirit of Fascism, though accepted for what use they can be in dealing with particular political situations, are all the international leagues and societies which, as history will show, can be scattered to the winds when once strong national feeling is aroused by any motive — sentimental, ideal, or practical. This anti-Pacifist spirit is carried by Fascism even into the life of the individual; the proud motto of the *Squadrista,* " Me ne Frego," written on the bandage of the wound, is an act of philosophy not only stoic, the summary of a doctrine not only political — it is the education to combat, the acceptance of the risks which combat implies, and a new way of life for Italy. Thus the Fascist accepts life and loves it, knowing nothing of and despising suicide: he rather conceives of life as duty and struggle and conquest, life which should be high and full, lived for oneself, but above all for others — those who are at hand and those who are far distant, contemporaries, and those who will come after.

The " demographic " policy of the régime is the result of the above premise. Thus the Fascist loves in actual fact his neighbor, but this " neighbor " is not merely a vague and undefined concept, this love for one's neighbor puts no obstacle in the way of necessary educational severity, and still less to differentiation of status and to physical distance. Fascism repudiates any universal embrace, and in order to live worthily in the community of civilized peoples watches its contemporaries with vigilant eyes, takes good note of their state of mind and, in the changing trend of their interests, does not allow itself to be deceived by temporary and fallacious appearances.

The Fascist State is an embodied will to power and government: the Roman tradition is here an ideal of force in action. According to Fascism, government is not so much a thing to be expressed in territorial or military terms as in terms of morality and the spirit. It must be thought of as an Empire — that is to say, a nation which directly or indirectly rules other nations, without the need for conquering a single square yard of territory. For Fascism, the growth of empire, that is to say the expansion of the nation, is an essential manifestation of vitality, and its opposite a sign of decadence. Peoples which are rising, or rising again after a period of decadence, are always imperialist; any renunciation is a sign of decay and of death. Fascism is the doctrine best adapted to represent the tendencies and the aspirations of a people, like the people of Italy, who are rising again after many centuries of abasement and foreign servitude. But Empire demands discipline, the coordination of all forces and a deeply felt sense of duty and sacrifice: this fact explains many aspects of the practical working of the régime, the character of many forces in the State, and the necessarily severe measures which must be taken against those who would oppose this spontaneous and inevitable movement of Italy in the twentieth century, and would oppose it by recalling the outworn ideology of the nineteenth century — repudiated wheresoever there has been the courage to undertake great experiments of social and political transformation; for never before has the nation stood more in need of authority, of direction and of order. If every age has its own characteristic doctrine, there are a thousand signs which point to Fascism as the characteristic doctrine of our time. For if a doctrine must be a living thing, this is proved by the fact that Fascism has created a living faith; and that this faith is very powerful in the minds of men, is demonstrated by those who have suffered and died for it.

Fascism has henceforth in the world the universality of all those doctrines which, in realizing themselves, have represented a stage in the history of the human spirit.

E. The New Liberalism and the Democratic Dilemma

25. Introduction

The basic unsolved problem with which modern liberal democratic thought has been faced is how it can salvage certain objective political standards while at the same time widening the range and the number of participants in the processes of political choice. The concept of an immanent criterion for political action has seemed to invite totalitarianism. Democracy has been faced with the challenge of producing a balance-wheel for freedom by creating a new sense of political responsibility. Most liberal democratic states have hastened to grant to all the electorate rights and privileges, only to find that these rights could survive only if they marched hand-in-hand with duties and responsibilities. In order to meet the tasks of a new era, moreover, democracies have been forced to revise their beliefs about the state as a night watchman. If the state had been constrained to do nothing beyond what had been proposed by the interests of the rising middle class in the seventeenth century, fascism and Marxism would in the twentieth century have undermined and destroyed its social foundations. Instead, democracies proved they could adapt. Finally, democracy has been required to resolve the dilemma of majority rule and minority rights. It has succeeded in this when some objective standard has been reintroduced, as has been true of the " Higher Law " in the American Constitutional System. The Supreme Court has stood watch over violations of these standards and possesses the power to invalidate a law passed by a majority in Congress which puts in jeopardy the constitutional rights of a minority. This power when abused, as we shall see, can become the power to perpetuate minority rule.

Herbert McClosky is Professor of Political Science at the University of Minnesota. We should observe that an answer to his essay " The Fallacy of Absolute Majority Rule " appeared in the succeeding volume of the *Journal of Politics* bearing the title " Prologemma to Majority Rule." The author was Professor Willmore Kendall of Yale. This exchange between Professors McClosky and Kendall is an example of the controversy going on between the so-called absolute and limited majoritarians.

26. On Majority Rule*

I

Perhaps no development of modern times has created so serious a dilemma for the theory and practice of democratic government as the rise of the totalitarian mass party. This type of party is distinguished by the fact that, while it is eager to exploit the opportunities afforded by the democratic process for persuasion and vote-seeking, it is nevertheless dedicated to a set of goals which, if attained, would destroy that process.

* From Herbert McClosky, " The Fallacy of Absolute Majority Rule," *The Journal of Politics,* Vol. XI (August, 1949), pp. 637–654. Reprinted by permission of Herbert McClosky and *The Journal of Politics.*

The dilemma now presents itself on at least two levels: *First,* is a democratic system obligated to make available the channels of participation even to parties whose undeniable objective is the destruction of the democratic process? And *second,* are democrats obligated to recognize as legitimate a government controlled by a totalitarian mass party that has succeeded in attaining office by clear majority vote? This paper will deal with the second of these questions, although it is recognized that the questions are closely related and that an analysis of one of them will necessarily have bearing upon the other.

The problem of the obligations required by the principle of majority rule will arise in coming European elections as it has already arisen in the recent Italian elections where, for a time, it appeared that the Communists might gain a majority of the votes cast. In the face of that possibility, western democratic opinion exhibited a confusion that disclosed, as the textbooks have never succeeded in doing, the profound uncertainty that attends the understanding of the majority principle. For, underlying the fear that the Communists might win the election was a tentative yet disturbing belief that the commitment to majority rule might compel democrats, both inside and outside of Italy, to recognize as a government-by-right even the dictatorship that the Communists would most certainly have established. Implicitly, those who held this belief were subscribing to a theory of political obligation — best designated perhaps as the theory of absolute majority rule — that is not without support in the literature of political theory. Essentially, this theory maintains (a) that a majority is, in a democracy, the highest authority, and its vote must therefore be final and absolutely binding; (b) that being the highest authority, no limits can logically be placed upon its power; and (c) that democracy and majority rule are, therefore, one and the same thing.

It is the burden of this paper to analyze the principle of majority rule and to demonstrate that a view of the majority principle which conceives the power of a majority as absolute is untenable on the ground that it does violence both to democracy and to logic. By way of attaining this, it will be necessary to examine the case for majority rule, to suggest the limitations that need to be imposed upon it, and to advance the empirical as well as the formal theoretical considerations which lead to a rejection of majority power conceived as absolute.

II

The principle of majority rule derives its status as an essential corollary of democratic theory from its association with the doctrine of popular sovereignty. The belief that the governed must be able to choose and to bring to account those who exercise authority has been characteristic of democratic thought throughout its modern history. Since every man, says Locke, is naturally free, nothing is "able to put him into subjection to any earthly power, but only his own consent. . . ." — an opinion, the latter part of which, at least, has been reiterated by almost every democratic thinker from Locke's days to ours. The doctrine of popular sovereignty, is, under democracy, made operationally meaningful through the implementation of the principle of consent and its twin principle, accountability. Consent and accountability are, in turn, made practicable through the implementation of the principle of majority rule.

The case for majority rule as a technique to make possible the accountability of rulers rests, first of all, on a set of postulates that have been implicit in virtually all theories of democracy. The *first* of these postulates is that man is either an end unto himself, or exists for purposes designed by God, but that in either case political and social arrangements exist to serve him, and not the reverse. The *second* is, that since, in civil affairs, each man must be regarded as an end, all men must therefore be accounted, for political and legal purposes, as equal. From this, a *third* postulate derives, namely, that all men being accounted as equal, the opinion (i.e., the vote) of each must, regarding his governance, be equal with that of every other man. *Fourth,* since every man is an end in himself, and the equal of every other man, those who govern him must do so as his agents — must do so, that is, with his consent — which requires, of course, that he can choose and remove them. *Finally,* if governance must rest on the principle of agency, and each man's vote regarding his governance must be accorded equal weight with that of every other man, the agent attaining the greatest number of votes cast shall be considered the popular choice and empowered either to make or enforce laws binding upon the entire citizenry. Fifty-plus-one must, then, take precedence over forty-nine, since this postulate assumes that the larger of these figures is, at the moment, the best possible approximation of the popular temper.

Over and above this set of postulates — largely *a priori* in character — a number of empirical judgments may be adduced in behalf of majority rule. It can, first of all, be pointed out that accountability is possible only where the rulers are chosen by the governed, for there is no effective way of implementing responsibility except choice. Where the exercise of power is sanctioned by birth, class, property, co-optation, force or any other principle except popular choice, the governed are, in effect, not consulted, and accountability is largely precluded.

Now, it is clear that the exercise of choice, where each participant is regarded as equal, requires — by virtue of arithmetic necessity — that either a majority or a minority shall prevail, unless, of course, unanimity is wanted. Where, however, unanimity is abandoned as unlikely or impossible of attainment, either *more* than half the equal members or *less* than half must be taken as potentially capable of settling the outcome of a given election. If the outcome is to be decided by less-than-half, one is presented with the difficulty that no grounds can be consistently established — where, for example, several minorities compete — by which one minority can claim to take precedence over another. If it is a minority that is to decide, then all minorities have an equal claim. Hence, " minority rule " effectively precludes choice and renders accountability impossible.

Moreover, it is obvious that minority determination is inconsistent with the postulates we have indicated as inherent in all democratic systems. We said that each member of democratic polity must be accounted as equal. Yet, to give to a minority final competence is to give special significance to its members, i.e., to treat its members not as equals of other men, but as their superiors. Similarly, the opinions they hold and the votes they cast are weighted differently from those of other men. Where, in addition, power resides finally in a minority, the authorization of government must rest not on consent, but on some arbitrary category of qualities enjoyed by that minority, like property or caste. Any minority that presumes to claim final power must, in effect, be self-appointed. For if it is not self-appointed, it is chosen; if it is chosen, it must be responsible to a majority; and if it is responsible to a majority it cannot presume to claim final power.

The empirical argument against lodging final power in a minority has, from the point of view of democratic values, still other aspects. Governments that are self-appointed or accountable to a privileged minority exhibit characteristic traits of behavior that contravene, in their results, the purposes to which democracy is dedicated. Such governments are, for example, invariably self-perpetuating and oligarchical, and hence callous to the needs and wishes of the governed. Since they cannot but be founded on privilege, it is privilege that they will generally serve. Such governments are likely, also, to read the interests of the governed in the image of their own special interests, accounting what is good for themselves as necessarily good for the rest of men. They will, as a rule, be unable, even with the best will in the world, to ascertain and weigh properly the true needs and wants of the governed, since, being oligarchi-

cal, they cannot permit the free expression of popular opinion, and, being privileged, they cannot successfully identify with those who are without privilege. The tendency of minority power is, moreover, generally suppressive and often tyrannical. That it will also be biased in favor of those upon whose sanction its power rests is sufficiently attested to by the history of such governments. It becomes clear, then, that minority rule is, so far as democratic values are concerned, quite unacceptable. And given the dichotomy indicated above, a democracy becomes inconceivable without the presence of the majority rule principle.

These arguments, more or less clearly articulated and understood, have provided grounds for the belief in majority rule and have helped, thereby, to bring western democrats to the state of anxiety they exhibited in the face of a possible Communist majority in Italy. That they should have this effect is understandable, for they are important questions of how the majority rule principle must be interpreted, and what limitations, if any, this principle allows us to place upon a majority or its government.

III

It may seem from the foregoing that, by positing a necessitous choice between majority and minority rule, and in rejecting the latter, the case for the absolute power of the majority has been conceded. This conclusion would, however, be unwarranted, for it remains now to define the majority principle and to determine whether or not the power of a majority must, under this principle, be qualified both in theory and practice.

The theoretical argument against a definition of the majority principle which grants unlimited power to the majority rests, to begin with, on the simple fact that it gives to a majority, or its government, the power to dispose of the rules that have given the majority its legitimate power in the first place. The legitimate power of a majority to rule in a democracy derives ultimately, as we have seen, from the necessity for establishing some procedure by which the will of the community may be assumed to be most closely approximated. Such a procedure obviously demands the elaboration of a set of rules, in order that the determination of what is assumed to be the proximate community will shall rest not on caprice but on an arrangement known and agreed to by all. The most important of these rules, and in fact the one under which all the other rules may be subsumed, is the rule that the majority must be *freely-arrived-at,* i.e., the opportunity must be kept open for individuals to form themselves, for legal purposes, into majorities, and *ipso facto,* into minorities. Where this opportunity is destroyed, the majority principle is itself destroyed.

What are some of the other rules that may be subsumed under the rule that majorities must be freely-arrived-at? In general, they are the rules that embody the political rights traditionally associated with democratic thought and practice. In order for individuals freely to form themselves into majorities and/or minorities, they must, for example, be free to speak and publish and criticize, to assemble and to associate. Where representative government is involved — as it invariably is in modern democracies — the rules require that they shall be free to choose and remove their rulers, and this presupposes, among other things, that they shall be free to cast their lot with the " government " or the opposition, to form parties, to choose among candidates and parties, to participate, in short, in free elections.

It is in such terms that the majority principle must be defined, for only if opportunity exists for majorities freely to determine their governance (and, hence, to dispose freely of a given government and replace it with another) can the principle of majority rule be made consistent with itself, as well as with democracy. It cannot be defined consistently if it grants to any majority the legitimate power to prevent the realization of new majorities, or if it grants to a government, elected by a majority, the power to forbid even that same majority from holding accountable the agents it has elected. There can be nothing in the majority principle that requires that a majority should have the power to destroy it, for it is the very nature of a principle that it prohibits its own negation. Moreover, such power as a majority enjoys derives precisely from the majority principle, and when that principle ceases to prevail, the legitimate power of the majority must cease also. On logical grounds alone, then, it becomes apparent that a majority, deriving its sanction from the principle of majority rule, is limited by that principle to the extent, at least, that it cannot abrogate the rules which authorize the power it can properly exercise.

It is not difficult to demonstrate, either, that the principle of majority rule can be made consistent with *democracy* only if it is defined as setting certain limits upon the majority. In the first place, to interpret the majority principle as requiring the unlimited authority of a majority is to preclude the possibility of limited government and to insist, in effect, that not only are there no proper limitations on political power, but that those who hold power may, if they like, prohibit recourse against its exercise. We need hardly be reminded that modern democracy *began* as a protest against unlimited authority and the power of absolute rulers excluded from the political process those whom they marked as dissidents. If, by virtue of its majority support, a government can legitimately prohibit the formation of an opposition, and forbid those who disagree to speak and publish, it can hardly be claimed that a democracy exists. Otherwise we should have had to account Nazi Germany a democracy if, instead of receiving thirty-three percent of the votes, the Nazis had attained, in 1932, fifty-one percent. This is, of course preposterous, just as it would be absurd to maintain that Soviet Russia or Fascist Italy are examples of (1) ma-

jority rule systems, and (2) democracies, because their governments attained huge majorities in popular elections. What makes spurious the claim of a modern totalitarian dictatorship to call itself democratic is largely the fact that it denies the majority principle as we have defined it. For if we define it as setting *no* limits upon the majority, we are compelled to admit that a dictatorial regime receiving majority support — either at its inception or subsequently — is in fact a majority rule system, and hence, presumably, a democracy. A definition of the majority principle that makes it possible to include within the category of majority rule systems the divergent governments of England and Russia, or Sweden and Argentina — that cannot, in short, distinguish a dictatorship from a democracy — is not only inadequate but self-evidently absurd.

The argument with which we are concerned here is in some ways like the argument that democrats have traditionally had with political thinkers of the Hobbesian school. It will be recalled that, for Hobbes, consent, once granted, became irrevocable, binding future generations for eternity, despite even the exercise of tyranny by the Sovereign. The Sovereign, once elected, was free to define or limit, however he pleased, the rights and duties of the citizenry. The original grant of consent was taken by Hobbes to justify the unqualified power of the Sovereign; nothing could require him to make available to the governed the opportunity to deliver themselves from his power. Against this, democrats have always insisted that consent is, by its very nature, revocable; that it must be periodically renewed; that a grant made by the father cannot bind the sons; that, in effect, the power of government must be limited at least by the requirement that the right to withdraw or renew consent cannot be annulled.

Were we to cast our argument in the language of the social compact school, we would contend that, under the principle of majority rule, the denial by a majority or its government of the basic political liberties that make consent possible is a violation of the compact and destroys the polity. The majority cannot, like Hobbes' Sovereign, violate the compact (i.e., the rules) that gives justification to its power. The " compact " implicit in every democratic system is that the majority shall prevail *providing it observes the rules which gave it, initially, the right to govern.* This is clearly recognized by Locke (as well as by other compact theorists) who, though he says at one point that " every man, by consenting with others to make one body politic under one government, puts himself under an obligation to every one of that society to submit to the determination of the majority, and to be concluded by it," nevertheless makes clear that consent must be ever renewed, which presupposes, of course, freedom. Moreover, for Locke, civil society is conceived as a means of protecting certain rights that are difficult to defend in the state of nature. Notice, too, such passage in Locke as the following:

For since it can never be supposed to be the will of the society that the legislative should have a power to destroy that which every one designs to secure by entering into society, and for which the people submitted themselves to legislators of their own making: whenever the legislators endeavour to take away and destroy the property of the people, or to reduce them to slavery under arbitrary power, they put themselves into a state of war with the people, who are thereupon absolved from any further obedience, and are left to the common refuge which God hath provided for all men against force and violence. Whensoever, therefore, the legislative shall transgress this fundamental rule of society, and either by ambition, fear, folly, or corruption, endeavour to grasp themselves, or put into the hands of any other, *an absolute power over the lives, liberties, and estates of the people, by this breach of trust they forfeit the power the people had put into their hands for quite contrary ends,* and it devolves to the people, who have a right to resume their original liberty, and by the establishment of a new legislative (such as they shall think fit), provide for their own safety and security, which is the end for which they are in society.

Was Locke contradicting himself by endorsing majority rule while at the same time viewing the majority, or its legislators, as limited? Not necessarily, for what is endorsed is *not* the power of a passing majority or its government to bind absolutely and eternally, but, rather, the power of a government, elected by a majority, to make laws *within a frame-*

work of rules established, and/or agreed to, by all. Also Locke seems implicitly to recognize that majority rule can be made consistent with the *purposes* it is designed to serve (namely, an approximation of the community will in order to protect the " lives, liberties and estates of the people ") only if limitations exist that forbid the majority or its government from contravening these purposes.

If Locke errs in his understanding of the limitations a democratic society imposes upon its legislators, the error lies in his failure to distinguish *political* freedoms, such as the freedom to participate in the choice of rulers, from *non-political* freedoms, like those often claimed for property or religion. The principle of majority rule recognizes no limitations on the power of the majority or its government except those that are essential to the attainment of freely-arrived-at majorities and to the maintenance of political consent and accountability. Freedoms associated with property, like, for example, freedom of contract, are from the point of view of the majority principle of an entirely different order from, let us say, the freedoms to speak and publish. The latter are political freedoms, without which a majority rule system is impossible; they cannot, therefore, be legitimately abridged. Freedom of contract, on the other hand, may, so far as the majority principle is concerned, be regulated and controlled in whatever fashion the majority or its government deems best. Whether industry shall be nationalized or privately owned;

whether wages shall be set by government or by private contract; whether polygamy shall be permitted within a monogamous society — these are matters that a democratic government, operating under majority rule, can if it likes, control. It cannot, however, properly determine whether political criticism will be tolerated or whether elections should be abolished, for the right to oppose and the right to elect are among those political freedoms from which its power derives. Empirically, of course, it would be folly for a democratic government to limit seriously the exercise of freedom in *any* matter about which the community feels strongly. It may be, too, that such matters as freedom of worship can be secured against governmental control by some principle other than the majority principle. It needs, however, to be made clear that while the majority principle imposes restraints on majority power, it does not sanction freedom from any sort of control. On the contrary, it *authorizes* the exercise of power, except over those matters upon which the authorization itself depends. Other matters that claim immunity from control must seek their sanction elsewhere.

IV

We have, so far, been examining the theoretical arguments against absolute majority rule. It remains now to take notice of some of the " practical " considerations that support the view of the majority principle that has been advanced here.

While we have employed, in the

course of this analysis, the phrase, "majority rule," it is important that we recognize the misleading suggestion contained in that phrase, i.e., the suggestion that majorities do in fact rule or govern. On the contrary, in all modern polities it is *governments,* and not *majorities,* that actually rule. Moreover, since governments are invariably minorities, the responsibility for running the affairs of a modern state falls largely to a minority in whose charge the offices of government are placed. Whatever it is a majority may appear to want requires for its implementation a government. Hence, to speak of a majority as being unlimited signifies *operationally* the grant of unlimited power to the minority that has gained access to the offices of government. The argument for absolute majority rule reduces itself *at the level of practice* to the endorsement of absolute governmental power by a minority.

The characteristic democratic arguments against unlimited governmental power are as cogent today as ever, and, given the enormous complexity of modern mass society, far more applicable. To suggest to a modern government that there are no proper limits on its power is to invite it to use, and, most likely, to abuse that power. Oligarchical tendencies are invariably present, as Michels has so brilliantly demonstrated, in even the most democratic governments. It is in the nature of power to seek generally to augment itself, as is clearly evident from the history of governments, and the most important brake on this tendency is,

in the last analysis, the *understanding* — among both rulers and governed — that power must be contained within agreed and fairly defined limits. Where the understanding is otherwise, there is little to check the self-aggrandizing tendencies of political power except the partisan consciences of those who hold it. It is precisely the recognition that a partisan conscience is inadequate security against the abuse of power that accounts for the dependence, in modern democracies, upon constitutions. Constitutions are the instruments by which communities formally define and delimit the powers of government to which they will be subject. Unlimited authority — when placed in a government or nominally, in the majority that lies behind — is the negation, therefore, of constitutionalism, rendering it impossible. What is even more important, however, is that *democracy* becomes impossible in practice where no rules are understood to delimit power.

What of the contention, sometimes offered against this view, that we must trust the majority to delimit itself, to establish the rules and abide [by] them? The first difficulty inherent in this contention is that the majority is, for practical purposes, unable to delimit itself, since the majority does not in fact *act*. It is *governments* that act, and what we in effect ask, when we assert this proposition, is that *governments* be trusted to judge their own powers. There are, moreover, a number of pertinent facts about majorities as such, and their relationship to government, that this contention overlooks:

The term majority refers, at its simplest level, to a mere arithmetical quality, namely, more-than-half. Political theorists have often, however, proceeded toward this term as though it implied something more: they have, in fact, infused the term with qualities it does not necessarily possess. There is a tendency, for example, to think of the majority as though it were (a) homogeneous, and (b) organic in its character. The arithmetical abstraction, majority, has, like so many other abstractions in politics, been reified and then proceeded toward as though it were a single anthropomorphic entity. The fact is, however, that a majority is neither organic nor usually homogeneous. On the contrary, there are frequently as wide differences in attitude and opinion among various members of " the majority " as there are between some members of the majority and some members of the minority. Under the American party system, for example, it is indeed *likely* that the candidate attaining majorities will have drawn support from virtually every section of opinion in the community. To assign, therefore, to so ambiguous an entity as the " majority " the ultimate power to determine without limitation the very foundations of the polity, is to sacrifice reality for formality.

We have fallen into the habit, too, of assuming that we must proceed toward the majority as though it were always right; as though there were some sanctity it enjoyed in matters of morality and truth. This grows out of the honorific status enjoyed by " the people " in democratic doctrine. Having hit upon the majority as the best possible working approximation of " the people," we have subtly transferred to the majority the quality of infallibility that democratic theory assigns to the people. Realistically, however, we must recognize that the infallibility of " the people " is, like the social compact and other such concepts, an operational myth, necessary, perhaps, as a theoretical presupposition, but hardly supportable empirically. " The people " cannot be infallible for the simple reason that the people is frequently divided. Nor, *a fortiori*, can a majority be so regarded, for not only is it also divided in numerous respects, but it represents at best only a crude approximation of " the people."

When it is said that the majority is always " right," what precisely does this mean? Obviously, it cannot mean that the majority always has the correct answers to social problems and issues that are posed to it since (1) different members of any given majority will invariably have a number of *different* answers to the same problem; and (2) it is obvious from our experience that some members of " the minority " have, on some questions, far more knowledge and insight than do many of those who happen to have voted with " the majority." Given the wide possibility of error in judgments about complex human affairs, we may certainly doubt that a case can invariably be made for the absolute superiority of the judgment of any 50.1 percent over those of the 49.9 percent. Suppose, however, that by " right " in this instance is meant that the majority always knows its own best interest and will act accordingly. Here again, however, we have a proposition that is empirically indefensible, for it is evident that not only do majority opinions sometimes shift back and forth on public questions and candidates (often, too, within brief spaces of time), but majorities suffer, often, the election of governments whose concern is primarily with the maintenance of established privilege and the dominant interests of powerful minorities.

Any realistic discussion of this problem must face the fact, too, that it has become exceedingly difficult, under the complex conditions of modern mass society, to choose courses wisely, or to discover one's best interest and find the means for its implementation. Considering the vast complexity of social issues, the difficulty of gaining insight into them, the enormous increase in governmental functions, the degree of specialization that is required to handle effectively the greatly augmented power of modern government — considering these, the opinion of the majority is at best an inadequate guide (even assuming that all who vote for the same set of candidates hold the same opinions, which they rarely do) to the discovery of the most efficacious social policy. There is, perhaps, no better guide, or at least no systematic method for producing better guides, but this should not blind us to the deficiencies that inhere in the guides and methods we do deem best.

Consider, also, the difficulties that attend our representative system. The voter in a modern democratic polity finds himself confronted with a number of huge party organizations, over which he has little control, and which present to him candidates he often does not know, has never seen, and is likely not to learn much about. To assume that there is a *necessary* consonance between his wants and desires and what he is likely to get from the candidate he votes for, is to mistake the myth for the reality. He may even find that, in terms of his social beliefs, all the candidates are objectionable, and his problem becomes, so far as he views it, a choice among evils. While there is, to be sure, a tendency for a party that seeks to win elections to respond ultimately to the temper of the many, it sometimes misreads that temper, and where it correctly gauges that temper, it resorts, not infrequently, to assuaging it by demagogy rather than action. Once elected, a candidate may go his way largely unobserved, and whether or not he can succeed in being re-elected may depend on variables quite irrelevant to his merits as a representative of the popular will. His election or re-election will in part be correlated with such extraneous factors as voice, personality, appearance, religion, national origins, and party label.

It becomes exceedingly difficult, in the light of all this, to interpret correctly the meaning of an election and to ascertain, with confidence, what it is the majority seems to have expressed when it selects one set of candidates over another. Where the issues themselves are complicated, unclear, and not adequately understood, and where, in any case, they constitute only one of the variables upon which the outcome of the election depends, no one can be certain what mandate, if any, the majority of the electorate has granted to its governors. Unfortunately, no better way is known to attain political accountability than to allow voters to select freely by whatever standards they deem important. To assume, however, that a government elected by a majority is justified, in the name of that majority, to exercise power unqualifiedly and to be made custodian of the very rules from which its power derives, is, in the face of the empirical considerations we have indicated, to fall victim to the dread formalism that seems so frequently to accompany theoretical systems.

Given these considerations, it becomes clear that there must exist in a democracy the opportunity to undo what previous majorities and their governments have done, for it must be granted that with the inevitable hiatus between the governed and their representatives, the complexity of issues, the difficulty of interpreting the meaning of an election, etc., — the potentiality for error, and even evil, has become, under the representative system, real. Nothing, either in its definition or operation, requires that democracy so trust its governors as to empower them to prevent the undoing of their work. It is very well to indulge ready aphorisms such as "Democracy is founded on trust." So, perhaps, in a sense, it

is. To trust a majority or its government is, however, one thing; to render it infallible, another. It is precisely because of its recognition that infallibility is not to be anticipated in human affairs that democracy insists on accountability and on keeping open the road to the correction of error. If the justification for government rests on the fact that men are not angels, the case for democracy and the majority principle resides in the fact that there are no Philosopher-Kings (and that even if there were, we should have no means of discovering them except by election). It is the essence of the majority principle that it insists that no one can be trusted with absolute power, not even half-plus-one of the people. We must, then, recognize "majority rule" for what it really is, namely, an imperfect mechanism for making consent and accountability possible, superior perhaps, to any other mechanism heretofore devised, but not, on that account, immune from criticism or from checks. On the contrary, the majority principle insists, as we have seen, on the recognition of limitations on the rule of the majority or its government.

It should also be clear from this that, on grounds both of theory and practice, democracy cannot be defined as merely the rule of the majority. The most that can be claimed is that majority rule, when limited by the majority principle as we have defined it, is a *necessary*, but not a *sufficient* condition for the existence of a democracy. Left unrestricted, majority rule must be regarded as a *sufficient condition for democracy* since if democracy is defined as equivalent with the *absolute* power of the majority, no other conditions, such as accountability or political freedom, are logically necessary to, nor can they enter into, the definition. Yet it is obvious from the actual history, as well as from the articulated theory, of democracy that it cannot be conceived apart from political freedom or from accountability.

To limit the majority does not mean that the minority shall be sovereign. Rather does it mean, in a democracy, that the minority that governs shall be empowered by a majority to act for a limited period of time within a framework of rules, established formally or traditionally, to which the community, in general, adheres. If we turn once again to experience, we shall discover that in virtually all modern democracies, (a) majority rule exists in some form, and (b) in even the clearest majority rule systems, it is never assumed that the power of the majority or its government is absolute and unqualified. The formal dichotomy, i.e., that either a majority or a minority must finally rule, fails to take into account the fact that, in practice, democracies have organized themselves so that neither majorities nor minorities have absolute power. Both are limited, though the majority, of course, prevails, or can prevail if it wishes, in those matters over which it has legitimate authority. All modern democracies have managed to make clear — either by specific constitutional limitation, by institutional checks, or most important, by the development of an *ethos* which requires that the rules of the game be respected — that there are certain things a government, no matter how wide its support, simply cannot do. Even in England, where, except for the remaining powers of the monarch and the House of Lords, there are no formal limitations on the majority of the House of Commons, it is nevertheless understood by virtually all who participate in or are subject to the political process that governmental power is limited and that actions which infringe the rules that make possible majority government cannot be abided. It is no accident that documents such as *Magna Carta* and the Bill of Rights of 1689 hold an honored place, even a constitutional status, in British law. Nor is it mere chance that those who sit opposite the Treasury Bench are designated the " Official Opposition," and that their leader is even paid a salary for " helping to make a Government possible." It would be utterly inconceivable to an Englishman that his commitment to the principle of majority rule would require him to recognize as legitimate an act by the Government that abolished, for example, all opposition. It would be no less inconceivable to the members of the Government itself that such powers might legitimately be assigned to them. The formalist, pointing to the fact that the constitution can in England be amended by mere statute, might insist that a government elected by a majority is therefore unlimited. This would be, however, to mistake the form for the substance. It is an occupational bias of lawyers, and of some political scientists, that what lacks formal legal status appears to them to lack also existence. Experience, however, compels us to recognize this bias as spurious and inadmissible.

If we are correct in believing that the principle of majority rule requires the existence of those rights that make democracy possible, then democrats would not, under this principle, be bound to recognize as legitimate the regimes that totalitarian parties may seek to establish in the name of the majority. A regime that will destroy the opposition, abrogate political freedom, or in any other way violate the conditions for the free expression of consent and accountability can rightfully make no claims on the loyalty of democrats, no matter how wide its support. The first obligation of democrats, *qua* democrats, would be, in fact, not to obey in this instance, but seek to maintain wherever they can, the possibility of choice, consent and accountability, for these are necessary prerequisites for any democracy. Just, for example, as we do not, under democracy, permit a citizen to sell himself into slavery (on the assumption that a man's freedom is the one quality he cannot dispense with as he pleases), so are we not bound to recognize as legitimate the yielding up of freedom by a *number* of men who happen to constitute an arithmetical quantity of more-than-half. Even more strongly are we bound not to recognize an attempt of fifty-one per cent to do likewise. It may appear a paradox, but democracy, though choice is of its essence, precludes one kind of choice: we cannot, under it, choose not to choose. We cannot, with democratic sanction, choose to cut ourselves off from those requirements that make all choice possible. Therein lies the essential fallacy of absolute majority rule.

3 ECONOMIC CHOICE IN MODERN SOCIETY

27. The Price System and Economic Choice in Modern Society

As we have seen in the last chapter, philosophical speculation about the proper role of political choice in society has had a long and sometimes tempestuous history. The political philosophies of democracy were forged in the crucible of the Hellenic-Christian tradition, but their articulation had to wait upon the slow movement of history — the relaxation of the spiritual grip of the medieval church, the rise of the nation-state out of the kingdoms and principalities of medieval Europe, and the establishment of strong and autocratic monarchs at the heads of these states. Then man could fix upon man the responsibility for injustice, tyranny, and corruption. Thus liberalism, the first philosophy of individual and democratic choice, was carried in the womb of the despotic monarchies of western Europe and born in the revolutions that destroyed the aristocratic monoply of political choice.

Liberalism did not hold the field unchallenged. Marx, in particular, took issue with its basic postulates. He denied the discreteness of man

and the utility calculus that allegedly motivates him and argued instead that man's position in the class structure determines his conduct. History, he argued further, is generated through the conflict of opposed behavior in the class structure. But, because Marx thought in historical categories of groups that were opposed to one another, individual choice had little, if any, place in his system.

As Marx attacked liberal theories of choice from the left, the Fascists attacked them from the right. Espousing the philosophy of political idealism, the Fascists contended that the individual can only exist in the state and is organically related to the state in the same way as a person's arm is related to his whole body. Subservient to the state, the individual can enjoy political choice only at the sufferance of the state. Whereas Marx had argued that individual choice has little meaning because of the class structure, the Fascists argued that individual choice interferes with the attainment of the higher good by the collectivity of the state.

173

Finally, liberalism has had to contend with defections from within its own ranks. Contemporary political philosophers, though free of the dogma of the extreme right or the extreme left, have been confronted with the inadequacies of a system which guarantees individual choice by placing beyond the pale of social policy certain so-called inalienable rights, e.g., private property, free speech, and free assembly. It sometimes seemed to be the case that a minority has used the doctrine of inalienable rights to oppress the majority — for instance, in the attack on minimum wage or social security legislation on the grounds that it abrogates rights in property. Should not the majority in democratic society make the essential decisions? If so, how do we guarantee that minorities will not be legislated out of existence.

In this chapter we are concerned with a particular aspect of choice — the decisions society has to make with respect to the allocation of scarce resources to particular uses, where the possible uses are virtually unlimited. The analysis of economic choice is of recent vintage relative to the analysis of political choice. It was not until the eighteenth century that there was a body of knowledge that could be designated as economics, then called political economy. Prior to that time economic inquiry was a part of philosophy.

The youth of economics cannot be ascribed to chance or the fortuitous circumstances of man's interests. Before economic choice could explicitly become the subject of study, a society had to develop in which economic decisions stood somewhat apart from other social decisions and therefore could be made consciously. Prior to the eighteenth century society in general was tradition-oriented. The things that people did were sanctioned by the conduct of previous generations. Under these circumstances decision-making as related to the utilization of resources was habitual or implicit in the way of life, and consequently there was no need to single out economic choice as a special field of study. The philosophers who attempted to uncover the essence of existence would necessarily deal with the rationale of economic choice.

The tradition-oriented society in the West broke down before the onslaught of the Renaissance, the Reformation, the Commercial Revolution, and the Industrial Revolution. In its place appeared the future-oriented society in which reason and progress were accorded high honor. Associated with this change was the rise of the capitalistic market. The capitalistic market permitted some distinctions between decisions concerning the utilization of resources and the other decisions that had to be made in society. In other words, individuals acquired roles as buyers and sellers that appeared to be distinct from their roles as parents or church members, for example. The market and the decisions reflected in the market then became the subject of explicit inquiry. Scholars attempted to discover the laws or tendencies governing its operations.

Although theories of economic

choice do not have the venerable history of theories of political choice, they display a similar lack of consensus. Today there are two competing systems of economic thought, the Western system on the one hand, and the Marxist system on the other. Both of these systems have their roots in the same institution, the capitalistic market. Whereas the Marxist system, however, analyzes the growth and development of capitalism and attempts to show its transitory nature and hence the inevitability of socialism, the Western system analyzes the market in an attempt to predict the consequences of economic decisions. The one is historically deterministic, the other is neutral with respect to historical causation.

In the article that follows, the price system, which is the basis of the capitalistic market, is explained. The author shows how resources are allocated among alternative employments in a price system and sets up standards for evaluating the performance of economic organization. Since both Western and Marxist economics originate in capitalism, an understanding of the price system is essential to an understanding of the systems of economic choice in Western and Communist countries.

28. The Price System*

I. THE ECONOMIC PROBLEM

Introduction. Commonplace things are seldom commonplace. Every day most of us engage in commercial transactions with little thought of their significance except when the transaction is the purchase of a new automobile or a passage on the *Queen Mary*. A suburbanite who works in the center of a city buys his train ticket and morning paper quite automatically. He much prefers to follow the earned run average of his favorite pitcher or the vicissitudes of his favorite stock rather than consider those intricacies of modern civilization which make his purchases possible. Similarly, the train trip into a crowded, noisy and often exasperat-

ing city impresses him, if at all, by its methodical drudgery, by its inevitableness.

If, however, the suburbanite had examined his routine existence in relation to the society in which he lived, he would have found it fraught with some rather extraordinary implications. He bought a morning paper for five cents and in that transaction procured the services of a high priced editorial staff, foreign correspondents, newspaper reporters and also, less obviously, typesetters, printing press operators, manufacturers of newsprint, paper boys. The purchase of a railroad ticket obtained for him the services of the conductor, the assemblers of railroad coaches, the producer of railroad ties, the miners of iron ore and so on. Everything he used within the course of a

* By Karl de Schweinitz, Jr., New Haven, Conn., 1948.

day, from the clothes he wore to the pencil sharpener in his office, represented the combination and culmination of a series of services. It is apparent, then, that behind the transactions in which people normally engage lies a systematic and not accidental organization which makes it possible for the commuter in New York to utilize the services provided by individuals in Pittsburgh, Duluth, Canada, England and other parts of the world.

The suburbanite, or any individual, has two capacities: first, as a consumer he buys goods and services; and second, as a producer he assists in the production of goods and services which eventually will be sold to consumers.

In his first capacity the commuter bought a train ticket. That transaction implied the making of a decision since he chose one of the many different methods of getting from suburb to city. He could have ridden by trolley, car, taxi or bus. That he chose one alternative to the exclusion of the others suggests that he had some basis for doing so. His choice of transportation by train might have indicated that he preferred that part of town through which the train passed or that he considered it most convenient to his home and place of business or that he liked the people who traveled by train. Whatever the basis for making the decision, the commuter chose to ride by train because, given his circumstances, it represented the most satisfactory way of getting to town.

In his second capacity an individual earns an income so that he can pay for the things he buys. The choice of job by which an individual earns income implies the making of a decision as much as the purchase of a railroad ticket since it represents a transaction between an individual supplying some sort of productive service and another individual buying that service. If the commuter works for a publishing house, he has chosen that occupation over other types of work. The fact that he elected to sell his services to the publishing firm suggests that he believed that occupation to be the best of the available jobs in the light of his capabilities, his income requirements and job requirements.

The necessity of making the above choices reveals that the world in which we live is complex not only in a technical sense, as in the processing of iron ore in a steel plant, but also in a social organizational sense. If the commuter buys a paper every morning, that transaction will require a continually functioning organization capable of coordinating the activities of the many individuals who, as producers, supply the services necessary for producing papers.

The Economic Problem in Brief. Society is a complicated institutional mechanism which has many purposes. One is the protection of its members against external invasion or internal violence. Another is the safeguarding of political democracy. Another is the preservation of religious freedom. Still another is the dissemination of knowledge through an adequate school system. And, finally, one of those purposes is economizing.

Everybody economizes. That is to say, the goods that people want exceed the goods that can be made from available resources. Therefore, individuals must use their income so that they get the goods they consider most important. Society as a whole must, therefore, also economize. That is, it must develop social institutions to allocate scarce resources to satisfy the most important wants.

On the one hand, wants are great. Human beings want steaks, eggs, vegetables, business suits, evening clothes, bathing suits, apartment houses, bungalows, movies, baseball games, concerts, automobiles and many other things.

In fact, wants are unlimited. A woman is happy with a wash board until her neighbor gets a washing machine, but a washing machine makes her happy only so long as her neighbor doesn't get an automatic washing machine. If a man buys a pin stripe suit, he will soon get a hankering to buy a new pair of shoes, a new tie and shirt to go with the suit. The wants of most people are insatiable.

On the other hand, resources are scarce. Resources consist of three elements: one, *the population:* its age composition, its level of education, its division between skilled and unskilled workers, its willingness to work; two, *the materials with which the earth is naturally endowed:* forests, iron ore, coal, copper, phosphorus, nitrogen etc.; and, three, an intermediate classification, *capital:* the machines, factories and other goods which are made by the services supplied by human and natural resources. Plentiful as resources are in the United States, there are not enough of any of them to make all the things that people want.

The scarcity of resources became apparent to everyone during the war. We were forced to convert from the production of peacetime goods and services to the production of guns, tanks and other war equipment. Furthermore, resources were inadequate to meet all our military needs. General Patton maintained that he could have reached the interior of Germany immediately after the breakthrough at St. Lo, France, in August 1944 if additional gasoline had been delivered to him rather than to the airforce. If resources were unlimited, the general would have had all the material he could possibly have used; and civilians would have been able to obtain butter without knowing the grip of the retailer's fraternity.

The scarcity of resources appears as limited income to individuals. The income an individual earns as a producer represents a claim against the goods and services created from the resources of the society and ultimately is limited by the scarcity of resources.

But what are economic wants? Wants have many aspects. Individuals want goods and services not only because they are essential for life, but because they yield many different types of satisfaction: physiological, emotional and familial. But these same wants are at the same time economic wants if their satisfaction requires the use of the society's limited resources.

The want for a Thanksgiving dinner and all its trimmings is a familial want because it is one of the rare occasions during the year when a family gathers together. It is a physiological want because the white wine and turkey are particularly pleasing to the palate. But it also is an economic want because its satisfaction requires the allocation of the society's scarce resources to the production of turkeys, cranberries, cashews and all the other things that go with a Thanksgiving dinner. An economic system, therefore, is not a system for satisfying economic wants as opposed to psychological, spiritual, or recreational wants. It is a system for satisfying any wants which require the use of scarce resources.

Is scarcity a permanent phenomenon or will it disappear as society develops and the fund of human knowledge increases? It is alleged by some people that human beings possess sufficient technical and scientific information to transform our economy into one of abundance. If we approach the problem of resource utilization from an engineering standpoint, it is said, we can squeeze so much out of resources that no one will be wanting. Proponents of this view unfortunately have interpreted scarcity in an absolute sense and have completely failed to understand the meaning of the economic problem.

Scarcity describes a relationship between human wants and resources and does not connote any particular standard of living. As society grows and the material level of living improves, human wants grow also. In the nineteenth century we econo-mized to provide people with what now we would consider the bare essentials of life. But in the century of the automobile, people want gasoline, good roads, week-end resorts, hot dog stands; and we economize to gratify those wants. We can reasonably expect scarcity to continue, although the nature of our wants will probably continue to change.

Thus, in brief, social economic organization is for the purpose of economizing, just as the military organization is for the purpose of preventing external invasion and the police system is for the maintenance of internal order. The Economizing Process is organized socially to get the most want satisfaction out of scarce resources.

II. Essentials of a Solution to the Economic Problem in Brief

A solution to the problem of economizing is contingent upon the fulfillment of several essential conditions.

The social economic organization must obtain information about wants and the means of satisfying wants so that individuals, as producers, will co-operate in producing the kinds of things that individuals, as consumers, want.

It also must evolve a system of choice since, if resources are insufficient to meet all the demands for their use, a choice must be made between the alternatives. Choice between alternatives does not mean choosing one to the exclusion of the other, but rather determining the proportions in which resources should be allocated to various uses. In the United States we do not have to choose between producing either automobiles or tractors; but we do have to choose between producing more automobiles and fewer tractors or fewer automobiles and more tractors. Economic choice is a problem of proportions.

But on what grounds should the organization facilitate choice? Why should resources be allocated to the additional production of automobiles rather than to the additional production of tractors? The choice could have been made for arbitrary reasons; but, if it were made to achieve the end of social economic organization, the value consumers attached to automobiles and tractors would have provided the rationale. If consumers find that additional automobiles satisfy want more than additional tractors, additional resources should be allocated to the production of automobiles. Choice, then, requires the comparison of values; and correct choice requires the apportioning of resources to alternative uses, or occupations, in the proportions that create the greatest value for consumers.

The values compared in decisions involving choice may be called marginal values. We do not have to know anything about the value to consumers of all the gloves and shoes produced with the resources allocated to those types of production. It is sufficient to compare the value to consumers of producing additional shoes, i.e., marginal value, with that of producing additional gloves. If the value obtained from producing

additional shoes is greater than that obtained from producing additional gloves, total value to the consumer will be increased by allocating additional resources to shoe production. The value lost in producing less of one will be more than made up by the value created by increasing production of the other.

Since consumers must choose between alternatives in order to satisfy want they also must compare, or balance, marginal values. Just as resource allocation is a problem of proportions, so is the allocation of consumer income among the alternative means of satisfying want. Consumers get more or less of things; they do not buy potatoes to the exclusion of bread, but rather more of one and less of the other, or *vice versa*. Consequently the consumer will compare the values of additional purchases, i.e., marginal value, and allocate his income in the direction of those commodities which he feels add most to want satisfaction.

When a consumer chooses between alternatives he adds something to want satisfaction, but to obtain that increase he has to give something up. As long as I can't have everything I can only get more of one thing by forgoing something else. I can only obtain more shirts by buying fewer shoes. The shoes I forgo to obtain more shirts represent a loss of want satisfaction and therefore are a value as much as the want satisfaction gained through the increase in my purchases of shirts.

Therefore, when a consumer economizes he chooses between alternatives. He balances the marginal values of the things he retains against the marginal value of the things he forgoes. He will have gotten the most out of his limited income, or maximized want satisfaction, if the additional want satisfaction obtained by purchasing any given item equals the additional want satisfaction forgone to obtain it. If the additional want satisfaction obtained from increased purchases of Hershey bars is greater than the additional want satisfaction forgone in consequence of the necessary reductions in the purchase of ice cream cones, total want satisfaction can be increased by getting still more Hershey bars and fewer ice cream cones. The loss of additional want satisfaction from the latter is more than compensated by the increase in additional want satisfaction from the former. The consumer would continue to improve his position by altering the proportions in which he gets Hershey bars and ice cream cones until the marginal values are equal, i.e., the marginal value of that retained equals the marginal value of that forgone.

In allocating its resources, an economy must choose between alternative uses and should add resources in one direction as long as the additional want satisfaction created is greater than the additional want satisfaction forgone. Suppose, for instance, that the people of an economy want more Bourbon and less pork. If the economic organization responds to this evaluation, it should facilitate the movement of men and grain into Kentucky from the hog producing areas. Total want satisfaction will be increased because the additional want satisfaction yielded by increased production of Bourbon will be greater than the loss of additional want satisfaction contingent upon the withdrawal of resources from the production of hogs. The movement of resources should continue until the marginal values are equal, i.e., what is gained just equals what is forgone.

The value of the alternative forgone as a result of allocating resources in a given way is called *cost*. The cost of increasing Bourbon production is the value of the reduced hog production necessary to bring about the increase in the output of Bourbon. Or the cost to the consumer of increasing his purchases of Hershey bars is the value of the ice cream cones he had to forgo in order to obtain more Hershey bars.

Therefore, the balancing of values conditional upon choice can be restated in terms of cost and value. Resources should be allocated among alternative uses in proportions that equate in each use the marginal value obtained with the marginal cost. Consumers must divide their income between alternative means of satisfying want in proportions that equate the marginal value obtained from any given commodity with the marginal cost. Choice is correct when at the margin cost equals value.

It would be very unwise for an economic organization to try to allocate resources in such a way as to increase the spread between marginal cost and marginal value, as has sometimes been suggested. If at the margin there is a divergence between cost and value, it means that consumers are not getting the things they want in the right proportions. If, for instance, the marginal value of additional pin stripe suits is greater than their marginal costs, i.e., the marginal value forgone by the diversion of resources from other occupations to the production of pin stripe suits, it indicates that consumers value resource utilization in the production of pin stripe suits more than in alternative occupations. Therefore, they want more pin stripe suits and fewer other commodities.

It should now be clear that a solution to the economic problem requires that the problem be recognized as one involving values, not engineering techniques. The study of social economic organization is in large part the study of the values on which choices, or economic decisions, are made. We want to know whether to produce more or less electric razors, more or less symphony concerts, more or less airplanes, more or less laundry delivery services and so on. We are, therefore, interested in the additions to and diminutions of production, or the margins. We can compare margins and determine whether one should be pushed out and another pulled in only if we reduce the physically incommensurable commodities produced in an economy to the common denominators of cost and value.

In a previous paragraph, we alluded to the opinion of those who believe that the problem of scarcity is symptomatic of our failure to apply our tremendous scientific and engineering knowledge to the transformation of physical resources into useful matter. The cult of Technocracy has expressed this belief in its ultimate form. Speciously using the terminology of the physical sciences, the Technocrats have translated economic problems into what they call energy problems; and they maintain that from our resources it is possible to create enough energy in ergs to overwhelm an economy with abundance.

Unfortunately, the Technocrats have only looked at one aspect of the problem of resource utilization and have consequently made invalid generalizations. Everyone would grant that in our economy advancing technology has increased the efficiency with which resources are processed, but technology *per se* can tell us nothing about the values upon which economic decision depends. Purely on the basis of energy relationships, the technocrats could reduce the quantity of resources allocated to agricultural pursuits by distributing to consumers pills that contained all the chemical ingredients essential for life. But whether consumers would be willing to eat the pills would depend upon the value they attached to them as satisfiers of want. People eat for many reasons other than the maintenance of life, and a pill would leave unsatisfied many of the wants that a plank steak satisfies. Without evaluation, physical relationships have little meaning for economizing organizations, simply because they provide no means of comparing values.

If there is no way of comparing values, it is impossible to know when labor should leave one industry and move to another. If consumers want more baseballs and fewer bowling balls, labor should be transferred from one industry to the other in order to effect the proper adjustment of production. But we have not attained a solution to this problem of allocation if we know only that one baseball can be produced by the expending of ten foot-pounds of energy and one bowling ball by the expending of twenty foot-pounds of energy. We must know the values that consumers ascribe to wants and resource utilization before we can obtain a proper allocation of resources.

The Basic Concepts as Illustrated in a Primitive Economy. It is difficult to discern the essentials of a solution to the economic problem in modern society because they are hidden under institutional developments such as banking, government, and large scale industrial enterprise. We will therefore examine the economic problem in primitive circumstances.

In his *The Mysterious Island,* Jules Verne tells the story of five prisoners of war, held by the Confederate Army in Richmond, who escaped in a balloon. Unfortunately for them and the dog they picked up at the last moment, the night chosen for the ascent was also the first night of a five day hurricane; and, contrary to their best calculations, they were blown far out into the South Pacific and marooned on an apparently uninhabited island. It soon became clear that the island was not located along one of the normal sea lanes and that there was little chance of a vessel picking them up. They settled down for a long stay on the island.

The castaways included Cyrus Harding, engineer; Gideon Spilett, newspaper reporter; Neb, Harding's servant; Pencroft, sailor, carpenter, tailor, gardener; Herbert Brown, a young student of natural science; and Top, the dog. Their combined resources on reaching the island consisted of two watches, a notebook, a metal dog collar and their own willingness to work (the balloon was lost in the ocean).

Since the wants of individuals arise from the circumstances in which they find themselves, their associations, in fact, the whole complex of living, these particular individuals had relatively simple wants, i.e., food and shelter. Nonetheless the means for gratifying those simple wants were scarce since they had no tools but their own hands with which to obtain food and shelter.

Conceivably, each man could have struck out on his own and have attempted to provide for his own wants, scouring the forest for edible berries and roots and the beaches for shellfish, etc. But this would not have been a very satisfactory way of providing for wants, because some of the men did not know an edible from a nonedible berry. If these men had to forage, all their time would have been consumed; and any talents they might have had for providing shelter would have gone to waste.

However, the group was under the aegis of Cyrus Harding and no activity was undertaken without prior consultation with the engineer. Having taken stock of the useful equipment in possession of his men, he conducted an exploratory expedition throughout the length and breadth of the island in order to ascertain the resources with which the island was endowed. The men discovered deposits of sulphur, iron ore, clay, limestone and sand.

The very process of discovery expanded the wants of the men. Whereas when they first landed they wanted food and shelter, they now had visions of processing the iron ore into iron and making tools with which they could construct a ship, a house and countless other items.

Now that he knew the resources with which he had to work, Harding was ready to organize the men for productive activity. He appointed Neb commissar of food procurement and supplied him with a crude weapon by breaking Top's metal dog collar in two and pointing each piece with the aid of a sandstone. The three other men, Gideon Spilett, Pencroft and Herbert Brown were set to work fashioning rough approximations of brick out of clay and sand. Harding made a fire by placing water between two convex watch crystals sealed with clay and using the contrivance as a burning glass on dry moss. The brick forms were then placed around the fire and baked, and the finished product was used to build a kiln. This operation took several days, and during that time Neb supplied the men with the food he had been able to find.

If Harding had organized his group for the purpose of obtaining food alone, assigning some of the men to the beach sector and others to the forest, he could undoubtedly

have procured more food for the men. Evidently there was a cost involved in the production of bricks, because an alternative was forgone in order to produce them. If the men had not produced bricks, they would have had more food; the cost, then, of producing the bricks was the food they gave up. Similarly, there would have been a cost if the men had done nothing but search for food; the loss of the alternative output from other possible occupations.

When the kiln was completed, Harding turned his men into potters; and for several days they made earthenware pots, plates and jars. The production of these utensils eased the pressure on Neb, since now a greater percentage of the food he procured could be effectively used; the carcasses of small game, instead of being thrown away, became the raw material of soup. But the new wants that arose concomitantly with the production of the pottery placed new demands on the time of the inhabitants of the Mysterious Island. Neb did not have to spend so much time grubbing for food, but he had to spend more time preparing it. Plates are only partially useful without their complements; hence the demand for forks, knives, spoons, tables, chairs, etc. became more significant.

By the time Harding converted his primitive economy from the production of pottery to the processing of iron ore, a relatively complicated structure of wants pressed down on the limited resources of the island. If each man had attempted to take care of himself, wants would have remained simple because each man's time would have been completely given to securing the minimal food requirements. As soon as individuals organize in a co-operative effort, the range of goods within reach of the individuals becomes much greater. However, at the same time, wants expand at a faster rate so that the problem of economizing becomes more urgent as the economy develops. Scarity, then, has no necessary relation to the standard of living; as the inhabitants of the Mysterious Island improved their material status, the problems associated with scarcity became more obvious because new occupations constantly opened up competing for their time and energy.

The technical problems Harding had to solve depended upon how the community decided to use its resources. Harding favored the processing of iron ore as the next objective of the community; and, to that end, contrived a technique for transforming the kiln into a blast furnace. He capitalized on the gaming instinct of his men and led a seal hunt in one of the island coves where seals were in the habit of taking a sun treatment. The expedition was rewarded with two seals whose hides, after skinning, were fashioned into a crude sort of bellows. The technical problem was how to combine the sealskins and a wooden frame in order to provide an airtight bellows. If the community had decided to obtain sealskins for shoe production the technical problem would have been somewhat different. Engineering technique, then, cannot solve the

economic problem; it can only facilitate the construction of those things that have value to individuals.

The refining of iron ore eventually provided the islanders with the raw material out of which hammers, levers, knives and other tools were made. These in turn permitted the production of more elaborate commodities since a greater variety of resources could be processed with tools than without them. Different preferences existed among the men as to what sort of good should be produced with the aid of their newly acquired tools. Some favored the construction of a ship so that they could leave the Mysterious Island, while others favored the construction of a suitable dwelling so that they could avoid the rigors of the approaching winter. Harding decided in favor of a dwelling and his guileless compatriots acceded to his decision without a murmur.

The engineer, not unmindful of the possibility that hostile natives might occasionally appear on the island, selected as remote a site for the dwelling as he could find. In the course of their explorations the castaways had discovered a large cavern which had been formed by the erosive action of a subterranean river. Harding, with his usual omniscience, estimated that this cavern was located behind the face of a high cliff which rose precipitously from the beach. He proposed to block the land entrance to the cavern and chisel windows and a door in the face of the cliff from which a retractable ladder would be dropped to the beach. Further, he intended to divide the cavern into rooms by building brick partitions and to construct a fireplace for the convenience of the cook.

Obviously, this ambitious project required a high degree of organization. On the beach when the men first turned their energies to the production of bricks the organizational problem was relatively simple. Given the lack of tools, there was really only one way of making bricks, molding the clay by hand and baking the rough mold beside the fire. But now the men had tools, materials with which to work and an infinite number of tasks to perform. This meant that there was an infinite number of combinations or methods for achieving the end of constructing a suitable dwelling.

On what basis did Harding organize his small economy for this task? His engineering knowledge provided the answers to technical questions, such as how metal should be tempered to insure a good knife blade and how long clay should be baked to obtain durable bricks; but it did not provide him with the value information required for production organization. If Harding managed his economy intelligently he would have examined the alternatives, or costs, of each job performed and distributed the productive effort of the men so that these costs did not outweigh the value created.

For instance, someone had to search for food each day. If Harding himself undertook to supply the community's food requirements, the cost would have been prohibitive. He was the coordinator of productive activity and without his direction production would have lagged. Similarly, Pencroft would not have been a wise choice since the loss of his carpentry skill and ability to make ladders out of bamboo reeds might possibly have created a bottleneck in operations. On the other hand, it does not follow that any unskilled man should have been spared for food procurement. Neb and Herbert with equal efficiency may have been carrying bricks from the kiln to the base of the cliff; but if Herbert could secure the same amount of food twice as quickly as Neb, it would not be economical to dispatch Neb for the food. The alternative loss of brick transport would be greater in that case than if Herbert searched for food.

What is required then is a balancing of values, the value an individual creates in an occupation against the cost of his working in that occupation; and the productive effort should be distributed so that one is not greater than the other.

The character of the costs is closely related to the wants that the community attempts to satisfy. Harding established the provision of shelter as a more urgent want than the construction of a ship. If there were a maverick in the group who did not accept the ranking given to the community's wants and appropriated the community ax so that he could fell a tree suitable for a ship's mast, the cost would have been high. Productive effort would have been lost from that activity upon which the community had placed its top priority. On the other hand, if the community expressed a preference for the construction of a ship over the provision of shelter, the cost of the same operations would have been considerably less. Cost, therefore, is closely related to demand.

Sufficient developments on the island have been examined to indicate the problems of economizing so that further advances such as the construction of a telegraph system, the cultivating of corn and tobacco, etc., can be passed over. The economic problem on the island was very much the same as the economic problem in modern societies. Any differences were of degree, and not of substance. The alternatives that Harding evaluated were quite precise; if he provided shelter he could not at the same time build a ship. In a modern economy one alternative is not obtained by completely foregoing other goods and services, but rather by reducing the volume of other goods and services produced elsewhere in the economy. To produce more houses the economy would reduce production of ships, not stop producing them altogether.

However, the institutional setting in which choices were made on the Mysterious Island was considerably different from the contemporary institutional background of economizing. Harding was able to gather all the men together so that they could discuss their mutual problems, and it was relatively easy to ascertain the way the men valued the alternative methods of resource utilization. Decision making on the Mysterious Island was similar to decision making in the modern family.

But in a modern economy it obviously is impossible to make economic decisions on the basis of face-to-face relations; and consequently an organization becomes necessary which can translate into meaningful terms the evaluations individuals place on wants and resource use, thus making economizing behavior possible.

III. The Essentials of a Solution in More Detail: The Functions of Economizing Organizations

An examination of the economic activity of the men on the Mysterious Island reveals new aspects of the conditions necessary for a solution to the economic problem. Five functions had to be discharged by decision-making based on values.*

First, the men had to decide what was to be produced. Clearly, the fulfillment of this function depends upon the evaluation which the members of the community place on their wants. The men placed their top priority on adequate shelter rather than on the construction of a ship. They did so because shelter was worth more to them than a ship.

Second, after it is known what the community wants, resources must be allocated in order to produce the goods that will satisfy the designated wants. In his capacity as leader, Harding allocated resources for production. Only if he compared the

---

* This particular classification is adapted from F. H. Knight, *The Economic Organization* (University of Chicago, 1933). [Author's note.]

values and cost of resource utilization could he have obtained an allocation that corresponded with the evaluation the men placed on their wants.

Conceivably, Harding could have ignored values in allocating the productive efforts of his men, but the resulting product would have been of little use to the men. He might have dispatched Gideon Spilett to one of the island coves to observe the social life of the seals, and he might have directed Pencroft to search for acorns. Or he might have ordered all the men to gather rocks for the construction of a memorial in honor of the safe arrival of the men on the Mysterious Island. But he tried to allocate resources in order to produce the things that the men wanted. Consequently, he had to decide whether the placing of one of his men in a given occupation added more to want satisfaction than the loss of want satisfaction from the alternative foregone.

Third, the goods and services produced from a particular allocation of resources must be distributed to the individuals of the economy. There was no obvious problem of distribution on the Mysterious Island. The men consumed the product of their joint efforts communally. When the men moved together into their cliff dwelling, each man was, in effect, receiving his share of the product.

But distribution implies a more intricate process than the mere equal division of a fixed amount of goods and services among the members of an economy. No two individuals

hold the same set of values. Some men may place a high evaluation on aspirin tablets, while others may have no use for them at all. If an economy produces aspirin tablets, it is no solution to the distributive problem to give all men the same amount. Some men will throw away what the others need to clear their heads. Only if distribution is guided by the diverse values that individuals place on the means for satisfying want will the right goods go to the right people in the right proportions.

Fourth, some method must be devised for adjusting consumption to production whenever production is not exactly as wanted. For example, when an economic organization starts adjusting to an expressed want, it will not initially produce the commodity that will satisfy that want in very large quantities. It may, therefore, be necessary to ration the goods that do appear. The demand of Harding's men for food was tremendous in relation to the amount of food forthcoming to accommodate that demand. Harding had to devise a method of rationing the available supply in order to prevent the strong from taking everything from the weak, or the deceitful taking everything from the trusting.

Fifth, a choice has to be made between the use of resources for immediate consumption and for enlarging the productive equipment. After they landed on the island, Harding's men could have obtained a much larger supply of food by devoting their energies exclusively to foraging. They chose, however, to allocate their time to other occupations in order to build for the future. The cost of building a dwelling was the reduction of food consumption it necessitated in the present. In other words, the men had to reduce their standard of living in the present so that resources could be used to raise their standard of living in the future. This phenomenon is called saving and investment.

At a later stage in the development of the island economy, grain was discovered. It was planted and carefully husbanded, and eventually it yielded five bushels. After the harvesting, the consumption of the community could have been increased, if Harding had attempted to transform the grain into bread. He chose to plant the five bushels of grain in order to obtain a bigger harvest in the future. The economy saved its resources by not using them for immediate consumption, and invested them for the purpose of having a larger supply of consumption foods in the future.

Whether or not individuals abstain from present consumption depends upon the value to consumers of present consumption as opposed to the value of the possible future benefits of the resources saved. Economic organizations must devise a means of transferring the resources saved to those who will use them for the building of capital equipment.

A subdivision of the fifth function is the repair of the community's capital equipment. This requires similar abstaining from the use of resources for consumption. The islanders' cliff dwelling could only be entered by climbing a long ladder, and the enjoyment of their home was contingent upon the maintenance of the ladder in good repair. But, it could only be serviced if someone were willing to take time off from other occupations, i.e., reduce output elsewhere in the economic organization.

The fulfillment of these five functions is the necessary condition for co-ordinating the economic activity of individuals, and any continually operating society must discharge each function in some manner.

In the United States the carrying out of the functions of economic organization is complicated by the great numbers of people. On the one hand, we must somehow find out the kinds of goods and services wanted by 140 million people with 140 million different sets of values. On the other hand, we should allocate 100 million people to the occupations in which the things that people want will be produced. We do not want arbitrarily to tell people where to work. We want individuals freely to choose their jobs. However, if we permit free choice of job, we should contrive a means of inducing individuals to take those jobs that consumers want filled. Similarly, the fact that the economy includes so many people makes it difficult to carry out the other functions of economizing organizations.

IV. Types of Economizing Organizations

The five functions of economic organizations outlined in the last chapter may be fulfilled in different types of institutional settings. Prior to the era of Mercantilism, the agrarian economy of Europe was organized on the basis of feudalism. Feudalism defined the relations between one individual and another and provided a framework within which the various functions of economic and social activity were specialized and co-ordinated.

The emphasis rested primarily on position or status rather than on function; and, in fact, status determined function. That is to say, a serf tilled his own strip in the common lands, gave his contractual service on the lord's land, and served his time repairing roads, not because he had a special facility in that type of work, but because he was born son of a serf. The whole pattern of relationships between serfs, villeins, vassals and lords established the means of executing the functions of an economic system. By and large, the economy recognized only those wants fixed by custom. Custom and tradition dictated the techniques of production and of resource allocation for the satisfaction of these traditional wants. Each individual's share in the product of the feudal economy was implicit in the position he occupied; status determined distribution. Feudalism hardly conforms to a modern criterion for good organization, but it did fix among individuals mutually recognized obligations which permitted the fulfillment of the five functions of economizing organizations.

A second possible type of organization, exemplified by the economy on the Mysterious Island, may be called an authoritarian system. In this case one man, or one group of men, determine what shall be produced, how it shall be produced, who shall receive the produce, how goods will be rationed, and the rate of economic growth. Harding made all these decisions in the island economy. The authority may or may not consider the wants of the individuals over which he exercises hegemony. As long as he has a variety of wants, or a scale of preferences, and only limited resources with which to satisfy those wants, he must economize in order to achieve his ends.

A third possible alternative for carrying out the functions of an economic system may be called planning by democratic political mandate. In this system the basic decisions are made consciously by a planning agency which is held directly responsible to the people. With the exception of labor, the ownership of the society's resources is vested in the state.

Obviously, a basic problem facing a planning board is the determination of what people want. Various methods such as periodic polls of consumer opinion, consumer legislatures and direct balloting have been suggested as suitable means for evaluating the preferences of the society for goods and services. In each case individuals would be called upon to make a choice between the various alternatives, whether they wanted more of A and less of B or *vice versa*.

The planning agency would direct the allocation of resources for consumer want satisfaction. Each industry would be assigned a priority in accordance with the consumer evaluation of its product. The quantity of machines, machine tools, factory buildings and other capital equipment allocated to each industry would depend on its priority, a high priority industry receiving more than a low priority industry. Labor would be allocated by political direction. That is to say, when consumers demanded more housing, the political authority would order additional allocations of labor to the building trades.

Similarly, the other functions of economizing organizations would be discharged by political decision. The authority would distribute the national product in a manner approved by the majority of the electorate. Rationing and the provision for economic growth would also depend upon conscious political decision.

A fourth method of organization is that of a simple exchange system, as in a frontier economy. The resources of the economy are owned by individuals who produce partly for their own needs and partly for a market. For instance, a farmer, who owns his land and farming equipment, will consume, with the assistance of his family, a large part of the annual yield of his farm. If he has extra grain, he will trade it in a market for something he cannot produce on his farm. A market is provided by the blacksmiths, tanners, shoemakers and other craftsmen who depend on the exchange of their services for agricultural produce in order to make a living.

Some of the functions of economic organization in a simple exchange system are carried out within the family unit. Wants are determined in the family councils. The allocation of resources depends upon the capabilities of the various members of the family. The husband and grown sons tend the crops, the wife and grown daughters prepare the meals and make the clothes and the children gather wood and take care of other small jobs. The product of the farm is distributed on a personal basis with need as the dominant criterion for proper distribution. Big appetites get big meals. Sick members of the family receive the benefits of what medicine the family has. Goods in short supply are rationed among the family members according to the traditions of the family. The head of the family saves that quantity of resources which he thinks he will need to meet the future needs of his family.

The United States and other industrial nations use elements of all of the above methods of economic organization. Status partially determines the allocation of labor in the United States. A bank president's son will often work in a bank simply because he is the son of a bank president. The son of a doctor or lawyer will enter a profession just to maintain the record of no business men in the family. Of necessity a large part of business organization depends upon authoritarian decision. The U.S. Steel Corporation could not reasonably be expected to operate efficiently if the executives had to depend upon voluntarism for the allocation of workers within a plant. Individuals frequently trade apartments or houses on a simple exchange basis. Many of the resources of the United States are owned by the Government, their utilization being subject to democratic nonmarket controls. The Post Office, TVA, and local public utilities are owned and operated by the state. The consumer is protected by his right to vote and his right to appear before utility commissions.

But obviously the United States relies more heavily on another form of economic organization which, without conscious direction, permits individuals and the society as a whole to economize by allocating scarce resources for the maximization of consumer want satisfaction. This formal organization is the *price system*.

A price system discharges the five functions of economic organization by co-ordinating individual decisions, not through planners or government authorities, but through a specialized institution — the market. Every commodity or service offered by firms to consumers has a price, and every resource offered to firms has a price. Buyers and sellers of both commodities and resources meet in the markets. The buying and selling decisions affect prices, and the behavior of prices in turn affects the decisions of individuals.

Individuals indicate their wants by freely buying goods or exchanging money for goods at a price. In effect, they vote with their dollars. Commodity prices rise and fall (or stocks of goods decrease or increase) as consumers buy more of one thing and less of another. These prices and inventory changes publicize consumers' wants.

The movement of prices also rations the available supply of commodities. If there is not enough steak to satisfy all consumers, its price will rise. Those consumers who do not value steak sufficiently to pay the price will be forced out of the market. On the other hand, if the supply of steak is too large in relation to consumer demand, its price will fall; and consumers will be encouraged to take an additional amount.

Price allocates resources to the firms that produce consumable commodities. When consumers buy more of a given commodity, the managers of the firms affected will offer a higher price to resource owners than prevails elsewhere in the markets. Owners of resources will be attracted to those firms by the higher price. When consumers reduce their purchases of a given commodity, the firms affected tend to reduce their purchases of the resources which produce that commodity. Resource prices will fall and make that occupation less attractive to the owners of resources.

The goods and services produced through a price system are distributed through the intermediate means of individual income. Income is a claim against goods and services. Individuals earn income by selling their resources to firms. The size of their income depends upon the price they receive and the quantity of their resources used.

Prices indicate wants, ration commodities among consumers, allocate resources and divide income because they represent values upon which individuals can make economizing decisions. For the consumer prices translate want satisfactions forgone and reserved into relatively objective terms. The prices of resources reflect the evaluation that consumers place on alternative occupations for resources, thus providing a means for allocating resources in response to consumer want indication.

The United States is a mixed economy, containing the elements of all types of economic organization; but price system organization is the most fundamental of these elements. Now, everyone is conscious of price, since in one capacity or another we constantly engage in transactions that involve price. But curiously, few are aware of the organizational features of prices. Consequently, we shall examine in subsequent sections the organizational role of prices.

To that end we shall explore the concept of a pure price system, which along with the traces of the status system, authoritarianism, planning and the simple exchange system describes the economy of the United States.

V. The Pure Price System

To develop an understanding of the price system, let us imagine that we are members of a planning agency charged with the responsibility of executing the functions of an economic system. The responsibility of the planners is such that they must allocate resources for maximum consumer want satisfaction. They can apply any method that they consider appropriate to this end.

Want Indication. The political scientists would undoubtedly press the advantages of political methods for determining wants. If we use the ballot in order to allow the people to elect governmental leaders, why not use a similar device for selecting the goods and services on which consumers place the greatest premium?

This proposal, however, encounters serious difficulties. The merely mechanical and administrative obstacles would be insurmountable. Casting the ballot would require impossible amounts of time, since the consumer would have to look through a ballot bigger than a Sears & Roebuck catalogue. Otherwise the voting consumer would not have all the alternatives before him. In a presidential election the alternatives are the Democratic candidate, the Republican candidate, and the standard-bearers of lesser parties such as the Vegetarians. The voter can cast his ballot, because he knows the alternatives and can choose one to his liking. Similarly, a consumer must know all the alternative commodities before he can make an intelligent choice.

Furthermore, the economic ballot would have to differ from the political ballot in that it must provide a means for a complicated weighted vote by each individual. As a member of the political electorate, you vote either for the Republican or Democratic candidates. As a member of the economic electorate, you would want to vote for more oranges and fewer steaks, or more toasters and fewer waffle irons. Consequently, it would not be sufficient to instruct voters to place x's beside the commodities they preferred; in voting they would have to indicate the proportion in which they wanted goods and services.

Some of the planners would object to such proposals because of the probability of less than 100% participation. The bother of going to the polls each Friday would deter a substantial percentage of potential voters, especially if the ballot contained several thousand items. The planning agency never could be sure that results obtained, if any, represented the consensus of all consumers. Also, the economy minded members of the planning agency would object to the tax burden of elaborate political voting mechanisms for consumers.

If these arguments failed to impress the political scientists, the economist would offer his basic criticism: that consumers would not be able to express their wants through political balloting even if all mechanical and administrative difficulties were overcome. They would not know what they were giving up, i.e., they would not know the cost, of the combinations of goods for which they were asked to state a preference.

I do not know whether I want an automobile until I know what I have to give up to get one. What I have to give up is cost. The cost, however, depends upon the number of people who want automobiles. For the more people who demand cars, the greater the amount of resources that must be withdrawn from alternative occupations to produce cars.

Hence, more demand for cars means higher cost. Therefore, I cannot know cost until everyone in the economy has expressed his preferences. If the cost is high, I may not find it worth while to obtain an automobile. What I give up may satisfy want more than the automobile. On the other hand, if the cost is low, it may be worth while to get an automobile.

What is required for choice, then, is a co-ordinated expression of wants by consumers. A social mechanism is needed to register constantly the results of all previous ballots so that each individual consumer will know cost when stating a want. This cannot be done by any political technique.

This fundamental criticism of political techniques for registering consumer wants applies to other nonmarket methods. The public opinion experts on the planning board might want to canvass consumer opinion by distributing questionnaires. Such a project, however, could not get far past the discussion stage, for the questionnaires could not be stated in terms meaningful to the consumer. If they were merely asked what they wanted, everyone would undoubtedly request diamond stick pins and Studebakers. Requests of that nature would not be an effective expression of wants, for no one would know the costs of the requests.

Political techniques have to be relied on for indicating particular types of wants such as the demand for an army and a navy or the demand for parks. As long as we know the cost of resource utilization in most lines of production, we can attain through political methods a reasonably close approximation of the cost of an army and navy to consumers. However, the bulk of consumers' wants cannot be expressed through political methods.

Having eschewed political methods for the determination of the majority of consumers' wants, the planners would be forced to find a satisfactory alternative. Fortunately a price system offers a solution — dollar voting with consumer markets as ballot boxes.

Each consumer is supplied with money. The spending of money for goods in the consumer markets accomplishes two purposes. First, in making a purchase a consumer takes a share of the national product. Everyone knows this. But second — and this is not widely realized — a consumer expresses his preference for the kinds of goods and services he wants produced. In other words, a purchase represents a consumer vote for a particular combination of goods and services. If I buy a pound of bacon, a dozen oranges, five loaves of bread and fifteen bottles of milk each week, my dollar votes are for the production of those sorts of things. As long as I buy them, I vote for them. I can change the nature of my vote simply by changing the proportions in which I buy goods and services.

Such a procedure, i.e., voting with money, solves the problem which precluded the universal use of the political ballot for want indication. Prices continually record the results of the balloting of the many individuals in the economy. When consumers want more of a given commodity, they demand more. The price of the commodity will rise, thus (1) informing producers that consumers want more output and (2) informing consumers that purchases of the commodity will involve a greater cost. When consumers want less of a given commodity, they demand less. The price of the commodity will fall, thus informing the producers that consumers want less and informing consumers that its purchase will involve less cost. Consumers, therefore, are continually informed of the terms of choice. They can express wants because prices indicate wants directly and at the same time express the cost of future purchases.

In casting his ballot, a consumer votes for more of one commodity and less of another. His problem is to determine how much of each commodity he should buy. He is, therefore, concerned with the marginal purchases. Consumer choice requires the comparison or balancing of the values of marginal purchases or marginal values. The consumer will successfully distribute his income so that he obtains the greatest want satisfaction if at the margins of all his purchases the value retained equals the value forgone. This means that a consumer has not purchased goods and services in optimum proportions unless the want satisfaction obtained by any additional purchase of a commodity equals the additional want satisfaction forgone.

Consumers, therefore, must constantly adjust their dollar voting in response to price changes, because price movements change the values of the alternatives forgone and the alternatives reserved. This proposition merely states precisely what everybody who has engaged in market transactions knows. When the price of eggs rises, consumers do not buy the same amount as before. They reduce their purchases or buy the same amount of lower quality eggs. Why? The consumer will tell you that he cannot afford to buy as many eggs as he used to, because the price is too high. That merely means that the additional want satisfaction from what formerly was his last dozen of eggs bought was less than the want satisfaction forgone to obtain it. Therefore, he decreases his purchases of eggs until the additional value he obtains equals the additional value he forgoes.

Thus the consumer not only votes but has the possibility of measuring and comparing values more or less objectively. That is, a price system affords consumers a vote and an intelligent vote. One consumer can indicate his wants because all consumers indicate their wants, thus providing him with the cost data on which measurement and comparison depend.

A price system thus accomplishes through the market mechanism of prices what planning groups cannot so comprehensively accomplish with nonmarket mechanisms.

Social Organizations for Resource Allocation. The planners have been directed to discharge the functions of

an economic system so that consumer want satisfaction is maximized. The market mechanism has informed them of the order of consumers' wants. Now they must allocate resources so that the goods and services produced correspond to the wants indicated. Their guide is the consumer. He is sovereign because he knows best the sorts of things that will satisfy his wants. If consumers prefer shirts and shoes in a ratio of five to one, the planners must allocate resources so that shirts and shoes are produced in that proportion.

Essentially the problems are, first, to develop some criterion which will permit us to judge when resources are in the right occupations; and, second, to devise a means for moving resources from one occupation to another. When consumers want additional output of typewriters, the criterion must immediately show that the resources in the typewriter industry are not adequate to produce typewriters in the quantity desired by consumers. Then, somehow, men and other resources must be transferred into the typewriter industry from other occupations.

Possibly they could discharge this function by building up a priority system. They could establish a hierarchy of industries from the most favored to the least favored according to consumer want indication and require all productive units seeking resources to submit their requirements to a priority board.

The problem of priorities would exasperate the most astute planner. He would have to decide whether bread producers deserved a higher priority than mattress producers. He knows from the behavior of prices whether consumers want more or less of those items. However, on the basis of that information alone, he does not know how much more or how much less.

Furthermore, the absolute level of prices does not provide the required information. Bread costs the consumer ten cents a loaf and a Rolls-Royce with leopard skin seat covers and a back-seat bar twenty thousand dollars. We do not conclude from those prices that consumers want more Rolls-Royces produced than bread.

But if the planners did draw up a priority that adequately reflected consumers' want indication, on what basis would the planners pass on the validity of the requests of productive units for resources? Suppose that a productive unit with a number one priority and another with a number fifteen priority both requested the planning board for fifty skilled mechanics. Should the planners accede to these requests, should they only grant a partial allocation, or should they give the unit with the number one priority fifty mechanics and the unit with the number fifteen priority twenty-five mechanics?

Assuming that somehow the planning board can determine hypothetically the right allocation of resources among the various occupations, how could it be sure that the owners of resources would care to be allocated in the prescribed way? Nobody likes to be drafted. If the board granted the request of a productive unit for fifty mechanics, it would have to disengage some mechanics from their present employment in order to make good its grant. Conceivably, some unemployed mechanics would be registered with the board. But even these men might not like being ordered into an industry about which they knew nothing or ordered to a new city or region.

Just as individuals as consumers are free to indicate their wants by casting their dollar ballots, ideally we want individuals as producers equally free to choose their occupations. There will, however, inevitably be a conflict between producer free choice and consumer free choice, a conflict which a planning board could only resolve on an arbitrary basis. Suppose that of a labor force of 60 million, 10 million want to be clerical workers, 15 million agricultural workers, 1 million civil servants, 10 thousand coal miners and 20 million industrial workers. But suppose also that consumers want a bundle of goods which can be best supplied by 5 million clerical workers, 2 million civil servants, 500 thousand coal miners and 10 million agricultural workers. How does one compromise these two contradictory patterns of choice? It would seem that either consumers or workers would have to give up their freedom. Lacking a means of compromise, the planning board would have to order workers from agricultural occupations into coal mines and government service. Clearly such orders would violate the freedom of the worker to choose his occupation. The equally unhappy alternative is to tell the consumer what to eat and what to wear.

Prices fortunately offer a means of compromising consumer free choice and producer free choice. Where consumers want more goods from an occupation than the people willing to work in that occupation can produce, price movements will adjust the discrepancy. The price of the commodity will rise thereby reducing the number of consumers who demand it. At the same time, the price paid resources in that line of production will also rise thereby attracting additional resources to it. Thus price movements compromise the patterns of consumer free choice and producer free choice by increasing the cost to consumers of the commodity wanted and increasing the attractiveness of the occupation to producers.

Another difficulty with a priority system is that under it the planners must attempt to allocate resources to the production of those things that consumers want without knowing the value of the resources they allocate. Consequently, they cannot know how resources should fit into the big picture. If you were trying to build a house but did not know the value of the resources used in constructing a house, you would not know how much labor to employ, whether to use brick, stone, or wood, and whether to build two or three stories.

What is needed for proper allocation is a system of resource valuation which will permit a comparison of (1) the value of resources used in a given occupation and (2) the con-

sumer want satisfaction arising from the products of that occupation. We do not want to allocate such a large quantity of resources to the production of Rolls-Royces that the value of all those resources in that use is less than the value in alternative uses.

Comparison requires a common denominator — value expressed in price — because in physical terms the demand for movies, for instance, and the services of unskilled labor are incomparable. But in value terms we can ask ourselves whether the value of movies to consumers is equal to the value that workers in the movie industry create.

Comparison is necessary for proper allocation of resources. The balancing by consumers of additional want satisfaction retained against that forgone requires an equivalent balancing of the use to which the sources of want satisfaction, i.e., resources, are put. If consumers increase their purchases of washing machines and reduce their purchases of scrub boards, the price of resources used in producing those commodities should, ideally, indicate the change in consumers' wants. The consumer will remain sovereign only so long as the values of resources in various uses can be altered to correspond to the balancing of consumer values.

Thus the planners again would be forced to accept a price system solution to the problem of allocation. It provides the means for valuation that makes possible comparison of the value of finished goods (prices) and the value of the alternative uses for resources (costs).

Costs are an evaluation based on

the relationship between the demand for resources and the availability of resources. High costs signify that the demand relative to the supply is great, and low costs the opposite. The price tag on Joe DiMaggio is high because there are not many baseball players that can perform the way he does. The price of the average major league baseball player is relatively low because there are many players in the bush leagues that can replace him when he wears out.

But costs, at the same time, measure the value of the alternative forgone. A skilled mechanic receives a high wage because many industries want his services. The industry that does employ him must pay him an amount sufficient to keep him from working for those other industries. Therefore, the price on his services measures the value of the alternative employment forgone to hold him in his present occupation. The low price of unskilled laborers reflects the relatively low value of the alternative employment forgone to employ them.

Since these propositions are probably unfamiliar to the student, they require restatement. Resources should not be placed in occupations in which the forgone alternative has a greater value than that which is gained. We do not want Arturo Toscanini mining coal, because the value of the coal he could mine would be considerably less than the forgone value of his services as a conductor. For the same reason we do not want labor producing additional ball point pens if consumers value their services more in the production of additional Parker 51's.

Whether the proper allocation of resources in relation to consumer wants has been obtained can be ascertained only by comparing the values of wants and resource utilization, or price and cost. These data provide the criterion for allocation that the planner who depends on nonmarket expedients lacks. Any disparity between these two values informs those responsible for allocation of the discrepancy between the consumers' evaluation of a commodity and of the resources utilized to produce it.

To continue: in resource allocation we are concerned with the margins of production. If, at the margins of production, cost is greater than price, it means that the value of the alternative forgone, as indicated by cost, is greater than the value retained, as indicated by price. In other words, consumers want less of the commodity costed and more of something else. If the cost of producing additional shoes is greater than the price consumers are willing to pay for those shoes, consumers value resources more in occupations other than shoe production. And, conversely, if the cost is less than the price consumers are willing to pay, they value resources more in the production of shoes than in other occupations. Consequently, the relationship of the values of cost and price determines the direction in which resources should move.

The two sets of value data, cost and price, provided productive units by a price system, obviate the need for a central planning board and priority system. Individual managers can tell by a comparison of those values whether they are justified in increasing or decreasing the quantity of resources they employ. *They can wisely employ additional quantities of resources as long as price at the margin is greater than cost and have not employed the correct quantity of resources until cost and price are equal at the margin.*

Fortunately the individual manager does not need to know anything about the big economic picture. He need not have the perspective of a planner. If he is a producer of peanut butter, he will neither know nor care about the production plans of shoe manufacturers. Nonetheless, the big picture is implicit in the relationship of his costs and of the price he receives for his product. Costs measure alternatives forgone and price measures the worth of the product to the consumer. When costs are greater than price at the margin, consumers prefer less of his product and more of something else. He doesn't have to know this fact or know what the " something else " is. All he has to do is to reduce the number of resources he employs so that they will be free to be employed by units where price at the margin is greater than cost.

The planners now possess a value criterion which indicates when resources are properly allocated for the maximization of consumer want satisfaction. But what motivates the movement of resources? When the price consumers pay for margarine is greater than the marginal costs of margarine production, what causes labor to move to the margarine in-

dustry? This is the second problem in the allocation of resources.

One way to solve the problem is to conscript labor. But prices provide a more acceptable solution. When consumers demand more margarine, the price of margarine will rise. Managers of margarine plants will offer labor a higher wage than prevails elsewhere in the labor markets. Those workers who are looking for an opportunity to increase their income will move to the margarine industry from less remunerative occupations. As workers move, the output of margarine will increase. The price of margarine will fall, or at any rate stop rising. If the price of margarine approaches the marginal costs of margarine production, the managers will no longer demand greater amounts of resources. The price of resources in that occupation will therefore become less attractive to resource owners; and the movement of men and materials will stop. Thus price allocates scarce resources by posting differential rates on alternative occupations for the same type of resource. Differential rates will continue until resources are allocated to those occupations in which consumers want them.

The effectiveness of price as an allocator of resources depends in large part upon the mobility of resources. Mobility depends upon two things, one, knowledge of opportunities, and, two, ability to take advantage of those opportunities. If the wages paid glass blowers increase, knowledge of the change may not get around. Or workers may know about the wage increase but not have the facilities for acquiring the needed skill. In either case, few can move into the occupation.

The longer the time period involved, however, the greater the mobility of resources. When the price paid glass blowers rises, there will be no change in the numbers employed at the outset. But because of the passage of time, people will become aware of the new wage level and have an opportunity to acquire the needed skill. Hence one would expect a gradual change in employment.

Resources other than labor are also sensitive to changes in their prices. If the return to a farmer for using his land in corn production increases relative to the return from other grain crops, he will shift acreage into corn. If the owner of urban real estate can obtain a higher rent by leasing his property to a manufacturer than to the present leasee, he will do so. Again the rapidity of the adjustment depends upon the mobility of land or, more precisely, upon the ability of other agents to transform the land from one use to another. Likewise the response of capital to changes in its return — interest — hinges upon the relative difficulty of transferring funds from one enterprise to another.

In summary, the allocation of resources for maximum consumer want satisfaction relies on two requirements: one, a criterion for determining when resources are in the right occupation, and, two, a means for moving resources into the right occupations. The values of cost and price provide the criterion, and the prices of resources provide the motive for allocation. Blind allocation is avoided as is a labor draft.

The Distribution of Income. The planners need not puzzle long for a systematic method of distributing income. The prices of resources which the planners use for allocative purposes at the same time distribute income to the owners of resources. Therefore, in allocating through prices the planners establish an automatic mechanism for distributing income.

To the owners of resources, the price of resources appears as income. The price, and hence the income received by a resource owner, depends upon the value of the goods and services a resource produces. But the value of goods and services depends upon consumers' wants. When consumers want more margarine, the resource owners who produce margarine receive increased income. In the first place, additional resources must be attracted to the margarine industry by a higher price. In the second place, the higher evaluation consumers place on margarine will be reflected in the higher evaluation of the resources which produce margarine.

It can be said, therefore, that the prices, through which income is distributed, measure the productivity of resources. A worker is paid for what he adds to the productive process. A floor sweeper at Willow Run adds relatively little to consumer want satisfaction and, therefore, receives a small wage. But the conductor of the Boston Symphony adds

a great deal to consumer want satisfaction and hence receives a high
wage.

Thus, income is distributed
through the prices of resources, but
the consumers' evaluation of wants
and of the means of satisfying want,
i.e., resources, determines those
prices. We thus use income to accomplish the allocation process.

**The Adjustment of Consumption
to Production.** The development of
a rationing system is a practical
problem that the planners must face.
When the demand for white shirts
increases, there will not immediately
be a corresponding increase in the
output of white shirts. It takes time
to hire the additional workers and
buy the additional raw materials necessary for the increased production of
shirts. The white shirts available
must somehow be distributed to consumers in an orderly way. In the
absence of a rationing system, the
shirts would be distributed haphaz-
ardly according to the whim of retailers or according to the ability of
the consumer to use "drag" with
the retailer.

Prices once again afford a solution.
When shirts are in short supply,
their price will rise. As the price
rises, those consumers will be driven
out of the market who place the least
value on additional shirts. The rationing function of prices assures
that the short supply will be distributed to those who place the greatest
value on the commodity.

On the other hand, if the demand
for shirts decreases, the stocks of
shirts held by retailers will increase
at the outset. Manufacturers will

not be able immediately to withdraw
resources from production. To keep
their stocks from becoming excessive, retailers will lower their prices.
Since the lower price entails a smaller sacrifice of alternatives than before, additional consumers will enter
the market for shirts. The gradually
falling price will line the consumers
up in descending order, from those
who place the highest value to those
who place the lowest value on additional shirts. One by one they
will enter the market as the price
falls.

**The Provision for Economic
Growth.** So far the analysis has focused on the development of a social
mechanism for the allocation of a
fixed quantity of resources in response to consumers' wants. Economic growth is dependent on an
increase in the volume of resources
with which an economy produces
goods and services. If we want to
increase production all around, we
will construct more factories, more
machines and increase supplies of
raw materials. If the labor force
works with increasing amounts of
capital, production will be increased.

Such a process requires abstaining
from using resources for consumption, or saving. It will be recalled
that when the men on the Mysterious Island harvested their first wheat
crop, they obtained five bushels of
grain. They could have consumed
that grain, but they chose to plant in
the hopes that the yield in the future
would be greater. They saved their
resources by reducing consumption
in the present.

The planners could arbitrarily indicate the amount of resources to be devoted to future production rather than to the production of goods and services for immediate consumption. This might be a perfectly reasonable procedure, but there is another way to do it through the role of individual decision. Consumers normally do not spend all their income on consumption goods. They place a certain amount in savings banks, insurance companies or old socks to cover their future needs. Refraining from consumption, or saving, reduces the demand for resource utilization in the production of consumption goods. It, therefore, liberates resources for use in further production. If it were possible, through individual decision, to transfer the resources liberated to the managers of productive units that produce machines and build plants, then economic growth could be obtained without arbitrary political decision.

That transference of resources can be accomplished if a special price is posted which will induce individuals to offer their savings to the men who will build plants and machines, i.e., investors. That price is the rate of interest, which measures the increase in income contingent upon the use of savings by investors.

The rate of interest also rations scarce savings to the best uses. At any given time there are series of investment possibilities whose realization depends on the acquiring of resources. An investor may want to construct a plant for the production of pre-fabricated houses. He can only construct the plant if he can bid resources away from other occupations.

If individuals turn over their savings to the investor, he has the means of offering prices to resource owners which will attract them to his industry. But to obtain the funds the investor has incurred an obligation to the saver, i.e., the payment of interest. He will incur that obligation only if the value of the capital goods he produces warrants the payment of the interest charges. The value of the capital goods, however, depends upon the consumers' evaluation of wants. Therefore, when interest rates rise, the available savings will be rationed among the best uses. Those investment projects will be dropped in which consumers do not condone the payment of interest.

Thus the rate of interest is similar to other prices. Just as the movement of wages induces laborers to allocate their services among the various occupations, so does the interest rate induce individuals to allocate their savings to investors. Just as commodity prices ration the available supply of a commodity to those who place the highest evaluation on that commodity, so does the rate of interest ration savings to the best uses. And by posting the rate of interest a price system provides for economic growth through individual decision.

Resumé of the Features of a Price System. We have examined the way in which a price system discharges the five functions of economic organization. In a price system, the planners have found practical solutions to economic problems. In this section we shall review the features of a price system that recommend it to the planners as a method of social organization.

A price system is a value system. But the values are not set arbitrarily by a governmental authority or by any one group in the economy. The consumer-public determines values by freely casting dollar ballots in consumers' goods markets for the things they want.

The managers of productive units are the representatives of the consumers. Government officials supply the electorate with political goods such as bills protecting democratic rights. If the administration does not provide the type of political good that the electorate wants, it can be voted out of office. Similarly the managers of productive units supply consumers with economic goods. If the managers do not produce the goods and services that consumers want, they also can be voted out of office. Consumers merely have to change their dollar votes in the market in order to change the values of price and cost which are the managers' guide to production.

As long as the representatives of the consumer are held responsible to the consumer, resource allocation will be rational. That is, through the enforcement of the standard of price-cost equality at the margins, consumers will obtain from resources a supply of goods and services in the right proportions. If consumers want one million automobiles and two million radios produced a year, resources will produce those amounts.

The rational allocation of resources, however, is obtained, not through arbitrary political decision, but through voluntary movement by resource owners. When the demand for industrial products increases relative to that for agricultural products the wages offered agricultural workers will fall relative to the wages received by industrial workers. Thus a price system provides an incentive for workers to move from farm to factory.

Any discrepancy between the pattern of consumer choice and producer choice is compromised through the movement of prices. Most individuals as consumers like the convenience of the Holland Tunnel as a means for getting from New Jersey to Manhattan. Not many individuals, however, would care to do the work of the sand hog that is essential for the construction of underwater tunnels. If some consumers want the tunnel badly enough, they will pay a high price for the use of the tunnel. Consequently, high wages will be offered to sand hogs, and some workers will decide that they do not mind doing that type of work.

Thus the planners have solved the economizing problem by planning a price system. We have seen its practical advantages.

Special Points for Recapitulation and Clarification. A lecturer has an advantage over the writer of a text. When he deals with concepts that are particularly abstruse, he can rephrase the problem and use many clarifying examples. Furthermore, he can determine whether his students have grasped the point by the simple expedient of asking questions. Here we can only guess that certain aspects of the discussion of the price system are not perfectly clear. We therefore turn to a recapitulation of these most difficult points of the analysis.

Margins significant rather than totals. In the course of a week a consumer buys a bundle of goods. He may buy two pounds of potatoes, one pound of steak, seven quarts of milk, two dozen eggs, four loaves of bread and five onions. The next week the consumer will buy the same bundle but with the goods in different proportions. He may buy one pound of potatoes, no steak, ten quarts of milk, three dozen eggs, three loaves of bread, and four onions. In other words, each time he goes to the market, a consumer does not choose an entirely different bundle of goods. The consumer, therefore, is not interested in the total satisfaction he gets from a bundle of goods. He is interested in the marginal satisfaction of getting more of one thing and less of another. The consumer, then, pushes some margins out and pulls others in.

Consequently, industries must constantly increase or decrease their output in response to changes in consumers' purchases. A producer will seldom transform his plant from the production of one thing to the production of something entirely new. Our interest, therefore, is in the additions to and reductions in production, i.e., the margins, rather than in the whole quantity of a commodity produced.

In order to obtain maximum consumer want satisfaction, margins must be continually balanced. That is to say, we must balance the marginal value of goods to consumers against the marginal value of the resources used to produce those goods. Consumers receive goods and services in the right proportions only when these marginal values are equal.

Marginal cost equals price. The argument of the previous section can be restated in terms of price-cost equality at the margins. For convenience we shall refer to that relationship as "marginal cost equals price."

Marginal costs measure the value of the alternatives forgone to obtain an addition to output of the commodity costed. To the manager of the productive unit they measure the additional amount he must pay to resources to obtain their services for an increase in production. The value of the alternative forgone, and hence the amount that managers have to pay for additional resources, depends upon the demand for resources in relation to their availability. The cost of employing additional night watchmen at the local water works is low for there are plenty of workers who can meet the needs of other productive units for night watchmen. The employment, therefore, of one or two more watchmen at the water works deprives other industries of relatively little in terms of value. On the other hand, the employment of additional chemists for analyzing the water supply costs more. Many industries demand chemists. To employ a chemist in one occupation necessitates the forgoing of the value that the chemist could have created in alternative occupations. That value is great if many industries demand his services.

Marginal costs will rise when the managers of many productive units increase their demands for a particular resource. To employ that resource in one occupation requires the payment of an amount sufficient to keep that resource from going to other occupations. Rising marginal costs, therefore, indicate an increasing value of the alternative forgone as the result of employing a resource in one occupation.

But the demand of productive units for resources reflects the demands of consumers for goods and services. A meat packing plant will hire more labor because consumers want more meat. The value of the alternative forgone, therefore, in employing more workers in meat packing actually represents the consumers' evaluation of the uses to which resources can be put. High marginal costs mean that consumers are forgoing a great deal of want satisfaction from alternative uses for resources as the result of the employment of additional resources in one occupation. Low marginal costs mean that consumers are giving up relatively little when more resources are employed in an occupation.

Now just as cost measures the value of the forgone alternative, so price measures the worth to consumers of additional amounts of a commodity. In buying goods and services a consumer balances marginal values. He will buy eggs, butter, or bread so that the value from the additional purchases of each will equal

the value foregone. If, however, the price of eggs is $.80 per dozen, the price of butter $.40 per pound, and the price of bread $.20 a loaf, the additional purchases of each entails the foregoing of different degrees of value. The consumer gives up more to get another dozen eggs than to get another pound of butter. If he gives up more to get additional eggs than additional butter, then he must obtain a greater marginal value from eggs than from butter. Price measures these different values. At the above prices, a consumer will get twice as much value from an additional dozen of eggs as from an additional pound of butter. He will get twice as much value from an additional pound of butter as from an additional loaf of bread. If this were not true, he would not pay what he does.

No two consumers will buy the same quantities of goods and services. In the course of a week one consumer might buy three dozen eggs, two pounds of butter, and five loaves of bread. Another consumer might buy two dozen eggs, one pound of butter, and seven loaves of bread. Each consumer buys goods and services according to his own tastes. For each consumer, however, the last purchase of each commodity will yield a satisfaction in proportion to its price. Price, therefore measures the worth to consumers of additional amounts of a commodity.

It then follows that, if marginal cost measures value forgone and price measures value received at the margin, the equality of marginal cost and price is a social ideal. For if all productive units adjust output on such a basis, consumers will receive the goods and services they want in the right proportions. Allocation will thus be ideal. If the price consumers are willing to pay for additional bicycles is greater than the marginal costs ,of producing those bicycles, consumers value the additional bicycles more than they value the alternatives forgone to obtain the increase in bicycle production. That is, they want more bicycles and less of something else. On the other hand, if the price consumers are willing to pay for additional bicycles is less than the marginal costs of production, then they value the alternatives forgone more than the increment to bicycle production. They want fewer bicycles and more of something else. Only when marginal cost equals price in all productive units do resources produce want-satisfying goods and services in the right quantities.

When allocation is ideal, consumers have obtained the optimum amount of want satisfaction consistent with their limited incomes. They cannot increase want satisfaction by transferring dollar expenditures from one commodity to another. They have purchased eggs, bacon, shirts, shoes, and suits in the proportions that get them the most for their money. If they buy more of one item and less of another they forego a greater value than they obtain.

Furthermore, ideal allocation places resources in the occupations in which they make their greatest contribution to production, i.e. the productivity of each resource is optimal.

Workers cannot add more to want satisfaction by transferring from automobile plants to airplane plants. Salesmen cannot increase their productivity by selling bonds instead of insurance. In each case the productive contribution lost would be greater than that gained by transfer.

Clearly the allocation contingent upon the equality of marginal cost and price does not make low price an ideal. It is often said that the performance of a productive unit can be judged by the lowness of the price at which it markets its product. But price is only significant in relation to cost. The absolute level of an individual price does not provide an adequate criterion for passing on the performance of productive units. A high price is correct if the value of the resources used to produce the commodity is high. A low price is correct if the value of the resources used to produce the commodity is low. Consequently, it is proper to price Cadillacs high and paper napkins low. Prices may be low or high, but whether they are correct prices can only be ascertained by comparing them to cost.

And it is equally true that correct costs are not necessarily low costs. Costs measure the value of the alternatives forgone. Low costs are therefore proper only when that value is low. We price resources on an alternative cost basis so that we will have a means of comparing the value of resources in alternative occupations. If we placed an artificially low cost on the resources used to produce Cadillacs, consumers would be led to believe that they were giving up less than they actually were to get additional output of Cadillacs. Costs are correct, then, only when they accurately represent the value of the alternatives forgone.

Pricing according to supply and demand. In the last section, we saw that ideal allocation is obtained when the managers of productive units adjust their output so that marginal cost is made equal to price. "Marginal cost equals price," is therefore a production rule. It is not a price rule. At any given price the manager produces that output which makes marginal cost equal to price, whatever price is. If price rises, the manager will increase output. If it falls, he will decrease output. Consequently, the production rule fixes the relationship between price and the amount supplied by productive units.

It is equally clear that at various prices demand will vary. When the price of eggplant rises, consumers will buy less than before. When it falls, consumers will buy more. A relationship, therefore, exists between price and the amount that consumers will demand. Such a relationship, however, does not itself set price.

Clearly, there will then be a price at which supply equals demand and this is the correct price. For at this price the market is cleared; there are no shortages and no surpluses. Each consumer in the market can find a seller, and each seller can find a buyer. Pricing according to supply and demand is therefore a convenient solution to pricing problems, because it assures that the rate of production will equal the rate of consumption.

The things produced will be sold without some consumers in the market going unsatisfied.

But more than this, when supply equals demand, suppliers are not frozen out of the market. That is, usable resources are not kept from producing the things which consumers want. For at that point, the consumers' evaluation of the product at the margin equals their evaluation of the resources at the margin. No resource not being used for producing A is capable of producing a value of A greater than the value of the resources in alternative uses.

Suppose that onions are priced so that the amount demanded is less than the amount supplied. Onions will tend to accumulate in retailers' vegetable bins, which must mean that consumers value additional onions less than the resources used to produce them. Otherwise they would buy the product which the resources produce. Price will fall. The production of onions will decrease, thus releasing resources for more valued employment. On the other hand, if onions are priced so that the supply cannot accommodate all the consumers in the market, consumers must value the product more than the resources which produce it. The price of onions, therefore, will rise, and an additional supply of onions will come into the market as additional resources move into the production of onions.

Thus price is correct when supply equals demand, because at that price the markets are cleared and resources produce the things that consumers want.

The problem of sunk costs. " Marginal cost equals price " is the ideal production rule because, if followed, no productive unit will increase output beyond the point where the additional value it creates equals the additional value forgone. This is so because the rule permits the comparison of the use of resources in alternative occupations. Additional resources will be employed in any one line only so long as the price consumers are willing to pay for the product covers the cost of the additional resources.

But some resources, once built, are sunk. They have no alternative uses except as they wear out and are replaced. A factory building, for instance, after it has been constructed, does not have an alternative use in short periods of time. That is, a Ford plant cannot suddenly be converted from the production of automobiles to the production of an alternative product. However, as the Ford plant wears out, it can be replaced, substantially as it was or adapted for new types of production. In other words, in long periods of time factory buildings and other fixed resources have alternative occupations.

Ideally, then, the cost of fixed resources, i.e., fixed cost, should be considered as marginal cost in long periods of time. But in short periods of time, because fixed resources have no alternative occupations, they should not govern production decisions. This is so because in the short period increased utilization of a factory building does not cause a diminution of alternative production, as

would be the case over the long run when the resources have alternative uses. Only temporarily, therefore, or in the short run, should the cost of a fixed resource not necessarily be covered.

Does the production rule of " marginal cost equals price," correctly take care of these considerations? The answer is yes. For fixed costs are actually marginal in the long run, but not in the short run. In the short run, output cannot be increased by changing factory size, and, consequently, there can be no addition to fixed cost — that is no marginal cost for fixed assets. But in the long run, when factories wear out and are replaced, plant sizes can change. And these changes in plant size, affect the volume of output. Hence, in the long run, fixed assets are marginal costs.

The Circular Flow. The framework of price system may be viewed quite simply as a circular flow of real goods and services and money, with the real goods and services moving in one direction and the money in the other. Individuals as consumers enter into transactions with productive units in the consumers goods markets. They receive real goods on the one hand and, on the other, create money income for the productive units. The productive units enter into transactions with individuals as owners of resources. On the one hand, they obtain the services of resources and, on the other, create income for the owners of resources. Thus real goods and services move from resource owners through productive units to consumers. Money moves from consumers through protective units to resource owners. However, since individuals are both resource owners and consumers, the whole process becomes circular.

The circular flow of a price system differs substantially from economic processes in other types of economic organization. For instance, in a simple exchange system individuals produce real goods for themselves. They obtain want satisfaction by consuming those goods or exchang-

high for effective dollar voting. But, nonetheless, people want education for themselves and for their children. Other wants cannot be satisfied, because private firms cannot produce the want-satisfying commodity. An army and navy uses a tremendous quantity of resources. People want resources to be used for military purposes, but they cannot express that want in a price system. Still other wants cannot be expressed, because consumers would not trust private

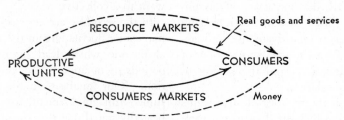

ing them for other consumable goods. But in a price system there is an intermediate step between production and want satisfaction. As producers, individuals receive claims against the means for want satisfaction, i.e., the goods and services produced. Then as consumers, they exchange those claims in the consumption goods market for want-satisfying goods and services.

Evaluation of a Price System. In the analysis thus far we have stressed the things that a price system can do; we have talked about its positive accomplishments. It is only fair, therefore, to point out that there are many things that a price system does not do.

In the first place, a price system does not permit individuals to express some wants. The price of private educational services is too

firms as suppliers. The provision of police protection is a public function. No individual would be happy if there were many police systems with many different standards of law enforcement in a single city. Finally, some wants can be satisfied only if the want-satisfying service can be consumed communally. The demand of an individual for fire protection is ineffective unless all individuals demand it. One person might lay asbestos floors and even keep a fire engine in his garage, but if the house next door catches fire and the fire spreads, his efforts will have been to no avail.

These are the collective wants of society as opposed to individual wants. We express individual wants by buying goods in the consumers markets. But collective wants cannot be expressed in the market, because the market does offer the individual the alternatives among which to choose.

Individuals, therefore, who cannot express their preferences through a price system turn to other organizations such as the government for satisfaction. In the case of education, consumers indicate their wants through the political ballot rather than the dollar ballot. In consequence governments will satisfy the demands of their constituents by modifying the operations of an unalloyed price system, withdrawing resources from private use and applying them to the construction of school buildings and the paying of teachers' salaries.

Even if the area of collective wants in relation to individual wants were constant, this would still be a serious criticism of a price system.

However, with the growth of population and the concomitant increase in specialization, collective wants expand. Early in the development of the United States the demands for education were satisfied in the home or through the co-operative efforts of the small communities. But advancing technology changed the content of the demand for education and placed a premium on professional teachers equipped to disseminate the increasing fund of human knowledge. Before the rise of the large cities, the closeness of the country to the home provided unlimited space for recreation and relaxation. The modern metropolis, however, deprives its inhabitants of the country. Since private firms ordinarily do not supply park services, city dwellers cannot express their preference for fresh air and green grass.

In all probability collective wants will continue to grow at the expense of individual wants. The expense of modern medical treatment necessitates charges that the average consumer can ill afford; and already Capitol Hill reverberates with the invective of the representatives pro and con Group Health, the sort of discussion that always accompanies the metamorphosis of an individual want to a collective want.

In the second place, a price system may cause fluctuations in the national income which lead to alternate periods of unemployment and inflation. Our analysis implicitly assumed full employment, for we repeatedly stated that the cost of utilizing resources in one use was the production forgone in alternative occupations, i.e., that many jobs were available to resource owners. But the level of employment, and hence the availability of jobs, depends upon the size of the national income. This in turn depends upon the volume of spending in the economy.

In our analysis consumer spending is a function of three variables, wants, commodity prices, and income. Any change in one or more of those variables will induce changes in spending. Business spending on capital goods, the other component of aggregate spending in a pure price system, is a function of two variables, the prices of resources and of finished goods.

In the real world, however, another element affects spending decisions, the state of expectations. A price reduction will not necessarily induce consumers to buy more of the commodity, because they may anticipate further price reductions. A business man will not purchase a machine now if he thinks that in the future it will cost him less. On the other hand, rising automobile prices will not reduce automobile purchases if consumers believe that the prices will be still higher in the future. Unfortunately, expectations seem to bunch and everyone evaluates the future course of events in roughly the same way. If everyone in the economy believes that "things are tough all over," things will be tough all over. Consumers and business men alike will husband their dollars, and reduced spending will reduce the volume of employment, confirming the original gloomy outlook.

On the other hand, if consumers and business men entertain opposite expectations, there may be such a deluge of spending that prices rise precipitously, a rise reflecting not a change in consumers' wants, but the pressure of redundant expenditures.

In the third place, ideal allocation will often conflict with the desires of the members of society for security. The ideal adjustment of production to consumption implies that consumers' wants control the allocation of resources. If wants change there must be a corresponding change in allocation. In terms of industrial operations this places upon managers the responsibility of increasing production in some industries, reducing it in others, and shutting down plant capacity in still others. These adjustments hurt be-

cause workers will lose their jobs. Eventually they will be re-employed in other occupations, but in the interim they lack the means of paying rent and buying food.

The success of an economy in our analysis depends upon the extent to which firms produce the things that consumers want. The requisite for success is a flexible price structure which adequately reflects the consumers' evaluation of their wants and of the resources that can satisfy them. But it is no comfort to a worker to know that his services are priced properly, if that price is so low that he does not receive enough income to make ends meet. A flexible price is an insecure price. It may go up, but it may just as easily go down.

In the fourth place, costing in a price system does not as accurately represent the terms on which a given commodity is produced as we might wish. Steel producers build blast furnaces and converters, hire labor, purchase coal and iron ore, and the payments they make for these resources in real terms evaluate the alternatives foregone to obtain steel production. But in addition to the obvious costs of steel production, there are hidden costs which do not appear in the accounting data of the industry. The smog that hangs over Pittsburgh, a by-product of the steel industry's coking ovens, forces its citizens to mobilize resources to combat the damage inflicted on home and personal equipment. In the absence of smog, resources would be free to engage in occupations which would increase alternative output. In other words a discrepancy between private and what may be called social costs misrepresents the sacrifice steel production entails; consumers actually give up more for a given output of steel than private cost figures indicate.

It is difficult to ascertain the extent of this discrepancy in costing, but it is probably fair to say that hidden costs accompany most kinds of industrial activity. The private costs of beer production do not include the payments that must be made to the officers of the law who have to arrest the drunks and maintain order in the tap rooms. Obviously the significant value data for ideal allocation are social costs which supply the full information about the terms of choice. If social costs exceed private costs in the production of a given commodity, consumers aware of this discrepancy would want a smaller volume of production. In the more infrequent case of private costs exceeding social costs, consumers would want a greater output.

A fifth criticism of a price system concerns its effect on the distribution of income for there is a strong tendency for a pure price system to accentuate distributive inequality. The income the owner of a resource receives depends upon the value of his productive contribution to the economic process, and the productive contribution of the many individuals of society will vary tremendously. Those people with high incomes can put the money to work that they cannot spend. Money gets money through the process of savings and investment. More money gets still more money. Thus the very rich become richer while the poor just hold their own.

Furthermore, there is nothing inherently good or bad about income distribution according to productive contribution. A peddler of hashish may receive a tremendously high income while a garbage collector receives relatively little. We cannot determine, therefore, whether distribution is good or bad by a productivity criterion. Such a judgment depends upon ethics.

In the presence of great inequality, consumer sovereignty is not democratic. Consumers do not have an equal voice in the determination of the composition of production for the rich man can vote many times more than the poor man. Consequently, the degree of inequality markedly affects the type of good produced; resources will turn out one Cadillac or five Fords, one private ocean-going yacht or one thousand outboard motor boats, depending upon the distribution of the voting power among the consumers.

Moreover a most disturbing aspect of a price system is its effect on human behavior. Life in a price system is a never-ending process of price-watching. Consumers balance marginal values expressed in price. Producers change the tempo of industry when marginal costs diverge from price. Resources owners constantly scan the market for the price that might increase their income. An overly price-conscious populace, however, may not be a pleasant populace. Some critics feel that people become money mad and that dollar chasing becomes the national pastime.

When all economic values are reduced to the common denominator of price, price becomes the dominant theme of the society. Price leaves no room for sentiment or the other values which bind people together in friendship. When marginal costs rise above price, managers must fire workers. It makes no difference to the manager whether or not the workers fired have the means of getting along. The manager, in fact, has no alternative; price and cost are his guide, and other considerations have no relevancy for the decisions he has to make.

The resource owners, who bear the human costs of changing economic values, must scrap and compete in the markets in order to keep their heads above water. When differential resource prices appear, the scramble is on. The man who gets the high paying job must beat someone else to it. A premium is placed on competitivism and individualism.

Now some may say that it is the love of the competitive game that made America as rich as it is. This may be true, but apparently few people like the force of the game when it touches them. One seldom sees a family where the mashed potatoes of the evening meal are distributed to those who get to the table first. Family life is co-operative rather than competitive. And it is this spirit of co-operation that human beings like. Its absence in the market place is a source of repeated objections to the competitive price system. A price system forces people to treat each other like automatons. Do we therefore not lose the values that really make life worth while?

VI. The Competitive Price System

In this and the next chapter we shall examine a price system in two different institutional settings and see to what extent the shortcomings of a pure price system are modified or accentuated by its institutional setting. In this chapter we shall examine the competitive price system, in the next the socialist price system.

The competitive price system does not differ from the socialist price system in the discharging of the first and fourth functions of economizing organizations. In both systems consumers indicate their wants by freely spending money for the things they want in the consumers goods markets. In both systems the movement of prices adjusts consumption to production. As we shall see in the next chapter, the arrangements for changing prices differ in the two price systems, although the function of the changing prices is the same. But the competitive price system differs from the socialist price system in the way it discharges the remaining functions of economizing organizations.

Of these others, the most important is the allocation of resources. An essential element in successful schemes for resource allocation is the development of a proper motive for top management. In all price systems, that motive must make managers adjust output so that marginal cost equals price. In the competitive price system this is done by rewarding successful managers with profits, bonuses, or attractive salaries. The penalty for failure is business losses and ultimately bankruptcy. There is a similar system of punishments and rewards in the socialist price system. Top management is explicitly instructed to adjust output according to marginal cost and price. Reward or penalty is directly related to the ability of the socialist manager to obtain that output.

Many motives may compel a manager, or entrepreneur, in the competitive price system to produce a particular commodity. He may have inherited a business from his family. He may like the idea of producing shiny gadgets. Or he may think that he is performing a public service by producing a drug guaranteed to kill the common cold. But within the limits established by these and similar considerations, entrepreneurs will attempt to obtain through production and sales as large a profit as possible.

Profits are the difference between costs (prices of resources $\times$ the amount of each used) and revenues (price of the product $\times$ the amount sold). In the competitive price system, therefore, price and cost mean to the entrepreneur something different from the evaluation of wants and of the means of satisfying want. They indicate the state of profits.

It can easily be shown that profits are greatest when marginal cost equals price. If marginal cost is less than price, increasing output will add more to revenues than to costs. If marginal cost is greater than price, reducing output will subtract more from costs than from revenues. Only when marginal cost equals price will profits be at a maximum. Thus the competitive price system assures an ideal allocation of resources by motivating top management, through profits, to produce where marginal costs equal price.

But the allocation motivated by profits will be ideal only if entrepreneurs are unable to manipulate price. That is to say, the entrepreneur must adjust output to price and not maximize profits by raising price. This condition will be satisfied if there are many sellers in a market. In that case one entrepreneur will be unable to raise price. If he does, he will lose business to his rivals and bankrupt his company.

Most industries in the United States are not, of course, perfectly competitive. Aluminum is produced by one company. Relatively few firms account for the total output of steel. Automobile production is largely confined to the big three, General Motors, Ford, and Chrysler. But this does not always preclude relatively effective competition. ALCOA has no rivals who produce aluminum, but it has rivals who produce plastics, wood, steel, and other metals. If ALCOA prices aluminum too high, consumers will buy commodities such as steel which are suitable substitutes for aluminum. Therefore, competitive conditions are more prevalent than it appears at first glance for every commodity produced in the United States has effective substitutes.

In using profits to make marginal cost equal to price, the competitive price system makes the entrepreneur accountable to the consumer. Consumers distribute profits to the entrepreneurs who produce the things they want and losses to those who do not. When an entrepreneur adjusts output so that marginal costs equal price, he has done the best he can, given the state of consumers wants. If consumers value the commodity he produces sufficiently, he will have maximized profits. If consumers do not find it worth much, he will have minimized losses. But losses and profits cannot exist for long. The entrepreneur who has minimized losses may be happy about the minimization, but he will not be happy about the losses. He will, therefore, transfer his plant into the production of those things for which consumers are willing to pay a profit-making price. The transfer of men and resources into the profitable industries will increase supply, lower price, and reduce the level of profits. The withdrawal of resources from unprofitable industries will reduce supply, raise price, and reduce losses. Resources will continue to move until profits are comparable in all industries. In short, profits are not an end — they are a useful social device — a means.

The third function of economizing organizations, the distribution of income, is discharged by the competitive price system just as we have explained it is in the pure price system. Resource prices, which allocate, also distribute income. In the socialist price system, the state distributes income through social dividends and social security plans to adjust the inequality of the distribution according to productive contribution. This inevitably also happens in a competitive price system, because people will not tolerate the inequality of the initial distribution characteristic of rigorous competition. As it is approximated in the real world, the competitive price system has the distributive scheme of the socialist price system.

In the United States, for instance, income inequality is so great that the government, reflecting the demand of the electorate, has socialized large parts of the distributive process. We have a progressive income tax which takes a greater proportional share of the rich man's income than the poor man's income. The taxes received by the government are used to supply many services consumed primarily by the lower income groups: parks, education, social security, and other similar benefits of government.

As for the fifth function of economizing organizations, the provision for economic growth, the competitive price system relies on individual decision. A special price, the rate of interest, is posted which induces savers to transfer their savings to investors. The investors use the funds for the construction of the capital equipment necessary for economic growth. This is as explained for the pure price system.

Evaluation of the Competitive Price System. Again we have explained a system in terms of what it can do, and have ignored its shortcomings.

The criticisms brought against a pure price system also hold for the competitive price system. Some wants cannot be expressed, income fluctuates causing alternate periods of prosperity and depression, ideal allocation may conflict with the goal of security, private costs diverge from social costs, income inequality is accentuated, and human beings tend to be reduced to mechanical robots chasing dollars. In addition there are other criticisms of the price system.

Entrepreneurs may tamper with the wants of consumers in order to influence them to their own advantage. Advertising has become deeply ingrained in enterprise society. Nonetheless, it is difficult to see what social function the announcement of Stan Musial's endorsement of Camels fulfills. Obviously entrepreneurs hope to establish their product as the only adequate satisfier of a want. If the makers of Wheaties can mobilize the children of America for Wheaties by the judicious use of pearls cast by Jack Armstrong and Superman, it will be difficult for parents to buy any other types of breakfast food. Consumers, therefore, no longer choose freely or intelligently between alternatives, but partially in response to the pressures of advertising.

Moreover the cost of advertising is great. When Lucky Strike hires Jack Benny and Speed Riggs to push its product, Camels and Chesterfields must hire similar talent to secure their own clientele. Consequently, a given output of cigarettes will cost more than previously for a greater number of resources are allocated to the tobacco industry. If advertising expenditures were reduced, resources would be liberated for the production of other types of goods and services.

The competitive price system may conflict with rapid economic progress. The factors which compel resource allocation to conform to the wants of consumers may destroy the conditions for progress. Progress requires the marketing of new types of commodities which can stimulate new consumers' wants. But consumers cannot express their preferences for new goods until they appear in the markets. Thus, the entrepreneur who manufactures an untried product has no guide. He risks complete failure and he may not be willing to assume that risk unless he anticipates the possibility of great reward, i.e., large profits. But the competitive price system precludes the maintenance of large profits since they have no social function other than that of a device for allocation. There is, therefore, a conflict between adjustment and economic progress.

Finally, the very process of competition may destroy the institution upon which it depends. The entrepreneur who maximizes profits will very quickly tire of the quest for the kind of profits that slip through his fingers. If he manufactures a commodity that strikes the consumers' fancy, they will only grant him profits long enough to get additional entrepreneurs into the production of that commodity. However, if the entrepreneur can block entry into his industry, he can secure profits for long periods of time.

Consequently, there is a constant tendency for entrepreneurs to attempt to gain control of the market. If they can buy up other firms, block entry, or withhold production techniques from competitors through patent devices, they can gain control of the substantial percentage of industry output. But when productive units become large, entrepreneurs have a chance to manipulate price. This is the antithesis of competition, since the competitor takes price as given and produces as much as is consistent with his costs.

This destroyer of competition is monopoly. With monopoly we lose some of the features of the competitive price system. Resources no longer are allocated according to the rule of the equality of marginal cost and price. The consumer has no effective control over the power of the entrepreneur to ignore wants. That is, the change from the competitive price system to monopolistic organization means the transference of sovereignty from the consumer to the entrepreneur. Since the consumer is a member of a larger economic group than the entrepreneur, it may be said that the shift to monopoly from competition is undemocratic; control now rests with the few instead of the many.

On the other hand, a slight degree of monopoly may be the answer to the tendency of the competitive price system to destroy the incentive for risky investment. If profits exist over long periods of time, entrepreneurs may have the incentive to develop new products and new industries. In the presence of slight monopoly we have sacrificed the adjustment of resource allocation to consumers' wants. But we may have obtained more economic progress. This is a dilemma. We cannot have ideal allocation with monopoly. And perhaps we cannot have rapid progress without it.

VII. THE SOCIALIST PRICE SYSTEM

With the exception of labor, all resources in a socialist state are owned by the government. The forests, agricultural land and urban real estate, coal and other mineral deposits, factories, machines, and everything with which labor produces want-satisfying goods and services are held in common ownership for the people by the representatives of the people, i.e., the government.

The utilization of resources, therefore, becomes directly a matter of public policy. If the policy makers are instructed by the members of the socialist state to allocate resources for maximum consumer want satisfaction, and if, further, they are aware of the difficulties that nonmarket planners encounter, they will plan a price system.

We shall assume that policy in a socialist state is made by a representative body such as our own Congress, or by committees acting for the representative body. Economic policy is made by the committee for economic affairs. Such a group establishes the basic criteria for the price and production decisions that must be made in the economy. Two rules provide those criteria. One, *prices must be set so that supply equals demand.* Two, *production must be adjusted so that marginal costs equal price.* Two groups of agencies are set up to carry through these rules: the price authorities and the production authorities.

The importance of these rules cannot be overstated. Only if the rules guide price and production decisions will allocation be rational and in response to consumers' wants. For then at the margins of every line of production the values of the alternatives foregone will equal the values of the alternatives received. Consumer-want satisfaction will be maximized.

The authorities must apply these rules to various categories of goods, each one of which presents a different problem.

We first consider consumers goods and services. Consumers indicate their wants by spending money freely in the consumers goods markets as explained in the pure price system. The purchases of consumers will depend upon price. When the price of eggs rises, consumers' purchases will fall. When the price falls, purchases will increase.

There will also be a relationship between price and the amount which government productive units will supply in the markets. The production authorities order managers to produce that output which will make their marginal costs equal to price. When the price of eggs rises, therefore, managers will increase output. When the price falls, they will decrease output.

Now since both purchases and sales are seen to depend on price, the price authorities will set that price which will make the demand equal to the supply. At that price the market will be cleared with no surpluses or shortages. Just as in a competitive price system, such a price is ideal in terms of resource allocation.

Since price is set to equate supply and demand and output is determined by the rule that marginal costs must be made equal to price, an ideal allocation is achieved. For the marginal values foregone (marginal cost) are equal to the marginal values received (price), and no willing buyer is without a seller and no willing seller is without a buyer.

Similarly producers' goods, i.e., machines and processed raw materials, will be priced and produced according to the rules.

Again, the demand for producers goods will depend on price. The government manufacturer of typewriters must produce where marginal cost equals price. If the price of the punch presses he utilizes falls, he will buy more. For to the manager of the typewriter plant, the price of punch presses is part of his marginal costs. Hence, if marginal costs fall relative to the price of output, he must increase output. He will therefore buy more punch presses. On the other hand, if the price of punch presses rises, he will buy less.

The demand for punch presses reflects the value consumers receive at the margin. If typewriter plants buy additional punch presses according to the rule of marginal cost and price, it means that consumers value additional punch presses more in the production of typewriters than in alternative uses.

The supply of producers goods also depends on price. The production authorities will instruct the managers of punch press plants to produce the output which will make their marginal costs equal to the price of punch presses. If the price of punch presses rises, therefore, managers will increase output. If it falls, they will decrease output.

Again, it will therefore be possible for the price authorities to find a price for producers goods which will make supply equal to demand. This is the correct price. And again the correct output is achieved by the rule which makes marginal costs equal to price. Under these conditions the value that additional producers goods can create in alternative uses are balanced. Punch presses will not be able to add more to consumer-want satisfaction in any other use than their present one.

The pricing of labor is similar to the pricing of producers goods and consumers goods. There is no equivalent production rule, however, for labor, because the labor offered to a productive unit does not depend on its marginal cost. In fact, there is no marginal cost of labor, because labor is not manufactured.

The demand for labor varies with its price (the wage rate) as does the demand for producers goods. As the wage rate rises, the managers of productive units whose product prices do not meet the higher marginal costs of operation will decrease their demands for labor. But if wage rates fall, their demand for labor will increase. The demand for labor reflects the demands of consumers for goods and services. The wage rate, therefore, reflects the value to consumers of additional workers in a given occupation.

The supply of labor also depends upon the wage rate. If the wage rate of masons increases, additional workers will enter the trade. On the other hand, if the wage rate of masons falls, workers will leave the trade, some to retire and others to transfer to other occupations. Wage rates also indicate the value of alternatives foregone. If a contractor has to offer a mason a higher wage rate in order to attract him to his employment from other occupations, it means that the value of the foregone alternatives is greater. This is so, because more productive units are demanding the services of masons, reflecting the increased value consumers place on this type of labor.

Again, the price authorities will set wage rates so that supply equals demand. The labor markets will be cleared: no workers will be unemployed and no productive units in the market for labor will be without workers. But, in addition, at those wage rates the marginal values will be balanced. The value of additional workers to consumers in any given occupation will equal the value foregone to employ them in that occupation.

The final category of goods, government owned capital such as land, coal, or oil, differs from the previous categories in that the supply offered in the markets is determined by political decision. Political decision is necessary because natural agents, i.e., land, cannot be produced according to marginal cost and price. Also supply cannot be determined on the basis of free individual decision, as in the case of labor, because the resource is owned by the government.

Rule one, however, still applies. The demand for land, for instance, responds to price in the same way as the demand for producers goods, consumers goods, or labor responds to their prices. When the price of land rises, demand falls; when it falls demand increases. Supply, however, is fixed. The price authorities will still set that price which equates supply and demand.

Such a price will be correct if it can be shown that margins are balanced at that price. In the first two categories of goods, the rule of "marginal cost equals price" permitted a balancing of the values of alternatives. Consumers goods were produced in the right proportions according to the value of consumers' wants. Producers goods were allocated to productive units so that no producer good could create a greater value for consumers in alternative occupations. In the third category, wage rates represented values received as well as values foregone and therefore could be balanced.

In this final category of good, values are also balanced, but the balancing is done by a political group. If the authority is determining the quantity of coal to be mined in a year, it must balance the value of using a certain amount of coal now against the value of conserving that

coal for the future. As far as the utilization of government owned capital is concerned, therefore, a political group balances values, whereas in the utilization of the other categories of goods, individuals balance values.

For all these categories, the ability of the socialist government to obtain ideal allocation depends upon observance of the rules. The price authorities have tangible evidence to guide their pricing policies. When there are shortages in a commodity or resource market, they know price is too low. When there are surpluses, they know price is too high. The production authorities, however, will have more difficulty in compelling observance of the production rule. For the function of production decision is decentralized; there are as many different output decisions made in the socialist economy as there are productive units. It will be necessary, therefore, to develop a system of punishments and rewards to motivate socialist managers, as was mentioned in the last chapter. The rewards may be in the form of attractive salaries or of prestige ranks, and the punishments of an opposite nature. At any rate, the socialist manager must be motivated to produce the output which makes marginal costs equal to price.

Distribution in a socialist price system differs from distribution in a genuinely competitive price system. Since the state owns all resources with the exception of labor, individuals will receive through the market only that income which they earn through their personal labor. No interest or dividends are received. But, as we have seen, in the so-called competitive system of the United States, distribution is in large part socialized. In our own economy and in the socialist price system, in addition to earned market income, one receives free educational services, the use of parks, unemployment insurance, and other benefits of government.

If doctrinaire socialists held power and insisted on absolute equality in income distribution, the allocative function of price would break down. Suppose that the socialist government distributed its income from nonlabor resources so that everyone in the economy received exactly the same income, regardless of his employment, what incentive would a man have to move from one job to another? If by moving from the men's suits industry to the hat industry, a worker increases his wages from 40 dollars to 50 dollars a week, but reduces his government income from 20 dollars to 10 dollars, he is neither better nor worse off. Why, then, should he move? Under these conditions, price will not allocate labor.

With absolute income equality, the socialist government would have to draft labor in order to obtain an allocation consistent with consumers' wants.

This, however, is a remote possibility. The socialist government will reduce income inequalities but will not level income. The democratic socialist is concerned with the freedom of workers to choose their occupations. In reducing income inequalities, therefore, he will want to maintain sufficient inequality to preserve the allocative function of price.

Evaluation of the Socialist Price System. Effective consumer control in the socialist price system depends upon the strength of political democracy. In the competitive price system, the consumer controls resource allocation by distributing profits and losses. In the socialist price system, the consumer will control resource allocation only if the price authorities translate the consumers' evaluation of wants into objective criteria upon which the production authorities can act. Everything depends upon whether the two rules are followed. The consumers' protection against negligence in the application of the pricing and production rules is the vote. They can vote out of office any administration that falls down on the job.

If we assume that consumers can compel their representatives through observance of the rules to allocate resources for maximum want satisfaction, the socialist price system becomes less vulnerable to criticism than other price systems.

Income inequality can be reduced. The state has jurisdiction over a part of the economy's income, which can be distributed to offset the inequalities of market distribution. The greater the degree of income equality, the more democratic consumers' sovereignty becomes. If consumer voting power is distributed on an equitable basis, resources will produce automatic washing machines for many instead of supplying services of personal maids to a few.

The state could control the excesses of competitive advertising and permit truly informative advertising only. The greater the consumer's knowledge of the alternatives offered for sale in the consumers goods markets, the more chance he has of satisfying his wants. Consequently, advertising informing consumers of the alternatives available in the markets would make for more intelligent consumer choice.

Insecurity resulting from the adjustment of resource allocation to consumers' wants would be more effectively treated in the socialist price system than in the competitive price system. In the first place, there may be less resistance to measures designed to cope with insecurity. The competitive philosophy of each man for himself is not conducive to the development of government programs to help out those who have lost out in the competitive struggle. But a socialist government is dedicated to the reduction of income inequality and to the provision of security for working people. There would be a more sympathetic attitude therefore towards security proposals. In the second place, and probably less important, the socialist government is less dependent on taxation for financing security schemes for it has a nonlabor source of income.

Income fluctuations could be controlled, for investment expenditures would be a function of government policy and not subject to volatile individual decision. The amount consumers spend, which with investment expenditure determines the total volume of spending and hence the size of the national income, is usually relatively stable. Income fluctuations are, therefore, due primarily to changes in investment expenditure. With the decision to invest the responsibility of one group, it is possible to plan a level of investment which will minimize income fluctuations.

As for social costs, which are not measured in the competitive price system, they can be accounted for in a socialist price system. The government managers of steel plants, for instance, would add to their obvious costs the hidden costs of resource utilization in the cleaning of home and equipment soiled with steel's dirt. If production decisions are made on the basis of marginal social costs and price rather than marginal private costs and price, resource utilization will more fully satisfy consumers' wants.

Whether there would be a clash between adjustment and rapid economic progress would depend upon the type of men in government. If the government officials were imaginative and willing to exercise initiative, they might develop new commodities and new industries. In the past, men in government have displayed the type of thinking and acting required for such development. The production of atomic energy is a governmental project, and atomic energy certainly opens up new vistas. On the other hand, if the socialist government rejects new ideas in favor of the traditional way of doing things, it may obtain an ideal allocation of resources, but develop nothing new. It may produce horses and buggies in the right proportions but never produce automobiles.

On the debit side, consumers would no more be able to express collective wants in the socialist price system than in the competitive price system. The socialist government would be compelled to modify the operations of their system in order to provide consumers with park services or a military establishment. Such wants cannot be expressed in a socialist price system because of the inability of individual productive units to supply the service or of the inability of the consumer to express the want individually.

VIII. Is a Price System Necessary?

We have explained in abstract terms what a price system is. We then examined a price system in two particular institutional settings. The competitive and socialist price systems, however, are not the only types of price systems. It is possible to conceive of a price system in which business is privately owned and prices are set by the government. Or it is possible to conceive of one in which the productive units are organized like consumers or producers co-operatives. But we have investigated price systems sufficiently to understand their similarities.

The competitive and socialist price systems differed in some respects, but in others they displayed similar characteristics. In the first place, in both systems wants were indicated by individual consumers spending money in the consumers goods mar-

kets. In the second place, resources were valued on the basis of alternative cost. That is to say, the price of a resource in a particular occupation represented the value foregone to employ it. In the third place, resource allocation was governed by the rule of price equals cost at the margin. In the socialist price system government managers were explicitly instructed to adjust output according to the equality of marginal cost and price. In the competitive price system entrepreneurs maximized profit by producing that output which equated marginal costs and price. These three features common to both the socialist and competitive price systems are the essential distinguishing characteristics of any price system.

We have seen that the incorporation of these features of a price system in an institutional setting such as socialism or competition does not ever lead to completely satisfactory results.

It is also clear that the system of economic organization in the United States does not depend solely on the competitive price system or the socialist price system but rather on elements of both. In addition, there are nonmarket forms of organization in the United States. We buy stamps at state stores at a fixed price, we buy gas and electricity from municipally owned utilities, we send our children to state universities, we join trade unions whose business it is to raise the price of labor above its alternative cost, we provide free lunches to school children, we require certain people to buy social security benefits, we pass laws that place a floor under wages, we allocate a tremendous volume of resources for the maintenance of a military establishment, and do many other things that either violate the requisites of a price system or place economic functions outside of the price system.

In view of the mixed nature of our economic organization, is a price system necessary? The answer is that, if we are interested in measuring the consumers' evaluation of goods and services, then one aspect of a price system is necessary. If we are interested in the maintenance of certain liberties such as freedom for producers to choose their occupations, we must rely on another aspect of a price system.

A complete price system as a method of social organization conflicts with some goals which people cherish. Consumers cannot adequately express their wants for education under a price system, but for that reason we do not forego the whole mechanism for the indication of consumer wants. Where a price system conflicts too harshly with other human purposes, we modify it through political processes in order to achieve a better balance between economic and noneconomic goals.

It is not a question of using a price system or not using a price system for social organization. It is one of deciding how its features can be combined usefully where conflicts exist between the maximization of want satisfaction and freedom to choose and other goals human beings hold.

For instance, resource evaluation according to alternative cost places a premium on flexible resource prices. This means that income recipients dependent on flexible prices never can be sure that their income will be the same from day to day. Partly for this reason the institution of the trade union has grown into prominence in the past fifty years. Its avowed economic purpose is to raise the price of labor above its market value so that labor can obtain a larger and steadier share of the national income.

Trade unionism has received the active support of the government since 1932, because the majority of the people in the United States were in sympathy with the goals of the trade union movement. But as union leaders organized more and more workers, wage rates became further divorced from alternative cost. The union wage became synonymous with a noncompetitive wage.

But because trade unionism precludes the realization of the second feature of a complete price system, we do not deny a place to the others in our economic organization. Consumers still indicate their wants by casting dollar votes. Resources still are allocated according to the criterion of marginal cost and price equality. In the presence of trade unionism, a partial price system has provided a means for determining what people want and allocating resources in response to those wants.

We accept the modifications trade unions force on a price system because most people in the United States feel that the trade union is a democratic institution, worth its cost to society. But if trade unionism also compelled us to drop the other features of a price system, we might decide it was not worth the cost. How, for instance, in the absence of a price system mechanism for registering consumers' wants, would we decide what to produce? Our discussion of the difficulties facing the nonmarket planners made it clear that without the facilities of value and price such a decision would be completely arbitrary.

Trade unionism, then, where it operates destroys one feature of a complete price system but we still incorporate the other two features in our economic organization and gain the advantages of choice and rational allocation that are contingent upon them.

Or resources may not be allocated to hospitals on the basis of marginal cost and price because of the grant by the state to the hospital of a subsidy in some form. In the absence of the subsidy the hospital would supply fewer services to the members of the community. We do not cut the hospital off from the other features of the price system because its operations violate the third. The hospital must still employ a clerical and medical staff and must still purchase various supplies. To that extent it must enter markets, and it can only purchase rationally if the values of the alternatives are stated clearly.

When the government enters agricultural markets in order to support farm prices, the want-indication mechanism of a price system is vitiated. A falling price informs producers that consumers want less of the commodity; but, if the price is prevented from falling by the government, the producer will tend to produce more than consumers want. It is still of positive value to price resources on an alternative cost basis. Otherwise there would be no way of rationing resources to their most valued use. Even if farmers draw a disproportionate amount of resources into agricultural pursuits, alternative cost will distribute those resources among agricultural users in the most effective way. Similarly allocation of resources according to the rule of the equality of marginal cost and price will produce the maximum amount of want satisfaction possible in the light of the disproportionate amount of resources devoted to agriculture.

Clearly our economic organization does not and cannot fulfill all the requirements of a complete price system, but we depend heavily on some of its features. Where one of the features is lacking the other two will often be present. Sometimes all three features are lacking. Other times two are lacking. But the greater part of our economy relies on one or more features of a price system.

As a minimum, a price system has practical value in discharging the five functions of economizing organizations. And, more than that, since a price system is basically an institutional device for measuring values and providing for the expression of free choice, it is difficult to see how either efficiency or liberty can be enjoyed without heavy reliance on some kind of price system.

4 THE ROLE OF COMMUNICATION

29. The Problem of Public Opinion

We have established the necessity of making certain decisions in society. This implies the necessity of developing channels of communication that can disseminate the information upon which decisions are made. The price system, for instance, can be viewed as an elaborate communication mechanism. The posting of prices on consumers goods and on productive services supplies the information about the terms of choice without which it would be impossible to make rational economic decisions. The movement of relative prices in the consumers' markets informs entrepreneurs of the preferences of consumers, while the movement of relative prices in the markets for productive services informs entrepreneurs of the preferences of resource owners for employment. The dissemination of this information thus permits the making of the many decisions which can adjust the pattern of resource allocation to the preferences of the individuals in society.

Democratic political organization is similarly dependent on a communication system, for the citizen cannot be expected to vote intelli-gently unless he is aware of the issues at stake in elections, and the elected officials cannot formulate public policy if they do not know the preferences of the citizens. The problem of the voter is more complex than the problem of the consumer. The latter can choose more effectively, the greater the information he has about the alternatives available in the market. That is to say, the consumer can satisfy a higher level of preferences if he increases his knowledge of the prices of consumer goods. The voter, however, must apply qualitative judgment to the information he receives about issues and candidates. He is not necessarily better off if he has more information because it may be conflicting and inconsistent. His knowledge is gleaned, not only from newspapers, magazines, and radio, but from his associations at work and at play. These diverse sources give the voter a picture of the world which is at once complex and oversimplified. And it is against this background that the voter must choose.

As society grows the problem of choice becomes even more difficult for the individual's direct contact with the experiences that constitute the basis of society must necessarily shrink. He becomes, therefore, more dependent on the channels of communication for his picture of life. In the article that follows, Mr. Walter Lippmann, whose political analyses have been read by newspaper readers both in this country and Europe for more than twenty years, discusses this "pseudo-environment" which separates the objective world from man's interpretation of the world. Since the choices man makes reflect his subjective view of the world, the "pseudo-environment" which transmits objective reality to the minds of men is an integral part of any study of decision-making.

30. The Foundations of Choice in Society*

I.

There is an island in the ocean where in 1914 a few Englishmen, Frenchmen, and Germans lived. No cable reaches that island, and the British mail steamer comes but once in sixty days. In September it had not yet come, and the islanders were still talking about the latest newspaper which told about the approaching trial of Madame Caillaux for the shooting of Gaston Calmette. It was, therefore, with more than usual eagerness that the whole colony assembled at the quay on a day in mid-September to hear from the captain what the verdict had been. They learned that for over six weeks now those of them who were English and those of them who were French had been fighting in behalf of the sanctity of treaties against those of them who were Germans. For six strange weeks they had acted as if they were

friends, when in fact they were enemies.

But their plight was not so different from that of most of the population of Europe. They had been mistaken for six weeks, on the continent the interval may have been only six days or six hours. There was an interval. There was a moment when the picture of Europe on which men were conducting their business as usual, did not in any way correspond to the Europe which was about to make a jumble of their lives. There was a time for each man when he was still adjusted to an environment that no longer existed. All over the world as late as July 25th men were making goods that they would not be able to ship, buying goods they would not be able to import, careers were being planned, enterprises contemplated, hopes and expectations entertained, all in the belief that the world as known was the world as it was. Men were writing books describing that world. They trusted the picture in their heads. And then over four years later, on a Thursday

* From Walter Lippmann, *Public Opinion*, excerpts from Chapter 1. Copyright 1922 by The Macmillan Company and used with their permission.

morning, came the news of an armistice, and people gave vent to their unutterable relief that the slaughter was over. Yet in the five days before the real armistice came, though the end of the war had been celebrated, several thousand young men died on the battlefields.

Looking back we can see how indirectly we know the environment in which nevertheless we live. We can see that the news of it comes to us now fast, now slowly; but that whatever we believe to be a true picture, we treat as if it were the environment itself. It is harder to remember that about the beliefs upon which we are now acting, but in respect to other peoples and other ages we flatter ourselves that it is easy to see when they were in deadly earnest about ludicrous pictures of the world. We insist, because of our superior hindsight, that the world as they needed to know it, and the world as they did know it, were often two quite contradictory things. We can see, too, that while they governed and fought, traded and reformed in the world as they imagined it to be, they produced results, or failed to produce any, in the world as it was. They started for the Indies and found America. They diagnosed evil and hanged old women. They thought they could grow rich by always selling and never buying. A caliph, obeying what he conceived to be the Will of Allah, burned the library at Alexandria. . . .

2.

Great men, even during their lifetime, are usually known to the public only through a fictitious personality. Hence the modicum of truth in the old saying that no man is a hero to his valet. There is only a modicum of truth, for the valet, and the private secretary, are often immersed in the fiction themselves. Royal personages are, of course, constructed personalities. Whether they themselves believe in their public character, or whether they merely permit the chamberlain to stage-manage it, there are at least two distinct selves, the public and regal self, the private and human. The biographies of great people fall more or less readily into the histories of these two selves. The official biographer reproduces the public life, the revealing memoir the other. The Charnwood Lincoln, for example, is a noble portrait, not of an actual human being, but of an epic figure, replete with significance, who moves on much the same level of reality as Aeneas or St. George. . . .

3.

Worldwide concentration of this kind on a symbolic personality is rare enough to be clearly remarkable, and every author has a weakness for the striking and irrefutable example. The vivisection of war reveals such examples, but it does not make them out of nothing. In a more normal public life, symbolic pictures are no less government of behavior, but each symbol is far less inclusive because there are so many competing ones. Not only is each symbol charged with less feeling because at most it represents only a part of the population, but even within that part there is infinitely less suppression of individual difference. The symbols of public opinion, in times of moderate security, are subject to check and comparison and argument. They come and go, coalesce and are forgotten, never organizing perfectly the emotion of the whole group. There is, after all, just one human activity left in which whole populations accomplish the union sacrée. It occurs in those middle phases of a war when fear, pugnacity, and hatred have secured complete dominion of the spirit, either to crush every other instinct or to enlist it, and before weariness is felt.

At almost all other times, and even in war when it is deadlocked, a sufficiently greater range of feelings is aroused to establish conflict, choice, hesitation, and compromise. The symbolism of public opinion usually bears, as we shall see, the marks of this balancing of interest. Think, for example, of how rapidly, after the armistice, the precarious and by no means successfully established symbol of Allied Unity disappeared, how it was followed almost immediately by the breakdown of each nation's symbolic picture of the other: Britain the Defender of Public Law, France watching at the Frontier of Freedom, America the Crusader. And think then of how within each nation the symbolic picture of itself frayed out, as party and class conflict and personal ambition began to stir postponed issues. And then of how the symbolic pictures of the leaders gave way, as one by one, Wilson, Clemenceau, Lloyd George, ceased to be the incarnation of human hope, and became merely the negotiators and administrators for a disillusioned world. . . .

The only feeling that anyone can have about an event he does not experience is the feeling aroused by his mental image of that event. That is why until we know what others think they know, we cannot truly understand their acts. I have seen a young girl, brought up in a Pennsylvania mining town, plunged suddenly from entire cheerfulness into a paroxysm of grief when a gust of wind cracked the kitchen windowpane. For hours she was inconsolable, and to me incomprehensible. But when she was able to talk, it transpired that if a window-pane broke it meant that a close relative had died. She was, therefore, mourning for her father, who had frightened her into running away from home. The father was, of course, quite thoroughly alive as a telegraphic inquiry soon proved. But until the telegram came, the cracked glass was an authentic message to that girl. Why it was authentic only a prolonged investigation by a skilled psychiatrist could show. But even the most casual observer could see that the girl, enormously upset by her family troubles, had hallucinated a complete fiction out of one external fact, a remembered superstition, and a turmoil of remorse, and fear and love for her father. . . .

In all these instances we must note particularly one common factor. It is the insertion between man and his environment of a pseudo-environment. To that pseudo-environment his behavior is a response. But because it *is* behavior, the consequences, if they are acts, operate not in the pseudo-environment where the behavior is stimulated, but in the real environment where action eventuates. If the behavior is not a practical act, but what we call roughly thought and emotion, it may be a long time before there is any noticeable break in the texture of the fictitious world. But when the stimulus of the pseudo-fact results in action on things or other people, contradiction soon develops. Then comes the sensation of butting one's head against a stone wall, of learning by experience, and witnessing Herbert Spencer's tragedy of the murder of a Beautiful Theory by a Gang of Brutal Facts, the discomfort in short of a maladjustment. For certainly, at the level of social life, what is called the adjustment of man to his environment takes place through the medium of fictions.

By fictions I do not mean lies. I mean a representation of the environment which is in lesser or greater degree made by man himself. The range of fiction extends all the way from complete hallucination to the scientists' perfectly self-conscious use of a schematic model, or his decision that for his particular problem accuracy beyond a certain number of decimal places is not important. A work of fiction may have almost any degree of fidelity, and so long as the degree of fidelity can be taken into account, fiction is not misleading. In fact, human culture is very largely the selection, the rearrangement, the tracing of patterns upon, and the stylizing of, what William James called " the random irradiations and resettlements of our ideas." The alternative to the use of fictions is direct exposure to the ebb and flow of sensation. That is not a real alternative, for however refreshing it is to see at times with a perfectly innocent eye, innocence itself is not wisdom, though a source and corrective of wisdom.

For the real environment is altogether too big, too complex, and too fleeting for direct acquaintance. We are not equipped to deal with so much subtlety, so much variety, so many permutations and combinations. And although we have to act in that environment, we have to reconstruct it on a simpler model before we can manage with it. To traverse the world men must have maps of the world. Their persistent difficulty is to secure maps on which their own need, or someone else's need, has not sketched in the coast of Bohemia.

4.

The analyst of public opinion must begin then, by recognizing the triangular relationship between the scene of action, the human picture of that scene, and the human response to that picture working itself out upon the scene of action. It is like a play suggested to the actors by their own experience, in which the plot is transacted in the real lives of the actors, and not merely in their stage parts. The moving picture often emphasizes with great skill this double drama of interior motive and external behavior. Two men are quarreling, ostensibly about some money, but their passion is inexplicable.

Then the picture fades out and what one or the other of the two men sees with his mind's eye is re-enacted. Across the table they were quarreling about money. In memory they are back in their youth when the girl jilted him for the other man. The exterior drama is explained: the hero is not greedy; the hero is in love.

A scene not so different was played in the United States Senate. At breakfast on the morning of September 29, 1919, some of the Senators read a news dispatch in the *Washington Post* about the landing of American marines on the Dalmation coast. The newspaper said:

FACTS NOW ESTABLISHED

"The following important facts appear already *established*. The orders to Rear Admiral Andrews commanding the American naval forces in the Adriatic, came from the British Admiralty via the War Council and Rear Admiral Knapps in London. The approval or disapproval of the American Navy Department was not asked. . . .

WITHOUT DANIELS' KNOWLEDGE

"Mr. Daniels was admittedly placed in a peculiar position when cables reached here stating that the forces over which he is presumed to have exclusive control were carrying on what amounted to naval warfare without his knowledge. It was fully realized that the *British Admiralty might desire to issue orders to Rear Admiral Andrews* to act on behalf of Great Britain and her Allies, because the situation required sacrifice on the part of some nation if D'Annunzio's followers were to be held in check.

"It was further realized that *under the new league of nations plan foreigners would be in a position to direct American Naval forces in emergencies* with or without the consent of the American Navy Department. . . ." etc. (Italics mine.)

The first Senator to comment is Mr. Knox of Pennsylvania. Indignantly he demands investigation. In Mr. Brandegee of Connecticut, who spoke next, indignation has already stimulated credulity. Where Mr. Knox indignantly wishes to know if the report is true, Mr. Brandegee, half a minute later, would like to know what would have happened if marines had been killed. Mr. Knox, interested in the question, forgets that he asked for an inquiry, and replies. If American marines had been, it would be war. The mood of the debate is still conditional. Debate proceeds. Mr. McCormick of Illinois reminds the Senate that the Wilson administration is prone to the waging of small unauthorized wars. He repeats Theodore Roosevelt's quip about "waging peace." More debate. Mr. Brandegee notes that the marines acted "under orders of a Supreme Council sitting somewhere," but he cannot recall who represents the United States on that body. The Supreme Council is unknown to the Constitution of the United States. Therefore Mr. New of Indiana submits a resolution calling for the facts.

So far the Senators still recognize vaguely that they are discussing a rumor. Being lawyers they still remember some of the forms of evidence. But as red-blooded men they already experience all the indignation which is appropriate to the fact that American marines have been ordered into war by a foreign government and without the consent of Congress. Emotionally they want to believe it, because they are Republicans fighting the League of Nations. This arouses the Democratic leader, Mr. Hitchcock of Nebraska. He defends the Supreme Council: it was acting under the war powers. Peace has not yet been concluded because the Republicans are delaying it. Therefore the action was necessary and legal. Both sides now assume that the report is true, and the conclusions they draw are the conclusions of their partisanship. Yet this extraordinary assumption is in a debate over a resolution to investigate the truth of the assumption. It reveals how difficult it is, even for trained lawyers, to suspend response until the returns are in. The response is instantaneous. The fiction is taken for truth because the fiction is badly needed.

A few days later an official report showed that the marines were not landed by order of the British Government or of the Supreme Council. They had not been fighting the Italians. They had been landed at the request of the Italian Government to protect Italians, and the American commander had been officially thanked by the Italian authorities. The marines were not at war with Italy. They had acted according to an established international practice which had nothing to do with the League of Nations.

The scene of action was the Adriatic. The picture of that scene in the Senators' heads at Washington was furnished, in this case probably with intent to deceive, by a man who cared nothing about the Adriatic, but much about defeating the League. To this picture the Senate responded by a strengthening of its partisan differences over the League.

5.

Whether in this particular case the Senate was above or below its normal standard, it is not necessary to decide. Nor whether the Senate compares favorably with the House, or with other parliaments. At the moment, I should like to think only about the world-wide spectacle of men acting upon their environment, moved by stimuli from their pseudo-environment. For when full allowance has been made for deliberate fraud, political science has still to account for such facts as two nations attacking one another, each convinced that it is acting in self-defense, or two classes at war each certain that it speaks for the common interest. They live, we are likely to say, in different worlds. More accurately, they live in the same world, but they think and feel in different ones.

It is to these special worlds, it is to these private or group or class, or provincial, or occupational, or national, or sectarian artifacts, that the political adjustment of mankind in the Great Society takes place. Their variety and complication are impossible to describe. Yet these fictions determine a very great part of men's political behavior. We must think of perhaps fifty sovereign parliaments consisting of at least a hundred legislative bodies. With them belong at least fifty hierarchies of provincial and municipal assemblies, which with their executive, administrative and legislative organs, constitute formal authority on earth. But that does not begin to reveal the complexity of political life. For in each of these innumerable centers of authority there are parties, and these parties are themselves hierarchies with their roots in classes, sections, cliques and clans; and within these are the individual politicians, each the personal center of a web of connection and memory and fear and hope. Somehow or other, for reasons often necessarily obscure, as the result of domination or compromise or a logroll, there emerge from these political bodies commands, which set armies in motion or make peace, conscript life, tax, exile, imprison, protect property or confiscate it, encourage one kind of enterprise and discourage another, facilitate immigration or obstruct it, improve communication or censor it, establish schools, build navies, proclaim " policies," and " destiny," raise economic barriers, make property or unmake it, bring one people under the rule of another, or favor one class as against another. For each of these decisions some view of the facts is taken to be conclusive, some view of the circumstances is accepted as the basis of inference and as the stimulus of feeling. What view of the facts, and why that one?

And yet even this does not begin to exhaust the real complexity. The formal political structure exists in a social environment, where there are innumerable large and small corporations and institutions, voluntary and semi-voluntary associations, national, provincial, urban and neighborhood groupings, which often as not make the decision that the political body registers. On what are these decisions based?

" Modern society " says Mr. Chesterton, " is intrinsically insecure because it is based on the notion that all men will do the same thing for different reasons. . . . And as within the head of any convict may be the hell of a quite solitary crime, so in the house or under the hat of any suburban clerk may be the limbo of a quite separate philosophy. The first man may be a complete Materialist and feel his own body as a horrible machine manufacturing his own mind. He may listen to his thoughts as to the dull ticking of a clock. The man next door may be a Christian Scientist and regard his own body as somehow rather less substantial than his own shadow. He may come almost to regard his own arms and legs as delusions like moving serpents in the dream of delirium tremens. The third man in the street may not be a Christian Scientist but, on the contrary, a Christian. He may live in a fairy tale as his neighbors would say; a secret but solid fairy tale full of the faces and presences of unearthly friends. The fourth man may be a theosophist, and only too probably a vegetarian; and I do not see why I should not gratify myself with the fancy that the fifth man is a devil worshiper. . . . Now whether or not this sort of variety is valuable, this sort of unity is shaky. To expect that all men for all time will go on thinking different things, and yet doing the same things, is a doubtful speculation. It is not founding society on a communion, or even on a convention, but rather on a coincidence. Four men may meet under the same lamp post; one to paint it pea green as part of a great municipal reform; one to read his breviary in the light of it; one to embrace it with accidental ardour in a fit of alcoholic enthusiasm; and the last merely because the pea green post is a conspicuous point of rendezvous with his young lady. But to expect this to happen night after night is unwise. . . ."

For the four men at the lamp post substitute the governments, the parties, the corporations, the societies, the social sets, the trades and professions, universities, sects, and nationalities of the world. Think of the legislator voting a statute that will affect distant peoples, a statesman coming to a decision. Think of the Peace Conference reconstituting the frontiers of Europe, an ambassador in a foreign country trying to discern the intentions of his own government and of the foreign government, a promoter working a concession in a backward country, an editor demanding a war, a clergyman calling on the police to regulate amusement, a club lounging-room making up its mind about a strike, a sewing circle preparing to regulate

the schools, nine judges deciding whether a legislature in Oregon may fix the working hours of women, a cabinet meeting to decide on the recognition of a government, a party convention choosing a candidate and writing a platform, twenty-seven million voters casting their ballots, an Irishman in Cork thinking about an Irishman in Belfast, a Third International planning to reconstruct the whole of human society, a board of directors confronted with a set of their employees' demands, a boy choosing a career, a merchant estimating supply and demand for the coming season, a speculator predicting the course of the market, a banker deciding whether to put credit behind a new enterprise, the advertiser, the reader of advertisements. . . . Think of the different sorts of Americans thinking about their notions of " The British Empire " or " France " or " Russia " or " Mexico." It is not so different from Mr. Chesterton's four men at the pea green lamp post.

6.

And so before we involve ourselves in the jungle of obscurities about the innate differences of men, we shall do well to fix our attention upon the extraordinary differences in what men know of the world. I do not doubt that there are important biological differences. Since man is an animal it would be strange if there were not. But as rational beings it is worse than shallow to generalize at all about comparative behavior until there is a measurable similarity between the environments to which behavior is a response.

The pragmatic value of this idea is that it introduces a much needed refinement into the ancient controversy about nature and nurture, innate quality and environment. For the pseudo-environment is a hybrid compounded of "human nature" and "conditions." To my mind it shows the uselessness of pontificating about what man is and always will be from what we observe man to be doing, or about what are the necessary conditions of society. For we do not know how men would behave in response to the facts of the Great Society. All that we really know is how they behave in response to what can fairly be called a most inadequate picture of the Great Society. No conclusion about man or the Great Society can honestly be made on evidence like that.

This, then, will be the clue to our inquiry. We shall assume that what each man does is based not on direct and certain knowledge, but on pictures made by himself or given to him. If his atlas tells him that the world is flat he will not sail near what he believes to be the edge of our planet for fear of falling off. If his maps include a fountain of eternal youth, a Ponce de Leon will go in quest of it. If someone digs up yellow dirt that looks like gold, he will for a time act exactly as if he had found gold. The way in which the world is imagined determines at any particular moment what men will do. It does not determine what they will achieve. It determines

their effort, their feelings, their hopes, not their accomplishments and results. The very men who most loudly proclaim their "materialism" and their contempt for "ideologues," the Marxian communists, place their entire hope on what? On the formation by propaganda of a class-conscious group. But what is propaganda, if not the effort to alter the picture to which men respond, to substitute one social pattern for another? What is class consciousness but a way of realizing the world? National consciousness but another way? and Professor Giddings' consciousness of kind, but a process of believing that we recognize among the multitude certain ones marked as our kind? . . .

The chief difficulty in adapting the psychoanalytic scheme to political arises in this connection. The Freudians are concerned with the maladjustment of distinct individuals to other individuals and to concrete circumstances. They have assumed that if internal derangements could be straightened out, there would be little or no confusion about what is the obviously normal relationship. But public opinion deals with indirect, unseen, and puzzling facts, and there is nothing obvious about them. The situations to which public opinions refer are known only as opinions. The psychoanalyst, on the other hand, almost always assumes that the environment is knowable, and if not knowable then at least bearable, to any unclouded intelligence. This assumption of his is the problem of public opinion. Instead of taking for granted an environment that is readily known, the social analyst is most concerned in studying how the larger political environment is conceived, and how it can be conceived more successfully. The psychoanalyst examines the adjustment to an X, called by him the environment; the social analyst examines the X, called by him the pseudo-environment.

He is, of course, permanently and constantly in debt to the new psychology, not only because when rightly applied it so greatly helps people to stand on their own feet, come what may, but because the study of dreams, fantasy and rationalization has thrown light on how the pseudo-environment is put together. But he cannot assume as his criterion either what is called a "normal biological career" within the existing social order, or a career "freed from religious suppression and dogmatic conventions" outside. What for a sociologist is a normal social career? Or one freed from suppressions and conventions? Conservative critics do, to be sure, assume the first, and romantic ones the second. But in assuming them they are taking the whole world for granted. They are saying in effect either that society is the sort of thing which corresponds to their idea of what is normal, or the sort of thing which corresponds to their idea of what is free. Both ideas are merely public opinions, and while the psychoanalyst as physician may perhaps assume them, the sociologist may not take the products of existing public opinion as criteria by which to study public opinion.

7.

The world that we have to deal with politically is out of reach, out of sight, out of mind. It has to be explored, reported, and imagined. Man is no Aristotelian god contemplating all existence at one glance. He is the creature of an evolution who can just about span a sufficient portion of reality to manage his survival, and snatch what on the scale of time are but a few moments of insight and happiness. Yet this same creature has invented ways of seeing what no naked eye could see, of hearing what no ear could hear, of weighing immense masses and infinitesimal ones, of counting and separating more items than he can individually remember. He is learning to see with his mind vast portions of the world that he could never see, touch, smell, hear, or remember. Gradually he makes for himself a trustworthy picture inside his head of the world beyond his reach.

Those features of the world outside which have to do with the behavior of other human beings, in so far as that behavior crosses ours, is dependent upon us, or is interesting to us, we call roughly public affairs. The pictures inside the heads of these human beings, the pictures of themselves, of others, of their needs, purposes, and relationship, are their public opinions. Those pictures which are acted upon by groups of people, or by individuals acting in the name of groups, are Public Opinion with capital letters . . . the chief factors which limit their access to the facts . . . are the artificial censorships, the limitations of social contact, the comparatively meager time available in each day for paying attention to public affairs, the distortion arising because events have to be compressed into very short messages, the difficulty of making a small vocabulary express a complicated world, and finally the fear of facing those facts which would seem to threaten the established routine of men's lives. . . .

INDUSTRIAL SOCIETY AND
THE PROBLEM OF CHOICE

PART II

INDUSTRIAL SOCIETY AND
THE PROBLEM OF CHOICE

5 INDUSTRIALIZATION THROUGH INDIVIDUAL CHOICE

31. Individualism and Inventions in Industrialization

We live in an industrial society. We live in a world in which big business manipulates millions of dollars of invested capital, big labor unions negotiate contracts for millions of workers, big government taxes and spends billions of dollars of the national income, big colleges and universities manufacture thousands of educated citizens. Bigness is an outstanding characteristic of industrial society.

And because industrial society is big, it is socially complex. Its many institutions pursue ends by means that often conflict. Yet the very size of these institutions precludes a reliance on personalized, face-to-face relationships for the resolution of these conflicts. In consequence new institutions proliferate as man strives to make of the divergent parts a stable and coherent whole.

Although big and complex, industrial society is young, a child of not more than 150 years. Its burgeoning in western Europe, however, at the turn of the nineteenth century was the outcome of long but inex-

orable historical processes, which destroyed the institutions that had held in check man's potential energy-creating capacities. The Industrial Revolution stepped up the tempo of life and induced more changes on the face of the earth in the subsequent 150 years than had taken place in the previous history of mankind.

There are many parts of the world in which industrial society cannot take roots. The geographic and climatic conditions of a large part of Africa, for instance, prevent the accumulation of capital that industrialization implies. Yet it has by no means appeared in all those countries whose physical environment is amenable to the processes of industrial society. Starting in England, industrialization spread southward into western and central Europe and westward across the Atlantic to the United States. Its transmission into eastern Europe and Russia was temporarily blocked by the tenacity of feudal institutions whose inflexibilities were impervious to change. Not until the Revolution destroyed Tsarist society was it possible for Russia to absorb the industrial techniques of the West. Today countries such as India and China are experiencing the first shocks contingent upon the metamorphosis of a rural into an industrial society.

One hundred and fifty years of industrial society has revealed two basically different methods of achieving the end of industrial growth. On the one hand the countries in the west relied in the main upon the capitalistic market to organize economic activity. The emphasis therefore was on individual decision-making, with a minimum of governmental direction of resources. On the other hand Russia and the countries now closely associated with it have relied upon governmental allocation of resources, with a minimum of control left to the discretion of individual decision-making. The one we call industrialization through individual choice, the other industrialization through collective choice.

In this chapter the first article, "Industrialization and the Rise of the Market," by Karl de Schweinitz, Jr., discusses the historical forces that gradually eroded the foundations of traditionalistic authoritarian societies in the West and thus made possible the growth of an individualistic ethic, which provided the motive power for industrial expansion. In the second article Professor Witt Bowden describes the concrete results of this historical transformation in terms of the flowering of inventions in England during the last half of the eighteenth century. Our third selection is taken from what is generally considered to be a classic of historical analysis, *Religion and the Rise of Capitalism*. Professor Tawney analyzes the influence of Protestantism, particularly Puritanism, on business behavior and tries to show that the Reformation acted like a catalytic agent on the acquisitive instincts liberated in the commercial and industrial revolutions.

32. Industrialization and the Rise of the Market*

The development of economic organization in the western world for the past 150 to 175 years has been unique in the history of mankind. During this relatively brief instant in the history of civilization man for the first time lived according to the precepts of economic liberalism and individualism. Man was free to pursue his own ends as he conceived of

* By Karl de Schweinitz, Jr.

them so long as he did not wantonly destroy his neighbor. The economic restrictions of an older society were raised and replaced in the main by the restraints implicit in the behavior of individuals.

The burgeoning of individualism released human energies that had long been confined within societies ruled by status or prescription. The release manifested itself in a tremendous increase in the output of goods and services. So large in fact was the increase in the output of goods and services that customarily we refer to the changes that made it possible as the industrial revolution.

Revolution implies a sharp break in the continuity of a society — the creation of new social configuration by the ruthless destruction of the old. In the French Revolution Danton, Robespierre, and the Jacobins tore asunder the traditional order of the *Ancien Regime*. In the Russian Revolution Lenin, Trotsky, and the Bolsheviks overthrew the effete Tsarist government. Violence and terror accompanied these upheavals as the revolutionary leaders tried to impose the principles of their revolution on the shells of the old societies.

The economic changes wrought at the end of the eighteenth century were a revolution of a somewhat different order from either the French or the Russian revolutions. There were no tumbrels daily clattering through the streets of London yielding their victims to the guillotine. There were no forcible seizures of government buildings or governmental officials. Nonetheless, the industrial revolution destroyed an old and created a new way of life.

The old way of life was predominantly agrarian and feudal. The bulk of the population tilled the soil and its complete energies were required to provide the people with a subsistence standard of living. The individual members of society were bound to one another through a series of status relationships so that

there was a sort of group responsibility for the condition of each. A peasant had certain rights and obligations by virtue of the estate to which he was born. Similarly a landowner had certain rights and obligations. This network of rights and obligations created a primitive division of labor; some individuals planted, husbanded, and harvested the grain, others cared for the roads, and still others provided for the defense of a community against predatory attack.

Such a society is unfree, but it is secure. The individual is not free to do what he wants. Regardless of his capabilities his assignment in the division of labor is determined by the status to which he happens to belong. If he is a peasant he will farm the land and care for the roads. But so long as he lives up to his obligations he will be secure in employment and in defense. For the discharging of his responsibilities is contingent upon the discharging of other responsibilities, which are his rights. Thus a member of this type of society is secure in the same sense that a small child is secure in the family.

In addition to being feudal and agrarian the old way of life was traditional. The forward look of contemporary western civilization had no place in the old society. There was no concept of progress. People looked back into the past for their inspiration. Authority was age and tradition the resolver of dilemmas.

Where authority and tradition predominate there can be no experimentation for the former cannot tolerate confutation. Thus a traditional society will threaten a Galileo with excommunication for proving hypotheses that refute received authority. In short, prior to the industrial revolution the scientific method was latent in the minds of men.

The objective manifestation of the belief in tradition is a lack of perceptible change. Each generation goes about its business in the same way. In economic terms an individual would consume the same bundle of goods at the end of his life as he did at the beginning of his life. To be sure, changes take place, but not because of a conscious search for new methods and techniques. Rather change is forced. A natural catastrophe or the threat of destruction by hostile neighbors may compel the society to make technological adaptations in order to survive. These changes then become a permanent part of the tradition of the society.

In contrast the new way of life as typified by western civilization glorifies experimentation and change. A new idea is the hallmark of distinction. Suggestion boxes are standard equipment in most factories. Industries subsidize research in their own factories and in the universities. A large part of academic research is devoted to the stating and testing of hypotheses about natural and human phenomena. In consequence change is such an integral part of the fabric of western society, particularly the United States, that it imparts an aura of restlessness to western life. Automobile models change yearly. The length of women's dresses rises and falls on the tides of fashionable opinion. The metamorphosis worked in one generation changes the face of the earth. At the end of life the individual has an entirely different consumption pattern from that at the beginning of life.

The industrial revolution, then, refers to the historical transition from the old traditional society to the new forward looking society. The transition was industrial because of the increased emphasis on capital accumulation and hence roundabout methods of production. It was revolutionary because of the destruction of the status system implicit in the old way of life by the new belief in individualism.

As a revolution the transition was unique. The destruction and ruthlessness implicit in the revolutionary process was not guided and directed by leaders who espoused some positive set of principles which served as criteria for ferreting out the counter-revolutionaries, the implacable opponents of change. A feudal aristocracy or a bourgeoisie did not become the victims of revolutionary ardor. But the industrial revolution wreaked as great a vengeance on existing society as either the French or Russian revolutions. A whole class of people, the most numerous in society, was withdrawn from the protection of the status system and thrown into the jungle of the factory system. And like the jungle the strong prevailed and the weak perished. The individual lost his rights in society and therefore won his freedom from society. It was, however, a spurious sort of freedom. The individual now could freely sell his services to an employer in return for the receipt of money income. He could bargain and accept the terms of the highest bidder. What might have been true in theory was hardly true in fact. For the employers, the owners of the growing factories, had the advantage of financial strength and knowledge. The owners no longer had a set of obligations to society as had a dominant class in an older society. The obligation of the owner was to produce for profits, to buy cheap and sell dear. He therefore had a vested interest in purchasing labor for as little as possible. Furthermore he was in a position to do so for the worker having been recently torn from the security of an older world was ignorant of the ways of the new world. More often than not he had no alternative but to submit to the terms of the employer.

Although the industrial revolution did not necessarily destroy lives, it destroyed personality and individual stature. The expanding working classes became a sort of amorphous and expressionless mass much like the child who is brought up in an institution away from the security of the family. The worker was on his own, but he had nothing to go on. Formerly he relied on the communal organization which implicitly at least stated his purpose in life and gave him a role to play which was an integral part of the society. Now he was told that he could shape his own life. But shaping his own life meant selling his labor services for a subsistence income. This apparently became the end of his existence, an end devoid of any larger meaning.

To repeat, the industrial revolution was unique because it destroyed life not through the machinations of a revolutionary tribunal but through the philosophy of individualism which forced an unprepared people to rely on their own resources.

Individualism which propelled the industrial revolution lies in the main stream of the development of western political thought. It is important to an understanding of planning. The latter stands at the end of the stream just as the philosophy of the medieval church fathers and the ancient Greeks stands at its headwaters. Individualism is an anarchic form of the belief in individual rationality and in so far as it is rationalistic it contains the seeds of the collective rationality implied in planning.

Rational behavior implies the adjustment of means to ends with minimum effort. An individual is rational if, given his ends, he uses the means available to him so that he reaches his ends with a minimum expenditure of effort. The theoretical entrepreneur of the firm in economic analysis behaves rationally when he maximizes profits, selects that output which gives him the greatest spread between total costs and total revenues.

Prior to the industrial revolution the philosophical basis of the typical society precluded the belief in individual rationality. A society rooted in authority and tradition provides an alternative method of making choices. The society acting upon received tradition prescribes both the means and the ends — in short, it dictates the bounds of appropriate behavior. From the point of view of the individual this system obviates choice and hence there is no chance for the individual to behave rationally. He must do things in the traditional way whether or not the traditional way involves a minimum expenditure of effort.

A large part of the history of the western world in the Christian era has been the gradual struggle of mankind to throw off the shackles of traditionalism. In the early centuries of the Christian era progress was imperceptible and was not a positive movement in the direction of the liberation of the individual through a philosophy of rationality. Rather there tended to be an increasing multiplicty of the authorities and traditions to which groups appealed. Since it is often the case that authority claims universality, the fact that there are competing universal cosmologies is likely to place doubts in the minds of men about the validity of any one system. Why am I not capable of choice if there is no agreement among the interpreters of authority about the appropriate way to behave? The initial progress then toward the development of a philosophy of rationality is somewhat negative — the breakdown and splintering of systems of authority.

A Christian dogma never attained a complete universality in the western world. The Catholic Church which claimed the apostolic succession at Rome and which later was declared the leader of organized religion in the Roman Empire by the Emperor Constantine was plagued throughout its early growth by internal schisms and struggles with temporal authorities. With the demise of the western Roman Empire in 476 the patriarchs of the church in the eastern empire, particularly the patriarch of Constantinople, claimed independence from papal authority. In the succeeding centuries the eastern church although nominally subordinate to Rome actually maintained independence. This schism was officially recognized in the middle of the eleventh century so that the Christian world was divided between the Roman Catholic Church and the Eastern Orthodox Church.

Within the Roman Catholic Church the great schism of 1378 in which two rivals claimed papal authority and which established two papal lines until their reconciliation at the Council of Constance a generation later epitomized the difficulty of maintaining unilateral spiritual hegemony over large numbers of people. The great schism and lesser earlier schisms encouraged the political rulers of Europe to contest the authority of Rome. Thus Europe reverberated to the struggles between the *sacerdotium* and the *imperium*.

Although the papacy from time to time gained an uneasy ascendancy over temporal rulers, it was destined to lose out in the struggle between the church and state. The centralization of an ecclesiastical power in Rome which claimed precedence over the temporal rulers of the expanding states of Europe created a hard irreconcilable core of conflict between church and state. Furthermore in the late medieval period certain corrupt practices appeared within the church which stimulated the growth of religious deviationist movements which the temporal rulers found expedient to support.

The Renaissance marked the high water mark of corruption within the church. From the point of view of our theme this is not merely coincidence, but the latter is a reflection of the pervasive influence of the former. The Renaissance refers to the rebirth of classical antiquity first in Italy and later in northern Europe. As such it represented a further splintering of the authorities which guided people's lives. The ancient Greeks replaced the church fathers as the arbiters of human values. In other words the tradition of the authoritarian society became older; it was not cut off at the first year of the Christian era.

With the replacement of the Christian tradition by the Greek tradition came a deprecation of the authority of the former. Perhaps this is best illustrated by the autobiography of Benvenuto Cellini who was a sort of Renaissance Scott Fitzgerald. Cellini epitomized this agnostic age and gloried in both its artistic achievements and its licentiousness. The murderers, lechers, and confidence men who imparted to this period of artistic revival the qualities of the " roaring twenties " were symptomatic not so much of the growth of the classical tradition but rather of the breakdown of medieval morality as represented by the church.

Inevitably the lay revolt affected the church. Nepotism, the commercialization of the sacraments, and Machiavellian concepts of control corroded the inner foundations of the papacy. In this period a Cesare Borgia could rise to the high estate in the papal hierarchy.

The corrupt practices within the church stimulated the revolt of religious leaders who now were supported by temporal leaders. What formerly was schism now became separation. Thus in the early sixteenth century Martin Luther and later John Calvin led successful revolts against the papacy. The Protestant Reformation, it is important to note, was not a protest against the concept and role of authority in the guidance of individual behavior. Rather it was a protest against the corruption of authority. The leaders of the Protestant Reformation were saying, " The papal authority is bad. We will give people a good authority." One only has to contemplate the rigors of life in Puritan New England during the seventeenth and eighteenth centuries to realize that Protestantism did not initially stand for a positive affirmation of the philosophy of individualism and the self-sufficiency of the individual.

The Renaissance and Reformation destroyed the universality of authority in western Europe by creating many competing authorities. The expansion of trade and commerce which accompanied these revolts made the system of authority a less tenable method of governing and bringing order to society. For with the growth of local trade to intra-Europe trade and then to inter-continental trade increasing numbers of decisions had to be made by increasing numbers of people for which the traditional life provided no criteria. The owners of a shipping firm which dealt in North American furs and Madras linens could hardly find precedents for governing their actions in the agrarian life of feudal Europe. Expanding trade then forced men to rely on their own resources.

Protestantism lent support to this new self-reliance. As opposed to Catholicism which emphasized salvation through the administration of the sacraments by the ecclesiastical representative of Christ, Protestantism tended to emphasize salvation through performance in the mundane world. That is to say, man glorified himself in the sight of God by working hard, living frugally and consequently accumulating wealth. One's passport to heaven was industry.

This is the so-called Protestant ethic. The Protestant ethic arises from the authoritarian prescriptions of Protestant society. What constitutes industry is not for the individual to choose. The sixteenth century counterpart of the industrious American baseball player would hardly have qualified for high heavenly reward. The important thing, however, in this connection is that once having prescribed what industrious behavior consists of the authority left it up to the individual to prove his qualifications for heavenly reward.

If Protestantism opened the door to a greater emphasis on individual choice in the rather narrow realm of commercial behavior, the Renaissance opened the door to greater scepticism in the wide realm of philosophical speculation. The rediscovery of ancient Greece revived interest in the Greek philosophers and the eternal questions with which they dealt. Inevitably this led to a re-examination of the philosophical tenets of the then existing societies.

The Renaissance, the Protestant Reformation, and the expanding commercialism loosened the fetters of traditional society and made society more susceptible to change and new ideas. Such an environment produced men like Bacon, Descartes, and Galileo at the end of the sixteenth and the beginning of the seventeenth centuries and later Newton who laid the cornerstones of the scientific method. This period marks the rapid growth of the deductive and inductive methods of logic which tended to destroy the presuppositions upon which traditional society was based. For the scientific method gave man grounds for questioning the received explanations of natural and human phenomena when the latter did not square with observation. If this was the case the scientific method required the construction of a new hypothesis which could stand the test of empirical verification. It was no longer satisfactory to say that the sun moves in an orbit around the earth if observation confutes this hypothesis.

Confronted with such a method the importance of tradition shrinks. For all ideas, regardless of how many centuries had sanctioned them, had to pass in review before the court of the scientific method. No longer was it sufficient to cite ancient authority in support of one's ideas. The test now was what we can observe today and what we can observe of yesterday in the light of today's knowledge. The hold of tradition on society then was attenuated for the paramount strength of tradition was unquestioned acceptance of authority.

The scientific method flowered in the period of the eighteenth century enlightenment and gave to western man a belief in individual rationality. Perhaps in retrospect this may appear to be the youthful optimism of a new cosmology. Nonetheless such a belief arose and not accidentally. The scientific method not only destroyed the old ways of thinking but also destroyed the traditional methods of ordering society. It became incumbent on man therefore to replace tradition with some new ordering concept. Such a new concept was the belief that individuals if given the appropriate knowledge could adjust means to ends and achieve the greater good for all of society. If man appeared to behave in an anti-social way it was not because he was inherently irrational but because he had not been adequately informed about the alternative methods of behavior. The technique then for maintaining the order of society was not the forcible imposition of authority, but rather the reform of society so that the capabilities of individuals for rational behavior could be maximized.

We return now to the industrial revolution. The evolution of the belief in individual rationality which culminated in the eighteenth century enlightenment gradually engendered a social environment more conducive to change. Individuals were not inhibited by tradition to the extent that they formerly had been; they were, then, encouraged to try new ways of doing things. Possibly more important individuals were not quite so concerned about the consequences of change for they felt that the rational powers of man give him a high degree of adaptability. A dramatic manifestation of this new attitude toward change was the tremendous increase in mechanical inventions during the last half of the eighteenth century.

The belief in rationality and change created reinforcing factors which greatly stimulated industrialization. Of particular importance from our point of view was the growth of the market and the economic philosophy about the market.

By the market we refer to a method of economic organization in which buying and selling in interrelated markets serves as a method for controlling the allocation of resources. Each individual is free to purchase the goods and services he wants and is free to sell his labor services or the services of other resources he owns. It is assumed that each transaction is motivated by the desire to maximize some value. The transactions or decisions made in each market then control the allocation of resources. If many consumers want peanuts then resources will be allocated to the production of peanuts for the owners of resources will find that they can maximize their return in peanut production.

In a subsequent chapter we shall analyze the market more closely, but for our present purposes this brief description should suffice. Above all the market is a rationalistic organization which conforms with the pattern of thought which developed with the enlightenment. The market provides an institution for exercising rational choice. Furthermore within the limits that it establishes it leaves the choice of ends and means to the individual. That is to say, each individual is the best judge of the types of goods that will satisfy his wants and also of the type of work that will maximize his money return. If left free in the market to make these decisions the individual can reach the highest level of satisfaction possible.

The economic organization prior to the industrial revolution was not rationalistic for decisions were not made consciously by individuals in organized market. Rather decisions were either made implicitly as in a feudal system or by prescription as in a mercantilist system. There was no room for the individual determination of ends and means. The traditional societies, then, were at odds with the developing philosophy of rationality and something had to give. The environment no longer reflected men's ideas of how men *ought* to live.

We cannot pick one date in history and designate it as the first year of the market and the last year of feudal and/or mercantilistic organization. For each period in history represents some combination of the past, present, and future. Some institutions advance while others recede. Some individuals adhere to the old institutions while others espouse the new institutions. The changes that occur in society come slowly as the balance tips in favor of one group as opposed to another. Only with the perspective of history can one acquire a dramatic consciousness of the change in basic organizations.

With this in mind we shall mark the nineteenth century as the era of the market particularly in England and to a lesser extent in Western Europe. The transition from the eighteenth to the nineteenth century saw the destruction of those remnants of feudal organization which hampered the development of well organized markets. An adequate supply of labor was insured through the continued enclosure of the common land from which the peasantry was accustomed to earning their living and the abrogating of those laws such as the poor laws and apprenticeship laws which restricted the mobility of labor. Thus on the one hand a potential source of labor was pushed off the land and on the other nothing tied workers down to any particular location. The geographical limits of England became the labor market. Again in England the corn laws were abolished; thus a cheap source of grain from foreign countries became available to the economy.

The change mentioned in the previous paragraph reflected a change in the political balance of power within the countries concerned.

That the corn laws in England were abolished was symptomatic of the fact that power had shifted to those groups in England who were interested in the repealing of the corn laws. The owner of agricultural land could not be expected to favor measures which would reduce the price at which grain could be sold. He had a vested interest in the old society because it happened to favor his property holdings. But the growing manufacturers who had to meet payrolls which more often than not were calculated in terms of the price of grain were very much interested in the lowering of the price of grain. The extension of the franchise to the middle classes by the reform bill of 1832 passed the control of English society to those groups which were sympathetic with the vested interest of the manufacturer.

The market became a tremendous catalytic agent for capital accumulation and hence industrialization. The test now for new ideas and new techniques was acceptance in the market place. Before an idea could be tested, however, it had to be embodied in concrete form. Then it could be screened by the impersonal appraisal of buyers and sellers. The criteria applied in this appraisal were not some set of social goals, but rather individual goals. Will the purchase of this product add to my satisfaction or reduce my costs of production to a sufficient extent to warrant the payment of the purchase price?

The significant point is that the market placed a premium on " doing." In the traditional society the new idea was rejected in anticipation of the changes it would bring. There could be no experimentation, no testing of ideas because the whole concept of change was abhorrent to the tradition of society. Now the market induced people to make changes because their acceptability could not be tested until the change was, in fact, made.

Furthermore since the market was central to the larger organization of society, the values of the market tended to permeate society. Prestige, social acceptability, came to be associated with the success of individual ventures in the market. The measuring rod of success became income. To achieve high status in society, then, required high income. To obtain high income required the development of new ideas which would receive the profitable sanction of the market.

Capital accumulation is the utilization of resources to produce goods that will yield satisfaction in the future. When society allocates resources to the production of steel mills and automatic machine tools it does not currently increase the production of consumption goods. Future output, however, will be increased because the production of this type of capital equipment will increase the productivity of the labor force and hence their future output. What ultimately limits the rate of capital accumulation is the rate of technological change. If this latter rate were zero there would be no reason to expect significant increases in productivity through capital accumulation for the labor force would be working with the same type of equipment period after period. It does not follow that if the rate of technical discovery is greater than zero that the rate of capital accumulation will be greater than zero. For technical discoveries must first become an integral part of the economic organization and in order to do this man must be motivated to make the changes in the industrial processes that such adaptations require.

For reasons mentioned in a previous paragraph the market provided this motivating stimulus. Released from the shackles of the overt social controls of former societies the enterprising man was no longer bound by tradition. In a sense this was the negative stimulus of the market. Man was not kept from "doing." But positively man was promised high reward if he broke into the market with a new idea or technique that received its confirmation.

Thus motivated man commercialized mechanical inventions and replaced man power with steam power. The number of factories increased as entrepreneurs found it easier to coordinate production processes when workers were concentrated under one roof and found it economical to centralize their mechanical equipment around the source of steam power. Railroads expanded, knitting the economy into an interrelated unit and increasing the size of the market in which each component part of the economy did business. With these changes productivity increased and the wealth of nations expanded at a greatly accelerated rate.

The expansion of the wealth of nations was obtained at high cost. In order to release the energies of individuals for the necessary adaptations of technological change into industrial processes the old society had to be destroyed. This was the revolutionary aspect of the industrial revolution which we have previously discussed. The majority of people were torn from the security of an agrarian community and thrown into the insecurity of factory life. There was then a harsh ambivalence imposed on society by the industrial revolution. On the one hand one group rode the crest of the waves of change and exacted a high monetary reward and consequently earned an enviable status in society. On the other hand another and more numerous group fell into the troughs of the waves of change and could only flounder in helpless anonymity. The society built around the market honored the first group and vilified the second group.

Such discrepancies in the status of the individuals of society cannot pass unnoticed. No man is self-sufficient. The fortunate man who earns the accolades of society cannot ignore the misery of society. He must have some explanation of the travail of others even if it is only terms of his own success. He cannot cut himself off from the experiences of others because it is through these experiences that he has achieved success.

In an older society it was possible to justify a status hierarchy by deference to supernatural authority. Some people were born to high estate and some to low estate — these things were ordained by God. The order of man within society was beyond the control of society and consequently no individual needed to be unduly concerned about his particular position. This was given to him by a far greater power than man.

Such a philosophy was no longer tenable when a belief in individual rationality has permeated society. It was inconsistent to say on the one hand that man was capable of choosing his ends and then adjusting available means so that he achieved these ends. The latter implied what the former denied — that man was a free agent in the determination of his life's path. This philosophical dilemma was very neatly resolved by the development of economic liberalism.

Economic liberalism provided the philosophical justification of the market economy and therefore the social relationships which arose from the market. Economic liberalism was the philosophy of individualism. It was rooted in the enlightenment and the belief in rationality but in its mature growth it tended to deny the individual the opportunities that were held out to him by the enlightenment. The economic liberal maintained that the market provided a mechanism through which individuals could strive to attain their ends and by which the conflicts among individuals and hence between the individual and society could be resolved. Competition was the force that performed this unique function. Although the interests of the seller and the interests of the buyer were inalterably opposed because the for-

mer sought a high price and the latter a low price, the competition of many buyers and many sellers made this a latent conflict. So long as there were many sellers competing for buyers the price of a commodity could not be too high for in order to attract buyers the individual seller would be tempted to lower prices. The interaction of the buyers and sellers yielded a price and a quantity of goods exchanged which represented the consensus of many. No one individual dominated the market. Rather the market dominated all individuals and led them to behave in a socially desirable way by encouraging the production and exchange of goods which could increase total welfare.

Fundamental to this faith was the belief in economic liberty. If individuals were free to choose employment for the resources they owned they would allocate them to the production of those things from which they could secure the greatest return for their effort. But this depended upon the things that consumers were demanding in the market, for profits could only be obtained if consumers were willing to buy commodities in sufficient quantities to yield profits. If individuals were free to purchase goods and services, the available supply of goods would be distributed among the people in such a way as to maximize consumer satisfaction. For no individual would buy a commodity from which he did not anticipate adequate satisfaction.

In stimulating economic activity and arbitrating the conflicts of individuals the market assigned values to the contribution each individual made to the national product. These values took the form of income received for services rendered. Thus the man who received $50,000 a year had added $50,000 to the national product whereas the man who received $1,000 a year had only added $1,000 to the national product. The market rewarded individuals in accordance with their productive effort. This then became the rationalization of the cruel disparities in status and income that developed with the industrial revolution. If a man received a subsistence income it was because his contribution to society was only worth that amount. He had not been discriminated against because no one individual had personally made this judgment and used the arbitrary criteria of personal opinion. What the man looked like, how he talked, and what he wore were irrelevant. The whole society working through the impersonal institution of the market passed judgment. And so it was with the rich man. A $50,000 a year income denoted a contribution to society valued at that amount.

From this position it was easy to take the next step and make value judgments on the capabilities of individuals in terms of their accomplishments in the market. Then not only did the society not place much value on the contribution of the poor man but the poor man himself was held responsible. Since he was free to make the most of his own resources, he must have been incapable if he failed. The onus for individual failure in the industrial society fell on the shoulders of the individual rather than on society. This position was the polar extreme of the status and secure society. There the individual was secured by the status relationships which imposed responsibilities on each member of society for the welfare of all. Here there was no status except that associated with income and since each individual was responsible for his own status there was no interrelated system of rights and obligations which provided individuals with security.

The philosophy of economic liberalism which arose from the market provided the leaders of society with a justification for the inequities that appeared in the social life. It also provided grounds for believing that the market form of economic organization benefited the whole society and not just those who reaped large rewards. For this philosophy hypothesized the harmony of all in the interests of all. Society would operate smoothly if the market was permitted to work.

Perhaps we can best conclude this chapter by drawing up a balance sheet for the industrial revolution and the century and a half of economic expansion that has followed it — its achievements and its social consequences.

The achievements of the industrial revolution can be stated quite simply — increased output. The capital accumulation stimulated by the release of individual energies through the rise of the market so increased the productivity of labor that the national output of the countries involved increased many times. Increased output, though a correct description of the achievements of the industrial revolution, is a colorless phrase for indicating the positive impact of this profound phenomenon. We must therefore spell out in a little more detail the implications of increased output for society.

First, and most obviously, the goods and services available for consumption proliferated at a remarkable rate. The development of steam, automotive, and air transport and the production of electrical home appliances, books, motion pictures, telephones, canned goods, bicycles, ready-made clothes, typewriters, baseballs, and hundreds of other commodities caused a greater metamorphosis in the society of the past one hundred and fifty years than in the whole span of history previous to the industrial revolution. Usually this increase in the availability of consumption goods is called a rise in the standard of living. Since the concept of the standard of living implies a value judgment as between two different standards, we prefer to state this achievement simply in terms of increased production of consumption goods. Whether or not the American or British society is better off in 1950 than in 1800 because of the increased output is an unprofitable question. It certainly cannot be answered within the confines of economics.

Second, industrialization has made possible a far greater control over the natural environment than had been possible before. To take but one instance, the Tennessee Valley Authority has set up a network of dams in the Tennessee Valley which have geared the turbulent flood waters of the Tennessee River to the useful purposes of mankind. Without the steel and concrete that industrialization makes available in large quantities the Tennessee River would have continued to erode the land and carry away the livelihood of the people with its floods.

Third, and clearly this is a mixed blessing, the national strength of nations has grown in direct proportion to the ability of economies to expand industrially. The armed forces of a nation are no longer self-sufficient units which can carry the means of war on their backs. Rather they are an extension of the industrial economy. The tremendous fire power fielded by a modern American division is an achievement of industrialization as is the application of atomic energy to warfare. In consequence the industrial revolution has caused a profound shift in the centers of world political power. Spain, Holland, and Sweden gave way before France, England, and Germany as industrial power became an increasingly important component of national strength. And now partially for the same reason the world has become polarized between the United States and the U.S.S.R.

Fourth, industrialization initially engendered rapid increases in the rate of growth of population. On the one hand the increase in productivity exorcised the Malthusian bogey. On the other hand the increased production of laboratory equipment permitted scientists to learn more about disease, and the increased production of hospitals and the development of modern systems of sanitation permitted the wide dissemination and application of this knowledge. Population spurted upward as mortality rates decreased.

Fifth, for the first time in the history of mankind mass education became a possibility. Books no longer had to be laboriously copied by hand. The printed word could be mobilized through the printing presses. Books, magazines, and newspapers became available at relatively low cost. Colleges and universities went into business on a large scale as the expansion of textbooks and classroom facilities permitted the handling of larger numbers of students. Furthermore the growth of radio, movies, and television accentuated the rate at which knowledge could potentially be disseminated.

Sixth, the revolution in transport and communication reduced the effective size of the world. North America, now only seconds removed from Europe by radio and only hours by air transport, was isolated from Europe prior to the industrial revolution. Consequently the external affairs of nations have become increasingly interdependent. No longer can nations afford the luxury of isolation — industrialization has knit the world too close together.

These are not the only achievements of the industrial revolution, but they are sufficient to suggest the pervasive influence of the changes which started to transform the world around the turn of the nineteenth century. As we have already implied the changes worked by indus-

trialization were by no means completely positive. They were only obtained at a cost — the creation of new social problems.

Of these new social problems the shattering of the old class structure and the erection of a new class structure is probably the most familiar. Karl Marx and the Marxists who followed him were the first to appreciate the relevance of this change. Indeed Marx made this an integral part of his theory of historical and revolutionary change, the rise of one class and the demise of another being an objective manifestation of the dialectical movement of history. In this particular epoch the changing techniques of production fathered a new propertied class, the bourgeoisie, which rose to power through its ownership of the means of production, i.e., capital equipment. As the star of the bourgeoisie ascended that of the landed interest, the remnants of the feudal barons, descended. The bourgeoisie destroyed the power of the land owner but such is the perverseness of the " dialect " that this ascendant class carried the seeds of its own destruction, the antithesis or the proletariat. The proletariat was distinguished by its negative relationship to the means of production. That is to say, the proletariat or worker had to sell his services to those who owned the means of production. In effect he was owned by the means of production.

The phenomenon of class is by no means as simple as Marx believed. According to him class is an objective condition rooted in the mass society and in the relation of each individual to the means of production. If an individual owned a factory he was a member of a homogeneous group, the bourgeoisie or capitalists, and consequently held a set of beliefs determined by this relationship. Similarly the worker who sold his services to the factory owner was a member of a homogeneous group whose views were molded by its subservient relationship to capital. We know now that there are subjective considerations in the class structure that influence man's attitudes and opinions. Therefore it is not possible to pose a simple dichotomy of classes, the bourgeoisie on the one hand, and the proletariat on the other. Rather there is a stratification in society which consists of many gradated status positions.

Although the class structure may not have been changed quite so dramatically as Marx thought, it is true that the stratification system of society was fundamentally changed by the industrial revolution. The business leader achieved the highest status in society and was accorded all the honors and privileges which go with that position. The industrial workers became more numerous and relatively the number of agricultural workers declined. The professional classes increased as more teachers, lawyers, doctors, and engineers were needed to service the increasingly complex society.

The increasing range of the stratification system created new social problems because of the multiplicity of interests which now had to be coordinated to permit the smooth functioning of society. No longer did tradition dictate the proper adjustment of classes. Ushered in on the wave of rationality the industrial revolution created many new groups which could appeal to rationality to achieve their interests. How then could society compromise these many interests?

A more obvious problem raised by the industrial revolution was the alteration in the habitation pattern of society. The factories were hungry for workers and sucked them away from rural areas. Since the industrial economy dictated the location of plants near the market, the source of raw material, or cheap means of transport, the population became increasingly concentrated. Thus the familiar problem of urbanism accompanied industrialization. Crowded living conditions generated slums and slums generated disease and crime. The city stood as the symbol not only of industrial might but also of the disparities in well-being of the very rich and the very poor.

Urbanism institutionalized squalor in large concentrated doses. The growing industrial processes obliterated one means of escape from this urban squalor. The effectiveness of the factory system depends upon the subdivision of skills which are hard to acquire into skills that can easily be taught to workers. The machine spreads the skill of one man to many men. But the process of specialization in production destroys it as an act of creation. Production is depersonalized. Each worker becomes an expert in the handling of a minute component of the total product and consequently has little consciousness of the creation of the total product. Man becomes an automaton and can no longer express himself in his work. Industrial labor then denied to man that type of creative expression which could effectively mitigate the harshness of his urban surroundings.

Finally, and the most crucially important of all the problems created by the industrial revolution, the energies of mankind released in the past 150 years have manifested themselves in differential rates of progress in the physical sciences and the social sciences. On the one hand progress in the physical sciences has provided an expanding base for the fantastic developments in industry. In the chain of causation the brain of the physicist, chemist, or electrical engineer ultimately lies behind the production of airplanes, nylons, and television. On the other hand progress in the social sciences is painfully slow. The rationale of human behavior does not yield easily to the probings of the human mind. In spite of the proliferation of disciplines and interest in the social sciences we cannot honestly say that we are about to develop a theory of human behavior which will permit us to predict and hence control behavior. In fact, many social scientists will deny that this is even a possibility.

The gap between the physical and social sciences would not be such a serious problem if it were not for the appalling destructive potential created by the former. Man has always displayed a commendable inventiveness except in the control of his own behavior. But in the past the in-

ability to control behavior did not threaten civilization because the technological base of civilization did not provide human beings with the means of ultimate destruction. This is no longer true. The astonishing success of nuclear physicists provides substance for the Armageddon. Mankind can destroy itself.

In summary, the industrial revolution was the product of the eighteenth century belief in rationality which in turn was the culmination of the centuries-old struggle of mankind to throw off the fetters of traditionalism and authoritarianism. The release of individual capabilities from their traditional bonds stimulated a tremendous outburst of inventive and productive activity. The cost was high, however, for individuals lost the security of the status system when they were thrown into the squalor of industrialization. That society accepted the cost and apparently maintained its stability was due partially to the change in the stratification system which shifted the political balance of power to the bourgeoisie and partially to the market philosophy which provided the bourgeoisie with a moral justification for the new order. The philosophy made it possible for the new " vested interest " to believe not only that existing relationships were good for itself but also for all of society.

Whether or not the social consequences of the industrial revolution outweigh its positive achievements, the creation of problems in a rationalistic age turns men's minds to the possibility of a conscious and rational solution of these problems. Planning is one solution devised by man. Planning therefore is part of the main stream of western social thought. It represents an attempt to substitute collective rationality for individual rationality.

33. The Age of Inventions*

1. HISTORICAL PERSPECTIVE

The rapid rise, since the latter part of the eighteenth century, of classes connected primarily with industry rather than with agriculture or commerce is a phenomenon familiar to all who are acquainted with economic history. But this great social transformation was in its earlier stages silent, lacking in the dramatic and the spectacular, overshadowed in contemporary imagination by politics and war. Records of the social forces of the time are meager and often remote from the main highways of historical study, and their meaning is in many cases obscure. Because of the consequent neglect, there is ample reason for further exploration of the field, and particularly of the obscure but decisive generation preceding England's engulfment in the wars of the French Revolution. It was during this earlier period that modern industrial society began to assume the distinctive forms and to acquire the peculiar significance that it has since retained.

Economic society in England, viewed in historical perspective, begins (after the obscure and primitive village and tribal economy) with the age of the great landlords. Before

*From Witt Bowden, *Industrial Society in England Toward the End of the Eighteenth Century* (New York, 1925), pp. 1–24, 51–69.

the sixteenth century, England was much more nearly self-sufficient than during later centuries. The country as a whole depended little on other countries, and the local communities and landed estates had slight intercourse even with other parts of the country. Towns were small and widely scattered, trade was insignificant, wants and tastes were simple and crude, and most of the commodities used were produced on the farms and manors. The violence and confusion of the long period of conquest from the fifth to the eleventh century, and the turbulent and aggressive military organization of society under feudalism, involved a process of concentrating land ownership in a few powerful families, with the subjection of the masses of the people as servile workers on the land. Governmental institutions, whether associated with the crown, or with the church, or with feudalism, were dominated by the greater landlords, lay and clerical.

But during the fourteenth and fifteenth centuries, this agrarian society was undergoing transformation. Feudal landlordism was being undermined. The Black Death of the middle of the fourteenth century decimated the population and gave to the surviving laborers an economic bargaining power which the hostile, landlord-controlled government could not entirely counteract. This, combined with other factors, obscurer but perhaps more significant, enabled the servile workers to become wage laborers and in many cases free tenants and independent yeomen. The Hundred Years' War with France and the later civil wars, the Wars of the Roses, carried off, in fratricidal conflict, a large proportion of the feudal aristocracy. The strong Tudor monarchy at the end of the fifteenth century turned more and more from the older landed aristocracy and tapped sources of strength in a new aristocracy not exclusively agrarian and in the urban and commercial classes.

The second period in the history of English economic society extends from the sixteenth century to the eighteenth, and is marked by the rise of the mercantile classes. The trading interests came into prominence at the time of the disruption of the feudal aristocracy. New wants and more elaborate tastes were introduced by the Renaissance and by the enlarged contacts of Englishmen with the Continent. The simple processes of production connected with the medieval manor no longer sufficed to gratify the expanding wants and tastes. The age of discovery and exploration gave a new and powerful impetus to commercial expansion. Henry VII and later rulers, in the development of a strong national government centering around the monarchy, were no longer able to depend on feudal revenues and feudal military and political services, and were increasingly dependent on a monetary income. A money economy supplanted the older feudal economy in the conduct of public affairs. The securing of money for the maintenance of hired armies and for the carrying on of the increasingly diversified and expensive functions of government became therefor a matter of utmost urgency. The landlords were wealthy, but their wealth was in fixed capital, and in the produce of their lands, and the most effective means of increasing their taxable money was by encouraging the exportation of their surplus. The revenues of the government came to be increasingly dependent on the fluid wealth brought into the country by means of mercantile enterprises and the semi-piratical activities of the sea rovers. In consequence, the rulers came to look with increasing favor on those who were connected with maritime activities.

But when imports were greater than exports, money was going out of the country to pay the "unfavorable" balance of trade. The policy of the government came, therefore, to be fixed upon the maintenance of an excess of exports over imports. Foreigners (Venetians, Flemings, the German Hansards) who had controlled English trade were by degrees ousted in favor of Englishmen. Commercial treaties were entered into from time to time, with the object of promoting English exports. Charters were granted to numerous companies of Englishmen, the Merchant Adventurers, the Baltic company, the Muscovy, Levant, East India, Virginia, Hudson Bay companies, and various others, with monopolistic trading rights and with extensive political and military powers, for trading with various regions of the Old World and for making settlements and developing markets in the New World. A long series of navigation acts, notably those of the middle of the seventeenth century, sought to check the Dutch and other rivals and to monopolize the commerce and resources of the overseas possessions. For the maintenance and enlargement of these possessions, which were acquired in the first instances more or less by accident, an imperialistic policy was by degrees developed and worked out largely in connection with the numerous wars in which England engaged. The outstanding feature of this policy of imperialism and expansion was the maintenance of the balance of power among Continental countries — a policy which enabled England to secure control of the choicest regions of the world and to develop them advantageously while her Continental rivals were consuming their energies and resources in the waging of devastating European conflicts. The imperial aim was to develop complementary economic relations between the home country and the colonies, by which the colonies were to furnish cheap raw materials not produced in England, and to buy from England more costly manufactured goods, thus increasing the " favorable " balance of trade.

The power of the mercantile classes was further augmented by greater mobility not only of their wealth but of their intelligence. Men of varied contacts, alert, resourceful, concentrated in towns where interchange of ideas and pooling of interests and energies were relatively easy — with such advantages, their influence in furnishing the dynamic forces and in determining the direction of progress, was out of all proportion to their numbers and their wealth.

These various tendencies and forces enabled the merchant princes to rival in power if not in social prestige the landed aristocracy of ancient lineage, and led in fact to an enlargement of the economic basis of aristocracy by the inclusion of mercantile wealth. Many of the more recently created members of the aristocracy had much in common with the classes connected immediately with trade, and the resulting alliance (an alliance out of which grew the Whig party) led to an increasing ascendancy of mercantile and imperial interests.

During the period of the rise of the mercantile classes, the manufacturers were petty in economic character, and were dominated by the merchants. Industrial capital was subordinate to. commercial capital. The period since the eighteenth-century revolution in technique, by which industrial capital and the industrial classes were emancipated from mercantile domination, is the third of the major periods in the history of English economic society.

The above statement, it is to be observed, assumes a causal connection between the revolution in technique and the transition from the mercantile to the industrial era of economic society. And yet the complexity of causal relations provides in this as in most instances a perplexing and at the same time a fascinating problem of historical study. So intricate are the forces which determine human events, and so variable are the conditions under which the forces operate, that the laws of historical causation transcend the utmost reaches of knowledge yet attained by historians. The formulation of general laws of causation seems at present impossible; it is sufficiently difficult to fix upon the causes of a particular historical occurrence. We may ask the astronomer what brings about eclipses of the sun, or the meteorologist what natural forces are responsible for a storm, and the explanations appear to be definite and final. But if the historian is asked for the causes of any familiar historical phenomenon, as the rapid rise of new economic groups in England toward the end of the eighteenth century, his explanation will seem tentative and perhaps vague.

Although attainment of finality and completeness in the study of historical causation may never be possible, yet, in the case of the phenomenon mentioned — the rise of new types of industrial society — the problem is relatively simple. It is true that there were already in existence tendencies toward more highly organized activities in manufacturing as well as trade; and it has been assumed that the concentration of industrial capital and the regimentation of industrial labor somewhat as in the modern factory system

would have come about independently of the introduction of machinery. It has been assumed that spinners (by way of illustration) would ultimately have been separated from their other employments, gathered together in large establishments, and set to work with spinning wheels under conditions not unlike those of the modern spinning factory. To this the reply may be made, by way of analogy, that if Napoleon had not assumed control in France during the later revolutionary period, probably some other commanding personality would have risen to power and directed events into substantially the same channels, because prevailing conditions were favorable. But this assumption cannot be said to nullify the important fact that it was Napoleon, and not someone else, who actually did direct affairs. It is interesting to consider what might have been the developments in English economic life had not the era of invention intervened, but it is certain that the forms actually assumed by industrial society were decisively molded by machinery.

Robert Owen in his autobiography (a priceless document of early industrialism as well as a record of a remarkable personality) gives an account of the beginning of his career as a cotton manufacturer. While employed as a common workman at Manchester in 1787, when only sixteen years old, he met a mechanic, a maker of wire frames for women's hats. Through him Owen became interested in the new spinning machinery. This mechanic, he relates, " began to tell me about great and extraordinary discoveries that were beginning to be introduced into Manchester for spinning cotton by new and curious machinery. He said he was endeavoring to see and get a knowledge of them, and that if he could succeed, he could make a very good business of it." The desired knowledge was secured, and a partnership was formed. As his share of the joint capital, Owen managed at length to get together the sum of £100. This humble beginning of the career of one of Great Britain's richest and most noted early " cotton lords " is a valid illustration of the close causal connection between the invention of machines and the rise of the new industrial capitalists. The most important, most characteristic source of this new group, ultimately the most powerful in England and indeed in the world, was in the wealth created by the " great and extraordinary discoveries " and the " new and curious machinery " by means of which Owen made his fortune.

Equally noteworthy was the influence of the new industrial technique on the rise of that other distinctive group of recent times, the employees of the great industrialists. To the toiling masses of the time, as well as to the few who rose into the ranks of the great, the mechanical improvements brought economic opportunity which vastly increased their numbers. The fears of many of the workers that labor-saving machines would take bread out of their children's mouths by robbing them of work was opposed by argument and allayed by fact. " Population,"

it was contended, " must go on in proportion to subsistence and in proportion to industry: now the machine eats nothing, so does not diminish subsistence," but rather, in fact, increases it, and therefore potentially creates population. Such arguments, though frequently advanced, naturally made little impression on the workers. But the logic of facts prevailed, as more than one writer made haste to point out. Thus the demand for labor at Bolton was so great, as a result of the spinning factories, that the population more than doubled in a decade, and in consequence " the opposition of the populace to the use of machines for shortening labor has been quelled." Similar conditions furnished convincing arguments throughout the region. Machines, " so far from tending to diminish unemployment, . . . must, when judiciously applied, be the means of multiplying it. . . . It is this which, almost in our own days, has expanded the villages of Lancashire into towns next to the metropolis in size."

The era of invention brought to the workers new conditions of work as well as new opportunities for work — conditions which made possible a rapid process of molding the inert mass of industrial labor into mobile shape and of animating it with group life and consciousness. The new opportunities were proclaimed by many champions of mechanical methods; but the ultimate effects of the new conditions were discerned by few.

While machinery has produced economic commodities infinite in variety and in extent beyond the power of calculation or conception, it has at the same time been the decisive factor in the formation of what is far more important — namely, the two outstanding economic groups of the modern industrialized regions. Among those who seek an understanding of present-day social forces, the age of invention is justly a subject of perennial interest.

2. THE PREVAILING SPIRIT OF INVENTION

In the study of the progress of invention, it would be a pleasant task to recount the lives of individual inventors, and to try to give due credit to men as to the work of Pitt or Washington or Napoleon. But the task, however pleasant to contemplate, is impossible to perform. Most of them were humble and obscure, and the boldest and most patient of historical architects who have adventured on the task of reconstructing their careers have been rewarded with the merest fragments of materials.

A most careful search of available records rewards the student with little that is important in the personal history of most of the great inventors, but the search is extremely fruitful in showing that the individual inventors were after all merely the focal points in a well-nigh universal interest in mechanical progress. Hargreaves, Arkwright, Crompton, Cartwright, Cort, Brindley, Watt, Wedgwood — these are the names that are commonly associated with the inventions and technical im-

provements that transformed the country; but while these men were engaged at their particular tasks, literally thousands of others were working with equal ardor to solve the same or similar problems. At the same time, national and local societies were organized for stimulating and rewarding inventive activity; and the government paid large sums in recognition of the work of inventors, and passed laws to prevent foreigners from using English inventions. So varied and extensive was the interest in technical progress, so unprecedented was the prevailing spirit of improvement in methods of doing things, that one may properly characterize the latter part of the eighteenth century as the age of invention.

In order to appreciate the significance of this aspect of the period, it is necessary to contrast it not with the progress of more recent times but with the earlier lack of progress and absence of interest in technical improvement. The nineteenth and twentieth centuries have been kaleidoscopic in their rapidity of change. Inventions and discoveries such as would have startled the minds and revolutionized the lives of former generations are multiplied, great factories are put up and straightway rebuilt to make way for improved machinery, gigantic warships are constructed and declared obsolete well-nigh before they are manned for the trial cruise, imagined miracles of yesterday are the commonplace realities of today. The conscious aim alike of a multitude of empirical workers and of thousands of scientific investigators is to effect improvements in machinery and technique.

It was not so in the middle of the eighteenth century, when (to cite a sufficient illustration and symbol of the prevalence of primitive methods) even "Manchester goods" were transported to Bristol, to the metropolis, and to the nearby port of Liverpool by means of the ancient packhorse. Interest in technical improvement was not unknown, to be sure, but the prevailing spirit was one of conformity to methods approved by age and precedent. Workingmen with a turn for invention feared that labor-saving devices would reduce employment, as when one Lawrence Earnshaw, a north-of-England tailor's apprentice, turning mechanic, invented, about 1753, a machine to combine the operations of spinning and reeling cotton, but destroyed it, saying that "he would not be the means of taking bread out of the mouths of the poor." Men of science and learning, as the faculties of the universities and the gentlemen of the Royal Society, were interested in improvements in the technique of pure science, but any idea of the application of their knowledge in the devising of inventions useful in the ordinary affairs of life was rarely entertained. Agriculture, to be sure, being the pursuit of the aristocracy, was viewed in a somewhat different light, and no less a person than Viscount Townshend was a pioneer, as early as 1730, in the introduction of technical improvements in farming by such means as seed drilling, marling, and horse hoeing. Serious efforts had also been made to im-

prove the use of navigation — which was directly connected not so much with "useful" economic life as with naval and imperial affairs. In general, the relation of the government to inventions was confined to the formality of issuing letters patent. Individual inventors with genius superior to that of Watt, Arkwright and Wedgwood had arisen in earlier times (asserted a popular writer), but their genius shone, "amid an ignorant and idle people, like a flambeau in a fog." The relatively inferior abilities of Watt and his contemporaries were effecting unique results because of the enlightened and active interest of the people of their time.

For the validity of the contrast between earlier times and the days of Watt and Arkwright, appeal may be made to the evidence of the patent records. Letters patent were granted in the Tudor period and in the time of James I for monopolies of various kinds, but patents for monopolies in the use of new machines and new processes were not differentiated from the general body of monopolies till late in the reign of James. Records of patents of invention since that time are fortunately accessible in the compilations made by Bennett Woodcroft of the Patent Office about the middle of the nineteenth century. Woodcroft's indexes reveal some interesting facts. The number of patents issued from 1617 to 1760, nearly a century and a half, was smaller than the number issued during the succeeding twenty-five years — 697 as contrasted with 776. Though the number issued previous to 1760 varied considerably from decade to decade, there was in general a surprising uniformity. During no ten-year period preceding the year 1760 did the number exceed 100, with the sole exception of the years 1690–1699, and the number was then only 102. In the decade beginning in 1760, the number was 205, and each succeeding ten-year period was marked by a rapid increase. Going back a hundred years, to the time of the Restoration, and compiling the numbers by decades, we have the following results:

1660–1669	31
1670–1679	51
1680–1689	53
1690–1699	102
1700–1709	22
1710–1719	38
1720–1729	89
1730–1739	56
1740–1749	82
1750–1759	92
1760–1769	205
1770–1779	294
1780–1789	477

As might naturally be expected, the momentum of inventive activity beginning about 1760 was in no whit abated after 1790. But the significant fact is that the momentum was acquired, the vital phase of the age of invention as evidenced by the patent records was inaugurated, during these decades.

The records of the Patent Office give evidence of the new mechanical interests by indicating a greater variety as well as an increase in the number of inventions. Woodcroft's elaborate classification for use in official publications recognized 396 distinct types of inventions patented during the years 1700 to 1785, and of these, 168 types were added during the years 1760 to 1785.

The patent records are significant in another way. In 1661 the Marquis of Worcester (reputed to have been the foremost mechanical genius of his time) secured a patent for " an invention to make a boat that roweth, draweth, or setteth even against wind or stream, yea, both, and to any part of the compass, which way soever the stream runs or wind blows, and yet the force of the wind or stream causeth its motion, nothing being required but a steersman, and whilst the boat stayeth to be loaded or unloaded, the stream or wind shall perform such work as any watermill or windmill is capable of." A patent was granted in 1692 to two men for " their new invention of taking fish by a light, which they can cause to burn some fathoms under water, with which, and a light above water, they can draw the fish which are in the compass of a league in the sea to one place." These two cases are cited because they illustrate the fact that the early patents were issued in many cases not for definite, finished inventions but for mere ideas and suggestions, for vaguely defined processes or devices, in some instances not far removed from the occult arts of the middle ages. Worthless or unfinished inventions were patented after 1760 as well as before; but in the later period the tendency to patent mere mechanical dreams is less and less observable. The contrast may be explained in part, no doubt, by the general increase in scientific and technical knowledge. Fanciful claims like those of earlier times, based upon misconceptions of natural laws, were less apt to be made, and when made were more readily discerned and repudiated. This increase of knowledge was accompanied by more rigorous rules for the submission of definite specifications, drawings, and models in order to secure valid patent rights. Nor should one fail to observe, on the basis of the evidence of the patent records, that the later patents in contrast with those issued before the middle of the eighteenth century, put the emphasis on the invention of new machines rather than on the introduction of new industries; and that in the later period a smaller proportion of the patentees were foreigners. These facts afford significant and cumulative evidence of the sudden outburst of inventive activity in the later decades of the eighteenth century.

Having examined the statistical and prosaic evidence of public documents concerning patents, we may now for a moment attend to the more picturesque but none the less valid testimony of contemporary journalists and other writers, concerning unpatented as well as patented inventions, and concerning the mechanical interests of the people generally.

The student of the past occasionally finds it possible to be honestly grateful even to the appallingly dull pseudo-classic muse of the eighteenth century. Dull, indeed, as poetry, is *The Patent*, published in 1776; but as a facetious expression of the in-

ventive spirit of the time it has lively interest and real significance. " Hail to the Patent! " exclaims the author; and after enumerating by way of illustration some of the varied performances attributable to patented inventions, he asks:

What man would scruple to resign his
    breath,
Provided he could die a patent death?

At length he grows prophetic:

The time may come when nothing will
    succeed
But what a previous Patent hath de-
    creed;
And we must open on some future day
The door of nature with a patent key.

It will be observed that the rimester spoke of *patented* inventions; and the public records mentioned above were concerned solely with patents. But the securing of a patent was itself an expensive proceeding, and yet it was merely the initial step in the protection of the rights of the inventor. There developed during this period, especially in the north of England, in connection with textile inventions, an organized and effective opposition to patents as a method of rewarding inventors, and various other methods were devised or suggested. Because of these facts, and also because of the generosity of many inventors and societies in giving inventions to the public, there was an immense inventive activity unrecorded in the patent office. A survey of the various types of literature current at the time reveals innumerable unpatented devices and processes, some of them very successful; and it reveals, also, a widespread public interest in mechanical improvement.

In 1764 a new periodical, the *Wonderful Magazine,* was founded with the purpose of recording things " out of the common road." In 1779 the editors of the *Gentlemen's Magazine* emphasized as an important part of their policy the announcement of " the discovery of every new invention and the improvements in every useful art." A correspondent of the same magazine suggested that readers exchange through its columns their knowledge of the progress of invention. The *Annual Register* had a department regularly devoted to " Useful Projects." The *Museum Rusticum et Commerciale,* begun in 1764 under patronage of members of the Society of Arts, and devoted to the recording of new and valuable discoveries, was of such interest, according to the editors, that " there was scarcely a newspaper or magazine in the kingdom " that had not reprinted portions of its contents. The publications of the Society of Arts, to which further reference will presently be made, were so popular as to call repeatedly for reprinting.

This was the period, too, of the rise and rapid development of encyclopedias, dictionaries of arts and sciences, and similar semi-technical compilations. Their popularity, evidenced by their numbers and their frequent editions, is an obvious indication of widespread interest in technical progress.

The literature of the time describes so vast a number and variety of inventions that to venture upon the briefest analysis would take this essay far beyond its proper limits. Suffice it to say that there was a lively interest not only in the well-known and successful inventions of the time, such as spinning machines and the steam engine, but as well in various lines of mechanical achievement commonly associated with much later periods.

So great was the interest in ballooning that in 1786 was published a book entitled *Airopaidia,* claiming to be " an introduction to the science of aerial navigation." Popular journals introduced departments dealing with " aerostatic experiments." A play produced at Covent Garden in 1784 was entitled *Aerostation,* and the plot centered around " the passion of a lady of fortune for balloons." According to a rimester of the time, " admirals forsake the swelling tide," and " surgeons leave their patients to their fate," in order " high on the wings of mighty winds to ride." The " celebrated aeronauts " of the time were " sumptuously entertained." The exploits of a balloonist in 1785 were said to have been witnessed by more than 40,000 persons. Not content with the amusement thus afforded, those of prophetic inclinations foresaw the time when " the inquisitive turn of mind which distinguishes the present era will improve . . . the art of ascending and exploring the upper regions . . . (so as to apply it) to many useful purposes of which at present we have no conception."

Two other inventions not successfully developed till much later times — the submarine and the " horseless carriage " — also exercised over ingenious minds a fascination which seems to have been little abated by the not infrequent fatality of the hazards of experiment.

Not the least important of the varied manifestations of mechanical interest was connected with popular amusements. Readers of Edmund Cartwright's account of the origin of the power loom will recall how he refuted the arguments of the Manchester manufacturers against the possibility of a power loom " by remarking that there had lately been exhibited in London an automaton figure which played at chess. Now you will not assert, gentlemen, said I (he continues), that it is more difficult to construct a machine that shall weave, than one which shall make all the variety of moves which are required in that complicated game." The outcome of this unique idea, he asserted, was his power loom. During the rise of inventive activity, there seems to have been a veritable vogue of exhibits such as that referred to by Cartwright. In periodicals and in booklets and circulars, varied and elaborate mechanical shows were extensively advertised. In one of these booklets, *A Descriptive Catalogue of the Several Superb and Magnificent Pieces of Mechanism and Jewelry Exhibited at Mr. Cox's Museum* (London, 1772), twenty-two exhibits are described. The following is an illustrative quotation from this curious document: — " Piece the Fifteenth " is a chronoscope in the form of an obelisk under a great and magnificent canopy, with profuse ornaments and with " a pro-

digious variety of motions. It stands in the center of a rich gallery, upon a table, . . . upon which an elephant . . . moves round the obelisk; upon his back is a castle of gold; . . . within the castle is a curious clock with three dials; above the clock, on the top of the castle, . . . are automaton figures, playing various tunes on twelve bells; over the music gallery is a figure that strikes the hours and quarters; above that, a pyramid of moving stars, which terminate with four dolphins, in the middle of which is an animated dragon, dropping pearls into one of the dolphin's mouths, moving his wings at the same time. The pedestal consists of four bulls, in contrary directions, . . . upon a ground . . . upon which dragons, storks, lizards, and various ornaments are placed."

It is probable that the prevailing ideas and interests of a given period, especially those that are of relatively recent and sudden development, find spontaneous and therefore significant expression in the popular amusements of the period. An ingenious student might profitably try to test the validity of such a generalization in wider fields. In any case, the extensive patronage given to these " museums " and traveling shows seems to have been an unconscious reflection, during the period of the present study, of popular mechanical interest.

The prevailing spirit of technical progress, while more or less active throughout the country, found most intensive and successful expression in the regions of Birmingham and Manchester.

A rimester of Birmingham writing as early as 1751, described "beneath a fable's thin disguise the virtues its inhabitants display"; these virtues were the "spirit of industry" and "bright inventive genius."

The "inventive genius," particularly of the north of England, found expression in the work of a large number of men interested in a wide variety of projects — men whose obscurity is due in part, no doubt, to the fact that they were in most cases members of the so-called lower classes. "It is generally allowed," wrote Richard Townley of Manchester in 1784, "that more ingenious improvements and useful inventions in machinery have taken their rise in these northern parts . . . than in all others throughout the kingdom; . . . (and) that most of these inventions and improvements have been struck out by such as are usually denominated the inferior ranks of mankind." To recount briefly the work of two or three north-of-England mechanics of this obscure type will perhaps not be without significance as illustrating an important phase of popular interest in problems of technical advance.

One of these was a tenant farmer of Belford, Cuthbert Clarke, whose work was recorded by Arthur Young in his *Northern Tour*. This man, wrote Young, "is very famous in the north for his knowledge of mechanics." Among his inventions were a machine for draining swamps, for which he received an award from the Society of Arts; a mechanical turnip slicer (important on account of the prevalent feeding of turnips to live stock); and "the grand machine on which he builds his reputation, . . . one for the threshing of corn." To his various activities in connection with mechanics he added another — experimentation with electricity for stimulating the growth of plants; and Young declared that his experiments afforded "strong proof that the electric fire had a remarkable power in promoting and quickening the vegetation." The mechanical and experimental interests of Farmer Clarke are not without interest in themselves; but they are mentioned here because they illustrate the "great spirit of improvement" and experimentation which Young and others found to be characteristic of the region.

Young's tour of the north, when the observations just mentioned were recorded, was made before Arkwright's cotton factories were built. The mechanical interests of the people in the newly developing northern industrial regions before the introduction of machinery are illustrated even more significantly by the career of another self-taught mechanic of that part of the country, Adam Walker. At his home on the border between Westmoreland and Lancaster counties, he was set to work at a very early age, but while a boy he found time to acquire (according to a contemporary) a remarkable mechanical ability by making devices for his own amusement. "He copied corn mills, paper mills, fulling mills, etc., and had them all going in model in the brook near his father's dwelling, to the great terror of strangers who passed them in the night." Though deprived by his father's poverty of schooling (so we are told), he nevertheless by his own efforts prepared himself by the age of fifteen to begin his career as a teacher; and at the age of eighteen, "was elected writing master and accomptant to the free school of Macclesfield in Cheshire." This was about 1750. Later he located at Manchester and "conceived a system of education more adapted to a town of trade than the monkish system still continued in our public schools (at least thought so by many)," and he put his ideas into effect in the form of a course of lectures which met with popular approbation. He continued his studies along mechanical and scientific lines, and at length embodied his knowledge in a series of public lectures which he gave in the regions of Manchester, Liverpool, Halifax, Leeds and Birmingham, his fame in the provinces preparing him at length, by 1778, for a successful career in the metropolis. So popular were his lectures in the north of England that in some of the smaller towns rooms large enough to accommodate his audiences could not be secured. By 1792, eight editions of his published lectures on mechanics had been issued. Nor was he merely a theorist and lecturer; his knowledge of mechanics he applied in the field of invention. Contemporaneous records attribute to him more than a score of inventions, some of them extremely elaborate, only two of which are said to have been patented.

The high esteem enjoyed by Clarke and Walker was shared quite generally by men of their type. On many occasions and in varied ways the country was urged " to record and publish inventions . . . and to take care that the fame of singular ingenuity do not expire with the possessor," both " for the honor of the discoverers," and for insuring " a rich harvest of future discoveries." It is true that occasions, as in 1779 during the period of unemployment and suffering accompanying the war against the American colonies, the workers held inventors of labor-saving machines partly responsible for their misfortunes. But the workers had no opportunity for education in self-restraint and foresight, no control over the machines, and no share in the profits save their meager wage, which was cut off entirely in times of depression and unemployment; and in view of these circumstances, their occasional hostility toward inventors was natural and inevitable.

The statement that inventors generally were held in high esteem should be qualified in another way. That is, a distinction should be made between public esteem and financial reward. It is unquestionably true that some of the inventors were not adequately rewarded financially, but the injustice has been exaggerated. John Kay, the inventor of the flying shuttle, is frequently cited as an instance of unrewarded genius. His career was in a somewhat earlier period, however, the flying shuttle having been patented as early as 1733, and his ill treatment he himself attributed to the attitude prevailing about 1740. Kay's misfortunes, and those of other inventors, mostly of earlier times, were utilized in exaggerated form by writers who were trying to counteract the occasional hostility of the workers to machines. When Arkwright was trying to maintain his monopoly of his patented machines for spinning, he resorted to the same device, seeking sympathy by comparing his own case with the exaggerated misfortunes of other inventors, and particularly of Hargreaves. The tradition that Hargreaves died in a workhouse has been traced directly to the statements by Arkwright. Hargreaves was perhaps rewarded inadequately for the invention of the spinning jenny (though the obscurity of the records makes judgment difficult), but in any case, instead of being forced to pass his last days in a workhouse, he was able to spend them in comfort. His estate at the time of his death amounted to several thousand pounds. Nor does the case of Samuel Crompton, inventor of the spinning "mule," afford unqualified evidence of ill-treatment of inventors. An attempt to patent it would probably have involved him in difficulties with Arkwright, because of the use of rollers, common to the "mule" and to Arkwright's patented "water frame." In any case a patent would have been expensive, and difficult to utilize. The importance of the invention seems not to have been fully recognized at first, either by Crompton or by his contemporaries; and indeed the machine, as it came from Crompton's hands, was crude and far from satisfactory. Crompton's personal idiosyncrasies also had something to do with his failure to profit

fully from his invention. Finally, it should be remembered that he received a small subscription as early as 1780; that Robert Peel offered him a partnership; and that ultimately he and his family received, in the form of subscriptions and grants, aside from business profits, several thousand pounds in recognition of his services.

The unjust treatment of inventors has been exaggerated, and yet there was injustice. Inventors as well as people generally, unless possessed of wealth and position, had precarious legal rights (as witness the laws against debtors, the game laws, and the Draconian penal code for the protection of property); and they commonly experienced great difficulty, unless patronized by some one of position, in maintaining such legal rights as they possessed. This condition seems to be an inevitable accompaniment of a differentiation of social classes such as existed in eighteenth-century England. The inventors belonged for the most part to the unprivileged classes; and in securing the enactment of laws as well as in taking advantage of legal rights, they encountered the difficulties inseparable from rigorous class rule in society and government. Furthermore, many inventors were working at the same time on similar problems, and justice was often complicated by rival claims.

3. Causes of the Revolution in Technique

This remarkable and widely diffused outburst of inventive activity

constitutes one of the major phenomena of history. From this judgment few students of history would
be inclined to dissent. As to its
causes, there is less uniformity of
judgment. Many, indeed, have ven-
tured no explanation, contenting
themselves rather with a study of the
attendant facts. But this attitude in
its extreme form leads to an undue
emphasis upon details. Mastery of
details is not in itself the worthiest
of ends but may be made the means
of formulating generalizations. Ignorant men seek vainly and oftentimes claim pretentiously to pierce
the veil of truth; while men of learning, having climbed to the vantage-
ground of facts, where alone the truth
is discernible, oftentimes needlessly
deny themselves the vision thereof.
Students have too often bowed down
to the facts of history as to idols,
forgetting the supreme reverence due
to the truth of history.

In the study of the spirit of invention suddenly arising in England in
the second half of the eighteenth
century, it is less difficult, to be sure,
to describe its manifestations than to
explain its causes or evaluate its importance. Its causes are indeed so
obscure, and the results of inquiry
are so uncertain, as to lend color of
justification, in this case to those students who would content themselves
with a statement of details. In order
to simplify the problem if possible,
we may approach the subject from
the point of view of the people of the
time, and see how they explained the
remarkable changes going on in their
midst. This inquiry, aside from being worth while in itself, ought to

put us on a vantage ground for an
independent view.

There is apparently no carefully
thought out, rational explanation of
the mechanical revolution that is
contemporaneous with the event in
its earlier stages, but as might naturally be expected, the nearest approach to such an explanation is to
be found in the *Wealth of Nations*.
Adam Smith in one of his most
noted passages tells us that " the invention of all those machines by
which labor is so much facilitated
and abridged seems to have been
originally owing to the division of
labor." This, he explains, is a result
of the whole attention of each worker being directed " towards some one
very simple object. It is naturally to
be expected, therefore, that some one
or other of those who are employed
in each particular branch of labor
should soon find out easier and read-
ier methods of performing their own
particular work." The same principle of division of labor is made to
account for those machines invented
by others than the workmen who use
the machines, for the making of
machines becomes in time, by division of labor, a business in which
specialization leads to ingenuity.
Furthermore, in the progress of society there arise " philosophers, or
men of speculation, whose trade is
not to do anything, but to observe
everything "; and at length this
trade, like others, " is subdivided into
a great number of different branches,
each of which affords occupation to
a peculiar tribe or class of philosophers; and this subdivision of employment in philosophy, as well as

in every other business, improves dexterity," and often leads to a rational inventiveness in contrast with the empirical and spontaneous ingenuity of the workman.

Adam Smith's interesting interpretation leaves many questions unanswered. Is it a fact of history, the critic may inquire, that the division of labor had increased so greatly and so suddenly as to be the source of the veritable deluge of inventions during and soon after the writing of the *Wealth of Nations?* And if so, how may one account for the increased division of labor?

What was in the minds of Smith's contemporaries an explanation of the era of invention? One of the favorite methods of accounting for the invention of particular devices was by resort to chance, as the flying shuttle attributed to Kay's lame back; the automatic valve, to the string tied by a boy to a valve handle; and the spinning jenny, to the accidental overturning of a spinning wheel by Jenny Hargreaves. But even when chance was believed to have been the immediate cause, an underlying human motive was recognized, as when the Society of Arts offered premiums in 1760 for a spinning machine because it had been informed that " manufacturers of woollen, linen, and cotton find it extremely difficult, in the summer season, when the spinners are at harvest work, to procure a sufficient number of hands."

A more comprehensive explanation is found in the curious suggestion that " the spirit of invention " was an outgrowth of the maritime experiences of Englishmen. " Mariners are, in general, not only the boldest and most enterprising, but also the most inventive of men: the frequent difficulties to which they are reduced in the course of the many adventures they go through, sharpen their wits; . . . hence they are fertile in contrivances." Others offered an explanation connected with maritime activities but in another way: inventive activity was attributed to commercial competition. " In manufacturing and commercial countries, when demands from abroad slacken, and foreign competitors working cheaper endanger the loss of a manufactory, then necessity sharpens the human intellect; men's geniuses awake and are animated; and discoveries are made that astonish the world."

It is probable, as will be observed later, that invention resulted from expansion rather than from contraction of foreign markets. And yet the earlier steps in England's mechanical progress were taken in imitation of foreigners, during periods when English manufacturers and merchants were at the mercy of superior Continental craftsmanship. There were Englishmen who were not deterred by national pride from some acknowledgment of the debt owed to foreigners, as when Arkwright's inventions were attributed to his study of the silk mills at Derby, which in turn had been erected from models introduced from Italy.

Although imitation of foreigners can hardly account for the surpassing of foreigners so apparent in the latter part of the eighteenth century, yet the indebtedness of Englishmen to the peoples of the Continent for technical skill is greater than Englishmen of that period realized or perhaps cared to admit. The skill and ingenuity of foreigners was utilized by England in two ways: by means of the direct importation of machines and new industries, and by means of foreign immigration into England. This immigration was in large part the result of age-long disturbances on the Continent. The Protestant Reformation, religious persecution, and the long-continued wars, strangely mixed and varied in their motives but uniform in their dismal, devastating results — from all these disturbances England was relatively free, and by the middle of the eighteenth century, innumerable peace-loving and enterprising craftsmen had brought to England the long-accumulated skill and ingenuity of the Continent.

These immigrants naturally found greater freedom and opportunity for plying their trades in the unincorporated towns than in those where corporate and gild restrictions tended to maintain monopoly and prevent change; and enterprising but unprivileged natives also naturally sought out the towns relatively free from the network of regulations and monopolies connected with corporations and gilds. The government of the towns of England had in earlier times been regulated largely by charters which were precious instruments of municipal liberty. They checked the aggressions of feudal barons and of despotic kings. But by degrees the charters of liberty were them-

selves transformed in many cases into instruments of oppression. The powers of government came to be exercised by small, self-perpetuating groups; and the forms of government came to be increasingly out of harmony with the needs engendered by the growth of towns and the changing conditions of town life. Similar in some respects to the history of the chartered and incorporated town governments was that of the industrial gilds and the commercial companies. These organizations, especially the gilds, maintained in earlier times what was in many respects an admirable economic system. Their members enjoyed monopolies of the local markets as against both " foreigners " and non-member townsmen. At the same time, the abuses of monopoly were largely avoided by public regulation of prices and wages; by public control of standards of workmanship; by the cultivation of pride of workmanship; and by the ideal of an income sufficient simply for comfort as opposed to the unrestrained accumulation of riches. Producers were protected from the ruthless forces of competition, and they were at the same time restrained from the unscrupulous gratification of the acquisitive instinct. In comparison with modern society's riotous and disastrous orgy of competition and wealth-accumulation, the earlier organization of urban economic life undoubtedly possessed many excellencies. But it had also a serious defect. It was too static. It lacked adaptability. It developed elaborate regulations which, while affording protection, fettered initiative and barred the way of progress.

Town and industrial activities in the north of England developed when the vogue of charters and gilds was declining. Urban growth in the north was in fact stimulated by the shifting to that region of elements of the population which were hostile to the restrictive and monopolistic regulations of corporations and gilds. The relative freedom of northern counties in these respects was early recognized and confirmed by national statutes. "Towns where manufactures are most flourishing," wrote Thomas Walker, one of Manchester's great early manufacturers, " are seldom bodies corporate, commerce requiring universal encouragement instead of exclusive privileges to the natives and freemen of a particular district. Those who first introduced the cotton manufacture into Lancashire were Protestant refugees, who probably found small encouragement for themselves and their industry amongst the corporate towns of England." It was this condition of municipal and industrial freedom which, in the view of many contemporaries, gave rise to the unparalleled ingenuity and enterprise of the north of England. Manchester is described by an enthusiastic visitor as a place of such note " that to name it is sufficient," and its position is attributed to its freedom: — " Such is the force of industry unfettered by any restrictions! Such the vigor of ingenuity unrestrained by fine-spun regulations! " The sentiments thus voiced were echoed and re-echoed; the belief found expression in many forms that

the mechanical and industrial progress of the country was due to the opportunity of ingenious aliens and enterprising natives to escape from the monopolies and fettering regulations of gilds and corporations.

Obviously a negation — the absence of corporate and gild restrictions and monopolies — could not of itself create a spirit of invention; it was merely a condition favorable for ingenuity and novel enterprise. Nor did the people of the time fail to observe that there were various other favorable conditions which had been lacking in earlier periods. It seems to have been taken for granted that many men are naturally ingenious, but that in past ages ingenuity had remained latent or unappreciated, and was active and successful in that generation because the prevailing state of mind and social tendencies were auspicious.

It was indeed an age of social change and innovation. Styles and manners remained formal and urbane, and as yet the smooth surface of society was little disturbed. But in the depths there were ferments varied and active. Agitation for political changes, especially for reform of Parliament, was extremely widespread and intellectually stimulating. The evangelical movement centering around Whitefield and the Wesleys, though ultra-conservative in its reverence for the existing social régime, was powerful nevertheless in stirring the too often languid sensibilities and in rousing masses of men out of their accustomed lethargy of mind. There was vigorous and promising agitation for prison reform, for the relief of debtors, for the abolition of the slave trade, for the amendment of the poor law, for the education of the masses, and for the amelioration of the state of Roman Catholics and of Dissenters. Especially in the north there was observable a breaking away from religious traditions and social conventions which, whatever may have been their historical importance, were nevertheless barriers in the way of change and therefore of progress.

It was a period when men were in a measure freeing themselves from the agelong grip of supernaturalism; a period when thought and action were being directed more generally by reason; and this tendency created a favorable, even a necessary condition for a spirit of invention. In order to appreciate its importance, one needs only to call to mind the experiences of Roger Bacon, Bruno, and Galileo, as well as a host of lesser innovators, in ages when supernaturalism prevailed over rationalism as a test of social sanction. It is true that not only supernaturalism but custom, tradition, and social privilege are in many cases inconsistent with rationalism. But the adherents of these are less likely to make war on rational changes than are the proponents of supernaturalism, because, on the one hand, they are not committed to the defense of any principle of absolute truth likely to be endangered by innovation; and on the other hand, they more readily find it possible to utilize changes engendered by reason for the maintenance of irrational privileges or conditions.

Supernaturalism has its origin in a primitive reaction to the unknown: thunder is the voice of the sky-god, the lightning his weapon. Rationalism is an outgrowth of experience and knowledge, as when Franklin, utilizing the accumulated store of information, made tests of his own, and explained the phenomena of the clouds on natural grounds; and even thought out an invention for protection against what had been deemed in earlier ages the invincible agency of a supernatural power. There had been promise of the substitution of rationalism for supernaturalism centuries earlier; for during the age of the recovery of ancient culture and of the discovery of the New World, knowledge expanded almost incredibly, and experience became diversified as never before. But there intervened, perhaps inevitably, the long struggle between rival camps of supernaturalists. The primitive dogmas and taboos of the middle ages, crowded into the background by the expanding knowledge and experience of the age of the Renaissance and of exploration, were again marshaled in the forefront by the unreasoning passions of the age of religious conflict. Much of the bitterness of the conflict resulted from old customs disrupted and the uprooting of long-flourishing privileges; but men were deeply disturbed by what to them was a grave question of life and destiny. The problem they wrestled with for two centuries was the problem of the source of authority for determining the proper form of supernaturalism. At length men began to realize the alternatives before them: they must go back to the medieval system of an all-inclusive ecclesiastical authority, or else they must go forward to the authority of individual reason. With the acceptance of the latter alternative, involving the principle of religious freedom, men's thoughts began to run once more, as during the Renaissance, in rational channels; the old fear of innovation as the enemy of absolute truth was no longer strong enough to keep in check the spirit of change and readjustment; and theological speculation and controversy were more and more trenched upon by experimental and applied science.

Dr. Priestley's lament over the destruction of his laboratory manuscripts by a " church and king " mob in 1791 brought to him at least a pathetic realization of the fact that rationalism is a tender plant cultivated in the midst of the jungle of elemental passions and superstitions which press relentlessly on all sides to regain complete sway over the human mind. But it was with profound satisfaction that sympathetic observers before the French Revolution noted the growth of rationalism from Newton's age to the time of Priestley. This comparatively unhindered growth culminated in an unprecedented curiosity of mind, a rationalizing of all phenomena, a habit of experimentation, a desire for readjustment when sanctioned by reason. Theories were decried as " little more than ingenious amusements; a series of well-made experiments can alone establish matters of fact "; it is by this method that " new

discoveries ought to be attempted." Men rejoiced that " theory " no longer prevailed, but that " experiment (had) regained its true honors "; and that new discoveries were in consequence being made " such as the human mind had hitherto no conception of." The tendencies of the age found characteristic expression in Arthur Young's boast that he had no fixed principle except " the principle of change " based on experience — " the only principle worthy of an experimenter."

It is to be supposed, on first thought, that tendencies so prominent would find expression in the education of the period. But the theological origin and the ancient endowments of the leading schools combined to make them (so Adam Smith tells us) " sanctuaries in which exploded systems and obsolete prejudices found shelter and protection, after they had been hunted out of every other corner of the world." To the same effect was Arthur Young's criticism: " The universities are curious to teach whatever is perfectly useless," while useful knowledge is avoided with extreme care. Shall educational establishments be exempt from change, he asks, " because they are ancient? Shall considerable revenues remain thus misapplied without at least turning a small part into a channel that may disperse its streams to the general fructification of the kingdom? " Not content with negative criticism, he desired that experimental and applied science be introduced; and that " practical agriculture " be taught in each institution by a professor acquainted with practical and experimental farming, in association with professors of the sciences able to explain the connections between agriculture and such subjects as chemistry, botany, mineralogy, and mechanics.

Many other writers emphasized the dependence of the " useful arts " on the sciences, and desired equally far-reaching changes in the system of education. The government was urged to establish institutions " open to all of every rank, religion, or nation," in which " the study of the useful arts and sciences and of modern languages should certainly be preferred . . . to the study of the languages and the works of taste of *decayed* nations; especially as both the histories and the moral writings of these nations, when thought of any peculiar utility, may easily be translated for the general advantage." There were proposals also for the establishment of agricultural schools with experiment farms and courses in the sciences under the auspices of the societies interested in agriculture and the arts. These were to be attended by " smart boys selected by each society," and these, returning to their several communities with knowledge of new and improved methods, would become centers of community education. " Like smaller rivulets, branching from the main stream, they would water and fertilize those lands where a large river cannot . . . expand." Nor was industrial education for the children of the poor without its advocates, as Jonas Hanway, an early humanitarian, [proves]. He believed in " the lowest of mankind " being taught not only to read but to work properly. He favored the establishment of " schools wherein children should turn their hands to every useful work," by the utilization of the natural inclination of the young toward the manipulation of material objects. These and many similar criticisms and suggestions had no great effect on the work of the schools and universities, except perhaps at Manchester, where, as has been seen, the College of Arts and Sciences was organized. Its purpose was not merely to promote mechanical improvements, but in general to supply the practical educational needs of a " town of trade." But even here conservatism obstructed the way.

Tradition, in spite of vigorous criticisms, maintained its control of educational institutions, but throughout the range of economic activities, a spirit of experimental change and rational readjustment prevailed. In Young's *Tours,* in periodicals, in various books on agriculture and related subjects, and in the publications of societies many thousands of agricultural experiments and improvements were recorded; and yet Young complained that " the present imperfection of agriculture does not arise from a want of experiments, but from the backwardness of gentlemen taking any care to make known those which are every day tried." " New undertakings " or " projects " were said to be " more frequent in this than in any other country in the world." Many of these enterprises, being connected with roads, bridges, canals, harbors, paving and other parochial and municipal developments, were authorized by Parliament; and the laws connected with such undertakings increased immensely in numbers after the middle of the century.

Of these various undertakings, the most important was canal construction of a new type, beginning with Brindley's epochal canal opened in 1761. Canals were immediately significant in the revolutionizing of transportation, but they also had an indirect result of incalculable importance — the stimulation of interest in material improvements of all kinds. For the canals were then most marvelous feats of engineering skill. It was said at the time that most of the nobility and gentry of the entire country visited Lancashire in order to see the early canals; and indeed they commanded " the attention and admiration of all Europe." " Such wonders are abroad," wrote Arthur Young concerning his anticipated visit to the Bridgewater canal, that " if only half are true I shall be not a little entertained." Nor was he disappointed with the view: he and other travellers who described their sensations seem to have exhausted their store of superlatives. A man with Brindley's " inventive genius . . . moves in a sphere that is to the rest of the world imaginary, or at best a *terra incognita.*" As for Bridgewater, his canal will " convey his name with peculiar brilliancy to the latest posterity." The work is " amazing," but it is after all in keeping with the spirit of the time: " By such noble undertakings is the present age peculiarly distinguished." Intelligent and self-disciplined observers were smitten with amaze-ment; the sensations of the common people we can only imagine. We read, for example, that on June 4, 1777, " the grand canal from Leeds to Liverpool was opened into the River Aire, at the former place, amidst such a concourse of people as was never seen in that town before; some computed them at 20,000, others at 30,000." How keen must have been the interest; how rudely shocked must have been faith in the old, unchanging ways of doing things, when vessels in the canals were

Seen and acknowledged by astonished crowds
From underground emerging to the clouds.

Since it was generally believed that one of Brindley's new engineering devices had " eased the expense " of his employer, the Duke of Bridgewater, " at least 5,000% " and that another " was better than £20,000 in the Duke's pocket ": since he was beheld doing such profitable as well as marvelous things, it is not at all surprising that vast numbers of people were stimulated to follow the great engineer's example by seeking new and better ways of doing things.

Many circumstances thus combined to create a condition favorable for mechanical improvements. The incoming of independent-minded and skilled artisans from the Continent; the escape, especially in the north, from the monopolistic restrictions of corporations and gilds; the social ferments tending to dissolve the traditions opposed to change; the rise of rationalism and experimental and applied sciences; the application of experimental change and rational readjustment to a wide variety of "useful projects," especially important in the case of canal construction because of the accompanying nation-wide stimulation of mechanical ingenuity: these are some of the elements in a complex of forces which had long been gathering momentum and which made inevitable a great increase of inventiveness.

But there is one other factor more positive, more decisive probably, in its influence than any that have been mentioned. The circumstances already described undoubtedly stimulated interest in technical progress, but the determining factor was the opportunity for the profitable use of mechanical inventions. Naturally, the profitable use of new and improved instruments of production depended largely on the demand for the output. It was in respect to the demand for English goods that the eighteenth century differed most radically from earlier periods. Pressure for goods was felt alike by the manufacturer, the trader, and the farmer. It was the pressure of excess of goods demanded over goods available by existing methods of production that made profitable the exercise of inventive ingenuity which otherwise would have remained in a measure dormant. Englishmen were at first not clearly conscious of the operation of this force; but they were not long in assigning to the machine its proper place in the control of the world's markets. With clear-sighted adaptation of means to ends, invention was then consciously and pub-

licly promoted, and the mechanical transition became a matter of national policy.

An important element in the situation was the very great increase of wealth and consequent expansion of demand for consumption goods at home. "That our riches are in fact amazingly increased within a few years," declared an Englishman in 1767, "no one who is in the least acquainted with this country can entertain a doubt; whoever will cast his eyes on our public works, our roads, our bridges, our pavements, and our hospitals, the prodigious extension of our capital, and in some proportion that of every considerable town in Great Britain; whoever will look into the possessions and expenses of individuals, their houses, furniture, tables, equipages, parks, gardens, cloths, plate, and jewels, will find everywhere round him sufficient marks to testify to the truth of this proposition." The merchant, acquiring a fortune far more rapidly than ever before, "vies all the while with the first of our nobility in his houses, table, furniture, and equipage." Wealth and luxury have even infected the "lower orders." The shopkeeper who used to be well contented with one dish of meat, one fire, and one maid, has now two or three times as many of each: his wife has her tea, her card parties, and her dressing room; and his apprentice has climbed from the kitchen fire to the front boxes at the play houses."

How may this increase of wealth and expansion of demand at home for consumption goods be accounted for? The same observer attributes it in part to the funding of the debt following the Seven Years' War. The "enormous sums" then expended are now "annually return-ing into the pockets of the merchants contractors, brokers, and stockjob-bers," and these "lend it again to the public on a new mortgage the fol-lowing year." But more dependable sources of prosperity are described. If one calls to mind "the immense riches daily flowing in since . . . (the Seven Years' War) from our commerce extended over every quar-ter of the globe, from the new chan-nels of trade opened with America, and the amazing sums imported from the East Indies, it will not be difficult to account for the opulence of the present time."

The increase of wealth, diffusion of prosperity, and widening of con-tracts led to an expansion of wants and to the introduction of new tastes. In consequence, the increase in pur-chasing power was accompanied by an even greater increase in demand for goods.

To the pressure of increasing de-mand in the home markets was add-ed the unparalleled expansion of English control over foreign mar-kets. France, the great imperial rival of England, was defeated and crip-pled. Her territories and commer-cial monopolies in America and the Far East were taken over by Eng-lishmen. Shipping facilities had been enlarged and made more effi-cient. There had been rapid prog-ress in the making of the great im-perial network of fortifications in strategic locations controlling the maritime trade routes. England's ad-

vantages were the greater because of her relative freedom from invasion and internal disturbance while her Continental rivals were exhausting themselves by wars. England, to be sure, had just emerged from the Seven Years' War, but her direct par-ticipation was relatively so slight as to give color of justification to the statement that the imperial French dominions were won from France in Germany, by means of English subsidies to the Prussian enemies of France. There were Englishmen, in-deed, who were dubious of war as an instrument of commercial expansion, who deplored "the amazing and un-natural height to which the com-merce of this country was carried by the war — being literally erected on the ruins of that of half our neigh-bors."

So large was the demand at home, and so extensive were the overseas markets controlled by Englishmen, that without new methods of pro-duction, "no exertions of the manu-facturers could have answered the demands of trade." Therefore, "the animating influence of large de-mand," bringing liberal rewards to the producers of goods, is observable "in a variety of inventions . . . and in works of ingenuity and taste."

The mechanical revolution, set in its proper historical background, is seen to assume the form of a natural inevitable result of gradually devel-oping forces; it becomes an integral, rationally explicable part of the age. Men had long been stirred by a strong, yet rational, sense of change and readjustment, which at length penetrated to the material foundations of society. This was the first phase of the mechanical revolution — the desire to bring about a more effective utilization of the material environment. To that end, as the second phase, new instruments and processes were devised. The final phase was the application of these inventions to productive processes.

In none of its aspects was this revolution the work of a few unappreciated individuals. It was rather the creation of social forces finding expression, to be sure, in the work of individuals, but far more significantly in governmental patronage and in organized co-operative activities intended primarily to promote not the fortunes of individuals but the welfare of the nation. The men who seized upon the new machines and by means of them attained wealth and power in a newly rising industrial society — the great industrialists — appropriated instruments which in their origins were distinctly social.

34. The Triumph of the Economic Virtues *

"One beam in a dark place," wrote one who knew the travail of the spirit, "hath exceeding much refreshment in it. Blessed be His name for shining upon so dark a heart as mine." While the revelation of God to the individual soul is the center of all religion, the essence of Puritan theology was that it made it, not only the center, but the whole circumference and substance, dismissing as dross and vanity all else but this secret and solitary communion. Grace alone can save, and this grace is the direct gift of God, unmediated by any earthly institution. The elect cannot by any act of their own evoke it; but they can prepare their hearts to receive it, and cherish it when received. They will prepare them best, if they empty them of all that may disturb the intentness of their lonely vigil. Like an engineer,

who, to canalize the rush of the oncoming tide, dams all channels save that through which it is to pour, like a painter who makes light visible by plunging all that is not light in gloom, the Puritan attunes his heart to the voice from Heaven by an immense effort of concentration and abnegation. To win all, he renounces all. When earthly props have been cast down, the soul stands erect in the presence of God. Infinity is attained by a process of subtraction.

To a vision thus absorbed in a single intense experience, not only religious and ecclesiastical systems, but the entire world of human relations, the whole fabric of social institutions, witnessing in all the wealth of their idealism and their greed to the infinite creativeness of man, reveal themselves in a new and wintry light. The fire of the spirit burns brightly on the hearth; but through the windows of his soul the Puritan,

* From R. H. Tawney, *Religion and the Rise of Capitalism*, copyright, 1926, by Harcourt, Brace and Company, Inc., pp. 227–273.

unless a poet or a saint, looks on a landscape touched by no breath of spring. What he sees is a forbidding and frost-bound wilderness, rolling its snow-clad leagues towards the grave — a wilderness to be subdued with aching limbs beneath solitary stars. Through it he must take his way, alone. No aid can avail him: no preacher, for only the elect can apprehend with the spirit the word of God; no Church, for to the visible Church even reprobates belong; no sacrament, for sacraments are ordained to increase the glory of God, not to minister spiritual nourishment to man; hardly God himself, for Christ died for the elect, and it may well be that the majesty of the Creator is revealed by the eternal damnation of all but a remnant of the created.

His life is that of a soldier in hostile territory. He suffers in spirit the perils which the first settlers in America endured in body, the sea behind, the untamed desert in front, a cloud of inhuman enemies on either hand. Where Catholic and Anglican had caught a glimpse of the invisible, hovering like a consecration over the gross world of sense, and touching its muddy vesture with the unearthly gleam of a divine, yet familiar, beauty, the Puritan mourned for a lost Paradise and a creation sunk in sin. Where they had seen society as a mystical body, compact of members varying in order and degree, but dignified by participation in the common life of Christendom, he saw a bleak antithesis between the spirit which quickened and an alien, indifferent or hostile world. Where they had reverenced the decent order whereby past was knit to present, and man to man, and man to God, through fellowship in works of charity, in festival and fast, in the prayers and ceremonies of the Church, he turned with horror from the filthy rags of human righteousness. Where they, in short, had found comfort in a sacrament, he started back from a snare set to entrap his soul.

We receive but what we give,
And in our life alone does Nature live.

Too often, contemning the external order as unspiritual, he made it, and ultimately himself, less spiritual by reason of his contempt.

Those who seek God in isolation from their fellowmen, unless trebly armed for the perils of the quest, are apt to find, not God, but a devil, whose countenance bears an embarrassing resemblance to their own. The moral self-sufficiency of the Puritan nerved his will, but it corroded his sense of social solidarity. For, if each individual destiny hangs on a private transaction between himself and his Maker, what room is left for human intervention? A servant of Jehovah more than of Christ, he revered God as a Judge rather than loved him as a Father, and was moved less by compassion for his erring brethren than by impatient indignation at the blindness of vessels of wrath who " sinned their mercies." A spiritual aristocrat, who sacrificed fraternity to liberty, he drew from his idealization of personal responsibility a theory of individual rights, which, secularized and generalized, was to be among the most potent explosives that the world has known. He drew from it also a scale of ethical values, in which the traditional scheme of Christian virtues was almost exactly reversed, and which, since he was above all things practical, he carried as a dynamic into the routine of business and political life.

For, since conduct and action, though availing nothing to attain the free gift of salvation, are a proof that the gift has been accorded, what is rejected as a means is resumed as a consequence, and the Puritan flings himself into practical activities with the dæmonic energy of one who, all doubts allayed, is conscious that he is a sealed and chosen vessel. Once engaged in affairs, he brings to them both the qualities and limitations of his creed in all their remorseless logic. Called by God to labor in his vineyard, he has within himself a principle at once of energy and of order, which makes him irresistible both in war and in the struggles of commerce. Convinced that character is all and circumstances nothing, he sees in the poverty of those who fall by the way, not a misfortune to be pitied and relieved, but a moral failing to be condemned, and in riches, not an object of suspicion — though like other gifts they may be abused — but the blessing which rewards the triumph of energy and will. Tempered by self-examination, self-discipline, self-control, he is the practical ascetic, whose victories are won not in the cloister, but on the battlefield, in the counting-house, and in the market.

This temper, of course with infinite varieties of quality and emphasis, found its social organ in those middle and commercial classes who were the citadel of the Puritan spirit, and whom, "ennobled by their own industry and virtue," Milton described as the standard-bearers of progress and enlightenment. We are so accustomed to think of England as *par excellence* the pioneer of economic progress, that we are apt to forget how recently that rôle has been assumed. In the Middle Ages it belonged to the Italians, in the sixteenth century to the Netherland dominions of the Spanish Empire, in the seventeenth to the United Provinces and, above all, to the Dutch.

The England of Shakespeare and Bacon was still largely medieval in its economic organization and social outlook, more interested in maintaining customary standards of consumption than in accumulating capital for future production, with an aristocracy contemptuous of the economic virtues, a peasantry farming for subsistence amid the organized confusion of the open-field village, and a small, if growing, body of jealously conservative craftsmen. In such a society Puritanism worked like the yeast which sets the whole mass fermenting. It went through its slack and loosely knit texture like a troop of Cromwell's Ironsides through the disorderly cavalry of Rupert. Where, as in Ireland, the elements were so alien that assimilation was out of the question, the result was a wound that festered for three centuries. In England the effect was that at once of an irritant and of a tonic. Puritanism had its own standards of social conduct, derived partly from the obvious interests of the commercial classes, partly from its conception of the nature of God and the destiny of man. These standards were in sharp antithesis, both to the considerable surviving elements of feudalism in English society, and to the policy of the authoritarian State, with its ideal of an ordered and graded society, whose different members were to be maintained in their traditional status by the pressure and protection of a paternal monarchy. Sapping the former by its influence and overthrowing the latter by direct attack, Puritanism became a potent force in preparing the way for the commercial civilization which finally triumphed at the Revolution.

The complaint that religious radicalism, which aimed at upsetting the government of the Church, went hand in hand with an economic radicalism, which resented the restraints on individual self-interest imposed in the name of religion or of social policy, was being made by the stricter school of religious opinion quite early in the reign of Elizabeth. Seventeenth-century writers repeated the charge that the Puritan conscience lost its delicacy where matters of business were concerned, and some of them were sufficiently struck by the phenomenon to attempt an historical explanation of it. The example on which they usually seized — the symbol of a supposed general disposition to laxity — was the indulgence shown by Puritan divines in the particular matter of moderate interest. It was the effect, so the picturesque story ran, of the Marian persecution. The refugees who fled the continent could not start business in a foreign country. If, driven by necessity, they invested their capital and lived on the proceeds, who could quarrel with so venial a lapse in so good a cause? Subsequent writers embellished the picture. The redistribution of property at the time of the Dissolution, and the expansion of trade in the middle of the century, had led, one of them argued, to a great increase in the volume of credit transactions. The opprobrium which attached to loans at interest — " a sly and forbid practice " — not only among Romanists and Anglicans, but among honest Puritans, played into the hands of the less scrupulous members of " the faction." Disappointed in politics, they took to money-lending, and, without venturing to justify usury in theory, defended it in practice. " Without the scandal of a recantation, they contrived an expedient, by maintaining that, though usury for the name were stark naught, yet for widows, orphans and other impotents (therein principally comprising the saints under persecution) it was very tolerable, because profitable, and in a manner necessary." Naturally, Calvin's doctrine as to the legitimacy of moderate interest was hailed by these hypocrites with a shout of glee. " It took with the brethren like polygamy with the Turks, recommended by the example of divers zealous ministers, who themselves desired to pass for orphans of the first rank." Nor was it only as the apologist of moderate interest that Puritanism was alleged to reveal the cloven hoof. Puritans themselves complained of a mercilessness in driving hard bargains, and of a harshness to the poor, which contrasted unfavorably with the practice of followers of the unreformed religion. "The Papists," wrote a Puritan in 1653, "may rise up against many of this generation. It is a sad thing that they should be more forward upon a bad principle than a Christian upon a good one."

Such, in all ages, is history as seen by the political pamphleteer. The real story was less dramatic, but more significant. From the very beginning, Calvinism had comprised two elements, which Calvin himself had fused, but which contained the seeds of future discord. It had at once given a whole-hearted *imprimatur* to the life of business enterprise, which most earlier moralists had regarded with suspicion, and had laid upon it the restraining hand of an inquisitorial discipline. At Geneva, where Calvinism was the creed of a small and homogeneous city, the second aspect had predominated; in the many-sided life of England, where there were numerous conflicting interests to balance it, and where it was long politically weak, the first. Then, in the late sixteenth and early seventeenth centuries, had come the wave of commercial and financial expansion — companies, colonies, capitalism in textiles, capitalism in mining, capitalism in finance — on the crest of which the English commercial classes, in Calvin's day still held in leading-strings by conservative

statesmen, had climbed to a position of dignity and affluence.

Naturally, as the Puritan movement came to its own, these two elements flew apart. The collectivist, half-communistic aspect, which had never been acclimatized in England, quietly dropped out of notice, to crop up once more, and for the last time, to the disgust and terror of merchant and landowner, in the popular agitation under the Commonwealth. The individualism congenial to the world of business became the distinctive characteristic of a Puritanism which had arrived, and which, in becoming a political force, was at once secularized and committed to a career of compromise. Its note was not the attempt to establish on earth a "Kingdom of Christ," but an ideal of personal character and conduct, to be realized by the punctual discharge both of public and private duties. Its theory had been discipline; its practical result was liberty.

Given the social and political conditions of England, the transformation was inevitable. The incompatibility of Presbyterianism with the stratified arrangement of English society had been remarked by Hooker. If the City Fathers of Geneva had thrown off by the beginning of the seventeenth century the religious collectivism of Calvin's régime, it was not to be expected that the landowners and *bourgeoisie* of an aristocratic and increasingly commercial nation, however much Calvinist theology might appeal to them, would view with favor the social doctrines implied in Calvinist discipline. In the reign of the first two Stuarts, both economic interests and political theory pulled them hard in the opposite direction. "Merchants' doings," the man of business in Wilson's *Discourse upon Usury* had observed, "must not thus be overthwarted by preachers and others that cannot skill of their dealings." Behind the elaborate façade of Tudor State control, which has attracted the attention of historians, an individualist movement had been steadily developing, which found expression in opposition to the traditional policy of stereotyping economic relations by checking enclosure, controlling food supplies and prices, interfering with the money-market, and regulating the conditions of the wage contract and of apprenticeship. In the first forty years of the seventeenth century, on grounds both of expediency and of principle, the commercial and propertied classes were becoming increasingly restive under the whole system, at once ambitious and inefficient, of economic paternalism. It was in the same sections of the community that both religious and economic dissatisfaction were most acute. Puritanism, with its idealization of the spiritual energies which found expression in the activities of business and industry, drew the isolated rivulets of discontent together, and swept them forward with the dignity and momentum of a religious and a social philosophy.

For it was not merely as the exponent of certain tenets as to theology and church government, but as the champion of interests and opinions embracing every side of the life of society, that the Puritan movement came into collision with the Crown. In reality, as is the case with most heroic ideologies, the social and religious aspects of Puritanism were not disentangled; they presented themselves, both to supporters and opponents, as different facets of a single scheme. "All that crossed the views of the needy courtiers, the proud encroaching priests, the thievish projectors, the lewd nobility and gentry . . . whoever could endure a sermon, modest habit or conversation, or anything good — all these were Puritans." The clash was not one of theories — a systematic and theoretical individualism did not develop till after the Restoration — but of contradictory economic interests and incompatible conceptions of social expediency.

The economic policy haltingly pursued by the Government of Charles I bore some resemblance to the system of which a more uncompromising version was developed between 1661 and 1685 by Colbert in France. It was one which favored an artificial and State-promoted capitalism — a capitalism resting on the grant of privileges and concessions to company promoters who would pay for them, and accompanied by an elaborate system of State control, which again, if partly inspired by a genuine solicitude for the public interest, was too often smeared with an odious trail of finance. It found its characteristic expression in the grant of patents, in the revival of the royal monopoly of exchange business, against which the City had fought under Elizabeth, in attempts to enforce by administrative action compliance with the elaborate and impracticable code controlling the textile trades and to put down speculation in foodstuffs, and in raids on enclosing landlords, on employers who paid in truck or evaded the rates fixed by assessment, and on justices who were negligent in the administration of the Poor Laws. Such measures were combined with occasional plunges into even more grandiose schemes for the establishment of county granaries, for taking certain industries into the hands of the Crown, and even for the virtual nationalization of the cloth manufacture."

"The very genius of that nation of people," wrote Strafford to Laud of the Puritans, "leads them always to oppose, as well civilly as ecclesiastically, all that ever authority ordains for them." Against this whole attempt to convert economic activity into an instrument of profit for the Government and its hangers-on — against, no less, the spasmodic attempts of the State to protect peasants against landlords, craftsmen against merchants, and consumers against middlemen — the interests which it thwarted and curbed revolted with increasing pertinacity. Questions of taxation, on which attention has usually been concentrated, were in reality merely one element in a quarrel which had its deeper cause in the collision of incompatible social philosophies. The Puritan tradesman had seen his business ruined by a monopoly granted to a needy courtier, and cursed Laud and his Popish soap. The Puritan

goldsmith or financier had found his trade as a bullion-broker hampered by the reëstablishment of the ancient office of Royal Exchanger, and secured a resolution from the House of Commons, declaring that the patent vesting it in Lord Holland and the proclamation forbidding the exchanging of gold and silver by unauthorized persons were a grievance. The Puritan money-lender had been punished by the Court of High Commission, and railed at the interference of bishops in temporal affairs. The Puritan clothier, who had suffered many things at the hands of interfering busy-bodies despatched from Whitehall to teach him his business, averted discreet eyes when the Wiltshire workmen threw a more than usually obnoxious Royal Commissioner into the Avon, and, when the Civil War came, rallied to the Parliament. The Puritan country gentleman had been harried by Depopulation Commissions, and took his revenge with the meeting of the Long Parliament. The Puritan merchant had seen the Crown both squeeze money out of his company, and threaten its monopoly by encouraging interlopers to infringe its charter. The Puritan member of Parliament had invested in colonial enterprises, and had ideas as to commercial policy which were not those of the Government. Confident in their own energy and acumen, proud of their success, and regarding with profound distrust the interference both of Church and of State with matters of business and property rights, the commercial classes, in spite of their attachment to a militant mercantilism in matters of trade, were, even before the Civil War, more than half converted to the administrative nihilism which was to be the rule of social policy in the century following it. Their demand was the one which is usual in such circumstances. It was that business affairs should be left to be settled by business men, unhampered by the intrusions of an antiquated morality or by misconceived arguments of public policy.

The separation of economic from ethical interests, which was the note of all this movement, was in sharp opposition to religious tradition, and it did not establish itself without a struggle. Even in the very capital of European commerce and finance, an embittered controversy was occasioned by the refusal to admit usurers to communion or to confer degrees upon them; it was only after a storm of pamphleteering, in which the theological faculty of the University of Utrecht performed prodigies of zeal and ingenuity, that the States of Holland and West Friesland closed the agitation by declaring that the Church had no concern with questions of banking. In the French Calvinist Churches, the decline of discipline had caused lamentations a generation earlier. In America, the theocracy of Massachusetts, merciless alike to religious liberty and to economic license, was about to be undermined by the rise of new States like Rhode Island and Pennsylvania, whose tolerant, individualist and utilitarian temper was destined to find its greatest representative in the golden common sense of Benjamin Franklin. "The sin of our too great fondness for trade, to the neglecting of our more valuable interests," wrote a Scottish divine in 1709, when Glasgow was on the eve of a triumphant outburst of commercial enterprise, "I humbly think will be written upon our judgment. . . . I am sure the Lord is remarkably frowning upon our trade . . . since it was put in the room of religion."

In England, the growing disposition to apply exclusively economic standards to social relations evoked from Puritan writers and devines vigorous protests against usurious interest, extortionate prices and the oppression of tenants by landlords. The faithful, it was urged, had interpreted only too literally the doctrine that the sinner was saved, not by works, but by faith. Usury, "in time of Popery an odious thing," had become a scandal. Professors, by their covetousness, caused the enemies of the reformed religion to blaspheme. The exactions of the forestaller and regrater were never so monstrous or so immune from interference. The hearts of the rich were never so hard, nor the necessities of the poor so neglected. "The poor able to work are suffered to beg; the impotent, aged and sick are not sufficiently provided for, but almost starved with the allowance of 3d. and 4d. a piece a week. . . . These are the last times indeed. Men generally are all for themselves. And some would set up such, having a form of religion, without the power of it."

These utterances came, however, from that part of the Puritan mind which looked backward. That which looked forward found in the rapidly growing spirit of economic enterprise something not uncongenial to its own temper, and went out to welcome it as an ally. What in Calvin had been a qualified concession to practical exigencies appeared in some of his later followers as a frank idealization of the life of the trader, as the service of God and the training-ground of the soul. Discarding the suspicion of economic motives, which had been as characteristic of the reformers as of medieval theologians, Puritanism in its later phases added a halo of ethical sanctification to the appeal of economic expediency, and offered a moral creed, in which the duties of religion and the calls of business ended their long estrangement in an unanticipated reconciliation. Its spokesmen pointed out, it is true, the peril to the soul involved in a single-minded concentration on economic interests. The enemy, however, was not riches, but the bad habits sometimes associated with them, and its warnings against an excessive preoccupation with the pursuit of gain wore more and more the air of afterthoughts, appended to teaching the main tendency and emphasis of which were little affected by these incidental qualifications. It insisted, in short, that moneymaking, if not free from spiritual dangers, was not a danger and nothing else, but that it could be, and ought to be, carried on for the greater glory of God.

The conception to which it appealed to bridge the gulf sprang from the very heart of Puritan theology. It was that expressed in the characteristic and oft-used phrase, " a Calling." The rational order of the universe is the work of God, and its plan requires that the individual should labor for God's glory. There is a spiritual calling, and a temporal calling. It is the first duty of the Christian to know and believe in God; it is by faith that he will be saved. But faith is not a mere profession, such as that of Talkative of Prating Row, whose " religion is to make a noise." The only genuine faith is the faith which produces works. " At the day of Doom men shall be judged according to their fruits. It will not be said then, Did you believe? but, Were you doers or talkers only? " The second duty of the Christian is to labor in the affairs of practical life, and this second duty is subordinate only to the first. " God," wrote a Puritan divine, " doth call every man and woman . . . to serve him in some peculiar employment in this world, both for their own and the common good. . . . The Great Governour of the world hath appointed to every man his proper post and province, and let him be never so active out of his sphere, he will be at a great loss, if he do not keep his own vineyard and mind his own business."

From this reiterated insistence on secular obligations as imposed by the divine will, it follows that, not withdrawal from the world, but the conscientious discharge of the duties of business, is among the loftiest of religious and moral virtues. " The begging friars and such monks as live only to themselves and to their formal devotion, but do employ themselves in no one thing to further their own subsistence or the good of mankind . . . yet have the confidence to boast of this their course as a state of perfection; which in very deed, as to the worthiness of it, falls short of the poorest cobbler, for his is a calling of God, and theirs is none." The idea was not a new one. Luther had advanced it as a weapon against monasticism. But for Luther, with his patriarchial outlook on economic affairs, the calling means normally that state of life in which the individual has been set by Heaven, and against which it is impiety to rebel. On the lips of Puritan divines, it is not an invitation to resignation, but the bugle-call which summons the elect to the long battle which will end only with their death. "The world is all before them." They are to hammer out their salvation, not merely *in vocatione,* but *per vocationem.* The calling is not a condition in which the individual is born, but a strenuous and exacting enterprise, to be undertaken, indeed, under the guidance of Providence, but to be chosen by each man for himself, with a deep sense of his solemn responsibilities. "God hath given to man reason for this use, that he should first consider, then choose, then put in execution; and it is a preposterous and brutish thing to fix or fall upon any weighty business, such as a calling or condition of life, without a careful pondering it in the balance of sound reason."

Laborare est orare. By the Puritan moralist the ancient maxim is repeated with a new and intenser significance. The labor which he idealizes is not simply a requirement imposed by nature, or a punishment for the sin of Adam. It is itself a kind of ascetic discipline, more rigorous than that demanded of any order of mendicants — a discipline imposed by the will of God, and to be undergone, not in solitude, but in the punctual discharge of secular duties. It is not merely an economic means, to be laid aside when physical needs have been satisfied. It is a spiritual end, for in it alone can the soul find health, and it must be continued as an ethical duty long after it has ceased to be a material necessity. Work thus conceived stands at the very opposite pole from " good works," as they were understood, or misunderstood, by Protestants. They, it was thought, had been a series of single transactions, performed as compensation for particular sins, or out of anxiety to acquire merit. What is required of the Puritan is not individual meritorious acts, but a holy life — a system in which every element is grouped round a central idea, the service of God, from which all disturbing irrelevancies have been pruned, and to which all minor interests are subordinated.

His conception of that life was expressed in the words " Be wholly taken up in diligent business of your lawful callings when you are not exercised in the more immediate service of God." In order to deepen his spiritual life, the Christian must be prepared to narrow it. He " is blind in no man's cause, but best sighted in his own. He confines himself to the circle of his own affairs and thrusts not his fingers in needless fires. . . . He sees the falseness of it [the world] and therefore learns to trust himself ever, others so far as not to be damaged by their disappointment." There must be no idle leisure: "those that are prodigal of their time despise their own souls." Religion must be active, not merely contemplative. Contemplation is, indeed, a kind of self-indulgence. " To neglect this [i.e., bodily employment and mental labor] and say, ' I will pray and meditate,' is as if your servant should refuse your greatest work, and tye himself to some lesser, easie part. . . . God hath commanded you some way or other to labour for your daily bread." The rich are no more excused from work than the poor, though they may rightly use their riches to select some occupation specially serviceable to others. Covetousness is a danger to the soul, but it is not so grave a danger as sloth. " The standing pool is prone to putrefaction: and it were better to beat down the body and to keep in subjection by a laborious calling, than through luxury to become a castaway." So far from poverty being meritorious, it is a duty to choose the more profitable occupation. " If God show you a way in which you may lawfully get more than in another way (without wrong to your soul or to any other), if you refuse this, and choose the less gainful way, you cross one of the ends of your Calling, and you refuse to be God's steward." Luxury, unrestrained pleasure, personal extravagance, can have no place in a Christian's conduct, for " every penny which is laid out . . .

must be done as by God's own appointment." Even excessive devotion to friends and relations is to be avoided. " It is an irrational act, and therefore not fit for a rational creature, to love any one farther than reason will allow us. . . . It very often taketh up men's minds so as to hinder their love to God." The Christian life, in short, must be systematic and organized, the work of an iron will and a cool intelligence. Those who have read Mill's account of his father must have been struck by the extent to which Utilitarianism was not merely a political doctrine, but a moral attitude. Some of the links in the Utilitarian coat of mail were forged, it may be suggested, by the Puritan divines of the seventeenth century.

The practical application of these generalities to business is set out in the numerous works composed to expound the rules of Christian conduct in the varied relations of life. If one may judge by their titles — *Navigation Spiritualized, Husbandry Spiritualized, The Religious Weaver* — there must have been a considerable demand for books conducive to professional edification. A characteristic specimen is *The Tradesman's Calling,* by Richard Steele. The author, after being deprived of a country living under the Act of Uniformity, spent his declining years as a minister of a congregation at Armourers Hall in London, and may be presumed to have understood the spiritual requirements of the City in his day, when the heroic age of Puritanism was almost over and enthusiasm was no longer a virtue. No one who was writing a treatise on economic ethics today would address himself primarily to the independent shopkeeper, as the figure most representative of the business community, and Steele's book throws a flood of light on the problems and outlook of the *bourgeoisie,* in an age before the center of economic gravity had shifted from the substantial tradesman to the exporting merchant, the industrial capitalist and the financier.

Like Baxter, he is acquainted with the teaching of earlier authorities as to equity in bargaining. He is doubtful, however, of its practical utility. Obvious frauds in matters of quality and weight are to be avoided; an honest tradesman ought not to corner the market, or " accumulate two or three callings merely to increase his riches," or oppress the poor; nor should he seek more than " a reasonable proportion of gain," or " lie on the catch to make [his] markets of others' straits." But Steele rejects as useless in practice the various objective standards of a reasonable profit — cost of production, standard of life, customary prices — which had been suggested in earlier ages, and concludes that the individual must judge for himself. " Here, as in many other cases, an upright conscience must be the clerk of the market."

In reality, however, the characteristic of *The Tradesman's Calling,* as of the age in which it was written, is not the relics of medieval doctrine which linger embalmed in its guileless pages, but the robust common sense, which carries the author lightly over traditional scruples on a tide of genial, if Philistine, optimism. For his main thesis is a comfortable one — that there is no necessary conflict between religion and business. " Prudence and Piety were always very good friends. . . . You may gain enough of both worlds if you would mind each in its place." His object is to show how that agreeable result may be produced by dedicating business — with due reservations — to the service of God, and he has naturally little to say on the moral casuistry of economic conduct, because he is permeated by the idea that trade itself is a kind of religion. A tradesman's first duty is to get a full insight into his calling, and to use his brains to improve it. " He that hath lent you talents hath also said, ' Occupy till I come! ' Your strength is a talent, your parts are talents, and so is your time. How is it that ye stand all the day idle? . . . Your trade is your proper province. . . . Your own vineyard you should keep. . . . Your fancies, your understandings, your memories . . . are all to be laid out therein." So far from their being an inevitable collision between the requirements of business and the claims of religion, they walk hand in hand. By a fortunate dispensation, the virtues enjoined on Christians — diligence, moderation, sobriety, thrift — are the very qualities most conducive to commercial success. The foundation of all is prudence; and prudence is merely another name for the " godly wisdom [which] comes in and puts due bounds " to his expenses, " and teaches the tradesman to live rather somewhat below than at all above his income." Industry comes next, and industry is at once expedient and meritorious. It will keep the tradesman from "frequent and needless frequenting of taverns," and pin him to his shop, "where you may most confidently expect the presence and blessing of God."

If virtue is advantageous, vice is ruinous. Bad company, speculation, gambling, politics, and "a preposterous zeal" in religion — it is these things which are the ruin of tradesmen. Not, indeed, that religion is to be neglected. On the contrary, it "is to be exercised in the frequent use of holy ejaculations." What is deprecated is merely the unbusinesslike habit of "neglecting a man's necessary affairs upon pretence of religious worship." But these faults, common and uncommon alike, are precisely those to be avoided by the sincere Christian, who must not, indeed, deceive or oppress his neighbor, but need not fly to the other extreme, be righteous overmuch, or refuse to "take the advantage which the Providence of God puts into his hands." By a kind of happy, pre-established harmony, such as a later age discovered between the needs of society and the self-interest of the individual, success in business is in itself almost a sign of spiritual grace, for it is proof that a man has labored faithfully in his vocation, and that "God has blessed his trade." "Nothing will pass in any man's account except it be done in the way of his calling. . . . Next to the saving of his soul, [tradesman's] care and business is to serve God in his calling, and to drive it as far as it will go."

When duty was so profitable, might not profit-making be a duty? Thus argued the honest pupils of Mr. Gripeman, the schoolmaster of Love-gain, a market-town in the county of Coveting in the north. The inference was illogical, but how attractive! When the Rev. David Jones was so indiscreet as to preach at St. Mary Woolnoth in Lombard Street a sermon against usury on the text "The Pharisees who were covetous heard all these things and they derided Christ," his career in London was brought to an abrupt conclusion.

The springs of economic conduct lie in regions rarely penetrated by moralists, and to suggest a direct reaction of theory on practice would be paradoxical. But, if the circumstances which determine that certain kinds of conduct shall be profitable are economic, those which decide that they shall be the object of general approval are primarily moral and intellectual. For conventions to be adopted with wholehearted enthusiasm, to be not merely tolerated, but applauded, to become the habit of a nation and the admiration of its philosophers, the second condition must be present as well as the first. The insistence among men of pecuniary motives, the strength of economic egotism, the appetite for gain — these are the commonplaces of every age and need no emphasis. What is significant is the change of standards which converted a natural frailty into a resounding virtue. After all, it appears, a man can serve two masters, for — so happily is the world disposed — he may be paid by one, while he works for the other. Between the old-fashioned denunciation of uncharitable covetousness and the new-fashioned applause of economic enterprise, a bridge is thrown by the argument which urges that enterprise itself is the discharge of a duty imposed by God.

In the year 1690 appeared a pamphlet entitled *A Discourse of Trade, by N. B., M. D.* Notable for its enlightened discussion of conventional theories of the balance of trade, it is a good specimen of an indifferent *genus*. But its authorship was more significant than its argument. For N. B. was Dr. Nicholas Barbon; and Dr. Nicholas Barbon, currency expert, pioneer of insurance, and enthusiast for land-banks, was the son of that Praise-God Barebones, by the parody of whose alluring surname a cynical posterity recorded its verdict on the brief comedy of the Rule of the Saints over Laodicean Englishmen. The reaction from Puritan rigor to Restoration license is the most familiar of platitudes. The reaction to a mundane materialism was more gradual, more general, and ultimately of greater significance. The profligacy of the courtier had its decorous counterpart in the economic orgies of the tradesman and the merchant. Votaries, not of Bacchus, but of a more exacting and more profitable divinity, they celebrated their relief at the discredit of a too arduous idealism, by plunging with redoubled zest into the agreeable fever of making and losing money.

The transition from the anabaptist to the company promoter was less abrupt than might at first sight be supposed. It had been prepared, however unintentionally, by Puritan moralists. In their emphasis on the moral duty of untiring activity, on work as an end in itself, on the evils of luxury and extravagance, on foresight and thrift, on moderation and self-discipline and rational calculation, they had created an ideal of Christian conduct, which canonized as an ethical principle the efficiency which economic theorists were preaching as a specific for social disorders. It was as captivating as it was novel. To countless generations of religious thinkers, the fundamental maxim of Christian social ethics had seemed to be expressed in the words of St. Paul to Timothy: "Having food and raiment, let us be therewith content. For the love of money is the root of all evil." Now, while as always, the world battered at the gate, a new standard was raised within the citadel by its own defenders. The garrison had discovered that the invading host of economic appetites was, not an enemy, but an ally. Not sufficiency to the needs of daily life, but limitless increase and expansion, became the goal of the Christian's efforts. Not consumption, on which the eyes of earlier sages had been turned, but production, became the pivot of his argument. Not an easy-going and open-handed charity, but a systematic and methodical accumulation, won the meed of praise that belongs to the good and faithful servant. The shrewd, calculating commercialism which tries all human relations by pecuniary standards, the acquisitiveness which cannot rest while there are competitors to be conquered or profits to be won, the love of social power and hunger for economic gain — these irrepressible appetites had evoked from time immemorial the warnings and denunciations of saints and sages. Plunged in the cleansing waters of later Puritanism, the qualities which less enlightened ages had denounced as social vices emerged as economic virtues. They emerged as moral virtues as well. For the world exists not to be enjoyed, but to be conquered. Only its conqueror deserves the name of Christian. For such a philosophy, the question " What shall it profit a man? " carries no sting. In winning the world, he wins the salvation of his own soul as well.

The idea of economic progress as an end to be consciously sought, while ever receding, had been unfamiliar to most earlier generations of Englishmen, in which the theme of moralists had been the danger of unbridled cupidity, and the main aim of public policy had been the stability of traditional relationships. It found a new sanction in the identification of labor and enterprise with the service of God. The magnificent energy which changed in a century the face of material civilization was to draw nourishment from that temper. The worship of production and ever greater production — the slavish drudgery of the millionaire and his unhappy servants — was to be hallowed by the precepts of the same compelling creed.

Social development moves with a logic whose inferences are long delayed, and the day of these remoter applications had not yet dawned. The version of Christian ethics expounded by Puritanism in some of its later phases was still only in its vigorous youth. But it sailed forward on a flowing tide. It had an unconscious ally in the pre-occupation with economic interests which found expression in the enthusiasm of business politicians for a commercial *Machtpolitik*. The youthful Commonwealth, a rival of Holland " for the fairest mistress in the world — trade," was not two years old when it made its own essay in economic imperialism. " A bare-faced war " for commerce, got up by the Royal African Company, was Clarendon's verdict on the Dutch war of 1665–7. Five years later, Shaftesbury hounded the City against Holland with the cry of *Delenda est Carthago*. The war finance of the Protectorate had made it necessary for Cromwell to court Dutch and Jewish, as well as native, capitalists, and the impecunious Government of the Restoration was in the hands of those syndicates of goldsmiths whose rapacity the Chancellor, a survivor from the age before the deluge, when aristocrats still despised the upstart plutocracy, found not a little disgusting.

The contemporary progress of economic thought fortified no less the mood which glorified the economic virtues. Economic science developed in England, not, as in Germany, as the handmaid of public administration, nor, as in France, through the speculations of philosophers and men of letters, but as the interpreter of the practical interests of the City. With the exception of Petty and

Locke, its most eminent practitioners were business men, and the questions which excited them were those, neither of production nor of social organization, but of commerce and finance — the balance of trade, tariffs, interest, currency and credit. The rise of Political Arithmetic after the Restoration, profoundly influenced, as it was, by the Cartesian philosophy and by the progress of natural science, stamped their spontaneous and doctrineless individualism with the seal of theoretical orthodoxy. Knowledge, wrote the author of the preface to a work by one of the most eminent exponents of the new science, "in great measure is become mechanical." The exact analysis of natural conditions, the calculations of forces and strains, the reduction of the complex to the operation of simple, constant and measurable forces, was the natural bias of an age interested primarily in mathematics and physics. Its object was "to express itself in terms of number, weight or measure, to use only arguments of sense, and to consider only such causes as have visible foundations in nature; leaving those that depend upon the mutable minds, opinions, appetites and passions of particular men to the consideration of others."

In such an atmosphere, the moral casuistry, which had occupied so large a place in the earlier treatment of social and economic subjects, seemed the voice of an antiquated superstition. Moreover, the main economic dogma of the mercantilist had an affinity with the main ethical dogma of the Puritan, which was the more striking because the coinci-

dence was undesigned. To the former, production, not consumption, was the pivot of the economic system, and, by what seems to the modern reader a curious perversion, consumption is applauded only because it offers a new market for productive energies. To the latter, the cardinal virtues are precisely those which find in the strenuous toils of industry and commerce their most natural expression. The typical qualities of the successful business life, in the days before the rise of joint-stock enterprise, were intensity and earnestness of labor, concentration, system and method, the initiative which broke with routine and the foresight which postponed the present to the future. Advice like that of the Reverend Mr. Steele to his City congregation was admirably calculated to give these arduous excellences a heightened status and justification. The lean goddess, Abstinence, whom Mr. Keynes, in a passage of brilliant indiscretion, has revealed as the tutelary divinity of Victorian England, was inducted to the austere splendors of her ascetic shrine by the pious hands of Puritan moralists.

Such teaching fell upon willing ears. Excluded by legislation from a direct participation in public affairs, Dissenters of means and social position threw themselves into the alternative career offered by commerce and finance, and did so the more readily because religion itself had blessed their choice. If they conformed, the character given them by their critics — "opinionating, relying much upon their own judgment . . . ungrateful, as not holding themselves beholden to any man . . . proud, as thinking themselves the only favorites of God, and the only wise or virtuous among men " — disposed them to the left in questions of Church and State. The names of the commercial magnates of the day lend some confirmation to the suggestion of that affinity between religious radicalism and business acumen which envious contemporaries expressed in their sneers at the "Presbyterian old usurer," " devout misers," and " extorting Ishban." The four London members elected in 1661 had not only filled the ordinary civic offices, but had held between them the governorship of the East India Company, the deputy-governorship of the Levant Company, and the masterships of the Salters and Drapers Companies; two of them were said to be Presbyterians, and two Independents. Of the committee of leading business men who advised Charles II's Government on questions of commercial policy, some, like Sir Patience Ward and Michael Godfrey, represented the ultra-Protestantism of the City, while others, like Thomas Papillon and the two Houblons, were members of the French Hugenot church in London. In spite of the bitter commercial rivalry with Holland, both Dutch capital and Dutch ideas found an enthusiastic welcome in London. Sir George Downing, Charles II's envoy at the Hague, who endeavored to acclimatize Dutch banking methods in England, and who, according to Clarendon, was one of the intriguers who prepared the war of 1665–7, had been reared in the Puritan severity of Salem and Harvard, and had been a

preacher in the regiment of Colonel Okey. Paterson, who supplied the idea of a joint-stock banking corporation, which Michael Godfrey popularized in the City and Montagu piloted through Parliament, was, like the magnificent Law, a Scotch company promoter, who had haunted the Hague in the days when it was the home of disconsolate Whigs. Yarranton, most ingenious of projectors, had been an officer in the Parliamentary army, and his book was a long sermon on the virtues of the Dutch. Defoe, who wrote the idyll of the *bourgeoisie* in his *Complete English Tradesman,* was born of nonconformist parents, and was intended for the ministry before, having failed in trade, he took up politics and literature. In his admirable study of the iron industry, Mr. Ashton has shown that the most eminent ironmasters of the eighteenth century belonged as a rule to the Puritan connection. They had their prototype in the seventeenth century in Baxter's friend, Thomas Foley, " who from almost nothing did get about £5,000 per annum or more by iron works."

To such a generation, a creed which transformed the acquisition of wealth from a drudgery or a temptation into a moral duty was the milk of lions. It was not that religion was expelled from practical life, but that religion itself gave it a foundation of granite. In that keen atmosphere of economic enterprise, the ethics of the Puritan bore some resemblance to those associated later with the name of Smiles. The good Christian was not wholly dissimilar from the economic man.

THE NEW MEDICINE FOR POVERTY

To applaud certain qualities is by implication to condemn the habits and institutions which appear to conflict with them. The recognition accorded by Puritan ethics to the economic virtues, in an age when such virtues were rarer than they are today, gave a timely stimulus to economic efficiency. But it naturally, if unintentionally, modified the traditional attitude towards social obligations. For the spontaneous, doctrineless individualism, which became the rule of English public life a century before the philosophy of it was propounded by Adam Smith, no single cause was responsible. But, simultaneously with the obvious movements in the world of affairs — the discrediting of the ideal of a paternal, authoritarian Government, the breakdown of central control over local administration, the dislocation caused by the Civil War, the expansion of trade and the shifting of industry from its accustomed seats — it is perhaps not fanciful to detect in the ethics of Puritanism one force contributing to the change in social policy which is noticeable after the middle of the century.

The loftiest teaching cannot escape from its own shadow. To urge that the Christian life must be lived in a zealous discharge of private duties — how necessary! Yet how readily perverted to the suggestion that there are no vital social obligations beyond and above them! To insist that the individual is responsible, that no man can save his brother, that the essence of religion is the contact of the soul with its Maker, how true and indispensable! But how easy to slip from that truth into the suggestion that society is without responsibility, that no man can help his brother, that the social order and its consequences are not even the scaffolding by which men may climb to greater heights, but something external, alien and irrelevant — something, at best, indifferent to the life of the spirit, and, at worst, the sphere of the letter which killeth and of the reliance on works which ensnares the soul into the slumber of death! In emphasizing that God's Kingdom is not of this world, Puritanism did not always escape the suggestion that this world is no part of God's Kingdom. The complacent victim of that false antithesis between the social mechanism and the life of the spirit, which was to tyrannize over English religious thought for the next two centuries, it enthroned religion in the privacy of the individual soul, not without some sighs of sober satisfaction at its abdication from society. Professor Dicey has commented on the manner in which " the appeal of the Evangelicals to personal religion corresponds with the appeal of Benthamite Liberals to individual energy." The same affinity between religious and social interests found an even clearer expression in the Puritan movement of the seventeenth century. Individualism in religion led insensibly, if not quite logically, to an individualist morality, and an individualist morality to a disparagement of the significance of the social fabric as compared with personal character.

A practical example of that change of emphasis is given by the treatment accorded to the questions of Enclosure and of Pauperism. For a century and a half the progress of enclosing had been a burning issue, flaring up, from time to time, into acute agitation. During the greater part of that period, from Latimer in the thirties of the sixteenth century to Laud in the thirties of the seventeenth, the attitude of religious teachers had been one of condemnation. Sermon after sermon and pamphlet after pamphlet — not to mention Statutes and Royal Commissions — had been launched against depopulation. The appeal had been, not merely to public policy, but to religion. Peasant and lord, in their different degrees, are members of one Christian commonwealth, within which the law of charity must bridle the corroding appetite for economic gain. In such a mystical corporation, knit together by mutual obligations, no man may press his advantage to the full, for no man may seek to live " outside the body of the Church."

Sabotaged by the unpaid magistracy of country gentlemen, who had been the obstructive agents of local administration, the practical application of such doctrines had always been intermittent, and, when the Long Parliament struck the weapon of administrative law from the hands of the Crown, it had ceased altogether. But the politics of Westminster were not those of village and bor-ough. The events which seemed to aristocratic Parliamentarians to close the revolution seemed to the left wing of the victorious army only to begin it. In that earliest and most turbulent of English democracies, where buff-coat taught scripture politics to his general, the talk was not merely of political, but of social, reconstruction. The program of the Levellers, who more than any other party could claim to express the aspirations of the unprivileged classes, included a demand, not only for annual or biennial Parliaments, manhood suffrage, a redistribution of seats in proportion to population, and the abolition of the veto of the House of Lords, but also that " you would have laid open all enclosures of fens and other commons, or have them enclosed only or chiefly for the benefit of the poor." Theoretical communism, repudiated by the leading Levellers, found its expression in the agitation of the Diggers, on whose behalf Winstanley argued that, " seeing the common people of England, by joynt consent of person and purse, have caste out Charles, our Norman oppressour . . . the land now is to returne into the joynt hands of those who have conquered, that is the commonours," and that the victory over the King was incomplete, as long as " wee . . . remayne slaves still to the kingly power in the hands of lords of manors."

Nor was it only from the visionary and the zealot that the pressure for redress proceeded. When the shattering of traditional authority seemed for a moment to make all things new, local grievances, buried beneath centuries of dull oppression, started to life, and in several Midland counties the peasants rose to pull down the hated hedges. At Leicester, where in 1649 there were rumors of a popular movement to throw down the enclosures of the neighboring forest, the City Council took the matter up. A petition was drafted, setting out the economic and social evils attending enclosure, and proposing the establishment of machinery to check it, consisting of a committee without whose assent enclosing was not to be permitted. A local minister was instructed to submit the petition to Parliament, " which hath still a watchful eye and open ear to redress the common grievances of the nation." The agent selected to present the city's case was the Rev. John Moore, a prolific pamphleteer, who for several years attacked the depopulating landlord with all the fervor of Latimer, though with even less than Latimer's success.

Half a century before, such commotions would have been followed by the passing of Depopulation Acts and the issue of a Royal Commission. But, in the ten years since the meeting of the Long Parliament, the whole attitude of public policy towards the movement had begun to change. Confiscations, compositions, and war taxation had effected a revolution in the distribution of property, similar, on a smaller scale, to that which had taken place at the Reformation. As land changed hands, customary relations were shaken and new interests were created. Enclosure, as Moore complained, was being pushed forward by means

of law suits ending in Chancery decrees. It was not to be expected that City merchants and members of the Committee for Compounding, some of whom had found land speculation a profitable business, should hear with enthusiasm a proposal to revive the old policy of arresting enclosures by State interference, at which the gentry had grumbled for more than a century.

In these circumstances, it is not surprising that reformers should have found the open ear of Parliament impenetrably closed to agrarian grievances. Nor was it only the political and economic environment which had changed. The revolution in thought was equally profound. The theoretical basis of the policy of protecting the peasant by preventing enclosure had been a conception of landownership which regarded its rights and its duties as inextricably interwoven. Property was not merely a source of income, but a public function, and its use was limited by social obligations and necessities of State. With such a doctrine the classes who had taken the lead in the struggle against the monarchy could make no truce. Its last vestiges finally disappeared when the Restoration Parliament swept away military tenures, and imposed on the nation, in the shape of an excise, the financial burden previously borne by themselves.

The theory which took its place, and which was to become in the eighteenth century almost a religion, was that expressed by Locke, when he described property as a right anterior to the existence of the State, and argued that "the supreme power cannot take from any man any part of his property without his own consent." But Locke merely poured into a philosophical mould ideas which had been hammered out in the stress of political struggles, and which were already the commonplace of landowner and merchant. The view of society held by that part of the Puritan movement which was socially and politically influential had been expressed by Ireton and Cromwell in their retort to the democrats in the army. It was that only the freeholders constituted the body politic, and that they could use their property as they pleased, uncontrolled by obligations to any superior, or by the need of consulting the mass of men, who were mere tenants at will, with no fixed interest or share in the land of the kingdom. Naturally, this change of ideas had profound reactions on agrarian policy. Formerly a course commending itself to all public-spirited persons, the prevention of enclosure was now discredited as the program of a sect of religious and political radicals. When Major-General Whalley in 1656 introduced a measure to regulate and restrict the enclosure of commons, framed, apparently, on the lines proposed by the authorities of Leicester, there was an instant outcry from members that it would "destroy property," and the bill was refused a second reading. After the Restoration the tide began to run more strongly in the same direction. Enclosure had already become the hobby of the country gentleman. Experts advocated it on economic grounds, and

legislation to facilitate it was introduced into Parliament. Though its technique still remained to be elaborated, the attitude which was to be decisive in the eighteenth century had already been crystallized.

The change of policy was striking. The reason of it was not merely that political conditions made the landed gentry omnipotent, and that the Royalist squirearchy, who streamed back to their plundered manors in 1660, were in no mood to countenance a revival, by the Government of Charles II, of the administrative interference with the rights of property which had infuriated them in the Government of Charles I. It was that opinion as to social policy had changed, and changed not least among men of religion themselves. The pursuit of economic self-interest, which is the law of nature, is already coming to be identified by the pious with the operation of the providential plan, which is law of God. Enclosures will increase the output of wool and grain. Each man knows best what his land is suited to produce, and the general interest will be best served by leaving him free to produce it. "It is an undeniable maxim that every one by the light of nature and reason will do that which makes for his greatest advantage. . . . The advancement of private persons will be the advantage of the public."

It is significant that such considerations were adduced, not by an economist, but by a minister. For the argument was ethical as well as economic, and, when Moore appealed to the precepts of traditional morality to bridle pecuniary interests, he provoked the retort that a judicious attention to pecuniary interests was an essential part of an enlightened morality. What the poor need for their spiritual health is — to use the favorite catchword of the age — "regulation," and regulation is possible only if they work under the eye of an employer. In the eyes of the austere moralists of the Restoration, the first, and most neglected, virtue of the poor is industry. Common rights encourage idleness by offering a precarious and demoralizing livelihood to men who ought to be at work for a master. It is not surprising, therefore, that the admonitions of religious teachers against the wickedness of joining house to house and field to field should almost entirely cease. Long the typical example of uncharitable covetousness, enclosure is now considered, not merely economically expedient, but morally beneficial. Baxter, with all his scrupulousness — partly, perhaps, because of his scrupulousness — differs from most earlier divines in giving a qualified approval to enclosure "done in moderation by a pious man," for the characteristic reason that a master can establish a moral discipline among his employees, which they would miss if they worked for themselves. What matters, in short, is not their circumstances, but their character. If they lose as peasants, they will gain as Christians. Opportunities for spiritual edification are more important than the mere material environment. If only the material environment were not itself among the forces determining men's capacity to be edified!

The temper which deplored that the open-field village was not a school of the severer virtues turned on pauperism and poor relief an even more shattering criticism. There is no province of social life in which the fashioning of a new scale of ethical values on the Puritan anvil is more clearly revealed. In the little communities of peasants and craftsmen which composed medieval England, all, when Heaven sent a bad harvest, had starved together, and the misery of the sick, the orphan and the aged had appeared as a personal calamity, not as a social problem. Apart from a few precocious theorists, who hinted at the need for a universal and secular system of provision for distress, the teaching most characteristic of medieval writers had been that the relief of the needy was a primary obligation on those who had means. St. Thomas, who in this matter is typical, quotes with approval the strong words of St. Ambrose about those who cling to the bread of the starving, insists on the idea that property is stewardship, and concludes — a conclusion not always drawn from that well-worn phrase — that to withhold alms when there is evident and urgent necessity is mortal sin. Popular feeling had lent a half-mystical glamour both to poverty and to the compassion by which poverty was relieved, for poor men were God's friends. At best, the poor were thought to represent our Lord in a peculiarly intimate way — "in that sect," as Langland said, "our Saviour saved all mankind " — and it was necessary for the author of a religious manual to explain that the rich, as such, were not necessarily hateful to God. At worst, men reflected that the prayers of the poor availed much, and that the sinner had been saved from hell by throwing a loaf of bread to a beggar, even though a curse went with it. The alms bestowed today would be repaid a thousandfold, when the soul took its dreadful journey amid rending briars and scorching flames.

If ever thou gavest hosen and shoon,
   Everie nighte and alle,
Sit thee down and put them on,
   And Christe receive thy saule.

If hosen and shoon thou gavest nane,
   Everie nighte and alle,
The whinnes shall prickle thee to the
   bare bane,
   And Christe receive thy saule.

If ever thou gavest meate or drinke,
   Everie nighte and alle,
The fire shall never make thee shrinke,
   And Christe receive thy saule.

If meate or drinke thou gavest nane,
   Everie nighte and alle,
The fire will burne thee to the bare
   bane,
   And Christe receive thy saule.

This ae nighte, this ae nighte,
   Everie nighte and alle,
Fire, and sleete, and candle-light,
   And Christe receive thy saule.

The social character of wealth, which had been the essence of the medieval doctrine, was asserted by English divines in the sixteenth century with redoubled emphasis, precisely because the growing individualism of the age menaced the traditional conception. " The poor man," preached Latimer, " hath title to the rich man's goods; so that the rich man ought to let the poor man have part of his riches to help and to comfort him withal." Nor had that sovereign indifference to the rigors of the economic calculus disappeared, when, under the influence partly of humanitarian representatives of the Renaissance like Vives, partly of religious reformers, partly of their own ambition to gather all the threads of social administration into their own hands, the statesmen of the sixteenth century set themselves to organize a secular system of poor relief. In England, after three generations in which the attempt was made to stamp out vagrancy by police measures of hideous brutality, the momentous admission was made that its cause was economic distress, not merely personal idleness, and that the whip had no terrors for the man who must either tramp or starve. The result was the celebrated Acts imposing a compulsory poor-rate and requiring the able-bodied man to be set on work. The Privy Council, alert to prevent disorder, drove lethargic justices hard, and down to the Civil War the system was administered with fair regularity. But the Elizabethan Poor Law was never designed to be what, with disastrous results, it became in the eighteenth and early nineteenth centuries, the sole measure for coping with economic distress. While it provided relief, it was but the last link in a chain of measures — the prevention of evictions, the control of food supplies and prices, the attempt to stabilize employment and to check unnecessary dismissals of workmen — intended to mitigate the forces which made relief necessary. Apart from the Poor Law, the first forty years of the seventeenth century were prolific in the private charity which founded alms-houses and hospitals, and established funds to provide employment or to aid struggling tradesmen. The appeal was still to religion, which owed to poverty a kind of reverence.

It was Thy choice, whilst Thou on earth didst stay,
And hadst not whereupon Thy head to lay.

" What, speak you of such things? " said Nicholas Ferrar on his death-bed to one who commended his charities. " It would have been but a suitable return for me to have given all I had, and not to have scattered a few crumbs of alms here and there."

It was inevitable that, in the anarchy of the Civil War, both private charity and public relief should fall on evil days. In London, charitable endowments seem to have suffered from more than ordinary malversation, and there were complaints that the income both of Bridewell and of the Hospitals was seriously reduced. In the country, the records of Quarter Sessions paint a picture of confusion, in which the machinery of presentment by constables to justice has broken down, and a long wail arises, that thieves are multiplied, the poor are neglected, and vagrants wander to and fro at their will. The

administrative collapse of the Elizabethan Poor Law continued after the Restoration, and twenty-three years later Sir Matthew Hale complained that the sections in it relating to the provision of employment were a dead letter. Always unpopular with the local authorities, whom they involved in considerable trouble and expense, it is not surprising that, with the cessation of pressure by the Central Government, they should, except here and there, have been neglected. What is more significant, however, than the practical deficiencies in the administration of relief, was the rise of a new school of opinion, which regarded with repugnance the whole body of social theory of which both private charity and public relief had been the expression.

" The generall rule of all England," wrote a pamphleteer in 1646, " is to whip and punish the wandring beggars . . . and so many justices execute one branch of that good Statute (which is the point of justice), but as for the point of charitie, they leave [it] undone, which is to provide houses and convenient places to set the poore to work." The House of Commons appears to have been conscious that the complaint had some foundation; in 1649 it ordered that the county justices should be required to see that stocks of material were provided as the law required, and the question of preparing new legislation to ensure that persons in distress should be found employment was on several occasions referred to committees of the House. Nothing seems, however, to have come of these proposals, nor was the Elizabethan policy of "setting the poor on work" that which was most congenial to the temper of the time. Upon the admission that distress was the result, not of personal deficiencies, but of economic causes, with its corollary that its victims had a legal right to be maintained by society, the growing individualism of the age turned the same frigid scepticism as was later directed against the Speenhamland policy by the reformers of 1834. Like the friends of Job, it saw in misfortune, not the chastisement of love, but the punishment for sin. The result was that, while the penalties on the vagrant were redoubled, religious opinion laid less emphasis on the obligation of charity than upon the duty of work, and that the admonitions which had formerly been turned upon uncharitable covetousness were now directed against improvidence and idleness. The characteristic sentiment was that of Milton's friend, Hartlib: "The law of God saith, ' he that will not work, let him not eat.' This would be a sore scourge and smart whip for idle persons if . . . none should be suffered to eat till they had wrought for it."

The new attitude found expression in the rare bursts of public activity provoked by the growth of pauperism between 1640 and 1660. The idea of dealing with it on sound business principles, by means of a corporation which would combine profit with philanthropy, was being sedulously preached by a small group of reformers. Parliament took it up, and in 1649 passed an Act for the relief and employment of the poor and the punishment of beggars, under which a company was to be established with power to apprehend vagrants, to offer them the choice between work and whipping, and to set to compulsory labor all other poor persons, including children without means of maintenance. Eight years later the prevalence of vagrancy produced an Act of such extreme severity as almost to recall the suggestion made a generation later by Fletcher of Saltoun, that vagrants should be sent to the galleys. It provided that, since offenders could rarely be taken in the act, any vagrant who failed to satisfy the justices that he had a good reason for being on the roads should be arrested and punished as a sturdy beggar, whether actually begging or not.

The protest against indiscriminate almsgiving, as the parade of a spurious religion, which sacrificed character to a formal piety, was older than the Reformation, but it had been given a new emphasis by the reformers. Luther had denounced the demands of beggars as blackmail, and the Swiss reformers had stamped out the remnants of monastic charity, as a bribe ministered by Popery to dissoluteness and demoralization. "I conclude that all the large givings of the papists," preached an English divine in the reign of Elizabeth, "of which at this day many make so great brags, because they be not done in a reverent regard of the commandment of the Lord, in love, and of an inward being touched with the calamities of the needy, but for to be well reported of before men whilst they are alive, and to be prayed for after they are dead . . . are indeed no alms, but pharisaical trumpets." The rise of a commercial civilization, the reaction against the authoritarian social policy of the Tudors, and the progress of Puritanism among the middle classes, all combined in the next half-century to sharpen the edge of that doctrine. Nurtured in a tradition which made the discipline of character by industry and self-denial the center of its ethical scheme, the Puritan moralist was undisturbed by any doubts as to whether even the seed of the righteous might not sometimes be constrained to beg its bread, and met the taunt that the reputation of good words was the cloak for a conscienceless egoism with the retort that the easy-going open-handedness of the sentimentalist was not less selfish in its motives and was more corrupting to its objects. "As for idle beggars," wrote Steele, "happy for them if fewer people spent their foolish pity upon their bodies, and if more shrewd some wise compassion upon their souls." That the greatest of evils is idleness, that the poor are the victims, not of circumstances, but of their own " idle, irregular and wicked courses," that the truest charity is not to enervate them by relief, but so to reform their characters that relief may be unnecessary — such doctrines turned severity from a sin into a duty, and froze the impulse of natural pity with the assurance that, if indulged, it would perpetuate the suffering which it sought to allay.

Few tricks of the unsophisticated intellect are more curious than the naïve psychology of the business man, who ascribes his achievements to his own unaided efforts, in bland unconsciousness of a social order without whose continuous support and vigilant protection he would be as a lamb bleating in the desert. That individualist complex owes part of its self-assurance to the suggestion of Puritan moralists, that practical success is at once the sign and the reward of ethical superiority. "No question," argued a Puritan pamphleteer, " but it [riches] should be the portion rather of the godly than of the wicked, were it good for them; for godliness hath the promises of this life as well as of the life to come." The demonstration that distress is a proof of demerit, though a singular commentary on the lives of Christian saints and sages, has always been popular with the prosperous. By the lusty plutocracy of the Restoration, roaring after its meat, and not indisposed, if it could not find it elsewhere, to seek it from God, it was welcomed with a shout of applause.

A society which reverences the attainment of riches as the supreme felicity will naturally be disposed to regard the poor as damned in the next world, if only to justify itself for making their life a hell in this. Advanced by men of religion as a tonic for the soul, the doctrine of the danger of pampering poverty was hailed by the rising school of Political Arithmeticians as a sovereign cure for the ills of society. For, if the theme of the moralist was that an easy-going indulgence undermined character, the theme of the economist was that it was economically disastrous and financially ruinous. The Poor Law is the mother of idleness, " men and women growing so idle and proud that they will not work, but lie upon the parish wherein they dwell for maintenance." It discourages thrift; " if shame or fear of punishment makes him earn his dayly bread, he will do no more; his children are the charge of the parish and his old age his recess from labour or care." It keeps up wages, since " it encourages wilful and evil-disposed persons to impose what wages they please upon their labours; and herein they are so refractory to reason and the benefit of the nation that, when corn and provisions are cheap, they will not work for less wages than when they were dear." To the landowner who cursed the poor-rates, and the clothier who grumbled at the high cost of labor, one school of religious thought now brought the comforting assurance that morality itself would be favored by a reduction of both.

As the history of the Poor Law in the nineteenth century was to prove, there is no touchstone, except the treatment of childhood, which reveals the true character of a social philosophy more clearly than the spirit in which it regards the misfortunes of those of its members who fall by the way. Such utterances on the subject of poverty were merely one example of a general attitude, which appeared at times to consign to collective perdition almost the whole of the wage-earning population. It was partly that, in an age which worshiped property as the foundation of the social order, the

mere laborer seemed something less than a full citizen. It was partly the result of the greatly increased influence on thought and public affairs acquired at the Restoration by the commercial classes, whose temper was a ruthless materialism, determined at all costs to conquer world-markets from France and Holland, and prepared to sacrifice every other consideration to their economic ambitions. It was partly that, in spite of a century of large-scale production in textiles, the problems of capitalist industry and of a propertyless proletariat were still too novel for their essential features to be appreciated. Even those writers, like Baxter and Bunyan, who continued to insist on the wickedness of extortionate prices and unconscionable interest, rarely thought of applying their principles to the subject of wages. Their social theory had been designed for an age of petty agriculture and industry, in which personal relations had not yet been superseded by the cash nexus, and the craftsman or peasant farmer was but little removed in economic status from the half-dozen journeymen or laborers whom he employed. In a world increasingly dominated by great clothiers, iron-masters and mine-owners, they still adhered to the antiquated categories of master and servant, with the same obstinate indifference to economic realities as leads the twentieth century to talk of employers and employed, long after the individual employer has been converted into an impersonal corporation.

In a famous passage of the *Communist Manifesto,* Marx observes that

" the *bourgeoisie,* wherever it got the upper hand, put an end to all feudal, patriarchal, idyllic relations, pitilessly tore asunder the motley feudal ties that bound man to his ' natural superiors,' and left remaining no other bond between man and man than naked self-interest and callous cash payment." An interesting illustration of his thesis might be found in the discussions of the economics of employment by English writers of the period between 1660 and 1760. Their characteristic was an attitude towards the new industrial proletariat noticeably harsher than that general in the first half of the seventeenth century, and which has no modern parallel except in the behavior of the less reputable of white colonists towards colored labor. The denunciations of the " luxury, pride, and sloth " of the English wage-earners of the seventeenth and eighteenth centuries are, indeed, almost exactly identical with those directed against African natives today. It is complained that, compared with the Dutch, they are self-indulgent and idle; that they want no more than a bare subsistence, and will cease work the moment they obtain it; that, the higher their wages, the more — " so licentious are they " — they spend upon drink; that high prices, therefore, are not a misfortune, but a blessing, since they compel the wage-earner to be more industrious; and that high wages are not a blessing, but a misfortune, since they merely conduce to " weekly debauches."

When such doctrines were general, it was natural that the rigors of economic exploitation should be preached as a public duty, and, with a few exceptions, the writers of the period differed only as to the methods by which severity could most advantageously be organized. Pollexfen and Walter Harris thought that salvation might be found by reducing the number of days kept as holidays. Bishop Berkeley, with the conditions of Ireland before his eyes, suggested that " sturdy beggars should . . . be seized and made slaves to the public for a certain term of years." Thomas Alcock, who was shocked at the workman's taste for snuff, tea and ribbons, proposed the revival of sumptuary legislation. The writers who advanced schemes for reformed workhouses, which should be places at once of punishment and of training, were innumerable. All were agreed that, on moral no less than on economic grounds, it was vital that wages should be reduced. The doctrine afterwards expressed by Arthur Young, when he wrote, " every one but an idiot knows that the lower classes must be kept poor, or they will never be industrious," was the tritest commonplace of Restoration economists. It was not argued; it was accepted as self-evident.

When philanthropists were inquiring whether it might not be desirable to reestablish slavery, it was not to be expected that the sufferings of the destitute would wring their hearts with social compunction. The most curious feature in the whole discussion, and that which is most sharply in contrast with the long debate on pauperism carried on in the sixteenth century, was the resolute refusal to admit that society had any responsibility for the causes of distress. Tudor divines and statesmen had little mercy for idle rogues. But the former always, and the latter ultimately, regarded pauperism primarily as a social phenomenon produced by economic dislocation, and the embarrassing question put by the genial Harrison — "at whose handes shall the bloude of these men be required?" — was never far from the minds even of the most cynical. Their successors after the Restoration were apparently quite unconscious that it was even conceivable that there might be any other cause of poverty than the moral failings of the poor. The practical conclusion to be drawn from so comfortable a creed was at once extremely simple and extremely agreeable. It was not to find employment under the Act of 1601, for to do that was only "to render the poor more bold." It was to surround the right to relief with obstacles such as those contained in the Act of 1662, to give it, when it could not be avoided, in a workhouse or house of correction, and, for the rest, to increase the demand for labor by reducing wages.

The grand discovery of a commercial age, that relief might be so administered as not merely to relieve, but also to deter, still remained to be made by Utilitarian philosophers. But the theory that distress was due, not to economic circumstances, but to what the Poor Law Commissioners of 1834 called "individual improvidence and vice," was firmly established, and the criticism on the Elizabethan system which was to inspire the new Poor Law had already been formulated. The essence of that system was admirably expressed a century later by a Scottish divine as "the principle that each man, simply because he exists, hold a right on other men or on society for existence." Dr. Chalmers' attack upon it was the echo of a note long struck by Puritan moralists. And the views of Dr. Chalmers had impressed themselves on Nassau Senior, before he set his hand to that brilliant, influential and wildly unhistorical Report, which, after provoking something like a rebellion in the north of England, was to be one of the pillars of the social policy of the nineteenth century.

It would be misleading to dwell on the limitations of Puritan ethics without emphasizing the enormous contribution of Puritanism to political freedom and social progress. The foundation of democracy is the sense of spiritual independence which nerves the individual to stand alone against the powers of this world, and in England, where squire and parson, lifting arrogant eyebrows at the insolence of the lower orders, combined to crush popular agitation, as a menace at once to society and to the Church, it is probable that democracy owes more to Nonconformity than to any other single movement. The virtues of enterprise, diligence and thrift are the indispensable foundation of any complex and vigorous civilization. It was Puritanism which, by investing them with a supernatural sanction, turned them from an unsocial eccentricity into a habit and a religion. Nor would it be difficult to find notable representatives of the Puritan spirit in whom the personal authority, which was the noblest aspect of the new ideal, was combined with a profound consciousness of social solidarity, which was the noblest aspect of that which it displaced. Firmin the Philanthropist, and Bellers the Quaker, whom Owen more than a century later hailed as the father of his doctrines, were pioneers of Poor Law reform. The Society of Friends, in an age when the divorce between religion and social ethics was almost complete, met the prevalent doctrine, that it was permissible to take such gain as the market offered, by insisting on the obligation of good conscience and forbearance in economic transactions, and on the duty to make the honorable maintenance of the brother in distress a common charge.

The general climate and character of a country are not altered, however, by the fact that here and there it has peaks which rise into an ampler air. The distinctive note of Puritan teaching was different. It was individual responsibility, not social obligation. Training its pupils to the mastery of others through the mastery of self, it prized as a crown of glory the qualities which arm the spiritual athlete for his solitary contest with a hostile world, and dismissed concern with the social order as the prop of weaklings and the Capua of the soul. Both the excellences and the defects of that attitude were momentous for the future. It is sometimes suggested that the astonishing outburst of industrial activity which took place after 1760 created a new type of economic character, as well as a new system of economic organization. In reality, the ideal which was later to carry all before it, in the person of the inventor and engineer and captain of industry, was well established among Englishmen before the end of the seventeenth century. Among the numerous forces which had gone to form it, some not inconsiderable part may reasonably be ascribed to the emphasis on the life of business enterprise as the appropriate field for Christian endeavor, and on the qualities needed for success in it, which was characteristic of Puritanism. These qualities, and the admiration of them, remained, when the religious reference, and the restraints which it imposed, had weakened or disappeared.

THE SPREAD OF INDUSTRIALIZATION TO THE UNITED STATES

6

35. Industrialization: the American Experience

Industrialization cannot take place until the strictures of the old and traditional society are broken down and a new group interested in advancing the techniques of industrial change rises in the social structure. In Western Europe the strictures of the traditional society were gradually dissipated as authority splintered and faltered and man came to believe that he could control and adapt the physical environment for his own ends. There was no single *denouement* but rather a succession of developments, such as the Renaissance and the Reformation, which had an accumulative effect in destroying man's belief in tradition.

With the relaxing of the grip of authority new groups rose to prominence. In England the bourgeoisie and the entrepreneurial class secured the franchise in the Reform Act of 1832 and thus broke the power of the landed interests. Across the Channel in France the transition was more violent — the Revolution of 1789 forcibly ejected the aristocracy from positions of responsibility and brought the middle classes to the fore.

The industrialization of the United States differed from the industrialization of Western Europe in several important respects. In the first place, no strongly established civilization existed in North America which could impede the growth of new social forms. The early settlers in the colonies had to combat the wilderness but they did not have to face the much more formidable foe of an established vested interest. The American Revolution was not directed against the internal structure of American society but against the subservient position of the colonies to England. In short, an industrial society could grow *de novo* without having to graft into its structure the remnants of an old social order.

This is not to imply that the transition in the United States from a rural to an industrial society was painless. One has only to recall that the Civil War was between the industrial North and the agricultural South to realize that the costs of transition were high. But the Civil War was qualitatively different from those eruptions in Europe that brought the middle classes to power. It was a sectional struggle between parallel political forces and consequently did not assume the proportions of an internal class struggle. The north did not rally its forces with the cry — Liberty, Equality, Fraternity. The cause was on the surface — the Union shall not be divided. The Civil War undoubtedly stimulated the rate of industrial development in the United States, but it was not essential to the structuring of society that made industrial development possible in the first instance.

In the second place, the United States benefited from the lag between its development and the industrial development of Western Europe. The skills of the labor force were constantly replenished by the arrival of successive waves of immigrants who carried with them the training acquired in the older societies of Europe. It was therefore a sophisticated labor force, which could positively influence the shape of American industrial development.

As important as the skill of the workers was their mobility. Having broken their ties with an old society, they had to become mobile to find roots in the new society. But the new society itself was so fluid in organization that mobility per se became an important value. Many people could find roots only by moving with the expanding tide of American civilization. Thus, the American people acquired a degree of mobility

and hence flexibility unknown in Europe.

Just as the more mature economies of Europe were able to supply America with a labor force, so they were able to transfer nonlabor resources, or capital, to the expanding industries of the young economy. Capital formation did not have to take place completely at the expense of consumption. The current cost of industrial development was minimized by borrowing from the European economies.

In the third place, the extensive geographical limits of the United States, relative to the available supplies of labor, placed compulsive pressures on entrepreneurs to adapt labor saving devices in industrial processes. In contrast, Europe faced the reverse situation — an abundance of labor relative to land. Consequently, in Europe it was economical to use labor intensively. The agricultural implement industry, for instance, flourished in the United States in advance of its counterpart in Europe, because the conditions of agricultural production required the use of heavier and more intricate capital equipment than in Europe.

Finally, the philosophy of individualism transplanted from Europe flowered as it never had before. In Europe individuals were held in bounds by well established and confined societies. It was difficult to hold an unequivocal faith in the ability of the individual to control his own destiny and in its corollary the necessity of a laissez-faire governmental policy when society crowded around and engulfed the individual.

For it was too obvious that the behavior of each individual profoundly affected the behavior of other individuals and that consequently what each individual did, his successes or failures, was partially dependent on the other members of society. In the United States a fluid society, restricted neither by geographical barriers nor hampering social conventions, flowed restlessly and steadily from the Atlantic to the Pacific. Here it was not obvious that society molded man. Rather the converse seemed to hold — that individuals molded society. Man's worth, then, might be justifiably measured by the imprint he made on society.

American individualism was a caricature of the nineteenth century European belief in rationality and progress. The belief that man could progress to higher levels of civilization by the rational application of his abilities to social problems degenerated into a belief that man was responsible only to himself and that success depended upon what one could get away with.

Unfettered and rugged though it was, American individualism had a lasting influence on the growth of the industrial economy. It stimulated and goaded men to make their mark in society. An entrepreneurial class adapted into the economy the techniques that increased productivity and income. The rail network expanded, heavy industry developed, and manufacturers produced for mass markets. The rewards for engineering this industrial growth were high. Not only did the entrepreneur receive large income but he acquired the prestige of the highest status in the American class structure. In the absence of an old and traditional aristocracy, the entrepreneur became the native aristocrat.

Like the British economy the American economy was organized around a capitalistic price system, which was eminently suited to the peculiar conditions of American society. The population, which was mobile to begin with, could be coherently directed by the movement of relative prices in labor markets. Profits guided the allocation of capital investment, and the capital markets provided a link between willing savers and those responsible for investment. The price system was flexible and uncontrolled. Like Topsy it just grew, and in its growth it reflected the flexible and uncontrolled state of American society.

Since industrial growth in the United States has been so intimately associated with capitalism, the selections in this chapter are concerned with the nature of capitalism. The first selection is from *The Robber Barons* by Matthew Josephson. It describes the business ethics which prevailed in the United States during the last half of the nineteenth century. Its purpose is to portray the spirit of restless striving that dominated the business community and to suggest the aristocratic aura acquired by the men of big business. The capitalism of mid-twentieth America is no longer unfettered and dominated by the type of capitalist described by Matthew Josephson. The repeated financial panics during the nineteenth century and early twentieth century and the prolonged depression of the 1930's compelled government to assume a greater responsibility for the economic state of the Union. The Antitrust laws at the beginning of the present century have been more than matched by the social and economic reforms of the New Deal and Fair Deal. Capitalism, consequently, has changed as has the nature of business leadership. The second selection, from *USA — the Permanent Revolution* by the editors of Fortune Magazine, describes this transformation of business leaders from robber barons to responsible industrial statesmen.

36. Industrialization and the American Character*

The cannonading that began at Charleston with the dawn of April 12, 1861, sounded the tocsin for the men of the new American union. The fatal clash of the two economic nations within the republic could no longer be escaped; the "irrepressible conflict" was at hand. When the trivial siege of Sumter was over, the North rallied from its stupor, its breathless waiting. A people who had barely known themselves a nation were unified at last by danger. The North, with a passion no less bitter than the South's, moved to crush the rebel who had ruled the national policy for generations, and stubbornly barred the way of industrial growth as if he would halt inevitability itself.

In legions, the recruits, the young men of '61, marched away to Bull Run for the three months' war. On both sides they were the soldiers of a people without tradition or gift for military heroics; a people which had come out to attend three earlier wars

only in small numbers, with remarkable apathy. The frontier democracy had known as little of the rule of the military captain as of the feudal noble or the prince of the Church. Its sons were no soldiers, yet possessed deathless courage, it had few battle leaders; most of these must rise up from disaster. Therefore the conflict would be long, the most stubborn, the most sanguinary in all the history of the West, and colossal in its scale of operations.

If the South did not truly estimate its powers for such a contest, neither did the North know its strength, its wealth, its destiny. Not many in either camp could have pictured the incredible transformations which would accompany those thundering years. And fewer still knew or sensed what the Civil War was really fought for.

The epoch of martial glory and martial stupidity need concern us but little here. We observe only that its grand blood-letting fixes a turning point at which the trend of our history declares itself: the opening of the Second American Revolution, that "industrial revolution" which

* From *The Robber Barons*, copyright 1934, by Matthew Josephson. Reprinted by permission of Harcourt, Brace and Company, Inc., pp. 3–31.

worked upon society with far greater effect than the melodramatic battles. After Appomattox, in 1865, it is widely and conveniently assumed, the Old Order was ended.

"Had they been Tyrian traders of the year 1000 B.C., landing from a galley fresh from Gibraltar," writes Henry Adams concerning his family's return from diplomatic duties abroad, "they could hardly have been stranger on the shore of a world so changed from what it had been ten years before." All this is true figuratively. But literally the symptoms of the future order of things, all the new shapes and forces existed vigorously in the days of Jefferson, side by side with the institutions and conditions of pre-capitalist or feudal eras. The process of change, the departure from the old ways toward large-scale industry, toward giant capitalism, toward a centralized, national economy, was long in preparing, gradual, and not too perceptible. When the abyss of the Civil War suddenly yawned before men's eyes it but registered a "lag" which had existed already during the whole of the preceding generation. Where England had officially recognized its economic transition peacefully by the repeal of the Corn Laws, America, through blood and iron, consecrated its own industrial revolution by the end of what had been comparatively free trade. . . .

All this we see in retrospect. But besides the young men who marched to Bull Run, there were other young men of '61 whose instinctive sense of history proved to be unerring. Loving not the paths of glory they slunk away quickly, bent upon business of their own. They were warlike enough and pitiless yet never risked their skin: they fought without military rules or codes of honor or any tactics or weapons familiar to men: they were the strange, new mercenary soldiers of economic life. The plunder and trophies of victory would go neither to the soldier nor the statesman, but to these other young men of '61, who soon figured as "massive interests moving obscurely in the background" of wars. Hence these, rather than the military captains or tribunes, are the subject of this history.

Shortly before or very shortly after 1840 were born nearly all the galaxy of uncommon men who were to be the overlords of the future society. They were born at a historical moment when by an easy effort one could as well look back at the mellow past as scan the eventful future. Their parents could remember the disturbed but very simple and light-hearted times of Mr. Jefferson, when pigs wandered unmolested at the steps of the Capitol; and it was only a comparatively few years since Mr. Jackson had "driven the money-changers from the temple."

It was not true of course that the early Republic was a millennium of free farmers and artisans; yet in the simplicity of its organization and of its mercantile economy, the nation belonged almost to a pre-capitalist age. Over great regions of the country men still worked for a "livelihood" rather than for "money." This man of the mercantile age, certainly contrasted with his successors, a few generations later, "did not stand on his head or run on all fours," but was a "natural man" and in himself was "the meteyard of all things." The handicrafts were widespread; little shops and factories were interspersed among the farms of New England. And it was still true, in many parts of the earlier America, that the artisan, as in olden times, loved his work and feared more that it might not be worthy of him than that he might not put a high enough price upon it. It was also true that goods circulated at a slow rate. The ingenious Yankee and his wife wove their cloth, turned their own furniture, molded their own pottery, in a manner now considered quaint but then truly economical. As their traffic in goods and moneys, while limited to narrow regions, was carried on at the pace of the horse-drawn post, the ox-cart, the river or canal vessel, so their opportunities were narrowed, while differences in station were correspondingly moderate. Thus although there were instances enough of large inequalities of wealth and power, there was more individual equality than in other countries. And of the possessors of great fortunes we note that their wealth was based on ownership of land. This was true of New York as of Virginia. In New England and elsewhere along the coast, the shipping trade was the medium of great fortune; but in this commerce too the pace of trade was long-breathed, temperate, at first.

In such spacious and leisurely days the art of politics and the art of rhet-oric tended to flourish. Many documents testify to the charm of ideas and talk in the circle of Jefferson, Madison, Gallatin and Marshall, who held forth almost daily in the incompleted presidential "palace" of the village of Washington. These statesmen were latter-day Romans; in their own eyes, at least, their role was high. With an acrid passion, they, and behind them the mass in town dwellings and log cabins, the lowliest immigrants from Scotland and Germany, upheld the notions of a free republic upon which Napoleonic Europe and even English opinion habitually heaped its contempt. Proud of having cast off the incubus of feudal and aristocratic institutions, each toiler with "every stroke of the ax and the hoe" knew himself a gentleman and his children gentlemen. Where monarchies clerical and temporal and theatrical military adventurers sucked the nourishment of Europe, here was a land where government was simply to be a judicature and a police. In the mind of the tall, negligently dressed but eloquent statesman from Virginia, little more was necessary to make the happiness and prosperity of the people than *a wise and frugal government which shall restrain men from injuring one another, which shall leave them otherwise free to regulate their own pursuits of industry and improvement, and shall not take from the mouth of labor the bread it has earned. This is the sum of good government, and this is necessary to close the circle of our felicities.*

Thus, under the lax political institutions, society would be wholly directed by *interests,* rather than by outworn traditions, or by the appetites of autocrats. Under favoring circumstances the Americans threw themselves into their tasks with a revolutionary zeal. And though Jefferson had hoped that only the *" agricultural capacities of our country "* would be furthered, rather than industry which would lead to the " mimicry of an Amsterdam, a Hamburg, a city of London," it was soon evident that the outcome was to be a different and unattended one. It was the qualities of trade and industry, in most predatory form, and not the " agricultural capacities " that flourished in the turbulent laissez-faire society of the frontier democracy. This was one of the first effects that struck the eye of visiting foreigners, such as Alexis de Tocqueville.

The Americans, and no less the newly arrived immigrants, were soon living in the future, filled with a large excitement over solid mountains of salt and iron, of lead, copper, silver and gold; over cornfields waving and rustling in the sun, over " limitless riches, un-imaginable stores of wealth and power " — none of which the cultured satirists who frequently journeyed here could see. But the poor who came here saw those mountains of gold. These wandering Yankee traders, these " projectors," these pioneers and immigrants remembered only how hungry and naked their forbears had been through the centuries, and were ravished by the future. To their minds, every new method which led

by a shorter road to wealth, every machine which spared labor, diminished the cost of production, facilitated or augmented pleasure, seemed the grandest effort of the human intellect. Hence the two strains in the national character: political freedom and idealism, abetting a " sordid and practical " materialism, which asked nothing of ideas, of the arts, and of science, but their application toward ends of use and profit.

When we search for the springs of the national character we can never long forget that the original settlers were English Protestants. In the worshipers of the Reformed Church the individual conscience had been liberated from Catholic and Anglican formula and tradition; was freer to adjust itself flexibly to new hazards and opportunities. Among the New Englanders, for a time, and among the widely scattered Scotch-Irish, Calvinism was dominant and its influence was widespread in nearly all the colonies. And though it was not true that Calvin had introduced usury, as so many suppose, he had recognized its existence more candidly than the Catholic Church; and, as shown by R. H. Tawney, in his *Religion and the Rise of Capitalism,* Calvin liberated the economic energies of the rising bourgeoisie of Europe by his teachings. By the Calvinist scale of moral values, the true Christian " must conduct his business with a high seriousness as in itself a kind of religion." By his sober ideal of social conduct the members of the merchant and artisan class, the roturiers, found their " soul "; saw all careers " open to character " rather than to the well-born; became welded into a disciplined social force. Hence the combination of business address and discipline noted among the early New Englanders, as in similar milieux of the mother country whence they came. So many sayings of the time show how " among the Reformed, the greater their zeal, the greater was their inclination to trade and industry, as holding idleness unlawful." Others commemorate the amalgam of piety and ruse which made the best of both worlds: " *The tradesman meek and much a liar. . . .*" We feel in the Puritan type that the will is organized, disciplined, nerved to the utmost, as Tawney concludes; and if his personal life is sober, then it is also true that he enjoys freedom in the deepest sense; he ends by utterly opposing the authority even of church officers to police him; in the end his own individual conscience is his final authority.

For the people of the Reformed Church (as for the Jews) money was long ago the sole means to power. We find early economists in the time of Charles II saying of the nonconformists that " none are of more importance than they in the trading part of the people and those that live by industry, upon whose hands the business of the nation lies so much."

The first colonists, then, were brimming with the developed " middle-class virtues "; their strict sumptuary laws and domestic habits seemed to lead always to diligence, to cheerless self-restraint, and finally culminated in the parsimony and " holy economy " of the Quakers.

Among those who won notable triumphs by pursuing the Puritan economic virtues was no other than the free-thinking Benjamin Franklin who was the son of Puritans; and none more than he was the representative and container of the national character in the early period of the republic. He was Defoe's wise shopman, his " Compleat English Tradesman," for whom " trade was not a ball where people appear in masque and act a part to make sport . . . but 'tis a plain, visible scene of honest life . . . supported by prudence and frugality." It was not for nothing that Franklin, even more than Washington, was held up as model for succeeding generations; indeed he was a paragon for the entire bourgeois world, inasmuch as no man of his time was more widely read than he, millions of copies of his " Poor Richard " and his " Autobiography " circulating in scores of languages, in all continents, at the outset of the nineteenth century. In him, as a result of the long slow process of economic and religious liberation there had crystallized what we may call the " bourgeois spirit," as opposed to the feudal; he was the *homo economicus* of the new times. The usefulness of his virtue and thrift are all the more significant inasmuch as we now have the strongest reasons to believe they were public; for the rest he showed strong tendencies to relapse into little uninjurious vices in private, or when abroad in foreign lands. . . .

It was Franklin, philosopher of the new middle class, inventor of a stove and the lightning rod, who lamented that we lose so much time in sleep; who framed the immortal dictum: "Time is money"; whose whole life was one long worship of "holy economy." It was he who wrote:

. . . The way to wealth, if you desire it, is as plain as the way to market. It depends chiefly on two words, industry and frugality; that is waste neither time nor money, but make the best use of both. Without industry and frugality nothing will do, and with them everything. He that gets all he can honestly and saves all he gets will certainly become rich, if that Being who governs the world, to whom all should look for a blessing on their honest endeavors, doth not, in His wise providence, otherwise determine.

Franklin believed that given personal restraint and prudence in the conduct of his affairs, God would oversee the rest. This Yankee was avid of novelty and invention, free of prejudices, ingenious mechanically, skillful with his hands, quick of wit. And, finally, he was respectable, his respectability being designed, as he said candidly, to impress his clients.

"In order to secure my character and credit as a tradesman, I took care not only to be in reality industrious and frugal, but to avoid the appearance to the contrary. I dressed plain, and was seen at no places of idle diversion; I never went out a-fishing or shooting."

This respectability, this honesty toward customers, this conservatism, in good quality, small volume, high prices, was also a strong trait of the earlier capitalism which was already departing toward 1840. The keeping of clients, the avoidance of encroachment upon others' trade, was part of the atmosphere of those unhurried times which referred back to a world already passing, in which man and his life were "the measure of all things" and, to a greater extent than ever afterward, of his business.

Franklin, the historic Yankee, the legendary Self-made Man, owed his success as a printer as much to this strict attention to new machinery studied in London as to his good and prudent business management; just as in journalism he owed his success to enterprise in the current of new ideas. Typical of the old order of early capitalism, he was in his own person a man of enterprise, a skilled artisan of nimble and strong hands; he was also a "small master" who, having made his "primary accumulations," held command over a little troop of apprentices and craftsmen whose associated toil represented the "division of labor" which was the momentous contribution of his century.

As in the case of Franklin, so in the other early Self-made Men of the young Republic we may study the naked process of change from the early stages of industrialism to the more advanced. We see Samuel Slater removing from England to the United States at the close of the eighteenth century, carrying in his brain the memory of Richard Arkwright's machinery designs. Bounties had been offered for power-carding machinery by our government and the ingenious British craftsman by his skill and of course his want of scruples about the pirating and exporting of patents — then forbidden by English law — sets up at Pawtucket the first successful cotton-spinning mill. He is aided, to be sure, by local capital in the person of the pious Moses Brown of Providence who had written to him in 1790:

"If thou canst do this thing, I invite thee to come to Rhode Island, and have the credit of introducing cotton-manufacture into America."

So with his own hands the Derbyshire master craftsman had set up numerous mills, employing numerous companies of workmen (whose labor as far as possible in those days was carefully divided into simple, routine motions), and had become by his technical talent a man of great wealth. Together with Moses and Obadiah Brown, the philanthropic Quakers, he had finally become a commander of armies of workmen whose mechanized and accelerated labor produced mountains of cotton and woolen cloth. But note how, while diligent and aggressive, these early masters of capital are godly men as well, giving their tithe to the Lord. Slater established in one of his mills in 1796 a Sunday-school for the improvement of his work people, "the first, or among the first, in the United States"; while Obadiah Brown, dying childless, left the stupendous sum of $100,000 to Quaker charities.

Thus at a time when most of the great fortunes were yet derived from the ownership of large landholdings, as in the Virginia of Washington or even along the Hudson River Valley, where the descendants of the Dutch patroons lived in feudal state, the first successes in manufacture and in use of natural resources revealed the significant symptoms of the new order of society.

The history of John Jacob Astor, legend of the poor boy risen to riches, was immortalized by Washington Irving in his romance of "Astoria" and was in everyone's eye. With empty hands the German butcher's son had arrived in New York in 1783 and apprenticed himself to a furrier; then with alternate boldness and parsimony made his first important accumulations. He himself had gone up the Mohawk Valley to trade with the Indians; then he had lived in frugal style over his own shop at Broadway and Vesey Street for two decades, he and his wife laboring over the stinking furs and skins, close-fisted, weighing every penny, secretive of his plans as of his possessions, until with his great means he was enabled to expand his trading to the wildest outposts of the frontier. The American Fur Company of Astor ranged in its quest of furs from Missouri to Oregon and farthest Canada. It was not only said that its canny agents were vendors of liquor demoralizing the Indians who brought skins, but according to Congressional reports of 1821–22, even debased the liquors they sold to the aborigines!

Out of the trading posts of drunkenness and misery came much of the great accumulations of an Astor. Then his wealth had been translated into city land, into bonds, into banks, above all, land — so that his heir, William B. Astor, after 1848, was called " the landlord of New York." Thenceforth tens of thousands of city dwellers collectively paid tribute to the grandees of the Astor family, which was likened to that of the Rothschilds of Europe.

There were other famous nouveaux riches. Had not Alexander Stewart, arrived in 1823 from Belfast, and dealer in Irish laces and linens, become within several years the lord of a great marble emporium which towered above Broadway and dispensed dry goods of every sort to the multitude? Soon two thousand persons labored in association for the modern merchant prince whose income was above a million a year!

And finally when had the world ever seen the like of " Commodore " Cornelius Vanderbilt, most astonishing of all the famous parvenus of the 1840's and 1850's? The hulking, Silenus-like figure of an old man, in his eternal fur coat and " plug hat," winter and summer, with the handsome, bald head, and the profane language of a sea-dog, was known and liked by all New York. Remembered as a Staten Island ferry-boy, untutored, unable to spell correctly, he was the pure type of the modern captain of industry flourishing along the frontier of a new world. He was born of poor Dutch peasants in 1794, when a landed baron and a soldier commanded the republic, and his career spanned the flight of time into a new epoch. At his death, the steamship, the railroad, the magnetic telegraph, the iron and steel industry had worked their changes upon so-ciety; changes which even if he did not comprehend them, he had the good fortune to turn to his use eventually, so that he would prosper to a grand old age, to a time that the Jeffersons and Gallatins of his youth could never have dreamed, with his hands always at the levers of the new power. But if Vanderbilt had much of Franklin's parsimony, he had something of John Hawkins's ferocity too. Engaged in the shipping trade of New York harbor from boyhood, Cornelius Vanderbilt had known no other school than that of the dock and the forecastle. His herculean strength, his dexterity, his mixture of fierce courage and shiftiness had gradually brought him to the fore as a master of river and coastwise sailing vessels. His early years were filled with long savage struggle against the dominant Eastern shipping interests, the Fulton-Livingston group, whom he would underbid perpetually in the competition for freight. And since they often had the law on their side in the dispute, Vanderbilt was driven to many wiles at times to avoid process-servers; at others to sudden violent aggressions, worthy of an old-time corsair, whereby his enemies and their minions were overwhelmed.

Possessed of a sharp wharf-rat's tongue and a rough wit, according to his early biographers, he took joy in combat. " His foible was opposition," we are told. " Wherever his keen eye detected a line that was making a large profit . . . he swooped down and drove it to the wall, by offering a better service and lower rates " — for a time. Then with the opposition driven out, he would raise his rates without pity, to the lasting misery of his clients.

The career of Vanderbilt shows little of that triumphant enterprise of " vision " for which he has been applauded so long. As a master of sailing vessels, he despised the newly arrived paddle-wheelers of 1807, holding that they were merely good enough for Sunday picnics. When they proved their value for passenger service, he was among those who insisted that the new steamboats could never be used for freight " because the machinery would take up too much room." But when the hazardous experimental period had been survived by the steamship, then he judged the time ripe for intrusion; he had the best steamboats built for his lines and became a dominant factor in the ocean and coastwise trade. In waiting for the steamboat to be perfected, he showed the shrewd capacity of the great entrepreneur whose undertakings are always larger, but tardier, safer and more profitable than those of the early inventor or pioneer.

The " heroic period " of Vanderbilt was undoubtedly the time of the California gold rush, when he moved heaven and earth to throw a competing line — against the Collins line — by ship and stagecoach across Nicaragua. Here he overcame unheard-of dangers of tide, of native revolutions and filibusters, of tropical heat and plague. In person he drove his men to the breaking point, setting the example for fourteen to sixteen hours a day of sleepless vigilance and labor. In an emergency he once took the helm of the side-wheel steamboat which must be sent up the San Juan River rapids to Lake Nicaragua, firing up the boiler to the utmost. His biographer, Croffut, relates:

" Sometimes he got over the rapids by putting on all steam; sometimes . . . he extended a heavy cable to great trees up stream and warped the boat over. . . . The engineers reported that he " tied down the safety-valve and ' jumped' the obstructions, to the great terror of the whole party."

But out of the traffic to California he drew the bulk of his sudden fortune, in the ripeness of age. In the 1850's when American shipping was supreme, he had over a hundred vessels afloat, and earned $100,000 each month. At the time of the " shipping subsidy " scandals, aired in the Senate in 1858, it was seen that Vanderbilt and E. K. Collins of the Pacific Mail Steamship Line were the chief plunderers, sometimes conciliating, sometimes blackmailing each other. To keep Vanderbilt silent and inactive, while he drew a government mail subsidy of $900,000 a year, and quadrupled steerage rates, Collins paid Vanderbilt the large sum of $56,000 a month. Thus the vigorous old privateer was enabled to boast in 1853 of a fortune of $11,000,000 which he kept invested at 25 per cent.

But though fabulously rich and engaged in numerous complex undertakings the Commodore carried all his bookkeeping accounts in his own head and trusted no one with them. His own son, William H.

Vanderbilt, declared that he knew nothing of his father's methods. He clung to his wealth. The carpet in his small home on Washington Place was long threadbare; his long-suffering wife, who had lived in terrible frugality with him, was for a long time denied anything resembling luxury. The nine children she had borne him grew up under a parent now brutally indifferent, now cruel with a fierce parsimony. His eldest son, William Henry, who was to be his heir, a meek and sluggish character, was consigned to a farm on Staten Island until he was of middle age: his father thought him an idiot and often told him so to his face. Another less patient and calculating son, Cornelius, was disowned for his extravagance. His pathetic wife, who at last became permanently distracted, the Commodore finally committed to Bloomingdale Asylum; while at the age of senility he pursued young women insatiably.

In an age of free struggle and fierce competition for power, this old buccaneer, who was almost a septuagenarian at the outbreak of the Civil War, was admired most of all for his unflagging aggressiveness. One incident was generally known of, in which associates had tried to take advantage of his absence upon a European journey to seize control of one of his properties. He wrote them:

Gentlemen:

You have undertaken to cheat me. I will not sue you, for law takes too long. I will ruin you.

Sincerely yours,
CORNELIUS VAN DERBILT.

And he did.

A characteristic expression of his, in another emergency, also became celebrated. "What do I care about the law?" he had exclaimed. "Hain't I got the power?"

In one respect, Vanderbilt foreshadowed the new conceptions of large-scale capitalism in his shipping business. His tactics were often directed to obtaining a great volume of traffic at lower rates than his competitors gave — in any case, until he obtained the upper hand, when he might safely give way to greed again. Once the great shipper Collins reproached Vanderbilt for making the federal government a lower offer for the mail-carrying privilege than seemed necessary. "I can't make it pay as it is," Collins had concluded.

"Then you are probably in a business that you don't understand," rejoined the Commodore.

Vanderbilt, then, combined in himself the new and the old social traits at once. Something of a sea-dog and a pioneer, endowed with physical courage and high energy as well as craftiness, he was the Self-made Man, for whom the earlier ruder frontier America was the native habitat. At the same time his individual conscience was already free of those prescriptive, restraining codes, as of the habitual prudence of Franklin's age of early capitalism. Though he kept no complicated books he had the taste for ever larger affairs such as men used to undertake only under the patronage of monarchs. In seeking quickened activity, great volume and lower prices

— instead of honest but limited services at high tariffs — he gave intimations of a new personal departure from the older bourgeois order. And though he had succeeded earlier as a craggy pioneer, he learned to employ the capital he possessed in the vast labyrinth of the modern marketplace. In short, he became originally a leader of men and undertakings, an owner of capital, because he was strong; but he learned to thrive in an age when men became commanders of industry because of their command of capital itself.

In the arts of buying and selling capital itself men grew both more subtle and more daring. Progress was registered not only in water power and steam engines, but in the rise and spread of "joint-stock companies" before 1840, in the growth of bourses or exchanges which dealt in such capital. The most notable of these at the time of the Civil War was the Stock Exchange of the City of New York, which by its natural advantages became the seaport and commercial metropolis of the nation. A century earlier, Wall and Water Streets were the haunt of pirates and slave-traders, and especially of the immortal William Kidd; here a market flourished already which differed in no wise from the old 'changes of Amsterdam, Frankfurt, Paris and London. Out of the neighboring coffeehouses where merchants of the shiftier kind, gamblers, lottery-players, touts and politicians had been wont to gather, the personnel of the marketplace was recruited in the days of the Revolutionary War. Un-

der the shade of a famous old buttonweed tree at 68 Wall Street there congregated those shrewd, lynx-eyed, slit-mouthed speculator-politicians who participated in the "bull" movement in "continentals" of the 1790's — a crowd bearing a close enough resemblance to the grave, secretive traders who walked in the Florence of the Medicis, or in seventeenth-century Edinburgh, or on the London Exchange whose "stock-jobbers" Defoe has described.

Robert Morris had been the leader of the first manipulative campaign for selling dear the rescued government scrip and securities which had been bought so cheap. The "stock-jobbers" who dealt in these peculiar wares were a perennial, hardy and resourceful race. In good times they did a flourishing business; even before the War of 1812 it often seemed that "stock and scrip were the sole subject of conversation" among the commercial-minded freemen, as Madison complainingly wrote to Jefferson. The press of the early republic spoke of the "raving madness bordering on insanity" of the mercantile public. And when the exaltation was succeeded by the cathartic cycle of depression, of tragic disillusionment, the society of brokers which had formed itself in Wall Street showed, ever since 1791, a wonderful poise, a "calm detachment toward the public ruin" which was to be one of the undying traditions of Wall Street.

The character of the Wall Street market had become definitely fixed after it had housed itself indoors in the Merchants' Exchange Building at Wall and William Streets, with solemn rules, initiation fees, and regular charges to outsiders. All its swift, smooth-running machinery — especially after the introduction of the telegraph — for dealing in pieces or shares of capital, as an "open and free securities market" were much as they are now, and had the same function. Even the "bear" had appeared in Jacob Little, who sold stocks "short" on six months' options in 1837. And as it is now so Wall Street was then a huge whispering gallery, vibrant with a thousand rumors, fears and passions, emotional and mercurial, or now impassive and inscrutable; a place of restless tides and bewitching calms, or howling hurricanes, a place as unfathomable as the sea, as impenetrable as the jungle.

In the 1850's another of the picturesque, weather-beaten figures who ruled as a king of the marketplace was Daniel Drew ("The Great Bear"), sometimes an associate, sometimes rival of Vanderbilt, and no less celebrated than the hardy Commodore. Tall, thin, bearded, rustic and "negligently dressed like a drover," Drew was renowned both for his piety and for his terrible market prowess, by which he dominated stock-gambling for almost a generation. This "Sphinx of the Stock Market" was as suspicious as Vanderbilt, also kept all his accounts in his head and considered the whole paraphernalia of bookkeeping a confounded fraud. Timid and mistrustful, he always believed the worst of men and their business ventures. He said: "Never tell no-body what yer goin' ter do, till ye do it."

Born in 1797, in the village of Carmel, New York, in the rural fastnesses of Putnam County, he had grown up to be a cattle-drover and lived a life of terrible privation in youth, which may have contributed to his "bearish" view of life. The cattle that he gathered up from farmers to drive to New York, purchased on credit, he often never settled for, according to the natives of Carmel; a practice which was the cause of his removing the base of his operations as far as Ohio. To him is also credited the invention of "watered stock," his cattle being kept thirsty throughout the journey, and only given drink immediately before arrival at the drovers' market uptown. Once, in bringing cattle at night over the Allegheny Mountains during a lightning storm, a tree had fallen upon Daniel Drew, killing his horse under him. But as Henry Clews relates, "No hardships or privations could deter him from the pursuit of money."

After having prospered in the cattle trade by his particular methods he had become the owner of the Bull's Head Tavern in the Third Avenue drovers' center; then a money-lender, an owner of Hudson River steamboats, and finally a stock-broker, head of the house of Drew, Robinson & Co., which bought and sold not only bank and steamboat shares, but also the new railroad shares which were already immensely popular in the '50's. In 1854 he had loaned the Erie Railroad, of which he was a director,

$1,500,000 in return for a chattel mortgage on its rolling stock.

The Erie was then a great trunk line, nearly 500 miles long, plying between the harbor of New York and the Great Lakes. It had been built at a cost of $15,000,000, partly through state subsidies; great celebrations, tremendous barbecues, had attended its completion, which was considered an enormous boon for the economy of the country at large as well as one of the marvels of modern science. But its capital had soon been watered until it stood at $26,000,000. Its rickety, lamp-lit trains, its weak iron rails had brought disaster and scandal, such as clung to its whole career; and when Daniel Drew, by virtue of his loans to the company, became its treasurer and master after the panic of 1857, it was soon clear that the flinty old speculator was not in the least interested in the Erie Railroad as a public utility or highway of traffic.

His strategic position gave him intimate knowledge of the large railroad's affairs which he used only to advance his private speculations. The very decreptitude of the rolling stock, the occurrence of horrendous accidents, were a financial " good " to the Speculative Director, who used even the treasury of his railroad to augment his short-selling of its own stock.

Nevertheless Drew, like Vanderbilt, became a character of renown, possessing a fortune of many millions, a model for the rising generation. His sayings were repeated everywhere and his more famous tricks were rehearsed by younger disciples. There was for instance the " handkerchief trick." In an uptown club one hot day, at a moment when he was supposed to be hard pressed in the market, Old Daniel pulled out his proverbial red bandanna handkerchief to mop his brow before sitting down with some fellow speculators. A slip of paper bearing a " point," or tip, fell to the floor; a bystander put his foot on it. As Drew left, apparently not noticing the incident, the others pounced upon the piece of paper, which proved to be an order. They bought Erie stock in large quantities, and were soon gulled. This is the " handkerchief trick."

According to Clews he cared not a fig what people thought of him, or what newspapers said. " He holds the honest people of the world to be a pack of fools. . . . When he has been unusually lucky in his trade of fleecing other men, he settles accounts with his conscience by subscribing toward a new chapel or attending a prayer meeting." And when unlucky, he would retreat to his house in Bleecker Street, " shut himself up, stuff up all the windows, bar all the doors, go to bed, swathe himself in blankets, pray and begin drinking."

For Drew was devoutly religious; and against the view held in money quarters that he never hesitated to sacrifice a friend, illustrated by innumerable anecdotes, his admirers pointed to his " genuine piety " as refuting his " closeness." Had he not given the immense sum of $250,000 to found a Methodist theological seminary in New Jersey? But in truth, it turned out in the end that he had given only his note, which after many years, in the shifting fortunes of new times, was never to be honored. . . .

Upon the customs of the market, upon its principles of negotiation and trading which an Astor, a Vanderbilt, a Drew exemplified other decisive influences were at work to give them their special American character. Immigrants or natives, these masters of the market soon absorbed the genius of the Yankee. But the Yankee was changing. We must look for him elsewhere than in the foot-worn marketplaces of the "civilized" East; we must observe the Yankee in process of transformation under the particular climate of the untamed frontier.

The legend of the Yankee Trader also formed a significant part of the composite national portrait, in which the mellow features of Franklin are prominent. . . . He was Uncle Jonathan, or Jonathan Slick or Sam Slick, as Miss Constance Rourke describes him in her recent inquiries into American folklore. He was long and lean and weather-beaten; never passive, he was "noticeably out in the world; it was a prime part of his character to be 'a-doin'.'" He pulled strings, he made shrewd and caustic comments; he ridiculed old values; "the persistent contrast with the British showed part of his intention." And to the British especially he had always appeared homely and "rapacious," but never slow-witted. If you met him in a tavern and he drew you into a trade, he

soon quietly stripped you of everything you had. In the South, superstitious colored folks and even white folks, according to tradition, locked their doors piously at the approach of the long, flapping peddler's figure.

This ingenious Yankee, quick to adapt himself everywhere, easily extricating himself from situations, and by religion and training profoundly rational, his passions under control, his reason dominating his natural inclinations, "plain and pawky," over-assertive, self-assured, moving everywhere, he had left his mark upon the society and leavened it. But in the give and take of the frontier he was at home naturally; he easily bested all others.

Those who looked for "noble savages" at the frontier looked in vain. (Two or three appeared in the most sophisticated region of the country, in Concord, outside of Boston, the products of much book-learning.) Freed of the restraints of organized society, at liberty to possess himself of all the riches of nature, the far-wandering Yankee or immigrant pioneer was deeply transformed, but not ennobled. The effect of the frontier movement was a "constant" in the conditioning of the nation, its recurrent waves and upheavals deeply marking the national character along with the low-church religion and the democratic institutions, until its cycle was ended in 1893.

The American frontier, as Frederick J. Turner holds, was as the outer edge of a wave, "the meeting place of civilization and savagery." Here the wilderness mastered the colonist. "It finds him a European.

. . . It strips away the garments of civilization." So periodically, in the Old Northwest (Ohio, Indiana, Illinois), in the Mississippi Valley, the farther Western prairies and the Pacific Slope, the frontier worked deeply upon the national character. It gave its measure of independence and optimism through the continued advantage of free land and the opportunity of a competency to all.

The immigrant (who came in a swarm of seven millions, between 1820 and 1870, chiefly from Great Britain and Germany), blended his character with that of the far-wandered New England Ulysses. The immigrant, in general, was the most aggressive, the coolest head, the least sentimental among his people, the least fettered by superstition or authority; he had no ties with any place or with the past, but lived only in the future. Having risked all, and crossed the ocean in search of pecuniary gain, he was stayed by few scruples, he feared no loss from a bold stroke. A stranger, like the others all about him, whose past, whose credit was unknown, he often dealt with the others as strangers. Thus, in the rude, loosely controlled commonwealths of the frontier, the pioneer became, as Turner concludes, " strong in selfishness and individualism, intolerant of . . . experience and education, and pressing individual liberty beyond its proper bounds." Here the national character assumed traits of " coarseness and strength "; it was " rooted strongly in material prosperity "; it tended toward a unity, a nationalism or Federalism rather than intense sectional-

ism of spirit; it would be lax in its business honor, its government affairs; it set at a premium acquisitiveness (crying always anew for free land) under a Jackson, a Lincoln, a Grant; it showed an inventive grasp of material things; it ranged to lawlessness and violence in the predations of those who sought either to " brave " the natural elements or to best each other.

The Yankee Trader, puritan though he was, and imbued with the " Poor Richard " principles of a mercantile capitalism, underwent a sea-change at the frontier, as Turner suggests. Civilized yesterday, he became half-savage in the wilderness, the deserts, the mountain gullies. To the traits of parsimony and prudence and calculation must be added those protective ones of force, swiftness and animal cunning, something of the " muffled bound of the wild beast." Else he was lost, trampled over, in the rush for the gold fields or the town-site claims.

In the recurrent, frenzied waves of land speculation, gold rushes and railroad booms, you saw the American at work, at his best and at his worst, prospector, pioneer, trader and settler.

" Were I to characterize the United States," writes an English traveler, William Priest, as early as 1796, " it would be by the appellation of the land of speculations." The very Fathers of the Republic, Washington, Franklin, Robert Morris and Livingston and most of the others, were busy buying land at one shilling or less the acre and selling it out at $2, in parcels of 10,000 acres or more. The very occasion of choosing a site for a National Capitol had been the outcome of collusion between the great land-grabbers, securities speculators, and the statesmen. Even before 1800 " land offices " were opened up, orators harangued the populace and sold shares or scrip, lots and subdivisions to settlers, often without deed or title. Cities like Cincinnati and Cleveland were laid out in the trackless wilderness and "jobbed." "Remember that lot in Buffalo! " cried the landjobbers. "Remember that acre in Cleveland! that quarter-section in Chicago! " Only promptness, speed, enthusiasm, vision were needed to wrest such a fortune as an Astor had taken from his acres in Putnam County, New York.

But though it was true that land speculations had given rise to the greatest fortunes in America up to about 1840, it was also true, as another distinguished foreigner remarked toward 1800, that " they have . . . been the cause of total ruin and disastrous bankruptcy." In 1795 the first great and typical panic had swept through the country with the failure of Robert Morris's colossal land projects. Such cruel disillusionments were to occur again and again. Yet mindless of this the roving Americans, as Emerson wrote to Carlyle, were bent only upon their " sections and quarter sections of swampland," kept "the country growing furiously, town and state . . . new Kansas, new Nebraskas, looming these days . . . vicious politicians seething a wretched destiny for them already in Washington." The pio-

neer kept moving westward toward the moving frontier, much as Mark Twain's Si Hawkins and his family, shiftless, voluble and happy-go-lucky, moved along from Kentucky to Missouri, where numberless acres could be bought at $2 apiece.

" But some day people would be glad to get it for twenty dollars, fifty dollars, a hundred dollars an acre! What should you say to (here he dropped his voice to a whisper and looked anxiously around to see that there were no eavesdroppers) a thousand dollars an acre!"

Such was the legend of the land boom, faithfully caught in " The Gilded Age " by Mark Twain and Charles Dudley Warner.

The sequel to the Mexican War was an orgy of land-grabbing and speculation in which the origin of the war is not hard to trace. A young army-officer of engineers, Grenville Dodge, later to be a distinguished general and railroad-builder, writes: " I can double any amount of money you've got in six-months. . . . To start with buy a couple of Mexican War land warrants."

More illuminating still was it to see the frontiersman in the railroad boom of the '40's and '50's. You saw him scheming, sometimes in collusion with men of capital, or with men of politics, to open the markets of inexhaustible coal fields or untold millions of feet of lumber. Along the right of way of the new railroad line, as along the canal lines a decade or so earlier, the directors would purchase town sites in the prairies. Thus when in 1850 the Illinois Central Railroad was awarded a vast land grant by the federal government of 2,600,000 acres in alternate sections between Chicago and Mobile, the affair was looked upon primarily as a land-jobbing project. Abraham Lincoln, heading a Western group of promoters, contended in vain against a ring of Massachusetts capitalists, who seizing the affair were able to sell land to their friends at $2.50 an acre along the line, while the public fought for town sites, to be had only at ten or fifteen times the price tomorrow. . . .

Anthony Trollope, visiting American during the Civil War, commented that the railroad companies " were in fact companies combined for the purchase of land . . . looking to increase the value of it five-fold by the opening of the railroad. It is in this way that the thousands of miles of railroads have been opened." And Mark Twain accurately pictures the process in his " Gilded Age ": as Mr. Bigler unfolds his scheme for the " Tunkhannock, Rattlesnake & Youngstown Railroad ":

" We'll buy the land on long time . . . and then mortgage . . . for enough money to get the road well on. Then get the towns on the line to issue their bonds for stock. . . . We can then sell the rest of the stock on the prospects of the business of the road . . . and also sell the land on the strength of the road at a big advance."

But the furor of Si Hawkins, as he looks toward the unknown and trackless Missouri, is even more instructive:

" Nancy, you've heard of steam-

boats, and maybe you believed in them — they're going to make a revolution in this world's affairs that will make men dizzy to contemplate. . . . And this is not all, Nancy — it isn't even half! There's a bigger wonder — the railroad! Coaches that fly over the ground twenty miles an hour — heaven and earth, think of that, Nancy! It makes a man's brain whirl. . . ."

He saw not only farm lands and towns. He saw

mountains of ore there, Nancy — whole mountains of it. . . . Pine forests, wheat lands, corn land, iron, copper, coal — wait till the railroads come, and the steamboats!

But in 1849 mountains of gold had suddenly surged up before the avid eyes of these restless people — such as the Spanish Conquerors had dreamed. In the gold rush, in the mining camp, the frontiersman, certainly by protective coloration, lost the historic conservative bourgeois traits; created the morale of violent speculation with his possessions and life itself. You saw him, as Mark Twain again reveals in " Roughing It ";

" It was a driving, restless population, in those days. There were none of your simpering, dainty, kid-glove weaklings, but stalwart, muscular, dauntless young braves, brimful of push and energy. . . . For all the slow, sleepy, sluggish-brained sloths stayed at home — you never find that sort of people among pioneers."

The frenzy and thunder of gold rushes, silver rushes, oil rushes, were to repeat themselves decade after decade, as this richest continent of the world opened up its underground to all comers, to the swift and the strong, to *fourrer dans le sac,* to take what he willed, till his arms tired. In the history of the frontier, the gaudy and tragic drama of the settlement of California is the eternal parable of the nation of pioneers.

Before 1849, the Pacific Slope is a garden of paradise. Hearing of its blessed climate, its soil and fruits, the mild Sutter, after long wanderings, enters the bay of San Francisco. He settles not far away in the Sacramento Valley, to dwell upon his ranch as a hidalgo, among his happy natives and Indians, in the peace of a medieval sleep.

Suddenly a man stumbles upon the glittering quartz in the brook gravel; the alarm is given. The gold lust sweeps not only the United States but the remotest corners of the civilized world. The bookkeeper in New York, the farmer of Pennsylvania, the Yankee tin-peddler, the waiter in New Orleans, all rush toward California, by land and by sea, around Cape Horn, or over Panama and Nicaragua, or the Great American desert. The mob of gold-seekers come in tens of thousands; Sutter's enchanted ranch is overrun by the desperadoes, his land is seized, his claims derided.

San Francisco, the beautiful Spanish port, is turned overnight into a shambles by the latter-day Argonauts. Within a year or two, literally, it is a " metropolis " of the Pacific, holding some 25,000 souls. From its wharves along the water front there stretches out an endless expanse of unpainted, rude frame dwellings, ramshackle warehouses, false-fronted shops and saloons, marked off by wooden-planked streets which straggle up toward Telegraph Hill.

A strange world; a strange social order. At night there are few lamps, burning whale-oil; only the " rumholes " send out a dull glow of light. A man arrives — it is more rare now — with buckskin poke heavy with gold dust; he drinks like a god, stakes his whole bag on a single throw of cards; there is a stabbing affray, and quickly he is taken and strung up. Before he has ceased kicking two men of the mob steal away, leap upon horses, and go galloping off to " jump " the unfortunate's claim. Those who owned provisions or land must watch them with unremitting vigilance against the rough squatters or Sydneymen who might expropriate them at any moment, with the help of gunplay by officers of the peace or justice no less unscrupulous or violent than they. And when the expropriations, the knifing or gunplay become intolerable, the great fire-bell is rung, sounding alarm to the thousands of Vigilantes, secretly banded together to preserve " law and order." They come running, armed, disciplined, impassive. Sometimes they err: but on the whole it is better so.

Soon the first rich placer claims on the western slope of the Sierra seem stripped, and deeper mining, needing both capital and technical skill, must now be attempted. The golden flood seems exhausted; and since the region offers at first nothing but its ore, the spoilers fall upon each other, in a kind of despair, robbing, fighting, cheating each other. An exodus begins; many more leave, broken in spirit and pocket, than those who come in.

Misery rises. The local gazette (Alta California) by February 12, 1853, comments:

"There has never been so deplorable an exhibition of mendicancy in our streets as may be witnessed daily at this time . . . hundred of destitute men and scores of women . . . little girls are to be found in front of the city saloons at all hours of the day, going through their graceless performances."

And eggs are still three dollars a dozen, milk 50 cents a quart; a rude dinner of fried pork and fried potatoes and molasses may be had at the heavy cost of a whole dollar. Civilization and the existing forms of capitalism have come to Eldorado — a swarm of shrewd, rough-joking entrepreneurs, tapsters, horse-traders, madames, dance-hall girls, dry-goods merchants have come to serve and to feed voraciously upon the care-free, high-hearted gold-seekers. As in San Francisco and Sacramento, so in the neighboring mining camps or communities, civilization has bloomed mushroom-like, in " Jackass Gulch," or " Hangtown," or " Slum Gullions" where the names give the moral tone. Here the heritage of puritanism has shrunk to its original core; only the puritan economic philosophy remains " strong in selfishness and individualism, intolerant of administrative experience," or tradition, or learning or social values, as Turner has noted, " and pressing in-

dividual liberty beyond its proper bounds," breeding new and incalculable dangers.

These sunbaked mining towns of the western slope, upon which the economic civilization of the time fixed itself, their single sandy street sprawling up the side of the Sierra Nevada, their unpainted weather-beaten shacks already grown old, their weary population of some two thousand red- and blue-shirted miners, bartenders, black-smiths, gamblers, Chinamen and Mexicans, dance-hall girls and tired mothers and unkempt, scrawny children — how often and untruthfully they have been pictured by the native historians. The frontier evolution, romanticized by a Bret Harte, was caught with a shrewd, veritably poetic vision by a Mark Twain. Out of the cycle of perpetual feverish gold-rushes, in the years after the Forty-niners, there was the renewed stampede to the Comstock Lode, at the western edge of Nevada. Here Mark Twain pictures to us the historical process of " Hell-On-Wheels." The " van-leader of civilization " is always whiskey.

" Look history over and you will see. The missionary comes after the whiskey — I mean, he arrives after the whiskey has arrived. Next comes the poor immigrant with ax and hoe and rifle; next, the trader, next the miscellaneous rush; next the gambler, the desperado, the highwayman, and all their kindred in sin of both sexes; and next the smart chap who has bought up an old grant that covers all the land; this brings in the lawyer tribe; the vigilance committee brings the undertaker. All these

interests bring the newspaper; the newspaper starts up politics and a railroad; all hands turn to and build a church and a jail — and behold, civilization is established forever in the land."

So in the second decade of the Pacific Slope's terrestrial paradise, the cycle is already completed, the arc defined. Out of the strenuous milling of free frontiersmen, two or three Yankee shopkeepers emerge, a derelict lawyer from the East, a pair of practical Irish miners in collaboration with a pair of Irish saloonkeepers, an English invalid gambler, a land-jobber, a drover and innkeeper from Indiana — these have banded together to form a ruling class, by something equivalent to an imperceptible process of *coup d'état* have seized all power, all economic control. For them the gold and silver flood of the Comstock; for them a great railroad leaps the Sierras and in spreading network penetrates into every smiling valley to levy toll and carry off the produce of the deep rich soil. The banking institution which dominates the Pacific Slope is in their hands; the mines, the water front, the terminals, a vast section of the land as right-of-way grant; also invaluable franchises, a heavy portion of all tax receipts in the communities are theirs. An industrial society is established; but under the ruder, simpler frontier conditions, it is done as if overnight, in the twinkling of an eye. The human mass of free pioneers who came yesterday plodding over the desert route, with its trail of ox and horse skeletons and wrecked wagons, its numerous

mounds of graves, braving storms, flooded rivers, thirst, hunger, heat, and Indian raiders — these and their children and their children's children are all in subjection to princely and dynastic overlords, who rule by "use" and "wont," who "own" because they own, and are well seized of so much land, forest, mineral deposits, harbor rights and franchises and rights of way because they have seized.

The story of this seizure of power — mightier than all the transient gains of hilarious and rudderless gold-seekers — a power and authority, a seizure, to remain vested forever, consecrated by law and custom, legalized by statute, confirmed by long undisturbed possession, this story has scarcely been told; though in parable, almost in caricature form and concentrated within a brief generation of California life, it epitomizes dramatically the historic process through which the nation in general passed over a somewhat longer period.

In a brief cycle, the *laissez-faire* political philosophy of a Jefferson, having given free reign to self-interest, would stimulate the acquisitive appetites of the citizen above all. These, whetted by an incredibly rich soil, checked by no institutions or laws, would determine the pattern of American destiny. The idealism of Jefferson's Declaration of Independence, as of his Inaugural Address of 1801, would be caricatured in the predatory liberty of the "Valley of Democracy" where, as Vernon Parrington has said, Americans democratic in professions, became "mid-

dle-class in spirit and purpose ";
where freedom came to mean " the
natural right of every citizen to satisfy his acquisitive instinct by exploiting the national resources in the
measure of his shrewdness." And
the strong, as in the Dark Ages of
Europe, and like the military captains of old, having preëmpted more
than others, having been well seized
of land and highways and strong
places, would own because they
owned. Chieftains would arise, in
the time-honored way, to whom the
crowd would look for leadership, for
protection, finally for their very existence. They would be the nobles
of a new feudal system, for whom
the great mass of men toiled willingly. These barons resembled their
forerunners, since they traced their
ownership back, as Veblen has said,
to the " ancient feudalistic ground of
privilege and prescriptive tenure . . .
to the right of seizure by force and
collusion."

Only the material conditions, the
instruments of such sovereignty,
would be changed owing to the advanced material standards of the society. Instead of armament, mercenary soldiers, serfs, the weapons
of offense and defense might be a
fleet of ships (as with the Merchant
Adventurers), fur-trading stations in
the frontier, finally railways which
were to be the arteries of trade,
mines, factories laboring for a continental or a world market.

All this transformation and " progress " the young men of '61 could
look back upon as a momentous part
of their history while the democratic
spirit of the laws still blessed them:

the conquest of the Frontier was always in their eye, whether it was
the virgin prairies of the Mississippi
Valley, the mineral deposits of the
Sierras, or the " Frontier " of new industries and of projects and speculations in the East, all about them. If
the doctrine of the nation favored
an ideal of free and equal opportunity for all, so its current folklore
glorified the freebooting citizen who
by his own efforts, by whatever methods feasible, had wrested for himself
a power that flung its shadow upon
the liberties and privileges of all the
others.

It was not surprising that a Livingston in New York, a Washington
in Virginia should wield great influence in the republic. That men
who were penniless, ignorant, without antecedents or influential connections, who knew neither the arts of
war nor those of the forum, but only
of the marketplace and counting-
house should have acquired grandiose wealth within their own lifetime, which the human imagination
then could scarcely spend, this was
one of the wonders of the time, and
the favorite legend held up before
the new generations, the young men
of '61. It bespoke also the new structure of society — finally crystallized
— the triumph of bourgeoisedom. In
olden days, mercenary captains, hereditary princes, landed nobles or
mighty prelates of the Church would
have preyed on the tradesmen, held·
him down with their contempt; now
all society protected him, government
policed his property, paid him hom-
age — and tomorrow in the sequel to
the national crisis the country would

change its laws, its Constitution, sacrifice a million lives for him and the economic force he represented.

In the meantime the paddle-wheels of Progress which typify the age were turning as always; steaming up the river valleys busily — though sometimes " snags " were struck and overheated boilers without safety valves blew up all hands. Then in all directions upon iron rails held by wooden " sleepers " the first Iron Horses, red and black brass-ornamented, puffing and rattling, named " Old Ironsides " or " Best Friend " or " Stourbridge Lion," were cutting their trail of destiny. By 1840, over 9,000 miles of railroad had been constructed, and they had climbed the difficult barrier of the Alleghenies, which had so long separated the settlers of Ohio, Indiana and Illinois from the Eastern market they panted for. Abandoning the river, the turnpike and canal the farmers of the West turned to using the railroad, as they would soon turn to use McCormick's horse-drawn reaper and thresher. Thus the whole tier of Northern states was linked closer than ever in a vast intercourse. The axis of trade had shifted away from the Mississippi by 1860, when 30,000 miles of railroad existed; so that with the river closed the following year there was little hardship. The settler was part of the orbit of a national market, in which goods circulated at a new speed. He found prosperity in free labor rather than in the routine effort of slaves. His spirit called for national unity, for freely circulating capital, and above all for a Pacific Railroad. The new political party clamored against the blockade of its future prosperity held by the South, as the Manchester industrialists of yesterday had clamored for the repeal of the Corn Laws in England. Its leader, a lawyer for Western railroads, included a Pacific Railroad bill and a protective tariff for native industries in his platform. Such overwhelming economic needs, confronted with the alarmed passionate resistance of the agrarian, slave-owning, static South, must burst the dam at last in the inevitable social cataclysm of the Civil War.

37. The Transformation of American Capitalism*

What we have here called the Proposition, together with what we have called the System, constitute the basis for the permanent revolution that was brought about in the eighteenth century and for which the U.S.A.

* From Fortune, USA — The Permanent Revolution, pp. 65–88. Reprinted from the February 1951 issue of Fortune magazine by Special Permission; Copyright 1951 Time Inc.

has ever since acted, or tried to act, as the vehicle. Yet, were this the end of the matter, the revolution would never have come about. For the revolution was not and is not a mere exercise in political theory. It was the revolution, as already explained, of the individual human being, and it consequently involved the transformation of all aspects of human society — not only the political, but also the cultural and economic. Thus, having reviewed its major political applications, we can only understand it if we now turn to an examination of its applications in these other fields.

With regard to this necessity, however, the authors have made a somewhat arbitrary decision. We have decided not to enter into a consideration of the application of the revolution to the important cultural field. Our reasons are, in general, twofold. First, we consider this field, which includes the great questions of religion, the arts, education, learning — all that which pertains to the development of the individual, as such — so important that it requires a whole study of its own if it is to be adequately represented. It could not be covered with any hope of success in one or two chapters. But secondly, while the authors confess to certain ideas in this field, they feel that their unique contribution, both in terms of theory and reporting, lies in that area which is usually referred to as " the economy." This word, we take it, includes something much more than economic theory: it includes business and industry, technology and science, politics and sociology, and so forth. It is an area in which the authors have to a great degree specialized. Moreover, it has been the major domestic battleground of our time. Probably the fundamental problem of freedom is cultural, but for the last quarter-century the struggle for freedom has manifested itself chiefly in questions of political economy all over the world.

This area, therefore, we believe, is the strategic one to choose in showing how the permanent revolution is being carried out by Americans in the modern world.

Nothing demonstrates this better than the theory of American capitalism itself. Fifty years ago American capitalism seemed to be what Marx predicted it would be and what all the muckrackers said it was — the inhuman offspring of greed and irresponsibility, committed by its master, Wall Street, to a long life of monopoly. It seemed to provide overwhelming proof of the theory that private ownership could honor no obligation except the obligation to pile up profits. It was, indeed, close to the capitalism that Andrei Vishinsky today keeps on denouncing so laboriously and humorlessly. And it was the capitalism that millions of people abroad and many even at home, to the immense aid and comfort of the Communists, still think American capitalism is.

But American capitalism today is actually nothing of the kind. There has occurred a great transformation, of which the world as a whole is as yet unaware, the speed of which has outstripped the perception of the historians, the commentators, the writers of business books — even many businessmen themselves. No important progress whatever can be made in the understanding of America unless the nature of this transformation is grasped and the obsolete intellectual stereotypes discarded.

Many evidences of the transformation are at hand, though they have never yet been drawn together into what is very urgently needed — a restatement of capitalistic theory in modern American terms. Take, for example, the all-pervasive character of American capitalism, as stressed in The American Way of Life. There has been a vast dispersion of ownership and initiative, so that the capitalist system has become intimately bound in with the political system and takes nourishment from its democratic roots. What might be called the influence of Main Street has become vastly more important than the control of Wall Street. U.S. capitalism is *popular* capitalism, not only in the sense that it has popular support, but in the deeper sense that the people as a whole participate in it and use it.

But perhaps the transformation can best be understood by looking at what has happened to "Big Business," which once was supposed to have controlled the economy from its headquarters in Wall Street. The fact is that Wall Street no longer wields much power over Big Business, which in turn is far from being the most powerful sector of the economy. For economic power boils down to the ability to decide who makes what and who gets what and in what proportions, and business no longer decides this. "The class struggle in America," wrote Professor Clair Wilcox in the *Harvard Business Review*, "is not a struggle between the proletariat and the bourgeoisie. It is a struggle between functional groups possessing concentrated power — a struggle to control the products of industry." These groups, as Professor Wilcox de-

scribed them, are Big Labor, Big Agriculture, Big Little Business, and Big Business. Of them all, Big Business, if only because it is subject to the most pressures, exercises its power with a strong and growing sense of responsibility. It has led the way to the formation of a kind of capitalism that neither Karl Marx nor Adam Smith ever dreamed of.

At the bottom of the change is simple morality, which has concerned the U.S. throughout its history, sometimes to the point of fanaticism. "The American," H. L. Mencken once said, "save in moments of conscious and swiftly lamented deviltry, casts up all ponderable values, including the value even of beauty, in terms of right and wrong." Like the European who described moral indignation as suppressed envy, Mencken scorned it as the mark of the peasant; and the American's capacity for moral indignation *has* resulted in many "uncivilized" excesses like prohibition. But it has also made him the most omnivorous reformer in history. Karl Marx based his philosophy on the fatalistic assumption that what he described as the inherent defects of capitalism are above the will of men to affect them. It has remained for the history of U.S. capitalism, beginning as early as the 1870's, to show that the moral convictions of men can change the course of capitalistic development.

And it would have been strange if a nation that had only recently fought a terrible war over the question of slavery had *not* got indignant about the excesses of its "robber barons." People, of course, do not necessarily rise up voluntarily and act on moral indignation. What is essential is their capacity for it; given a free, lively press and plenty of politicians, the action follows. Action followed in the U.S. because a whole school of commentators, from novelists to reporters, from historians to cartoonists, rose up to expose the financial and industrial scandals of the day. There were the Ida Tarbells and Henry Demarest Lloyds, the Upton Sinclairs and Frederick Oppers, backed by the Hearsts, McClures, and Munseys. Some were hypocritical and others wholly sincere, but all operated on the effective principle that the public could be fetched by an earnest appeal to its moral standards.

In their zeal the muckrakers paid little attention to the great economic role played by "robber barons" in forming the capital to lay the rails, erect the factories, build the machinery for a new and expanding economy. Naturally the muckrakers were concerned not with the amoral economics but with immoral practices. Their pictures of the American economic brigandage of the later nineteenth and early twentieth centuries became stereotypes all over the world — Daniel Drew feeding his cattle salt to make them drink heavily the day before market; Cornelius Vanderbilt bragging how "we busted the hull damn legislature"; foxy Jay Gould, whom Vanderbilt called the smartest man in America, cornering the national gold-coin supply through his White House connec-

tions, and systematically and openly robbing the Erie; gelid old John D. Rockefeller perfecting the trust system and eliminating competitors like clay pigeons. Here was the principle of property ownership carried to its absurd conclusion, capitalism going berserk. But here also was the moral indignation of the American people. Fanned by lurid accounts in the press and by politicians and publicists of almost every persuasion, from Populists to Republicans, it started the transformation of American capitalism.

Popular resentment of the railroad rate-making came early, even before the muckraking school was in full swing. The Interstate Commerce Act was passed in 1887. And only three years later there occurred what is probably the most portentous single legislative act in the history of American capitalism: the passage of the Sherman Act against monopolies and combinations "in restraint of trade." Although endorsed by all parties, its birth was inauspicious, and the bill was amended almost to death. Senator John Sherman himself, the story goes, never read the final version. And for several years, under Cleveland and McKinley, the act was used little, and then ineffectively. In 1901 J. P. Morgan disregarded it and put U.S. Steel together. "What looks like a stone wall to a layman," said Mr. Dooley, "is a triumphal arch to a corporation lawyer." But the muckrakers began to make themselves felt. In 1902 Teddy Roosevelt, a man who not only understood the public mind but judged almost everything in terms of righteousness, whipped out the Sherman Act and used it as a "big stick" on what he was the first to call the "malefactors of great wealth." He wielded it so effectively against the Northern Securities Co. that the legislation became a power in American life.

The defects of the Sherman Act were soon and widely recognized. "No law can make a man compete with himself," observed J. P. Morgan characteristically. Others noted the great paradox of the antitrust conception: a strong company that really obeyed the law and competed strenuously would end up as a monopoly, violating the law. Contemplating such contradictions, the "realistic" Europeans abstained from trust-busting; they left it to the naive Americans, who in their preoccupation with right and wrong were foolish enough to take so seriously and apply so dogmatically their notions of fairness and justice.

The antitrust law nevertheless acquired stature and authority. However patent its imperfections, however hollow its victories, however vitiated by later acts like Miller-Tydings and Robinson-Patman, it became, in the words of Justice Holmes, "a brooding omnipresence in the sky." Even when businessmen are puzzled and irritated by the letter of the law, they respect its spirit. Even when their lawyers tell them how to get around it, they know they *are* getting around it. The law, in the last analysis, amounts to nothing less than the successful extension of the Anglo-Saxon common law, the basis of the whole English-speaking

world's unique liberty, into the realm of business. And its success is among the chief reasons why American business is today so vastly different from European business.

Other reforms came sporadically. The American's moral indignation, naturally enough, did not burn with a steady flame. In good times he tended to overlook violations of his basic notions; in bad times he looked for something to blame things on, and demanded that something be done about them. During the 1920's popular demand for reform was almost nonexistent. For one thing, the scorn of some of the nation's most effective writers made preoccupation with moral issues unfashionable if not ludicrous. For another, business seemed to be doing fine, and seemed to deserve not reform but praise. As the immensely popular *Saturday Evening Post* demonstrated in almost every issue, as Herbert Hoover himself phrased it, "The slogan of progress is changing from the full dinner pail to the full garage."

The catastrophe of depression blasted this dream. The shocked and angry people, seeing their livelihood disappear, put the Right of Life above the other rights. Their natural tendency to blame the bust on those who only yesterday were taking credit for having started an eternal boom was strengthened by revelations such as those of the Pecora congressional investigation into Wall Street financial practices. So they embraced the latter-day Populism of the New Deal, and demanded that something be done. Writers and intellectuals took up the cudgels. Some were merely inclined to condemn what they had for so long contemned, but many tried to find out how and why it had happened, and how to keep it from happening again.

Many of the ensuing reforms survived. Immediately after the Pecora investigation, Congress passed a law divorcing investment banking from deposit banking. And a year later it passed the well-intentioned Securities Exchange Act, which put the Stock Exchange under federal regulations, gave the Federal Reserve Board authority to limit speculative margins, required all officers and stockholders of big companies to report their dealings in their companies' securities, and created the Securities and Exchange Commission to watch over the investment market.

Other attempts at reform were less successful. NRA, for example, went to a well-deserved death. As for the famed Temporary National Economic Committee, much of what it investigated was beside the point by the time it was in print — and not only because of the impending war. Even while the committee was mulling over the power of big business, and the intellectuals were in full cry on the trail of finance capitalism, business initiative had been dispersed among hundreds of enterprises; business power in the aggregate found itself confronted by the rising power of the unions on the one hand, the farmers on the other; and Wall Street had ceased to be a valid symbol of great tyranny.

The decline of Wall Street actually began long before the reforms of the New Deal. It began when corporations grew rich and independent. The rights to their profits, of course, were by traditional economics vested in the stockholders. But their managers saw no point in paying, say, $20 a share in dividends on their stock, when $10 was enough to sustain the company's credit rating. They also reasoned that it was *they,* and not the stockholders, who were directly responsible for the profits. So they began to hold back on the stockholders and put the money into corporate reserves. As early as 1905 the Santa Fe, under Edward Ripley, adopted the policy of a dollar for the stockholder, a dollar for the property. Owen Young of G.E. and others, some years later, further developed the idea of self-capitalization, arguing that the money plowed back would in the long run enhance the stockholder's equity. Whether it did or not, it enabled a large part of business to do its own banking.

Wall Street did not feel the change at first. In the boom of the 1920's the issue of new securities passed the $500-million-a-year mark, and a rich time was had by all. But even then the bulk of the Street's effort was going into the buying and selling of old issues (and new issues of holding companies that used the money to buy old issues), the promotion of dubious foreign bonds, and the lending of money at, say, 7 per cent for the speculative purchase of stock paying, say, 5 per cent. And even then corporations were putting up to ten times as much money into their reserves as all companies were raising in new stocks and bonds. And the depression hit the Street's new-issue function even harder than it hit the trading function. High income taxes and the growing corporate practice of financing new issues through insurance and trust companies trimmed the new-issue business almost to the vanishing point.

Except as its opinions still influence investment policies, Wall Street today exerts only a fraction of the power it once wielded. Industry now plows back 60 per cent of its profits, as against 30 per cent in the 1920's, and the bulk of money used in capital formation comes from corporate earnings or from internal sources such as depreciation. The largest brokerage house on the Street, accounting for 10 per cent of the stock trading on the Stock Exchange, is Merrill Lynch, Pierce, Fenner & Beane, 90 per cent of whose customers are small-fry out-of-towners.

The House of Morgan is still one of the large commercial banks of the country (its underwriting business was passed over to Morgan Stanley in 1935), with total resources of about $667 million; and the phrase "Morgan Company" still evokes images of the old days when Morgan did direct U.S. business. But the working capital of General Motors, by contrast, is more than $1.6 *billion,* and G.M. not only finances itself but recently loaned money to Jones & Laughlin. As for leadership and control, Robert Young's defiance of Morgan in buying control of the C. & O. years ago was more a feat of derring-do than genuine audacity. And when the "Morgan" directors of Montgomery Ward found themselves disapproving Sewell Avery not long ago, they shortly afterward found themselves resigning. The power and the glory had vanished. The dynamic leadership of the economy had moved to the big corporate offices in midtown New York, Schenectady, Chicago, Pittsburgh, and points west and south. It is indeed hard to believe that only thirty-nine years ago J. P. Morgan, the one-man center of the American business universe, was candidly laying his cards on the table at the Pujo investigation: "I like a little competition, but I like combination better . . . Without control you cannot do a thing."

The cataclysm of the depression, which forever broke apart the old business universe, also heaved up the bright new stars of the unions and the farmers. With between 14 and 16 million members in labor unions, labor leaders now enjoy tremendous industrial power. This power is exercised through the familiar method of tying up an entire industry in order to win certain gains for the workers, whether these gains be "economic" or not. In the face of such power, industry is impotent; and since the national welfare is often enough at stake, the White House itself becomes directly involved. The danger of such power is obvious, and was recently accented by John L. Lewis, who put his miners on a three-day week, not merely to enforce a wage demand, but to keep the price of coal up by creating a scarcity. Here, indeed, is a problem that the permanent revolution has not yet solved, although certain solutions are beginning to emerge, as described in the next chapter. The point to note here is that the power of Wall Street, which has declined in any case, has been met, and sometimes overmatched, by the power of modern labor; a development that has played an enormous role in the transformation of American capitalism.

The power of the farmer, if less direct than that of labor, is likewise formidable. Represented in Congress out of proportion to his numbers, the farmer has been championed by legislators and bureaucrats who have effectively insulated him from the law of supply and demand. By restricting output, fixing prices, and storing up surpluses at government expense, they have done for agriculture what a watertight cartel would do for a group of manufacturers of widely varying efficiency. They have not only saddled the public with high prices, they have, of course, tended to prevent American farming from becoming as efficient as it ought to be and can be. For they have spread a price umbrella over the farmers that has enabled the worst of them to do all right and the best of them to make fantastic and undeserved profits without necessarily encouraging any of them to become more efficient. The $23-billion farm industry, furthermore, is hardly comparable to any one industry; it is more comparable to all industry — to all industry cartelized, subsidized, and rigidified. In terms of deciding who makes what and who gets what, it is one of the most powerful blocs in American history.

And where, in this regrouping of U.S. economic power, do we find the sense of responsibility that ought to go with the power if the nation is to increase its productivity? Labor, with a few exceptions, does not yet show much of it, and agriculture shows even less. The only place it can be found in any force is in the individual business enterprise, which now has the initiative that might have remained in Wall Street had not the transformation taken place.

One of the two chief characteristics of big modern enterprise is that it is run by hired management. As Berle and Means show, the power inherent in the control of the " active property " — the plant, organization and good will — has superceded the power inherent in " passive property " — the stocks and bonds. Even companies whose owners are managers may be described as management-run. The Ford company, for example, behaves not as an organization solely dedicated to earning the maximum number of dollars for the Ford family, but as an organization dedicated first of all to its own perpetuation and growth.

The other chief characteristic of the big modern enterprise is that management is becoming a profession. This means, to begin with, that a professional manager holds his job primarily because he is good at it. Often he has begun at the bottom and worked his way up by sheer merit. Or more often he has been carefully and even scientifically chosen from a number of bright and appropriately educated young men, put through an executive-training course, and gradually insinuated into the activities for which he shows the best talent. Since even at the top he generally functions as a member of a committee rather than as a final authority, his talents are so well balanced that none of them protrude excessively. He lives on what he makes, and even when he is well paid he doesn't have much left after taxes. Generally he is gregarious, and usually he is not a colossal " personality." But if he is not a General MacArthur, neither is he a Mr. Milquetoast. And if he is expected not to give arbitrary orders, he is also expected not to take them. In most well-run big enterprises, an executive is by definition a man who would object officially to a policy decision he disapproved.

More important, the manager is becoming a professional in the sense that like all professional men he has a responsibility to society as a whole. This is not to say that he no longer needs good, old-fashioned business sense. He does, and more than ever. The manager is responsible primarily to his company as a profit-earning mechanism, and current talk about the corporation as a nonprofit institution is more than a little naive. Any self-respecting businessman would rightly suspect a colleague who allowed he was in business not to make money. The modern enterpriser *should* be in business to make money. His ability to make money is the prime measure of his company's efficiency. If it cannot prosper in the service it supplies to society, or if it cannot persuade society to pay it enough to prosper, it does not deserve to stay in business. Moreover, the good, efficient manager *likes* to make money, and it is mainly because he likes to make money that he does a first-rate job. As the Russians have discovered, when the profit motive does not exist it has to be invented.

But the great happy paradox of the profit motive in the American system is that management, precisely because it is in business to make money years on end, cannot concentrate exclusively on making money here and now. To keep on making money years on end, it must, in the words of Frank Abrams, Chairman of the Standard Oil Co. of New Jersey, " conduct the affairs of the enterprise in such a way as to maintain an *equitable and working balance* among the claims of the various directly interested groups — stockholders, employees, customers, and the public at large." Not all pundits have understood this vital point. In his romantic *Managerial Revolution,* for example, James Burnham described the trend accurately enough but conveyed the idea that somehow the corporate manager is destined to become the Western equivalent of a King Farouk or perhaps an unusually favored commissar. The corporate manager neither is, nor is becoming, anything of that kind. He is part of a group that enjoys power only so long as it does not abuse it — in other words, precisely so long as it does not exercise power the way men and groups of men used to before the capitalistic transformation.

Thus it is not too difficult to define management's responsibility to the stockholder. Management is no longer occupied exclusively with the interests of the stockholder, who often has become a kind of contingent bondholder rather than a part owner, and who rarely exerts any direct influence on the affairs of the company. But management cannot flagrantly disregard the stockholders' interests, at least not for long. As the management of Bethlehem and U.S. Steel know well, stockholders can be a considerable nuisance. Even when widely dispersed, they can be induced to take a point of view by proxy. And on the whole, management is treating the stockholders well — despite " abuses " like the habit of holding annual meetings in some out-of-the-way railway station or in Wilmington, Delaware. Almost any good manager can honestly argue that the growing importance of the hired management and its policy of self-capitalization have been to the benefit of the stockholder. Above all, he can argue that the stockholder's long-term interests lie in letting competent, responsible management build up the company and deal justly with employees, customers, and the public.

But modern management exhibits also a sense of responsibility toward its employees, not only to prevent or anticipate the demands of labor unions (though this motive has often been strong) but for the simple, obvious, and honest reason that a satisfied, loyal group of employees is at least as much of an asset as a modern plant or a vital piece of machinery. The trend toward more enlightened employment policies has been growing for years, and while there is still a great distance to go, an old-style capitalist would be appalled by the wide variety of benefits that modern corporations offer those who work for them. There is a growing tendency on the part of blue-chip management to regard a job in the company as a kind of employment package, complete with pensions, savings plan, and numerous " fringe " benefits such as severance pay, maternity leave, hospitalization and medical insurance. Other managements specialize in certain types of benefits. Some, for instance, go in for stabilization of employment. ATF, Inc., as an example, which recently bought into the furniture business, has succeeded in almost eliminating the highly seasonal character of that work. Some companies (Proctor & Gamble, Nunn-Bush, Hormel) carry employment stabilization to the point of guaranteeing an annual wage. Others have developed forecasting techniques to anticipate trends and to stabilize employment by leveling out production. Almost every important company now has a pension plan or is in the process of getting one. Many, like Sears, Roebuck, combine pensions with savings plans, so that when an employee retires he takes with him a sizable capital sum. Others, backed by the Council of Profit-Sharing Industries (276 members), give the workers a cut of profits, with annual bonuses running up to 100 per cent of base wages.

But material benefits, as Elton Mayo and others have demonstrated, are often not as important as job satisfaction — the feeling of having done a good job, and of having it recognized by people who know what a good job is. Related and equally important is the question of real participation in the company's affairs. The problem involved here is tremendous, and it cannot be solved merely by the resolution to do something about it. In one of the Standard Oil affiliates, for example, management was stumped by a case of group dissatisfaction until the president of the company began to talk to the men informally about some of the problems that were plaguing him and his board. "The men showed an immediate and extraordinary interest, and that gradually revealed the source of their dissatisfaction," recalls Frank Abrams. "They had been 'left out of things.'" The point to be noted here is that not every president could have done that. This president obviously had the "something" it takes to put a man across with his employees. And the gradual cultivation of that something is one of the unfinished tasks ahead of management.

This fundamental point is met, and is combined with material incentives, by the "participation" school, which is growing, and whose most promising development is that fostered by Joseph Scanlon of M.I.T. The Scanlon approach actually brings the worker into the enterprise system by giving him a share in productivity decisions and a cut in productivity profits. Since January, 1950, at least a dozen firms, including Stromberg-Carlson of Rochester, New York, have adopted the Scanlon system, and many more are preparing for it. This approach can hardly fail to revolutionize American industrial relations and thus carry further the great transformation in which American capitalism is engaged.

How well American management has actually done by its employees is a question that leads to inevitable debate. The fact is incontestable, however, that it has done better than management anywhere else — and, for that matter, better than management ever dreamed it could, under the old form of capitalism. The problem, indeed, may be to prevent management from becoming over-generous. For when a company distributes employee benefits that are not compensated by rising productivity, it must in the long run pass the cost increase on to the consumer. Obviously a company *can* be tempted to win employee cooperation easily; a few producers and a single union can combine to gang up on the public.

Thus far, however, it is the modern manager's sense of responsibility to his customer and the general public that gives him his best claim to being progressive. More goods at lower costs (and prices) is the basic principle of American industry, and even companies regarded as anything but socially-minded have built themselves upon it. Many a chemical, for example, has been sold at a progressively lower price without the spur of competition, simply to encourage the market. And most modern managers do worry a good deal about the related subjects of prices, monopoly, and competition. Competition has come a long way since the time of Lord Dewar, who cracked that " competition is the life of trade, and competition is the death of profits." The alternatives today are not monopoly or all-out competition. The Darwinian concept of all-out competition has given way to the concept of pragmatic or " workable " competition, which, far from being the death of profits, provides, as smart companies know, the soundest way to ensure survival.

Aside from its value as a foil to antitrust, which can be exaggerated, healthy, workable competition provides a good check on how a company is doing. Take du Pont, which, though almost unique, may well set a precedent. Pursued by the hounds of antitrust (unjustly, it maintains), du Pont spent more than a year looking for a competitor willing to put $20 million into a cellophane plant. Having found one in Olin industries, it is building the plant for Olin and supplying the necessary technical assistance. And that is not all. Because du Pont was the only market source for sodium metal, it induced National Distillers to make the stuff. And recently it turned over its nylon patents to the Chemstrand Co.

Other companies have learned that a similar self-discipline is the best price policy in the long run. The recent furor about rolling back the prices of automobiles obscures the fact that the automobile companies had conducted themselves with a notable respect for public opinion. Had they let the law of supply and demand take its course in the sellers' market of the past four or five years, they could have priced their cars much higher. Their dealers, it is true, sometimes did extract a premium from eager buyers. But it was the manufacturers' list prices that in the main determined the price level, and the auto makers' refusal to charge what the traffic would bear must be reckoned as an extraordinary example of the transformation of the capitalistic mind.

One of the most pressing concerns of almost every large company today is what people are going to think about it. Board meetings often turn into self-examination sessions, with managers defending or explaining their actions as if before accusing judges. At a recent board meeting of a large consumer-goods company, the president rose up and remarked that the foremen had in effect built up a block between management and labor, and that management was mostly at fault. Fully two hours were devoted to soul-searching and discussion. There was also the matter of closing an old mill in a small town. Not only was the specific situation explored thoroughly, but the history of other similar cases was brought up. This problem was solved, after a full hour's discussion, by the decision to move a storage plant into the town and thus absorb nearly all the displaced employees. As one executive remarked, "At least half our time is taken up with discussing the repercussions of what we propose to do. And this is what the boys who write the books call the managerial revolution."

What may set a new high in business' concern with fundamental values and questions is a current project of Corning Glass Works, which is celebrating its centennial in 1951. On the premise that "As long as there are men making and operating machines, there will be a humanistic problem as well as a scientific and technological problem in an industrial society." Corning has joined the American Council of Learned Societies in sponsoring a conference on "Living in Industrial Civilization." The conference was held in May, 1951, at the Corning Glass Center, and attended by academicians and men of affairs from all over the world. They discussed such topics as Work and Human Values; Leisure and Human Values; the Individual's Sense of Community; Confidence in Life.

Nothing perhaps is more indicative of the corporation's awareness of its responsibilities than the growth of public-relations activities. Upwards of 4,000 companies now go in for public-relations "programs." Although many of them are hardly more than publicity campaigns, more and more managers understand tolerably well that good business public relations is good perform-

ance publicly appreciated, because adequately communicated. Now the mere comprehension of a moral axiom, as all parents know, does not guarantee its observance. But its constant reiteration does make the subject more and more acutely aware of its importance, and thus eventually influences his behavior. As Paul Garrett of G.M. has been saying for years, "Our program is finding out what people like, doing more of it; finding out what people don't like, doing less of it."

All of which should not be interpreted to mean that business is already rolling us down the six-lane, high-speed highway to economic paradise. We have concerned ourselves here with the pace-setters of American management, and do not presume to imply that all managers and all other companies are doing as well. Many still give precedence to the big, quick profit. Many incline to regard the stockholder mainly as a convenient personification of the profit goal, labor as a lamentably sensitive kind of commodity, and the customer as the man who gets rolled. Like many a labor and agricultural leader, these businessmen try to increase their share of the national product regardless of their contribution to that product. What Professor Wilcox calls Big (or organized) Little Business, for example, is responsible for or protected by most of the fair-trade laws, licensing systems, local bidding laws, and other legal devices that maintain prices independently of the market.

Big Business, too, has something to answer for. Just how much power it has, for example, to fix prices, and to what extent it uses or abuses that power are right now the subjects of much expert contention. Some economists maintain that "Oligopoly is by all evidence the ruling market form in the modern economy" — i.e., since the nation's corporate assets are concentrated in a relatively few companies, the market is made up of a few sellers, who can administer prices. Other economists, attacking the statistics on which such conclusions are based, maintain that only 20 per cent of the national income is provided by unregulated monopoly, and that an analysis of competition in terms of market realities, which nobody has yet completed, will show that the American economy is be-

coming more, not less, competitive. It is hoped that such an important analysis will be undertaken soon. But whatever its results, it is not likely to reveal that business, socially speaking, has yet attained perfection.

What counts, however, is that certain business leaders *are* setting the pace, and *are* being followed. What counts is that old concept that the owner has a right to use his property just the way he pleases has evolved into the belief that ownership carries social obligations, and that a manager is a trustee not only for the owner but for society as a whole. Such is the Transformation of American Capitalism. In all the world there is no more hopeful economic phenomenon.

7 THE SOCIAL CONSEQUENCES OF INDUSTRIALIZATION

38. The Price and the Problems of Industrialization

The industrialization of the Western world increased the income of nations many times, but it was not an unmixed blessing. Although income abounded it was distributed unequally — the few received the lion's share and the many the scraps. If the inequality of income were attributable solely to the varying inherent capacities of men to contribute to society, one might not be concerned about inequality. But such is not the case. Income also is gained through inheritance, the inside tip, the exploitation of monopoly power, the influencing of public officials, and even mere chance, none of which are necessarily related to man's inherent abilities.

Although morally offensive to many, income inequality does not yield gracefully to social policy because it is integrally related to the production of income. The capitalistic market, through which the West industrialized, inculcates in man money and material values and must therefore reckon with these values in motivating man. There is some strategic point beyond which reductions in the degree of income inequality will impair the capacity of society to produce income.

If income has been unequally distributed it also has been unstable. Periodic crises have haunted the path of capitalistic development, now throwing workers out of employment, then diminishing their real income through inflation. These crises are inherent in the pure system of Western capitalism because the crucial decisions that determine the level of income and employment are made by all the people who meet as buyers and sellers in the markets. In other words, choice is decentralized, and so it can only be chance that causes the thousands of decisions made to yield the correct solution from the point of view of the maintenance of income. Yet the very decentralization of decision-making, which causes income instability, is the strength of the system in terms of maximizing the freedom of individuals.

Perhaps even more serious are the agglomerations of private power, which have grown in the wake of industrialization. Business has expanded horizontally and vertically,

351

exerting monopoly power over consumers and suppliers of resources. In response labor has organized, and a relatively few union leaders wield the collective power of millions of workers. Not to be outdone the farmer has formed organizations to seek ends which he cannot attain by himself. Indeed the outstanding characteristic of the modern industrial age is the growth of groupism. Only the consumer has been unable to avail himself effectively of the organized power of groups.

Private power blocs are a threat to democratic society because they are in a position, as they pursue their own ends to negate public policy. Society, having determined a course of action through the democratic political process, may find its course thwarted by the struggle of private interests. Thus the United States is hard put to maintain the stability of the price level in the face of the insistent upward pressures on costs and prices that seem to follow from the collective bargaining procedure between labor and management.

Underlying all these economic consequences of industrialization is an abrupt shift in population patterns. The urban population has expanded relative to the rural population, for the increasing productivity of agricultural production and the expanding demand of industry for labor has permitted the movement of workers from the farm to the city.

The city itself is almost as old as the history of man. What is new in industrial society is the concentration of population in cities — approximately one-quarter of the people in the United States live in the top ten metropolitan areas of the country (ranging from New York City to Washington, D.C.). So great is the magnitude of this change that it has brought to society a new way of life — urbanism.

The urban way of life is the symbol of industrial society. It contains the harsh contrast between slum and penthouse. It forces people into close physical association and yet destroys the social intimacies that bind families in rural communities. It segments and departmentalizes man so that he must move from one role to another, constantly shifting as it were the gears of his personality. The urban way of life undermines the community and the community spirit which can integrate man into society and make him feel part of something that is permanent and lasting. Or conversely, the urban way of life turns the individual loose in the welter and confusion of a depersonalized existence.

The first article in this chapter by Robert L. Heibroner describes the pattern of income distribution in the United States of the mid-twentieth century. The remaining articles are devoted to the urban way of life, which is perhaps the most dramatic focus of income inequality in the United States today. Louis Wirth (1897–1952), late Professor of Sociology at the University of Chicago, describes the social organization of the city in his article, *Urbanism as a Way of Life*. In *The Gold Coast and the Slum*, Harvey W. Zorbaugh graphically depicts the striking and cruel contrasts between the dwellings of the rich and the dwellings of the poor. He also discusses urban morphology and tries to uncover the basic structure of urban organization. Finally, we include a selection by Dr. Erich Fromm which, employing the psychoanalytic approach, analyzes the influence of the urban way of life on the personality of the individual.

39. The American Poor *

IN 1948 — A YEAR WE ARE GOING TO look back on fondly for quite a few to come — a hundred and forty-odd million Americans, digging and blasting, making and planting, clipping coupons, cornering markets, and begging on street corners, pulled down the staggering total personal income of $212,000,000,000.

If 212 billion is too large a number for you to imagine comfortably, you can settle for the fact that we received the largest amount of purchasing power ever distributed in any nation in history and that our average standard of living was the highest ever achieved by any civilization of which we know.

All that is true and very reassuring.

But at the same time that our aggregate national income was making us the economic wonder of the age, these facts about our national state of well-being were also true and somewhat less reassuring:

One out of every two single-dwelling individuals lived on less than $1,000.

One family out of 10 got along —

* From Robert L. Heilbroner, " Who Are The American Poor? ", *Harper's Magazine*, June 1950, pp. 27–33. Reprinted by permission.

to the extent that a family could get along — on $20 a week or less.

Out of 40 million families in the nation, 10 million shared in the greatest boom in history with an income of less than $40 a week — just over $13 per person.

These alarming statements should put you in a frame of mind to examine a curious table of statistics: the distribution of income among American families and individuals in 1948. . . .

It is an odd picture, both impressive and disturbing. Here is an industrial society that not so many years ago would have been thought Utopian: the better-off actually outnumber the poor. Here is the only society with a mass market for luxury goods: there are more Americans with incomes over $5,000 than the total populations of Canada and Australia put together. Here is also an unresolved hard core of poverty which in 1948 limited one-quarter of our citizens to a standard of living far short of that which we required for our national health, our social morale, or the mass market necessary to keep our farms and factories running at full production.

It is because our total national income is so large that the thinness of 30 million slices of the income cake at the bottom is disturbing and provoking.

What is disturbing is not that there is poverty in America — everyone with eyes to see knows that for himself. The provoking fact is that there is so much poverty, so much

vide a decent living for so large a fraction of its citizens.

One final word. You will want to know how much credence to place in the statistics themselves. They are the facts reported by a subcommittee of the Joint Committee on the Economic Report of the Congress of the United States, a subcommit-

THE DISTRIBUTION OF INCOME IN THE UNITED STATES IN 1948

Total Income received during the year	Total number of families	Total single individuals, not living with families	Total number of people (family members plus individuals)
Under $1,000	4,020,000	4,090,000	16,220,000
$1,000–$2,000	5,580,000	1,830,000	20,060,000
$2,000–$3,000	7,950,000	1,240,000	28,470,000
$3,000–$5,000	12,970,000	810,000	
$5,000–$10,000	6,900,000	140,000	76,260,000
Over $10,000	1,110,000	30,000	

marginal living amidst so much plenty. One child in five lives in the heap of families in the bottom two layers of the nation's pile of incomes; something like five elderly persons out of ten scrimp along on a level well below the needs, not to say the rights, of the aged. . . .

But there is no point in dramatizing further the fact that the statistical picture of America differs a good deal from the advertising man's conception of it. Nor are we ready for panaceas or polemics or politicking. These are unpleasant facts, to be sure, but before we lose our balance in outraged indignation, let us inquire why a country as rich and productive as our own can yet fail to pro-

tee which is looking into the question of our low-income families. The data have been gathered by the Bureau of the Census. . . .

At the bottom of the nation's pile of incomes lie nearly ten million families and almost six million individuals whose earnings in 1948 averaged under — well under — $40 a week. But low incomes are all these people seem to have in common. For if you should take a family or an individual at random and look behind the bare statistics of their wealth, you would probably find that you were looking at Americans in one or more of six quite separate social or economic groups:

They Might Be Rural Poor. Just

where the threshold of rural poverty lies is not an easy thing to say: $2,000 goes a lot further in rural Abilene, Kansas, than in urban Albany, New York, and most farm families provide some of their own food (not all, by a long shot) and usually they own their own homes and pay no rent. . . .

But I think we can agree that an income of $1,000 is too little to keep a farming family of even the simplest tastes in decent food and clothing and medicine — not to mention feed and seed. There are over 1,700,000 farm families with incomes under that, a quarter of them with five or more mouths to feed. Counting only rural Americans with less than $1,000 income, there are well over six million farming poor — blacks, whites, sharecroppers, Dust Bowlers, tenants.

They Might Be Aged. Four and one-half million families in the United States are headed by a person over 65 (who is not just " living with the family ") and there are another two million single older folk who must live on what they make or get. *One out of every four elderly families and two out of every three single older men or women got along in 1948 on less than $20 a week.* The Social Security Administration tells us that in June 1949 there were a quarter of a million Old-Age beneficiaries subsisting on less than $500! Here is one such case:

After working 33 years for the same company as a marble-worker, Mr. N. quit his job because of failing health and became entitled to monthly (Old-Age) benefits of $10.93. The benefici-ary, who is a widower, lives alone in an attic apartment for which he pays $10 a month rent. During the survey year he received $229 from public assistance and the payment of a $10 doctor bill by a lodge. He stated he needs more medical assistance but hesitates to ask for more as he feels he is getting enough from public assistance. The beneficiary's only asset is a $200 bank account and a life-insurance policy with a face value of $250 on which he is still paying premiums.

They Might Be Negroes. Five million Negroes — mostly not on the farm — crowd into families in the brackets under $2,000; two of the five million have only half of that. Not only is the Negro poor, but the fact that his chances for advancement are so closely circumscribed more or less condemns him to a permanent continuance of his marginal economic status.

They Might Be Broken Families. No one knows exactly how many broken families are to be found in America — families headed by a widowed or deserted or divorced parent or even by an oldest child. We do know that out of 6.3 million urban families with incomes of less than $2,000, 1.5 million were headed by women, and that half a million of these families (with over one million children) depended in whole or in part on relief to stay alive. Even worse, half of these families on relief had total incomes of under $1,000.

They Might Be Disabled. Disabled people — industrial casualties, social derelicts, the mentally and physically ill — number at any time about 4,500,000 people — and that excludes both the aged and the very young. Many of the disabled are living on charity, others are using up their savings; too many are destitute. About one-third of the pool will mend its strength, rejoin the working force, and leave the lowest income brackets; another third will move up the economic scale *if* it receives the rehabilitative training that it needs. A final third — one and a half million people — will be wards of the community as long as they are alive.

Or They Might Belong to a Sixth Group. . . . But the sixth group is different because it is not the victim of social circumstances. It is simply a group that fails to earn a decent keep because the jobs it does are not sufficiently productive to warrant a decent wage.

In 1948, for every four workers who earned over one dollar for an hour of work in a manufacturing industry, there was one worker who did not. Aside from the truly marginal jobs — the sweepers and the janitors and the cleaning women — here is just a sample of a few low-wage industries:

PERCENTAGE OF WORKERS MAKING LESS THAN $1 PER HOUR

Men's seamless hosiery business
male workers 48%
female workers   84

Fertilizer plants
all workers   69

Grain-milling industry
all workers   54

Wood furniture industry
all workers   60

Men's shoe industry
male workers   30
female workers   64

And these are only small and scattered segments of our industrial machine. There are the tobacco plants where the *average* wage in 1950 was under $40. Among the poorest paid jobs in the country are broad sections of the textile industry, the hotel industry, the retail stores, the cleaning and dyeing industry, and still others.

If you take an average low-income American and look behind the statistics, that is the picture you are likely to see. Not that all poor Americans fall into these categories or that there are not other contributing or principal causes of poverty: merely consider the fact that one-third of the people heading our 10 million lowest-income families never went beyond grade school. But these half-dozen categories will help us comprehend the basic shapes in which our poverty is manifested, and we will find them useful in analyzing more fully the strange co-existence of prosperity and scanty living.

Now we must look more deeply still. For although poverty is poverty, it makes a difference what *kind* of poverty we face when we seek to find a remedy for our ills. Penicillin is of little use to a man with arthritis and a wholesale dose of public works may likewise be of slight value to an economy with encysted pockets of tenant farmers and indigent older folk.

.   .   .

Poverty is nothing new to us Americans; we still have clear memories of breadlines and Hoovervilles and the stagnation of the thirties. But this poverty of which we have written is different. For in 1948 — to all intents and purposes — there was no large-scale unemployment in America. At any time during the year the number of people without jobs averaged just over two million, and this included the normal shifting about from job to job as well as the irreducible burden of the unemployables. It was rock-bottom unemployment for a dynamic economy.

So the fact that we suffered poverty amidst plenty was not an indictment of a system which did not work. On the contrary, from the point of view of the number of job opportunities offered, it never worked better. This was poverty that resulted from bumping up against the hard physical limits of an economy which many of us think of as incredibly bountiful and inexhaustibly rich.

It isn't. Despite our billions of dollars of aggregate income, we are cramped and bound and sharply limited in the amount of real wealth we can scrape up and fashion from the resources at our command.

Nor is this an indictment of our distributive system. Fifty-five per cent of us lived on more than $3,000 a year — a figure that may seem modest enough, but which represents a new epoch in economic engineering. And although the few who were very rich received far more than the many who were very poor, the fact remains that many of the lower-income groups were subsidized by the transferred incomes of the wealthy. If it can truthfully be said that not many moguls could justify their enormous (pre-tax) incomes before a court of social justice, it can also be maintained that many a typist, many a delivery-boy, many a salesgirl was grossly overpaid in that year of superboom, in terms of the services which they actually rendered the community.

No, the distributive system was not too bad, and after taxes it was better yet. The fault must lie some where else.

The fault — if it is a fault, for no one is directly responsible — is not spectacular. It lies partly in the fact that our economy has not moved forward at an even pace throughout the ranks, that there have been laggard sectors that have failed to keep up with the general advance toward a better way of life. By now some of these sluggish backwaters of inactivity are almost detached from the rush of the main current. The old and the disabled, the victims of discrimination and rural isolation and decay, these and other groups will for many years need programs of special care if they are to share in our national prosperity. Few of us have squarely faced the scope and extent that these programs (if they are to be effective) must necessarily attain.

But there is another reason for our plight.

That reason is the low level of

productivity at the bottom of the economic pyramid. By productivity I do not mean industriousness; low productivity does not just come from lazy backwoods farmers and unskilled workers who do nothing but lean on their shovels. Productivity means the ability to produce; and the ability to produce, in this industrialized world, means a chance to work with capital goods, with equipment and machines. After all, no one works harder than the Asiatic peasant who toils all day to stay alive. And yet no one is less productive. Add a little capital — in the shape of a bullock — to the primitive farmer, and watch his output shoot up 10- and 20-fold. Add a couple of machines to our ditch-diggers and they will become crane operators, our share-croppers will become combine mechanics.

And underneath the whole, behind the 10 million neediest cases, the misfits and the unproductive workers, lies the basic fact of scarcity. For what we are stricken with — at the lower levels of our economic structure — is the same disease that is eating all the world: a shortage of productive apparatus. We Americans — the most prodigious capital-builders the world has ever known — still lack the wealth — the real, hard, physical wealth, not the stocks and bonds — to make us all productive. And because the capital we have is unevenly spread from trade to trade, some sectors of the nation are badly undeveloped. Three-quarters of America has grown to an impressive stature; it can not only sustain itself in style but help the outside

world as well. A laggard fourth remains. And in that fourth are not just those whose plight is age or weakness or ill health. There are also those for whom there is insufficient steel or electricity or education or managerial skill to raise them to the level of the rest.

So much for diagnosis. The question that interests us now is what to do. It is easier perhaps to point out what we should *not* do. This is no simple matter of patching a leak and pumping air into a deflated economy as we did back in the thirties: let us not rely too much on the medicines of public works and work relief. For the depression gave us a different sort of poverty from the round pegs and square holes and economic zeros we have been describing. The thirties gave us the poverty of idle men and idle machines; what we have now is the poverty that is left over when everything is running at top speed. There is a time for public pumping — but not when our economy is fully inflated to begin with, for the chances are that we would pump three-quarters of us higher and leave the bottom quarter sitting where it is. Do not forget that in 1948 the searching pressures of thousands of booming enterprises could not harness the abilities or use to much advantage the labor of one-quarter of the nation. What reason is there to suppose the blunter instrument of public works would succeed where the varied ends and impetus of private enterprise have not?

And let us be wary of another

tempting cure: the cure of national charity and relief. For alleviating poverty is not curing it, and there is a vast deal of difference between supporting the underprivileged and making it possible for them to support themselves. No matter how fancily we wield the fiscal knife, thinner slicing does not make a bigger pie, nor does fairer sharing provide a substitute for self-support. There is a need for sharing and a need for help, but merely spreading incomes thinner does not make us richer than we are.

The disagreeable fact is that for this poverty of scarcity there are no miracle drugs. But that does not mean that nothing can be done — far from it. It means we need tonics more potent than relief and more specific than mere pumping, and that we must distinguish palliatives from cures.

Take, for example, the problem of our rural poor. We can help the blighted farmer by jacking up the prices of the crops he grows. . . . But for most of us it is nothing but a transfer of wealth from the nation at large to one small corner of it; if the potato-growers are better off, it is because our income taxes have made them so.

But we can help the farmer in another way. When we bring in power to counties which have been without electric lights or pumps or generators, when we upgrade an entire region with a TVA, when we curb floods, terrace slopes, revitalize the soil — that is welfare of a different sort. That's the sort of welfare that does more than prop the farmer up: it puts him on his own two feet.

Or think about the question of our aged. We can face up to the problem of indigent old age by ladling out purchasing power with Old-Age Benefits and we can buy options on the future with old-age pension schemes. . . .

But can we do nothing better than give the old a helping taken from the plates of others? We are not as young a nation as we were and the curve of average age is moving up: there is a limit to what we can afford. Already in Louisiana four-fifths of all the aged depend on Old-Age Benefits to get along; humanitarian considerations aside, these old folk are little more than economic parasites.

Is it not possible to have our aged *contribute* to our national wealth at the same time that we gladly contribute to their welfare? For example could we not — as Professor Slichter has suggested — pay to those employers who keep older workers on the job a portion of the Old-Age pensions the government would save? Surely everyone might benefit from such a plan. And can we not find part-time work and special tasks to tap the earning power of those who want to supplement the pittance of government support? There must be some better way of using our old workers than making them night watchmen — and it is these better ways that we must plan (business and union leaders willing) if old age itself is to help us bear the cost of growing old.

It is apparent that the disabled need retraining if they are to generate their own support: yet in 1948 we rehabilitated only 50,000 and left 1,500,000 on relief. And the Negro needs a foothold too: how can we build a market up when we hold a twelfth of the nation down? . . .

But there is one group that we cannot help with welfare — the workers at the margin who do not earn enough. For while we can bolster up the chambermaids, the millhands, and the bellhops by legislating higher minimum wages, we cannot legislate 10 millions at the margin into better jobs. And while we can encourage the exploited to form unions, and pave the roadway of advance with wider education, we shall not budge the economic margin by these means alone. It is the stubborn lack of productivity that must be remedied, for higher wages without higher output may only price the worker at the margin out of any job at all.

To raise the margin, to make 10 million better jobs, we have to grow. And growth is not an economic process that we can take for granted.

. . . .

Our economy may be mature, but it is far from senile; perhaps it was the shock of the depression that made us myopic toward our past and caused us to forget the history of American production. For if any single feature characterizes our past 100 years, it has been growth. Since 1850 we have given jobs to 50 million workers, cut their working time by nearly half, and upped the output of each man by 600 per cent.

And our technology has not lost its vigor: since the end of the war we have engineered at least two new *industries* — plastics and television — and the incalculable investment opportunities of an atomic age are dimly visible for the future. . . .

But the fact that growth can give us what we need does not mean that we should lean back and wait for our salvation. *If* we keep on growing at our present pace — 2 per cent per year — we *can* double our real earnings in our lifetimes, and before the next decade is out the average family *can* enjoy an income of $5,000. The opportunities for growth are there: the man who operates a bulldozer worked with pick and shovel yesterday, and the man behind the hoe today *can* some day sit behind a tractor. The troubling challenge is whether we will *in fact* push against our boundaries.

And for that no complacent answer can be given.

For the real danger is that we will lose the fight against our poverty by default; not because our motors fail to deliver enough power, but because we fail to run them to capacity. Growth will only be a tantalizing vista unless we march resolutely down the road; if we do not find the sticks and carrots to keep us on the march, the problem of our poverty will be infinitely worse. We are the richest nation that the world has ever known, and yet we are not rich enough to give us all a decent living. If America at full production has 30 million poor, how will we fare at three-quarters speed ahead?

40. Urban Society*

The beginning of what is distinctively modern in our civilization is best signalized by the growth of great cities. Nowhere has mankind been further removed from organic nature than under the conditions of life characteristic of great cities. . . . The distinctive feature of the mode of living of man in the modern age is his concentration into gigantic aggregations around which cluster lesser centers and from which radiate the ideas and practices that we call civilization.

The degree to which the contemporary world may be said to be " urban " is not fully or accurately measured by the proportion of the total population living in cities. The influences which cities exert upon the social life of man are greater than the ratio of the urban population would indicate, for the city is not only in ever larger degrees the dwelling-place and the workshop of modern man, but it is the initiating and controlling center of economic, political, and cultural life. . . .

The shift from a rural to a predominantly urban society, which has taken place within the span of a single generation in such industrialized areas as the United States and Japan, has been accompanied by profound changes in virtually every phase of social life. . . . Since the city is the product of growth rather

* From Louis Wirth, " Urbanism as a Way of Life," The American Journal of Sociology, Vol. 44 (July 1938), pp. 1–3, 10–17, 21–23. Reprinted by permission.

than of instantaneous creation, it is to be expected that the influences which it exerts upon the modes of life should not be able to wipe out completely the previously dominant modes of human association. To a greater or lesser degree, therefore, our social life bears the imprint of an earlier folk society, the characteristic modes of settlement of which were the farm, the manor, and the village. This historic influence is reinforced by the circumstance that the population of the city itself is in large measure recruited from the countryside, where a mode of life reminiscent of this earlier form of existence persists. Hence we should not expect to find abrupt and discontinuous variation between urban and rural types of personality. . . .

Since the population of the city does not reproduce itself, it must recruit its migrants from other cities, the countryside, and — in this country until recently — from other countries. The city has thus historically been the melting-pot of races, peoples, and cultures, and a most favorable breeding-ground of new biological and cultural hybrids. It has not only tolerated but rewarded individual differences. It has brought together people from the ends of the earth *because* they are different and thus useful to one another, rather than because they are homogeneous and like-minded. . . .

The bonds of kinship, of neighborliness, and the sentiments arising out

of living together for generations under a common folk tradition are
likely to be absent or, at best, relatively weak in an aggregate the
members of which have such diverse
origins and backgrounds. Under
such circumstances competition and
formal control mechanisms furnish
the substitutes for the bonds of solidarity that are relied upon to hold a
folk society together. . . .

The multiplication of persons in a
state of interaction under conditions
which make their contact as full personalities impossible produces that
segmentalization of human relationships which has sometimes been
seized upon by students of the mental life of the cities as an explanation
for the " schizoid " character of urban
personality. This is not to say that
the urban inhabitants have fewer acquaintances than rural inhabitants,
for the reverse may actually be true;
it means rather that in relation to the
number of people whom they see and
with whom they rub elbows in the
course of daily life, they know a
smaller proportion, and of these they
have less intensive knowledge.

Characteristically, urbanites meet
one another in highly segmental
roles. They are, to be sure, dependent upon more people for the satisfactions of their life-needs than are
rural people and thus are associated
with a greater number of organized
groups, but they are less dependent
upon particular persons, and their
dependence upon others is confined
to a highly fractionalized aspect of
the other's round of activity. This is
essentially what is meant by saying
that the city is characterized by sec-

ondary rather than primary contacts.
The contacts of the city may indeed
be face to face, but they are nevertheless impersonal, superficial, transitory, and segmental. The reserve,
the indifference, and the blasé outlook which urbanites manifest in
their relationships may thus be regarded as devices for immunizing
themselves against the personal
claims and expectations of others.

The superficiality, the anonymity,
and the transitory character of urban-
social relations make intelligible,
also, the sophistication and the rationality generally ascribed to city-
dwellers. Our acquaintances tend to
stand in a relationship of utility to
us in the sense that the role which
each one plays in our life is overwhelmingly regarded as a means for
the achievement of our own ends.
Whereas, therefore, the individual
gains, on the one hand, a certain degree of emancipation or freedom
from the personal and emotional controls of intimate groups, he loses, on
the other hand, the spontaneous self-
expression, the morale, and the sense
of participation that comes with living in an integrated society. This
constitutes essentially the state of
anomie or the social void to which
Durkheim alludes in attempting to
account for the various forms of social disorganization in technological
society.

The segmental character and utilitarian accent of interpersonal relations in the city find their institutional expression in the proliferation
of specialized tasks which we see in
their most developed form in the
professions. The operation of the

pecuniary nexus leads to predatory relationships, which tend to obstruct the efficient functioning of the social order unless checked by professional codes and occupational etiquette. The premium put upon utility and efficiency suggests the adaptability of the corporate device for the organization of enterprises in which individuals can engage only in groups. The advantage that the corporation has over the individual entrepreneur and the partnership in the urban-industrial world derives not only from the possibility it affords of centralizing the resources of thousands of individuals or from the legal privilege of limited liability and perpetual succession, but from the fact that the corporation has no soul.

The specialization of individuals, particularly in their occupations, can proceed only, as Adam Smith pointed out, upon the basis of an enlarged market, which in turn accentuates the division of labor. This enlarged market is only in part supplied by the city's hinterland; in large measure it is found among the large numbers that the city itself contains. The dominance of the city over the surrounding hinterland becomes explicable in terms of the division of labor which urban life occasions and promotes. The extreme degree of interdependence and the unstable equilibrium of urban life are closely associated with the division of labor and the specialization of occupations. This interdependence and instability is increased by the tendency of each city to specialize in those functions in which it has the greatest advantage.

In a community composed of a larger number of individuals than can know one another intimately and can be assembled in one spot, it becomes necessary to communicate through indirect mediums and to articulate individual interests by a process of delegation. Typically in the city, interests are made effective through representation. The individual counts for little, but the voice of the representative is heard with a deference roughly proportional to the numbers for whom he speaks. . . .

On the subjective side, as Simmel has suggested, the close physical contact of numerous individuals necessarily produces a shift in the mediums through which we orient ourselves to the urban milieu, especially to our fellow-men. Typically, our physical contacts are close but our social contacts are distant. The urban world puts a premium on visual recognition. We see the uniform which denotes the role of the functionaries and are oblivious to the personal eccentricities that are hidden behind the uniform. We tend to acquire and develop a sensitivity to a world of artifacts and become progressively farther removed from the world of nature.

We are exposed to glaring contrasts between splendor and squalor, between riches and poverty, intelligence and ignorance, order and chaos. The competition for space is great, so that each area generally tends to be put to the use which yields the greatest economic return. Place of work tends to become dissociated from place of residence, for the proximity of industrial and commercial establishments makes an area both economically and socially undesirable for residential purposes. . . .

The different parts of the city thus acquire specialized functions. The city consequently tends to resemble a mosaic of social worlds in which the transition from one to the other is abrupt. The juxtaposition of divergent personalities and modes of life tends to produce a relativistic perspective and a sense of toleration of differences which may be regarded as prerequisites for rationality and which lead toward the secularization of life.[1]

The close living together and working together of individuals who have no sentimental and emotional ties foster a spirit of competition, aggrandizement, and mutual exploitation. To counteract irresponsibility and potential disorder, formal controls tend to be resorted to. Without rigid adherence to predictable routines a large compact society would scarcely be able to maintain itself. The clock and the traffic signal are symbolic of the basis of our social order in the urban world. Frequent close physical contact, coupled with great social distance, accentuates the reserve of unattached individuals toward one another and, unless compensated for by other opportunities

[1] The extent to which the segregation of the population into distinct ecological and cultural areas and the resulting social attitude of tolerance, rationality, and secular mentality are functions of density as distinguished from heterogeneity is difficult to determine. Most likely we are dealing here with phenomena which are consequences of the simultaneous operation of both factors.

for response, gives rise to loneliness. The necessary frequent movement of great numbers of individuals in a congested habitat gives occasion to friction and irritation. Nervous tensions which derive from such personal frustrations are accentuated by the rapid tempo and the complicated technology under which life in dense areas must be lived.

The social interaction among such a variety of personality types in the urban milieu tends to break down the rigidity of caste lines and to complicate the class structure, and thus induces a more ramified and differentiated framework of social stratification than is found in more integrated societies. The heightened mobility of the individual, which brings him within the range of stimulation by a great number of diverse individuals and subjects him to fluctuating status in the differentiated social groups that compose the social structure of the city, tends toward the acceptance of instability and insecurity in the world at large as a norm. This fact helps to account, too, for the sophistication and cosmopolitanism of the urbanite. No single group has the undivided allegiance of the individual. The groups with which he is affiliated do not lend themselves readily to a simple hierarchical arrangement. By virtue of his different interests arising out of different aspects of social life, the individual acquires membership in widely divergent groups, each of which functions only with reference to a single segment of his personality. . . .

Partly as a result of the physical

footlooseness of the population and partly as a result of their social mobility, the turnover in group membership generally is rapid. Place of residence, place and character of employment, income and interests fluctuate, and the task of holding organizations together and maintaining and promoting intimate and lasting acquaintanceship between the members is difficult. This applies strikingly to the local areas within the city into which persons become segregated more by virtue of difference in race, language, income, and social status, than through choice or positive attraction to people like themselves. Overwhelmingly the city-dweller is not a home-owner, and since a transitory habitat does not generate binding traditions and sentiments, only rarely is he truly a neighbor. There is little opportunity for the individual to obtain a conception of the city as a whole or to survey his place in the total scheme. Consequently he finds it difficult to determine what is to his own "best interests" and to decide between the issues and leaders presented to him by the agencies of mass suggestion. Individuals who are thus detached from the organized bodies which integrate society comprise the fluid masses that make collective behavior in the urban community so unpredictable and hence so problematical. . . .

The low and declining urban-reproduction rates suggest that the city is not conducive to the traditional type of family life, including the rearing of children and the maintenance of the home as the locus of a whole round of vital activities. The transfer of industrial, educational, and recreational activities to specialized institutions outside the home has deprived the family of some of its most characteristic historical functions. In cities mothers are more likely to be employed, lodgers are more frequently part of the household, marriage tends to be postponed, and the proportion of single and unattached people is greater. Families are smaller and more frequently without children than in the country. The family as a unit of social life is emancipated from the larger kinship group characteristic of the country, and the individual members pursue their own diverging interests in their vocational, educational, religious, recreational, and political life. . . .

On the whole, the city discourages an economic life in which the individual in time of crisis has a basis of subsistence to fall back upon, and it discourages self-employment. While incomes of city people are on the average higher than those of country people, the cost of living seems to be higher in the larger cities. Home ownership involves greater burdens and is rarer. Rents are higher and absorb a larger proportion of the income. Although the urban-dweller has the benefit of many communal services, he spends a large proportion of his income for such items as recreation and advancement and a smaller proportion for food. What the communal services do not furnish the urbanite must purchase, and there is virtually no human need which has remained unexploited by commercialism. Catering to thrills and furnishing means of escape from drudgery, monotony, and routine thus become two of the major functions of urban recreation, which at its best furnishes means for creative self-expression and spontaneous group association, but which more typically in the urban world results in passive spectatorism on the one hand, or sensational record-smashing feats on the other.

Being reduced to a stage of virtual impotence as an individual, the urbanite is bound to exert himself by joining with others of similar interest into organized groups to obtain his ends. This results in the enormous multiplication of voluntary organizations directed toward as great a variety of objectives as there are human needs and interests. While on the one hand the traditional ties of human association are weakened, urban existence involves a much greater degree of interdependence between man and man and a more complicated, fragile, and volatile form of mutual interrelations over many phases of which the individual as such can exert scarcely any control. Frequently there is only the most tenuous relationship between the economic position or other basic factors that determine the individual's existence in the urban world and the voluntary groups with which he is affiliated. . . .

It is largely through the activities of the voluntary groups . . . that the urbanite expresses and develops his personality, acquires status, and is able to carry on the round of activities that constitute his life-career. It may easily be inferred, however, that the organizational framework . . . does not of itself insure the consistency and integrity of the personalities whose interests it enlists. Personal disorganization, mental breakdown, suicide, delinquency, crime, corruption, and disorder might be expected under these circumstances to be more prevalent in the urban than in the rural community. This has been confirmed in so far as comparable indices are available.

41. The Skyscraper and the Community*

. . . . It is a veritable Babel, in which some thirty or more tongues are spoken. . . . Gunmen haunt its streets, and a murder is committed in them nearly every day in the year. It is smoke-ridden and disfigured by factories and railway yards, and many of

* From Harvey W. Zorbaugh, *The Gold Coast and the Slum,* pp. 1–13 and pp. 229–37. Reprinted by permission of the University of Chicago Press.

its streets are ill-paved. Moreover, the people who throng them are more carelessly dressed than those in Fifth Avenue, and their voices not so well modulated as those of the inhabitants of Boston. Their manners, too, are of the kind the New Yorker defines as western. — CHATFIELD-TAYLOR, *Chicago*

The Chicago River, its waters stained by industry, flows back upon itself, branching to divide the city into the South Side, the North Side, and " the great West Side." In the river's southward bend lies the Loop, its skyline looming toward Lake Michigan. The Loop is the heart of Chicago, the knot in the steel arteries of elevated structure which pump in a ceaseless stream the three millions of population of the city into and out of its central business district. The canyon-like streets of the Loop rumble with the traffic of commerce. On its sidewalks throng people of every nation, pushing unseeingly past one another, into and out of office buildings, shops, theaters, hotels, and ultimately back to the north, south, and west " sides " from which they came. For miles over what once was prairie now sprawls in endless blocks the city.

The city's conquest of the prairie has proceeded stride for stride with the development of transportation. The outskirts of the city have always been about forty-five minutes from the heart of the Loop. In the days of the horse-drawn car they were not beyond Twenty-second Street on the South Side. With the coming of the cable car they were extended to the vicinity of Thirty-sixth Street. The electric car — surface and elevated — again extended the city's outskirts, this time well past Seventieth Street. How far " rapid transit " will take them, no one can predict.

Apace with the expansion of the city has gone the ascendancy of the Loop. Every development in transportation, drawing increasing throngs of people into the central business district, has tended to centralize there not only commerce and finance, but all the vital activities of the city's life. The development of communication has further tightened the Loop's grip on the life of the city. The telephone has at once enormously increased the area over which the central business district can exert control and centralized that control. The newspaper, through the medium of advertising, has firmly established the supremacy of the Loop and, through the news, focused the attention of the city upon the Loop. The skyscraper is the visible symbol of the Loop's domination of the city's life. The central business district of the old city — like that of modern London — with its six- and eight-story buildings, sprawled over an unwieldy area. But the skyscraper, thrusting the Loop skyward thirty, forty, fifty stories, has made possible an extraordinary centralization and articulation of the central business district of the modern city. Drawing thousands daily into the heart of the city, where the old type of building drew hundreds, the cluster of skyscrapers within the Loop has become the city's vortex.

As the Loop expands it literally submerges the areas about it with the traffic of its commerce. Business and industry encroach upon residential neighborhoods. As the roar of traffic swells, and the smoke of industry begrimes buildings, land values rise. The old population moves slowly out, to be replaced by a mobile, shifting, anonymous population bringing with it transitional forms of social life. Within the looming shadow of the skyscraper, in Chicago as in every great city, is found a zone of instability and change — the tidelands of city life.

A part of these tidelands, within ten minutes' walk of the Loop and the central business district, within five minutes by streetcar or bus, just across the Chicago River, lies the Near North Side, sometimes called "North Town." Within this area, a mile and a half long and scarcely a mile wide, bounded by Lake Michigan on the east and by the Chicago River on the south and west, under the shadow of the Tribune Tower, a part of the inner city, live ninety thousand people, a population representing all the types and contrasts that lend to the great city its glamor and romance.

The first settlers of Chicago built upon the north bank of the Chicago River, and Chicago's first business house and first railroad were on Kinzie street. But early in Chicago's history destiny took its great commercial and industrial development southward, and for several decades the North Side was a residential district, well-to-do and fashionable. The story of early Chicago society centers about homes on Ohio, Erie, Cass, and Rush streets; and street after street of old stone fronts, curious streets some of them, still breathe an air of respectability reminiscent of earlier and better days and belying the slow conquest of the slum.

Here change has followed fast upon change. With the growth of the city commerce has encroached upon residential property, relentlessly pushing it northward or crowding it along the lake shore, until now the Near North Side is chequered with business streets. Into this area, where commerce is completing the conquest of the community, has crept the slum. Meantime great industries have sprung up along the river, and peoples speaking foreign tongues have come to labor in them. The slum has offered these alien peoples a place to live cheaply and to themselves; and wave upon wave of immigrants has swept over the area — Irish, Swedish, German, Italian, Persian, Greek, and Negro — forming colonies, staying for a while, then giving way to others. But each has left its impress and its stragglers, and today there live on the Near North Side twenty-nine or more nationalities, many of them with their Old World tongues and customs.

The city's streets can be read as can the geological record in the rock. The old stone fronts of the houses on the side streets; old residences along lower Rush and State, crowded between new business blocks, or with shops built along the street in front of them; a garage with "Riding Academy" in faded letters above its doors; the many old churches along La Salle and Dearborn streets; an office building growing out of a block of rooming-houses; "Deutsche Apotheke" on the window of a store in a neighborhood long since Italian — these are signs that record the changes brought about by the passing decades, changes still taking place today.

The Near North Side is an area of high light and shadow, of vivid contrasts — contrasts not only between the old and the new, between the native and the foreign, but between wealth and poverty, vice and respectability, the conventional and the bohemian, luxury and toil.

Variety is the spice of life, as depicted in the books of the Board of Assessors; autocracy and democracy mingle on the same pages; aphorisms are borne out; and "art for art's sake" remains the slogan of the twentieth century.

On one page of North District Book 18, the record of the worldly holdings of James C. Ewell, artist, 4 Ohio Street, is set down as "Total personal property, $19." So-and-so, artists, are reported thruout the district with this notation: "Attic room, ill-furnished, many paintings: unable to estimate."

The art colony is located in this section, as is the colony of the rich and the nearly rich. And on the same page are the following three entries which span the stream of life:

Cyrus H. McCormick, 50 E. Huron St., $895,000; taxable assessment, $447,-500.

Mary V. McCormick, 678 Rush St., $480,000; taxable assessment, $240,000.

And then — as another contrast — the following entry appears on record:

United States Senator Medill McCormick, guest at the Drake Hotel, $____,000,000,000.[2]

At the corner of Division Street and the Lake Shore Drive stands a tall apartment building in which seventeen-room apartments rent at one thousand dollars a month. One mile west, near Division Street and the river, Italian families are living in

[2] *Chicago Herald and Examiner,* July, 1923.

squalid basement rooms for which they pay six dollars a month. The greatest wealth in Chicago is concentrated along the Lake Shore Drive, in what is called the "Gold Coast." Almost at its back door, in "Little Hell," is the greatest concentration of poverty in Chicago. Respectability, it would seem, is measured by rentals and land values! [3]

The Near North Side is not merely an area of contrasts; it is an area of extremes. All the phenomena characteristic of the city are clearly segregated and appear in exaggerated form. Not only are there extremes of wealth and poverty. The Near North Side has the highest residential land values in the city, and among the lowest; it has more professional men, more politicians, more suicides, more persons in *Who's Who,* than any other "community" in Chicago.

The turgid stream of the Chicago River, which bounds the Near North Side on the south and the west, has played a prominent part in its history. A great deal of shipping once went up the river, and tugs, coal barges, tramp freighters, and occasional ore boats still whistle at its bridges and steam slowly around its bends. This shipping caused commerce and industry to locate along the river, and today wharves, lumber and coal yards, iron works, gas works, sheet metal works, light manufacturing plants and storage plants, wholesale houses for

[3] United Charities of Chicago: *Sixty Years of Service.* In 1920–21 there were 90 contributors to the United Charities in less than a square mile on the Gold Coast, and 460 poverty cases in the square mile behind it.

spices, furs, groceries, butter, and imported oils line both sides of the river for miles, and with the noise and smoke of the railroads make a great barrier that half encircles the Near North Side, renders the part of it along the river undesirable to live in, and slowly encroaches northward and eastward.

"North Town" is divided into east and west by State Street. East of State Street lies the Gold Coast, Chicago's most exclusive residential district, turning its face to the lake and its back upon what may lie west toward the river. West of State Street lies a nondescript area of furnished rooms; Clark Street, the Rialto of the half-world; "Little Sicily," the slum.

The Lake Shore Drive is the Mayfair of the Gold Coast. It runs north and south along Lake Michigan, with a wide parkway, bridle path, and promenade. On its western side rise the imposing stone mansions, with their green lawns and wrought-iron-grilled doorways, of Chicago's wealthy aristocracy and her industrial and financial kings. South of these is Streeterville, a "restricted" district of tall apartments and hotels. Here are the Drake Hotel and the Lake Shore Drive hotel, Chicago's most exclusive. And here apartments rent for from three hundred fifty to a thousand dollars a month. Indeed, the Lake Shore Drive is a street more of wealth than of aristocracy; for in this midwest metropolis money counts for more than does family, and the aristocracy is largely that of the financially successful.

South of Oak Street the Lake Shore

Drive, as it turns, becomes North Michigan Avenue, an avenue of fashionable hotels and restaurants, of smart clubs and shops. North Michigan Avenue is the Fifth Avenue of the Middle West; and already it looks forward to the day when Fifth Avenue will be the North Michigan Avenue of the East.

On a warm spring Sunday "Vanity Fair" glides along "the Drive" in motor cars of expensive mark (sic), makes colorful the bridle-paths, or saunters up the promenade between "the Drake" and Lincoln Park. The tops of the tan motor busses are crowded with those who live farther out, going home from church — those of a different world who look at "Vanity Fair" with curious or envious eyes. Even here the element of contrast is not lacking, for a mother from back west, with a shawl over her head, waits for a pause in the stream of motors to lead her eager child across to the beach, while beside her stand a collarless man in a brown derby and his girl in Sunday gingham, from some rooming-house back on La Salle Street.

For a few blocks back of "the Drive" — on Belleview Place, East Division Street, Stone, Astor, Banks, and North State Parkway, streets less pretentious but equally aristocratic — live more than a third of the people in Chicago's social register, "of good family and not employed." Here are the families that lived on the once fashionable Prairie Avenue, and later Ashland Boulevard, on the South and West sides. These streets, with the Lake Shore Drive, constitute Chicago's much vaunted Gold Coast, a little world to itself, which the city, failing to dislodge, has grown around and passed by.

At the back door of the Gold Coast, on Dearborn, Clark, and La Salle streets, and on the side streets extending south to the business and industrial area, is a strange world, painfully plain by contrast, a world that lives in houses with neatly lettered cards in the window: "Furnished Rooms." In these houses, from midnight to dawn, sleep some twenty-five thousand people. But by day houses and streets are practically deserted. For early in the morning this population hurries from its houses and down its streets, boarding cars and busses, to work in the Loop. It is a childless area, an area of young men and young women, most of whom are single, though some are married, and others are living together unmarried. It is a world of constant comings and goings, of dull routine and little romance, a world of unsatisfied longings.

The Near North Side shades from light to shadow, and from shadow to dark. The Gold Coast gives way to the world of furnished rooms; and the rooming-house area, to the west again, imperceptibly becomes the slum. The common denominator of the slum is its submerged aspect and its detachment from the city as a whole. The slum is a bleak area of segregation of the sediment of society; an area of extreme poverty, tenements, ramshackle buildings, of evictions and evaded rents; an area of working mothers and children, of high rates of birth, infant mortality, illegitimacy, and death; an area of pawnshops and second-hand stores, of gangs, of " flops " where every bed is a vote. As distinguished from the vice area, the disintegrating neighborhood, the slum is an area which has reached the limit of decay and is on the verge of reorganization as mission, settlements, playparks, and business come in.

The Near North Side, west of Clark Street from North Avenue to the river, and east of Clark Street from Chicago Avenue to the river, we may describe as a slum, without fear of contradiction. For this area, cut off by the barrier of river and industry, and for years without adequate transportation, has long been a backwater in the life of the city. This slum district is drab and mean. In ten months the United Charities here had 460 relief cases. Poverty is extreme. Many families are living in one or two basement rooms for which they pay less than ten dollars a month. These rooms are stove heated, and wood is sold on the streets in bundles, and coal in small sacks. The majority of houses, back toward the river, are of wood, and not a few have windows broken out. Smoke, the odor from the gas works, and the smell of dirty alleys is in the air. Both rooms and lots are overcrowded. Back tenements, especially north of Division Street, are common.[4]

---

[4] A five-room house on Hill Street, the rooms in which are $9 \times 12 \times 10$ feet high, has thirty occupants. Another nurse told the writer of being called on a case on Sedgwick Street and finding two couples living in one room. One couple worked days, the other nights; one couple went to bed when the other couple got up. Mrs. Louise De Kowen Bow-

Life in the slum is strenuous and precarious. One reads in the paper of a mother on North Avenue giving away her baby that the rest of her children may live. Frequently babies are found in alleyways. A nurse at the Passavant Hospital on North La Salle tells of a dirty little gamin, brought in from Wells Street, whose toe had been bitten off by a rat while he slept. Many women from this neighborhood are in the maternity ward four times in three years. A girl, a waitress, living at the Albany Hotel on lower Rush Street, recently committed suicide leaving the brief note, "I am tired of everything. I have seen too much. That is all." [5]

Clark Street is the Rialto of the slum. Deteriorated store buildings, cheap dance halls and movies, cabarets and doubtful hotels, missions, "flops," pawnshops and second-hand stores, innumerable restaurants, soft-drink parlors and "fellowship" saloons, where men sit about and talk, and which are hangouts for criminal gangs that live back in the slum, fence at the pawnshops, and consort with the transient prostitutes so characteristic of the North Side — such is "the Street." It is an all-night street, a street upon which one meets all the varied types that go to make up the slum.

The slum harbors many sorts of people: the criminal, the radical, the bohemian, the migratory worker, the immigrant, the unsuccessful, the queer and unadjusted. The migratory worker is attracted by the cheap hotels on State, Clark, Wells, and the streets along the river. The criminal and underworld find anonymity in the transient life of the cheaper rooming-houses such as exist on North La Salle Street. The bohemian and the unsuccessful are attracted by cheap attic or basement rooms. The radical is sure of a sympathetic audience in Washington Square. The foreign colony, on the other hand, is found in the slum, not because the immigrant seeks the slum, nor because he makes a slum of the area in which he settles, but merely because he finds there cheap quarters in which to live, and relatively little opposition to his coming. From Sedgwick Street west to the river is a colony of some fifteen thousand Italians, familiarly known as "Little Hell." Here the immigrant has settled blocks by villages, bringing with him his language, his customs, and his traditions, many of which persist.

Other foreign groups have come into this area. North of "Little Sicily," between Wells and Milton

---

en (*Growing Up with a City*), reminiscing of her United Charities experiences, tells of a woman who for three years existed on the food she procured from garbage cans and from the samples of department store demonstration counters. She adds:

"Sometimes fate seems to be relentless to the point of absurdity, as in one case I remember of an Italian family. . . . The man was riding on a street car and was suddenly assaulted by an irate passenger. . . . His nose was broken and he was badly disfigured. . . . A few days later, on his way home from a dispensary where he had gone to have his wound dressed, he fell off a sidewalk and broke his leg. The mother gave birth to a child the same day. Another child died the following day, and the eldest girl, only fourteen years old, who had been sent out to look for work, was foully assaulted on the street." Such is the life of the slum!

[5] *Chicago Evening American,* December 21, 1923.

Streets, there is a large admixture of Poles with Americans, Irish, and Slavs. The Negro, too, is moving into this area and pushing on into "Little Hell." There is a small colony of Greeks grouped about West Chicago Avenue, with its picturesque coffee houses on Clark Street. Finally, there has come in within the past few years a considerable colony of Persians, which has also settled in the vicinity of Chicago Avenue. The slum on the Near North Side is truly cosmopolitan.

In the slum, but not of it, is "Towertown," or "the village." South of Chicago Avenue, along East Erie, Ohio, Huron, and Superior Streets, is a considerable colony of artists and of would-be artists. The artists have located here because old buildings can be cheaply converted into studios. The would-be artists have followed the artists. And the hangers-on of bohemia have come for atmosphere, and because the old residences in the district have stables. "The village" is full of picturesque people and resorts — tearooms with such names as the Wind Blew Inn, the Blue Mouse, and the Green Mask. And many interesting art stores, antique shops, and stalls with rare books are tucked away among the old buildings. All in all, the picturesque and unconventional life of "the village" is again in striking contrast to the formal and conventional life of the Gold Coast, a few short blocks to the north.

One has but to walk the streets of the Near North Side to sense the cultural isolation beneath these contrasts. Indeed, the color and picturesqueness of the city exists in the intimations of what lies behind the superficial contrasts of its life. How various are the thoughts of the individuals who throng up Michigan Avenue from the Loop at the close of the day — artists, shop girls, immigrants, inventors, men of affairs, women of fashion, waitresses, clerks, entertainers. How many are their vocational interests; how different are their ambitions. How vastly multiplied are the chances of life in a great city, as compared with those of the American towns and European peasant villages from which most of these individuals have come. What plans, plots, conspiracies, and dreams for taking advantage of these chances different individuals must harbor under their hats. Yet they have little in common beyond the fact that they jostle one another on the same street. Experience has taught them different languages. How far they are from understanding one another, or from being able to communicate save upon the most obvious material matters!

As one walks from the Drake Hotel and the Lake Shore Drive west along Oak Street, through the world of rooming-houses, into the slum and the streets of the Italian Colony one has a sense of distance as between the Gold Coast and Little Hell — distance that is not geographical but social. There are distances of language and custom. There are distances represented by wealth and the luster it adds to human existence. There are distances of horizon — the Gold Coast living throughout the world while Little Hell is still only slowly emerging out of its old Sicilian villages. There are distances represented by the Gold Coast's absorbing professional interests. It is one world that revolves about the Lake Shore Drive, with its mansions, clubs, and motors, its benefits and assemblies. It is another world that revolves about the Dill Pickle Club, the soap boxes of Washington Square, or the shop of Romano the Barber. And each little world is absorbed in its own affairs.

THE EXPANSION OF THE CITY

The most overt of the processes exhibited by the city's growth is that of expansion.

The expansion of the city from the standpoint of the city plan, zoning, and regional surveys is thought of almost wholly in terms of its physical growth. . . . No study of expansion as a process has yet been made, although the materials for such a study and intimations of different aspects of the process are contained in city planning, zoning, and regional surveys. The typical processes of the expansion of the city can best be illustrated, perhaps, by a series of concentric circles, which may be numbered to designate both the successive zones of urban extension and the types of areas differentiated in the process of expansion.

Such a chart represents an ideal construction of the tendencies of any town or city to expand radially from its central business district — on the map, the Loop.[6] Encircling the downtown area

there is normally an area in transition, which is being invaded by business and light manufacture (II). A third area (III) is inhabited by the workers in industries who have escaped from the area of deterioration (II), but who desire to live within easy access of their work. Beyond this zone is the "residential" area (IV) of high-class apartment buildings or of exclusive "restricted" districts of single family dwellings. Still farther, out beyond the city limits, is the commuters' zone — suburban areas, or satellite cities — within a thirty- to sixty-minute ride of the central business district.

This chart brings out clearly the main fact of expansion, namely, the tendency of each inner zone to extend its area by the invasion of the next outer zone. This aspect of expansion may be called *succession,* a process which has been studied in detail in plant ecology. If this chart is applied to Chicago, all four of these zones were in its early history included in the circumference of the inner zone, the present business district. The present boundaries of the area of deterioration were not many years ago those of the zone now inhabited by independent

6 This conception is perhaps implicit in some of the literature of the "muckrake," e.g., in Lincoln Steffen's *The Shame of the*

Cities. But the first notable approximation to a natural history of the city was a small book by a real estate man, Richard M. Hurd, entitled *Principles of City Land Values* (1903). In attempting to generalize the fluctuations of land values in the city, Hurd found it necessary to describe certain processes typical of city growth, to treat of the city's growth in generalized terms. The surveys made by the Bell Telephone Company, and other public utilities, to predict the city's growth in anticipation of extension for future service, and the Plan for the Study of New York and its Environs, as well as the Chicago Regional Planning Association, are other attempts to analyze and manipulate the natural processes involved in the growth of the city.

URBAN AREAS

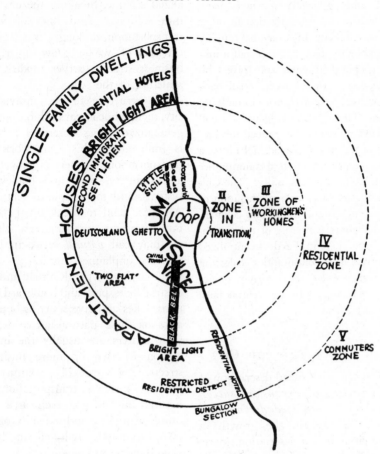

THE ANATOMY OF THE CITY. The above chart discloses the gross anatomy of the city, the typical zones into which every city segregates as it expands. The chart shows, further, the segregation of typical cultural areas of Chicago within these zones (chart after Burgess).

wage-earners, and within the memories of thousands of Chicagoans contained the residences of the " best families."

Besides extension and succession, the general process of expansion in urban growth involves the antagonistic and yet complementary processes of concentration and decentralization. In all cities there is the natural tendency for local and outside transportation to converge in the central business district. In the downtown section of every large city we expect to find the department stores, the skyscraper office buildings, the railroad stations, the great hotels, the theaters, the art museum, and the city hall. Quite naturally, almost inevitably, the economic, cultural, and political life centers here. The relation of centralization to other processes of city life may be roughly gauged by the fact that over half a million people daily enter and leave Chicago's Loop. More recently sub-business centers have grown up in outlying zones. These " satellite loops " do not, it seems, represent the " hoped for " revival of the neighborhood, but rather a telescoping of several local communities into a larger economic unity. The Chicago of yesterday, an agglomeration of country towns and immigrant colonies, is undergoing a process of reorganization into a centralized decentralized system of local communities coalescing into sub-business areas visibly or invisibly dominated by the central business district.[7]

THE STRUCTURE OF THE CITY

Such is a generalized description of the processes of *expansion, succession,* and *"centralized decentralization"* displayed in the growth of every city. It is a description, moreover, of the gross anatomy of the city. The concentric circles, or zones, represent the typical structure of a modern commercial and industrial city. Of course, no city quite conforms to this ideal scheme. Physical barriers such as rivers, lakes, rises of land, and the like may modify the growth and structure of the city, as is strikingly demonstrated in the cases of New York, Pittsburgh, and Seattle. Railroads, with their belts

[7] E. W. Burgess, " The Growth of the City," in R. E. Park and E. W. Burgess, *The City*, pp. 50–51.

of industry cut through this generalized scheme, breaking the city up into sections. And lines of local transportation, along the more traveled of which grow up retail business streets, further modify the structure of the city.

The structure of the individual city, then, while always exhibiting the generalized zones described before, is built about this framework of transportation, business organization and industry, park and boulevard systems, and topographical features. All these tend to break up the city into numerous smaller areas, which we may call *natural areas,* in that they are unplanned, natural product of the city's growth. Railroad and industrial belts, park and boulevard systems, lakes and rivers, act as boundaries of these natural areas; while their centers are usually the intersection of two or more business streets. By virtue of proximity to industry, business, transportation, or natural advantages, each area acquires a physical individuality of its own, accurately reflected in land values and rents.[8]

[8] These natural areas, which are usually " trade areas," are not to be confused with communities. They are the result of the economic rather than of the cultural process. Communities may or may not conform to natural areas, and natural areas may exist without corresponding communities, as the Near North Side clearly illustrates. Natural areas, moreover, are not always so well defined as this ideal scheme might seem to indicate. In a city like Chicago, where natural barriers are few, a natural area may be defined almost wholly in terms of land values, as is the case of the area occupied by the Gold Coast on the Near North Side.

Zoning ordinances may create natural areas by forming " barriers " to movements of population. However, a study of the relationship

Within the limits of these broader zones and of these natural areas, competition, economic and cultural, segregates the population.[9] There is no phenomenon more characteristic of city life, as contrasted with the life of the rural community or the village, than that of segregation. The village is relatively undifferentiated; its population is relatively of one economic and social class; the business area is the general store; the characteristic areas within the village are confined to a few shacks along the railroad, or to a " darky town." But the sharp contrasts of the city, emphasized as they are by segregation over given areas, are familiar to everyone: the great central business district, with its towering buildings and thronged streets; the railroads lined with smoking industries; slums and foreign colonies; the " bright light area " and the " red light district "; bleak areas of deteriorated dwellings, small businesses and " furnished rooms "; mile after mile of apartment houses; outlying districts of single homes and dormitory suburbs. Nor is this segregation ac-

of zoning ordinances to the physical structure of the city, in the cases of Chicago and Cleveland, for example, indicates that zoning ordinances tend merely to add a legal definition to pre-existing natural areas. The Gold Coast has been guaranteed for another decade, at least, against the press of business and the rooming-house, by the recent zoning ordinance of Chicago.

9 The modern city, industrial or commercial, like the plant or animal community, is largely an ecological product; that is, the rate and direction of the city's growth, the distribution of city features, the segregation of communities within the city, are by-products of the economic process — in which land values, rents, and wages are fixed — and the unintended result of competition.

cidental. It is the result of competition and the economic processes which fix the utility and value of the land, determine the rent the land will derive, and consequently precribe more or less rigorously the usage to which the land will be put.

Physical geography, natural advantages, and the means of transportation determine in advance the general outlines of the urban plan. As the city increases in population, the subtler influences of sympathy, rivalry, and economic necessity tend to control the distribution of population. Business and manufacturing seek advantageous locations and draw around them a certain portion of the population. There spring up fashionable residence quarters, from which the poorer classes are excluded because of the increased value of the land. Then there grow up slums which are inhabited by great numbers of the poorer classes who are unable to defend themselves from association with the derelict and vicious. Every great city has its racial colonies, like the Chinatowns of San Francisco and New York, the Little Sicily of Chicago, and various other less pronounced types. In addition to these, most cities have their segregated vice districts, like that which recently existed in Chicago, and their rendezvous for criminals of all sorts. Every large city has its occupational suburbs, like the stockyards of Chicago, and its residence suburbs, like Brookline, in Boston, each of which has the size and the character of a complete separate town, village, or city, except that its population is a selected one. Undoubtedly the most remarkable of these cities within cities, of which the most interesting characteristics is that they are composed of persons of the same race, or of persons of different races but of the same social class, is East London, with a population of two million laborers.

In the course of time every section and quarter of the city takes on something of the character and qualities of its inhabitants. Each separate part of the city is inevitably stained with the peculiar sentiments of its population.[10]

Through this process of segregation each natural area in the city takes on a color which sets it off from adjoining areas, and the city becomes a mosaic of neighborhoods, " communities," and little cultural worlds. But these areas are not distributed throughout the city at random. The striking contrasts and the heterogeneity which these numerous segregated areas of the city present, resolve, upon analysis, into the more generalized zones which we have already discussed. Segregated areas of a given type, wherever they may be located in a given city with respect to other such areas, invariably fall, in every city, within one of these larger and well-defined zones. And this follows from the fact that, important as cultural factors are in the ultimate segregation, the broad outlines of segregation within the city are fixed within the economic proccss. Because of the character that attaches to these segregated areas, lends them a certain identity, and tends to set them off from one another, it has been customary to look upon these

10 Adapted from Robert E. Park, " Suggestions for the Study of Behavior in the Urban Environment," *The City*, pp. 6, 12.

areas as communities. But other processes which are a part with the growth of the city run counter to these tendencies, and have made many of these local areas within the city anything but communities.

PHYSICAL CHANGE AND SOCIAL CHANGE

The very march of the city, as commerce and industry push out from its center, encroaching upon residential neighborhoods, turning the population back upon itself, results in a physical instability and change which has significant implications for local life. We have seen how commerce and industry are constantly expanding, at once creating and reorganizing the slum; how the slum eats its way into adjacent areas, converting apartments into tenements and rooming-houses, wiping out whole communities before it; how apartment areas push their way into outlying residential areas which, giving way in turn, sprawl out into the country. The history of the Near North Side has shown that no area or group can long withstand the pressure of this relentless succession, fashionable residential districts giving way as rapidly as slums.[11]

11 A generation is as long a period as any area has been able to maintain itself as a fashionable residence area. In the slum, both on the Near West Side and on the Near North Side, the Irish, Swedes, Germans, and Italians have maintained their original communities not more than a generation (see *Hull House Maps*).

On the Near North Side during the writer's two years of residence there has been a startlingly rapid physical change which has completely altered the outward aspect of many neighborhoods and presages further cultural succession.

Fashionable residential streets have become the heart of the rooming-house district; rooming-houses have become tenements; tenements have been reclaimed for studios and shops. Group has succeeded group; the world of fashion has become the world of furnished rooms, and into this world have come the slattenly residents of the slum. The Irish Kilgubbin has become the Swedish Smoky Hollow; the Swedish Smoky Hollow, a Little Sicily; and now Little Sicily becomes a Negro quarter.

As the physical growth of the city carries before it the little cultural worlds, the local groups, which make up its population, it wipes out the physical symbols of their identity. The town has its old church, in which everyone has been christened, married, and buried for generations. In the town cemetery are the graves of its heroes; the town finds there its history graven in stone, and each family finds there symbols that are the basis of emotional bonds of solidarity. The homes of the town's founders and notables stand as visible symbols of the past, and are pointed to each succeeding generation. About these and other symbols gather the traditions, rituals, and sentiments that make up the community's history and are the core of its self-consciousness and solidarity. They are visible and permanent symbols which serve as the physical basis of the community's continuity. But local groups in the city have no such symbols. As the succession of the city pushes the groups farther and farther from its center, these physical symbols are abandoned and destroyed. The physical basis of local cultural unity ceases to exist, and with it many of the local group's unifying and controlling traditions.[12]

We have already seen that the same competitive process which has made of the city a mosaic of cultural units, and which has resulted in the succession of these cultural units over given local areas, has also resulted in a grosser segregation which has taken business and industry outside the community and has located it in well-defined belts or zones. Now practically the entire population of the city goes outside the community, often eight and ten miles outside the community, every day of the year, to a diversity of occupations concentrated in the Loop or in outlying manufacturing districts.[13] There are no longer common economic activities carried on by the community as such; men who live side by side no longer spend the hours of the day working at tasks that bring them together. Economic activities, which

[12] The Swedish colony which formerly centered at the corner of Elm and Sedgwick streets, where stood its original church, has in fifty years moved four times, each time building a new church and making an attempt to maintain itself as a distinct community. But it has repeatedly been invaded by migrations of other national groups. Its last move has taken it beyond Cicero Avenue on the North-west Side. Even here it is finding difficulty in maintaining its identity. The present community has no history. The younger generation is drifting away, as it has tended to do each time the colony has moved (see Document 72).

[13] On the Near North Side, for example, the entire population of the world of furnished rooms, such part of the population of the Gold Coast as has occupation, and practically the entire population of the slum, go to work outside the community.

were in the village a source of much of the community's common body of experience, serve in the city community, more often than not, to draw men apart, to give them separate interests and points of view.

In like fashion recreation has ceased to be a spontaneous communal activity, and has become a commercialized affair segregated in the Loop or in a few so-called "bright light" areas. Whereas the hours of leisure brought together the members of the village community in a group of common activities, these same leisure hours now disperse them in a diversity of activities and areas without the community. The fact that occupational and recreational activities have been taken outside the community has important consequences for local life. A common group of activities out of which may grow a common body of experience and a common set of traditions and attitudes is the *sine qua non* of community life and collective action. Without this common group of activities, the community of tradition and attitudes of the local group in the city rapidly disintegrates.

Another aspect of the growth of the city equally significant in its consequences for local life is the increasingly detailed division of labor which it entails. The outstanding economic phenomenon of the industrial society and the great city is this ever more minute and more rigidly defined division of labor. In Chicago, according to the 1920 census, approximately 1,000,000 persons gainfully employed reported 509 occupations, and the 1,000 and more men and women in *Who's Who* gave 116 different vocations.[14]

This division of labor, resulting in occupational differentiation, combined with the segregation of commerce and industry which has taken economic activities outside the community, has produced an organization of sentiment and interest along occupational rather than along local lines. Every occupation, in the life of the city, tends to assume the character of a profession. The discipline required for success in specialized vocations and the associations which it enforces emphasize this tendency.

42. The Marketing Orientation *

The marketing orientation developed as a dominant one only in the modern era. In order to understand its nature one must consider the economic function of the market in

* From *Man For Himself*, Copyright 1947 by Erich Fromm, and reprinted by permission of Erich Fromm and Rinehart & Company, Inc., Publishers. Pp. 67–76.

modern society as being not only analogous to this character orientation but as the basis and the main condition for its development in modern man.

[14] E. W. Burgess, "The Growth of the City," in R. E. Park, and E. W. Burgess, *The City*, p. 57.

Barter is one of the oldest economic mechanisms. The traditional local market, however, is essentially different from the market as it has developed in modern capitalism. Bartering on a local market offered an opportunity to meet for the purpose of exchanging commodities. Producers and customers became acquainted; they were relatively small groups; the demand was more or less known, so that the producer could produce for this specific demand.

The modern market is no longer a meeting place but a mechanism characterized by abstract and impersonal demand. One produces for this market, not for a known circle of customers; its verdict is based on laws of supply and demand; and it determines whether the commodity can be sold and at what price. No matter what the *use value* of a pair of shoes may be, for instance, if the supply is greater than the demand, some shoes will be sentenced to economic death; they might as well not have been produced at all. The market day is the "day of judgment" as far as the *exchange value* of commodities is concerned.

The reader may object that this description of the market is oversimplified. The producer does try to judge the demand in advance, and under monopoly conditions even obtains a certain degree of control over it. Nevertheless, the regulatory function of the market has been, and still is, predominant enough to have a profound influence on the character formation of the urban middle class and, through the latter's social and cultural influence, on the whole population. The market concept of value, the emphasis on exchange value rather than on use value, has led to a similar concept of value with regard to people and particularly to oneself. The character orientation which is rooted in the experience of oneself as a commodity and of one's value as exchange value I call the marketing orientation.

In our time the marketing orientation has been growing rapidly, together with the development of a new market that is a phenomenon of the last decades — the "personality market." Clerks and salesmen, business executives and doctors, lawyers and artists all appear on this market. It is true that their legal status and economic positions are different: some are independent, charging for their services; others are employed, receiving salaries. But all are dependent for their material success on a personal acceptance by those who need their services or who employ them.

The principle of evaluation is the same on both the personality and the commodity market: on the one, personalities are offered for sale; on the other, commodities. Value in both cases is their exchange value, for which use value is a necessary but not a sufficient condition. It is true, our economic system could not function if people were not skilled in the particular work they have to perform and were gifted only with a pleasant personality. Even the best bedside manner and the most beautifully equipped office on Park Avenue would not make a New York doctor successful if he did not have a minimum of medical knowledge and skill. Even the most winning personality would not prevent a secretary from losing her job unless she could type reasonably fast. However, if we ask what the respective weight of skill and personality as a condition for success is, we find that only in exceptional cases is success predominantly the result of skill and of certain other human qualities like honesty, decency, and integrity. Although the proportion between skill and human qualities on the one hand and " personality " on the other hand as prerequisites for success varies, the " personality factor " always plays a decisive role. Success depends largely on how well a person sells himself on the market, how well he gets his personality across, how nice a " package " he is; whether he is " cheerful," " sound," " aggressive," " reliable," " ambitious "; furthermore what his family background is, what clubs he belongs to, and whether he knows the right people. The type of personality required depends to some degree on the special field in which a person works. A stockbroker, a salesman, a secretary, a railroad executive, a college professor, or a hotel manager must each offer different kinds of personality that, regardless of their differences, must fulfill one condition: to be in demand.

The fact that in order to have success it is not sufficient to have the skill and equipment for performing a given task but that one must be able to " put across " one's personality in competition with many others shapes the attitude toward oneself. If it were enough for the purpose of making a living to rely on what one knows and what one can do, one's self-esteem would be in proportion to one's capacities, that is, to one's use value; but since success depends largely on how one sells one's personality, one experiences oneself as a commodity or rather simultaneously as the seller *and* the commodity to be sold. A person is not concerned with his life and happiness, but with becoming salable. This feeling might be compared to that of a commodity, of handbags on a counter, for instance, could they feel and think. Each handbag would try to make itself as " attractive " as possible in order to attract customers and to look as expensive as possible in order to obtain a higher price than its rivals. The handbag sold for the highest price would feel elated, since that would mean it was the most " valuable " one; the one which was not sold would feel sad and convinced of its own worthlessness. This fate might befall a bag which, though excellent in appearance and usefulness, had the bad luck to be out of date because of a change in fashion.

Like the handbag, one has to be in fashion on the personality market, and in order to be in fashion one has to know what kind of personality is most in demand. This knowledge is transmitted in a general way throughout the whole process of education, from kindergarten to college, and implemented by the family. The knowledge acquired at this early stage is not sufficient, however; it emphasizes only certain general qualities like adaptability, ambition, and sensitivity to the changing expectations of other people. The more specific picture of the models for success one gets elsewhere. The pictorial magazines, newspapers, and newsreels show the pictures and life stories of the successful in many variations. Pictorial advertising has a similar function. The successful executive who is pictured in a tailor's advertisement is the image of how one should look and be, if one is to draw down the " big money " on the contemporary personality market.

The most important means of transmitting the desired personality pattern to the average man is the motion picture. The young girl tries to emulate the facial expression, coiffure, gestures of a high-priced star as the most promising way to success. The young man tries to look and be like the model he sees on the screen. While the average citizen has little contact with the life of the most successful people, his relationship with the motion-picture stars is different. It is true that he has no real contact with them either, but he can see them on the screen again and again, can write them and receive their autographed pictures. In contrast to the time when the actor was socially despised but was nevertheless the transmitter of the works of great poets to his audience, our motion-picture stars have no great works or ideas to transmit, but their function is to serve as the link an average person has with the world of the " great." Even if he cannot hope to become as successful as they

are, he can try to emulate them; they are his saints and because of their success they embody the norms for living.

Since modern man experiences himself both as the seller and as the commodity to be sold on the market, his self-esteem depends on conditions beyond his control. If he is " successful," he is valuable; if he is not, he is worthless. The degree of insecurity which results from this orientation can hardly be overestimated.. If one feels that one's own value is not constituted primarily by the human qualities one possesses, but by one's success on a competitive market with ever-changing conditions, one's self-esteem is bound to be shaky and in constant need of confirmation by others. Hence one is driven to strive relentlessly for success, and any setback is a severe threat to one's self-esteem; helplessness, insecurity, and inferiority feelings are the result. If the vicissitudes of the market are the judges of one's value, the sense of dignity and pride is destroyed.

But the problem is not only that of self-evaluation and self-esteem but of one's experience of oneself as an independent entitiy, of one's *identity with oneself.* As we shall see later, the mature and productive individual derives his feeling of identity from the experience of himself as the agent who is one with his powers; this feeling of self can be briefly expressed as meaning *"I am what I do."* In the marketing orientation man encounters his own powers as commodities alienated from him. He is not one with them but they are masked from him because what matters is not his self-realization in the process of using them but his success in the process of selling them. Both his powers and what they create become estranged, something different from himself, something for others to judge and to use; thus his feeling of identity becomes as shaky as his self-esteem; it is constituted by the sum total of roles one can play: "I am as you desire me."

Ibsen has expressed this state of selfhood in Peer Gynt: Peer Gynt tries to discover his self and he finds that he is like an onion — one layer after the other can be peeled off and there is no core to be found. Since man cannot live doubting his identity, he must, in the marketing orientation, find the conviction of identity not in reference to himself and his powers but in the opinion of others about him. His prestige, status, success, the fact that he is known to others as being a certain person are a substitute for the genuine feeling of identity. This situation makes him utterly dependent on the way others look at him and forces him to keep up the role in which he once had become successful. If I and my powers are separated from each other then, indeed, is my self constituted by the price I fetch.

The way one experiences others is not different from the way one experiences oneself. Others are experienced as commodities like oneself; they too do not present themselves but their salable part. The difference between people is reduced to a merely quantitative difference of being more or less successful, attractive, hence valuable. This process is not different from what happens to commodities on the market. A painting and a pair of shoes can both be expressed in, and reduced to, their exchange value, their price; so many pairs of shoes are "equal" to one painting. In the same way the difference between people is reduced to a common element, their price on the market. Their individuality, that which is peculiar and unique in them, is valueless and, in fact, a ballast. The meaning which the word *peculiar* has assumed is quite expressive of this attitude. Instead of denoting the greatest achievement of man — that of having developed his individuality — it has become almost synonymous with *queer*. The word *equality* has also changed its meaning. The idea that all men are created equal implied that all men have the same fundamental right to be considered as ends in themselves and not as means. Today, equality has become equivalent to *interchangeability,* and is the very negation of individuality. Equality, instead of being the condition for the development of each man's peculiarity, means the extinction of individuality, the "selflessness" characteristic of the marketing orientation. Equality was conjunctive with difference, but it has become synonymous with "in-difference" and, indeed, indifference is what characterizes modern man's relationship to himself and to others.

These conditions necessarily color all human relationships. When the individual self is neglected, the relationships between people must of necessity become superficial, because not they themselves but interchangeable commodities · are related. People are not able and cannot afford to be concerned with that which is unique and "peculiar" in each other. However, the market creates a kind of comradeship of its own. Everybody is involved in the same battle of competition, shares the same striving for success; all meet under the same conditions of the market (or at least believe they do). Everyone knows how the others feel because each is in the same boat: alone, afraid to fail, eager to please; no quarter is given or expected in this battle.

The superficial character of human relationships leads many to hope that they can find depth and intensity of feeling in individual love. But love for one person and love for one's neighbor are indivisible; in any given culture, love relationships are only a more intense expression of the relatedness to man prevalent in that culture. Hence it is an illusion to expect that the loneliness of man rooted in the marketing orientation can be cured by individual love.

Thinking as well as feeling is determined by the marketing orientation. Thinking assumes the function of grasping things quickly so as to be able to manipulate them successfully. Furthered by widespread and efficient education, this leads to a high degree of intelligence, but not of reason. For manipulative purposes, all that is necessary to know is the surface features of things, the superficial. The truth, to be uncovered by penetrating to the essence of phenomena, becomes an obsolete concept — truth not only in the prescientific sense of "absolute" truth, dogmatically maintained without reference to empirical data, but also in the sense of truth attained by man's reason applied to his observations and open to revisions. Most intelligence tests are attuned to this kind of thinking; they measure not so much the capacity for reason and understanding as the capacity for quick mental adaptation to a given situation; "mental adjustment tests" would be the adequate name for them. For this kind of thinking the application of the categories of comparison and of quantitative measurement — rather than a thorough analysis of a given phenomenon and its quality — is essential. All problems are equally "interesting" and there is little sense of the respective differences in their importance. Knowledge itself becomes a commodity. Here, too, man is alienated from his own power; thinking and knowing are experienced as a tool to produce results. Knowledge of man himself, psychology, which in the great tradition of Western thought was held to be the condition for virtue, for right living, for happiness, has degenerated into an instrument to be used for better manipulation of others and oneself, in market research, political propaganda, advertising, and so on.

Evidently this type of thinking has a profound effect on our educational system. From grade school to graduate school, the aim of learning is to gather as much information as possible that is mainly useful for the purposes of the market. Students are supposed to learn so many things that they have hardly time and energy left to *think*. Not the interest in the subjects taught or in knowledge and insight as such, but the enhanced exchange value knowledge gives is the main incentive for wanting more and better education. We find today a tremendous enthusiasm for knowledge and education, but at the same time a skeptical or contemptuous attitude toward the allegedly impractical and useless thinking which is concerned " only " with the truth and which has no exchange value on the market.

43. The Elements of Social Structure*

There persists a notable tendency in sociological theory to attribute the malfunctioning of social structure primarily to those of man's imperious biological drives which are not adequately restrained by social control. In this view, the social order is solely a device for " impulse management " and the " social processing " of tensions. These impulses which break through social control, be it noted, are held to be biologically derived. Nonconformity is assumed to be rooted in original nature. Conformity is by implication the result of an utilitarian calculus or unreasoned conditioning. This point of view, whatever its other deficiencies, clearly begs one question. It provides no basis for determining the nonbiological conditions which induce deviations from prescribed patterns of conduct. In this paper, it will be suggested that certain phases of social structure generate the circumstances in which infringement of social codes constitutes a " normal " response.

The conceptual scheme to be outlined is designed to provide a coherent, systematic approach to the study of socio-cultural sources of deviate behavior. Our primary aim lies in discovering how some social structures *exert a definite pressure* upon certain persons in the society to engage in noncomformist rather than conformist conduct. The many ramifications of the scheme cannot all be discussed; the problems mentioned outnumber those explicitly treated.

Among the elements of social and cultural structure, two are important for our purposes. These are analytically separable although they merge imperceptibly in concrete situations. The first consists of culturally defined goals, purposes, and interests. It comprises a frame of aspirational reference. These goals are more or less integrated and involve varying degrees of prestige and sentiment. They constitute a basic, but not the exclusive, component of what Linton aptly has called " designs for group living." Some of

* From Robert K. Merton, " Social Structure and Anomie," *American Sociological Review*, Vol. III (October, 1938), pp. 672–682. Reprinted by permission of Robert K. Merton and the *American Sociological Review*.

these cultural aspirations are related to the original drives of man, but they are not determined by them. The second phase of the social structure defines, regulates, and controls the acceptable modes of achieving these goals. Every social group invariably couples its scale of desired ends with moral or institutional regulation of permissible and required procedures for attaining these ends. These regulatory norms and moral imperatives do not necessarily coincide with technical or efficiency norms. Many procedures which from the standpoint of *particular individuals* would be most efficient in securing desired values, e.g., illicit oil-stock schemes, theft, fraud, are ruled out of the institutional area of permitted conduct. The choice of expedients is limited by the institutional norms.

To say that these two elements, culture goals and institutional norms, operate jointly is not to say that the ranges of alternative behaviors and aims bear some constant relation to one another. The emphasis upon certain goals may vary independently of the degree of emphasis upon institutional means. There may develop a disproportionate, at times, a virtually exclusive, stress upon the value of specific goals, involving relatively slight concern with the institutionally appropriate modes of attaining these goals. The limiting case in this direction is reached when the range of alternative procedures is limited only by technical rather than institutional considerations. Any and all devices which promise attainment of the all important goal would

be permitted in this hypothetical polar case. This constitutes one type of cultural mal-integration. A second polar type is found in groups where activities originally conceived as instrumental are transmuted into ends in themselves. The original purposes are forgotten and ritualistic adherence to institutionally prescribed conduct becomes virtually obsessive. Stability is largely ensured while change is flouted. The range of alternative behaviors is severely limited. There develops a tradition-bound, sacred society characterized by neophobia. The occupational psychosis of the bureaucrat may be cited as a case in point. Finally, there are the intermediate types of groups where a balance between culture goals and institutional means is maintained. These are the significantly integrated and relatively stable, though changing, groups.

An effective equilibrium between the two phases of the social structure is maintained as long as satisfactions accrue to individuals who conform to both constraints, viz., satisfactions from the achievement of the goals and satisfactions emerging directly from the institutionally canalized modes of striving to attain these ends. Success, in such equilibrated cases, is twofold. Success is reckoned in terms of the product and in terms of the process, in terms of the outcome, and in terms of activities. Continuing satisfactions must derive from sheer *participation* in a competitive order as well as from eclipsing one's competitors if the order itself is to be sustained. The occasional sacrifices involved in institutionalized conduct must be compensated by socialized rewards. The distribution of statuses and roles through competition must be so organized that positive incentives for conformity to roles and adherence to status obligations are provided *for every position* within the distributive order. Aberrant conduct, therefore, may be viewed as a symptom of dissociation between culturally defined aspirations and socially structured means.

Of the types of groups which result from the independent variation of the two phases of the social structure, we shall be primarily concerned with the first, namely, that involving a disproportionate accent on goals. This statement must be recast in a proper perspective. In no group is there an absence of regulatory codes governing conduct, yet groups do vary in the degree to which these folkways, mores, and institutional controls are effectively integrated with the more diffuse goals which are part of the culture matrix. Emotional convictions may cluster about the complex of socially acclaimed ends, meanwhile shifting their support from the culturally defined implementation of these ends. As we shall see, certain aspects of the social structure may generate countermores and antisocial behavior precisely because of differential emphases on goals and regulations. In the extreme case, the latter may be so vitiated by the goal-emphasis that the range of behavior is limited only by considerations of technical expediency. The sole significant question then becomes, which available means is most efficient in netting the socially approved value? The technically most feasible procedure, whether legitimate or not, is preferred to the institutionally prescribed conduct. As this process continues, the integration of the society becomes tenuous and anomie ensues.

Thus, in competitive athletics, when the aim of victory is shorn of its institutional trappings and success in contests becomes construed as " winning the game " rather than " winning through circumscribed modes of activity," a premium is implicitly set upon the use of illegitimate but technically efficient means. The star of the opposing football team is surreptitiously slugged; the wrestler furtively incapacitates his opponent through ingenious but illicit techniques; university alumni covertly subsidize " students " whose talents are largely confined to the athletic field. The emphasis on the goal has so attenuated the satisfactions deriving from sheer participation in the competitive activity that these satisfactions are virtually confined to a successful outcome. Through the same process, tension generated by the desire to win in a poker game is relieved by successfully dealing oneself four aces, or, when the cult of success has become completely dominant, by sagaciously shuffling the cards in a game of solitaire. The faint twinge of uneasiness in the last instance and the surreptitious nature of public delicts indicate clearly that the institutional rules of the game *are known* to those who evade them, but that the emotional supports of these rules are largely vitiated by cultural exaggeration of the success-goal. They are microcosmic images of the social macrocosm.

Of course, this process is not restricted to the realm of sport. The process whereby exaltation of the end generates a *literal demoralization*, i.e., a deinstitutionalization, of the means is one which characterizes many groups in which the two phases of the social structure are not highly integrated. The extreme emphasis upon the accumulation of wealth as a symbol of success in our own society militates against the completely effective control of institutionally regulated modes of acquiring a fortune. Fraud, corruption, vice, crime, in short, the entire catalogue of proscribed behavior, becomes increasingly common when the emphasis on the *culturally induced* success-goal becomes divorced from a coordinate institutional emphasis. This observation is of crucial theoretical importance in examining the doctrine that antisocial behavior most frequently derives from biological drives breaking through the restraints imposed by society. The difference is one between a strictly utilitarian interpretation which conceives man's ends as random and an analysis which finds these ends deriving from the basic values of the culture.

Our analysis can scarcely stop at this juncture. We must turn to other aspects of the social structure if we are to deal with the social genesis of the varying rates and types of deviate behavior characteristic of different societies. Thus far, we have sketched three ideal types of social orders constituted by distinctive patterns of relations between culture ends and means. Turning from these types of *culture patterning,* we find five logically possible, alternative modes of adjustment or adaptation *by individuals* within the culture-bearing society or group. These are schematically represented in the following table, where (+) signifies "acceptance," (−) signifies "elimination" and (±) signifies "rejection and substitution of new goals and standards."

	Culture Goals	Institution-alized Means
I. Conformity	+	+
II. Innovation	+	−
III. Ritualism	−	+
IV. Retreatism	−	−
V. Rebellion	±	±

Our discussion of the relation between these alternative responses and other phases of the social structure must be prefaced by the observation that persons may shift from one alternative to another as they engage in different social activities. These categories refer to role adjustments in specific situations, not to personality *in toto.* To treat the development of this process in various spheres of conduct would introduce a complexity unmanageable within the confines of this paper. For this reason, we shall be concerned primarily with economic activity in the broad sense, "the production, exchange, distribution and consumption of goods and services" in our competitive society, wherein wealth has taken on a highly symbolic cast. Our task is to search out some of the factors which exert pressure upon individuals to engage in certain of these logically possible alternative responses. This choice, as we shall see, is far from random.

In every society, Adaptation I (conformity to both culture goals and means) is the most common and widely diffused. Were this not so, the stability and continuity of the society could not be maintained. The mesh of expectancies which constitutes every social order is sustained by the modal behavior of its members falling within the first category. Conventional role behavior oriented toward the basic values of the group is the rule rather than the exception. It is this fact alone which permits us to speak of a human aggregate as comprising a group or society.

Conversely, Adaptation IV (rejection of goals and means) is the least common. Persons who "adjust" (or maladjust) in this fashion are, strictly speaking, *in* the society but not *of* it. Sociologically, these constitute the true "aliens." Not sharing the common frame of orientation, they can be included within the societal population merely in a fictional sense. In this category are *some* of the activities of psychotics, psychoneurotics, chronic autists, pariahs, outcasts, vagrants, vagabonds, tramps, chronic drunkards and drug addicts. These have relinquished, in certain spheres of activity, the culturally defined goals, involving complete aim-inhibition in the polar case, and their adjustments

are not in accord with institutional norms. This is not to say that in some cases the source of their behavioral adjustments is not in part the very social structure which they have in effect repudiated nor that their very existence within a social area does not constitute a problem for the socialized population.

This mode of "adjustment" occurs, as far as structural sources are concerned, when both the culture goals and institutionalized procedures have been assimilated thoroughly by the individual and imbued with affect and high positive value, but where those institutionalized procedures which promise a measure of successful attainment of the goals are not available to the individual. In such instances, there results a twofold mental conflict insofar as the moral obligation for adopting institutional means conflicts with the pressure to resort to illegitimate means (which may attain the goal) and inasmuch as the individual is shut off from means which are both legitimate *and* effective. The competitive order is maintained, but the frustrated and handicapped individual who cannot cope with this order drops out. Defeatism, quietism and resignation are manifested in escape mechanisms which ultimately lead the individual to "escape" from the requirements of the society. It is an expedient which arises from continued failure to attain the goal by legitimate measures and from an inability to adopt the illegitimate route because of internalized prohibitions and institutionalized compulsives, *during which process the supreme value of the success-goal has as yet not been renounced.* The conflict is resolved by eliminating *both* precipitating elements, the goals and means. The escape is complete, the conflict is eliminated and the individual is asocialized.

Be it noted that where frustration derives from the inaccessibility of effective institutional means for attaining economic or any other type of highly valued " success," that Adaptations II, III and V (innovation, ritualism and rebellion) are also possible. The result will be determined by the particular personality, and thus, the *particular* cultural background, involved. Inadequate socialization will result in the innovation response whereby the conflict and frustration are eliminated by relinquishing the institutional means and retaining the success-aspiration; an extreme assimilation of institutional demands will lead to ritualism wherein the goal is dropped as beyond one's reach but conformity to the mores persists; and rebellion occurs when emancipation from the reigning standards, due to frustration or to marginalist perspectives, leads to the attempt to introduce a " new social order."

Our major concern is with the illegitimacy adjustment. This involves the use of conventionally proscribed but frequently effective means of attaining at least the simulacrum of culturally defined success, — wealth, power, and the like. As we have seen, this adjustment occurs when the individual has assimilated the cultural emphasis on success without equally internalizing the morally prescribed norms governing means for its attainment. The question arises, Which phases of our social structure predispose toward this mode of adjustment? We may examine a concrete instance, effectively analyzed by Lohman, which provides a clue to the answer. Lohman has shown that specialized areas of vice in the near north side of Chicago constitute a " normal " response to a situation where the cultural emphasis upon pecuniary success has been absorbed, but where there is little access to conventional and legitimate means for attaining such success. The conventional occupational opportunities of persons in this area are almost completely limited to manual labor. Given our cultural stigmatization of manual labor, and its correlate, the prestige of white collar work, it is clear that the result is a strain toward innovational practices. The limitation of opportunity to unskilled labor and the resultant low income can not compete *in terms of conventional standards of achievement* with the high income from organized vice.

For our purposes, this situation involves two important features. First, such antisocial behavior is in a sense " called forth " by certain conventional values of the culture *and* by the class structure involving differential access to the approved opportunities for legitimate, prestige-bearing pursuit of the culture goals. The lack of high integration between the means-and-end elements of the cultural pattern and the particular class structure combine to favor a heightened frequency of anti-social conduct in such groups. The second consideration is of equal significance. Recourse to the first of the alternative responses, legitimate effort, is limited by the fact that actual advance toward desired success-symbols through conventional channels is, despite our persisting open-class ideology, relatively rare and difficult for those handicapped by little formal education and few economic resources. The dominant pressure of group standards of success is, therefore, on the gradual attentuation of legitimate, but by and large ineffective, strivings and the increasing use of illegitimate, but more or less effective, expedients of vice and crime. The cultural demands made on persons in this situation are incompatible. On the one hand, they are asked to orient their conduct toward the prospect of accumulating wealth and on the other, they are largely denied effective opportunities to do so institutionally. The consequences of such structural inconsistency are psychopathological personality, and/or antisocial conduct, and/or revolutionary activities. The equilibrium between culturally designated means and ends becomes highly unstable with the progressive emphasis on attaining the prestige-laden ends by any means whatsoever. Within this context, Capone represents the triumph of amoral intelligence over morally prescribed "failure," when the channels of vertical mobility are closed or narrowed *in a society which places a high premium on economic affluence and social ascent for all its members.*

This last qualification is of primary importance. It suggests that other phases of the social structure besides the extreme emphasis on pecuniary success, must be considered if we are to understand the social sources of antisocial behavior. A high frequency of deviate behavior is not generated simply by "lack of opportunity" or by this exaggerated pecuniary emphasis. A comparatively rigidified class structure, a feudalistic or caste order, may limit such opportunities far beyond the point which obtains in our society today. It is only when a system of cultural values extols, virtually above all else, certain *common* symbols of success *for the population at large* while its social structure rigorously restricts or completely eliminates access to approved modes of acquiring these symbols *for a considerable part of the same population,* that antisocial behavior ensues on a considerable scale. In other words, our egalitarian ideology denies by implication the existence of noncompeting groups and individuals in the pursuit of pecuniary success. The same body of success-symbols is held to be desirable for all. These goals are held to *transcend class lines,* not to be bounded by them, yet the actual social organization is such that there exist class differentials in the accessibility of these *common* success-symbols. Frustration and thwarted aspiration lead to the search for avenues of escape from a culturally induced intolerable situation; or unrelieved ambition may ventuate in illicit attempts to acquire the dominant values. The American stress on pecuniary success and ambitiousness for all thus invites exaggerated anxieties, hostilities neuroses and antisocial behavior.

This theoretical analysis may go far toward explaining the varying correlations between crime and poverty. Poverty is not an isolated variable. It is one in a complex of interdependent social and cultural variables. When viewed in such a context, it represents quite different states of affairs. Poverty as such, and consequent limitation of opportunity, are not sufficient to induce a conspicuously high rate of criminal behavior. Even the often mentioned "poverty in the midst of plenty" will not necessarily lead to this result. Only insofar as poverty and associated disadvantages in competition for the culture values approved for *all* members of the society is linked with the assimilation of a cultural emphasis on monetary accumulation as a symbol of success is antisocial conduct a "normal" outcome. Thus, poverty is less highly correlated with crime in southeastern Europe than in the United States. The possibilities of vertical mobility in these European areas would seem to be fewer than in this country, so that neither poverty *per se* nor its association with limited opportunity is sufficient to account for the varying correlations. It is only when the full configuration is considered, poverty, limited opportunity and a commonly shared system of success symbols, that we can explain the higher association between poverty and crime in our society than in others where rigidified class structure is coupled with differential class symbols of achievement.

In societies such as our own, then, the pressure of prestige-bearing success tends to eliminate the effective social constraint over means employed to this end. "The end-justifies-the-means" doctrine becomes a guiding tenet for action when the cultural structure unduly exalts the end and the social organization unduly limits possible recourse to approved means. Otherwise put, this notion and associated behavior reflect a lack of cultural coordination. In international relations, the effects of this lack of integration are notoriously apparent. An emphasis upon national power is not readily coordinated with an inept organization of legitimate, i.e., internationally defined and accepted, means for attaining this goal. The result is a tendency toward the abrogation of international law, treaties become scraps of paper, "undeclared warfare" serves as a technical evasion, the bombing of civilian populations is rationalized, just as the same societal situation induces the same sway of illegitimacy among individuals.

The social order we have described necessarily produces this "strain toward dissolution." The pressure of such an order is upon outdoing one's competitors. The choice of means within the ambit of institutional control will persist as long as the sentiments supporting a competitive system, i.e., deriving from the possibility of outranking competitors and hence enjoying the favorable response of others, are distributed throughout the entire system of activities and are not confined merely to the final result. A stable social structure demands a balanced distribution of affect among its various segments. When there occurs a shift of emphasis from the satisfactions derived from competition itself to almost exclusive concern with successful competition, the resultant stress leads to the breakdown of the regulatory structure. With the resulting attenuation of the institutional imperatives, there occurs an approximation of the situation erroneously held by utilitarians to be typical of society generally wherein calculations of advantage and fear of punishment are the sole regulating agencies. In such situations, as Hobbes observed, force and fraud come to constitute the sole virtues in view of their relative efficiency in attaining goals, — which were for him, of course, not culturally derived.

It should be apparent that the foregoing discussion is not pitched on a moralistic plane. Whatever the sentiments of the writer or reader concerning the ethical desirability of coordinating the means-and-goals phases of the social structure, one must agree that lack of such coordination leads to anomie. Insofar as one of the most general functions of social organization is to provide a basis for calculability and regularity of behavior, it is increasingly lim-ited in effectiveness as these elements of the structure become dissociated. At the extreme, predictability virtually disappears and what may be properly termed cultural chaos or anomie intervenes.

This statement, being brief, is also incomplete. It has not included an exhaustive treatment of the various structural elements which predispose toward one rather than another of the alternative responses open to individuals; it has neglected, but not denied the relevance of, the factors determining the specific incidence of these responses; it has not enumerated the various concrete responses which are constituted by combinations of specific values of the analytical variables, it has omitted, or included only by implication, any consideration of the social functions performed by illicit responses; it has not tested the full explanatory power of the analytical scheme by examining a large number of group variations in the frequency of deviate and conformist behavior; it has not adequately dealt with rebellious conduct which seeks to refashion the social framework radically; it has not examined the relevance of cultural conflict for an analysis of culture-goal and institutional-means malintegration. It is suggested that these and related problems may be profitably analyzed by this scheme.

INDUSTRIALIZATION THROUGH COLLECTIVE CHOICE

8

44. The Collective Form of Industrialization

The historical processes that prepared the way for the expansion of capitalism in the last half of the eighteenth century in Western Europe did not penetrate the whole world or even all of Europe. Russia, for instance, in the nineteenth century was untouched by those changes in Western Europe that enthroned the individual and raised new elites to positions of authority. The Russian aristocracy tenaciously maintained its place of dominance and held the vast majority of people in feudal bondage. Russia, therefore, marked time while Western Europe and the United States expanded their industrial capacities with the releasing of the energies of the individual.

Although the techniques of the Industrial Revolution did not immediately spread to Russia, Russian society was by no means unaware of the changes taking place in the West. One group was particularly alert to these developments — the Russian Marxists. Many Russian intellectuals who were dissatisfied and

restless under the despotic rule of the Romanovs accepted Marxism when it appeared in Russia during the last quarter of the nineteenth century, as the oracle of the new society which would replace the archaic social and economic organization of Tsarist Russia. These people fervently hoped and assiduously worked for the destruction of the old order.

The new society envisaged by the Marxists would be free of the oppressions of capitalism — the social consequences of capitalism discussed in the last chapter. The class struggle would disappear and with it the coercive functions of state, as the proletariat seized title to the ownership of the means of production. The new productive relationships in socialist society would release new human energies that had been held in check by a system in which the means of production were owned privately, and human beings would rise above the drudgery of economic necessity and be able to inscribe on their banner: " to each according to his need, from each according to his ability."

The Russian Revolution of 1917 brought to power the Russian Marxists, a group dedicated to the creation of this new society. Whether or not the new society has been achieved by the leaders of the Soviet Union is an open question. One thing is clear, however: the path of development chosen by the Soviet Union is markedly different from the path of development followed in the West. Having reacted against the capitalism of the Western world the Soviet leaders were not willing to rely on the organizational features of capitalistic society to achieve their objectives. Consequently, Soviet economic organization is differentiated from that in the West through the use of collective methods of making decisions. Russia today is the Russia of Five-Year-Plans.

Since Russia stood outside of the Western tradition and was not part of the evolution which elevated the status of the individual in society, it is not surprising that Russia has eschewed the economic methods of the West in favor of a pattern of eco-nomic organization more congenial to the indigenous values of Russian society. In the West the basic economic decisions are made by all the people who meet as buyers and sellers in the market; in Russia these same decisions are made by central governmental authority. In the West the means of production are owned by private individuals; in Russia the means of production are owned collectively by the state. In the West, therefore, the state has been on the periphery of economic growth, in Russia at the center of economic growth.

The first article in this chapter describes the evolution of Russian planning, or the evolution of the system of collective choice. The second suggests some of the adjustments individuals must make in changing from a collective to an individualistic system. And, because it is sometimes difficult for people brought up in a democratic, capitalistic environment to believe that non-capitalistic organization can really function, the third article presents some empirical evidence about the growth of the Soviet economy.

45. Planning in the USSR *

I. Pre-Soviet Russia

The economic problem is universal — every society must evolve institutions for allocating scarce resources among competing uses. Economiz-

* By Karl de Schweinitz, Jr.

ing institutions, however, are specific; they vary from society to society depending upon the peculiar social conditions from which the economic problem arises. Economic organization to be effective must reflect the values that people conceive to be important. If its operation depends upon methods that are offensive to the values of people it must be altered or face destruction. Thus the American economy has continually adjusted to the changing attitudes of the American people. By the same token we cannot expect capitalism to be congenial to the peoples of Tanganyika. In this respect economic organization is in no way different from the other institutions which compose society. The family must adhere to certain culturally determined conventions in order to remain respectable and therefore a functioning unit. Religious organizations must conform to what is generally considered appropriate behavior. A church would be censured for offering a bottle of Haig & Haig to every fifth person who entered its portals on Sunday.

In order to understand the Soviet planning system, therefore, we must briefly consider the historical development of Russian society and suggest the conditions which have influenced the values of the leaders of the Soviet Union. Such a treatment of the subject does not imply that the values of society are assiduously sought after and that an economic organization is then erected to satisfy these values. The institutions of society are mutually interdependent, with one another and with the prevailing beliefs and attitudes of the members of society. Nonetheless, it is convenient to break into the circle of interdependence with a search for value-forming conditions. We recognize, however, that causation is not a one-way street

and that we may sacrifice a certain degree of reality in order to establish a logical explanation of the Soviet planning mechanism.

Perhaps the single most important factor in the background of the Soviet Union was the economic backwardness of Tsarist Russia. It would not be much of an exaggeration to say that nineteenth-century Russia stood in relation to Western Europe in this respect as twentieth-century India stands in relation to the United States. At a time when the nations of Western Europe and the United States were rapidly industrializing, Russia was mired in an antiquated social system which precluded a similar development of its economic organization. Consequently, Russia fell far behind in the production of transport, iron and steel, coal, and the other ingredients that are the basis of strong industrial economies.

Economic backwardness has a number of important implications. First, and most obvious, the standard of living for the majority of people in Russia was abysmally low. The predominantly agricultural population eked out a subsistence living from the meager offerings of the soil. And yet the contrasts between the rich and the poor were greater than in those countries where industrialization had permitted a partial diffusion of the fruits of high productivity among the whole people. There was no large middle class which relentlessly pushed up the margins of productivity through enterprise and capital accumulation. An aristocratic class consumed what surplus the quasi-feudal peasant produced but in return did not contribute its energies to the creation of national product.

Second, the economic backwardness of Russia so weakened the structure and power of the Tsarist government that it was not able to successfully resist the military incursions of unfriendly powers. In 1904–1905 Russia was defeated by a much smaller but more energetic Japan. Twelve years later in 1917 the Russian army cracked from the pressure exerted by Germany from the west. These disastrous military defeats underlined the poor position in which Russia stood in relation to its industrially stronger neighbors. So long as the military organization was self-sufficient, the organization of the society it represented was not too important. In the twentieth century, however, the military organization is an extension of industrial society; without a strong industrial base the modern army cannot survive.

To the future leaders of the Soviet Union, brought up under the conditions of life during the Tsarist regimes, it was patent that economic development must be a fundamental part of any program designed to improve the life of the Russian citizen. This much was clear. Not so clear were the appropriate methods of stimulating economic development. The Marxian ideology, about which we shall say more later, did not provide an answer except at such a high level of abstraction that it was meaningless in any concrete situation. Some of the Russian Marxists felt that a bourgeois revolution was essential to the development of Russia, that the restraints of feudalism could only be loosened through the utilization of the propertied interests of the middle class. Others felt that a proletarian revolution would somehow unleash the energies of the vast majority of the population which had been held in check by the exploitation of the aristocracy, and that wealth would rise from the ashes of the old society. It would not be until the Marxists in Russia had achieved power and were compelled to face the responsibilities of administering a sovereign state that they would come to grips with the problem of economic development and of achieving the material wealth implied by communism.

The economic backwardness of Russia, especially when juxtaposed to the utopia of communism, emphasized the need for economic development in Russia. The traditional lack of freedom in Tsarist Russia suggested, if only vaguely or intuitively, the use of administrative techniques for achieving ends that relied to a large extent on overt coercion. This may seem paradoxical — that a people oppressed by one arbitrary and dictatorial system should destroy and replace it with one equally willing to use the methods of the mailed fist. It was not, however, an illogical development. In the first place, the Russian peasantry had never known the amenities of political freedom. The reforms in nineteenth-century Russia came too late to create a large class of independent farmers. The emancipation of the serfs in 1861 and the

Stolypin reforms in the early part of the twentieth century had undoubtedly improved the lot of the peasant. The number of farmers producing and selling for a market, and therefore acquiring a money income which could be used to buy industrial products, increased. The Tsarist government was turning its attentions to the problems of the peasants and was obtaining results. But — and this is the significant point — the reforms of the Tsarist regime did not rise from a functioning and flexible democratic system. The opinion of the peasant was not continuously solicited and acted upon. Rather the Tsarist reforms represented the attempts of the few in power to relieve the pressures that were building up in the constrained Russian society of the nineteenth century. In short, reforms were promulgated not because it was felt right that the people should be controlling the direction of change but because it was felt that the ruling few would suffer if the ungratified desires of the peasantry were not assuaged. The Crimean War forced the emancipation reforms as the revolution of 1905 forced the Stolypin reforms.

If the peasants lacked the political freedom to press for the solution of their own problems within the framework of nineteenth-century Russian society, the intelligentsia and professional groups within the attenuated middle class lacked the freedom to carry on the fight for them. The Russian intellectual, sensitive to the plight of Russia and eager to propose methods of solving its economic and social problems, could not receive much comfort from the political traditions of the West. Constitutionalism or gradual reform was not a program he could realistically espouse. The Tsarist bureaucracy was adamant and intransigent and would only consider constitutionalism when it was apparent that the only alternative was its own demise. And, as was the case in 1905, when the danger seemed past the authoritarian hand of the Tsar reasserted itself.

In this type of political milieu it is not surprising that the reformer, who finds himself frustrated by the constraints on his conduct, turns to extremism and supports revolution as the solution of the particular evils of his society. Thus many nineteenth-century Russians, who in the environment of liberal democratic government might have turned their energies to the institution of reform within the framework of existing society, went underground or into voluntary exile in order to carry on the fight against the Tsarist government. If these revolutionists had not voluntarily removed themselves from Russian society they would have been involuntarily incarcerated by the Tsarist government.

Nikolai Lenin was by no means the first Russian who chose to forego a life of conformity in favor of the ascetic existence of the nonconformist. Before him N. S. Chernyshevsky, Alexander Herzen, Michael Bakunin, and George Plekhanov, to name but a few of the outstanding nineteenth-century Russian revolutionists, broke with the amenities of their life in Russia in order to bring the better life to the Russian people. These men were not in doctrinal agreement; each of them espoused a somewhat different solution to the peculiar problems of Russia. We need not concern ourselves with the fragmentation of the left wing — the important point is that lack of political freedom in their own country drove each of them to take positions which undermined the structure of Russian society.

Having taken the irrevocable step and having maintained the integrity of his political conscience, however, the revolutionist becomes peculiarly suspectible to a belief in omniscience. He has broken with the society in which he lives because he thinks it is unjust and oppressive. He has, so it might easily seem to him, placed himself at one with the downtrodden many in one magnificent gesture of defiance. Yet this very attitude, which is inextricably bound up with his own sufferings as an exile, can very easily degenerate into one of knowing what is best for people. " I have suffered for you; therefore, I know what is best for you."

There was then a generation of revolutionists prior to the Russian Revolution of 1917 who were living under conditions which fostered a belief in the justification of a unilateral solution of social problems. At the best such men sincerely believe in the worth of the individual but think that his salvation lies in the conscious direction of his activities. At the worst such men hold the people in contempt because they

need the help of the endowed few. As we shall see subsequently these beliefs tend to be accentuated by the Marxian ideology.

To spin these consequences from the lack of political freedom may press the reader's credulity. We are not, however, trying to assert that the lack of political freedom in Tsarist Russia is the sole explanation of the planning system which eventually evolved in the Soviet Union. We are simply saying, one, that the lack of freedom among the peasants, the predominant class in Tsarist Russia, established a basic group in Soviet society, which, possibly, did not stand to lose much by the application of coercive methods if these methods resulted in a material improvement in the conditions of life, and, two, that the lack of political freedom in Tsarist Russia molded a group of leaders who were susceptible to the methods of the conscious control of economic and social life.

Although the actions of the Russian citizens were severely proscribed during the nineteenth century, the government was not wholly able to prevent the outbreak of violent protest against its policies. The experience of these abortive outbreaks of violence provided the future leaders of the Soviet Union with a guide book to revolution. They learned what methods were inappropriate for the achievement of the revolutionary end and, positively, learned what had to be done. From the point of view of the organization of the economy the nineteenth-century revolts emphasized the necessity of a rather comprehensive control —

that Bolshevik control could not be secure unless the appendages of the economy came under central direction.

In 1825, at the conclusion of the reign of Alexander I, a group of young Russian officers, who had come under the influence of the ideology of the French and American revolutions, attempted to compel the new sovereign, Nicholas I, to accept the limitations of constitutionalism. The revolt failed, and the reprisals decimated the ranks of the aristocracy. This revolt was essentially a palace revolution. It was, therefore, from the point of view of the Bolsheviks at the end of the century a superficial attempt to modify the authority of the Tsar. There was no systematic reordering of society, but merely an attempt to reshuffle the leaders at the top of the social hierarchy.

A half a century later some young members of the intelligentsia turned to the methods of terror in a vain effort to obtain the reform of society. The Narodniki, members of The Will of the People, believed in the spiritual and social regeneration of Russia through the peasant communities. Furthermore, they believed that the removal of key officials in the Tsarist bureaucracy, notably the Tsar, through violent means would lift the reign of oppression that lay upon the land. The assassination of Alexander II in 1881 was the culmination of their activity. Like the Decembrists before them the Narodniki were destroyed by the Tsarist police. To the Bolshevik the Narodniki pressed home the futility of seeking reform through terrorism. The failure of their isolated acts of terrorism emphasized the basic organizational problem which beset Tsarist Russia. The root of the difficulty, so thought the Bolsheviks, lay in the structure of society and to expect the revival of Russia to come from the agrarian and native socialism of the peasant was naive. The Narodniki forever memorialized for the Bolsheviks the failure of agrarian revolution.

The first proletarian revolution in Russia in 1904–1905 also had its lesson and therefore influenced the values of the future Soviet communists. Unlike the activities of the Decembrists and the Narodniki, which affected relatively small numbers of Russian citizens, the Revolution of 1905 had an important impact on the urban centers of Russian society. It was a unique revolution because it was spontaneous. By 1905 the ranks of the professional revolutionists had grown to respectable proportions. Lenin, Trotsky, Stalin, Bukharin, Martov, Plekhanov, and others were underground or in exile working for the overthrow of the existing Russian regime. Perhaps these men were out of touch with the developments in Russia, or perhaps their energies were too much devoted to the factional disputes in the Russian Social Democratic party which caused the split between the Bolsheviks and Mensheviks. Nonetheless, the professional revolutionists were caught unawares. And the organization of soviets proceeded apace in St. Petersburg and Moscow under the direction of workers and other amateurs who were not tempered in the polemics and asceticism of the exiles' existence. (A notable exception is Leon Trotsky who first achieved fame for his activities in the St. Petersburg Soviet.)

The revolution was a failure. Ignited by the indiscriminate and indiscreet armed assault by soldiers upon a crowd of citizens who were seeking to petition the Tsar for an amnesty for political prisoners, it flickered out because of the irresoluteness of the proletariat and the promises of constitutionalism made by the Tsar to the middle classes. To the Bolshevik the lesson was obvious: do not leave the proletariat to its own devices and do not trust the intentions of the middle classes. The Revolution of 1905 was, therefore, an experience which reaffirmed the belief that central direction of the economic and social life must be an integral part of a revolutionary program in Russia. In the first place, the sympathetic proletariat must be guided so that it will not become the dupe of the pious intentions of the middle classes. In the second place, the middle classes must be controlled so that they will not be tempted to sabotage the revolutionary effort.

The factors discussed thus far have been objective conditions in the development of nineteenth- and early twentieth-century Russia. Each of these objective conditions tended to reinforce the authoritarian values of the future leaders of the Soviet Union. We must now add the ideological element — the influence of Marxism. As indicated in an earlier chapter the Marxian analysis did not hold out much hope for Russia in the immediate future. Marx looked to the advanced countries of Western Europe to lead the revolution. It was in Germany, France, and particularly England that the capitalistic industrial processes had had their greatest success and, therefore, according to Marxian analysis, had created the strongest antithetical reactions. The proletariat were becoming more class-conscious because of their increasing misery, the system was becoming more susceptible to those periodic crises which eventually would cause the dethronement of the capitalistic class. In Russia, however, during Marx's time the society was only starting to throw off the shackles of a feudal organization. Russia, therefore, had to pass through the essential capitalistic stage of economic development. The revolution was indeed far away.

Marx influenced the future Soviet leaders not because of his prescriptions, which did not have an immediate relevance in Russia, but because he captured their minds and provided them with a methodological approach to social problems. To put it another way, Marx articulated a body of doctrine which apparently placed time on the side of the Bolsheviks. He gave them certitude, a peek behind the curtain of time, so that they believed they knew where the world was moving. Thus Marxism in Russia became an absolute, the symbol of a new religious fervor. And unlike life in Western Europe, life in Russia did not provide the evidence for refuting the absolute.

In the last half of the nineteenth century the national income of the countries of Western Europe not only rose but was distributed more equitably. The workers did not become greater in number and more miserable in circumstances as Marx had predicted. Productivity increases apparently exorcised the specter of communism. Russia, on the other hand, which in the late nineteenth century was just beginning to move into the early stages of capitalism, could bear witness to the squalor of an incipient factory system but not to the fruits of its productivity.

The Marxian system was extended and refined by Lenin so that it became, as compared with its pristine state, more of a rationalization for direct revolutionary action. According to Lenin the dialectical struggle between the capitalists and the proletariat was aided and abetted by the imperialistic competition among capitalistic nations for world markets. Such competition degenerated into armed conflict which sapped the energies of the warring nations and broke down the lines of capitalistic control, thus making room for the salients of the proletariat advance. The concept of the imperialistic stage of capitalistic development minimized the significance of the stage of economic development within any one country by explicitly projecting capitalism to the world stage. The relative backwardness of the Russian economy, therefore, was not a deterrent to revolutionary activity in the eyes of Lenin. The important thing was to ignite the flame of the proletarian revolution. If the light were

struck in Russia, the fire would spread to Western Europe.

Not only did Marxism provide an ideological basis for the revolutionary activities of the Russian Bolsheviks, but it inculcated in them a particular attitude about social and economic organization. The writings and theories of Karl Marx were largely a reaction against the squalor of capitalism, which he saw rising around him in Western Europe and in England. The burden of his analysis fell on capitalism. He was not concerned with the utopia of the future but with the principles that governed the development of the past into the present and, he hoped, the present into the future. In searching for these principles he subjected capitalism to the scalpel of his incisive mind and concluded that its demise was only a matter of time. Since Marxism was a reaction against the methods of Western capitalism, the adherents to Marxism were led to reject the self-regulating market and all its political and social implications. Thus the Russian Marxists eschewed the automatism of the West in favor of the conscious direction of economic and social processes.

It is important to note that prior to the Revolution in Russia "the conscious direction of economic and social processes" was a pious hope more than a program on which to base action. Marx had little idea of what planning involved — his energies were too absorbed in laying to rest the system of capitalistic enterprise to permit him to contemplate the problems of the socialist state. Lenin contemplated these problems but with a naivete that was later swept away during the baptism of the Soviet regime. On the eve of the October Revolution Lenin wrote:

Capitalist culture has created large-scale production, factories, railways, the postal service, telephones, etc., and on this basis the great majority of functions of the old " state power " have become so simplified and can be reduced to such simple operations of registration, filing, and checking that they will be quite within the reach of every literate person, and it will be possible to perform them for " working-men's wages," which circumstance can (and must) strip those functions of every shadow of privilege, of every appearance of " official grandeur." (*State and Revolution*, p. 38)

In Lenin's view, then, the direction of the social and economic life of the nation was a relatively easy task. The important job was to gain control of the state.

To summarize, the objective conditions in Russia of the nineteenth century, such as the lack of political freedom and the poverty of the economy plus the Marxian ideology, created for the Bolshevik leaders a compulsion to increase the economic wealth of Russia by conscious methods of control, which in some sense were distinguishable from the methods of capitalistic enterprise. What these methods consisted of was not clear. Indeed the early history of the Soviet Union is in considerable part one of the gropings and fumblings for the unique form of Soviet economic organization.

It was not until 1928 when the first Five-Year Plan was inaugurated that the Soviet Union developed the form of economic organization that since has become uniquely associated with Russia. The years between the Revolution of 1917 and the first year of the Five-Year Plans provided the experience out of which Soviet planning evolved. These years can be conveniently divided into two periods: the period of War Communism, 1918–1921, and the period of the New Economic Policy (NEP), 1921–1928. We shall consider each of these periods in turn and point up the factors which led the Soviet leaders to organize the economy around the Five-Year Plans.

II. WAR COMMUNISM AND THE NEW ECONOMIC POLICY

The most difficult economic problem that the Soviet leaders have had to face during the years of their regime has been the exchange relationship between town and country. Obviously, an urban population is dependent upon an agricultural population that can produce enough both for its own needs and the needs of city residents. Likewise industry in considerable part depends upon the movement of industrial raw materials from the farm to the factory. In a well-ordered market economy an agricultural surplus is exchanged for industrial products that the farmer either cannot produce himself, or can acquire more cheaply by raising and trading agricultural commodities. If industrial products are not forthcoming the farmer is likely either to increase his consumption of his own output or restrict the quantity he produces. In both cases the surplus available to the urban and industrial population is reduced, thus limiting the output potential of industry. It is in the context of this central economic problem that we shall consider the move toward planning in the Soviet Union.

The economy that the Bolsheviks seized in the fall of 1917 was an empty shell. Three years of war had strained the meager resources of an economy that even at the outset, had lacked the strength to compete with the industrial nations of the West. The collapse of the Russian front and the internal disorders created conditions favorable for revolution but unfavorable for the orderly utilization of what resources Russia did have. Already disorganized, the economy was further hampered by its isolation from the industrial West and the loss of territories (the Ukraine) rich in agricultural and industrial resources to Germany.

Against this background of devastation a group of men came into power in Russia who had little, if any, experience with the problems of public administration. The Bolsheviks were schooled in the polemics of Marxian theory and experienced in the uncertain life of an underground or exiled existence. Up until the Revolution the life of these men had been negative in the sense that they were combating established authority and, consequently, they had not had to face the positive task of administering a society. Furthermore, the Bolsheviks drew their chief support

from the proletariat, but in Russia the proletariat was a small minority relative to agrarian groups. In 1917 communism was not widely rooted in Russian society. Finally, to compound the difficulties faced by the new government, the preponderance of managerial and technical personnel was carried over from the Tsarist regime and therefore was suspect by the Bolsheviks. They, in turn, were not always sympathetic with the objectives of the new leaders. But it was from these groups that the Bolsheviks had to obtain the practical experience necessary for manning the machinery of state and economy.

In spite of these problems, or possibly because of them, the Bolsheviks proceeded with little delay to consolidate their position. Recognizing the anomaly of a proletarian revolution in an agrarian society, they nationalized the land and through local soviets or committees distributed the large state, church, and private estates to the land-hungry peasants. This was deemed necessary in order to win the support of the peasant, and indeed without this precipitous action the subsequent civil war might well have been decided against the Bolsheviks. It was the unwillingness of the White Russians to commit themselves on land policy which gave many of the peasants a preference for the Red Russians. "Land to the peasants" became a supporting slogan for the Bolsheviks.

The distribution of land to the peasants was matched in the industrial centers by the formation of workers' committees in the factories whose function it was to supervise and control the decisions being made by management. In the confusion of the Revolution the workers' committees often got out of hand and took it upon themselves to dispossess managerial and owner groups as a symbol of their revolutionary fervor. There was, in consequence, a wave of spontaneous, decentralized, and unco-ordinated acts of nationalization.

The Russian economy already staggering under the blows of war and political revolution suffered anew from these manifestations of economic revolution. The distribution of land among the peasants reduced the agricultural surplus available for the urban and industrial centers. The estates which had previously produced the surplus now were split up into many small holdings whose output went into increased peasant consumption. The factories in many instances were in the charge of men who had not the least idea how production should be organized. The quantity and quality of goods produced fell off. And because the output of industry diminished the peasant had less of an incentive to offer his products in exchange for industrial products.

Real income fell precipitously during this early period of the Soviet Union. Money income, however, rose explosively. The ruble already inflated by three years of war finance depreciated further as the quantity of goods available for exchange diminished and as the new government ran the printing presses to supplement its almost nonexistent tax revenues.

The young Soviet regime had not made an auspicious start. Yet the worst was still to come. In the summer of 1918 civil war broke out in Russia. The Bolsheviks were literally beset on all sides by hostile forces, which were attempting to break the back of Soviet control. The early successes of these hostile forces deprived the Bolsheviks of much of Russian territory and left them holding the inner core of what approximately corresponded to ancient Muscovy. In one sense this was a blessing in disguise because it reduced the area of control to the limits of the Bolsheviks' power to control. Yet in most other senses the Civil War was a major catastrophe. Much of the territory lost to the White Russians was vital to the economy. A Red Army had to be mobilized from a peasantry which had just suffered through three years of World War I. And as the army was mobilized the number of men available for agricultural and industrial occupations was reduced. Yet the exigencies of war placed new demands on the economy which was depleted by men and resources.

The Bolsheviks met the challenge of the Civil War by inaugurating the period of what is now called War Communism. Basic industries were formally nationalized and brought under the centralized control of government finance (that is, what at that time could be recognized as finance). Man power was conscripted both for the Red Army and for industry. The government attempted to control the rationing of consumer goods through state stores.

The government could nationalize industry and it could conscript labor, but it could not control the peasant. The provision of grain and other agricultural products for the urban population was the most ineluctable problem of all those faced by the Bolsheviks during this period of War Communism. At first grain was requisitioned from the peasants by the government. When this measure failed to yield adequate supplies of grain, the government authorized trade unions and other groups to organize detachments for seizing grain from the peasants at fixed prices. For an incentive these groups were permitted to hold half of the grain they collected, the balance being turned over to the government for state distribution. Later, the poor peasants were organized into similar detachments for securing the grain of the kulak, the rich peasant. Still later armed detachments of workers and soldiers scoured the countryside for surplus grain.

On the positive side the Bolsheviks encouraged the formation of collective farms. The compulsions of revolution forced the Bolsheviks to distribute the land to the peasants, but this policy ran counter to their desire to develop large-scale agriculture. Not only did they fear the vested interest of a propertied peasantry but they were apprehensive about the effects of small peasant holdings on productivity. Therefore, the Bolshevik government established a special fund for supporting through financial aid those groups in rural areas that desired to pool their energy and resources in collective agriculture.

Neither the negative nor the positive agricultural measures were particularly successful. If the peasant could not hide grain from the detachments of workers and soldiers he could reduce the acres he cultivated to take care only of his own and his family's needs. Nor did the peasant display any spontaneous enthusiasm about collective farming. Having won in the Revolution the land that he had always thought rightfully belonged to him, he was loath to cede it to a collective entity about which he knew nothing.

And hovering above the whole problem of agricultural-industrial exchange was a galloping inflation, which further restricted the government's ability to control the peasant's output. In keeping with the doctrinaire intentions of communism the Bolsheviks established a distribution system of state stores, which rationed consumers' goods, mainly food products, at fixed prices. Inflation, however, continued to plague the economy. The peasant, therefore, had a monetary incentive for withholding his grain from the prescribed channels of collection and distribution. If he did so, he could sell his excess grain at much higher prices in the black market. As the Civil War continued and the ruble depreciated, the state stores became an increasingly unimportant part of the distribution system. Eventually these stores distributed their supplies without charge, or what amounts to the same thing, the inflation having proceeded so far that the fixed state price was merely a token charge. But the bulk of goods passed through the black market. In fact, the government was dependent on the black market for supplying the cities with food and so closed its eyes to these supposedly illegal operations.

The inflation had its most enervating effect on the urban population. With the ruble hardly worth the paper it was printed on — it is alleged that 10,000 workers were employed in supplying the new government's currency needs — payments in kind gradually were substituted for payments in money. Workers received their wages in the products they produced and then bartered them for their consumption needs. But this was a period of severe deprivation and the worker did not produce enough to provide a subsistence income for himself. The government, therefore, often leased to factories land that could be used for the cultivation of subsistence crops. Lacking this, the workers had to be granted time off to forage in the country surrounding the cities. These expedients may have kept the workers alive but they meant a loss of productivity that the economy could ill afford. Time off from work was time off from production.

With the development of payments in kind the rural-urban pattern of population changed. Many of the workers, most of whom were not even a generation removed from the countryside, returned to their rural homes. It was easier to keep alive close to the soil than in centers of population. From 1917 to 1919 the population of Petrograd, for ex-ample, fell from 2,300,000 to 700,000.

It is interesting to note that the period of War Communism which in retrospect can only be described as chaos, a period in which stocks were run down and capital equipment drastically depreciated, was viewed by some Bolsheviks as the triumphant order of communism. Some argued that the inflation was an important technique for destroying those elements of the bourgeoisie who still might offer resistance to the new regime. Others argued that the inflation brought about the moneyless economy, the ideal of communism, in which distribution was governed by need.

Fortunately for the Soviet Union, Lenin did not take a doctrinaire attitude about War Communism. He realized that it was the crudest of expedients and one that could not be continued without jeopardizing the very existence of the economy. The Civil War was concluded in the fall of 1920 with victory for the Red Army. Thus the Russian economy was relieved of the extraordinary demands of war. In the following spring Lenin announced the introduction of the New Economic Policy at the Tenth Congress of the Communist Party with the following statement:

We are living in such conditions of impoverishment and ruin, of overstrain and exhaustion of the principal productive forces of the peasants and the workers, that for a time everything must be subordinated to this fundamental consideration — at all costs to increase the quantity of goods. . . . On the economic front, in our attempt to pass over to Communism, we had suffered, by the spring of 1921, a more serious defeat than any previously inflicted on us by Kolchak, Denikin or Pilsudsky. Compulsory requisition in the villages and the direct Communist approach to the problems of reconstruction in towns — this was the policy which interfered with the growth of productive capacity of the country and proved to be the main cause of a profound economic and political crisis which confronted us in the spring of 1921. The new economic policy means the substitution of a food tax for requisitioning, it means a transition to the restoration of capitalism in no small degree. In what degree we do not know. . . . The fundamental question, from the point of view of strategy, is, who will the sooner take advantage of this new situation? Who will win? The capitalist whom we are now letting in through the door or even through several doors which we ourselves ignore and which will open independently of us and against us? Or the proletarian sovereign power. (Quoted by Alexander Baykov, *The Development of The Soviet Economic System,* p. 48.)

As Lenin stated in his announcement the New Economic Policy was a retreat towards capitalism. Industry which had been highly centralized under War Communism was ordered to operate autonomously without the aid of governmental financial assistance. In other words, the state trusts were to use the methods of private capitalistic accounting, balancing revenues against cost in an effort to operate profitably. Some

industries were leased to private operators. Private trading, both wholesale and retail, was permitted. Peasants were allowed to lease land, hire agricultural labor, and produce for a market. Finally, labor was relieved of the draft and could seek employment in labor markets.

For many Communists NEP was a bitter blow. Since it was a move away from what was vaguely thought to be communist social and economic organization, it seemed to be a betrayal of the Revolution. The market was to be substituted for the conscious administration of economic processes; an unplanned economy was to replace a planned economy. But the reasons for the change were too compelling to be ignored.

First and foremost, the peasant had to be appeased. The grain requisitioning of War Communism had failed. The peasant struck back at the government by reducing the acreage he cultivated. Without adequate food supplies moving into the cities the Bolsheviks could not hope to maintain the productivity of industry, let alone increase it. And with hunger stalking the towns, the population was moving back to the country. This was an intolerable situation — the proletarian revolution was de-proletarizing Russian society. The Revolution could only be saved by yielding to the peasant and providing him with a positive incentive for supplying his products to the towns.

Second, NEP in considerable part simply officially sanctioned practices that unofficially came into existence during War Communism. The black market is a sub rosa form of capitalism, which develops during periods of stringent price control. During War Communism the volume of food products moving through the black market was greater than the volume moving through the state stores. Thus NEP acknowledged the facts of Soviet existence.

Third, the Bolsheviks did not have the trained and loyal technical and managerial personnel necessary for any other possible solution to the problems they faced in 1921. They had to resort to methods which would minimize the responsibilities of a bureaucracy. The market eminently fulfills this purpose by decentralizing the decisions that have to be made in economic society, thus giving many people a small role to play in economic organization instead of a few people a large role.

NEP was successful in achieving its primary purpose of stimulating the recovery of the Russian economy. By 1926 agricultural and industrial output were approaching their prewar levels. Productivity, however, had fallen off so that real income per capita was lower than it had been in 1913. The ruble had finally been stabilized after a series of currency reforms. Even those Communists who depreciated the use of money in the socialist state saw the necessity of establishing a stable unit of account in an economy that was relying on the methods of the market. Thus the Soviet Union turned to orthodox methods of finance and banking in order to stay the rise of the price level. With the recovery of produc-

tion and the stabilization of the currency, the time had come to consider ways and means of increasing the industrial capacity of the economy.

Although successful in promoting recovery NEP had never been fully acceptable to the Communist Party. It was too much of a compromise with forces that were out of step with the ideology of the Bolsheviks. To encourage the Kulak and private commercial interests was to encourage those groups who posed the threat of counterrevolution. Throughout NEP the treatment of the peasant provided a focal point for Party discussions about the future of economic organization in the Soviet Union.

These discussions were doubly important in view of the fact that the economy continued to be plagued by the problem of exchange between town and country. During the early period of NEP, 1922, there was a marked disparity between industrial prices and agricultural prices. The widespread and catastrophic famine of 1921 placed a premium on agricultural products the following year. Industry, cut adrift from the governmental support of War Communism, found itself perpetually short of working capital. Firms were consequently compelled to liquidate stocks at sacrifice prices in order to obtain the funds to finance current operations. Industrial prices tended to lag behind agricultural prices.

In a supposedly proletarian society looking forward to industrial development this was an undesirable situation. It reduced the real wages of the workers, the main support of the regime, who found their ability to buy farm products diminished by the relative rise of agricultural prices. Also unemployment in the industrial centers accompanied these price changes and thus presented the Communist Party with the curious paradox of a reserved army of unemployed in a socialist state. The adverse price movements prevented the accumulation of investment funds by industry as income tended to be channelized toward the rural sector of the economy. Finally, as suggested above, the income of those groups who were most likely to be hostile to the Bolshevik regime was increased.

By 1923, however, the price scissors started to open up in the opposite direction. The supply of agricultural goods increased in response to the price situation of the previous year which was favorable to the peasant. On the other hand industrial prices moved up as the state trusts organized marketing syndicates to prevent the disorderly competition which had damaged them the previous year. In other words, the trusts exerted monopoly power over price.

From the ideological point of view this was a more congenial price pattern for the party leaders, but from the economic point of view it posed a further dilemma. The movement of prices in favor of industry reduced the return the peasant received from a given output of agricultural produce. The now familiar problem faced the Party — the reduction in the movement of grain from the farm to the city.

What could be done to break out of this vicious circle? In particular, what part should planning play in the attempts to resolve the problem? NEP, as we have seen, was a move away from the conscious control by central authority of economic and social processes. Nonetheless, there were elements of planning in the economy of this period. A state economic planning commission (Gosplan) had been organized early in 1921 almost simultaneously with the birth of NEP. Although its inception was overshadowed by NEP and the return to the market, Gosplan accumulated economists and technical personnel, studied the comprehensive economic problems that faced the Soviet Union, and passed on plans submitted to it by economic ministries. It supervised the work of an electrification plan about which Lenin was particularly enthusiastic, an enthusiasm which led him to remark that "communism is Soviet power plus electrification." Also there was a concerted effort during NEP to rationalize production as a means of reducing costs. Surveys were made of the efficiency of competing plants. The most inefficient plants (or mines) were closed and production concentrated in the most efficient.

Some elements in the Communist Party, however, looked upon what planning there was during NEP and the discussions of planning as essentially non-socialist and in no way different from policies that would be compatible with capitalism. These groups, which came to be known as the left wing of the party (the outstanding personality associated with the left wing was Leon Trotsky), felt that planning should be actively and consciously directed towards achieving comprehensive economic goals, in this case the industrialization of Russia. They argued that agriculture should be collectivized and bent to the task of providing the surplus necessary to support a rapid rate of capital accumulation. Likewise labor should be directed into those occupations necessary to develop the industrial strength of the nation. In their view the plan to electrify Russia, for instance, was a particular plan, which was all very well, but it did not go far in achieving the objectives of a socialist society.

In opposition to the left-wing group, a right-wing group contended that planning was essentially the guiding of the economy along a trend line extrapolated from past economic development. In the context of NEP, this would mean that the peasant would determine the rate of industrialization because the size of the surplus he was willing to supply to industry would control the rate of capital accumulation. It would further mean a greater emphasis on light industry than on heavy industry because the extrapolation of past trends would implicitly place a heavy weight on consumers' decisions and their preferences for consumers goods.

The left wing, then, supported an active concept of planning, which would force a rapid rate of industrialization. The right wing supported a passive concept of planning, which would achieve a rate of indus-

trialization consistent with the economic decisions being made by consumer, worker, and peasant.

The dispute over planning was part of the larger political struggle for control of the Party after the death of Lenin. The latter is not our particular concern. Suffice it to say that both the left wing and the right wing lost out in the struggle and that Stalin emerged triumphant. It is of concern to us, however, that Stalin, having consolidated his power, adopted the economic program of the left-wing group and launched the Soviet Union into the era of Five-Year Plans and the collectivization of agriculture, a period that is sometimes referred to as the second Bolshevik revolution. Planning as we now know it in the Soviet Union started after eleven years of vacillating policy following the seizure of power by the Bolsheviks in the fall of 1917.

Before we go on to consider the planning method in the Soviet Union we must first ask what prompted Stalin to promote the method of Five-Year Plans and the forcible collectivization of agriculture. First, it became clear during NEP that a satisfactory rate of industrialization could not be achieved on the basis of the agricultural output the peasants would voluntarily produce. The land units were too small to permit the effective use of capital equipment, for example combines, in the raising of agricultural products. Large-scale farming seemed to be the solution to this particular problem and to this end Stalin ordered the collectivization of agriculture, the making of big farms out of small farms. Second, to continue NEP would strengthen the hand of those the Party consider unfriendly to the regime. Being revolutionists themselves, the Bolsheviks were particularly sensitive to the threat of counterrevolution. The Kulak and private commercial interests were, therefore, suspect.

Third, the failure of world revolution threw the Soviet Union completely on its own resources and thus made it unlikely that it could borrow resources to facilitate industrialization. In the early days after the Russian Revolution the Bolsheviks had high hopes that they had ignited the flame of world revolution and that the nations of Western Europe would become proletarian states. In that event Russia could have expected material assistance from the industrial West in their effort to increase the industrial capacity of their economy. But the failure of revolution in Germany after World War I frustrated these expectations. By 1928 it was clear that Russia would have to proceed alone.

Fourth, for ideological reasons it was deemed necessary to differentiate the economy of the Soviet Union from those in capitalistic nations. The Bolsheviks believed that the economic laws of socialism were different from the economic laws of capitalism and that to continue NEP would be a betrayal of the Revolution. Finally, eleven years of Communist rule had provided cadres of personnel who had sufficient experience in administration to permit the Party to attempt the ambitious form

of planning epitomized by the Five-Year Plans.

III. THE SOVIET PLANNING SYSTEM

Before entering upon a detailed discussion of the Soviet planning system it is worth while to remind the reader of the outstanding characteristics of the market economy, because the latter will serve as a foil for our examination of the former. The market is a decentralized form of economic organization, for all the significant economic decisions are made by all the members of society, who meet in the markets as buyers and sellers. On one side of the market consumers express their preferences by the way in which they divide money income among the alternative consumers' goods offered for sale. On the other side of the market resource-owners sell the services of their resources, including labor, to those firms which will yield the maximum income, income taken to include preferences for employment. Straddling both sides of the market is the entrepreneur who tries to maximize the spread between the costs he pays out to resource-owners and the revenues he receives from consumers for sale of product. The allocation of resources is guided by the changing prices which are formed in consumers' markets and resources markets. Thus the goods produced in the market can be said to represent the complex interaction of the preferences of consumers and producers.

In contrast, the basic economic decisions are centralized in governmental authority in the Soviet planning system. The pattern of resource-allocation, therefore, represents the policy preferences of the Communist Party. It may well be the case that these preferences correspond to those of the majority of citizens of the Soviet Union. This is not the place to investigate this difficult and intriguing question. Nonetheless, it is important to note that economic policy originates ultimately in the councils of the Party and not in the preferences of the people.

For reasons suggested in the previous sections of this chapter the Communist Party has a marked preference for a rapid rate of economic development or industrialization. Many of the characteristics of the Soviet planning system spring from this desire to accelerate the growth of the productive capacity of the Soviet economy.

In order to achieve this end the Soviet authorities establish their objectives in terms of real production and subordinate the planning of money values to the achievement of these objectives. Thus the attempt is made to prevent disturbances in monetary phenomena from jeopardizing the realization of real production quotas.

This system of planning, though emanating from the preferences of the Communist Party and couched in terms of real production objectives, cannot be divorced from that reality which is the behavior of people. Planning is conceived of as a continuous interaction between the subjective element of policy formulated by the planners and the objective conditions of production, which limit and control the possibilities of plan-fulfillment. It would be futile to devote 50 per cent of the nation's resources to the production of investment goods if by doing so the energies of people were sapped and their interest dulled by a dearth of consumers' goods. Soviet planning, then, must always deal with the possible regardless of the preferences of the Party leaders.

It is convenient to conceive of Soviet planning in two phases: one, the formulation of the plan, and, two, the execution and enforcement of the plan. Clearly this is a conceptual distinction for the purposes of exposition, which is hard to draw in practice. For if there is truly an interaction between planning and objective reality a plan must yield and change to a certain extent even as it is being enforced. Nonetheless, we shall consider Soviet planning in these two phases.

The highest planning agency in the Soviet Union is Gosplan, or the State Planning Commission, which as we have seen was organized in 1921. Gosplan occupies a central position in the Soviet planning apparatus, its primary task being to formulate the plans that adjust the data of Soviet economic existence to the policy objectives of the Communist Party. Gosplan is not itself an executive agency but rather is attached in an advisory capacity to the highest executive organ in the economy, Sovnarkom or the Council of People's Ministers. The planning decisions of Gosplan, however, become binding on the units in the economic hierarchy through the executive powers of Sovnarkom.

Gosplan is divided into a number of departments some of which deal with problems that are common to all industry and some of which deal with the problems of particular industries. In dealing with common economic problems the former departments are discharging the co-ordinating function of the planning agency. In fact, however, the distinction between these two different types of departments in Gosplan cannot be strictly adhered to. A department responsible for co-ordinating the investment program in the Soviet Union must necessarily work in conjunction with those departments that are concerned with the particular industries that will be affected by an investment program.

More important than the internal organization of Gosplan is the communication system which supplies Gosplan with the economic data upon which plan construction depends. The communication link between Gosplan and the production plants is the economic administration which supervises production. Although the organization of the economic administration has changed frequently during the period of the Five-Year Plans it has apparently assumed a reasonably consistent pattern. Heavy industry, or industry in which the production units are large, such as the iron and steel industry or the aircraft industry, are centrally administered by All-Union Ministries. That is to say, the management of

iron and steel mills is directly connected with the Ministry for Ferrous Metallurgy without the intervention of any sort of administrative sub-group. Light industry, generally industry producing for a consumer market, is subordinated to a Republic Ministry, which in turn is supervised by a Union Ministry. In some cases where production is carried on in numerous small plants an administrative sub-group called the Trust may separate the operating plants from the Republic Ministries. Finally, local industry, that industry depending largely upon the utilization of local resources, is controlled by the province or municipality in which it happens to be, the latter being under the jurisdiction of the Republic Ministries for Local Industry. Standing above the whole hierarchy of All-Union Ministries and Republic Ministries is Sovnarkom, to which as we have previously indicated Gosplan is attached.

Each of the units in this administrative hierarchy has a planning division. Thus each plant producing iron and steel will have a planning section attached to it as will the Ministry for Ferrous Metallurgy. These planning divisions at all levels of the economy provide the data which Gosplan co-ordinates into the comprehensive plan which controls the economy. These lower divisions are Gosplan's link with reality.

The data which Gosplan receives through the economic hierarchy relate to the availability of labor and raw materials, the size of plant inventories, the progress of capital construction. Gosplan then fashions these data into a complex series of balances. The method of balances is an attempt to relate the input-output relationships of all plants in such a way as to avoid surpluses or shortages of particular goods or resources. Not only must Gosplan ensure that plant A receives adequate allocations of resources to produce its projected output, but it must ensure that the output of plant A and all similar plants is adequate to satisfy the demands of plants B, C, D, and E, which are the users of the output of plant A. The output of coal must balance against the demands of the railroad, steel, power, and heating industries, which utilize coal. The method of balances, then, is essentially a means for checking the internal consistency of a plan.

In the market economy the internal consistency of the pattern of resource-allocation, which Gosplan seeks consciously from its position at the top of the economic administration, is maintained more or less unconsciously by the accommodating behavior of buyers and sellers. If a material shortage threatens the economy the price of that material rises, rationing the available supply among those who can buy. If a commodity is in excess supply at existing prices, the price of that commodity will fall until enough buyers are induced to absorb the surplus. In consequence, the product-mix changes, more of some commodities and less of others being produced.

For Gosplan the balance in resource-utilization is crucial. Since the Soviet Union in its planning system has chosen to consciously direct economic development, the balance must conform to the developmental objectives of the Communist Party. A fortuitous balance is not sufficient.

Once having achieved a balance among the uses to which resources can be put, the plan can be issued as a series of input-output directives to the constituent units of the economic hierarchy. This entails the distribution of the plan through the economic organization we described previously. Each production ministry receives that part of the plan which is relevant to the operations for which it is responsible. Thus the Ministry for Non-Ferrous Metals would receive the plan directives concerned with the production of copper, manganese, aluminum, or silver. This Ministry in turn would send the appropriate parts of the plan that it had received to the plants or Trusts producing particular non-ferrous metals.

At each administrative level the planning division reviews the projected plan in terms of its estimate of its ability to achieve the prescribed quotas. Criticisms and suggestions are made, these being reviewed in the first instance by the administrative unit immediately superior to that making the suggestions. During this process of review and criticism the plan moves back through the economic hierarchy to Gosplan where all acceptable revisions are coordinated in order to maintain the balance of the plan.

The plan leaves Gosplan and moves from top to bottom for the last time as binding directives on administrative and managerial personnel.

With the accumulation of experience and knowledge the trips of the production plan can be minimized. Much of the plan can be initially formulated at the bottom of the economic hierarchy. Those plants that have been in operation for a period of time can establish production objectives for themselves on the basis of their knowledge of the supplies of raw material available and past increases in labor productivity. Gosplan, then, balances plan objectives sent up to it from the operating plants.

In addition to this all-important co-ordinating function Gosplan also initiates new capital construction. Although operating plants can take the initiative in planning current production, they cannot take the initiative in determining new investment except within narrow limits. For in the Soviet system the investment decision does not necessarily depend upon the productivity of the operations of a particular plant, but rather on the over-all objectives of the economy. In other words, an indication at the plant level that capacity could be doubled or tripled with profitable results is not binding on the planning authority. The expansion of the particular plant may not conform with the investment program of Gosplan.

The investment decision can be broken down into two separate but related parts: one, the determination of the total volume of resources to be devoted to investment, i.e., the production of goods that will yield satisfactions in the future but not in the present, and, two, the allocation of this total volume of resources among alternative investment opportunities.

This first aspect of investment is primarily a political decision in the Soviet Union depending upon the values that the Communist Party is trying to maximize and the social background against which the decision is made. The leaders of the Party want to increase the industrial strength of Russia as rapidly as possible, but the amount of resources they can allocate to the production of investment goods which will increase industrial capacity is limited by the necessity of allocating resources to the production of consumption goods. The latter is necessary to prevent political unrest and to maintain the productivity of the labor force. Just how one determines what output of consumption goods will be sufficient to maintain an optimum rate of labor productivity is a moot question. Conceivably some concept of a subsistence minimum might be employed to estimate the quantity of consumption goods required, but a subsistence minimum is a highly flexible condition which will vary with the objective conditions of work and the subjective attitudes of the worker. The coal miner needs a greater caloric intake in his diet than the bureaucrat, but the work of the bureaucrat may require a higher consumption standard than the work of the coal miner.

This problem is complicated by the twenty-year existence in the Soviet Union of full employment. When resources are fully employed the cost of increasing the output of investment goods is the reduction in the output of consumption goods. If resources are not fully employed the output of both investment goods and consumption goods can increase simultaneously. In the early stages of Soviet planning experience, unemployment existed either overtly or covertly in the form of the inefficient use of labor resources. In the rural areas the abundance of labor reduced the marginal product of farm labor to at least zero and possibly below zero. Consequently, it was feasible to withdraw labor from agricultural pursuits into the production of investment goods without diminishing the output of farm products. The passing into history of four Five-Year Plans has destroyed both forms of unemployment and hence has increased the real cost of investment.

The allocation of a total volume of investment, however, is susceptible of economic calculation and therefore is a legitimate function of Gosplan. It must be admitted at the outset that the criteria used by Gosplan to make this aspect of the investment decision are not clear. Several choices are involved in this decision. First, a choice must be made between different types of investment output, e.g., diesel engines or coal-burning engines. Second, a choice must be made between different methods of producing the same investment output. Finally, a choice must be made about the size of plant in which the output is to be produced.

In the market economy these decisions are made by each firm decentrally on the basis of a comparison of the expected rate of return from an investment plan and the market rate of interest. Those investment projects are feasible in which the expected rate of return is greater than the market rate of interest. Investment, then, is allocated through changes in the rate of interest, a rise choking off investment and a fall stimulating investment. In effect, this type of calculation lines up investment projects in order of their priority and ensures that preferred investment comes first. Since the calculation is a form of profit maximization with respect to future output, each firm will estimate its expected rate of return on the basis of that combination of variable factors of production and of plant which minimize cost. The three choices mentioned in the previous paragraph are therefore included in the market-investment decision.

Because of the Marxian origins of the Soviet economy, the rate of interest is looked upon with something less than respect. It therefore cannot be explicitly used in the allocation of investment among alternative uses. Nonetheless, there is implicit in the decisions that Gosplan must make some concept of a rate of return. For, in fact, choices are made and we can infer that there are some criteria to guide these choices. On the strength of the record of Soviet planning we can suggest that those criteria favor the use of capital-intensive methods of industrial development, the expansion of hydroelectric power or iron and steel capacity. We cannot stipulate criteria of selection which correspond to the theoretical criteria of capitalism.

As we have implied, it is through the investment function that Gosplan influences the development of the Soviet economy. The construction of new industries, the expansion (or the contraction) of old industries, and the location of industry depend upon the decisions made by Gosplan. Gosplan in a sense, then, is the location of the entrepreneurial function in the Soviet Union. It does not formulate the over-all objectives of the economy — this function belongs to the Communist Party — nor does it develop ideas independently of the economic hierarchy to which it is attached — presumably there is a continuous give and take between Gosplan and the units in the economic order which are close to the actual production process — but it does shape concrete plans out of policy objectives and economic data which change the production functions upon which economic development depends. In this respect the position of Gosplan in relation to the Communist Party and the economic hierarchy is somewhat similar to the position of top corporation executives in relation to a board of directors and the managers of the various corporation production departments. The executive may receive general policy directives from the board of directors, but it is his responsibility to develop concrete means of achieving these policies. To do so he must have ideas and know the potential of his plant, which requires an administrative organization which brings the plant into his office.

In the planning and, therefore, the influencing of the future the time factor is obviously important. In the immediate present Gosplan is restrained by the relative immobility of resources, but as the time period is extended and resources become more mobile it gains control over the variables which determine the future. In other words, during a present period resources are committed to various uses which cannot quickly be altered. Short-run planning, therefore, must function within the limits set by this immobility. In the long run, however, mobile resources accrue to Gosplan, which then can plan the margins of economic development. Today the construction of additional steel capacity commits Gosplan to a given line of action. Tomorrow when the additional steel capacity bears fruit, Gosplan can allocate the additional steel among an almost unlimited number of alternatives.

The time factor is explicitly recognized in the Soviet planning mechanism. The Five-Year Plans state the long-run objectives of the economy, for instance, the increase in the output of consumers' goods or the increase in the capacity of the power-supplying industries. Within the Five-Year Plans there are annual plans and quarterly plans. These latter are way stations on the road to the larger objectives. They provide at once a means of checking progress towards fulfillment of plan objectives and a limited amount of flexibility for adjusting the economy to unforeseen contingencies.

In our discussion of plan formulation thus far we have been speaking only about a real production plan.

We have said nothing about values, price, or cost. In practice the Production Plan will be paralleled by a Financial Plan. We have chosen to place the Production Plan at the forefront of our discussion because it is supposedly controlling of the direction of change of the Soviet economy, and value or money data are but the servants of these changes.

The Financial Plan is an integral part of the Soviet planning scheme. In the first place, a unit of account is essential to the calculations that must be made by the producing units. For this purpose the physical dissimilarities of resources and finished goods must be translated into the common denominator of value. In the second place, money values are important for plan control about which we shall have more to say later. Finally, if it is considered desirable to grant consumers freedom of choice, as it apparently is, money is an indispensable means for facilitating choice.

The Financial Plan accomplishes two basic purposes: one, it controls the aggregate level of expenditures, and, two, it attaches money values to the real values of the Production Plan. If the quantity of money were not controlled, the expenditures of consumers on consumption goods would distort the planned allocation of resources. If, for example, the money demand for consumers goods was in excess of the supply of consumers goods at the prices established in the plan, a black market would develop, which would draw resources away from planned uses. This would not be a problem if

wages and salaries were only paid out to workers employed in the production of consumers' goods. Then the value of consumers' goods produced would always equal the money demand for consumers' goods (assuming wages to be the whole part of cost and no savings by consumers). But in the Soviet Union, as in any industrial society, wages and salaries are paid out to workers who produce investment goods as well as consumer goods. Therefore, the money income paid out to workers will be greater than the costs of producing consumption goods. In capitalistic society the discrepancy between these values is adjusted through price changes and voluntary savings. In Soviet society the Financial Plan, theoretically, assures that sufficient consumer income will be channelized into the government budget to prevent the demand for consumers' goods from being greater than the supply at the prices established by the planning authority.

Equally as important as the control of aggregate expenditures is the costing and pricing of real production. The Financial Plan fixes the selling price of output and the cost of resources, including labor. As we have already implied, the point of departure for the financial calculations is the Production Plan. The allocation of resources delineated in the Production Plan determines the real cost of using resources in any given occupation. In planning real output Gosplan implicitly sets up demand and supply schedules for particular resources — this is what the method of balances consists of. With these schedules, or in Soviet terms balances, determined, the financial authorities can translate the real cost of resources into relative money values.

Costs provide the data upon which selling prices are fixed. For any given production unit A, the selling price of its output is calculated by adding to the costs of labor, raw material, depreciation, and overhead a figure known as planned profit. This selling price then becomes a cost to the production units B, C, and D which buy the output of A. If A is a wholesaler or distributor selling to state stores, the latter add to the costs of obtaining goods from the former their own costs of operation plus a figure known as the turnover tax, about which we shall say more subsequently.

From the point of view of the manager of a production unit the Financial Plan means that he has no discretionary control over the price he must pay for resources or the price he receives for his product. Just as the entrepreneur in a perfectly competitive market is constrained by the prices determined in the markets, so the plant manager in the Soviet Union is constrained by the prices established in the Financial Plan. The incidence of the restraint, however, differs in the two cases, for the entrepreneur in perfect competition is restrained by the decisions of innumerable people while the plant manager in the Soviet Union is restrained by the decisions of central authorities.

Because of the fixed prices set by the Financial Plan the Soviet plant manager cannot improve the financial position of his plant by manipulating price. Theoretically, at least, he lacks what we would recognize in capitalism as monopoly power. He can only increase profits by increasing the efficiency with which he utilizes resources. If he can get more out of the resources allotted to him than anticipated in the plan he can improve the financial position of the plant. In order to do this the manager would have to improve the organization of the plant, raise the morale of the labor force, introduce new methods, or make some change internal to his organization that would increase the productivity of labor.

The manager is further controlled by being prohibited from receiving money or credits directly from other production units in inter-firm transactions. All transactions between firms are recorded as bookkeeping entries in the state bank (Gosbank). Money transactions are confined to the payment of workers. If, for instance, plant A delivers one thousand screw drivers valued at four thousand rubles to plant B, plant A receives a credit in Gosbank for that amount and plant B receives a debit of a like amount. On the other hand when plant A purchases steel rod valued at three thousand rubles from plant C, it receives a debit at Gosbank of three thousand rubles and plant C receives a three thousand ruble credit. Thus Soviet trade is facilitated through the use of a gigantic system of state bookkeeping.

Gosbank, the seat of this bookkeeping system, becomes a key point in the Soviet planning system for examining the financial position of producing units and, therefore, for checking on progress towards plan fulfillment. Suppose that plant A is having difficulty in meeting its production commitments because the punch presses used to press the screw driver shaft into the screw driver handle consistently drive the shaft in one end of the handle and out the other end. Plant A, then, will not build up credits from its sales to plant B at a sufficient rate to offset the debits it incurs in its purchases from plant C. The account of plant A at Gosbank, therefore, will fall. The auditor who checks the financial position of the producing units will know simply by glancing at the account of plant A in Gosbank that all is not well with the progress of plant A towards its planned objectives. On the other hand if plant A's account is rising over a period of time it would suggest that its production record is good.

In addition to making possible this auditing function, Gosbank is the bank of issue and the short-term credit institution in the Soviet Union. The units in the economic hierarchy receive cash for their payroll disbursements from Gosbank. The total quantity of cash that Gosbank is permitted to pay out is, of course, controlled by the Financial Plan. Under certain circumstances Gosbank is allowed to grant short-term credit to the producing units. To revert once again to our screw driver plant, if upon investigation it is shown conclusively that the difficulties of plant A are in no way attributable to the management of plant A,

that the punch presses were faulty when they left the plant that was responsible for producing them and that they had to be returned for extensive repairs, plant A would be in line for a credit grant. Lacking a grant of credit, plant A would have insufficient working capital to finance its current operations. The granting of credit, however, is closely controlled by the Financial Plan. Gosbank has no independent powers to grant credit but must conform to the directives of the Financial Plan. This aspect of financial control relates to the problem of the control of the aggregate money supply, which we discussed previously. If credit is extended indiscriminately as snags and bottlenecks develop in the production process, the quantity of money might exert an independent influence on the allocation of resources. This does not conform to the Soviet intention of making real production the controlling element in the planning system.

Thus far we have been discussing those aspects of the Financial Plan that pertain to current operations. But the Financial Plan also facilitates the realization of the investment program. First of all, the Financial Plan estimates the supply of investible funds which will accrue to the state in the course of a fiscal year. These funds come from a number of sources: one, direct taxation, two, deductions for social security, three, personal savings, four, subscriptions to state loans, five, profits of production units, and six, proceeds of the turnover tax. Secondly, the Financial Plan stipulates how and to what enterprises these investible funds shall be distributed through the specialized long-term credit institutions (e.g., Prombank) of the Soviet Union.

There are several things to note about this savings-investment mechanism. From a conceptual standpoint it is similar to the savings-investment mechanism in capitalism. In both economies consumers' money income is restricted in order to release resources for the production of investment goods (and/or government goods). In spite of the divergent economic ideologies that separate these economies, they both labor under the necessity of restricting consumption in favor of investment. Moreover, the Soviet mechanism is similar to its capitalistic counterpart in that Soviet citizens can save and receive a premium for their savings. Savings banks exist in Russia and pay their depositors a rate of interest. It is also possible for individuals to buy state bonds and hence increase their future income. Typically these bonds are sold by the state on a lottery basis. In buying a bond one takes a chance; one might receive zero interest, but, on the other hand, one might receive ten or twenty per cent interest. The Soviet Union capitalizes on the gaming instincts of its citizens to assure that its bond issues are fully subscribed.

Although the savings-investment mechanism is similar to that of capitalism in these respects, the differences are probably more striking. There is no such thing as a private capital market in the Soviet Union. The individual production unit can-

not go before the Soviet citizen with private investment plans and seek private financing. It is dependent on the state for its investment program and the financing of its investment program. One reservation should be made, however. The manager of a plant can use part of his earned profits for investment purposes. These profits are held to his credit, or the credit of his plant, in either Gosbank or Prombank. When drawing upon these funds the manager must receive approval of the planning authority and the use to which the funds are put must be included in the Financial Plan. Nevertheless, the manager has initiatory powers with part of the profits his unit earns. This aspect of Soviet investment operations is similar to the plowing back of profits by American business firms.

Finally, we must note the regressive effect of the Soviet savings-investment mechanism on the distribution of income. Of the sources of investible funds by far the most important is the turnover tax. Direct taxation, or income taxation, accounts for only a small percentage of the revenue of the state. The tax rates are not steeply graduated. The turnover tax is similar to a sales tax and therefore bears more heavily on the low-income recipients than the high-income recipients of Soviet society.

It is, perhaps, an anomalous situation that the Soviet Union, whose leaders in the early days of the regime had a doctrinaire bias in favor of equality, should now be using regressive methods of taxation to finance its investment program. The exigencies of economic reality have forced the Soviet leaders to reorder their value preferences. They apparently discovered that it was not possible to maximize economic development and income equality at the same time. In order to develop the nation's industrial capacity, the consumption of consumers had to be restricted. But if the income of a poor society were distributed equally each individual in society would attempt to consume all of it. Furthermore, to rely upon progressive income taxation with high marginal tax rates would deprive the individual of much of the material incentive for producing wealth. The Soviet tax policy, then, is a concession to the requirements of economic development in a relatively poor country. Savings are forced out of the members of Soviet society through the regressive turnover tax, but the Soviet citizen is not deterred by progressive income taxation from earning high income through high productivity.

The Production Plan provides the output targets for the Soviet economy, the Financial Plan the means for facilitating the achievement of the targets. We must now consider the execution or enforcement of the plan. The enforcement of the plan is primarily a matter of motivating the members of society to carry out the directives of the plan. In general there are two aspects of motivation: negative and positive inducements to conformance and performance.

About negative inducement we can say relatively little. We know

that man responds to the fear of loss or deprivation. We also know that the Soviet Union relies to a large extent upon a capitalistic system of motivation. In capitalism the fear of loss of income is an important goad, which stimulates economic activity. In the Soviet Union the same thing holds. Implicit in the planning mechanism are devices for checking performance. The planned profit is a norm against which the performance of a plant manager can be measured. Consistent failure to achieve the planned level of profits might result in dismissal with the consequent loss of income and prestige.

Piecework is the standard basis upon which wage rates are determined in the Soviet Union. A norm, therefore, exists for workers, below which they can only fall at the risk of dismissal or reduction of income.

To say more than this would be to go beyond the scope of this chapter. It is only fair, however, to make a few comments about the existence of forced labor in the Soviet Union. This type of labor is certainly a negative inducement to performance. But the incidence of forced labor in the Soviet Union is a closely guarded state secret. "Informed" guesses made by Soviet experts outside the USSR have ranged from two million to fifteen million and more. Even if we knew how many workers were enrolled in the forced labor camps we would still not know how vital this institution is to plan enforcement. Conceivably, forced labor could be purely a political phenomenon — a device for controlling the opponents of the Soviet regime.

It is likely to be the case, however, that forced labor is a useful adjunct to the Soviet planning mechanism in that it relieves the planning authority of the necessity of constructing a wage pattern that will attract workers into employment that is essential to the economy but that also is highly distasteful, e.g., gold mining in northern Siberia. This is conjecture. We can only tab the question of forced labor as an unknown in the Soviet planning mechanism.

As far as positive inducements are concerned we have already stated the existence of the capitalistic incentive system in Russia. Productivity is the important criterion in the distribution of income.

The manager of an enterprise, for instance, has a very real material interest in increasing the level of profits his firm earns. Planned profits are split three ways, one part going to the government's budget for use throughout the economy, another part going to Prombank for the capital development of the enterprise, and the last part going to a manager's or director's fund to be used within the plant for bonuses or welfare purposes at the discretion of the manager. Of profits earned over and above planned profits, the director's fund receives a much larger percentage share than in the division of the normal profit. Thus the manager can improve his own position and the position of his firm by stimulating productivity and raising the level of profits.

The manager whose money income is likely to be high in the Soviet distribution scheme may receive in addition real income of considerable value. The use of an automobile or the lease of an apartment may accompany his position as plant director. His annual vacation may be spent in the Crimea. In an economy that has not placed a conspicuous emphasis on the production of consumers' goods these benefits of the managerial position are likely to represent an important increase in real income.

The worker has similar inducements to work hard for the fulfillment of the plan. Since piecework is the standard basis of the wage system, income is directly related to productivity. The worker can earn more by producing more. If he can enroll in the ranks of the Stakhanovites he can receive in addition the honorific status of top worker. A. G. Stakhanov was a coal miner who during the thirties made some changes in the organization of production on his shift, which resulted in a tremendous increase in productivity and output. The Soviet Union for a number of years had been encouraging so-called Shock Workers, who worked harder and longer hours in order to increase output. The idea of workers' spontaneously making suggestions that effected changes in the production function and stimulated output without additional physical effort appealed to the Soviet authorities, and they established the Stakhanovite movement on a nationwide basis in order to induce Soviet workers to emulate the example of A. G. Stakhanov. The Stakhanovites are the highest paid workers in the Soviet Union.

Apart from monetary rewards, both managers and workers can receive non-monetary rewards for excellent service to industry. The Order of Socialist Toil or the Order of Lenin are honors that may stimulate the Russian citizen to high achievement. It is difficult to say how important this form of motivation is. The philosophical and ideological background of the Soviet Union is sufficiently different from that in the United States to make invalid judgments about the Soviet citizen on the basis of the presumed behavior of Americans in similar circumstances. The gold watch after fifty years' service or the picture in the company newspaper after twenty-five years' service have probably not been notable motivation devices in the American economy. Yet similar techniques may be more important in a collective society. The badge for distinguished service to the community may elevate the status of the Soviet citizen and so make him strive positively for a socialist honorary award.

For reasons discussed below, it is appropriate to consider the role of the Soviet trade union in this section on plan-enforcement. In capitalistic society the trade union is independent of all groups except its own membership. Its policy objectives are determined by the union leaders who supposedly act in the interests of the rank-and-file. Generally these policies are designed to increase the money income of the union members and to improve their conditions of work. The means for achieving these policies is collective bargaining with management, backed up by the

threat of the strike. Since the union is bargaining with management over wage rates, the bargain struck will affect the level of industrial costs and hence will influence the price of the product, profit rates and other non-labor income. Consequently, the activity of many independent unions alters the distribution of income and the allocation of resources.

In contrast the union in Soviet Russia is dependent on the government and does not have an independent influence on the allocation of resources. Clearly, independent unions and central planning are incompatible. Gosplan plans the output of consumption goods. It also fixes the money wage-bill. With these data fixed by central authority there is nothing for the union to bargain about. The total real income of the labor force is represented by the planned output of consumers' goods and the distribution of that total among the members of the labor force is determined by the money wage-bill. Conceivably trade union officials can exert pressure at the top levels of policy formation before a plan takes concrete form. They might try to use their influence to obtain a planned expansion in the output of consumers' goods. Once the plan has crystalized, however, the union official has lost the power to influence the allocation of resources in favor of union members.

Having been deprived of the functions of the typical Western union by the development of central planning, the Soviet trade union has been absorbed into government and has become concerned primarily with problems of plan-enforcement. In short, Soviet trade unions are productionist unions.

During the years of the Five-Year Plans the trade unions at the direction of the government have addressed themselves to the solution of problems that have interfered with the efficiency of the planning system. In the early days of the Five-Year Plans during the great influx of the rural population into the industrial centers the union acted as a recruiting agent in attracting the peasant to particular employments. It thus facilitated the carrying out of the contracts between production managements and collective farms, which stipulated the reserves of rural population available for industrial employment. The unions not only recruited workers but supervised their transition to industrial labor, implanting in them industrial skills and discipline and doing what they could to find the raw peasant housing and to protect him from unfair discrimination.

With the absorption of unemployment in the planning process the Soviet Union lost the goading threat of unemployment which traditionally enforced labor discipline in capitalistic society. During the thirties the Soviet economy suffered from a sizable, drifting labor force. Workers could go from job to job seeking improved conditions of living because the existence of full employment guaranteed a job in the next factory or town. In consequence, the development of labor productivity was impaired because many workers did not stay on the job long enough to acquire the requisite skills.

The union was urged to take measures against labor drifting, such as the enforcement on workers of the obligation to take employment for specific periods of time and the revocation of union membership from those workers who consistently deserted the production lines. When these measures did not bring satisfactory results the government and unions jointly decreed (December 1938) that holidays would be granted only after eleven months of continuous employment, that persistent absenteeism would be punished with dismissal or loss of pay ratings, and that insurance allowances would depend upon length of employment. These are not unusual steps for instilling discipline in a labor force. What is unusual is that they should be sponsored by a trade union.

It is almost gratuitous to state that the Soviet trade unions have eschewed the use of the strike which is such an important weapon in the tactics of the unions in capitalistic society.

As if to compensate the trade union for its loss of independent status in Soviet Russia, it was given the function of administering the social insurance program (1933). The union also owns rest homes and holiday resorts, which can be used by its members. Finally, the union maintains staffs of inspectors who supposedly see to it that management devotes adequate funds to the protection of workers against industrial accidents. These welfare measures, however, cannot obscure the most important aspect of the obligations of the Soviet trade union — the enforcement of planned production objectives.

We have considered industrial planning first in our analysis of the Soviet planning system because the second Soviet "revolution" in 1928 placed industrial development at the forefront of economic policy. Prior to 1928 the peasant and agricultural organization had limited the scope of Soviet planning aspirations. After 1928 agriculture was reorganized with the avowed purpose of subordinating it to the requirements of industrial growth. The collectivization drive in the early years of the first Five-Year Plan was an attempt to obtain quickly the economies of large scale agricultural production so that, one, agricultural output could be increased, and, two, labor could be liberated for use in the expanding industrial centers.

Agricultural planning is at once more difficult and less difficult than industrial planning. It is more difficult because of the agricultural industry's dependence on favorable weather conditions. In spite of the so-called Stalin plans to change nature, the Soviet planners cannot control the elements. It is less difficult because the variables dealt with are not so complex. For example, in planning industrial output all factors of production are variable in the long run. The planners must therefore be concerned with the economies of location to ensure that plants are located at the optimum points between markets and resources. In agriculture, however, land is immobile —

the planner only has to be concerned with what land should or should not be brought into cultivation.

The basic agricultural units are the Collective Farm (Kolkhoz), the Machine Tractor Station (MTS), and the State Farm. The kolkhoz and the MTS are the most important units in the production of agricultural output for industrial and urban consumers, the State Farm being primarily an agricultural experimental station. Just as the industrial production units are subordinated to Republic and Union Economic Ministries, so these agricultural units are subordinated to agricultural ministries, which establish a chain of command from the smallest kolkhoz to the policy makers at the top of the economic hierarchy.

It is through this economic hierarchy that the plan directives are transmitted to the kolkhoz. Agricultural planning does not prescribe the conditions of production as closely as industrial planning. In part this is because the nature of farming sharply limits production possibilities. Soil and climatic conditions have a greater influence on the choice of the appropriate crop for cultivation than the preferences of the planners. Also the Soviet planners discovered through experience that the kolkhoz functions more effectively if given discretion in the control of particular agricultural operations.

The planned directives submitted to the kolkhoz generally specify its basic specialization (for example, grain or meat), the system of crop rotation, the cultivation of new land, the crop yield, the level of mechanization, the expenditures for new construction, and the dates for the completion of assigned tasks. With these general directives as guides the kolkhoz draws up its own production plan specifying the particular grain or meat it will raise, the subsidiary crops it will rotate against its basic specialization, the organization of kolkhoz members for work, the arrangement with the MTS for achieving its planned levels of mechanization, plans for the cultivation of new areas, plans for the development of domestic industry, the nature of new construction, the schedule of deliveries to the state, and the income distributed to its members.

The kolkhoz plan then must pass through the agricultural ministries where it is discussed and criticized and fitted into the national plan for agriculture. On being accepted by the administration it becomes binding on the kolkhoz.

In the execution of the plan there are two aspects of agricultural organization which facilitate production and therefore deserve attention; one, the work and incentive system of the kolkhoz, and, two, the relationship of the kolkhoz to the MTS. The kolkhoz is a peculiar compromise between the desires of the Soviet leaders to proletarize the peasant and the desire of the peasant to own the product of the land. The kolkhoz consists of a number of farm families — in 1938 the average number of households in a kolkhoz was seventy-eight — who lease land from the state in perpetuity and cultivate it cooperatively or collectively.

Collective cultivation entails the division of agricultural production into a series of tasks and the assignment of the responsibility for performing each of the tasks to groups called brigades. The brigades are in charge of brigade leaders who further subdivide their tasks into operations assigned to squads and squad leaders. There is, then, a military chain of command on the kolkhoz reaching down from the kolkhoz chairman through the brigade leader to the squad leader. In concrete terms, in a kolkhoz specializing in the production of wheat one brigade might be assigned the task of cultivating the grain during its life cycle, another the cultivation of the non-specialty crops in the rotation system, still another the construction of storage bins for the grain, and finally another the construction and maintenance of roads. The size of the brigade would depend on the nature of the task as would the subdivision of brigades into squads.

This work plan is motivated by a system which utilizes both collective and individual incentives. The gross income of the kolkhoz consists of the value of its output of agricultural produce. The bulk of this output is delivered to the state at fixed prices and this exchange constitutes the money income of the kolkhoz. From this money income the kolkhoz is obliged to pay taxes to the government and also to make deductions for the purposes of capital construction and cultural needs. From the real output not delivered to the state the kolkhoz must make deductions for seed and fodder reserves. The net money income and the net real income are available for distribution to the members of the kolkhoz.

The net income of the kolkhoz is distributed on the basis of the work-credits that the members have accumulated during the month. The work-credit is a value attached to a job, which varies with the skill required for the job. Thus a squad leader might receive three work-credits a day for his job while a man working on road maintenance might receive only one-half work-credits a day. At the end of the accounting period, say a month, the work-credits of the members are added up and divided into the net income available for distribution. The resulting figure is the income value of one work-credit. The income of the individual, then, is that value times the number of work-credits he has accumulated.

With this system for differentiating income the individual has a material incentive for acquiring the skill which will give him a job with higher work-credits. But in addition bonuses are granted to the squads and brigades which over-fulfill their production quotas. Consequently, each member of the kolkhoz has a collective incentive to cooperate with his group in the attainment of production quotas.

Aside from the material incentives the usual non-material incentives stimulate the kolkhoz member. The eager chairman may receive a trip to Moscow for his outstanding services or be pictured in the regional newspaper as the model chairman who overcame the individualistic tendencies of the kolkhoz members.

Socialists orders are available to those who have demonstrated the capacity for outstanding service to farm and community.

The collective organization of agriculture satisfies the production and doctrinaire needs of the Communist Party. The peasant's desire for the individual ownership of land is satisfied by granting to him the right to the use of one to one and a half acres of land. Here the peasant may build his house, raise crops, keep a certain amount of poultry and cattle. The agricultural produce his homestead yields can either be sold in the peasant markets or consumed.

This form of quasi-private ownership clearly was a concession to the peasant who did not always positively embrace the principle of collective farming, and it was thought that a remnant of the past would compensate him for the unaccustomed methods of rural communism. It was a concession, however, that sometimes caused difficulty for the kolkhoz chairmen and the agricultural ministries. The peasant frequently discovered that he received a greater return from working on his own homestead than from working on collective production. He had an incentive, therefore, to default on his obligations to the collective farm. This was particularly true when the government take from the kolkhoz gross income so diminished the income available to the members that there was only a tenuous link between collective effort and individual return. This problem was met negatively by compelling peasants through legal enactment to live up to their labor obligations to the kolkhoz and positively through the demonstration to the peasant of the efficiency of collective agriculture in terms of increasing output.

The second unique feature of Soviet agriculture is the Machine Tractor Station. The MTS is the service unit that maintains and operates agricultural equipment such as combines or harvesters for the collective farms. It is separate and distinct from the kolkhoz, which must contract with the MTS in order to obtain the use of agricultural equipment. Since the MTS is the agent of the state it is the symbol of the nationalization of the means of agricultural production.

This system was an adaptation to the backward conditions of Russian agriculture. The peasants lacked the technical knowledge to understand the functioning of complex agricultural equipment. To turn the tractor and combine over directly to the untutored peasant would be to reduce the effective life of the equipment. Therefore, the MTS was conceived of as an institution which could economize on the use of technical personnel by servicing a number of collective farms. Not only would technical personnel be strategically located but the equipment itself would be worked closer to its capacity.

Since its inception the MTS has become a center where technical assistance of all kinds can be obtained. The kolkhoz chairman, for instance, can obtain help from the MTS in the formulation of his production plan and in fact has become dependent on it. For the level of mecha-

nization that the former plans depends upon the schedule that the latter maintains in the use of its agricultural equipment. It is also a check point for observing progress towards the fulfillment of production quotas.

The kolkhoz and the MTS, then, are the significant units in Soviet agriculture. There are two additional points to be made. The state farm was originally conceived of as the agricultural counterpart of the industrial factory. They were tremendous farms employing wage labor and devoted to one crop specialities, for instance, wheat production. During the late twenties and early thirties the state farms expanded rapidly. Between 1928 and 1932, for instance, the state farms devoted to the production of grain increased eight times over and accounted for approximately one-tenth of the total sown area in Russia. With the rise of the kolkhoz and the accumulation of comparative statistics the inefficiency of the state farms became quite clear. They were too large and unwieldy for effective administration. In the mid-thirties the state farms lost their place in the sun to the kolkhoz, much of their land being turned over to the latter. Now the state farms are primarily agricultural experimental stations concerned with the improvement of crop yields.

Finally, it should be noted that for the past two years Soviet agriculture has been undergoing a new reorganization. The collective farms are being collectivized into Agro-towns. The Soviet Union apparently is continuing its drive to urbanize and proletarize the Russian peasant. The collective farms have been reduced in number and consequently the land units are larger as are the rural centers of population. As of now little information about this new agricultural organization is available to the West.

IV. THE PERFORMANCE OF THE SOVIET PLANNING SYSTEM

In the previous section we have analyzed the Soviet planning system in ideal terms; we have tried to explain how it functions and, consequently, we have only occasionally mentioned difficulties that the system has encountered. It is appropriate now to ask whether the planning system has operated effectively. This is a difficult question to answer for two reasons: one, the statistical evidence upon which one might measure performance is wholly inadequate, and, two, it is not clear what criteria should be used in evaluating performance.

The statistical information emanating from the Soviet Union is so vague that it is difficult to form a picture of the growth of the Soviet economy. Some of the important production indices are not maintained in continuous series. Much of the Soviet value data covering the periods of the Five-Year Plans is expressed in terms of 1926–27 prices, which give an upward bias to the data. Some goods produced in relative abundance during the Five-Year Plans were produced in small quantities and at high cost during the period 1926–27. If these goods were an im-

portant part of output, they would unduly weight the statistics in periods subsequent to 1926–27. Moreover, much of the economic data is quoted only in relative terms without the anchor of an absolute base. Finally, since World War II much information has been withheld from the Western world for strategic reasons. Indeed since the conclusion of the fourth Five-Year Plan in 1950 the West has not received any definitive data about the Soviet intentions for the fifth Five-Year Plan.

Even if the statistical information were adequate, what standards should be used in evaluating it? By standards derived from the capitalistic market one might reach one conclusion, by standards indigenous to Russia another. We shall follow out the logic of the development of this chapter and evaluate Soviet performance in terms of the criteria important to the Soviet leaders. It should be clear from the analysis in the previous section that the Soviet system would not satisfy Western values. In organizing resources through the mechanism of a central planning authority the Soviet Union has substituted a public economic bureaucracy for the more or less impersonal organization of markets. Political authority ultimately controls the allocation of resources and political coercion becomes an explicit part of the economic design. Since the Communist Party exercises authoritarian powers over the political process, the individual, so important in Western society, has little control over the development of the Soviet economy. But this is not to say much more than that the Soviet economy is different from the American economy or the British economy. We must return, therefore, to Soviet standards for judging Soviet performance.

The first Five-Year Plan (1928–32) was formulated by Gosplan in the years between 1926 and 1928 and in its final version was designed to carry out the decision of Stalin to speed up the tempo of industrialization in Russia. Accordingly a large part of the national income, between one-quarter and one-third, was allocated to the production of investment goods and of this amount three-quarters was devoted to the production of heavy capital equipment, e.g., blast furnaces or hydro-electric plants. This meant that the Soviet planners intended to lock up a large quantity of resources in the construction of equipment that would not yield results for a period of two or three years.

The percentage of resources devoted to the production of consumption goods was to decline over the five-year period from 75 per cent to 65 per cent, but in absolute terms consumption was planned to increase by approximately 70 per cent.

In general the investment program was successful and the consumption program unsuccessful. From 1928 to 1933 the output of electric power increased from 5 to 16.4 billion kilowatt hours, of coal from 35.5 to 76.3 million tons, of oil from 11.7 to 22.5 million tons, of steel from 4.3 to 6.9 million tons, and of cement from 1.8 to 2.7 million tons. During the same period, however, the output of cotton

textiles fell from 2,742 to 2,422 million meters, of woolen textiles from 93 to 86.1 million meters, and of sugar from 1,283 to 995 thousand tons. On the other hand, grain production increased from 73 to 88.4 million tons and the output of shoes increased from 29.6 to 80.3 million pairs. The targets for the output of producers' goods were not all reached — the goal for steel was 10 million tons — because the Soviet planners underestimated the gestation period for construction in the producers' goods industries. Relative to the output of consumers' goods, however, the producers' goods industries fared well.

The reasons for the lagging behind of consumption output are important for they may throw light on some of the output biases of the Soviet planning system. During the first Five-Year Plan the Russian countryside was transformed in the collectivization drive. As we suggested in the previous section the upper and middle Russian peasants resisted the coercive efforts of the state to herd them into collective farms. Their resistance was not notably successful except in a peculiar negative sense. Rather than turn over their livestock to a collective authority many peasants slaughtered them. In consequence, from 1929 to 1932 the number of horses fell from 34.6 to 19.6 million, of cattle from 67.1 to 40.7 million, of sheep and goats from 147.0 to 52.1 million, and of pigs from 20.7 to 11.6 million. The Soviet Union suffered the overwhelming disaster of losing approximately half of its livestock, a disaster from which they are just recovering today.

Not only were the supplies of meat and milk drastically reduced but the collective farms lost what at that time was an important part of their tractive power — horses. Presumably this is a non-recurring cause of low consumption since the battle for collectivization was fought and won by the Soviet authorities. One would not expect now after twenty years of the kolkhoz the same sort of resistance to the Agro-towns.

The first Five-Year Plan paralleled the spread of the great depression in the Western world. The depression did not spread to Soviet Russia but it did affect the terms on which Russia traded with the outside world. Russia was then an exporter of raw materials and an importer of industrial equipment. Since the world prices of the former fell more than the world prices of the latter, the terms of trade turned against Russia. It could not receive as much for a given volume of exports as it had received before the depression. Forced to reduce its imports the Soviet authorities chose to restrict purchases of goods and resources that went into consumption. The planners, then, were consistent in giving top priority to the investment program.

In addition to the slaughtering of livestock and the worsening of the terms of international trade, the Soviet planners miscalculated the increase in labor productivity over the five years. These were the years of the great influx of labor into the expanding industrial centers. The labor force, exclusive of kolkhoz members, grew from 11.6 million in 1928 to 22.3 million in 1933. It was also during these years that the phenomenon of drifting labor mentioned in the previous section was so common. Thus the efforts to increase labor productivity were hampered by the new and untutored peasant-worker. More workers were required to obtain production targets than was originally anticipated and because the investment program had the top priority, the consumption program had to suffer.

Finally, because of international complications the Soviet authorities thought it was essential to allocate resources to the production of military goods.

All these factors combined to create the so-called goods famine. Because productivity had not increased as predicted and because the labor force expanded more than predicted the wage payments to workers were in excess of the value of consumers' goods at the prices planned by the authorities. A system of rationing, therefore, was used to make the demand fit the supply. Different ration categories were set up and the particular ration card one carried depended upon the type of work one did. Within this rationing system prices were raised by the imposition of the turnover tax through which the government received the major part of its revenues for the support of the capital expansion program.

The first Five-Year Plan was not a definitive test of the efficacy of the Soviet planning system. The planning mechanism was still in the process of growth and this was the first real attempt to consciously direct resource allocation. Without hesitation one can say the system was effective in forcing a rapid rate of industrialization, and this was one of the primary objectives of the Communist Party. It was less successful in achieving a balanced allocation of resources and in preventing monetary phenomena from disturbing the real production indices. Perhaps it is fair to say that one can perceive in the experience of the first Five-Year Plan a willingness to press for the achievement of investment objectives regardless of the effect of this effort on the balance of resource-allocation in the other sectors of the economy. Finally the first Five-Year Plan forced the Soviet authorities to sacrifice their equalitarian predilections in the struggle for production. After 1931 equalitarianism was a form of left-wing deviationism.

The second Five-Year Plan (1933–37) emphasized qualitative improvements and the mastering of the new techniques of production. Production targets were not as ambitious as the targets of the first Five-Year Plan. Approximately 24 to 30 per cent of the national income was to be devoted to investment and once again three-quarters of this was allocated to the production of capital equipment for the producers' goods industries. It was anticipated that over the five years the output of consumers' goods would be increased by 133 per cent — a more than twofold increase.

The investment program was complicated by the necessity of paying particular attention to the development of the transport system, which after the first Five-Year Plan became a bottleneck in the industrialization program. The expanding urban population required the transport of much larger volumes of grain from the farm to the city than had ever before been the case. Parts of Siberia became grain surplus areas shipping grain to the deficient areas of European Russia, and much of the grain production in the Black Sea area, which was formerly exported through the Black Sea by ship, was now sent into the interior. The new industrial centers were not always well integrated, and raw materials and product had to be transported over long distances.

During the second Five-Year Plan resources were allocated to transport in order to break the transportation bottleneck. Railroad roadbeds were improved, heavier rails installed, gradients reduced, and some lines double-tracked. The output of locomotives increased from 941 in 1933 to 1,626 in 1938. The inland water system was expanded with the construction of the Moscow-Volga canal and the widening of old canals linking the Volga with the Baltic. These projects loosened the transportation bottleneck and incidentally facilitated the movement of industry eastward, which was the intention of the Soviet planners.

These and similar construction projects were made possible by the expansion of the producers' goods industries. By 1938, 39 billion kilowatt hours of electric power were being generated which was a sevenfold increase over 1928. Coal output expanded to 133 million tons, approximately four times greater than the output of 1928. Oil production increased from 11.7 million tons in 1928 to 32 million tons in 1938, a threefold increase. Over the same period steel output increased four times from 4.3 million tons to 18.0 million tons, and cement output increased three times from 1.8 million tons to 5.7 million tons.

The output of consumption goods increased enough to raise living standards to the highest point yet attained in Russian economic development (Tsarist and Soviet). Cotton textiles expanded to one and one-third times their pre-plan capacity, making up the losses of the first Five-Year Plan. Similarly, woolen textiles expanded their output above the pre-plan levels. In 1938 the leather shoe industry was producing at the rate of 213 million pairs of shoes a year, an output almost nine times larger than that in 1928. Sugar capacity doubled until in 1938, 2,519 thousand tons of sugar were being produced. Grain output reached its highest point in history, 95.0 million tons, 30 per cent larger than the 1928 output and close to 20 per cent larger than the best grain year in pre-Soviet Russia, 1913.

Living standards might have risen further had not the familiar theme of international complications dictated the re-allocation of investment from light industry to heavy industry. This time the rise of Hitler and Nazi Germany was the cause for alarm. Nonetheless, the Soviet Union had overcome the goods famine and the Soviet citizen was benefitting. By 1934, it has been estimated, the level of food consumption

had been restored to the level of 1928 and by 1937 food consumption in urban centers was up 20 per cent over the 1934 level.

Rationing ended in 1935. Food supplies had increased, but possibly more significantly the Soviet planning authorities found that rationing interfered with the incentive system. To encourage income inequality, on the one hand, and ration goods, on the other, was self-defeating. The limiting of real consumption through rationing destroyed the lure of added money income.

With de-rationing the prices of consumers' goods were raised. In spite of the relatively small increase in the labor force — 18 per cent during the second Five-Year Plan as compared with almost 100 per cent during the first Five-Year Plan — and a satisfactory increase in labor productivity, the wage-bill expanded more than anticipated. The money demand had to be restricted in order to avoid the recurrence of the goods famine.

On the basis of the Soviet experience during the second Five-Year Plan one begins to suspect that in the construction of the production plan the planners do not obtain an economy-wide balance. The capital construction of the first Five-Year Plan increased the flow of goods to such an extent that the transport capacity of the economy had to be increased during the second Five-Year Plan. If resource-allocation had been balanced, transport-capacity would have grown with the need of the economy for transport. Economic growth through the Soviet planning mechanism is lumpy and discontinuous. Attention is devoted to one sector of the economy and within this sector a production balance may be achieved, but this sector concentration is likely to create bottlenecks in the links among sectors. It is conceivable that this is considered desirable by the Soviet authorities. If the act of planning always creates sector bottlenecks, then the authorities have concrete grounds on which they can dramatize the coming national effort. In other words, the crisis may stimulate a type of inspired performance that is not possible when the economy grows smoothly and continuously.

Also it is evident during the second Five-Year Plan that the Financial Plan cannot always control the inflationary bias of the fully employed economy. Perhaps it would be more correct to say that with the tremendous emphasis on the investment program it was found desirable not to place primary emphasis on the control of the price level. As we know from our experience in this country, it is easier to finance a heavy program of government expenditures through an inflationary price rise than through a rigorous tax program that maintains the level of prices. The same apparently holds for the Soviet Union. Prices rose with the expanding capital demands of Soviet industry.

Finally, it should be observed that during this period of relative prosperity for 'the Soviet consumer, the Soviet authorities found it expedient to give increasing emphasis to local and regional industry producing for the consumers' markets. It was found that decentralization in the organization of the consumers' goods industries made it easier to plan output that would satisfy consumers' needs.

Little can be said about the third Five-Year Plan (1938–1942). Whatever the original intentions of the planners the outbreak of the European War in 1939 forced their hand. Investment priorities favored heavy industry and special attention was paid to the chemical industry, the production of non-ferrous metals and high quality steels, and the expansion of transport facilities. The geographical center of industry continued to be pushed to the east. Whether or not in the absence of the war the output of consumers' goods would have received increasing attention is fruitless conjecture. The fact is that the gains that the consumers made in the late thirties were lost in the holocaust of war.

The fourth Five-Year Plan (1946–1950) was designed to restore the war-torn Soviet economy to its prewar capacity. The war had reduced consumption to an abysmally low level. A large part of the productive capacity of European Russia was destroyed or damaged. The monetary system was disrupted by the exigencies of wartime finance.

Once again the emphasis was on investment in heavy industry and consequently the plan targets in the output of producers' goods were more ambitious than the plan targets for the output of consumers' goods. By 1950 the plan called for the production of 82 billion kilowatt hours of electric power as compared with 39 billion in 1938, 250 million tons of coal as compared with 133 million in 1938, 35.4 million tons of oil as compared with 32 million in 1938, 25.4 million tons of steel as compared with 18.0 million in 1938, and 10.5 million tons of cement as compared with 5.7 million in 1938. Among consumers' goods the plan anticipated that by 1950 the output of cotton textiles would have increased to 4,-686 million meters as compared with 114 million meters in 1938, of woolen textiles to 159 million meters as compared with 114 million meters in 1938, of leather shoes to 240 million pairs as compared with 213 million pairs in 1938, of grain to 127 million tons as compared with 95 in 1938. The target for sugar was 2,400 thousand tons as compared with an output of 2,519 in 1938.

The large increase in the capacity to generate electric power was to come from the construction of hydro-electric plants on the Volga at Stalingrad and Kuibyshiev and on the Dnepr at Kakhovka. The output of coal, oil, and iron was to expand in the Urals and Siberia relative to output in the Ukraine, the Caucasus and the older industrial centers. Transportation was given emphasis to facilitate this geographical change in the centers of production.

The evidence about plan fulfillment is fragmentary since the Soviet Union has guarded its production and economic data rather closely during the postwar period. The investment program seems to have yielded better results than the consumption

program. Once again the consumer has had to take second place to the construction requirements of the economy. Nonetheless, by the end of the fourth Five-Year Plan the real income of consumers seems to have risen to approximately the prewar level.

During this plan the inflationary trend of the Soviet price level seems to have been arrested. In September, 1946 a drastic monetary reform drained the Soviet citizens of the excess liquid assets they had accumulated during the war years. The ruble was revalued at rates which discriminated against those who had large holdings of rubles, principally the peasants who had acquired large money income from sales in the peasant markets. In short, the quantity of money in circulation was quickly and ruthlessly reduced. At the same time the prices of consumers' goods were raised. By December of the following year the output of consumers' goods had increased enough to warrant the abolishing of the wartime ration controls. In each of the years since the abolishment of rationing the Soviet Union has announced general reductions in the prices of consumers' goods. Although these price reductions have not yet offset the official price rises of 1946, they suggest that during the fourth Five-Year plan the price level was brought under control.

After this necessarily cursory look at the evidence, what can we say in conclusion about the effectiveness of the Soviet planning system? It is clear that the Soviet Union is able to produce and produce well those things on which it sets its top priority. It has been able to induce a rapid rate of economic growth so that now it is an industrial nation second only to the United States. In order to do this, however, the leaders of the Soviet Union have had to sacrifice some values that at one time were important to them. Equalitarianism has passed into oblivion in the rush to increase the industrial strength of the economy. The power of the state has increased.

This subordination of all values to the industrialization effort manifests itself in planning as a marked preference for the expansion of heavy industry. In each successive plan circumstances arise, some of which are internal to the economy and some of which are external, that compel the allocation of resources to the production of heavy producers' goods. One suspects that in this type of planning there is a bias in favor of intensive capital development, for in expanding the output of coal, oil, and steel the chances of making serious mistakes are minimized. The economy can always use more coal, oil, or steel. On the other hand, to place primary emphasis on the production of consumers' goods is to plan in an area where mistakes can be made more easily. The preferences of consumers as income rises become increasingly capricious and therefore it becomes increasingly difficult for central authorities to correctly elicit these preferences. To decentralize the control of the economy in order to meet consumers' demand more effectively would represent the partial abdication of the planners' role of conscious directors of economic activity. Thus there seems to be a willingness on the part of the planners to concentrate on heavy investment and let the other sectors of the economy adapt to the requirements of such a program.

In closing, one might predict that if circumstances convince the Soviet leaders that the consumer should re-receive top priority, the Soviet planning mechanism would decentralize so that it could better respond to the preferences of consumers. Up to the present it has served Soviet purposes admirably, but it has not been primarily concerned with serving the consumer.

46. A World Away*

Daniel Lang

Although Soviet citizens have long been taught that the American way of life represents a doomed and de-

* From Daniel Lang, "A Reporter at Large," The New Yorker, February 16, 1952. Reprinted by permission. Copyright 1952 The New Yorker Magazine, Inc.

cadent culture, it is only within the last five years that any but a relatively few specially certified political emissaries have had a chance to check up on this official view. These people, the first Russian émigrés to reach this country since the exodus that immediately followed the Bolshevik Revolution in 1917, owe their look at the other of the so-called "two worlds" to the accidents of war, rather than to any relaxing of the Kremlin's tight passport control. So far, counting children, they number about ten thousand. All the adults, except for some Red Army deserters, were hauled away from their homeland by the Nazis, who conscripted them as workers in factories and mines in Germany or German-occupied territory. At the end of the war, finding themselves in the American Zone, or hurrying to it from other sections of Germany, they were able to avoid repatriation and to continue their westward movement.

The other evening, I spent several hours with three of these fairly recent arrivals — Igor and Zina Soben, formerly of Leningrad, and their son Vadi, who was two weeks old when, in October, 1943, he and his parents were shipped by cattle car to a labor camp in Poland. After a brief stay there, the family was shipped, again by cattle car, to another camp, in Germany, and then, in April, 1944, to Franzensbad, Czechoslovakia, where the Nazis set the father to mining coal and the mother to serving as a charwoman in a miners' barracks. From the Sobens, who finally found their way here in August, 1946, I heard an account of the difficulties experienced by a Soviet family in adapting itself to the ways of a capitalist democracy and was given a picture of an odd kind of pioneering, which has confronted them with moral puzzles and brought about marked changes in them. We dis-

cussed a wide range of subjects, including television, the Russian soul, and Vadi's former teacher at P.S. 86, in the Bronx. Igor and Zina — they suggested that we use first names before the evening was very old — are in their late thirties, and they are products of the Soviet regime in the very real sense that for a quarter of a century they were exposed to only those schools, clubs, plays, movies, and newspapers whose purpose it was to indoctrinate them permanently with the Communist outlook. Igor, to be precise, was five at the time of the Revolution and Zina three.

My meeting with the Sobens was arranged, somewhat reluctantly, by a friend of mine, M. K. Argus, who is a writer for *Novoye Russkoye Slovo,* an anti-Communist Russian-language daily published in New York. Argus, an expansive, quixotic man in his fifties, said he wasn't sure which of his many newly arrived countrymen he preferred to have me meet. "Any one of them is liable to say something horrible," he told me at lunch one day. "I was a Russian immigrant myself a long time ago, but this batch — they're different. Last week, I asked one of them how he was getting along here, and he answered, 'How do I know you're not a spy?' Some of those who are out of work have come up to the office and threatened to go back to the Soviet Union and denounce America if my colleagues and I don't find them jobs. And many of them have legally changed their names — even some who have no relatives in Russia to protect. But, ah," he went on, suddenly turning wistful, "they are all true Russians! They come calling on us with poems in their hands. They tell us how they are related to this grand duke and that prince. We, too, were all poets and nobles when we arrived." Argus asked himself aloud whom he should send me to. "Go talk with the Sobens," he told me at last. "A changed name, of course, since in their case I believe they do have relatives in the Soviet Union. Don't ask me why I suggest them rather than any of the others. I have no idea what they think of the United States. Now that we have decided, we must become practical. Two things. Go with a bottle of vodka. And when Igor introduces you to his wife, say that Argus considers her the prettiest of the new immigrants. These things will help you very much."

A few days after my lunch with Argus, I arrived, a bottle of vodka under my arm, at the Soben home, a two-story, one-family brick house in a row of almost identical dwellings on 150th Street, in a tidy neighborhood of Queens. Igor, a stocky, sandy-haired, blue-eyed man, opened the door, shook hands with me gravely, and ushered me into the living room. It was early evening, and Vadi, a thin, blond boy with a pleasant face, was sprawled on the floor before a television set, watching Captain Video. He turned to size me up briefly, then went back to his watching. Igor called out in Russian to his wife, and she hurried out of the kitchen-dinette, adjoining the living room, to greet me. A hand-

some, spirited woman with light-brown hair and expressive brown eyes, she, like her husband, speaks English with a marked accent. "Excuse me for not being at the door, but I was making *pelmeny* for dinner," she said. "It is a Siberian dish. I hope you will like it." I handed her the bottle of vodka and both of them thanked me politely. I also delivered Argus's message, and they were delighted. Igor became less reserved. "We have just bought this house," he told me. "Fifteen years in which to pay! Clearly, the lady who sold it to us is not worried about revolutions."

Zina suggested a tour of the house. "Our living room," she said, indicating the lamps, easy chairs, and sofa that surrounded us. In a corner stood an upright piano, its top adorned with framed snapshots of, I presumed, relatives. We went down to the cellar, where, Igor said, he was planning to set up a rumpus room. "It will be necessary to buy a ping-pong table," he remarked. On the second floor were two bedrooms of modest size and a peach-tiled bathroom. We were soon in and out of the bedrooms, but Zina lingered by the basin in the bathroom. "Hot water whenever we want," she said, turning the faucet on for a moment. "In Leningrad, we never had that." "In Leningrad," Igor said, "we had one small room in a small five-room apartment. Four families were in the other rooms. We all shared the kitchen." We went back downstairs and through the living room and kitchen to the rear door. Zina opened it wide. "Our yard," she said proudly. I looked out at a patch of ground, perhaps ten feet square, bounded by a white picket fence. The view took in a street corner, a few maples, and several replicas of the Soben house. While we were standing in the doorway, a sleek bus, with fluorescent lights, stopped at the corner to pick up a passenger. "Such a beautiful bus!" Zina exclaimed.

"We have become members of the American middle class," Igor said earnestly. Zina looked at him with a questioning expression. "It is the truth," he assured her. "We must face it."

Igor opened the bottle of vodka and filled two jiggers, and he and I sat down at the table in the dinette. Zina, fussing over the *pelmeny* at the stove, a few feet away, was too busy to join us. Igor raised his glass. "*Khorosho!*" he said, and we downed our drinks. "Vodka in Queens," he said with a shrug. "It is sometimes still hard to believe that we are not leading our lives in Leningrad." Zina, he told me, was born and raised there and he moved there with his family from the city of Kuznetsk, his birthplace, at the age of ten. Zina's father was a journalist of note and Igor's father a professor of forestry. "I am of the nobility," Zina put in eagerly, momentarily neglecting her cooking. She mentioned some vague connection, through her maternal grandmother, with the Georgian throne. Igor went on to say that he and Zina were married in 1933, in a civil ceremony. Zina was an office worker at the time, and Igor was a student at the Leningrad Mining Institute, where he subsequently earned the Russian equivalent of a Master of Science in mining engineering. Even before he had his degree, he joined the staff of a mining-research organization in Leningrad, which sent him on research missions to mines in the Arctic Zone, the Urals, and Siberia. In 1937, Zina gave up her office job and enrolled in the Herzen Institute, where she majored in Russian history, expecting someday to teach that subject.

When Russia was invaded, the government dispatched Igor to the Donets Basin mines, in the Ukraine, to help supervise the stepping up of coal production there. Zina joined him six months later. In 1941, Panzer divisions overran the region, and the Sobens were trapped. Igor continued to work as a mine supervisor, only now, of course, he was a servant of the Nazis. Two years later, just after Zina had her baby, the Germans, feeling the pinch of the manpower shortage, rounded up the Sobens, and a lot of other Russians, and the family found itself embarked upon the cattle-car journey that took them eventually to Franzensbad. "Thank God I escaped the Leningrad siege!" Zina said, crossing herself. "Two million people starved to death there." I asked her how she felt about religion. "I attended the Russian Orthodox Church until I was thirteen," she replied. "Then the regime became very antireligious and we children stopped going. Now I go to church only occasionally. I believe in God in my own way. Igor is the same."

After American troops captured Franzensbad, in 1945, the Sobens remained there for a while, picking up a smattering of English from the G.I.s and trying to decide whether to return to the Soviet Union. During the next three months, their minds were made up for them by the hundreds of their fellow-citizens who streamed through the town. These Russians had been liberated by the Red Army, but instead of being repatriated, as they had hoped, they had been denounced as Nazi collaborators by Red Army officers and kept at their jobs in German mines and factories, the output of which was being shipped back to the Soviet. Bitter and angry, they had escaped from their liberators, and their flight had brought them to Franzensbad.

Igor said that he and Zina kept asking these fugitives if the regime in Russia had changed. "We hoped that maybe the sacrifices of the Russian people during the war had softened Stalin's outlook," he said. "We talked to Tartars, fishermen from the Black Sea, Ukrainian peasants, intellectuals from Moscow and from our own city. Naturally, the details of each individual's experiences had been different, but basically they all understood our question, and the answer was always the same — no change. In my own case, when I asked them if the regime had changed I was asking if the mines were still being inefficiently operated in an atmosphere of political terror and if an engineer might still be accused of sabotage because his reports were not flowery enough or were too

flowery. I was asking if my sister was still in a concentration camp for refusing to divorce her husband. The regime had ordered her to divorce him because his origin was wrong. His father, you see, had been a wealthy paper manufacturer in czarist times. I was asking if my closest friend, a musician, was still in the concentration camp to which he had gone just to visit his brother, who was a prisoner there. Zina and I had always managed to stay out of trouble ourselves, but now we knew that if we went back, we would risk facing charges of collaborating with the Nazis. Even if that did not happen, it would be recorded in our dossiers that we had been outside our country. We would always be suspected of not believing that the Soviet Union is Paradise."

"It was the regime we wanted to escape, not our country," Zina said. To her, she went on, the regime meant entrenched power; her country meant a language, landscapes, familiar customs, and friends. "On vacations, we used to feel this difference distinctly," she said. "That was the only time the regime left people to themselves. We used to go to Gagri, a beautiful resort in the Caucasus, on the northeast shore of the Black Sea. On the beach, picnicking with friendly strangers, we would talk about anything that came into our minds — music, art, philosophy. I think we could even have talked about the regime, but who wanted to? We were all tired of politics. In Gagri, we had a glimpse of what Russia could have been like the whole year round if it were not for the regime. But the minute people got aboard the trains to go home, their masks were back on. They were no longer willing to talk with strangers. They were afraid anyone they spoke to might be either a spy for the regime or about to be arrested by it."

In August, 1945, a major attached to the American command in Franzensbad told Igor that the Americans were withdrawing from the town and that their place was likely to be taken by the Russians. Accordingly, the Sobens set out for the American Zone — on foot, like nearly all other uprooted Europeans on the move. Their particular trek involved pushing Vadi in his baby carriage a hundred and twenty miles to Bavaria. "Whenever we were near water, we bathed Vadi," Zina said. After ten days, they arrived at the border of the American Zone, in a driving rainstorm. There they were stopped by an American sentry, who apparently had orders to deny entry to anyone without proper papers. "We had nothing," Igor recalled. "But he just looked at Vadi, fast asleep in the rain, and said, 'He's a good boy.' After looking around to see if anyone was watching him, he gave a sharp little whistle, like when Americans call taxicabs, and waved us by. No lecture about freedom, or anything like that. Just a little whistle. We pushed the carriage until we came to a big rock. We sat down there. The rain was still pouring down, but we didn't care. I think that we both realized at last that we had thought enough about home."

Zina served the *pelmeny,* a kind of *pasta,* which we dunked in saucers of sour cream. She tried in vain to coax Vadi into having some. As a compromise, he took a bottle of Coca-Cola out of the refrigerator, and then returned to the television set. Zina, who hardly ate anything, pressed second helpings of the filling stuff on Igor and me. After the meal, we moved to the living room. We had scarcely sat down when from the television set came the penetrating screech of an electric organ; an ugly old man was strangling a pretty ingénue. Igor barked at his son in Russian, and the boy turned the set off. Then, evidently still heeding paternal instructions, he walked to a bookshelf and took down a volume of Pushkin's "Fairy Tales." Before long he was contentedly stretched out on the floor in front of us, absorbed in the book.

After watching his son fondly for a few minutes, Igor resumed the story of the family's migration. Once safely in American-occupied territory, he said, they proceeded to Frankfurt. There he made them a rickety apartment in the ruins of a bombed building and got a menial job in an American Army kitchen. It didn't pay much, but there was always leftover food, which he took home to his wife and child. Life in Frankfurt was dreary but safe, and the Sobens plodded along there until the spring of 1946, when a Russian friend told them that the American Christian Committee for Refugees, an organization set up to help people like themselves reach the United States, had opened an office in the city. Igor and Zina discussed the idea of coming to this country. Zina was not enthusiastic. " I believed that there was a small clique of powerful individuals in the United States who would make it difficult for people with our background to earn a living," she told me. Igor was hardly more enthusiastic, but he had a hunch that a good engineer could get along in any prosperous country. They both were convinced that Germany offered no future, and that was what eventually decided them.

Even after the Sobens had made up their minds, they continued to have misgivings. " You see, we had read many bad things about the United States in Soviet publications," Igor told me. " Sometimes, though, we had been able to read between the lines. For example, Ilya Ilf and Eugene Petrov, two Soviet journalists, once wrote a book about a visit they had made to America. They wrote that a Social Security system had been set up there that was going to give old people a mere thirty dollars a month — scandalous, they tried to make it appear. Still, we knew that in the Leningrad black market a dollar was worth fifty rubles, so we figured that these old people were going to receive fifteen hundred rubles a month. But I, a hard-working engineer, earned only six hundred rubles a month. Also, Ilf and Petrov wrote that poor people in America had to stand on the highways with their thumbs in the air if they wanted to ride from one place to another. To Zina and me, that meant two things. First, there must be a great many automo-

biles in America, and, second, Americans must be a very polite people to stop and give somebody a ride." Zina held up a rigid thumb. " In the Soviet Union," she said, " you could stand like this for two years and you'd still be standing."

Igor and Zina finally went to talk matters over with an A.C.C.R. representative in Frankfurt. He assured them of the organization's good will; it would advance them the price of their boat passage and enough money to keep them going in the United States until they got on their feet. But, he added, they would have to have visas before they could move on to this country as displaced persons. Vadi, then nearly three, solved that problem. One day, accompanying his parents to the local American consulate, where they had been going repeatedly in an effort to procure the necessary credentials, the boy caught his finger in an office door and yowled. A man on the staff of the consulate happened to be passing and went to his rescue. The man took a fancy to the boy and became interested in the Sobens' case. Two months later, the Sobens, equipped with visas, went to Bremerhaven, where, with a dozen of their fellow-countrymen and several hundred other passengers, they boarded the American transport Marine Perch. " Just as the ship got under way, an electrician from Kiev made a joke," Igor told me. " He said that we were on a Soviet ship that was taking us to Murmansk. Everybody laughed."

When the Sobens landed here that August, the A.C.C.R. put them up in a large room at the Hotel Diplomat, on West Forty-third Street, and allowed them seven dollars a day for expenses. The organization also set about finding Igor a job by circularizing mining firms with photostatic copies of a citation, and a translation of it, that he had received from his chief at the research organization in Leningrad. (The citation stated, among other things, that Igor had "never been fined for mismanagement.") The Sobens were dazzled by New York. "So many oranges on sale in the streets!" Zina said to me. "So many big, shiny cars! And your department stores, with all those crowds in them! In the Soviet Union, they would be like museums."

"And me jumping up and down on the bed at the hotel," Vadi said, looking up from his Pushkin.

"It was his first bedspring," Igor explained. "He says he remembers nothing that happened to him before then."

The Sobens' sightseeing produced a number of surprises. As they were coming out of the Diplomat one morning, Igor said, they saw three men with signs on their backs walking up and down in front of a barbershop near the hotel, and, upon inquiring, learned they were pickets proclaiming that the barbers were on strike. "We had never known that men could refuse to work," Zina said. "In the Soviet Union and Nazi Germany, of course, those pickets would have been arrested." The same morning, Igor and Zina, passing a newsstand on Forty-second Street near the Public Library, were amazed to see copies of *Pravda* on sale. "We felt like tearing up every copy," Igor said. A few days later, they were chatting on a Sixth Avenue bus when another passenger, a friendly middle-aged woman, struck up a conversation with them in Russian and invited them to a farewell meeting she was organizing for two American priests of the Russian Orthodox Church who were about to leave for the Soviet Union. At the meeting, which was held in St. Nicholas Cathedral, at Ninety-seventh Street and Madison Avenue, the Sobens heard several speakers hail the priests' departure as proof that the war, which had ended only the year before, had changed Stalin's attitude toward religion. At an informal reception after the meeting, Igor and Zina expressed the belief to their hostess and other members of the audience that Stalin's apparent pact with God was no more than a temporary political expedient. "We made them angry," Igor told me. "And they disgusted us. These people were not Communists — they were just kindhearted — but they disgusted us. After all, Zina and I had lived under a dictatorship — or rather under two of them — nearly all our lives."

After six weeks here, the Sobens took out their first citizenship papers. "I don't know why we did that so soon," Igor said. "We wanted to be citizens of some country, but we did not yet really know anything of the American form of government. I didn't even have a job, although I had certainly tried to find one." At the end of three months, Zina found temporary work packing toys at F. A. O. Schwarz during the Christmas-shopping season, and this made Igor more restive than ever about being unemployed. Now that there was a wage-earner in the family, their allowance was cut off, and Igor almost decided to take a laborer's job, but an A.C.C.R. representative counselled him against getting off on the wrong foot. He did, however, chuck the idea of finding work with a mining company, and made the rounds of the local civil-engineering offices. He visited a hundred firms in a month's time, but his then rudimentary English discouraged prospective employers. He got his break one morning in December, 1946, when he walked into the offices of Madigan-Hyland, an engineering firm in Long Island City, where he presented a copy of his citation to a man who happened to be standing in the outer office. The man glanced at the document and held out his hand. " Come in," he said to Igor, in Russian. " I also had a hard time getting a start when I came here. But that was thirty-two years ago." Igor's new-found benefactor was the chief engineer of Madigan-Hyland's structural division. He put Igor to work at a drafting board alongside an Irishman with a heavy brogue. " Don't worry about your English," the chief engineer advised Igor. " Nobody understands his, either."

Once Igor had a job, the Sobens checked out of the Diplomat and rented a seventeen-dollar-a-month one-room furnished apartment in a tenement on Kingsbridge Terrace,

in the Bronx. The room was no larger than their home in Leningrad had been, Igor said, but it was a beginning. " As soon as we moved in," he told me, " we made a kind of Five Year Plan, although all we could think of at first that we needed was something we believed we might be able to scrape together in three years — enough money to buy furniture for a two-room apartment. The reason we decided we ought to have a plan was that we thought it would help us save money each week. Nobody ever saves money in the Soviet Union — when you have money there is nothing to buy there and when there is something to buy you don't have the money. And besides, we wanted to start paying back the A.C.C.R. what we owed it."

The rate of the Sobens' savings was considerably improved in June, 1947, when Zina, after arranging to have the tenement superintendent's wife take care of Vadi during the day, took a job at the Horn & Hardart Commissary, at Fiftieth Street and Eleventh Avenue. The job, which Zina still has (Vadi pretty much takes care of himself these days under the benevolent supervision of a neighbor), requires her to weigh salads from 7 A.M. until noon, and to keep count from 1 to 3:30 P.M. of the fish-cake and chow-mein orders sent in by the firm's cafeterias. She hadn't been at the commissary very long, Zina said, before her fellow-workers started calling her " the Russian flower," because her name sounded to them like " Zinnia." The congenial atmosphere of the establishment impressed her. " In the Soviet Union, people don't talk at work," she said. " To do so can mean arrest for sabotage. But at Horn & Hardart, just so long as we do our work, we can talk and even joke. Yes, and sing, too. One afternoon, maybe four months after I started working there, I suddenly thought how pretty my uniform was — my gray dress and white cap and white apron. Then I started to sing softly to myself. A girl from the salad section was passing and she heard me. She said to me, ' Well, well, the Russian flower is happy today.' Her remark startled me. Russians usually sing to themselves when they are sad, not happy. I wondered what was the matter with me — singing happily like that, and in a place where one worked, too."

Along about November, 1948, Igor told me, he decided upon an elaboration of the family's Five Year Plan; they would work toward buying a car. "One night," he said, "I was walking up the stairs to our room when a neighbor asked me to come in and have a glass of tea. I was glad he did. This man had puzzled Zina and me for a long time. We could not understand why he and his family were living in such a tenement. He looked like the cartoons of capitalists that we had seen so many times in Soviet publications — fat, with loud suits and always a long cigar. Every Sunday, we would see this man drive off with his family in a shiny car that was almost big enough for a member of the Politburo. Zina did not think he was a capitalist. She thought he was an American gangster hiding

from the police. The last few weeks, she had become sure of this, because he never seemed to go to work. Anyway, I sat down with him and we talked. I found out that he was a house painter and that this was his slack season. It was 'a nice talk. So he was no longer a puzzle to me, and I had made the discovery that here anyone can own a car. Someday, I thought, I will own one, too."

From the material point of view, the Sobens said, their first two years here were gratifying. Igor proved himself a competent engineer, switched jobs several times, and doubled his salary. Zina received a small raise. Vadi had both winter and summer clothes. The couple was steadily repaying the money advanced by the A.C.C.R. In December, shortly after Igor's talk with the house painter and a year ahead of their plan, the Sobens moved into larger quarters — two rooms in a six-room apartment that they shared with six other Russian immigrants, in the basement of the Kingsbridge Terrace tenement.

This prosperity confused the Sobens. They were troubled by the realization that they were committing *meshchanstvo* — an offense, in Russian eyes. Igor defined it for me as " living for oneself, without regard for one's brother." In Russia, he said, a person guilty of *meshchanstvo* is definitely looked down upon, particularly among the intelligentsia. For decades, he said, *meshchanstvo* had been a target for Russian writers. " Instead of *meshchanstvo,* one must be willing to make *zhertvy* — sacrifices," he told me. "One must live for some spiritual concept like self-sacrifice, not just for personal comfort."

"Willingness to make *zhertvy* is the heart of the Russian soul," Zina broke in. "To Russians, one's private life should be no more than a respite from making sacrifices, and never an end in itself. From what I have learned of Russian history, I would say that this tradition is a result of the many invasions of the motherland from both Asia and Europe. The invasions have been constantly expected. And the invasions have made sacrifices essential."

The Sobens became increasingly convinced that in this country the accumulation of personal comforts was the primary objective, the accepted order of things. "The people here seemed to us to be living for themselves," Zina said. "They went to work, made money, and bought gardenias for their kitchens. We found we were living the same way, and it worried us. We wondered why we were becoming citizens of a country that seemed to lack a common purpose." In Russia, the atmosphere had been different; there, Igor said, Stalin, exploiting the taboo against *meshchanstvo,* kept exhorting his subjects to make the regime their life. "In Leningrad, we hardly ever went home when we finished work," Igor said. "We went to political demonstrations or government-sponsored sports contests, and especially to meetings of our *yacheiki* — our communal societies. Often, Zina and I would not have a chance to talk to each other for three or four days, we were so busy with our *yacheiki.*" Night after night, he said, they attended meetings of these societies — the Friends of the Victims of Capitalism, the Chemical Warfare Defense Society, the Bulletin Board Committee, which was devoted to getting out notices that were posted in offices and factories to give workers the latest word from above about production goals, and many others. "And, of course, we were assured that by living for the government we were living for a common purpose — the building of Socialism," Igor said. "We looked on the hardships Stalin imposed on us as idealistic sacrifices that were helping to make a better life for the whole Russian people. We had to believe that. Life was so hard it would have been impossible to endure it otherwise. A feeling of intimacy with the regime became an ingrained part of our existence. Do you remember the escape, three years ago, of Peter Pirogov and Anatoli Barsov? They were two Soviet Air Force lieutenants who flew their plane to the American Zone in Austria and then came on to the United States. Pirogov is still here, but Barsov isn't. He was unhappy in the United States. He could not live without his *yacheiki.* He went back to the Soviet Union, where, I've heard, he was shot." Igor shrugged. "At first, we, too, missed our *yacheiki.*"

Igor and Zina tried to atone for their prosperity by creating for themselves a life based on *yacheiki* of another kind, right here in New York. For one thing, they helped found the Society of New Immigrants from

Russia. The activities of this organization, which met in the Russian Orthodox Church of Christ the Savior, on 121st Street near Madison Avenue, included shipping food parcels to Soviet émigrés in Germany and helping the émigrés make their way to the United States by finding jobs or sponsors for them. The Sobens also busied themselves with the Association of Lovers of Russian Art, frequently appearing in plays it presented in various small auditoriums around town. "It made us feel good to come home tired," Igor said. "In fact, we did not like to spend our evenings alone at home. It made us think we were leading selfish lives. When we had no meetings to go to, we would have some of our Russian friends in or go to visit them. If we *did* have to spend a quiet evening at home, we would try to give it significance by devoting ourselves to study — engineering in my case, and American history in Zina's."

Zina told me that during the months she and Igor were wrestling with the problem of *meshchanstvo* she even attempted to imbue her fellow-workers in the commissary with a spirit of sacrifice. Igor smiled. "Zina wanted to become an *udarnitsa* — a heroine of labor — at Horn & Hardart," he said. His wife, he went on, had called on her colleagues to increase production, and they replied with a general invitation to her to relax. One day, Zina said, while she was lunching with the chef and some other employees in their cafeteria at the commissary, she held forth on the great responsibility they all had to help keep thousands of residents of the city healthy by supplying them with good food. "When we left the table," Zina recalled, "the chef bowed low to me and said sarcastically, 'Don't be a boss, Russian Princess.' He always calls me that when I annoy him, but I do not mind." She glanced shyly at the floor. "After all, I *am* of the nobility."

Late in March, 1949, the Cultural and Scientific Conference for World Peace convened at the Waldorf-Astoria. It was sponsored by the National Council of the Arts, Sciences, and Professions and was attended by a substantial number of delegates whose praise of the Soviet Union's foreign policy had been as undiscriminating as their condemnation of this country's. A counter-demonstration, sponsored by the Russian League for People's Freedom, was held at the City Center Casino, at Fifty-fifth Street and Seventh Avenue. Igor and Zina, having become prominent in New York's Russian community because of their organizational activities, were two of the speakers at the latter gathering, along with, among others, Alexander Kerensky, the former Russian premier whose government was overthrown by the Bolsheviks, and Peter Pirogov, who, accompanied by the unhappy Barsov, had arrived in America a month earlier. After the League's meeting, which took place on a Sunday afternoon, the Sobens and Pirogov strolled down to Times Square, then cut over to Eighth Avenue and proceeded uptown. At Forty-ninth Street, they encountered some pickets protesting a rally that was being held in Madison Square Garden as the final session of the Cultural and Scientific Conference for World Peace. "Pirogov wanted us to go inside and beat up some of the audience," Igor said. "He hadn't been here two and a half years, like Zina and me. He had just come from the Soviet Union. I took him by the arm and led him away."

The three resumed their walk. As they came out on Columbus Circle, they saw four soapbox orators, their makeshift platforms draped with American flags and surrounded by groups of listeners. Neither the Sobens nor Pirogov had ever seen Columbus Circle on a Sunday afternoon before and they approached the scene curiously. The first speaker they listened to was a Communist, a middle-aged, bald man who was shouting in praise of what he professed to be the peace-loving tendencies of the Soviet Union. Two boys, Zina remembered, were sailing paper airplanes at him. "Pirogov wanted to do something more violent than that," she said. "He was growling in an angry way. Igor and I left him there, because we were eager to hear what the other speakers had to say."

Twenty feet away, Igor and his wife listened for a while to a man who said he represented the Hoboes of America and was advocating a three-hour workday, explaining that the rest of man's waking hours should be devoted to music, games, and making love. Igor lingered to hear more of what was on the hobo's

mind, while Zina moved on to the fringe of another crowd, which was gazing up at a speaker who was arguing in favor of the single tax. "I did not know then what the single tax was," Zina told me, smiling. "It must be, I thought, that he does not want married people to be taxed. A very fine speaker, I said to myself. Then I listened to an atheist — an old man with long gray hair who looked like God. He was saying, 'God hasn't helped you yet and He never will.' He talked about the measurements of a whale's mouth to prove that no whale could have swallowed Jonah."

Eventually, Igor and Zina spotted each other in a group that was forming around a newcomer — an apostle of vegetarianism. "We were both very excited by then," Zina told me. "Igor said to me, 'It is better this way than to arrest these people. To allow this is a sign of strength.' Then he asked me what I thought, but I did not feel like talking. I was afraid that if I talked, I might lose a happy feeling I had. As we left Columbus Circle, we passed the Communist's platform. Pirogov was still standing there, his face just as angry as before."

After their visit to Columbus Circle, Igor said, he and Zina decided to take a second look at Americans. "We stopped going so often to our *yacheiki*," he continued. "We realized that although we were in America, we had been trying to live like Soviet citizens. Now we wanted to try to understand Americans. Our half hour with the soapboxes had made us feel that there was, after all, some worth-while idea guiding this country. Wherever we looked, we were reminded of Columbus Circle. Not that people were talking like hoboes, but to us everyone seemed to be trying to do and say what he pleased." Igor smiled reminiscently. " There was this young draftsman I met, not long after our walk with Pirogov," he said. " We were both working on the construction of the Pelham Parkway Housing Project. He amazed me. I had never heard anyone with so many plans for his personal future. I had hardly shaken hands with him before he was telling me that he wanted to make enough money to go back and finish college. Then he was going to marry a lawyer's secretary he was engaged to. But they weren't going to have children right away. They would both work for the first five years of their marriage and save money to buy a small house in Mount Vernon. Listening to him, I remembered a cousin of mine, a girl in Leningrad, who, after she got married, set a private goal for herself. This was unheard of there. Couples in the Soviet Union never know when they will be separated by labor assignments. But my cousin wanted nice furniture for herself and her husband, who was a mining engineer, like me. So they ate little, lost weight, didn't take vacations, and put aside rubles. They had just bought their last chair when the husband was sent to some phosphate mines in the Urals. He stayed there three years. My cousin was so put out that she sold her furniture and ate better than anyone else.

When her husband came back, he was very happy. He said that he liked new furniture, but that he liked a wife with flesh on her bones better." Igor shook his head. " That draftsman on the housing project," he said. " He probably has his plans even for his old age. Maybe his desire for personal happiness was a case of *meshchanstvo,* but he was one of the hardest workers I ever met. And all because he wanted to live in a house more than five years later with a girl he hadn't even married yet."

Igor went on to say that he had also been impressed by a newspaper story he read one day in the summer of 1949. It dealt with a Texan who, while driving along a highway with his wife nine months after the 1948 Presidential election, happened to ask her which candidate she had voted for. " She told him Truman," Igor said, " and he stopped the car, threw her out into the road, which broke her arm, and drove away. My God, I thought, what a country, where a wife doesn't have to tell her husband who she is going to vote for! "

Zina said she would never forget Mrs. Sarah Mandel, who had been Vadi's first-grade teacher in the Bronx. The two women met one afternoon at the school, when Zina, who happened to have a day off, stopped by for Vadi, and Mrs. Mandel showed her a batch of the pupils' paintings. " Most of them were done in several different colors, but one was just a red blotch," Zina told me. " I said that in Russia there is a proverb — an old one that has

nothing to do with the regime —
that goes, 'A fool always chooses
red.' Mrs. Mandel was shocked.
She said that the blotch was a form
of self-expression that was helping
the child find his personality. Personality! In the Soviet Union, Mrs.
Mandel would have made Vadi an
Octobrist — a little boy marching
with all the little boys and girls in
front of big pictures of Stalin."

Early in 1950, Zina went on, she
was changing into her uniform in
the commissary locker room one
morning when she heard a fellow-
employee mention to another girl
that it looked as if long day dresses
would continue to be the fashion in
the coming year. The other girl replied that she didn't care what the
vogue was — she was much too short
to wear long dresses, and wouldn't.
"In the Soviet Union, she would
have had to care," Zina said. "The
regime dictates styles, and Soviet
women know that if they do not
follow the style of the moment, they
will be stared at as individualists.
And to be thought an individualist
in Russia is not wise. In 1932, I remember, the style was very short
dresses, and even women with fat
legs wore them. In 1934, it was a
flat, Cossack-type hat, and round-
faced women wore them even
though they made their faces look
still rounder. Then, there was the
year when women's heels had to be
exactly four and a half inches high.
Even the tallest women wore them.
I don't think there was a man in
Russia as tall as his wife was that
year."

Signs of personal freedom such as
these were sobering, rather than exciting, to the Sobens. It struck them
as a difficult, lonely sort of freedom.
"It meant that whatever happened
to us, good or bad, would be our own
responsibility," Igor said. "In the
Soviet Union, the regime was responsible for everybody, and we had
freedom to do only one thing — to
help the regime. We did not have
to think what to do next. Our lives
were planned for us and we asked
no questions. Still, it is a better freedom here — a more honest one, in
which people can ask questions and
have opinions." He checked his
growing enthusiasm, paused, and
then added slowly, "I do not say
that everything is perfect in this
country."

Igor glanced at Zina. Her face
had become drawn. "We have our
own reservations," she said anxiously to me. "We were just talking
about them just before you came."

"It is not good when one person
calls another 'a dirty Russian Communist' just because the other person happens to have been born in
Russia or to have Russian parents,"
Igor said. "I haven't been called
that, but Zina and Vadi have. Zina
slapped the woman who said it.
Vadi cried when it happened to
him."

"Both boys were bigger than me,"
Vadi said, putting aside his book.

"The beaches are a disgrace,"
Zina joined in, with seeming reluctance. "So many short bathing
suits, so much kissing. And many
television programs are too abnormal for children. But Vadi told us
all his friends had sets, so how could

we say no? He's been through so much. We don't think the Metropolitan Opera is very good, either. It is not nearly as modern as Russian opera."

"Children under sixteen should not be permitted to attend stupid love movies," Igor said. "That was a good Soviet law. And American parties are dull. All the guests do is worry about their baby sitters. Russian parties are gay. We forget Vadi when we go to a party."

"We have complained enough, Igor," Zina said anxiously. "Maybe too much. Maybe we will be deported."

Igor shook his head. "No, Zina, we have not complained too much," he assured her. "Why should anybody think so? In this country, one must say what one thinks."

During the past two years or so, the Sobens said, their guilty feeling about *meshchanstvo* has gradually subsided. They started planning to buy a house of their own in May, 1951, and had moved to Queens only a few weeks before I saw them. Igor, now well established in his profession, has settled down as a design-

er for Devenco, Inc., an engineering firm at 150 Broadway, which he also represents as a consultant to the Port of New York Authority. The couple's hour of greatest trial in shedding the old ways and adopting the new — an ordeal they think they took in their stride — came in May, 1950. Igor and Zina were spending a Sunday afternoon at home when a friend of theirs, a Russian pianist whom they met aboard the Marine Perch and who has become a mechanic here, burst in on them and announced that they had been stewing long enough about buying an automobile. The time had come for action, he said. Igor and Zina, hypnotized, followed him to a used-car lot, where he talked them into buying a 1940 Dodge coupé. When the sale was completed, the dealer held the door open for Igor to get in and take the wheel. At that point, Igor recovered sufficiently from his confusion to recall that he didn't know how to drive. The friend, disgusted, got in the car and drove them back to Kingsbridge Terrace. Three months and two road tests later, Igor had a license.

47. Soviet Economic Progress*

I. PRODUCTION UNDER THE POSTWAR PLAN

The statistical office of the Soviet Government has published its report on economic development in 1950,

* From *The Economist* (*London*), CLX (1951), pp. 436–37, 494–96, 549–52. Reprinted by permission of *The Economist*.

without insisting on the fact that this was the last year of the first postwar Five-Year Plan. Thus the Plan has reached its end without the Soviet authorities having drawn up a general account for the period. This is the more surprising because the Plan has been, on the whole, successful. It may be that the overall balance will still be officially announced with the appropriate publicity and ado. In the meantime, a fairly clear picture emerges from a comparison of the five annual reports published between 1947 and 1951.

overfulfilment of the original targets and the modest claims made for 1950 — which were obviously related to the new targets — suggests that the raising of the sights was of the order of 10 per cent, at least in the output of basic materials.

COMPARISONS OF PRODUCTION

| | | Index of Industrial Production | (In Million Long Tons) | | | | Electricity (billion kWh.) |
			Pig Iron	Raw Steel	Coal	Oil	
		1940=100					
	USSR	.....	15.0	18.3	166.0	31.0	48.0
1940............	USA	.....	41.9	59.8	457.4	178.0	141.8
	UK	.....	8.2	13.0	224.3	.....	28.8
	USSR	.....	8.8	12.4	150.0	19.5	45.0
1945............	USA	.....	48.4	71.2	509.4	227.9	225.5
	UK	.....	7.1	11.8	206.3	.....	37.3
	USSR	118.0	13.8	18.9	210.0	29.2	65.5
1948............	USA	153.2	54.3	79.1	610.1	272.4	282.7
	UK	116.0*	9.3	14.9	209.4	.....	46.5
	USSR	141.5	16.4	23.6	238.0	33.3	77.5
1949............	USA	140.5	48.4	69.6	429.1	248.1	291.1
	UK	123.4*	9.5	15.6	215.1	.....	49.1
	USSR	174.0	19.2	27.6	264.0	37.6	86.7
1950............	USSR†	148.0	19.5	25.4	250.0	35.4	82.0
	USA	159.3	58.2	86.3	491.3	263.9	328.9
	UK	134.5*	9.6	16.3	216.3	.....	55.0

* 1938=100.   † Planned target.

The first two years of the Plan were taken up by painful efforts at rehabilitation accompanied by bad harvests. In the third year the pre-war levels of output were reached and slightly exceeded. At the end of 1949 the targets set for the end of 1950 were nearly reached. But it was not decided to proclaim the fulfilment of the Five-Year Plan in four years: instead, the final objectives of the Five-Year Plan were raised but no details were made public. A comparison between the considerable

The general progress is shown in the increase in the national income, which is claimed to be 60 per cent higher than in 1940, compared with a planned increase of 38 per cent. This is a startling claim; but it appears less so when it is compared with the huge rise in employment since the war. Total employment is said to exceed now 39 million, which is some 8¾ million more than in 1940, although another computation shows the increase as amounting to only 6.7 million. The number of workers and employees has certainly grown by about 25 per cent, which may be partly explained by the continued employment of great masses of women. To this must be added the lengthening of working hours; for the Soviet Union has not gone back to the five-day week and seven-hour day which were in force before the war.

The rise in employment and the lengthening of hours have resulted in an increase of man-hours worked by about 45 per cent. A rise in efficiency by 10 per cent over the last ten years would account for the claimed increase in the national income. On the other hand, Soviet sources claim an increase in productivity of labour by 40 per cent. Whatever "productivity of labour" may mean, it certainly does not mean sheer efficiency; for if it did, the rise in the national income should have been much steeper, in view of the higher employment. Incidentally, although Soviet statistics lump together workers and employees, Soviet economic theory considers only the former to be productive.

Industrial production was rising pretty steeply during the five-year period, particularly in its second half; according to the index in the accompanying table gross industrial output in 1950 was higher by nearly three-quarters than before the war.

This index also shows the rising tempo of development, and it indicates that 1948 was the year in which the prewar level was reached and exceeded. Yet, while for the whole of Russia that year's output was 18 per cent higher than before the war, output in the territories formerly occupied by the Germans was only three-quarters of the prewar volume. This shift from west to east, accelerated by the war, continued. Its strategic implications are clear.

For the first time it is now possible to compute a table showing in *absolute* figures, and not as has been customary in enigmatic percentages, the production of basic materials since the war. Here, too, the increase was relatively slow up to 1948 and was gaining in tempo from then onwards. In iron and steel the rate of increase approximately doubled in 1948.

Generally speaking, the output reached by 1950 does not differ considerably from the targets set before the war for the end of 1942 which was to be the last year of the third Five-Year Plan. In other words Soviet industrial output has reached only now the level it should have reached by 1942, if the war had not intervened. Even so, the USSR has now an output of basic materials superior to the German production of 1938. Obviously output a head of population is incomparably lower; and this affects the Soviet standards of living. From the power-political angle, however, aggregate output, rather than output a head, is decisive.

Basic Industry Moves East

Another glance at the table shows that, while coal output has risen by roughly three-quarters during the Plan and oil and electricity have nearly doubled, pig iron and ingot steel have more than doubled, while rolled steel has risen by nearly one and a half. The latter point indicates the great emphasis placed on the production of machinery.

The extent of the shift to the east is reflected in the following figures: Before the war the " West," i.e., the Donbass and the Moscow basin, produced nearly 100 million tons of coal out of a national total of 166 million, thus accounting for roughly 64 per cent of the total. In 1950 total output rose by nearly 100 million tons and the East (the Kuzbas, Kazakhstan, the Urals and Siberian basins) was responsible for most of this increase. In fact, eastern output rose twofold from 70 to 140 million tons and now accounts for more than half of the total.

The same is true of steel. The Ukraine (the Donbass) produced before the war more than 8½ million tons of steel, while total output was slightly over 18 million tons. For 1950 the Plan foresaw a rise of some 7 million tons over that figure (this was in fact exceeded), but output in the Ukraine was to increase only by 200,000 tons.

The output of oil in the strategically vulnerable Caucasus has declined both relatively and absolutely. Before the war the Caucasus produced 27.5 million tons, nearly 90 per cent of the total. At the end of 1950 the Caucasian output was 6,000,000 tons less. Oil extraction in the east, on the other hand, rose to some 16 million tons. These came from the so-called " Second Baku " (the region between the Volga and the Urals), Central Asia (Turkmenia and Uzbekistan) and from the Far East (Sakhalin, which is, of course, highly vulnerable).

In spite of this substantial increase in oil extraction the Soviet Union still has less oil than it was planned to extract by 1942 according to pre-war targets. An ever-growing number of tractors needs fuel; " save oil " is the order of the day and the shortage is one of the major motives behind the present electrification drive. By the end of 1950 one-third of the Soviet collective farms were to be electrified. Plans also exist for the introduction of electrically, instead of petrol-driven, agricultural machinery. The output of electrical current was nearly doubled during the five years, but 90 billion kWh fall far short of requirements; and the Soviet authorities plan to press electrification with the utmost vigour.

For cement and timber no absolute figures of production are to be found. For cement a very steep rise is claimed: between 1945 and 1950, according to Soviet sources, output has increased five and a half times. To this rise the transfer of East German cement works to Russia as reparations may have contributed. The timber target of 280 million cubic metres, on the other hand, has not been reached, since the Ministry of Timber and Paper Industry was almost every year censured for not fulfilling its plan. Timber output was slightly more than doubled during the five years, but development is hindered by shortage of manpower in the far north, by insufficient mechanisation and by transport difficulties.

II. Capital *versus* Consumer Goods

The Soviet Government had promised an abundance of consumer goods for 1950. Yet from the figures now published on the Fourth Plan it

sumers' wants, and are granted first call on the existing resources. Soviet planners would certainly adhere to a slogan: "Machine tools, tractors and lorries before clothing."

This contrast may be partly seen in the following tables showing the

GROWTH OF SOVIET PRODUCTION, 1946–1950

	Index Numbers 1945 = 100					Planned (in '000s) for 1950
	1946	1947	1948	1949	1950	
Engineering & Chemicals						
Tractors................	172	359	732	1,135	1,396	112
Lorries.................	138	160	257	334	435	428
Electrical motors: —						
Of less than 100 kw....	169	257	404	541	650	624
Of more than 100 kw...	138	192	292	400	480	9
Machine tools...........	134	174	245	292	327*	74
Artificial fertilisers.......	152	205	293	384	457	5.100,000 tons
Dye stuffs..............	129	186	251	281	306	43 "
Consumer Goods						
Cotton fabrics..........	117	156	192	219	236	4.686 million metres
Woollen fabrics.........	130	173	220	262	270	159.4 " "
Leather footwear........	128	176	215	262	325	240,000 pairs
Paper..................	161	201	241	306	367	1.340,000 tons
Meat...................	118	138	173	183	247	1.300,000 "
Sugar..................	100	210	357	439	540	2.400,000 "
Animal fats............	169	189	255	270	289	0.275,000 "
Vegetable fats..........	119	167	220	290	331	0.880,000 "
Soap..................	100	128	182	309	343	0.870,000 "
Retail sales............	130	152	200	240	312	

* Production of Ministry of Machine Tools only.

is quite clear that during the last five years priority was once again given to capital goods; while from statements now made, it may be gathered that this emphasis on producer goods is to be continued in the years to come. Soviet citizens are still made to save for future benefits. The increase in the capacity of the industrial plants and the mechanisation of agriculture are still considered as more important objectives than the immediate satisfaction of the con-

growth over the last five years of the engineering and chemical industries on one side and the consumer goods industries on the other.

For consumer goods with the exception of sugar, 1950 indices range between 200 and 350. The real difference is probably even greater than it appears. Generally the high indices for 1950 are to be explained by the very low level of the base year (1945), when the switchover from war to peace had only begun and war damages were scarcely repaired. This, of course, applies also to engineering — e.g., the fourteenfold rise in the output of tractors can only be understood with this reservation in mind. But it is even truer for consumer goods. In wartime heavy industry is always more fully exploited. By 1945 the drop in the output of consumer goods was certainly much greater than for capital goods. For both producer and consumer goods Russian statistics are not lavish with absolute figures and the few data supplied are often contradictory. Soviet sources lead one to believe that for most branches the targets have not only been fulfilled but exceeded. Since the claims of over-fulfillment, however, are usually couched in ambiguous terms it is safer, in most cases, to assume that targets have simply been reached.

Among producer goods greatest stress is laid on machine tools. Outwardly the threefold rise in production since 1945 is small compared with other engineering indices. But the production of machine tools was very high even during the war. The Soviet press always emphasises any topic connected with these basic instruments of industrial development and it seems that it is in this sphere that greatest efforts are made " to reach and exceed America." In 1950 probably more than 74,000 tools were produced and, partly thanks to the lend-lease supplies, the Soviet Union may well have now 1,300,000 machine tools. This was the target set for 1950 by Mr. Voznesensky, who claimed that with this number the USSR will have as many machine tools as American industry had in 1943. Of course, there may be very great variations in the size and the complexity of the tools. Still, in this sphere great progress has certainly been made.

Great efforts have also been made to build up the production of lorries. The Russians have drawn their conclusions from the bitter lesson of the war, when even in the army the shortage of lorries was painfully felt. Then the 400,000 lorries sent to Russia under the lend-lease agreement were invaluable. Now this year's output alone has probably exceeded that number. This is a good example of the advance made. Since 1945 output has risen more than fourfold. Since 1940 five new plants have been built, in Dniepropetrovsk, Minsk, Novosibirsk, Ulianovsk and Kutais. During the last Five-Year Plan diesel lorries have been produced for the first time in the USSR, as part of the general fuel-saving campaign.

The tractor industry was another branch treated with special care, but in spite of that, production here seems to have lagged behind the targets. True these are not clear, since it is not always known whether the figure is translated into units of 15, 30 or other horse power. The target for 1950 was 112,000 units of unspecified power. At the same time it was planned to supply 720,000 tractors, translated into 15-hp units, during the five years of the plan. It is this latter figure which was not reached, as will be seen in the following table of tractor supply: —

SOVIET TRACTOR PRODUCTION

('ooo of 15-H.P. Units)

1945	1946	1947	1948	1949	1950
13.2	22.5	47.5	96.8	150	184

The number supplied over the five years of the plan was thus only slightly more than 500,000 15-hp units. This figure, though inferior to the planned target, is very high and nearly equals the total Soviet tractor park of 1940. The figure is even more impressive, since demand for tractors should be falling with the progressive introduction of larger collective farms.

Achievements in consumer goods are certainly not so spectacular. In fact, the targets for cotton and woollen fabrics set for 1950 were actually lower than the end-targets set (though not fulfilled) for all previous Five-Year Plans. The discrepancy between the promises of great abundance and the relatively low targets, particularly for textiles, may have been partly made up by imports. Considerable imports from the west are obviously ruled out. But immediately after the war it became clear that the Soviet authorities were going to rely in their computations on the output of the light industries of east European countries. Commercial treaties to that effect were signed. For instance, according to the agreement with Poland, Lodz, the Polish textile centre, was to receive raw cotton from Russia and send cotton fabrics in return. Part of the raw cotton was to be left behind as payment for the manufacture.

The size of the imports of consumers' goods from the countries within the Soviet orbit is not known, but foreign observers in Moscow say that the Muscovite is now incomparably better clothed and shod. This is largely to the credit of the Czech shoe factories and the East German (Saxon), Polish and Czech textile mills.

According to the plan, Russian factories should now be producing annually more than one pair of shoes and somewhat less than three pairs of socks or stockings per inhabitant. This is very little by western standards. In Russia, on the other hand, where many peasants had only recently put on their first pair of shoes and where there is a large Asiatic population, this is quite an achievement. The share of sugar per person — over 2 lb. per month — would be quite considerable even by non-Russian standards. Another striking figure is that for soap. The average Russian should now be getting roughly 11.5 ounces of soap per month, i.e., not very much less than the recent British ration. Even if this figure has not been reached, but only approached, it certainly means a very notable rise in the level of Russian hygiene.

Generally speaking, Russia is certainly not yet a land of plenty and even the western standards are quite distant, whatever propagandists may say. On the other hand, over the five years of the Plan, and probably with the help of countries within the Soviet orbit, the supply of consumers' goods has been increased and the Russian consumer must have felt a real improvement after the very low postwar level.

III. Lag in Agriculture

During the last five years progress in agriculture was not comparable with the achievements in industry. Here the Plan has not been fulfilled, except in cotton and sugar-beet, where it has even been exceeded. The grain crop of 1950 fell short of the targets; in livestock, although the position was even worse, the Government raised somewhat the targets in a special new Plan published in 1949.

The ravages of war, shortages of machinery and the calamitous drought of 1946 offer part of the explanation. Since 1946, however, climatic conditions have improved and there has been a steady flow of machinery to the collective farms. At the close of 1948 the number of tractors in the countryside was already roughly the same as before the war. In 1950, 90 per cent of ploughing and sowing was done with tractors, and more than half the crop was gathered by harvester-combines. Yet, as the table below shows, the dramatic recovery of agriculture in 1947–48 was followed by relative stagnation in subsequent years, when the equipment of the farms was much better: —

Grain Production

(000.000 Metric Tons)

1940........	119	1948	118
1945........	80	1949	124
1946........	70	1950	124
1947........	110	1950*	127

* Planned.

The yield per acre has not risen very substantially and seems to be somewhat less than the 4.85 quintals, which is claimed to be the average. The total area under cultivation is still less than before the war. In 1950 the total cultivated area was nearly 15 million acres greater than the year before, yet the crop was exactly the same in both years. The lower average yield in 1950 may be partly explained by the drought which hit the Caucasus.

The Government does not seem to be unduly alarmed by this situation. The grain crop was still approximately 5 million tons higher than in the prewar record harvests (1937, 1940), which had enabled the Soviet authorities to build up reserves for the war. The rise since 1940 has been proportionately greater than the growth of population. The supplies to the state of the so-called commercial grain may be estimated at nearly 40 per cent of the total crop, i.e., roughly some 50 million tons. This should be sufficient to feed the more than 70 million urban dwellers, to supply bread to the farms which do not produce grain, and to leave a big surplus for stocks. But the non-fulfillment of the Plan may have prevented the Soviet Union from increasing the export of grain, which might have served as a political trump card, particularly in Asia.

Rising Urban Population

But the problem of agricultural expansion is fairly acute. The urban population of the Soviet Union is growing fast. Between 1926 and

1939 it rose by nearly 30 million. The process was slowed down by the war, though even then 67 new towns were built, 53 of these behind the Urals. Further urbanisation is planned; but it may be hampered by the inadequate growth of agriculture, especially in Asiatic Russia.

The gap between the original plans and the actual achievements is even wider in livestock. Shortage of cattle has been a chronic illness of Russian agriculture since the October Revolution. The Civil War, the famine of 1921, the mass slaughter of cattle and horses by the peasants during collectivisation greatly depleted stock. To restore it the Government organised before the war special cattle-rearing farms, and even encouraged private rearing. A cow in every rural household was Stalin's slogan. Then came the losses of the war. Hitherto these have not been made good, and the Plan has not been fulfilled: —

LIVESTOCK

(In Millions)

	Horses	Horned Cattle	Sheep and Goats	Pigs
1916........	35.8	60.6	121.2	20.9
1940........	20.6	71.0	108.5	36.1
1945........	10.5	47.0	69.4	10.4
1950........	13.7	57.2	99.0	24.1
1950 (targets)	15.3	65.3	121.5	31.2

These figures cast some doubt on Marshal Bulganin's recent statement that the supply of meat, sausage and butter was in 1950 more than 30 per cent higher than before the war. The quantities of meat and milk supplied to the towns may have increased, but this could not outweigh the actual drop in livestock.

Sugar beets and cotton are the only agricultural products in which both the prewar level and the targets have been exceeded: —

(In Million Tons)

	1940	1950	1950 Target
Sugar beets....	21.8	27.25	26.0
Cotton.......	2.7	3.65	3.1

Large scale cultivation of cotton started in the Soviet Union only in 1928. Now Uzbekistan is the main cotton producer, accounting for more than half of the total crop. The collective farms of that region are amongst the richest in the Soviet Union. Generally, there is much scope for further development of cotton cultivation in Soviet Central Asia.

The most publicised features of new agricultural development are those designed to protect Soviet farming from the periodical natural calamities and to reclaim desert land. A 15-year plan of afforestation was proclaimed in 1948. It received the imposing title of "Stalin's Plan for Changing Nature." Forests were to be planted as a protection against sand drifts; snow reservoirs and ponds were to be built to preserve moisture. Soviet propaganda was mobilised to bolster this venture; the composer Shostakovich was even commissioned to produce a symphony on this topic. But it soon became clear that the "Stalin Plan" was inadequate. New plans to combat drought and increase the area under cultivation have now been launched. These are to be combined with a huge programme for the development of power stations. In addition, 65 million acres of desert or other land perpetually threatened with drought in the Volga region, in Central Asia, in the northern Crimea and Southern Ukraine are to be irrigated by canals.

DEVELOPMENT OF CENTRAL ASIA

The greatest works are to be carried out in the region of the Caspian Sea between the rivers Volga and the Ural (some 30 million acres are to be irrigated here) and on the river Amu Darya in Turkmen SS.R., where the desert, covering 87 per cent of the land, is to be prepared for cotton cultivation. The scope of plans for this region may be gauged from the project to build a canal nearly 700 miles long through the Kara Kum desert. The irrigation plan covers also the European provinces — e.g., it provides for the linking of the Volga and the Don near Stalingrad, which is not quite a new project — yet the main stress is on the development of Central Asia. Similar projects were already being considered before the war. Some attempts at fighting drought in Central Asia were made, particularly in the Fergana Valley. But the methods were still primitive. Now the job is to be carried out with the aid of modern machinery, which is to be supplied through the new Five-Year Plans. Local manpower, from state and collective farms, is to be used for these gigantic works.

These agricultural plans, coupled with the scheme for "agrotowns," are not less ambitious or less difficult of attainment than are Stalin's objectives for industry for 1965 or even 1960: 60 million tons of steel, 60 million tons of oil, and 500 million tons of coal. The fulfillment of these targets, it is proclaimed, should mark the beginning of a new era, "the transition from socialism to communism."

9 THE PROBLEM OF THE BACKWARD AREA

48. Industrialization in the Backward Areas

Since World War II the so-called backward, or underdeveloped, areas of the world in an outburst of nationalistic spirit have been attempting to achieve independence of the foreign nations that formerly dominated them. India and Indonesia have been successful. The struggle continues in French Indo-China, Egypt and Tunisia.

Whether or not these countries attain their formal goal of political independence, they must face the ineluctable problems of poverty, disease, and squalor. Obviously the solution to these problems is the raising and in many cases the redistributing of the nation's income. This solution, easily stated, is not so easily realized. In most instances the supply of labor is unskilled and more significantly, immobilized by systems of values that bind it to place and status. The internal supply of capital is limited and more often than not used unproductively. Moreover, the underdeveloped areas of the world are plagued with large populations of high growth potential, i.e., high birth rates and high death rates. Increased income, therefore,

might produce an increased population rather than higher standards of living, or indeed its very achievement might be smothered in population growth.

The question that we **are** raising in this chapter — but that we do not intend to answer — is: what is the appropriate system of economic choice for breaking out of the vicious circle of poverty and low productivity? Undoubtedly there is an ethnic propensity for people to answer this question in the image of their own solutions. Thus, some people in the United States propose the extension of the free market to these blighted areas. Let the profit system operate in a market, they say, and the people will exert themselves to generate income. They fail to realize, however, that materialistic motivation is not universal — some people do not respond to changing profit and wage rates. On the other hand, the Soviet Union acting upon their own experience, urges the revolutionary restructuring of society as the proper means of destroying the Philistines and bringing to the front that group that can raise living standards. But this method is ruthless and destructive of life and liberty.

For the West the underdeveloped countries pose a dilemma. The methods of liberal capitalism and democratic socialism may not be suited to conditions in countries with subsistence living standards. Because of the competition from the Soviet Union, time is of the essence. Programs of international economic aid, such as the Point IV program sponsored by the United States, are consistent with the liberal method but they require time and forbearance on the part of both the grantor of resources and the grantee. The former must be willing to forego the use of the resources exported and the latter must be willing to accept the assistance and supervision of the grantor. The liberal method is inevitably slow and gradualistic. To some of the patriots of these countries it may seem too slow and lead them to espouse revolutionary methods. Yet the revolutionary solution, which conceivably might speed up the process of economic development, is offensive to the Western standard of values. The West cannot compete with the Soviet Union on the latter's terms without making a mockery of much that it cherishes.

The following article on "Communism in Asia" explores the appeal of communism in the East and points up the weaknesses of the appeal of liberal capitalism in those countries that are right on the margin of subsistence. The point of the article is to raise a question the West must face. It does not propose a solution. In the same spirit, Professor Wilbert E. Moore of Princeton University analyzes the problem of native labor and its attitudes toward industrial activities in the final article of this chapter.

49. "Communism in Asia"*

Communism in Asia is not like Communism in Europe. The doctrine and the end may be the same, the causes are almost entirely different. In Europe, Communism is an answer to frustrations that are more often spiritual than physical; in Asia it is the direct result of poverty, though very often poverty working at one remove. The most effective Communists are often not

* From *The Economist* (*London*), CLIX (1950), pp. 1147–48 and 1205–06. Reprinted by permission of *The Economist*.

the poor themselves, but those who are disgusted by the corruption, inflation and injustice which poverty produces. In Asia the revolutionary fact is that it is getting steadily poorer. The consequent erosion of all hope in the future makes men ready for any desperate course; the Soviet Union's success suggests that terror and Five-Year Plans can enable even a backward society to pull itself up by its own bootstraps. If Mao Tse-tung can increase China's national income in any visible way (which might not be too difficult), while elsewhere in Asia the rot goes on, the future of Asian liberalism might well be bleak.

Communism in Europe is many things to many men. It is an interpretation of history which provides an alternative inevitability for those who no longer accept the will of God. It is a value judgment in economics which restores its self-respect to a working class too often left out and despised by Europe's hierarchical society. It is a technique of revolution, offering early power to the intelligentsia and the factory workman of whose interests Governments with a military and rural bias have usually taken far too little account.

None of these is of any importance in Asia. There is no anti-clericalism. Traditional religion still retains its hold, and, where it does not, it turns into agnosticism rather than militant atheism. Asian religions have no powerful hierarchies to serve as a focus for attack — in Europe Communism is a phenomenon of Catholic and Orthodox rather than of Protestant countries. Certainly Asia's societies are even more hierarchical than those of Europe; but for that very reason Communism is deprived of one of its most effective weapons. All European creeds appear to the Asian, by contrast with his own stratification, to have equality as their base; it is Liberalism, not Communism which is breaking caste. Communism appears only as the extreme statement of a general attitude. Indeed, the reactionary Asian is more afraid of the easy-going democracy of American social customs than of a Communism which permits the Russian official and manager full Brahmin privilege. Nor does Communism have the same appeal as a technique of gaining power in Asia as in Europe. The intelligentsia has had its interests very satisfactorily served by liberal nationalism; the proletariat barely exists; and Marx had only a nodding interest in peasants.

Tide of Babies

People in Asia go Communist primarily because they see no hope in the present system and feel that any change can only be for the better. That conditions in Asia are in fact desperate over very wide areas should need no emphasis. The Indian gets only 1,600 calories a day, the Pakistani and the Filipino only 1,800. In the countryside, the three-acre holding and work for only three or four months in the year are usual; in many areas there is a steady increase in the landless — in India there may be some 60 million of them. In the towns, hundreds of thousands sleep in the street because the tenements will not accommodate more than ten to a room. There are still islands of relative sufficiency and content — Siam and parts of Sumatra for example — but even they are being gradually engulfed by the tide of babies.

In the past this poverty had limited political importance. It was accepted as fate, and there was all the authority of religion to emphasise the illusoriness of material wants. But for fifty years now liberalism and nationalism have been undermining this resignation. The nineteenth century west believed above all in material progress. Therefore colonial governments felt the need to justify themselves in terms of increased welfare; therefore too the rising nationalist movements had to prove that the west had made them poorer, not richer. They found plenty of material to hand. They pointed out to the masses their poverty, and the masses responded.

WEAKNESS OF THE LIBERAL TRADITION

Once again, this has not been an undiluted advantage to Communism. One of Communism's strengths in Europe is its capacity for the organisation and exploitation of grievances. But in Asia no Communist outside China has been as effective in this way as the nationalists, Nehru or Soekarno or, above all, Jinnah whose whole career was built on the successful exploitation of a sense of grievance; and there has never been a strike organiser like Gandhi. Communist methods, with their slavish adherence to doctrine, lack the flexibility of a nationalism which could blame the grievances of capitalist and worker alike on the ruling alien.

The liberal nationalists were experts in opposition; their weakness now is that they are now in power. They have promised their followers, in all sincerity, in the best European style, the welfare state; they did not realise — they often still do not realise — that European welfare requires the surplus over subsistence of European national incomes. The men in power, therefore, whose efforts have made them national heroes, seem to grope and lose their way, and the regime loses its moral hold. Yet in Asia it needs a hold much firmer than in Europe. In the west, most people have cause for relative contentment. In Asia poverty gives nearly everyone reason for discontent, and so the whole atmosphere is " agin " the Government. This position is sometimes made worse by the fact that neither people nor ministers are quite adjusted yet to power; they do not always remember that the Government is now their own, not an alien, if sometimes benevolent, machine. This atmosphere of opposition might, however, not matter if there were a liberal opposition to take advantage of it. But Asian liberalism seems to have exhausted itself in furnishing the great nationalist parties which now hold power; nowhere, not even in the Indian Socialists, has it been able to create an opposition too.

So far, indeed, the Communists have not succeeded in doing so either. Outside China and such special cases as Viet-Minh and the Hyderabad trouble, the Communist parties have neither effective organisation nor mass following. They are always being disrupted by the changes in the Cominform line and discredited by their obedience to Moscow. Nevertheless, because Communism is to-day one of the two great world doctrines, there is everywhere the feeling that the spread of discontent must eventually benefit them, and them only; and this feeling in itself saps not so much the will as the ability to resist.

Discontent *is* spreading, because of poverty. It is not only that wider and wider classes of the population are awakening to the misery of their condition. Unless there is also economic equality, poor countries are always corrupt countries; every little privilege, even the most ill-paid jobs, is so desperately needed. But an awakening Asian public opinion is no longer prepared to tolerate corruption. It may well be no worse today than it used to be, but people find it much harder to bear, and everybody has read of the unheard-of honesty of Mao's soldiers.

In Asia poverty has caused the whole of society to be rotted not only by corruption but also by inflation. Partly, of course, inflation is the consequence of the war and its devastation. But beyond that there is in Asian society a perpetual tendency towards inflation. Governments which have promised the impossible, and which also realise how desperate is the need of their society for capital investment, are always being tempted to finance welfare and investment alike by a budget deficit. Moreover, the modern social conscience demands that nobody should starve or die of unnecessary disease. There is, therefore, always a tendency for income to outrun production, and the economy is deprived of the correctives of famine and plague.

Inflation, by its gross aggravation of social injustice, also destroys the moral effect of the liberal reforms Asian governments have recently been so extensively making. In many places, the tenant is being given ownership; everywhere rents and interest have been controlled. Everywhere, too, taxation has been made sharply progressive. The resultant benefits in extra social stability would be more obvious if at the same time the black market were not constantly furnishing new examples of the wicked flourishing like the green bay tree. No system which does not command the moral respect of the people can survive. Capitalism is, therefore, dependent on the good behaviour of capitalists. A main reason why England has no Communism, where France and Germany have, is the Nonconformist conscience. Inflation and black market create a world where the big cars and the pretty women go to those who let wages lag behind prices, who sell under the counter and whose transactions are conducted in cash.

No wonder that the young and the idealist begin to hanker for more violent courses, that Parliamentary processes begin to appear too cumbersome for the cleaning of augean stables. The common law tradition of protecting the accused itself seems somewhat old fashioned when its main beneficiaries become profiteers.

Production Must be Expanded

In a normal society, the ideals of youth fade away with age and family cares and a secure job. But in an inflation even the able find themselves chasing the pot at the end of the rainbow. No matter how hard they work, no matter how many promotions they receive, taxes and the cost of living seem to go up as quickly as their pay, while the average member of the middle class faces a slow squeeze of all his standards, a slow destruction of all his hopes for his own future and those of his sons. When the shopkeeper flourishes and the clerk starves, revolution is round the corner, for the educated middle class will tolerate only so much.

All these problems could be solved if production could once be set on the road of expansion. There would be less corruption, for the struggle for life would become less grim. There would be a cure for inflation, because supply would rise. There would be room for welfare, since there would be a surplus with which to pay for it. Everywhere in Asia the first enthusiasm for the welfare state has died in disillusion, and men are beginning to talk of production. But so far the liberal state has shown no sign that it knows how to increase production. Its combination of large promises with small performance, inappropriate welfare with freedom for the profiteer, talk of nationalization with the practice of private enterprise, is the worst possible atmosphere for development. Most of Asia — Malaya is the only notable exception — has been getting poorer for twenty years; much of it has been getting poorer for fifty. Whatever test one takes one always gets the same answer of increasing poverty. India has 25 percent less textiles per head than before the war, Japan has had its housing shattered, the Philip-

pines have 1,800 calories per head per day against 1,900 in 1938. In 1880, India probably had its full requirements of 2,500 calories; its present 1,600 leave no margin for millions above the basic requirements. Production and more production must then be the cry. Without it Asian societies risk becoming a madhouse where the starving fight for scraps. Already in Calcutta the great landowner's grandson is a clerk and his grandson will be lucky to be a doorman. Against such conditions people must eventually revolt.

WHERE ARE THE SAVINGS?

Liberalism has, indeed, so far done well in Asia. It has given freedom and independence, a new respect for the dignity of man and a new concern for the under-privileged. But it is not very well equipped to solve the problem of production, for its whole assumption is that production is to be left to individual initiative; and in societies without entrepreneurs or adequate savings, individual initiative, without aid from outside, in management and risk-taking ability as well as in money, cannot possibly do the job.

Yet the job must be done and done quickly. These societies have lost the stability which came from the belief that poverty was the will of God. Karma can no longer satisfy even the Hindu of the incorrectness of the western idea that man can improve his material condition by his own efforts. It is here, therefore, that poverty gives Communism its best chance. Free capitalism will fail without aid. Then Asia will turn to the capitalism-cum-terror of the Communists. As Asia sees it, the Soviet Union has shown that if the population is squeezed by enough liquidations and enough forced labour camps, even the most backward society can produce the savings necessary for development. Every western tremble before Soviet might is in Asia an argument for Communism — it is rarely realized that the Soviet Union was a great power even before 1917. If China should be able to follow the Soviet example, then liberalism will be irretrievably lost in Asia unless enough aid to permit the other countries to match the Chinese achievement is given at once. In order to meet the increase in population and give a margin for hope, an improvement in national income of 2 1/2 –3 per cent a year is required. To attain that, aid would not need to exceed £250 million a year, of which £150–£175 million would be for India, which has over half the population of the region (ex-cluding China) and is the strategic and political key of the whole area.

The Soviet Union and China are dangerous examples for reasons which are wider than the merely economic. Asia has observed how profound is the western respect for force. It is remembered that the quality of the Japanese Navy made Japanese honorary white men in a dozen countries and it has been remarked that Mao is treated more gingerly than Chiang ever was. Certainly nobody doubts that there would be no South African Group Areas Act if India and Pakistan had an American-size air force. Asia is profoundly sensitive about colour; and colour prejudice is fundamentally the result of the colored man's poverty, with its concomitant ignorance and squalor.

Liberalism is today fighting a losing battle in Asia. It is not made for forced draft economies. The forced draft must come from elsewhere. If the West does not provide it through aid, the Soviet Union and terror will.

50. Native Labor in Industry*

No part of the earth is now wholly untouched by industrialism or its consequences. Many areas are only

* From Wilbert E. Moore, " Primitives and Peasants in Industry." *Social Research* (March 1948) pp. 44–81. This and a second article, plus bibliographies, are part of a more comprehensive treatment to be found in the author's *Industrialization and Labor: Social Aspects of Economic Development* (Ithaca: Cornell University Press, 1951). Reprinted by permission of Wilbert E. Moore and *Social Research*.

now beginning the process of economic modernization, and many others are still affected by it only indirectly, but even the most " backward " areas have started the fateful " forward " march, under foreign or local impetus, and the pace will certainly accelerate rather than slacken. In this veering toward factory production and the protean machine a great many influences converge to affect the tempo and effectiveness of the change. Underlying them all, however, is the character of the labor force — not merely its size, but its attitudes toward disciplined, rationalized endeavor, its response to given conditions of existence. These responses, however changeable they may be, are crucial determinants of industrial development.

The extensive literature on the spread of industrialism contains numerous direct investigations into the cultural and psychological factors involved in that process; it contains also many incidental comments on this subject by students primarily concerned with other aspects of economic development. Further field work will assuredly be necessary for a thorough analysis of primitives' and peasants' responses to industrialization, but the fact remains that it would be uselessly wasteful to ignore the knowledge already gained. The following pages, therefore, present a brief survey of the information to be derived from existing works.

This information is contained almost solely in area studies, and thus pertains to specific peoples and places and times. It is necessary, therefore, to determine the rubrics under which the mass of material can be examined most effectively in order to discover and appraise any general principles that it may contain. In the larger study from which the present survey is drawn, one of the principal objects will be to determine the significance of cultural differences, and thus it will be necessary there to consider the material primarily with reference to the various kinds of so-

cial systems that it represents. For the purposes of the present survey of the existent literature, however, it has been decided to put primary emphasis on the general conditions and attitudes that impede or induce a shift toward industrial labor.[1]

Two lines of warning are worth emphasizing. First, it is of course only for the purposes of systematic analysis that broad social conditions and attitudes can be thus defined and isolated; in their actual operation they are intertwined in infinite variations. And second, since the choice of this method makes a considerable degree of generalization unavoidable, it cannot be too strongly stressed that the nonindustrial economies have a very wide range of technical and organizational complexity; that the form and degree of the impinging industrialism differ greatly in different localities, ranging from plantation agriculture and mining to the complex economies of Japan and the Soviet Union; and that there is a considerable variety in the modes of intercurrence that have thus far been evolved between nonindustrial and industrial ways of life. Less a warning than a regret is the fact that any information on "attitudes" and their causes is subject to the hazards of interpretation and deduction; scientific exactitude is difficult to achieve in regard to the nature and sources of personal feelings, and the literature is notably lacking in the concrete, objective data whereby in-

[1] Bibliographical documentation has been omitted from the present summary for reasons of space, but a list of works that have provided material for this survey is presented at the end of the original article.

ferences might be supplemented and confirmed.

BARRIERS TO INDUSTRIAL EMPLOYMENT

Before considering the various conditions and attitudes that cause primitives and peasants to accept industrial life, it is worth outlining the principal reasons why they do not do so. Aside from sheer ignorance of the industrial way of life as a possible alternative — which is to be found today in very few areas of the world — the barriers to acceptance of the new ways lie fundamentally in the disparities between the old and the new. These could be differentiated in many ways, but they will be considered here under the two simplest possible headings.

Attachment to the old forms. Attachment to traditional forms that offer security and the pleasure of familiarity is certainly not limited to undeveloped areas of the earth, but in those areas it is very pronounced. In one form or another, depending on the interplay of local conditions, it is found among primitive and peasant societies everywhere: in Africa, where the casual laborers among the Tale people of the northern Gold Coast, and among the Bantu groups farther south, return to their native villages after a period of work in mines or plantation agriculture or even factories, and continue to find in their tribal customs the source of social and economic security and family stability; in the Netherlands Indies, where again the pattern of casual labor and mainte-nance of community ties is conspicuous; in Indo-China, where the natives require considerable pressure or strong inducements to leave family connections, village relations, and claims on the land, however meager these may be; in Peru, where substantial employment needs, in urban manufacturing as well as in agriculture and mining, are predominantly filled by resort to various forms of indenture, providing for temporary or limited periods of service; in the old peasant economies of eastern and southern Europe, where long-established patterns of village cooperation and also property interests in the land, based on the rule of equal inheritance, give the peasant a sense of security that reduces the appeal of urban employment, even though these communities have for a long time been in relatively close contact with industrial life; in India, where industrial workers in general tend to return to their native villages, and where the existence of village ties is an important source of morale even for those who stay in urban employment; in China, where the kinship structure offers such protection that factory employment, if accepted, is likely to be only a temporary expedient.

This strong tendency to cling to, or return to, old forms and habits does not mean that the primitive or the peasant is actively opposed to any change. But the evidence strongly indicates that he is much more inclined to accept changes operating within the structure he knows than changes regarded as a threat to that structure. And on this matter his fears are not unjustified. A shift, for example, from self-sufficient agriculture, or from a communal village economy, to commercial agriculture or wage labor on plantations may not mean a sharp change in technical procedures, but it is likely to be a greater break than is commonly supposed by the naïve administrator. It has far-reaching implications not only for the network of social relations within which the labor was formerly performed, but also for basic economic security: in industrial enterprise, dependent on the world market, employment is not as stable as it is in a primitive economy based on mutual aid.

This central problem of combining traditional security and economic change has given rise to a wide variety of transitional or compromise arrangements for the use of indigenous labor. The most common of these arrangements is the system of casual labor, whereby the native enters outside employment from time to time and meanwhile maintains his relations with his own community. This practice is prevalent not only in colonial areas but also in Latin America, China, and India. Although it may be a convenient means of recruitment where there is at best only a half-hearted interest in new forms of economic activity, it is a wasteful and inefficient system. In some places, as in parts of Africa, where there is a deliberate policy of segregating natives in limited reserves, the practice of using casual labor is based not only on economic opportunism but also on attitudes of racial discrimination.

Among these compromise methods of grafting modern economic organization on to nonindustrial social organizations, one of the most interesting was that worked out in Japan. There the archaic familial and hierarchical controls, rather than being disrupted by the introduction of industry, were consciously utilized, as part of the policy of economic transition by deliberate plan. Labor recruitment was carried on through the families, and employment was frequently in small units formed on kinship bases. Here, too, industrial labor was commonly regarded as a temporary expedient, not only in the early stages, but to a remarkable degree even after the rise of great urban industries: the son entered a shop, often under the supervision of a relative, in order to give temporary financial help to the family, or the daughter worked in a factory long enough to accumulate a dowry. But the basis of the whole system, even in the larger establishments, was a quasi-feudalistic paternalism, with emphasis on the ultimate security of the rural family structure. In its degree of labor turnover and in its minimum development of skills this system was not efficient, and continued rural poverty helped to undermine its premises. Even before World War II it was unmistakably giving way to less personal arrangements, evidenced in the growth of a permanent urban proletariat. Nevertheless, this utilization of existing customs and forms of social life undoubtedly eased the transition to industrialism.

As a means of coping with the difficulties of economic transition in undeveloped areas, many experts have urged the establishment of decentralized and small-scale consumer-goods industries. This course, it is contended, would reduce to a minimum the interference with traditional patterns, and would avoid some of the less fortunate effects of the industrial revolution in the west, particularly the disadvantages of urban concentration. And in fact, whether for these reasons or for others, the idea has been put into practice to a considerable extent. In Indo-China, for example, small plants were set up in rural areas by European administrators and enterprisers, apparently in response to the natives' reluctance to move long distances to urban centers; and they have been established in various parts of China, either as rural industries located near the supply of raw materials and surplus rural labor, or as fairly mobile industrial cooperatives operating in the interior during the Japanese occupation.

This method of introducing industrial work undoubtedly makes for easier recruitment of labor, and constitutes a smaller threat to traditional patterns of integration, than do larger and less personal enterprises. On the other hand, it may have certain disadvantages: the very acceptance of forms that developed in another context may operate to diminish purely technical efficiency; in small plants and domestic industry, demoralizing " sweating " practices are not unlikely to develop, as has frequently occurred in China; and the substitution of a new kind for an old kind of protective paternalism is not likely to promote among the workers a capacity for independence and self-reliance. The latter point raises, of course, a most complex question. It appears that individual autonomy is in some degree an essential aspect of the flexibility and dynamic drive that characterize industrialism; and at the same time it may well be that in western industrial life this autonomy, this divorcement from established controls and responsibilities and protections, has gone so far as to be subversive of its own ends. This is a problem in the philosophy and policy of industrialization, not a matter of concern in a factual review of existing conditions, but thoughtful observers in newly developing areas have been aware of its implications.

Lack of interest in the new forms. In turning now to the problems raised by a disinclination to accept new ways of life, we are not merely restating in negative terms what has been said about attachment to the old. Logically these are the two sides of the same coin, but functionally they entail different problems. The one arises from the fact that the familiar bases of assurance have no counterpart in the new life; the other arises from the fact that what is offered in the new life, whether in the form of income and activity or in the form of intangibles such as personal relations and status, has no relation to the accustomed standards. Again the problem is not the absolute differences between the two ways of life in isolation, but their interrelations in active competition.

The most obvious reward of industrial life is wages, but the desire for wages depends on the desire for the things that money will buy — and also on whether the wages are sufficient to buy the things desired. In a society where status is based on attributes, inherited or acquired, or on goods that are not purchasable, or are not purchasable with money, wages alone can offer small inducement. To be sure, the situation is not so simple when money standards have once begun to replace the older values, or where commercial penetration has gone so far that some needs or desires can be fulfilled only with money. Then, as will be emphasized in a later section, wages may be a positive incentive to employment. But it may also be true that not all the members of the group have an interest in wage employment, and that the interest even of those who accept it is only limited or sporadic. Thus it is not infrequently found that natives are interested in industrial employment only long enough to acquire wages for the satisfaction of particular wants or needs that are important in their own society; higher wages then merely reduce the length of employment. Or the wages offered, and the range of goods and services that they will buy, may be considered insufficient to make up for the effort and estrangement involved.

Other, nonmonetary rewards of industrial employment may fail to be appreciated in much the same way. The particular kind of rational, technically precise adaptation of means to ends which is characteristic of industrialism produces a

working milieu and a way of life that are not congenial to an individual who is unaccustomed to rational efficiency of this kind. An especially striking example is evident in India, where the caste system has resulted in a rigid definition of status and of the levels of consumption and types of occupation that are permitted to each stratum. Many of these distinctions are now breaking down, but caste orientation is still a considerable barrier to acceptance of the more flexible and individualistic standards of industrial life; it is significant that in India industry obtained its first recruits largely from those who had nothing to lose, from the untouchables and the low-caste underlings. An interesting sidelight on the complexity of this problem is that in a colonial area the governing administrators may adhere to values quite comparable with those held by the upper strata of natives; thus productive labor was no more disdained by high-caste Hindus than by many of their British governors, the main difference being that for the Hindus it was frequently the only alternative to starvation.

Unlike India, China has no rigid system of stratification which acts as a barrier to new forms of social relations and social distinctions, yet the traditional Chinese social order was no more conducive to individualism. In China the family and kinship organization, not the individual or his caste, provided the effective social unit. In one respect, however, even the impersonal aspect of individualism is familiar to the Chinese and is respected by him: the socially honored civil servant was traditionally recruited by examination, and at least nominally the competition was open to everyone. It has been suggested that despite the many differences between industrial activity and the role played by the civil servant, this tradition of open competition for respected position might serve in some way to diminish the reluctance to change from reward-by-family to reward-by-merit. The continued effectiveness of the government-official ideal is evident in the fact that some workers have entered employment in government-operated factories under the mistaken impression that they were being admitted to the civil service.

Closely comparable to the dislike of industrialism for its disruption of familiar status arrangements and personal relations is dislike of its particular kind of discipline and routine. Life in a nonindustrial community may be subject to a great many controls and responsibilities, but their operation is familiar: the rules are known and are regarded as legitimate. In industrial life the rules are based on principles that are strange and remote, and their legitimacy may be less evident than their power. Evidence on native restiveness under industrial discipline is not clear-cut, however, as it is difficult to distinguish between opposition to authority and opposition to particular abuses, or supposed abuses, in its exercise. Uprisings have occasionally occurred — even in Africa, where a work stoppage is a criminal offense — but it is uncertain that they signify any fundamental antipathy to the industrial process. There is not even any evidence of general hostility to the machine itself, as occurred in the early stages of western industrialization.

It cannot be overemphasized that the attitude toward industrial work depends on the specific situation: the nature of the particular preindustrial economy and of the new economic forms that are being introduced into that particular area. It is likely to vary also among the different groups in the indigenous community. The young, the unprivileged, the disaffected are probably the most amenable recruits, but their perseverance in industrial employment depends partly on whether it offers positive advantages as well as mere change. Older individuals, or those in a position of greater prestige, if they accept employment at all, may attempt to retain their former status and to view the new more rigorously in terms of the old.

Briefly, in each set of circumstances the new activities, and the rewards and relationships that accompany them, not only must compete with the accustomed ways, but also must show some promise of living up to their own potentialities. There is no ground for believing that there is in undeveloped areas an antipathy to industrialism as such. The interplay of two contrasting systems of values is too complex to allow of any such monistic interpretation. What we find is a dislike for certain aspects of industrialism, manifested with varying emphasis by different groups with different types and degrees of experience.

PROPELLANTS TOWARD IN-
DUSTRIAL EMPLOYMENT

Despite the barriers that may cause indifference or dislike for industrial employment, the fact remains that it is accepted, for longer or shorter periods, by larger or smaller numbers. In some measure the reasons for this acceptance are positive — active inducements that are strong enough to overcome any hesitation that may exist on other grounds. But the reasons may also be negative — a thrust of circumstances which causes wage employment to be a reluctant choice among evils. Whether in the west or in the east, whether among "civilized" or among "primitive" peoples, workers may be more pushed than pulled into new employments. Hunger and fear, acting as propellants, may be as powerful as the positive interests that act as magnets.

The circumstances that serve thus to push native workers into new productive activities as a reluctant choice among evils are of three general descriptions: decline of alternative economic opportunities; political pressures; and uncongenial social pressures in the native community. Under each of these general headings several different kinds of factors can be distinguished.

Pressure of population. In the decline of economic alternatives for nonindustrial peoples no factor is more important than the "pressure" of population which ultimately develops when given land resources are worked with given techniques — a pressure that is increased if western influence has raised the average life expectancy. Rural poverty and the periodic threat of famine are especially characteristic of mature civilizations built upon the economic foundation of agriculture and petty trade. Thus in India, Indo-China, and preindustrial Japan, for example, the limited employment capacity of the land was a significant factor in pushing workers out of rural villages into whatever factory employment they could find.

This result may in some instances be directly traceable to modes of inheritance that prescribe succession by a single heir (as was the case in England and Ireland). Equal inheritance by all heirs — a rule that is widespread in China, as it is in eastern and southern Europe — is likely to prolong the period in which at least a minimum level of subsistence can be wrested from the land. Thus it is only in very recent times that the pressure of rural population in China has become so inescapable as to push workers into factory employment, despite the poverty and successive famines of agricultural life. The Chinese family system has also played a role in keeping the potential industrial worker on the land, for as a rule impoverishment must extend to the family unit as a whole before the individual is forced to the wall.

In colonial areas there have sometimes been more or less deliberate efforts to increase labor supply through governmental restrictions of the land available for native cultivation. Colonial policies on native land rights have varied widely, but except in the British West African colonies it has been a common practice to pre-empt at least part of the land for plantation agriculture or other uses by foreign employers. This policy pushes native agriculturists into employment under European management, and if it is carried out on a large enough scale, or despite a rising population, it may have this effect even if new land is set aside for native cultivation. Labor supply has been thus increased in the Netherlands Indies, for example, especially in Java. The same result occurs where natives are segregated in " reserves," as in British South and East Africa; as a rule these reserves are the poorer lands, and in addition they are continually subject to further reduction in the interests of European occupancy.

Even if land resources become inadequate, or have been made inadequate by colonial policy, a pressure of population would at least be postponed if agricultural techniques were concurrently improved to yield higher production with less land. But native agriculture is generally wasteful, of fertility and of area as well as of manpower, and it is not easily subject to change. In fact, uneconomic practices are sometimes rooted in requirements of the social structure itself. Thus in the South and East Africa native reserves the agriculture of the Bantu, which is based on cattle, has proved highly resistant to change because cattle are a badge of prestige and an integral element in the marriage and kinship structure. What is sought is number rather than quality, and the result is overgrazing, deterioration of breeds,

and increasing poverty that might have been mitigated by more rational methods. Thus it is from these areas that native laborers for the mines are most extensively recruited.

Loss of markets. No known economy is so completely agricultural that there is no development of specialized craft skills, if only as a part-time occupation; in old and complex though nonindustrial societies such skills may even be integrated in a true market exchange. When outside manufactured goods appear in the community the native craftsmen, unable to compete in price or in quality or perhaps only in the appeal of novelty, may be forced to other employment. This development, familiar in eastern and southeastern Europe, has occurred also in the interior of China and in Indo-China. In India too, despite Gandhi's efforts to encourage domestic production of cloth and clothing, village artisans have been deprived of their function by the competition of manufactured goods, especially textiles. This displacement of artisans has been much less frequent in Latin America, but only because many of the Indian villages there are physically and economically isolated; as soon as market roads are built the process is as evident there as elsewhere.

Not only artisans, of course, but also individuals in more " professional " positions — such as chiefs, priests, witch doctors — may lose the market for their services through the intrusion of new ways. And very similar to the loss of markets for craft and professional skills is the loss of employment as a commercial trader. This development has little actual importance, however, for it is only in complex areas like India and China that nonindustrial economies have significant market exchanges, and where such markets exist, competition from outside traders is less likely to displace native traders than competition from outside manufacturers is likely to curtail native production.

Direct coercion. The political, as contrasted with the economic, pressures that push primitives and peasants into industrial employment are often directly coercive, particularly in colonial or dependent areas. In fact, a direct compulsion to labor, exercised by governing authorities or by private organizations under government sanction, has been a conspicuous characteristic of colonial, as of western, history. Forced labor in colonial areas is now imposed mainly for public works, but in the not very remote past it was also possible for private enterprise to benefit from government conscription, or even to conscript natives for its own purposes.

The direct coercion of native manpower has taken various forms. As a governmental practice it is likely to consist in a flat requirement that natives work at stipulated jobs, for longer or shorter periods, with or without pay — a requirement that has sometimes, especially in Africa, been carried out with the more or less strong-arm methods of impressment; the role of direct coercion in African labor recruitment is certainly declining, but it was reintroduced

rather widely, and perhaps unnecessarily, as an emergency measure during World War II. In some areas, notably in certain Dutch colonies, much the same result has been achieved by imposing a "labor tax" — a levy payable in labor. Debt servitude systems such as peonage, under which individuals are involved in debt and are forced to work as a means of payment — often a quicksand endeavor — have been very widespread, especially in Latin America, where peons have been used on haciendas, in mines, and even in factories. But probably the most frequent method of compelling natives to work has been through the long-term indenture, often supported by penal sanctions.

Nominally an indenture is a voluntarily-entered contract governing the period of work, rather than a coercive method of acquiring labor, but actually force and fraud often reduced freedom of choice to a mere technicality. The possibility of delusion was increased by the fact that the place of work was distant, often overseas, from the locality where the indentured laborers were sought. Recruiters made all manner of assurances that were not part of the contract, and among illiterate peoples the contract itself was often more a formal than an actual protection for the worker. Once he entered into the agreement and was transported far from his native village he had no effective possibility of escape from unforeseen conditions. The contract might not even include a time limitation, or it might be illegitimately extended without the worker's consent. In the past half century the possible abuses of indenture have been widely recognized, widely condemned, and widely prohibited, and the practice is now of diminishing significance. But it has not wholly disappeared. In Peru, for example, a form of indenture, nominally illegal, has still been practiced in recent years, not only in agriculture and mining but also in industry, and force and fraud have been common. The penal sanction for enforcing employment contracts was in effect in the Netherlands Indies until 1940, and is still widely used in Africa, especially for workers in the mines, and in Indo-China.

It may be worth stressing that also in Europe and North America various forms of direct political coercion (and even private coercion with political sanction) have in some periods been common as a means of obtaining labor, and even today conscription for military service, or for industrial service in wartime, leaves the individual little choice but to obey. In many countries labor is exacted from convicts, and even free citizens are often required to work on public roads. In the Soviet Union compulsory labor for prescribed purposes has been an important factor in the nation's spectacular industrial development. There the coercive recruitment of peasant labor for factory production has been partly an emergency measure for rapid internal development and wartime needs, but it is also, of course, a corollary of state control over the productive organization.

The effectiveness of compulsion as a means of recruiting labor is entirely dependent on the personal and institutional circumstances. Under some conditions the power exercised by the governing authorities, or by employers and their agents, may be a legitimate exercise of authority, and be so regarded; and at the other extreme it may be, and be regarded as, an outright coercion by superior force. As a permanent measure for overcoming reluctance to work, compulsion is likely to be wasteful as well as callous, through high costs of recruitment. Even as a temporary measure intended to shift manpower into new economic patterns it may lose much of its effectiveness, as it has in parts of Africa, by inducing an active antipathy to the new forms where there was formerly merely ignorance or indifference.

Indirect coercion. Indirect political pressures on potential workers in undeveloped territories are exercised mainly through taxation, backed by penal sanctions for nonpayment. Head taxes or hut taxes which can be paid only in cash have been an almost universal practice in British Africa, and they have proved effective in drawing the natives into wage employment. This use of the tax power fits into European conceptions of law and ethics, but it may be resented by the native, and, like other "push" factors, it provides no assurance that the native, once employed, will be a satisfactory worker.

A rather different way in which political coercion may work indirectly to push potential workers into industry is through military conscription. Thus in the interior of China a considerable number of the local population chose to enter factory employment during the recent war, in order to avoid the army.

Traditional social controls. Even in primitive and peasant societies there may be some who rebel against certain customary social pressures, particularly if it is known that other customs exist. There are some South African natives, for example, who have left their villages for urban employment in order to escape certain religious and magical practices. In India, villagers have sometimes accepted labor in factories or mines rather than endure the ostracism resulting from infractions of caste rules; and those on the lowest rungs of the caste ladder have turned to industrial employment in considerable numbers, with the hope of improving their lot if only in small degree.

On the whole the traditional kinship organization of society acts as a barrier to industrial development, as it encourages the individual to rely on its security rather than on his own devices, but there are indications that its influence is occasionally resented. Thus in many areas — South Africa, the African Gold Coast, China — individuals have turned to industrial work as an escape from the kinship structure, with its claims on goods and services, its personal supervision, and its dictation of status and function. It is noteworthy that in China, where the wife came into the home of the husband's family, considerable numbers of women entered factories in order to escape the friction with the moth-er-in-law which was widely characteristic of this arrangement; possibly this factor is even a contributing reason for the predominant role of female labor in the developing factories of China, which sharply contrasts with the situation in India.

Such instances of rebellion are more likely to indicate a dissatisfaction with the personal situation than a hostility toward the kinship system as such; thus the female factory workers in China tried to duplicate the traditional family structure in their informal associations in the factory. And it is important to emphasize that the family itself, rather than any restiveness it may produce, may push the individual into industrial employment. This is particularly true in Japan, where it was not uncommon for employers to make a contract with the father for the labor of his sons and daughters — an example of how preindustrial social customs can themselves be used to facilitate the development of an industrial economy.

ATTRACTIONS OF INDUSTRIAL EMPLOYMENT

The various pressures that drive an individual into industrial employment are essentially negative and possibly unstable. A reluctant decision to leave familiar types and contexts of work may be reversed by very slight changes in the real or fancied balance of alternatives. Thus it may be a fragile basis for labor recruitment unless there are also positive inducements. Needless to say, there is only an analytical distinction between the conditions and attitudes that push and those that pull an individual into new economic activity; in the actual decision the skeins of motivation are likely to be so closely interwoven that they have no individual identity. Granted this, however, it is possible to distinguish the positive incentives from the negative thrusts, and to describe them according to the familiar economic-political-social differentiation.

Monetary wages. Among the primarily economic incentives the most effective is certainly wages. It is widely believed that primitives and peasants are characteristically contented with their lot and have little interest in turning to wage employment. In some circumstances this is undoubtedly true, yet there are few parts of the world where there has not been at least some commercialization of values under western influence.

In this connection Africa is particularly interesting, largely because of the variety of its technical and cultural development. It was mentioned above that in most of the Bantu societies of South and East Africa cattle are the standard of wealth, but the practice of payment in money has become familiar, and the result is a variety of compromises, transitional forms, and occasionally outright adoption of monetary standards. A quick review of some of the variations is probably the best way of describing the comparative importance of money wages as an incentive to employment.

Among the Bemba of Northern Rhodesia, with their rather informal political structure, aspirants for power as lesser chiefs have customarily attracted a following by distributing goods, and it was soon found that a period of wage service in the mines gave access to a new and different supply of commodities. Subsequently cotton clothes, available only through money wages, began to replace home-produced bark-cloth, which was inferior both in wearing quality and in comfort. Thus money has entered into the social, if not the economic, structure of the villages, though it is still regarded as useful only for specific kinds of purchases, and the natives do not try to accumulate it. In other parts of Northern Rhodesia, where the natives have been engaged in wage labor more generally and for longer periods, monetary calculation and exchange have been more widely adopted.

In East Africa money has become quite generally a symbol of prestige, and its individualizing effects are evident in aspirations for greater monetary success. The Baganda of Uganda, who were formerly one of the most politically advanced of the African societies, have gone so far in adopting monetary standards that they pay wages to agricultural laborers and domestics from neighboring tribes, though even there cows have still a disproportionate value as symbols of wealth. Natives in the Ulanga Valley, in Tanganyika Territory, first entered wage employment in order to buy money with labor for the purpose of paying taxes, but now there are individuals who employ other natives at wage labor, rather than relying on the older forms of mutual aid; there, as among the Ngoni of Nyasaland, money has on the whole become a general standard of value and is not limited to specific purposes.

Perhaps the most extensive, and the most varied, adaptation to monetary exchange is in the Union of South Africa and its immediate recruiting areas (especially Basutoland, Swaziland, and Mozambique). At first the demand for native labor was primarily for domestic service and agriculture, but then came the tremendous and concentrated labor demand of the Witwatersrand gold mines, with the workers recruited mainly through the indirect coercion of the hut tax. The necessity for considerable numbers of young males to leave native agriculture for work in the distant mines has caused far-reaching disruptions in the traditional village cattle economy. There is a high turnover of laborers, which means that new recruits are constantly being brought into the wage system while former recruits carry some of the new attitudes back to their villages — a development that has a cumulative effect even though the villages that produce the laborers are mainly in areas that have been least affected by European contacts. Moreover, most contracts run for at least a year, and during that time the worker is not only separated from his home and kin but is living in a very substantial urban center.

In the resultant development toward a money orientation four stages can be roughly discerned. At first the young natives seek employment only to pay the tax, and the village is little affected except that it is deprived of their labor. Subsequently it is no longer possible for families — through obligations of the father and gifts or loans from other kinsmen — to supply enough cattle for the bride price, and then the young men may seek work not only to pay taxes but to buy cattle, in order to complete the marriage agreement. The next step is the complete commutation of the bride price into its monetary equivalent, but this deprives the whole arrangement of its functional meaning in the village economy. The customs and rituals of marriage and kinship, the symbols of family cohesion, have been essentially altered, and finally the young men who leave the villages for wages must, if they return, work out new family arrangements without the buttressing of precedent and tradition.

In general it appears to be a mistaken notion that the earning of money is no incentive to native workers, and that their wants lie outside the area of commercial goods and services. Their uses of money may be different from those of the European, and may not conform with what the European thinks is good for the native, but certainly the uses exist. On the other hand, the amount of money that is commonly paid in wages is so little that many natives find its advantages unequal to the effort and uprooting that it requires. In their own villages they may have no access to the things they could buy with wages, but in the industrial centers their wages are not sufficient to buy much, and even that little may have less attraction when part of its price is disciplined and uncongenial living conditions.

In old peasant civilizations, where some degree of monetary exchange has long been part of customary practices, the situation is somewhat different. The peasant needs no sweeping change of attitude in order to be interested in wages as such — though again a minor monetary advantage may not be enough if there are no other factors that push or pull him into a new occupation. Here the Soviet experience with rapid industrialization of a peasant economy is relevant. In the Soviet Union a complicated system of remuneration has developed, based partly on monetary wages and partly on privileges and other perquisites, and in its gradations an important factor is the quantity and quality of performance. Also, there are certain price differentials favoring the urban over the rural areas, and until very recently there was another multiprice system operating with various categories of closed markets. Such practices have certainly been intended partly to induce the peasants to enter industry, and to develop the ways of efficiency in the place of more leisurely rural habits. There is evidence that for this latter objective it has been found useful to increase wages in accordance with attempted rather than actual increases in productivity. It is not possible to know explicitly how successful these various measures have been in changing the peasants' attitudes toward industrial work, mainly because so many other factors are involved. Part of the efficiency and cooperative support that might otherwise arise from the wage inducements may possibly be negated by the complications of the market machinery and the absolute shortage of consumer goods.

In China the peasants' interest in money as a means of exchange has been increased by the introduction of cheap manufactured goods, with its disruptive effect on home production and village markets. It is difficult to know how important the monetary incentive has become as a basis for industrial recruitment, because economic pressures have produced a large supply of unskilled labor and wages are low. An interesting practice that serves to facilitate the orientation toward monetary standards is that of supplementing the workers' wages by "gifts," in the form of especially desired commodities, and subsequently commuting the gifts into outright money payments. In India, too, unskilled labor is cheap, and the importance of the monetary incentive as such is hard to distinguish. It is noteworthy, however, that in India the effectiveness of that incentive is reduced where caste traditions limiting individual aspirations are effective in the urban environment.

On the whole there has been no effort to examine analytically the comparative importance of different wage rates as an inducement to attract primitives and peasants into modern economic activity. The problem is complicated not only by the fact that preindustrial peoples are not familiar with monetary values but also by the low-wage policy that is generally practiced, and by the pressures that dictate acceptance of whatever is offered. When the potential worker has some choice about accepting employment, wages may have direct importance as an incentive. When he has no choice, his incentive is survival, and the wage is merely a means toward that end. Whether it acquires additional importance, and thus serves as an inducement toward better performance or longer service, depends on the complex of personal and cultural factors involved — including the amount of the wage and the availability of desired goods and services on which to spend it.

Specialized skills. Not dissimilar to the ambiguity of wages as an incentive is the ambiguity of another inducement that may be considered economic, even though it is not directly monetary; the opportunity to develop and exercise specialized skills. Here too the potential importance of the incentive is blurred by the fact that it is seldom offered in any quantity, as well as by the fact that it involves unfamiliar standards. Indeed, in some areas this incentive is not offered at all. In parts of Africa, for example, natives are deliberately prevented from occupying more advanced positions. To be sure, the complex technology of industrialism demands talents and skills not characteristic of primitive societies, but there is abundant evidence that such relegation of the native to unskilled labor is not due to any intrinsic lack of ambition or ability, but rather to the color sensi-

bilities or the economic self-assertion of the Europeans. Throughout southern Africa the demand for education exceeds the supply of schools and teachers. Also in the Netherlands Indies, before World War II, there was a strong interest in education but very little opportunity to make use of it.

In general, it is unlikely that primitives or peasants in any considerable number turn to industrial employment primarily in order to learn new skills or utilize old ones. The tasks available to the worker untrained in industrial technology are for the most part routine and unlikely to constitute, in themselves, much inducement to the artisan, or even to a native who merely desires to develop a skill. But once the worker has turned to industrial labor, the possibility of using and increasing his skill may be an incentive to continued employment — provided the possibility exists at all, and he is not arbitrarily prevented from moving into higher positions as his ability increases.

National needs and aspirations. Political, as contrasted with economic, considerations may work in two main ways as an incentive to enter industrial employment. One is through the desire to support the political community in a time of emergency, specifically in wartime. Only for the Soviet Union and China, however, has this question been studied. In both countries this incentive seems to have had some importance in the recruitment as well as in the productivity of labor during World War II, though it is of course impossible to know how generally it was a decisive consideration in recruitment. In China it undoubtedly prompted many skilled workers from the coast to make the long and hazardous journey to the interior, whither the factories were removed, but its role in inducing new workers to enter the factory is uncertain.

Similar to patriotism in a time of national emergency is the response to purposes glorified through education and official propaganda in a time of rising national ambition. Thus in Japan's thrust to world power the notion of racial destiny was deliberately promoted to aid the process of industrial development, and it was tailored to fit the requirements of such powerful social traditions as the developed family structure and the cult of the emperor; as a result of the combination of emotions thus invoked, service in the factories became a matter of familial, patriotic, and religious duty. In the Soviet Union, enthusiasm for socialist construction has been promoted with quite different appeals — emphasis on quantity and number in presenting collective goals, glorification of "socialist competition," the offering of honorific titles and public rewards — but there, too, national aspirations have been made incentives to individual labor.

This potentially powerful incentive cannot, of course, be expected in dependent and colonial territories. Whether the natives in those territories today are stimulated by aspirations for independence from the governing powers is a different ques-

tion; but even if such aspirations exist, they are scarcely likely to be expressed in enthusiastic labor for the industries controlled by those powers. And even in independent nations there may be no nationalistic enthusiasm for industrial labor. Thus in China, where industrialization is promoted with some reluctance, and largely because it is considered unavoidable in an industrial world, there is little effort to endow industrial tasks with a nationalistic emotional aura that would serve as a motivation for the individual.

New opportunities. Among the incentives that may be called social, rather than primarily economic or political, is the desire for new opportunities — more chance for independence, for prestige, for individual achievement. Here we have the positive expression of the merely negative desire to escape customary social controls, discussed above. The desire for new opportunities may be effective even if the economic incentive of earning monetary wages has no importance, but if the two exist together their separate outlines are scarcely distinguishable: it is impossible, for example, to assess the comparative importance of a desire for prestige and a desire for the money that provides that prestige.

In most primitive and peasant societies the individual's status and function are fixed, or change only according to a fixed process, the determinants being mainly factors outside his control, such as age, sex, the position in the kinship or class structure; the preservation of the established structure is all-important, and change from within is strongly resisted. But once the members of such a society have acquired some knowledge of industrial life they are confronted with a quite different system of controls and values, in which status and function are much more susceptible of change, and are determined largely by what the individual does, rather than by who he is. The desire to benefit from the new possibilities is largely dependent on the degree to which the industrial way of life has modified the old forms. Moreover, the opportunities actually made available to the new industrial worker may be meager indeed in absolute terms, and perhaps also in terms of his own valuation, as was stressed above: the possibility for individual achievement may provide small inducement to enter industrial employment if workers are not fully admitted to the system of reward by merit. Nevertheless, the desire for new opportunities is an incentive that can be considerably influential.

Thus in the Soviet Union the possibilities for social and occupational advancement — evident in the system of rewards for outstanding individual performance and in the abolition of traditional class restrictions of opportunities (albeit new inequalities have been introduced) — have acted as a strong inducement to participate in industrial development. And in China, where women have held an inferior position in the traditional social order, work in the factories has the attraction of offering increased independence, and recognition as economic assets rather than liabilities; to some extent the same may be true for younger sons. Little evidence is available regarding the direct importance of this incentive among more primitive peoples, but it appears that sometimes industrial employment as such, regardless of its possibilities for individual achievement, may acquire a prestige value, especially if traditional avenues of achievement are no longer open. In Northern Rhodesia, for example, the prestige formerly accorded the successful warrior is now given — especially by marriageable girls — to the adventurer who leaves his village for work in the mines.

Free choice of associates. Another aspect of industrial life that may have an appeal in recruitment is the possibility it offers of choosing one's companions. At least among primitive peoples this may well be less a primary incentive than an incidental result of a decision reached on other grounds, but the importance of personal associations has occasionally been stressed by observers of native workers; it is reported, for example, as significant among South African natives who have left tribal villages for the towns, and among the Tale peoples of the northern Gold Coast. There is also some evidence that if industrial employment offers little chance for personal relationships, or for choice in determining them, African natives are less likely to enter or to remain in modern enterprise. It may be that the motivating factor is a desire to continue existing personal relationships, rather than a desire for new ones. Thus in Northern Rhodesia the personal influence of natives already experienced in the mines may be a factor in recruiting new workers, and also in the associations that develop on the job.

MORALE AND EFFICIENCY ON THE JOB

Thus far we have discussed the various conditions and attitudes that impede or further a decision to enter or remain in industrial employment. It remains now to consider the worker as a functioning part of the new productive system. We are not concerned here with such matters as capital equipment and managerial organization and the quality of materials, even though they are essential factors in productivity, and to some extent affect the attitudes of the worker as well. The following pages will consider only the main working conditions, as distinct from technical and political conditions, which affect the productivity and the attitudes of labor in areas not yet fully industrialized. It would be merely frivolous to try to define how far these factors are causes and how far they are effects of job morale and efficiency.

Wages. This cause-and-effect reciprocity is very conspicuous in the matter of wages. The very low wages that are characteristic of industrial enterprises in areas of economic transition have various causes, not the least of which is the relatively low productivity of labor in such areas. But it seems that this works both ways, with low productivity due in part to the low wages

offered. Among the factors that drive primitives and peasants into employment, the most prevalent, in all areas, is probably poverty, and numerous investigators have concluded that it is largely poverty which keeps their efficiency at a low level — whether for physiological reasons, as may be true in the very lowest levels of wages, or for psychological reasons, as may be true when meager pay seems worth only meager effort. Thus there develops a vicious-circle situation in which the employer is not likely to forgo the advantage in a plentiful supply of cheap labor, and the very factors that make labor cheap serve to diminish some of the advantage gained.

It would seem that a solution to this situation could be sought by offering higher wages as a reward for better performance. But for various reasons, including racial or ethnic discrimination, this is seldom attempted in undeveloped areas. Such encouragement becomes increasingly important as industrialization grows from small to large scale and as the native population becomes the source for all levels of labor, as in Japan and the Soviet Union; and those countries, particularly the latter, have largely succeeded in breaking the closed circuit of low productivity, low wages, low productivity. In such complex developments, however, the specific importance of the wage incentive cannot be distinguished from that of other influences that also help to develop skill and productivity. The Soviet Union has probably gone further than Japan in deliberately encouraging the unskilled to improve their efficiency, but there the wage incentive, while it has been strongly relied on, is only one of several that work in the same direction.

Skill. Except in the crudest forms of gang labor, modern enterprise demands a particular technical competence and a range of general knowledge that are not provided in the training and development of nonindustrial peoples. And certainly a fundamental reason for low productivity among primitives and peasants, and thus for low wages, is their lack of training and skill in the tasks of industrial work. But this too is not a static fact, to be regarded as given and unchanging. If it is true that a worker is poorly paid because he is unskilled, it may also be true that he is unskilled because he has no possibility of using old abilities or of developing and using new ones.

As has been indicated, there is in newly developing areas little tendency to encourage better workmanship. It is seldom attempted to adapt for use in industry any handicraft skills that the workers may already possess — although some efforts of this kind were made in India during the war. And training in new techniques is likely to be extremely limited. Even where it exists, the opportunity of learning and the rewards in advancement may depend on the supervisor's preconceptions rather than on effort. In many areas advancement is next to impossible, or is possible only within a very narrow range — and even ambitious workers are not likely to apply

themselves to increasing their effort and efficiency when there is little prospect of thereby improving their position. On the whole, it seems safe to believe that the level of skill and aspiration is in some measure dependent on the area of opportunity for their exercise.

There is ample evidence on this general failure, in undeveloped areas, to make full use of the potential capacities of indigenous labor. In India the caste system is partly responsible, for to some extent it has been carried over into industry, with resultant arbitrary limitations on position and type of work. In Africa the native worker is confronted with really unbridgeable barriers to advancement. It is reported that in China many employers are passively or actively opposed to job training, or even to the extension of literacy, for fear that the workers will become less tractable in accepting low pay and long hours. Even in Japan, despite the high value placed on craftsmanship, there was little possibility of advancement, partly because of hierarchical restrictions and partly because of the peculiar decentralized organization of work; it is interesting to note, however, that the resultant narrowing and overspecialization of skills seems to have been, in Japan, less harmful to workers' morale than to industrial efficiency.

Ethnic discrimination. In the areas of economic transition the strongest barrier to workers' development on the job is the prevalence of ethnic discrimination, sanctioned by custom or even by law. By this practice, caste distinctions in work and in wages are introduced into an economic system that is basically incompatible with arbitrary limitations. The justification that there are racial or ethnic differences in the capacity to learn and use industrial skills has no shred of scientific validity. Cultural differences certainly exist — differences in training and attitudes — but these are neither innate nor immutable. Ethnic discrimination is most flagrant in colonies and in other areas of European commercial and industrial interest, but it sometimes develops even among the indigenous peoples themselves.

The consequences that follow from the practice of setting an arbitrary limitation to the position and type of work that are attainable are too familiar to require elaboration. It is sufficient to say that this policy in large measure reflects and augments the hazards to morale and efficiency that have already been discussed — the disadvantages proliferating from low productivity, low wages, and undeveloped skills.

Industrial discipline. The controls, requirements, and gradations of authority that accompany industrial routines are of quite a different order from those to which primitive and peasant workers are accustomed, and frequently they are a cause of restiveness, if only because they are unfamiliar — a situation, again, that is reflected in low productivity. Cultural differences in regard to conceptions of time, quantity, space, unquestionably make for differences in the orientation toward methodical work and punctuality. The Bemba of Northern Rhodesia, to mention an extreme example, have no conception of equal units of time, and thus find it difficult to fit into the time discipline of industrial activity. And even where cultural differences are not so extreme, the disciplinary hierarchy of industrial life is generally of quite a different order from the traditional patterns of authority, and, particularly in factory work, newcomers are likely to have difficulty in adjusting to it. Loitering and rule-breaking, in defiance of factory discipline or in mere unconcern, are particularly notable in India and China.

It is noteworthy that in Japan the family basis of industrial recruitment and organization removed this particular cause of disaffection, at least until very late in the industrialization process. The importance of this factor in the Soviet Union is impossible to assess, as the tremendous and highly-rewarded increases in productivity associated with the shock brigades and Stakhanovites have overshadowed any difficulties that may exist in new workers' adjustment to industrial discipline. But it is at least open to speculation whether the attitude called wrecking is not as much a reflection of these difficulties as it is a matter of ideological significance.

Systemic inequities. The existence of favoritism and other inequities in the relations between management and workers would require no special emphasis in the present discussion were it not that this universal failure of practice to conform with theory takes various special forms in newly developing economies. In this context the special treatment accorded those who follow a prescribed line, be it political or religious or any other — such as the situation in the Soviet Union, where it appears that party membership and activities play some role in industrial recruitment and advancement, despite efforts to consider merit alone — is of less interest than those inequitable practices that are integral in a system of organization.

In large part these arise from the fact that, except in Japan and the Soviet Union, industrialism in undeveloped areas has usually been established under foreign capital and control. This fact is indeed an element in many of the problems that we have considered: the sharp distinction between foreign executives and technicians and native labor is one of the reasons why the workers' opportunities for advancement are so limited; the disparity between traditional and industrial patterns is in some measure due to the fact that foreign managers have shown a tendency to follow policies and forms of organization that are based on their experience at home, imposing them on situations where they do not fit; foreign domination is also an essential element in the problem of ethnic discrimination; and it has the additional result that any real or potential antagonism between management and labor is supplemented by the further antagonism between foreign and native. But a more specific result of foreign control is worth special emphasis in the present context. Sometimes the barriers of language and custom make it necessary to rely on local personnel for the lower managerial ranks, and this practice, despite its potential advantages, has frequently only augmented the difficulties of transition. Selection for such positions tends to be on grounds of convenience in communication rather than on technical capacity, and the behavior of these intermediaries is not always an aid to satisfactory industrial relations.

Thus in China and India it has been a common practice of administrators unfamiliar with local language and custom to use natives in the lower levels of management, and very frequently the result has been a systematic abuse of authority. In China the recruitment of labor through self-seeking intermediaries — who might keep as much as 80 percent of the wages they were paid for each worker — was widely practiced by the early European enterprisers, and was continued unofficially long after the system was abolished by law. In India under British rule there developed a " managing agency " system, under which the worker was recruited and supervised by Indian intermediaries; often the same individual performed both functions, and thus he was in a position to collect a fee for each worker hired, to exact a bribe from the worker himself, and then in his role as foreman to fire the worker in order to repeat his collections. The situation is similar where native bosses are relied on in agricultural undertakings, as in Indo-China.

Whether the favoritism and extortion of buffer functionaries drive the workers into active resentment or only into fatalistic resignation, their morale and efficiency are not thereby improved.

A somewhat different form of inequity has been particularly prevalent in China. It was stressed in an earlier section that the impersonal, reward-by-merit character of industrial life is not congenial to the Chinese peasant, who is accustomed to family hierarchy as the determinant of status. For this very reason, however, industrial enterprises in China have frequently taken over the family principle and made family connections the basis for any opportunities that are offered. Such nepotism is congenial enough to those who are favored, but it does not make for industrial efficiency or for strong working morale among those who fail to benefit from it.

Looking backward. Throughout the undeveloped areas, industrial enterprises have difficulty in maintaining a reasonably constant working force — even if poverty or other factors provide a continuous new supply. And no problem reveals more conspicuously than this with the intertwining of the causes and effects of industrial morale. All the various factors that have been mentioned — and certainly more could be added — make it difficult for the workers to find security and satisfaction in the life around them, and therefore encourage them to stay away from the job or to throw it over altogether. But on the other hand, the various influences that make primitive and peasant peoples cling to their accustomed ways of life, or feel indifferent toward new ways, tend to make them look backward toward family and native village rather than actively seeking new roots in the new system.

Thus in the Netherlands Indies absenteeism averages more than half of the ordinary working time; in China and India it is not so great, but still substantial; it exists, in fact, even in the Soviet Union, among peasants unaccustomed to urban and industrial constraints. And labor turnover, resulting from the abandonment of jobs, is almost as great in China, India, and Japan, where workers are presumably recruited on a comparatively permanent basis, as it is in the South African mines, where temporary service is the official policy. Both in absenteeism and in job abandonment a considerable factor is the stronger claim of nonindustrial pursuits and home ties. Very often the job was accepted in the first place only as a temporary necessity.

In Japan, as we have seen, this family orientation was deliberately utilized in the method of recruitment and the organization of work — a policy that made transition less abrupt but for that very reason made it easier to revert to rural security. To be sure, a considerable part of industrial activity was carried on in small-scale family enterprises in the cities, but this development of the principle, whatever its psychological advantages may have been, did not make for efficiency of operation, and in the period between the wars it was giving way to less personal and more centralized organization of industry.

When the old pattern of security has crumbled, or for some other reason is no longer a possible refuge, the worker must continue as best he can. And then, as we have seen, the chances are that his efficiency suffers from his dissatisfaction and his dissatisfaction is increased by the results of his inefficiency. It may be significant that opium smoking and the use of other narcotics are reported as being most common among displaced and dissatisfied workers; this observation refers particularly to Southeast Asia, but there is reason to believe that it has general relevance. And one further cause-and-effect interrelationship is worth mentioning. The widespread tendency of workers to remain oriented toward their native villages has been a factor in the neglect of urban living conditions for workers, as it has been regarded as a justification for failure to provide permanent and decent living quarters. And the wretched living conditions have served in turn to encourage the nostalgic tendencies.

New integrations. On the development of positive factors that might serve, through the workers themselves, to mitigate both the causes and the effects of low morale and inefficiency, very little has been observed. Voluntary associations have of course developed among the workers — ranging from the banding together of African natives around a more experienced worker from the same village to the full-

fledged labor organizations that began to develop in Japan between the wars, under strong government opposition. On the whole, associations that might have any relevance for labor discipline have been looked upon unfavorably by western employers in undeveloped areas. And at the same time, the western-style trade union has met little enthusiasm among primitive and peasant workers. The associations formed around the nucleus of the factory are likely to be informal and to follow the lines of preindustrial allegiances and cleavages, rather than focusing on the problems and requirements of the job itself. It may be that some form of association will develop which will synthesize the vestiges of the old patterns and the requirements of the new, but this is at present only conjectural. As was mentioned in an earlier section, collective aspirations reaching beyond the job situation to the society as a whole are capable of serving as a galvanizing factor. Quite possibly these may play a larger role than they have thus far — but the integrating effects of collective goals can hardly be looked upon as an advantage without knowledge of the nature of the goals.

The literature that has been reviewed in this survey makes it very clear that the introduction of industrial enterprise into hitherto nonindustrial areas entails many and sober difficulties in addition to the technical problems involved — difficulties that reach into the very roots of personal and group existence. In some directions solutions have been sought, with a greater or lesser degree of concerted effort. But in large measure the difficulties have been ignored and allowed to multiply; thus past practices have produced a formidable barrier to continued development along present lines. A transformation of economic relations, in the direction of greater understanding for the needs and aspirations of the indigenous peoples, is not, however, beyond possibility; in fact, there are indications, here and there, that the attempt has been started. And while this process of reformulation may well be somewhat less than peaceful and gradual in the especially critical areas, there is nevertheless reason to believe that it will be increasingly attempted, for the morale and efficiency of workers are matters whose significance is not limited to the workers alone.

10

BUREAUCRACY: THE ADMINISTRATION OF CHOICE

A. The Administrative and Political Process

51. Introduction

In 1944 an Austrian who had spent a major part of his life in England and the United States published a book entitled *The Road to Serfdom*. The burden of the argument that the author Friedrich von Hayek attempted to convey was that the liberal democracies were abandoning their birthright of freedom. The growing complexity of public affairs was serving as a façade for the invasion of democracy by the hosts of socialism. Mr. Hayek asserted: "We are rapidly abandoning . . . one of the salient characteristics of Western Civilization as it has grown from the foundations laid by Christianity and the Greeks and Romans. Not merely nineteenth- and eighteenth-century liberalism, but the basic individualism inherited by us from Erasmus and Montaigne, from Cicero and Tacitus, Pericles and Thucydides, is progressively relinquished." This charge has been heard in treatises and polemics on every hand here in this country and abroad. The concentration of power in government even when wisely employed has become a foremost issue. It is perhaps the most serious problem faced by peoples who are organized in large industrial societies.

As we have seen, the bureaucratization and routinization of decision-making is a persistent characteristic of life in all mass industrial societies. In this sense the troublesome problems by which the executors of big government periodically are confounded are essentially no different from those which face the rest of society. Specialization has been the dynamic process by which our society has advanced and progressed, but in every realm the multitudinous units created in this process have required some form of synthesis or integration. Somewhere within our public and private systems control towers are needed to coordinate and integrate the separate activities of all the particular units.

Public administration has grown up as a separate and vital branch of the field of political science. The expansion of functions of the public service has evoked great concern for improving these services. In general the importance which societies give to bureaucracy is a consequence both of the quality and quantity of governmental affairs. From a qualitative standpoint, we have observed the wide extension of governmental activity into areas which, in earlier years, had been *territorium nullius* for public officials. The business of government has extended into the most vital domains of the individual's life including his employment and status in old age. Quantitatively, the numbers of governmental activities have increased so rapidly that more and more personnel have been called for to administer them.

The vital character and broad range of the functions of government have aroused the mass of people to demand that bureaucrats be held accountable to the Congress or to their state legislatures. Yet Congressional control of administration is fraught with difficulties and problems. The tasks that are performed by administrators are often complex and difficult, with a high degree of special and technical knowledge required. For many positions that appear on the civil service list, for example, we find specifications indicating that only wide experience and training can equip men for understanding fully their duties. The increasing rationalization of functions,

which has been the source of unparalleled achievement in the factory, in the office and in commerce, has likewise contributed to the more skillful operation of the highly intricate and complicated public system. There are numerous public servants who conceive of their roles in professional and scientific terms and who devote themselves for a lifetime to particular responsibilities. To control and supervise in detail the activities of these individuals would demand new agencies of government or the reorganization of procedures and functions on the part of Congress. It would call for nothing less than a parallel bureaucracy in Congress equipped by profession and training to implement the laws which their opposite numbers, the law-maker, had passed. There are sound reasons for believing that were the legislature to supply itself with full-time experts to do the work of the public administrator, this practice would break down the separation of politics and administration, which has come about as a result of trial and error in the past century and a half. The history of administration by pseudo-legislative officials elected for short terms hardly encourages the belief that such practices, even under the best and most simple conditions, can be made effective. And the objective expansion of some government departments to a size that has exceeded 100,000 employees demonstrates the fact that public affairs are the most vast and extensive of enterprises.

Therefore public administration has to avoid the critical points of the tyranny of bureaucrats on the one hand and the tyranny of uninformed public or legislative opinion on the other hand. The risk of dominance by trained public servants, with designs for preserving or extending their spheres of authority, has become a subject for serious comment and scholarly inquiry. Max Weber was one of the first to argue, perhaps with some exaggeration, that in practice the bureaucracy had become the dominant organ of government. He declared in 1918: "In the modern state the real government effectuates itself neither in parliamentary debates nor in royal proclamations but in the exercise of administration in daily life, necessarily and unavoidably in the hands of the Civil service." This emphasis was carried further by James Burnham, who in 1941 in his book *The Managerial Revolution* asserted that the center of power in the private as well as the public sphere had shifted from lawyers, industrialists, and clergymen, who in past eras had dominated society, to a new managerial class. The managers of business and government, he argued, are the bureaucrats who see to it that policies are interpreted and put into practice. This gives them a power out of all proportion to other powers in modern society. The managers, it is said, have become the new ruling class.

If the shoals of excessive centralization and bureaucratization are one of the points on which democratic administration can flounder, another grave risk is the practice of arbitrary and indiscriminate legislative intervention. From one viewpoint it is necessary that the administration of government be carried on in the public eye, for the public trust is vital to any efficient and responsible administration. Yet the demand for public accountability presents serious problems, not least among them the question of how to evaluate public administration.

We have considered in some detail the operation of the price system or economic choice in a free and competitive market. We have gone on to observe that essentially the same general principles operate in regard to political choice. But in one respect at least this analogy must be modified, for the state in mass industrial societies has generally renounced the idea that the consumer should pay a direct price for every good duly received. Instead the chief aim of governmental service is to provide all the people with services for which there is a common need. The state is not in the habit of charging what the market will bear, nor can its efficiency be measured directly by the preference among consumers for alternate goods. In a free and open market the comparative values of varying amounts of goods which the society produces is registered by the response to the sale of these commodities at particular prices. The state undertakes to provide society with certain goods and services considered to be vital to its well-being and indeed its survival. They include education, protection against unemployment and old age, and survivors benefits. In these areas a society's output in terms of the contributions of these services to its collective well-being cannot be so readily balanced in quantitative terms against the expenditures it has made for these vital services.

Furthermore, between the consumers and the producers or the citizens and the state there are intermediaries like political parties and legislators. They interpret at a distance once removed the wishes and desires of the people. Their judgment is affected by vulnerability to special pressures, the unequal influences of regions or groups, and their own frames of reference for conceiving what the people are telling them. Thus the activities of a bureaucracy are resistant to measurement on the simple economic basis of profit and loss — at least in the short run. In the long run it is possible for opinion to be registered on fundamental alternative policies, but by then societies will have moved forward imperceptibly on the basis of short-term decisions.

There are four unsolved problems for bureaucracy in modern society. In the first place it is true, as recent scandals affirm, that public officials live in a goldfish bowl. They are accountable to the public and most liberal democrats would consider this to be a good thing. Yet the unceasing pressure of ambitious politicians, secretly bent on acquiring reputations for themselves as arch-defenders of the public treasury or as leaders in a political crusade against inequity in another party's administration, can evoke an administrative psychology that is sometimes as dangerous as overt mismanagement. Bureaucrats in a de-mocracy are often portrayed as pallid creatures but one stage removed from *rigor mortis*. The fear of a public investigation frequently produces an excessive concern for legality and creates a spirit of servility that is quite inappropriate for an age of far-reaching social change. Men of independence and courage are driven from administrative posts by an overemphasis on blind conformity. The first unsolved problem of bureaucracy in a democracy is that of perpetuating a spirit of creativity and resolution at the same time that public accountability is maintained.

Secondly, the problem for most democracies has been that of attracting to the public service men of character and stature, who can be expected to remain at their posts at least until their immediate tasks are completed. In the United States, however, the low public esteem for civil servants in general, the problem of inferior financial and material rewards, and the tendency to abuse and defame men of honor have placed serious obstacles in the path of this goal.

Thirdly, bureaucracy from one viewpoint is essentially conservative. In practice there are conditions peculiar to administrative behavior that encourage the maintenance of the *status quo*. The psychological incentives which highly competitive situations almost inevitably invoke are frequently absent from government. Inter-group rivalries are blunted over in the vast administrative hierarchy. It is of course essential to a permanent and continuing civil service that individuals be safe-guarded against arbitrary removal. Yet the safeguards established may dampen enthusiasm and weaken instincts for progress and change.

Finally, the proper area and purpose of bureaucracy in industrial societies are generally construed in the false terms of laissez-faire on the one hand or collectivism on the other. Most disputes on bureaucracy swing with rash violence from one of these extremes to the other. While the intellectuals have wrangled, however, practical men have attempted to wrest from our present position some kind of honest and tolerable compromise whereby the freedom which liberalism would preserve could be wedded with the security about which collectivists are wont to discourse. Perhaps this is the supreme challenge of administrative choice. President Woodrow Wilson (1856–1924) in an essay which has become almost a classic explores some of these problems. Professor Leonard D. White of the University of Chicago, in the judicious little essay which was his Presidential Address to the American Political Science Association in 1945, deals with the problem of the relation of the administrative and legislative branches.

At the heart of the administrative process is a hard core of civil servants called the bureaucracy. At the heart of the political process is the political party. The number of voters in major countries is so vast and heterogeneous and their interests and needs are so diverse that they can make their voices heard only through large groups and associations. In part political groupings or parties are based on common beliefs and convictions. As the Spanish philosopher Ortega y Gasset has observed " people are inclined to believe in company." In addition, political parties are often temporary coalitions of diverse groups joined by no other cohesive element than a desire to achieve political power. Historically, there have been in American politics combinations of groups whose differences seem to far exceed their similarities. Thus on occasion great urban bosses and their political machines, Southern conservatives, intellectuals and idealists, and strong labor unionists have joined hands.

Groups and individuals associate in political parties on the basis of one of three principles of organization. Some parties are formed on the basis primarily of *patronage*. The paramount objective of some leaders and workers is in the political jobs they hope to obtain, and for them policies or principles are entirely secondary. The American political parties at the turn of the century were examples of this " ideal type."

Then there are *class-status* parties, of which the old Tory party in England and particular socialist parties in Europe before World War II may be taken as examples. This form of party organization is generally more resistant to change and accommodation than the patronage party. Once having risen to power, it must overcome the tendency to regard politics solely from the standpoint of its class and must establish a national outlook on issues. The Tories in England enjoyed an advantage which class-status parties have generally lacked, as they were from the start a ruling class accustomed to think in national terms.

A third party is the *Weltanschaung* or ideological type. Of these, the parties with the longest history and tradition have been European Catholic and Protestant parties and coalitions of parties like the *Centrum* in Germany or the Christian People's Party in Norway. Parties organized around a central, all-pervasive doctrine or purpose, including parties in the United States like the Municipal Reform Party, have tended to be rigid in their practices and inflexible in accommodating themselves to other groups.

Outside the Soviet Union, Communist Parties not infrequently have displayed great flexibility through combining with other forces in "popular fronts" or through an invasion and domination of particular trade union movements. Indeed in Western and Eastern Europe, Communist Parties, which would appear to be the representatives *par excellence* of ideological parties, have become class-status parties following their capture of positions of leadership in the trade union movement. Thus even the most doctrinaire parties can in practice shift from one party-type to another.

In the same way as membership and association in political parties reflect these three patterns, the basis for authority and compliance within party structures suggests three possibilities. Leaders are related to the rank and file on the basis of tradi-

tion, bureaucratic organization and procedures, or faith in the leader. Tradition was the cohesive force in the Tory Party in England. The special social status of its leaders had been fixed by tradition and was generally accepted by members of the Party. The active groups in politics remained for some time the aristocracy and gentry even after the suffrage was extended. The lower classes in England remained for some time under the social domination of privileged elements in society whose status was assumed to entitle them to the role of political leadership.

Bureaucratic organizations for party action emerged concomitantly with the growth of democracy. It became essential, with the extension of the suffrage to mobilize loyalties by means of some formal kind of organization and control. Rules and laws were enacted providing means whereby this control could be made effective. Committees and officers were established to administer them.

A final pattern, which has been especially prominent in time of crisis, is the "charismatic" pattern wherein the rank and file of the party acquiesce because of a mystical and unquestioning faith in the leader. The closest examples to this "ideal type" have been the Fascist and National Socialist Parties. In time of crisis, when the membership of a party is composed of irregulars and when the formal controls are at a minimum, there frequently appear in both democratic and authoritarian parties men of great apparent natural ability possessing a sense of mission and calling. The masses in society are willing and able to place their faith unreservedly in men of this kind and the control which develops is frequently as rigid as that of the traditional party. In both cases the control is exercised from the top down and deviation is punished through a wide range of pressures and controls.

Robert A. Dahl, of the Department of Political Science of Yale University, discusses the role of political parties in the Marxist tradition and by implication contrasts this pattern with the one that exists in most of the liberal democracies. It may be useful to employ the conceptual scheme we have first summarized in thinking about the Marxist idea of political parties. Perhaps we perceive our own party system most clearly by comparing it directly with other systems that are radically unlike it.

52. On Bureaucracy*

In a modern state, actual domination which is manifested neither in parliamentary speeches nor in the pronouncements of monarchs but rather in the day-to-day functioning of the administrative machine rests necessarily and inevitably in the hands of the officialdom. This holds for the military as well as the civil officialdom. For it is indeed from his office that the higher officer nowadays directs his battles. We are used to measuring the extent of the modernization of an economic system by the degree to which it has become capitalistic since the Middle Ages. In the same way, we measure the modernization of the state by the extent to which it has become bureaucratized, i.e., the extent to which it has an officialdom based on appoint-

ment, salary, pension, promotion, specialized training and division of functions, stipulated jurisdiction, acts, decisions and rules recorded in writing and hierarchical sub and superordination. (This applies to monarchies as well as to democracies [republics].) And it is especially so when the state is not a small canton with a rotating administrative personnel but is rather a large, mass-state. Democracy, just like the absolute state, replaces administration by feudal, patrimonial, patrician or other honorarily or hereditarily functioning unpaid amateurs with appointed officials. Appointed officials decide on all of our daily needs and troubles. In this respect there is no difference between the civil official and the wielder of military domination, i.e., the officer. The modern mass army is a bureaucratic army, and the officer is a particular kind of official as distinguished from the knight, *condottiere,* chieftain, or Homeric hero. The fighting power of

* Max Weber, " On Bureaucracy," translated by Edward A. Shils, *Social Science 3: Syllabus and Selected Readings,* Vol. I, fifteenth edition (Chicago: University of Chicago Press, 1950), pp. 385–391. Reprinted by permission of Edward A. Shils and the University of Chicago Press.

the army rests on the discipline of its personnel. The advance of bureaucracy in municipal administration goes on in practically the same way. Its bureaucratization is in proportion to its size or the extent to which as an inevitable consequence of technically or economically necessitated rational-purposeful activities it has transcended its organic autochthonous parochialism (*Zweckverbandsbildungen*).

In the church the really important element in the encyclical of 1870 was not the much discussed dogma of infallibility but the universal episcopacy. It created the "priestocracy" and in contrast with the Middle Ages, it made the bishops and parsons into mere officials of the central authority of the Papal See (Curia). The situation is not different in the great private enterprises of the present day — and the larger they are, the more bureaucratized they are. Bureaucracy in private industry is growing at a faster rate than the manual labor force and it is quite ludicrous to believe as some of our literati do that brain work in a business office differs even slightly from brain work in a government office.

Fundamentally they are both the same. From the standpoint of social science the modern state is an "organization" just as much as a factory is. In fact its "organized" character is what gives the modern state its historical uniqueness. And the domination-relationships within the organization are very similar in the state and in the factory. The relative independence of the artisan or domestic worker, of the peasant on the estate, of the warrior captain, of the knight and the vassals was a function of their ownership of the tools, supplies, money and arms by means of which they performed their economic, political, and military functions. The hierarchical dependence of the worker, clerk, technician, academic assistant on the one hand and the public official and the soldier on the other is a function, conversely, of the fact that the tools, supplies and money which are indispensable for the organization and for economic existence are in the hands, in the one case, of the enterpriser, and, in the other, of the political ruling group. The Russian soldiers (in the First World War) did not in the main want to continue the war. But they had to because the material instruments for carrying on the war and the supplies on which they had to live were under the control of persons who by the use of those instruments and supplies forced the soldiers into the trenches just as the capitalistic owner of the means of production forces the workers into the factories and mine pits. This decisive economic fact: the "separation" of the workers from the instruments of operation — in economic life, from the instruments of production; in military organization, from the instruments of warfare; in public administration, from the material means of administration — in all these spheres, non-possession of the money necessary for operation — and finally, in the research institutes of universities and in scientific laboratories, from the devices required for research — in all these varied fields of activity, " separation " is the basic feature, common both to the modern state in its power-wielding, cultural and military phases, and to the capitalistic private enterprise. In both these situations, disposition over these instrumentalities is held by that group or body which the bureaucratic apparatus (judge, official, officer, foreman, clerk, subaltern) obeys directly or to whose call it responds. The bureaucratic apparatus is equally characteristic of all these structures; and its existence and function are inextricably connected as cause and as effect with this concentration of the instruments of organizational operation. " Increased socialization " today necessarily carries with it increased bureaucratization.

Historically, " progress " towards the bureaucratic state in which judicial and administrative activities are carried on in accordance with rationally promulgated laws and rationally devised rules has been very closely connected with the development of modern capitalism. The structure of modern capitalistic organization rests on calculation. It requires for its existence a judicial and administrative system the operation of which can, at least in principle, be predicted in accordance with fixed general norms — just as the predictable productivity of a machine can be calculated. The capitalistic system is no more compatible with what is popularly called cadi-justice; i.e., adjudication according to the judge's sense of justice in the concrete case or according to other irrational means and principles of ad-

judication (such as were universal in the past and which are still widespread in the orient) than it is with the patriarchal administration of the theocratic or patrimonial systems of social organization of Asia and of our own past in which uncontrolled discretion and grace, and furthermore uninfringeable sacred and irrational tradition constitute the bases of administration and adjudication. The circumstance that this kind of cadi-justice and its related types of administration can even, because of its irrationality, frequently be bought and paid for facilitates the emergence and existence of that type of capitalism in which merchants and government contractors are the main figures, as well as, of all those forms of pre-rationalistic capitalism, which have been known for four millenia, namely robber — and freebooter-capitalism which find their sustenance in politics, war and government administration as such. Indeed these types of capitalism often owe their prosperity to cadi-justice. The specific characteristic of modern capitalism is the rigorously rational organization of labor on the basis of rational technique and it never has arisen nor can it ever arise in an irrationally coordinated political system. Modern forms of industrial organization with their fixed capital and exact calculation are much too sensitive to irrationality in law and administration. They can arise in situations where either, as in England, the practical formation of the law actually lay in the hands of lawyers, who in the service of their capitalistic clients devised the appropriate business forms on the basis of which judges bound by precedents, i.e., by predictable schemes could proceed. They can also emerge where the judge, as in the bureaucratic state with rational rules, is more or less a "legal machine" into one end of which one put the laws and fees and which turns out at the other end the decision together with the more or less plausible reasons for it. Capitalistic institutions can, in other words, develop only where the functioning of the legal and administrative system is, in the main, predictable.

Finally, the advance of bureaucratization in political parties is no different from what it is in economic life or in governmental administration. Parties are not provided for or recognized by any constitution and (at least in Germany) they are not regulated by law although they are by all odds the most important form of expression of the political preferences of the subjects of the bureaucracy, i.e., of the citizenry. Parties are — whatever may be the means by which they attach their followers to themselves — essentially voluntarily formed organizations based on free canvassing or recuitment. In these respects they are to be contrasted with all statutorily contractually circumscribed corporate bodies. Their goal is always the attraction of votes for political offices or for non-elective balloting. A stable nucleus of interested persons, under a leader or a group of unpaid amateurs and of varying degrees of formal organization — which today often takes the form of a complex bureaucracy — looks after the finances of the party with the help of party maecenases, economic interests, or groups seeking political patronage or with members' dues. Usually all of these sources of income are drawn on. This nucleus determines the program of the moment, the *modus operandi* and the candidates even in very democratic forms of mass parties. All this always and necessarily involves a complicated salaried bureaucracy.

Naturally the state bureaucracy is quite different from the party bureaucracy and within the former, the civil bureaucracy is different from the military. They in their turn are different from bureaucracy in a municipal government, in a church, in a bank, in a cartel, in an occupational association, in a factory, or in an interest group (like an employers', or farmers' association). The extent to which amateurs or materially interested persons fill the offices of these groups varies considerably from one to another. In the party the "boss" is not an "official," nor is the "director" in a corporation. In the diverse forms of "self-administration," all sorts of unpaid amateurs or elected representatives of the dominated or compulsorily burdened interested parties may collaborate in making decisions, may exercise supervisory, advisory and even occasionally executive functions *vis-à-vis* the officials. In this capacity, they may be subordinate, coequal or superordinate to the official in either corporate or individual forms. It is especially likely that they will stand in a superordinate relation in municipal governments. . . . But what concerns us here primarily is the fact that in the administration of large scale organizations, an officialdom with stipulated salaries and specialized education constitutes the nucleus of the apparatus, and its "discipline" is absolutely indispensable for its success. And what is more — as the organization increases in size and as its tasks grow more complex with the increasing dependence of its existence on power (be it power in the market, in elections, or on the battlefield) the more indispensable this type of bureaucracy becomes. It is the same with parties. A party system is doomed when as in France (the entire parliamentary disorder of which is due to the absence of bureaucratized parties) and in part as in Germany, there are still parties which still cling to a system of local administration by unpaid amateurs. It is true that this system was universal during the Middle Ages in all sorts of organizations and even today it still persists in small and middle-sized municipalities. "Eminent citizens" and "leading scientists" are useful to parties only as advertisements and not as performers of important day-to-day tasks — in the same way that all sorts of decorative dignitaries serve on the boards of directors of corporations, or in which dukes of the church function at Catholic Congresses. Or to cite further instances: pure and impure aristocrats at the meetings of the landowners' associations, or leading historians, biologists, and similar completely apolitical talents in the campaigns of the all-German associations of munitions producers or of those interested in elec-

toral privileges. The real work in all organizations is done by the paid employees and agents. Everything else is or is becoming a "front." Just as the Italians, and following them the English, developed the modern capitalistic economic organization, so the Byzantines, then the Italians, then the territorial states of the Age of Absolutism, French revolutionary centralization and finally, exceeding them all the Germans with high virtuosity developed the rational, functionally differentiated, specialized bureaucratic organization of all human associations, involving dominance relationships, from the factory to the army and the state. Only in the sphere of party organization have the Germans permitted themselves to be bested, for the time being, at least by other nations, particularly by the United States. The present World War signifies above all the triumph of this form of organization over the world. It was of course well under way already. Universities, technical and commercial colleges, industrial schools, military academies, specialized training schools of every conceivable sort (even schools of journalism!) specialized examinations as the precondition for all remunerative and therewith above all of "secure" private and public employment; the diploma as the basis of all claims to social status (marriage and social contact with those circles who designate themselves as "society"); whenever possible the secure salary with its prospect of a pension and its "appropriateness" to one's social status; improvement and advancement in accordance with seniority — all these have for some time been the true " demand of the hour " manifested in the enrollment in colleges and in the search for " livings " on the part of their products. This has gone on inside the state as well as outside it. Here we are only concerned with its consequences for political life. The harsh reality of universal bureaucratization is in truth contained in the so-called " German ideas of 1914," in what *litterateurs* call the " socialism of the future " in the slogan of " organization " in the " cooperative economy," and in all similar slogans. All of them result in the furthering of bureaucracy (even when they strive to achieve the opposite). It is of course true that bureaucracy is not the only modern form of organization by any means, just as the factory is by no means the only form of industrial organization. But they are the organizational forms of the present age and the foreseeable future. To bureaucratization belongs the future. . . .

In contrast with other historical manifestations of the modern rational mode of life, bureaucracy is characterized by its pre-eminent indispensability. There is no historical instance of its disappearance in any situation in which it achieved exclusive domination except where the entire civilization disintegrated. This is true for China, Egypt, the late Roman Empire (in a less thorough-going form) and Byzantium. And yet these represented a relatively irrational form of bureaucracy, namely, " patrimonial bureaucracy." Modern bureaucracy is distinguished from these older examples by virtue of a feature which only re-enforces its indispensability and its indissolubility, namely its rational professional specialization and training. The ancient Chinese mandarin was not a professional official; he was rather a gentleman educated in the humanities. The Egyptian, late Roman, and Byzantine officials were bureaucrats in something like our sense. But the governmental tasks for which they were responsible, were as compared with those of our day, infinitely simpler and more modest, and their behavior was regulated in part traditionally and in part patriarchally and was thereby irrationally oriented. They proceeded by empirical rule of thumb like the industrial enterpriser of the past. The modern official is becoming, in accordance with the rationalized character of modern life, increasingly more professionally trained and specialized. All bureaucracies — in all parts of the world — are moving in this direction. The fact that they did not complete this process before the war gave our bureaucracy its superiority over the rest of them. The older American official, for example, who obtained his post by party patronage was a real " connoisseur " of electoral struggle and all the devices which it required but he was in no way a professional with specialized preparation. American political corruption was due to this and not to democracy, as our literary gentlemen would like us to believe. The professional official with university training who is now emerging in the Civil Service of the United States is just as free from corruption as the modern English bureaucracy, which is increasingly supplanting " self-government " by unpaid amateurs ("gentlemen "). Once the modern trained professional official has achieved dominance, his power is unbreakable, because the entire organization of even the most elementary necessities is integrated with and dependent on his performance. An ever further-reaching elimination of private capitalism is certainly theoretically conceivable — although that is not the minor matter which many of our *littérateurs* who know nothing about it, think it is — and it certainly will not be a consequence of this war. But even if it does happen, what will be the practical result? Will the steel frame of modern industrial life be broken? No! The outcome would be that the management of the nationalized or " communal " enterprises would be bureaucratized. Is the mode of life of the white collar and manual workers in the Prussian State mining or railroad administration tangibly different from that of their counterparts in the large private capitalist enterprises? It is perhaps less free because any struggle for power which they undertake against the state bureaucracy is hopeless from the start and further because there is no authority which in principle has interests contrary to the state bureaucracy and whose power can be invoked against it. This would be the entire difference. If private capitalism were entirely eliminated, then the state bureaucracy would rule alone. There would be a fusion of the two, private and public bureaucracies, which at pres-

ent exist alongside one another and at least have the possibility of working against one another, which, in other words, can to some extent hold each other in check. The result would be like Ancient Egypt except that the modern form would be incomparably more rational and therefore all the more difficult to get rid of.

A physical machine is a rigidified product of the intellect. The fact that it is such gives it its power to force human beings into its service and to determine the course of their working life as, e.g., in the factory. The rigidified product of the mind is also represented in the " living machine " constituted by the bureaucratic organization with its specialization in trained professional work, its determination of jurisdictions, its rules, and its bureaucratically graded obedience relationships. The living machine which is bureaucracy, in co-operation with the inorganic — physical — machine, is bringing about the structure of super- and subordination which will characterize the future. In that structure human beings will be forced into impotent obedience like the fellaheens in the ancient Egyptian State. . . .

In view of the fundamental fact of the unstoppable advance of bureaucratization, the question regarding the future form of political organization can only be formulated as follows:

1. In view of the powerful tendency toward bureaucratization, how is it possible to preserve some remnant of "individualistic" freedom? For it is a very crude self-delusion to believe that we (even the most con-

servative among us) can continue to live without these values which have come down to us from the age of "the rights of man." But we will not concern ourselves with this question right now, since there is another one to which we must give our attention.

2. In view of the increasing indispensability, and the power therewith involved, of the state bureaucracy, how is it possible to obtain some assurance that groups will exist which will hold within limits and effectively control the tremendous power of this increasingly important system. What are the possibilities of democracy even in this restricted sense? But even this question is not our primary concern.

3. A third question — the most important of all — emerges from the examination of those things which the bureaucracy as such does *not* do. It is, of course, easy to establish the fixed subjective limitations of its capacity for achievement in the sphere of public governmental organizations as well as in that of private enterprise. The leading spirit — in the former the politician, in the latter the enterpriser — is not a bureaucratic official, not so much formally as substantively, since even the enterpriser sits in an "office" and the military leader no less. The military leader is an officer and formally he is no different from other officers. If the general director of a great enterprise is an appointed official of a joint-stock company, his legal status is, in principle, the same as that of the other officials. The same is true of the leading political personage in the government. The head official of a department is formally a salaried official with a right to a pension. The circumstance that in all legal systems over the whole world he can be dismissed at any time and can resign, distinguishes his service in an external manner from most officials but not all. More important, however, is the fact that there are no prescribed training requirements for him as there are for other officials. This signifies that his position is meant to be somewhat different from that of the other officials — like the enterpriser and the general director in the business firm. . . . And so it often is in reality. If a leader does his work with the attitude of a bureaucratic official, then however diligent he is — regardless of whether he is a man who is used to doing his work dutifully and honorably, following rules and orders — there is no use for him either at the head of a private business organization or at the head of a state. In our own political history, we have unfortunately often seen the truth of this.

The difference does not consist entirely in the type of expected achievement. Independent decision and organizational ability on the basis of his own ideas in matters of detail, and often in larger matters, are frequently expected from "bureaucrats" as well as from "leaders." Even the conception that the bureaucrat is exclusively occupied with subordinate humdrum routine while the leader is concerned with "interesting" tasks requiring high intellectual achievements is peculiar to *littérateurs* and is possible only in a country where there is a complete lack of insight into the nature of its leadership and the achievements of its bureaucracy. The real difference lies in the type of responsibility called for from each — and this in turn determines the type of requirements made of each. A bureaucrat, who receives a command which is, in his opinion, wrong, can — and should — raise objections. But if his superior insists on adherence to his order, then it is not only obligatory, it is required by the bureaucrat's honor, to carry it out as if it embodied his own most firmly held convictions. In doing this he shows that his feeling of responsibility to his office is higher than his devotion to his own preferences. It makes no difference whether the superior from which he receives the imperative is an " office," an " association " or an " assembly," — such is the requirement of his office. But a political leader who acted in that way would deserve nothing but contempt. He will often be compelled to compromise — i.e., to sacrifice the more important to the less important. If he is incapable of saying to his superior (be it the king or the people): either I receive *this* mandate or I resign — then he is a wretched piece of putty — and not a leader. The bureaucrat should stand "above parties," which means outside the arena of struggle for his own power. Struggle for his own power and responsibility for the policy which derives from this power should be the soul of the political leader and of the enterpriser.

53. The Study of Administration *

I suppose that no practical science is ever studied where there is no need to know it. The very fact, therefore, that the eminently practical science of administration is finding its way into college courses in this country would prove that this country needs to know more about administration, were such proof of the fact required to make out a case. It need not be said, however, that we do not look into college programmes for proof of this fact. It is a thing almost taken for granted among us,

* From Woodrow Wilson, *Political Science Quarterly*, II (1887), pp. 197–222. Reprinted through the courtesy of Mrs. Woodrow Wilson and *Political Science Quarterly*.

that the present movement called civil service reform must, after the accomplishment of its first purpose, expand into efforts to improve, not the *personnel* only, but also the organization and methods of our government offices: because it is plain that their organization and methods need improvement only less than their *personnel*. It is the object of administrative study to discover, first, what government can properly and successfully do, and, secondly, how it can do these proper things with the utmost possible efficiency and at the least possible cost either of money or of energy. On both these points there is obviously much need of light among us; and only careful study can supply that light.

Before entering on that study, however, it is needful:

I. To take some account of what others have done in the same line; that is to say, of the history of the study.

II. To ascertain just what is its subject-matter.

III. To determine just what are the best methods by which to develop it, and the most clarifying political conceptions to carry with us into it.

Unless we know and settle these things, we shall set out without chart or compass.

I

The science of administration is the latest fruit of that study of the science of politics which was begun some twenty-two hundred years ago. It is a birth of our own century, almost of our own generation.

Why was it so late in coming? Why did it wait till this too busy century of ours to demand attention for itself? Administration is the most obvious part of government; it is government in action; it is the executive, the operative, the most visible side of government, and is of course as old as government itself. It is government in action, and one might very naturally expect to find that government in action had arrested the attention and provoked the scruntiny of writers of politics very early in the history of systematic thought.

But such was not the case. No one wrote systematically of administration as a branch of the science of government until the present century had passed its first youth and had begun to put forth its characteristic flower of systematic knowledge. Up to our own day all the political writers whom we now read had thought, argued, dogmatized only about the *constitution* of government; about the nature of the state, the essence and seat of sovereignty, popular power and kingly prerogative; about the greatest meanings lying at the heart of government, and the high ends set before the purpose of government by man's nature and man's aims. The central field of controversy was that great field of theory in which monarchy rode tilt against democracy, in which oligarchy would have built for itself strongholds of privilege, and in which tyranny sought opportunity to make good its claim to receive submission from all competitors. Amidst this high warfare of principles, administration could command no pause for its own consideration. The question was always: Who shall make law, and what shall the law be? The other question, how law should be administered with enlightenment, with equity, with speed, and without friction, was put aside as " practical detail " which clerks could arrange after doctors had agreed upon principles.

That political philosophy took this direction was of course no accident, no chance preference or perverse whim of political philosophers. The philosophy of any time is, as Hegel says, " nothing but the spirit of that

time expressed in abstract thought";
and political philosophy, like philosophy of every other kind, has only
held up the mirror to contemporary
affairs. The trouble in early times
was almost altogether about the constitution of government; and consequently that was what engrossed
men's thoughts. There was little
or no trouble about administration,
— at least little that was heeded by
administrators. The functions of
government were simple, because life
itself was simple. Government went
about imperatively and compelled
men, without thought of consulting
their wishes. There was no complex system of public revenues and
public debts to puzzle financiers;
there were, consequently, no financiers to be puzzled. No one who
possessed power was long at a loss
how to use it. The great and only
question was: Who shall possess it?
Populations were of manageable
numbers; property was of simple
sorts. There were plenty of farms,
but no stocks and bonds: more cattle
than vested interests.

I have said that all this was true of
"early times"; but it was substantially true also of comparatively late
times. One does not have to look
back of the last century for the beginnings of the present complexities
of trade and perplexities of commercial speculation, nor for the portentous birth of national debts. Good
Queen Bess, doubtless, thought that
the monopolies of the sixteenth century were hard enough to handle
without burning her hands; but they
are not remembered in the presence
of the giant monopolies of the nine-

teenth century. When Blackstone
lamented that corporations had no
bodies to be kicked and no souls to
be damned, he was anticipating the
proper time for such regrets by full
a century. The perennial discords
between master and workmen which
now so often disturb industrial society began before the Black Death
and the Statute of Laborers; but
never before our own day did they
assume such ominous proportions as
they wear now. In brief, if difficulties of governmental action are
to be seen gathering in other centuries, they are to be seen culminat-
ing in our own.

This is the reason why administrative tasks have nowadays to be so
studiously and systematically adjusted
to carefully tested standards of policy,
the reason why we are having now
what we never had before, a science
of administration. The weightier
debates of constitutional principle
are even yet by no means concluded;
but they are no longer of more immediate practical moment than questions of administration. It is getting
to be harder to *run* a constitution
than to frame one.

Here is Mr. Bagehot's graphic,
whimsical way of depicting the difference between the old and the new
in administration:

In early times, when a despot wishes
to govern a distant province, he sends
down a satrap on a grand horse, and
other people on little horses; and very
little is heard of the satrap again unless he send back some of the little
people to tell what he has been doing.
No great labor of superintendence is

possible. Common rumour and casual report are the sources of intelligence. If it seems certain that the province is in a bad state, satrap No. 1 is recalled, and satrap No. 2 sent out in his stead. In civilized countries this process is different. You erect a bureau in the province you want to govern; you make it write letters and copy letters; it sends home eight reports *per diem* to the head bureau in St. Petersburg. Nobody does a sum in the province without some one doing the same sum in the capital, to " check " him, and see that he does it correctly. The consequence of this is, to throw on the heads of departments an amount of reading and labor which can only be accomplished by the greatest natural aptitude, the most efficient training, the most firm and regular industry.

There is scarcely a single duty of government which was once simple which is not now complex; government once had but a few masters; it now has scores of masters. Majorities formerly only underwent government; they now conduct government. Where government once might follow the whims of a court, it must now follow the views of a nation.

And those views are steadily widening to new conceptions of state duty; so that, at the same time that the functions of government are every day becoming more complex and difficult, they are also vastly multiplying in number. Administration is everywhere putting its hands to new undertakings. The utility, cheapness, and success of the gov-

ernment's postal service, for instance, point towards the early establishment of governmental control of the telegraph system. Or, even if our government is not to follow the lead of the governments of Europe in buying or building both telegraph and railroad lines, no one can doubt that in some way it must make itself master of masterful corporations. The creation of national commissioners of railroads, in addition to the older state commissions, involves a very important and delicate extension of administrative functions. Whatever hold of authority state or federal governments are to take upon corporations, there must follow cares and responsibilities which will require not a little wisdom, knowledge, and experience. Such things must be studied in order to be well done. And these, as I have said, are only a few of the doors which are being opened to offices of government. The idea of the state and the consequent ideal of its duty are undergoing noteworthy change; and " the idea of the state is the conscience of administration." Seeing every day new things which the state ought to do, the next thing is to see clearly how it ought to do them.

This is why there should be a science of administration which shall seek to straighten the paths of government, to make its business less unbusinesslike, to strengthen and purify its organization, and to crown its duties with dutifulness. This is one reason there is such a science.

But where has this science grown up? Surely not on this side of the sea. Not much impartial scientific method is to be discerned in our administrative practices. The poisonous atmosphere of city government, the crooked secrets of state administration, the confusion, sinecurism, and corruption ever and again discovered in the bureaus at Washington forbid us to believe that any clear conceptions of what constitutes good administration are as yet very widely current in the United States. No; American writers have hitherto taken no very important part in the advancement of this science. It has found its doctors in Europe. It is not of our making; it is a foreign science, speaking very little of the language of English or American principle. It employs only foreign tongues; it utters none but what are to our minds alien ideas. Its aims, its examples, its conditions, are almost exclusively grounded in the histories of foreign races, in the precedents of foreign systems, in the lessons of foreign revolutions. It has been developed by French and German professors, and is consequently in all parts adapted to the needs of a compact state, and made to fit highly centralized forms of government; whereas, to answer our purposes, it must be adapted, not to a simple and compact, but to a complex and multiform state, and made to fit highly decentralized forms of government. If we would employ it, we must Americanize it, and that not formally, in language merely, but radically, in thought, principle, and aim as well. It must learn our constitutions by heart; must get the bureaucratic fever out of its veins; must inhale much free American air.

If an explanation be sought why a science manifestly so susceptible of being made useful to all governments alike should have received attention first in Europe, where government has long been a monopoly, rather than in England or the United States, where government has long been a common franchise, the reason will doubtless be found to be twofold: first, that in Europe, just because government was independent of popular assent, there was more governing to be done; and, second, that the desire to keep government a monopoly made the monopolists interested in discovering the least irritating means of governing. They were, besides, few enough to adopt means promptly.

It will be instructive to look into this matter a little more closely. In speaking of European governments I do not, of course include England. She has not refused to change with the times. She has simply tempered the severity of the transition from a polity of aristocratic privilege to a system of democratic power by slow measures of constitutional reform which, without preventing revolution, has confined it to paths of peace. But the countries of the continent for a long time desperately struggled against all change, and would have diverted revolution by softening the asperities of absolute government. They sought so to perfect their machinery as to destroy all wearing friction, so to sweeten their methods with consideration for the interests of the governed as to placate all hindering hatred, and so assiduously and opportunely to offer their aid to all classes of undertakings as to render themselves indispensable to the industrious. They did at last give the people constitutions and the franchise; but even after that they obtained leave to continue despotic by becoming paternal. They made themselves too efficient to be dispensed with, too smoothly operative to be noticed, too enlightened to be inconsiderately questioned, too benevolent to be suspected, too powerful to be coped with. All this has required study; and they have closely studied it.

On this side of the sea we, the while, had known no great difficulties of government. With a new country, in which there was room and remunerative employment for everybody, with liberal principles of government and unlimited skill in practical politics, we were long exempted from the need of being anxiously careful about plans and methods of administration. We have naturally been slow to see the use or significance of those many volumes of learned research and painstaking examination into the ways and means of conducting government which the presses of Europe have been sending to our libraries. Like a lusty child, government with us has expanded in nature and grown great in stature, but has also become awkward in movement. The vigor and increase of its life has been altogether out of proportion to its skill in living. It has gained strength, but it has not acquired deportment. Great, therefore, as has been our advantage over the countries of Europe in point of ease and health of constitutional development, now that the time for more careful administrative adjustments and larger administrative knowledge has come to us, we are at a signal disadvantage as compared with the transatlantic nations; and this for reasons which I shall try to make clear.

Judging by the constitutional histories of the chief nations of the modern world, there may be said to be three periods of growth through which government has passed in all the most highly developed of existing systems, and through which it promises to pass in all the rest. The first of these periods is that of absolute rulers, and of an administrative system adapted to absolute rule; the second is that in which constitutions are framed to do away with absolute rulers and substitute popular control, and in which administration is neglected for these higher concerns; and the third is that in which the sovereign people undertake to develop administration under this new constitution which has brought them into power.

Those governments are now in the lead in administrative practice which had rulers still absolute but also enlightened when those modern days of political illumination came in which it was made evident to all but the blind that governors are properly only the servants of the governed. In such governments administration has been organized to subserve the general weal with the simplicity and effectiveness vouchsafed only to the undertakings of a single will.

Such was the case in Prussia, for

instance, where administration has been most studied and most nearly perfected. Frederic the Great, stern and masterful as was his rule, still sincerely professed to regard himself as only the chief servant of the state, to consider his great office a public trust; and it was he who, building upon the foundations laid by his father, began to organize the public service of Prussia as in very earnest a service of the public. His no less able successor, Frederic William III, under the inspiration of Stein, again, in his turn, advanced the works still further, planning many of the broader structural features which give firmness and form to Prussian administration to-day. Almost the whole of the admirable system has been developed by kingly initiative.

Of similar origin was the practice, if not the plan, of modern French administration, with its symmetrical divisions of territory and its orderly gradations of office. The days of the Revolution — of the Constituent Assembly — were days of constitution-*writing,* but they can hardly be called days of constitution-*making.* The Revolution heralded a period of constitutional development — the entrance of France upon the second of these periods which I have enumerated — but it did not itself inaugurate such a period. It interrupted and unsettled absolutism, but did not destroy it. Napoleon succeeded the monarchs of France, to exercise a power as unrestricted as they had ever possessed.

The recasting of French administration by Napoleon is, therefore, my second example of the perfecting of civil machinery by the single will of an absolute ruler before the dawn of a constitutional era. No corporate, popular will could ever have effected arrangements such as those which Napoleon commanded. Arrangements so simple at the expense of local prejudice, so logical in their indifference to popular choice, might be decreed by a Constituent Assembly, but could be established only by the unlimited authority of a despot. The system of the year VIII was ruthlessly thorough and heartlessly perfect. It was, besides, in large part, a return to the despotism that had been overthrown.

Among those nations, on the other hand, which entered upon a season of constitution-making and popular reform before administration had received the impress of liberal principle, administrative improvement has been tardy and half-done. Once a nation has embarked in the business of manufacturing constitutions, it finds it exceedingly difficult to close out that business and open for the public a bureau of skilled, economical administration. There seems to be no end to the tinkering of constitutions. Your ordinary constitution will last you hardly ten years without repairs or additions; and the time for administrative detail comes late.

Here, of course, our examples are England and our own country. In the days of the Angevin kings, before constitutional life had taken root in the Great Charter, legal and administrative reforms began to proceed with sense and vigor under the impulse of Henry II's shrewd, busy, pushing, indomitable spirit and purpose; and kingly initiative seemed destined in England, as elsewhere, to shape governmental growth at its will. But impulsive, errant Richard and weak, despicable John were not the men to carry out such schemes as their father's. Administrative development gave place in their reigns to constitutional struggles; and Parliament became king before any English monarch had had the practical genius or the enlightened conscience to devise just and lasting forms for the civil service of the state.

The English race, consequently, has long and successfully studied the art of curbing executive power to the constant neglect of the art of perfecting executive methods. It has exercised itself much more in controlling than in energizing government. It has been more concerned to render government just and moderate than to make it facile, well-ordered, and effective. English and American political history has been a history, not of administrative development, but of legislative oversight — not of progress in governmental organization, but of advance in law-making and political criticism. Consequently, we have reached a time when administrative study and creation are imperatively necessary to the well-being of our governments saddled with the habits of a long period of constitution-making. That period has practically closed, so far as the establishment of essential principles is concerned, but we cannot shake off its atmosphere. We go on criticizing when we ought to be creating. We have reached the third of

the periods I have mentioned — the period, namely, when the people have to develop administration in accordance with the constitutions they won for themselves in a previous period of struggle with absolute power; but we are not prepared for the tasks of the new period.

Such an explanation seems to afford the only escape from blank astonishment at the fact that, in spite of our vast advantages in point of political liberty, and above all in point of practical political skill and sagacity, so many nations are ahead of us in administrative organization and administrative skill. Why, for instance, have we but just begun purifying a civil service which was rotten full fifty years ago? To say that slavery diverted us is but to repeat what I have said — that flaws in our constitution delayed us.

Of course all reasonable preference would declare for this English and American course of politics rather than for that of any European country. We should not like to have had Prussia's history for the sake of having Prussia's administrative skill; and Prussia's particular system of administration would quite suffocate us. It is better to be untrained and free than to be servile and systematic. Still there is no denying that it would be better yet to be both free in spirit and proficient in practice. It is this even more reasonable preference which impels us to discover what there may be to hinder or delay us in naturalizing this much-to-be-desired science of administration.

What, then, is there to prevent?

Well, principally, popular sovereignty. It is harder for democracy to organize administration than for monarchy. The very completeness of our most cherished political successes in the past embarrasses us. We have enthroned public opinion; and it is forbidden us to hope during its reign for any quick schooling of the sovereign in executive expertness or in the conditions of perfect functional balance in government. The very fact that we have realized popular rule in its fulness has made the task of *organizing* that rule just so much the more difficult. In order to make any advance at all we must instruct and persuade a multitudinous monarch called public opinion — a much less feasible undertaking than to influence a single monarch called a king. An individual sovereign will adopt a simple plan and carry it out directly: he will have but one opinion, and he will embody that one opinion in one command. But this other sovereign, the people, will have a score of differing opinions. They can agree upon nothing simple: advance must be made through compromise, by a compounding of differences, by a trimming of plans and a suppression of too straightforward principles. There will be a succession of resolves running through a course of years, a dropping fire of commands running through a whole gamut of modifications.

In government, as in virtue, the hardest of hard things is to make progress. Formerly the reason for this was that the single person who was sovereign was generally either selfish, ignorant, timid, or a fool — albeit there was now and again one who was wise. Nowadays the reason is that the many, the people, who are sovereign have no single ear which one can approach, and are selfish, ignorant, timid, stubborn, or foolish with the selfishnesses, the ignorances, the stubbornnesses, the timidities, or the follies of several thousand persons — albeit there are hundreds who are wise. Once the advantage of the reformer was that the sovereign's mind had a definite locality, that it was contained in one man's head, and that consequently it could be gotten at; though it was his disadvantage that that mind learned only reluctantly or only in small quantities, or was under the influence of some one who let it learn only the wrong things. Now, on the contrary, the reformer is bewildered by the fact that the sovereign's mind has no definite locality, but is contained in a voting majority of several million heads; and embarrassed by the fact that the mind of this sovereign also is under the influence of favorites, who are none the less favorites in a good old-fashioned sense of the word because they are not persons but preconceived opinions; i.e., prejudices which are not to be reasoned with because they are not the children of reason.

Wherever regard for public opinion is a first principle of government, practical reform must be slow and all reform must be full of compromises. For wherever public opinion exists it must rule. This is now an axiom half the world over, and will presently come to be believed even in Russia. Whoever would effect a change in a modern constitutional government must first educate his fellow citizens to want *some* change. That done, he must persuade them to want the particular change he wants. He must first make public opinion willing to listen and then see to it that it listen to the right things. He must stir it up to search for an opinion, and then manage to put the right opinion in its way.

The first step is not less difficult than the second. With opinions, possession is more than nine points of the law. It is next to impossible to dislodge them. Institutions which one generation regards as only a makeshift approximation to the realization of a principle, the next generation honors as the nearest possible approximation to that principle, and the next worships as the principle itself. It takes scarcely three generations for the apotheosis. The grandson accepts his grandfather's hesitating experiment as an integral part of the fixed constitution of nature.

Even if we had clear insight into all the political past, and could form out of perfectly instructed heads a few steady, infallible, placidly wise maxims of government into which all sound political doctrine would be ultimately resolvable, *would the country act on them?* That is the question. The bulk of mankind is rigidly unphilosophical, and nowadays the bulk of mankind votes. A truth must become not only plain but also commonplace before it will be seen by the people who go to their work very early in the morning; and not to act upon it must involve great and pinching inconveniences before these same people will make up their minds to act upon it.

And where is this unphilosophical bulk of mankind more multifarious in its composition than in the United States? To know the public mind of this country, one must know the mind, not of Americans of the older stocks only, but also of Irishmen, of Germans, of Negroes. In order to get a footing for new doctrine, one must influence minds cast in every mould of race, minds inheriting every bias of environment, warped by the histories of a score of different nations, warmed or chilled, closed or expanded by almost every climate of the globe.

So much, then, for the history of the study of administration, and the peculiarly difficult conditions under which, entering upon it when we do, we must undertake it. What, now, is the subject-matter of this study, and what are its characteristic objects?

II

The field of administration is a field of business. It is removed from the hurry and strife of politics; it at most points stands apart even from the debatable ground of constitutional study. It is a part of political life only as the methods of the counting-house are a part of the life of society; only as machinery is part of the manufactured product. But it is, at the same time, raised very far above the dull level of mere technical detail by the fact that through its greater principles it is directly connected with the lasting maxims of political wisdom, the permanent truths of political progress.

The object of administrative study is to rescue executive methods from the confusion and costliness of empirical experiment and set them upon foundations laid deep in stable principle.

It is for this reason that we must regard civil-service reform in its present stages as but a prelude to a fuller administrative reform. We are now rectifying methods of appointment; we must go on to adjust executive functions more fitly. and to prescribe better methods of executive organization and action. Civil-service reform is thus but a moral preparation for what is to follow. It is clearing the moral atmosphere of official life by establishing the sanctity of public office as a public trust, and, by making the service unpartisan, it is opening the way for making it businesslike. By sweetening its motives it is rendering it capable of improving its methods of work.

Let me expand a little what I have said of the province of administration. Most important to be observed is the truth already so much and so fortunately insisted upon by our civil-service reformers; namely, that administration lies outside the proper sphere of *politics*. Administrative questions are not political questions. Although politics sets the tasks for administration, it should not be suffered to manipulate its offices.

This is distinction of high authority; eminent German writers insist upon it as of course. Bluntschli, for instance, bids us separate administration alike from politics and from law.

Politics, he says, is state activity "in things great and universal," while "administration, on the other hand," is "the activity of the state in individual and small things. Politics is thus the special province of the statesman, administration of the technical official." "Policy does nothing without the aid of the administration"; but administration is not therefore politics. But we do not require German authority for this position; this discrimination between administration and politics is now, happily, too obvious to need further discussion.

There is another distinction which must be worked into all our conclusions, which, though but another side of that between administration and politics, is not quite so easy to keep sight of: I mean the distinction between *constitutional* and administrative questions, between those governmental adjustments which are essential to constitutional principle and those which are merely instrumental to the possibly changing purposes of a wisely adapting convenience.

One cannot easily make clear to every one just where administration resides in the various departments of any practicable government without entering upon particulars so numerous as to confuse and distinctions so minute as to distract. No lines of demarcation, setting apart administrative from nonadministrative functions, can be run between this and that department of government without being run up hill and down dale, over dizzy heights of distinction and through dense jungles of statutory enactment, hither and thither around "ifs" and "buts," "whens" and "howevers," until they become lost to the common eye not accustomed to this sort of surveying, and consequently not acquainted with the use of the theodolite of logical discernment. A great deal of administration goes about *incognito* to most of the world, being confounded now with political "management," and again with constitutional principle.

Perhaps this ease of confusion may explain such utterances as that of Niebuhr's: "Liberty," he says "depends incomparably more upon administration than upon constitution." At first sight this appears to be largely true. Apparently facility in the actual exercise of liberty does depend more upon administrative arrangements than upon constitutional guarantees; although constitutional guarantees alone secure the existence of liberty. But — upon second thought — is even so much as this true? Liberty no more consists in easy functional movement than intelligence consists in the ease and vigor with which the limbs of a strong man move. The principles that rule within the man, or the constitution, are the vital springs of liberty or servitude. Because dependence and subjection are without chains, are lightened by every easy-working device of considerate, paternal government, they are not thereby transformed into liberty. Liberty cannot live apart from constitutional principle; and no administration, however perfect and liberal its methods, can give men more than a poor counterfeit of liberty if it rest upon illiberal principles of government.

A clear view of the difference between the province of constitutional law and the province of administrative function ought to leave no room for misconception; and it is possible to name some roughly definite criteria upon which such a view can be built. Public administration is detailed and systematic execution of public law. Every particular application of general law is an act of administration. The assessment and raising of taxes, for instance, the hanging of a criminal, the transportation and delivery of the mails, the equipment and recruiting of the army and navy, etc., are all obviously acts of administration; but the general laws which direct these things to be done are as obviously outside of and above administration. The broad plans of governmental action are not administrative; the detailed execution of such plans is administrative. Constitutions, therefore, properly concern themselves only with those instrumentalities of government which are to control general law. Our federal constitution observes this principle in saying nothing of even the greatest of the purely executive offices, and speaking only of that President of the Union who was to share the legislative and policy-making functions of government, only of those judges of highest jurisdiction who were to interpret and guard its principles, and not of those who were merely to give utterance to them.

This is not quite the distinction between Will and answering Deed, because the administrator should have and does have a will of his own in the choice of means for accomplishing his work. He is not and ought not to be a mere passive instrument. The distinction is between general plans and special means.

There is, indeed, one point at which administrative studies trench on constitutional ground — or at least upon what seems constitutional ground. The study of administration, philosophically viewed, is closely connected with the study of the proper distribution of constitutional authority. To be efficient it must discover the simplest arrangements by which responsibility can be unmistakably fixed upon officials; the best way of dividing authority without hampering it, and responsibility without obscuring it. And this question of the distribution of authority, when taken into the sphere of the higher, the originating functions of government, is obviously a central constitutional question. If administrative study can discover the best principles upon which to base such distribution, it will have done constitutional study an invaluable service. Montesquieu did not, I am convinced, say the last word on this head.

To discover the best principle for the distribution of authority is of greater importance, possibly, under a democratic system, where officials serve many masters, than under others where they serve but a few. All sovereigns are suspicious of their servants, and the sovereign people is no exception to the rule; but how is its suspicion to be allayed by *knowledge?* If that suspicion could but be clarified into wise vigilance, it would be altogether salutary, if that vigilance could be aided by the unmistakable placing of responsibility, it would be altogether beneficent. Suspicion in itself is never healthful either in the private or in the public mind. *Trust is strength* in all relations of life; and, as it is the office of the constitutional reformer to create conditions of trustfulness, so it is the office of the administrative organizer to fit administration with conditions of clear-cut responsibility which shall insure trustworthiness.

And let me say that large powers and unhampered discretion seem to me the indispensable conditions of responsibility. Public attention must be easily directed, in each case of good or bad administration, to just the man deserving of praise or blame. There is no danger in power, if only it be not irresponsible. If it be divided, dealt out in shares to many, it is obscured; and if it be obscured, it is made irresponsible. But if it be centered in heads of the service and in heads of branches of the service, it is easily watched and brought to book. If to keep his office a man must achieve open and honest success, and if at the same time he feels himself intrusted with large freedom of discretion, the greater his power the less likely is he to abuse it, the more is he nerved and sobered and elevated by it. The less his power, the more safely obscure and unnoticed does he feel his position to be, and the more readily does he relapse into remissness.

Just here we manifestly emerge upon the field of that still larger question — the proper relations between public opinion and administration.

To whom is official trustworthiness to be disclosed, and by whom is it to be rewarded? Is the official to look to the public for his meed of praise and his push of promotion, or only to his superior in office? Are the people to be called in to settle administrative discipline as they are called in to settle constitutional principles? These questions evidently find their root in what is undoubtedly the fundamental problem of this whole study. That problem is: What part shall public opinion take in the conduct of administration?

The right answer seems to be, that public opinion shall play the part of authoritative critic.

But the *method* by which its authority shall be made to tell? Our peculiar American difficulty in organizing administration is not the danger of losing liberty, but the danger of not being able or willing to separate its essentials from its accidents. Our success is made doubtful by that besetting error of ours, the error of trying to do too much by vote. Self-government does not consist in having a hand in everything, any more than housekeeping consists necessarily in cooking dinner with one's own hands. The cook must be trusted with a large discretion as to the management of the fires and the ovens.

In those countries in which public opinion has yet to be instructed in its privileges, yet to be accustomed to having its own way, this question as to the province of public opinion is much more readily soluble than in this country, where public opinion is wide awake and quite intent upon having its own way anyhow. It is pathetic to see a whole book written by a German professor of political science for the purpose of saying to his countrymen, " Please try to have an opinion about national affairs "; but a public which is so modest may at least be expected to be very docile and acquiescent in learning what things it has *not* a right to think and speak about imperatively. It may be sluggish, but it will not be meddlesome. It will submit to be instructed before it tries to instruct. Its political education will come before its political activity. In trying to instruct our own public opinion, we are dealing with a pupil apt to think itself quite sufficiently instructed beforehand.

The problem is to make public opinion efficient without suffering it to be meddlesome. Directly exercised, in the oversight of the daily details and in the choice of the daily means of government, public criticism is of course a clumsy nuisance, a rustic handling delicate machinery. But as superintending the greater forces of formative policy alike in politics and administration, public criticism is altogether safe and beneficent, altogether indispensable. Let administrative study find the best means for giving public criticism this control and for shutting it out from all other interference.

But is the whole duty of administrative study done when it has taught the people what sort of administration to desire and demand, and how to get what they demand? Ought it not to go on to drill candidates for the public service?

There is an admirable movement towards universal political education now afoot in this country. The time will soon come when no college of respectability can afford to do without a well-filled chair of political science. But the education thus imparted will go but a certain length. It will multiply the number of intelligent critics of government, but it will create no competent body of administrators. It will prepare the way for the development of a sure-footed understanding of the general principles of government, but it will not necessarily foster skill in conducting government. It is an education which will equip legislators, perhaps, but not executive officials. If we are to improve public opinion, which is the motive power of government, we must prepare better officials as the *apparatus* of government. If we are to put in new boilers and to mend the fires which drive governmental machinery, we must not leave the old wheels and joints and valves and bands to creak and buzz and clatter on as best they may at bidding of the new force. We must put in new running parts wherever there is the least lack of strength or adjustment. It will be necessary to organize democracy by sending up to the competitive examinations for the civil service men definitely prepared for standing liberal tests as to technical knowledge. A technically schooled civil service will presently have become indispensable.

I know that a corps of civil servants prepared by a special schooling and drilled, after appointment, into a perfected organization, with appropriate hierarchy and characteristic discipline, seems to a great many very thoughtful persons to contain elements which might combine to make an offensive official class — a distinct, semi-corporate body with sympathies divorced from those of a progressive, free-spirited people, and with hearts narrowed to the meanness of a bigoted officialism. Certainly such a class would be altogether hateful and harmful in the United States. Any measures calculated to produce it would for us be measures of reaction and of folly.

But to fear the creation of a domineering, illiberal officialism as a result of the studies I am here proposing is to miss altogether the principle upon which I wish most to insist. That principle is, that administration in the United States must be at all points sensitive to public opinion. A body of thoroughly trained officials serving during good behavior we must have in any case: that is a plain business necessity. But the apprehension that such a body will be anything un-American clears away the moment it is asked, What is to constitute good behavior? For that question obviously carries its own answer on its face. Steady, hearty allegiance to the policy of the government they serve will constitute good behavior. That *policy* will have no taint of officialism about it. It will not be the creation of permanent officials, but of statesmen whose responsibility to public opinion will be direct and inevitable.

Bureaucracy can exist only where the whole service of the state is removed from the common political life of the people, its chiefs as well as its rank and file. Its motives, its objects, its policy, its standards, must be bureaucratic. It would be difficult to point out any examples of impudent exclusiveness and arbitrariness on the part of officials doing service under a chief of department who really served the people, as all our chiefs of departments must be made to do. It would be easy, on the other hand, to adduce other instances like that of the influence of Stein in Prussia, where the leadership of one statesman imbued with true public spirit transformed arrogant and perfunctory bureaux into public-spirited instruments of just government.

The ideal for us is a civil service cultured and self-sufficient enough to act with sense and vigor, and yet so intimately connected with the popular thought, by means of elections and constant public counsel, as to find arbitrariness or class spirit quite out of the question.

III

Having thus viewed in some sort the subject-matter and the objects of this study of administration, what are we to conclude as to the methods best suited to it — the points of view most advantageous for it?

Government is so near us, so much a thing of our daily familiar handling, that we can with difficulty see the need of any philosophical study of it, or the exact point of such study,

should it be undertaken. We have been on our feet too long to study now the art of walking. We are a practical people, made so apt, so adept in self-government by centuries of experimental drill that we are scarcely any longer capable of perceiving the awkwardness of the particular system we may be using, just because it is so easy for us to use any system. We do not study the art of governing: we govern. But mere unschooled genius for affairs will not save us from sad blunders in administration. Though democrats by long inheritance and repeated choice, we are still rather crude democrats. Old as democracy is, its organization on a basis of modern ideas and conditions is still an unaccomplished work. The democratic state has yet to be equipped for carrying those enormous burdens of administration which the needs of this industrial and trading age are so fast accumulating. Without comparative studies in government we cannot rid ourselves of the misconception that administration stands upon an essentially different basis in a democratic state from that on which it stands in a non-democratic state.

After such study we could grant democracy the sufficient honor of ultimately determining by debate all essential questions the public weal, of basing all structures of policy upon the major will; but we would have found but one rule of good administration for all governments alike. So far as administrative functions are concerned, all governments have a strong structural likeness; more than that, if they are to be uniformly useful and efficient, they *must* have a strong structural likeness. A free man has the same bodily organs, the same executive parts, as the slave, however different may be his motives, his services, his energies. Monarchies and democracies, radically different as they are in other respects, have in reality much the same business to look to.

It is abundantly safe nowadays to insist upon this actual likeness of all governments, because these are days when abuses of power are easily exposed and arrested, in countries like our own, by a bold, alert, inquisitive, detective public thought and a sturdy popular self-dependence such as never existed before. We are slow to appreciate this; but it is easy to appreciate it. Try to imagine personal government in the United States. It is like trying to imagine a national worship of Zeus. Our imaginations are too modern for the feat.

But, besides being safe, it is necessary to see that for all governments alike the legitimate ends of administration are the same, in order not to be frightened at the idea of looking into foreign systems of administration for instruction and suggestion; in order to get rid of the apprehension that we might perchance blindly borrow something incompatible with our principles. That man is blindly astray who denounces attempts to transplant foreign systems into this country. It is impossible: they simply would not grow here. But why should we not use such parts of foreign contrivances as we want, if they be in any way serviceable? We are in no danger of using

them in a foreign way. We borrowed rice, but we do not eat it with chopsticks. We borrowed our whole political language from England, but we leave the words " king " and " lords " out of it. What did we ever originate, except the action of the federal government upon individuals and some of the functions of the federal supreme court?

We can borrow the science of administration with safety and profit if only we read all fundamental differences of condition into its essential tenets. We have only to filter it through our constitutions, only to put it over a slow fire of criticism and distil away its foreign gases.

I know that there is a sneaking fear in some conscientiously patriotic minds that studies of European systems might signalize some foreign methods as better than some American methods; and the fear is easily to be understood. But it would scarcely be avowed in just any company.

It is the more necessary to insist upon thus putting away all prejudices against looking anywhere in the world but at home for suggestions in this study, because nowhere else in the whole field of politics, it would seem, can we make use of the historical, comparative method more safely than in this province of administration. Perhaps the more novel the forms we study the better. We shall the sooner learn the peculiarities of our own methods. We can never learn either our own weaknesses or our own virtues by comparing ourselves with ourselves. We are too used to the appearance and procedure of our own system to see its true significance. Perhaps even the English system is too much like our own to be used to the most profit in illustration. It is best on the whole to get entirely away from our own atmosphere and to be most careful in examining such systems as those of France and Germany. Seeing our own institutions through such *media,* we see ourselves as foreigners might see us were they to look at us without preconceptions. Of ourselves, so long as we know only ourselves, we know nothing.

Let it be noted that it is the distinction, already drawn, between administration and politics which makes the comparative method so safe in the field of administration. When we study the administrative systems of France and Germany, knowing that we are not in search of *political* principles, we need not care a peppercorn for the constitutional or political reasons which Frenchmen or Germans give for their practices when explaining them to us. If I see a murderous fellow sharpening a knife cleverly, I can borrow his way of sharpening the knife without borrowing his probable intention to commit murder with it; and so, if I see a monarchist dyed in the wool managing a public bureau well, I can learn his business methods without changing one of my republican spots. He may serve his king; I will continue to serve the people; but I should like to serve my sovereign as well as he serves his. By keeping this distinction in view — that is, by studying administration as a means of putting our own politics into convenient practice, as a means of making what is democratically politic towards all administratively possible towards each — we are on perfectly safe ground, and can learn without error what foreign systems have to teach us. We thus devise an adjusting weight for our comparative method of study. We can thus scrutinize the anatomy of foreign governments without fear of getting any of their diseases into our veins; dissect alien systems without apprehension of blood-poisoning.

Our own politics must be the touchstone for all theories. The principles on which to base a science of administration for America must be principles which have democratic policy very much at heart. And to suit American habit, all general theories must, as theories, keep modestly in the background, not in open argument only, but even in our minds — lest opinions satisfactory only to the standards of the library should be dogmatically used, as if they must be quite as satisfactory to the standards of practical politics as well. Doctrinaire devices must be postponed to tested practices. Arrangements not only sanctioned by conclusive experience elsewhere but also congenial to American habit must be preferred without hesitation to theoretical perfection. In a word, steady, practical statesmanship must come first, closet doctrine second. The cosmopolitan what-to-do must always be commanded by the American how-to-do-it.

Our duty is, to supply the best possible life to a *federal* organization, to systems within systems; to make town, city, county, state, and federal governments live with a like strength and an equally assured healthfulness, keeping each unquestionably its own master and yet making all interdependent and co-operative, combining independence with mutual helpfulness. The task is great and important enough to attract the best minds.

This interlacing of local self-government with federal self-government is quite a modern conception. It is not like the arrangements of imperial federation in Germany. There local government is not yet, fully, local *self*-government. The bureaucrat is everywhere busy. His efficiency springs out of *esprit de corps,* out of care to make ingratiating obeisance to the authority of a superior, or, at best, out of the soil of a sensitive conscience. He serves, not the public, but an irresponsible minister. The question for us is, how shall our series of governments within governments be so administered that it shall always be to the interest of the public officer to serve, not his superior alone but the community also, with the best efforts of his talents and the soberest service of his conscience? How shall such service be made to his commonest interest by contributing abundantly to his sustenance, to his dearest interest by furthering his ambition, and to his highest interest by advancing his

honor and establishing his character? And how shall this be done alike for the local part and for the national whole?

If we solve this problem we shall again pilot the world. There is a tendency — is there not? — a tendency as yet dim, but already steadily impulsive and clearly destined to prevail, towards, first the confederation of parts of empires like the British, and finally of great states themselves. Instead of centralization of power, there is to be wide union with tolerated divisions of prerogative. This is a tendency towards the American type — of governments joined with governments for the pursuit of common purpose, in honorary equality and honorable subordination. Like principles of civil liberty are everywhere fostering like methods of government; and if comparative studies of the ways and means of government should enable us to offer suggestions which will practicably combine openness and vigor in the administration of such governments with ready docility to all serious, well-sustained public criticism, they will have approved themselves worthy to be ranked among the highest and most fruitful of the great departments of political study. That they will issue in such suggestions I confidently hope.

54. Role Conceptions in Bureaucracy*

The social scientist has traversed the subject matter of bureaucracy with a variety of problems and interests, ranging from the historical descriptions of concrete instances of bureaucratic structures to theoretical frameworks designed to order the essential bureaucratic mechanisms. Its importance as an area for study increases with the realization that this form of organization [1] is becoming increasingly typical of the structures of American society as evidenced in the bureaucracies of government, education, labor, politics, and industry.

One of the major problems with which the sociologists has grappled in his approach to the subject has been that of clarifying the relation of the *informal* organization and social processes to the *formal* relationships and status positions as ordered by the bureaucratic rules. Any separation by the researcher of these two areas, which are in fact so functionally interrelated, leads to a limited or partial presentation of the real subject matter.

Phrased around the concept of "social role," the empirical study which is here presented seeks to accomplish two objectives: 1) to present data on American bureaucrats — a stratum of professionally-trained specialists in a State civil service; [2] and 2) to present the theoretical framework within which this study was conducted, as a suggested resolution of the methodologically created dichotomy of informal-formal structures in the study of bureaucratic organizations.[3]

THE THEORETICAL FORMULATION

An adequate sociological presentation of bureaucracy must include the formal structure, the interpersonal relationships within it, and the effects of the surrounding social milieu. These three aspects can be interrelated in the " social role " which the bureaucratic official fulfills, as that role mirrors both the formal and informal structures, as well as the culture of which he is obviously a part. The following quotation from George H. Mead presents the social psychological mechanism of role-taking, where " role " is defined as the expected or recurrent behavior in a given situation:

[2] This might be considered as the middle stratum, between the policy-makers at the top and the highly routinized clerical workers at the bottom.

[3] *Cf.* Philip Selznick, " An Approach to a Theory of Bureaucracy," *American Sociological Review*, 8: 47–54 (February 1943), as an example of emphasis upon the informal structures. Also, Robert K. Merton, " Bureaucratic Structure and Personality," *Social Forces*, 18: 560–68 (May 1940), as an example of emphasis upon the formal structure and the personality characteristics to be deduced from it.

* From Leonard Reissman, *A Study of Role Conceptions in Bureaucracy.* *Social Forces*, XXVII (1949), pp. 305–10. Reprinted by permission of Leonard Reissman and *Social Forces*.

[1] H. H. Gerth and C. W. Mills, " A Marx for the Managers," *Ethics*, 52: 200–15 (January 1942).

. . . the human organism may arouse the same response . . . in itself which it aroused through its gesture in the other form (other human organism) and it finds itself, therefore, in the attitude of the other in so far as this attitude which it calls out in another is called out in itself.

Such a pattern would only be present in so far as it served a function. The advantage of the individual approaching his own response from the standpoints of those also involved in the same conduct is evident enough. It would need to be present in the emphasis which it would give to appropriate responses of the individual. . . .

A matter of very great importance in connection with this consideration is *the organization of the conduct of the individual about this pattern of group activities, and in so far as these group activities are interrelated, about the pattern of the group conduct as a whole. . . . The self, then, would inevitably be organized about the pattern of the group activities in so far as they are unitary.* In various respects this is the case, and those respects are particularly important to the individual. They are those in which the individual has specific functions, duties, rights, and privileges in the group.[4]

Two factors are important in the use of the concept of " social role." First, the social role must always be seen in terms of a given social situation. Secondly, allowance must be made for a range of individual role fulfillment based upon that person's experiences and values, if the *concept* of a social role is to be more adequately expressive of an *acting* individual. The alternative is rejected —that of structuring the social role exclusively in terms of the situation and ideal behavior patterns derived therefrom with little or no concern for modifications due to individual definitions. Such an approach would lead to formulations of behavior based solely upon logically derived extensions of an ideal-type concept of bureaucratic organizations.[5]

The problem posed by this study was to determine what the civil servant conceived his social role to be. In addition to " role," a corollary conceptual tool was introduced. The content of the responses given by the bureaucrats was viewed as constituting a synthesis of three functionally interrelated levels of defining the situation in which the role is performed. The first consists of the culturally prescribed behavior which conforms to the normative standards of the society. The respect for individuality, the altruistic submergence of individual ends for the good of the group, and the qualities of amiability in dealing with people are indicative of such values to which the civil servant, as a member of society, gives credence. The second level consists of the bureaucratically defined behavior required by the formal structure of the organization. The duties, the authority, and the responsibilities which inhere in the office

---

[4] George H. Mead, *Philosophy of the Act,* edited by Charles W. Morris and others (Chicago: University of Chicago Press, 1938), pp. 448–49. (Italics mine).

[5] The reasoning followed in this instance derives the personality characteristics most suited for a given ideal form of bureaucratic organization. *Cf.* Merton, *op. cit.*

occupied by the individual civil servant carry with them highly explicit definitions of relationships and functions. The third level is that of the individually defined behavior which takes into account not only the requirements already distinguished, but also adds to it the unique individual elements. This includes the final synthesis of the individual's experience and the conception upon which he acts.[6]

The situational background against which this particular social role was performed was the bureaucratic form of administrative organization, which has been given its most explicit theoretical treatment by Max Weber.[7] Briefly, it is characterized by an emphasis upon a rational organization ordered by rules, a high degree of disciplined behavior, an established office hierarchy, clearly-defined areas of power for each office, and appointed specialists to fill these offices. The civil servant of this study then, is seen as a bureaucratic official or specialist in a midwestern State government. He has shown qualifications (by means of a technical examination) to fulfill the duties ascribed to the given office which he holds.

[6] It would be unreal to omit the individual category in our framework. Even though it is methodologically necessary to concentrate upon a single role among the many which individuals fulfill, there is obviously a psychological unity (the total individual) throughout this segmentalized behavior.

[7] From Max Weber: *Essays in Sociology*, transl. & edited by H. H. Gerth and C. W. Mills (New York: Oxford University Press, 1946), chap. VIII. *The Theory of Social and Economic Organization*, transl. by A. M. Henderson and T. Parsons (New York: Oxford University Press, 1947), pp. 329–41.

Seven areas of investigation were delineated to obtain necessary content on the role conceptions of this stratum of bureaucratic officials:

1. The reasons given by the civil servant and the surrounding conditions for his entry into the service.
2. His evaluation of his contact with the public in his official capacity.
3. The content and pattern of his interaction with fellow employees both within and outside of the office situation.
4. His occupational aspirations and life plans, and a self evaluation of his achievement in both spheres.
5. The mores of behavior in the office and in the community.
6. His intellectual dilemmas interpreted as possible or actual conflicts between the job and a professional ethos, and/or between the job and expressed public opposition.
7. The extent to which the civil servant identifies himself with the public bureaucracy.

METHODOLOGY OF THE STUDY

A note on the methodology of this study will serve not only to relate the theoretical framework presented above with the findings which follow, but also to present more concretely the characteristics of those bureaucrats being dealt with.

Information as to salary, job assignment, education, place and extent of public contact was already available from the personnel records of a 10 percent random sample (705 cases) of the seven thousand civil service employees of the State.[8] Three discriminating criteria, whose use was dictated by the nature of the problem, were then applied against the sample 705 cases. The first criterion, evidence of successful completion of a course of college work, was applied as the only expedient and reasonably accurate measure of possession of certain technical and professional skills. The second criterion, evidence of contact with the public, was employed because it was felt that the highest degree of role awareness would be found among those who daily were being made conscious of their bureaucratic positions by such official public contact. A final criterion selected only those civil servants whose office headquarters were in the capital city, inasmuch as the expense involved in covering all areas of the State was prohibitive.

A universe of 263 cases thus was obtained for this study, focusing on that corps of bureaucrats charged with the interpretation and daily administration of the policies handed down to them by the elected legislators in the Capitol Building. The army of highly routinized stenographic and clerical workers was excluded from the limits of the problem. The universe was stratified according to salary and place of public contact (office or community) and a sample was drawn conforming to these proportions. Intensive interviewing was accomplished for 40 cases (15 percent),

although certain statistics were obtained for an additional 60 cases from this universe.[9] Further characteristics of the bureaucrats of this study show them to average 49.8 years of age, earning $321 per month, with 17 years of continuous service.

The civil servants were interviewed on the job and their responses were recorded verbatim, except for the material gained during a free conversation period immediately following each interview. The data were analyzed by delineating categories for each question asked in the interview, and testing for the significance of the difference of the frequencies thus obtained. Replies to several questions were juxtaposed for the purposes of analysis, although they had been separated in the interview schedule to serve as cross-checks.

Findings of the Study

An informative result of this study appeared when the concept of a single individual type was broken down to order the greater flexibility which was found to exist. In the literature, the trend has been to blot out individual differences in favor of a single type which fails to capture the subtle and complex background of the individual in the bureaucratic situation. In reviewing the interview data it was found that the subjects of this study exhibited allegiances not only to their job and the gov-

[8] Prof. Useem had drawn this sample after excluding those who were assigned either to: 1) state hospitals, penal institutions, and colleges; or 2) an agency which had less than 10 persons assigned to it.

[9] Tests of significance between those cases interviewed and the additional 60 cases were computed for differences in age, place of birth, year of entry into civil service, and salary. These tests further assured the representativeness of the sample interviewed.

ernment which employed them, but also to professional organizations, to particular groups who were serviced or regulated by their bureau, and to other social constellations within the community. The seven areas of investigation noted above were treated first as discrete units in each individual case to determine the direction and nature of the subject's allegiance. Abbreviated examples of the direction followed at this point will serve to clarify this procedure.

Under the first section of the interview, the reasons given for entry into civil service showed either a positive and planned decision by the subject, or a negative one such as: " It was during the depression years and this opportunity came along." From other questions in this section the extent of activity in professional societies (holding office, attendance of conventions and meetings, etc.) was determined. Finally, the subject was asked to indicate whether he would derive more satisfaction from being recognized for the work he was performing by the people in his own department or by those in a similar profession.

Responses given in the second section of the interview were surveyed to determine whether the subject insisted upon a high degree of formality in dealing with the public with whom he came into contact or whether such contact rather was characterized by a greater informality. Here, too, the extent to which the civil servant felt the public made him aware of being " a government official " was sought, and the effect which such awareness played

in his relations with that public.

In the third section, the following points were focused upon: whether the source of satisfaction with the job was basically oriented toward " things " or " people ";[10] from which groups were close friendships sought (other civil servants, other professions, business men, etc.); and finally was the strength of the individual's feeling of belonging with other office personnel high or low as reflected in frequent identity of interests and exchange of invitations for meeting outside of the office.

The content and self-rating of the individual's aspirations and achievements were sought in the fourth section of the interview. Did he plan to remain in civil service or was he still speaking of leaving at the first opportunity to accept employment elsewhere? Were his future aspirations tinged with concerns for promotion within the service, or with attaining greater status among members of his own profession, or did they focus more directly upon " private " aspirations of owning a home or a car? Did he feel that he ranked favorably or not when he compared himself to like professionals who were privately employed?

In the fifth section, the responses were grouped to determine whether the individual defined the " good " civil servant principally according to a standard of job proficiency or according to one of general personal qualities such as amiability, sincerity, and the like. Also surveyed here

[10] Cf. Alexander H. Leighton, The Governing of Men (Princeton: Princeton University Press, 1943).

was whether a high or low degree of "rule consciousness" was present, and whether or not the conduct of civil servants in the community was predicated upon a standard which was peculiar to them as an occupational group.

The information obtained in the sixth section exhibited the strength which the requirements of the job exercised when compared with the felt demands of a professional group and of the public generally. That is, the direction in which the civil servant would tend when confronted with such a series of choices.

Finally, the limits of the individual's conception of his place in the bureaucracy were appraised as to whether he was aware of the problems of other departments in the government and what he defined as "bureaucracy."

Each individual's responses were then charted to show whether his selection of means in performing the job and the stated goals to which he felt his job was contributing were directed toward or away from the bureaucratic structure. In other words, was he appraising himself *primarily* as a civil servant or did this particular job situation rather enter into the configuration as modified and secondary to other lines of affiliation? For example, the bureaucrat who has conceived his role about a strong professional ethos considers his government employment as just a place to do the work for which he has been trained. The bureaucrat who is more deeply imbedded psychologically in the service, on the contrary, is consciously and continually aware of his position as a government official and acts accordingly. The orientation of these two extreme types toward the matter of "rules" for example, are similarly opposed and a degree of leniency in the first instance and overstrictness in the second were evident.

The substantive content for each of the four bureaucratic types which follow represents only a beginning formulation in that the necessary criteria for delineating the individual in each empirical instance have not been sufficiently sharpened in this study. They represent more accurately a potential tool in the analysis of the "bureaucratic personality"; in capturing more adequately the ranges of real variation with the formal organization. They also present a means of ordering the data within the informal organization and indicate the consequences which the behavior of each type presents. They are included as ideal-types at present for these reasons.

The first type is the *Functional Bureaucrat* — one who is oriented towards and seeks his recognition from a given professional group outside of rather than within the bureaucracy. He may be portrayed as a professional who "just happens to be working for the government." His evaluations of success and accomplishment are not measured in terms of satisfactorily fulfilling a given bureaucratic policy or aim (over and above that required of him in the position), but rather in terms of the professional quality with which he does his job. Psychologically he is facing outward and away from the bureaucratic structure. He entered civil service because it offered material advantages and allowed him to do unique or specialized professional work. He is active in his professional societies and seeks appreciation and recognition on the basis of his professional specialities. Avoiding any identification with the office group, he declines any such intimacy with other civil servants because it is based only upon a common work situation. His future plans include doing research along lines of professional interests. His standards for the "good" civil servant are the standards of success in the profession, and not necessarily related to success in the bureaucracy. He feels no conflict between his professional ethics and his job because only the former standard exists for him. The bureaucracy imposes certain well-defined limitations upon him, but within these he is professionally biased.

The second type is the *Specialist Bureaucrat*. Though he resembles the first type in his professional orientations, he exhibits a greater awareness of an identification with the bureaucracy. He seeks his recognition from the department and the people with whom he works rather than from like-professionals who are privately employed. He entered civil service for "negative" reasons, i.e., he was forced in because of the depression or a business failure. Though he contacts other professional people, he remains aware of the difference between them and himself as a government employee. The ambivalent nature of his position is evident throughout — the orientation

to his professional status on the one hand, and his position within the bureaucratic hierarchy on the other. This is more pointedly shown in his aspirations which evidence a desire to "get ahead" in his profession, yet realizing that this must occur through the mechanism of the bureaucratic promotion system. Overly meticulous about the rules and regulations, he attempts always to remain safely within these limits.

The third type is the *Service Bureaucrat*. Here too, as noted in the preceding type, a position of ambivalence is created. He is oriented in terms of the bureaucratic structure, but seeks recognition for the job he does from a group outside of it. He entered civil service primarily to realize certain personally-held goals which center about rendering service to a certain group.[11] The bureaucracy offers a framework through which he can best function and his task is one of utilizing that mechanism to achieve his goals.

The last type is the *Job Bureaucrat*. He is immersed entirely within the structure. Professional skills only provide the necessary entrance qualifications and determine the nature of the work to be done. He seeks recognition along departmental rather than professional lines. Satisfactions are found in the technical aspects of the work itself, and improvement of the operating efficiency of the bureau becomes an end in itself. His aspirations consist of achieving material re-

[11] He need not himself be a member of that group as, for example, in the case of the civil servant who renders service to handicapped children.

wards and increased status through promotions. He strongly adheres to the rules and the job constitutes his full center of attention and the end to be served.

The over-all role conceptions as they mirror the three levels of situational definitions presented in the theoretical formulations above present additional data.[12] The civil servant readily identifies himself as working for the goals of the bureaucracy at those points which explicitly embody the ideal cultural values to which a democratic form of government is traditionally dedicated. He feels, therefore, that in his position he is "working for the good of the public" and that he is constantly "aware of the best interests of the public." Such values, however, undergo modification and interpretation as the bureaucrat is faced with fulfilling the requirements of his job. Hence, he is most pleased with those people who cooperate, follow instructions, and take the advice he offers, i.e., allow *him* to determine which course of action is to the "best interests of the public." He feels, too, that "the public" treats him as "just another government official" according to popular evaluations of government administration, instead of as an individual. This situation poses a dilemma for him, in that he desires on the one hand to be treated as an individual rather than as a cog in a machine, and yet on the other hand desires to retain his superordinate position which the bureaucratic rules reserve for him in his public contacts.

The bureaucratic structure also imposes certain values which must be incorporated into these role conceptions. Hence, we find that the "good" civil servant is one "who can get along with people," who is "honest" and "loyal" to the department, and who is not so ambitious that he is constantly striving to "get ahead" even though promotions might not be immediately available. There is the recognition that higher supervisory positions carry with them more discretionary power to modify existing regulations in certain cases. Such changes will be made more readily while working in the field rather than in the office, although the civil servant feels no greater psychological tension in one place as compared to the other. It is significant to note that his conceptions of bureaucratic organization are similar to those held by the public. He believes, for example, that government administration is less efficient than that of private organizations, and that personal merit and faithful service are more readily recognized in private employment. Also, the term "bureaucracy" is for him descriptive of the operation of the Federal government and he does not believe that "we have any 'bureaucracy' in this State."

That part of the role conceptions which incorporates the values on the individual level have been partly implied in the presentation of the bureaucratic types. Personal aspirations center about raising one's standard of living rather than specifically

---

[12] These conclusions are based upon a statistically significant frequency of responses in each generalization.

about job promotions. However, the level of achievement is appraised most often on a standard based upon psychic as contrasted with material rewards. Accordingly, the civil servant can rate himself equally with a similar age and professional stratum in the community. However, when he uses a standard of material rewards, he ranks himself below average as a consequence. He frequently speaks of changing to private employment or going into business for himself, but such mobility is often verbalized but rarely acted upon.[13]

Finally, the civil servant does not feel that he is part of a "government class" but instead indentifies himself with other class and status groups in the community. This is bolstered by seeking his close friendships from professional and business people who are not employed by the government.[14] Naturally, the civil servant feels quite certain that there is no difference in the personalities attracted to civil service as contrasted to private organizations.

[13] This generalization is limited by the fact that the sample interview obviously includes only those civil servants who have chosen to remain in the service.

[14] All responses to this point indicated that those who are employed in the State university are not considered as "other civil servants" although a strict definition would most certainly include them.

Conclusions

The concept of "role" offers a valuable tool for the study of bureaucracy in at least two important ways. First, it serves to focus upon the basic content and processes in the bureaucratic situation through the individuals actually involved. A range of individual variation is thus more easily grasped from which empirically derived types can then be constructed. Secondly, it serves to synthesize information gained from other relevant areas. White's studies[15] of the public's evaluations of the prestige of government employment and Kingsley's work[16] on the historical dynamics surrounding civil service reforms in England are but two examples of valuable corollaries against which the bureaucrat's role conceptions can be placed and interpreted.

Too often the personalities are overlooked as important data in the analysis of bureaucracy, although the individuals on all administrative levels who make the mechanism function are quite obviously an integral part of such study.

[15] Leonard D. White, *Prestige Value of Public Employment* (Chicago: University of Chicago Press, 1929); *Further Contributions to the Prestige Value of Public Employment* (Chicago: University of Chicago Press, 1932).

[16] J. Donald Kingsley, *Representative Bureaucracy* (Yellow Springs: Antioch Press, 1944).

55. Congressional Control of the Public Service*

Since the English Revolution of 1688, it has been a part of the Anglo-American tradition that elected representative assemblies control the policies and acts of the executive branch of the government. This doctrine was firmly embedded in the American state and federal constitutions. With some wartime reservations, it has been universally accepted throughout our country. At the present time, however, there is an uneasy feeling that practice does not square with theory. There is even a suspicion that practice contradicts theory — that a vast body of officials has in fact escaped the possibility of control by the people's representatives.

The trends of the last half-century have certainly complicated the problem of congressional authority over administration. This has occurred in part because administration has made impressive gains in effective organization and operation, while relatively Congress has stood still. Within the administrative system there has developed a capacity for self-direction which might well challenge the dominance of Congress, if Congress continues to be the laggard partner in the governmental team.

The fact that Congress has declined in public esteem and in com-

* From Leonard D. White, *The American Political Science Review*, XXXIX (1945), pp. 1–11. Reprinted by permission of Leonard D. White and *The American Political Science Review*.

parison with the executive branch is so apparent that Congress itself is preparing to take reformatory steps. I do not propose to discuss the difficult problem of congressional organization. I merely argue that reform is essential if Congress intends to control administration. I must, however, make some assumptions about the future organization of Congress, since if it remains unreformed I despair of effective and intelligent control over the public service. For the purpose of this discussion, I therefore assume (1) that the majority party in each House will assert more effective power to control its own members and the business of Congress; (2) that congressional committees will be reduced in number and made responsible to each House; and (3) that the seniority rule will be abolished. These are minimum requirements, however difficult of realization.

I

Some contend that no improvements in Congress are likely to be enough; that the range and complexity of public administration are such that its control by a representative assembly has become impossible. The author of *The Managerial Revolution* argued that officials have already usurped the very essence of congressional power by determining public policy. Officials are certainly active participants. Some believe that Congress has lost the capacity to arrive at a formulation of policy except under compulsion from outside, especially the compulsion of the executive branch. There is much in the record to support this view. Some claim that the "bureaucracy" has acquired a capacity for resistance which puts it beyond the reach of amateurs. There is evidence to sustain this contention. We can all agree that the mere existence of a federal civilian army probably destined to remain at not less than a million and a half, armed with wide discretionary powers and possessing both intelligence and a sense of direction, presents a problem of control. If we intend to remain citizens of a republic and masters of our future, we may well take note.

I assert, nevertheless, that congressional control of the administrative system is not only democratically essential but also technically feasible. It is not feasible, however, on the pattern of the eighteenth and nineteenth centuries, projected into the twentieth. The forms of control which Congress now understands and tries to use are not especially good for control and are sometimes bad for administration. They need to be thoughtfully reconsidered.

The indictment against the existing system of congressional control is impressive. It is basically control over details, not over essentials. It is negative and repressive rather than positive and constructive. It reflects fear rather than confidence. It is sometimes irresponsible. It is based on no rational plan, but is an accumulation of particulars whose conse-quences are seldom seen in perspective. Congress has done both too much and too little in trying to discharge this phase of its responsibilities. It needs a Committee on Congressional Management to do for it what the President's Committee on Administrative Management did for him.

Without presenting the specifications of the indictment, a few particulars may be suggested by way of illustration. The *Statutes at Large* and the annual appropriation acts are cluttered with a mass of detailed prohibitions and limitations upon administrative action. They represent in part a process of legislation by exasperation. Unfortunately, these often petty restrictions tend to continue and to accumulate. They hamper good administration and miss the mark as a means of control.

The mass of legislation governing the housekeeping activities of government departments became so great by 1930 that escape was necessary for the pioneering ventures of the New Deal. Congress deliberately released the Tennessee Valley Authority and some other government corporations from part of the restrictions placed upon older established agencies. The General Accounting Office and Congress itself have both looked upon this freedom with a jaundiced eye, and it tends gradually to disappear. One may take the view that a degree of freedom was good for the T.V.A. and would also be good in due measure for the whole federal system. Congress has apparently taken the view that freedom is progressively less good for the

T.V.A. and is dangerous in principle.

Obviously, Congress is in error when it asserts control by making particular administrative decisions. This temptation, however, continues to be strong. For example, Congress requires senatorial confirmation of appointments of certain middle management officials. This is an invasion of an area definitely administrative, not policy-making. It is motivated either by a taste for patronage or by the natural desire of congressmen to protect themselves against the political consequences of administrative bungling in their states or districts. The attempt of Congress to force the removal of three named persons — Messrs. Lovett, Dodd, and Watson — is an example of congressional interference at its lowest level. In still another direction Congress recently invaded the proper field of administrative decision by reserving the right to decide from time to time how much oil could be produced from certain naval reserves. The President protested this action, but was forced to yield.

These criticisms of some of the forms of congressional control of the administrative system are not intended to cast any doubt on the desirability or necessity of such control. I would argue, indeed, that we need increasingly effective supervision by Congress as the powers of officials increase, their discretion expands, and their numbers multiply. My argument is that we are likely to get progressively less effective supervision unless Congress changes its tactics and strengthens its own position.

The task is to devise a system of congressional control which will be adequate to democratic purposes without at the same time impairing the capacity of public officials to operate efficiently. This balance cannot be attained by any simple formula. A solution is complicated by the fact that Congress (the controlling body) is " a numerous assembly " unaccustomed to close internal discipline, with a changing personnel periodically absent from the seat of government, whereas the public service (the agency to be controlled) constitutes a vast permanent heirarchy of trained, professional, and relatively disciplined officials.

The two essential objects which Congress must achieve are, first, to ensure that its mandates on public policy prevail, and, second, to ensure that the execution of public policy avoids waste, incompetence, and the unnecessary public inconvenience. I propose to explore each of these essentials in turn.

II

Congress in theory has, of course, complete control of public policy, at least in the domestic field. Some congressmen believe that they are losing control of policy, because bills originate elsewhere, because departments and agencies are developing their rule-making powers on an ever-increasing scale, because they suspect their policy is not always fully observed in the course of administration, and because they fear administrative action may foreclose a future policy decision by Congress.

Although it is important to conserve congressional control of policy, it is not necessary or desirable to require congressmen to originate all the bills. Congress first shared this duty with officials in September, 1789, when it asked Alexander Hamilton to bring in recommendations on the public revenue and discharged its own committee from further consideration of this subject. In recent years, the administrative agencies have carried an ever larger part of the task of policy initiation and first formulation, and properly so.

The need for effective coördination of administrative rules with statutes presents a more important consideration. One of the most effective means of securing an appropriate control of the rule-making power, without hampering administrative operations, is to follow the procedure applied in 1939 in connection with plans for administrative reorganization. Here the initiative lay with the President, who was authorized to prepare plans for submission to Congress. Each plan was to lay on the table for sixty days and to become effective unless, within this period, the two Houses disapproved by a concurrent resolution.

Except in emergency cases, Congress might properly require basic administrative rules imposing obligations upon citizens to be reported to it in this manner, and to be subject to a legislative veto. This practice has long been accepted by the British House of Commons in dealing with provisional orders.

It is also important to ensure that administrative action accords with congressional policy and to give Congress a more effective sense of participation in early stages of policy formation. The policy conferences which Secretary Hull held with members of the Senate Foreign Relations Committee suggest a useful line of experiment. A large part of the major issues of public policy could be included within a small number of such conferences: for example, foreign policy, including military and naval programs; fiscal policy; social security policy and veterans' benefits; business policy; and resources policy.

This proposal assumes, let me repeat, that the committee system has been reformed, that the seniority rule has been abandoned, that the majority party has accepted effective responsibility for directing the business of Congress, and that consequently confidential discussions of policy will not be reported to the press. Policy conferences would be seriously handicapped as long as the seniority rule prevails; length of service on a committee is no guarantee of party confidence or personal restraint. Such conferences would be devoted to broad policy orientation rather than to the terms of a particular bill; indeed they should normally precede the stage of bill-drafting. They would occur at frequent intervals, and would be participated in only by members of the majority party. On the administrative side, the participants would include department and agency heads and their policy advisers; members of permanent staffs would be present only to furnish data, otherwise their status would be undermined with a change of party.

It is unnecessary to argue that Congress can secure firmer control of policy by enacting laws which are neither vague nor ambiguous. These criteria are impossible to achieve when the mind of Congress is confused or divided. Unfortunate is the lot of the official who has then to decide his course of action; he must make his own contribution to policy with the high probability that he will offend one section of congressional opinion. To congressmen may be commended the moral virtue of charity as they review the decisions of their agents.

Apart from the gains arising from greater precision in drafting legislation, I would therefore argue that Congress may be better assured of genuine control of policy by adopting the provisional-order technique as a means of reviewing administrative rules, and by cultivating policy conferences with top executive officials in the most important and most controversial areas of public action.

The House Select Committee to Investigate Executive Agencies recently recommended another type of policy control: a permanent joint standing committee to ascertain whether the laws are executed according to the intent of Congress. I doubt whether any single committee can advise the departments and agencies of the intent of Congress throughout the length and breadth of public policy as stated in federal legislation. There are other and better ways of determining the intent of Congress; and it is not necessary to set up a standing committee to prevent deliberate neglect or defiance of the will of Congress by any administrative agency.

III

The second major objective of congressional control is to ensure that public policy is executed efficiently, without waste, and without undue public inconvenience. Congress has a duty to watch the course of administration, consult with officials, criticize administrative policies and performance, and conduct formal investigations. But it can make its contribution to efficiency only by a substantial degree of abnegation — by giving up the practice of criticizing details in favor of a genuine over-all supervision achieved through a few really effective administrative controls within the executive branch.

If Congress must, in its own interest, forego control of details, what form of action can it undertake to compel high standards of performance? The answer is, it must concern itself with the improvement of the administrative system, and with creating the conditions of employment which attract a superior type of public official. Congress needs to face the task of creating a *system* which tends to produce competence rather than incompetence, responsibility rather than irresponsibility. If incompetence does occur, the essential question for Congress to ask is: What is wrong with the system of administration or the quality of management which permitted it to develop? The essential remedy for Congress to apply is not to discipline individuals or agencies (although discipline may sometimes be necessary), but to insist upon the improvement of the system and the quality of management. Only by bringing the administrative system to a high point of perfection can official stagnation or incompetence be reduced to the minimum which an imperfect world must tolerate.

The historic instrument of congressional criticism and investigation is the standing or special committee. The Interstate Commerce Committee of the Senate, the Civil Service Committee of the House, and the Truman Committee illustrate what can be achieved under favorable circumstances and with stable leadership. These forms of legislative control are pervasive and important. An intelligent public official proceeds on the assumption that he may have to explain his every act before a congressional committee. While this is a salutary climate for official life, it can quickly induce an insidious form of sleeping sickness unless Congress exercises its power with restraint, and constructively. A hostile remark by a congressman in a committee hearing, or even worse on the floor of the House, induces tremors throughout the official world. But congressional wrath is not necessarily control, and official trepidation not necessarily conformity. The problem remains of translating undoubted congressional influence on administrative performance into intelligent ultimate control of standards of administrative excellence.

It has been proposed to increase the influence of the present commit-

tees by attaching to each of them a small staff of experts, who could balance the influence of the experts who speak for the departments and agencies. The proposal to equip committees with technical staffs raises some serious questions. It would probably increase the potential rivalry between the subject-matter committees and the Appropriations Committees. It would also lessen the probability — remote enough at best — of substituting joint committees for separate, independent, and sometimes hostile committees of the two Houses. It would set the stage for conflict between two sets of " experts," or potentially three — one in the House, one in the Senate, and one in the department. It would incur the danger of administrative management by a committee chairman and his experts. Much worse, it would fasten the present committee structure upon Congress; for the existing vested interests of chairmen would be buttressed by those of technical staffs. I do not, therefore, favor staffs for congressional committees until the committee system itself has been reformed. A rational committee system, however, would strengthen the case for small committee staffs. I do not need to add that a system which allotted one committee to each department, agency, authority, office, corporation, and commission would not be rational; it would be positively dangerous.

Parenthetically, one improvement is greatly needed in committee contacts — an improvement too subtle to be subject to legislation or standing orders. I refer to the need for protecting officials and citizens against the unintelligent and intemperate attacks to which they are sometimes subjected by committee members. Two instances will illustrate my point: the attacks upon officials of the Tennessee Valley Authority at hearings in the Senate, and the recent investigation of the Federal Communications Commission in the House. Congress can ill afford to allow such displays of arrogance or such punitive expeditions. They impair respect for Congress and for congressmen, and raise questions about congressional powers which ought not to be open to discussion.

To keep congressional use of the power to criticize on the level of decency is a responsibility of Congress itself. It can be achieved best by the unwritten code of each House. The prescriptions of this code derive from practice — but practice is molded by leadership and by the behavior of the men who have earned the respect of their colleagues. In ways which are subtle but none the less compelling, the behavior of a small minority who do not understand the ordinary courtesies of human contact and the purposes of congressional control can be curbed and ought to be disciplined.

To return to my principal theme — Congress cannot through fifty committees or fifteen become a board of efficiency engineers. No board of directors of a great business organization would undertake to solve its operating problems. The directors do enough when they require a system of management properly de-

signed to produce results, and secure top business executives of a high order of competence. The control function of Congress is analogous. Congress should bend its efforts to create a system of administration based on the best known practice and should provide conditions of employment which will attract able men and women. If then incompetence or official arrogance appears, Congress should find out where the system is at fault and insist upon a remedy.

Congress needs some means other than private complaint to keep informed of official incompetence. It is now moved to action principally by complaint — sometimes justified and sometimes not. As a complaint bureau, Congress might take itself less seriously than it has at times. Like its presumed agent, the General Accounting Office, it has been known to waste endless time and energy on inconsequential trivialities while serious waste and mismanagement went unnoticed. The problem at this point is to devise institutional means of bringing to the attention of Congress the really important issues of administration, and to aid Congress in finding genuinely effective solutions.

The House Select Committee to Investigate Executive Agencies recently proposed to place this function in a joint standing committee on appropriations, with the help of a joint legislative staff.[1] This recommendation is entitled to respect. It might, however, have the unde-

[1] House Report No. 1912, 78th Cong., 2nd Sess., Nov. 20, 1944.

sirable effect of diverting the Appropriations Committee from its main functions — to weigh the great competing claims upon the Treasury in the scales of the general interest and to adjust the volume of public expenditures to safeguard the public economy. These tasks are so important and so different in kind from the task of considering administrative performance that it is open to question whether they should be combined.

There is an acceptable alternative. Congress has an established agency of its own which is in touch with every unit of the administrative machine, the General Accounting Office. It has been permitted to operate on the level of details, not on the level of principle, and to extend its authority far beyond an audit. In consequence, Congress may have acquired a sense of security against embezzlement, but it has been gained at a heavy and unnecessary cost in economy and efficiency. The President's Committee on Administrative Management proposed to convert this office into one concerned only with an audit. Such a change is long overdue. If the General Accounting Office could be induced to abandon the search for petty errors and devote itself to advising Congress on major administrative problems revealed by the audit, it would become an instrument of far greater value to the American people. It could then perform for our government the function that the British Comptroller and Auditor General performs for his government — responsible criticism of administrative

operations on the broadest scale. Congress can bring this reform to pass only by new directives involving important changes in the character of the General Accounting Office. Furthermore, Congress itself should select the Auditor General and make him fully responsible to it. A new congressional Joint Committee on Executive Agencies and Procedures would then have a significant and challenging opportunity to improve administration by dealing with principle rather than with the complaints of disappointed and disgruntled individuals.

IV

The apparent dilemma presented by the need for legislative control of a powerful public service and the need for relative freedom of official action to secure sound management is in truth a perplexing one. As a student of public administration, I probably am more sensitive to the need for a free hand for officials, at least in the service functions of government. But Congress must have ultimate control of policy and its execution. I urge that it settle on principle and avoid detail. To control policy as it is defined in administrative rules, the provisional-order technique deserves attention. To participate in policy in its formative stages, the device of congressional-executive policy conferences might be useful. To ensure high standards of administrative performance, Congress can make its greatest contribution by building up the administrative system and by depending largely on its internal controls. A reformed committee system would continue the function of consultation, criticism, and occasional investigation; but as committees become more powerful, they need to be on guard lest they take over in fact some of the responsibilities of administration. The greatest single asset of Congress to guarantee sound administration might be a transformed General Accounting Office, restricted to an audit but strengthened to become an office of administrative intelligence acting on behalf of the two Houses. These innovations would, in my judgment, help achieve a satisfactory balance; they would go far to strengthen Congress without impairing the necessary authority of the executive branch of the government.

In closing this paper, I reëmphasize familiar ground — the great objectives to be secured by congressional control of administration. They are close to the heart of democratic institutions, since an uncontrolled body of permanent officials and employees would almost certainly degenerate into a bureaucracy, with all the unpleasant connotations of that word. It is the duty of Congress to be ever on guard against official sloth, stupidity, arrogance, or corruption. Apart from the courts, the elected representative is the principal protection of the humble citizen against abuse of the great powers which officials possess. We must always remember, however, that power may be beneficent; and in a democracy it is presumed to be directed toward beneficent ends. Congress faces, therefore, a delicate problem of balance — it must control with enough certainty of touch to guarantee a responsible and responsive public service; but it must refrain from impairing the capacity of the public service to achieve the great social purposes to which it is dedicated.

56. Marxism and Free Parties*

The centennial of the publication of the *Communist Manifesto* is a reminder of the diverse and unreconciled aspirations of 1848. Since that critical year, and particularly since the death of Marx and Engels, a number of far-reaching developments have taken place in democratic theory and practise — develop-

ments that run sometimes far beyond and sometimes directly counter to the basic concepts of the two great philosophers of socialism.

An important case in point is the contrast and even outright contradiction between (a) the modern conception of political parties widely accepted by democratic theorists, both socialist and non-socialist, in England and America, and (b) the views on this subject, or often the lack of them, of Marx and Engels.

* From Robert A. Dahl, *The Journal of Politics*, X (1948), pp. 787–813. Reprinted by permission of Robert A. Dahl and *The Journal of Politics*.

The current "democratic" assumptions about political parties, constituting a doctrinal position often defended with almost religious intensity, may be summarized roughly as follows:

Proposition I: Conflicts in interests or freely expressed wants seem to be inevitable in any complex society.

Proposition II: (a) Such conflicts ought ultimately to be resolved by a majority rule.

(b) Government by majority rule necessarily includes the "right" of a minority to attempt by persuasion to become a majority.

Proposition III: These propositions, together with the difficulty of "securing" a majority view in a large and complicated society, indicate the need for freedom to form political parties, and for freedom of competition among political parties, as the well-nigh indispensable means for determining and enforcing what the majority wants.

If we examine the works and letters of Marx and Engels, we discover little that throws any direct light on these propositions, and particularly on the third.

Be it noted, Marx and Engels did not fail to concern themselves with parties in their practical activities. Marx, for example, was interested in one revolutionary party or another from the age of 30 until his death. He never questioned the need of political instruments for achieving the social objectives to which he so completely dedicated his life. "The philosophers have only interpreted the world in various ways; the point, however, is to change it" — and to change the world requires political organization. Marx's address to the Communist League in 1850 furnishes a picture of the 32-year-old intellectual as a leader of the revolutionary party: intense, angry, uncompromising, cocky, no doubt rather typical of the intellectual revolutionary intent on power for himself and his cause — and too much aggrieved by the enemy's misuse of power to be concerned with the way power might endanger the ultimate realization of his own objectives.

Yet there is little evidence that his experience with parties caused him to reflect much on the role, if any, that such organizations were to play *within the socialist society* of the future. We find Engels in his old age — and after an experience with parties greater than that of Marx — reflecting briefly on the significance of political parties and the electoral struggle *as means to power*. But the integration of these reflections into the corpus of the earlier, basic writings of Marx and himself is a task for which Engels apparently saw no need. Certainly he did not attempt it.

So we are left with two questions. First, why did Marx and Engels, two of the most original and inventive minds of the 19th century, fail to deal with this problem? And second, the more fundamental question: is there a conflict between the Marxism of Marx and Engels (as distinct from that of their successors) and the propositions of democratic theory set forth above?

It is no part of my purpose here

to defend the validity of the propositions of modern democratic theory
given above, but simply to explore
the relationship between these propositions and Marxist theory. *A priori,*
there are at least these possible answers to the questions just given:

1. Marx and Engels avowedly opposed
   the general objective of popular control over government. I.e., they
   were explicitly opposed to " democracy " itself.
2. They assumed that conflicts of interest or want would not exist in a
   socialist society. I.e., they rejected
   Proposition I.
3. They did not accept the validity of
   majority rule as a device for resolving conflict in a socialist society.
   I.e., they rejected Proposition II a)
   and II b).
4. They accepted one or both of these
   propositions, but rejected (or failed
   to draw) the conclusions drawn
   from them by many modern democratic theorists. I.e., they rejected
   Proposition III.

I. MARXISM AND POPULAR CONTROL

That Marx and Engels thought
they were engaged in a struggle for
some form of " democratic " government, is, on any careful reading
of their works, undeniable.

Although even as early as the
Communist Manifesto Marx and
Engels were speaking in general
terms of the need " to win the battle
of democracy," their writings before 1871, the year of the Paris Commune, shed little light on their conception of a working class democ-

racy. The Commune, in many ways
the great historic event of their lives,
elicited not only the clearest but also
the first full statement they ever
made on proletarian democracy.
More than once, Marx and Engels
were to speak of the political forms
of the Paris Commune as a true
representation of what they meant
by the dictatorship of the proletariat.
" Its true secret," Marx said of the
Commune in 1871, " was this. It was
essentially a working-class government, the product of the struggle of
the producing against the appropri-
ating class, the political form at last
discovered under which to work out
the economical emancipation of Labour." In 1891, eight years after
Marx had died and four years before
his own death, Engels looked back
on the Commune and, doubtless
with an old man's nostalgic remembrance of his life's great events, was
able to say: " Of late the German
Philistine has once more been filled
with wholesome terror at the words:
Dictatorship of the Proletariat. Well
and good, gentlemen, do you want
to know what this dictatorship looks
like? Look at the Paris Commune.
That was the Dictatorship of the
Proletariat."

To Marx and Engels, the Paris
Commune created a wholly new
form of state that guaranteed control
by the proletariat. Both expressed
an enthusiasm for certain forms of
direct democracy practised in the
commune, forms that in Marx's and
Engels' view wholly transformed
the state. These were: (1) the election of all officials — administrative,
judicial, educational — by universal

suffrage. (2) " The right of electors to recall their delegates at any time." (3) The payment of all officials at worker's wages. (Engels spoke of these three as " infallible expedients " against " transformation of the State and the organs of the State from the servants of society into masters of society — a process which had been inevitable in all previous States.") (4) " The fusion of administrative and legislative at the sametime," said Marx. (5) Free public education. (6) " Suppression of the standing army, and the substitution for it of the armed people." (7) Disestablishment of " disendowment " of all churches. (8) Performance by a central government of " the few but important functions which would still remain " after the country was fully organized into Communes like the one in Paris. The central government was to be conducted by a National Delegation in Paris, chosen by district assemblies composed of delegates from rural and urban Communes. The national delegate was to be a " strictly responsible agent " and " at any time revocable and bound by the *mandat imperatif* of his constituents."

What is significant by contrast with modern democratic theory is the point at which the analysis of Marx and Engels abruptly halts. That they saw and approved in the Commune a wide variety of instrumentalities for democratic control is evident. *What they neither asserted nor anywhere implied was the need for political parties to operate within the democratic framework of the Commune.*

Both Marx and Engels were aware that conflicts of interest and opinion occurred in the Commune — conflicts that in a ·democratic system, according to our propositions, would be handled by means of competing parties operating through the electoral process and majority rule. Even while the Commune was still in existence, Marx saw that the Commune was beset with conflicting points of view. " The Commune," he wrote in May, 1871, " seems to me to be wasting too much time in trivialities and personal quarrels. One can see that there are other influences besides that of the workers." Ten years later Marx pointed out that the " majority of the Commune was in no sense socialist." And a decade later, in his eulogy of the Commune, Engels referred in some detail to the conflicting viewpoints even among the socialists; the majority, he said, were followers of Blanqui, and even the minority (members of the International) were disciples of Proudhon rather than of Marx.

Yet, having recognized these conflicts, Marx and Engels stopped; they never concerned themselves with the crucial problem in all known societies of how to handle the conflicts between the various groups. By majority rule? If so, does this imply the formation of parties and an appeal to the electorate on all the critical issues? By minority coercion? If so, who is to apply the force — one wing of the proletarian movement against the rest of the proletariat and the whole burgeoisie? Or may conflicts be expected to vanish, after any future revolution, because of the universal acceptance of Marxism? Still, as Marx himself was wholly aware, even " Marxists " may differ over programs and policies.

In fact, Marx and Engels never considered these problems. Their endorsement of the democratic techniques of the Commune would seem to suggest that they would have approved the resolution of conflict by the democratic process of party competition at the polls. But they offered no concrete proposals in this sense.

For this neglect, a number of explanations suggest themselves.

II. MARXISM AND THE DOCTRINE OF HARMONY

According to the propositions of democratic theory set forth above, political parties are needed in a " democracy " only because there are conflicting purposes and outlooks within the corresponding society: in a society in which such conflicts exist there must be machinery for crystallizing majority support for policies and programs in the disputed areas. But political parties would be superfluous in a society without significant disagreements or conflict; policy decisions would then no longer divide the citizens, and parties would have no function to perform. Was this latter, perhaps, the view of Marx and Engels?

A. Harmony and the dialectic. A condition of social harmony is one of civilized man's oldest dreams, one so recurrent that surely it must appeal to some persistent inner needs

of the social man — or at least to those of the intellectual. This dream had suffused the writings of St. Simon, Fourier, and Owen, as, for that matter, it had pervaded much of eighteenth century thought. In sharp contrast to their immediate predecessors, Marx and Engels, like Hegel and Darwin, helped to substitute for the static, mechanistic, Newtonian concepts of the eighteenth century and the socialist Utopians, a view that runs in terms of a long evolution, marked by struggle, conflict, contradiction, and even annihilation. And yet, by one of their most impressive and influential paradoxes, they retained the older harmony ideal side by side with their destruction of all logical basis for such an ideal.

Thus we find Engels insisting on the one hand that the dialectical process of development is a permanent feature of human history, embedded in the very structure of the universe, and describing the " negation of the negation " as " an extremely general — and for this reason extremely comprehensive and important — law of development of nature, history and thought, a law which . . . holds good in the animal and plant kingdom, in geology, in mathematics, in history and in philosophy." On such a showing, it would be reasonable to suppose that society, like nature, would develop through conflict; and that even a socialist or communist society would contain inner conflicts forcing its continual development. We find Engels arguing, on the contrary, that with adequate knowledge and economic reconstruction social conflict could be eliminated.

Moreover, Marx and Engels never really tried to reconcile the dialectical process with their versions of the "social harmony" that ought to follow the completed revolution. They were prepared to argue that man, by recognizing and understanding the laws of social development, would be able to *control* social relationships for the first time; yet they never faced up to the fact that just as the discovery of "laws" operating in the physical universe to control it did not change those laws, by the same token there is no reason to expect the discovery of the "laws" of development in history to suspend the operation of those laws. Either, that is to say, dialectical development is a permanent aspect of society, in which case conflict must be forever characteristic of social organization; or dialectical development is *not* a permanent characteristic of society, in which case it is nonsense to say that the science of dialectics applies equally to history and to nature. The democratic theorist might conceivably reconcile his theory of democracy with one or the other of these positions but obviously not with both at the same time.

B. The Harmony Ideal in Marxism. At one level of analysis, Marx and Engels, like their Utopian predecessors, regarded social conflict as a product of man's institutions, and held that a revolutionary transformation of these institutions would ultimately so reduce social contention that no instruments of political coercion like the state would be needed. "In place of the old bourgeois society, with its classes and class antagonisms," Marx and Engels forecast in the *Communist Manifesto,* "we shall have an association in which the free development of each is the condition for the free development of all." Or as Engels put it thirty years later in *Anti-Dühring,* "As soon as there is no longer any class of society to be held in subjection; as soon as, along with class domination and the struggle for individual existence based on the former anarchy of production, the collisions and excesses arising from these have also been abolished, there is nothing more to be repressed which would make a special repressive force, a state, necessary." And the Apocalyptic vision goes on: "The interference of the state power in social relations becomes superfluous in one sphere after another, and then ceases of itself . . . the state is not 'abolished,' *it withers away."*

Although it is by no means obvious that this conclusion can live at ease with the ubiquitous dialectic, it does follow logically from certain assumptions of Marx and Engels about the nature of political conflict. In their view, political conflict is a reflection of the relationships between economic classes. "Political power, properly so called," they said in the *Communist Manifesto,* "is merely the organized power of one class for oppressing another." To say that political power determines economic relations, Engels later argued in criticising Dühring's theory of force, is to put the cart before the horse. "All political power is originally based on an economic, social function," and when political power comes into opposition with economic development " the contest has always ended with the downfall of the political power." Do away with economic classes, then, and in the long run you will do away with " politics " and political coercion. " When, in the course of development," runs the *Communist Manifesto,* " class distinctions have disappeared, and all production has been concentrated in the hands of a vast association of the whole nation, the public power will lose its political character." To sum up: if political conflict stems from class conflict, if class conflict results from the mode of production, if at a certain state of development the transformation of the means of production into state property " puts an end to all class differences and class antagonisms," then it follows that political conflict will disappear. And if political conflict disappears, there will be no need for a state.

What bearing do these assumptions and conclusions of Marx and Engels have on the role of political parties? Two logical inferences suggest themselves. In the first place, *until* the disappearance of class conflict, parties must either reflect that conflict or their rivalry has no historical significance. Either, that is to say, party conflict is a sort of optical illusion; or else it is an expression, direct or indirect, of the underlying conflict of economic classes. As we shall see later, when Marx and Engels observed the party conflicts of contemporary Europe, they seemed to find great empirical support for these

alternatives. Either party disputes appeared to be mere quarreling, among a fundamentally united bourgeoisie, over the spoils derived from capitalist exploitation, and were therefore, to Marx and Engels, without historical importance, or else the conflict was only a reflection of the basic struggle between bourgeoisie and proletariat. On neither view was the question of preserving the free party system in a transitional socialist order likely to appear as a problem worth speculating about.

And in the second place, *after* the disappearance of class conflict, parties would cease to have any function. Machinery for arriving at a " political " decision (i.e., a state-enforced decision) is, by definition, necessary only so long as there are social conflicts in the arbitration of which state power must be employed. If the new economic organization ultimately renders the state obsolete, *a fortiori* it will make parties and party conflict superfluous. While Marx and Engels never explicitly developed this last conclusion about parties, it is a clear inference from their basic view of the withering away of the state. Such a conclusion, nevertheless, leaves open several questions of significance to democratic theory.

1. On Marx's own assumption that the proletariat comes into power after acute conflict with the bourgeoisie, what happens politically to the bourgeoisie? Will the limitation of the *economic* power and functions of the bourgeoisie during the transitional socialist stage eliminate the *political* opposition of individual members of the

bourgeoisie? If not (and Marx pretty clearly assumed that such opposition was to be expected) then: (a) will (or ought) these individuals be physically restrained from engaging in any political opposition to " the proletariat," even including peaceful persuasion? Or rather (b) will (or ought) they be given full freedom to attempt the peaceful persuasion of a new majority against " the proletariat "?

2. Let us assume that socialization of the means of production and exchange is completed and the conflict with the bourgeoisie is ended somehow. (a) Is there really any reason for supposing that new conflicts of aims, wants, and purposes will not appear? In other words, is unanimity achievable on every issue, even given agreement on " ultimate ends "? If not (b) what " rights " and " obligations " ought the new minorities and majorities to have?

Quite evidently the content and meaning of the new society, to anyone who has *political* values of any kind, depends crucially on the answers to these essentially *political* questions. Specifically, one committed to the propositions of democratic theory set forth above, whatever one's economic objectives, will find a major incompleteness in the Marxian theory of transitional socialism, and an unresolved (although not necessarily unresolvable) contradiction between the " democratic " hypothesis that society is inevitably beset by conflicting interests or wants, and the Marxist portrayal of the completed socialist society as one in which conflict is absent.

III. MARXISM AND MAJORITY RULE

From one limited point of view, Marx and Engels were the great majoritarians of their day. They always assumed that when the transition to the socialist society took place, the proletariat was bound to constitute a majority, even an overwhelming majority, of the population. Moreover, they frequently condemned Blanqui and other conspiratorial revolutionaries who proposed to establish the new society by the revolutionary action of a small group.

The important point, however, is this: within the framework of their own philosophy, Marx and Engels had no grounds for defending majority rule, either as a means to socialism or as an aspect of political society under socialism, except in so far as it promised " success " in the historic struggle. Blanqui was heading in the wrong direction because minority dictatorships promised failure. But the crucial question is: in what sense must minority movements " fail "? Because of inability to achieve and hold power? Or to destroy private property in the means of production? If either of these, then Marx's view is merely a prediction of what would in fact happen in a particular historical period, and, from the vantage point of the contemporary world, a rather bad prediction at that. Or must minority movements fail, in Marx's view, because of their inherent inability to achieve certain valued results, such as freedom in some sense or equality of power, that were necessary to the ends for which socialism itself was but the means? Or to put it differently, were socialism and majority rule equally necessary means to certain ends that Marx and Engels valued?

Let us put the point this way: Majority rule is a means by which a political society (given certain cultural pre-requisites) may determine its ends in situations where unanimity is lacking; it may also be, and in practice commonly is, a method of determining broadly what means are to be employed to achieve those ends. If I want a political society to employ regularly the method of majority rule, it must be because I believe some kind of constant relation obtains between that method and some of the ends I value. On the minimal rational assumption, this implies a relation such that there is a better probability of my values being achieved by majority rule than by any probable alternative; on the maximum assumption, it implies a relation such that my values can be achieved by majority rule and in no other way. But in either case it implies that I want the society to employ majority rule because of the close relation between that method and the ends I value. It follows that unless I have a relatively clear conception of the ends I value and of what is involved in them, I cannot rationally support majority rule.

Now in their views on the "means-end" problem, Marx and Engels never did much more than open up questions which, from the standpoint of the majority rule democrat, they failed to answer.

In the first place they reduce the "problem" of values to a purely sociological question of explaining the social genesis of values. This sociological problem is solved rather simply by Marx and Engels. Values to them are the products of class conditioning, and from the "scientific" point of view they have no other significance. We might paraphrase one of Marx's statements by saying it is not values that determine the development of history, but historical forces that determine the development of values.

Engels, at least, contended that a time might come, "at a stage of society which has not only overcome class contradictions but has even forgotten them in practical life," when "a really human morality which transcends class antagonisms" would become possible. But evidently he regarded this as a goal so distant that it raised no problems demanding immediate analysis — such as the question whether a "really human morality" would imply the utilization of majority rule as a political means. Yet it seems obvious that one of the first problems facing a socialist society would be that of making collective decisions on questions that failed to command unanimous agreement. Marx and Engels provided no grounds on which the primary problem might be answered one way or another; for to say that the "values" of the proletariat, like those of the bourgeoisie, are determined by the circumstances of the class struggle, gives no hint as to how the proletariat "ought" to resolve differences on the morrow of victory.

In the second place, insofar as

Marx and Engels attempted to specify the consequences of socialism, they merely exaggerated their ambiguity on the subject of majority rule. For at least one of those consequences would be, in their view, to enlarge the area of man's freedom, to enhance man's control over himself and over his environment. "The objective, external forces which have hitherto dominated history, will then pass under the control of men themselves . . . Men, with full consciousness, will fashion their own history . . . It is humanity's leap from the realm of necessity into the realm of freedom."

There are at least two possible interpretations of this concept of freedom — each with a set of consequences profoundly different from the other. There is no way of knowing what Marx and Engels really meant, even assuming that both meant the same thing; and yet one historically important interpretation of what they meant leads (under the firm guidance of the Bolsheviks) in the direction of the one party state, while another view poses questions to which one answer lies in the direction of majority rule and free parties. The two later streams of Marxism, the one totalitarian, the other seeking somehow to keep within "democratic" channels, both find their seminal source in this confusion.

The one view is deterministic and stems directly from Engels' interpretation of Hegel. "Freedom is the appreciation of necessity." The more fully you understand the laws of social development, the more "free" you are to arrive at a judg-

ment based on the inherent necessity of the social situation. From such a view it is by no means a lengthy step to the position (which Marx and Engels neither asserted nor denied) that the desires of the majority need have relevance to political leadership in a socialist society only insofar as these desires coincide with the innate necessity of the social situation as revealed by the tools of "scientific" analysis. This may be taken to imply that wherever the majority cannot be expected to understand "the laws of social activity," it is irrational to base social choice on what the majority want. And it might be held to follow, as the Bolsheviks have argued, that a sense-making society would tolerate the existence only of the party or parties capable of a "scientific" (i.e., Marxist and ultimately Bolshevik) understanding of society. Once the party of "scientific socialism" achieves power, then, it might use its power to suppress all "unscientific" parties for precisely the same reasons that it would employ state power to forbid quack doctors from practising medicine or improperly trained pharmacists from filling prescriptions, and with precisely the same justification.

On the other hand, careful reading of Engels' views in *Anti-Dühring* (on which we have to rely almost exclusively for any insight into what he, and presumably Marx, meant to say on this point) indicates pretty clearly that he did not conceive the development in the future proletarian society to be predetermined. Man can make social laws work toward the ends he sets. "Freedom does not consist in the dream of independence of natural laws, but in the knowledge of these laws, and in the possibility this gives of systematically making them work towards definite ends." Or as he says later, once we have recognized the forces operating in society and understood how they work, "the use of them for the attainment of our aims depends entirely upon ourselves."

What does Engels mean? Does his assertion imply that society may be molded to alternative aims? If so, *whose* aims? Or will there be unanimous agreement on aims in the socialist society? If so, no problem of majorities and minorities will exist, at least with respect to aims. But if there is anything less than unanimity on aims, whose views are to be accepted? Those of a majority or of some particular minority? If the former, why do the aims of a majority have some special validity? And if the latter, assuming that a genuine freedom of alternative choices is available to members of a socialist society, why should the aims of some particular minority prevail? Moreover, even assuming agreement as to aims, and assuming that it is possible to distinguish means from ends, the same problems arise with respect to means — including the problem of who is to decide in any given case whether a difference is really one of means or of ends.

I am not arguing here that these questions either are or are not answerable by non-Marxists. It is sufficient to point out that:

1. The theory of majority rule democracy presupposes an answer and this answer is of central importance to the majority rule democrat. (Whether or not the theory of majority rule democracy is defensible on ethical, sociological or other grounds is, it need scarcely be repeated, another question.)

2. Marx and Engels, on the other hand, (a) not only do not provide an answer, but (b) remove much of the ground on which any answer at all is possible. Marx the "scientific" socialist to a very large extent undermines Marx the potentially democratic socialist. For if every ethic is a class ethic, the product of class conditioning, then no proposition about who *ought* to rule, even in a completely socialist society, makes much sense. Majority rule is "right" when the historical forces make it inevitable that the majority will rule, but it cannot be "wrong" for a minority to rule if it has the power to do so.

3. Thus, because Marx and Engels do not provide any comprehensive theory of political means, or any unequivocal grounds on which one may be constructed, there can be no *inherent* contradiction between Marxism and totalitarianism from the point of view of their respective assumptions about the means by which political power is to be wielded.

IV. MARXISM AND THE SIGNIFICANCE OF PARTIES

Not much conceptual basis is left on which Marx and Engels could have erected a defense of political parties in the transitional socialist society. But there are still other reasons why they should have failed to do so.

For one thing, they were generally skeptical about resolving the problems of a socialist society in advance. Marxism is a study and prognosis of the tendencies of capitalism against the background of an analysis of feudalism; it attempts little prognosis about the tendencies of socialism. Discussions of the Commune aside, almost all of the present-day Marxist dogma about the nature of society after the revolution is based on the single letter by Marx, written in 1875 and not published until 1891, criticizing the Gotha program of the German Social Democratic Party. Furthermore, Marx and Engels were familiar with the history of Utopian Socialism, and made no secret of their contempt for efforts to paint a picture of the future society.

In addition, the hypothesis that political parties are indispensable to democracy was not widely accepted during the lifetime of Marx and Engels even by those who set democracy, agrarian or capitalist, as their ideal polity. As late as the end of the nineteenth century, political parties were regarded by many as disagreeable evils of popular politics rather than a necessary means of eliciting and securing consent.

But perhaps the most important reason why Marx and Engels were effectively blocked from a creative analysis of parties as devices in a new society lay in the interpretation of party reality inherent in their own ideology.

Just as Marx's economics has been characterized as a reaction to the specific evils of 19th century capitalism, so too his view of politics is based on the particular qualities of the bourgeois state of the 19th century. All the major ideas of Marx and Engels were formed, at least in outline, by 1848, when Marx was 30 and Engels was 28. By 1859, when Marx, at 42, published the *Critique of Political Economy,* the matrix was fully finished. Throughout this period, there was much to support the Marxian view of the class-exploitative nature of the state and the puppet role of political parties. Democracy could indeed be regarded as a bourgeois luxury: from the point of view of a worker, excluded from the franchise, "popular government" was a device for deciding conflicts within the bourgeoisie. Anyone like Marx or Engels who identified himself with the excluded groups in society might well view the political conflicts of bourgeois democracy as sham battles. On the continent the occasional parliaments were dominated by spokesmen of the bourgeoisie. Even in England the electoral reforms of 1832 had merely extended the political prerogatives of the landed aristocracy to the oligarchy of commerce and manufacturing; the narrow limitation of the franchise and the harsh legislation in which the "liberals" and the manufacturers embodied their ideas (as in the Poor Law Reform of 1834) were, from the worker's point of view, concrete instances of the class character of the existing regime.

Even in America, where the franchise reforms of the Jacksonian period had resulted in a near approach to universal suffrage, there was from a worker's point of view little to choose between Republican and Democratic parties in the post-Civil War period. In 1891 Engels described American parties in terms not far from the realities of American politics of the period.

There is no country in which " politicians " form a more powerful and distinct section of the nation than in North America. There each of the two great parties which alternately succeed each other in power is itself in turn controlled by people who make a business of politics. . . . It is precisely in America that we have the best example of the growing independence of the State power in opposition to society, whose mere instrument it was originally intended to be. Here there was no dynasty, no nobility, no standing army, beyond the few men keeping watch on the Indians; no bureaucracy with permanent posts or the right to pensions. And nevertheless we find here two great groups of political spectators, who alternately take possession of the State machine, and exploit it by the most corrupt means and for the most corrupt ends — and the nation is powerless against these two great cartels of politicians, who are ostensibly its servants, but in reality exploit and plunder it.

The oppressive state, the sham parliaments, the bogus party conflicts — these were matters of direct experience to Marx and Engels, especially during their formative twenties. At 24, Marx (not yet a Marx-ist) became editor of the *Rheinische Zeitung* in Cologne, a liberal and highly critical journal written by young intellectual rebels like himself. Within five months, the paper was suppressed. Not long afterward, the German government succeeded in getting Marx expelled from France. Within three years, he had been run out of Belgium; and when Jenny, his wife, tried to find out what had happened to her husband, she was arrested and thrust into a cell with common prostitutes. Meanwhile Engels, faced with the immediate prospect of being thrown into jail for his Communist activities, felt it wise to leave Barmen, his birthplace.

The revolutions of 1848 provoked all over Europe an enormously powerful display of the oppressive power of the state and the weaknesses of parliamentary institutions. Returning to Cologne, Marx and Engels set up the *Neue Rheinische Zeitung* and daily castigated the Prussian State for its oppressiveness and the revolutionary bourgeois assembly at Frankfurt for its ineffectiveness. Naturally Marx provoked the authorities and alienated the bourgeoisie; he was hounded by the police, hailed into court, and finally expelled.

Marx saw the failure of the Revolution in France and Louis Bonaparte's coup as proof that the state was an instrument of repression, and that political parties and parliamentary government are, from a democratic point of view, of little significance. In *The Class Struggles in France* (1840–50) and *The 18th Brumaire of Louis Bonaparte* (1852),

Marx offers a brilliant concrete analysis that underscores, with regard to the situation in France, both the reality of the class struggle as the dominant force in politics, and the frothy irrelevance of parliaments and political parties. In *The 18th Brumaire* he affirms that in the conflict with the working class republicans, 3,000 workers had been killed and 15,000 had been transported without trial. The lesson was clear enough to him: " The defeat of the June insurgents . . . had revealed that here *bourgeois republic* signifies the unlimited despotism of one class over other classes."

As a man in his early thirties, therefore, Marx had much reason to regard parties and parliaments as reflections of the class struggle or, failing that, as insignificant and meaningless.

Moreover, Marx's experience gave him scant grounds for distinguishing between the "reactionary" states of the European monarchs and the "liberal" states of the bourgeoisie. The manner in which the bourgeois government of Thiers treated the Paris Commune of 1871 seemed to Marx a confirmation of his central thesis. That government, to all appearances, preferred the triumph of the German army to a victory of the proletarian forces in the Commune, and pursued the defeated Communards with a cruel and bloody Terror that proletarian leaders would not forget as conveniently as the bourgeoisie.

The introduction of universal suffrage in Germany in 1866, the electoral reforms in England in 1867 and 1884, and the subsequent growth of socialist parties might, conceivably, have caused Marx and Engels to reconsider their view of the state and of party competition. These developments pointed to a potential contradiction between (1) the view of the state as a device by which a bourgeois minority oppresses the proletarian majority, and (2) the opportunity apparently now presented to the proletarian majority to capture control of the state by winning a majority of the votes. But the dogma had crystallized by the time the great democratic reforms began. Marx, preoccupied with finishing *Capital* before he died, had neither time nor wish to revise his premises; and Engels was not sufficiently independent of Marx to amend the dogma, however congenial to his own temperament a restatement in a form more friendly to democracy might have been. After Marx's death, when German Social Democracy showed great gains each year, Engels set forth his conviction that the older methods of revolution had been superseded — at least in countries where the working class could vote — because of the opportunity now extended to workers to rally a majority of voters around a party program and put it into effect. In 1891, Engels wrote to Kautsky: " If one thing is certain it is that our Party and the working class can only come to power under the form of the democratic republic. This is even the specific form for the dictatorship of the proletariat, as the great French revolution has already shown." And in 1895, the year of his death, the old man made a significant concession to the importance of the party process as a means to power:

With this successful utilisation of universal suffrage, an entirely new mode of proletarian struggle came into force, and this quickly developed further. It was found that the state institutions, in which the rule of the bourgeoisie is organised, offer still further opportunities for the working class to fight these very state institutions. They took part in elections to individual diets, to municipal councils and to industrial courts; they contested every post against the bourgeoisie in the occupation of which a sufficient part of the proletariat had its say. And so it happened that the bourgeoisie and the government came to be much more afraid of the legal than of the illegal action of the workers' party, of the results of elections than those of rebellion.

For here, too, the conditions of the struggle had essentially changed. Rebellion in the old style, the street fight with barricades, which up to 1848 gave everywhere the final decision, was to a considerable extent obsolete.

To a mind less bound by the formalisms of the Marxian dogma, this new attitude toward the struggle for power might conceivably have led to a frank endorsement of party competition and majority rule as inherent characteristics of a democratic order — even of a socialist democracy. Yet Engels never went on to repair the gap that Marx had left. Nowhere in the writings of Marx and Engels, therefore, is there any definite indication of support for majority rule and free parties *except as tactical de-*

vices for gaining power. As Engels wrote to Bernstein in 1884: " In my opinion what should be said is this: the proletariat too requires democratic *forms* for the seizure of political power, but, like all political forms, these serve it as means." Means, then, to be abandoned upon the seizure of power? Or were dissidents to have the same broad right in a socialist society that socialists were allowed, on Engels' own admission, in a capitalist society? After the " inevitable " triumph of the socialist party, could opposition groups organize into parties and attempt to unseat the socialists by majority vote? Or for that matter, could opposition socialists organize into a rival party? These are crucial questions — just how crucial, probably neither Marx nor Engels ever foresaw. But from the point of view of the modern democrat, no political theory that does not answer them can be regarded as adequate for the contemporary world.

To sum up:

1. If one accepts the propositions of democratic theory set forth in the beginning of this essay, one logically cannot, even if one is a socialist, accept Marxism as an adequate *political* theory.

2. There is a hiatus between the proposition of democratic theory about conflicts of interests or wants, and the Marxist conception of social conflict and harmony. In the first place, because Marx and Engels leaped over the basic political problems stemming from the probable persistence of group conflict during the socialist " transition " from capi-

talism to anarcho-communism, Marxism is, for the democratic socialist, a wholly incomplete guide to the problem of maintaining, in any foreseeable future, the institutions implied by the propositions of democratic theory above. And, secondly, the Marxist assumption that group conflict stems from a class structure, which by definition is eliminated when social ownership is completely substituted for private ownership, leaves the democratic socialist incapable of explaining, without self-contradiction or extraordinary hair-splitting, a situation (as in the USSR) where the total elimination of private property in the means of production and exchange has virtually taken place. To "explain" the USSR, the democratic socialist must either deny the democratic propositions, or revise the Marxist hypothesis as to the origin of social conflict.

3. There is an unresolved contradiction between the essentially moral or prudential or derivative proposition of democratic theory that political conflicts ought ultimately to be resolved by majority rule, and the absence in Marx and Engels of any extensive grounds on which to defend not only majority rule but any other proposition about how political power *ought* to be distributed in a socialist society. Here again the conclusion seems unavoidable that the democratic socialist must either (1) modify the absoluteness of the majority rule principle or (2) modify or reject certain aspects of Marxism in such a way as to make possible a rational defense of majority rule.

4. There are in Engels' later writings grounds for developing a more systematic view of parties. But, for the reasons already indicated, such a development appears impossible without a significant modification of Marxism and an abandonment of some of its central doctrines.

B. The Arms of Government

57. Introduction

On January 28, 1950, in a speech at Woodford, Mr. Winston S. Churchill declared: "The wisdom of our forebears for more than 300 years has sought the division of power in the Constitution. Crown, Lords and Commons have been checks and restraints upon one another. The limitation of the power of absolute monarchy was the cause for which as Liberals used to say, 'Hampden died in the field and Sidney on the scaffold.' . . . The British race have always abhorred arbitrary and absolute government in every form. The great men who founded the American Constitution expressed this same separation of authority in the strongest and most durable form. Not only did they divide executive, legislative, and judicial functions, but also by instituting a federal system they preserved immense and sovereign rights to local communities. . . ."

This general principle of separation of powers is set forth for our American system in *The Federalist* [Papers] No. 51. There the author, who was either James Madison or Alexander Hamilton, asked the question: what expedient can be devised to maintain the separation of powers among the separate departments? He replied: " The only answer that can be given is, that as all these exterior provisions are found to be inadequate, the defect must be supplied, by so contriving the interior structure of the government as that its several constituent parts may, by their mutual relations, be the means of keeping each other in their proper places."

It was not the belief of the framers of the Constitution that the principle of dividing power among the departments was a feature peculiar to national government. For, the author of Federalist No. 51 continued: " This policy of supplying, by opposite and rival interests, the defect of better motives, might be traced through the whole system of human affairs, private as well as public. We see it particularly displayed in all the subordinate distributions of power, where the constant aim is to divide and arrange the several offices in such a manner as that each may be a check on the other — that the private interest of every individual may be a sentinel over the public rights. These inventions of prudence cannot be less requisite in the distribution of the supreme powers of the State."

Not only in the structure of government as such but likewise in the elements comprising society power would be divided among many groups. " Whilst all authority in it will be derived from and dependent on the society, the society itself will be broken into so many parts, interests and classes of citizens, that the rights of individuals, or of the minority, will be in little danger from interested combinations of the majority. In a free government the security for civil rights must be the same as that for religious rights. It consists in the one case in the multiplicity of interests, and in the other in the multiplicity of sects. The degree of security in both cases will depend on the number of interests and sects; and this may be presumed to depend on the extent of country and number of people comprehended under the same government."

The political philosophy underlying this declaration is the belief that an equilibrium of power must be maintained in all societies. This belief has been fortified and strengthened by recent experiences where power has been concentrated in one agency, department, or leader. It is one of the hallmarks of modern totalitarianism that while ostensibly providing for limited government, the constitution becomes a mere façade obscuring the real source of power and responsibility. It is true that in democracies a government of limited and divided powers has sometimes appeared capable of plunging the whole society into a coma. One criticism raised against the American form of government has been that it provides for all checks and no balance and that progress is retarded because of the restraints one recalcitrant branch can place on the whole system. Yet there has been an alternation among the various branches in the roles they have played within the constitutional system. If the Supreme Court has been opposed to social change at particular times, it has on other occasions been a defender of the advancement of civil rights.

We have undertaken to illustrate the characteristic functions ascribed to the executive, legislature, and judiciary under the American Constitution and to show through the words of scholars and statesmen how these functions have actually been interpreted in practice. We have included the debate carried on in the journal *Public Administration Re-* *view* between Don Price, well-known writer on public administration in the United States and Harold Laski (1893-1950), who was a famous British political scientist and leader in the British Labour Party. In conclusion, we have included classic statements of the arguments for and against judicial review. Chief Justice John Marshall (1755-1835) was responsible in 1803 for the classic statement in *Marbury vs. Madison* introducing the precedent for the right of the Supreme Court to declare unconstitutional action taken by the Congress. Morris R. Cohen (1880-1947), late Professor of Philosophy at the College of the City of New York, puts the case for the opponents of judicial review. It is argued that such a power gives to the Court supreme instead of co-ordinate powers with the Congress.

58. The Parliamentary and Presidential Systems*

To keep the administration of government under the control of the people, to invigorate it for effective action in their behalf, and to adjust national policy and its administration to the needs of various regions and institutions — these are urgent problems in this time of crisis.

While in Great Britain as well as in the United States new political and administrative institutions are being worked out to meet the needs

* From Don K. Price, *Public Administration Review*, III (1943), pp. 317-34. Reprinted by permission of Don K. Price and *Public Administration Review*.

of the hour, it is curious that much of the academic and journalistic criticism of government in America is based on a desire to imitate the classic parliamentary system of government. This is all the more curious since the British long ago abandoned the classic parliamentary system as definitely as they abandoned the classic theories of political economy.

Perhaps only a psychoanalyst could explain America's peculiar nostalgia for the obsolescent political institutions of the mother country, but the persistence of her obsession with the parliamentary system makes it not only an interesting theoretical problem but a practical political and administrative issue.

It is easy to understand why Woodrow Wilson started the fashion. When he wrote *Congressional Government* as a graduate student (even before he ever set foot in the United States Capitol), the memory of Johnson's impeachment and the scandals of Grant's administration were fresh in his mind, in sharp contrast to the leadership of Gladstone and Disraeli over the House of Commons that they dominated and the electorate that they were creating. And he had undoubtedly read Walter Bagehot's monumental study, *The English Constitution,* which gave the classic description of the parliamentary system.

Bagehot pointed out in 1867 that the term "Her Majesty's Government" had become only a polite fiction, although a very useful one. Under the parliamentary system, which he preferred to call Cabinet government, the executive and legislature were not independent of each other as in the American presidential system; the House of Commons virtually elected the Cabinet and could force it to resign whenever it lost confidence in its policies or its efficiency. Thus the executive was always responsible to the legislature, and through it to the people. On the other hand, the executive was assured of enough power to discharge its responsibility because, if the House refused to vote funds and enact laws as it recommended, it could dissolve the House and call for a new election. "It" meant the

Cabinet, the Government of the Day, the committee of legislators who individually served as ministers of departments and collectively were dismissed if the action of any one of them was not supported by the House. Thus the parliamentary system provided immediate political responsibility and at the same time gave the executive enough power to make all special interests balance into a coherent national policy.

Wilson found this system far preferable to the presidential system, which seemed to encourage continual squabbles between the executives and the Congress. Senator Pendleton, the author of the civil service reform act, had proposed several years before that the President's department heads be given seats in Congress, in order to defend their administration before the legislators. The idea of adopting an outright parliamentary system by constitutional amendment or of giving Congress or its committees some sort of control over the appointments of department heads has persisted, and is stronger now than it has been for many years.

"If we had a parliamentary form of government," says Mr. David Lawrence, ". . . we would be able to hold to accountability all the various bureaucrats who nowadays do as they please under presidential appointment." Mr. Lawrence is one of many who have followed the lead of Mr. Henry Hazlitt, of the *New York Times,* who wants us to adopt a parliamentary system by constitutional amendment. Others are for limited action. Mr. Walter Lippmann has suggested that "when the voters turn against an administration in midterm, the cabinet officers responsible in the field where the issue was drawn will as a matter of course resign," since a department head " has lost his usefulness when he no longer has the confidence of the people's representatives."

Supported by this assumption that members of Congress are representatives of the people while the President is not, that Congress should govern while the President should be restrained as a threat to our liberties, some members of Congress have undertaken to pinch off bits of the executive function. Representative Hendricks helped kill the National Resources Planning Board, while trying to create a House committee on postwar problems, because he thought that Congress should be doing the planning. Senator Tydings has suggested that Congress and not the President should control the Budget Bureau. Senator McKellar wants more executive appointments " confirmed " by the Senate. Congressman Ramspeck does not believe that administrative officials should remain in office unless approved by a majority of the people, by which, unless he means to propose a popular referendum on each official, he must mean a majority of Congress or one of its houses or committees.

This tendency is not supported as a whole by anybody in particular, or opposed by anybody in particular. It simply goes on because we use terms and ideas, in thinking about the President's relations with Congress, that we have borrowed from the British. Congressmen are supposed to represent the people, while the President is not, because the British House of Commons is elected while the British King is not. Department heads are not supposed to be responsible unless a legislature can discharge them. We, the people, could hold ministers responsible through a legislature, but we, the people, look on a President's appointees as bureaucrats — especially if we do not happen to like the policies they carry out with money voted them year after year by Congress.

But perhaps the facts on which Bagehot based his logic are no longer so. Perhaps the classic parliamentary system, even though it were ideal for Great Britain, might not fit the United States. Perhaps the United States should consider its system of legislative-executive relations in the light of the world as it is today and may be tomorrow. To do so it will have to ask some critical questions about the classic theory of parliamentary government.

THE LEGISLATIVE FUNCTION

Much of the sentiment for the parliamentary system in the United States springs from a dislike of executive influence over legislative proceedings. For this reason it is pleasant to recall that in Great Britain " must " legislation is always enacted and very few other statutes are, while the " purges " of party members who refuse to follow their leaders are almost always successful.

In the British system the nice balance between the Cabinet and the Commons has long since been upset. A half-century ago it was not too unreasonable to argue that the power of the House to dismiss the Cabinet, balanced against the power of the Cabinet to dissolve the House, would always result in a perfect balance of democratic control and executive authority. Within limits, the system worked that way; the Cabinet could never outrage public opinion for fear of losing the support of the House, the members of which went home every week end to get the opinion of the county families if not of the people; the House would never yield to minority interests, for the Cabinet would have the House dissolved if defeated on a policy question, and the members, not wishing to risk their seats in a general election, would not vote against the Cabinet. The equation balanced until a new factor — the electorate — became continuously instead of only potentially effective.

The British in effect did to the House of Commons what the Americans did much earlier to their Electoral College: they made it an automatic machine for registering the vote of the people, as organized into parties, for a Prime Minister. Once the Prime Minister is in office, with the Cabinet that he selects, the House remains in session to enact the bills proposed by the Cabinet, and to serve as the place where Cabinet ministers make speeches for the newspapers to report to the public but rarely remain to listen to the speeches of other members.

In theory, the House has the power to turn the Cabinet out of office or to refuse to enact the laws it proposes. But that constitutional power seems to be going the way of the King's power to appoint ministers and to veto legislation. Theoretically it exists, but politically it is rarely exercised. Since 1895 only two Cabinets have been refused a vote of confidence and turned out of office by the House, and neither of them had majority support to begin with. A political machine does not elect men to vote against its boss, and the Prime Minister is leader of the party and boss of the machine.

By invading and taking over the executive power the House of Commons destroyed its own independence. The very privilege of holding the Cabinet responsible makes it impossible for the House to think independently. No members of the House will accept office and serve in the Cabinet if the House will not support them. After taking office they will not accept defeat by the House without dissolving the House, calling for a new election, and appealing to the voters to return members who will support them. Because this is constitutionally possible, the members of the House who select and support a Cabinet put the desire to keep their men in office ahead of all minor considerations. The party machinery therefore controls the members fairly rigidly; if the Cabinet wants a measure passed, it will be passed, according to the schedule of debate which the Cabinet considers expedient. As soon as the House of Commons took away the power of the House of Lords by the

Parliament Act of 1911 it had to surrender its independence to its leaders; in the cautious words of Sir William Anson, on that date "legislative sovereignty may be said to have passed to the Cabinet."

The day of the independent landed gentry, holding seats in the Commons as a matter of family privilege, is gone, and the discipline of parties, especially of the Labour Party, over their members goes far beyond American practice. There is no tradition that a legislator should live in his own district in Great Britain; it is a matter of course to elect a candidate who never visited the district before in his life. The party leaders could therefore defeat nearly any of their members in his own constituency by withdrawing their support, or even by sending in a strong national leader to oppose him. The "purge" of members who do not support the national organization is taken for granted, but members are generally co-operative enough to make it unnecessary.

This control by party machines over the political fortunes of members is a corollary of the similar control by the Cabinet over the legislative procedure. The Cabinet takes for its legislative program just as much of the time of the House as it needs, and during the 1920's and 1930's that was about seven-eighths of the total. The remainder went to consideration of measures proposed by private members (private members are all those except the seventy-odd members who are a part of the "Government" as ministers or assistants to ministers), who drew lots

for the privilege of getting their bills considered by the House. No private member's bill could be passed if the Cabinet opposed it, and in practice private members who drew the right to introduce a bill would often ask the Cabinet (or its Whips) for a bill to introduce. Since the war, however, the time allotted to private members has been entirely abolished; no bill can be introduced except by a minister.

The House of Commons has no committees, in the sense that Congress understands that term. At one stage a bill is referred to a committee — one of several large committees which do not deal with any specialized subject matter, which do not have any fixed membership, and which have no initiative or influence whatever of their own, being little more than devices to permit interested parties to testify. Funds are appropriated and statutes enacted without any independent review, and as the Cabinet requests.

The House votes the funds requested by the Cabinet; it does not have the constitutional power to vote more money for any purpose than the Cabinet asks for, and it has never during this century voted any less. In theory the private member may offer amendments to legislation proposed by the Cabinet, but in practice, as Mr. W. Ivor Jennings puts it, "Members appeal to the minister to accept amendments; they do not compel."

In short, through the party machinery the Cabinet controls the House of Commons on every question that is important enough to be called policy, and it *must* control the House as long as it is "responsible" to the House.   The British short-cut the House of Commons to elect their executive as effectively as American voters short-cut the Electoral College. But between elections, since they have reduced their legislature to a voting machine under the control of the Cabinet, they have to rely on the executive to take complete charge of legislation, restrained and guided effectively only by public opinion as it is expressed through the press and through a multitude of private organizations as well as in the House. This is what Mr. Lloyd George meant when he told a Select Committee on Procedure on Public Business in 1931 that "Parliament has really no control over the Executive; it is a pure fiction." (This select Committee of the House of Commons heard extensive testimony on the operations of the parliamentary system; its proceedings will be described more fully hereafter.)

Now "control" has at least two meanings. One is to restrain or check, and the House of Commons, by acting as a sort of barometer of public opinion (though not the only one, and perhaps not even the most important one) certainly exercises an effective though impalpable restraint on the Cabinet. The other meaning is to direct, and in this sense of "control" Mr. Lloyd George was right in saying that the House does not control the Cabinet. For the essence of the cabinet system is that the Cabinet must be supported on every issue not only by a majority but by the *same* majority. If the Conservatives are

in power, the Conservative member dares not vote against the Cabinet on any issue even if he disagrees, because if he and others like him do so they might make up a majority against the Cabinet and force it to resign. Likewise, the Labour Party member cannot afford to vote with a Conservative Cabinet even if he approves of one of its actions, because that issue might be his own party's chance of getting into power. This line of reasoning and the type of party discipline that it brings about makes independent voting extremely rare. The idea that a major tax bill could be passed with a majority of the administration party against it and a majority of the opposition party for it would be unthinkable in Westminster.

The merit of this arrangement is that it makes impossible a national policy that seems inconsistent to the Cabinet or the Prime Minister. If two groups of members of the House, even two majority groups, want the Cabinet to follow policies that the Cabinet considers inconsistent, they cannot have their way. To take a hypothetical example, if a majority of the House wished to protect a system of private enterprise, but also wished to build a public power project in a certain depressed area, it would not be able to do so if the Cabinet considered the two purposes inconsistent.

From one point of view, this system brings about an admirable coherence of policy; if a Cabinet is engaged in carrying out a certain program, it has a right to insist that its responsibility not be hampered by the enactment of measures that are inconsistent with it. But, from another point of view, the issue whether certain policies are consistent with each other is the most important issue to be decided, and the most important issue ought to be decided by the supreme authority. And if a Cabinet should tell the House that it could not be held responsible for (for example) the encouragement of private enterprise if the House should insist on building a public power project, it would be putting its view of administrative practicality ahead of the legislature's view of public policy. The system that lets it do so puts the Cabinet over the House for most practical purposes, no matter which body elects the other.

In practice, a legislature cannot exercise control or take an independent line unless it can set up committees to make investigations and recommendations. Under the parliamentary system, the Cabinet is the committee to end all committees; it can tolerate no rivals. It can let other committees conduct investigations and hearings or propose minor amendments, but on any question that a minister chooses to consider policy the House must fall into line. This lets the Cabinet define the scope of "policy," and it is not inclined to leave any controversial issue of importance outside the definition that it formulates.

This difficulty was brought out clearly in the testimony to the 1931 Select Committee. Several members proposed that the House create specialized committees and that the Cabinet refrain from considering every question a question of policy, but they were apparently unable to convince the Select Committee that a committee could do anything significant without supplanting the minister concerned. As one of them asked Mr. Lloyd George, "Do you not think you would get back to exactly the same position we are in now, that if the Minister and the Cabinet supported the Minister in one line and the Committee took another you might have a more interesting debate, but ultimately the decision would rest with the Cabinet, and you would not really control your Executive?" Even Mr. Lloyd George could think of no formula (within the limits of the Cabinet system) which would let a committee successfully oppose the Cabinet on policy. Everyone assumed that "ultimately the decision would rest with the Cabinet."

Thus the House cannot itself make decisions on the several major issues of policy that exist at any one time; constitutionally it can only choose which Cabinet to entrust those decisions to, and as a matter of practical politics it can only keep in office the men it is elected to keep in office.

What is true of policy is even more true of administration. The outlines of departmental organization are fixed by Cabinet action, without legislation, and so are the principal procedures of management, such as budgeting, planning, and personnel. The Cabinet itself now operates through a hierarchy of committees and subcommittees which have no hard-and-fast membership and no formalized existence; any decision on which agreement cannot be reached by common consent is passed on up the line to the War Cabinet, to be settled in the last analysis by the Prime Minister. The freedom of the Cabinet to handle administrative questions with this degree of independence undoubtedly makes for a high degree of coordination.

It is no wonder that even Mr. Stanley Baldwin admitted to the Select Committee in 1931 that (in Mr. Hore-Belisha's words) members of the House of Commons felt that they had "nothing much to do of a responsible nature." This lack of function was reflected in practical arrangements. The pre-war House had enough seats for only about half its members. Most of the members carried on their other occupations by day, and to let them do so the more important sessions of the House were held in the late afternoon and evening. As Sir Austen Chamberlain complained, the leading Cabinet members, who in the nineteenth century would have spoken at the climax of debate at eleven o'clock and then waited to hear their opponents, had taken to reading their speeches (usually prepared for them by others) early in the evenings in time to be reported by the morning papers and then leaving the House immediately, so that debate, "the essence of Parliamentary government," had become a lost art. Members could not make up for the decline in debating by detailed work as members of committees, for the committees had no independent function. As individual members they were not ex-

pected to make any great contribution, or even to work full time. The members were not paid at all until 1911, and in 1937 they were raised to £600 ($2,400) per year — a salary one-fifth that of the top rank of civil servants. The only private accommodation each member had was a locker in the corridor. On this point, one member of the 1931 Select Committee remarked in what must have been a wistful tone of voice, "I think that in the American Congress every Member has a small room."

In this contrast, the accommodations that the Congressmen enjoy are significant of their function. Congress, since it has not taken over control of administration, has not had to feel responsible as an organization for getting the work of government accomplished. For that reason it has not had to organize itself into a tightly disciplined body, controlled by a single small committee that can act in a businesslike way. If it should do so, the individual members would have to surrender to their organization the individual freedom of action and decision that now enables them to criticize and restrain at their discretion even an administration that they generally propose to support.

During the Napoleonic war, according to Lord Mountararat in *Iolanthe,*

The House of Lords throughout the war
Did nothing in particular
And did it very well.

The House of Commons, which was forced by the bombing of its own quarters to move into those of the House of Lords a couple of years ago, has succeeded to the role which Mr. W. S. Gilbert described with his usual precision of language. The House of Commons has influence, it does an important job, and it does it very well. But it does not control things "in particular." Its control has become so general, it is exercised through so rarefied a medium, that the Commons seem to be following the Lords into the status of one of the "theatrical elements" of the British constitution.

THE EXECUTIVE FUNCTION

During the past century the British have had the problem of bringing under popular control a civil service that was formerly under royal domination, while the Americans have had the totally different problem of creating a national administration devoted to the national service rather than to factional or particular interests.

The tenure of the civil service, like the sovereignty of the King, was undisturbed by the British as they converted themselves into a democracy. This feat was unique; no other major power managed to become a democracy without a revolution, and some countries backslid even after a revolutionary conversion. But the British conversion was accomplished so subtly that the theories which describe and justify it will hardly fit the countries that became democracies by more forthright methods.

A democratic country has two problems in controlling its public service: how to get it to do what the people want, and how to keep it from doing what the people do not want. One is the problem of avoiding red tape and lethargy; the other, of preventing oppression.

Americans have been so long accustomed to using the British civil service as an example of rectitude and impartiality while reproaching their own government for partisan patronage that it is a little disconcerting to them to read that the British are showing considerable dissatisfaction with the record of their administrators during the present war and the years before it. This comes as no surprise, however, to those who have been following the self-criticism of British statesmen for some years. In 1931, the Permanent Undersecretary of State for the Colonies, Sir Samuel Herbert Wilson, complained to an official commission that the higher civil service had all the negative virtues, but was static, unadventurous, inflexible, and impractical. Similar criticisms have been made many times before and since. There may be room for disagreement on a question of degree, but the more ardent defenders of the permanent officials who are administrative heads of departments under the ministers say that their primary qualities are "stoical realism" or "moderation and prudence," while the severer critics of these gentlemen say they are merely cynical opportunists. Fervor and enthusiasm, at any rate, are not their primary characteristics.

Some Labour Party critics of the

civil service are apt to blame its caution on the economic predilections and the family and educational backgrounds of its leading members. Even though many of the most vigorous advocates of the social services came from much such English backgrounds (Sir William Beveridge was educated at Charterhouse and Balliol in classical literature and philosophy), there is much in this explanation. But it is not the whole story; it will not explain, for example, why Oxford University and the headmasters of public schools have reported that the more energetic and ambitious men among their better graduates were avoiding the civil service for more adventurous occupations, or why some of the more energetic and ambitious men who reached the top of the civil service between the two world wars left the government to go into private business, like Sir Josiah Stamp, or into politics, like Sir John Anderson. All Englishmen take the parliamentary system for granted, like the air they breathe; perhaps they overlook a tendency of the system itself to overdevelop the caution of the civil servants.

The parliamentary system, for one thing, requires a permanent civil service. This requirement fits in with British tradition, but it is also inherent in the institutional arrangements. For given the constitutional possibility of an unexpected change at any time in all the ministers who head departments, it is necessary to have the departments staffed by men who can carry on the job. It is unsettling enough to change the chief executive at stated intervals, but when change may come at any moment permanent tenure is necessary both to keep the work going and to attract first-rate men to the jobs. Thus, in normal times, it is difficult under the parliamentary system and unheard of in British practice to bring men in from universities or private business to high administrative positions in the government departments. The top administrators are recruited as they leave the universities and spend all their lives in the government offices in Whitehall.

For another thing, the parliamentary system puts the ministers and the top civil servants on the defensive. The minister is primarily a legislative leader, not an administrator. He is normally chosen for his ability in commanding the support of members of the House and in defending party policy before the House. He must therefore have distinguished himself in debate or by leadership in the party organization. If he has done so it does not matter much which department he heads, and it is quite customary for him to change from one department to another. The minister, from the historical point of view, has elbowed himself into a spot between the King and the civil service, a spot which he occupies as a representative and one of the leaders of the House. In this spot he must agree to take the blame for anything that his department does wrong, in exchange for getting the credit for anything it does right. This is necessary to safeguard the permanence of the civil service; it is a tacit arrangement between the Cabinet and the civil service that the civil service will always obey the Cabinet ministers and let them be considered responsible for whatever is done, in exchange for a virtual guarantee of undisturbed tenure.

Unless the minister has an exceptional interest in a certain policy and exceptional determination, he is likely to insist above all things that his subordinates keep him out of trouble. His eye is always on the political barometer of the House; if he can avoid doing anything that will cost the Cabinet any undue criticism or loss of votes, he will be a success among his colleagues. Whether he is more concerned with a positive program or with political protection, however, it is pretty clear to civil servants in his department that they stand to lose more by making mistakes for which the minister may be called down than they stand to gain by initiative and enterprise for which their superiors would probably get most of the credit anyway.

Official caution is common to all large organizations to some extent, but the essential feature of the parliamentary system serves to intensify it. Because any decision on a question of policy may be discussed in the House as an issue on which (at least in constitutional theory) the minister's job will depend as a result of a vote on party lines, every policy question is potentially the cause of a general election. A British civil servant simply must remain noncommittal on policy questions in order to keep out of party politics.

For this reason, a civil servant must not publicly take credit for anything he proposes or accomplishes; the minister has to take the credit or blame in order to give the "ins" and the "outs" in the House of Commons a fair chance to debate a possible vote of confidence on the question. Moreover, the civil servant must anticipate serving under other ministers. A Permanent Secretary of the Treasury who is serving under a Conservative Chancellor of the Exchequer today may be under a Socialist one tomorrow — or under the parliamentary system he must at least pretend to think so. Accordingly, he may not write or say anything publicly that might embarrass him or his political superior if he had to change policies.

The minister's role is much like that of the chairman of a congressional committee in the United States, except that he probably has not had the long service in a single subject matter that the congressional seniority system requires. His time is taken up so much with political and legislative affairs that he cannot serve as the administrative chief of his department. That role falls to a permanent undersecretary, assisted by a number of staff assistants who, like himself, were recruited after a classical education and trained in general administration. The advantages of having men with a general administrative interest in the top positions of a department are only beginning to be appreciated in the United States. But, except for the peculiar needs of the parliamentary system, it is something of a disadvantage to have a public service headed by men who have had to restrain most systematically their political and social ideals in order to be acceptable to any political group that might come to power.

British statesmen and students have made two interesting proposals to make the civil service less inbred, but neither has been adopted. One is to make a special arrangement to give young civil servants some experience outside the government, or at least outside the capital, so that they will have a better appreciation of the thinking of the private citizen and a keener interest in practical problems. Another is to devise some scheme by which civil servants could be recognized publicly by the Cabinet or the House for specific achievements, as well as honored by the Crown for their general service.

No artificial measures are needed to accomplish these purposes under the presidential system. The United States has a constitutional series of Four Year Plans, during each of which the President can assure his subordinates of a chance to make a record for themselves. Since the President is to be in office for four years and has control over the tenure of his subordinates, he can call to the government service men from private business, universities, or state and local governments. This process keeps the federal service from becoming a closed corporation; it always includes men with a wide variety of prejudices and it has never developed a guild spirit.

American department heads themselves have a function and status quite different from that of parliamentary ministers. The use of the term " Cabinet member " to refer to both is extremely misleading. The American department head is chosen for executive ability or leadership in a certain field of interest, not for legislative influence. Only one President's Cabinet since the Civil War has had a majority of ex-Congressmen. The ex-Republicans who were in the Roosevelt administration even before the war illustrate the President's selection of department heads for their leadership in subject matter rather than in party politics — Wallace in agriculture, Hopkins in welfare, Ickes in conservation.

The administrative official in the United States government — whether a Cabinet member or a bureau chief or one of their assistants or advisers — has a vital interest in making a positive record for himself. He does not take it for granted that he will be in the federal service forever; he probably keeps a close acquaintance with private organizations and his specialized field of interest, whether it is agriculture or banking or law, and his reputation among his colleagues in the field — in both public and private positions — depends on what they think of his ability to get a job done. That ability will depend partly on his leadership in his professional organization, among the leaders of the trade association concerned, or with the general public.

It is not at all unusual for career civil servants, or public officials temporarily in the service, to help build up support for policies. For example, soil-conservation officials in the United States, whether employed by federal, state, or local governments, whether Democrats or Republicans, will unite in advocating their programs among the people and before Congress under the leadership of the specialists in the Department of Agriculture, headed by the chief specialist, the Secretary of the Department. It is significant that Great Britain, which has far more effective organizations of public officials for the protection of their own interests than does the United States, has far less effective organizations of officials devoted to the improvement of their service to the public.

There is not much doubt that American public officials lack the political inhibitions of the British civil servants. But one of the most persistent ideas that Americans in general have picked up from the parliamentary system is that there is something improper about this kind of positive attitude of the public official toward his job. Frequently an executive official is criticized for proposing or advocating a policy on the grounds that he is thereby infringing the prerogatives of Congress or violating some essential principle of democratic government. Civil servants under a parliamentary system of democracy remain anonymous and deferential to the legislature as a matter of principle; it is almost essential for them to have permanent tenure of office, and a set of permanent officials at the top of the administrative hierarchy would seriously unbalance the democratic process if it took a leading role in the public discussion of policies. They have to be neutral for the same reason that the British King has to be

neutral; he too is in a position where he could make democratic control of policy impossible, and he too has retained his permanent position in a democracy as a result of a tacit bargain to stay out of policy and politics.

But under the presidential system the public official is under no such restraint. The popular control of the executive is a double control; the people elect the President and the President holds his appointees responsible, retaining the power to discharge them at his discretion; and the people elect the Congress, which controls the executive by statutes, by appropriations, and by investigations. For failing to comply with congressional legislation, a public official is subject to legal penalties; for being so zealously opposed to administration policy that his administrative usefulness is ended, he is subject to removal by his administrative superiors. But since the advocacy of policy by the administrative official does not threaten the tenure of Congressmen, it does not need to be prohibited. Unlike the House of Commons, the Congress retains the power to regulate and control the executive in detail, without putting at stake on any issue the tenure of office of its own members or the President or (generally speaking) subordinate executives. For this reason, it largely divorces questions of policy from questions of party politics in its own proceedings, and executive officials are therefore free to participate in discussions of policy as much as they like — if they are willing to risk their jobs by making themselves no longer useful to the President or his successor. In public discussions of policy they are no more bound as a matter of democratic principle by the restrictions that apply to the British civil service than the President is bound by the restrictions that apply to the King — and for exactly the same reason.

Democratic control over a public official is most effective if it is backed up by the sanction of dismissal and if that sanction is a practical, not merely a theoretical, weapon. In the Middle Ages the English barons, when mortally offended at some act of the King's, felt obliged to protest their loyalty to his person, to blame his acts on bad advice, and to punish the advisers. History does not lead us to believe that this system had much effect on the character of kings as long as kings had real power. The parliamentary system operates on the same theory with respect to the civil service; you must not fire leading civil servants, for the minister is "responsible" if they are wrong. And the political ascendancy of the Cabinet over the House of Commons has made it nearly impossible to fire the minister on the mere judgment of the members of the House — it takes a considerable revulsion of popular feeling.

In enforcing the responsibility of public officials, the parliamentary system has another practical disadvantage in addition to the difficulty of dismissal. That disadvantage, like several others, springs from the Cabinet's inevitable jealousy of any rivals within the legislature: it is that the minister could permit his civil servants to testify before a committee on any question in which policy was involved. The "question hour" lets the members of the House of Commons put the minister on the spot, but the questioning is emasculated by a procedural etiquette which no committee of Congress would tolerate for a moment. The parliamentary system draws clear lines between the House and the Cabinet, between the minister and the administrator, between the administrator and the technician, and these lines are barriers to the transmission of information and the operation of democratic control over the details of policy.

The presidential system, although it unifies responsibility for the execution of a program, does not unify responsibility for the preparation and enactment of a legislative program, as does the parliamentary system. Thus the voters are less able to hold a party clearly responsible for its administration of the program as a whole. On the other hand, the voters have a double check on their government — administratively through the President, their only national representative, and legislatively through the Congress. And they know that, however poorly the President and the Congress are carrying out their responsibilities, they are not kept from exercising their controls by a system of mutual deference that results from the fear of disturbing each other's tenure of office.

CONSTITUTIONAL FEDERALISM

It is easy to arrange complete harmony between executive and legislature by unifying them. But that only covers up the problem; any differences then appear within the legislature itself, and if they are serious enough the several factions, merely by refusing to cooperate, can simply bring government to a standstill. There is nothing automatic in the process by which various political groups combine in a two-party system. That process has to be impelled by a positive community of interest and a positive loyalty to a central symbol. If even a significant minority has different interests and no loyalty and wishes only to make the existing system of government impossible, there can be no orderly opposition, no gentlemanly alternation of " ins " and " outs."

During the nineteenth century there was little friction in the British parliamentary system because it reflected accurately the concentration of political influence. The two previous centuries had been different. In the seventeenth, England had the first modern revolution, by which an alliance of merchants and religious dissenters abolished the monarchy and experimented with written constitutions, legislative committees, and a republican chief executive — three political developments that died in their native soil but were transplanted to America with great success. Even in the eighteenth century it was still the theory that the British constitution provided a balance of power between the King, who headed the government, the Lords, who represented the great landowners, and the Commons, the lesser landowners and mercantile interests. There are even respectable historians who

argue that it was in theory a federal system, in which the King was legally supposed to govern such areas as Ireland, the Channel Islands, and the American colonies through their own assemblies, the Houses at Westminster having no jurisdiction over them. Over these differences of interest many battles royal were fought among the executive and the two Houses of Parliament.

But by the early nineteenth century it was clear as a matter of practical politics that the union of the English landed and mercantile gentry was predominant over all other interests in England, in the United Kingdom, and in the Empire as a whole, and that areas like Ireland and the colonies would have to admit their subordination. The constitutional theory that followed this fact was that Parliament was omnipotent and unrestricted, and that in Parliament supremacy was held by the House of Commons, the most exclusive gentlemen's club in Europe. If there were to be no separation of powers, one house of the legislature had to yield to the other.

Since the House of Commons assumed full control, the government could be directed only by a committee of members who could lead the House from inside. As legislative leaders, the one thing they could not do was to admit any restrictions on the constitutional power of the House. Throughout the Empire its power had to be absolute as long as it existed at all. At the same time, members were not in a position to urge local points of view effectively unless they were willing to back them up by a threat not to support the government.

The tendency of this system was consequently toward a uniform national program in essential matters of policy. The uniformity of the program reflected the tight unity of the parliamentary system and the tight unity of the governing class which supported that system — a class produced by a national system of education which taught the gentry to think and talk alike throughout England.

The advantages of such a system were obvious; it prevented such parochialism as the pork-barrel appropriations of the American Congress. On the other hand, it had the disadvantage of providing no formula by which the national government could authoritatively handle national interests, while subordinate areas could deal with their own problems. The Dominions were too distant, perhaps, to be represented in a central legislature, but Ireland was not; and if the theories of royal divine right and then of parliamentary omnipotence had not existed, who knows but that Ireland might have been given control over her own local affairs throughout the nineteenth century and come into the twentieth without her inheritance of hatred against all things English?

A more serious difference between regions more evenly matched in power occurred in the United States without effecting a permanent separation. In the United States, however, an independent executive surmounted the confusion in Congress and held the Union together. He

did not have to say, with Dogberry, "Bid any man stand, in the prince's name," and, if he will not stand, "Why, then, take no note of him, but let him go; and presently call the rest of the watch together, and thank God you are rid of a knave." Significantly enough, the only flagrant sectional oppression in the history of the United States came with the congressional usurpation of executive power during Reconstruction.

A federal constitutional republic needs a separation of powers to keep its federalism adjusted to the wishes of the people. If a single national representative body is omnipotent, it is likely to disregard subordinate loyalties in carrying out its program. Much of the friction that arises between the President and Congress grows out of the conflict between the national program as planned by the executive branch and the impulse of the legislators who modify it in the interests of their constituencies. Since the American executive is not a part of Congress, members of Congress have no institutional incentive to nationalize our system and to ignore the rights and interests of state and local governments. Their lack of individual responsibility for the administration of any federal program enables them to protect local interests and often to overemphasize them.

Senators and Representatives alike may be called to account more effectively by state and local interests than by their national party organizations. The existence of equal representation in the Senate, which the Constitution provides shall be permanent except by the consent of the states, would make it almost impossible to adopt a parliamentary system; it is difficult to imagine the more powerful of the two houses giving control over the executive to the lower house alone, and it is equally fantastic to imagine them acting jointly on every question.

Neither house of Congress has yet been willing to handle legislation by a committee system which is immediately responsible to the wishes of the house as a whole. If the isolationist Senator Reynolds heads the Military Affairs Committee during a world war, the Senate simply puts up with him. The advocates of " responsible " government will know they are making progress when either house decides to remove the chairman of any committee that differs with the house as a whole on a question of policy. And when both houses agree to hold each other's committees mutually responsible, and to discharge their chairmen whenever they disagree with each other, then we shall really be well along toward minimizing local differences and adopting the tightly knit system of parliamentary government.

But in the meantime, the flexibility of the presidential system has its advantages. We can make progress piecemeal, without waiting for a whole program to get approval in principle. The chief executive can get a majority from these groups on one issue, from those groups on another. The party discipline can be relatively loose; groups that oppose the administration on one issue for local or special reasons need not op-

pose it on the next. A parliamentary cabinet, by tending to command the same majority on all issues (since that majority wants to keep its administration in office) also tends to keep the opposition always against it. If that minority is concentrated in national or regional or social groups that appeal strongly enough to the loyalty of their members, such opposition is apt to become uncompromising and irreconcilable.

The kind of flexibility that the presidential system permits may be useful in dealing with various types of institutions, as well as with various regions or political groups in the state.

The neat logic of the parliamentary system requires the legislature to hold the executive responsible for a little issue in the same way as for a big one, for a technical detail or a subordinate's error in judgment in the same way as for a major policy decision. This was tolerable enough when government had very little to do with the daily lives of people. But now the dividing line between governmental and other institutions has become very shadowy, all sorts of hybrid agencies and corporations exist, and many private corporations and institutions carry on functions for governmental agencies. In such a situation, if a legislature is to keep the whole organism working in the public interest, it cannot depend mainly on a power to hire and fire the head of it, but it must approve one action and condemn another, encourage here and reprove there, expand this agency and restrict that one.

Under the parliamentary system the legislature must always hold a sword over the head of the executive and cannot stoop to slap his hand. To keep a discussion of the British Broadcasting Corporation from bringing up a vote along party lines on which the Cabinet might be ousted, the Cabinet had to set it up by a statute that makes it generally impossible for the House to control its detailed operations or even to ask questions about them. If an executive and a legislature have a degree of mutual independence, the legislature may review the budget of a government corporation and force it to change its policy without conflicting with the chief executive at all.

In their system of legislative control over the executive the British have let the Americans outdo them in refusing to conform to an abstract theory. The omnipotence of the House of Commons, the absolute responsibility of the ministers to Parliament — these ideas are so mystical that they can be explained only in terms of nostalgia for the nineteenth century. They are corollaries to other absolutes of the nineteenth century that we now see melting away — the idea of the absolute sovereignty of each nation, the idea of the complete freedom of private business from governmental interference. In the years that lie ahead, we shall probably work out a great many compromise adjustments between the world program and the interests of nations and their component parts; between governmental policy and the freedom of private corporations and institutions. If a legisla-

tive body is going to play an active role in such developments, it will need to be able to make up its collective mind coherently and responsibly, as the parliamentary system has been supposed to require it to do. But it will also need freedom to be inconsistent, to restrain the executive even when it wishes to support him, and to keep people and institutions from being fitted to the Procrustean bed of unified policy. Every step toward unification with the executive is a step toward the loss of that freedom.

THE SANCTIFICATION OF A SUBTERFUGE

What Bagehot wrote about the parliamentary system was not a constitutional dogma, but a description of how an informal political arrangement really operated in 1867. Legally and theoretically, the government of Great Britain was Her Majesty's Government; the ministers kissed Her Majesty's hand on taking office and were dismissed by her when they resigned; the House still voted supplies to the Crown and debated the Queen's address when Parliament came into session. But Bagehot explained that these "theatrical elements" of the monarchy only appealed to the "ruder sort" of subjects, while the effective part of the system — the responsibility of the Cabinet to the House of Commons — made the government work.

The parliamentary system was originally a sort of refined blackmail by which log-rolling groups in the House of Commons conspired to take control of the executive branch away from the Crown by threatening to refuse supplies if their demands were not met. This process was considered somewhat indecent in the eighteenth century; ministers like the first Pitt were still servile to the King in person and deplored the existence of parties. But when the idea of popular representative government developed, the blackmailers found they had a respectable case; nineteenth-century English liberals gave up the republican idea of abolishing royalty (which was making considerable headway in the early nineteenth century) for the compromise expedient of nullifying royal influence by the parliamentary system. Bagehot considered the British system only " ' a disguised republic ' . . . suited to such a being as the Englishman in such a century as the nineteenth," but Bagehot's rationalization led students to consider this makeshift system the classic form of representative government.

Bagehot himself, of course, looked on it as a sort of temporary compromise with democracy, not as an institution to venerate for all time. Only five years after he published *The English Constitution* he wrote an introduction to its second edition explaining that the system as he described it was already ceasing to exist.

For in 1867, the year in which *The English Constitution* was published, Disraeli's reform bill lowered the property qualification for the franchise, and Great Britain began to be a democracy. But Bagehot pointed out that parliamentary government (or, as he preferred to call it, Cabinet

government) would simply be impossible under a system of universal franchise; it is, he said, " only possible in what I may venture to call *deferential* nations . . . in which the numerous unwiser part wishes to be ruled by the less numerous wiser part. . . . A country of respectful poor," he observed, " though far less happy than where there are no poor to be respectful, is nevertheless far more fitted for the best government." As the franchise was repeatedly extended, the British poor became somewhat less like the " miserable creatures . . . politically contented as well as politically deferential," on whom Bagehot built his theory. Just as Bagehot feared, their demand that the government improve their economic welfare led both political parties to " bid for the support of the working-man " and even brought about " a political combination of the lower classes." Thus the end of laissez faire and the end of Bagehot's parliamentary system were parts of the same process.

In one other respect Bagehot deserves credit for understanding better than his followers the limitations of the parliamentary system. He made it clear that the system worked best in a restricted area with uniform standards of wealth and education. New England alone could make a parliamentary system work even better than England itself, he said, but the United States as a whole could not make it work at all.

Bagehot understood clearly that the parliamentary system was the result of the British people's failure to take the clean-cut step of assuming direct control of the executive. Cabinet government, he said, is possible only where the people believe that the executive is not their own agent, and not to be trusted. "We are not in this respect," he said, "'*un vrai peuple moderne*,' like the Americans," who "conceive of their executive as one of their appointed agents. . . . The French, the Swiss, and all nations who breathe the full atmosphere of the nineteenth century, think so too." But the English, he pointed out, can get a strong executive only by the subterfuge of Cabinet government, since by "the very nature of our Government our executive cannot be liked and trusted as the Swiss or the American is liked and trusted."

This statement no longer rings true. The British have obviously liked and trusted their government, they have brought it under popular control with a system of universal franchise, and they have called on it to administer a wide range of social services that America is just beginning to copy. (Sir William Beveridge has even predicted to America that she will fail to establish an adequate system of social security after the war because "we aren't so afraid of government as you are.") As all this has happened, however, a subtle transformation has taken place. It is as subtle as the earlier transformation by which His Majesty's Government effectively became parliamentary or Cabinet government. Bagehot described the earlier change and gave the new system a new name. The parliamentary system, the effective system of Bagehot's day, has

now become one of the "theatrical elements" of the British constitution, like the monarchy itself. W. Ivor Jennings has described the new system by which parties, newspapers, trade unions, and associations of many types collaborate to determine the course of public policy. He has described this system of popular government as thoroughly as Bagehot described the parliamentary or Cabinet system. But he lacked Bagehot's willingness to give a new name to a new thing; he called his two most important books *Parliament* and *Cabinet Government*.

Some of the official observers who testified before the Select Committee on Procedure on Public Business in 1931 were less cautious in their comments on what had happened to the parliamentary system. They testified in 1931, in the last few months before Mr. Ramsay MacDonald disbanded Great Britain's last party government and founded an allegedly temporary National Government to deal with the economic emergency. The creation of the Committee gave the more independent statesmen of all shades of political opinion (Mr. Winston Churchill among them) a chance to propose to imitate the American system of legislative committees and to express their opinion that the parliamentary system made it impossible in practice for the House to hold the ministers responsible for their actions.

Let us recall for a moment their testimony. (We probably overlooked it at the time, for we were too preoccupied with the fate of economic institutions to notice our political ones; the London *Times* reported none of the testimony, and American scholarly journals took no notice whatever of the Select Committee's existence.) All those who appeared before the Committee agreed that representative institutions were on trial throughout the world and that the House of Commons had lost a great deal of prestige and authority. Here, however, the agreement ended. Three main types of testimony were given.

One witness, speaking on behalf of the party he headed, proposed to carry the parliamentary system to its logical conclusion: he proposed to create a small emergency cabinet, like the War Cabinet of the First World War, and to give it extensive power to act by executive orders, rather than by legislation. As long as Parliament has "the power to dismiss the Government of the day by vote of censure," he insisted, "it is absurd to speak of Dictatorship." The War Cabinet of 1943, acting by orders such as he proposed, is now keeping the gentleman in question, Sir Oswald Mosley, in jail, and most of his party leaders with him.

The second type of testimony came from the chiefs of the Labour and Conservative parties, supported by a few traditionalists and by the Comptroller and Auditor General, the principal agent of the House in supervising the legality of public expenditure. Mr. MacDonald, who had in earlier years protested against the extent of the Cabinet's control over the House, now proposed to extend it still further. Mr. Baldwin had no idea to offer; he said that he had "been far too busily occupied in the last ten years in trying to run the machine to have ever attempted the reform of Parliament." He had never, he added, "given any consideration to the academic question of whether you could have a better system."

The chiefs of the Labour and Conservative machines were supported by Lord Eustace Percy, whose view (historically quite a correct one) was that it was not "the business of the House of Commons to 'control' the King's Ministers, if by that is meant to control the detail of their administration or even of their expenditure," and that "many of its present defects probably arise from the recent 'democratic' tendency to convert it into a sovereign parliamentary assembly." The noble lord's closing prescription for reform was that "if we could go back to the middle of the Nineteenth Century it would be immensely better."

On the other hand, both the machine and the traditional views were opposed vigorously by independents of all parties. All the leading Liberals, such as Mr. Lloyd George, Sir Herbert Samuel, Sir Archibald Sinclair, and Mr. Ramsay Muir; the Independent Labour Party as a whole, led by Mr. F. W. Jowett; and a few dissenting Conservatives, led by Mr. Winston Churchill, proposed ways by which the House of Commons could reassert its control over the executive. All these critics agreed on one point; that the doctrine of ministerial responsibility — the theory that the power of the House to dismiss the ministers provided a system of democratic control over them — in some ways prevented the House of Commons from controlling the administration. They agreed that this doctrine should be relaxed by permitting the House to vote against the Cabinet's wishes without dismissing the Cabinet and having the House itself dissolved, on many questions which the Cabinet had been considering "questions of confidence." They wished to make this change in order to make it possible for the House to set up committees like those of the Congress in the United States. Most of them, furthermore, were in favor of the creation of regional or functional assemblies of one kind or another, so that Parliament could delegate to other bodies certain types of legislation.

In appraising their systems of legislative-executive relations, the British and the Americans are both inclined to make the classic theory of parliamentary government their touchstone. Neither nation can really make it work under twentieth-century conditions, but both are curiously fascinated by it and judge the systems as they actually exist in terms of patterns that are now dead. But the effects of this spell on the two nations are different in one respect. In Great Britain, the innovators are fairly free of it; it is the traditionalists who are eager to go back to the middle of the nineteenth century. The innovators, at least, are in a position to propose something practical, as did Mr. Ramsay Muir in 1931 when he argued for a hierarchy of Cabinet committees much like the one which now exists under the War Cabinet. But in the United States the traditionalists and the innovators, among our academic and journalistic critics, argue for what will amount to the same thing. Our traditionalists want to go back to the American practice of the days of Buchanan and Grant and Harding — a weak executive and government by congressional committees — while our innovators, who always seem to turn to the classic theory of parliamentary government for their arguments, want to go back with Lord Eustace Percy to the House of Commons of the middle of the nineteenth century; but the specific steps that they usually propose could only serve to weaken the executive and lessen the unity of the legislature.

Those who were arguing in 1931 in Great Britain for innovations in the system of legislative-executive relations did not achieve any immediate practical results. When the economic crisis led to the resignation of the MacDonald Labour Government and the creation of the National Government in August, 1931, the Select Committee handed in its Minutes of Evidence without any report or recommendations. But the independent critics had at least made some realistic observations about the responsibility of the Cabinet to the House of Commons in relation to twentieth-century conditions inside Great Britain, and asked some searching questions.

The last few years have added to the changes that the Select Committee observed. The collective responsibility of the Cabinet seems a curious myth when we remember that the storm of disapproval over the Hoare-Laval pact led the other appeasers in the Cabinet to drop Sir Samuel Hoare, much as an American President drops a subordinate who is a political liability, and remain comfortably in power. Or that members of the House now insist again and again that Mr. Churchill stay in office himself but discharge certain of his colleagues. Or that the Secretary of State for War can be a former civil servant who was obviously not chosen for parliamentary leadership. The control of the Cabinet by the House of Commons seems equally mythical when we remember that the idea of a " National Government " replaced that of party responsibility in 1931, and that Mr. Neville Chamberlain could be made to resign in 1940 while still commanding an overwhelming majority in the House, being succeeded not by an opposition leader but by Mr. Churchill, who on questions like armaments and empire had been considered more imperialist than the Conservative leaders themselves. And as for the future, Mr. Churchill has predicted the continuance, at least during the period just after the war, of " a national government formally representative of the three parties in the state or . . . a national government comprising the best men in all parties who are willing to serve."

The British have been pretty enterprising since the war began in discarding the dogmas of the parliamentary system. In their peculiar informal way, they seem to be putting into effect something more like the presidential system. At least

their political issues now revolve around a single chief executive, who may rely for support on members of all parties while selecting and dismissing department heads at his discretion and who is more concerned with his following in the country at large than with that in the legislature. These changes have certainly not been planned that way, but at least one British authority has found the American Presidency an institution worthy of emulation. It was not to the House of Commons, but to the Senate and the House of Representatives of the United States in Congress assembled, that Mr. Churchill recently spoke of "the Chief Executive Power which the President derives from his office, and in respect of which I am the accredited representative of the Cabinet and His Majesty's Government."

The wisdom of the founders of the American Constitution (he went on to say) led them to associate the office of Commander in Chief with that of the Presidency of the United States. In this they followed the precedents which were successful in the case of George Washington. It is remarkable that after more than 150 years this combination of political and military authority has been found necessary not only in the United States, but in case of Marshal Stalin in Russia, and of Generalissimo Chiang Kai-shek in China. Even I, as majority leader in the House of Commons, in one branch of the Legislature, have been drawn from time to time — not perhaps wholly against my will — into some participation in miliary affairs. Modern war is total, and it is necessary for its conduct that the technical and professional authorities should be sustained and if necessary directed by the heads of governments who have knowledge which enables them to comprehend not only the military but the political and economic affairs at work, and who have the power to focus them all upon the goal.

There was never a more striking contrast between Prime Ministers than is shown by a comparison of this statement with Mr. Baldwin's remark that he had been so busy making a nineteenth-century set of institutions work that he had never considered the " academic question " whether it could be improved. And there has rarely been a more timely tribute to the wisdom of those Americans of the eighteenth century who deliberately rejected both hereditary monarchy and the election of an executive by a legislative assembly, but created instead a new thing — the presidential form of government.

It is odd enough to find Americans who seek to increase legislative control over the executive arguing for the system that in Britain has given the executive control over the legislature, or Americans who seek to remove unpopular department heads arguing for a system that in Britain keeps the administrative heads from being known, much less responsible, to the people. But it is even more peculiar, at a time when people are thinking about the creation of international federal institutions, to find Americans proposing to discard the presidential system

that has been associated with constitutional federalism, in favor of a system that has never proved its ability to accommodate the interests of diverse areas and populations in a federal republic.

America is a federation that is becoming a nation; the institutional system that has helped her do so will be of interest to the whole world as it moves toward greater unity. She gets her job of government done by popular control over two cooperating branches — an executive that provides unity and enterprise, a legislature that furnishes independent supervision and the restraining influence of local interests. Members of her public service are as varied in their origins and experience as the mixture of public and private institutions in her society itself; the leading members of that service come from private life and return to it freely, looking on the government as the people's agency open to their participation.

The assumptions that the legislature alone represents the people and that the administrative officials and departments are responsible to the people only through the legislature served the cause of democratic government well when the executive departments were under a hereditary monarch. They are the classical assumptions of the parliamentary system. Under the presidential system they can only set up an impossible relationship as the ideal to be attained and handicap the legislative and executive branches alike in their efforts to work together to meet the demands of a new age.

59. The Parliamentary and Presidential Systems*

On the issue of whether the parliamentary or the presidential system is more suited to the circumstances confronted by the United States at the present time, it is clearly a matter for Americans only to pronounce; and I have therefore no concern with the debate between Mr. Don K. Price and those with whom, like Mr. Henry Hazlitt, he differs. My purpose is the very different one of attempting to annotate some of his conclusions, both on the British system and on the American — for, as it seems to me, his account of the first is hardly aware of the changing social order of which it is the expression; and his account of the second, if a foreigner may judge, suffers somewhat seriously from those sins of omission in description which it is the natural temptation of a patriot to exhibit as virtues. And the whole argument, if I may say so, is built upon a series of unexplored and unstated assumptions which have an importance far beyond anything that Mr. Price is ready to recognize. I am, therefore, in no way seeking to eulogize the parliamentary system at the expense of the presidential, or vice versa; each seems to me to have its own special merits, and neither is likely to be capable of transference to another environment, where alien traditions are deep-rooted, without becoming something very different from

* From Harold J. Laski, *Public Administration Review*, IV (1944), pp. 347–59.

what it was in the country of its origin.

I begin by noting that the "classic" parliamentary system, which Mr. Price is so emphatic this country "long ago" abandoned, has never existed outside the imagination of the publicists. In each epoch of its history since the time of Bagehot, the character of parliamentary government has changed with the problems it has had to solve. It was one thing in the days of Gladstone and Disraeli; it was another thing in the ten years when Mr. Balfour led the House of Commons; and it was different again in the years of the Liberal government from 1906 to 1914. The adaptation of Parliament to the demands of the First World War was of a profound character; and in the years from 1919 to 1939, no small part of its character changed in terms of a party situation which was, in its turn, a reflection of issues raised by political and economic matters outside the walls of Westminster. Nor must it be forgotten that a parliamentary system under the leadership of Mr. Baldwin or Mr. Neville Chamberlain can only be regarded by formalists as the same as when it is directed, as by Mr. Churchill, by a man whom only three men since Palmerston can rival in the complex art of mastering the House of Commons.

The function of a parliamentary system is not to legislate; it is naive to expect that 615 men and women can hope to arrive at a coherent body of policy unless they are organized for this purpose. Its function is essentially threefold in our time. It must ventilate grievance and thereby scrutinize the executive's policy as a process of administration; it must so discuss the principles upon which the government of the day proposes to proceed that the virtues and defects are fully known to the electorate of the time; and it must exercise that selective function which, in its ultimate form, may mean the withdrawal of its confidence from ministers and, as a result, a general election. And it must so perform each of these functions that it shows awareness and responsiveness to public opinion outside, that intricate amalgamation of parties and interests to which it owes its authority and by whose will it is able to maintain itself as a going concern.

I do not think that Mr. Price could seriously analyze the parliamentary history of Britain in the last generation and conclude that the system has failed in any of these regards. If there is a better vindication of the power to ventilate grievance than the Savidge case of 1928, with all its important consequences, I do not know it. Even the secrecy which necessarily enshrouds the operations of war has not prevented questiontime in the House of Commons from remaining a vital check on the habits of the executive, and no one knows better than the prime minister that his colleague who cannot survive the ordeal of "supplementaries" with undimmed reputation is not likely to survive at all. So far

as the making of policy is concerned, nothing is more false, than to believe that cabinet initiative is imposed upon an army of faithful slaves. Mr. Chamberlain (as Mr. Pride has forgotten) had still a majority in the Narvik debate; but he did not survive the trenchant criticism of his policy. Mr. Churchill has an overwhelming majority as head of the Coalition government; but he has had to give way on such urgent matters as ministry of production, the allowances to the dependents of serving men and women, our relations with Marshal Tito, and the thorny problem of an excess profits tax which, despite the shrill lamentations of businessmen, remains at one hundred per cent. I select examples only; there is a host of other instances to prove that, even in the angry crisis of war, no prime minister may strain too far the allegiance out of which he has become prime minister. And, in my judgment, there is no aspect in which the House of Commons appears to better advantage than in its performance of the selective function. It will always listen with respect to some member who has something to say; its benches will always empty when a member, even if he be a minister of the crown, is talking, not of the real business in hand, but either to his constituents, or, as the member thinks, in a few cases of outstanding vanity, to History. It is not easy for a prime minister, however autocratic, to keep a colleague whom the House refuses to respect; and it is not easy for him to maintain his authority if he tempts the House to that temper where a minister is looked upon with dislike or with distrust.

Mr. Price writes as though the intensity of party allegiance turned most members of the House, differently from in the "classic" period, into little more than units in a division lobby. But that, I submit with respect, could only be held by someone who knows the House of Commons from books and not from direct observation. Perhaps the foreign critic is always tempted to be a *laudator temporis acti*. The present House of Commons is, I think, with but one exception, the poorest in the quality of its personnel since the parliament described in a famous sentence by Lord Keynes in his *Economic Consequences of the Peace,* a quarter of a century ago. Like every House there has ever been it contains dull men and stupid men and bad-tempered men; there are even some who seem to me malignant in habit and evil in purpose. But there is no party whip that could crack loudly enough to bring to heel some thirty members of the Labour party and perhaps as many on the Tory side. I do not think Earl Winterton compares in intellectual stature with Lord (Robert) Cecil; but I do not, either, think that the whip's office has yet been invented which could make him vote against his conscience. I do not share most of the political views of Sir George Schuster, but I am pretty confident that he makes up his own mind in his own way. And I suspect that if Mr. William Whiteley, the chief Labour whip, were to compare his experiences with the secretary of the treasury in the time of Lord North, or with those of Sir William Sutherland when Mr. Lloyd George was prime minister, he would be unable to repress his sense of envy at the ease with which the earlier generation marshalled its battalions in the proper lobbies. There is a significant moral in the lessons taught by men like Mr. Shinwell and Mr. Aneurin Bevan. There is a moral perhaps even more significant in the fact that the standing orders of the Labour party not only permit abstention from the division lobby but affirm the right of the private member to speak against what the caucus of the party has decided to support.

Mr. Price is distressed by the fact that the House cannot make policy but is restricted to the choice of men to whom the making of policy is entrusted. Upon this view, there are certain observations to be made. In the first place, the Cabinet (emergency apart) does not produce a policy as a conjurer produces a rabbit from his hat. It produces the policy that, at least in its large outlines, is likely to satisfy the established expectations of the majority by which it is supported. A cabinet does not come into office without a pretty clear notion in the public mind of the line it is likely to follow. Mr. Price admits that the system produces "an admirable coherence of policy." It is difficult to think of a legislative object that is more important in a modern community. For coherence, after all, means, first, that the direction in which it is moving is clearly defined;

and it means, second, that the source of responsibility for action is beyond mistake. It is difficult to think of anything more important in a democratic society than the achievement of clear responsibility; for nothing else does so much to enable the electorate to make up its mind. Compared to this, the independence of the private member is a matter of lesser import. As Burke said, nearly two hundred years ago, if a member of Parliament cannot, after election, find a body of members with whom he wishes to work, he must be either a beast or a god. Mr. Price is able to quote a good deal of evidence, some of it from politicians of long experience, who take the view that members of the House of Commons have little responsible work to do. It is, of course, no easy matter to pit one's judgment against men who, like Lord Baldwin and Sir Austen Chamberlain, knew parliamentary life for over a generation. But my own impression is that this view is disproportionate to the facts. The private member has little responsible work to do if that is his own inclination. But a good deal depends on what we agree to regard as responsible work. I think it is true that a lazy member will have a full opportunity to be lazy. It is also true that any member who is deeply interested in the personal problems of his constituents, in their pensions, in the working of the Rent Restriction Acts, in the location of industry in the area, will find that he has plenty of work on his hands. And if he is wise enough to specialize on a theme which evokes public interest, he be-

comes the center of a body of pressure groups all of which will seek to influence the action he chooses to take. And few governments, even when they have a comfortable majority, can afford to neglect such men. The questions they put, not least their supplementary questions, the points they make in debate, have an influence it is very easy to underestimate. Mr. Price seems to think that debate has become a lost art. If by that he means the great occasion when the galleries are packed and the orators on both sides of the House feel that they are addressing posterity, the answer is twofold. First, debates of this character were always pretty rare; it is an illusion cultivated by the biographers of great parliamentarians that world history was altered by what their heroes said. Most speeches are dead within a week of their delivery. It must, in fact, be so save in those rare periods when the speeches from either front bench are almost duds; and a constitutional democracy is unlikely to survive if those periods are frequent in its history.

The other answer is the elementary one that the substance of parliamentary discussion has changed. The franchise, Ireland, and religious toleration have given place to the future of the export trade, the ownership and control of the mining industry, and the amount of the allowances for the dependents of men and women in the forces. This change of substance means in a large degree, that most parliamentary business turns upon problems of quantity rather than problems of quality. As soon as this is the case, the type of oration which as with Burke, was a spoken book, or, with Mr. Gladstone, was like a Bach cantata, is utterly unsuited to the medium involved. If such occasions do arise, as in the debate over the Revised Prayer Book, or the issues implied in the illegal arrest of Mr. Art O'Brien, I do not think Mr. Price would find that the House of Commons of our own day is in any way inferior to its predecessors. I should, indeed, go further and argue that on the really great occasion the level of debate in our own day compares favorably with the past. Let Mr. Price read, speech by speech, the discussion in that Narvik debate which caused the down-fall of the Chamberlain government with the famous debates between Pitt and Fox over the French Revolution, or between Gladstone and Disraeli over British foreign policy in southeastern Europe, and I suggest that the Narvik debate does not suffer by comparison. And I suspect that Mr. Price would agree with me that the speech of Lord Cranborne, at the time of his resignation with Mr. Eden, or of Mr. Churchill, or Mr. Chamberlain's return from Munich in 1938, are likely to rank high in any collection of documents which seek to illustrate these times.

I suspect, in short, on this head, that just as Mr. Price thinks that Woodrow Wilson, when he wrote *Congressional Government,* was overinfluenced by the impeachment of President Johnson and by the scandals of the Grant administration and so became the easy victim of

Bagehot's brilliance, he has, in his turn, been gravely misled by his belief that what Wilson described was a species in the morphology of institutions not subject to the laws of evolution. The British state of this generation is not the British state of 1900 even; and the change in its purpose and its habits has naturally altered the character of its institutions.

I agree with Mr. Price's account of the defects of the British civil service between the two wars. I do not, however, accept his view that Lord Stamp and Sir John Anderson left the civil service for business and politics respectively because they were "more energetic and ambitious" than their colleagues. Lord Stamp went into private business because he wanted a large income; Sir John Anderson, near the close of his career as a civil servant, was promoted by Lord Baldwin to be the governor of Bengal; when he returned from his five years of office in India the Conservative party immediately offered him a seat in the House of Commons. The real reason for Mr. Price's general conclusion lies in British history in the interwar years. Partly, the civil service, in the administrative grade — itself a reflection of the general social structure of British life — reflected a series of prime ministers whose main ambition it was to safeguard the historic traditions of this country against any invasion of revolutionary ideas from the European continent and, especially, from the Soviet Union; partly, the social composition of the civil service made it tend to be attracted by this attitude. Mr. Price seems to forget that from 1906 to 1918 the civil service had a great record, not least in the First World War, and this record, in which the "energy and ambition" of its leading figures is outstanding, is very largely the reflection of a government which was engaged in the greatest measures of social reform Great Britain has ever known. It is an elementary principle of administration that a government with an enterprising program attracts a spirit of enterprise among its officials; while a government which seeks to make the degree of change weak and tepid will tend to give a character of weakness and tepidity to the civil service.

Mr. Price is, I think, quite mistaken in assuming that a permanent civil service of the British type would be "unsettled" if its chief officials were brought in from the outside. It is important, first, to note that businessmen have rarely made a success of civil service work; and the main reason appears to be their curious inability to work out reasons for the policy they recommend. They are accustomed to issue orders which they do not have to defend in public; the essence of the British system is that the House of Commons is entitled to receive a reasoned explanation from the minister of the policy he adopts.

Nor can I accept Mr. Price's view that the minister is "primarily a legislative leader, not an administrator." The successful minister in the parliamentary system is a man who can do three things. First, he must have ideas; second, he must know how to make his officials an effective team for carrying out those ideas; and, third, he must be able to secure support for them from Parliament. These have been the characteristics of all great ministers in modern times. They were the qualities of Sir Robert Peel; they were the qualities of Lord Cardwell; they were the qualities of Lord Haldane; they are, today, the qualities of Mr. Churchill and of Mr. Herbert Morrison. And the outstanding thing about any minister who wants a big job done is his ability to find the officials who will do it, with a determination to get rid of the chief administrators he has inherited if he does not think they fit in with his purposes. That was true of Lord Haldane's great army reforms; it was true of Mr. Arthur Henderson's remarkable record as a foreign secretary; and it is true of almost every stage in Mr. Churchill's administrative career in the last forty years. In the context of Mr. Price's remarks, it is worth recalling that when Mr. Churchill became president of the Board of Trade in 1908 he brought Sir William Beveridge from Toynbee Hall and the *Morning Post* to be the director of the labor exchange system he inaugurated. And it is an important footnote to these matters that when Sir William Beveridge left the civil service in 1919 to become the director of the London School of Economics and Political Science he had had a number of years as the very successful second secretary and then permanent secretary of the Ministry of Food.

There are, I think, two main reasons why the permanent civil service has been, since 1870, hostile to the acceptance of outsiders except in wartime. The first is historical: entrance by competitive examination ended that era of corruption and patronage which made so much of the British civil service a means of enabling the privileged classes in this country to provide for their indigent relatives; and there has always, quite intelligibly, been the fear that to tamper with open competition would mean a return to a system in which patronage would gain the upper hand. I say "intelligibly" because no one can analyze the war-time appointments made by nomination to the civil service without seeing how important a part influence plays in securing a post. The second reason is that the civil service, naturally enough, no more likes to see the limitation of its hopes of promotion by the choice of outsiders than do doctors like to see the recognition of osteopaths, or practicing lawyers in England the choice of eminent jurists for the Bench.

But there is no inherent reason at all why this attitude should be accepted. There is a great deal to be said for the appointment to the civil service of men and women who stay in a department for periods up to four or five years, or for the choice of specialists in a given field (Lord Keynes is a good example in this war) to do some special piece of work. Nor is there any reason at all why the official should be tied to his desk. Already, there are departments, of which the Colonial Office is a good example, in which field-work is done by the young official as part of his normal training; and the Asheton Committee has just reported in favor of periods of leave of absence for the purpose of study or research. If, to this, there is added a real effort to make service in local spheres of government interchangeable with service in the national spheres, most of Mr. Price's criticisms would seem to me to have been met.

There is one other aspect of Mr. Price's comments on the civil service which, I think, deserves a word. Admitting, though he does, that " official caution is common to all large organizations to some extent," he yet seems to regard it as a defect in the British system that " a British civil servant simply must remain noncommittal on policy questions in order to keep out of party politics." On this, I submit, there are two observations at least to be made. The British official must not *publicly* commit himself; I should have thought that the reasons for this habit of conduct were made sufficiently obvious when General MacArthur publicly committed himself on the New Deal in his letters to Congressman Miller. It would hardly have made for effective administration if, when Lord (then Sir) Robert Vansittart was chief diplomatic adviser to his Majesty's government, he had, with his typical ardor of phrase, written letters to *The Times* angrily denouncing, say, the foreign policy of Mr. Neville Chamberlain and Lord Halifax. Nor do I think it would have contributed to the smooth running of a department if Lord Keynes's brilliant pamphlet on the " Economic Consequences of Mr. Churchill" had been written by him not as a Cambridge don but as an official of the Treasury upon whom Mr. Churchill, as chancellor of the exchequer, relied for advice.

A British civil servant must remain *publicly* noncommittal. But few civil servants of any vigor or determination are lacking in a political philosophy which they express with remarkable freedom in the minutes of the departments or in conversation with their political chiefs. Mr. Price must have read some of the memoranda of Sir Eyre Crowe when he was at the Foreign Office; their pungency seems to me to exclude the prospect that they could be regarded as "noncommittal." Sir Kingsley Wood, when he was postmaster-general, found the peculiar eighteenth-century Whiggism of his permanent secretary incompatible with the positive policy he had decided upon; and Sir Evelyn Murray exchanged St. Martin's le Grand for the quieter atmosphere of the Board of Customs and Excise. Lord Welby, Lord Farrer, Sir Warren Fisher, Sir Horace Wilson — to take some examples from both the dead and the living — can hardly seriously be regarded as men who avoided the expression of their convictions "in order to keep out of party politics." They did not address public meetings, nor did they write to the press about the policy of their ministers. But I do not think any minister was ever in doubt about their outlook. And where there was some policy they wished to forward, or some legislation to which they were hostile,

they fought for it, or against it, with a tenacity it is impossible to mistake.

It is, no doubt, true that the ultimate decision is in the minister's hands, and that, once he has made the decision, it is the duty of his officials to do all they can to make it effective at its best. But Mr. Price must surely realize that this quality of loyalty to the ministerial decision is a fundamental safeguard against the evils of bureaucracy; it is why men of the type of the Baron von Holstein in Berlin are as rare as men of the type of Sir Horace Wilson in Whitehall. And to this must be added that Mr. Price's comparison of the minister's role to that of the chairman of a congressional committee save that the rule of seniority gives the latter an experience in the subject-matter to which the former cannot pretend seems to me an elementary confusion of antiquity with wisdom. All in all, I hazard the guess that Lord Haldane, who knew nothing of military matters when he became secretary of state for war in 1905, would compare pretty favorably with Senator Reynolds, the chairman of the Senate Committee on Military Affairs. I was not a great admirer of Lord Halifax' record as foreign secretary; but I prefer that record, with all its limitations, to the record of the late Senator Lodge, as chairman of the Senate Committee on Foreign Affairs. Lord Halifax, no doubt, was profoundly Conservative; but at least he fought in the open, and with a clean sword.

One final remark on the British system is perhaps worth making in the light of Mr. Price's comments. " It is not at all unusual for career civil servants, or public officials temporarily in the (United States) service," he writes, " to help build up support for policies." It is no more unusual in Great Britain than in the United States. The influence of Sir James Stephen on colonial policy was profound; we owe our system of secondary education and our health insurance system more to Sir Robert Morant than to any other person; Sir Charles Trevelyan, the brother-in-law of Macaulay, Sir Antony MacDonnell, Sir Michael Sadler, in the days when he directed research at the Board of Education, Lord Hankey when, as Sir Maurice Hankey, he was secretary both of the Cabinet and of the Committee of Imperial Defense, Sir Henry Tizard, as secretary of the Department of Scientific and Industrial Research, Sir Walter Morley Fletcher, as secretary of the Medical Research Council — all of these, to take but a few names almost at random, have exercised an influence at least as profound as any American civil servant since at least the Civil War. Their methods may have been different in the sense that they have not publicly " lobbied " for the policies in which they believed. But to suggest of any of these that they would have regarded a " positive " attitude to their jobs as " something improper," only means, I think, that Mr. Price is making his comparisons in terms of " inarticulate major premises " which he has not related to the facts he ought to have considered.

I must not be taken from all this to be arguing for a moment that the parliamentary system, both on its legislative and on its executive side, is not in need of drastic reform. I think it is in such need; but I think the grounds for that need arise out of quite different considerations from any Mr. Price puts forward. For the most part, I suggest, he is arguing not from life but from literature. The real problem the British system confronts is born of the fact that its institutions presuppose, both in the legislature and in the executive, government by the gentlemen in the age of the positive state. And, as most of Mr. Price's quotations from the Select Committee of 1931 make clear, he thinks that nothing can be done because gentlemen like Mr. (now Lord) Baldwin and Sir Austen Chamberlain thought that nothing could be done. He has omitted to notice that they were not anxious that anything should be done, for that simplest of reasons — that they were, broadly speaking, satisfied with things as they were. More than that: I do not doubt for a moment that their successors will insist that nothing can be done. Yet, already, Mr. Herbert Morrison has created a standing committee of the House of Commons to examine and report on all orders and regulations made under delegated legislation; and he has announced the forthcoming establishment of a permanent consultative committee of the Home Office on prisons and prison treatment. Large-scale changes of a comparable kind are on the way in the Ministry of Labour and the Colonial Office. I do not think it is a rash prophecy to suggest that, with victory, there will be large-scale institutional adaptation in the parliamentary system to meet the demands of a new world undreamed of in 1931 or, indeed, in 1939, by the "gentlemen of England" who have ruled Great Britain, with barely an interval, since 1688. At any rate, it is relatively obvious that either the adaptations must be made, or the foundations of the system itself will be in jeopardy.

II

If I venture some remarks upon Mr. Price's picture of American tendencies, I do so, first, with the sense that few foreigners can ever understand from within the "feel" of a system that is not their own, and, second, because, as I think, the congressional system raises vital problems with which Mr. Price has omitted to deal. He writes:

America is a federation that is becoming a nation; the institutional system that has helped her do so will be of interest to the whole world as it moves toward greater unity. She gets her job of government done by popular control over two cooperating branches — an executive that provides unity and enterprise, a legislative that furnishes independent supervision and the restraining influence of local interests. Members of her public service are as varied in their origins and experience as the mixture of public and private institutions in her society itself; the leading members of that service come from private life and return to it freely, looking on the government as the people's agency open to their participation.

It is difficult for a foreigner not to feel that these remarkable sentences belong less fully to the literature of political science than they do to the realm of poetry. It is true that Mr. Price elsewhere lays stress on the "parochialism of the pork-barrel" and that lack of individual responsibility for the federal program in Congress which "often" overemphasizes "local interests." But he likes the "flexibility" of the presidential system, the ability it confers "to make progress piecemeal," and the looseness of party discipline that it permits. It prevents, he surmises, the kind of opposition which is "apt to become uncompromising and irreconcilable." In modern society, "if a legislature is to keep the whole organism working in the public interest, it cannot depend on a power to hire and fire the head of it, but it must approve one action and condemn another, encourage here and reprove there, expand this agency and restrict that one." The assumptions of the parliamentary system, he thinks, would in the United States "handicap the legislative and executive branches alike in their efforts to work together to meet the demands of a new age."

I hope these quotations do justice to Mr. Price's point of view. I note with some surprise the thesis that the executive provides "unity and enterprise"; that may have been true of President Franklin Roosevelt and of perhaps the first two years of Woodrow Wilson's first term. But it does not seem to me a very accurate description of the president's function as that was conceived by Harding or Coolidge or Mr. Hoover. And the "independent supervision" that is "furnished" by Congress could not unfairly, I think, be described in a different way. Partly, of course, the description depends upon whether the president has a majority in both houses of Congress; if that is absent, there is certainly supervision of his policies, but to describe it as "independent" then seems to me the tribute of formalism to geniality. And if the president has a majority, the description seems to omit certain relevant factors. Supervision has one degree of intensity when the patronage is undistributed; it has another degree if the presidential term of office is nearing its close.

The "unity and enterprise" of which Mr. Price speaks is operative in the American system only when there is genuine presidential leadership, and when Congress is prepared to cooperate in its acceptance. What Mr. Price calls "independent supervision" seems to me only too often an attempt on the part of Congress to destroy the effectiveness of that leadership. I do not find it easy to accept that phrase as a fair description of the activities of men like Senator Holman, of Oregon, or of Congressman Thorkelson. Indeed, I think a strong case could be made out for the view that when cooperation between the president and Congress is lacking there is, behind either the one or the other, a "sinister interest," in Bentham's sense of the term, which deprives the people of the

United States of the legislation to which it is entitled. The "parochialism" to which Mr. Price refers seems to an outsider like myself to have many and more evil results than he notes. It can arrest the development of great projects, as when the hostility of Senator McKellar to Mr. Lilienthal holds up the progress of the TVA. It maintains the evil practice of "senatorial courtesy," which only too often has been no more than a polite name for enabling a particular senator to insist that the power of patronage be used to protect his hold upon the party machine in his own state. It results in a considerable wastage of public funds in the fulfilment of works projects which are not seldom indefensible in conception and inadequate in execution, and when the "independent supervision" of the executive by Congress results in investigating committees like that of Mr. Martin Dies, the abyss between the purpose Mr. Price attributes to the system and the consequences actually achieved seems to me far wider than he seems to admit.

It is easy to say lightly that the United States is "a federation that is becoming a nation"; that seems to pass over not only the degree in which American federalism is obsolete but, also, the degree in which the presidential system intensifies that obsolescence. That emerges, I suggest, in the vastly different standards of education, factory conditions, public health, to take three examples only, in the different parts of the Union. That infant mortality in San Antonio should be worse than in any great city save Shanghai is a serious comment upon the results of the division of powers. That the level of educational opportunity in the South should be so different from what it is in the North or in the West raises issues of the first importance for a democratic society. Mr. Price emphasizes the urgency of keeping "the administration of government under the control of the people, to invigorate it for executive action in their behalf," especially in this time of crisis. But he does not inquire whether there is in fact that popular control, nor whether the presidential system is a method of invigorating the administration.

He would, no doubt, agree that there is good reason to suppose that the under-privileged in the United States — not merely the Negro people but poor whites, like the share-croppers of Arkansas — have a relatively small part in the popular control of the administrative process. He would, I suggest, find it difficult to prove that the action of Congress over matters of war taxation or its abolition of the National Resources Planning Board are contributions to "invigorating the administration." It may well be, as he says, that the scandals of Grant's presidency turned Woodrow Wilson's mind towards the theme of Bagehot's *English Constitution*. But it would be no more surprising if the scandals of President Harding's brief period of office raised the question of whether the American institutional pattern was adequate to the problems it confronted. It is at least open to debate, for example, whether it ought

perpetually to require a grave emergency to give the American commonwealth an effectively coherent policy. It is not less open to doubt whether a party system that becomes effectively national only during election time enables the people really to know what men they are choosing and what issues they are deciding. I see no reason to suppose that there is any real advantage in a cabinet system upon which so able a man as Secretary Franklin Lane can make the incisive criticisms that his letters reveal. And the "independent supervision" of the Senate in foreign affairs which drives any president with an important problem on his hands to the use of *"eminences grises"* like Colonel House, or to those "agreements" and "understandings" which, by falling short of the status of treaties, enable him to by-pass that supervision, at least makes one reflect that President Wilson may not have been without some ground for the choice he made in his Congressional Government.

Nor do I find it easy to be enthusiastic about Mr. Price's praise for a public service in which "the leading members . . . come from private life and return to it." I note, in the first place, that the quality of administration in the United States has, in the main, improved in the degree that the spoils system has given place to the merit system. I note, in the second place, that as soon as the head of a government department has really learned how to handle his office, he is only too likely to return to private life, so that most departments contain some permanent official upon whose advice and judgment his minister is compelled to rely. And I note, in the third place, that every member of the executive, from the president downwards, is driven, as he makes his plans, to bear in mind not merely the objective he may have in view but the fact that, just because it is his objective, the legislature will want to shape it differently lest the full credit for its achievement be accorded to the executive, and not to the legislative, branch of the government. Mr. Price may be content with an administrative process in which the Teapot Dome scandal was exposed and overcome because the under secretary of the interior, Mr. Harry Slattery, gave the late Senator La Follette the material for his resolution by which Senator Fall was broken. He can hardly feel that it is satisfactory that Senator Stephens of Mississippi should be able to prevent the appointment of Dr. Willard Thorp as the head of the Bureau of Foreign and Domestic Commerce in 1933–34, seemingly on the ground that political fidelity is more important than technical competence; and I submit that his dissatisfaction ought to be even greater if it be true that Senator Stephens was merely the instrument of the postmaster-general, Mr. James A. Farley, who was in quest of posts for "deserving Democrats."

I omit from these observations that most remarkable of the institutions in the presidential system — the Supreme Court of the United States. But it is at least necessary to remark that this third chamber of the American legislature has amply justified the comment of Chief Justice Hughes upon its working. " The spirit of the work of the Supreme Court," he has written, " permeates every legislative assembly and every important discussion of reforms by legislative action. We largely subject our political thinking to the conception of law, not as an arbitrary edict of power, but as governed by the fundamental conceptions of justice." Few better methods could easily be found than that of judicial review for keeping the people in political tutelage, on the one hand, or of slowing down, save in the gravest emergency, both the pace of social change and the interest in attaining it. For once the final word, the cumbrous process of amendment apart, was placed in the hands of the Supreme Court, the American Constitution entrusted the shaping of its final character not to the operation of some abstract principles but to a body of men who are nominated to the court either on political grounds or because they have been successful lawyers. Only the reader of the massive volume of the hearings before the Senate Judiciary Committee on Mr. Justice Brandeis' appointment can appreciate the full implications of this confidence. And when he thinks of Chief Justice Hughes's " fundamental conceptions of justice," he should study the resounding rhetoric of Mr. Joseph H. Choate in the income tax case, or the dissents of Mr. Justice McReynolds in the springtime of the New Deal, to discover how those conceptions are determined.

Mr. Price does not discuss the Supreme Court in his interesting article, though I should have thought that no account of the presidential system was complete without a survey of its implications. In one sense, perhaps, he was wise to omit the court from his comparison, for it raises issues — about the application of the Fifth, Fourteenth, and Fifteenth Amendments, for example — which cast a vivid light upon the relations between the court and public opinion. Universal suffrage has its defects, no doubt, but at least in the British parliamentary system it is in fact universal. It is, at least to an outsider, significant that all the combined efforts of the Constitution in the United States have not been able honestly to confront what Professor Myrdal, in his remarkable book, calls the " American Dilemma."

Nor is it entirely fair to leave out of account in any discussion of the presidential system the quite special influence it offers to pressure groups by reason of the separation of powers. Julius Caesar Burrows of Michigan and General Sickles were the precursors of that titan with feet of clay, the American Legion, which makes the modest demands upon the British Treasury of the eighteenth-century English aristocrat seem almost childish by comparison. Lobbying in Whitehall is not, of course, any more unknown than lobbying in Washington. But there is, I think, the significant difference between the two places that, in the one, the responsibility for the result is direct and unmistakable, while in the other it is so thinned out by dispersion that it is often beyond the reach of the

elector's insight. It would be an illuminating task to discover what interests precisely were responsible for the character and level of the Hawley-Smoot tariff; in Britain, there is little difficulty in concluding that our protective tariff was a wreath deposited by the Tory party, through the agency of Mr. Neville Chamberlain, on the tomb of his distinguished father. It would be still more interesting to know by what influences a progressive Democrat, like President Roosevelt, was led to acquiesce in policies which could have no other result than the overthrow of the nascent Spanish democracy in the interest of that Franco whose status as a puppet of Hitler and Mussolini was clear even when the President helped to pave his way to Madrid. And, in some ways, it would be most interesting of all to know why American patronage was preferred, first to Pétan and Darlan when they built the evil regime of Vichy, then to Darlan when he achieved his second piece of treachery, and then to that Peyrouton whom every element in the French resistance movement united to hate. Mr. Churchill's patronage of King George of the Hellenes and King Peter of Jugoslavia is, after all, of a piece with all his character; he is an eighteenth-century Whig who has strayed by chronological accident into a twentieth-century war, and in his mind, " republic " and " revolution " are almost interchangeable terms. But why this outlook should at least equally dominate the mind of President Roosevelt and his advisers in the State Department is, pretty clearly, a longer more complicated story.

It is, further, significant enough that Mr. Price makes no serious comment on the rule requiring local residence for congressmen and senators. It is a rule that has vast influence, almost wholly evil, on American public life. For, in the first place, it excludes from politics a large number of citizens, except in an indirect way; and, in the second, it makes the congressman or senator balance the alternatives between, for example, a small law practice in a backwoods township and the interest and excitement of life in Washington. The result is twofold; it makes him a perpetual candidate living by the favors he can secure for his district or his state; and, in most instances, it compels him to build or use a machine in his support, lest he be ousted by some ambitious rival. And to this must be added that the very fact that so large a number of people to whom politics is a natural métier are excluded from it, multiplies the number of pressure groups through which they may hope to win alternative influence. And the rule of local residence gives by its nature a secret source of power to the great economic interests of America. The Du Ponts in Delaware and the Anaconda Copper Corporation in Montana are only classical examples of this kind. And where there arises this relationship, there is almost bound to arise also intermediate machines to collect " brokerage," as it were, on the service they can render the politicians or the corporations. The Kelly machine in Chicago, the

Hague machine in New Jersey, the late Senator Huey Long in Louisiana, the late Senator Penrose in Pennsylvania are only the most striking examples of an underworld of politics which breeds corruption wherever its influence extends. The result is not merely the " parochialism " which Mr. Price deplores; the result is the far more mischievous consequence that the politician and the businessman are engaged either in joint corruption or in mutual conflict at the expense of the common welfare. Judge Pecora's exposure of the practices of Wall Street is one link only in the long chain which reaches back to the classic bargain whereby the capital of the United States was placed on the banks of the Potomac.

III

These annotations have, I hope, established the thesis that the problems involved in any comparison between the parliamentary and the presidential systems are far more complicated than Mr. Price is willing to concede. I should not for one moment claim that one system is better than the other, still less that the parliamentary system is more suited to the genius of the American people than the presidential. A system of government is very like a pair of shoes; it grows to the use of the feet to which it is fitted. But it is well to remember of governments what is true, also, of footwear — that the shoes must be suited to the journey it is proposed to take. It ought, I think, to occur to Mr. Price that if

Lord Baldwin did not examine whether the British system of nineteenth-century institutions could be improved, he himself failed to examine whether improvement was possible in the American system of eighteenth-century institutions.

It is essential for both our countries to realize that we face, in the coming years, problems of a scale and an intensity far greater than any we have known at least in our own lifetime. We shall, neither of us, confront them in a constructive way unless we make up our minds about the purposes we want to fulfill as communities and the methods that are appropriate to those purposes. Both Great Britain and the United States have achieved political democracy; neither has in a serious way approached a democratic way of life in either our social or our economic institutions. As the Second World War draws to its close, we ought at least to have learned certain lessons that are implied in its grim experience. Whether the form of our political institutions be parliamentary or presidential, it is quite certain that they will not remain on a democratic foundation unless we deliberately set out to conquer mass unemployment. It is no less certain that democracy will lose the spirit that gives it meaning unless our citizens have that sense of hope and exhilaration which is born only of an economy that, by its power to expand, is capable of raising the standard of life for all our citizens. It is in a high degree probable that the power of successful expansion depends upon the planning of production for community consumption. Free enterprise, in the American sense of the phrase, is only too likely, on our experience, to make the tragic process of boom and slump once more endemic in our societies. That process is a threat to any political system which seeks to make persuasion, and not force, the main method of social change. If we are to avoid this threat, our task is, above all, to give men and women an equal claim upon what there is of common welfare and to create in them that power to make their experience of life articulate which alone gives reality to their citizenship. If we feel entitled to ask millions to risk their lives for freedom, at least we have the obligation to make the freedom for which they fight come to have significance in their lives. The one thing to which we are not entitled is the purchase of our own freedom at the price of their servitude.

I do not need to point out that by no one was this more clearly seen or more effectively enunciated than by Thomas Jefferson; nor do I need to argue that the significance of America in the last three hundred years has lain in the fact that it made this dream a source of spiritual renovation to millions of poor and oppressed men and women in Europe and Asia and even on the African continent. Those for whom that dream came true were, alas, far fewer in numbers than those who were sustained by what it evoked of hope. In any attempt to give it a wider fulfilment the first necessity, as I think, is to see life as a whole, to refuse to divorce it into categories which are firmly separated from one another. From this angle, therefore, the attempt to measure political institutions in one country against political institutions in another is a method of analysis which cannot lead to fruitful results. For the political cannot be separated from the economic, and both are set in a context to which history and the material resources of a community give a special meaning. My own main consciousness is of the certainty that we are living in an age which will compel enormous changes. In some ways it will seem a smaller world, and it may well find that the annihilation of physical space means the assimilation of spiritual difference. The vital thing is to make our categories of thought the outcome of examining nature and not the result of imposing a pattern upon it in the belief that it must conform to our ways. For only in the degree that we understand how definitively freedom is the recognition of necessity can we adjust our hopes to our destinies.

60. Marbury v. Madison, 1 Cranch 137 (1803)

[On March 2, 1801, two days before the close of his term, President John Adams appointed William Marbury, among others, as a justice of the peace in the District of Columbia. The appointment was confirmed by the Senate, the commission was signed by the President, countersigned by the Secretary of State and the seal of the United States was affixed. Through some inadvertence the commission was left on the desk of the Secretary of State when President Adams' term expired at midnight, March 3rd. Upon Thomas Jefferson's accession to the presidency, he directed his Secretary of State, James Madison, to refuse delivery of the commission. Marbury appealed to the Supreme Court sitting as a court of original jurisdiction for a writ of mandamus to compel delivery of the commission. This specific writ was sought under a section of the Judiciary Act of 1789 which provided that, "The Supreme Court . . . shall have power to issue . . . writs of mandamus in cases warranted by the principles and usages of law, to any persons holding office, under the authority of the United States." Chief Justice John Marshall, speaking for the entire court, held this provision unconstitutional as an attempt to enlarge the original jurisdiction of the Supreme Court beyond that provided by Article III, Section 2 of the Constitution of the United States which reads in part as follows: " In all cases affecting ambassadors, other public ministers and consuls, and those in which a State shall be Party, the Supreme Court shall have *original jurisdiction*."]

The following opinion of the court was delivered by the CHIEF JUSTICE [MARSHALL]. . . .

The question, whether an act, repugnant to the constitution, can become the law of the land, is a question deeply interesting to the United States; but, happily, not of an intricacy proportioned to its interest. It seems only necessary to recognize certain principles, supposed to have been long and well established, to decide it. That the people have an original right to establish, for their future government, such principles as, in their opinion shall most conduce to their own happiness, is the basis on which the whole American fabric has been erected. The exercise of this original right is a very great exertion; nor can it, nor ought it, to be frequently repeated. The principles, therefore, so established, are deemed fundamental; and as the authority from which they proceed is supreme, and can seldom act, they are designed to be permanent.

This original and supreme will organizes the government, and assigns to different departments their respective powers. It may either stop here, or establish certain limits not to be transcended by those departments. The government of the United States is of the latter description. The powers of the legislature are defined and limited; and that those limits may not be mistaken, or forgotten, the constitution is written. To what purpose are powers limited, and to what purpose is that limitation committed to writing if these limits may, at any time, be passed by those intended to be restrained? The distinction between a government with limited and unlimited powers is abolished, if those limits do not confine the persons on whom they are imposed, and if acts prohibited and acts allowed, are of equal obligation. It is a proposition too plain to be contested, that the constitution controls any legislative act repugnant to it; or that the legislature may alter the constitution by an ordinary act.

Between these alternatives, there is no middle ground. The constitution is either a superior paramount law, unchangeable by ordinary means, or it is on a level with ordinary legislative acts, and, like other acts, is alterable when the legislature shall please to alter it. If the former part of the alternative be true, then a legislative act, contrary to the constitution, is not law; if the latter part be true, then written constitutions are absurd attempts, on the part of the people, to limit a power, in its own nature, illimitable.

Certainly, all those who have framed written constitutions contemplate them as forming the fundamental and paramount law of the nation, and consequently, the theory of every such government must be, that an act of the legislature, repugnant to the constitution, is void. This theory is essentially attached to a written constitution, and is, consequently, to be considered, by this court, as one of the fundamental principles of our society. It is not, therefore, to be lost sight of, in the further consideration of this subject.

If an act of the legislature, repugnant to the constitution, is void, does it, notwithstanding its invalidity, bind the courts, and oblige them to give it effect? Or, in other words, though it be not law, does it constitute a rule as operative as if it was a law? This would be to overthrow, in fact, what was established in theory; and would seem, at first view, an absurdity too gross to be insisted on. It shall, however, receive a more attentive consideration.

It is, emphatically, the province and duty of the judicial department, to say what the law is. Those who apply the rule to particular cases, must of necessity expound and interpret that rule. If two laws conflict with each other, the courts must decide on the operation of each. So, if a law be in opposition to the constitution; if both the law and the constitution apply to a particular case, so that the court must either decide that case, conformably to the law, disregarding the constitution; or conformably to the constitution, disregarding the law; the court must determine which of these conflicting rules governs the case; this is of the very essence of judicial duty. If then, the courts are to regard the constitution, and the constitution is superior to any ordinary act of the legislature, the constitution, and not such ordinary act, must govern the case to which they both apply.

Those, then, who controvert the principle, that the constitution is to be considered, in court, as a paramount law, are reduced to the necessity of maintaining that courts must close their eyes on the constitution, and see only the law. This doctrine would subvert the very foundation of all written constitutions. It would declare that an act which, according to the principles and theory of our government, is entirely void, is yet, in practice, completely obligatory. It would declare, that if the legislature shall do what is expressly forbidden, such act, notwithstanding the express prohibition, is in reality effectual. It would be giving to the legislature a practical and real omnipotence, with the same breath which professes to restrict their powers within narrow limits. It is prescribing limits, and declaring that those limits may be passed at pleasure. That it thus reduces to nothing, what we have deemed the greatest improvement on political institutions, a written constitution, would, of itself, be sufficient, in America, where written constitutions have been viewed with so much reverence, for rejecting the construction. But the peculiar expressions of the constitution of the United States furnish additional arguments in favor of its rejection. The judicial power of the United States is extended to all cases arising under the constitution. Could it be the intention of those who gave this power, to say, that in using it, the constitution should not be looked into? That a case arising under the constitution should be decided, without examining the instrument under which it arises? This is too extravagant to be maintained. In some cases, then, the constitution must be looked into by the judges. And if they can open it at all, what part of it are they forbidden to read or to obey?

There are many other parts of the constitution which serve to illustrate this subject. It is declared, that " no tax or duty shall be laid on articles exported from any state." Suppose, a duty on the export of cotton, of tobacco, or of flour; and a suit instituted to recover it. Ought judgment to be rendered in such a case? ought the judges to close their eyes on the constitution, and only see the law?

The constitution declares " that no bill of attainder or *ex post facto* law shall be passed." If, however, such a bill should be passed, and a person should be prosecuted under it; must the court condemn to death those victims whom the constitution endeavors to preserve?

" No person," says the constitution, " shall be convicted of treason, unless on the testimony of two witnesses to the same overt act, or on confession in open court." Here, the language of the constitution is addressed especially to the courts. It prescribes, directly for them, a rule of evidence not to be departed from. If the legislature should change that rule, and declare one witness, or a confession out of court, sufficient for conviction, must the constitutional principle yield to the legislative act?

From these, and many other selections which might be made, it is apparent, that the framers of the constitution contemplated that instrument as a rule for the government of courts, as well as of the legislature. Why otherwise does it direct the judges to take an oath to support it? This oath certainly applies in an especial manner, to their conduct in their official character. How immoral to impose it on them, if they were to be used as the instruments, and the knowing instruments, for violating what they swear to support!

The oath of office, too, imposed by the legislature, is completely demonstrative of the legislative opinion on this subject. It is in these words: " I do solemnly swear, that I will administer justice, without respect to persons, and do equal right to the poor and to the rich; and that I will faithfully and impartially discharge all the duties incumbent on me as ——, according to the best of my abilities and understanding, agreeably to the constitution and laws of the United States." Why does a judge swear to discharge his duties agreeably to the constitution of the United States, if that constitution forms no rule for his government? if it is closed upon him, and cannot be inspected by him? If such be the real state of things, this is worse than solemn mockery. To prescribe, or to take this oath, becomes equally a crime.

It is also not entirely unworthy of observation, that in declaring what shall be the supreme law of the land, the constitution itself is first mentioned; and not the laws of the United States, generally, but those only which shall be made in pursuance of the constitution, have that rank.

Thus, the particular phraseology of the constitution of the United States confirms and strengthens the principle, supposed to be essential to all written constitutions, that a law repugnant to the constitution is void; and that courts, as well as other departments, are bound by that instrument.

The rule must be discharged.

61. An Evaluation of Judicial Review*

The power of the Supreme Court to declare acts of Congress unconstitutional does not, as a practice, exist in any other civilized country. One or two cases in Australia and Canada, under unusual conditions, are the exceptions which prove the general rule. Those who argue for its *necessity* rely on old fictions and ignore the facts. Thus, they claim that it is a necessary part of our Anglo-Saxon liberties, but Anglo-Saxon England has never allowed this power to its courts. Marshall's argument that it follows from the nature of written constitutions, is obviously refuted by the constitutions of France and of other countries where life, liberty and property are as safe, if not safer than they are here; and the argument that Federal Government is impossible without it, ignores the Swiss and other Federal states.

But the main fallacy is the argument that since the Constitution declares itself to be the supreme law of the land, therefore Congress and the Executive must accept the Court's interpretation of it, though they are supposed to be coordinate and not subordinate powers. This is the fallacy of *non sequitur*. A Constitution is adopted by the people, who ought to know what they vote for, and this cannot exclude the people's repre-

* From Morris R. Cohen, "Is Judicial Review Necessary?" the *New Leader*, XIX (1936), p. 5. Reprinted with permission of the administrators of the estate of Morris Raphael Cohen and the *New Leader*.

sentatives in the Congress and in the Executive, mostly lawyers in any case. What the Constitution in fact does say, is that *it and the laws and treaties of the United States made in pursuance* of it, should be the supreme law of the land. Now, the members of Congress and the Executive swear to obey the Constitution, and how can they make laws and treaties under it without interpreting its meaning? And why must they disregard their own conscientious reading of the Constitution because a different opinion is held by a majority of the Supreme Court, which may not be a majority even of all the judges that pass on the act? The notion that the court must necessarily have the *exclusive* and final power to declare what the Constitution means is neither historically nor logically tenable. Indeed, the Supreme Court itself abandons it when it admits that the meaning of the term "republican form of government" in the Constitution must be left to Congress and to the Executive.

Let us get behind legalistic hair-splitting and look at the question in the light of common sense and the logic that is no respecter of traditional dogmas. No one really believes that the human beings who adopted the Constitution in the 18th century foresaw all our modern conditions and made unmistakable provision as to what Congress may or may not enact into law. And the notion that they laid down certain principles from which every decision of the Supreme Court is deduced with absolute rigor and without regard to the personal opinion of the judges, must be pronounced ridiculous by the logic of modern science. History shows unmistakably that decisions on constitutional issues depend upon the political, social and economic opinions of the judges. Taney differed from Marshall, Field from Waite, and McReynolds from Holmes. And who honestly doubts that if the personnel of the court were to change tomorrow, its decisions would be different? It is certainly not through the will of the people and the express words of the Constitution that the power to regulate interstate commerce includes the power to prohibit lotteries but not to regulate insurance, to prohibit the passage of liquor from some States to others or to compel railroads to install certain safety appliances, but not to prohibit them from posting notices that they will discharge their men who join trade unions. Only recently this power to regulate interstate commerce was held to include the power to order a system of workmen's compensation but not a pension system. These and a thousand other subtle distinctions are points on which well-informed men and even judges honestly differ, and how the court will rule on any actual act of Congress, is largely a matter of guess work even for lawyers. It is unbelievable that the framers of the Constitution in 1787 had settled these matters beyond a reasonable doubt. When, therefore, a mere majority of the court insists that no rational being can doubt that

Congress has misread or violated the plain provisions of the Constitution, their sense of humor as well as of courtesy to their fellow judges and to the coordinate powers of the government is rather esoteric.

Consider now the practical arguments for judicial review.

It has been defended as a necessary appeal from the passion and haste of Congress to the calm and deliberate judgment of the Courts; but this rests on a number of untenable assumptions. It is psychologically weird to suppose that judges are not human or free from human passions. One has only to recall Justice McReynolds dissent in the Gold Case or the passionate outburst of Chief Justice Chase and the minority in connection with the second Legal Tender Case. Even more important is the fact that our courts are so constituted that their deliberation cannot possibly be based on adequate knowledge. For the court cannot institute investigation. It cannot hold prolonged hearings. The life of the judge does not permit him to be fully cognizant of all that is going on in our modern complicated civilization. And the fiction that judges only pass on the law and not on the actual facts makes them satisfied to decide fateful questions of public policy by listening to two lawyers argue for a few hours on submitted briefs, which is hardly an intelligent way of determining any great issue or the affairs of a nation.

Moreover, the assumption that all restraints on Congressional action are good is utterly thoughtless. One might well say that it is a good thing to tie us to stones so as to prevent us from running and possibly breaking our necks. Safety often depends upon quick action, as when our house is on fire or someone is to be rescued from danger. Indeed, this argument for the necessity of restraints on the people's representatives is precisely the one that used to be advanced in England for the House of Lords. When, however, the English people discovered that such restraints were in fact exercised in the interests of a given class, and against the popular will, they curbed that power to delay legislation. So we may likewise curb the power of our courts to suspend Congressional legislation until the people go through the elaborate process of a Constitutional Amendment. The trouble with Congress is not only its haste but more often its cumbrous slowness. In any case, it is safer to be subject to accidental majorities of a Congress that is in touch with and responsive to popular needs than to be at the mercy of an accidental and very small majority of the Supreme Court. For the mistakes of Congress can be corrected more quickly, while to overcome the mistakes of the Supreme Court, as in the Income Tax Case of 1895, took eighteen years. Actually there have been very few acts of Congress that have been felt to be unjust or unconstitutional by a majority of our people, and from which the courts have saved us. The liberties which the courts have enforced have more often been the liberty of powerful vested interests to exploit the poor who work for a living — witness the minimum wage

cases, the child labor case, the enforcement of yellow dog contracts and iniquitous injunctions, and the like. In the two cases where Congress did admittedly violate the plain command of the Constitution, to wit, in refusing from 1922 to 1932 to reapportion representation according to the latest census or to reduce representation in accordance with the plain provision of the 14th Amendment, the courts have done nothing or have been helpless. The rights and liberties of the people are safe only in the hands of a vigilant and intelligent electorate.

The power of the courts to declare legislation unconstitutional has in fact made our law uncertain and has degraded our political life. For when a law is planned no one knows with reliable certainty how the courts will rule on a Congressional enactment, and the result is that instead of discussing issues on their merits, we discuss them in terms of what a few elderly gentlemen on the Supreme Court bench will think of their constitutionality. *The worst of all possible systems of government is that which divorces power from responsibility, and that is what we do when we give the last word to judges who are not answerable to any earthly authority.*

It is vain to say the people can amend the Constitution. Not only is that process very cumbrous, requiring three-quarters of the States rather than a majority of the people, but no one knows what the courts will make of the Amendment when it is passed. Thus, when the people adopted the 11th Amendment prohibiting a foreign citizen from suing a State, it was practically nullified by Marshall permitting such suits against the officers of the State. When the people, after the Civil War, adopted the 14th Amendment to safeguard the rights of the negroes, the latter got very little real protection from it, but it became instead an instrument to prevent the former free States from protecting their white laborers by regulating hours, wages and the like. The people recalled the court's decision of 1895 when they empowered Congress to tax incomes *from whatever source derived*. Nevertheless, the courts do not allow the taxing of incomes from child labor and other sources, thus creating a privileged class free from taxation. The words *from whatever source derived* are as plain as human words can be, but the courts pay more attention to obsolete political theories and Marshall's dictum that the power to tax is the power to destroy — a dictum, however, which they disregard when they allow Congress, through heavy taxation, to drive out oleomargarine and State notes.

The arbitrary assumption that federal government cannot exist without the judicial review, ignores the fact that the harmonious adjustment between the constituent States of a federal union depends upon changing social, economic and political conditions and cannot be absolutely fixed in advance in purely legal terms. It is, therefore, properly a matter for a federal council, as Jefferson, indeed, suggested for the United States. If the distinctive virtue of a federal law is that it allows the different States to try diverse provisions for a common good, that virtue has been nearly killed by the way our Supreme Court has stretched the 14th Amendment — intended by the people to protect the negroes — to prohibit all legislation that does not appeal to elderly and conservative gentlemen who refuse to think in terms of the actual conditions of today.

It has frequently been urged that since the judicial review has been our accepted tradition since the beginning of our national life, and since we have prospered under it, it is unpatriotic to try to change it. Even if the historic facts here assumed were true, the conclusion would not follow in logic or ethics. But the history thus assumed is not quite accurate. In the early days of the Republic the matter was by no means settled, as can be seen by Chief Justice Gibson's refutation of the arguments advanced by Marshall in *Marbury* v. *Madison*. The first case in which the Supreme Court undertook to set aside a Congressional enactment of general interest was really the Dred Scott case, and it was certainly not tacitly accepted. It is only since the Civil War that this power has become an active and important factor in the affairs of our country.

As a student of philosophy, I must decline the challenge to name the exact alternative to the mode prevailing today. There are many possible alternatives and we shall probably not anticipate the actual historic consequences of proposed changes any more accurately than those who adopted the 14th Amendment. But there can be no doubt that the strength of judicial review rests on the popular misconception that the Constitution is some esoteric document which in some mysterious way contains a solution to every problem, revealed only to a majority of the judges on the Supreme Court Bench. When the people at large begin to discount sanctimonious fictions and to look at the naked facts — as our advanced legal scholars and progressive jurists are already doing — they will see what all honest thinkers have seen all along, namely, that constitutional law is just what the judges make it, that our Supreme Court is, in fact, a continuous Constitutional Convention, and that the people or their elected representatives ought to have an effective way of ratifying or rejecting the results. Otherwise the will of the majority will continue to be frustrated and representative government exist in name only.

C. Politics as Science and Art

62. Introduction

What is the essential nature of politics? What is the relationship between politics and ethics? What are the chances of eliminating through science rivalries and struggles among contending groups? The viewpoint that is currently most prominent in western society has confidently predicted that politics would yield to scientific studies and has looked for its replacement by scientific techniques of organization. Two of the selections which follow are sharply opposed to the prevailing scientific attitude and view. They suggest that politics must be construed as an art wherein prudent adjustments are the best to be hoped for or expected. The first selection is taken from an essay by one of the editors pertaining especially to international politics but relevant for politics in general. Winston S. Churchill was the wartime Prime Minister of England and was returned to power with the triumph of the Conservatives in 1951. It was his purpose in this address to show that politics is not and can never become a pure science. Our third selection is drawn from the great German sociologist Max Weber (1864–1920), whose writings have furnished the foundation for sociological inquires into politics. It will be challenging for students to consider to what extent these three essays are based on common assumptions regarding the nature of politics and to what extent they proceed on the basis of opposing beliefs. By exploring this question, the agreement and conflict existing between present-day political science and sociology will perhaps be illustrated concretely.

63. Three Theories of International Political Behavior*

It is frequently said that one test of the independent character of a discipline or field of study is the presence in the field of theories contending for recognition by those engaged in thinking and writing. It may be significant that underlying the study of contemporary international politics are two general theories of human nature and politics. Moreover, there are already the first signs of the origin of a third way of conceiving the nature of international affairs. At this time, however, political idealism and political realism are the major competitors for recognition as *the* theory of international behavior. In the past there has been no coherent political theory evolved from the ancients which deliberately sets forth to explain politics within a system that is not ordered and controlled by an all-powerful central authority. Indeed idealism and realism as conceived and defined in political theory from Greek times to the present have little in common with the assumptions and premises of the two philosophies of contemporary international politics. Each in its sphere has its own tacit or explicit assumptions. In world politics, the philosophy of idealism or utopianism so-called includes most of the thinking which

* From Kenneth W. Thompson, "The Study of International Politics: A Survey of Trends and Developments," *The Review of Politics*, Vol. 14 (October, 1952), pp. 443–57. Reprinted by permission of *The Review of Politics*.

was done in the intervening years between the two World Wars. The philosophy of realism which had prevailed throughout most of the eighteenth and nineteenth centuries has been revived both in theory and practice especially in the years following World War II. The currently most useful and original literature has been contributed primarily by those concerned with testing the assumptions of realism. Yet it is fashionable especially in circles of older scholars to proclaim that the distinctions between realism and idealism are unreal and exaggerated. Moreover, there are many who contend that both terms are fraught with emotions and value judgments and thereby are disqualified from use in social studies. In contrast, great diplomats in the West including the most distinguished representatives in 1952 have rarely been seized by such fears and doubts. Our wisest diplomats and statesmen have taken idealism and realism for granted. For example, the most learned and perceptive of American diplomats and the present Ambassador to Moscow, Mr. George F. Kennan, has declared: " I see the most serious fault of our past policy formulations to lie in something that I might call the legalistic-moralistic approach to international problems. This approach runs like a red skein through our foreign policy of the last fifty years. . . . It is the belief that it should be possible to suppress the chaotic and dangerous aspirations of governments in the international field by the acceptance of some system of legal rules and restraints. . . . It is the essence of this belief that instead of taking the awkward conflicts of national interest and dealing with them on their merits with the view to finding the solutions least unsettling to the stability of international life, it would be better to find some formal criteria of a juridical nature by which the permissible behavior of states could be defined." Mr. Kennan concludes his estimate of the philosophy of utopianism by pointing to the beliefs and attitudes in the United States which have made this viewpoint meaningful and creditable. "Behind all of this, of course, lies the American assumption that the things for which other peoples in this world are apt to contend are for the most part neither creditable nor important and might justly be expected to take second place behind the desirability of an orderly world, untroubled by international violence. To the American mind, it is implausible that people should have positive aspirations, and ones that they regard as legitimate, more important to them than the peacefulness and orderliness of international life."

Another wise statesman, a young Conservative Member of Parliament, Captain Peter Thorneycroft, who in 1951 was to become the youngest member of Prime Minister Churchill's Cabinet, voiced on February 28, 1945, essentially the same beliefs that Mr. Kennan was to express in 1951. In a debate in the House of Commons on the issues arising from the Polish settlement agreed to by Prime Minister Churchill, President Roosevelt and Premier Stalin at the Crimean Conference, Captain Thorneycroft chose the occasion to cast his specific comments in the mold of general principles of international politics.

I believe the real difficulty in which my hon. Friends find themselves is not so much Poland at all. I believe it is in the apparent conflict between documents like the Atlantic Charter and the facts of the European situation. We talk to two different people in two different languages. In the East we are talking to the Russians. The Russians are nothing if not realists. . . . I believe that the Russian Foreign Office is perhaps more in tune with the advice which would be given to the Tsars than to the potentates of the twentieth century. In such circumstances we talk in language not far removed from power politics. In the West we are faced by the Americans. They are nothing if not idealists. To them we talk in the polite language of the Atlantic Charter. Somehow or other we have to marry those two schools of thought. If I could persuade the Americans, particularly in the Middle West, to have something of the Russian realism in international relations, and persuade the Russians to have the idealism that exists on the East coast of America, we might get somewhere, but let us face the fact that the process will be a long and painful one. You do not move suddenly from a world in which there are international rivalries into a world

where there is international cooperation. It is the world that we are in
that the Prime Minister has to deal
with. We could not come back from
Yalta with a blueprint for a new
Utopia. . . . The right of small nations are safeguarded by a mixture of
diplomacy and military power. . . .

These two expressions of an American and British conception of the
nature of international politics are
significant because of the strong clear
light they throw on the two opposing theories. They indicate that professional diplomats and statesmen are
unable to indulge themselves the
luxury of shying away from the facts
of international life. The assumptions underlying the two points of
view may be enumerated in relatively
simple terms. For the political realist, rivalry and some form of strife
among nation-states is the rule and
not a mere accident of backwardness in the past. There are harmonies as well as disharmonies to be
sure but the failure of every scheme
for world peace in the past must be
sought in the conditions which have
created the disharmonies and not
through comparisons with a blueprint of a commonwealth of absolute
world harmonies. In all social
groups, whether in states or in smaller more intimate communities, a contest for influence and power goes on
unceasingly. On the international
scene, however, rivalries among states
are uncontrolled by effective law or
government. The business of statesmanship and diplomacy under the
conditions of present-day international society is to limit the struggles

and restrict their extent and scope.
The means available in the absence
of government are the unceasing pursuit of new balances of power and
rough equilibriums among contending parties. The aims include adjustment and accommodation on the
basis of mutual recognition that an
equilibrium does exist. The realist
strives to mitigate the rivalries among
nations, through checks and balances
and by compromise and bargaining.
Abstract moral principles may be the
ultimate object and purpose of the
bargain or agreement but an abstract
principle is not an essential part of
the bargain itself. Realism would
prepare the student of international
politics for the tragic and stubborn
discrepancy of means and ends in
international politics. It accepts for
the guide and premise of its thought
the permanence and ubiquity of the
struggle for power. But it strives unceasingly through every means at its
disposal to contain and limit concentrations of power and to compose and
relieve tensions which could lead to
a situation of war.

The utopian philosophy has little
in common with political realism
nor has it shown much patience or
understanding for this brand of
thinking. It chooses to abjure the
toils of power politics since at most
they are considered an abnormal and
passing historic phase. In fact, with
the creation of one universal society,
so primitive and barbaric a form of
international politics, if not indeed
politics itself, will be eliminated.
Political realism, it is claimed, is a
distortion and cynical corruption of
the true meaning of history. It is

claimed by the spokesmen of political idealism that if there have been group controversies throughout history, these struggles have centered not in political rivalries for influence and power but in the clash between incompatible ideals and principles. A concrete example which is offered is the aggression of fascism against democracy. At such time, therefore, as fascism and the other philosophies whose aims have made conflict inevitable have been permanently smashed and destroyed, power politics and war will disappear. Historically, utopianism has offered three alternatives for moral nations confronting the practical problems of survival in a world of archaic power politics. Ultimately, power politics must be eliminated through instituting a universal world government. Practically, power politics will be abolished when their main exemplars, the totalitarian states have been erased from the face of the earth. Provisionally, their evil influence will be progressively and decisively undermined by the example of moral and upright nations foreswearing relations with corrupted, power-seeking nations, pursuing neutrality policies and abstaining from all forms of traditional power politics.

In practice, moreover, the nations of good will who have accepted the philosophy of utopianism have pursued foreign policies reflecting precisely these three alternatives. It is not by accident that the United States as the nation over recent decades that has yielded most readily to utopianism has pursued a foreign policy that has vacillated between these three possibilities. For in these terms we can account for the neutrality policy of the United States before both World Wars. In each pre-war period, we tried to abstain and withdrew from the impure and corrupted power politics of the European continent. Any concession in terms of territorial guaranties against German expansion would have been unworthy of the philosophy we espoused. Any intervention in the affairs of Europe for the purpose of bolstering and strengthening the Weimar Republic would have weakened our moral position. When at length we were driven by the inherent logic of utopianism to justify our role in World War II, we turned from neutrality to a holy crusade against the evil incarnate in fascism. When through no fault of our own war became unavoidable — for had we not meticulously avoided any political action that could have invited the conflict — we gave unstintingly of our resources and our principles. We engaged in the world struggle not selfishly or for political advantage but in order to end conflict in the west and destroy and eliminate those evil men and ideals who had been responsible. These wars were not ordinary struggles for more territorial adjustments, new balances of power or specified political gains but were crusades for advancing the spread of democracy. They were holy wars of " unconditional surrender " against solitary infidels and troublemakers. For these men and ideas had caused the catastrophies; therefore, with their elimination, aggrandizement and rivalry would disappear.

The third stage in the utopian journey, however, has been for us the most basic, fateful and far-reaching. After the war, it was clearly essential that what had been undertaken and achieved in war be sealed and perfected in peace. The agents of power politics lay mortally wounded; now the climate in which their nefarious policies had thrived must be cleansed and transformed and international organization substituted for politics. In this new commonwealth, the problem of power would disappear. What this meant in concrete terms was that the *status quo* with its prevailing lawfulness based on the relative satisfaction of the victorious powers must be made permanent through the regularized procedures of new international organizations. Thus through our policies of neutrality, moralistic crusades and the substitution of organization for anarchic world politics, we have consistently pursued in recent times the aims of political idealism.

Hence the crucial difference and the real point at which political idealism and political realism diverge is with respect to the positions they take regarding the problem of power. Power is an attribute of an archaic and transitory international situation for idealists who have chosen not to recognize it as enduring. Power for the realist is the single most stubborn social psychological factor by which international behavior is influenced. Only through understanding this phenomenon can man hope to improve the melancholy status of his present situation. There is a third general approach or theory, however, which departs explicitly from both of these theories of politics. A viewpoint which is perhaps best designated *eclectic* has been asserted to represent a new synthesis. Thus in the second revised edition of George Schwarzenberger's voluminous *Power Politics,* the author rejects both idealism and realism as unscientific. Neither, he claims, has seen fit to state its major premise which he finds on the one hand in the case of realism to be that of pessimism and on the other hand with idealism that of optimism. Mr. Schwarzenberger concludes: "What is actually required is a primarily empirical approach to international affairs." Eclecticism in these terms asks the student to start without any *a priori* assumptions in making his inquiries in the field. The eclectic point of view has shown a preference for a sociological approach to the problems of world politics. There would appear to be three reasons alleged for this practicality. First, only present-day sociology with its separation of facts and values and its resistance to *a priori* judgments is equipped with a tradition of having pursued truly empirical studies. Also, the sole catholic and inclusive approach to the study of international politics is that of sociology. For example, in the case of tariff legislation, the international lawyer can discuss the legal and normative implications of treaties and treaty observance; the economist can assess the purely economic aspects of the problem; and the political scientist will contribute to an understanding of the political conflicts going on within a certain nation. Yet the only discipline which will cover all these separate facets under the enveloping umbrella of a single conceptual framework is sociology. Thirdly, sociology alone is capable of providing tests or clues by which to separate subject matter that is clearly international in character from what is essentially domestic in nature. It finds this test in the general principle of whether or not a given issue or episode affects the growth or the disintegration of international society. A new unity called the international society which by definition falls short of a true community but in effect exceeds a condition of anarchy is the guidepost by which we must measure whether a thing is international or not. At the present stage of development international society is an emerging embryonic movement that is measurable. Any event must be examined and assessed in light of its effect on the degree of integration and disintegration in international society. In American foreign policy, for example, the scientific way in which to think about the Truman Doctrine or the Marshall Plan would be to estimate their effects on the integration or disintegration of international society.

Of the three approaches or theories of international politics, eclecticism has come on to the scene most recently. Its claim that it foreswears the espousal of one viewpoint or another regarding human nature and politics is hardly substantiated in concrete studies by scholars like Professor Schwarzenberger. For that author, after disclaiming the assumption of realism that man is competitive and possesses a lust for power as well as the belief of idealism that he is rational and good, actually proceeds throughout most of his analysis to employ the working concepts of political realism. Indeed the illusion of much of contemporary social science that the student can in fact approach his inquiry with a *tabula rasa* is hardly supported by the undertakings of Schwarzenberger or any of his colleagues. Yet this view is central to eclecticism as a theory of international politics. If this assumption is false, then much of the work of this approach will in all likelihood be seriously undermined. At this stage, however, the presence of three separate theories each avowing qualitatively distinct assumptions tends to give to the study of world politics the character of something approaching a discipline.

THE NORMATIVE ASPECTS OF INTERNATIONAL POLITICS

Probably the area of international studies which has evolved most painfully and slowly are studies in the relationship of morality and norms to international practice. Only in comparatively recent times has there been any evidence of a serious and deliberate attempt to approach this question objectively and systematically. The literature of the inter-war period is barren of conscious attempts to deal "scientifically" with the problem. Following World War II, a handful of philosophers and scholars turned their attention to this problem. Among them the most noteworthy have been the theologian Reinhold Niebuhr, the Cambridge historian Herbert Butterfield, and the political scientists Hans J. Morgenthau and E. H. Carr.[1] Their contributions can be understood most fully in the perspective of the fundamental problem of ethics and politics as it exists at all levels of politics but especially at the level of international politics. It is an indisputable fact that ethics and politics are in conflict wherever man acts politically. This is the case because it is the essence of politics that man chooses goals and objectives which are limited and therefore equitable and just only for particular groups and nations. For example, in practice those things which are done in the interest of labor will frequently work an injustice upon management. Indeed only in pure thought and reflection can policies and acts remain uncorrupted and undefiled by some margin of injustice. This universal aspect of the corruption of absolute justice in the realm of politics finds its outstanding expression in international morality. There my nation's justice means oftentimes your nation's injustice; my nation's security

and the requirements assigned thereto may appear as the cause of your nation's insecurity. For the allies, armaments and spheres of influence essential to safety as viewed through my eyes may represent a threat to security when seen through your eyes. So the tendency everywhere present for ethics to be separated from politics, reaches its culmination in international affairs.

Three answers to this dilemma have been provided in modern thought. They are the answers of *moralism, cynicism* and *political wisdom*. It will be our purpose now to review their main characteristic: first, it is tempting to seek to bridge the gulf and resolve the discrepancy between ethics and politics in simple moralistic terms. Moralism as a political philosophy maintains that at present men pursue a double standard of conduct in their private and public lives. Privately, man is honest and ethical; publicly he covers his acts with a tissue of lies and deception. His virtue in private affairs is seen as the conquest of culture over barbarism, of a moral age over an immoral one. At an earlier stage in man's evolution, his conduct in private affairs had been corrupted by violence. And in the same way in international affairs the cultural lag from which nations now suffer is being quickly erased. The forward march of history is carrying nations from a retarded condition into a new and enlightened era when private standards will become public rules. The same conception of ethics which determines the conduct of individuals will influence hereafter the behavior of

---

[1] Herbert Butterfield, "The Tragic Element in Modern International Conflict," Review of Politics, Vol. 12, No. 2 (April, 1950), pp. 147–64; E. H. Carr, *Conditions of Peace* (New York: The Macmillan Company, 1944); Hans J. Morgenthau, *Scientific Man vs. Power Politics* (Chicago: University of Chicago Press, 1946); Reinhold Niebuhr, *Christianity and Power Politics* (New York: Charles Scribner's Sons, 1940); "Democracy as a Religion," *Christianity and Crisis*, Vol. 7, No. 14 (August 4, 1947), pp. 1–2.

nations in one universal society of nations. This was the faith of President Woodrow Wilson and more recently of Secretary of State Cordell Hull.

The sanguine hopes and expectations of this moralistic outlook bear little resemblance to the conduct of nations. The melancholy unfolding of the past four decades has left the most ardent of the believers in this faith shaken and uncertain of its assumptions. Therefore in practice simple moralistic viewpoints have tended to induce the emergence of their opposite, namely, cynicism. Herein it is argued that when politics and ethics diverge it is only because they are unlike quantities. Politics are means and ethics are ends; means may be evil, but good ends, to which means are subordinated, can endow acts which are morally ambiguous with their own ethical content. The dictum which claims that the end justifies the means seems particularly in the realm of politics to furnish a simple clue to our problem. Yet for men and for nations, it is universally the practice to justify every evil measure by claiming it serves an ethical goal. For Stalin the brutality of liquidating the kulaks found its justification in communist eschatology; for Hitler the cremation of so-called inferior races was excused as a necessary hygienic measure if Teutonic virility were to continue unimpaired. Since nations in the present anarchic world society tend to be repositories of their own morality, the ends-means formula has prevailed as an answer to the moral dilemma, for it is undeniably a concealed but essen-

tial truth that nations tend to create their own morality. In its extreme form, however, this development has found nations accepting as ethical whatever redounded to their own material advantage and judging whatever was detrimental to their purposes as being immoral and evil. Yet by the nature of man and politics, statesmen and nations never wholly escape the judgment of elementary ethical standards. The history of politics discloses that no peoples have divorced completely politics from ethics but have generally agreed that men were required to conform in their deeds to standards more objective than those of success.

One sign that ethics are accepted as relevant in most societies and cultures is the apparent compulsion felt by political actors to justify their deeds in moral terms. This tribute to a moral order has its consequences both in words and deeds. There is a striking dialectical movement of expediency and morality which has its impact on international politics. Moves in practical politics must be articulated in such a way as to pay tribute to moral principles. However limited and particular, acts of political expedience must seem to carry forward aims of justice and the common good. Thus political morality in these modest terms, forces the statesman who would justify expediency with ethics to choose his measures so that on some points at least the practical and moral march hand in hand. It is political wisdom to act successfully in accord with the interests of state. It is political and moral wisdom to choose the most moral of several alternatives through which both expedience and ethics may be served. The margin which separates cynicism from this form of wisdom is frequently narrow indeed but by it the statesman is saved from a fatuous " moralism " or the despair of unqualified expediency. It is the essence of moral judgment to transcend the limits of expediency and narrow self-interest in this one sense at least.

The development of a rational concept of international morality is illustrated best in the recent attempts to construct a concept of international morality possessing three dimensions or layers. The heart or core of this conception is the idea of the moral dignity of national interest. Whereas it is obvious that the first duty of a nation's foreign policy must be to safeguard the interests of its citizens and of past and future generations, it must follow that the moral values of that state are defended and promoted in this way. In practice a nation can indulge itself the private virtues of generosity and self-sacrifice only if its survival is not endangered thereby.[2] If in fact its external acts are restricted because of the threats to its security, the nation as a community of men of good will can as a minimum pursue moral ends and purposes at home and in this way contribute to international order and peace.

A second dimension of this conception of the norms and morality of international politics is the opposite side of the shield we have designated the national interest. It is the concept of reciprocal or mutual national interests. The practical importance of this phase of morality is inherent in the statement of Governor Adlai E. Stevenson of Illinois whose deep wisdom and realism are becoming widely known. "The United States will find support among peoples in the free states to the degree that they believe we do not simply consult our own interests but give consideration to their interests as well — that we in truth have ' a decent respect for the opinions of mankind.' Other nations have a reciprocal obligation to give weight to our interests too. There is no doubt that our power gives us an advantage in this process, but neither is there room to doubt that if we wish allies who will go forward with us with courage and fortitude into the risks of the future, they must be willing and confident allies."[3]

The one thing which saves the idea of the national interest from itself is its essential reciprocity. To the extent that nations are in earnest not alone about their own self-interests but in their recognition of the application of similar criteria by others, the national interest as a guide escapes any temptation to conceal real designs for world aggrandizement. The English political philosopher Edmund Burke declared: " Nothing

[2] Hans J. Morgenthau and Kenneth W. Thompson, *Principles and Problems of International Politics* (New York: Alfred A. Knopf, 1950), pp. 33–41.

[3] Adlai E. Stevenson, *Korea in Perspective* (Stamford, Connecticut: The Overbrook Press, 1952), p. 16.

is so fatal to a nation as an extreme of self partiality, and the total want of consideration of what others will naturally hope or fear." [4] After a nation has determined its own objective interests in terms of its national security, it has an obligation to draw back as it were and appraise coolly and realistically the interests of its neighbors. In this way alone can nations decide if their interests are compatible or can be adjusted. There is no other basis for true coexistence. It is as tempting as it is hazardous to treat other peoples as pawns in the struggle to preserve one's own national interest. There is a tendency to treat other nations as means instead of as ends embodied in their own national purposes. Yet in relations particularly with those societies in Asia and Africa which have most frequently been treated as instruments to be used and exploited by others, their claims upon international society to accord them means of national recognition and personal self-respect make such a tendency well-nigh fatal. It is essential that every nation pursue wisely its own best interests but the pathway for each nation must not be strewn with the remnants of the interests of others that were forgotten in its headlong drive to attain national security. Among nations with decent intentions there must be a reciprocal process of recognizing each other's vital interests and avoiding collisions and conflicts *in so far* as it

[4] Edmund Burke, "Remarks on the Policy of the Allies with Respect to France," (1793), *Works* (Boston: Little, Brown, and Company, 1889), Vol. IV, p. 447.

is possible through the compromise of divergent interests.

There are four reasons why the arch of international morality is properly conceived of as being the mutuality of national interests. The first of these we have discussed. As we have seen, mere national egotism without realistic attention to what other countries conceive their vital interests to be leads to the corruption of a nation's power and values. The second reason for the importance of this aspect of morality is inherent in the nature of international politics. Interests we know are capable of being compromised; principles can never be made the object of bargains. Yet if nations are to survive somehow they must find ways of compromising their differences while at the same time they succeed in protecting and safeguarding their interests. For as it is the essence of politics that individuals possess the capacity to compromise their differences, the art of diplomacy merely raises this process to the level of nations and founds it upon a structure of multiple national interests. Peace and order rest on the identification and accommodation of interests. Thirdly, the unequivocal lesson of history is that conflicts which seem at the time to present to the parties a clear case of right and wrong, almost without exception have appeared to future historians, less blinded by passion and loyalty, as something infinitely more tragic than good men fighting bad ones. The real pattern of conflict and war is one of minor differences hardening into intractable political divisions, of men faced by terrible dilemmas and of nations eventually driven by the inner dialectic of events to wars which no one desired. The difference between a struggle between good and evil and actual struggles in world politics in which every party in some way is at fault but is unable to disengage itself from the tragic predicament of fearing others but never comprehending their counterfears is the difference between the substance of "heroic" and "revisionist" or scientific history. In this predicament, each party has a sense of its own insecurity but never imagines that its own righteous efforts could have anything to do with the insecurity of others. After each military conflict, the minds of the early or "heroic" historians are locked in the combat expounding their own nation's cause. Their judgments are generally the kind that stem from self-righteousness. Subsequently, it remains for "revisionist" historians to re-write the narrative in terms of the mutual fear of each side for the power of the other. In their histories of conflict the revisionist schools have frequently proved we have muddied the waters and darkened our minds about the true nature of a struggle when it has been interpreted in terms of certain accidental characteristics. In the present crisis between East and West, for example, historians may show that the ideological aspect of the struggle was accidental in comparison to the more profound and underlying political struggle. In this tragic predicament, the one source of relief from the struggle can come from the accommodation of conflicting political interests. The first step in this process is to discover what are the vital interests of the foe. The one escape from this human predicament is the patient quest of mutually compatible national interests if they are found to exist. And fourth and finally, a firm and steady endeavor to find out what are the interests of the other party to a crisis provides any nation with some basis for predicting its actions and in the same way of anticipating the faithfulness of its allies.

The third layer of international morality comprises such general moral principles as opposition to tyranny. Although politics are primarily power politics, human beings obstinately reject the view that state behavior is not in some ways a fit subject for moral judgment. Even one of the most brilliant of our contemporary analysts who has been in the vanguard of those who have contributed realist critiques of western political thought, has stated repeatedly that realism in statecraft was not enough. Mr. E. H. Carr, the well-known English author of *The Twenty Years' Crisis*, has exposed relentlessly the hollowness of utopianism in the inter-war years with its hazardous practice of identifying limited experiences and national policies with universal good. But he has also insisted that any mature outlook must contain elements of utopianism and realism, purpose and analysis, ethics and politics. "Consistent realism excluded four things which appear to be essential ingredients of all effective political thinking; a finite goal, an emotional appeal, a right of moral judgment, and a ground for action." [5] It is the task of the statesman to supply these deficiencies but no task is fraught with greater danger or perils. Whereas loyalty to the nation is morally tolerable only if it includes values which are wider than the nation, there is the baffling problem in means and ends of discovering what those values are and how they can be sustained by nations with limited power. The story of political realists who have discovered the primacy of power and national interest and then gone in search of moral principles by which to transcend them has too often been the melancholy account of an Odyssey in which the true goal of the journeyer is sacrificed for the early exhilaration of too simple, good-hearted moral positions. In practice most attempts to provide moral meaning for international affairs have been tainted with self-interest and hypocrisy. The realist turned moralist with the aim of providing a disinterested standard with concrete applications for the conduct of world affairs tends almost invariably to propose general principles such as the easy harmony of interests of a universal collective security system which are not principles at all but unconcious reflections of one party's national interests.

Yet most accounts of political action show quite plainly that realism is not enough and that there is a certain sphere in which moral principles must be operative. In any full and complete political system there must be room for both philosophy and action. There can be no more serious error than to confound these two. The realms of ideals and practice are not the same. However, it is equally false to imagine that they are two planes that never touch nor meet. For if the vertical dimension be conceived of as the line of ideals, it plainly intersects at certain points in history the horizontal dimension of political practice. In this sense, general moral principles, though often inoperative and always subservient to national interest, affect and influence international behavior. Yet in the impingement of these three layers of international morality and in their careful study would seem to reside the key to a better understanding of the scope and limits of the normative aspects of international morality. (. . .)

64. Politics as an Art*

One of the questions which we are debating here is defined as "The

[5] E. H. Carr, *The Twenty Years' Crisis, 1919–1939* (London: Macmillan and Company, 1949), p. 89.

* From Winston Churchill, "Address at the Massachusetts Institute of Technology. *The New York Times*, April 1, 1949, p. 10.

Failure of Social and Political Institutions to Keep Peace With Material and Technical Change." Scientists should never underrate the deep-seated qualities of human nature and how, repressed in one direction, they will certainly break out in another. The genus homo — if I may display my Latin — is a tough creature who has traveled here by a very long road. His nature has been shaped and his virtues ingrained by many millions of years of struggle, fear and pain, and his spirit has, from the earliest dawn of history, shown itself upon occasion capable of mounting to the sublime, far above material conditions or mortal terrors. He still remains as Pope described him two hundred years ago:

Placed on this isthmus of a middle
    state,
A being darkly wise and rudely
    great;
Created half to rise, and half to fall —;
Great Lord of all things, yet a prey to
    all — ;
Sole judge of truth, in endless error
    hurl'd;
The glory, jest, and riddle of the
    world!

In his introductory address, Dr. Burchard, the Dean of Humanities, spoke with awe of " an approaching scientific ability to control men's thoughts with precision." I shall be very content if my task in this world is done before that happens. Laws just or unjust may govern men's actions. Tyrannies may restrain or regulate their words. The machinery of propaganda may pack their minds with falsehood and deny them truth for many generations of time. But the soul of man thus held in trance or frozen in a long night can be awakened by a spark coming from God knows where and in a moment the whole structure of lies and oppression is on trial for its life. Peoples in bondage should never despair. Science no doubt could, if sufficiently perverted, exterminate us all; but it is not in the power of material forces in any period which the youngest here tonight need take into practical account, to alter the main elements in human nature or restrict the infinite variety of forms in which the soul and genius of the human race can and will express itself.

How right you are in this great institution of technical study and achievement to keep a Dean of Humanities and give him so commanding a part to play in your discussions! No technical knowledge can outweigh knowledge of the humanities in the gaining of which philosophy and history walk hand in hand. Our inheritance of well-founded slowly conceived codes of honor, morals and manners, the passionate convictions which so many hundreds of millions share together of the principles of freedom and justice, are far more precious to us than anything which scientific discoveries could bestow.

Those whose minds are attracted or compelled to rigid and symmetrical systems of government should remember that logic, like science, must be the servant and not the master of man. Human beings and human societies are not structures that are built, or machines that are forged. They are plants that grow and must be tended as such. Life is a test and this world a place of trial. Always the problems, or it may be the same problem, will be presented to every generation in different forms. The problems of victory may be even more baffling than those of defeat. However much the conditions change, the supreme question is how we live and grow and bloom and die, and how far each life conforms to standards which are not wholly related to space or time.

Here I speak not only to those who enjoy the blessings and consolation of revealed religion but also to those who face the mysteries of human destiny alone. The flame of Christian ethics is still our highest guide. To guard and cherish it is our first interest, both spiritually and materially. The fulfillment of spiritual duty in our daily life is vital to our survival. Only by bringing it into perfect application can we hope to solve for ourselves the problems of this world and not of this world alone.

65. Politics as a Vocation *

What do we mean by "politics"? The term is unusually comprehensive and refers to every type of independent leadership activity. We speak of the bills of exchange policy [1] of banks, of the discount policy of the Reichsbank, of the policy of the trade union in a strike. One can speak of the educational policy of a village or of a municipal government, of the leadership policy of the executive committee of an association, indeed one can even speak of the policy of a clever woman who is concerned with managing her husband. Such a comprehensive term does not really indicate the subject matter of our discussion of this evening. By politics, *we will hence-*

* From Max Weber, "Politics as a Vocation," translated by Edward A. Shils from *Politik als Beruf*, 2nd edition, Munich and Leipzig, 1926. Copyright, University of Chicago Press, 1950. Reprinted by permission of Edward A. Shils and the University of Chicago by courtesy of the Social Science staff.

[1] In German the word "Politik" covers the meaning of both the English words, "policy" and "politics." (Translator)

forth mean only: the control over a political association or activities influencing that control. And right now the political association with which we are concerned is the State.

But what sociologically is a "political" association? What is a "state"? The State can not be defined sociologically on the basis of what it does. There is no function which at one time or another has not been performed by some political association. At the same time, there is no function of which it could be said that it has always been performed exclusively and peculiarly by political associations which today we call "the State" or which are the historical antecedents of the modern State. The modern State can ultimately be characterized only in terms of the one method which is peculiar to it, and which signalizes all political association, namely, the use of physical violence. "Every State is founded on violence": said Trotsky at Brest Litovsk. It is quite correct to say that when only social structures exist in which violence as a method is unknown, then "the State" will no longer exist and a condition which we call anarchy in the special sense of the term will have emerged. Violence is naturally neither the only nor the normal method used by the State. There is no question about that. But it is the method which distinguishes it from other forms of association. Indeed today the relationship between violence and the State is especially close. In the past the most diverse kinds of association, beginning with the kinship groups, utilized physical violence as an entirely normal method. In contrast with this we must say today that the State is that human association which within the boundaries of a certain area (the "area" is part of the defining criteria) lays effective claim to a monopoly of legitimate physical violence. What is unique to the modern situation is that all other associations or individuals are accorded the right to use physical violence only insofar as the State has permitted it. The State is the exclusive source of the right to use violence. Hence, politics will mean for us that striving for power, or for influence over the exercise of power, be it between states, or be it within a state, between the groups which it comprises.

This corresponds fairly closely with the customary linguistic usage. When a problem is called a "political" problem or whenever a cabinet member or an official is said to use a political official or when a decision is said to be "politically" deter-

mined, it means that interests bearing on the maintenance or change of the distribution of power are decisive for the solution of a problem, or that they determine the decision or condition the activity of the official in question. Whoever engages in politics is seeking power either as a means to certain ends, be they ideal or egoistic, or for its own sake or for the enjoyment of the feeling of prestige which it confers.

The State — just like the historically antecedent political associations — is a power relationship between individuals based on legitimate (i.e., what is regarded as legitimate) force. For its existence, those over whom power is exercised must bow before the authority claimed by those who are dominant at the time. Why do they do it? On what justifications and on what material instruments does it rest?

There are in principle three types of justification, i.e., bases for the legitimacy of a power relationship. First, the authority of the "eternal past": i.e., custom which is sanctified by immemorial validity and habitual attitudes. This is "traditional" authority of the type exercised by the patriarch or the patrimonial prince of the old style. Second, the authority of the unusual personal gift of grace, charisma, i.e., the entirely personal devotion to and personal confidence in the revelations, heroism or other leadership traits of an individual. This is "charismatic" authority such as is exercised by the prophet or — in the political sphere — the chosen warlord or the plebiscitary party leader.

Third, authority on the bases of legality, by virtue of belief in the validity of legal promulgation and in the jurisdiction derived from rationally enacted rules, i.e., orientation towards obedience in the fulfillment of enacted obligations. This is the authority which is exercised by the modern " public servant " and all those wielders of power who resemble him in this respect. It is of course obvious that in reality very powerful motives of fear and hope — fear of the vengeance of magical powers or of the power-holder, hope of otherworldly or earthly rewards — and therewith interests of the most various sort, condition obedience. We shall discuss this shortly.

But if one inquires into the basis of legitimacy of this obedience, then one comes back to these three types. These conceptions of legitimacy and their subjective bases are of very considerable significance for the structure of authority. The pure types are seldom found in reality, and in today's lecture we are unable to treat the very intricate deviations, transitions and combinations of these pure types. (This belongs to the general theory of the state.) We are particularly interested in the second of these three types: authority by virtue of the devotion of the dominated to the purely personal " charisma " of the " leader." For here we find the sense of *vocation* in its most extreme form. Devotion to the charisma of the prophet or of the leader in war or the great demagogue in the church or in parliament means that he is personally accepted as the truly " called " leader of men and that the latter do not obey him because of custom or enactments but because they believe in him. He himself lives for his task, " is concerned with his work," if he is more than a narrow-souled and vain upstart of the moment. His personal qualities are what hold the devotion of his followers, his disciples, his following (*Gefolgschaft*), his personal party hangers-on. The two types in the past who were most important, the magicians and prophets, on the one hand, and the chosen war-lords, gangleaders and condottieri, on the other hand, were prominent as leaders in all times and all places. But what we are most interested in is what has been unique to the Occident: political leadership, first in the form of the free " demagogue " who emerged only in the soil of city state (itself unique to the Occident, particularly to the Mediterranean culture area) and later in the form of the parliamentary " party leader " who arose in the constitutional state which too is unique to Occidental culture.

These politicians by " vocation " in the more special sense of the term are of course by no means the only significant figures in the struggle for political power. Very decisive are the types of auxiliary devices which are available to them. How do the politically dominant groups exert their authority? The problem exists for every type of authority and accordingly for all the forms of political authority, for the traditional as well as for the legal and charismatic.

Every hierarchically organized structure which requires continual administration must have on the one hand an attitude of obedience to the persons who claim to be the bearers of legitimate power, and on the other hand in consequence of this obedience, control over those material goods which in any given case are necessary for the exercise of power; in other words, the administrative personnel and the material means of administration.

The administrative staff, which is the external form of the organization of political authority (as well as of every other kind of authority), is naturally not bound in obedience to the wielders of authority merely through beliefs about legitimacy. There are also two means which touch personal interests, namely, material rewards and social honor. Dues of the vassal, the prebends of the patrimonial official, and the salary of the modern state official — the honor of a Knight, status privileges and official honor constitute the wages, and the fear of losing them constitutes the ultimately decisive conditions for the solidarity of the administrative staff with the wielder of power. This is true for charismatic leadership as well: military honor and booty for the military following, and "spoils," i.e., exploitation of the ruled by the monopoly of official positions, politically determined profits and the gratification of their vanity for the demagogic following.

The maintenance of every organization of authority requires certain material goods, just as in the case of an economic organization. All states may be classified in accordance with (a) whether the administrative staff,

be they "officials" or others on whose obedience the power holder must count, own the instruments of administration themselves regardless of whether they consist of money, buildings, ammunitions and military supplies, trains, horses, etc., or (b) whether the administrative staff is "separated" from the instruments of administration in the same way that the white collar employee and the proletarian in a capitalistic organization are today "separated" from the material instruments of production. In other words, the decisive criterion is whether or not the power holder runs the administration through a system of management which he himself has organized and allows the administration to be carried on by personal servants, appointed officials or personal favorites and confidants who are not owners in their own name of the material means of administration but are directed by the chief. This distinction is to be found in every administrative organization known to history.

A political organization in which the material instruments of administration are entirely or partially the property of the dependent administrative staff will be called a "status"-differentiated organization. The vassal, for example, in the feudal organization takes care of the administration and adjudication of the district which has been enfeoffed to him out of his own purse, he equips and provisions himself for war and his own sub-vassals do the same. This naturally has consequences for the power-position of the lord who depends only on the personal loyalty of the vassals and on the fact that their feudal tenure and social honor derives its "legitimation" from him.

But we also find throughout history, even in the earliest forms of political organization, the personal administration of the lord. Through personal dependents, i.e., slaves, household officials, servants, personal "favorites," and prebendaries whom he compensates from his own stores with emoluments in kind or money, he strives to hold the reins of administration in his own hands; he undertakes to defray the expenses from his own purse, from the product of his partimonium; he tries to create an army which is purely personal in the sense of being dependent on him, and drawing its supplies from his warehouses and armories. In an organization based on status (*Ständischer Verband*) the lord rules with the aid of an autonomous "aristocracy," i.e., shares power with it. There, however, the lord makes use of bondservants or plebians, i.e., propertyless persons who are members of a class enjoying very little deference, who are materially entirely dependent on the lord and who possess no autonomously competitive power. All forms of patriarchal and patrimonial domination from sultanic despotism to the bureaucratic state-system are of this type, particularly the latter in its most rational form as found characteristically in the modern state.

The modern state has everywhere arisen through the lords' expropriation of the independent "private" agents of administrative power: i.e., those proprietors of the instruments of administration and war, of fiscal resources and all sorts of politically usable goods. The whole process is a complete parallel to the development of the capitalistic enterprise through the gradual expropriation of the independent producer. At the culmination of this process we see that in the modern state control over the instruments of political operation is consolidated in a single center. No single official is any longer personal owner of the money which he expends for state purposes or of the buildings, stores, tools, or military machinery which he controls. The modern state is characterized — and this is essential to the definition — by the complete separation of the administrative staff, i.e., the administrative officials and workers from the material means of operating the organization. The most recent stage of political development has witnessed the expropriation of these expropriators of the political means therewith of political power. The Revolution [2] has accomplished at least this: it has supplanted the reigning authorities with leaders who through usurpation or election have acquired control over the political personnel and the material apparatus of the state and who legitimate their claims to power — the rightness of their legitimation is immaterial in this context — in the name of the will of the ruled. It is another problem whether on the basis of this — at least apparent — success, the revolutionary groups can hope to bring

[2] This lecture was delivered during the revolutionary days of the winter of 1918–1919. (Translator)

about the expropriation of the capitalistic enterprises, the direction of which, despite very considerable internal similarities, operates according to principles quite different from those of political administration. But this does not concern us today. For us the important thing is the definition of the modern state as a power-controlled organization (*Herrschaftsverband*) which within a certain territory, effectively monopolizes legitimate physical violence as a means of domination and to this end, brings together the control of the material instruments of operation in the hands of its leading personnel but expropriates the autonomously privileged feudal functionaries who previously had enjoyed such autonomy, while placing itself in their stead at its very peak.

In the course of this process of expropriation which has transpired in all countries with varying success, there emerged at first in the service of the princes the first professional politicians — "professional" in a sense different from that already mentioned. They were persons who did not themselves, like the charismatic leaders, seek to be lords but who entered the service of the wielders of authority. In the struggles for the political expropriation of the nobility they worked for the princes and made the execution of their policies a means of livelihood and an ethical ideal. This type of professional politician is found only in the Occident, serving not only the prince but other powers as well. In the past they were the most important agents in the expropriation process.

Let us first make unambiguously clear to ourselves what is involved in the existence of such professional politicians. One can participate in "politics," i.e., one can try to influence the distribution of power within and between political organizations, as an "occasional" activity as well as in part-time or full-time capacities — just as in occupations of the more usual sort. We are all "occasional" politicians casting our ballot or in some similar expression of political preferences, i.e., in assenting or protesting in a "political" meeting, in delivering a political speech, etc. For many persons, all of their contact with politics is restricted to this kind of occasional participation. "Part-time" politicians comprise all those "reliables" who perform their activities only when needed and neither materially nor ideally draw their sustenance primarily from them. Part-time politicians also comprise those members of state councils and similar advisory bodies who come into action only when called upon. Similarly, they include those rather broad groups of parliamentarians who are politically active only when parliament is in session. In the past such groups were found among the estates. ("Estates" are autonomously privileged owners of military or administrative apparatus or personal sovereignty.) A great many of them were far from devoting their lives to politics entirely, partially or even more than occasionally. They used their power to rule for the sake of acquiring rents or even profit and they became politically active in the service of the political organization only when the lord or their status-equals made a particular request. It was no different with a section of those auxiliaries from whom the prince drew support in his struggle for the consolidation of his power. The "household councils" and, more remotely in the past, a significant proportion of the advisors in the "Curia" and the other advisory councils of the prince possessed this character. But this occasional or part-time assistance was insufficient for the prince. He had to build a staff of aides who were exclusively dedicated to his service on a full-time basis. Wherever this occurred, the structure of the emerging dynastic political structure and, not only it, but the entire culture were very pronouncedly influenced thereby. It was only the same necessity which was experienced by those political organizations which, completely disregarding or considerably restricting the princely power, constituted themselves "free" communities — free, not in the sense of free from power exercised through force, but rather in the sense of the absence of traditionally legitimated (mainly religiously consecrated) princely power as the exclusive source of authority. Historically these communities are found solely in the Occident, and their seedbed was the city as a political organization, in which form it first emerged in the Mediterranean culture area. What was the "full-time professional politician" like in these instances?

One can make politics his vocation in two ways. He can either live "for" politics or "by" politics.

These are not mutually exclusive. As a rule, one does both, at least ideally, but mostly materially. One who lives "for" politics "makes it his life" in a subjective sense: he either enjoys the naked exercise of power or he maintains his subjective equilibrium and sense of dignity by the knowledge that he is giving meaning to his life by serving a cause, by doing his duty (*Dienst an einer "Sache"*). In this subjective sense every serious person who lives for a "cause" also lives "by" his cause. The distinction refers really to a more material aspect of the subject: namely the economic. One lives "by" politics when one seeks to make it a stable source of income. One lives "for" politics when such is not the case. In order for a person to be able to live for politics, as long as the system of private property prevails, certain very trivial conditions are necessary: he must normally be economically independent of the income which political activity brings. This means quite simply that he must be quite opulent or must have some private position which supplies him with an adequate income. This is the situation at least under normal conditions. The followers of the warrior prince are not, it is true, concerned with the normal conditions of economic life any more than the followers of the revolutionary heroes of the street. Both live by plunder, robbery, contributions, forced levies — which are essentially all the same. But these are necessarily extraordinary occurrences; in ordinary economic life, only a private income serves the function. But this is not enough: in addition it is necessary to be economically "independent," i.e., the acquisition of his income should not be a function of the continuous day-to-day application of his working powers and thought. The purest embodiment of this independence is the *rentier* who receives an income entirely without working — be it like the lord of the past or the land owner or nobleman of the present day from ground rents (in antiquity and the middle ages from slave or serf payments), or from securities or similar modern sources of income. Neither the worker nor, it should be noted, the enterpriser, especially the modern large scale enterpriser is independent in this sense. The enterpriser particularly — the industrial much more than agricultural enterpriser due to the seasonal character of farming — is bound to his enterprise and can not get free of it. It is usually very difficult for him to have someone substitute for him, even temporarily. It is no less true of the physician in proportion to his eminence and the size of his clientele. It is easier for the lawyer simply by virtue of the technical aspects of his business and on that account the lawyer has played a much greater and often even a predominant role as a professional politician. We will not pursue this analysis but will try to make explicit a few conclusions.

The leadership of a state or a party by persons who, in the economic sense, live for and not by politics necessarily signifies the plutocratic recruitment of the leading political strata. This does not imply the reverse: i.e., plutocratic leadership does not imply that the politically dominant stratum is not seeking to live "by" politics, in the sense of trying to use its political power to achieve its private economic aims. There is naturally no question about this. It only means that the professional politicians of plutocratic derivation are not under direct necessity of being paid for their political work as would be the case with those who are without independent means. On the other hand it does not mean that politicians without a private fortune are exclusively or even only primarily concerned with gaining their livelihood through politics, nor does it mean that they do not view politics as a responsibility. Nothing would be more incorrect. Concern for his economic security is a cardinal point in the outlook of the man of private means, while utterly consistent and unconditional political idealism is found, if not exclusively then at least characteristically, in those strata the members of which in consequence of their low income position stand outside the circle of those concerned with the maintenance of the existing economic order. This is particularly true in extraordinary situations such as revolutions. However, it is still true that nonplutocratic recruitment of political leaders and their active followers necessarily involves the acquisition of a regular and adequate income by those leaders and followers from their political activity.

Politics can be carried on by *honoratiores* and that implies by persons of "independent means," i.e. well-to-do persons, especially *rentiers*. Otherwise, political activity must be made accessible to those without large fortunes and in that case they must receive remuneration. The professional politician who lives by his political activity can be either a pure "prebendary" or a paid "official." In that case his income derives from fees and perquisites (tips and graft are only an unregulated and formally illegal subtype of this category of revenues) or else he receives a fixed payment in kind or a salary in money or else both simultaneously. He can assume the character of an "enterpriser" like the condottiere or the purchaser or farmer of official positions in former times or like the American "boss" who views his costs as a capital investment which provides a return thru the exploitation of his influence. Or he can receive a fixed salary, like an editor or party secretary or a modern minister or political official. In the past, enfeoffments, grants of land, benefices of all sorts and with the development of a money economy, perquisite-prebends were the typical form of remuneration of princes, conquerors or successful party chiefs. Today there are positions of all sorts in parties, newspapers, cooperatives, sickness-insurance funds, municipalities and states which are granted by party-leaders for loyal services. All party struggles are struggles not merely for material goals but above all, for patronage as well. All conflicts between the particularistic and centralistic tendencies in Germany turn about the question whether Berlin or Munich or Karlsruhe or Dresden will control the distribution of patronage. Reductions in their share of positions is felt by political parties to be a greater deprivation than the frustration of their strivings for achieving their substantive goals. A shift in the party composition of the prefects in France is always interpreted as a greater revolution and causes more of an uproar than a change in the program which is of almost exclusively rhetorical significance. Many parties and particularly those in the United States since the end of the older conflicts on the interpretation of the constitution have become strictly job-hunting parties which change their substantive program in accordance with the vote-getting prospects which the various alternatives offer. In Spain up until recently the two major parties rotated as if by agreement by means of the "elections" handed down from above in order to provide their followers with positions. In the Spanish colonial territories in the so-called "elections" just as in the so-called "revolutions" it is always a question of the public treasury from which the victors want to feed. In Switzerland the parties divide the jobs peacefully by means of proportional representation and many of our "revolutionary" drafts for a constitution, e.g., the first one recommended in Baden, sought to extend this system to the ministerial positions and treated the state and its posts as an institution for the provision of benefices. The Center Party was especially enthusiastic about this scheme, and Baden made the proportional distribution of jobs in the government, in accordance with the religious composition of the population without regard for qualification, a plank in its platform. This tendency becomes more pronounced for all parties with the increase in the number of positions consequent on general bureaucratization and with the increased demand for those positions as a form of a secure livelihood. For their followers the parties become a means of gaining a secure livelihood thru state employment.

In counter-action against this however there stands the modern bureaucracy developed into a specialized, highly skilled intellectual labor force, trained for many years and possessing a highly developed sense of status-honor centering about the maintenance of integrity. Without this professional bureaucracy we are threatened with the danger of frightful corruption and a fate of common philistine boorishness (*Banausentum*). Even the purely technical achievements of governmental activity would be endangered without it. The significance of this professional bureaucracy for the economic system, especially with increasing socialization, has steadily increased and will continue to increase. Dilettante administration by spoils politicians which in the United States used to allow the replacement of hundreds of thousands of officials, down as far as mailmen, after each presidential election and which was completely ignorant of the professional official who made a career out of government service, has long since been breached by the Civil Service Reform. Purely technical administrative necessities which can not be put off or disregarded have facilitated

this development. In Europe the professional bureaucracy with a differentiated allocation of functions is the gradual product of a process which has gone on for five centuries. The Italian cities and *signori* made a beginning: among the monarchies. The Norman States of Southern Italy did the same. The decisive step was taken in the fiscal administration of the princes. In the administrative reforms of Kaiser Max one could see how difficult it was, even under pressure of the most extreme urgency and the threat of Turkish domination, for the professional administrator to displace the princes in an area which was least capable of supporting the dilettantism of a ruler who was at that time a knight before everything else. The development of military technique gave rise to the specialized officer; the refinement of legal procedure to the trained jurist. In these three spheres specialized bureaucracy finally triumphed in the more developed states by the 16th century. Concurrently with the rise of the absolutism of the princes vis-a-vis the estates, there began the prince's gradual abdication of his autonomous power in favor of the professional bureaucrat who had first made possible his victory over the estates.

Simultaneously with the rise of the bureaucrat with specialized training, there developed also — though much more gradually — the "guiding statesman." Such *de facto* decision-making advisors to rulers have obviously existed always and everywhere. In the Orient the necessity of freeing the sultan from the burden of personal responsibility for the success of the government as much as possible created the typical figure of the "Grand Vizier." In the Occident diplomacy in the age of Charles V — the age of Machiavelli — became for the first time a deliberately cultivated art, the predominantly humanistically educated practitioners of which treated each other as an educated class of initiates, similar to the humanistic Chinese statesmen of the last dynasty of the age of the segment-states. The necessity of a formally unified direction of all policy, including the domestic, by a leading statesman, became decisive and urgent only as a result of certain constitutional developments. Until then, there were always of course certain individuals who served as advisors or rather, in point of fact, guides of the prince. But the organization of councils moved, even in the most progressive states, in other directions. In theory, and to a decreasing extent in fact, they assembled personally under the chairmanship of the prince who made the decision. By means of this collegial system which led to opinions, counteropinions, and votes of the majority and minority and by surrounding himself with purely personal confidants, i.e., the "cabinet" (in addition to the officially highest councils) by means of whom he made up his mind on the resolutions of the State council or whatever else the highest state body was called, the prince who was falling more and more into the status of a dilettante sought to protect himself from the inevitably growing weight of the bureaucrats'

specialized training and to keep the ultimate power in his own hands. This latent struggle between the professional bureaucracy and the autonomous power of the prince existed everywhere. The situation changed only when the struggle was turned against the parliamentary assemblies and the aspirations for power of the party-leaders. Very different conditions thus led to externally similar results. There were of course certain differences. Wherever the dynasties held real power in their hands, as was the case in Germany, the interests of the princes were bound up quite closely with those of the bureaucracy against the parliamentary bodies and their demands for power. The bureaucrats were interested in having the leading offices including the ministerial posts filled by members of their own ranks — in other words, they wanted them to become accessible to the bureaucracy. The monarch for his part was interested in appointing his ministers according to his own wishes and from among the officials who were devoted to him. Both were interested in opposing to parliament a closed and unified political leadership. Hence, the collegial system was supplanted by a single cabinet chief. In order to remain formally detached from party conflicts and party attacks, the monarch required, in addition to this, an individual who would be responsible to him, who would answer to parliament and treat with the parties. All these interests led in the same direction: unified political leadership exercised by a bureaucratic minister.

Even more influential in contributing to unification was development of parliamentary power where — as in England — it got the upper hand over the monarchy. In this situation there developed the " cabinet," with the individual parliamentary leader at the head, as a committee of the majority party which, though ignored in official laws, in actuality is the decisive political power. The official collegial bodies were not, as such, organs of the really ruling power, i.e., the party, and hence they could not constitute the real government. A dominant party in order to exercise power at home and to carry on politics on the grand scale in foreign affairs requires a forceful body, composed exclusively of its really leading men managing their affairs confidentially, namely the cabinet. To deal with the public, especially the parliamentary public, it requires a leader who will be responsible for all decisions, namely, the cabinet leader. The English system was adopted on the continent in the form of parliamentary ministries. Only in America and the democracies influenced by it was a quite different system set up in which the chosen leader of the victorious party, elected by direct vote, was placed at the head of the body of officials whom he himself appointed, and was made dependent on the consent of the legislative only in budgetary and legislative matters.

The tendency of political activity to become organized, requiring training in the struggle for power — e.g., the modern party system, has brought about a distinction between two types of public functionaries which though not completely clear-cut is still relevant: namely the distinction between professional officials on the one hand and " political officials " on the other. The " political officials " in the narrow sense of the term are externally distinguishable by the fact that they can be appointed or dismissed at will or at least " are subject " to dismissal, like the French prefects and their counterparts in other countries, as compared with the " independence " of the officials with judicial functions. In England the former included those officials who by fixed convention resigned whenever there was a shift in the parliamentary majority and accordingly in the cabinet. This particularly included those whose jurisdiction involved the " home administration," the " political " component of which imposes the task of maintaining " order," i.e., the existing distribution of power. In Prussia following the decree of Putkammer, these officials were obliged under the pain of discipline to espouse the policies of the government and they were, like the French prefects, used as a governmental apparatus to influence elections. In the German system, unlike other countries, most " political " officials resembled the professionals inasmuch as the attainment of these posts presupposed academic training, specialized examinations, and a certain preparatory service. In Germany only the chief of the political apparatus, the minister, lacked this specific characteristic of the modern professional bureaucracy. Even under the old regime it was possible to become the Prussian minister of culture without ever having attended an institution of higher learning, while to be a councillor who makes reports (*Vortragender Rat*) was possible only on the basis of the prescribed tests. The professionally trained department chief and reporting councillor were obviously — e.g., under Althoff in the Ministry of Education — far better informed regarding the technical problems of the work than their superior. It was no different in England. They were consequently more powerful than their superior in the treatment of all routine problems. Nor was this wrong in itself. The minister was the representative of the existing constellation of political power. He had to act according to these political standards. He had to apply them to the recommendations of his professional subordinates or he had to give them the corresponding directives of a political character. . . .

What does the spoils system — the turning over of all government jobs to the followers of the victorious candidate — mean for the formation of parties today? One result is that entirely conscienceless parties, pure job-hunting organizations face each other, changing their programs in the various elections in accordance with their prospects of catching votes — changing them to an extent unparalleled anywhere despite all analogies. The parties are primarily oriented towards the electoral battle which is most important for job patronage, namely the presidential and gubernatorial elections. Programs and candidates are arranged at the "national conventions" of the parties without the intervention of members of Congress. The conventions are formally, very democratically, made up of delegates who derive their mandates from the "primaries" of their parties. Even in the primaries the delegates are chosen according to the names of the candidates for the presidency. Within the individual parties the most ferocious struggles are carried on over the "nomination." The President has 300,000 to 400,000 jobs which he hands out in the consultation with the senators of the individual states. The senators are also powerful politicians. The House of Representatives on the other hand is relatively powerless politically because it has no patronage to distribute. The cabinet members are aides of the president who is himself legitimated by the people and can run their posts without regard for the confidence or lack of confidence of Congress, thanks to the "separation of powers."

The spoils system resting on these foundations was technically possible in the United States because the youthfulness of American culture could bear a system of Administration by dilettantes. For 300,000 to 400,000 such party men who have no qualifications for their parts other than having rendered faithful services to their party obviously cannot work in a government without bringing about frightful disorders — corruption and waste without equal — which only a country with unlimited economic resources could afford.

The individual who emerges with this plebiscitary party machinery is the " boss." What is the " boss "? A capitalistic enterpriser in the political sphere whose business is the production of votes. He might have obtained his first contacts as a lawyer or tavern keeper or as the operator of a similar kind of enterprise or as a money lender. From there on he spins his web further until he is able to " control " a certain number of votes. Once he has gone that far, he enters into connection with the neighboring bosses and by his zeal, ability and discretion wins the attention of those whose careers are already further advanced. Then he ascends. The boss is indispensable for the organization of the party which, centralized, lies in his power. On the whole he produces the means for running it. How does he get them? Partly from the dues of members and particularly by a levy on the salaries of those officials who got their posts through him and his party. Then through bribes and tips. Whoever wants to infringe on one of the numerous laws with impunity must have the connivance of the boss and must pay for it. Otherwise he will face irresistible unpleasantnesses. However, this alone does not supply the capital necessary for the enterprise. The boss is indispensable as the direct receiver of the money given by the great financial magnates. These latter would not trust any paid party officials or any other person, who might give a public accounting, with money for electoral purposes. The boss with his clever discretion in money matters is obviously just the man for those capitalistic circles which finance the elec-

tions. The typical boss is an absolutely matter-of-fact man. He is not after social honor; the " professional " is despised in " good society." He is after power, power as a source of wealth and as an end in itself as well. He works in obscurity; thus distinguishing him from the English leader. He is not to be heard speaking in public; he suggests to the speakers what it is expedient for them to say but he himself remains silent. As a rule he does not accept any office outside the Federal Senate. For since the senators are constitutional participants in the distribution of patronage, the leading bosses often sit in the Senate in person. The grant of jobs takes place primarily according to services for the party. But there are many instances in which they are granted for money and certain jobs involve definite levies on their incumbents. This is a system of job selling which was widely known in the monarchies of the 17th and 18th centuries including the pontifical states.

The boss has no firm political " principles." He has no conscience and is concerned only with the problem " What will get the votes." Not seldom he is a rather poorly educated man but his private life is unobjectionable and correct. Only in his political ethics naturally does he adapt himself to the prevailing ethics of political activity, as many of us have done in the sphere of economic ethics during the age of greed. Being socially despised as a professional politician does not trouble him. The fact that he does not aspire to and has no chance for the higher positions of the Federal government has the advantage that sometimes intellectuals who have no relations with the party and who are persons of eminence — and not as in Germany where it is always the old party *honoratiores* — become candidates when the bosses expect votes to be won in that way. Indeed, the system of these ideologically indifferent parties with their socially despised power-holders often helps arise to the Presidency able men who in Germany would never get very far. Of course the bosses resist an outsider who might endanger their sources of power and money. But in the competition for the voter's favor they have not infrequently had to bring themselves to accept candidates who were reputed opponents of corruption.

Thus in the United States there exists a strongly capitalistic party organization rigorously organized from top to bottom, supported by the thoroughly solid clubs, which are organized like " orders " on the style of Tammany Hall. These parties strive for profit via political power particularly in municipal governments which in America too are the most important objects of plunder. It is possible that that type of party system is the result of the advanced democracy of the United States as a " new country." This accounts for the fact that this system is now gradually dying. America can no longer be administered by dilettantes. Fifteen years ago, one still encountered American workers who in response to the question why they allowed themselves to be ruled by such politicians whom they themselves despised explained:

" We would sooner have as officials persons on whom we can spit than a bureaucratic caste like you have in Germany, which would spit on us." This was the traditional attitude of American " democracy," but the socialists even then thought of things differently. The situation will not last. Administration by dilettantes is no longer adequate and the Civil Service Reform is creating positions with life tenure and pension rights in increasing numbers. In consequence, the government positions are now being filled with university trained officials who are just as uncorruptive and as able as ours. About 100,000 positions are no longer objects of plunder by means of the ballot box and are instead pensionable and accessible only through the demonstration of qualifications. This will lead to the gradual disintegration of the spoils system, and the party system will then probably undergo a transformation in ways that we do not yet know.

In Germany the decisive features of the political system hitherto have been the following. First: Parliament was impotent. As a result no one with leadership qualities entered it to stay. Given the case that one wanted to enter — the question was: What could one do there? If a position in the chancellery became empty one might approach the appropriate administrative chief and say " I have a very able man in my electoral district who is fit for the position. Will you take him? " And this is what happened. But that was about all that a German parliamentarian could do to satisfy his demand for power — if he had it. In addition to this — this second factor influenced the first — a trained professional bureaucracy has been of extraordinary significance in Germany. In this respect Germany leads the world. But the importance of this trained professional bureaucracy was such that it claimed not only the positions in the bureaucracy but the ministerial posts as well. In the Bavarian *Landtag* during the discussion of parliamentarization it was said that talented persons would no longer be entering the bureaucracy if the ministerial posts were to be filled by parliamentarians. Furthermore, bureaucratic administration in Germany systematically escaped from such types of control as the British Committee System afforded and thus rendered the parliament usable — disregarding a few exceptions — to develop really useful administrative chiefs.

The third factor is that in Germany, in contrast with the United States, we have " *Weltanschauung* " parties, the subjective *bona fides* of which are provided by the fact that their members do have a " self-conscious " attitude towards the world (*Weltanschauung*). The two most important of these *Weltanschauung* parties, the Center, on the one hand and the Social Democratic, on the other, were originally minority parties and were so even intentionally. The leaders of the Center Party never tried to disguise the fact that their anti-parliamentary attitude was based on the fear of being in a minority which would make more difficult for them the business of providing jobs for job-hunters through pressure on the Government. The Social Democratic Party was a minority party out of principle and it was a hindrance to parliamentarization because it did not want to sully itself by contact with the prevailing bourgeois political system. The parliamentary system was made impossible by the self-exclusion of these parties from it.

What then became of the German professional politician? He had no power, no responsibility and could play the role only of a rather minor *honoratior*. As a result he has most recently been possessed by those hopes for the future which are typical everywhere. It has been impossible in these *honoratiores*-circles which get their livings from holding a minor post for a man of superior ability to rise high above them. I know of many men in every party, including naturally the Social Democratic Party, whose political careers are tragedies because they had leadership qualities and were for this very reason not tolerated by the *honoratiores*. All of our parties have traversed this path of development into a guild of *honoratiores*. Bebel for example was a leader in temperament and in purity of character, however limited he was in intelligence. The fact that he was a martyr, that he never abused the confidence of the masses (as far as they knew) put them behind him unconditionally and as a further consequence no power in the party was able seriously to oppose him. This situation came to an end with his death and then began the rule of the functionaries. Trade union officials, party secretaries, and journalists ascended; bureaucratic attitudes dominated the party. It was an honorable bureaucracy — honorable to a degree rarely found if one looks at other countries, especially at the United States with its often corrupt labor leaders — but the consequences of rule by bureaucracy which we have discussed took their toll in the party.

Since the 80's the bourgeois parties were entirely *honoratiores*-guilds. Occasionally, it is true, the parties for purposes of publicity had to take in some non-party intellectual in order to be able to say: "We have so and so in our party." They tried as much as possible to prevent these people from entering the electoral race and allowed them to do so only where it was unavoidable. That is, where the person in question would not have it otherwise.

In the *Reichstag* the same spirit prevailed. Our parliamentary parties were and are guilds. Every speech which is delivered at a session of the *Reichstag* is thoroughly reviewed beforehand by the party. That is what makes them so unbelievably boring. Only the person who has been designated to speak is allowed to take the floor. A sharper contrast with the English and the French custom in this regard is scarcely conceivable. (In the case of the French, the divergence is due to quite different causes.)

Perhaps a change is now occurring as a result of the violent breakdown which is referred to as a revolution. Perhaps, but not certainly. At first incipient forms of new types of party organization appear. Amateurism is in evidence, especially in the activity of students of the various higher schools who say to a man to whom they ascribe leadership qualities: "We will invest you with important tasks; you carry them out." We also see tendencies toward a businessman's organization in the party system. Persons will come to a man to whom they impute leadership qualities and will offer to undertake to obtain votes for him at fixed sum per vote. If you seriously and honestly ask me which of these two systems I regard as more reliable from a purely technical-political point of view, I would, I believe, prefer the second. But both are rapidly rising bubbles which will quickly disappear. The existing forms of party organization are making some readjustments and continuing. These incipient forms are only a symptom of the fact that the new forms would take root — if their leaders would be available. But the technical peculiarities of proportional representation excludes their emergence. Only a few street-corner dictators arose and then fell, and only the following of these street-corner dictatorships is rigorously organized — hence the power of these disappearing minorities.

If we believe that changes are occurring, then we must make clear what has already been said: the leadership of the parties by plebiscitary leaders is a function of the "depersonalization" of the followers — one might say, of their intellectual proletarization. In order to be useful for the leaders, they must give blind obedience, they must be machines in the American sense, undisturbed by the vanity of *honoratiores* or by pretentions to having one's own opinions. Lincoln's election was possible only through this kind of party organization and with Gladstone, the same emerged in the caucus. It is indeed the price one pays for guidance by leaders. Our only choice is: leadership-democracy with the " machine " or leaderless democracy, i.e., the rule of the " professional politician " without a *calling,* without the inner charismatic qualities which make a leader. And this only means what party rebels call the " rule of a clique." For the time being, we have only the latter in Germany. Its persistence in the future, at least in the *Reich,* is furthered by the fact that the Federal Council (*Bundesrat*) will probably be revived, which will necessarily limit the power of the *Reichstag* and its significance as a selective mechanism for leaders. It will be promoted furthermore by proportional representation as it now exists: a typical product of leaderless democracy, not only because it favors cattle trading in jobs by the *honoratiores* but also because it gives the interest-organizations the possibility of bringing about the inclusion of their functionaries into the voting lists. Thus they will create an *apolitical* parliament in which there can be no genuine leadership. The only place where the need for leadership can find expression is in the *Reichs*-presidency — if it is the object of plebiscitary and not parliamentary election. Leadership on the basis of the testimony of achievement can arise and be selected best when in the great municipalities — as is done everywhere in the United States

when an assault against corruption is seriously undertaken — the plebiscitary city manager appears on the scene with the right to organize his bureaus himself. This would require a party organization oriented toward such elections. But the thoroughly petit bourgeois hatred of leadership to be found in all parties, including above all the Social Democrats, obscures the coming form of party organization and accordingly all these chances for the emergence of leadership.

It is not yet possible to see what will be the external form of political activity as a " vocation " in the future, and even less, in which ways opportunities will open for persons with political talent to be brought into relations with politically satisfying tasks. Those who must, because of their private situation, live " by " politics will probably always have to confront the alternatives: a) journalism or b) a position as a party functionary as the typical direct path or c) service for some interest group: trade unions, chambers of commerce, agricultural associations, craftsmen's associations, labor chambers, employers' associations, etc., or d) suitable municipal jobs. Nothing more can be said about the external aspects than that the odium of being déclassé is attached to the party functionary and journalist. " Writer for wages " and " speaker for wages," even though not so explicitly said, are the epithets which occur to every one. Whoever is subjectively defenseless against these charges and who is unable to answer his own conscience against them should stay away from this career, which is in every case not only a serious temptation but a path to perpetual disillusionment. What then are the inner joys which it offers and what personal qualities does it presuppose in those who turn toward it?

First, it affords a sense of power. Even in formally minor positions, the professional politician can be conscious of his influence on human beings, of participation in the exercise of power over them. He can have the feeling of holding in his hand a thread of historically important events, of being above the ordinary routine of daily life. But the question for him is: through which qualities can he hope to be adequate to this power (be it ever so slight) and the responsibility which it imposes? Herewith we enter the area of ethical questions. For the question: what sort of person should one be to lay one's hands on the spokes of the wheel of history, is an ethical question. One can say that three qualities are pre-eminently decisive for the politician: passion, sense of responsibility and good judgment. Passion in the sense of matter-of-factness: passionate devotion to a "task"—to the god or daemon who sets it, but not in the sense of the subjective excitement which my deceased friend George Simmel called "sterile agitation" and which used to characterize certain, especially Russian, intellectuals (though not all of them) and which in this carnival which is being decorated with the proud name of "revolution" is playing such a great role among our intellectuals today. With the latter it is only a "romanticism of the intellectually interesting" running off into nothing and totally devoid of any sense of responsibility. For with mere passion, however genuinely experienced, nothing is to be accomplished. Passion does not make the politician if, in service to a task he does not make responsibility toward this task the guiding star of his conduct. And for this, it is necessary to have — this is the decisive psychological trait of the politician — good judgment, the ability to let realities impinge on one with poise and detachment. In other words, it requires the maintenance of perspective on human beings and on events. The lack of detached perspective in itself is a mortal sin for a politician and one of those qualities the cultivation of which in the coming generation of our intellectuals will doom them to political impotence. The problem is: how can fiery passion and cool judgment be brought together in the same person? Politics is brain work and not physical or spiritual work. Yet, devotion to it, if it is not to be viewed as a frivolous intellectual game but is intended to be a genuine and honest human activity can be born and nurtured only out of passion. That strong discipline of his spirit which characterizes the passionate politician and which distinguishes him from the political dilettante with his merely sterile agitation is only possible through the cultivation of this detached perspective in every sense of the word. The "strength of a political personality" consists primarily in the possession of these qualities.

Hence the politician must daily and hourly struggle against a quite trivial all-too-human enemy, namely, the ordinary variety of vanity which is the mortal enemy of all sober devotion and all detachment — in this sense detachment vis-a-vis oneself.

Vanity is a very widespread trait and no one is perhaps free from it. In academic and scholarly circles it is a sort of occupational disease. But in the case of the scholar, however disagreeable it may be, it is relatively harmless in the sense that it does not as a rule disrupt the course of scientific activities. This is not the case with the politician. He strives for power as an indispensable means. The " power instinct " as it used to be called is accordingly one of his normal qualities. The sin against the holy ghost of his vocation begins when this striving for power loses its substantive goal and becomes a means of purely personal self-intoxication, instead of being put to the exclusive service of the " task." In the last analysis, there are only two mortal sins in politics: lack of sobriety and what is often but not always identical with it — irresponsibility. Vanity, the demand to make oneself as visible as possible, leads the politician to commit one or both of these sins. Since the demagogue is forced to consider " effectiveness," he is on that account in perpetual danger of becoming an actor as well as taking too lightly his responsibility for the consequences of his actions and of being concerned only with the impression which he makes. His lack of sobriety leads him to mistake the glamorous externalia of power for real power but his irresponsibility forces him to enjoy power for its own sake without reference to any substantive goals. For although, or perhaps because, power is the indispensable means, and the striving for power is one of the driving forces of politics, there is no more ruinous distortion of political power than the swaggering of a parvenu power holder and the vain self-admiration in the feeling of power — and in general every form of adoration of power itself. The mere " power politician " whom in Germany, too, a zealous cult tries to glorify, may make a strong impression but in point of fact his effectiveness is empty and meaningless. In that sense the criticisms of " power-politics " are right. The sudden collapse of certain typical representatives of this attitude has provided us with insight into the subjective weakness and impotence which was hidden behind those pretensions and empty gestures. It is the product of an impoverished and superficial blaséness toward the meaning of human action and it has no connection whatsoever with insight into the tragic elements which repose in all action and especially in political action.

It is an entirely true and fundamental proposition of history — which we will not attempt to confirm any further here — that the final results of political action often, nay, regularly stand in a completely inadequate and indeed frequently in quite a reverse relationship to the original intentions of the action. But on this account, this intention of " service to a task " should not be lacking if the action is to have a moral basis. What the "task" should be in the service of which the politician strives for and uses power is a matter of faith. It may serve national, or universal or social or ethical or cultural or earthly or religious goals; it can be borne in firm belief in "progress" — whatever its meaning — or it can reject this belief, it may claim to serve an "idea" or it may seek to serve certain everyday ends while rejecting the claims of the "idea" in principle — in any case, there must be an element of belief. Otherwise the curse of earthly nothingness will burden even the externally most successful political action.

With the last statement, we have entered on the last of the problems which concern us this evening: the ethos of politics as a "task and duty." What vocation can it fulfill, independently of its goals, in the total system of the conduct of life? What, so to speak, is its ethical status? Here ultimate points of view come up against each other, between which a choice must be made. Let us resolutely face this problem which has once more been opened — in my opinion in a quite confused way.

First let us free ourselves from a rather trivial falsification. Ethics can be introduced in a morally very fatal way. For example: you will seldom find a man whose love for one woman has been withdrawn and redirected towards another, who does not find it necessary to legitimate himself to himself by saying she was not worthy of his love or she disillusioned him or by citing some other reasons. He ungraciously adds a lack of gallantry to the plain fact that he no longer loves the woman and that she must bear it, "legitimating" himself by claiming righteousness for himself and shifting to her the blame as well as the misfortune. The successful competitor in erotic matters proceeds in the same way: the opponent was less worthy for otherwise he would not have been beaten. Obviously it is no different when after some victorious war, the victor in undignified self-righteousness declares: "I won because I was on the side of Right"; or when under the pressure of the horrors of war, a person breaks down psychologically and then instead of simply saying: "It was too much for me," finds it necessary to legitimate his war-weariness to himself by saying: "I couldn't bear it because I was forced to fight for a morally wrong cause." And the same applies to those who lose in war. Instead of looking for the "guilty" like gossiping old women — when the social structure produced the war — a manly, hardheaded attitude requires that the enemy be told: "We have lost the war. You have won it. This is now settled. Let us now discuss which conclusions are to be drawn from these facts in accordance with the interests which were involved, and — this is the main thing — in view of the responsibility to the future which weighs especially heavily on the victor." Anything else is undignified and self-defeating. A nation pardons injury to its interests but not to its honor, least of all injuries inflicted by preacherish self-righteousness. Every new document which comes to light after decades revives the undignified scolding, the hatred and the fury, instead of allowing it to be at least morally buried once it is over. This is possible only on the basis of sobriety and chivalry, but above all, dignity. It cannot be done through an "ethics" which in truth signifies only the unworthiness of both sides. This type of "ethics" instead of concerning itself with the only things which should occupy the politician; namely, the future and his responsibility to it, busies itself with questions of past guilt which are politically sterile because they can not be settled. It is a political crime if ever there was one, to be doing this. Furthermore the inevitable falsification of the entire problem is being overlooked out of very material interests: the interests of the victors in the greatest possible gain — morally and materially — and the hopes of the vanquished to gain some benefits by acknowledging their guilt. If there is anything "base," it is just this — and it is the result of utilizing "ethics" as an instrument of "self-righteousness."

What are the relationships between ethics and politics? Are they, as has often been said, not related in any way? Or is it just the opposite: do the "same" ethical norms which apply in all other spheres of life also apply to political action? It has often been asserted that these were two mutually exclusive alternatives, either one or the other being correct. But is it true that any ethical system in the world can provide materially the same ethical imperatives governing erotic, business, familial, and official relations, relations with one's wife, with one's storekeeper, son, competitor, friend, or defendant? Is the fact that political action employs a particular means, namely, power, and as a last resort, violence, ethically indifferent? Do we not see that the Bolshevist and Spartacist ideologists, by using these political instruments, have brought about exactly the same results as those achieved by any military dictator? How, apart from the differences in their personal characteristics and in their dilettantism, are the leaders of the workers and soldiers councils distinguished from any of the power-wielding figures of the old regime? How are the polemics which most of the spokesmen of the allegedly new ethics direct against their opponents any different from those of any other demagogue? By their lofty purposes, it is said. Good! But here we are speaking of means, and the warring antagonists both insist with the utmost sincerity on the loftiness of their ultimate ends. "He who takes the sword shall perish by the sword" and conflict is always conflict. Are they then professing the Sermon on the Mount? The Sermon on the Mount (i.e., the absolute ethic of the Gospels) is a more serious affair than those who evoke these norms are willing to believe. It is not to be taken lightly. It has been said that causality in science is not a cab which one can stop at will, to enter and to leave whenever one wishes. The same is true of the ethics of the Sermon on the Mount. If it means anything more than a mass of trivialities, it must be fully realized or not at all. Otherwise we have the case of the wealthy youth — " he went about tearfully because he was so wealthy." The imperatives of the Gospel are unconditional and straightforward: give up all your possessions — absolutely all. The politically active person would say that it is a socially senseless demand as long as it is not realized for everyone; as long, in other words, as taxation and confiscation — i.e., discipline and order — are not exercised against everyone. The ethical imperative does not concern itself with such questions — that is its essence. For instance it commands " turn the other cheek," without raising any question as to why it is the right of the other person to strike. For all but the saintly, it is an ethic of abjectness (*Würdelosigkeit*). To be a saint, one must be a saint in every respect, and especially in one's intentions. One must live like Jesus, like the Apostles, like Saint Francis and others like them for this ethic to be meaningful and expressive of dignity. When it follows from the acosmistic ethics of love that " one should not resist evil with force " — the politically active person takes the other position which asserts that one should resist evil with force, for otherwise one will be responsible for its triumph. Those who wish to live according to the Gospel should not participate in strikes — for they involve compulsion. They should enter the yellow trade unions; and they should not speak of revolution, for the gospel ethic does not teach that civil war is the one legitimate

form of war. The pacifist who follows the Gospel will reject or throw down his arms. This is being proposed in Germany today as an ethical duty in order to put an end to the war and therewith to all war. The participant in politics would say that the one sure way to discredit war for the foreseeable future is to make a peace which preserves the *status quo*. Then the nations would ask, " Why did we fight this war? " It would then be reduced to an absurdity. This however is impossible now, since something else is profitable to the winners — at least to a part of them. And for this, those actions which made our resistance impossible are responsible. Now, in consequence of this — once the period of exhaustion is over — peace will be discredited rather than war. This is a result of absolute ethics.

Finally, we should comment on the obligation to speak the truth. It is an unconditional imperative in the *absolute* ethical system. This was the reason why some people demanded the publication of all war documents, especially those incriminating their own country, and a one-sided, unconditional confession of the guilt, proved by these documents, regardless of the consequences. The politically active person finds, however, that truth is not actually advanced in this way but is rather obscured by abuse and by the stimulation of the emotions. Only a more widespread and better planned establishment of the truth by nonpartisans would be effective. Any other procedure will have irreparable consequences for the nation which uses it. But absolute ethics does not concern itself with consequences.

This is the decisive point. We should understand that all ethically-oriented action is guided by either of two fundamentally different, irreconcilably opposed maxims. These maxims may assert either absolute, unconditional values (*Gesinnungsethik*) or values the status of which is determined by their costs of attainment in terms of other values (*Verantwortungsethik*). We will call the former the ethics of absolute values and the latter the ethics of responsibility or instrumentalist ethics. This does not mean that the absolute-value ethic is identical with irresponsibility and that the responsibility ethic has no values. Naturally we do not mean this. But there is an unbridgeable gulf between action following the absolute-value maxim — expressed in religious terms, "The Christian acts rightly and leaves the consequences of his actions with God" — or action following the maxim of the responsibility ethics: Everyone has to answer for the predictable consequences of his own actions. You may demonstrate to a convinced syndicalist most conclusively that the consequences of his action will lead to an increase in the chances for reaction, to the intensified oppression of his class and to the blocking of its ascent, and still not make any impression on him. If an action undertaken with good intentions has evil consequences, the actor places the responsibility not on himself, but on the environment, the stupidity of other people or the will of God who created things so. The person who acts according to the ethics of responsibility takes the average deficiencies of man into account — he has no right, as Fichte correctly said, to take their goodness and perfection for granted; he does not seek to shift the consequences of his actions, to the extent that he could foresee them, onto the shoulders of others. He will say, "These consequences are charged to my action." The person who acts according to absolute-value ethics feels "responsible" only for keeping alive the right attitudes, e.g., an attitude of protest against an unjust social order. His actions, which are irrational from the viewpoint of expediency, are intended only to stimulate this attitude. They have and are intended to have only exemplary value.

But the problem is not yet settled. No ethics in the world can dodge the fact that the attainment of good goals is frequently dependent on the utilization of morally dubious or at least dangerous means and involve the possibility or even the probability of disagreeable subsidiary consequences. No ethics in the world can decide when and to what extent ethically good ends "justify" ethically dangerous means and subsidiary consequences.

Force is the decisive means in politics. The magnitude of the ethical contradiction between means and ends may be gathered from the fact that during the war the revolutionary socialists (the Zimmerwald wing) adhered to a principle which might be stated as follows: " If we were confronted by the choice of a few more years of war and then a revolution or immediate peace and no revolution, we should choose the few more years of war." If one asks the further question, " What will be the results of this revolution? " every scientifically trained socialist would have answered that there could be no question of a socialist economy, but that the result would be a bourgeois economic system freed from feudalism and dynastic vestiges. This would be the very modest result of " a few more years of war." It might well be compatible with very firm socialistic convictions to reject the end which requires such means. But this nonetheless is the attitude which we find among Bolshevists, Spartacists, indeed among all types of revolutionary socialists — and it is ludicrous to see these circles denounce the " politicians of violence " of the old regime in ethical terms because of their use of the same means. We do not, of course, deny the justness of the rejection of the ends pursued by these " politicians of violence."

The absolute value ethic must, it seems, collapse in the face of the problem of the justification of means by ends. As a matter of fact, it logically has only one possible path open to it: it must reject every action which applies ethically dangerous means. Here we are speaking of logical possibilities; but in the world of reality, we often find the proponents of absolute value ethics suddenly turn into chiliastic prophets. Those, for example, who preached

" love against violence " now call out for violence — the final use of violence which will bring an end to all violence — just as our generals told the soldiers at every offensive: " This will be the last one; it will bring us victory and then peace." The proponents of the absolute value ethic do not tolerate the ethical irrationality of the universe. They are " rationalists " in the cosmic-ethical sense. Those of you who know Dostoievski will recall the scene of the Grand Inquisitor, where the problem is very aptly analyzed. It is impossible to reconcile the ethics of absolute value with the ethics of responsibility. Once one has admitted at all the principle that ends justify means, it is not possible to limit its application.

Prof. F. W. Foerster, whom I esteem most highly for his sincerity but whose political views I totally reject, is of the opinion that he has overcome this difficulty by the simple proposition that from good only good can come, and from evil, only evil. If this is so, then our whole problem is nonexistent. But it is really astonishing that such a view can be asserted 2500 years after the Upanishads. Not only the whole course of world history but any clearsighted analysis of every-day experience points to the contrary. The development of every known religion rests on the truth of the exactly contrary proposition. The age-old problem of theodicy consists precisely in the question as to how a power which is said to be omnipotent and good, could create an irrational world of undeserved suffering, of unpunished injustice, and of unimprovable stupidity. Either it is neither the one nor the other, or life is governed by quite different principles of reward and retribution which we can interpret metaphysically or which we can never understand in any way. The problems raised by the irrationality of the world have always been the driving force in all religious developments. The Hindu theory of *Karma,* Persian dualism, original sin, predestination, and the *deus absconditus* were all answers to these problems. Even the early Christian knew that the world was ruled by demons and that anyone who entered into politics, i.e., dealt with power and violence as means, concluded a pact with diabolical forces. The early Christian also saw that the proposition that the good produces only good, and evil only evil, did not hold for such persons but just the opposite. Whoever fails to see this is, in fact, a child.

Religious ethics have dealt in various ways with the fact that we are involved in different orders of life, each governed by different laws. Hellenic polytheism sacrificed to Aphrodite as well as to Hera, to Dionysius as well as to Apollo, while fully aware that they were often in conflict with one another. The Hindu system of conduct subjected each occupation to a particular ethical law, a *Dharma,* and separated them from one another into castes. It placed them in a fixed hierarchy, from which those who were born into it could not escape except through rebirth in a subsequent life. Thus it placed them at various distances from the highest values of salvation. It was thereby possible to work out the regulations proper to each occupation in accordance with the *Dharma* of each caste, from the ascetics and the Brahmans to the thieves and prostitutes. Politics and war were included therein. The integration of war into the value system takes place in the *Bhagavadgita,* in the conversation between Krishna and Arduna: " Do what is required," i.e., what is obligatory according to the *Dharma* of the warrior-caste and its rules, and correspondingly expedient for military purposes. This does not interfere with religious salvation but promotes it. India's heaven was just as sure for the Hindu soldier who died a hero as Valhalla was for the German warrior. The former would have despised Nirvana just as much as the latter would have sneered at the Christian paradise with its choirs and angels. This type of specialization permitted Hindu ethics to deal with the royal art of politics with complete consistency allowing for, and even intensifying an expediential attitude toward the immanent practical requirements for political success. A really thoroughgoing " Machiavellianism " in the popular sense is expounded in Hindu literature in the *Kautilya Arthasastra* (dating from the pre-Christian era, allegedly from the period of Chandvagupta). By contrast, Machiavelli's *Prince* is quite innocent. In Catholic ethics, to which Professor Foerster is otherwise rather close, the *consilia evangelica* represent a special ethic for those endowed with the charisma of saintliness. In contrast with the monk who may neither shed blood nor carry on gainful employment, the knight is allowed to do the former and the citizen the latter. The gradation of ethical imperatives and their integration into a systematic doctrine of salvation is less consistent than in India. And according to the presuppositions of the Christian faith, it must and should be so. The corruption of the world by original sin easily allows the incorporation of force into ethics as a means of discipline against sin and against the soul-endangering heretics. The purely absolute-value oriented, acosmistic imperatives of the Sermon on the Mount and the religious natural law as an absolute imperative which is derived from it, however, conserved their revolutionary drive and in periods of social upheaval almost always emerged with elemental force. They brought forth the radical-pacifistic sects, one of which in Pennsylvania tried to establish a polity which eschewed all violence in external relations. The results of this were tragic since when the War of Independence broke out, the Quakers could not participate in it in a military way although the war was being fought for their ideals. In contrast with this attitude, Protestantism, on the whole, legitimates authority, and therewith the use of violence, as a divine institution. It gives particular legitimation to the use of force by the legitimate authority. Luther freed the individual from ethical responsibility for war and imposed it on the authority,

obedience to whom in matters other than faith can never be wrong. Calvinism accepted violence in principle as a means of defending the faith, thereby justifying religious war which has been integral to Islamic culture from the very beginning. Thus we see that the problems of political ethics are not peculiar to modern times. They are not products of the unbelief which grew up in the soil of the Renaissance cult of the hero. Every religion has struggled with these problems — and with various degrees of success. Nor, after what we said above, could it have been otherwise. The peculiar feature of all ethical problems in politics centers about the specific instrument of legitimate violence resting in the hands of human associations.

Whoever has any traffic with these instruments, whatever the purpose, is put at the mercy of certain consequences. This applies to every person participating in politics. It applies in an especially high degree to warriors for a faith, be it religious or revolutionary. Let us examine the present period as an example of this. Whoever wishes to use violence as means to establish justice on earth, must have followers, i.e., an organization or a " machine." These followers must have the prospect of material and symbolic rewards — either in heaven or on earth — or else they will not function. On the psychological and symbolical side, given the existence of the modern class struggle, these rewards must comprise the satisfaction of hatred and revenge, above all, resentment and the demand for pseudo-ethical self-righteousness including the demand for insulting and injuring the enemy. On the material side, they include adventure, conquest, booty, power and patronage. The leader is entirely dependent for his success on the functioning of his organization. Thus he is dependent on *their* motives and not on his own. His success is dependent on the permanence of the supply of rewards demanded by his followers, be they Red Guards, spies, or agitators. Hence it is not entirely a result of anything that he himself does that certain results are achieved. Rather the results are determined by the ethically base motives underlying the actions of his followers, who can be held in check only as long as at least a part of them — probably never a majority — honestly believe in him and in his aims. But this belief, even where it is subjective, is in most cases only an ethical "legitimation" of the demand for revenge, power, booty, and patronage. We will not be dissuaded from this insight for the materialistic conception of history is not a cab which can be halted at will and it does not stop even for revolutionaries. It is important to remember that emotional revolutionism is succeeded by traditionalistic routine; the heroic believer and even the belief itself disappears — or what is more significant — becomes a part of the conventional phrase-mongering of the political philistine and wire-puller. This development is especially rapid in the case of conflicts of belief because these are ordinarily led or inspired by genuine leaders, i.e., revolutionary prophets. For here, as in the case of every kind of organization, depersonalization and routinization, in other words, psychic proletarization in the interests of "discipline" is a condition of success. The victorious following of an ideologically motivated leader is especially likely for this reason to degenerate into a stratum of mere beneficiaries of patronage.

Whoever wishes to participate in politics and especially those who wish to make a career in politics, must be aware of these ethical paradoxes and of his responsibility for what he does under their pressure. He is dealing with the diabolic forces which lurk in every act of violence. The great *virtuosi* of acosmistic humanitarianism and goodness, regardless of whether they came from Nazareth, from Assisi, or from royal Indian castles, did not operate with the political instrument of violence, their kingdom was "not of this world." Still they influenced and continue to influence this world, and the figures of Platon Karatajev and the saints of Dostoievski are their best reproductions. Those who are trying to save their own souls and those of others should not try to do so through politics, the solution of the problems of which can be effected only by the use of violence. The genius or the daemon of politics stands in deep and perpetual conflict with the God of Love and even with the Christian God in His ecclesiastical form — a conflict which can break out into the open at any moment. This was known even

during the periods of church supremacy. Time and again, the papal interdict was applied to Florence,
whose citizens continued to fight
against the hierocracy. And at that
time the papal interdict had much
greater importance for men and the
salvation of their souls than, as
Fichte said, the " cool approbation "
of the Kantian ethical judgment. It
was with reference to such situations
that Machiavelli — in the *History of
Florence,* if I am not mistaken —
had one of his heroes praise those
citizens who prize the greatness of
their native city higher than the salvation of their soul.

But if instead of " native city " or
" fatherland " — which is at present
an ambiguous term for some people
— we substitute " the future of socialism " or " international peace,"
then we confront the problem in its
contemporary form. Everything
which is striven for by political
means, which uses violence and
which treads the path of responsibility ethics, endangers the " salvation
of the soul." But if it be striven for
in accordance with the ethics of absolute value and by means of a war
of beliefs, then it can suffer damages
and discredit which will not be repaired for generations, just because
responsibility for consequences was
lacking. In such cases, the diabolical forces which are at work remain
unknown to the actor. These forces
are relentless and they generate consequences in the face of which he is
helpless if he does not perceive them.
The proverb, " The Devil is old, so
become old in order to understand
him," does not refer to chronologi-

cal age. I have never permitted myself to be vanquished by the dates
entered on birth certificates. The
mere fact that someone is twenty
years old and I am fifty does not impress me as an achievement worthy
of much reverence. Age is not decisive. What counts rather is a carefully cultivated relentlessness in analyzing the problems which we confront and the capacity to face the
realities of life and to measure up to
them.

It is true that intelligence is the
chief requirement in politics — but
not intelligence alone. In this the
ethics of absolute value are right.
But whether one should follow the
dictates of absolute value ethics or of
responsibility ethics, and when one
and when the other, cannot be prescribed to anyone. Only one thing
can be said: When, in these excited
days, which you believe are not
sterile — and it should be remembered that excitement is not necessarily genuine devotion or passion —
when in such a period as this, those
whose political activity follows the
standards of absolute value ethics declare, " The world is stupid and base
— not I. The responsibility for consequences falls not on me but on the
others whom I wish to serve and
whose stupidity or baseness I would
eradicate " — then I say openly that
I would first enquire into the degree
of personal integrity underlying
these absolute-value pronouncements.
I am of the impression that in nine
cases out of ten, we would discover
windbags who do not really appreciate the responsibilities they are assuming but who are intoxicating

themselves with romantic sensations. I am not very much attracted by this and it leaves me unmoved. But it is tremendously moving when a mature person — regardless of whether he is old or young — who realizes his responsibilities, accepts them with complete self-awareness and acts accordingly, states in a certain situation: " Here stand I. I can do no other." This is something genuine. All of us, if we are not subjectively ossified, must face the possibility of confronting such a situation. In this sense, absolute value ethics and responsibility ethics are not in complete conflict. They are rather mutually complementary, and together they produce the genuine person who really can experience the " *vocation* of politics."

Ten years from now we will discuss this point again. It must, unfortunately, be feared that by then, because of a whole complex of causes, the wave of reaction will have long since broken over us, and of the many things which many of you — and I too, confess — wished and hoped for, little, at least according to external appearances, will have been realized. I will not be crushed by it, but it is a hardship to have to know it. I will be greatly interested at that time, to see what has become of those of you who think of yourselves as active in politics on behalf of an ethic of absolute values, and who are sharing in the intoxication signified by this revolution. It would be fine if things turned out in such a way as to make Shakespeare's 102nd sonnet to the point:

Our love was new, and then but in the
   spring,
When I was wont to greet it with my
   lays
As Philomel in summer's front doth
   sing
And stops her pipe in growth of riper
   days.

But the situation is not like that. We are not entering the bloom of summer but rather a polar night of icy darkness and hardness, regardless of which group triumphs externally. For where nothing exists, then not only the Kaiser but the proletarian as well has lost his rights. When this night gradually softens, who will still be alive of those for whom spring is now in such bloom? And what will your attitude be then? Bitterness or unreflective philistinism, dumb and dull acceptance of the world and your occupation, or thirdly and not least frequently: mystical flight from reality by those who are capable of it or — as it is both frequent and unpleasant — an attempt to follow this fashion. In all such cases, I will conclude that you did not measure up to the actions which you undertook, that you did not measure up to the world as it really is, that you really have not experienced in the deepest sense, the vocation of politics which you thought you discovered in yourselves. You would have done better had you simply concerned yourself with practicing brotherliness in personal relations and with doing your daily task in a sober way.

Politics is a slow and strenuous boring of hard boards and it requires both passionate devotion and perspective. It is, of course, true, and history provides ample evidence for the fact that we would not achieve the possible if we did not strive for the impossible. But the man who can do this must be a leader — and not only a leader but a hero as well — in the very literal sense. And those who are neither must equip themselves with that steadfastness of heart which is capable of bearing the complete failure of all one's hopes. If already now they fail to do this, then they will not even be able to do that which is practicable today. Only those who are certain that they will not collapse if the world, from their viewpoint, is too stupid or too base for the things they offer it — who can say "nonetheless" in the face of this — only those who have been "called" to a political career.

PART III

TENSIONS IN
MODERN SOCIETY

11 TENSIONS WITHIN NATIONS

66. Conflicts and Tensions in Industrial Societies

In the modern society of large industrial organizations, urban concentrations, and large public bureaucracies the individual lives with and among groups of conflicting interests. Some of these group conflicts, or tensions, are seemingly far removed from the milieu in which the individual pursues his own interests. The conflict among nations, for instance, makes its impact on the individual through the communication channels, which report the convening of international conferences, the departure of diplomatic missions, and the sending of notes of protest to foreign governments and which also issue analytical reports about the motives of governments and officials who function in the rarefied atmosphere of international politics. Only when diplomatic procedures break down and nations resort to war do individuals become visibly and immediately affected by the conflict among nations.

The tensions within nations do, however, continually affect the individual, for in his daily experience he is constantly reminded of the forces in society that contravene the interests with which he identifies himself. If he is a worker, he knows he may be at odds with the decisions made by management. As a member of a family, he is constantly fighting the battle of the generations. Much of the life of an individual, in fact, is spent in adjusting himself to the social tensions surrounding him.

Karl Marx placed one particular tension at the center of his social system and explained historical development in terms of the conflicts of opposed classes. The position of the individual in society and hence his behavior, i.e., the decisions he makes, are determined by his relationship to the means of production. In the historical epoch of capitalism there are, according to Marx, essentially two of these relationships: one, individual ownership of the means of production, and, two, individual subservience to the means of production. Marx assumed that all the individuals in one of these categories would behave the same way. He thus hypothesized a rigid type of class behavior in which the interests of the capitalistic class runs counter to the interests of the proletariat. And from this concept of the class struggle Marx spun theories which purported to show the imminence of the demise of capitalism.

The Marxian theory of class is an objective theory. Marx contended that there are certain objective conditions in society, one's relationship to the means of production, that determine behavior. It is also a theory rooted in the mass society. The position of the individual in his local community, for instance, is superseded by his position as an industrial worker or owner of large enterprise.

Sociologists do not accept the Marxist concept of class, for it grossly oversimplifies the complicated social structure of modern society. One simply cannot assume that all workers or employers will behave in the same way. In the first place, there are significant subjective elements in the decisions that people make and the objective conditions of employment and income do not necessarily control these elements. In the second place, man performs numerous roles in society, all of which influence his behavior. To single out one role as determinant, i.e., worker or employer, is to ignore a large part of man.

The first article in this chapter on Tensions Within Nations points up the complexities of the class structure and thus casts doubt on the validity of the Marxian class theory as a basis for predicting behavior. Professor Paul Hatt suggests that a class structure consists of many statuses with varying prestige values attached to each. The proletariat and the bourgeoisie, therefore, are not clearly defined groups in society but rather a range of stages in a stratified continuum.

Although Marx's theory of class is inadequate, he recognized more clearly than most people of his time the profound influence of industrialization on the structure of society. New groups have thrust themselves forward as advancing technology increased the size of industrial units and decreased the size of the world in which they function. Management executives have acquired prestige and power with the divorce of ownership from the control of corporate enterprise. Unions have become large enterprises in their own right catering to the demands of the workers who man the apparatus of industrial organization. Their leaders wield a power that matches and possibly overmatches the power of the leaders of corporate enterprise. And along with these groups the influence of the professions has grown as they minister to the legal, medical, and educational growing pains of society.

The rise of unions in the United States has focused attention on the struggles of management and labor. Casual acquaintance with newspaper headlines reveals the existence of this struggle and the question inevitably arises whether it is the prototype of the Marxian class struggle. The article on labor taken from Fortune's *USA — the Permanent Revolution* argues persuasively that the American labor movement by and large is pragmatic and non-doctrinaire and consequently not concerned with the strategy and polemics of class warfare. If this is true, then, it is because both parties to the struggle accept a set of values that transcends each of their own immediate interests. Both labor and management take democratic capitalistic society as given and attempt to achieve their objectives within this framework.

This is not to deny the reality of the conflict. Clearly diverse interests, which are difficult to adjust, meet head-on at the collective bargaining table. Labor views wage rates as income while management views them as costs. The one is interested in maximizing income, the other in minimizing costs. The proximate ends of labor and management therefore conflict. Neither can obtain all it desires. Tensions are at the lowest point when both sides are willing and able to accept compromises.

In the article " The Clash between Security and Progress," Professor Allan Fisher attempts to prove that excessive concern about security may destroy a desirable rate of economic growth. This issue, security versus progress, is at the core of the conflict between labor and management. Labor, understandably concerned about fluctuating income and contingent insecurities, strives to secure high and continuous income and pension benefits to protect itself against the day when it no longer will earn current income. If it cannot attain these ends through collective bargaining it will turn to government and try to mobilize the collective power of society for its own purposes. Management, on the other hand, is responsible for those investment decisions that increase the productivity of society and hence bring material progress. Investment decisions are made on the basis of a profitability criterion, and understandably management will resist those demands of labor that reduce profit prospects and encroach on what it considers to be its decision-making prerogatives. Like labor, management will turn to government if unsuccessful in protecting its interests.

Collective bargaining, therefore, is a public issue in a very real sense. The struggle over security and progress is constantly carried on before the bar of public opinion. In the large society, issues such as this can only reach the public audience through the channels of communication. As we have seen in Part I, communication is a screen through which reality is filtered. The nature of this screen then is tremendously important in influencing people's attitudes. The last article of this chapter is an excerpt from the report of the Commission on Freedom of the Press. The Commission addressed itself to the problem of the bias of the free press. Does the private ownership of newspapers unduly prejudice the reporting of news? Are minority points of view fairly represented? Do advertisers exert unfair pressures on newspaper policies? The answers to these questions obviously have some bearing on the type of compromise that is struck between the conflicting interests of labor and management. An understanding of the institutional organization of communication, therefore, is important to an understanding of the conflicts of choice, or tensions, within nations.

A. The Class Structure

67. Stratification in Modern Society*

It is a commonplace to state that the study of social stratification is in a chaotic state. One writer has recently said that "There is no general agreement among sociologists at the present time as to what factor or combination of factors delineates the social class. All concur that the concept of class deals with the horizontal stratification of a population, but whether it is based on economic power, occupation, status feelings, culture differences, or their combination, and to what extent separate group life is indicated by the term, are questions on which there is no substantial agreement." [1] And another has commented that "Although well aware of social class, social scientists have been more concerned with their theories and with quarrelling among themselves about what social class is than studying its realities in the daily lives of people." [2]

It is impossible not to agree with the general tenor of these statements. However, all is not lost so long as it is possible to place the varying theoretical and empirical materials in any sort of sensible order. And this at least does seem possible. Moreover, it is the thesis of this paper that once placed in this order, the materials do reveal a promising amount of convergence. As widely variant as sociologists may have been with respect to this problem, the consequences of their thinking and research are adequate to provide some identification of a common frontier, or frontiers, which now should and can be penetrated.

SOURCES OF DIFFICULTY

There seem to be five major interrelated areas of disagreement which revolve around: (1) terms, (2) whether the determinants of stratification are subjective or objective, (3) whether class is classificatory or substantive, (4) the variety of institutional matrices within which stratification occurs, and (5) the question as to the extent to which stratification is to be regarded as occurring on the local community level and the extent to which it is to be seen on the level of the mass society.

1. *Terms.* Although a frequent source of annoyance this problem should not require attention at this point, since an arbitrary solution is possible.

2. *Objective vs. Subjective Con-*

---

* From Paul K. Hatt, "Stratification in the Mass Society," *American Sociological Review*, XV (1950), pp. 216–22. Reprinted by permission of the *American Sociological Review*.

[1] Milton M. Gordon, "Social Class in American Sociology," *American Journal of Sociology*, LV (November, 1949), 265.

[2] W. Lloyd Warner, Marchia Meeker, Kenneth Eells, *Social Class in America* (Chicago: Science Research Associates, 1949.)

ceptualization of Stratification. The subjective point of view focuses primarily upon the term " social class " and assumes classes to be substantive in nature. This is illustrated by the statement: "No matter what objective criterion we use, we do not have a *social* class unless class consciousness is present." [3] This point is also made by Centers who states that "Class, as distinguished from stratum, can well be regarded as a psychological phenomenon in the fullest sense of the term, that is, a man's class is a part of his ego, *a feeling on his part of belongingness to something; and identification with* something larger than himself." [4] The objective view on the other hand maintains that classes, economic or social, are determined outside the consciousness of the individual. It can thus be seen that the question of objectivity versus subjectivity depends upon the existence of substantive classes and hence further discussion of it must await fuller treatment of the more general problem, stratification.

3. *Conceptualization of Stratification as Classificatory or Substantive.* As in the case of the second point, this source of disagreement refers to a highly specialized aspect of stratification, that is, social class, and consequently must also wait upon further clarification of stratification itself. [5]

4. *The Variety of Institutional Matrices.* This difficulty in the understanding of stratification has been stated in a variety of ways. One of the oldest and certainly one of the clearest is Max Weber's formulation of the three orders of stratification. [6] To him the differential distribution of power is the essential basis of stratification and power is defined as the ability to control the behavior of others. The sources of power are found, according to Weber, in three major social institutions. First, there is the legal order associated with the use of physical or psychical compulsion with the intent of obtaining conformity with the order or of inflicting sanctions for violations of it. The unit of stratification within the legal order is the political party, a category so defined that it may be found in any group which is " societalized," that is, which has a rational order and a staff to enforce that order.

Second, there is an economic order which is directly conditioned by differing relations to the market and hence to material production. The units of stratification within this order are considered to be " classes." Class is thus defined by Weber as a collectivity possessing similar life chances determined by the operation of the market in the differential distribution of material property.

[3] R. M. MacIver and Charles H. Page, *Society* (New York: Rinehart & Co., 1949), p. 350.

[4] Richard Centers, *The Psychology of Social Classes* (Princeton: Princeton University Press, 1949), p. 27.

[5] Llewellyn Gross, " The Use of Class Concepts in Sociological Research," *The American Journal of Sociology,* LIV (March, 1949), 410–11.

[6] The following discussion of Weber's thought on this point is taken from H. H. Gerth and C. Wright Mills, *From Max Weber* (New York: Oxford University Press, 1946), Ch. 7.

The third structure within which stratification occurs is considered to be the " social " order. This is based upon the differential distribution of " social honor," and the units within this order are termed " status groups." These Weber defines as groups characterized by a specific style of life linked to restrictions on social intercourse, that is intercourse which is not subservient to economic or business ends.

It must, of course, be made clear that for Weber, the three orders of stratification are very closely intertwined and that any one may affect or be affected by any other, or any combination of orders. It is this fact which has made an agreement upon the nature of stratification difficult. Weber has posed, but not solved, the problem of analyzing the net effects of each of these three highly interrelated systems. It has, however, unquestionably aided in our understanding of stratification by positing a series of areas within which work should be done.

5. *The Problem of Community Matrices.* The question as to whether stratification is to be considered a function of the local community or of the mass society is, of course, merely a segment of the larger theoretical question concerning the nature and significance of the differences between these two aspects of society as determinants of human behavior. This problem has been raised by Redfield in his statement that " Anthropologists commonly used the terms ' community,' ' society,' ' culture ' interchangeably; while the distinctions among these

concepts may be of significance in dealing with the modern urbanized and industrialized society." [7] The context in which this quotation is found makes it clear that the distinctions referred to are not concerned with the larger abstractions of culture, community and society but rather with the essential problem of dealing with what sociologists have in mind when distinguishing between the primary and secondary community.

On the taxonomic level, sociology is by no means unaware of the significance of these differences. Even introductory textbooks contain one or more of the common dichotomies, such as *gesellschaft* and *gemeinschaft, connubium and commercium,* social segment and social organ, primary and secondary communities, or some other variant of this notion. It is not so clear, however, that the significance of this distinction with respect to research and theory is always understood, or at least it is frequently not made explicit. For example, local communities are used in one way when they are employed mechanically as primary sampling units in a large statistical study. In such a case there is no need of being concerned with the primary-secondary community differences. Local communities are, however, also used in an entirely different fashion, which does call for specific elaboration of the theoretical relationship when the study takes what Redfield has called the anthropological view — sees the

[7] Robert Redfield, " The Folk Society and Culture," *Eleven Twenty-six* (Chicago: University of Chicago Press, 1940), pp. 46–47.

local community and society as one. Stratification seems to be one field in which this has been notably true. Reference is made here to those cases in which the community is taken as a replica of the larger society. In these, the local community is not a sample but a universe — and more, the universe is taken to be that of the larger society. This procedure is illustrated by Warner's conception of the role of Jonesville: "Jonesville has been our laboratory for studying Americans. The social structure governing American capitalism lies within the actions of its people, for the lives of the ten thousand citizens of Jonesville express the basic values of 140 million Americans."[8] This ignores the problem raised by Redfield and, in fact, fails to consider some of the most fundamental characteristics of a complex society. Theoretical problems which immediately rise from such an assumption of the identity of the local community with the national life are that modern industrial society is characterized by, among other things, regional specialization, local differentiation, impersonality and mobility. These are factors which cannot by definition exist on the level of the local community. To this extent, Jonesville *cannot* be taken as America. Any satisfactory theoretical conception of stratification in the mass society must, therefore, allow not only for its local impact, but also for its significance in the patterns of the larger society.

6. *Summary of the Sources of Dif-*

[8] W. Lloyd Warner and Associates, *Democracy in Jonesville* (New York: Harper & Bros., 1949.)

ficulty. If, then, the problem of nomenclature is temporarily ignored and the questions of subjective-objective and classificatory-substantive conceptualizations are deferred for subsequent consideration, it is possible to summarize the problems in stratification theory in a sentence or two. There are six (or perhaps more, if institutional contexts in addition to those listed by Weber are chosen) possible orders within which stratification develops. These may be seen as a paradigm containing Weber's three orders of stratification, each one of which in turn may be viewed as existing on either the level of the local group or the level of the secondary society. This paradigm can serve as a frame of reference within which to examine alternative formulations.

ALTERNATIVE SOLUTIONS

When the modes of solution to the problem posed by the foregoing are analyzed they appear to fall into two general types. One may be called "solution by correlation." This includes those conceptualizations which employ an index, or indexes, correlating highly with all the possible orders of stratification. The second is "solution by summation" and embraces those attempts to solve the problem by assuming that all of the elements in the paradigm suggested earlier in this paper can somehow be combined into a single status system.

1. *Solution by Correlation.* The chief difficulty with these solutions lies in their lack of validation and

standardization. In general it may be said that the extent to which high correlations characterize all elements in the paradigm is unknown. In addition, most of these solutions have not been demonstrated to be applicable in cross-regional or cross-community (in terms of size of community) studies. In so far as this is true such solutions are incomplete and in need of further refinement.

A. *Single Factor Indexes.* Income, education, area of residence and occupation have been the chief factors employed in this approach to stratification. The most systematic work on these has unquestionably been done in the field of occupational classification, of which Alba Edwards' socio-economic scale of occupational classification using primarily distinctions between "head and hands" types of employment is perhaps the most frequently used.[9] Another type of classification of eighty-eight occupations has been suggested by an NORC survey using the prestige ratings given by a representative sample of the United States.[10]

B. *Multiple Factor Indexes.* A wide variety of multiple factor indexes exists. Some are adapted to rural regions as, for example, the work of Sewell,[11] while others, such as Chapin's social status scale,[12] are applicable only to urban conditions. Composite scales may employ as few as two indexes, or several, as the case may be. These indexes may in turn represent either one or a combination of the cells in the paradigm of stratification. C. Wright Mills, for example, has usefully combined income and occupation,[13] both characteristic of the *economic* order. Chapin's, Sewell's and similar scales, on the other hand, have all drawn upon the *social* order and local community values as well as upon the economic order. Such multiple factor solutions may appear on the basis of common sense to be measurably superior to the single factor indexes but this has yet to be definitively demonstrated and, in any case, the correlations of both types with all possible orders of stratification need still to be investigated.

2. *Solution by Summation.* This mode follows two general lines. One of these is essentially a theoretical description of the way in which the orders of stratification are integrated within a society; the other is an empirical application of the hypothesis that all orders contribute to a single status system.

A. *Analysis by Role and Status.* Any approach to the solution of the problem through the analysis of role

---

[9] Alba M. Edwards, *Comparative Occupational Statuses for the United States* (16th Census, 1940), U. S. Government Printing Office, 1943.

[10] Cecil C. North and Paul K. Hatt, "Jobs and Occupations: A Popular Evaluation," in Logan Wilson and William A. Kolb, *Sociological Analysis* (New York: Harcourt, Brace & Co., 1949), pp. 464–73.

[11] William H. Sewell, *The Construction and Standardization of a Scale for the Meas-*

urement of the Socio-economic Status of Oklahoma Farm Families, Oklahoma A. & M. Agricultural Experimental Station, 1940 (Technical Bulletin No. 9).

[12] Louis Guttman, "A Review of Chapin's Social Status Scale," *American Sociological Review*, VIII, 3 (June, 1943), 362–69.

[13] C. Wright Mills, "The Middle Classes in Middle-Sized Cities," *American Sociological Review*, 10 (April, 1945), 42–249.

and status elements in social position must undertake the responsibility of relating these to each of the possible orders of stratification. From among those who have selected this approach, Kingsley Davis' statement of the position is chosen as the most complete.[14] Status is defined as the expectations of society around given functions and statuses have the quality of differential value. In this way statuses confer a *prestige* value upon their occupant. *Role,* on the other hand, refers to the manner in which the occupant of a status fulfills the status expectations and thus contributes an *esteem* value to one's total social position, which is thus seen as some type of summation of a wide variety of statuses and roles. Social position is thus regarded as a personal quality rather than a locus in a social structure. Strata are composed of individuals possessing social positions with approximately equivalent values.

The manner in which this approach combines the increments of positional value from all possible cells of the paradigm of stratification, may perhaps be represented by the formula:

$$SP = f(P_1, P_2 \ldots P_n), g(E_1, E_2 \ldots E_n)$$

in which SP is the total social position, P_1 is the prestige value of any one status and E_1 the esteem value of the role associated with that status; P_2, E_2, etc., represent prestige and esteem values associated with an indefinite number of statuses. If, however, recognition of the different na-

[14] Kingsley Davis, *Human Society* (New York: Macmillan, 1949), pp. 91–96.

ture of positional values on the local level from those values on the mass society level is desired, the formula requires some elaboration, such as the following:

$$SP = f(P_1, P_2 \ldots P_i), f'(E_1, E_2 \ldots E_i),$$
$$f''(p_1 p_2 \ldots p_i), f'''(e_1 e_2 \ldots e_j)$$

in which the symbols represent the prestiges and esteems as before but in this instance the upper case letters stand for the values in the context of the mass society and the lower case for local community values.

The empirical test of such a formula is not yet possible, because three very difficult values must be supplied, that is, the number and value of prestiges, the number and value of esteems, and the nature of the functions which unite them into the single expression of social position. Its utility is primarily making explicit one manner in which the complexities of stratification may be viewed as a unified whole.

In one sense this approach is the opposite of solution by correlation. In the latter case a large body of empirical data have been gathered with, however, a rather unsatisfactory theoretical framework; while in role-status analysis a satisfactory body of theory is presented, but one which makes empirical testing difficult.

B. *Community Reputational Analysis.* The assumption underlying this approach is that the separate orders of stratification all contribute to one over-all status system, and that this system finds its expression in a graded series of substantive social classes. Because these classes include " social honor " as a basis of judgment, they exist only within the local community. Warner puts the first part of the assumption this way: " . . . societies must have rank orders to perform certain functions necessary for group survival. . . . When societies are complex and service large populations they always possess some kind of status system which by its own values places people in higher and lower positions." [15] The second part of the assumption, that is, that social classes are found on the local community level, can be seen in the definition of social class given by Allison Davis: " The crucial tests of class position are certainly the same all over America, in both white and Negro society. People are of the same class when they may normally (1) eat or drink together as a social ritual, (2) freely visit one another's family, (3) talk together intimately in a social clique, or (4) have cross-sexual access to one another outside of the kinship group. These relationships are the basic privileges of class equals, and it is to limit the range of such contacts that the class pressures are exerted." [16]

This definition of social class is very closely related to Weber's concept of the status group, placed upon the local community level, and also to one element in role-status analysis.

The actual method of locating social classes employed in this approach is most fully stated in Volume I of the Yankee City Series [17] and in *Elm-*

town's Youth. [18] A shorter method of approximating the classes in the community is described in a more recent volume by Warner in which six techniques are outlined. [19]

The reason for the development of the simplified technique, according to Warner, is that the original method is too expensive, time consuming, difficult to communicate explicitly, and imprecise for adequate comparative study of communities. This concern over the comparative study of communities indicates that one of Warner's aims is to go beyond the local community by securing values more broadly applicable in mass society. This indicates a turn in Warner's thinking allowing for the possible integration of his work with other approaches.

The shorter method of community reputational analysis is based upon the following techniques:

1. *Rating by Matched Agreements.* This technique involves two steps: (a) securing the opinion of a group of informants as to the number and names of classes recognized in the community, and (b) the assignment of class statuses to actual persons within that community.

2. *Rating by Symbolic Placement.* In this method an individual is assigned a class position on the basis of symbolic reference made to him by the informants. These symbolic statements will include such things as (a) struc-

[15] W. Lloyd Warner, Marchia Meeker, Kenneth Eells, *Social Class in America,* p. 8.

[16] Allison Davis, *Children of Bondage,* American Council on Education, 1940, p. 201.

[17] W. Lloyd Warner and Paul S. Lunt, *The Social Life of a Modern Community,* Vol.

I, " Yankee City Series," (New Haven: Yale University Press, 1941).

[18] A. B. Hollingshead, *Elmtown's Youth* (New York: John Wiley & Sons, 1949).

[19] W. Lloyd Warner, *Social Class in America.*

tural-family, social or clique terms, (b) regional or area terms, and (c) trait characterized, derogatory or eulogistic phrases.

3. *Rating by Status Reputation.* This assigns status by virtue of the reputation an individual has in the mind of the informant as a result of engaging in activities or possessing certain traits which have a definite class value.

4. *Rating by Comparison.* Here an individual is placed by a judgment on the part of the informant that he is superior, equal or inferior to someone else whose position is already known.

5. *Rating by Simple Assignment to a Class.* Class position is estimated in this instance by a simple statement of class position by the informant.

6. *Rating by Institutional Membership.* Class position is ascribed by the informant through reference to participation in cliques, churches and associations.[20]

This shorter method of class analysis is termed the method of Evaluated Participation, known familiarly as EP. There is little indication that this technique will contribute anything to increasing the cross-community comparability of Warner's earlier methods. The EP is still basically a function of the local community even though it does include the effects of all three of the institutional matrices of stratification.

[20] Paraphrased from W. Lloyd Warner, *Social Class in America,* pp. 37–38. Attention may be called here to the fact that the six methods of placing an individual are not so much separate methods, or techniques, as they are probing questions to secure an accurate answer from the informant.

From the EP, however, Warner does move on toward indexes applicable throughout the larger society. This method, then, should not be considered as a part of the community reputational approach but rather as an attempt at methodological and theoretical extension beyond the limits of community reputation.

3. *The Relationship Between Community Reputational Analysis and Solution by Correlation.* The EP, in this analysis, was used as the criterion of validity of the simpler mode of analysis which Warner terms the Index of Status Characteristics, hereafter referred to as the ISC. The ISC was originally composed of six items which were transformed into a composite scale of a type quite similar to those discussed earlier in this paper. The elements utilized were as follows: occupation, amount of income, source of income, house type, dwelling area, and education. The zero order of coefficients of correlation between each of these and the EP of the Jonesville sample ranged from 78 to 91 and the total ISC reached .97.[21] Since so high a value could scarcely be increased, simplification of the index provided the next task. This was achieved by the process of weighting the individual indexes with the value of their respective $b's$ as found in the multiple regression equation, between them and the EP. Items were then eliminated until the optimum in simplicity in combination with predictive value was achieved. The outcome of this was an index composed of occupation, source of income, house type,

[21] *Ibid.,* p. 168.

and dwelling area. The multiple correlation of these items with the EP reached .972.[22] It is not apparent why a still simpler method was not used, inasmuch as three characteristics, also dropping out either source of income or dwelling area, still produce a multiple coefficient of .964 and .966 respectively, which are certainly not measureably below the coefficient for the four-item scale.[23] In fact, occupation alone has a zero order coefficient of correlation with the EP of .91. From the point of view of sheer scientific parsimony one might be inclined to feel that occupation alone yields an index of stratification sufficiently accurate for most practical purposes.

If, however, it is felt important to raise the coefficient from .91 to, let us say, a level of .95, it is still possible to deduce from these data an index which would reach this level and yet be applicable in cross-community comparisons. As the four-item ISC now stands, it is composed of two items whose value can be shown to be generalizable — source of income, and occupation. With respect to the former we have commonsense agreement that source of income is constant as a value throughout our society, and with respect to the latter we may refer to the NORC study cited earlier.[24] The findings in this case indicate an extraordinary amount of agreement on the prestige value of occupations, regardless of region or size of community.

22 W. Lloyd Warner, *Social Class in America*, p. 168.
23 *Ibid.*
24 Cecil C. North and Paul K. Hatt, *op. cit.*

The other two components of the ISC, *i.e.,* house type and dwelling area, are expressed in terms of the local community and this impairs their value as cross-community indexes. It has become accepted as a general principle by ecologists that rental values or rental equivalent are stable and reliable indexes of both the quality of housing and the quality of neighborhood. The suggestion, therefore, would seem to be inevitable that a combination of occupation, source of income and rental value would allow a correlation with the EP of approximately .95. They would have the additional value of rating individuals not only in terms which would be meaningful in the local community but which would also be meaningful in cross-community comparisions within the mass society. It is, of course, true that varying population pressures and other factors produce a situation in which comparable residential properties are valued at differential rates in various regions and among various sizes of communities. A correction for this should, however, not be too difficult a problem to solve.

In short, Warner's recent work has opened up the possibilities of greater agreement in the field of stratification through its indication of the validity of a multiple factor or even a single factor index based upon values which can be applied both within the local community and the mass society. What is being suggested here is that a prestige scale of occupations plus a simple rental index seems adequate to replace the laborious and expensive technique of community reputational analysis. This fact also indicates the likelihood that while class positions exist in the local community, they are local expressions of determinants in the mass society. This is not, however, to imply that the classes stand simply for economic level. An occupational scale based on prestige allows for variation in terms of other than financial rewards. This point has been made in some detail in an earlier paper.[25]

Such a hypothesis could be checked rather simply from available data. If the social class materials available in the studies mentioned were checked by the application of a simplified ISC, and the differences between this analysis and the original analysis in terms of community reputational classes were assessed, we should then be in a position to know what *net loss,* if any, is consequent upon the use of the simpler mode. If a loss is found in terms of the consequences of class position, that is, if the consequences in differential life chances of positions determined by the two methods are different, then detailed research could illuminate the differences between class on the local level (presumably class values on the national level plus idiosyncratic clique values) and class as it is determined throughout the mass society. If no differences appear then a simple measure such as that indicated could easily be put into relatively standard use.

Moreover, if the application of the two methods of classifying did not yield substantial differences the point would be made that solution by summation and solution by correlation yield substantially the same results. At this point the question as to the substantive or classificatory nature of class could be investigated, and perhaps even the question of the objective versus the subjective determination of class position be given at least an approximate answer.

B. The Impact of Industrialism on Class

68. "The U.S. Labor Movement" *

The transformation of American capitalism has been due in large part,

[25] Paul K. Hatt, "Occupation and Stratification," forthcoming in *The American Journal of Sociology.*

* From *U.S.A. — The Permanent Revolution,* pp. 89–108. Reprinted from the February 1951 issue of *Fortune* Magazine by Special Permission; Copyright 1951 Time Inc.

as just pointed out, to the rising power of labor, which has forced a revision of capitalist thinking and capitalist practices. Yet the fact that this change has been no more than a *transformation,* the fact that capitalism in America has not been overthrown or seriously damaged by the power of the workers, is of equal importance to a real understanding of America. And this fact, which can scarcely be duplicated anywhere in the world, can be accounted for only by reference to the U.S. labor movement itself.

What utterly baffles the European intellectual concerning the American labor movement is its stubborn refusal to behave in accordance with the so-called "laws of history." American labor has exhibited none of the ideological uniformity that characterizes continental or British labor. A vast philosophical distance separates arch-Republican Bill Hutcheson of the carpenters from ex-Socialist Dave Dubinsky of the ladies' garment workers; yet they work together as vice presidents of the American Federation of Labor. And while the younger Congress of Industrial Organizations shows greater cohesion, the differences between Emil Rieve of the textile workers and Walter Reuther of the automobile workers might be enough to disrupt most European trade-union organizations. This diversity runs all the way to the individual local. Within the same union, within the same industry, within the same city, union practices, union policies, and even union oratory vary all over the lot.

American labor is not "working-class conscious"; it is not "proletarian" and does not believe in class war. Some parts of it are as uncompromisingly wedded to rugged individualism as the National Association of Manufacturers. Others want to "reform capitalism." If there were a standard or typical labor view

on this subject, it would probably come close to that of George W. Brooks of the strong and tough pulp, sulfite, and paper-mill workers (A.F. of L.), who says "labor's objective of 'making today better than yesterday' is predicated on its acceptance of capitalism."

Yet the American union is a militant union — more militant, perhaps, than its European counterparts. Not only can the average union point to steadier gains for its members in the form of wages and benefits than any counterpart of it elsewhere; it has also been demanding for itself more and more managerial power within the business enterprise. And it is capable of fighting for both its economic and its power demands with a ferocity and bitterness (to say nothing of a vocabulary) that could hardly be matched by any class-war union.

For however much similarity there may be between the objective conditions that gave rise to unionism throughout the industrialized world, the American union is unique in the meaning it has for its member, in the purpose and function it serves for him: *it is his tool for gaining and keeping as an individual the status and security of a full citizen in capitalist society*. That the union has made the worker to an amazing degree a middle-class member of a middle-class society — in the plant, in the local community, in the economy — is the real measure of its success. The existence at the same time of real hostility to enterprise, management, and the economic system among the American workers is not only the measure of its failure; it is the greatest danger to the American labor movement — and perhaps also its greatest opportunity.

Twenty years ago it was easy to dismiss the peculiar characteristics of the American labor movement as signs of the "immaturity" of the American worker. The U.S. at that time, next to Japan, was the least unionized of the major industrial countries. Surely, so the argument ran, a bigger union movement in America would be as proletarian and as much dedicated to class war, as much anti-capitalist and socialist, as the union movements of Europe. The most confident expression of this view came from Harold Laski, the lord high keeper of leftist illusions. But the same view had been held inside the American labor movement itself all during the twenties — for instance, by the young men around the Brookwood Labor College, many of whom later on showed up among the moving spirits of the C.I.O.

Today the U.S. may well be the most unionized of the free countries. Practically all production employees in "big" and "middle" industry are organized. Union contracts determine wage rates everywhere in the land, in unorganized as well as in organized businesses, for clerical as well as for production employees. This switch from an open-shop to an organized economy took only twelve years — from 1933 to 1945. They were years of depression and war, of tension and upheaval. Yet today's successful, strong, and militant labor movement is as little "proletarian" or "socialist" as the small and unsuccessful labor movement of twenty years ago.

Since 1941 there have been three major developments within American labor, all illustrating the same drift: the renascence of the A.F. of L.; the strong anti-ideological shift within the C.I.O.; and the eclipse of left-wing ideologies and philosophies within the labor movement itself.

All through the thirties and right up to World War II the A.F. of L. was the "sick man" of American labor, if not given up for dead. It was obsolete, if not senile; hidebound, unprincipled, inflexible, corrupt, and — worst swear-word of all — "petty bourgeois." Yet today the A.F. of L. has some eight and a half million members — twice as many as it had in 1941. In addition, the bulk of the "independent" unions are A.F. of L. unions in their philosophy, their tactics, and their structure, though not in formal affiliation. Almost two out of every three American union members — 10 million out of a total of 15 million — are thus organized on the A.F. of L. basis and in unions that derive in unbroken descent from Samuel Gompers.

Neither economic developments nor the small changes in tactics that have occurred within the A.F. of L. fully explain this renascence. Perhaps it is too much to claim, as some A.F. of L. men do, that it is precisely its anti-proletarian, pro-capitalist character that has been attracting the American worker. But one thing at least is sure: that the A.F. of L.'s middle-class character has proved no obstacle to its success, let alone, as was so confidently predicted only ten years ago, fatal to its very survival.

The C.I.O. at its start was hailed as the fulfillment of the intellectual's dream of a " class-conscious " and " proletarian " labor movement. What has actually been happening to the C.I.O. may be read in the career of the one bright young C.I.O. radical of fifteen years ago who actually made good, the automobile workers' Walter Reuther, by all odds the most dynamic personality in American labor today.

Where Walter Reuther stood politically was never exactly clear. He was certainly not just an " ordinary socialist." There was always a strong resemblance to the Henry Ford of thirty years ago — the Henry Ford who sent the " Peace Ship " to Europe to stop World War I, who had an opinion on anything and everything, and whom the Chicago *Tribune* once called an " anarchist." There was also a bit of the technocrat in Walter Reuther, this being the element of continuity in his many " Reuther Plans." But there was no doubt whatever that he also believed in the class struggle, in some form of socialism, and in a labor party to bring about the " necessary change in the system." These beliefs (rather than his ability and competence as a union leader) gained him the admiration of all the sentimental " friends of labor " among the intellectuals, from the *New Republic* to the amateur politicians of Americans for Democratic Action.

Yet the biggest labor event of 1950 — if not of the entire post-World War II period — was a contract negotiated by Walter Reuther that goes further in its affirmation both of the free-enterprise system and of the worker's stake in it than any other major labor contract ever signed in this country. The General Motors contract is the first that unmistakably accepts the existing distribution of income between wages and profits as " normal," if not as " fair." This at least was the interpretation that was given within the U.A.W. itself to the acceptance of the existing wage structure as the basis for the next five years. It is the first major union contract that explicitly accepts objective economic facts — cost of living and productivity — as determining wages, thus throwing overboard all theories of wages as determined by political power, and of profit as " surplus value." Finally, it is one of the very few union contracts that expressly recognize both the importance of the management function and the fact that management operates directly in the interest of labor.

The G.M. contract probably reflects what Reuther himself has come to believe over the last few years — though he will surely continue to talk his old line and to ride it hard in his two union publications, the *United Automobile Workers* and *Ammunition* (two of the liveliest pieces of aggressive journalism in the country today). But his own beliefs or words are really none too relevant. The important thing is that this contract — whose significance everyone in the labor movement grasped immediately — has become the program on which Reuther hopes to unify American labor under his own leadership. This is strong evidence of the C.I.O.'s shift toward the George Brooks concept of unionism, "predicated on its acceptance of capitalism." And the force behind the shift is precisely the C.I.O.'s success in gaining for the unskilled and semiskilled worker in the mass-production industries what has been the goal of American labor in general: middle-class status and full citizenship.

Never have left-wing ideologies had so little influence on the American labor movement as they have today. The Communists still control a small but strategic sector of American labor and have scattered but dangerous beachheads elsewhere, notably in the Ford local of the automobile workers. But in glaring contrast to twenty or even to ten years ago, the Communists stay in control only by claiming to be "bona fide unionists"; the mask is dropped only in the closed conventicles of the faithful. David Dubinsky pointed out in 1950 that the old radical, socialist, and idealist movements which formerly were the source of union leaders have been drying up. There are no Wobblies today, no Jewish Bund, no Italian anarchists, no Debs, no Mother Jones. If there is any ideological influence in American labor today it is Catholic union theory — spread by a growing number of labor priests and Catholic labor schools. It is of considerable importance in several C.I.O. unions as well as in the building trades of the A.F. of L.

In historical perspective it appears that the flare-up of left-wing ideologies in the middle thirties was a freak, no more typical of the basic trends of American unionism since the 1890's than the economic stagnation of the period was typical of the basic trends of the American economy. In origins (Knights of Labor, etc.) the American labor movement was more socialist than the British, and in 1902 the A.F. of L. convention barely defeated a resolution endorsing socialism (4,897 to 4,171). This date corresponds to the date when British labor took the opposite turning — 1899, when Keir Hardie committed the T.U.C. to the borning Labor party. Since then British labor has been increasingly dominated by the socialist intellectual. By contrast, the creed of the American labor movement, as summed up in that famous sentence of the Clayton Act of 1914, "The labor of a human being is not a commodity or article of commerce," traces back not to the *Communist Manifesto* but to that blackest of "black Republicans," Mark Hanna, whom Gompers joined in the leadership of the National Civic Federation.

This anti-proletarian and non-ideological character of American unionism is the key to its unique achievement, to its greatest danger, and to the method by which it may extend the achievement and avoid the danger. Let us first consider the achievement, which is the democratic one of integrating unionism with American community life.

Any proletarian union movement,

with its class-war creed, regards the existing community and its institutions as " instruments of oppression." All European union movements, including the British, have sought to build their own community organizations in competition with, if not in opposition to, those of " capitalist society." The American union movement, by contrast, accepts the community and its institutions.

In 1942 the C.I.O. was represented on ninety community-service programs; last year the number was 7,000. In Akron alone — the bloody labor-management battleground of the thirties — sixteen C.I.O. people serve on various boards of the Community Chest. " We're in about everything in this town except the Portage Country Club," said one C.I.O. leader to John Dos Passos. There is still plenty of resistance by " polite society " against accepting the union leader. But the resistance is hardly more strenuous today than that always offered to the newcomer — for example, the resistance of the New York " society " of merchants and bankers in the 1870's and 1880's to the new industrial magnates.

In some places — one-industry towns with a strong union like Saginaw, Michigan, and the paper and pulp towns of Wisconsin — even this resistance is disappearing. There union men are accepted by the groups that run the communities and set the mores: the Parent-Teacher Association and the school board, the elders of the churches, the hospital board, the volunteer firemen, and the dramatic society. Even the " service

clubs " of the small businessman, such as Rotary or the Lions — once strongholds of anti-union sentiment — are beginning to bring union men in as members. There is also increasing acceptance of union men as normal and regular members in management workshops and panels. For years, of course, union leaders have delivered set speeches to such groups as the American Management Association and the National Industrial Conference Board. But now they are coming more and more into the small, informal, off-the-record groups where the real work is being done — and as men who have something to contribute to a common problem, not just under a flag of truce as emissaries of an enemy power. And there has been full union support for the Joint Council of Economic Education, an amazingly successful group of educators, businessmen, and unionists who are trying to educate Americans in the facts of the free-enterprise system through teaching high-school teachers.

There is a price for these achievements of democratic unionism. The less class war, the more group greed: a quiet division of loot or assumption of privilege at the expense of less organized members of society. Here is the peculiar danger posed by American labor to a free and mobile society: the danger of social thrombosis, of union feudalism.

Last November, Pan American Airways pilots threatened to strike. Their objective was not higher wages, shorter hours, or different working conditions. It was to deny jobs and benefits to a group of fellow pilots. Pan American had just acquired American Overseas Airlines. But the Pan American pilots refused to let the American Overseas pilots come in except at the very bottom. Union leaders and government agencies both urged full acceptance of the seniority gained by the American Overseas men during their years of service — in vain. The demand of the Pan American pilots was not motivated so much by fear of damage as by desire to gain a better position for themselves — at the expense of fellow pilots who had been unlucky enough to work for the less successful company.

The pressure for *exclusive* kinds of job security usually comes from the men and is often resisted by union leaders. It is in part an instinctive assertion of the property right — a property right in a certain job. The blame, if blame there be, lies not at the door of unionism but in the technical conflict between machine modes of production and American democratic ideals. It seems harder nowadays (though it may not be) to reach the top through individual effort in an industrialized economy. The workers respond to this supposed sacrifice of vertical mobility by claiming more security — and when this claim is asserted in a particular job, the result may be a real loss of horizontal mobility.

Union policy is not responsible for this danger, but the structure of U.S. unionism has paralleled and sharpened it. The value of the union card is highest in a small unit: there is one local per company, if not per plant or even per department. Seniority rights tend to be bounded by the local's membership. So are the "fringe benefits" — pension rights, severance pay, vacations, sick pay, profit shares, life insurance, etc. — benefits worth as much as 30 cents in some companies for every dollar paid in straight wages. The growing demand for these benefits is in itself a sign of the middle-class character of the American worker and of his union. They are among our major tools of integrating the worker into industrial capitalism as a full and responsible citizen. And they are necessarily grounded in his membership in one particular enterprise or in one particular industry. But these privileges and benefits are usually not transferable. They thus create the danger of tying the worker to his job. After a few years of service a man has amassed too big a stake to be willing to leave, even for a better job. They may also tend to convert the job into a property and the work group into a closed guild. In the typographical union a "priority system" protects a preferred job for a linotype operator even if the worker is forced out for years by illness — or, as in the last war, even leaves the industry for a defense job. Companies with generous pension or profit-sharing plans are under increasing pressure to restrict the hiring of new workers to sons or relatives of their present employees. The fear of just such "un-American" developments was partly responsible for the no-closed-shop provision of the Taft-Hartley Act.

But to halt or reverse this trend will require more than restrictive legislation. It will require considerable imagination in devising new techniques and procedures — above all, techniques to make job benefits transferable. It may also require enabling legislation, the kind that encourages and rewards voluntary action. In attempting to solve this problem we will have to be careful not to weaken the desire of the American worker and of his union for a stake in the enterprise.

We also must not sap the strength of the local unit of unionism. For the vigor and autonomy of the local constitute one of the distinctive traits of American labor, indispensable to its development along democratic rather than proletarian lines. The local has grown strong because American labor, like so many other of our institutions, found it necessary to organize itself on the hallowed American principle of federalism. This followed from the physical nature of the country, from the spirit of its society, and from labor's approach to its task. The English, French, or German union can be satisfied with one national center of power and authority. The American union demands two centers of about equal strength and vigor, the local union and the national union.

A *national,* or industry-wide, organization of real strength is needed to prevent domination of the locals by management. It is needed to set policy, to develop standards for wages and contracts, to represent the union to public and government, and to accept responsibility for the economic and social effects of labor's actions. For every management that feels it would have no labor-relations problems if only it could work exclusively with the " local boys," there is another that has had to ask for the help and intervention of the national officers to settle a local situation that had got out of hand.

National policies and wage rates, however, are no more than the skeleton of American labor-management relations. The local is their flesh and blood. The local develops the spirit of the relationship as well as the rapidly growing " common law," the body of grievance settlements and arbitrator's decisions that define the rights and responsibilities of both parties. As with the federal structure of our system of government, so in the labor movement: local autonomy makes experimentation possible. While bad labor-management relations can be caused by national union officers alone, good union relations require good locals. Even in large companies such as General Motors, in which mutual distrust is profound, and in which as a result all authority is apparently concentrated in the hands of top-management and top-union leadership, patterns of living and working together are quietly but steadily being developed by local union leaders and by the local plant managements with whom they deal day by day.

Federalism is a difficult political system, and many or most American unions have not yet learned how to use it. The national leader is greatly tempted to centralize all power in his own hand, if only to remove threats to his tenure of office. In a few unions, notably John L. Lewis' coal miners, this has led to an all but complete destruction of local life and local autonomy; the locals are not much more than administrative units. Equally great is the temptation for the local leader to declare himself independent; in some of the railroad brotherhoods this has almost fragmented the union into a loose league of warlords whose feuding makes responsible unionism impossible. While unionism was struggling for recognition, these inherent constitutional problems could be brushed aside. Now they are coming to the fore — so much so that more than one union has hired a professional management consultant to strengthen its internal structure.

When that structure is stronger, American labor will have the right machinery for consolidating and extending its traditional goal and for avoiding the danger of feudalism ahead of it. It can fulfill the worker's desire for full citizenship in a non-class society, and keep that society open and mobile. It can — if that is what the worker continues to want.

Many signs point to his still wanting these goals. All kinds of sociological studies reveal his desire to take pride in his job, in his product, and in the company he works for. As his income rises he wants to buy stock in that company through some form of payroll deduction — a desire that has been voiced in companies large and small such as the Bell System, G.M., and Cleveland Graphite Bronze. One of the best popular guides to the reading of corporate balance sheets and corporate profit-and-loss statements was printed two years ago in the A.F. of L. house organ, *Labor's Monthly Survey;* and the Detroit *Labor News* recently ran an admirable treatise on investment and small-estate management. The visiting teams of businessmen and union leaders who have been studying American productivity under ECA auspices were all struck hard by the American worker's acceptance of increased productivity as in his own interest, by his pride in being a worker, but also by his acceptance of the management function as necessary to his own effectiveness.

All this is true — truer than ever. Yet it is not the entire truth. There is also another picture of the American worker — and it is the one major discord in the harmony of the American Proposition. We cannot assert that the big job of industrial society has been done, or that the industrial worker will surely remain " deproletarianized " in the U.S. For there undoubtedly runs a powerful undercurrent of hostility to management and to enterprise, to competitive economy and to profits, throughout the American working class. There are only a handful of conscious collectivists in American labor. But throughout it there is a strong acceptance of anti-enterprise union oratory, a steady support of collectivist and anti-business legislation. And an attitude that sees in enterprise and management THE ENEMY — rather than the opposing team in a rough and competitive game — is a proletarian attitude.

We cannot blame this attitude on the "foreign agitator corrupting the good American workingman" as management was wont to do only a few years ago. It is indigenous, and shared by the skilled "aristocrat of labor" as well as the unskilled man on the assembly line. We cannot explain it away as "economic illiteracy" that will yield to high-powered campaigns of "economic education." But we equally cannot explain it as expressing the "real" desires of the American worker, as the left-wing intellectual is prone to do; the evidence is all the other way. The explanation does not even lie in past management sins. It lies in something much more difficult to change: lack of imagination on the part of managements and union leaders.

The American worker definitely wants to be a part of the business enterprise. He wants to consider it "his" business, its future "his" future, its prosperity "his" prosperity. But his everyday experience is one either of conflict or of lack of relationship between the interests, the prosperity, the profitability of the business and his own interests, his own prosperity, his own future.

The worker is told that his wage, his standard of living, and his job depend on the profitability, stability, and productivity of the enterprise. He knows that. But this relationship is not immediate, not visible, not part of the daily relationship between man and company. It has no impact on the worker's experience. What is real is all too often the opposite: conflict, or the total lack of mutuality of interest.

One illustration must suffice. It is possible to understand why managements were caught so unprepared by the 1949–1950 pension wave. But what is totally impossible to understand is why managements did not use the pension demands to make crystal-clear the connection between the company's prosperity and the employee's old-age security. There are proved ways in which this could have been done, simply and dramatically. Yet, as a result of management's handling of the issue, pensions to the worker have become another experience of conflict between his needs and the objectives of business, between "human values" and "greed."

It is the biggest challenge to American management today to design institutions that will tie the needs of business and of the capitalist system (profitability, independent management, investment of risk capital, productivity) directly and visibly to the major interests of the worker (income, job security, recognition and participation, promotional opportunities). Until this is done the American worker will not be able to be what he wants to be, a full citizen in a free-enterprise industrial society. Despite his beliefs he will be pushed by his daily experience into pressing for more and more anti-business laws, more anti-business taxes, and more government welfare. He may even, in an economic or political emergency, develop a susceptibility to that very collectivist infection to which he has hitherto shown such singular resistance. But the development of new and positive policies that will institutionalize the worker's stake in the business enterprise and his responsible citizenship in capitalist society is equally a major challenge to union leadership. The anti-business undertow is a danger to American unionism as well as to business. It tends to push the union leader into opposition to the spirit of American society — a position in which he cannot function. But above all it is only in and through such policies that the American labor movement can develop what it so conspicuously lacks today: the appeal of ideals and of moral leadership. The very strength of the anti-business undertow is proof that it is not enough for a union movement to be free from a class-war and proletarian ideology. It has to have positive beliefs — or it will be in constant danger of infiltration by the very ideologies it rejects.

The left-wing critics of the American labor movement were wrong when they predicted its conversion into a European-type proletarian movement. But they were right in their assertion that it is not enough for labor to define its beliefs and aims in Sam Gompers' famous answer to the question as to what labor wants: "More." Only a positive acceptance of the American Proposition, a positive creed, will strengthen both American society and the American labor movement. Only positive policies will make the union

an instrument for the worker's responsible citizenship in capitalist society rather than just a device for getting more from it.

There are labor leaders who realize this and who work devotedly to develop such a policy. There is Clinton Golden — formerly of the steelworkers, now Labor Adviser to ECA — who has directed the research for *Causes of Industrial Peace*. There is Joseph Scanlon — also formerly of the steelworkers, now at M.I.T. — whose exciting work, already referred to in the previous chapter, has been discussed in FORTUNE, January, 1950. There is the work done by the unions in the once strife-torn pulp and paper industry in the Pacific Northwest. But by and large today's union leadership cannot do the job. It has — almost without exception — risen to leadership in the bitter and violent fight for union recognition. Their very background makes it all but impossible for these men to take the lead in integrating the worker and the enterprise into one industrial society. As judicious and as conservative a man as Philip Murray, for instance, cannot help using the usual hate rhetoric of union negotiations, though it both embarrasses and frightens him.

But today's labor leaders are largely at the end of their careers. Even in the young C.I.O., few unions have a young leadership. The majority will retire or die within the next ten years. Mostly their places will be taken by new men, unknown today. These leaders of tomorrow will be men of a very different background:

men who have come up in the leadership of a local rather than in organizing a national union, who have learned their unionism after recognition, rather than in the battle for it, and who have served their apprenticeship in day-to-day living and working with management. It is to those men that we will have to look for the resolution of the major conflict within American society.

Looked at one way, American labor has reached maturity. The last decade has proved the validity of its basic concept — the concept that was formulated fifty years ago when the young and small A.F. of L. turned its face against socialism. Looked at another way, the history of American labor is just about to begin. For it is only now that it has achieved power and recognition that it faces its real challenge: to make fruitful its beliefs, its aims, and its power. The potential at least is there.

C. Industrial Classes and the Conflict of Means and Ends

69. The Clash Between Progress and Security*

In whatever terms the proposition is put, everybody seems to agree that the greatest hope for the postwar world is a higher standard of living for all. An acquaintance who visited the New York World's Fair has described to me the great General Motors exhibit called "Highways and Horizons" and the immensely long queues of spectators waiting impatiently for admission. If those spectators had been asked whether they wanted a higher standard of living, some of them, perhaps, might have wondered what you meant; but there seems to have been no doubt

* From Allan G. B. Fisher, "The Clash Between Progress and Security." *Harper's Magazine*, July, 1944. Copyright, 1944, by Harper & Brothers. All Rights Reserved. Reprinted by permission of Allan G. B. Fisher and *Harper's Magazine*.

about their enthusiasm once they were inside the General Motors Building and found themselves borne along through the darkness in upholstered chairs while spread below them was the landscape of the future with marvelous speed highways, orchards under glass, dream cities of modern architecture, and streamlined cars and busses and trucks and planes. This, by implication, was what the United States was going to be, this was the happy land which the children of the spectator could look forward to — a land with a higher standard of living for all.

It is not inconceivable that the landscape of the United States may come to resemble the dream of the General Motors Company, but this will never be if the passion for security that one senses on every hand is permitted to paralyze the country. Sometimes in the open, sometimes far below the surface, there is a violent war going on between the forces of progress and the forces of security. The purpose of this article is to examine the character of the clash.

Not long ago Paul G. Hoffman, chairman of the Committee for Economic Development, urged us to "strive with all our might for an increase of productivity of not less than 30 per cent" as compared with the prewar level. This echo of an almost unanimous enthusiasm for productivity does not, by itself, get us very far. An increase of 30 per cent in the production of corn, radio sets, terra-cotta tile, and cocktail shakers would be meaningless unless people wanted to increase their purchases of these articles at the same rate.

A very different sort of picture would be presented if *average individual income* rose by 30 per cent after the war. The new purchases which people would make would be distributed over a wide range of goods and services. Some persons might want twice as many clothes as they used to buy; some others might want larger houses with more bathrooms; still others might want to go to twice as many concerts as before. But there would be few, even among the poorest, who would care to eat twice as much as they had been accustomed to eat.

If Mr. Hoffman's 30 per cent is to have any useful meaning it must therefore be interpreted as an average covering the widest diversity in

rates of expansion for some businesses and contraction for others. In some businesses there would be relatively little increase; in others, where low-quality goods are dropped by persons who can now afford better ones, there would be a decrease; in others there would be varying degrees of expansion. Talk about increased production and a rising standard of living is actually talk about a series of changes in the relative importance of the various enterprises which constitute the national economic system. This is nothing new. The whole of economic history is marked by such changes. Sometimes the change is violent, as in war, when so much labor and capital is rapidly shifted to military production. Sometimes the change is gradual, as, for example, the steady decrease throughout American history in the proportion of the population engaged in agriculture and the corresponding increase in the proportion of those employed in industry or who earn their living by providing various services.

If, in the postwar period, an attempt is made to shift back from military to civilian production and to increase the nation's average productivity by 30 per cent — more or less — the problems encountered are going to be very considerable. It would help if a picture could be drawn of what our economy will look like. What proportion of the working population will be engaged in producing food, in manufacturing automobiles and refrigerators, or in providing the numerous services which in recent years have become increasingly important fields for employment and investment? These questions cannot be answered precisely, but a useful impression can be formed of the trends that will inevitably develop in the important fields of economic activity.

It will become clear that there can be no progress if, at the same time, an attempt is made to freeze the economy in any structural pattern; it will be clear that some businesses will have to retrench or fold up entirely while others expand; that many persons will have to shift from familiar occupations to new and strange ones. It will be possible to get a rough idea of those who stand to lose — in the short run, at least — as a result of these changes *and will therefore resist them*. Finally, it will be clear how important it is that both private action and public policy assist these changes rather than obstruct them, as has so often happened in the past.

Is there, at bottom, any justification in expecting an overall increase in production? Numerous persons doubt it, regarding such an increase as a promoter's dream. But continued growth of the sciences justifies the belief — despite all the losses of the war — that the long-term trend of increasing production and rising income levels can be resumed. But it cannot be resumed unless the character of the changes necessary in the structure of our economy is understood. And the current controversies between the "planners" and the champions of "free enterprise" obscure and hinder any such understanding. The real point at issue is,

or ought to be, which form of organization is most likely to encourage the varying rates of expansion and contraction of production and keep them moving toward an overall increase of productive activity.

Many people think that the growing burden of debt is a sufficient reason to discount any optimism. War debts are certainly troublesome things, and their indirect effects, through the transfer of income by means of taxation and through their repercussions upon monetary policy, may so clog the machinery for increasing production as to make realities fall far short of possibilities. But the burden of debt does not involve any *net* subtraction from national income; it means a redistribution of income. The process of redistribution may stimulate some people to increase their contribution to national income; others may find their energies sapped and their eagerness diminished. However, the so-called burden of debt need not prevent us from achieving increased production and higher standards of living, so long as the essential elements are present upon which increased production depends. The most important of these is the knowledge which enables us to control and make use of our material environment.

In the early stages of economic history most human effort was devoted to agricultural occupations. Science was primitive, people were poor, and capital for trying out new ideas was scarce. Most of the money was spent on food and simple necessities, and the production of these things provided most of the jobs. The Malthusian population pressure was a real thing, and technical improvements were urgently needed as a safeguard against the constant threat of famine.

The era of manufacture and industry — which began in England toward the end of the eighteenth century — changed the character of production and consumption. Not only were more people employed in making textile and iron and steel products; revolutionary improvements in the technique of agriculture at the same time made it possible for a smaller fraction of the population to feed the whole people. In due course, and in the same way, the refinement of manufacturing methods made it possible for the current requirements of the people for many goods to be satisfied by the labors of a smaller fraction of the working population. Later — with the growth of great cities like London, New York, Sydney, Buenos Aires, and Yokohama — an increasing share of the community's resources came to be devoted to services of various kinds and to what had previously been regarded as luxuries. Such luxuries include everything from public education and municipal garbage removal to scientific research, permanent waves, the arts, and amusement parks.

Recognition of the economic importance of these and other services has been strangely delayed, but during the inter-war period the census returns from all countries with high standards of living showed clearly that a large part of the population was engaged in them. The level of remuneration in these fields is extremely varied, as is the return on capital investment. The demand for some of them is uncertain and ephemeral, and many people deplore the standards of taste which some of these " services " satisfy. But the important fact is that *they represent the growing-points of modern economic systems,* and healthy and steady development for the economy as a whole inevitably depends on healthy conditions at the growing-points.

These trends in economic organization as outlined briefly here are what anyone would expect in a community whose income level was steadily rising. (The poorest countries throughout the world still have the highest proportion of working population employed in producing bare necessities.) As income increases an even larger portion of it is naturally devoted to industrial products, and as income rises further *the economic importance* of things previously regarded as luxuries becomes very great. Countries which have the highest standards of living ought to pay increasing attention to the production of the amenities of life. These are the changes which in the past have been the essence of material progress. They must be carried still further if material progress is to continue in the future.

II

What are the obstacles in the way of further development along these lines? The main obstacle is the fact that while most people want to enjoy the advantages of a higher income, many are afraid of the insecurity which often seems to be associated with the process of raising the general income level. Throughout the whole of economic history there has been a succession of transfers of the resources of production from one type of work to another. Carriages and wagons are doomed when the automobile appears, and those who have jobs or investments in carriages bitterly resist the change. Some, of course, recognize the inevitable and jump while the jumping is good.

However unanimous the feeling may be that increased production and a higher standard of living after the war are highly desirable, it is an ironical fact that the chief fear of the future is that there will be unemployment on a grand scale. Where are the jobs to come from? Obviously the biggest part of the answer lies in the transfer of thousands of persons from agricultural, industrial, and manufacturing enterprises — where the productivity of machinery has been so enormously expanded and where the changes effected by applied science have been most profound — to the service industries, professions, and trades.

Against any such transfer are:

1. The inertia of many of those thousands who are past their youth and no longer have the adaptability which they had when young.

2. The vested interests of those whose fortunes depend upon the maintenance of what, in many instances, are outmoded forms of production.

3. The vested interests of those who have jobs in trade unions, trade associations, political organizations, and other groups whose reasons for being are these same outmoded forms.

This opposition can and will exert very great pressure against change. Anyone who presses upon our attention any general economic policy should be urged to explain how he proposes to handle this opposition. In the past such changes brought bankruptcies in their train and doubtless they will again. It is easy to tell an individual farmer attached to his holding in Iowa or Rumania or New South Wales that he ought to abandon his farm and prepare to earn his living as a member of an orchestra or as an employee of a rapidly expanding aviation company. For many individuals such a change is quite impossible. But the problem in real life is seldom so impossibly difficult as this illustration might suggest — as has been shown during the present war, in which men from the farms have piled into the aircraft plants and men from a dozen trades and professions have gone to work in precision instrument factories. If it is impossible for a middle-aged coal miner to adapt himself to the requirements of an aviation company, it may be quite easy for his son.

It would be misleading to suppose that any unwillingness of wage-earners to change their jobs is the main obstacle to material progress. Some men hate to move, of course, but in the United States, anyway, the alacrity with which people will migrate to better themselves is proverbial. On August 16, 1943, *Life* published a photograph of a farm family which had moved to the Northwest for wartime employment. All told, the family was earning $50,000 a year!

No; the responsibility for resistance to structural change may be much more fairly placed upon the shoulders of the controllers of capital investment — a group in which government has a strong representation and influence now — than upon the wage-earners whom they employ. It is not only the man who tries to protect an obsolete investment who blocks the path to progress; much more dangerous are those who (whether they be manufacturers, labor leaders, or whatever), having got an early start in performing some scarce and highly paid service, presently attempt to bar the field to later comers. People hate to give up privileges and, unless they are checked, they will take steps to hinder or completely prevent the adjustments necessary if the potentialities of economic progress are to be realized.

Monopolistic resistance to changes in economic structure is a commonplace. All of us have heard of the purchase and suppression of inventions by corporations whose product is threatened; all of us know how unions have spread-the-work and feather-bedded useless jobs. But the resistances go a great deal deeper. For the higher income groups, material progress of a general character often demands significant changes in some of the elements of real income to which traditionally they have come to attach great importance. These changes are annoying to them, and if they feel that the loss of certain customary personal conveniences is inadequately compensated by the increased opportunities for the enjoyment of new things, they will probably add the weight of their influence to the other resistances to structural adaptation.

Personal services, for example, traditionally have been paid at low rates. Cheap personal services are always most abundantly available in countries with a low general level of income. Unskilled labor, male or female, is relatively plentiful in such communities, whereas in wealthier countries there are numerous alternative outlets for low-paid labor, whose price thus tends to rise. In normal times the proportion of working women employed in domestic service in the United States is only half the corresponding proportion in Great Britain. This is not a matter of chance, but an inexorable consequence of the more rapid material progress of this country. If the general income level rises, wealthy people accustomed to a great deal of personal service soon begin to complain that they cannot get what they want, or indeed, as they are apt to put it, what they ought to have. During the war we have heard of people regretting the " good old days " of the Great Depression, when personal services were abundant and cheap! Such complaints are really identical with complaints that production is becoming more efficient, for that is the most significant explanation of rising incomes. The amount of time spent by members of the middle classes in all highly developed countries in discussions of " the servant problem " is merely a reflection of a widespread social outlook which finds it difficult to stomach the inevitable consequences of material progress. From many people with great economic and political influence, material progress demands significant changes in their mode of life. Some would find the changes, once made, quite agreeable. But timid people often dislike the prospect of being obliged to make them. If they successfully resist the structural changes which the economic system needs, they are at the same time checking the general improvement in standards of living which ought to be the normal consequence of scientific and technical progress.

III

A progressive and healthy economic system requires a steady flow of resources into types of economic activity which less wealthy economies cannot afford. The growing-points of the economy must be invigorated by new investment and expanding employment. But this means insecurity for some people, and *seems* to mean insecurity for many more.

Security cannot be attained by frantically clutching at it and sitting tight. If we sacrifice progress we usually find, and without having to wait very long, that security itself has also eluded us.

These are not new problems, but they seem to have become more acute in our own time. " For the past ten or twenty years," as Thurman Arnold said in a speech to the Economic Club some months ago, " and I don't blame this on the Democrats because I have heard more of it from Republicans and business men than any other source, we have been obsessed with the economics of security. We have been thinking of stabilizing profits, keeping a fool from losing his money, social security, ironing out depressions, creating a situation where anybody who remained sober and didn't run off with somebody else's wife was assured of a comfortable old age." This obsession with security has been carried so far that some people have elaborated a theory of a " mature economy " to explain the slowing-down of the normal processes of economic development which had been characteristic of the last century and a half.

It is, of course, both true and important that an " advanced " economy necessarily differs in many important respects from a more " primitive " one, but analogies based on the life history of individuals are in this connection quite misleading. The character and quality of our economic growth must be different in the future from what it has been in the past, but when we observe the low standards of living which still prevail among many citizens of even the most " advanced " economies, it is difficult to take seriously the suggestion that normal growth must from now on inevitably slow down.

The exponents of the mature economy theory frequently seek a way out through programs of public works. In certain circumstances there is much to be said for public works, as a subordinate instrument of policy, but it betrays a woeful ignorance of the real economic possibilities of the modern world to put them in the forefront of our policy. For this means that, despairing of the possibility of organizing the production of things which consumers would be eager to buy, we fall back on the production of things which, though they are sometimes quite useful in themselves, no one is very anxious to have.

The decline in the rate of population growth has something to do with our reluctance to encourage structural change — for when population is comparatively stable there is less likelihood that the necessary structural changes can be made merely by slowing down the rate of entry into certain occupations. But this factor is not so important as many people have supposed, and is certainly less significant than the obsession with corporate and personal security, which is the natural consequence of the depression years and their violent fluctuations in employment. Mr. Ernest Bevin, the British Minister of Labor and National Service, has gone so far as to say that his war aim is summed up in the phrase, "The motive of our life must be social security." The longing for security has always been with us, of course; but it has now become a much more significant factor in economic and political life than formerly because those who emphasize security now know, or think they know, how to attain it.

The fundamental question re-

mains, however, *whether these devices can be effective for anything more than the short run.* Is it possible to allay the natural apprehensions of those who fear that economic change may harm or even ruin them without at the same time checking the structural changes which our economic system must undergo if the people as a whole are not to be condemned to unnecessarily low standards of living — in other words, without deferring to the antisocial prejudices of privileged groups?

It is from this point of view that the claims of both the planners and the supporters of private enterprise should be assessed. Before we approve of any planner's program, we ought to examine with a highly critical eye the possibility that planning may be used merely to bolster up traditional positions and therefore to impede necessary processes of adjustment. Such a policy cannot succeed, for the power of technical progress is too great to be kept permanently in check. The effort to impose a stability which runs counter to the adjustments demanded by progress may, however, build up a rigid economy whose ultimate disruption — when the effort finally fails, as fail it must — will also destroy the security which has been the immediate objective.

But our suspicion of "plans" should not lead us to accept protestations of devotion to "private enterprise" as a guarantee that essential structural changes will not be resisted. Some of the most vociferous clamorers for free enterprise are interested only in free enterprise for themselves. They too want to control the economy and parcel out the labor (on a tidy basis convenient to themselves) — which would be no less damaging to progress than some forms of the planning which they so vigorously oppose. The emphasis should be placed less on "privacy," with the opportunities which privacy has already too often given for restriction of production and obstruction of necessary adaptations, and much more on "enterprise" — that is, on the prompt acceptance of new techniques and the readiness to assist those transfers of resources which expansion entails. From this point of view there is often little to choose between the planners and the supporters of private enterprise. Both are aiming to protect everyone from the changes which the advance of science will make inevitable. Such tactics will serve only to arrest progress and dam up vital economic forces until at last they break through the obstructions and the whole concern bursts. It is not only hard, it is also arrant folly to kick against the pricks. Struggle as we may against the adjustments which a changing world imposes upon us, they must at last be made. If we refuse to accept them and attempt to freeze an existing situation, we shall presently find the whole machinery slowing down or falling to pieces.

IV

In the nature of things, no simple clear-cut remedy can be offered which we could pretend would clear up all these difficulties. Action must be taken simultaneously on many fronts. To many ardent supporters of particular remedies, the scriptural injunction may appropriately be applied, "These ye ought to have done, and not left the other undone." The forces of resistance to structural adaptations in our economy are so powerful that no useful device for countering them can safely be neglected. Here we shall mention only two or three outstanding points.

In the first place, the problem of "social security" cannot be seen in proper perspective unless we have firmly fixed in our minds the argument here outlined. The adjustments demanded by the public interest carry with them obvious risks for certain individuals and groups. The days are past when intelligent people could regard unemployment merely as the personal responsibility of the unemployed man. He is often the innocent victim of trends and changes quite outside his control. But while the case is strong for measures against the risk of being sacrificed in the public interest, the form and purpose of such measures will be quite different according as we think in narrow terms of provisional aid until "recovery" — i.e., until things improve and everyone is right back where he used to be — or *in the wider terms of maintaining a flexible and healthy economy by continuously encouraging the development of new kinds of work*. We will get nowhere — and incidentally fail to get "social security" — if we aim first at stabilizing progress. *The proper approach is to put progress in the forefront of our thinking and action, and then to provide supplementary measures for those who are unfairly penalized in the process.*

The second point is the importance of educational policy as a constructive element in economic development. Extensions of education have frequently been more or less forced by the pressure of economic changes. Widespread illiteracy is obviously intolerable if the efficient performance of the ordinary man's tasks demands that he be able to read and write. This, of course, is a very low ground on which to put a case for universal primary education, but even on this low plane, the increases in production which scientific advances and increased demand for services will make possible simply cannot occur without a more widespread dissemination of higher educational facilities than even the most advanced countries today provide for their citizens. If a rapidly progressing economy needs considerable additions to the ranks of its musicians, medical men, and other purveyors of skilled personal services, our educational policy must be molded to make possible a larger supply of these people. Unless a larger proportion of the population is trained to understand and use new industrial and agricultural techniques, we cannot hope to make the most of our opportunities in industry and agriculture.

The social resistances discussed earlier are often a clogging influence at this point. Some ten years ago a minister of the Crown in New Zealand expressed his doubts about the wisdom of further extensions of sec-ondary education. For, if everybody received a secondary education, " who, then," he asked, " would do the dirty work? " This obstructive attitude is widespread elsewhere, though seldom so clearly and crudely expressed. We cannot seriously claim to favor higher standards of living unless we are prepared to face and overcome such resistances.

Finally — and this above all — there can be no progress if special interests — government or private — are allowed to check the expansion of investment in enterprises which produce goods and services that people with rising incomes would be likely to want in increasing quantities. It is impossible here to deal adequately with the many intricate technical questions involved in determining the best methods of preventing monopolistic restrictions. It is unlikely that any single method will be suitable in all economies or even in all parts of a single economy. In Great Britain it has been urged that monopolistic organizations and cartels would become less dangerous if they were granted statutory authority to exclude or control potential competitors in return for submission to some kind of public supervision. Interested parties have approved of this idea, no doubt in the confident expectation that they themselves could, in the last resort, control the supervisors. No doubt there are interested parties in the United States who feel exactly the same way and, in some quarters, the " inevitability " of the extension of international cartels after the war is often discussed. The demand for authorized monopolies doesn't at present attract open support in the United States, but it was not so long ago that many business men welcomed the opportunity afforded by the NRA to control the entry of new competitors into their spheres of operations. It may not be entirely cynical to suppose that in some cases American business men forego the advantages of legislative checks on competitors because the informal but real checks are quite effective enough without the backing of any statutory authority.

We shall enjoy neither the full measure of progress which is possible nor the benefits of security unless we keep the path clear for those who are competent to supply the new goods and the new services which a progressive economy will demand. The critical spots in any economy will always be the points where growth ought to be taking place, and anything which impedes development at these points will have harmful repercussions on the economy as a whole. New institutional devices may well be needed in the new circumstances which arise *when services become more important fields of employment than agriculture or industry*. The organization of the capital market evolved for the latter fields may not be in all respects suitable for the needs of the newer types of production. There is, however, nothing fixed or eternal about the constitution of the capital market at any given point of time. The process of evolution of which it is the product is continuous and never-ending. In asking for further adap-

tation, therefore, we are not asking for anything revolutionary, but merely for a continuation of the same developments which enabled Western countries to reach their present position.

Thousands of people today are worried and fearful about their economic prospects in the postwar years. In the face of these fears, is a rational man entitled to be optimistic? The general picture of the growth of a progressive economy justifies a cautious optimism, but it cannot give us any certainty. Everything depends on whether we do the right things, and the most important right thing is to provide conditions which will encourage the production of the goods and services which people living in a progressive economy would wish to buy in increasing quantities. Such conditions do not spring up automatically. The resistances provoked by the attempt to create them are numerous and powerful, and it is an unfortunate consequence of the otherwise legitimate interest in social security that it so easily diverts attention from them and their baneful consequences.

There is one important short-term qualification to be noted. Though the effects of the losses inflicted by the war ought not to be exaggerated, those losses are nevertheless very real. The United States has not suffered as much as some other countries where capital equipment has been destroyed or its maintenance neglected. But the United States cannot avoid repercussions from other economies, and the capital structure of all belligerent countries, including the United States, has been so violently distorted to meet the requirements of totalitarian war that its redirection to meet the requirements of peace will present great difficulties. The solution of all the tasks arising in this situation will take time. We may reasonably expect after the war to resume the movement of progress which marked the nineteenth and early twentieth centuries, but we must not expect too much too quickly. Some of our troubles during the interwar period can be traced back to the impatient expectations of those who, after the last war, thought wartime losses could be neglected.

Nevertheless, the very profundity of the disturbances of the war justifies some hope that we may be able to snatch from this catastrophe an opportunity to direct our economic structure into more expansive channels. Nearly everywhere before the war there was too little flexibility in industry. The war brought flexibility to an unprecedented degree. The structure has been thoroughly loosened. It will take more shoving to get it into working order for peace conditions. We must not allow the desire for security to reinforce an effort to restore something resembling the prewar layout of employment.

The truth is, however, that it would take no more effort to construct a working basis adapted to the new conditions of production techniques and consumer demands than it would to restore the prewar status quo. If an effort toward a new working basis is made, then we shall be in a better position than ever before to begin the further and continuous structural adjustments which will always be needed so long as our knowledge is expanding and there are still people dissatisfied with their existing standards of living.

70. The Responsibilities of a Free Press

THE INSTRUMENTS

The new instruments which technology has given the press have enormously increased the range, variety, and speed of mass communications. They have also contributed to the growth of huge business corporations. The development of new tech-

* From The Commission on Freedom of the Press, *A Free and Responsible Press*, pp. 30–68. Copyright 1947 by The University of Chicago. Reprinted by permission of The University of Chicago Press.

niques and growth in the size of units are not peculiar to the press. They have occurred in almost all industries. Moreover, the changes in the press are closely related, partly as cause and partly as effect, to the technological and industrial changes elsewhere. The technical-industrial development in other areas made possible the new machinery of mass communication which permits, and even requires, operation on a continental scale. The minutely timed reactions of the new industrial society depend, in turn, on the service supplied by the vast network of the agencies of mass communications.

THE TECHNOLOGICAL REVOLUTION

Mass communication began with the invention of the steam-driven press in the early nineteenth century. This was followed by the high-speed rotary press, the linotype machine, and photoengraving, which were accompanied by the appearance of the land-line telegraph, the oceanic cable, and the land-line telephone.

Our generation has seen the development of moving — then moving and talking — pictures, of wireless transmission used for telegraph, telephone, and voice broadcasting; of airplane transport; of offset and color printing. Together they have changed the character of mass communication, adding to the printed word the broadcast word and the moving image, and bringing the remote corners of the world within a few hours of one another.

We are now in the midst of this technological revolution. It is far from completed. The war put into military use a new series of inventions. Their possibilities have not been fully realized, partly because of delays resulting from reconversion from war work and partly because of the need for further experiment. Technological advance creates its own inertia because investment does not disappear so rapidly from the balance sheet as new inventions render the equipment obsolescent. The investments of users of existing machinery and the vested interests of skilled employees slow down change.

The fullest use at lowest prices of radio telegraph was retarded, and still is retarded, because of the huge investment in ocean cables and land lines; direct international radio voice broadcasting from the United States languished for want of interest by advertisers until the war compelled its exploitation and proved its value to the American people. Linotype machines which can do the job of four or five ordinary machines are held back by the opposition of the unions; apprenticeship rules are holding back improvements in engraving. It is admitted that frequency modulation (FM) radio has been delayed not only by war priorities but also by AM (standard broadcasting) owners and by the unions. It remains to be seen whether similar delays will be encountered, for similar reasons, by television and the facsimile newspaper.

But full utilization of these inventions is clearly in the offing, and their potential influence is enormous.

A world-wide voice broadcasting network over which the deliberations of the United Nations as they take place could be transmitted to every citizen on the planet is mechanically possible at the present time. Such a network has been recommended by the United States National Commission for U.N.E.S.C.O.

Air mail and air express are technically at the point where films or periodicals can be delivered anywhere on the inhabited earth in two or three days. Light plastic plates of magazine pages can be flown to printing plants anywhere so that a complete periodical may come off the press on five continents forty-eight hours after it has been assembled in the originating office.

Through new processes of book manufacturing the people of the world can be supplied with the best literature of all countries at twenty-five cents a copy or less. Experimental work on printing presses is expected to reduce the cost of manufacture still further, particularly for the smaller plants.

Frequency modulation radio is now mechanically ready for general use. It is expected to replace the standard broadcasting systems, except for high-powered clear channels reaching sparsely settled areas. FM's technical superiority over AM is that it gives better tone, free from static. FM provides an opportunity for more stations, each serving its local community on equal terms as to volume, and makes possible new and more widely distributed station ownership.

An even newer device, pulse-time modulation, though not yet clearly established as a means of broadcasting to home receivers, will undoubtedly make it possible within a few years to broadcast more than one program simultaneously over one channel. It will cut down the cost of broadcasting any program and at the same time increase the variety of programs available to a community at a given time.

Of immediate importance are the advances which the war produced in long-distance wireless transmission.

Speeds up to eight hundred words a minute (as compared with average cable speeds of forty to sixty words a minute) have been attained, and interruptions resulting from atmospheric conditions are slowly yielding to the ingenuity of the engineers. Four-color facsimile, by which text or photographs or both are transmitted by wireless, has reached the point where whole pages of books and periodicals with their illustrations are now being instanteously sent in any language halfway round the earth.

The war also gave impetus to multiple-address press transmission, by which news is distributed by wireless, not from point to point, but from a single originating station to receivers in an entire region. Just how radically this reduces costs appears from an application to the F.C.C. of a subsidiary of the International Telephone and Telegraph Company, recently approved. The cost to the users of this multiple-address press system will be a cent and a half a word. This is four to ten times cheaper than any previous service. It is as cheap for the obscure editor in a distant outpost of civilization as for the metropolitan publisher in a European capital. It is as cheap — and it is of the same quality. Within the next decade or two this kind of service will be a major means of communicating news across national borders. Only national regulations and the habits of press associations prevent its general adoption today.

The facsimile newspaper is equally practicable now. Such a newspaper would go to press at the local radio station at 5:00 A.M., say, would be broadcast from FM transmitters, and would drop, automatically folded, from the home radio receiver ready for the family breakfast table. It can be distributed more quickly and more frequently than the standard newspaper. No expensive power presses will be required to print it and no newsstands, new dealers, trucks, trains, or airplanes to distribute it. The farmer and the city dweller will have access to news of the same quality.

The facsimile newspaper need not be expensive. John V. L. Hogan, one of the ablest experts in the facsimile field, estimates that receivers may come down to the price of radio phonographs, say $100–400. The paper, to be provided by the reader, at present costs four cents for a four-page facsimile edition. But Hogan estimates that it eventually may cost only a penny — actually cheaper than the printed newspaper.

Television is more familiar to the layman, but his conception of it does not altogether reflect the importance of the invention. Television is not just a better or different form of radio. It is a combination of radio and motion picture which adds new dimensions to mass communication. The form, color, and sound of events will sooner or later be re-enacted by television before enormous household audiences all over the world. People in remote parts of the globe will be permitted the same face-to-face observation of each other that is now limited to the citizens of small communities.

The speed, quantity, and variety of mass communication will continue to increase. Long since, the volume and variety of words and images have exceeded the capacity of any individual consumer to assimilate them. The press has an increasing responsibility for the organization and selection of the material it distributes. But the citizen, who has always had to sift the material he has received, will now have a more complicated task than ever.

We cannot assume that the mere increase in quantity and variety of mass communication will increase mutual understanding. It may give wider currency to reports which intensify prejudice and hatred. Nevertheless, the new instruments exist and will be used in any case. The cure for distorted information would seem to be more information, not less — the full and responsible use of the new instruments of communication to get before the peoples of the world a true picture of one another and of what goes on among them.

THE ORGANIZATION

These technological changes have in one sense resulted in a greater diversity of communication. Information and discussion are now supplied through different channels by different managements. Television and the broadcast newspaper may introduce still further diversity of ownership and management, for it is not certain that these new instruments will become the property of those who control the old ones.

But the outstanding fact about the

communications industry today is that the number of its units has declined. In many places the small press has been completely extinguished. The great cities have three or four daily newspapers each, smaller cities may have two; but most places have only one. News-gathering is concentrated in three great press associations, and features are supplied from a central source by syndicates. There are eight majors in motion pictures, four national radio networks, eight to fifteen giants among magazine publishers, five to twenty-five big book houses. Throughout the communications industry the little fellow exists on very narrow margins, and the opportunities for initiating new ventures are strictly limited. The detailed picture of concentration in each medium is as follows.

NEWSPAPER CONCENTRATION

For a considerable period (since 1909) the number of daily English-language newspapers has fallen at a fairly constant rate. At the same time there has been a growth in literacy, in total population, and in total circulation. The peak of 2,600 dailies reached in 1909 has been steadily reduced to the present 1,750. Dr. R. B. Nixon, who has done the most recent research on this subject, reported in the *Journalism Quarterly* for June, 1945, that only 117 (approximately one out of twelve) of the cities in which daily newspapers are published now have competing dailies. He also found that in ten states of the Union no cities have compet-

ing dailies; in twenty-two states no cities have competing Sunday newspapers. Altogether 40 per cent of the estimated total daily newspaper circulation of forty-eight million is noncompetitive. Rival newspapers exist only in the larger cities.

Twenty-five hundred of the 16,000 and more weekly newspapers of the nation disappeared between 1910 and 1920, another 1,300 between 1920 and 1930, and 1,750 more in the next decade. Fewer than 10,000 now survive.

MAGAZINE AND BOOK CONCENTRATION

A few big houses own the magazines of largest circulation. The eight leading publishers include the so-called "Big Five": Curtis, with the *Ladies' Home Journal, Saturday Evening Post, Country Gentleman,* and the new *Holiday;* Time-Life, Inc., with *Life, Time, Fortune,* and *Architectural Forum;* Crowell-Collier's, with *Collier's, American* and *Woman's Home Companion;* Hearst, with *Good Housekeeping, Harper's Bazaar, House Beautiful,* and the new *Junior Bazaar;* and McCall's, with *McCall's Magazine* and *Red Book.* To these should be added the *Reader's Digest,* which had at the end of the war an estimated domestic circulation of 8,500,000, plus Spanish, Portuguese, Swedish, Arabic, Danish, and Finnish editions totaling another 1,500,000; all but the last of these had the largest circulations in their languages. Among the giants must be included also the Capper group of farm periodicals and the separately owned *Farm Journal,* which together have a circulation over six million. Very recently the Coronet-Esquire group, with a reported circulation of four million for *Coronet,* has jumped into the higher brackets.

Thirty years ago there were nearly two dozen major women's magazines and a group of six large magazines which was just emerging. Now the six largest in a reduced field have nearly nine-tenths of the total circulation.

Though there is still a lively interest in new ventures in magazines and the attempt to launch one is frequently made, the advantages in promotion posssessed by the big groups give their publications a head start in the race for readers.

In book publishing the competitive area is comparatively broad. New book houses appear frequently, and some rapidly achieve financial success. Approximately two hunderd houses provide 90 per cent of the books published in the United States each year. More than a quarter of the annual titles are produced by the ten largest publishers.

There is a Big Five in trade or general publishing. They are headed by Doubleday-Doran, which printed forty million volumes in 1945, with gross receipts somewhere near thirty million dollars. The next four, Macmillan, Pocket Books, William Wise, and Harper's, do not approach this size. (The Book-of-the-Month Club could be included in this group.) In the textbook and subscription book field a small number of still other publishers do a large percentage of the total business which equals or exceeds the trade publication total.

In the field of technical books Mc-Graw-Hill deserves special mention. It accounts for approximately 25 per cent of such books and, in addition, dominates the field of business and industrial magazines. The importance of these magazines, and hence of concentration in this area, should not be underestimated.

RADIO COMPETITION AND THE NETWORKS

The situation in radio is distinguished by the fact that the number of stations which can broadcast without interference is limited by nature and the further fact that the maintenance of competition among these stations is enjoined by law. The result is that the number of stations at present is just over a thousand, of which only twenty-five are Class 1A clear channel stations, and that single ownership of more than one in any locality or more than eight in all is effectively prevented by the Federal Communications Commission. In spite of these facts, however, the prevalent trend in the communications industry has dominated radio. The broadcasting networks which provide programs to the stations are outside the regulative power of the F.C.C., except as they own stations subject to regulation, or except as regards their contracts with affiliated stations. Over the last twenty years, four great networks have emerged — the National Broadcasting Company, the Columbia Broadcasting System, the American

Broadcasting Company, and the Mutual Broadcasting System. The natural tendency of national advertisers to gravitate toward the networks has induced nearly eight hundred of the thousand stations to become affiliated with the chains.

MOTION PICTURE CONCENTRATION

The eight major motion picture companies are Loew's (M-G-M), RKO, Warner Brothers, Paramount, and Twentieth Century-Fox, which five produce, distribute, and exhibit pictures; Columbia and Universal, which produce and distribute alone; and United Artists, which distributes for a group of independent producing companies and exhibits in England. Approximately a fifth of the theater capacity of this country has been affiliated with the five producing companies among the eight majors. The theaters in the best city locations with the largest audiences, the highest admissions, and the longest runs have been controlled by the eight major companies.

CHAINS

Large individual units in a single medium are not the only types of Big Press that have grown up. Another kind of development, especially in the newspaper field and in motion pictures, is the ownership of more than one newspaper or other mass medium in one or several cities by a single person or corporation. These are technically called chain ownerships.

The number of papers controlled by national chains has actually declined in recent years, the papers included in the Hearst chain having dropped from twenty-six to seventeen in the ten depression years, and those in the Scripps-Howard chain from twenty-three to eighteen. At present only a dozen chains among newspapers extend beyond seven dailies, and all but three or four are limited to a single region.

The number of regional chains or, more properly, single ownership of papers in two to a dozen different communities has, however, increased. In 1935 there were 63 such combined ownerships, and in 1945, 76. Fourteen were cases of single ownership of 8 or more papers. The 76 chains — national, regional, and local — own 375 dailies altogether, or 25 per cent of all English-language dailies. In addition, there are 174 localities in which there are partial combinations of separately published newspapers through joint use of the single printing establishment, so that a Republican and a Democratic newspaper run peacefully through the same press but at different times of day.

Whatever the tendency is, the fact remains that the local and regional chains, together with the Hearst, Scripps-Howard, and McCormick-Patterson ownership groups, control more than half (53.8 per cent) of the total newspaper circulation of the nation. Fourteen newspaper owners control 25 per cent of the daily circulation, with less than fifty owners controlling nearly half the total Sunday circulation.

LOCAL NEWS MONOPOLIES

Monopoly, in the strict sense of single control of all current information coming into an area, does not exist in the communications industry. The nearest thing to it — and it is too near for comfort — is unitary ownership in a single locality. This does exist. Ninety-two per cent of the communities in this country, all but the bigger cities, have only one local newspaper. In a hundred small communities the only newspaper owner also owns the only radio station. This creates a *local* monopoly of local news. Joint newspaper-radio ownership is increasing. About a third of the radio stations in the United States are controlled by newspapers, and the applications for FM licenses so far received exceed this ratio.

THE COMMUNICATIONS EMPIRES

The Commission doubts that any regional or national monopoly of communications by a single owner is possible. Mr. Hearst at the top of his fortunes, not many years ago, had accumulated twenty-six newspapers, thirteen magazines (mainly with large circulation), eight radio stations, a newsreel company, a substantial interest in a motion picture feature producing company, a leading feature syndicate, and one of the three press associations, for a total of an estimated thirty million readers and a huge motion picture and radio audience. But at this peak Hearst's organization was in brisk competition with rivals in each medium. It was a communications empire of great size and influence; but it was no monopoly. And it has visibly decreased in size in recent years.

The Luce interests, the Cowles interests, and the Marshall Field interests are powerful combinations in the various media. The Radio Corporation of America, if not an empire in the Hearst sense, was at its moment of greatest extent a mass communications principality of extraordinary scope.

The Luce interests have owned, at one time or another, a weekly news magazine (*Time*), a weekly picture magazine (*Life*), two monthly magazines (*Fortune* and *Architectural Forum*), a documentary motion picture producing company and a radio program ("March of Time"), and interest in a metropolitan radio station (WQXR) and a radio network (A.B.C.) — the two latter now sold. The Cowles brothers own four midwest newspapers, four radio stations, and a weekly picture magazine. The Radio Corporation of America, which is a leading manufacturer of radio and sound and color equipment, owns the National Broadcasting Company, had a substantial interest in RKO-Radio Pictures, Inc., and is one of the two leading American companies handling the international radio telegraph business to and from the United States.

Big money made in other fields is now going into communications. The Atlas Corporation has recently bought *Liberty Magazine,* with a circulation of a million and a half, and has a substantial interest in RKO-Radio Pictures, Inc., and Walt Disney Productions, as well as three movie-fan magazines. Marshall Field owns two metropolitan dailies, four radio stations, a farm journal, and a Sunday newspaper magazine supplement used by more than forty papers. He also has a controlling interest in a large book publishing house and its related reprint house. Edward Noble used money from the sale of Lifesavers to buy the Blue network. The Pew interests (Sun Oil) control one of the biggest farm journals, a group of trade papers including *Iron Age,* and *Pathfinder* magazine with a large circulation in small town and rural areas.

News Agencies, Features, and Syndicates

The press associations and some one hundred and seventy-five companies offer feature services with nation-wide coverage, so that, as compared with fifty years ago, an increasing sameness appears in news stories, photographs, cartoons, and columns. Even editorials are mass-produced for certain categories of papers. Almost all of the ten thousand weekly newspapers still surviving, for example, have for a long time used the services of the Western Newspaper Union, a manufacturer of editorials, features, and columns, owned by John H. Perry, the so-called "Boiler Plate King." Nearly three thousand of them use an eight-page paper provided by Western Newspaper Union, four of the pages of which are pre-written, pre-edited, and pre-printed by syndicate. Perry is also developing a chain of small

papers including seven dailies, fourteen weeklies, and four radio stations. He owns the principal trade magazine for the weekly press and has an interest in plants producing printing machinery which he sells to his clients.

Of the 1,750 remaining general English daily newspapers in the United States, 95 per cent, serving all but one-fifth of 1 per cent of the total daily circulation, take the services of one or more of the three major press associations — the Associated Press, United Press, and International News Service. This standardization is made more uniform still by the fact that International News Service is owned by interests identified with Hearst, United Press by interests identified with Scripps-Howard, and the Associated Press by a limited, and until recently self-limiting, group of newspaper publishers. (Radio stations and news magazines are now admitted to associate membership without a vote.)

The same interrelationship within an interrelationship appears in the syndicate news and photo feature business which sells photographs, comic strips, feature columns, and the like, thus providing a central control of content far more extensive than any control through ownership. Perry's Western Newspaper Union is itself one of the country's biggest newspaper syndicates in terms of papers served. Of the five or six biggest syndicates, among the hundred-and-seventy-odd now operating, King Features is connected with the Hearst interests; United Features and Newspaper Enterprise

Association, with the Scripps-Howard interests. Associated Press operates one of the largest and most complete feature services. Large syndicates are owned or controlled by metropolitan newspapers; the *Chicago Tribune* and the *New York Daily News* (jointly), one of the largest of all the syndicates, the *New York Herald Tribune,* the *Des Moines Register* and *Tribune,* the *Chicago Sun, PM,* the *New York Evening Post,* and the *Chicago Times.*

MONOPOLISTIC PRACTICES

The main causes of the trend toward concentration in the communications industries have been the advantages inherent in operating on a large scale using the new technology. High labor costs have also contributed to the elimination of the smaller, marginal owner.

Other forces are at work as well. They are *personal* forces; they have nothing to do with technological change. They exist, and always have existed, in all branches of the economy, and the communications industries are no exception. These forces are those exaggerated drives for power and profit which have tended to restrict competition and to promote monopoly throughout the private enterprise system. As in other industries, the means employed in specific instances have varied all the way from complicated economic pressures down to the simple instruments of physical violence.

Hearst and McCormick fought an epic newsstand war in Chicago early in the present century, which involved not only the destruction of papers but also the shooting of employees. These battles, and the private armies which fought on either side, were a factor in promoting the gang warfare which has distressed the city since. Violence as a curb on competition has not, however, been confined to Chicago. The New York papers, including the *Times* and the *Herald Tribune,* had newsstand fights in the thirties; and *PM* faced serious difficulties in finding a place on the newsstands.

Potential competitors have divided territory as Hearst, Gannett, and Block did in upstate New York and as motion picture theaters have done elsewhere. Small publishers are now complaining that giant concerns, such as Time-Life and Curtis, have pre-empted paper stocks and printing facilities under long-term contracts. In recent litigation the Associated was compelled to give up a practice which the Supreme Court found monopolistic, since it permitted one publisher to deny the Association's service to a competitor. Antitrust actions, now on appeal, against the eight great motion picture companies are designed to separate the control of production from exhibition, a combination which is claimed to amount to monopoly. These companies have produced 80 per cent of American feature films and distributed 95 per cent of the films reaching the public.

THE COST OF NEW VENTURES

Monopolistic practices, together

with the cost of machinery and the momentum of big, going concerns, have made it hard for new ventures to enter the field of mass communications. Although there is no such thing as a going price for a great city newspaper, it is safe to assume that it would cost somewhere between five and ten million dollars to build a new metropolitan daily to success. The investment required for a new newspaper in a medium-sized city is estimated at three-quarters of a million to several million; for a small-town paper, $25,000–$100,000. Radio stations have been sold at figures well over a million dollars, though such prices must include, in the words of Commissioner Durr, " something (the sellers) do not own and have no right to sell; namely, the use of a radio channel." The equity needed for a new feature motion picture producing company would probably be at least $100,000, but this is merely a shoestring; one cannot sensibly initiate a producing unit without a contract with one of the major distributors. A publisher should not start a magazine aimed at the mass market unless he is prepared to lose two or three million dollars at the outset. On the other hand, a book publishing house might be established for as little as $100,000.

Our survey of the instruments and the organization of the communications industry leaves us with certain questions. To what extent has the reduction in the number of units of the press reduced variety? Has the reduction in the number of units cut down the opportunity to reach an audience on the part of those who have something to say? Has the struggle for power and profit been carried to such a point in this field that the public interest has suffered? Have the units of the press, by becoming big business, lost their representative character and developed a common bias — the bias of the large investor and employer? Can the press in the present crisis rise to its responsibility as an essential instrument for carrying on the political and social life of a nation and a world of nations seeking understanding? If not, will its irresponsibility deprive it of its freedom?

These questions require an examination of the actual performance of the American press today.

THE PERFORMANCE

Private enterprise in the field of communications has great achievements to its credit. The American press probably reaches as high a percentage of the population as that of any other country. Its technical equipment is certainly the best in the world. It has taken the lead in the introduction of many new techniques which have enormously increased the speed and the variety of communications. Whatever its shortcomings, the American press is less venal and less subservient to political economic pressure than that of many other countries. The leading organs of the American press have achieved a standard of excellence unsurpassed anywhere in the world. It is necessary to keep these general comments in mind in order to see the criticisms which follow in the proper perspective.

The economic logic of private enterprise forces most units of the mass communications industry to seek an ever larger audience. The result is an omnibus product which includes something for everybody. . . .

Information and discussion regarding public affairs, carried as a rider on the omnibus of mass communication, take on the character of the other passengers and become subject to the same laws that governed their selection: such information and discussion must be shaped so that they will pay their own way by attracting the maximum audience.

Scoops and Sensations

Hence the word " news " has come to mean something different from important new information. When a journalist says that a certain event is news, he does not mean that it is important in itself. Often it is; but about as often it is not. The journalist means by news something that has happened within the last few hours which will attract the interest of the customers. The criteria of interest are recency or firstness, proximity, combat, human interest, and novelty. Such criteria limit accuracy and significance.

The eager pursuit of these qualities is undoubtedly captivating to the participants, but to the world at large it seems often to lead to unfortunate excesses. . . .

The effort to attract the maximum audience means that each news account must be written to catch head-lines. The result is not a continued story of the life of a people, but a series of vignettes, made to seem more significant than they really are. The sum of such discontinuous parts does not equal the whole, because the parts have not been represented in their actual size and color in relation to the whole.

This was illustrated at the San Francisco Conference. This gathering necessarily followed a course governed by protocol; it involved proposal and counter-proposal, preparation of texts, amendments and revisions, and eventual agreement by compromise.

On many days during the weeks the Conference was in session there was nothing to report. But the reporters had to send in their stories. Somehow there had to be news. The result on the lower levels was a series of personal items modeled after the Hollywood fan magazine and on the higher levels a distorted account of what took place. Because drama and tension were demanded by the editorial desks back home, drama and tension were manufactured at San Francisco. Hence calm was turned into the calm-before-the-storm. Silence became the silence-of-impending-conflict. The passage of time became a portentous period of delay. So completely was the task of manufacturing suspense performed that, when after some weeks an acceptable charter was signed, the effect on newspaper readers was one of incredulous surprise. (A detailed study of the treatment given the Conference by the press has been made by Milton D. Stewart of the Commission staff and will be published under the title, *The American Press and the San Francisco Conference.*)

The worst offenders in this direction are to be found among the newspaper columnists and radio commentators. The members of this craft have come to perform an indispensable function in American public discussion. But they must attract the maximum audience, too. Some of them have thought that the way to do this is to supply the public with keyhole gossip, rumor, character assassination, and lies.

THE PRESSURE OF THE AUDIENCE

People seldom want to read or hear what does not please them; they seldom want others to read or hear what disagrees with their convictions or what presents an unfavorable picture of groups they belong to. When such groups are organized, they let the press know their objections to remarks concerning them. The press is therefore caught between its desire to please and extend its audience and its desire to give a picture of events and people as they really are.

The motion picture industry offers the most elaborate example of accommodation to the pressure of the audience. (The Motion Picture Code is described in a study by Ruth Inglis, a member of the Commission staff, published by the Commission under the title, *Freedom of the Movies.*) This accommodation may not have gone quite so far as the present Code executive says it would have to go to satisfy all protestors: it has not limited the villain of the screen to "a native-born, white, American citizen, without a job, and without any political, social, religious, or fraternal affiliation of any kind." But pressure groups, because they have or are thought to have influence on attendance, have shaped the motion picture to their desires. Hollywood's efforts to develop the documentary film may be thwarted by its habit of yielding to this kind of intimidation. . . .

THE BIAS OF OWNERS

The agencies of mass communication are big business, and their owners are big businessmen. The American consumers just prior to the war paid the forty thousand mass communication establishments nearly two and a half billion dollars for their services, representing one dollar out of every twenty-seven spent that year for all goods and services. The press is a large employer of labor. With its total wage and salary bill in the same year nearly a billion dollars, it provided about 4 per cent of the country's total salary and wage expenditures. The newspapers alone have more than 150,000 employees. The press is connected with other big businesses through the advertising of these businesses, upon which it depends for the major part of its revenue. The owners of the press, like the owners of other big businesses, are bank directors, bank borrowers, and heavy taxpayers in the upper brackets.

As William Allen White put it: "Too often the publisher of an American newspaper has made his money in some other calling than journalism. He is a rich man seeking power and prestige. He has the country club complex. The business manager of this absentee owner quickly is afflicted with the country club point of view. Soon the managing editor's wife nags him into it. And they all get the unconscious arrogance of conscious wealth. Therefore it is hard to get a modern American newspaper to go the distance necessary to print all the news about many topics." In the last thirty years, in Mr. White's opinion, newspapers "have veered from their traditional position as leaders of public opinion to mere peddlers and purveyors of news . . . the newspapers have become commercial enterprises and hence fall into the current which is merging commercial enterprises along mercantile lines."

The same point is made with equal force by another distinguished editor, Virginius Dabney of the *Richmond Times-Dispatch* writing in the *Saturday Review of Literature:* "Today newspapers are Big Business, and they are run in that tradition. The publisher, who often knows little about the editorial side of the operation, usually is one of the leading business men in his community, and his editorial page, under normal circumstances, strongly reflects that point of view. Sometimes he gives his editor a free hand but far oftener he does not. He looks upon the paper primarily as a 'property' rather than as an instrument for public service." . . .

We need to project across all groups, regions, and nations a picture of the constituent elements of the modern world. We need to clarify the aims and ideals of our community and every other.

These needs are not being met. The news is twisted by the emphasis on firstness, on the novel and sensational; by the personal interests of owners; and by pressure groups. Too much of the regular output of the press consists of a miscellaneous succession of stories and images which have no relation to the typical lives of real people anywhere. Too often the result is meaninglessness, flatness, distortion, and the perpetuation of misunderstanding among widely scattered groups whose only contact is through these media.

As we have said, the American press has great technical achievements to its credit. It has displayed remarkable ingenuity in gathering its raw material and in manufacturing and distributing its finished product. Nor would we deny that extraordinarily high quality of performance has been achieved by the leaders in each field of mass communications. When we look at the press as a whole, however, we must conclude that it is not meeting the needs of our society. The Commission believes that this failure of the press is the greatest danger to its freedom.

12 TENSIONS AMONG NATIONS

A. The Nature of Politics Among Nations

71. The Theory and the Problems of Contemporary International Politics

No area of human relations has suffered so deeply as has international relations from the impoverishment of theoretical understanding of which we have spoken above (Supra, pp. 1–10). This defect has been manifested in three important ways. The nature of international relations has been conceived of in *non-political* terms, although the core of the problem all along has been profoundly political. It has been politics and the struggle for power which have confounded ideal programs of philosophers and statesmen for centuries. Yet politics at best have been considered incidentally as the flaw in an older and inferior type of international relations.

The nature of international relations has, further, been conceived of in *idealistic* terms. Under a new and ideal legal and institutional order, nations could formulate foreign policies without regard for their own vital national interests. Yet this order and the expected liberation of states from anxious measures for na-

tional security has not yet materialized. And the discovery by practical men that these ideal assumptions are logically false and politically unacceptable has called for their replacement or an imaginary rationalization of their faults. In practice, this discrepancy between theory and practice has merely encouraged the search for some scapegoat more flagrantly self-oriented than all the rest. To some leader or nation or group of nations — a Kaiser, a Soviet Union, or the European nations, whose relations alone have been constantly marred by power politics — is attributed the failure of the international order. Since, according to this viewpoint it was only a minority which stood athwart the achievement of the ideal world, no occasion has been found for any re-examination of the underlying and persistent characteristics of international politics.

Finally, the nature of international relations has been construed in *unhistorical* terms. Each new experiment in international organization

705

or new code of international behavior has been presented as something entirely novel and unique.
Woodrow Wilson declared that a
brave new world would follow the
ratification of the Covenant of the
League of Nations, and Cordell Hull
proclaimed that the Charter of the
United Nations was ushering in a
new day. Each was a revolution,
the first against foreign policies
founded on selfish interests and the
second against the whole structure
of European power politics. But
each, as proclaimed in these unhistorical terms, was destined to be ill-
fated and illusory.

In truth, both the League and the
United Nations are points on a continuum in the history of international politics. Neither is unique any
more than the Delian League or the
Concert of Europe was unique.
Their points of difference are less
basic than their common point of
reference. All are embedded in an
environment corresponding to the
sociologist's conception of an "international society." Not mutual
confidence and law and order, but
fear and rivalry shape the actions
of individuals and nations huddling
together in the temporary and provisional cooperation and harmony of
world politics. The United Nations,
offered to the world as the vaunted
alternative to the evil order of strife
and suspicion, has become the stage
on which the actors from the rival
nations play their sordid parts. Anyone who has considered this latest
adventure in cooperation among
states could have found the proto-
types of the United Nations at the

outset. In the principle that its action depended on the unanimity of
the Great Powers, the United Nations is based on the principles of
the Concert of Europe. In other respects, it derives from the League of
Nations. The one thing that has
been certain is the fact that the
United Nations is merely a step in
the unfolding of a pattern of interstate relations which has prevailed
for almost four hundred years.

The pattern of relations among
states in modern society is one of
inequality in their relative power.
The first truth of contemporary international politics is that its actors
are not equal. The differences in
the influence and power of individuals *within* any society are modest
indeed compared to the differences
between the United States and Ecuador. This disproportion of power
has meant that the voice of the
United States in the United Nations
would carry infinitely more weight
than Ecuador's. Indeed Ecuador's
voice may become essentially an echo
of the big brother who is at the same
time the protector and benefactor.

At any peace treaty, disarmament
conference, or meeting of foreign
ministers the basic disparity between
representation and power is apparent. The Japanese Peace Treaty
signed in 1951 is a product of diplomacy through power in which the
influence Mr. Dulles was able to exert reflects the radical inequality, for
example, of the United States and
Indonesia. Equality of opportunity
under law is a basic moral principle
of Western democracies. Since,
however, there is no general system

of law on the world scene and since war as the final arbitration lurks always in the background, the great powers play overwhelmingly the most important roles. In the absence of world law and world government, the policies of those nations who by persuasion and force can influence and rally to their side other powers determines the course of international history. On the national scene, this state of affairs prevails when a civil war is raging or when locally the forces of law and order decay. The condition that Hobbes described as *bellum omnium contra omnes* (the war of each against all) is the permanent condition of contemporary international society. The first problem which students of international relations stubbornly disregarded throughout most of the inter-war period is the enormous gap between the legal rights and status of most sovereign states and their actual role and influence. Theories of law have dealt exhaustively with status; only in recent times has equal attention been given to power.

This disparity between law and practice, rights and responsibility, status and power confounds numerous fields of human relations. It deals its most deadly blows, however, to actions in contemporary world politics. The influence of states as competitors in the struggle for power rests mainly on permanent and material resources such as strategic location and natural resources and the organized power and influence comprising its government, diplomacy, and industry. Their influence derives further from human elements, such as population and the quality and stamina of their people. If we may use an analogy with human beings, the fist of a nation's power is its military preparedness. This power, in turn, is dependent on the vitality of the whole man — economic, social, and political. These elements, fused inseparably together, constitute an aggregate of power difficult to estimate, measure, or study but vital to an understanding of the pattern of politics as it is expressed in international practice.

1. The Concert of Powers

In history, the prevailing influence of power in world politics can hardly be overlooked or denied. It can be traced throughout the nineteenth century in the operation of " the European System." In general terms this was the international order from 1815–1914. In the democratic West, the illusion has in recent times been sedulously cultivated that it was the most disastrous of world systems. Today it is contemptuously dismissed as anarchical, lawless, and anti-democratic. Yet one great historian of diplomacy, Professor Mowat, maintains that this system succeeded in preventing at least seven great European wars between 1871 and 1914. The most peaceful of modern centuries attained security through the informal but effective instrument of " the Concert of Europe." Moreover this century of peace was achieved in an era where war was still recognized and accepted as a legitimate and appropriate instrument of national policy.

The point to be stressed is the fact that the principles of the Concert of Europe squared with the facts of the time. It more nearly identified power and responsibility than any international system in modern history. Nations with the greatest stake and the widest experience in preserving peace conferred together when threats to the peace arose. Their leaders formed an aristocratic elite with a common interest in avoiding violence and destruction. Austria, France, Russia, Spain and England were powers who had attained such influence that there was common agreement that more would be lost than could be gained through a disturbance of the *status quo*. Their system had little or no constitutional foundation. Its sole basis was a wise merger of force with interests, since the nations who stood to profit most from preserving the peace were also the nations powerful enough to exert pressure to dissuade those who would disturb it. War was opposed not on moral grounds but in terms of enlightened self-interest. Its uncertainty, wastefulness and the disproportionate burden it placed on more advanced nations were unmistakable reasons for limiting its occurrence. The Concert of Europe emerged from the necessities of the situation. In the same way and for the same reasons, in 1945 the principle of the unanimity of the Great Powers was written into the Charter of the United Nations. It provided for a veto by the permanent members of the Security Council. Disputes among great powers must be settled by them. The veto is a safety-valve permitting a cooling-off period if no settlement can be reached within the Security Council chambers. The first characteristic of the nature of international relations historically, as well as at this moment, is the inequality of power among its participants.

2. THE BALANCE OF POWER

The nature of international politics is related, furthermore, to the stabilizing element through which order is achieved. Some system of political dynamics operates in every society to preserve its identity. In domestic societies this purpose is generally served by regulated political competition among parties and pressure groups. Among nations where a number of mutually independent states strive for influence and power, one ordering force is in the balance of power. The agony and pathos of contemporary world politics is commonly attributed to the balance of power. Some have discovered in it the true cause of war. Many asserted after World War II that the great game of the balance of power had been forever exposed and discredited. Yet today serious students of international politics set forth another less absolute view. They maintain that it was the early abandonment rather than the blind pursuit of a balancing policy which hastened and made inevitable both World Wars. Before World War I, the fruits of three Bismarckian Wars led to so great an accumulation of power in German hands that war alone could re-establish the balance. Even England whose foreign policy has become a by-word for prudence and political wisdom remained passive and indifferent to threats to the equilibrium of the "Europe System." Only in 1900 did it stir and, responding to the challenge of a new German navy, emerged from its coma of "splendid isolation." There followed overtures to Japan and to France. The Entente which resulted was no longer an effort to re-establish an equilibrium of power but rather an attempt belatedly to bolster the military strength of the allies for the impending conflict. When Lord Grey sought to reassert the principles of the Concert and the balance of power this was merely a frantic and hopeless gesture. So powerful was Germany by this time that no counterpoise could be found to equalize the scales of the balance now overweighted by the elements of German national power. What failed in this instance was not the balance of power but the policy of indifference and isolationism which had taken its place.

What is the idea of the balance of power? What are its underlying assumptions? Its traditional definition is in terms of the maintenance of such an approximate equilibrium between nations or groups as to prevent any member or combination of members from attaining the power that would enable them to impose their will upon the rest. The "great unconscious tradition" of British foreign policy has been to forestall the domination of all Europe by any single power. The principle is broader and more far-reaching than international politics. Some social scientists maintain there is a general social principle underlying the relations of independent units, which provides that stability can be achieved through a tendency of the separate units to establish and re-establish some kind of equilibrium. This equilibrium is uncertain, precarious, and temporary, for life can never be kept in balance or equilibrium but is subject to unceasing change and variation. A rough stability is achieved from time to time, however, through forces which combine to re-establish the lost equilibrium.

This social "law" has sometimes been formulated in the broadest if not universal terms as in the following general statement by Julian Huxley: "If one species happens to vary in the direction of greater independence, the inter-related equilibrium is upset and cannot be restored until a number of competing species have either given way to the increased pressure and become extinct, or else have answered pressure with pressure and kept the first species in its place, by themselves too discovering means of adding to their independence." [1]

The balance of power manifests itself particularly in three dimensions of modern society. It can be observed in the functioning of the human body, the operation of the national government, and the history

[1] Julian S. Huxley, *The Individual in the Animal Kingdom* (London: Cambridge University Press, 1912), pp. 115–116.

of international politics. If some organ or tissue of the human body becomes diseased or injured, other organs seek to repair this loss or assume part of the burden. In this way, blind people develop an extraordinary sensitivity to sound and substitute this capacity for the function that was at one time performed by the disabled organ. The human body is the scene of ever-shifting states of equilibrium as adjustments within the organism are continuously being made.

In our national government, a similar process is in evidence. Ours is a government of limited powers and systems of checks and balances. Underlying our system are political beliefs which perhaps are best contained in the aphorism: If men were gods, government would not be necessary; if men were devils, government would be impossible. Since they are somewhere between these extremes, governments of limited powers are the best means of attaining relative justice (see above, p. 446). The legislature has acted traditionally as a brake on the executive; the judiciary, in turn, restrains the legislature. Interest groups have throughout history worked through one or the other branch to press their ambitions. During the Civil War period, the Northern interests found an ally in the Supreme Court. In a more recent period, the executive-legislature became the voice of labor and the judiciary spoke in behalf of the business community.

Finally, the balance of power has been most conspicuous and overt from the first century of the modern era in international relations. From 1075–1475 A.D. among the little North Italian city-states, a system of pressures and balances operated to preserve the independence of individual states and prevent their domination by any would-be conqueror. In the sixteenth and seventeenth centuries there were regional systems of the balance of power, as in Northern Europe against Sweden; in the eighteenth and nineteenth centuries the system became Continental in extent. Then the objective of England as "balancer" was to maintain the equilibrium of Europe. At last in our own day there are only two major weights in the balance, the United States and the Soviet Union. But the fundamental process of the balance of power, whatever its changing forms, has been an enduring feature of the pattern of world politics. Its recurrence should suggest that its roots are more than superficially embedded in the preferences of a handful of diplomats or leaders.

It is appropriate to note that the balance of power bears marked resemblances to the contemporary system called collective security. Both systems seek to apply sanctions, one through the action of a "balancer" or combination of power, the other theoretically by the whole family of nations. These differences in techniques are less significant in practice. Balancing is achieved by a combination or collectivity of nations; the much vaunted collective security system of the League and the United Nations has in practice become a process of collective self-help by fewer than all the nations. Decisions as to troops and assistance remain with sovereign states despite constitutional provisions in the Charter.

If the techniques of the two systems are not qualitatively different, however, the same can hardly be said with regard to timing. The rule by which action is taken is different in each case. The commandment to be upheld for the balance of power is: "Thou shalt not grow too formidable"; for collective security it might read: "Thou shalt not make war." The most fundamental difference is the attempt by the traditional system to meet the challenge at an earlier stage before conditions have been created that only war can change. Moreover, the objective of the older system is to prevent only those struggles that involve unpleasant consequences for the whole family of nations, and to localize the others. It is not our purpose to become an advocate for one system or the other. But the relative successfulness of the older system should teach us some measure of humility regarding our political inventions or at least make us less disdainful of past political practices.

3. NATIONALISM

There is a third force which distinguishes the pattern of international politics. Nationalism is at present the most powerful determinant of international behavior. It is a man-made phenomenon and yet it has achieved enduring characteristics. In some respects it is not novel, for there have been primitive societies in which men worshipped the political community as today modern societies glorify the nation. There were few signs of nationalism anywhere in Europe during the Middle Ages. The way was prepared for it, however, by the quickening of national consciousness inspired by the Crusades. Frenchmen, Castilians, Portuguese, and Catalans were brought into contact with people who spoke their language or dialect. These contacts served to inspire a feeling of pride in their own nationality and a consciousness of rivalry with others. Loyalty to an area or locality and the growth of a spirit of community among a people through the spread and effects of a language or dialect were some of the seeds from which nationalism was to grow. The fundamental nature of modern nationalism is the demand of such a group for a state or an independent political organization of its own. The achievement of this stage in modern nationalism awaited the popular revolutions in the late eighteenth and nineteenth centuries.

There were, however, traces and signs of a precocious nationalism somewhat earlier than this. The development of contemporary nationalism was foreshadowed in the North Italian city-states of the fifteenth and sixteenth centuries. Their origin corresponded with the breakup of the seamless web of universal Christendom. In Florence, Milan, and Venice this new crop of Central and North Italian city-states revived the pagan religion of "tribalism." These tiny city-states constituted in microcosm the modern nation-state. The same rules for the art of politics which Machiavelli perceived and described for the city-states have become the accepted principles for the practice, if not the theory, of politics among nations. These miniature city-states served as laboratories for proving and testing techniques of diplomacy and power politics.

Subsequently in the seventeenth and eighteenth centuries a new form of nationalism, which was half-hearted in character, appeared. If one identifies this at all with contemporary nationalism it must be distinguished as a much weaker and more diluted form. It is in the nature of this form of nationalism that its followers were partly starved of any plausible object of worship. In the dynastic nationalism of this period the idol had to be the vested interest of the dynasty. This hardly compares as a wellspring of emotion and loyalty with the incarnation of a sovereign people.

This is one side of the coin of dynastic nationalism. The other is the fact that dynastic regimes were drawn together by the firm bonds of common membership in an " aristocratic international." There was more community between two princes or rulers than there was between a prince and his own subjects. Frederick the Great of Prussia spoke the French language more fluently than German, which he confessed he always spoke as a coachman. Since rulers and ruled were essentially indifferent to the symbols of nationalism, it should not be surprising that this era did not produce strong nationalist sentiments among their citizens and subjects.

The late eighteenth and nineteenth centuries heralded the birth of a new epoch. In a series of revolutionary convulsions, which racked the world from 1775 to 1918, nations were substituted for dynastic states. The uninspiring figures of monarchs such as Louis XIV and George III were replaced by the effulgent images of " France," " England," and " America." These incarnations of national communities were to acquire the same splendor as Ancient Rome or Athens. They furnished an object of worship which no " Prince " could supply.

A series of events mark this change. Fanaticism and ruthlessness toward foes and former friends is foreshadowed in the harsh treatment of the Loyalists by the Americans in 1783. The same emotional pattern is continued throughout Europe beginning with the French revolutionary *levée en masse*, the *German Befreiungskrieg*, the Belgian Revolution of 1830, the burning of Moscow, and the Italian *Risorgimento*. International politics since these days has become increasingly infected with the virus of unqualified national loyalty and mutual hostility until the old forms of moderation and accommodation have disappeared. A signpost of this development is the contrast between the last moderate peace treaty of 1866 (we might say that the Japanese Peace Treaty of 1951 is an exception only because of the demands that both sides acquire allies in the " Cold War ") and the Peace Treaty of 1871 between France and

Germany. The latter treaty was the direct consequence of a German nationalism which, under the fostering hand of Bismarck, had become so strong by 1871 that it was his master rather than his servant. Because of this pressure and against his better judgment, Bismarck was compelled to inflict a rankling wound on the French national consciousness by tearing away Alsace-Lorraine from the French body-politic.

Nationalism today has become a political religion. In the days of Giuseppe Mazzini, intellectual spokesman for Italian unity in the nineteenth century, and Thomas Masaryk, first President of the Republic of Czechoslovakia, nationalism was characterized by its humanitarianism and moderation. The aim of ethnic and national groups was to establish their own independent state. But correlative to this idea was the widely acknowledged view that other groups in turn had the right to set out to achieve this same goal and purpose. Thus Mazzini wrote in the "Pact of Fraternity of young Europe": "Every people has its special mission, which will cooperate towards the fulfillment of the general mission of humanity. This mission constitutes its *nationality*. Nationality is sacred." [2]

Humanitarian nationalism of this easy-going variety has been supplanted by the new universalism of present day nationalism. Three conditions have led to the almost unlimited concentration of power in the hands of the state. They are

[2] *Life and Writings of Joseph Mazzini,* III (Smith, Elder and Company, 1905).

technological, psychological, and politico-religious factors. The most astounding changes of modern history, indeed of all history, are those surrounding the Industrial Revolution. Within the past half-century and even the past decade, the globe has been shrunken by changes in transportation and communication. It is possible to circle the globe in 1952 in the same time that was required to travel from Philadelphia to Washington in 1790. Whereas the range of weapons was only a few hundred yards in the sixteenth century, in the twentieth century bombers have attained an operational range of 7,000 miles. The social-psychological development which accentuates national fervor is the increase in unfulfilled ambitions in modern society. The tasks of present day industry are specialized and fragmentary and the laborer who spends his days performing minor tasks in assembly-line production must realize his thirst for influence and prestige elsewhere. By projecting his unfulfilled aims and aspirations into the world actions of the great nation of which he is a citizen, he experiences a vicarious fulfillment of his needs and desires, which contemporary society would otherwise have thwarted. The claims he makes upon his nation in world affairs are therefore less moderate than those the eighteenth century diplomat would require. Finally, the role of nationalism has been secured by the disappearance of supernational forces which might compete successfully for the minds of men. Religion as a universal force had at one time an equal claim on men's loyalties. The doctrine of the "Two Swords" was the philosophy which ascribed equal influence in their own spheres to church and state. Today the emotional fervor which once characterized loyalty to the spiritual order has been united with the patriotism of the past. Compounded together, religious fervor and patriotism have become the most powerful and dynamic force of our day.

Together these changes in technology, psychology, and religion have created the Leviathan. They have strengthened the state and made it nearly invulnerable to popular revolutions. Not only does it possess a monopoly over the means of violence but its power has become so overwhelming that over wide regions or areas popular rebellions can be stamped out with great effectiveness. Control within the Soviet empire, for example, is easier to maintain than in any earlier empire. Dissension can be crushed by massive air squadrons carrying atomic bombs almost instantaneously to the scene of the trouble, whereas at the beginning of the nineteenth century revolts in the provinces of Spain or Italy against Napoleon required full-fledged military campaigns. Nationalism has absorbed the dynamics of industrialism in the sense that production in every country is geared to preserving the products and resources of the state for the eventuality of war. Nationalism, moreover, has played a more decisive role in determining the ultimate loyalties of workers than socialism. For example, the French laborers fought

German workers in the World Wars despite visions of a workers international. Finally, in the case of Titoist Yugoslavia, loyalty to the nation outlasted allegiance to Moscow-dominated world Communism. It should be clear that plans for rapid change through new international institutions must recognize the power of contemporary nationalism or suffer failure, disillusionment, and despair. We are merely deceived if we conceive of present-day nationalism as brittle, fragile, and transitory.

The prevailing philosophy of international relations in Western society has looked for approaches to peace in plans and blueprints for the future. The idealistic outlook has achieved its great force and influence by pointing the way toward new and better forms of international relations unfettered by past institutions and practices. These programs have been formulated in deep sincerity and high moral dignity and have captured the hopes of millions, for whom traditional foreign policy has become corrupting and outmoded.

However, it should be recognized that only in the field of international relations has there been such bold and unqualified contempt for the lessons of the past. Historical method has moved through successive stages, law has broadened with the accumulation of precedents and contemporary economic theory finds wisdom as well as folly in Ricardo and Adam Smith. In contrast, the Wilsonian tradition in rejecting institutions and experience from past international politics set the stage for unparalleled disillusionment when claims made in behalf of novel institutions proved unrealized and unrealizable. The twentieth century has been a century of unexampled conflict. This is our supreme tragedy, for if Mr. Winston S. Churchill is right, both World Wars could have been prevented. One ray of hope in an otherwise gloomy picture is the fact that our peril has caused sensitive minds to re-examine the scroll of past centuries and compare our period of total war and " Fighting Faiths " with the underlying beliefs of other epochs and centuries.

If the twentieth century is the century of unparalleled bloodshed, the nineteenth century was one of unparalleled peace. Karl Polanyi, editor, author, and sometimes professor at Columbia University considers some of the forces that were operative during this extraordinary era from 1815–1914. For those who think primarily in terms of new and universal institutions and techniques, this penetrating study of the functioning of the balance of power in the nineteenth century should occasion new inquiries and studies based more firmly on history and the lessons of past international politics.

The second essay by one of the most distinguished of American diplomatic columnists lays bare the intellectual errors and false assumptions underlying much of twentieth century American foreign policy. Walter Lippmann explores the philosophy and practice of American foreign policy. In this philosophy, defective on all counts in meeting the problem of power, Mr. Lippmann

discovers the primary cause for the unparalleled breakdown in international peace and order. The strength and influence of the false philosophy about which Lippmann has written is reflected in the modest influence which his views and those of a handful of scholars and diplomats such as Hans J. Morgenthau and George F. Kennan, recently American Ambassador in Moscow, have had on the practice of American foreign policy in the " Cold War."

The third selection assesses an ancient conflict in modern form. The war between idealism and realism, which has been described in historical and logical terms, is being carried on today in the family clash between two rival Western political philosophies of conservatism and liberalism. Reinhold Niebuhr, Professor of Applied Christianity at Union Theological Seminary, analyses this struggle in terms of the theoretical foundations of conservatism and liberalism in our national community. The analysis of their inadequacies as vital political theories capable of accounting for the ambiguities of political power confirms the judgment of the preceding selection. It shows further that the false conception of the struggle for power among nations apparent in American foreign policy derives from errors in the two prevailing outlooks as expressed in American thinking on the nature of politics and political behavior. The destructive effects of particular aspects of these two philosophies make it essential that Americans strike a balance between truth and error in each great historic tradition.

72. The International System*

The nineteenth century produced a phenomenon unheard of in the annals of Western civilization, namely, a hundred years' peace — 1815–1914. Apart from the Crimean War — a more or less colonial event — England, France, Prussia, Austria, Italy, and Russia were engaged in war among each other for altogether only eighteen months. A computation of comparable figures for the two preceding centuries gives an average of sixty to seventy years of major wars in each. But even the fiercest of nineteenth century conflagrations, the Franco-Prussian War of 1870–71, ended after less than a year's duration with the defeated nation being able to pay over an unprecedented sum as an indemnity without any disturbance of the currencies concerned.

This triumph of a pragmatic pacifism was certainly not the result of an absence of grave causes for conflict. Almost continuous shifts in the internal and external conditions of powerful nations and great empires accompanied this ironic pageant. During the first part of the century civil wars, revolutionary and anti-revolutionary interventions were the order of the day. In Spain a hundred thousand troops under the Duc d'Angouleme stormed Cadiz; in Hungary the Magyar revolution

* From Karl Polanyi, *The Great Transformation*, pp. 5–9. Copyright 1944 by Karl Polanyi. Reprinted by permission of Karl Polanyi and Farrar and Rinehart, Inc., New York.

threatened to defeat the Emperor himself in pitched battle and was ultimately suppressed only by a Russian army fighting on Hungarian soil. Armed intervention in the Germanies, in Belgium, Poland, Switzerland, Denmark, and Venice marked the omnipresence of the Holy Alliance. During the second half of the century the dynamics of progress was [*sic*] released; the Ottoman, Egyptian, and the Sheriffian empires broke up or were dismembered; China was forced by invading armies to open her door to the foreigner and in one gigantic haul the continent of Africa was partitioned. Simultaneously, two powers rose to world importance: the United States and Russia. National unity was achieved by Germany and Italy; Belgium, Greece, Roumania, Bulgaria, Serbia, and Hungary assumed or reassumed, their places as sovereign states on the map of Europe. An almost incessant series of open wars accompanied the march of industrial civilization into the domains of outworn cultures or primitive peoples. Russia's military conquests in Central Asia, England's numberless Indian and African wars, France's exploits in Egypt, Algiers, Tunis, Syria, Madagascar, Indo-China, and Siam raised issues between the Powers which as a rule, only force can arbitrate. Yet every single one of these conflicts was localized, and numberless other occasions for violent change were either met by joint action or smothered into compromise by the Great Powers. Regardless of how the methods changed, the result was the same. While in the first part of the century constitutionalism was banned and the Holy Alliance suppressed freedom in the name of peace, during the other half — and again in the name of peace — constitutions were foisted upon turbulent despots by business-minded bankers. Thus under varying forms and ever-shifting ideologies — sometimes in the name of progress and liberty, sometimes by the authority of the throne and the altar, sometimes by grace of the stock exchange and the checkbook, sometimes by corruption and bribery, sometimes by moral argument and enlightened appeal, sometimes by the broadside and the bayonet — one and the same result was attained: peace was preserved.

This almost miraculous performance was due to the working of the balance of power, which here produced a result which is normally foreign to it. By its nature that balance effects an entirely different result, namely, the survival of the power units involved; in fact, it merely postulates that three or more units capable of exerting power will always behave in such a way as to combine the power of the weaker units against any increase in power of the strongest. In the realm of universal history balance of power was concerned with states whose independence it served to maintain. But it attained this end only by continuous war between changing partners. The practice of the ancient

Greek or the Northern Italian city-states was such an instance; wars between shifting groups of combatants maintained the independence of those states over long stretches of time. The action of the same principle safeguarded for over two hundred years the sovereignty of the states forming Europe at the time of the Treaty of Münster and Westphalia (1648). When, seventy-five years later, in the Treaty of Utrecht, the signatories declared their formal adherence to this principle, they thereby embodied it in a *system,* and thus established mutual guarantees of survival for the strong and the weak alike through the medium of war. The fact that in the nineteenth century the same mechanism resulted in peace rather than war is a problem to challenge the historian.

The entirely new factor, we submit, was the emergence of an acute peace interest. Traditionally, such an interest was regarded as outside the scope of the state system. Peace with its corollaries of crafts and arts ranked among the mere adornments of life. The Church might pray for peace as for a bountiful harvest, but in the realm of state action it would nevertheless advocate armed intervention; government subordinated peace to security and sovereignty, that is, to intents that could not be achieved otherwise than by recourse to the ultimate means. Few things were regarded as more detrimental to a community than the existence of an organized peace interest in its midst. As late as the second half of the eighteenth century, J. J. Rousseau arraigned trades people for their lack of patriotism because they were suspected of perferring peace to liberty.

After 1815 the change is sudden and complete. The backwash of the French Revolution reinforced the rising tide of the Industrial Revolution in establishing peaceful business as a universal interest. Metternich proclaimed that what the people of Europe wanted was not liberty but peace. Gentz called patriots the new barbarians. Church and throne started out on the denationalization of Europe. Their arguments found support both in the ferocity of the recent popular forms of warfare and in the tremendously enhanced value of peace under the nascent economies.

The bearers of the new " peace interest " were, as usual, those who chiefly benefited by it, namely, that cartel of dynasts and feudalists whose patrimonial positions were threatened by the revolutionary wave of patriotism that was sweeping the Continent. Thus, for approximately a third of a century the Holy Alliance provided the coercive force and the ideological impetus for an active peace policy; its armies were roaming up and down Europe putting down minorities and repressing majorities. From 1846 to about 1871 — " one of the most confused and crowded quarter centuries of European history " — peace was less safely established, the ebbing strength of reaction meeting the growing strength of industrialism. In the quarter century following the Franco-Prussian War we find the revived peace interest represented by that new powerful entity, the Concert of Europe.

Interests, however, like intents, necessarily remain platonic unless they are translated into politics by the means of some social instrumentality. Superficially, such a vehicle of realization was lacking; both the Holy Alliance and the Concert of Europe were, ultimately, mere groupings of independent sovereign states, and thus subject to the balance of power and its mechanism of war. How then was peace maintained?

True, any balance-of-power system will tend to prevent such wars as spring from one nation's failure to foresee the realignment of powers which will result from its attempt to alter the *status quo*. Famous instances were Bismarck's calling off of the press campaign against France, in 1875, on Russian and British intervention (Austria's aid to France was taken for granted). This time the Concert of Europe worked against Germany who found herself isolated. In 1877–78 Germany was unable to prevent a Russo-Turkish War, but succeeded in localizing it by backing up England's jealousy of a Russian move towards the Dardanelles; Germany and England supported Turkey against Russia — thus saving the peace. At the Congress of Berlin a long-term plan for the liquidation of the European possessions of the Ottoman Empire was launched; this resulted in averting wars between the Great Powers in spite of all subsequent changes in the *status quo,* as the parties concerned could be practically certain in advance of the forces they would have to meet in battle. Peace in these instances was a welcome by-product of the balance-of-power system.

Also, wars were sometimes avoided by deliberately removing their causes, if the fate of small powers only was involved. Small nations were checked and pervented from disturbing the *status quo* in any way which might precipitate war. The Dutch invasion of Belgium in 1831 eventually led to the neutralization of that country. In 1855 Norway was neutralized. In 1867 Luxembourg was sold by Holland to France; Germany protested and Luxembourg was neutralized. In 1856 the integrity of the Ottoman Empire was declared essential to the equilibrium of Europe, and the Concert of Europe endeavored to maintain that empire; after 1878, when its disintegration was deemed essential to that equilibrium, its dismemberment was provided for in a similarly orderly manner, though in both cases the decision meant life and death to several small peoples. Between 1852 and 1863 Denmark, between 1851 and 1856 the Germanies threatened to disturb the balance; each time the small states were forced by the Great Powers to conform. In these instances, the liberty of action offered to them by the system was used by the Powers to achieve a joint interest — which happened to be peace.

But it is a far cry from the occasional averting of wars either by a timely clarification of the power situation or by the coercing of small states to the massive fact of the Hundred Years' Peace. International disequilibrium may occur for innumerable reasons — from a dynastic love affair to the silting of an estuary, from a theological controversy to a technological invention. The mere growth of wealth and population, or, eventually, their decrease, is bound to set political forces in motion; and the external balance will invariably reflect the internal. Even an organized balance-of-power system can ensure peace without the permanent threat of war only if it is able to act upon these internal factors directly and prevent imbalance *in statu nascendi*. Once the imbalance has gathered momentum only force can set it right. It is a commonplace that to insure peace one must eliminate the causes of war; but it is not generally realized that to do so the flow of life must be controlled at its source.

The Holy Alliance contrived to achieve this with the help of instruments peculiar to it. The kings and aristocracies of Europe formed an international of kinship; and the Roman Church provided them with a voluntary civil service ranging from the highest to the lowest rung of the social ladder in Southern and Central Europe. The hierarchies of blood and grace were fused into an instrument of locally effective rule which needed only to be supplemented by force to ensure continental peace.

But the Concert of Europe, which succeeded it, lacked the feudal as well as the clerical tentacles; it amounted at the best to a loose federation not comparable in coherence to Metternich's masterpiece. Only on rare occasions could a meeting of the Powers be called, and their jealousies allowed a wide latitude to intrigue, crosscurrents, and diplomatic sabotage; joint military action became rare. And yet what the Holy Alliance, with its complete unity of thought and purpose, could achieve in Europe only with the help of frequent armed interventions was here accomplished on a world scale by the shadowy entity called the Concert of Europe with the help of a very much less frequent and oppressive use of force.

73. The Rivalry of Nations*

If we study the history of American foreign relations during the past forty years, we must be struck by an extraordinary paradox. During this period the United States has emerged from its long isolation. It has become one of the leading powers of the world. Not once but twice during this period the American people have had to face the awful issues of war and peace. Can it be said that during this momentous period we have ever succeeded in forming and agreeing on a foreign policy which foresaw correctly and enabled us to deal successfully with the actual course of events? The record is, I think, clear. We have won both wars. But on the crucial issues our diplomacy has thus far always miscarried. It has been unable to prevent war. It has been unable to avoid war. It has not prepared us for war. It has not been able to settle the wars when they have been fought and won.

At no critical phase in this epoch

* From Walter Lippmann, *The Atlantic Monthly*, CLXXI (1948), pp. 17–20. Copyright 1948 by The Atlantic Monthly Company. Reprinted by permission of Walter Lippmann and The Atlantic Monthly Company.

has the actual outcome conformed with our declarations and our expectations. Never has the country been able to achieve any of the principal objectives to which again and again it has been so solemnly and fervently committed.

Thus from 1914 to 1917 the country believed and hoped that it could avoid participation in the First World War. Yet it was compelled to participate. And when it did participate, it was unprepared because it had believed that it would not have to participate. During that war the country hoped and believed that by a victory it would achieve a lasting and democratic peace. The victory was attained. But the peace which had been promised was not achieved. After the First World War the country again believed that if there were another war, it would be able to remain out of it. Again it did not prepare for war. Once again it was unable to remain out of the war when it came.

During the Second World War the country again believed that with victory over the Germans there would begin an era in which all the victorious powers would agree and be harmonious and become unanimous on the terms and conditions of a just and durable peace. We have had the victory. But we have not been able to attain that peace.

Now, after two victorious world wars we find ourselves discussing the possibility of a third world war. And so we must ask ourselves whether we have become entangled in a degenerating cycle of wars that breed more wars, each more savage and more inconclusive than the last. It is a grim question. We must, however, face it; and I believe that we must answer it by saying that if our present estimates and calculations are no more correct than those on which we acted before, during, and immediately after the First and Second World Wars, then we shall be surprised and disappointed again. Once more we shall not know how to prevent war, or how to prepare for it correctly, or how, assuming we win it, to make peace after it. And if a second world war leads to the third — because we cannot make a settlement of the war we have just won — what ground is there to suppose that we could settle a third world war so that it did not lead to a fourth?

Is it not true that in the twentieth century we have witnessed on the one hand the rise of the United States to pre-eminence among the nations, to a position of great leadership and immense responsibility in shaping the destiny of mankind? And on the other hand, is it not also true that the course of events during the American rise to pre-eminence is strewn with the debris and wreckage of high and hopeful declarations of policy: with Wilson's neutrality, Wilson's Fourteen Points, and the Covenant of the League of Nations; with the Washington treaties of disarmament and the Kellogg Pact to outlaw war; with the Dawes Plan, the Young Plan, and the Hoover Moratorium to reconstruct the world after the First World War; with the Stimson doctrine to prevent aggression; with the Neutrality Act before the Second World War; with the quarantine speech of Franklin Roosevelt, and the Four Freedoms, and Hull's Seventeen Points, and the Atlantic Charter, and the Yalta Declaration, and the Truman Doctrine?

When we reflect on this series of declarations and the disappointments which followed them all, we must be struck by the contrast between our capacity as a people to develop national power, and our ability to use it and to manage it successfully. And is it not plain that our failures lie in the field of policy — that is to say, in deciding correctly when, where, how, and to what ends we shall exert the enormous power and influence which we are able to generate?

It cannot be argued that the miscarriages of American diplomacy during the past forty years are due to the weakness of the American nation. Among the powers of the world the United States is the least vulnerable to invasion, to blockade, or, with existing weapons, to decisive assault. The United States has the material resources and it has the productive capacity to develop enormous offensive power in time of war.

In time of peace it produces a great export surplus — a surplus above and beyond a high standard of life at home — which renders it economically invulnerable in the outer world. Two great wars have proved the valor of American troops, the fortitude of the American people, and the military competence of American military commanders. Our institutions and our traditions are respected. And on the whole our participation in world affairs is welcomed by the great masses of mankind as promising liberty, justice, peace, and plenty.

We must seek the cause of our diplomatic failures, therefore, in our own minds. We must look for the cause of trouble not in material circumstances but in our own habits of thought when we are dealing with foreign affairs and with the formation of American policy. In the period from Woodrow Wilson to Harry S. Truman our foreign policy has miscarried so regularly because there has been interposed within our own minds, between the outer world and ourselves, a collection of stereotyped prejudices and sacred cows and wishful conceptions, which misrepresent the nature of things, which falsify our judgments of events, and which inhibit the formation of workable policies by which our available means can be devoted efficiently to realizable ends.

We have brought along with us from our age of innocence, from the nineteenth century when we were isolated and when we were sheltered from the rivalries of states and empires, an ideological picture of the world, a philosophical framework of preconceptions. We think this picture of the world is real and noble. In fact it is imaginary and false. And because our philosophy of the nature of international life is imaginary and false our efforts to play an effective part in world affairs are frustrated.

II

What then is it in our philosophy which, instead of guiding us, misguides us continually? I think that the question can be answered. The point, as I have already indicated, where our declarations of policy have regularly miscarried is in avoiding war, in preparing for war, and in settling wars. We must ask ourselves whether there is here some common factor of error which confuses all of us on the issues of war and peace. I think there is. I think the error is a refusal to recognize, to admit, to take as the premise of our thinking, the fact that rivalry and strife and conflict among states, communities and factions are the normal condition of mankind. The popular American philosophy of international life refuses to recognize this fact. It denies that in the world as it is, the struggle for existence is fundamental and in the nature of things. This, I believe, is the philosophical error which prevents us from forming an effective foreign policy.

In the American ideology the struggle for existence, and the rivalry of nations for advantages, are held to be wrong, abnormal, and transitory. Our foreign policy throughout this period has been dominated by the belief that the struggle does not exist, or that it can be avoided, or that it can be abolished. Because of this belief our aim has not been to regulate and to moderate and to compose the conflicts and the issues, to check and to balance the contending forces. Our aim has been either to abstain from the struggle, or to abolish the struggle immediately, or to conduct crusades against those nations that most actively continue the struggle.

Yet in the world as it actually is, the struggle is not abnormal, and it is perpetually renewed. Twice during this period we have sought to abstain from the struggle by declaring our neutrality. We have not been able to stay out of it. Twice we have conducted victorious crusades against the chief troublemaker, believing what was soon disproved by events: that if he could be eliminated, we would then have eliminated all troublemakers. Twice we have sought, by forming universal societies like the League of Nations and the United Nations, to abolish the struggle. They have not abolished the struggle.

Our refusal to recognize the struggle for existence as the normal state of mankind in international affairs has resulted in the repeated miscarriage of American policies. Our efforts to deal with events, as if they conformed or could be made to conform with our ideological picture of what they ought to be, has been rather like using a map of Utopia to find your way around New York City.

The American refusal to recognize the struggle for existence has in this century crystallized in three recognizable patterns of conduct: in a neutrality which assumes that the struggle can be ignored and avoided; in crusades that assume that by defeating the chief troublemaker the struggle for existence will end; in the sponsorship of a universal society which assumes that the struggle can be abolished.

Since 1914 American relations with the outer world have oscillated among these three patterns of conduct. The great debates within this country have turned upon them. But the experience of these forty years shows conclusively, I think, that if we insist on treating the conflict of states, communities, and factions as abnormal, as exceptional, as transitory, we are unable to form an efficient foreign policy. Our American ideology, which we have brought over from a time when we did not have to play a responsible part among the powers of the earth, distorts our judgment when we deal with the problems of power. It distorts our judgment when we have to calculate how a balance can be struck between our aims and our power to realize them.

In practical judgments — and diplomacy, when the stakes are life and death, calls for very practical judgments — the criteria are always relative. There is no such thing as absolute power. Whatever the wealth, the power, and the prestige of a nation may be, its means are always limited. The problem of the maker of policy is to select objectives that are limited — not the best that could be desired but the best that can be realized without committing the whole power and the whole wealth and the very existence of the nation.

But if we examine the issues of foreign policy as they are presented to our people, we find an overwhelming disposition to regard the choices before us not as relative but as absolute. We are disposed to think that the issue is either this or that, either all or nothing, either isolationism or globalism, either total peace or total war, either one world or no world, either disarmament or absolute weapons, either pious resolutions or atomic bombs, either disarmament or military supremacy, either nonintervention or a crusade, either democracy or tyranny, either the abolition of war or a preventive war, either appeasement or unconditional surrender, either nonresistance or a strategy of annihilation.

There is no place in this ideological pattern of the world for the adoption of limited ends or limited means, for the use of checks and balances among contending forces, for the demarcation of spheres of influence and of power and of interest, for accommodation and compromise and adjustment, for the stabilization of the status quo, for the restoration of an equilibrium. Yet this is the field of diplomacy. These are the substance and the matter of an efficient diplomacy.

Our ideologists, however, regard the use of power to achieve and maintain an equilibrium of power as "power politics." And they regard the recognition of spheres of influence as "appeasement." Yet in the absence of a world state, and ex-

cept in a world dominated by one supreme power, there must be an equilibrium among several powers and a recognition of their spheres of influence. A diplomacy for the world as it is, which is not to expend itself in verbal declarations on the one hand, and on crusades of annihilation on the other, must deal with the balance of power and the determination of spheres of influence.

But under the spell of our ideological picture of the world, we exclude from our minds the very subject matter of diplomacy itself. We would exclude it, we would outlaw it, and we would excommunicate those who discuss it. We insist on treating the rivalry of nations as something that could not exist among right-thinking men. We do not regulate the rivalries because we hold that the rivalries ought not to exist. And so we are left with our three patterns of policy: to ignore the rivalries by proclaiming our neutrality, or to deny the rivalry and to believe it will disappear if the nations are members of a universal society, or to conduct crusades of annihilation against the lions who do not wish to lie down with the lambs.

III

How does what I have been saying bear upon the subject which preoccupies us all so anxiously and so profoundly — upon our relations with the Soviet Union, with which we are now engaged in a world-wide diplomatic conflict?

The beginning of wisdom on the Russian question is, I believe, to recognize the historic fact that the division between eastern and western Europe, the rivalry between Russia and the nations of the West, did not begin with Marx, Lenin, and Stalin, nor would it end if the Soviet regime were overthrown or defeated. The cultural and ideological division of Europe is as old as the division of Christendom between Rome and Byzantium. The imperial rivalry with Russia in the Baltic, in eastern and central Europe, in the Danube valley, in the Balkans, in the Middle East, and in the Far East did not begin with the Communists and will not end with Communism. It was one of the great fields of diplomacy under the Czars as it is under the Communists. Rivalry with Russia is a new problem for the United States. But the British Foreign Office has been preoccupied with it for a hundred and fifty years. We had better make up our minds that we shall now be preoccupied with it for a very long time to come.

That being the case, we must give up the notion that the choice is between one world, in which the Russians are our partners, and two worlds, in which we must annihilate the Russians or they must annihilate us. I do not believe that we must either marry the Russians or must fight them, that we must have either a perfect peace or a total war. I believe that the best policy is to recognize that the rivalry will remain, and not to expect it to disappear, and not to think it could be abolished by the United Nations, and not to think it could be abolished by a victorious war; and having recognized that the rivalry is a permanent fact, to use our whole power and influence to regulate it, to keep it within bounds, to establish spheres of influence which limit the rivalry, and a balance of power in the world which checks it.

I do not believe that we can settle the Russian problem once and for all. I do believe we have enough power and influence, if we use them efficiently, to bring about a settlement with Russia in this generation. But it will have to be a settlement which aims not at unanimity, not at ideological harmony, not at the abolition of all our differences and disagreements, but at a truce in the cold war, a *modus vivendi* during which the nations can recover from World War II, at treaties which end in the withdrawal of the armies of occupation in Europe, and the restoration of Europe to the Europeans.

This will not be easy to achieve. It will require the pressure of power — which will offend those among us who do not like power politics. It will require political and economic compromises — which will offend those who regard all compromise as appeasement. But if a truce, and a *modus vivendi*, and a treaty are hard to achieve by power and by compromise, it is certain that without power on the one hand, and compromise on the other, nothing can be achieved.

If we will not or cannot use the classic procedure of diplomacy — which is always a combination of power and compromise — then the best we can look forward to is an era of disintegration in the civilized world, followed perhaps by a war which, once it began, would be savage, universal, and indecisive.

That must not happen. And it need not happen if only our people will abjure their illusions about the nature of the world in which they have so recently become a leading power, and will permit and assist those who must form our policy, to go forward on the assumption that our aim is not to marry the Russians and then to live with them happily ever after, nor to fight them and let the whole world be devastated. Our aim is to transact our necessary business with the Russians, at arm's length, coolly, shrewdly, without fear and without extravagant hope, and with as much justice as may be possible where there is as yet no agreement on first principles and where the rivals do not live in the same moral order.

74. American Conservatism and the World Crisis: A Study in Vacillation*

American conservatism has been particularly inept in dealing with the foreign policy issues which confront our nation. These issues would have been difficult for the nation even if American conservatism had not made confusion worse confounded, for we have had world leadership thrust upon us very suddenly, with little opportunity to accustom ourselves to its vexing problems. We are, moreover, a paradise of plenty suspended in a hell of global insecurity, and our good fortune makes it difficult either to understand the needy world in which we have gained so precarious an eminence or to achieve the hardness of discipline required for the exercise of our leadership. But all these difficulties have been accentuated by the fact that American conserva-

* From Reinhold Niebuhr, The Yale Review, XL (1951), pp. 385–99. Copyright 1951 by Yale University Press. Reprinted by permission of Reinhold Niebuhr and The Yale Review.

tism is bereft of the resources of wisdom and imagination in foreign policy which are the rightful boast of traditional conservatism in the Western European tradition.

The superiority of traditional conservatism in foreign policy was not a moral superiority. Indeed, conservatism was usually uncritically nationalistic and imperialistic. It did, however, have the one advantage of clearly recognizing the complexities of power in political struggles. This is particularly important in foreign affairs, because the international community is unorganized or only partly organized; and the contests of power, which are an element of the social life of the human community on every level, are therefore more violent and naked on the international level. The realism of conservatism in the past may have been merely the achievement of men who actually wielded power, though they may have wielded it with little sense of justice.

Liberalism, on the other hand, was informed by a high sense of justice but had little understanding of the power which was required to attain just ends. The liberal creed was avowed either by idealists who had no experience with power or by the new economic overlords of society who wielded a form of power so covert that it betrayed them into sentimental illusions. Thus, in an earlier period, Disraeli was shrewder than Gladstone in the field of foreign relations, and Theodore Roosevelt's understanding of foreign affairs was certainly superior to that of William Jennings Bryan. More recently, when Britain was plunged into its deepest crisis, it had to supplant Neville Chamberlain, typical exponent of the business creed, with Winston Churchill, who was deeply rooted in the conservative tradition. Chamberlain thought that foreign policy was merely an extension of the field of commercial transactions of which Manchester is the perfect English symbol. He thought Hitler must have a price which reasonable men could pay. He could not understand the demonic fury in the Nazi movement. Incidentally, Churchill was helped to power by the Labor Party, though it had its own sad record of unrealism in foreign policy, having tried as late as April, 1939, to prevent conscription in Britain, to the consternation of France, which needed the assurance of British divisions then as surely as Europe needs the assurance of American divisions now.

This lack of realism on the left was also evident in the socialist movements of Scandinavia, which took pride in their disarmament policies but failed to recognize that their peace and security were parasitic on the British Navy. Yet this socialist illusionism was not very different from the thoroughly bourgeois politics of calculation which persuaded the Dutch that a meticulous neutrality might beguile Hitler from the threat to overrun Holland.

These distinctions between conservatism and liberalism in Europe have at times seemed to apply in America as well, and certainly American liberalism has revealed many defects arising from lack of realism. It generated a sentimental isolationism which did not scorn to make common cause with the cynical isolationism of the reactionaries. It talked glibly of defeating Hitler by the power of our superior democracy but had no answer to the challenge of Hitler's guns. There are still liberals who, even when they are not touched by Communist sympathies, think it possible and desirable to come to terms with Stalin. They do not understand the power elements involved in either a trade union or an international bargaining procedure. They are therefore oblivious to the futility of an immediate accord with a movement which is still " rolling " as successfully as the Communist movement and which would certainly ask as high a price of us for an accord at the present moment as Hitler asked of Chamberlain at Munich.

But whatever the weaknesses of

American liberalism in the understanding of foreign policy, it has nevertheless produced in Wilson and Roosevelt the two great architects of a responsible foreign policy, and has guided our nation in assuming responsibilities proportioned to its power in the world community. These achievements of American liberalism seemed for a time to be due primarily to chance personal factors — the vision of Woodrow Wilson and the political shrewdness of Franklin Roosevelt, who had the confidence of the liberal world sufficiently on domestic issues to be able to beguile it from its illusions concerning the hard realities of international relations. But now Roosevelt has passed from the scene; and yet a President who is not a political genius has managed to achieve a fairly consistent foreign policy that does some justice to the vast responsibilities which our power implies and is cognizant of the hazards of our age. The mistakes which have been made have frequently been forced upon the present Administration by pressure from a hysterical conservatism. In short, the liberalism of this generation, although unrealistic in some phases, has displayed in other phases a surprising capacity to grapple with brutal realities.

When one turns to examine the role of conservatism in American foreign policy, the distinctive trait appears to be a curious ambivalence between isolationism and imperialism, between a disavowal of the responsibilities of our power and an exercise of that power without a sense of its limits.

In the days of the "interventionist" debate before World War II isolationism and neutralism were drawn primarily from the conservative sector of the population. Sometimes isolationism was prompted by fear of the cost of war, thus refuting the Marxist theory that our "capitalists" drive us into war in order to gain profits. Sometimes it was informed by serious miscalculations of the breadth and the depth of the danger which we faced. In other cases it was informed by a simple parochialism arising in a vast economy so nearly self-sufficing that it had learned little of the outside world.

Perhaps it should be noted that some isolationism was derived from a certain tolerance in the conservative community for the Nazi creed. But this could not have been very powerful, for ultimately American conservatism shared unreservedly in the fight against Nazism. Today it is violently anti-Communist, but the violence of its anti-Communism has been little help to us. The conservative community thinks that it has uttered the final condemnation of Communism when it equates Communism with Nazism, thereby obscuring the fact that Communism is more dangerous than Nazism. For Communism is the corruption of a dream of justice (an inevitable and not a fortuitous corruption), and that dream is a source of political power to Communism, particularly in the Orient. And the violence of the conservatives' anti-Communism imparts to our reactions to world events a kind of apoplectic quality which militates against a shrewd calculation of possibilities. The hysteria of American conservatism is making it almost impossible to analyze the attractive power of Communism, not only in Asia but in such nations as France and Italy, and equally difficult to state the political and economic program which will eliminate the social conditions and resentments that are exploited by Communism.

But whatever its motivation, conservatism very nearly pursued isolation to the extreme of self-destruction. The Republican opposition to Roosevelt came within one vote of destroying our inchoate army before World War II. It fought the Lend-Lease Plan, which was probably Roosevelt's most imaginative contribution to Allied victory, since it saved our Allies from collapse before we entered the conflict. During the war it frequently endangered a well-conceived global strategy by seeking to subordinate the European to the Asiatic struggle before the time was ripe. Since the conclusion of the war it has been hesitant to support the Economic Recovery Program in Europe, by which the Communist tide has been stemmed. Most recently, it thought that a complete prohibition of East-West trade in Europe was a smart idea, though it is easy to prove that the health of Western Europe requires as much of such trade as is compatible with strategic necessities.

Isolationism was, however, but one aspect of the conservative reaction to world events a decade ago. Another portion of conservatives, once we were in the conflict (or perhaps it was the same portion after we had got in), insisted that the real strategic center of the conflict was Asia, rather than Europe. This special concern for Asia in conservative circles is something of a mystery. It must be noted that the pattern is repeating itself in this decade. Whatever lies behind it, it reveals an obvious lack of imagination in weighing the strategic factors on a world scale. One reason for this error is surely a tendency to measure our power too purely in terms of our military strength. This military strength is drawn from our economic power, so directly that it can be measured with logistic exactitude. But, of course, the power of a nation or of an alliance of nations consists of other factors than its military strength. The insistence, in the past decade, that Asia was the strategic center of the struggle failed to measure the technical military superiority of Germany over Japan. But it also failed to gauge the moral and political considerations which made Europe the center of the struggle.

Thus American conservatism, insofar as it has been isolationist, has shrunk from the overt application of power, and, insofar as it has conceived of intervention in purely military terms, has conceived of power in terms that are misleadingly simple. The one historic ability of traditional conservatism — its realistic understanding of the nature and application of power — has been conspicuously absent in both of the leading manifestations of American conservatism.

The conservative errors in foreign policy are so consistent in their inconsistencies and so manifestly based upon mistaken conceptions of the breadth and the depth of our historical crisis that they cannot be attributed to the vagaries of this or that statesman. Even if Senator Taft were more imaginative in foreign policy, the fact would still remain that American conservatism is singularly inept on foreign issues and that it is bereft of the virtues which were once the peculiar possession of Western conservatism. There must be a more profound cause for these weaknesses than the inadequacies of any particular politician.

Perhaps the answer to this question of the cause of the political incompetence of American conservatism can be most simply supplied by one sweeping generalization: American conservatism is not the traditional conservatism of Western political history. That conservatism was rooted in the aristocratic tradition; American conservatism is a decayed form of nineteenth-century "liberalism." It is the creed of the business community. This community was "liberal" in its historic contest with feudalism. It enlarged many liberties and opposed many traditional injustices. But in America the business community developed in a middle-class paradise without the background of an aristocratic past and therefore without the qualifications which the aristocratic tradition introduced into British politics, for instance. American conservatism is related to the liberalism of the nineteenth century as Herbert Hoover's book entitled "The Challenge to Liberty" is related to John Stuart

Mill's book "On Liberty." It has a common emphasis upon "liberty." But liberty for nineteenth-century liberals was a genuine passion. In our day "liberty" tends to become the ideological façade behind which men of great economic power seek to preserve their freedom against a more broadly-based political power and seek to arrest the one process by which modern democracies have achieved a measure of health and refuted the Marxist predictions of their doom.

American conservatism is thus an ossified form of liberalism. It lacks the virtues in domestic politics which the original liberalism had. But it preserves the vices of traditional liberalism in foreign policy.

Much of the weakness of original liberalism came as a result of the fact that original liberalism was identified with the business community and ever since has been colored by the business community's views. Such a community predicates its operation upon the containment of the various egoistic drives, individual and collective, within the nicely circumscribed balances of a competitive market. In this realm, life is neither noble, tragic, nor demonic, and the purposes of life are never incalculable. Realists in this world readily assume the force of human selfishness, but they also believe that it is confined to the desire for gain. Hence they are oblivious to the dynamic of the idolatrous political religions of our day, whether Nazi or Communist. The idealists of the same world find its chief moral glory in the fact that it repudiates the overt use of force — of which bourgeois culture has a horror — but they do not comprehend the endless complexities of power and the covert forms of force in a human community. Economic power — as distinguished from political and military power — is, in fact, so lacking in the symbols of force that it is easy to describe its operation in purely moral terms, and to hide, either sentimentally or hypocritically, the power elements in economic competition.

Actually the powers which are in cooperation and conflict in the human community are compounded of ethnic loyalties, common traditions, ancient sanctities, common fears, common hopes, and endless other combinations of human motives. The Western " Tory " tradition understands them, simply because it has manipulated them for generations. The business community has never fully understood them. In the Anglo-Saxon tradition the thought of Edmund Burke best summarizes this understanding, and his " Reflections on the French Revolution " represents a perfect refutation of the illusions to which a pure bourgeois rationalism is subject.

But American conservatism is not informed by this tradition. Instead, it is rooted in the business community and shares that community's lack of understanding of the complexities of international power. Therefore it displays a curious ambivalence between isolationism and imperialism, between sentimentality and cynicism. In one moment it is ready to discount all the perils in which we stand and to counsel the nation to " cut its losses " lest further involvement in world responsibilities increase our tax rate. In the next moment it is ready to use our economic power to force European nations into " free enterprise " patterns after our image, however irrelevant these patterns may be to the necessities of poverty-stricken nations.

Our conservatives are ready, moreover, to use our economically-based military power in Asia in such a way as to make our struggle with Communism appear a purely military venture, thus alienating such vast uncommitted Asiatic nations as India. In its sentimental moments it regards our high living standards as a validation of our " way of life " to the poor peoples of Asia. In its cynical moments it thinks we could solve the Asiatic problem if only we showed the Asians " what's what " by putting the Chinese Nationalist government back in power. The vast social convulsions of a continent in travail are such a mystery to this type of mind that even the most catastrophic upheavals are attributed to mistakes made in our State Department.

This defect of American conservatism is now manifesting itself again in almost frightening patterns of recurrence. The conservatives tell us that we will lose Europe if we lose Asia, though it is obvious that for both technical and moral-and-political reasons we cannot afford to have Communism inundate Europe, and that we run such a danger if we are too deeply involved in Asia. We are confronted again with the same ambivalence of the conservatives between a tendency to disavow the responsibilities of our power and another tendency to overestimate the degree of our moral authority in both Europe and Asia, but especially in Asia.

The impingement of American power upon Asiatic life without adequate comprehension in America of the vast complexities of Asiatic politics is one of the most frightening aspects of the present international situation. We refuse to believe that Asia is, in a sense, an uncommitted continent, and we do not know what to do about its indecision. Actually, Asians, even when anti-Communist, have little admiration for our cause. The fact is that Communism, designed for the industrial proletariat of the Western world, failed in the healthy Western nations, but has found fertile fields for its seed among the landless poor in decaying agrarian economies, particularly in Asia. Even when Asians understand the perils of Communism they are not particularly attracted by the ideals of a libertarian democracy.

But American conservatism, oblivious to all these complex elements in the situation, continues egocentrically to conceive of the disintegration of the Chinese Nationalist government as nothing more than the consequence of our failure to give this government adequate military support. Conservatives think even now that an adequate military assistance program would give the pathetic Chinese politicians who have taken refuge in Formosa a chance to master the Chinese nation. Having been reluctant to exploit the political and economic alternatives to a general war in Europe, they are not reluctant to involve us in vast military ventures in Asia. They have made it difficult for us to align ourselves with the legitimate national aspirations of colonial peoples and have helped the Communists to exploit nationalism in Asia for their own ends.

This ambivalence in conservative foreign policy between isolationism and imperialism, between the disavowal of the responsibilities of our power and the assertion of our power beyond our moral resources, has been perfectly illustrated in the debates of recent weeks and months. Mr. Hoover would make America a Gibraltar of democracy, including in our system of defense only peripheral islands like Japan and Britain, should Britain desire to flee to our bosom from the hazards of continental insecurity. This suggestion has naturally aroused deep apprehensions in Europe, for it means that we turn our back on the growing "Atlantic community." Though this community has grown into a political reality under the pressures of contemporary history, it has always been a spiritual community, for it embodies what we know as the traditions of "Western civilization." The only real communities are those which grow upon the foundation of common traditions, tasks, hopes, and fears. For these imponderables American conservative theory has little understanding. It moves quickly from economic to military calculations, leaving as a *terra incognita* the vast realm of political and spiritual realities which constitute the main stuff of man's common life.

At the other end of the scale in American conservatism is the theory best expressed in the opinions of Senator Knowland and symbolized in General MacArthur. It would counter communist pressure in Asia by a series of military ventures, including the arming of the Chinese Nationalists, the bombing of Manchuria, and all manner of strategies between the concepts of limited and unlimited war in Asia. This policy overestimates our moral resources in Asia as seriously as the Hoover policy underestimates our moral and spiritual affinities with Europe. The theory tends to reduce the struggle in Asia to purely military proportions. Actually Asia is in the throes of vast social convulsions due to the disintegration of the old colonialism, the impact of Western technology upon its agrarian economy, the resentment of a colored continent against the white man's arrogance, and, one may add, its lack of resources, spiritual as well as economic, for what we know as democracy. Our lack of moral authority in Asia means that when we use military power there we diminish, rather than augment, our moral and political authority. Military power without a moral base is always intolerable. Nor can we cover our moral nakedness by alliance with such regimes as that of Chiang Kai-shek. The reactions of the whole of India to such proposals are instructive.

Incidentally, liberal theory is almost as mistaken on Asia as conservative theory. For it reiterates monotonously that we must support the "democratic" forces of Asia instead of supporting Bao Dai, Chiang Kai-shek, and Syngman Rhee. It does not observe that there are no organized "democratic" forces in Asia. Perhaps the government of India is such a force, but that government has not yet proved that it can move creatively against the decaying feudal-agrarianism of India with sufficient speed to prevent a rapid expansion of Communism. This is also true of the government of the Philippines, which is supposed to be the beneficiary of our superior tutelage in the ways of democracy.

In this vast confusion of abject poverty and racial and political resentments, the "American way of life" is not the beacon light of truth that we imagine it to be. The American way of life has two connotations, both of which seem irrelevant to Asia. It means a high standard of living, which may excite the envy or prompt the scorn of Asia, but will not arouse its admiration; and it means a libertarian political theory that has little meaning on a continent on which an agrarian economy and pantheistic culture have united to prevent the emergence of the individual as the West knows the individual.

The fact that American conservatism can produce two contradictory political theories, one of which obscures the political complexities of Asia and overestimates our moral authority there, while the other counsels treason against the Atlantic community, is explicable only if we recognize that both policies are derived from the inability of American conservatism to recognize the political and moral forces which lie between the economic and the military dimensions of our collective life.

Perhaps we have been saved from the errors of American conservative policy by the very fact that it does produce contradictory theories. At the moment the policies of Mr. Hoover on the one hand and of Senator Knowland on the other neutralize each other, though each of them has done considerable harm to American prestige in both Europe and Asia. Nor has Senator Taft's effort to strike a balance between them by confining the exercise of American power primarily to the sea and the air done much to produce a reconciliation.

But it is more important to recognize that America's position in the world community has been established primarily by a political force which challenged the business community in domestic policy and which also elaborated a theory of American responsibility in foreign affairs. This political movement had its inception in Woodrow Wilson's Administration and reached its highest point in the Administration of Franklin Roosevelt.

The Wilson Administration established America's recognition of the responsibilities of its constantly increasing power. There were some vestigial " liberal " illusions in Wilson's approach to foreign policy. His type of idealism was hardly a match for Clemenceau's cynical realism or Lloyd George's shifty opportunism. Nevertheless, he did set America upon a new course. Or rather he would have done so, had not American conservatism succeeded in undoing what he had accomplished in organizing the League of Nations. We do not have to adopt the theory that the League would have succeeded had our nation remained loyal to it in order to appreciate the significance of the resurgence of national irresponsibility which our rejection of the League revealed. The neutralism which subsequently engulfed the nation, the almost psychotic fear of further commitments, the effort to attribute the peril of war to munition manufacturers (as in the Nye investigation), our frantic neutrality laws in which we tried to play the part of King Canute and cry " Back tides " to the vast forces of modern history, all these phenomena were too widespread to allow us to attribute them to American conservatism alone.

A balanced view of the relative effectiveness of liberal and conservative policies must recognize that not all conservatives fall within the pattern suggested here. The intelligent wing of conservatism, as symbolized, for instance, by Henry L. Stimson and Senator Vandenberg, has made important contributions. Some of the irresponsibility of conservative action is, moreover, the irresponsibility of a party in opposition rather than the irresponsibility of conservatism as such. Even Mr. Churchill has indulged in irresponsible utterances since he is free of the sobering influence of actual power. But the mistakes which American conservatism persists in making today are more than could be ascribed to the mere temptations of a party not in power.

The hysteria symbolized by the name of Senator McCarthy is a case in point. This hysteria satisfied a deep craving in the American heart to reduce the vast menace of a world-wide Communist movement to manageable proportions. If it could be made to appear that the danger is a local conspiracy, rather than a global movement that threatens us not simply by military force but by arraying a whole world against the remnants of what we know as Western civilization, we could then come to terms with it by the arts of prosecutor and politician, which we have mastered. The tolerance of the Republican high command towards the aberrations expressed in this sortie may well have been prompted by its own miscalculation of the actual perils we face in the world.

A balanced view must also recognize that the miscalculations and errors of our foreign policy did not all originate in the conservative camp. Roosevelt, for instance, made the mistake of believing that Russian intransigence could be beguiled by hearty good fellowship. But it must be remembered that his attempts in this direction expressed the longing of a whole world. In an effort to avoid Woodrow Wilson's sentimental idealism, he sometimes fell into cynicism, as, for instance, in his conception of the policy of "unconditional surrender."

Nevertheless, his achievements were enormous, particularly when measured against those of his critics. He not only dealt with the vast intricacies of global politics with a shrewd understanding of the various imponderables, which his critics lacked; but he also managed to beguile the left-of-center political movement of America from its "liberal" illusions and to establish a political force in America which would insist on a course accepting our full responsibility to a nascent world community, while pursuing a moderately reformist course in domestic politics. To do this he had to win the labor movement over from an isolationism which was almost as pronounced as that of the business community and which was informed by the same parochialism. It may be worth recording that Roosevelt was a kind of "renegade" Hudson Valley aristocrat, the product of one of the very few vestigial aristocratic traditions in America. Whether that had anything to do with his political insights is a question which could be answered in the affirmative only by making very far-fetched generalizations. It is worth mentioning only because it seems so obvious that the ethos of a purely bourgeois community is not conducive to wisdom in foreign affairs.

In one sense, the mistakes of American conservatism are the mistakes of our total community. They must therefore be measured, and blame apportioned, without too much party animus. We are a great business nation, without a past reaching deeply into European history with all its stored political experience. We have come to power very rapidly and without such a period of apprenticeship as that in which other powerful nations gained imagination adequate for their tasks. Our authority in the world rests primarily upon our military might; and that derives directly from our technical power in a day when technical power is the very basis of military power. Culturally, we are a remnant of the ethos of the nineteenth century, called upon to manage a world in which neither Europe nor Asia, for different reasons, is deeply persuaded of the validity of our regnant ideas and ideals.

Furthermore, we have been accustomed for generations to a constant expansion of our opportunities and our powers. Now we have been suddenly thrust into an historic situation in which there is frustration and the contraction of possibilities. We have been called upon to assume a major responsibility in making decisions in a situation in which historical destiny is less subject to the mastery of human decsions than we had assumed. A part of our hysteria is caused by this frustration.

Our difficulties in foreign policy do not, therefore, derive merely from the errors of American conservatism. But these errors are great enough to prompt gratitude that the same conservatism which understood our world so little also misunderstood the American scene sufficiently to lose the chance to guide our national destinies in a perilous period.

In any event we will be undone if we do not constantly overcome the two temptations of nations in our situation. One is the temptation to flee from the responsibilities which are inherent in our power. There is no safety for us in such a flight, for our power diminishes at every point when irresponsibility prompts us to sacrifice friend or ally to a ruthless foe. Furthermore, we have gone too far, culturally, morally, and religiously, to find it tolerable to gain our security at the expense of a nascent community of free nations.

The other temptation is to overestimate the degree of our power, more particularly our moral authority, in the calculations of world politics. This is true not only with reference to our position in the more intimate circle of our allies and friends in the Western community. It is also true in our relations to a world of uncommitted, or only partly committed, nations, who fear aggression and are therefore prepared for a general defensive alliance. But they are not prepared to accept us as the arbiters of their destiny or as the guides of their political pilgrimage.

The first temptation assails us in moods of despair; the second in moments of desperation. It is no sign of weakness if even strong nations learn to measure the limits of their power and the contingent character of their moral values. This kind of humility is an absolute prerequisite for our leadership if we are to engage successfully the shrewd and calculating foe who confronts us, and if we are to prevent both the spread of Communism and the outbreak of an atomic war.

B. The Nature of Foreign Policy

75. Two Theories of Foreign Policy and Their Consequences

No single charge is leveled against the public policy of the United States so often as the claim that we have no foreign policy. The domestic political arena rings perennially with angry charges that this lack can be traced to the moral dereliction of a certain administration or the irresponsibility of one set or the other of political leaders. These attacks, whatever their merits at any given moment, are based upon a false picture of the true nature of foreign policy. The prevailing philosophy of twentieth century Western society has interpreted the conduct of foreign policy almost exclusively in psychological terms, the motives of an administration or a leader being viewed as the sole determinant of policy. This philosophy has maintained that a democratic government would pursue one foreign policy, an autocratic government another, a communist government a third, and a democratic-socialist administration still another. Foreign policy has been considered a function of the political system in operation or the preferences and convictions of political leaders who put it into effect.

There is a second philosophy of foreign policy which has at least as respectable a heritage. It prevailed during much of the eighteenth and

nineteenth centuries. Its influence in our own day has been revived by a handful of analysts and scholars, most notable among them Walter Lippmann and Hans J. Morgenthau. However, what slight influence this philosophy exerts today comes about not as a result of its acceptance but because of the utter inadequacy of the psychological philosophy in accounting for current international developments. That philosophy has been shaken and discredited by its own inner contradictions, as, for example, when asked to deal concretely with present day British foreign policy. Its underlying assumptions make it unable to account for the continuity of objectives in the foreign policy of the Conservative and Socialist governments. In practice it is obvious that the Labor government has sought to protect — in Western Europe, in the British Commonwealth countries, in the Iberian Peninsula, and in the Near and Middle East — substantially those same interests that Tories and Whigs considered vital over several centuries. Methods and techniques have changed, but interests and objectives are relatively constant.

It is only a second philosophy which does justice to this characteristic of foreign policy. It maintains that the objective requirements of the national interest place certain irremovable limits upon any statesman who seeks to formulate foreign policy. That is, there are certain strategic interests intimately bound up with a nation's geographic position and its international role which must be safeguarded if independence is to be preserved. Not only are these interests permanent, but in addition there is continuity in the approach of a nation's statesmen who stand watch over their country's security and whose conception of that security has been formed and molded by the same institutions and traditions. The national mind, which interprets the national interest, is itself a factor in the permanence of foreign policy. Out of the interplay of a durable international position with permanent traditions and institutions the larger nation-states have fashioned foreign policies which, in their broad outlines, have been consistently maintained over long periods of time.

If one accepts the second philosophy of foreign policy, two additional issues invite discussion. Not only are the interests of a nation permanent in character but they range themselves in a hierarchy of greater and lesser interests. In a classic statement, which was intended for guidance in the formulation of Belgium's foreign policy but which has relevance for all foreign policy, Monsieur Paul-Henri Spaak observed:

There must be a hierarchy in international obligations. The nations of a continent cannot reasonably be asked to consider with the same realism and sincerity of judgment affairs which directly concern them and events which are taking place thousands of kilometres away in regions where they have neither interests nor influence.

There are certain interests which must be defended at all costs; there are others which should be safeguarded under particular circumstances; and there are some which almost never can be defended. It is the task of foreign policy initially to decide what this hierarchy of interests is and subsequently to examine the scale of interests in the principles or practice of other nations' foreign policies. Even though nations forswear the actual formulation of their hierarchy of interests, in the hard tests of actual practice their most vital interests emerge.

Moreover, the determination of interests provides the basis for the ultimate task of foreign policy, namely the negotiating of a political settlement and demarcation of spheres of influence. There can be compromise for both sides on less vital interests once these have been uncovered. There can be no compromise on abstract moral or psychological principles. Therefore, the first philosophy breeds nations pursuing foreign policies which inevitably come into conflict with one another, nations which advance without retreating and nations which operate with scarcely any attention to the limits of their own power.

The consequences of the two philosophies of foreign policy have great moral significance the character of which is infrequently appreciated.

If it is accepted that a nation's foreign policy is merely the creation of a certain philosophy or psychology of a leader or group, then the policies of nations become either good and moral ones or evil and aggressive ones. If evil, they must be destroyed for they alone make peace impossible. Thus the psychological theory of foreign policy by its very nature heralds inevitable conflict as the outgrowth of crises impossible to resolve. The tragic results of strife and open conflict are deepened by the nature of warfare itself. In wars fought for moral principles, the struggle can be terminated only in total victory or total defeat. The temperate character of war in the eighteenth and nineteenth centuries was influenced by the philosophy of foreign policy which required that nations define their vital national interests. The absolute brutality of modern warfare, with indiscriminate bombing of whole towns and populations, is likewise in part the outcome of a philosophy — the legalistic-moralistic philosophy, with its emphasis upon moral and immoral foreign policies.

The moral issue is indeed present but its expression is radically different from the utopian schema. For the moral values and principles which are championed by nations in ambitious moral crusades are eventually destroyed if a nation seeks peace through imposing its political ethics on others. A nation pursuing such a foreign policy either avoids contacts with other nations lest its moral superiority be contaminated, as the United States did after World War I,

or it engages in a fanatical crusade to purge from the world that political philosophy which alone has occasioned warfare. In the first instance, by abstaining from the struggle for power it presides at the destruction of moral values inherent in the loss of independence for little countries whose survival is dependent primarily on the zeal of a Great Power in protecting its vital interests. The United States was not guiltless on this score in the period before World War II. The annihilation of the Weimar Republic and of Belgium was fraught with grave ethical consequences. American foreign policy by its transcendent moral isolation contributed to this tragedy.

Again, a nation aiming at the destruction of another nation and its philosophy, will expend its resources and manpower, irrespective of cost, to earn victory and unconditional surrender. But if the nation engaged in the total effort is truly the citadel of moral principles it is endangering and indeed destroying those values for which it purports to be fighting. For to win total victories nations must employ total resources and this is possible only in a garrison state. States organized and geared to so exhaustive an objective can tolerate no irregulars, and thus freedom and liberty are sacrificed to total victory. Therefore, a foreign policy of total objectives, which is the logical foreign policy under the psychological philosophy, is profoundly unethical and immoral in its consequences.

The final and most tragic paradox of foreign policy in our day is the justification of this philosophy in purely moral terms. The most profoundly immoral of all foreign policies in practice has prevailed because it alone has been identified with morality. And yet the traditional philosophy of foreign policy is the one truly moral outlook, for its adherents, through compromises on less vital interests, pay a price for peace. Or when war comes they seek to localize it in one area. Through political means and indeed through the balance of power the preservation of moral values is made possible.

The following essay by Professor Morgenthau is a brilliant example of the traditional way of thinking about foreign policy. In it, for virtually the first time in present-day literature, timeless principles of foreign policy in the West are applied concretely to historic periods in American foreign policy. The two subsequent essays deal with the foreign policies of other nations.

76. The Nature of Foreign Policy*

It is often said that the foreign policy of the United States is in need of maturing and that the American people and their government must grow up if they want to emerge victorious from the trials of our age. It would be truer to say that this generation of Americans must shed the illusions of their fathers and grandfathers and relearn the great principles of statecraft which guided the path of the republic in the first decade and — in moralistic disguise — in the first century of its existence. The United States offers the singular spectacle of a commonwealth whose political wisdom did not grow slowly through the accumulation and articulation of experiences. Quite to the contrary, the full flowering of its political wisdom was coeval with its birth as an independent nation — nay, it owed its existence and survival as an independent nation to those extraordinary qualities of political insight, historic perspective, and common sense which the first generation of Americans applied to the affairs of state.

The classic age of American statecraft comes to an end with the physical disappearance of that generation of American statesmen. The rich and varied landscape in which they had planted all that is worthwhile in the tradition of Western political thought was allowed to go to waste. It became a faint and baffling remembrance, a symbol to be worshipped rather than a source of inspiration and a guide for action. Until very recently the American people seemed to be content to live in a political desert whose intellectual barrenness and aridity were relieved only by some sparse and neg-

* From Hans J. Morgenthau, "The Mainsprings of Foreign Policy: The National Interest vs. Moral Abstractions," *The American Political Science Review*, XLIV (1950), pp. 833–54. Reprinted by permission of Hans J. Morgenthau and *The American Political Science Review*.

lected oases of insight and wisdom. What in that period, stretching over more than a century, went under the name of foreign policy was either improvisation in the face of an urgent problem which had to be dealt with somehow, or — and especially in our century — the invocation of some abstract moral principle in the image of which the world was to be made over. Improvisation as a substitute for foreign policy was largely successful, for in the past the margin of American and allied power to spare generally exceeded the degree to which American improvidence fell short of the demands of the hour. The invocation of abstract moral principles was in part hardly more than an innocuous pastime; for embracing everything it came to grips with nothing. In part, however, it was a magnificent instrument for marshalling public opinion in support of war and warlike policies — and for losing the peace to follow. The intoxication with moral abstractions which as a mass phenomenon started with the Spanish-American War, and which in our time has become the prevailing substitute for political thought, is indeed one of the great sources of weakness and failure in American foreign policy.

It is, however, worthy of note that underneath this political dilettantism, nourished by improvidence and a sense of moral mission, there has remained alive an almost instinctive awareness of the perennial interests of the United States. This has especially been true with regard to Europe and the Western Hemisphere; for in these regions the national interest of the United States has from the beginning been obvious and clearly defined.

I

In the Western Hemisphere we have always endeavored to preserve the unique position of the United States as a predominant power without rival. We have not been slow in recognizing that this predominance was not likely to be effectively threatened by any one American nation or combination of them, acting without support from outside the Western Hemisphere. It was, then, imperative for the United States to isolate the Western Hemisphere from the political and military policies of non-American nations. The interference of non-American nations in the affairs of the Western Hemisphere, especially through the acquisition of territory, was the only way in which the predominance of the United States could have been challenged from within the Western Hemisphere itself. The Monroe Doctrine and the policies implementing it express that permanent national interest of the United States in the Western Hemisphere.

Since a threat to the national interest of the United States in the Western Hemisphere can come only from outside it, that is, historically from Europe, the United States has always striven to prevent the development of conditions in Europe which would be conducive to a European nation's interference in the affairs of the Western Hemisphere or to a direct attack upon the United

States. Such conditions would be most likely to arise if a European nation had gained such predominance that it could afford to look across the sea for conquest without fear of being menaced at the center of its power, that is, in Europe itself. It is for this reason that the United States has consistently — the War of 1812 is the sole major exception — pursued policies aiming at the maintenance of the balance of power in Europe. It has opposed whatever European nation — be it Great Britain, France, Germany, or Russia — seemed to be likely to gain that ascendancy over its European competitors which would have jeopardized the hemispheric predominance and eventually the very independence of the United States. Conversely, it has supported whatever European nation seemed to be most likely to restore the balance of power by offering successful resistance to the would-be conqueror. While it is hard to imagine a greater contrast in the way of thinking about matters political than that which separates Alexander Hamilton from Woodrow Wilson, in this concern for the maintenance of the balance of power in Europe — for whatever different reasons — they are one. It is by virtue of this concern that the United States has intervened in both World Wars on the side of the initially weaker coalition and that its European policies have so largely paralleled those of Great Britain; for from Henry VIII to this day Great Britain has invariably pursued one single objective in Europe: the maintenance of the balance of power.

With Asia the United States has been vitally concerned only since the turn of the century, and the relation of Asia to the national interest of the United States has never been obvious or clearly defined. In consequence, the Asiatic policies of the United States have never as unequivocally expressed the permanent national interest as have the hemispheric and European ones; nor have they for that reason commanded the bipartisan support which the latter have largely enjoyed. As a further consequence, they have been subjected to moralistic influences in a measure from which the European and hemispheric policies of the United States have been largely immune. Yet beneath the confusions, reversals of policy, and moralistic generalities, which have made up the surface of our Asiatic policy since McKinley, one can detect an underlying consistency which, however vaguely, reflects the permanent interest of the United States in Asia. And this interest is again the maintenance of the balance of power. The principle that expresses it is the "open door" in China. Originally its meaning was purely commercial. However, in the measure in which other nations, especially Japan, threatened to close the door to China not only commercially, but also militarily and politically, the principle of the "open door" was interpreted to cover the territorial integrity and political independence of China not for commercial but political reasons. However unsure of itself the Asiatic policy of the United States has been, it has always assumed that the domination of China by another nation would create so great an accumulation of power as to threaten the security of the United States.

II

Not only with regard to Asia, however, but wherever American foreign policy has operated, political thought has been divorced from political action. Even where our long-range policies reflect faithfully, as they do in the Americas and in Europe, the true interests of the United States we think about them in terms which have at best but a tenuous connection with the actual character of the policies pursued. We have acted on the international scene, as all nations must, in power-political terms; we have tended to conceive of our actions in nonpolitical moralistic terms. This aversion to seeing problems of international politics as they are and the inclination to viewing them instead in nonpolitical, moralistic terms can be attributed both to certain misunderstood peculiarities of the American experience in foreign affairs and to the general climate of opinion prevailing in the Western world during the better part of the nineteenth and the first decade of the twentieth centuries. Of these peculiarities of the American experience three stand out: the uniqueness of the American experiment, the actual isolation during the nineteenth century of the United States from the centers of world conflict, and the humanitarian pacifism and anti-imperialism of American ideology.

The uniqueness of the American experiment in foreign policy contains two elements: the negative one of distinctiveness from the traditional power-political quarrels of Europe and the positive one of a continental expansion which created the freest and richest nation on earth without conquest or subjugation of others.

That the severance of constitutional ties with the British crown was meant to signify the initiation of an American foreign policy distinct from what went under the name of foreign policy in Europe was a conviction common to the founders of the republic. As Washington's Farewell Address put it: "Europe has a set of primary interests, which to us have none, or a very remote relation. Hence she must be engaged in frequent controversies, the causes of which are essentially foreign to our concerns. Hence, therefore, it must be unwise in us to implicate ourselves, by artificial ties, in the ordinary vicissitudes of her politics, or the ordinary combinations and collisions of her friendships or enmities." In 1796, European politics and power politics were identical; there was no other power politics but the one engaged in by the princes of Europe. "The toils of European ambition, rivalship, interest, humor or caprice" were the only manifestations, on the international scene, of the struggle for power before the American eye. The retreat from European politics, as proclaimed by Washington, could therefore, be taken to mean retreat from power politics as such.

The expansion of the United States

up to the Spanish-American War seemed to provide conclusive proof both for the distinctiveness and moral superiority of American foreign policy. The settlement of the better part of a continent by the thirteen original states seemed to be an act of civilization rather than of conquest and as such essentially different from, and morally superior to, the imperialistic ventures, wars of conquest, and colonial acquisitions with which the history of other nations is replete. Yet it was not so much political virtue as the contiguity of the sparsely settled object of conquest with the original territory of departure, which put the mark of uniqueness upon American expansion. As was the case with Russia's simultaneous eastward expansion toward the Pacific, the United States, in order to expand, did not need to cross the oceans and fight wars of conquest in strange lands, as did the other great colonizing nations. Furthermore, the utter political, military, and numerical inferiority of the Indian opponent tended to obscure the element of power, which was less obtrusive in, but no more absent from the continental expansion of the United States than the expansionist movements of other nations. Thus it came about that what was in actuality the fortuitous concatenation of two potent historic accidents could take on, in the popular imagination, the aspects of an ineluctable natural development, a "manifest destiny," thus confirming the uniqueness of American foreign policy in its freedom from those power-political blemishes which degrade the foreign policies of other nations.

Yet American isolation from the European tradition of power politics was more than a political program or a moralistic illusion. As concerns involvement in the political conflicts of which Europe was the center, and the commitments and risks which such involvement of necessity implies, American isolation was an established political fact until the end of the nineteenth century. The actuality of this fact was a result of deliberate choice as well as of the objective conditions of geography. Popular writers might see in the uniqueness of America's geographic position the hand of God which had unalterably prescribed the course of American expansion as well as isolation. But more responsible observers, from Washington on, have been careful to emphasize the conjunction of geographic conditions and of a foreign policy which chooses its ends in the light of geography and which uses geographic conditions to attain those ends. Washington referred to " our detached and distant situation " and asked, " Why forego the advantages of so peculiar a situation? "

From the shores of the North American continent, the citizens of the new world watched the strange spectacle of the struggle for power unfolding on the distant scenes of Europe, Africa, and Asia. Since for the better part of the nineteenth century their foreign policy enabled them to retain the role of spectators, what was actually the result of a passing historic constellation appeared to Americans as a permanent condition, self-chosen as well as naturally ordained. At worst they would continue to watch the game of power politics played by others. At best the time was close at hand when, with democracy established everywhere, the final curtain would fall and the game of power politics would no longer be played.

To aid in the achievement of this goal was conceived to be part of America's mission. Throughout the nation's history, the national destiny of the United States has been understood in antimilitaristic, libertarian terms. Where that national mission finds a nonaggressive, abstentionist formulation, as in the political philosophy of John C. Calhoun, it is conceived as the promotion of domestic liberty. Thus we may " do more to extend liberty by our example over this continent and the world generally, than would be done by a thousand victories." When the United States, in the wake of the Spanish-American War, seemed to desert this anti-imperialist and democratic ideal, William Graham Sumner restated its essence: " Expansion and imperialism are a grand onslaught on democracy . . . expansion and imperialism are at war with the best traditions, principles, and interests of the American people." Comparing the tendencies of European power politics with the ideals of the American tradition, Sumner thought with Washington that they were incompatible. Yet, as a prophet of things to come, he saw that with the conclusion of the Spanish-American War America was irrevocably committed to the same course which was

engulfing Europe in revolution and war.

To understand the American mission in such selfless, humanitarian terms was the easier as the United States — in contrast to the other great powers — was generally not interested, at least outside the Western Hemisphere, in a particular advantage to be defined in terms of power or of territorial gain. Its national interest was exhausted by the preservation of its predominance in the Western Hemisphere and of the balance of power in Europe and Asia. And even this interest in general stability rather than special advantage was, as we know, not always recognized for what it was.

Yet while the foreign policy of the United States was forced, by circumstance if not by choice, to employ the methods, to shoulder the commitments, to seek the objectives, and to run the risks, from which it had thought to be permanently exempt, American political thought continued to uphold that exemption at least as an ideal — an ideal which was but temporarily beyond the reach of the American people, because of the wickedness and stupidity either of American or, preferably, of foreign statesmen. In one sense, this ideal of a free, peaceful, and prosperous world, from which popular government had banished power politics forever, was a natural outgrowth of the American experience. In another sense, this ideal expressed in a particularly eloquent and consistent fashion the general philosophy which during the better part of the nineteenth century dominated the Western world. This philosophy contains two basic propositions: that the struggle for power on the international scene is a mere accident of history, naturally associated with nondemocratic government and, hence, destined to disappear with the triumph of democracy throughout the world; and that, in consequence, conflicts between democratic and nondemocratic nations must be conceived not as struggles for mutual advantage in terms of power but primarily as a contest between good and evil, which can only end with the complete triumph of good and with evil being wiped off the face of the earth.

The nineteenth century developed this philosophy of international relations from its experience of domestic politics. The distinctive characteristic of this experience was the domination of the middle classes by the aristocracy. By identifying this domination with political domination of any kind, the political philosophy of the nineteenth century came to identify the opposition to aristocratic politics with hostility to any kind of politics. After the defeat of aristocratic government, the middle classes developed a system of indirect domination. They replaced the traditional division into the governing and governed classes and the military method of open violence, characteristic of aristocratic rule, with the invisible chains of economic dependence. This economic system operated through a network of seemingly equalitarian legal rules which concealed the very existence of power relations. The nineteenth century

was unable to see the political nature of these legalized relations. They seemed to be essentially different from what had gone, so far, under the name of politics. Therefore, politics in its aristocratic, that is, open and violent form, was identified with politics as such. The struggle, then, for political power — in domestic as well as in international affairs — appeared to be only an historic accident, coincident with autocratic government and bound to disappear with the disappearance of autocratic government.

It is easy to see how this general climate of opinion, prevailing in the Western world, nourished similar tendencies in the American mind, grown from the specific experiences of American history. Thus it is not an accident that nowhere in the Western world was there such depth of conviction and tenacity in support of the belief that involvement in power politics is not inevitable but only a historic accident, and that nations have a choice between power politics and another kind of foreign policy conforming to moral principles and not tainted by the desire for power. Nor is it by accident that this philosophy of foreign policy found its most dedicated and eloquent spokesman in an American President, Woodrow Wilson.

III

The illusion that a nation can escape, if it only wants to, from power politics into a realm where action is guided by moral principles rather than by considerations of power, not only is deeply rooted in the American mind; it also took more than a century for this illusion to crowd out the older notion that international politics is an unending struggle for power in which the interests of individual nations must necessarily be defined in terms of power. Out of the struggle between these two opposing conceptions three types of American statesmen emerge: the realist, thinking in terms of power and represented by Alexander Hamilton; the ideological, acting in terms of power, thinking in terms of moral principles, and represented by Thomas Jefferson and John Quincy Adams; the moralist, thinking and acting in terms of moral principles and represented by Woodrow Wilson. To these three types, three periods of American foreign policy roughly correspond: the first covering the first decade of the history of the United States as an independent nation, the second covering the nineteenth century to the Spanish-American War, the third covering the half century after that war. That this division of the history of American foreign policy refers only to prevailing tendencies and does by no means preclude the operation side by side of different tendencies in the same period, will become obvious in the discussion.

It illustrates both the depth of the moralist illusion and the original strength of the opposition to it that the issue between these two opposing conceptions of foreign policy was joined at the very beginning of the history of the United States, decided in favor of the realist position, and

formulated with unsurpassed simplicity and penetration by Alexander Hamilton. The memorable occasion was Washington's proclamation of neutrality in the War of the First Coalition against revolutionary France.

In 1792, the War of the First Coalition had ranged Austria, Prussia, Sardinia, Great Britain, and the United Netherlands against revolutionary France, which was tied to the United States by a treaty of alliance. On April 22, 1793, Washington issued a proclamation of neutrality, and it was in defense of that proclamation that Hamilton wrote the "Pacificus" and "Americanus" articles. Among the arguments directed against the proclamation were three derived from moral principles. Faithfulness to treaty obligations, gratitude toward a country which had lent its assistance to the colonies in their struggle for independence, and the affinity of republican institutions were cited to prove that the United States must side with France. Against these moral principles, Hamilton invoked the national interest of the United States:

There would be no proportion between the mischiefs and perils to which the United States would expose themselves, by embarking in the war, and the benefit which the nature of their stipulation aims at securing to France, or that which it would be in their power actually to render her by becoming a party.

This disproportion would be a valid reason for not executing the guaranty. All contracts are to receive a reasonable construction. Self-preservation is the first duty of a nation; and though in the performance of stipulations relating to war, good faith requires that its ordinary hazards should be fairly met, because they are directly contemplated by such stipulations, yet it does not require that extraordinary and extreme hazards should be run. . . .

The basis of gratitude is a benefit received or intended, which there was no right to claim, originating in a regard to the interest or advantage of the party on whom the benefit is, or is meant to be, conferred. If a service is rendered from views relative to the immediate interest of the party who performs it, and is productive of reciprocal advantages, there seems scarcely, in such a case, to be an adequate basis for a sentiment like that of gratitude. . . . It may be affirmed as a general principle, that the predominant motive of good offices from one nation to another, is the interest or advantage of the nation which performs them.

Indeed, the rule of morality in this respect is not precisely the same between nations as between individuals. The duty of making its own welfare the guide of its actions, is much stronger upon the former than upon the latter; in proportion to the greater magnitude and importance of national compared with individual happiness, and to the greater permanency of the effects of national than of individual conduct. Existing millions, and for the most part future generations, are concerned in the present measures of a government; while the consequences of the private actions of an individual ordinarily terminate with himself, or are circumscribed within a narrow compass.

Whence it follows that an individual may, on numerous occasions, meritoriously indulge the emotions of generosity and benevolence, not only without an eye to, but even at the expense of, his own interest. But a government can rarely, if at all, be justifiable in pursuing a similar course; and, if it does so, ought to confine itself within much stricter bounds. . . . Good offices which are indifferent to the interest of a nation performing them, or which are compensated by the existence or expectation of some reasonable equivalent, or which produce an essential good to the nation to which they are rendered, without real detriment to the affairs of the benefactors, prescribe perhaps the limits of national generosity or benevolence. . . .

But we are sometimes told, by way of answer, that the cause of France is the cause of liberty; and that we are bound to assist the nation on the score of their being engaged in the defence of that cause. . . .

The obligation to assist the cause of liberty must be deduced from the merits of that cause and from the interest we have in its support.

. . . . . .

An examination into the question how far *regard to the cause of Liberty* ought to induce the United States to take part with France in the present war, is rendered necessary by the efforts which are making (*sic*) to establish an opinion that it ought to have that effect. In order to a right judgment on the point, it is requisite to consider the question under two aspects.

I. Whether the cause of France be truly the cause of Liberty, pursued with justice and humanity, and in a manner likely to crown it with honorable success.

II. Whether the degree of service we could render, by participating in the conflict, was likely to compensate, by its utility to the cause, the evils which would probably flow from it to ourselves.

If either of these questions can be answered in the negative, it will result, that the consideration which has been stated ought not to embark us in the war. . . .

The certain evils of our joining France in the war, are sufficient dissuasives from so intemperate a measure. The possible ones are of a nature to call for all our caution, all our prudence.

To defend its own rights, to vindicate its own power, there are occasions when a nation ought to hazard even its existence. Should such an occasion occur, I trust those who are most averse to commit the peace of the country, will not be the last to face the danger, nor the first to turn their backs upon it.

But let us at least have the consolation of not having rashly courted misfortune. Let us have to act under the animating reflection of being engaged in repelling wrongs, which we neither sought nor merited; in vindicating our rights invaded without provocation; in defending our honor, violated without cause. Let us not have to reproach ourselves with having voluntarily bartered blessings for calamities.

But we are told that our own liberty is at stake upon the event of the war against France — that if she falls, we shall be the next victim. The combined powers, it is said, will never forgive in us the origination of those principles which were the germs of the French Revolution. They will endeavor to eradicate them from the world.

If this suggestion were ever so well founded, it would perhaps be a sufficient answer to it to say, that our interference is not likely to alter the case; that it would only serve prematurely to exhaust our strength.

But other answers more conclusive present themselves.

The war against France requires, on the part of her enemies, efforts unusually violent. They are obliged to strain every nerve, to exert every resource. However it may terminate, they must find themselves spent in an extreme degree; a situation not very favorable to the undertaking anew, and even to Europe combined, an immense enterprise.

To subvert by force republican liberty in this country, nothing short of entire conquest would suffice. This conquest, with our present increased population, greatly distant as we are from Europe, would either be impracticable, or would demand such exertions as following immediately upon those which will have been requisite to the subversion of the French Revolution, would be absolutely ruinous to the undertakers. . . .

There are two great errors in our reasoning upon this subject. One, that the combined powers will certainly attribute to us the same principles, which they deem so exceptionable in France;

the other, that our principles are in fact the same.

If left to themselves, they will all, except one, naturally see in us a people who originally resorted to a revolution in government, as a refuge from encroachments on rights and privileges *antecedently* enjoyed, not as a people who from choice sought a radical and entire change in the established government, in pursuit of new privileges and rights carried to an extreme, irreconcilable perhaps with any form of regular government. They will see in us a people who have a due respect for property and personal security; who, in the midst of our revolution, abstained with exemplary moderation from every thing violent or sanguinary, instituting governments adequate to the protection of persons and property; who, since the completion of our revolution, have in a very short period, from mere reasoning and reflection, without tumult or bloodshed, adopted a form of general government calculated, as well as the nature of things would permit, to remedy antecedent defects, to give strength and security to the nation, to rest the foundations of liberty on the basis of justice, order and law; who have at all times been content to govern themselves without intermeddling with the affairs or governments of other nations; in fine, they will see in us sincere republicans, but decided friends to the freedom of opinion, to the order and tranquillity of all mankind. They will not see in us a people whose best passions have been misled, and whose best qualities have been perverted from their true direction by headlong, fanatical, or designing leaders, to the perpetration of acts from which hu-

manity shrinks to the commission of outrages over which the eye of reason weeps, to the profession and practice of principles which tend to shake the foundations of morality, to dissolve the social bands, to disturb the peace of mankind, to substitute confusion to order, anarchy to government. . . .

It is therefore matter of real regret, that there should be an effort on our part to level the distinctions which discriminate our case from that of France, to confound the two cases in the view of foreign powers, and to pervert or hazard our own principles by persuading ourselves of a similitude which does not exist. . . .

But let us not corrupt ourselves by false comparisons or glosses, nor shut our eyes to the true nature of transactions which ought to grieve and warn us, nor rashly mingle our destiny in the consequences of the errors and extravagances of another nation.

Must a nation subordinate its security, its happiness, nay, its very existence to the respect for treaty obligations, to the sentiment of gratitude, to sympathy with a kindred political system? This was the question which Hamilton proposed to answer, and his answer was an unequivocal " no." Hamilton unswervingly applied one standard to the issues raised by the opposition to Washington's proclamation of neutrality: the national interest of the United States. He put the legalistic and moralistic arguments of the opposition, represented by Madison under the pseudonym " Helvidius," into the contest of the concrete power situation in which the United States found itself on the international scene and asked: If the United States were to join France against virtually all of Europe, what risks would the United States run, what advantages could it expect, what good could it do for its ally?

IV

Considerations such as these, recognized for what they are, have guided American foreign policy but for a short period, that is, as long as the Federalists were in power. *The Federalist* and Washington's Farewell Address are their classic expression. Yet these considerations, not recognized for what they are, sometimes even rejected, have determined the great objectives of American foreign policy to this day. During the century following their brief flowering, they have by and large continued to influence policies as well, under the cover, as it were, of those moral principles with which from Jefferson onward American statesmen have liked to justify their moves on the international scene. Thus this second period witnessed a discrepancy between political thought and political action, yet a coincidence in the intended results of both. What was said of Gladstone could also have been said of Jefferson, John Quincy Adams, Theodore Roosevelt, the war policies of Wilson and Franklin D. Roosevelt: what the moral law demanded was by a felicitous coincidence always identical with what the national interest seemed to require. Political thought and political action moved on different planes, which however, were so inclined as to merge in the end.

John Quincy Adams is the classic example of the political moralist in thought and word who cannot help being a political realist in action. Yet even in Jefferson, whose dedication to abstract morality was much stronger and whose realist touch in foreign affairs was much less sure, the moral pretense yielded often, especially in private utterance, to the impact of the national interest upon native good sense.

Thus during the concluding decade of the Napoleonic Wars Jefferson's thought on international affairs was a reflection of the ever-changing distribution of power in the world rather than of immutable moral principles. In 1806, he favored " an English ascendancy on the ocean " as being " safer for us than that of France." In 1807, he was by the logic of events forced to admit:

I never expected to be under the necessity of wishing success to Bonaparte. But the English being equally tyrannical at sea as he is on land, & that tyranny bearing on us in every point of either honor or interest, I say, " down with England " and as for what Bonaparte is then to do to us, let us trust to the chapter of accidents, I cannot, with the Anglomen, prefer a certain present evil to a future hypothetical one.

However, in 1812, when Napoleon was at the pinnacle of his power, Jefferson hoped for the restoration of the balance of power. Speaking of England, he said that it is for the general interest that she would be a sensible and independent weight in the scale of nations, and be able to contribute, when a favorable moment presents itself, to reduce under the same order, her great rival in flagitiousness. We especially ought to pray that the powers of Europe may be so poised and counterpoised among themselves, that their own security may require the presence of all their forces at home, leaving the other quarters of the globe in undisturbed tranquility.

In 1814, again compelled by the logic of events, he came clearly out against Napoleon and in favor of a balance of power which would leave the power of Napoleon and of England limited, but intact:

Surely none of us wish to see Bonaparte conquer Russia, and lay thus at his feet the whole continent of Europe. This done, England would be but a breakfast; and, although I am free from the visionary fears which the votaries of England have effected to entertain, because I believe he cannot effect the conquest of Europe; yet put all Europe into his hands, and he might spare such a force to be sent in British ships, as I would as leave not have to encounter, when I see how much trouble a handful of British soldiers in Canada has given us. No. It cannot be to our interest that all Europe should be reduced to a single monarchy. The true line of interest for us, is, that Bonaparte should be able to effect the complete exclusion of England from the whole continent of Europe, in order, as the same letter said, " by this peaceable engine of constraint, to make her renounce her views

of dominion over the ocean, of permitting no other nation to navigate it but with her license, and on tribute to her, and her aggressions on the persons of our citizens who may choose to exercise their right of passing over that element." And this would be effected by Bonaparte's succeeding so far as to close the Baltic against her. This success I wished him the last year, this I wish him this year; but were he again advanced to Moscow, I should again wish him such disasters as would prevent his reaching Petersburg. And were the consequences even to be the longer continuance of our war, I would rather meet them than see the whole force of Europe wielded by a single hand.

Similarly, in 1815, Jefferson wrote:

For my part, I wish that all nations may recover and retain their independence; that those which are overgrown may not advance beyond safe measures of power, that a salutary balance may be ever maintained among nations, and that our peace, commerce, and friendship, may be sought and cultivated by all.

It was only when, after 1815, the danger to the balance of power seemed to have passed that Jefferson allowed himself again to indulge in the cultivation of moral principles divorced from the political exigencies of the hour.

From this tendency to which Jefferson only too readily yielded, John Quincy Adams was well-nigh immune. We are here in the presence of a statesman who had been reared in the realist tradition of the first period of American foreign policy, who had done the better part of his work of statecraft in an atmosphere saturated with Jeffersonian principles, and who had achieved the merger of these two elements of his experience into an harmonious whole. Between John Quincy Adams' moral principles and the traditional interest of the United States there was hardly ever a conflict. The moral principles were nothing but the political interests formulated in moral terms, and vice versa. They fit the interests as a glove fits the hand. Adams' great contributions to the tradition of American foreign policy, freedom of the seas, the Monroe Doctrine, and Manifest Destiny, are witness to this achievement.

The legal and moral principle of the freedom of the seas was in the hands of Adams a weapon, as it had been two centuries earlier in the hands of Grotius wielded on behalf of the Low Countries, through which an inferior naval power endeavored to safeguard its independence against Great Britain, the mistress of the seas. The Monroe Doctrine's moral postulates of anti-imperialism and mutual non-intervention were the negative conditions for the safety and enduring greatness of the United States. Their fulfillment vouchsafed the isolation of the United States from the power struggles of Europe and, through it, the continuing predominance of the United States in the Western Hemisphere. Manifest Destiny was the moral justification as well as the moral incentive for the westward expansion of the United States, the peculiar American way

— foreordained by the objective conditions of American existence — of founding an empire, the " American Empire," as one of the contemporary opponents of Adams' policies put it.

V

Jefferson and John Quincy Adams stand at the beginning of the second period of American thought on foreign policy, both its most eminent representatives and the heirs of a realist tradition which continued to mould political action, while it had largely ceased to influence political thought. At the beginning of the third period, McKinley leads the United States, as a great world power, beyond the confines of the Western Hemisphere, ignorant of the bearing of this step upon the national interest and guided by moral principles which are completely divorced from the national interest. When at the end of the Spanish-American War the status of the Philippines had to be determined, McKinley expected and found no guidance in the traditional national interest of the United States. According to his own testimony, he knelt beside his bed in prayer, and in the wee hours of the morning he heard the voice of God telling him — as was to be expected — to annex the Philippines.

This period initiated by McKinley, in which moral principles no longer justify the enduring national interest as in the second, but replace it as a guide for action, finds its fulfillment in the political thought of Woodrow Wilson. Wilson's thought not only disregards the national interest, but is explicitly opposed to it on moral grounds. "It is a very perilous thing," he said in his address at Mobile on October 27, 1913,

to determine the foreign policy of a nation in the terms of material interest. It not only is unfair to those with whom you are dealing, but it is degrading as regards your own actions. . . . We dare not turn from the principle that morality and not expediency is the thing that must guide us, and that we will never condone iniquity because it is most convenient to do so.

Wilson's war-time speeches are but an elaboration of this philosophy. An excerpt from his address of September 27, 1918, opening the campaign for the Fourth Liberty Loan, will suffice to show the continuity of that philosophy:

It is of capital importance that we should also be explicitly agreed that no peace shall be obtained by any kind of compromise or abatement of the principles we have avowed as the principles for which we are fighting. . . .

First, the impartial justice meted out must involve no discrimination between those to whom we wish to be just and to whom we do not wish to be just. It must be a justice that plays no favorites and knows no standard but the equal rights of the several peoples concerned.

Second, no special or separate interest of any single nation or any group of nations can be made the basis

of any part of the settlement which is not consistent with the common interest of all.

Third, there can be no leagues or alliances or special covenants and understandings within the general and common family of the League of Nations.

Fourth, and more specifically, there can be no special, selfish economic combinations within the League and no employment of any form of economic boycott or exclusion except as the power of economic penalty by exclusion from the markets of the world may be vested in the League of Nations itself as a means of discipline and control.

Fifth, all international agreements and treaties of every kind must be made known in their entirety to the rest of the world.

Special alliances and economic rivalries and hostilities have been the prolific source in the modern world of the plans and passions that produce war. It would be an insincere as well as insecure peace that did not exclude them in definite and binding terms. . . .

National purposes have fallen more and more into the background and the common purpose of enlightened mankind has taken their place. The counsels of plain men have become on all hands more simple and straightforward and more unified than the counsels of sophisticated men of affairs, who still retain the impression that they are playing a game of power and playing for high stakes. That is why I have said that this is a peoples' war, not a statesmen's. Statesmen must follow the clarified common thought or be broken.

Yet in his political actions, especially under the pressure of the First World War, Wilson could no more than Jefferson before him discount completely the national interest of the United States. Wilson's case, however, was different from Jefferson's in two respects. For one, Wilson was never able, even when the national interest of the United States was directly menaced, to conceive of the danger in other than moral terms. It was only the objective force of the national interest, which no rational man could escape, that imposed upon him as the object of his moral indignation the source of America's mortal danger. Thus in 1917 Wilson led the United States into war against Germany for the same reasons, only half-known to himself, for which Jefferson had wished and worked alternately for the victory of England and of France. Germany threatened the balance of power in Europe, and it was in order to remove that threat — and not to make the world safe for democracy — that the United States put its weight into the Allies' scale. Wilson pursued the right policy, but he pursued it for the wrong reasons.

Not only did the crusading fervor of moral reformation obliterate the awareness of the United States' traditional interest in the maintenance of the European balance of power, to be accomplished through the defeat of Germany. Wilson's moral fervor also had politically disastrous effects, for which there is no precedent in the history of the United States. Wilson's moral objective required the destruction of the Kaiser's autocracy, and this happened also to be required by the political interests of the United States. The political interests of the United States required, beyond this immediate objective of total victory, the restoration of the European balance of power, traditional guarantor of American security. Yet it was in indignation at the moral deficiencies of that very balance of power, "forever discredited," as he thought, that Wilson had asked the American people to take up arms against the Central Powers! Once military victory had put an end to the immediate threat to American security, the very logic of his moral position — let us remember that consistency is the moralist's supreme virtue — drove him toward substituting for the concrete national interest of the United States the general postulate of a brave new world where the national interest of the United States, as that of all other nations, would disappear in a community of interests comprising mankind.

Consequently, Wilson considered it to be the purpose of victory not to restore a new, viable balance of power, but to make an end to it once and forever. "You know," he told the English people at Manchester on December 30, 1918,

that the United States has always felt from the very beginning of her history that she must keep herself separate from any kind of connection with European politics, and I want to say very frankly to you that she is not now interested in European politics. But she is interested in the partnership of right between America and Europe. If the future had nothing for us but a new attempt to keep the world at a right poise by a balance of power, the United States would take no interest, because she will join no combination of power which is not the combination of all of us. She is not interested merely in the peace of Europe, but in the peace of the world.

Faced with the national interest of the great allied powers, Wilson had nothing to oppose or support them with but his moral principles, with the result that the neglect of the American national interest was not compensated for by the triumph of political morality. In the end Wilson had to consent to a series of uneasy compromises which were a betrayal of his moral principles — for principles can, by their very nature, not be made the object of compromise — and which satisfied nobody's national aspirations. These compromises had no relation at all to the traditional American national interest in a viable European balance of power. Thus Wilson returned from Versailles a compromised idealist, an empty-handed statesman, a discredited ally. In that triple failure lies the tragedy not only of Wilson, a great yet misguided man, but of Wilsonianism as a political doctrine as well.

Yet Wilson returned to the United States, unaware of his failure. He offered the American people what he had offered the allied nations at Paris: moral principles divorced from political reality. "The day we have left behind us," he proclaimed at Los Angeles on September 20, 1919,

was a day of balances of power. It was a day of "every nation take care of itself or make a partnership with some other nation or group of nations to hold the peace of the world steady or to dominate the weaker portions of the world." Those were the days of alliances. This project of the league of Nations is a great process of disentanglement.

VI

While before Paris and Versailles these moral principles rang true with the promise of a new and better world, they now must have sounded to many rather hollow and platitudinous. Yet what is significant for the course which American foreign policy was to take in the interwar years is not so much that the American people rejected Wilsonianism, but that they rejected it by ratifying the denial of the American tradition of foreign policy which was implicit in the political thought of Wilson. We are here indeed dealing with a tragedy not of one man, but of a political doctrine and, as far as the United States is concerned, of a political tradition. The isolationism of the interwar period could delude itself into believing that it was but the restorer of the early realist tradition of American foreign policy. Did it not, like that tradition, proclaim the self-sufficiency of the United States within the Western Hemisphere? Did it not, like that tradition, refuse to become involved in the rivalries of European nations?

The isolationists of the twenties and thirties did not see what was the very essence of the policies of the Founding Fathers — that both the isolated and the preponderant position of the United States in the Western Hemisphere was not a fact of nature, and that the freedom from entanglements in European conflicts was not the result of mere abstention on the part of the United States. Both benefits were the result of political conditions outside the Western Hemisphere and of policies carefully contrived and purposefully executed in their support. For the realists of the first period, isolation was an objective of policy, which had to be striven for to be attained. For the isolationists of the interwar period, isolation was, as it were a natural state, which only needed to be left undisturbed in order to continue forever. Conceived in such terms, it was the very negation of foreign policy.

Isolationism, then, is in its way as oblivious to political reality as is Wilsonianism — the internationalist challenge, to which it had thought to have found the American answer. In consequence, they are both strangers not only to the first, realist phase of American foreign policy, but to its whole tradition. Both refused to face political reality either in realistic or ideological terms. They refused to face it at all. Thus isolationism and Wilsonianism have more in common than their historic enmity would lead one to suspect. In a profound sense they are brothers under the skin. Both are one in maintaining that the United States has no interest in any particular political and military constellation outside the Western Hemisphere. While isolationism stops here, Wilsonianism asserts that the American national interest is nowhere in particular but everywhere, being identical with the interests of mankind itself. The political awareness of both refuses to concern itself with the concrete issues with regard to which the national interest must be asserted. Isolationism stops short of them, Wilsonianism soars beyond them. Both have but a negative relation to the national interest of the United States outside the Western Hemisphere. They are unaware of its very existence. This being so, both substitute abstract moral principles for the guidance of the national interest, derived from the actual conditions of American existence. Wilsonianism applies the illusory expectations of liberal reform to the whole world, isolationism empties the realist political principle of isolationism of all concrete political content and transforms it into the unattainable parochial ideal of automatic separation.

In view of this inner affinity between isolationism and Wilsonianism, it is not surprising that the great debate of the twenties and thirties between internationalism and isolationism was carried on primarily in moral terms. Was there a moral obligation for the United States to make its contribution to world peace by joining the League of Nations and the World Court? Was it morally incumbent upon the United States, as a democracy, to oppose Fascism in Europe and to uphold international law in Asia? Such were the questions which were raised in that debate and the answers depended upon the moral position taken. The question which was central to the national interest of the United States, that of the balance of power in Europe and Asia, was hardly ever faced squarely, and when it was, it was dismissed on moral grounds. Mr. Cordell Hull, Secretary of State of the United States from 1933–1944 and one of the most respected spokesmen of internationalism, summarized in his *Memoirs* his attitude toward this central problem of American foreign policy in these terms:

I was not, and am not, a believer in the idea of balance of power or spheres of influence as a means of keeping the peace. During the First World War I had made an intensive study of the system of spheres of influence and balance of power, and I was grounded to the taproots in their iniquitous consequences. The conclusions I then formed in total opposition to this system stayed with me.

When internationalism triumphed in the late thirties, it did so in the moral terms of Wilsonianism. That in this instance the moral postulates which inspired the administration of Franklin D. Roosevelt happened to coincide with the exigencies of the American national interest was again, as in the case of Jefferson and of the Wilson of 1917, due to the impact of a national emergency upon innate common sense and to the strength of a national tradition which holds in its spell the actions even of those who deny its validity in words. However, as soon as the minds of the American leaders were freed from the inescapable pressures of a primarily military nature and turned toward the political problems of the war and its aftermath, they thought and acted again as Wilson had acted under similar circumstances. That is to say, they thought and acted in moral terms, divorced from the political conditions of America's existence.

The practical results of this philosophy of international affairs, as applied to the political war and postwar problems, were, then, bound to be quite similar to those which had made the allied victory in the First World War politically meaningless. Conceived as it was as a " crusade " — to borrow from the title of General Eisenhower's book — against the evil incarnate in the Axis Powers, the purpose of the Second World War could only be the destruction of that evil, transacted through the instrumentality of " unconditional surrender." Since the threat to the Western world emanating from the Axis was conceived primarily in moral terms, it was easy to imagine that all conceivable danger was concentrated in that historic constellation of hostile powers and that with its destruction political evil itself would disappear from the world. Beyond " unconditional surrender " there was, then, a brave new world after the model of Wilson's, which would liquidate the heritage of the defeated evil, not " peace-loving " nations and would establish an order of things where war, aggressiveness, and the struggle for power itself were to be no more. Thus Mr. Cordell Hull could declare on his return in 1943 from the Moscow Conference that the new international organization would mean the end of power politics and usher in a new era of international collaboration. Three years later, Mr. Philip Noel-Baker then British Minister of State, echoed Mr. Hull by stating in the House of Commons that the British Government was " determined to use the institutions of the United Nations to kill power politics, in order that by the methods of democracy, the will of the people shall prevail."

With this philosophy dominant in the West — Mr. Churchill provides almost the sole, however ineffective, exception — the strategy of the war and of the peace to follow could not help being oblivious to those considerations of the national interest which the great statesmen of the West, from Hamilton through Castlereagh, Canning and John Quincy Adams to Disraeli and Salisbury, had brought to bear upon the international problems of their day. War was no longer regarded as a means to a political end. The only end the war was to serve was total victory, which is another way of saying that the war became an end in itself. Hence, it became irrelevant how the war was won politically, as long as it was won speedily, cheaply, and totally. The thought that the war might be waged in view of a new balance of power to be established after the war, occurred in the West only to Winston Churchill —

and, of course, to Joseph Stalin. The national interest of the Western nations was, then, satisfied insofar as it required the destruction of the threat to the balance of power emanating from Germany and Japan; for insofar, the moral purposes of the war happened to coincide with the national interest. However, the national interest of the Western nations was jeopardized insofar as their security required the creation of a new viable balance of power after the war.

How could statesmen who boasted that they were not " believers in the idea of balance of power " — like a scientist not believing in the law of gravity — and who were out " to kill power politics," understand the very idea of the national interest which demanded above all protection from the power of others? Thus it was with deeply and sincerely felt moral indignation that the Western world, expecting a brave new world without power politics, found itself confronted with a new and more formidable threat to its security as soon as the old one had been subdued. There was good reason for moral indignation, however misdirected this one was. That a new balance of power will rise out of the ruins of an old one and that nations with political sense will avail themselves of the opportunity to improve their position within it, is a law of politics for whose validity nobody is to blame. Yet blameworthy are those who in their moralistic disdain for the laws of politics endanger the interests of the nations which are in their care.

The history of American foreign policy since the end of the Second World War is the story of the encounter of the American mind with a new political world. That mind was weakened in its understanding of foreign policy by half a century of ever more complete intoxication with moral abstractions. Even a mind less weakened would have found it hard to face with adequate understanding and successful action the unprecedented novelty and magnitude of the new political world. American foreign policy in that period presents itself as a slow, painful, and incomplete process of emancipation from deeply ingrained error and of rediscovery of long-forgotten truths.

The fundamental error which has thwarted American foreign policy in thought and action is the antithesis of national interest and moral principles. The equation of political moralism with morality and of political realism with immorality is itself untenable. The choice is not between moral principles and the national interests, devoid of moral dignity, but between one set of moral principles, divorced from political reality, and another set of moral principles, derived from political reality. The basic fact of international politics is the absence of a society able to protect the existence, and to promote the interests, of the individual nations. For the individual nations to take care of their own national interests is, then, a political necessity. There can be no moral duty to neglect them; for as the international society is at present con-

stituted, the consistent neglect of the national interest can only lead to national suicide. Yet it can be shown that there exists even a positive moral duty for the individual nation to take care of its national interests.

Self-preservation for the individual as well as for societies is not only a biological and psychological necessity, but in the absence of an overriding moral obligation a moral duty as well. In the absence of an integrated international society, in particular, the attainment of a modicum of order and the realization of a minimum of moral values are predicated upon the existence of national communities capable of preserving order and realizing moral values within the limits of their power. It is obvious that such a state of affairs falls far short of that order and realized morality to which we are accustomed in national societies. The only relevant question is, however, what the practical alternative is to these imperfections of an international society based upon the national interests of its component parts. The attainable alternative is not a higher morality realized through the application of universal moral principles, but moral deterioration through either political failure or the fanaticism of political crusades. The juxtaposition of the morality of political moralism and the immorality of the national interest is mistaken. It operates with a false concept of morality, developed by national societies but unsuited to the conditions of international society. In the process of its realization, it is bound to destroy the very moral values which it is its purpose to promote. Hence, the antithesis between moral principles and the national interest is not only intellectually mistaken but also morally pernicious. A foreign policy derived from the national interest is in fact morally superior to a foreign policy inspired by universal moral principles. Albert Sorel, the Anglophobe historian of the French Revolution, well summarized the real antithesis when he said in grudging admiration of Castlereagh:

He piqued himself on principles to which he held with an unshakable constancy, which in actual affairs could not be distinguished from obstinacy; but these principles were in no degree abstract or speculative, but were all embraced in one alone, the supremacy of English interests; they all proceeded from this high reason of state.

May as much be said by a future historian of the American foreign policy of our time!

77. Principles of Foreign Policy Around the Globe*

As with American foreign policy, certain permanent characteristics can be observed in the foreign policies of other nations. Because the objective foundations of, say, British foreign policy remain relatively constant, the principles of British foreign policy which obtained in the eighteenth century are more or less valid today. This section is merely an introduction to a subject that is infinitely complex in character. We have tried to provide a conceptual framework for thinking about the foreign policy of any nation. At this stage, principles or hypotheses regarding any particular nation are merely tentative and suggestive.

The foreign policy of a major nation in contemporary world politics should be examined in terms of: (1) The objective material and geographic foundations of its policy; (2) The historic policies it has pursued;

* By Kenneth W. Thompson.

and (3) Some of its vital interests in past generations. The great virtue of this approach to foreign policy is not that it provides short cuts or ready-made answers to baffling contemporary issues. What it provides is a basis for anticipating the behavior of particular nations that is somewhat more durable than casual opinions on the personality traits of its leaders. The objective conditions of any foreign policy place certain irremovable limits on its executors. Such an essential study was ruled out in most earlier writings because of the myth that only the political preferences of the administration then in power determined a nation's foreign policy.

THE PERMANENT ASPECTS OF BRITISH FOREIGN POLICY

1. **Objective Foundations.** British foreign policy is the classic example

of a foreign policy determined largely by objective conditions. It is begging the question to say that other nations who share certain geographic features with England, as for instance Denmark its insular position, have not produced comparable foreign policies. In fact there are five aspects and not one of the British situation which constitute the objective foundations of its policy. They represent a complex of geographic and strategic factors undergirding British policy. They are the objective conditions by which every administration is guided and limited in making foreign policy.

First, England is an *island state*. Therefore the threats to its security have not had their origin across nearby frontiers or boundaries. Hence England's problems contrast markedly with those of France. The security of France has traditionally been determined by its success in sealing off its northeast frontier against a German aggression. The insular position of England has determined its security requirements and affected its psychology in appraising them. It has helped to indicate the tools and techniques appropriate to the maintenance of its security.

Secondly, England is on the *ocean flank of a great continent*. This constitutes a source of attraction but also one of restraint. In these terms England's interests are in Europe but not of it, and thus one aim has been to keep for itself some measure of freedom of action. With modern technology and the welding of England to Europe, the basis for this freedom,

in theory if not always in practice, has been sharply limited. Someone has said that the English Channel has become no broader in subjective terms than a Dutch dyke in the age of William the Silent and the Atlantic is no wider today than the Channel at the time of Napoleon's encampment at Boulogne. Yet the mere presence of a barrier has influenced nations, as it did in the case of Hitler. Thirdly, England's position has meant that she controls the exits from the North Sea and the Baltic. Any military calculations by a would-be aggressor on the Continent had to take this into account.

Fourthly, Britain has become an empire with vast overseas possessions. If British commitments in foreign policy are viewed as a triangle, one angle has been its far-flung obligations to territories and colonies, and the other two have been its European and American interests. These interests have meant that survival is not merely a local or a regional but a world-wide issue. Moreover, these interests have stimulated a type of policy that can be bolstered and maintained by the power of the world's greatest navy.

Fifthly, the size and economic vulnerability of England have dictated that it avoid above all inspiring fear and jealousy among other nations. To avert this danger and the combining of nations to overthrow it, England has tried to harmonize its interests with the interests and ideals of the majority of nations. It became in the nineteenth century the champion of national independence. It posed as the protector of less powerful nations. The objective conditions of British foreign policy have never been as clearly summarized as in the great state paper of Sir Eyre Crowe:

The general character of England's foreign policy is determined by the immutable conditions of her geographical situation on the ocean flank of Europe as an island state with vast oversea colonies and dependencies. . . .[1]

2. Historic Foreign Policies. The objective conditions of British foreign policy are responsible in turn for its enduring historic policies. The first principle of British foreign policy since Henry VIII has been the maintenance of the European *balance of power*. For four hundred years England has opposed the strongest, most aggressive power which threatened to dominate the Continent. It has taken no account of which nation or what ideology was concerned. The only guide has been whether the balance of power was threatened. Mr. Churchill has observed: "The question is not whether it is Spain, or the French Monarchy, or the French Empire, or the German Empire, or the Hitler regime. It has nothing to do with rulers or nations, it is concerned solely with whoever is the strongest or potentially dominating tyrant." The wonderful unconscious tradition of

British policy has been to stand watch over the balance of power and especially to deny to any aggressive power the domination of the Low Countries. What Mr. Churchill could propose in March of 1936 regarding threats to the balance of power, he could reiterate again in 1948. *Plus ça change, plus c'est la même chose* here receives concrete meaning from the utter consistency of this principle of foreign policy. That the national interest and not abstract moral principles have motivated this consistency of policy is strikingly revealed by two alliances concluded in 1870 by Gladstone only two days apart. The first was with Prussia guaranteeing the neutrality of Belgium against its isolation by France; the second was with France and hinged upon an invasion by Prussia of this strategic area. The goal was the same in both cases. The security of Belgium was intimately bound up with British national interest. Therefore it proposed to defend this interest through every means.

A second historic principle is that of *supremacy of the seas*. England could exploit its geographic position primarily because it had the power. The sole power effective for a nation detached from Europe by the English Channel was a power that enabled it to defend this gulf. Naval superiority or the relative naval inferiority of one's foes in these waters made this geographic feature a most formidable obstacle. To the British navy, as well as to British diplomacy, can be ascribed the fact that from the fifteenth century to the present, with the exceptions of the American Revo-

---

[1] "Memorandum by Sir Eyre Crowe on the Present State of British Relations with France and Germany, January 1, 1907," British Documents on the Origins of the War 1898–1914, ed. by G. P. Gooch and H. Temperley (London: His Majesty's Stationery Office, 1928), Vol. III, p. 402.

lutionary War and the Afghan Wars, Britain suffered no military defeats or invasion. In 1688 it fell victim to a " political invasion " that some have called a liberation. But because of geography and strategy, it suffered no military invasion. Even today a deliberate policy is pursued of maintaining the high quality of the British navy and pursuing time-honored objectives through collaboration with others. British outposts and dependencies have been maintained through naval power and strategy.

A third principle of foreign policy is procedural rather than substantive in nature. The technique of " wait-and-see " has become so integral to British policy as to give it national characteristics all its own. British foreign policy burns with a slow-burning fuse. For critics this is an evidence of inertia; for sympathizers it is a mark of sangfroid. To unravel the baffling questions of policy the diplomat must be a man with ice water in his veins. The most difficult question in foreign policy is to discover the real threat and its nature. In 1919 the real threat had been promptly identified as Soviet Russia. It is questionable in the light of Germany's rapid recovery whether this estimate was sound or whether in this instance the fuse did not burn out too quickly. If foreign policy could be molded in the blinding light of good versus evil, none of these painful problems need be considered. Since it takes its shape in the gray dawn of the struggle for power, there can be no short cuts. The principles of a European balance

of power, supremacy on the seas, and caution in matters of political judgment are the tripod on which British foreign policy rests.

3. Vital Interests. The vital interests of England traditionally have begun and sometimes have been limited to the Low Countries. It has been axiomatic that "whoever controlled the Scheldt pointed a dagger at the heart of England." The integrity of France is today central to the British national interest, although sometimes this interest has been obscured by certain policy-makers but always to England's mortal peril. The Iberian Peninsula for centuries. has been considered vital to the maintenance of the British life-line. This interest has been protected by Britain's most ancient treaty, its agreement with Portugal. The Middle East and Hongkong have been crucial for both Conservative and Labor Governments. And British interests in the Iberian Peninsula have been served by its influence over Gibraltar in the same way that Suez has been a crucial link for its interests in the Middle East. Nor have obligations to the British Commonwealth ever been neglected in either political or military arrangements. In 1936 there was a majority whom it was said would have accepted the German proposal for a bargain over Eastern Europe. Manchuria five years earlier had been ruled out as a paramount vital interest. Whether justifiable or not it would seem that in practice British diplomacy has construed these two areas as less vital to British security than the others we have mentioned.

The Permanent Aspects of French Foreign Policy

1. The Objective Foundations. France is near *the heart of Europe*. This objective condition has made the task of maintaining security and independence different for France than for England. The French conception of the balance of power and of the role of alliances has its own unique character because France has found herself indissolubly welded to the Continent of Europe.

Since 1870 at least, the *northeast frontier* of France has constituted a boundary that is both vulnerable and exposed to aggression from Central Europe. The integrity of the Rhine Valley has become its most crucial geographic interest. No other aspect of France's objective position has influenced as markedly its foreign policy.

Politically and economically, France has *faced both east and west*. Its trade has included exchange with Poland and Eastern Europe. Its capital was vital in the early days of Russian industrialization. When guarantees of security from "natural allies" in the west were not forthcoming, France has turned eastward. Its changing east-west orientation, its vulnerability from the northeast and its inescapable role at the core of the European power vortex together make up a relatively permanent foreign policy environment.

2. Historic Foreign Policies. France is the nation whose foreign policy between wars could most nearly be summed up in one word, "*security*." France's fear has become an obsession, for even with its army on German soil in the twenties, there was unmistakable evidence of anxiety over a new invasion. The Germans had invaded France in 1914, 1870, 1814, in "the Thirty Years' War," and in the days of Julius Caesar. It was inconceivable that they would not invade again. The quest for security was blind and unreasoning to the point of overlooking the number of precedents for a French invasion of Germany. The sole threat was Germany and to meet the threat France piled alliance upon alliance and sanction upon sanction.

In the mid-twentieth century, France superficially appears to have abandoned its quest for security vis-a-vis Germany. On the surface the Franco-German *rapprochement* as it gives evidence of being worked out in the Schuman Plan and the Plevan Army Plan appears to throw overboard the traditional policy. But on the contrary, it is becoming increasingly clear that the policy of *securitée* is being pursued as sedulously today as it ever was. Only the means have changed for instead of alliances *against* Germany, an agreement is being worked out *with* Germany. It has been decided to join someone whose power is too great to permit its control. Through this "unholy wedlock," which is in the nature of politics, France seeks to preserve its integrity. If Germany is ultimately to dominate the economy of Europe, as the superiority of its natural resources makes almost inevitable, France's interests can best be served through a controlled and regularized pooling of skills and resources with its most powerful neighbor. This is a simple case of joining him whom one is unable to dominate.

Secondly, France's geographic location has inspired persistent efforts to establish an *intra-European balance of power*. France has been unable to indulge itself the detachment of British foreign policy but has sought, sometimes with wisdom and often with folly, to attain a balance within Europe itself. Following the rejection of membership in the League of Nations by the United States Senate, France sought to build up a balance against German potentialities through alliances in Eastern Europe. Sometimes it has found in the power of Russia a weight in the balance. Before and during World War I it was an objective of Delcassé and Poincaré to tighten relations with Russia. But when the psychological or moral outlook on foreign policy prevailed, as it did in regard to Bolshevik Russia after World War I, this vital counter in the balance was abandoned. Hamilton and Washington and Kennan stand for one tradition in American foreign policy. That same realist tradition is represented in France by Henry II, Richelieu, who in the seventeenth century united Catholic France and Protestant Sweden during the Thirty Years' War, Delcassé and Poincaré, who in 1892 combined democratic France and absolutist Russia, and Louis Barthou, who sought to tie Russia to France in 1934. France pursued successfully its aim of an intra-European balance in the periods when ideologies were held subordinate to vital political interests.

Over the past half century, France has followed a foreign policy of the *status quo*. She has sought not only to keep things relatively the same, but through an excessive legalism has justified her interests in terms of the sanctity of treaties. Whereas England favored concessions within the framework of the Versailles Treaty, France opposed any peaceful change that might drain from her one drop of strength for arresting the advance of Germany. One can conclude that historic French policy has had as its ends security, an intra-European balance of power, and recently the defense of the sanctity of treaties.

3. Vital Interests. As all nations, the paramount vital interest of France is its territorial integrity. By definition in French thinking, this can be assured only if its northeast frontier is secure. The Rhine valley must be safeguarded. The southern flank is vital in the sense that it should be neutralized. To this end, France has persistently pressed for alliances with Italy. If war was to come from the only conceivable foe, that is, Germany, it was essential that France's other flank not be endangered. Another type of interest is that in strong land defenses. Sometimes this has betrayed France into a self-defeating strategy, which was static in character. The Maginot Line was both a symbol of France's vital interest and of its error in judging how it might best be served. Finally, France has interests in the Mediterranean, in North Africa, in Indo-China, and in Eastern Europe, at least to a greater extent than England.

78. Permanent Aspects of Russian and Soviet Foreign Policy*

1. **Objective Foundations.** In geographic extent, the Soviet empire is the greatest landlocked empire in history. It is probably the strongest land power in the world today. No other nation in Europe has, over the centuries, acquired so vast a sway of power. Russian foreign policy, because of its geographic position and the orientation of its interests, has been the example *par excellence* of an expansionist foreign policy. Thus, for Europeans, and especially the British, for over a century and a half there has been a " Russian problem."

The objective conditions of Russian policy have been constant over long periods of history. Russia, as Germany, has occupied a middle position. This has permitted a freedom of action and maneuver which France, for example, never enjoyed. Sometimes Russia has found allies in Central Europe; at other times, especially in wars and crises, she has looked to the powers of Western Europe. At all times her location has facilitated the flexibility of her diplomacy. Russia, moreover, has been *landlocked*. The absence of ice-free ports in the north and of unchallenged access to the sea in the south has left her cribbed and confined within her enormous empire. Furthermore, she has found herself at *the end of a natural avenue for invasion* from Central Europe over the

* By Kenneth W. Thompson.

Eurasian plains. Poland has been a springboard for aggression into Russia. Thus Poland is conceived of as one outpost in the network of defenses today. Also, Russian strategy and tactics in war and peace are a function of her *immense territory*. The concept of defense in depth and retreat followed by counterattack is an obvious by-product of the permanent Russian position.

Also the objective conditions of the Russian and Soviet empires have influenced the mood and techniques of its foreign policy. It has shown violent fluctuations from isolationism to internationalism. For at least two centuries there has been evident, as in the shift from Bolshevik isolationism in 1917 to Litvinov's program for universal disarmament, a brooding concern for its own security. There is an isolationist core to Russian foreign policy. In history there has been an almost morbid anxiety about the defilement which might come from too much cultural contact with a Europe that was considered corrupt and effete. Russia's plains and vast spaces have inspired a xenophobia more deep-seated than the normal suspicions of one people for another. It is this characteristic of xenophobia that has contributed always to the aloof and conspiratorial outlook of Russia in 1815 and the Soviet Union since 1917 with reference to the institutions of contemporary diplomacy. This anxiousness

about foreigners has frequently over-
flowed into missionary crusades to
dominate and convert the heathen.
A Greek Orthodox world, which
escaped the influence of a reformation, has imposed a semi-religious
spirit of submission on the Russian
people.

2. **Historic Foreign Policies.** Traditionally Russian aims have remained essentially the same for several centuries. Russia's foreign policy
can best be characterized as an expansionist policy. As a great landlocked
empire, it has pushed out in numerous prongs of an expansionist drive
especially for " windows to the west."
Toward the southwest, there have
been thrusts into the Balkans reaching out especially for control of the
Bosporus and the Dardanelles. Another drive has aimed at filling the
void left by the contracting Ottoman Empire. To the southeast Russia has sought influence in Persia and
Afghanistan, but on these interests
she has reached settlements in the
past. A drive to the east has had as
its aim control in Outer Mongolia
and the Maritime Provinces. The
Baltic States to the northwest have
been considered crucial to Russian
security there. Not only for Stalin
at Yalta but for earlier czars and
ministers, Poland has been " a matter
of life and death." In Eastern Europe the policy of an inner security
zone, of a *cordon sanitaire* in reverse
has gradually emerged.

Moreover, Russia and the Soviet
Union have consistently invoked the
idea of foreign policy based on
spheres of influence. In all periods
there has been a willingness, contrary to the prevailing American
philosophy of foreign policy, to accept tentative sphere-of-interest settlements, which would register the
distribution of power in an area.
Russia has approved spheres of influence for Iran and the Near East.
It has shown willingness to consider
a far-reaching settlement with the
West on Central and Eastern Europe. Stalin and Churchill tenta-
tively adopted a three months settlement in Eastern Europe. Its leaders talked cynically with Hitler in
regard to a general settlement. It
is surely illuminating to consider
that the same predisposition toward
this technique has been manifested
both by czarist and Bolshevik regimes. Stalin on numerous occasions
since 1945 has supported the idea of
a political settlement, whatever the
underlying motives of his strategy
may have been.

Furthermore, traditional Russian
foreign policy has been based squarely on the balance of power. Particularly has the Soviet Union tried
to balance power in the Far East.
Before and during World War II
the threat to the balance of power in
Asia was Japan. The natural ally
of the Soviet Union here was the
Chinese Communists. Yet Moscow
never withdrew support or recognition from the Chinese Nationalists
nor threw its full weight to the Communists. Instead it walked hand in
hand with Chiang Kai-shek. The
sole purpose behind this policy was
the aim of balancing Japanese power in Asia. Yet this policy would
seem out of step with ideological
interests and the affinity of the doc-

trines of Stalinism and Mao Tsetung.

Russian foreign policy in general and Soviet policy in particular is one of marvelous *flexibility*. It gives practically unparalleled opportunities for changes and reversals. A first principle in Communist doctrine has been the inevitability of world revolution. But from the beginning Soviet international relations have been with non-Communist states. To survive, it has been forced to pursue a flexible policy in determining the moment for advance or retreat. The two objectives of world revolution and national interest have marched hand in hand. One has never been forgotten in any permanent use of the other. But when the relativities of power have limited freedom of action, world revolution has been subordinated to Russian national interest, as it was in the case of Tito in Yugoslavia and the recognition of the Nationalists in China in order to thwart Japan.

Four phases in the history of Soviet foreign policy before World War II dramatically illustrate its policy of advance and retreat. The first phase comes with Lenin's seizure of power in October of 1917. This was the honeymoon period in which a moratorium was declared on diplomacy with all non-Communist states, when czarist treaties were torn up and when uprisings throughout Europe and the rest of the world were confidently expected.

But these revolutions did not take place and in the spring of 1918 Soviet policy was altered as a second phase was inaugurated. From that time until the winter of 1921 a new blueprint of three worlds in foreign policy was drawn up. The first was the capitalist world, that world being identified with the victors in World War I. The second was the non-Communist world. This was the world of unreclaimed capitalist wilderness impoverished by capitalist aggression, but still not converted to a belief in Communist scripture. The third world was that of Communist peoples. The objective of this third world, as reflected in the conduct of Soviet foreign policy, was to recognize and strengthen common bonds with the non-Communist world. Treaties were completed with the Weimar Republic, with pre-capitalist Islamic powers including Turkey, Persia, and Afghanistan. Efforts were already being made at that time to stir up Asian distrust and unrest, particularly in China and the Netherland East Indies. Soviet policy-makers in this phase abandoned the theory that Communist nations should limit their diplomacy to relations with one another. They extended this concept to include contacts with the defeated Central Powers and with Oriental and primitive peoples.

In the third phase of Soviet foreign policy from 1921–33, the area of international relations was broadened to include contacts with a number of undeniably capitalist nations. Boundaries were settled by means of treaties with virtually all European countries. The one exception was its southernmost neighbor, Rumania, and the obstacle here was not any Marxian scruple about concluding treaties with capitalist countries but rather an unsettled dispute over Bessarabia. These treaty arrangements became a valuable instrument by which the Soviet Union sought to safeguard its own security. Not only bilateral but multilateral treaties were made with states from Estonia in the north to Persia in the south. Even Rumania ultimately joined in subscribing to the Litvinov Protocol, which anticipated the Briand-Kellogg Pact. Then in the Geneva draft of May 24, 1933, prepared mainly by the Soviet government, an even larger number of capitalist nations joined Russia in a regional agreement on the definition of "aggression." The concept of Soviet international relations now included most of the world.

The fourth phase of Soviet foreign policy was presaged by a speech of Molotov in March, 1931. The gist of it was that peace was the paramount objective of Communism. Although the two economic systems of capitalism and Communism would not both permanently exist, for the latter would inevitably supplant the former, yet for a certain historical period unavoidably there would have to be practical arrangements worked out between them. In the fourth stage, the Soviet Union began to behave as just another sovereign state. It no longer hesitated to carry on relations with other states if these served the national interest. Any support or friendship which could be obtained was accepted during this period, for Soviet planners had some serious worries over their chances for maintaining their na-

tional independence. It was during the early part of this period that a *rapprochement* with France was achieved and the most far-reaching action of all concluded, that is, the entry of the Soviet Union into the League of Nations.

The one constant element in these changes was the primacy as a motivating force of the national interest. In the first few years of the Bolshevik regime the propaganda of world revolution held sway, often with little attention to the political interests of the state. In the face of growing threats of aggression from Germany and Japan the Communists foreswore the simple policy of expecting and fostering world Communism to the more pedestrian task of painfully assuring their security through customary techniques of foreign policy. The climax was reached when the breakdown of understandings with France and England invited the consummation of the Soviet-German Non-Aggression Pact of 1939. Based on hard-boiled conceptions of *raison d'état*, it was nonetheless the logical outcome of the almost imperceptible change from a policy based on a fervent belief in early world revolution to a policy grounded in an acute fear for the safety of the Soviet Union itself.

These same characteristics of advance and retreat can be perceived in Soviet foreign policy since World War II. The problem regarding them is the difficulty of achieving full perspective on events in the immediate persent. It should be readily apparent that in its policy in Germany, and in particular Berlin, in Iran, in

Korea, in Greece, and at all points outside her inner security zone, the Soviet Union has maintained a flexible posture, pressing aggressively for universal ends when opposition appeared lacking and making concessions or retreating when it was necessary. This is the common thread that binds postwar Soviet foreign policy to prewar practice as it, in turn, was tied to traditional Russian interests.

3. Vital Interests. What are the vital interests most highly prized in the hierarchy of Russian and Soviet objectives? This is the question more baffling than any other in current international politics. Obviously, the first concern of Bolshevik policy is the security of the homeland. The Russian people's inbred fear of invasion from without or alien influences from within has been used and exploited for political ends by the Communist regime in power. Yet the territorial integrity of the Soviet state has been the guidepost of Soviet foreign policy since Chicherin. Since World War II, this interest in practice has rested on dual foundations. One has been the stability and friendly character of governments in an inner security zone. The other has been a balance of power outside this security zone. The military strategy of the Soviet Union was political in character through most of World War II. It sought the basis for a security zone in Eastern Europe. Partly because of its policy and power and partly because of Western military strategy, it was able to establish conditions for achieving this aim. Once its power was recognized in this zone, it was a mistake to expect that the political practices of the West, free elections, could be instituted in the sphere comprising the core of Soviet national interests.

Of special importance to the Soviet Union are the Ukraine and the status of Poland. It is an open question often debated whether Soviet foreign policy is oriented primarily eastward or westward. Obviously there has been expansion in both directions. In the thirties this brought it into conflict with both Germany and Japan. The issue, which arose then and which in different terms is present in the minds of Western statesmen today, is whether Russian vital interests were in fact concentrated most heavily in the West or in the East. The experiences of earlier periods are hardly more than inferentially valid, but the Soviet Union was forced to choose in this historic crisis. The menace on either flank was almost equally forbidding. Japan as a military power with " troops in being " might have appeared the more immediate threat. In war with Japan, Russians would be handicapped by unfavorable terrain and overextended lines of communication. Germany at this time was still disarmed. Yet the decision was that the greater threat was Germany for if the Ukraine should fall, a vital interest would be lost. Russia could lose the territory east of Lake Baikal and still survive, it was argued. But if the Ukraine were lost, with it would go the chief Soviet granary and workshop. It would be years and take numerous Five Year Plans before industry behind the Urals and wheat production in Western Siberia could replace these essential resources.

The vital interests of the Soviet Union include the integrity of the U.S.S.R. and the Ukraine and the security of Poland from the West, an inner security zone including most of Eastern Europe, access to the North Sea, to the Mediterranean and to the Pacific, spheres of influence in the Middle East and North and Northeast Asia. As a condition for the protection of its vital interests, it seeks a balance of power in the Far East and in Central Europe. Ultimately, Communist interests include more than this. Eventually they would encompass the world. But at present, analysts must depend on history in assessing paramount Soviet-Russian interests. Historically they have involved the areas of Russian vital interests which we have discussed. It is significant that again in 1951 the Soviet Union has itself foresworn open warfare in the Far East and continues to amass its greatest strength on the Continent of Europe.

C. Contemporary Diplomatic Problems

79. Introduction

One factor that is unique in the present "cold war" is the influence it exerts on political conflicts and issues in almost every area of the world. In this sense, problems that are exclusively municipal in character scarcely exist anymore. Elections in Germany, land reform in Italy, or famine in China are no longer conceived of as merely important events in local history. Instead, what takes place is interpreted on the basis of the effects it may have on the outcome of the East-West struggle. The present crisis has penetrated politics within states all around the globe.

Inasmuch as our international struggle is world-wide, the misconception has been fostered that so universal a rivalry must in its nature be everywhere the same. When this first error in judgment is defended and maintained, a second mistake must logically and inevitably follow. If the threat is identical everywhere throughout the world, then the remedies for allaying it should be substantially the same. The policies we ought to follow should be consistent, it is said, and everywhere the same.

In fact, the present crisis is not so simply dealt with or explained. There are in practice at least three discrete dimensions in the East-West struggle. First, there is an inner and tragically perilous dimension. Some writers have called it "the in-between zone." Here a great struggle for vital concentrations of industrial and military power is being waged constantly and unremittingly. The struggle for Germany is the best example at present, but the struggle for Japan could become just as grave and decisive an issue. Germany's resources, its skills, and its manpower and the political and military potential it provides make central Europe a critical focal point where the anxieties and ambitions of the Western powers, of the Soviet Union and its satellites, and of a reviving Germany all come together. Neither the United States nor the Soviet Union could afford to lose Germany decisively, permanently, and completely to the other side. Yet across sidewalks and provisional boundaries drawn through the center and soul of Germany, the contending antagonists face one another as only the shadow of their earlier agreement remains. For Europeans the development most laden with import and meaning for the future is the reappearance of the once prostrate but now reinvigorated Germany claiming rights and interests of its own. Its capacity to achieve these claims and demands by playing the protagonists against one another is something not lost on those who have a mind for Germany's past history.

The second layer of the conflict includes competition over areas which make up the hard core or center of both spheres. Parts of Eastern and all Western Europe make up this zone. For the United States the independence of Europe has been a traditional if unavowed objective for which we have gone to war in two major World Wars. Today we have expressed this same interest more decisively and directly through our policies of military and economic assistance. Yet whereas our accomplishments are occasions for pride, the far-reaching issues of European community remain one of the West's major unsolved problems.

The third dimension to be identified is the West's outer sphere, including the Far East. There has been far less of a positive program here for which we would care to take credit. Our failures in the Far East are primarily the failure of will as to action we knew should be taken. Having correctly appraised the nature of the struggle in the Chinese civil war, we proceeded to support with military assistance the side we had declared could not win. Having recognized the character of the movement throughout Asia as being of a genuine revolutionary nature, we proceeded to act as if only the support of our enemy were responsible for the uprisings within this vast and ancient world region. Having said that the situations in Asia and Europe were not essentially the same, we proceeded to act as if the same basis for democratic propaganda was present in both places.

In the selections which follow, G. A. Craig, Professor of History at Princeton University, discusses the problem of Germany in historic perspective. A more recent article which appeared in *The Economist* (London) brings his review up to date. Another article discusses Europe under the Marshall Plan. Harold R. Isaacs, Far Eastern correspondent, author, lecturer and analyst briefly appraises the dimensions of the crisis or revolt of Asia. The crisis Mr. Isaacs has described was characterized on January 8, 1951, by Governor Adlai E. Stevenson in the following way:

Pray heaven we can remember . . . that military force alone cannot win the day for us in Asia. Our moral authority there is low because we are white and Asia is colored. Desperately poor, struggling to shake off the shackles of white colonialism, Asia is just now passing thru the era of revolution, independence and self-determination that swept the western world long ago. It will take great patience, great insight, great restraint for us who see the whole world in our own image and likeness to win confidence and faith in the great uncommitted areas of Asia. It can't be done with the white man's sword. But it can be done; they can be convinced that communist imperialism is not liberation but a more deadly enemy of normal aspirations for freedom and social justice than colonialism.

In another setting he declared:

There was a day when we Americans believed that it was only necessary for the rest of the world to know about democratic freedom and they would desperately want it. We used to take it pretty much for granted that the oppressed and wretched masses of Asia, or even the primitive natives of Africa, would be yearning for the blessings of freedom and democracy. Forgetting our own stormy history and bitter struggles, in our blind faith and sometimes naive hope, we failed to recognize that words and platitudes, dreams and ideals, were not sufficient to win the interest of the hungry, oppressed and ignorant. We exported our speeches and our finished goods, but seldom offered a way for all to share in these goods or the tangible hope which would give concrete meaning to our ideas and free institutions.

But of late we have been awakening to the fact that people who have been hungry or oppressed are attracted by adroit, emphatic demagogues who offer them a blueprint of a new world without hunger and oppression. True, we know these blueprints don't disclose the price in terms of human rights and freedom, but to the native of Burma or the coolie of China who has never enjoyed and seldom even heard of these privileges of democratic life they have scarcely any meaning.

Almost too late we have learned that hope to many does not precede but follows tangible economic and social advance. So at last we are rapidly learning the facts of life and making the first beginnings of a realistic attack on the central problem of our time, which is victory in the war of ideas and peace. Now, belatedly, we are starting to export our most marketable and precious product, the " know-how " which has made this country the envy of the world and the greatest social and political force since the fall of Rome.

80. Germany: Satellite or Great Power?*

. . . Today we are confronted with a situation in which Germany is the main field of contention between the Eastern and Western Powers and in which the Germans are being ardently wooed by the very states upon whom they thrust war in 1939 and 1941.

The present tug-of-war over Germany involves great dangers for the Western world. The chiefest of these we all realize — namely, that Russia may win the struggle and dominate all Germany. But even if that does not happen — even if the Western Powers succeed in establishing a viable Western German state — there is the danger that, in doing so, we may forget the original objectives of our German policy, restore to power individuals and groups whose values have nothing in common with our own, and create a state which is a source of embarrassment and danger to the Western bloc.

It is important for Americans to assess the dangers inherent in their present policy in Germany; and one way for them to do so is to turn to history. For Germany once before was a defeated power — once before she stood between the East and the West — and, on that previous occasion, she was able to exploit her situa-

* From G. A. Craig, "Germany Between the East and the West," in *Proceedings of the Academy of Political Science*, Vol. 23. Copyright 1949 by the Academy of Political Science, New York. Reprinted by permission of G. A. Craig and the Academy of Political Science.

tion in order to escape the controls which military defeat had brought upon her and to involve the world in another war. There are obvious differences between the present situation and that subsequent to Germany's defeat in 1918; but there are enough similarities to justify some consideration of the earlier period.

I think it may be said that there has never been a time — except perhaps the present — in which "democracy," so called, was more popular in Germany than the period between the armistice of November 1918 and the acceptance of the peace terms in June 1919. In those troubled days, Germany lay powerless, her armies smashed by the Allied Powers, her country rent by a revolution which threatened to submerge the land in Bolshevism. In these circumstances, the groups which assumed political leadership in Germany chose to associate themselves with the principles of their victorious foe and called for a democratic parliamentary Germany.

The dominant political groups in Germany in 1918 were the Social Democratic party and the Left-wing elements of the old Progressive and Center parties; and their profession of faith in democratic principles was consistent with their record of opposition to Hohenzollern absolutism. This could not be said, however, of all or even the majority of the avowed democrats of 1918. The bulk of the German middle classes accepted Social Democratic leadership not because of democratic conviction but largely because that was the surest way of protecting their position against the threat of Bolshevism. And the foreign policy of the Social Democrats — acceptance of the Fourteen Points and orientation toward the West — was supported by many German Nationalists solely for tactical reasons, in the hope that expression of faith in democracy might win a lenient peace for Germany and make it possible for her to regain a measure of independence in international affairs. Indeed, in the period of peace negotiations, some German leaders thought it might even be possible to exploit the Allies' fear of Bolshevism to the advantage of Germany. On the eve of Brockdorff-Rantzau's departure for Versailles, General Groener of the High Command urged him to point out to the Allies that stringent peace terms might plunge Germany into general despair, and that communism would follow; and later, in his memoirs, Groener admitted that by such tactics he had hoped to persuade the Allies to rehabilitate Germany as a military power for the purpose of a joint crusade against Russia.

Such extravagant hopes came to nothing. Unconvinced by the late conversion of Germany to democratic principles, the Allies at Versailles imposed a peace which was far from lenient and which established controls designed to prevent German rearmament or the resurgence of aggressive nationalism. The outburst of fury which greeted the peace terms in Germany was followed by a perceptible weakening of the popularity of democracy. As long as Bolshevism remained a threat to propertied interests, there was no open manifestation of this. By the end of 1919, however, the Spartacist menace had been liquidated and internal security had been restored, and in the following year these facts and resentment against the peace treaty were reflected in a strong swing to the right in German domestic politics. The elections of June 1920 showed the evanescent character of the wave of democracy which had swept Germany in 1918. The middle classes which had temporarily supported the Weimar Coalition now gave their votes to the chauvinist parties of the Right and the prewar ruling groups came back to prominence.

This domestic revolution of June 1920 also brought an end to the predominantly Western orientation of German foreign policy. The professional diplomats, the soldiers, and the industrialists, whose influence in policy formulation was now reestablished, sought to restore Germany's freedom of diplomatic action as a first step toward restoring Germany's power; and, in furtherance of this intention, they had no compunction about turning away from the West and toward Soviet Russia.

The man whose name is most closely associated with the new Eastern orientation was General Hans von Seeckt, head of the German Reichswehr. Seeckt thought primarily in terms of military recovery, and it was his hope that collaboration with Russia might make possible the evasion of the military clauses of the peace treaty. As early as the fall of 1920, Seeckt, on his own initiative, was sending agents to Moscow to establish relations with the Russian General Staff; and, in September 1921, secret talks in Berlin laid the basis for a Russo-German agreement concerning production of war materials on Russian soil. In these meetings detailed plans were drawn up for the establishment of aviation and tank training schools and for the production inside Russia of aircraft, artillery grenades, and poison gas by German firms like Junkers, Stolzenberg and Krupp; and in 1922 German officers were despatched to Russia to set these plans in operation.

Seeckt's schemes were given full support by the politicians. To men like Josef Wirth and Walter Rathenau — who were discovering that the Western Powers were united in their insistence that the Versailles peace terms be observed — the new Eastern orientation offered a means of demonstrating that Germany was neither isolated nor completely helpless. It was Rathenau, indeed, who in April 1922 supplemented Seeckt's secret negotiations with the conclusion of the much publicized Treaty of Rapallo, in which Russia and Germany announced to the world that they were henceforth pledged to mutual peace and friendship.

The importance of Rapallo can scarcely be underestimated. It was, as the spokesman of the *Deutsche Volkspartei* announced, " a symptom of the resurrection of Germany's activity " in foreign affairs. It not only

surprised the Western Powers but tended to disunite them, making the British at least more receptive to German arguments against the Versailles Treaty. Thus, Ago von Maltzan was to claim later that Rapallo was the necessary prerequisite for the Dawes Plan and the relaxation of military controls on Germany. And finally, of course, Rapallo gave an impetus to the joint Russo-German military plans formulated earlier by Seeckt.

Had Seeckt had his way, Rapallo would have been followed by an actual military alliance between Russia and Germany. To the professional diplomats, however, who thought in terms of playing Russia off against the West and winning advantages from both, such a permanent tie seemed premature. Germany's first ambassador to Russia, Brockdorff-Rantzau, warned in September 1922 that it would be dangerous " for us to give ourselves into the hands of the wholly unscrupulous Soviet Government," that it would destroy the possibility of driving a real wedge between England and France, and that active alliances must be deferred to a later date. Here there is no doubt that the diplomat was wiser than the soldier. Given his head, Seeckt might very well have precipitated a general war in 1923 — it is known that he weighed seriously the possibility of joint Russo-German assaults on Poland and Czechoslovakia — and the results of such military adventures would have been disastrous. In a phrase used earlier by Walther Rathenau, Germany by such policy would merely have committed hara-kiri on the doorstep of France.

Instead of committing Germany definitely to the Eastern orientation, the Foreign Office maintained a flexibility of policy which made possible adjustment to changing needs. Thus, when the French invasion of the Ruhr involved Germany in the horrors of inflation, the Eastern orientation was jettisoned temporarily by the government and — despite the anguished cries of the Russians who warned against dangers of Western imperialism — a new approach was made to the West.

This new Western orientation of 1923 was no more bred of love of democracy or affection for the West than the Western orientation of 1918. It was a tactical shift made necessary by the collapse of the German currency, the spread of social disorder, and the dangerous resurgence of communism within Germany. It was designed to bolster up German industry by securing loans from the West and it succeeded in that purpose. It succeeded also in winning a degree of sympathy for the German cause in the Western world which had its logical culmination in the Locarno agreement of 1925, the entrance of Germany into the League of Nations, and the relaxation, despite French objections, of the military control system imposed upon Germany in 1918.

The formulator and executor of Germany's foreign policy from 1923 to 1929 was Gustav Stresemann, perhaps the greatest German diplomatist since Bismarck. Stresemann was perfectly sincere in his desire to break down what he called "the iron curtain between France and Germany," because he felt that a *détente* in Franco-German relations was the indispensable prerequisite for the attainment of Germany's legitimate policy objectives. These objectives he defined as a diminution of the reparations burden, the withdrawal of Allied troops from German soil, the general strengthening of Germany's diplomatic position, and, eventually, the rectification by peaceful means of Germany's frontiers to the east. But if these objectives were to be attained, Stresemann also insisted, Germany must not orient herself so completely to the West that she became a satellite of the Western Powers. In words which might almost be applied to the present situation, Stresemann in 1925 said that Germany must continue to balance between Russia and the Western Powers.

"The question of a choice between East and West [he wrote] does not follow from our entrance into the League of Nations. One can make such a choice only if he has military power at his disposal. In our case, unfortunately, that is lacking. We can neither become a continental dagger for England, as some desire, nor can we trust ourselves to a German-Russian alliance. I warn against the utopia of flirting with Russia. Once the Russians are in Berlin, the red flag will fly from the castle; and in Russia they will be satisfied with having bolshevized Europe to the Elbe and will allow the rest of Germany to be gobbled up by the French. On the other hand, we are perfectly ready to deal with the Russians on another basis in order to prevent selling ourselves to the West. . . . The most important [task of German foreign policy] is the liberation of German soil from any occupying force. We must get the stranglehold off our neck. On that account German policy will be one of *finassieren* [of finesse] and of avoiding the great decisions."

When, in 1926, the Russians themselves began to accuse Stresemann of selling Germany out to the West, and when their complaints were taken up by the German Nationalists, Stresemann found it expedient to modify his earlier doubts and to conclude a new agreement with Russia, the so-called Treaty of Berlin, which converted Russo-German friendship into a virtual alliance. The British ambassador in Berlin noted that the new treaty " shows how unwilling the Germans are to separate themselves in any absolute manner from the Russian connection." This was a correct conclusion. The policy of finesse demanded that Germany keep a foot in both the Eastern and Western camps.

Nor can there be any doubt that the policy of finesse worked, to the extent of restoring to Germany complete diplomatic freedom and a large measure of military power. The Western connection brought Germany not only loans to stimulate her heavy industry but also — despite French complaints — the progressive relaxation of military controls. In 1927, for instance, the work of the Inter-Allied Control Commission came to a complete stop; and there-

after Western military observers in Germany could report violations of the treaty but could scarcely expect anything to be done about them. At the same time, Germany's Eastern connection, strengthened by the Treaty of Berlin, enabled Germany to push forward the joint armament and training program laid down by Seeckt in 1921.

If, in these same years, the democratic forces inside Germany had grown in strength, the recovery of Germany which was effected by Stresemann might have contributed to the general pacification of Europe and the restoration of a balance of power not unlike that of the Bismarck period. History, however, was not so kind; and after the collapse of the German economy in 1929–1930 it was Adolf Hitler who emerged as the beneficiary of Stresemann's work. When Hitler assumed power, he found that the controls devised in 1918 to restrain ambitions like his own were already so weak as to be ineffective; his main contribution was to destroy what was left of them publicly and contemptuously. Hitler found also that the incompatibility of English and French views was so great that he need no longer place as much importance on a Russian tie as had his predecessors. But even Hitler, it should be noted, did not abandon the Eastern orientation completely. In 1939 when Western opposition to his designs began to harden, Hitler's ambassador in Moscow informed the Russians that Germany still considered the Berlin Treaty of 1926 as a valid instrument; and, thus, Stresemann's treaty served as the basis for the negotiations which led to the Nazi-Soviet Pact.

Seen as a whole, the period 1918–1939 is one in which Germany was able to recover from an isolated and powerless condition by using a shifting East-West orientation. In the adjustment of her policy from phase to phase, genuine conviction — real agreement with Eastern or Western ideals — played a very minor role. The game was one of expediency, designed to promote German interests, to build up German power and to free Germany from dependence upon others.

As I said before, there are, of course, great differences between the situation which obtained in Germany after 1918 and the situation in Germany today. Germany is at present in a state of total occupation, which was never true after 1918. Moreover, since — even in the West — there is no autonomous government with power to determine foreign policy, there has been little opportunity for Germans thus far to indulge in diplomatic maneuvering. One suspects, however, that these differences are not essential. The logic of events, by bringing on the current Soviet-Western duel, has made the problem of East-West orientation more vital for Germans than ever before. The Russians have already forcibly " oriented " their zone unto themselves; the Western Powers are frantically engaged in building up a Western German state as a bulwark against the Soviet.

As we go ahead with this objective, can we learn anything from the history of the earlier period? At the very least, it would seem that historical memory should make us more skeptical of German professions of democracy than we seem to be at present. The predominant political tendency in Germany today is orientation toward the West. Because of this, and in our eagerness to check Russia, we appear in recent months to have assumed that Western orientation is synonymous with democratic conviction; and we have been irritated because the French have been rather less convinced by this late conversion and rather more reluctant to reward it with a grant of powers of autonomy in government and industry. Yet we have little evidence to justify a belief that the present Western orientation is any different from the similar movements of 1918 and 1923 — a rally to the West on the part of a middle class motivated by fear of communism and by the desire to assume positions of power in any German state we may set up. Certainly all of the clamant German professions of faith in Western ideals are discounted by recent intelligence to the effect that, throughout the Western zones, there has been a revival of nationalistic parties, that former Nazis have been creeping back into public office, and that the leadership principle still exercises a fatal attraction among German youth. . . . There have been sufficient reports of this kind to suggest that there may be more " democrats in name " than " democrats in principle " in Western Germany.

Moreover, it is at least questionable that we ourselves have done much to encourage the genuine democratic elements which do exist in Germany. That there are such forces — in the trade-union movement, for instance, and in the Social Democratic party— is evident. But one suspects at times that our policy makers in Germany have been alienated by the advanced social doctrines advocated by these groups and have preferred to work with men whose political past may be suspect but whose views on free private enterprise are sound. Thus there is a real danger that we may be on the point of setting up an autonomous state in which political and economic power will be controlled by men who pay lip service to democracy but whose allegiance to democratic ideals will be as short-lived as it was in 1918–19 and in 1933. That such a state would be an effective bulwark against the Soviet threat is doubtful.

Indeed, a Western German state which was dominated by rehabilitated industrialists, disguised nationalists, ex-Party *Bonzen* and civil servants carried over from the old regime might well reward its creators by a speedy accommodation with Russia. Here again history provides a warning. If, in the 1920's, fear of communism was a prevalent middle-class reaction, willingness to deal with Russia was something which cut across class lines and inspired the activities of Germans of varying social status. So in the future, while middle-class fear of communism may be a factor in our favor it may not be sufficiently strong to weld Germany permanently to the West. The Germans, after all, remember their own history and are aware that, in the 1920's, Soviet Russia — as a counter-weight to the West — was a potent instrument in Germany recovery. The temptation to try to make history repeat itself may be too great to resist.

Thus, within our Western German state, we may see the emergence of a new Eastern school which comprises — as it did in the 1920's — not only professed Communists and Left-wing labor leaders, but also such diverse elements as: soldiers (like Seeckt) who hope for the rehabilitation of their profession through collaboration with Russia; ex-diplomats (like Ulrich von Hassell) who hope to try their hand at Stresemann's policy of finesse; businessmen (including some of the very industrialists who are currently recipients of American favors) who remember the profits made by the Junkers and Krupps in the 1920's; unsophisticated patriots who dream of becoming twentieth-century Yorck von Wartenburgs and freeing Germany from Western domination with Russian aid; and despairing aristocrats (like Brockdorff-Rantzau in his last years or like Adam von Trott zu Solz of the German resistance) who revolt against the "bourgeois prejudice and pharisaic theorizing" of the West and succumb to the blandishments of national bolshevism. . . . Unless the Western Powers exercise extreme caution in delineating the powers of their new German state and in selecting its rulers, it is quite likely that they may yet be rudely startled by a new Rapallo.

81. Germany as an Ally*

Bonn is losing no time over the ratification of the conventions ending the Allied occupation and of the treaty embodying the European Defence Community. The process may be held up by the German Social Democrats' appeal to the Federal Supreme Court, contesting the German Government's constitutional right to sign the agreements, but this is no more than a delaying action. The general view in Germany is that ratification will take place, even if the majority is small. That this should be likely will surprise only those who, like Mr. Michael Foot, claim to know " by plentiful evidence " that a majority of the Germans oppose the agreements. In fact, the ascertainable mood of the German people is far nearer to apathy, to the desire to be left alone and, like Louis Philippe's bourgeois, to enrich themselves. Any apprehension lest the new settlement may delay German unity and invite Russian counter-measures is more or less balanced by the knowledge that the EDC convention represents a formidable advance towards equality and freedom of action.

The West Germans, without an army or even the pretensions to one, receive completely equal status with the French whose military establishment is large, independent and already in being. Moreover, in the

* From *The Economist* (London), CLXIII (1952), pp. 721–22. Reprinted by permission of *The Economist*.

first stages, an agreement with the Americans offers the Germans the possibility of building up an army at bargain prices. At first, Germany will be responsible for nothing but maintenance costs. The United States is to provide the heavy equipment during the period of training and much light equipment. Later on, it is true, when the full cost of modern armies is realized by the Germans, and when, under EDC orders, the Ruhr may begin to produce tanks and guns, diverting heavy industry from civilian use, the matter may look different. But for the time being the path offered by EDC to the recovery of sovereignty and equality of arms is fantastically favorable to a nation which, only just over seven years ago, was still dragging itself and Europe down in a common destruction.

It would be encouraging to record that a realization of this fact is general in Western Germany and that the new vista of sovereignty and responsibility is showing up qualities of statesmanship in people and press at large. Unhappily, Dr. Adenauer's brave conception of Germany as a partner of the West and a good neighbor in Europe, is, like the agreements which give embodiment to the idea, received with considerable indifference. Interest concentrates upon the guarantees given Germany, not upon the responsibilities it assumes. There is little feeling that Germany needs allies. It is rather that Germany is being asked to sacrifice itself in someone else's cause.

A reaction of such narrow national self-interest is hardly promising for the growth of a European community. Now, therefore, that the immediate pattern of German sovereignty and rearmament is known and the first German reaction has been tested, it cannot be said that reassurance has taken the place of earlier fears among Germany's neighbors or that the spectacle of a rearmed and independent Germany chills the blood any less. Memories are not after all so short and it may well be that the real crisis over ratification will occur not in the German Assembly but in Paris. There is a similar reaction in Britain. The Labor Party, in demanding that fresh German elections should precede the ratification of the new agreements, is not in theory asking that they should be abandoned — that would not be too embarrassing for Mr. Attlee and Mr. Morrison. But that, nevertheless, would be the obvious result.

Admittedly, the political motives of those who have forced Mr. Attlee to accept this gloss upon German policy are probably domestic. They do not so much fear German rearmament as need some issue upon which to differ from the bipartisan approach to Western Europe evolved under Mr. Bevin and continued under Mr. Eden. Yet the rider is now included in Labor's official program for its autumn conference, and although the retreat from bipartisanship on this point will make no difference to British ratification, it will confuse further a public opinion already confused enough about putting weapons back into German hands.

It is, therefore, of supreme importance to remember that even now, when the contractual agreements have been agreed and signed, they cannot be left to speak for themselves. The real and overriding reasons for them must still be explained and repeated and insisted upon, in season and out. Short of world disarmament, there is no way in which the most powerful nation in Europe can be kept without sovereignty and without arms. Short of permanent occupation, there is no way in which a people, even a divided people, of nearly 70 million, can be deprived of the attributes of power which their neighbors possess. The great argument for the EDC and for the contractual agreements is that they are probably the last opportunity of persuading Germany to contribute, as the recent statement of Labor Party policy demands, "toward a system of collective security . . . within which German forces could serve without danger to their neighbors." In the long run, this can come about only if sufficient Germans wish it to come about. The present experiment is almost certainly the last opportunity of coaxing them into a collective system and of proving to enough of the new generation that the system works. Delay it, impede it, abandon it, and in its place will finally come the armed, united, sovereign Germany bargaining between East and West and owing no allegiance to anything save its naked self-interest.

Yet if the new agreements offer the last opportunity for securing German rearmament within a collective framework and with proper safeguards, this does not mean that the safeguards are already sufficient and that the framework is adequate at every point. In the House of Commons on Tuesday, Mr. Eden referred to the agreements as "a culmination" of the policy of bringing Germany into the western community. It would surely be wiser to refer to them as a beginning only. It is no use talking about the Atlantic community and the West European community as though they existed. They do not. In fact, on the economic front, both attempts at association are suffering grievous setbacks this year and are likely to suffer more. At the moment, it seems more certain that Western Germany will be rearmed than that the restraining collective framework will be made to work. The months ahead need to be a period of the most vigorous effort to ensure that the Allies' German policy does not go off at half-cock — with Western Germany sovereign and rearming and its neighbors no more united than they are today.

The needed line of advance lies first of all in Western Germany itself. There the processes of rearmament should not be hurried. In the military office of Herr Blank, working closely with Dr. Adenauer, there are men sincerely convinced of the ideal of European defense, anxious to keep German rearming clear of any taint of the old militarism, determined to maintain civilian and European control. They must be allowed to make the pace and form the cadres. If too much pressure for quick expansion is applied, they will be swamped by the old guard. There were only 40,000 ex-officers after 1918. Hitler's legacy was 400,000, among them thousands of generals. Dr. Adenauer must not be forced to throw down the dams against this turbulent tide. At the same time, Germany's allies need to continue in the excellent mood established by General Eisenhower, the mood not of war, but of peace through strength. The distinction is not yet familiar to Germans who, when asked whether they wish to defend themselves, tend to reply that they do not want war.

Within Europe, the need is to hasten forward with all speed the creation and functioning of the various "communities," whose existence is the best guarantee of a generally collective spirit and policy. If, for instance, the officers of the new Germany are to learn a European spirit, it is better that they should start, not finish, their training in European staff colleges. But the staff colleges have first to exist. All that Britain can do to hasten the process of unification and to participate in it within the political limits set by both parties should be set on foot at once. It is encouraging that Mr. Eden has himself taken the chairmanship of the Council of OEEC and that, at Strasbourg, his proposals to associate the Schuman Plan and the EDC with the Council of Europe were so well received and given such wide support. The need now is for Britain to become a pace-setter for Europe's advance toward unity.

The decisive arena is, however, the Atlantic world. No European arrangements, even with British participation, can do more than restore the balance of Stresemann, Locarno and the twenties. The overwhelming concentration of power necessary to bring Germany down decisively on the western side lies in the United States, and no caution over premature rearmament inside Germany, no advance toward unity in Europe, no British participation therein, can safeguard Europe against an irresponsible German resurgence unless the United States is a permanent partner in the Atlantic community. Any belief in America that Germany can be built up as a substitute for American commitments in Europe has in it the seeds of the next war. In fact, Germany should be a partner not only in the West European but in the North Atlantic community as well, so that its statesmen and its generals can be exposed day by day to the realities of American participation and American strength.

To say so much is no more than to repeat how long the road ahead still is before any equilibrium or stability can be secured in the western world. The negotiations are over, the papers are signed. The framework of a European policy exists. It is only now that the real work begins.

82. Last Act of the Marshall Plan*

The Marshall Plan is drawing to its close. Officially it ends next June, but already this week the American counterpart organization — the Economic Co-operation Administration — has changed its name to the Mutual Security Administration. This change will not affect the Organization for European Economic Co-operation, which is a permanent body. But it is an indication of the design of things to come. The concept of economic co-operation, in which the emphasis has been on Europe, is being transformed into the wider concept of mutual security, with the emphasis on the North Atlantic community.

It is ironical that Europe, after four years of co-operation, should find itself in what seems to be the same position as in 1947. Europe is still hungry for dollars; the overseas payment accounts of most countries are again markedly in the red; countries are still trying vainly to combat inflation, while the need to increase productivity is just as great as it was four years ago. Was, then, this generous gesture of the United States to no purpose? Has Europe

* From *The Economist* (London) (1952), pp. 8-9. Reprinted by permission of *The Economist*.

achieved nothing under the Marshall Plan?

Europe's recovery program was based on four aims. First, an expansion in output, particularly in agriculture, fuel and power, transport and modernization of equipment. Secondly, the creation and maintenance of internal financial stability.

sions which will be manageable through normal means without special aid.

Looking back on the events of 1950 and 1951, the architects of that report can be justifiably proud of their far-sightedness; for 1950 seemed to herald the fulfillment of recovery, a fulfillment that was frustrated by the

TABLE I — EUROPE'S ACHIEVEMENT IN AGRICULTURE

	Prewar	1950–51	Objective 1950–51
	(Million Metric Tons)		
All cereals...................	64.0	64.1	65.8
Bread grains................	34.0	34.5	34.0
Potatoes....................	59.6	72.4	68.2
Sugar......................	3.7	5.5	3.9
Meat.......................	9.7	9.7	8.1
Milk.......................	76.4	81.0	73.5
Oils and fats (incl. butter).....	3.0	3.7	2.9
	(Million Head)		
Cattle.....................	75.0	80.0	80.4
Sheep.....................	106.3	98.0	109.5
Pigs.......................	41.1	38.7	37.1

Thirdly, the development of economic co-operation between the participating countries and, fourthly, reducing Europe's deficit with the American continent particularly by increased exports. The committee of co-operation, which prepared the initial report in September, 1947, was under no illusions about the dollar problem. It maintained that the purpose of the recovery program was to reduce the dollar deficit as fast as possible. The report went on:

There will be some deficit in 1951. . . . But by the end of 1951, given reasonably favorable external conditions, the deficit should be of dimen-

scramble for commodities and the dramatic rise and fall in prices in late 1950 and early 1951.

Any assessment of Europe's achievement must be related to these four aims. Production has increased and most of the objectives have been reached. Four years ago the need to expand agricultural output was great. Food supplies were limited; most countries of Western Europe had rationing schemes in force, while the poor harvest of 1947, coupled with the lack of dollars, raised the specter of starvation. At the time the agricultural objectives were set, many people considered them unattainable. But only two have not been reached. Cereal production in 1950–51 amounted to 64.1 million metric tons compared with its objective of 65.8 million tons; it had, however, regained its prewar level. The production of bread grains was slightly above its objective while the output

tons. The main deficiency has occurred in Britain whose output was only 223 million tons compared with its goal of 249 million tons, though Germany, France and Belgium have also failed to reach their planned output for 1951. Europe's total coal

TABLE II — EUROPE'S ACHIEVEMENT IN INDUSTRY

	Prewar*	1951 †	Objective 1951
Hard Coal (million metric tons).	467.8	459.5	*510.8*
United Kingdom............	233.0	223.2	*249.0*
Germany, Federal Republic...	126.2	117.6	*121.1*
France....................	46.6	52.4	*62.5*
Belgium..................	28.5	29.1	*31.0*
Saar.....................	12.5	17.1	*16.8*
Electricity (billion kwh.)........	130.5	245.8‡	*236.8*
United Kingdom............	23.1	57.8	*54.2*
Germany, Federal Republic...	30.5	49.6‡	*36.1*
France....................	20.8	35.1	*37.0*
Italy.....................	15.4	28.1	*31.3*
Sweden...................	8.2	19.1	*19.3*
Norway...................	9.9	16.9	*15.0*
Crude Steel (million metric tons).	45.5	55.5	*55.4*
United Kingdom............	10.6	15.9	*15.0*
Germany, Federal Republic...	18.2	13.2	*10.2*
France....................	6.2	9.6	*12.7*
Belgium-Luxemburg........	3.8	8.0	*7.9*

* 1935–38 average for coal; 1938 for electricity and crude steel.
† Annual rate based on 9 months. ‡ Annual rate based on 8 months.

of potatoes, sugar, meat, milk and oils and fats were well above theirs. And in each case the prewar level was exceeded. Cattle numbers are close to their objective, while pig numbers have already passed theirs. The only other deficiency is in sheep numbers.

In industry, too, most of the objectives have already been achieved. The only blot on the record is coal, the production of which in 1951 (based on the first nine months) reached 460 million metric tons against the objective of 511 million

production is still below its prewar level. Electricity production in 1951 amounted to 246 billion kwh compared with the objective of 237 billion kwh and a prewar level of 130.5 billion kwh. All the major countries except France and Italy have more or less passed their goals. Steel production is also up to schedule and German output well above it. France, again, is the exception; its output in 1951 was still well below its objective.

In 1947 the shortage of locomotives and rolling stock was a major difficulty. Although no comparable figures are available to prove that this problem has been overcome, Europe is no longer beset with transport difficulties. The increase in motor vehicle production in Britain, France and Germany during the past four years has been almost phenomenal, while tractor production has also been maintained at a high level. Among the consumer goods, textile production has expanded, and the problem at the moment is not to find clothes for the people but to find people to buy the clothes.

Modernization of industry has also gone on apace, though again it is difficult to show the progress in specific figures. Total industrial production of Western Europe in 1949 was 13 per cent higher than in 1948; in 1950 it was 25 per cent higher and in 1951 35 per cent higher — a very significant increase. On the other hand, the working population increased by 1½ per cent in 1949 and by almost 1 per cent in each of the two succeeding years:

	Index of Industrial Production	Index of Working Population
1948	100	100
1949	113	101½
1950	125	102½
1951	135	103½

It is fair to conclude from the comparison of these two trends that productivity per man-year has increased so rapidly in Western Europe during the past four years, that improved equipment must have played a major role, even though a significant part of the increase in output was due both to the revival of Germany and to the use of previously unemployed resources.

On production, then, Europe has done well enough with the single exception of coal, adequate supplies of which are vital to European recovery. The fight against inflation, however, has been less successful. Most countries have experienced an almost continuous rise in prices since 1946, though until 1950 the rise has been generally moderate. But as was shown in an article on page 1380 in *The Economist* of December 8, 1951, even the sharp rise in the latter part of 1950 and in 1951 was helped by too ample credit facilities granted to manufacturers and traders to build up stocks. In all countries retail prices have increased more sharply than they would have done if higher import prices had been the sole cause, while in most countries wage-rates have kept pace with the rise in the cost of living. Europe has certainly warded off the dangers of "hyper-inflation" but it has remained a victim of "creeping inflation."

The progress on co-operation has not been very spectacular but it has been none the less real. The intra-European payments scheme followed by the European Payments Union are only two examples. The freeing of intra-European trade from quantitative restrictions is another and by the middle of 1951 most countries had freed at least 75 per cent of their private trade and had also adopted a common list of goods on which restrictions were abolished. This was a new step in economic co-operation. Previously countries were allowed to choose independently which goods they would free. This same technique of a common list has been employed in the prohibition of the use of certain scarce materials in the production of consumer goods. Again, the Schuman Plan for an integrated European coal and steel industry is at last coming to fruition.

$1.7 billion and in 1951 $2.4 billion. If the value of imports from the dollar area in 1951 had not been so large, Europe would, indeed, have reduced its dollar deficit to more manageable proportions.

The similarity between 1947 and 1951 is, therefore, only superficial. Europe has not squandered Amer-

TABLE III — TRADE OF WESTERN EUROPE

(Million Dollars)

Year	Imports (a)	Exports	Balance	Exports to USA and Canada
1948.......	22,163.6	16,835.5	− 5,328.1	1,289.3
1949.......	22,352.5	18,822.5	− 3,530.0	1,171.2
1950.......	21,788.1	19,736.2	− 2,051.9	1,655.8
1951 *	30,095.4	26,297.3	− 3,798.1	2,380.8

* Annual rate based on 9 months.   (a) Adjusted to f.o.b.

Even on its foreign trade Europe can record achievement. Its total trade deficit was reduced from $5.3 billion in 1948 to $2.1 billion in 1950. In 1951, owing to the sharp rise in the value of imports, it rose once more to $3.8 billion. But Europe's exports have increased at a surprising rate from $16.8 billion in 1948 to $26.3 billion in 1951. In volume, exports rose by 75 per cent during this period. Of more immediate concern for the dollar problem is Europe's expansion in exports to the United States and Canada. This was to be Europe's main method of reducing its dollar deficit. In 1948 exports to these two countries amounted to $1.3 billion; by 1950 they had reached

ica's generous gift. It has increased output; it has re-equipped its industry, it has worked as a unit in certain fields and it has expanded both its total exports and its exports to the United States and Canada. Its major deficiency has been its failure to bring under control its internal inflation. Without rearmament even this would not have had very serious consequences. From the United States' point of view the disbursement of $12 billion of aid under the Marshall Plan has been a successful investment, and it is worth remembering that the sum is only half of what was originally considered necessary.

83. The Dimensions of the Crisis*

There is almost no vantage point from which we can view the whole heaving panorama of present-day Asia. There is no secure height from which the contemporary historian, with wonder but with detachment, can look out and down upon the great opening fissures, the smoking craters, and the newly-rising peaks and mountain ranges. There is no such place because what is going on in Asia is part of a gigantic rearrangement of continents and nations and classes in which we, too, a hemisphere away, are profoundly involved. We, too, stand on a moving slope. Our own footing is too unsure, our view around us colored by our own danger and our attention wholly absorbed by our frantic reach for safety.

Asia, moreover, is a continent we never saw well or clearly, even in quieter times. We scarcely know what it looked like, what moved its peoples, or how its societies were put together before the great eruptions broke surface and filled the world with their obscurity and tumult. The savants of the past did not accumulate the knowledge or understanding that might have prepared us for the West's downfall in Asia. Scholars now reach desperately for monographs which are not there. Policy-makers devise expedients,

* From Harold R. Isaacs, "Asia's Multiple Revolution," *Saturday Review of Literature*, XXXIV (1951), pp. 13–16, 56. Reprinted by permission of Harold R. Isaacs and the *Saturday Review of Literature*.

which almost always fail for the reason that the people they are aimed at do not react in the expected manner.

On the other hand, the fact that Asia exists and is important has penetrated the American consciousness and is there to stay. This has been part of the process through which we have been forced in the last decade to discover and accept our inescapable links with the rest of the world. It has been a process of what we might call education-through-catastrophe. The Second World War finally jarred this country loose from its classic isolationism and transformed the American people in the main from complacent nationalists into reluctant internationalists. They discovered through an experience that entered in some degree into almost every American's life, that their future was bound up with the future of the peoples of Europe. A thousand affinities with Europe in American origins, culture, and history made this discovery less of a wrench than it might otherwise have been.

Without any such affinities, with much more difficulty and much more slowly, there has also come the knowledge that beyond Europe, insistent and clamorous, lay Asia. Not one but a series of shattering events stretched over ten years — Pearl Harbor, the Pacific war, the Communist conquest of China, the war in Korea — have finally fixed

Asia in the American's mind as a new base point for his thinking about world affairs and America's new world role.

This is a great new fact in our national history. It is not to be minimized because it is still an uninformed awareness or because it is developing amid such monumental confusion. A recent poll indicated that 80 per cent of the American people do not know where in Asia Manchuria is located. That shows that, among other things, we have some geography homework to do. But we do know that Manchuria is *in Asia*. Twice in ten years when crises erupted into war involving Americans the blow came upon us from Asia. One could think of easier educational methods. But this is, at any rate, the way we have learned that Asia *is*, that it has a bearing on all our lives, that we will persist in our ignorance about Asia only at our own utmost peril.

In the American mind especially the crisis in Asia has become inextricably bound up with the menacing expansion of Soviet totalitarianism. The two, to be sure, are linked in many important ways. But it has to be stressed again and again and again that the Asian crisis is not created by Russian totalitarianism but is exploited by it. In one form or another the Asian revolutions would be taking place if there were no such thing as Stalin's Russia. The forces of self-reassertion had begun to gather among the Asian peoples long before Communist Russia became a major power. The Western nations, with their depressions and wars, had begun to do a fair job of disembowelling themselves without Russia's help.

The Asian revolutions came tragically late, in part because the West resisted for so long and so stupidly the liquidation of its Asian empires. Because they are late, these revolutions swirl and eddy into blind passages, seeking to create new nations in an age no longer hospitable to nationhood. Because the long-retarded victory of nationalism can no longer bear fruit in effective social progress, revolutions that remain purely nationalist in content are abortive. The revolutionary pressures go far beyond the matter of national independence to the issues of the whole social structure, relations on the land and between classes, the terms and methods of economic development. These issues force themselves, in turn, far beyond national boundaries. They are soluble no longer within the confines of separate national economies; a new world economy is wanted. Thus the great forces in motion move blindly toward some new coherence. Communist totalitarianism responds to this need with a coherence of a kind, powerful even though it can only lead the peoples of the underdeveloped countries into still another blind passage. The Western world, for its part, has not yet been able to define what new coherence *it* might find to succeed its age of empire. This is the nub of the matter, the heart of the enigma.

To achieve this definition and to act upon it is not a matter of philanthropy. It is a matter of survival. For with the old European empires the whole world economic system based on them came crashing down. That system was based upon a particular relationship between Europe and its colonies. That relationship has been severed now and will never be restored. Empire is gone from Asia and is going in Africa. Whether we appreciate it or not, we are engaged in trying to create a new kind of world political economy, not merely because it would be a good thing to have but because we need it to survive and grow, we of the Americas, and the Asians, and the Africans, and the peoples of Europe. It is into this great context that we must somehow try to fit the crowded violence and confusion of present-day Asia and the circumstances of our own conflict with the new Soviet Russian empire. We have to try to see all these events as the loose segments of a great effort, vast and jagged and irregular and blind, to overcome the obsolete separateness of the nations. We have to find the way of moving along with Asia's revolutions toward some new and tolerable coherence in world affairs, moving into new channels of democratic growth which the United States alone can open. Unless we do, these revolutions and the peoples of Asia will be sucked either into the blind alley of Communist totalitarianism or will adopt other forms of tyranny equally grotesque and insupportable.

It is Russia's great initial advantage that the Asian revolutions are directed in the first place against the West. Russia, too, is in conflict with the West, and we represent it. The major emotional drives in Asia now are compounded of self-assertion against Western power and Western racism and rejection of the whole pattern of enforced inferiority imposed during the age of Western empire. No present avowal of Western good intentions can wipe out all this history and all this accumulated hostility. In this respect the present plight of the West in Asia brings strongly to mind the Biblical dictum about the sins of the fathers.

For beginning with the loot of the great European freebooting expeditions of two and three centuries ago, Asian wealth was fed as primary capital into the process of European industrialization. In the long colonial era, Asian growth was thwarted and deformed, its poverty deepened, and its problems multiplied as its population grew. Many of Asia's present problems are rooted in Asian soil, but the major fact remains that Asian economic development for nearly 300 years was a function not of Asian needs but of Western European requirements. This imposed an insupportable distortion on Asian life. It preserved obsolete social relations and institutions. While creating a thin layer of modernization to service the extraction of wealth, it also created and maintained subsistence economies for multiplying masses of people.

On one hand, Western power established racial mastery and social, economic, and legal superiority for tiny alien minorities, adding to the economic burden the emotional tensions created among people held and treated as helots in their own lands.

On the other hand, the West involuntarily opened up to Asia the immense vistas of modern economic development and democratic revolutionary thought and traditions. These were the explosive charges laid deep in Asian soil during the colonial era. These are the charges that have so recently exploded, one after another, in a gigantic chain reaction across the face of Asia in our own time. They have thrown China, after a tortured history of frustrated struggle, into the arms of a Communist dictatorship. Out of the colonies of southern Asia they have shaped the new republics of India, Burma, Indonesia, and the Philippines, the new dominion of Pakistan, and opened the conflict, still unresolved, in Indochina. Foreign rule has been left more or less intact only in Malaya, where the British sway holds only because the divided population cannot find any nationalist consensus.

We still know too little of all the history, remote and recent, that has gone into the making of these events. The adequate study of it remains a major challenge and task for both Western and Asian scholarship. All the Asian peoples now share their backwardness and their need to overcome it. They share also the legacy of the age of empire and the present anarchic state of the world. But there is a point, even in a summary meant to be brief and broad, where it becomes misleading to generalize about " Asia."

Vast differences among peoples and cultures are embraced in this one great continent, differences as great as the contrasts between its steaming tropical valleys and its Himalayan heights, its equatorial islands and its high, dry, northern continental reaches. Its peoples are of many ethnic varieties. Its civilizations include the Islamic, the Hindu, the Buddhist, the Chinese. Often these, though thousands of years old, are superimposed upon still older animisms which still play a vital and even a governing role in the lives of millions of people. Within each country contrasts and differences abound. Together and separately they condition the thinking and behavior of the people.

Only Asians examining themselves will eventually sort out the roots of their behavior, just as we are only now beginning to sort out our own. But we will all have stereotypes to shed. The Asians will have to get over the stereotype of the bloated Western capitalist, and the Westerner will have to get over such things as the legend of Asian inscrutability, a myth created by Westerners to cloak their own abysmal ignorance of the people they ruled for so long. Varying Asian attitudes and states of mind are a total product, like attitudes anywhere, of culture, environment, and contemporary pressures and circumstances. They remain mysterious only to those who make no effort to understand them. The present upheavals, to be sure, are taking place on a scale often too large for clear visibility. But starting from what we can grasp, we can discern at least some of the major paradoxes into which all this history has propelled the peoples of Asia and the rest of the world. For we can be sure that the resolution — or further complication — of these paradoxes will be the major content of the history that still lies ahead of us.

The first of these paradoxes is wrapped up in the fact that nationalism is triumphing in Asia in an age when nationalism as such is bankrupt. Nationalist self-assertion is still the primary emotion among Asia's dominant intellectuals and leaders, yet in the profoundest historical sense their nationalism is already obsolete and fruitless. They are desperately trying to find new dignity and new growth in nationhood but they are already discovering that nationhood is not enough, that it cannot begin to solve the people's needs. National sovereignty has become not a tool of progress but a brake upon it. If this is true for the older, stronger nations, it is even more cruelly true for these new nations, just emerging with all their accumulated burdens out of their colonial past. Unless they become part of a larger entity engaged in building a new world political economy they are doomed to frustration.

The problem of achieving new national identity, moreover, has been absorbed into the problem of achieving new social identity. The question is no longer: who shall rule, Westerner or Asian? It is rather: which Asian shall rule, peasant or landlord, worker or capitalist, plebeian or aristocrat, democrat or bureaucrat or despot? For the issue is not merely one of power at the summit but of the shape of the entire social fabric, of outworn social relations, of land systems retarding productivity, of the terms and methods of new

growth, of modernization and industrialization. It is a matter of renewing and reshaping superannuated societies, rich with age and tradition but incapable of solving the problems of poverty and ignorance for the masses of people. The friction between imbedded cultural patterns and irresistible pressure for social change will have to generate new syntheses and open new epochs whose shape we can now only dimly perceive.

It is the weakness of the non-Communist Asian nationalist today that he is in the main unable or unwilling to reach toward these new revolutionary perspectives. Often he is a man whose aspirations were satisfied by merely replacing the hated foreigner in the seat of power. More often he is also a man who wants change but does not want to upset existing property rights and social relations. Still more often he is a man who hopes to cope with problems with a gradualness that the times do not allow. And most often he is a man who tends, as the new pressures crowd in upon him, to place the blame for his weaknesses and limitations not upon himself but upon forces outside, on the legacies of empire, on the continuing power struggle which hems him in and deprives him of the aid he so urgently needs. Since these are in fact enormous obstacles in his path, he has ample basis for his new resentments; they lend a certain reasonableness to his increasingly unreasonable sense of frustration and helplessness.

Meanwhile the popular élan which swept nationalism forward in the

wake of the Japanese war has subsided into a dissatisfied apathy, a
deepening mass disillusionment, a
search for other means of achieving
the improvements which national independence was somehow magically
supposed to bring about. In the face
of his own ineffectualness and the
conservatism of the new regimes and
the inhospitableness of the Western
world, the displaced Asian, especially
the displaced Asian intellectual and
the hard-pressed member of the middle class, is being drawn to fanati-
cisms that seem to promise him some
release. This can, as in the case of
Hindu extremism in India, take the
form of religious fanaticism linked
to ultraconservative political and social outlooks. Often it includes a
blind and peculiarly hopeless reach
for a resurrection of the ancient glo-
ries and power that are gone forever;
there is much of this in the Islamic
political movements in Pakistan and
Indonesia. To an increasing extent
it assumes the form of an acceptance
of Communist totalitarianism as the
" wave of the future," as the only hope
of achieving the new national and
social identity and economic coherence the Asian needs and must have.

In this lies a second major paradox
of even more formidable proportions
than the paradox of abortive nationalism. For if conservtive nationalism
is a blind alley, so is Communist totalitarianism. The attractive power
of the Communist movement lies, in
the first place, in its readiness to
carry the revolutionary movement to
bold extremes. It lies, in the second
place, in the example of Russia itself; was not Russia a backward

country that transformed itself by
these means in a single generation
into a major power? Smash Western influence, demolish the old social
relations, create an absolutist power
mechanism, crush all dissidence, mobilize the people, and begin a mon-
ster series of harsh expedients designed to lift the land out of its backwardness by its own sandal-straps.
It can be done because Russia did it
and Russia is today close to ruling
the world. Such, in brief essence, is
the Communist promise and the
Communist claim. It has undeniable power, especially in the face of
faltering conservatism or plain oppression. Yet it is a siren promise,
a false claim. The question is how
much the peoples of Asia — and of
the rest of the world — are going to
have to pay in blood and sweat to
find this out.

That national freedom becomes
pure mythology in the Russian totalitarian empire is a fact of life that
a great many Asians have yet to
learn. It has been demonstrated
within the USSR itself and on a massive scale in Eastern Europe. Within this empire all national purposes
are subordinated to Russian power
strategy and Russian national aggrandizement. Thousands of Communists, not to speak of non-Com-
munists, have found this out in the
prisons and execution chambers of
the Stalinist power machine. In China a further demonstration of this
fact is in process, although its impact cannot yet be measured because
its full force has not yet made itself
felt. But consider, among many other
particulars, the consequences of the

Korean adventure for the new Communist regime. It doubtless had its own reasons for intervening in Korea, but the fact remains that it moved into a tactical operation in the power struggle that was dictated in the first place by the Russians and whose ultimate outcome depended in the end on Russian strategy decisions. The result was a grisly stalemate that cost the Chinese Communists heavily, not only in the tangibles of expended men and materials and deferred internal programs, but in the intangibles of growing internal stringency. Eighteen months after it had come to power amid almost general popular acquiescence the regime had to resort to mass terror. This year popular acquiescence and support for Peking has been transformed into submission, with the revolutionary élan of the people dropping away as the dictatorship claims its victims by the thousands on public execution grounds trampled by obscenely cheering masses of frightened people.

The promise of relative economic development in Asia under totalitarian auspices also fades under closer examination. Asian development on a scale comparable with the needs can take place only on the basis of a new kind of partnership with the advanced West. The Russian empire is not now and will not be for a long time in a position to play this role in relation to its Asian satellites. Russia is still engaged in its own form of primitive accumulation. It does not feed wealth to its empire; it drains it. It is sucking Europe dry and has already begun to exploit

even the meager resources of China to this same end. If it is possible to conceive of a stabilized totalitarian empire dominated by Russia for any extended period, the flow of industrial resources on the necessary scale into Asia will be indefinitely postponed. The condition of the peripheral countries in such an event is scarcely pleasant to contemplate. Even Russia's tyranny will have been a picnic compared to the weight that the power machine will have to exert to bear down on the mounting pressures in Asian lands. The extreme characteristics of the present Chinese mass purges is already an index of what might be expected.

Finally, there is the matter of time. Russia achieved its relative transformation in the first place because it had a resource pattern which no Asian country can match. But it was able to do so primarily because it bought time, thirty years of time, in which to sweat the necessary surpluses out of its own people and to extract what it could from the outside world by extended maneuvering both in the political and economic spheres. It accomplished its purposes at enormous cost both to the Russian people and the European revolutionary movements. It survived the war, thanks to a decisive margin of Western aid, and was able to rebuild itself in no small measure out of the loot of conquest, including the industrial loot it stripped from Manchuria in 1945. No country now drawn into the Russian sphere will be allowed to duplicate this experience or to buy by maneuvering even a fraction of the time that

Russia bought. This, too, is already being demonstrated on a massive scale in China, which needed time so desperately on the morrow of the Communist conquest. Instead, it was cut off from the West and sucked into a conflict that cost it so heavily in ponderable goods and in the imponderables of public support. How much more travail China and perhaps other parts of Asia may have to pass through before this lesson is fully learned, no one now can say.

This brings us to what is perhaps the ultimate paradox of all this history. It is that Asia's hopes for a tolerable epoch of growth and development depend in the final analysis on the West, which did so much to bring Asia to its present pass. These hopes, moreover, rest now with the further evolution of the United States. If there is a democratic alternative to totalitarian development in Asia, it rests with the rise of a new democratic revolutionary synthesis in Asian-American relations. But here, too, the paradoxes multiply. The United States was in a position at the end of the Japanese war to identify itself with the Asian revolutions. Instead, by its failure to grasp the significance of what was happening, by its stubbornly conservative and Europe-focused myopia, by its capitalist inertia and its own stubbornly persistent racialism the United States has managed to become in Asian minds the heir to Western imperialism. This is already a profound drag on American policy in Asia. But even this might yet be overcome if American behavior in Asia can still be based on dem-

ocratic revolutionary premises. Here again, as the need for a revolutionary world outlook mounts, the internal American trend is toward increasing conservatism and a tendency to reduce the terms of the Russian-American struggle to brute force alone.

Yet in Asia, as Korea has demonstrated, brute force is not enough. Force may have to be applied, but it can be applied productively only if it is a function of a total policy that opens up prospects of effective development, encourages democratic revolutionary forces in the Asian countries, and creates on a basis of common self-interest and mutual respect a new American-Asian partnership.

The fact that we have discovered Asia so late lays heavy burdens upon us. Our failure to grasp the meaning of the Asian upheaval has already since 1945 cost us heavily. We may have in these few but explosive years lost more ground than we may be able to retrieve for years to come. On the other hand, lessons learned the hard way are more adhesive. Nor are we alone in having lessons to learn. Millions of Asians are going through a series of shock treatments, discovering great new facts of life with pain, confusion and difficulty. They have at least as much ignorance and as many misconceptions to overcome as we have. This is only in small measure consoling, for it suggests how long and how painful our mutual education-through-catastrophe may be before we finally do stumble out onto common ground and get on with our common business of making the world over.

D. Approaches to Peace

84. Introduction

Five approaches to the problems of international order and peace have prevailed in modern international society. They are the balance of power, disarmament, world government, international organization and diplomacy. Each of them has been identified with a particular philosophy of international politics; each has conceived the resolution of the world's troubles as dependent upon particular methods or agencies without which universal conflict would be inevitable. Often two or more have been combined as essential ingredients of an integral approach. Indeed when any one has been elevated as the only technique, it has usually been the result of popular opinion that, inasmuch as traditional methods had culminated in war, novel techniques were essential to the pursuit of permanent peace.

The classical approach to the unchanging problems of rivalry and war is the balance of power. It provides that in any constellation of mutually independent and separate political entities there is a dynamic principle which operates to infuse order and stability through the tendency of units to establish and reestablish conditions of equilibrium. In the play of political forces, each unit and nation strives to promote a situation in which no single nation by achieving overwhelming power

can threaten at will the survival of all the others. In pursuing these ends, each nation attempts to increase its own power through resolute internal and external policies striving to combine its efforts with strong and faithful allies. The balance of power is always uncertain and temporary for no phase of life can be held in permanent equilibrium. But a rough stability has sometimes been attained through the persistent search for a balance of power with an ever-changing content. There are monuments to both success and failure in the long history of the balance of power, but its greatest contributions have been as an instrument of international order. Because of this principle of political dynamics no one state in modern times has permanently acquired such power that the independence of all others was placed in jeopardy. The modern state system through a system of pressures and balances has operated to prevent universal imperium. On the other hand, the contributions of the balance of power to world peace, although sometimes spectacular, have often been erratic and unpredictable and in general have been unsuccessful for any period of time, as the painful procession of ever-more destuctive wars attests. The balance of power while maintaining international order and the independence of the members of society has failed to preserve the peace. There have been exceptions as in the nineteenth century when the practice of the balance of power was faithfully and prudently cultivated. But nations in general have failed to avert wars through this approach either because they abandoned its enduring principles or misjudged and miscalculated the elements essential to its wise application.

Disarmament as an approach to international order and peace has been emphasized increasingly as war has become the scourge not of a handful of mercenaries but of men everywhere. Moreover, concomitant with the brutalization of war has been the growth of practical morality and respect for human life as expressions of the Age of the Enlightenment and the theory of political liberalism. The spirit of this age was responsible for the social and political reforms in which criminal law has been transformed, prison changes initiated, and electoral reforms concluded. The greatest humanitarian task which remained was the outlawry of war. To the rational man the path to this goal was to be found in the one simple, unambiguous step of proscribing or reducing the means of destruction and violence. The assumption, whether outright or tacit, was that men fight because they have arms and, with the elimination or modification of armaments, fighting would become impossible.

Yet the history of attempts at disarmament is a melancholy story of numerous failures and few successes. In practice, disarmament conferences have usually failed. On those rare occasions when agreements have been reached, an increase instead of a reduction in armaments has frequently resulted. This was the case with the Washington Treaty of 1922 whereby American, British and Japanese production of cruisers was temporarily limited, destroyers and submarines remaining outside the agreement. Only in those extraordinary instances where the underlying political problems have first been adjusted or resolved has disarmament or regulation of armaments resulted in any substantial pacification of international relations. In American experience the Rush-Bagot Agreement concluded in 1816 between the United States and Canada, which until its revision during World War II allowed each nation three naval vessels of equal tonnage and armament for use on the Great Lakes, is the outstanding example of the positive function disarmament can play. But its success is dependent upon the sequence of political settlement and disarmament, with the former providing the sole foundation on which arms control can stand and prosper.

The disarmament approach to peace can be profitable if nations have first taken the step of seeking a viable political understanding. So long as their purpose is to continue advancing mutually contradictory claims in the struggle for power, their claims for armaments must remain unresolved and contradictory. We may conclude in a word that disarmament or rearmament are symptoms of the nature of the contest for power. When nations have arrived at a tolerable understanding about the distribution of power among them, then an arms pact can reflect the easing of the burden of competition and rivalry which this accommodation has brought about. At this point the easing of the arms race can have the result of contributing still further to the lessening of political tensions and to the heightening of mutual confidence among nations.

However the movement which has eclipsed all others in popular and moral appeal is that of world government. It has made this appeal despite its failure to advance beyond the discussion stage. Its aims and high purposes have imparted to the broad masses a deeper sense of urgency than has resulted from any of the other approaches. It has found supporters in Europe and America, Asia and Africa. We may well ask the question: What accounts for the attractiveness of world government as a doctrine of political salvation among peoples and nations from such diverse backgrounds? Some would say that its force appears to rest in three factors or conditions which have in varying degree and at different times been compelling and persuasive to quite different peoples. Since the age of the Stoics and the first followers of Christianity the sense of the moral unity of all mankind in the West has expressed itself in programs and visions for the establishment of universal political institutions. In practice every attempt to create an institutional framework commensurate politically with the range of these moral sentiments, whether it has been the Ro-

man Empire or the Napoleonic Empire, has failed, been corrupted — sometimes at birth — and disappeared. But the moral and intellectual roots of the world government movement have perpetuated this residual Western belief in the essential unity of mankind.

The second basic factor which accounts for the movement is technological in character. Through vast and massive changes in transportation and communication, the separate parts of the world have been knit together. Yet this interdependence of the world's people wrought by the Industrial Revolution has not affected the international anarchy which obtains on the political scene. The argument for world government founded on this aspect of world affairs holds that since one economic world exists, the next urgent step is the creation of a single political universe. It is further true, of course, that the interdependence of nations in peace is matched by their close proximity in war. The modern conditions of warfare and the virtual elimination of distance as a limitation on strategy have stirred men to seek some kind of remedy for ever-recurrent wars.

Finally, the experiences of the nation-state in achieving order and amity domestically have invited men of good will to adapt its institutions to the world scene. War exists internationally alongside conditions of international anarchy; peace obtains within the nation-state side by side with organs of government. Therefore inasmuch as national societies owe their peaceful condition to a state endowed with supreme power and authority, the transference of sovereignty from national states to a world state is considered to be the sole means to achieve peace and order. The logic of this threefold argument for world government is unexceptionable so far as it goes, but the unresolved dilemma upon which every concrete plan has been impaled is the issue of whether what is necessary and desirable is therefore possible and acceptable. The aggregate of experience in the modern state system would indicate that up to now no sovereign nation-state has shown itself willing or able to pay the price that would be essential for a supra-national system.

There have been, in addition, actual experiments in harmonizing and integrating the manifold relations among sovereign nation-states. At least three international organizations have devoted themselves to the maintenance of international order and peace. The Concert of Europe was an informal expression of the European System, whose members met periodically to consult upon problems of safeguarding the *status quo* established by the Congress of Vienna in 1815. The League of Nations created in 1919 and the United Nations in 1945 have been full-fledged international agencies with permanent locations and secretariats. Indeed it has been customary to consider them the sole international organizations. Yet if peace and order are the real purposes of international organization the lessons to be gained from nineteenth century practice are no less vital than those of the twentieth century. For the nineteenth was a century of almost uninterrupted peace in which the six leading nations until the First World War engaged in general war with one another for only eighteen months, if we exclude the Crimean War as a semi-colonial struggle.

It was during this century of peace that the fifth approach was more assiduously cultivated and respected than it has been in recent times. For diplomacy is the ancient technique whereby two nations whose conflicting interests appear irreconcilable can discover if in fact their vital interests are incompatible and how far they can compromise on non-vital interests. If we apply this general concept to British foreign policy, we find that England has been willing to compromise on secondary issues in the Far East or in Africa, but on vital interests such as the territorial integrity of the Low Countries it has been unyielding. In an unorganized international society, diplomacy continues to be the one indispensable approach to world peace. But while in practice its success depends on prudent judgments regarding the balance of power, its use is also necessary to the fruitful activities of any international organization. Indeed, if in practice compromise and accommodation are wanting, competing states within or outside an international government have only the recourse of war itself.

The following selections illustrate four of these fundamental approaches to world peace. Ernest Gross is an official deputy-representative of the United States to the United Nations, and in his " Answer to the Critics of the U.N." he presents the viewpoint of an intelligent advocate. Robert M. Hutchins, former Chancellor of the University of Chicago and now of the Ford Foundation, presents the case for immediate world government. A companion article is the essay entitled " The Myth of World Government" by Reinhold Niebuhr. The editorial " Cross Purposes " considers the relationship between traditional diplo-

macy and collective security. Finally, the author of our final selection, Arnold J. Toynbee, concludes this section with a challenging essay " Can We Live and Let Live? " Students concerned with the problems of universal disarmament are urged to examine the transcripts of United Nations discussions. The contrast between the idealist and realist approaches is illustrated in the divergent conceptions of the United Nations and of the prospects for world government.

85. The United Nations and World Peace*

Today the United Nations is the target of a great deal of criticism. It is called a powerless debating society, a mere forum for propaganda. It is censured for not having dealt effectively with the cause of most of the world's present troubles, the deep conflict between Soviet Russia and the free world. It is blamed for " never settling anything." Not only its performance but even its basic aims are sometimes questioned.

These doubts must be cleared away. In the light of world actualities the U.N. is doing a good job — and a vital one.

What is the United Nations doing — what can it do — to fulfill the principles of the Charter and so help build the foundations of free-world strength? I see at least four differ-

ent ways in which the U.N. is making important progress toward this objective, as well as helping the free world to meet the menace of Soviet imperialism.

1. *The United Nations furnishes a continuous open forum for negotiation and discussion.*

Preoccupied as we are with the tensions created by the conflict between the Soviet system and the free world, it is easy to lose sight of the role which the U.N. constantly plays in respect to disputes and controversies arising within the free world itself. Some of the most striking successes of the U.N. have involved settlement of bitter and dangerous conflicts of this sort in which the U.N. has successfully brought to an end hostilities which, if unchecked, threatened to become widespread conflagrations. Kashmir, Palestine and Indonesia are but three examples.

* From Ernest A. Gross, " Answer to the Critics of the U.N.," *New York Times Magazine,* April 27, 1952. Reprinted by permission of Ernest A. Gross and *The New York Times.*

We Americans naturally tend to think of aggression or invasion in terms of the threat of Communist imperialism. However, for many other peoples and countries the most direct and immediate threat, real or imagined, may come from a next-door neighbor or may arise out of explosive disputes too long unresolved. The possibility of recourse to the United Nations is not merely a reassuring factor, but it is a means of obtaining protection or redress which removes a sense of compulsion to resort to force.

The United Nations reveals weak spots and important problems within the free world itself. Emergent nationalisms in many parts of the world find voice. They are not left to develop volcanic force under the surface which, in the past, has so often resulted in violent explosions. When international disputes arise covering these problems and efforts to seek solutions by negotiations have been exhausted, the United Nations can be used to promote and foster agreement.

In addition, the conflict between the Soviet system and the free world makes the existence of the forum even more imperative.

The Communists are discovering how difficult it is to continue to lie and cheat successfully in a public forum. Debates bring out the truth, questions are asked, representatives of many nations confer and exchange opinions as to the hidden purposes and meanings of Soviet maneuvers. The fact that Soviet leaders and their satellites are accountable to the United Nations deprives them of certain advantages which dictators in former periods of history have enjoyed: such as operating in dark corners and conspiring against intended victims one at a time.

Most of us during the last General Assembly felt that the Soviet representatives were on the defensive. The free world delegates were neither persuaded nor intimidated by Soviet lies and threats, which have largely lost their value as diplomatic currency. I think this is due to some extent to its constant debasement by Soviet representatives in United Nations exchanges.

The existence of a standing forum for discussion and negotiation is of crucial importance. We may dream of "global solutions," but the building blocks of peace will be the settlements of specific issues and the removal of specific causes of tension. Such settlements will be brought about, if at all, by patient, firm and continuous effort on the part of the free world, backed by sufficient strength to assure observance of specific agreements by the other side.

The United Nations, then, is an important forum for the exposure and discussion of problems of world concern and a forum in which Communist imperialism is constantly revealing its dangerous nature and purposes. Truth and knowledge in themselves create moral unity in the world. Nations need not cower in fear of the unknown.

2. *The United Nations provides the framework for increasingly effective collective action against aggression.*

The abuse of the veto by the Soviet Union in the Security Council has, of course, made it impossible to rely upon the Council as the sole United Nations instrument for the maintenance of security in all cases. But the United Nations can, nevertheless, play an important role in the age-old quest for collective security.

In the first place, the Charter itself formulates general standards and objectives by which national policies can be tested, both in the case of individual national action, such as the Truman Doctrine, and in the activities of regional organizations, such as the North Atlantic Treaty. One of the most important aspects of our program of aid to Greece and Turkey was the declaration by the Congress of the United States that the aid was to be administered in accordance with the United Nations Charter and that it would be terminated if and when the United Nations decided that the aid was no longer necessary to accomplish the purposes of the Charter. The moral influence of the program was vastly heightened by the fact that the Congress waived our right under the Charter to veto any such decision by the United Nations.

Secondly, the role of the General Assembly, where the majority will cannot be frustrated by the veto, has become increasingly important. We are bending our efforts to find methods for increasing its effectiveness.

One of the most important steps in this direction was the adoption by the General Assembly a year ago of the " Uniting for Peace " Resolution. The essential elements of the framework of a collective security system are contained in this Resolution: the means for determining the existence of and the responsibility for aggression (through the Peace Observation Commission); machinery for putting collective measures into operation (through emergency sessions of the General Assembly); and military forces in readiness to carry out those measures.

By the " Uniting for Peace " Resolution, the United Nations, drawing upon the constitutional powers inherent in the Charter, has put itself in postion to create an organized system of collective defense in spite of Soviet obstruction.

Whether this program fulfills its promise depends upon the will with which the task is approached. The first Report of the Collective Measures Committee was unanimous, revealing a full acceptance by the members of the Committee — in which the Soviet Union has refused to participate — of the principles upon which the " Uniting for Peace " Resolution was based.

There is much to be done and it will take time to do it. But the United Nations now has a veto-proof procedure for bringing a real collective defense program into being.

Thirdly, the work of the Disarmament Commission, established by the Sixth General Assembly, is of the greatest importance. The efforts to achieve disarmament are painfully difficult but are all the more essential for that very reason. They reflect the strong moral urge of people everywhere to build toward a future in which resources now being diverted to economically unproductive purposes can be used for the betterment of mankind. Our efforts for disarmament demonstrate that our objective in building strength is to defend freedom and is not a mere process of creating strength for the sake of power alone.

3. *The United Nations can focus pressures for human rights and political freedom.*

The expansion of human rights creates strength in support of the free world by satisfying one of the deepest human aspirations. The United Nations is a valuable instrument for observing, promoting and cultivating universal respect for human rights and fundamental freedoms.

There are hundreds of millions of people in the world today who are awakening to the urge for liberty and freedom. Seventy millions of them two years ago formed a new and independent state — with our help and that of the United Nations. The principles of the United Nations Declaration of Human Rights are incorporated into the Constitution of that new state — Indonesia.

Members of the United Nations which have responsibilities for the administration of territories whose peoples have not yet attained a full measure of self-government have pledged themselves in the Charter to insure the inhabitants of such territories political, economic, social and educational advancement, just treatment and protection against abuses.

The United Nations has not merely paid lip service to the broad principles of political independence. It has in the few brief years of its existence already supported the creation of new states — Indonesia, Israel, Libya and the Republic of Korea, and it is a remarkable fact that all this has been done in the face of Soviet obstruction or non-cooperation.

Apart from all its other values, if the United Nations did not exist today, there would develop tomorrow all over the world strong pressure to create an organization dedicated to the promotion of human rights and political freedom, with machinery to give effect to these principles.

4. *The United Nations helps to improve economic conditions so that free institutions can take root and grow.*

A large part of the work of the United Nations is devoted to an attack upon the natural enemies of man: poverty, disease and despair. The Economic and Social Council, the Trusteeship Council, and all the United Nations specialized agencies, are doing some of the essential work of the world.

The program of expanded technical assistance to underdeveloped areas has kindled the imagination of the world's people, simply because a steel plow will cut a deeper furrow than a lofty statement of good intentions.

The necessity for increased food production in vast areas of the world, and the necessity for land reform, is a problem engaging the attention of the members of the United Nations.

Conditions in Asia and the Middle East, which were once the almost exclusive concern of travelers, traders or missionaries, have now become matters of our national interest and security. The small farmer in Southeast Asia paying 50 per cent of his crop for rent and 60 per cent interest on his loans for fertilizer, seed and groceries, may or may not know about the Voice of America. But he cannot walk back to his hut without hearing the Whisper of Communism.

The United Nations can deal effectively with problems of unrest and instability in underdeveloped countries. It is essential that it do so, for these problems affect our military establishment, our trade and commerce, our sources of raw materials, and, what is more important, our basic friendship with other countries. They thus affect our own standard of living and our hopes for peaceful development.

Taken together, these advantages and values of the United Nations justify confidence in its future.

In the face of one of the greatest imperialist threats in history, the United Nations contributes to the process of making "peaceful coexistence" endurable and less risky for the free world while at the same time providing a continuously open forum in which the settlement of specific issues can be patiently explored.

Like all human institutions, the United Nations has a life and vitality all its own. This arises from the interplay of points of view exchanged in the forum, from group pressures and moral judgments, from the contributions of a devoted and efficient international civil service, and from the leadership of representatives of member governments who form a special diplomatic corps in the new field of "multilateral diplomacy."

However, in the last analysis, the United Nations is an instrument of policy of its member states. It is primarily an agency in which governments can speak and through which they can act. It is subject to misuse, abuse and nonuse. It is also capable of growth and improvement. This being so, much of the criticism which is directed against it is in reality self-criticism. Many of those who attack the United Nations or deplore its shortcomings might well consider whether they are not in fact criticizing the failure of their own governments to make the most effective use of the organization in accordance with its scope, its promise and its capabilities.

The future course of Soviet conduct will determine to a large extent whether and for how long the promises of San Francisco remain unfulfilled. In the meantime, the United Nations will serve as one of the major instruments for holding open the door to negotiation and for strengthening the free world by helping to build the foundations of freedom. That strength will, more than anything else, hasten the day of fulfillment.

86. Cross Purposes in Korea*

The Korean war and its consequences in the Far East will inevitably be a main subject of today's debate in the House of Commons. Inevitably, too, it will be discussed by many members in terms of a clash between British and American policies. Yet many of the difficulties in which the Western Powers now find themselves are the result not of a conflict between Britain and the United States but of a conflict between two policies which are widely held in both countries. These are the policy of collective security and the principles of traditional diplomacy. There are some, of course, who would deny that such a conflict exists. A system of collective security, they would say, is always and everywhere the best protection for national interests. That, indeed, is the view of which this country, like most others, is committed by its membership of the United Nations, though in fact the system of collective security embodied in the Charter is modified in many important — and realistic — ways by the right of veto given to the great Powers. However that may be, it is fair to say that in the present state of world affairs this conflict does exist and has not yet been given the attention it deserves.

Korea is not the first, though it is the best, example of this. When Mussolini threatened Abyssinia many people held that since Britain and France were not prepared to go to war and therefore could not save Abyssinia, it was foolish to take action which would merely annoy Italy and drive her into the arms of Hitler's Germany. The champions of collective security replied that if the League of Nations did nothing it would merely encourage other and more dangerous acts of aggression elsewhere. Clearly, if nations sign a declaration that they will resist any act of aggression in any part of the world, as they did in the Covenant of the League, and then fail to do so, it will reduce the value of their promise and raise doubts about its validity. Realists might say, however, that this is precisely the danger of making such declarations. In the bad old days, just because Britain took no action when Italy invaded Libya, it did not mean — and no one thought it meant — that she would not take action if Italy invaded Egypt.

The Korean war raised all these questions very clearly. Korea was not and is not a vital interest of any of the Western Powers. Even the American Chiefs of Staff apparently took this view when they agreed to withdraw all United States troops from South Korea, and one official, perhaps unwisely, said as much in a public statement in Tokyo. (General MacArthur himself is said to have told the President that any American general who thought

* From *The London Times*, Feb. 5, 1952, p. 5.

of committing American troops to the mainland of Asia should have his head examined.) There is little doubt that the Communists took this to mean that the United States would not intervene if the North Koreans invaded South Korea and indeed, on the basis of *Realpolitik,* it was a reasonable belief. The United States, however, was also a member of the United Nations and a firm believer in collective security. When, therefore, the North Koreans crossed the 38th parallel President Truman acted promptly to support the South Koreans in resisting " this later aggression in defiance of the Charter." The great majority of the United Nations, including this country, followed his lead with approval and admiration.

The value of this act was immense. It enormously strengthened the United Nations, which at that time appeared to be dying of inanition, and roused the western nations to a supreme effort. Some would say that it saved the world from a third great war in 1951. Yet realism, like nature, has a way of coming back when men think it has been expelled, and the action of the United Nations, brilliant and effective though it was, has left some awkward questions. To begin with, though it did repel North Korean aggression, it did not prove a deterrent to all aggression. Within six months China had invaded Tibet and joined in the Korean war. Indeed, so far from preventing Chinese aggression, it provoked it. Again, having fulfilled their original purpose by driving the Communists back to the 38th parallel, the United Nations found themselves without any clear policy. The Charter tells how to resist aggression but it does not say how to bring a war to an end or how to deal with the consequences. At present Chartists and Realists are equally at a loss, and Mr. Churchill's report on his visit to Washington [January, 1952] was an admirable expression of the dilemma in which the Western Powers are placed.

The ultimate problem is clear enough. For reasons of geography Korea will always fall under the influence of China unless some other Power of equal or greater strength is prepared to protect it, and has the means at hand to do so. If the Western Powers really wished to keep Korea out of Chinese hands they should not have taken it away from Japan at the end of the war. Then, however, Japan was an enemy and China a friend, so that it seemed safe to create an " independent " Korea. After the war the United States found herself taking the place of Japan, and was therefore forced to assume the role of defending South Korea when China and North Korea went Communist; but since she did not intend to stay permanently in Japan she withdrew from Korea by agreement with Russia before its independence was secure. Now, as the result of the war, she finds herself once more committed to stay in Korea at the very moment when Japan has become independent again and the American occupation there will be replaced by an American garrison. One solution of this problem might be to bring back Japan into Korea, but this is denied to the United Nations, partly because it would be an act of perfidy and partly because it would inevitably bring into effect the Russo-Chinese Treaty. (In any case Japan is not yet strong enough to sustain the role.) For the moment there is no protector of Korea except the United Nations themselves.

The burden of defending Korea will be less onerous if the United Nations can first come to some agreement with the Communists. Fortunately there is a good deal of evidence that the Communists are prepared to accept a division of the country which will give them the northern half and leave the southern half to the United Nations. They would plainly prefer the whole of Korea, but they will take half if they cannot get the rest. On the other hand they have shown that they will make the most strenuous efforts to prevent the United Nations — and therefore the Western Powers — from occupying the whole of Korea up to the frontier of Manchuria. After making one disastrous attempt to conquer the whole of Korea the United Nations forces have accepted this and are now trying to get an armistice on terms which they might easily have got over a year ago. Their failure to do so then was the result of a failure to decide what were the objects of the campaign; if they fail again now the reason may be the same.

For every reason a truce on the present lines is now the best hope.

If the Communists refuse to sign a truce, or break a truce once it has been signed, those who believe in collective security and those who prefer a more empirical approach to foreign policy would have an equal duty to reconsider the aims of their policy. Both would surely agree that the United Nations must now remain in and protect South Korea from Communist invasion; but while the advocates of collective security might urge that it was a moral duty to go on and punish the Chinese for their intervention, many would recoil from the logic of such an argument. Even on moral grounds it cannot conceivably be in the interests of the United Nations to turn every small war into a world war. Their true interests lie rather in limiting their commitments on the mainland of Asia by taking such action, and only such action, as is necessary to defend South Korea and south-east Asia. It is true, as the Americans argue, that this may require bombing targets outside the present frontiers of Korea, but there would be less risk of the war spreading if in that case the Communists understood the limits and aims of Western policy. Nothing is more dangerous than the present ambiguity which leaves them uncertain whether the United Nations are trying to protect South Korea or to reverse the Communist revolution in China. It would be an absurd paradox if the collective action which may have saved the world from war in 1950 were to threaten the peace of the world in 1952.

87. World Community and World Government*

The French observer André Sieg-fried thought several decades ago that America was coming of age. One hopes he was right; though it is worth noting that there are many stages of maturity and we seem hardly to have reached one commensurate with the responsibilities which have been thrust upon our very powerful if very young nation. At every turn we face decisions requiring us to use our power creatively to stabilize an inchoate community of nations in a civilization which can achieve stability only in global terms.

Our hesitancies and ambiguities reveal that we have not yet overcome our adolescent pride of power or our inner insecurities. It would be the rightful function of a "liberal" movement in such a situation to furnish the nation with mature counsel, assuming that liberalism, whatever else it may be, represents a measure of detachment from the shortsighted collective impulses of a community. It must be regretfully recorded, however, that the liberal movement of America has not risen to the occasion. It is, if anything, more infantile than the nation. It proves its lack of maturity by trying to solve the complex problems of our global existence in purely logical and constitutional terms. We do not yet

* From Reinhold Niebuhr, "The Myth of World Government," *The Nation,* Vol. 162 (1946), pp. 312–14. Copyright 1946 by *The Nation.* Reprinted by permission of Reinhold Niebuhr and *The Nation.*

have a world community — only halting and hesitant beginnings toward one. American liberals, however, insist that one be brought into being by legal, constitutional, and governmental means, disregarding the fact, which history attests on every page, that governments may perfect the order and justice of a community but cannot create a community — for the simple reason that the authority of government is primarily the authority of the community itself. If the community does not exist in fact, at least in inchoate form, constitutional instruments cannot create it. The authority of law as such is slight, and the fear of police power is useful only to suppress incidental recalcitrance against the will of the community. The community cannot be coerced into basic order; the basic order must come from its innate cohesion.

These obvious facts are obscured in almost all the educational propaganda on the problems of world government put out by our international organizations. They are rightfully concerned about the fact that unabridged national sovereignty is a principle of anarchy in an interdependent world. Their answer to this problem is to call for a constitutional convention of the world or to try to persuade the new United Nations Organization to pass a law which will abridge the sovereignty of nations. This solution takes legal symbols for social realities. The principle of national sovereignty is the legal expression of the fact that national communities regard themselves as morally and politically autonomous. They have become increasingly conscious of the claims of other nations upon them and of the necessity of a larger degree of mutual accord, but they will have to reach a much higher degree of implicit abridgment of their moral freedom before it will be possible to fix and extend this moral and social gain by law.

The present accord between the nations, as expressed in the United Nations Charter, contains a "veto" provision by virtue of which no great power can be voted down in the council of the nations. This fact fills our liberals with moral and political disgust. It does of course prove that the great powers are not ready to submit unreservedly to the authority of a world organization. But this merely means that in the present state of world affairs peace cannot be maintained by a majority imposing its will upon a minority. When the minority is not a group of individuals but a nation or a group of nations, it will use its social and military power to defy a decision which has not been reached with its consent. We have, therefore, no real security against war. But there is no reason to think we could gain this security by constitutional means after having failed to establish the minimum basis for it by political means.

All the great nations insisted upon the veto power, and the United Nations Charter would hardly have passed the United States Senate without this provision. Russia is more insistent upon retaining the veto than we are because it is in greater danger of being voted down in the United Nations Assembly or the Security Council. This fact does not deter our constitutional idealists from bombarding the ear of the Administration and the conscience of the nation with proposals for abolishing the veto. Here the constitutional answer to the problem of world peace obviously threatens the delicate and tentative degree of accord which has been achieved politically. We are professedly interested only in establishing a universal sovereignty, and we refuse to admit that we can afford greater devotion to the principle than Russia because we run less danger of being in the minority. This taint in our idealism is obvious enough to the Russians.

It must be observed in this connection that a great deal of enthusiasm for world government is explicitly anti-Russian — for instance, that of ex-Justice Owen Roberts and Clarence Streit. The theory is: let us set up a real world government; if the Russians fail to adhere so much the worse for them. These idealists are ready to bring on another world war in the name of world government. As consolation for the dire effects of so ironic a policy, we are assured that if we must have another world war it would be spiritually thrilling to fight it for the principle of world government. Some of the enthusiasm for world government is not explicitly anti-Russian but merely too naive to recognize that the effect of demanding a constitutionally perfect world order in the present situation must be to destroy the very tentative degree of mutual trust which has been achieved between the two great centers of power.

To say that there is no way of guaranteeing the peace of the world constitutionally is not to say that there are other ways of guaranteeing it. There are none. We are living in a very unsafe world; and it will be unsafe for a long time. To note the difficulty of bringing Russia into a world community does not imply that Russia's policies based on its fears are well justified. Some are; some are not. Some are reactions to our own policies, which are prompted by our own fears. Some seem to be derived from Marxist dogmatism. But there they are. They cannot be overcome by constitutional means unless they are first mitigated by a great deal more common counsel and common experience.

The excessive devotion to constitutional answers for world problems in America seems to be a dubious inheritance from the whole "social-contract" theory of government with which the liberal democratic movement began. According to this theory men and nations create communities by the fiat of government and law. That all human communities had a long history of organic cohesion before they ever began explicitly and consciously to alter or extend it is ignored. One reason why the idea of the social contract has special prestige in America is our belief that

we created a nation by constitutional fiat; and we think it is our special business to ask the world to do in macrocosm what we so successfully accomplished in microcosm. This analogy fails to consider that the cohesion of a national community is so different from the organization of a universal community that the difference is one of kind rather than degree. It also leaves out of account an important aspect of our history. If our Constitution created a "more perfect union," the union which the Constitution perfected had already been established. The fear of a common foe, the shared experiences of the battlefield, a very considerable degree of similar culture — these and many other factors provided the cohesion of the American colonies. The Constitution could not have created a unity which it had to presuppose.

Emery Reves in his *Anatomy of Peace,* which has become a kind of bible of American constitutional idealism, declares that the way to "prevent wars between nations once and for all" is to integrate "the scattered conflicting national sovereignties into one unified higher sovereignty capable of creating a legal order in which all peoples will enjoy equal security, equal obligations, and equal rights under the law." The "once and for all" gives one pause, for even our own Constitution could not prevent the Civil War. But a brilliant defender of pure constitutionalism recently explained that difficulty away. The Civil War, he declared, was caused by certain ambiguities in our Constitution which left some doubt whether we were in fact a nation or a loose federation of states. It is now our business to profit from the experience of the past and eliminate similar ambiguities from the world constitution. Unfortunately, to assume that the tortuous processes of history can thus be controlled by the power of constitutional logic is an infantile illusion.

American liberalism refuses to face the fact that there is a tremendous difference between the problem of community on the national and global level, a difference which no constitutional magic can overcome. National and imperial communities all have ethnic, linguistic, geographic, historical, and other forces of social unity. The universal community, however, has no common language or common culture — nothing to create the consciousness of " we." Modern democratic communities may be culturally and ethnically pluralistic, but they all possess a core of common spiritual possessions which the world community lacks.

The world community does, indeed, have some compelling motives toward unity. Technical civilization has created an economic interdependence which generates insufferable frictions if it is not politically managed. There is in the culture of every nation, moreover, a religious and philosophical sense of world community waiting to be actualized, and of moral obligations extending beyond the national community. There is, finally, the fear of mutual destruction. It is the thesis of the proponents of world government that the atomic bomb has so intensi-

fied the fear of mutual destruction that hitherto impossible constitutional goals now appear possible.

Undoubtedly fear may be a creative force. The scared man can run faster from the pursuing bull than he ever thought possible. But the creative power of fear does not increase in proportion to its intensity. Fear finally becomes paralyzing. Furthermore, the fear of mutual destruction easily degenerates into the fear of a particular foe. Even now it must be regretfully recorded that fear of Russia in the West and of the West in Russia seems more potent than the common fear of destruction.

These are tragic facts, and one could wish that they were not true; but it is hardly mature to deny what is so obvious. The world community lacks, in short, the potent elements of " togetherness " which national communities boast. Neither law nor police power can supply this defect. If one trusted to police power alone, the amount required by a universal state to maintain order in a community which did not cohere naturally and organically would be so great as to amount to tyranny. This was Thomas Hobbes's answer to the problem of community; the similarity between his answer and that of many of our modern constitutional idealists is instructive. Fortunately, national communities had a more organic unity than Hobbes supposed. Unfortunately, the international community corresponds at least partly to his picture.

These simple lessons must be

spelled out to American idealists, not to induce a mood of defeatism, but to get them to direct the impulses of their idealism to real rather than imaginary objectives. Many creative acts are required of America that are more difficult, though more immediate and modest, than espousal of world government. Will the British loan agreement pass? If it does not, America will have proved that it does not know how to relate its wealth to an impoverished world. Shall we find a way of transferring our dangerous knowledge of the atomic bomb to some kind of world judicator? If not, we shall have proved that we know how to resent, but not to allay, the world's fear of our power.

These immediate steps toward achieving a higher degree of mutuality among nations may be too modest to guarantee peace. But they are in the right direction. It would be intolerable if we again presented the world with a case of American schizophrenia, allowing our idealists to dream up pure answers for difficult problems while our cynics make our name odious by the irresponsible exercise of our power.

88. Constitutionalism and World Government*

We have a mystical notion that all the issues that perplex us are going to be settled by improvements in transportation. They will give us one world. A colleague of mine has asked, one world, but whose? We may also inquire, one world, but how long? And one world, but what kind? One world which brings in closer contact the sparks of greed and ambition is sure to be in constant explosion. One world under one tyrant, or one association of tyrants, would be worse than many. In many worlds there is at least the chance of escape from one to the other.

But let us suppose that by one world we mean one good world.

* From Robert Maynard Hutchins, *Foundations for World Order*, pp. 97–114. Copyright 1947 by Social Science Foundation, University of Denver. Reprinted by permission of Social Science Foundation.

Will we stop to ask what one good world involves? It involves, unless we propose to kill them all, such people as the Russians. The proposal to kill them all seems to be gaining in popularity. If we are going to do that we had better do it at once. Now we have a monopoly of the atomic bomb.

There are two propositions about the atomic bomb that are worth remembering. There is no secret. There is no defense. Since there is no secret, other nations will have the bomb almost any day. Since there is no defense, we cannot use the bomb after our monopoly ends to kill other people without being killed ourselves.

In a war in which both sides have atomic bombs the cities of both sides will be destroyed. Since one to ten atomic bombs can reduce any city in the world to ashes, superiority in atomic bombs will not give material advantage to the side possessing it. Superiority in land, sea, and air forces will mean little. The atomic bomb is a weapon directed against civilians. The economy which supports the military can be wiped out before the military can get started. As General Groves said in Chicago a few weeks ago, " I do not see how it will be possible to supply large armies in the field." When two nations have the atomic bomb, it will be impossible for either of them to win a war. The day of force as the determining factor in world affairs ends with the end of our monopoly of the atomic bomb.

Yet just as the day of force is waning, the official American attitude is to rely on it more than ever. In the greatest moral crisis in history we do not say, " Let us be good." We say, " Let us be powerful — and then we can compel other people to be good." Instead of saying, " Let us use our knowledge and our resources for the benefit of all mankind," we say, " Let us use our knowledge to make more terrifying weapons of destruction; and let us use our resources to usher in the American Century, in which we shall dominate the world." Instead of saying, " Let us feed the starving because all men are brothers," we say, " Let us feed the starving, if we feed them at all, so that they will not vote the Communist ticket." Instead of saying, " Let us have moral education in the United States," we say, " Let us have military training."

Three weeks ago the Chairman of the Federal Reserve Board said that we had spent twenty-five billions on military forces in the first two postwar fiscal years, compared with sixteen billion spent on foreign aid in that period.

Yet even before the atomic bomb it is possible that General Montgomery was right in saying, as he did the other day, that it is not weapons or large armies that win victories, but the character, that is, the education, of the people. A tremendous military establishment can be, and usually is, a Frankenstein; and all history confirms the doctrine that those who rely upon the sword shall perish by it. Power corrupts. A false sense of superiority leads to a false sense of security. Behind an impressive façade the building falls into ruins. The building can be no better than the character of the people who inhabit it.

Force is absolutely amoral, and therefore has no role, except in support of law, in a world that has any title to be called good. Force is almost certain to be immoral. The essence of fascism is pushing other people around; you frighten them into doing what you want them to do. A country composed of people who want to push other people around is a fascist country; a government which pursues a fascist policy will eventually produce a lot of fascist citizens. It will produce a population of immoral individuals who regard other individuals as means to their ends and who will seek the power to make other individuals serve their ends. Such a country cannot long remain strong; such a population cannot be happy. If the official American attitude is to rely upon force, it follows that the power and the happiness of America have already passed their zenith.

And, if the official policy of America is to rely upon force, it follows that the security of America cannot be guaranteed by force after the day of force is over. The day of force can last only a moment longer. There are only two possibilities: to use the bomb at once, or to create a situation in which nobody can ever use it.

Of these two possibilities, we hear more and more about the first and less and less about the second. The first possibility is a preventive war on Russia. If we seriously entertain this possibility, we ought first to make our apologies to the Nazis we hanged at Nuremberg.

If we are concerned to create a situation in which the bomb will not be used, we must recognize that international agreements for the control of atomic energy will simply mean that the next war will end with atomic bombs instead of beginning with them. The minute war breaks out, every nation that knows how will start making atomic bombs.

The *New York Times,* in its editorial on the second anniversary of the bomb, says that the ultimate protection against it can only be the abolition of war itself. The *Times* suggests that the final success of efforts to abolish war can be realized only in an ultimate world government.

I do not understand the use of the word " ultimate " in this connection. We have now arrived at the ultimate stage in history. We cannot do something intermediate now and ultimately do something ultimate. What is ultimately required of us is required of us now. If what is ultimately required of us is the abolition of war through a world government, then we had better set about trying to get war abolished through world government now.

Any proposal for a world atomic authority is a proposal for world government. Such an authority must have a monopoly of atomic bombs, which means that every nation would be at its mercy, and it must have the right to enter, inspect, and destroy atomic installations anywhere in the world. No nation could call itself sovereign in any usual sense under such conditions.

The major premise of all discussions looking toward agreements for the control of atomic energy has been that the nations retain their sovereignty. Hence, these discussions have not succeeded and cannot succeed. Either we have world federal government and real atomic control, or we have no agreements, or agreements that are meaningless, and eventually atomic war.

It will be said, of course, that if nations will not collaborate in an alliance or debating society or propaganda forum like the United Nations, they cannot be expected to come together or to stay together in a world state. The American states could not or would not collaborate under the Articles of Confederation before 1787, but they did come together, and, with the exception of one period, they stayed together under the Constitution.

It may be admitted that there were ties which united them which do not unite the nations today. Moreover, they were remote from the rest of the world. Both their enemies and their friends were too preoccupied to bother them. They had the safety valve of a new country and the western lands. On the other hand, we should not forget that many differences deeply divided the American states, so much so that, three months before the Constitutional Convention, Madison wrote that he "trembled for the issue."

Mr. Hooker has lately shown in the magazine *Common Cause* how serious the divisions among the states in the Confederation were. Virginia had twelve times as many people as Delaware. Georgia claimed a hundred times as many square miles as Rhode Island. There were so many Germans in Pennsylvania that Franklin feared they might make German the language of the state. It was impossible to get along in some sections of New York without knowing Dutch. The trip from Boston to New York, which now takes less than an hour, took four days to a week along the finest road, or longer than it takes now to go round the world.

Gouverneur Morris thought that a federal tax was impossible because of the extent of the country; and one member of the Convention asked, "How can it be supposed that this vast country, including the western territory, will, one hundred and fifty years hence remain one nation?"

When Washington took charge of the armies surrounding Boston, he wrote that the New Englanders were an exceedingly dirty and nasty people. On the other hand, Ephraim Paine of Vermont complained that the southern members of Congress regarded themselves as a superior order of animals. Tariffs were levied by New York, Pennsylvania, and Maryland on the goods of other states; and New Jersey taxed the New York lighthouse on Sandy Hook. New York, New Hampshire, and Massachusetts quarreled about Vermont, and Pennsylvanians battled Virginians on the Upper Ohio. It is no wonder that when the Constitution was completed by the Convention, the principal attack upon it was that it was utopian, a visionary project, an indigestible panacea.

And it barely was accepted. In the conventions in the critical states it just squeaked through. In Massachusetts it carried by twenty-nine votes; in Virginia by ten; and in New York by only three.

What we are talking about is the relation between world community and world law. Reinhold Niebuhr, whom I greatly admire, takes the view that we cannot discuss world government because we have no world community to support it. The discussion of world government, he thinks, may even retard the development of world community and hence retard world government.

It is true that one good world pre-supposes a world community. In one good world every man is our neighbor, because every man is our fellow citizen. The commands of the political community supplement the demands of charity. Three or four years ago the Council of the American Federation of Labor, in response to the suggestion that China was our ally, voted to reaffirm its support of the Chinese Exclusion Act. Mr. William Green took the occasion to announce that " A China-man is still a Chinaman." If this is so, the one good world at which Mr. Green doubtless aims is still far off.

Our traditional attitude toward the rest of the world has been ex-pressed in the old question, " Should foreigners be abolished, or should we save some to sell things too? " We have been dedicated to a policy of high tariffs and no immigration. Twenty years ago we regarded na-tional relief of the unemployed as revolutionary socialism. Our sys-tem of social security is only twelve years old. We are not yet com-mitted to give national aid to the education of under-privileged Amer-ican children. And yet, in one good world, we should be called on to support, to educate, to buy from, and to receive as fellow citizens, men of every race, creed and color, at every economic level, and at every stage of ignorance or enlightenment.

One good world requires more than the sacrifice of ancient preju-dices. It requires the formulation and adoption of common principles and common ideals. It requires that this be done on a world-wide basis. A world organization cannot be held together simply by fear. Not transportation but communication lies at the foundation of any durable community. By communication I do not refer to the means of com-munication, but to a common un-derstanding of what is communi-cated. The extraordinary develop-ment of the telegraph, the telephone, the radio, the motion picture, and airmail in our time has done as much as any single factor to disrupt international relations and exacer-bate wounded feelings throughout the world. A vice-president of the General Electric Company has late-ly commented on the benefits to civi-lization from television. He said that, since the principal market for television sets was taverns, what this triumph of technology had meant to society was more booze, less fresh air, and the same old ball-game. It would have been very fortunate if almost every speech made by repre-sentatives of great powers in the last two years, from Mr. Truman's Navy Day address of October 1945 to Mr. Vishinsky's recent outpourings, could have been heard or read only by their own people, and a very small fraction of them. Confucius remarked that men cannot work to-gether unless they have common principles. Common principles are essential to communication.

Here it will not do to say that com-mon principles cannot be found. They must be found. And they can be found in the common humanity of all mankind. By patience, toler-ance, and good will we can come to understand other human beings, because they are human beings like ourselves. The most salutary reflection about the Russians in which we can indulge is to imagine how we would feel about the United States if we were Russians. And it would do the Russians no harm to consider how Mr. Vishinsky's speeches would affect them if they were Americans. By patience, tolerance, and good will we can come to understand one another; understanding is essential to communication. Communication is the basis of community. Transportation hastens consolidation; there can be no doubt about that. In the last century it has hastened consolidation of the most unstable and disagreeable kind, consolidation by conquest. One good world presupposes that the moral, intellectual, and spiritual foundations of the community have been laid. Otherwise the improvement of transportation must simply mean more frequent and terrible wars leading to the despotism of that power which discovers how best to apply the latest inventions to the destruction of its neighbors.

But I am afraid that Mr. Niebuhr exaggerates the state of perfection which world community must achieve before world government can be considered. Before the atomic bomb we could take world government or leave it. We could rely on the long process of evolution to bring world community and world government hand in hand. Any such program today means another war, and another war means the end of civilization. The slogan of our faith today must be, world government is necessary, and therefore possible.

Furthermore, those who oppose discussion of world government on the ground that a world community must precede a world government seem to me to overlook the interaction between the two. This is what the Greeks had in mind when they said that law was an educational force and that the city educates the man. The Constitution of the United States has educated the people of this country to believe in and support the Constitution of the United States. We are so used to thinking of law as repressive and constitutions as the embodiment of pre-existing agreement that we neglect the tremendous force which any constitution and any system of law exerts in behalf of its own acceptance and perpetuation. Anybody who has studied the relation between the political institutions of a state and its educational system, for example, must agree with Aristotle that politics is the architectonic science. One of the reasons Aristotle gives for this conclusion is that politics determines what is studied in the state.

The way to promote world community is to have world government. But since we cannot establish a world government here tonight the next best thing we can do to promote world community is to talk about world government. World discussion of world government, far from disrupting the world, may have some chance of uniting it; for the consideration of what is necessary to unite the world, the discussion of a common problem of overwhelming importance, should lead to a growing sense of community among all peoples.

An important reason for talking about world government is that nobody knows what it is. Should a world government aim at limited measures designed to maintain what is called security, or is security itself dependent on the pursuit of broader purposes? Should a world state be federal or unitary, or should it, perhaps, contain the best features of each? What should be the relation of the world government to the citizens of extant states? What taxing powers shall the world state have, and what order of military forces, if any? This list of questions can be prolonged indefinitely, and there are countless possible answers to each of them. Yet people go around saying world government is wonderful or world government is impossible. It may be that many forms of world government would be something less than wonderful; and it may be that some form of world government is possible. The only way to find out whether any form of world government is possible and practicable in our time is to work at it and talk about it.

Such discussion cannot legitimately be interpreted as an attack upon the United Nations. We must support the United Nations; it is all we have. We support it, not because it can guarantee peace, but because it is a highly tentative first step toward world government and world law. To say that the discussion of world government is a criticism of the United Nations is like saying that to talk about buying an automobile is an attack on the baby-carriage industry. The notion that if only we don't say anything about it the United Nations will in some way, while nobody is looking, turn gradually into an effective world government is surely naive. Constitution framing is a highly technical problem. The organization of sentiment for a new constitution is a matter of time, thought, and effort. And when the task must be carried forward on a global scale we must realize that no matter how soon we start we may be too late.

Mr. Molotov defends the United Nations and proposes as a remedy for the ills of the world what he calls the peaceful competition of states and social systems. This is certainly better, if it may be taken at face value, than the stirring calls issued by our statesmen for the largest army, navy, and air force in the world. But Mr. Molotov overlooks or suppresses the fact that between states and social systems there cannot in the long run be peaceful competition unless peace is enforced by law. The history of our own country from the Gold Rush to the Chicago newspaper wars shows that competition between individuals can be made peaceful only with some difficulty, and then only within a framework of law. The competition of sovereign states is competing anarchy. It is peaceful only so long as all nations want it to be. When one nation thinks that its competitive position would be improved if it stopped being peaceful, it will engage in warlike, instead of peaceful, competitions, and there is no way for other nations to stop this process except to abandon peaceful competition, too. The United Nations is composed of independent, sovereign states. Their competition must be anarchical. Therefore, in the long run it cannot be peaceful.

Every alteration in the constitution of the United Nations looking toward making it a world government is to the good. But any important limitation on the powers of sovereign states means that the whole theory of the United Nations is changed. To allege that anybody who insists on the basic theory of the United Nations is in some way an enemy of world peace is unfair. This applies, for example, to criticism on constitutional grounds of the use of the veto. Such criticism assumes that the United Nations is a world government and assails Russia on the ground that it does not recognize this obvious fact. Actually, the United Nations was not designed to put an end to the competing anarchy of sovereign states, but to perpetuate it.

Does anybody imagine that the United States would consent to any modification of the veto which would endanger our present majority position? Suppose that we were in a minority in the United Nations. Would we part with the veto, which would be the only weapon with which we could protect ourselves against the majority? Does anybody imagine that we would consent to effective inspection by an interna-

tional body of atomic installation in this country? The United Nations is and is by its charter declared to be an association of independent, sovereign states. How can we complain if one of the members insists on asserting its independent sovereignty?

Tinkering with the United Nations will not help us, if we agree with the *New York Times* that our only hope is in the ultimate abolition of war through an ultimate world government. An entirely different constitutional foundation is required. A new set of commitments must be made. Commitments to an alliance can be transformed into allegiance to a government only by a change of heart which is embodied in a fundamental constitutional reform.

The most futile of all the things we can do is to speculate about the intentions of the Politburo. Even if we were sure at some given moment that we knew what these gentlemen were planning, we could not be positive that they would adhere to these plans for more than a few minutes. What we should be thinking about is what America should stand for, regardless of what other nations may have in mind. If that policy fails, we shall at least have the satisfaction of knowing that we have done the best we could and that the catastrophe cannot be laid at our door. The policies we have been following — peace by intimidation and peace by purchase — do not seem to be succeeding very well; and, if the catastrophe comes, we shall be unable to evade a large share of the responsibility for it.

The policy of peace by intimidation, otherwise known as "getting tough with Russia," has produced Mr. Vishinsky, who proclaims a policy of peace by vilification, which is the *reductio ad absurdum* of peace by intimidation. Peace by vilification is that version of peace by intimidation which can be adopted by powerful and remote nations who do not yet have the atomic bomb, but who, since they are powerful and remote, can respond to attempts to intimidate them by showing in as rude and noisy a fashion as possible that two can play at the game. The policy of peace by purchase may succeed temporarily in those portions of the world which are purchasable. In those areas it will last as long as the purchase price is being paid or as long as no other bidder will offer more or until the nations bought come to value their independence more than food, clothing, and houses. But we have really made no attempt to buy peace. We have been attempting to buy allies for the next war. Yet we cannot contemplate another war. Another war will mean the end of civilization. We have reached the point where we cannot have war and civilization, too.

If peace through intimidation and peace through purchase are failing and in the nature of things are bound to fail, we might try peace through justice. Justice means giving every man his due; it means not doing to others what you are unwilling to have them do to you. Justice is suggested to us by a well-known American document which states that all men are created equal. Justice is the cement which holds a political organization together.

If we will grant that what we want is peace, and that justice is the only way to peace, then we may begin dimly to perceive both the outlines of a policy for the present and the constitutional foundations of a future world order. We are required to abandon a policy of power and purchase and pursue a policy of justice at home and abroad.

In order to pursue this policy we have to make certain moral and intellectual commitments, commitments that threaten to take us, in fact, into the realm of metaphysics. We have to admit that men are different from the other animals and that their moral, rational, and spiritual qualities are the qualities that make them men. These characteristics prevent us from dealing with men as we are free to deal with other animals. Human dignity forbids us to apply force to men, except by law. It forbids us to regard other men as means to our ends, for every man is an end in himself. The prospects of a human community result from our common humanity.

To give every man his due, therefore, is to treat every man as a man, black or white, British or Russian, rich or poor, ignorant or educated. And we may remember, as John Stuart Mill pointed out long ago, that we cannot expect the slave to show the virtues of the free man unless we first make him free. To say that certain men cannot be treated as men means simply that they have never had a chance to be men, and they must be given that chance.

To give every man his due is to give him the Rights of Man. This means that he must be free from want as long as he is willing to work. It means that he must be free from the fear of tyranny, oppression, and exploitation. It means that his claims to life, liberty, and the dignity of the human person are inalienable. It means that the necessities of life must be the common property of the human race, and that the management of the necessities of life by individual owners is a trusteeship which such owners hold subject always to the common good. It means that a world government must be a democracy, because only democracy gives every man his due.

It will be said that a world government which is founded on justice goes further than world government has to go and that we should limit ourselves to those objects as to which there can be no debate, the principal one of which is security. It will be said that nobody wants war and that all that a world government should do is to try to prevent war. This it can do by securing a monopoly of arms. Why talk about justice, the rights of man, and the law of nature when all we want is peace?

The answer is that men will fight until they get their rights. The minimum structural requirements of world government are plain enough. A world government, so as to preserve the cultural values that now exist in the states and regions of the world. It must be a government which acts directly on the individual, wherever he may be; for otherwise it is merely a league of sovereign, and

hence ultimately warlike states. But these are minimum structural requirements. There are minimum moral and spiritual requirements, too; and these may be summed up in the single word justice. The advancement of man in spiritual excellence and physical welfare is the common goal of mankind. Universal peace is the prerequisite for the pursuit of that goal. Justice in turn is the prerequisite of peace. Peace and justice stand or fall together. Men will fight until they get their rights.

These are hard sayings; for if we are going to promote justice throughout the world we shall have to rely largely on the power of example. We shall have to start doing justice at home, and shall have to sacrifice many ancient prejudices that are very dear to us. And if we are to have a world government based on justice, we, as the most prosperous and powerful nation of the earth, shall have to give up many economic and political advantages. We shall have to give up also the notion that there are some people in the world who are sub-human and not qualified to participate in any government that will hold sway over us. If we are going to have peace we must pay for it; and the price of peace is justice. If it will cost us a good deal to have world government, it will cost us far more to have war.

We are in no present danger from Russia. We have the atomic bomb. We have the industrial power. We are in no present danger from communism. The people of this country could be made communistic only by conquest, and probably not then. At present we are our own worst enemy. The present danger to us lies in our own hysteria and inertia. Our hysteria means that we will not face the facts of life, and our inertia means that we will not do anything about them. We hysterically build up tremendous military preparations, oblivious to the fact that while we have a monopoly of the atomic bomb we do not need these preparations, and when other nations have the bomb these preparations will do us no good. These preparations are, in fact, a danger to us for they can be used to convince other nations that we are out to dominate the world. Because of our inertia we will not recognize that our first obligation is to make our own system work until it must commend the admiration and imitation of the world. We will not see that the atomic bomb puts all further talk of force out of the question and that the hope of civilization is in world government. The Pax Romana existed before the atomic bomb. The atomic bomb makes a Pax Americana a romantic dream. The attempt to get a Pax Americana will give us not one Rome, but two Carthages.

The task of this generation is to establish peace. Gibbon in a celebrated chapter seeks to relieve the fears of Europe by assuring his contemporaries that there can never be another barbarian conqueror. The reason is simple. War is now so far advanced and requires the knowledge of so many arts and sciences that only highly educated men can hope to wage war successfully. The in-ference is that if men are highly educated they will not be so stupid or so vulgar as to wage war. But the last war was the most barbarous in history precisely because so much knowledge was at the disposal of those who waged it; and the atomic bomb is the final refutation of Gibbon's comforting theory. It can be little consolation to the Japanese who died at Hiroshima and Nagasaki that they were killed by Ph.D's.

The crisis of our time may be summed up in the proposition that our knowledge now exceeds our capacity to use it for good. The solution is not to reduce our knowledge, or to halt the progress of science, but to make our moral stamina equal to it. We have now reached the point where the bad character, or even the momentary carelessness, of the human race may lead to its extermination by the tremendous discoveries which the human intellect has achieved. The problem of preserving our civilization is a moral problem. Our difficulty is not to get more knowledge or more goods, but to do the right thing with them when we get them. Today we are confident that every scientific question will in time be answered. We know that every material deficiency of mankind can with good will be supplied. The problem is obtaining the good will. This is a moral problem.

The task of our generation is to establish peace. We cannot establish it by power or by purchase. We can establish it only by justice which begins at home and extends throughout the world. If you ask, what good will it do for us to be just if other nations are unjust, I reply as Plato did 2500 years ago, that the unjust man and the unjust state bear within themselves the seeds of their own destruction; and as General Montgomery did the other day that the character of a people is its best defense. Character implies moral and intellectual conviction. We must know, understand, and believe in what we are defending. What we are defending is not the American Way of Life, by which we usually seem to mean All the Comforts of Home. We are defending the cause of suffering humanity everywhere. This is justice, which is the foundation of any constitutional order and the basis of one good world.

89. A Settlement with Russia?*

Can our Western world and the communist world live at peace with each other side by side? Is their peaceful coexistence something desirable from our western point of view? And, if we come to the conclusion that it is desirable, as well as possible, for these two worlds to put up with one another's presence on the face of the same planet, on what terms can we look forward to seeing them live and let live?

I suppose, among all current questions, these three are about the most highly controversial ones that anybody could pick out for discussion. The most that any of us can do is to say what he personally expects and personally hopes. I am going to start with a commonplace which, I believe, is very much to the point. After any great event — whether it is some experience in our private lives or a public event like a great war — one becomes alive, as one looks back on it, to the mistakes that one has made in trying to cope with it, and one says to oneself: "Now, if anything like that ever happens to me again, there is one thing that I will make sure of. Whatever I do about it this next time, I will take care not to repeat that awful mistake I made last time." This good resolution is a natural one as well as a sensible one; but there is a catch in it; for, unfortunately, in human life, last time's big mistake is, after all, only one out of a thousand possible mistakes that are lying in wait for us each time the crisis recurs. While keeping one's eye on a particular mistake that one happens to have made last time, it is important also to be on the look out not to fall into next time's different big mistake; for the chances may be a thousand to one against the possibility that history may exactly repeat itself.

Let me illustrate what I mean. After the First World War, the western peoples had on their consciences a feeling that that war might perhaps have been avoided if, when it

* From Arnold J. Toynbee, "Can We 'Live and Let Live?'" The Listener (1951) XLVI, pp. 885–86. Reprinted by permission of Arnold J. Toynbee.

was looming up, we had all shown a bit more wisdom, more forbearance, more generosity, more readiness for renunciation. So we tried all this in the nineteen-thirties and had the disillusioning experience of finding that appeasement, too, was of no avail for saving us from a repetition of the catastrophe. National Socialist Germany had made up her mind to fight a war of revenge in any case. The captured German official documents have now revealed to us, after the event, just how cold-bloodedly implacable Hitler's determination to have another war really was. So now we are perhaps inclined to say to ourselves: "Well, we have learnt that lesson anyway, and we shall take care not to repeat the foolish mistake that we made with Nazi Germany now that we are faced with a threat of aggression from Communist Russia. Appeasement did not save us from the Second World War; so far from that, it only made the second world war a certainty. So this time, now that we have to deal with Russia, let us make up our minds to it that we are in for a third world war. We cannot stop Stalin from bringing that catastrophe upon us, any more than we were able to stop Hitler. What we can do is to take care to neglect no precautions or preparations and to stand no nonsense."

Russian Expansion Yesterday and Today.

I suppose one of the few points on which all of us in the west are in agreement with each other today is just this point that we must be firm, that we must rearm, that we must be vigilantly on our guard. But it does not follow from any of this that we must resign ourselves to the prospect of a third world war as being something inevitable. As I see it, it is just as important for us now to keep on reminding ourselves that a third world war is really not inevitable, as it is important for us now to be firm and energetic and on the watch.

In saying this, I have another historical precedent in mind. I am thinking of the history of the Anglo-Russian relations during the thirty years 1856–1885. In the Crimean War the Western Powers had foiled an attempt of Russia's to put Turkey in her pocket. They had inflicted on Russia a humiliating defeat which the Russians naturally wanted to reverse, as the Germans, after 1918, wanted to reverse their defeat in the First World War. So, like Germany in the nineteen-thirties, Russia in the eighteen-sixties began to expand eastwards overland, in a quarter where the British Navy could not operate; and this expansion of Russia's in Asia in the nineteenth century, like her present expansion, was taken very hard in the liberal western world. At least twice within the thirty years ending in 1885, Great Britain found herself on the verge of going to war with Russia again. The first occasion was in 1878, when Russia had fought another war with Turkey and had beaten Turkey to its knees. The second occasion was in 1885, when the Russian advance in Central Asia reached the north-western frontiers of Afghanistan. At these two dates, at least, another Anglo-Russian war seemed inevitable. And then, after all, it did not happen this time. After reaching a final peak of intensity in 1885, the long-drawn-out nineteenth-century tension between Britain and Russia began to relax. Within twenty-two years the two powers had entered into an entente with each other in face of a new menace to both of them from Germany. And between 1907 and now they have twice been allies in a world war, first in 1914–1917 and then for a second time in 1941–1945.

My point in bringing up these episodes of past history is this. It is possible that our present tension with Russia may end in another war, as our tension with Germany after the first war ended in a second world war. It is also possible that our present tension with Russia may end in a relaxation of the tension, as after the Crimean War it eventually relaxed without ending in another war between the two powers. At the present moment it is impossible for us to foresee in which of these two possible alternative ways the present tension between the western world and Russia is going to end. We must be prepared for the less happy as well as for the more happy possibility; but we must surely be prepared for both possibilities. In facing the possibility of another 1939, we must not lose sight of the possibility of another 1885.

But is it possible for a democratic free western world and a communist totalitarian Russia to live and let live on the face of a planet that has now become physically " one world " as a result of " the annihilation of distance " by new-fangled methods of mechanical transport? This is possible, as I see it. I see this possibility in the light of another historical precedent. I am thinking of the one world, stretching from Britain to India, which was called into existence by the expansion of the ancient Greek civilization in and after the time of Alexander the Great. For about seven centuries, running from the last century B.C. to the seventh century of the Christian Era, that Ancient World was partitioned between a western and an eastern power: the Roman empire in the west and a rival oriental empire in Persia. It is true that Rome and her Iranian rivals did go to war with one another from time to time; but the point is that each of them soon discovered that it was beyond its strength to conquer, subjugate, and annex the other. Each of them did make the attempt, only to find that it must give it up because the effort was straining its own resources to the breaking point. So these two ancient powers resigned themselves to the necessity of their co-existing, and they did go on living in one world side by side for very nearly seven hundred years. When they fell into a life-and-death struggle with one another at last, they had to pay for the mistake, cash down, by both immediately succumbing to a common new enemy; the Saracens. Why should it not be possible, in our modern one world, for the west and Russia to repeat that episode of ancient history?

But, granting for the moment that this may be possible, do we want to see it happen? As I see it, the peaceful coexistence of our western civilization and a Russian communist society is not merely possible: it is also highly desirable. I will give you what seem to me to be two good reasons — one negative reason and one positive one — for this personal conviction of mine.

My negative reason is my belief that a third world war fought with atomic weapons would plunge our planet into a chaos which would be beyond even America's power to bring into order again. I am assuming that America would win a third world war hands down; and I will also make the further assumption that the United States would come out of such a war without grave damage to herself (though I find few Americans so optimistic as that about their country's prospects of coming through unscathed). But I take it for granted that, at the end of a third world war in which Russia had been knocked out by America, the whole of the old world would have been laid flat — not only Russia, but Europe, Asia, and Africa as well. And would even an undamaged United States have the strength by herself, to set the whole of the rest of the world on its feet again?

My positive reason for thinking a third world war undesirable is that, even if that fearful world-wide destruction could eventually be repaired by a victorious United States, it would not, as I see it, be healthy for the world, or healthy for America herself, for there to be only one

sole surviving power in the world. In order to keep morally fit, human nature needs to be exercised and kept in training by some devil or other; and our western world today is having this indispensable, though very disagreeable, service performed for her by Russia. The other way round, too, if we can submit with a good grace to the practical joke of seeing ourselves for a moment as Russian eyes see us: I fancy that the capitalist world, dressed up in horns, hooves, forked tail and the devil's other stage properties, is a bogy that communist Russia needs just as much as a democratic west needs the bogy of Russian totalitarianism to keep her up to the mark. In fact, neither of these two incongruous neighbors would find it easy to keep in good health if the other were entirely eliminated.

"The Other Party's Devil"

"But what kind of *modus vivendi* can you imagine?" you may ask me. As I see it, I cannot imagine any formal agreement between us to behave to each other as good neighbors; but I can imagine an unspoken determination on either side not to fall into a shooting war with the other party — though the kind of peaceful coexistence that consists merely in the avoidance of a shooting war between the principal parties may well prove to be a state of extremely painful stress, anxiety, and discomfort. There might be other local shooting wars like the war in Korea. And I personally feel sure that, even if we manage to avoid dropping atom bombs on each other, we shall continue to wage our present missionary war — I mean, the competitive propaganda of our rival ideas and ideals. This, I fancy, will go on until Asia becomes formidable enough to the rest of us to make the English-speaking peoples begin to look upon Russia as "the White Man's hope"; and, even if that eventually happens, we shall then merely be exchanging a Russian peril for an Asian one, as we have exchanged a Russian peril for a German one, and then a German peril for a Russian one.

You will see that I am not doing you the disservice of prophesying to you smooth things. I am prophesying a continuance of toil and trouble for as long as we can peer ahead into our future; and, as I see it, this prophecy is a safe one to make; for I personally agree with Eliphaz the Temanite's view that "Man is born into trouble, as the sparks fly upward." Indeed I will go farther than Eliphaz goes in the Book of Job. I will put it to you that, if ever man does manage to elude trouble, he merely brings trouble on himself, because trouble, after all, is the necessary salt of life without which life loses its savor. So perhaps the unwritten condition on which we and the Russians are going to coexist is that each party shall go on serving as the other party's devil.

13 THE INFLUENCE OF IDEAS IN MODERN SOCIETY

90. Introduction

In the preceding pages we have viewed three aspects of society: one, its permanent foundations, two, the political and economic decisions that must be made by the members of society, and, three, the tensions, or conflicts in the patterns of choice, that arise within and among nations. We have devoted Part II to the process of industrialization because of its lasting influence on each of these aspects of society. First, the industrial metamorphosis of society has enlarged the permanent foundations upon which contemporary institutions rest by making available to society large quantities of resources whose utilization formerly had been confined by the limits of technological knowledge. It also stimulated the growth of a population which could organize and fashion these resources into goods and services. Moreover, industrialization has become part of the tradition of Western society and, consequently, shapes the preferences and attitudes of the people who live within its orbit. And even those countries outside of its orbit aspire to the wealth, if not the methods, of the countries that have advanced along the road of industrial development.

Second, industrialization has made society socially complex so that the making of political and economic decisions requires the development of institutions which can relate discrete individuals to one another in a meaningful way and can disseminate the information upon which decisions can be made. Such an institution is the price system which coordinates the behavior of millions of people and thus facilitates the transformation of ultimate resources into want-satisfying goods and services. Similarly the democratic political system with its political parties, legislatures, and administrative bureaucracy is an elaborate mechanism for ferreting out and acting upon the preferences of the many people in the large society.

Third, industrialization has ramified tensions throughout society so that their relaxation is a matter of greater public concern than it has ever been before. Yet the very process of industrial growth makes this more difficult. The Industrial Revolution ushered in a period of unparalleled mobility both in the social structure and in economic markets by destroying the restraints on movement implicit in feudalistic and mercantilistic society. Man could seek employment in organized labor markets and could raise his social status by successfully producing for the market unique products which embodied his creative inspiration. The expanding society of the new industrial age welcomed change and rewarded its innovators as it had once frowned upon change and had been suspicious of innovators.

But as the industrial society has matured, new impediments interfere with its recently acquired mobility. Increasing specialization has impaired man's versatility or, more properly, extended the range of jobs and skills, so that the individual can only be familiar with an infinitesimal part of the industrial process. If the experience of the individual is limited by industrial expansion, the requirements for the successful operation of business enterprise have become more exacting. Technological advance precipitated the growth of large business units controlling millions of dollars of invested capital and calling for organizational talents beyond the capacity of most people. Likewise the expansion of the market has placed a premium on sales and marketing skills. Furthermore, even if the individual possesses the requisite knowledge and skills for industrial enterprise, it is not always possible for him to obtain financial support for his ideas. One has to be able to pass the screen of the capital markets. Thus the mature indus-

trial society tends to display rigidities that were not always present in its early phase. The industrial labor force expands and a private bureaucracy of white collar workers grows up to fill the gap between worker and management executive. In short, the industrialization process destroys one type of class structure, but creates another one in its place.

A unique feature of the present-day class structure in democratic society is the articulateness of some of its sub-groups. In the United States the worker, the business man, the farmer are members of highly organized groups, which assiduously pursue their ends. Since the ends of these groups are frequently contradictory, the groups are often in conflict, and since the groups are rooted in society at large, these conflicts are symptomatic of the tensions in mass industrial society. In contrast many of the tensions of an older society were sublimated in the status arrangements that bound people to place and occupation. Those tensions on the surface brought into conflict the top layers of society — for instance, the landed interests and the commercial interests — and hence were not embedded in society at large. One might say, then, that the industrialization and democratization of society have brought to the surface tensions that lay dormant in traditional and authoritarian society.

The tensions within society sometimes threaten its stability — civil war and revolution have by no means been unknown in the development of Western civilization — but the successful and stable society institutionalizes its tensions so that they can be dealt with by orderly and hence tension-easing procedures. The tensions among nations are not so easily dealt with and, consequently, are more likely to degenerate into overt war than domestic tensions into revolution or civil war. In an earlier era this was not a particularly alarming prospect. Wars were campaigns of maneuvers fought by mercenaries who were not too concerned about the goals or objectives of those who employed them. War was their livelihood and naturally they were interested in maintaining the repectability of their source of income. Loss of life, therefore, was minimized. Industrialization and the concomitant forces of democracy and nationalism, however, have laid to rest the mercenary and replaced him with the citizen-soldier, who is bound to defend his country against those forces that would destroy it. The military establishment is but an extension of industrial society, and war is a struggle between totally committed societies. And now for the first time the technological advances of industrial society raise the possibility of the sudden and swift destruction of civilization in a holocaust of atomic warfare.

In developing our study of modern society we have said relatively little about policy — the methods by which society can consciously reduce or minimize its conflicts. We have not analyzed labor legislation nor have we spent time on the fiscal and monetary measures that can be employed to iron out the unevenness that we saw accompanied the growth of income in the United States. We have shown that the distribution of income is unequal but have not talked about schemes for redistributing income. In the area of international politics we analyzed the interplay of nations in terms of the struggle for power. What we said about policy was always secondary to an attempt to develop principles which could explain and account for the conduct of nations in international politics.

Because we have not always explicitly considered problems of policy does not mean, however, that this study has no relevance for policy. On the contrary we would hope that it might prove profoundly relevant, for policy considerations can only have meaning when rooted in an understanding of the problems that policy is supposed to solve. We have, consequently, emphasized the ideas through which an understanding of social problems can be obtained. Many of these ideas are abstract and may at first seem unreal to the reader. We hope that he will not discount them for this reason. Despite frequent assertions to the contrary, the world of ideas is a tremendous moving force in the behavior of man. Lord Keynes stated this most forcefully when he said:

But apart from this contemporary mood, the ideas of economists and political philosophers, both when they are right and when they are wrong, are more powerful than is commonly understood. Indeed the world is ruled by little else. Practical men, who believe themselves to be quite exempt from any intellectual influences, are usually the slaves of some defunct economist. Madmen in authority, who hear voices in the air, are distilling their frenzy from some academic scribblers of a few years back. I am sure that the power of vested interest is vastly exaggerated compared with the gradual encroachment of ideas.[1]

Strikingly enough, the influence of Keynes' own economic philosophy would seem to corroborate his general belief.

Perhaps Lord Keynes himself exaggerated the power of ideas, but if so he was reacting against the crude pragmatism of men of practical affairs. The spread of communism in the mid-twentieth century, however, suggests that he has not overstated the influence of ideas on behavior. Karl Marx was, among other things, an " academic scribbler." Yet the ideas of Marx have precipitated revolutions and fathered a type of dedicated behavior that is not unlike religious fanaticism. The revolutionary activities of a Lenin or a Trotsky were sustained by the imperatives of historical development gleaned from the Marxian system of ideas. These men knew where the world was moving because they looked at the world through the prism of dialectical materialism — a proposition as abstract as Euclid's theorems.

Obviously, communism is not the only system of ideas that holds sway in the world. Indeed communism has had its most meager results in

those countries dominated by the ideals of liberal democracy. Liberal democracy does not purport to show its adherents the true road of historical development as does communism. Rather it inculcates in man a distrust of such dogma and a belief in the competition of ideas as the source of truth. Where the communist knows, the liberal democrat has to be shown. To be sure, even liberalism must be constantly on guard lest it erect its particular manifestations into absolutes. Where the Communist views the individual as a reflection of underlying historical forces, the liberal democrat sees the individual as the prime mover in social phenomena. The one, consequently, is deterministic, the other by comparison tends to be indeterministic.

Today the world is split by these systems of competing ideas. In a previous age a system of ideas established a consensus in the civilization which is now divided between Communism and democracy. The concept of Christianity stood athwart medieval Europe and provided a community of interests for all individuals regardless of their place of origin. Medieval Christianity was dogmatic on theological points in somewhat the same sense that contemporary communism is on politics. Based on the doctrine of original sin it assumed that man could not be left to his own devices and that he only could be saved by strict conformance to tradition and authority as determined by the Church. Man was born imperfect and could strive for perfection only by reaching for

[1] John Maynard Keynes, *The General Theory of Employment, Interest and Money* (New York: Harcourt, Brace, and Company, 1936), p. 383.

the past. Despite its distortions, however, medieval Christianity provides us with one of our few examples of an era marked by a community of beliefs.

Much of what we have included in this book has been designed to demonstrate the profound impact the world of ideas has had on the development of Western civilization. Furthermore, implicit in the book is a belief in a special role of ideas. In the previous paragraphs we have been talking about ideas that can best be described as cosmologies, or systems of thought which attempt to explain the universe of human action. On a less grandiose plane ideas are inextricably associated with intelligent thinking. Being part of the Western tradition we cannot help but absorb the belief — what essentially is a faith — in rationality. Not only do we believe that man can be rational but that as he is rational in terms that are appropriate to each setting and problem, he can help to relieve the tensions of society. Just as the psychologist relieves the anxieties of his patient by trying to make him aware of the source of his tensions, so the social scientist can contribute to the relieving of social tensions by increasing man's understanding of society. In short, when ideas explain phenomena the understanding imparted to man may dull the sharp edges of conflict-creating bias.

If, for instance, man believes that poverty is contrived by grasping monopolists who consciously strive to hold the poor in perpetual bondage, then he can only conceive of a so-lution to the problem of poverty in terms of the destruction of that group which he believes causes poverty, i.e., the monopolists. On the other hand, if he believes that poverty is a reflection of the fundamental scarcity of resources, he will seek solutions which attempt to enlarge the quantity of resources available to society.

Or to take another example, the belief that nations can be self-sufficient and that international trade is important only in so far as it permits a nation to unload its exportable surplus in foreign markets leads to a type of behavior — the erection of high tariff walls — that creates conflict in international affairs. The view that nations cannot be self-sufficient and that international trade is merely an extension of domestic trade, which will increase a nation's income, will cause man to seek means of promoting international harmony, upon which international trade rests.

We have analyzed society in terms of the social choices man must make. Our emphasis throughout the book has been on individual choice. Where we have considered collective choice, we have not intended to prove its inefficiency or its immorality but rather to use it as a foil for highlighting the unique features of systems of individual choice. We have tried to show that in the development of Western civilization the making of political and economic decisions has become increasingly complicated with the growth of industrial society and that the conflicts of society rise from the divergent aims of individuals, groups, and nations. To understand this is to understand a lot. For such understanding relaxes the grip of dogma and bias on the minds of man and permits him to seek rational solutions to and make appropriate judgments concerning social problems. We hope that this study of modern society has convinced the reader that ideas are not merely the playthings of academicians but are potent forces in the world of practical affairs. We hope further that the reader is now familiar enough with the world of ideas to be better able to understand the world in which he lives.

In our final selections we offer the reader, who is also a citizen in a most turbulent and anxious age, concrete examples of two pressing issues which illustrate the role of ideas and their relationship to institutions. More important, they illustrate how ideas may be adjusted to practical realities in politics and society. We have chosen to consider how we should deal with unfriendly and alien ideas and how best preserve our own ideals. The most immediate menace for us as Americans today is that of world Communism. How are we to meet this powerful if spurious idea, which is expressed through the acts of the Communist Party? One of our wisest statesmen and diplomats, the former Ambassador to Moscow, Mr. George F. Kennan, answered this on the occasion of his nomination to the Board of Trustees of Princeton University. There is perhaps no more urgent issue calling for sober thought and grave deliberation than that of safeguarding freedom while opposing tyranny. Yet the ultimate and final commitment to Communism, with all the brutality and ruthlessness this produces, is not the only peril with which the West is faced. Political ideas are vital in determining the direction a society will go. But the moral and spiritual values of a nation against which it must constantly measure its own institutions and beliefs are more crucial still. This is the point which a great American democrat and famous theologian, Professor Reinhold Niebuhr, makes in our concluding selection. In completing his survey of modern industrial society, the reader will have considered with a great diplomatist and a great churchman how false ideas may be combatted and abiding truths be preserved in the sphere of human existence where ultimate truth exists but is never attainable.

91. The American Position on Communism?*

WHERE DO YOU STAND ON COMMUNISM?*

" Where do you stand on communism?" This question was put recently to George F. Kennan, on the occasion of his nomination for the Board of Trustees of Princeton. The question came from a Princeton alumnus, and Mr. Kennan, who has served in the diplomatic service twenty-five years . . . recognized in the inquiry a matter of concern to many Americans. He answered his correspondent at some length, and his reply is printed here.

DEAR SIR:

The question you have asked me is, as I understand it: Where do I stand on communism?

I am glad you have asked this question, for it involves things that have a most important relation to the problems of our society at this time, and I should feel very badly if there were any misunderstanding of my position.

Your question is broadly stated, and I feel the need to outline my understanding of it before answering it.

My views on the issues of political philosophy that underlie the conflict between the Communist world and our own are publicly known, and I am sure that your question was not

* From George F. Kennan, " Where Do You Stand on Communism? " *The New York Times Magazine,* May 27, 1951, p. 7. Reprinted by permission.

intended to imply that I might be an adherent of the Soviet ideology, or an admirer of Soviet policy. I gather from the enclosure to your letter that what you are interested in is rather my attitude toward American citizens who belong to the Communist party or who are, or appear to be, Communist sympathizers.

The problem of the influence exercised in this country by the leaders of the Soviet Communist party is one with which, as it happens, I have been thrown into rather intimate contact for a number of years. As an official of the Government stationed for long periods in the Soviet Union or adjacent countries and charged off and on for a period of nearly two decades with reporting on Soviet phenomena, the significance of this problem has been brought home to me on a multitude of occasions and in the most varied ways. Actually I believe that it fell to me to be the first, or one of the first, of our civil servants to bring formally to the attention of our Government the problem of the misuse of the privileges and facilities of American citizenship by the agents of Soviet power.

That was even before the recognition by our Government of the Soviet Government. In the Thirties I enjoyed, together with a small circle of associates in the Government service, the experience of being frequently labeled one of " the reactionaries in the State Department " and strongly criticized generally from the Left Wing for advocating a firm and realistic attitude toward the Soviet Government. Following my return in 1946 from my last period of service in Moscow, I shared with Jim Forrestal for some time the curious distinction of being the leading target for the Cominform propaganda machine among persons in this country. This particular form of attentiveness on the Communist side endured as long as I remained in Government service. Only as recently as last spring [1950] my presence in Brazil was the occasion for organized hostile demonstrations on the part of the Brazilian Communists on a scale which I imagine must have been almost unprecedented, and which included the smearing of hundreds of walls in the city of Rio with inscriptions reading "To death with Kennan" and even a number of burials in effigy.

In the light of these experiences I think you can understand that the problem you have raised is not one which has been absent from my thoughts or the importance of which I would be apt to underrate.

Now as far as our country is concerned this problem has, as it seems to me, three major aspects: (1) the Communist Party itself; (2) the fellow-travelers and sympathizers; and (3) the rest of us.

With regard to the Communist Party, I think that we would have a complete moral justification for outlawing it and stamping membership in it as an offense to the country; but I doubt for several reasons that it would be wise or expedient to do

so. Accordingly, I approve the general line of conduct we have followed toward the party over the course of these past three decades, namely: not to dignify it or enhance its outward importance or make martyrs out of its adherents by trying to outlaw and suppress it, but rather to keep it in the open where it can be seen and its activities observed, where its very freedom of action demonstrates how little afraid of it we are, and where its outward activities provide anyone who cares to see with ever-fresh and current demonstrations of its extremism, its remoteness from the feelings and ideals of our people, and the extent to which it is beholden to its cynical and contemptuous foreign masters.

One reason why I doubt the efficacy of any attempt to outlaw the party by legislation is that no legal formula can really be fully accurate and comprehensive for this purpose. The operating flexibility of the Communist movement is such that if membership in the party is made the criterion of legal action, it will simply be arranged that most dangerous Communists will not formally be members of the party. This phenomenon of American communism, being in part a state of mind and of subjective loyalty and touching for this reason on situations of fact which are highly unstable and difficult to elicit, is not a suitable one for treatment by legal norms; it is better handled — as it has been over these past three decades — by the basic common sense of our people and their natural resistance to violent and extreme political movements.

With regard to the fellow-travelers, you have a more complicated and difficult problem. I take these to be the people who would not think of joining the Communist Party and who certainly do not consciously picture themselves as agents of Soviet power, but who feel sympathy for Soviet purposes as they see them, perceive no great conflict between those purposes and the purposes for which our own society was established and has lived, and are inclined to accept uncritically a substantial amount of the Soviet propaganda about our own country. That these people are a problem to us, I readily concede. That they are poor people to have in responsible and delicate governmental positions seems to me to be obvious, since they are apt to become subject to conflicts dangerous to the faithful and effective performance of their duties. I think it the business of our governmental leaders to see that they do not occupy such positions, and I know of no responsible Government administrators who have not tried faithfully, in recent years, to do just this.

But it does seem to me important that such matters should be arranged, if at all possible, quietly and tactfully and without unnecessary damage to the reputations and occupational possibilities of the persons concerned. People of this description are not criminals under the law. They have usually come by their beliefs honestly and out of a sincere preoccupation with the problems of our country. In many instances the attitudes which cause the trouble are passing phases, marking a given stage of intellectual and emotional growth. In such cases, what the people require is often a certain forbearance and firm intellectual resistance on the part of the rest of society — not public humiliation and ignominious rejection — in order to become constructive and useful citizens. Surely it is more important that they should become such citizens, enabled and encouraged to contribute again to the workings of our society, than that they should remain embittered outcasts.

In education, the presence of such people presents a more complicated problem than in government, because their elimination frequently brings up questions of the freedom of thought and inquiry infinitely greater in their importance than any individual situation of this sort. That persons really committed to the Soviet ideology have no place in our educational system seems to me to be obvious, for such persons cannot logically believe in the freedom of the mind or in the desirability of the quest for objective truth, and can therefore have no integral relation to the purposes of American education.

When you get into the realm of the sympathizers, however, you have a different problem. The worst you can formally charge these people with is poor judgment and muddy thinking. That is certainly a reason for not hiring them as educators in the first place, and I suppose there are certain categories of educational establishments in which it can properly and easily be a reason for letting them go, when they have once been hired. But there are other categories of establishments in which this last is more difficult to do without introducing ulterior questions and inviting serious misunderstandings. Here, it is always a question of circumstances; and I would know of no answer to such a question other than common sense and human wisdom applied to each individual case, coupled with a readiness to remember that the principles of academic freedom are absolutely basic to our American system, and that any inconvenience or danger brought on by the tolerance of an unhappy individual situation must always be weighed against the damage that may be done to those principles by too arbitrary and abrupt an approach in an individual case.

In general, precisely because things so vital to American ideals are here involved, I think we should be extremely careful to measure in each case the real extent of the danger and not risk prejudicing our principles for minor causes. It would be a serious situation indeed where we would have to conclude that sound teachings could not stand the competition of one or two challenging voices, however misguided we might think them to be. Our concern, after all, must be not to shelter our youth from destructive and ill-founded ideas but to arm it intellectually so that it will be capable of recognizing such ideas for what they are and playing its part in enabling our society generally to resist them. John Milton wrote: " He that can apprehend and consider vice with all her baits and seeming pleasures, and yet abstain, and yet distinguish, and yet prefer that which is truly better, he is the true warfaring Christian." Surely this is an American sentiment; and we have no greater reason than Milton did to wish to see in our youth a " fugitive and cloistered virtue, unexercized and unbreathed, that never sallies out and sees her adversary. . . ."

The third category to be taken into account here is, as I say, the rest of us. It may surprise you that I include this category in such a discussion, but I assure you that if it is the dangers of communism we are talking about, we have no choice but to include it. Our society today is in the throes of a peculiarly painful and difficult adjustment to demands placed upon it by its own growth and by the development of world realities. It is idle to argue how many of these problems are of our own making, and how many have been made for us by others. We are like an individual moving into the responsibilities of maturity: he may feel that these responsibilities are unjustly placed upon him and are greater than he ought to be asked to bear, but it will do him no good to approach them in a spirit of self-pity and recrimination against others. On the contrary, he probably faces no greater danger than precisely that habit of thought. It is not by accident that so much of individual mental trouble begins with a tendency to exaggerate the malevolence of others and the extent of its relevance to one's own difficulties, as compared with the elements of one's own responsibility.

Our situation, as a national society, is analogous, but bears in it a special danger. It is a fact that palpable damage has been done to our national interest in the past by agents of, or sympathizers with, Communist power. We have only recently become aware of that fact. If there is nothing more difficult for the individual to assess and to keep in perspective than his own responsibility for his troubled predicaments, as opposed to the injuries that may have been done him by others, this is doubly true in the case of a national society. Because some damage has been done to us by misguided or malicious people in our own midst, because we are not sure that we yet know the full measure of this damage and because we find our present conditions of life exasperating, frustrating and alarming generally, there is a natural tendency among us to go the whole hog, to assume that all our troubles stem from this single source, and to conclude that we have only to eliminate it from our society and everything will be all right.

I cannot overemphasize to you the danger which I think lies in this aberration. It is not just the danger of getting things out of proportion — of exaggerating the damage done to us in the past by Communist penetration, or failing to realize the degree to which this problem has already been countered and liquidated, of seeing bogey men for the future. It is a question of something much more important — of our retention of the ability to meet effectively the many and heavy problems we have before us which have nothing to do

with domestic Communism at all, in which we would not be materially aided if every Communist Party member and sympathizer were to be deported from our shores tomorrow, and for which we require the utmost restraint and realism in public action.

If our handling of the problem of Communist influence in our midst is not carefully moderated — if we permit it, that is, to become an emotional preoccupation and to blind us to the more important positive tasks before us — we can do a damage to our national purpose beyond comparison greater than anything that threatens us today from the Communist side. The American Communist party is today, by and large, an external danger. It represents a tiny minority in our country; it has no real contact with the feelings of the mass of our people; and its position as the agency of a hostile foreign power is clearly recognized by the overwhelming mass of our citizens.

But the subjective emotional stresses and temptations to which we are exposed in our attempt to deal with this domestic problem are not an external danger: they represent a danger within ourselves — a danger that something may occur in our own minds and souls which will make us no longer like the persons by whose efforts this republic was founded and held together, but rather like the representatives of that very power we are trying to combat: intolerant, secretive, suspicious, cruel, and terrified of internal dissension because we have lost our own belief in ourselves and in the power of our ideals. The worst thing that our Communists could do to us, and the thing we have most to fear from their activities, is that we should become like them.

That our country is beset with external dangers I readily concede. But these dangers, at their worst, are ones of physical destruction, of the disruption of our world security, of expense and inconvenience and sacrifice. These are serious, and sometimes terrible things, but they are all things that we can take and still remain Americans.

The internal danger is of a different order. America is not just territory and people. There is lots of territory elsewhere, and there are lots of people; but it does not add up to America. America is something in our minds and our habits of outlook which causes us to believe in certain things and to behave in certain ways, and by which, in its totality, we hold ourselves distinguished from others. If that once goes there will be no America to defend. And that can go too easily if we yield to the primitive human instinct to escape from our frustrations into the realms of

mass emotion and hatred and to find scapegoats for our difficulties in individual fellow-citizens who are, or have at one time been, disoriented or confused. If we cannot resist these tendencies, then we would be better off to go to the other extreme and to put the Communist problem out of our minds entirely, dismissing it from our thoughts as even a contributory cause of our difficulties; for this would mean that we were incapable of dealing with such a problem in a balanced way, and of the two dangers, the lesser one would be to stop thinking about Communism entirely.

But, personally, I feel that neither of these extremes is desirable or necessary; and I see no reason why we should not proceed on our course without either panic or complacency, recognizing our domestic Communists and their well-wishers for the genuine though limited problem that they are, but refusing to let this divert us from the greater problems we have before us or to lure us into reactions which threaten us with the loss of the national soul.

92. Democracy as a Religion*

If one may judge by the various commencement utterances of the past month, Americans have only one religion: devotion to democracy. They extol its virtues, are apprehen-

* From Reinhold Niebuhr, *Christianity and Crisis*, Vol. VII, No. 14 (1947), pp. 1-2. Reprinted by permission.

sive about the perils to which it is exposed, pour maledictions upon its foes, rededicate themselves periodically to its purposes and claim unconditioned validity for its ideals.

It happens that democracy is probably that form of society in which both freedom and order are brought most successfully in support of each other. It is not the only form of society in which justice prevails. The modern prejudice and illusion, that there is no middle ground between democracy and totalitarianism, is a very parochial viewpoint. Nevertheless democracy is worth preserving. It is a worthy object of qualified loyalty. But is it a proper object of unqualified loyalty? Is it an adequate religion? Does not the very extravagance of our devotion prove that we live in a religiously vapid age, in which even Christians fail to penetrate to the more ultimate issues of life?

Democracy cannot be the final end of life for various reasons. It is a form of human society, and man is only partly fulfilled in his social relations. Ultimately each individual faces not society but God as his judge and redeemer. Democrats talk very much about democratic individualism; but what does it profit a society to refrain from making ultimate claims upon the individual in principle; yet in fact make ultimate claims because it is the kind of society in which the individual is supposedly accorded higher rights than in other societies. And what does it profit an individual to be free of social compulsion if he lacks every ultimate point of reference for the freedom of his soul which exceeds the limits of his social institutions? Democracy is certainly a better form of society than totalitarianism. But many proponents of it share one mistake of communists at least: they know no other dimension of existence except the social one.

Another peril of democracy as a religion is that, without a more inclusive religious faith, we identify our particular brand of democracy with the ultimate values of life. This is a sin to which Americans are particularly prone. American conceptions of democracy are characterized by an excessive individualistic and libertarian note. A large number of parochial Americans are arriving at the absurd conclusion that we are the only surviving democracy in the world. They arrive at this conclusion because they think the emphasis upon community and upon "planning" which is prevalent in Europe is incompatible with democracy. This kind of devotion to a partial and parochial view of democracy might actually become democracy's undoing. There are no historic institutions, whether political, economic or religious which can survive a too uncritical devotion. Such devotion accentuates their vices and makes them incapable of adjusting themselves to new situations. There is actually a very ironic note in the current American devotion to democracy; because so much of it is a type of devotion which is a hazard to democracy's future.

But even if our democracy were more perfect than it is, and if our current notions of it were not so obviously drawn from the peculiar conditions of the world's wealthiest nation, devotion to democracy would still be false as a religion. It tempts us to identify the final meaning of life with a virtue which we possess, and thus to give a false and idolatrous religious note to the conflict between democracy and communism for instance.

John Middleton Murry, in a recent article in the British *Christian News-Letter,* went so far as to arrive at a practical identification of Christianity and a free society. He was, at least, quite confident that it was the primary business of Christianity to protect a free society against communism. The readers of this journal are not likely to suspect us of tardiness in the defense of democracy against communism. We are nevertheless highly critical of this approach. We have to make the best defense we can of our most cherished social and historical values against ruthless foes. But from the standpoint of our Christian faith we have to view such struggles in another dimension. We must recognize the ambiguous and tragic character of a struggle in which a contest of power between two great blocs of power in the world obscures the moral issues involved in the struggle and creates a vicious circle of mutual fear, from which there is no easy escape. We do not suggest that there is some simple pacifist solution for these mutual fears, created by power contests. But neither must we fall into the illusion that the foe alone is responsible for the fears and that we are merely virtuous defenders of a great cause, beset by scoundrels. There must be a dimension of faith in which, whatever our loyalties and however justified our defense of them, we recognize the tragic character of the human drama, including the particular drama of our own day, and call upon the mercy of God to redeem us not from the predicament of democracy but from the human predicament.

INDEX